UNIVERSITY CASEBOOK SERIES®

FIRST AMENDMENT LAW

EIGHTH EDITION

NOAH R. FELDMAN
Felix Frankfurter Professor of Law,
Harvard University

KATHLEEN M. SULLIVAN
Partner, Quinn Emanuel Urquhart & Sullivan, LLP
Former Professor of Law and Dean of the School of Law,
  Stanford University
Former Professor of Law, Harvard University

FOUNDATION
PRESS

University Casebook Series is a trademark registered in the U.S. Patent and Trademark Office.

© 1999, 2003 FOUNDATION PRESS
© 2007, 2010 by THOMSON REUTERS/FOUNDATION PRESS
© 2013 by LEG, Inc. d/b/a West Academic Publishing
© 2016, 2019 LEG, Inc. d/b/a West Academic
© 2023 LEG, Inc. d/b/a West Academic
        860 Blue Gentian Road, Suite 350
        Eagan, MN 55121
        1-877-888-1330

Printed in the United States of America

ISBN: 978-1-63659-365-4

For Mina Zipporah Feldman and Jaemin David Feldman

NRF

For my many students at Harvard and Stanford Law Schools,
who taught me as much as I taught them

KMS

PREFACE

This edition of the casebook reflects significant changes to major areas of First Amendment law made by the Supreme Court since the last edition, published in 2019. In the October 2021 Term, the Court decided Kennedy v. Bremerton, in which it remade the interpretation of the Establishment Clause, effectively overruling long-established doctrinal tests (the so-called Lemon test and the endorsement test) and replacing them with a historical approach. The Court in the same Term shifted the meaning of the Free Exercise Clause in Carson v. Makin, continuing the trend of treating the clause as an anti-discrimination provision. This shift was also demonstrated in earlier COVID-19-related decisions, most prominently Tandon v. Newsom.

In the law of free speech the Court also decided a number of very important cases that are incorporated in this edition. It addressed out-of-school, on-line student speech (Mahanoy Area School District v. B.L.); compelled disclosure of donor identity (Americans for Prosperity Foundation v. Bonta); and the distinction between government speech and private speech in a limited public forum (Shurtleff v. Boston). The Court also took steps to clarify what counts as content-based speech regulation (Austin v. Reagan National Advertising).

Since the last edition, the Court's composition changed. President Trump, who had already nominated Justice Neil Gorsuch to replace Justice Antonin Scalia, further nominated Justice Brett Kavanaugh (who replaced Justice Anthony Kennedy) and Justice Amy Coney Barrett (who replaced Justice Ruth Bader Ginsburg). President Trump's three confirmed Supreme Court appointments were the most of any president since Ronald Reagan, and the most of any one-term president since Herbert Hoover. President Joseph Biden nominated Justice Ketanji Brown Jackson to replace Justice Stephen Breyer. She was confirmed, and became the first Black woman justice in the Court's history when she was sworn into office on June 30, 2022.

This casebook, like its predecessors, contains in self-contained form the same material on the First Amendment freedoms of speech and religion that is presented in Chapters 11–14 of Constitutional Law (21st ed. 2022). In keeping with longstanding practice, deletions and alterations are marked by brackets rather than ellipses, and footnotes are renumbered from the original text opinions, with those from opinions by the Justices so designated.

As it has done since its first edition, the casebook aims to present First Amendment law as a species of law, informed by history, politics, and ideas but also marked by a deep, if contested, internal structure. Our goal is that any student learning the law of the First Amendment from this book will be readily equipped to practice it. The casebook attempts to uncover and explicate the rules, standards, and methodologies that inform practice before the Court as much as it seeks to make sense of the Court's evolving doctrine.

We are grateful to the many longtime faithful users of the casebook and to those who have joined their ranks with recent editions. Special thanks to Dan Coenen and Abner Greene for thoughtful, detailed comments on the whole manuscript; and to Charles Fried and Martha Minow for many helpful suggestions. Finally, we are thankful for excellent research assistance from

Alex Walker, John Acton, Joshua Freundel, Delaney Herndon, and Jazmine Phillips-Acie.

We hope that you will enjoy teaching from this edition of the casebook, and that Gerald Gunther would continue to recognize his great presence in its pages.

NOAH R. FELDMAN
CAMBRIDGE, MASSACHUSETTS

KATHLEEN M. SULLIVAN
NEW YORK, NEW YORK

November 2022

SUMMARY OF CONTENTS

TABLE OF CONTENTS

TABLE OF CASES

The principal cases are in bold type.

TABLE OF AUTHORITIES

FIRST AMENDMENT

ARTICLES IN ADDITION TO, AND AMENDMENT OF, THE CONSTITUTION OF THE UNITED STATES OF AMERICA, PROPOSED BY CONGRESS, AND RATIFIED BY THE SEVERAL STATES, PURSUANT TO THE FIFTH ARTICLE OF THE ORIGINAL CONSTITUTION.

AMENDMENT I [1791].

Congress shall make no law respecting an establishment of religion, or prohibiting the free exercise thereof; or abridging the freedom of speech, or of the press; or the right of the people peaceably to assemble, and to petition the Government for a redress of grievances.

UNIVERSITY CASEBOOK SERIES®

FIRST AMENDMENT LAW

EIGHTH EDITION

CHAPTER 1

FREEDOM OF SPEECH— CATEGORIES OF SPEECH— DEGREES OF PROTECTED EXPRESSION

SECTION 1. FREE SPEECH: AN OVERVIEW

The First Amendment to the United States Constitution provides: "Congress shall make no law abridging the freedom of speech, or of the press." As written, the First Amendment is simple and unqualified. But there has been a broad consensus that not all expression or communication is included within "the freedom of speech." The Court's first major encounters with free speech claims did not arise until after World War I. In the decades since, claimed infringements of First Amendment rights have become a source of frequent controversy and a staple of Court business.

Are some types of speech clearly covered by the First Amendment, while others are entitled to less protection, or excluded from protection altogether? What government interests are sufficient to justify lesser or no protection for speech? Chapter 1 explores these questions after this overview. It begins by reviewing the speech that the Court has deemed *not* protected by the First Amendment. Of course many speech acts receive no First Amendment protection: bribery, perjury, antitrust conspiracies and solicitation to murder are not considered protected speech, and such traditional exclusions are so uncontroversial as to go (mostly) unlitigated. But the Court has debated extensively the boundaries of several other categories of speech that it has held to be outside First Amendment protection: in particular, the categories of incitement, fighting words, libel, obscenity, and child pornography. The Court continues to hold such categories nominally unprotected, but the story of Chapter 1 is largely one of the shrinking of these categories' boundaries to avoid trenching upon speech that is considered clearly within the First Amendment, especially "political" speech and speech critical of governmental policies and officials. The Court has also grappled with the question whether to treat some speech as protected, but not fully protected. It has upheld various regulations of sexually explicit but nonobscene speech, and it has treated commercial speech (i.e., advertising) as explicitly enjoying lesser First Amendment protection. Chapter 1 concludes by exploring these "lower value" categories.

Chapter 2 turns from the question of the categories of speech to the modes or techniques of abridgement, and to their influence on the relevant standard of review. Chapter 3, the last of the free expression chapters, turns to several rights derived from the right of free speech, including the right to association and the right against being compelled to speak.

FIRST AMENDMENT HISTORY

In Palko v. Connecticut, 302 U.S. 319 (1937), Justice Cardozo characterized protection of speech as a "fundamental" liberty in part because "our history, political and legal," recognized "freedom of thought and speech" as "the indispensable condition of nearly every other form of freedom." Does history in fact support special protection of First Amendment rights? What is the scope of "the freedom of speech" enshrined by the Framers of the Bill of Rights? What evils of pre-Constitution history was the Amendment designed to avert?

1. ***Prior restraints.*** A prominent technique of restraint in English law after invention of the printing press had been the licensing of printers— the submission of publications to royal officials with the power to give or withhold an imprimatur of approval. It was this practice that the great poet, scholar, and political theorist John Milton protested in a tract called Areopagitica—A Speech for the Liberty of Unlicensed Printing (1664). As William Blackstone described the evils of the practice: "[To] subject the press to the restrictive power of a licenser [is] to subject all freedom of sentiment to the prejudices of one man, and make him the arbitrary and infallible judge of all controverted points in learning, religion, and government." 4 Blackstone, Commentaries on the Laws of England *151–52.

Prior restraint through licensing was abandoned in England a century before the adoption of the American Bill of Rights. Nevertheless, a barrier to licensing was at one time viewed as the major thrust of the First Amendment. Blackstone had expressed the view that "[t]he liberty of the press [consists] in laying no *previous* restraints upon publication, and not in freedom from censure for criminal matter when published." Justice Holmes, a great legal historian as author of The Common Law (1881), initially embraced the Blackstonian view that freedom of expression was protected solely against prior restraints. See, e.g., Patterson v. Colorado, 205 U.S. 454 (1907). Compare his grudging recognition 12 years later, in Schenck, below, that "[i]t well may be that the prohibition of laws abridging the freedom of speech is not confined to previous restraints, although to prevent them may have been the main purpose."

2. ***Seditious libel.*** In pre-Revolutionary England, hundreds of people were prosecuted and convicted for seditious libel—"the intentional publication, without lawful excuse or justification, of written blame of any public man, or of the law, or of any institution established by law." Viewing treason laws as too cumbersome to use against critics of government, the Stuart monarchs used seditious libel instead. The English judges held, on the question of what was "intentional publication," that it was sufficient to show that the defendant had intended to publish writings having a seditious tendency; the Crown did not have to prove that the defendant maliciously intended to cause sedition. Moreover, under English law it was the judge, not the jury, who decided whether the writing had a seditious tendency. Truth was not a defense.

In the colonies, trials for seditious libel were extremely rare. The best known was the prosecution of John Peter Zenger in New York in 1735. Zenger was tried for criticizing the Governor General of the colony in his weekly publication. The judge refused the pleas of Zenger's counsel that the truth of the alleged libel was an absolute defense and that the jury, not the judge, should decide the issues of seditious tendency and intent. The jury, disregarding the judge's instructions, found Zenger not guilty.

The English Bill of Rights of 1689 provided that "the freedom of speech and debates or proceedings in Parliament ought not to be impeached or questioned in any court or place out of Parliament." Although this provision only applied to speech and debate in Parliament, it provided some protection for members against seditious libel charges. Its language ("the freedom of speech") clearly influenced the drafting of the First Amendment.

The question whether the First Amendment embodied a general principle against the suppression of seditious libel has divided historians. Zechariah Chafee, Jr.'s influential work on free speech argued that the Framers of the First Amendment had more in mind than the banning of the long-gone censorship through licensing: he insisted that they "intended to wipe out the common law of sedition and make further prosecutions for criticism of the government, without any incitement to law-breaking, forever impossible." Chafee, Free Speech in the United States (1941) (revising Freedom of Speech (1920)). Compare, however, Leonard Levy's historical study denying that the First Amendment was "intended to wipe out the common law of sedition." Levy, Legacy of Suppression (1960). Levy's "revisionist interpretation" (which he later revised and softened in The Emergence of a Free Press (1985)), claimed that 18th century Americans "did not believe in a broad scope for freedom of expression, particularly in the realm of politics." He concluded that "libertarian theory from the time of Milton to the ratification of the First Amendment substantially accepted the right of the state to suppress seditious libel." For Levy, the First Amendment Framers' main concern was with states' rights and the fear of national power rather than with individual liberty, and he argued that a "broad libertarian theory of freedom of speech and press did not emerge in the United States" until the Jeffersonian battle against the Sedition Act of 1798.

3. ***The Sedition Act of 1798.*** The Sedition Act of 1798, enacted by the Federalists, barred the publication of "false, scandalous, and malicious writing [against] the Government of the United States, or either House of [Congress], or the President, [with] intent to defame [them]; or to bring them [into] contempt or disrepute; or to excite against them [the] hatred of the good people of the United States, or to stir up sedition within the United States. . . . " In order to eliminate the most criticized procedural aspects of English law, the Act provided that truth *would* be a defense, that malicious intent *was* an element of the crime, and that the jury *would* decide such issues as the seditious tendency of the publication. The Act was rigorously enforced, entirely against Jeffersonian Republicans, including their leading newspapers. The federal courts applying the act imprisoned publishers and writers and assessed large fines against them. Although the Supreme Court did not rule on the Act's constitutionality, it was upheld by several lower federal courts, in decisions written in some cases by Supreme Court Justices riding circuit. The Act was a major factor in the defeat of the Federalists by the Jeffersonian Republicans in the 1800 election. It expired of its own force in March 1801, and Jefferson, the new President, pardoned all of those convicted under it. Levy notes, however, that the Jeffersonians in power "were not much more tolerant of their political critics than the Federalists had been."

How did Congress pass such a speech restrictive law in the immediate aftermath of the enactment of the First Amendment? Historical context sheds some light: "[To] understand the [Sedition Act of 1798] we must appreciate the Federalists' view of 'the freedom of speech, or of the press.' In short, the Federalists had little faith in free and open debate. [The] Federalists believed that the common man could easily be manipulated and misled. [After] witnessing the violent aftershocks of the French Revolution, the Federalists had no doubt of both the power and danger of public opinion." Stone, The Story of Sedition Act of 1798, 14–17 in First Amendment Stories (Garnett & Koppelman eds., 2012). Following French aggression toward U.S. shipping vessels, Federalists were able to capitalize on the public's fear and resulting enthusiasm for war abroad. President Adams acted to further foment distrust of French sympathizers, warning in his public speeches that "the United States of America are at present placed in a hazardous and afflictive situation, by the unfriendly disposition, conduct and demands of a foreign power . . . ." It was the presence, whether real or imagined, of an external threat that permitted Congress to pass its first major restriction on civil liberties and free speech.

To Republicans, the Sedition Act was a flagrant violation of the Constitution and evidenced Adams' "appetite for tyranny." Jefferson, Madison, and other Republicans of the time rejected the English conception of freedom of speech, believing the First Amendment to prohibit more than merely prior restraints. Their hopes that the Court would intervene by finding the Act unconstitutional, however, were not realized. Justice James Iredell, while riding circuit only a few years earlier, had charged a Virginia grand jury to issue a presentment against several Republican Congressmen who had written public letters that attempted "at a time of real public danger, to disseminate unfounded calumnies against the happy government of the United States," articulating the British understanding of the Free Speech Clause in his opinion. See Thomas Jefferson to James Madison, Aug. 3, 1797, 17 Papers of James Madison 33 (quoting Richmond Gazette, May 24, 1797). Quoting Blackstone, Iredell had articulated the British understanding of the Free Speech Clause in his order: "The liberty of the press is indeed essential to the nature of a free state. And this consists in laying no previous restraints upon publications, and not in freedom from censure for criminal matter when published." To argue for their alternative interpretation, Jefferson and Madison turned to state legislatures: Jefferson to Kentucky and Madison to Virginia. Each drafted and submitted a set of resolutions to the respective states' legislatures. Madison's Virginia Resolutions asserted that the state legislature believed the Sedition Act to be unconstitutional and called on other states to make similar declarations, while Jefferson's Kentucky Resolutions would have had the states declare the law null and void. Yet other states ultimately rejected the resolutions and the Act went into effect.

4.   *Later history.* The century after the Sedition Act controversy witnessed efforts to suppress abolitionist literature during the slavery controversy, and attempts to suppress seditious publications during the Civil War, see Randall, Constitutional Problems Under Lincoln (rev. ed. 1951). But not until the World War I era did major free speech issues reach the Supreme Court. Why that was so constitutes a historical puzzle. For exploration of the antecedents of modern free speech jurisprudence in the years before World War I, see Rabban, "The First Amendment in Its Forgotten Years," 90 Yale L.J. 514 (1981); Rabban, "The Free Speech League, the ACLU, and Changing Conceptions of Free Speech in American History," 45 Stan. L. Rev. 47 (1992); Rabban, "The IWW Free Speech Fights and

Popular Conceptions of Free Expression Before World War I," 80 Va. L. Rev. 1055 (1994). For discussion on the relationship between labor organizing in the interwar period and the development of First Amendment rights, see Weinrib, The Taming of Free Speech: America's Civil Liberties Compromise (2016). Weinrib argues the concept of civil liberties was born as an adjunct to, and in service of, the radical labor movement after the First World War. However the ACLU began to reorient their agenda away from the rights of labor organizers towards a neutral vision of personal freedom of expression. Weinrib argues this latter vision, unhooked from its redistributive origins, became the modern conception of civil liberties we know today.

5. ***The right to petition.*** At a minimum, the Petition Clause ("Congress shall make no law . . . abridging . . . the right of the people . . . to petition the Government for a redress of grievances") protected an exception for speech critical of government that was formally presented to government officials. This provision had roots in Magna Carta, and a similar provision was codified in the English Bill of Rights of 1689. See Krotoszynski & Carpenter, "The Return of Seditious Libel," 55 UCLA L. Rev. 1239 (2008).

FIRST AMENDMENT THEORY

Philosophical justifications for the protection of free speech supplement the uncertain light cast by history. Free speech has been thought to serve three principal values: advancing knowledge and "truth" in the "marketplace of ideas," facilitating representative democracy and self-government, and promoting individual autonomy, self-expression and self-fulfillment. See Emerson, The System of Freedom of Expression (1970). Protection of free speech has also been defended based on a negative theory of government power, questioning both the competence and the incentives of state officials to regulate the flow of ideas among citizens. See Sullivan, "Two Concepts of Freedom of Speech," 124 Harv. L. Rev. 143 (2010). These values have animated much of the Court's reasoning in free speech cases, though not always articulately and not always consistently. What is the consequence of one emphasis or another for the implementation of First Amendment values in the decisions that follow?

1. ***Truth.*** The classic statements of the value of speech in the search for truth are those of John Milton and John Stuart Mill. John Milton wrote in 1644, protesting a licensing scheme for books: "And though all the winds of doctrine were let loose to play upon the earth, so Truth be in the field, we do injuriously, by licensing and prohibiting, to misdoubt her strength. Let her and Falsehood grapple; who ever knew Truth put to the worst, in a free and open encounter?" Milton, Areopagitica—A Speech for the Liberty of Unlicensed Printing (1644). John Stuart Mill's classic libertarian argument came two centuries after Milton's, in On Liberty (1859). Mill's central argument was that the suppression of opinion is wrong, whether or not the opinion is true: if it is true, society is denied the truth; if it is false, society is denied the fuller understanding of truth which comes from its conflict with error; and when the received opinion is part truth and part error, society can know the whole truth only by allowing the airing of competing views.

As Mill summarized his argument in Chapter II of On Liberty: "First, if any opinion is compelled to silence, that opinion may, for aught we can certainly know, be true. To deny this is to assume our own infallibility.

Secondly, though the silenced opinion be in error, it may, and very commonly does, contain a portion of the truth; and since the general or prevailing opinion on any subject is rarely or never the whole truth, it is only by the collision of adverse opinions that the remainder of the truth has any chance of being supplied. Thirdly, even if the received opinion be not only true, but the whole truth; unless it is suffered to be, and actually is, vigorously and earnestly contested, it will, by most of those who receive it, be held in the manner of a prejudice, with little comprehension or feeling of its rational grounds. And not only this, but, fourthly, the meaning of the doctrine itself will be in danger of being lost, or enfeebled."

Justice Brandeis echoed these truth-based rationales for speech protection in his concurrence in Whitney v. California, below: "freedom to think as you will and to speak as you think are means indispensable to the discovery and spread of political truth." Justice Holmes did so in a different, pragmatist vein in his dissent in Abrams v. United States, below: "[W]hen men have realized that time has upset many fighting faiths, they may come to believe even more than they believe the very foundations of their own conduct that the ultimate good desired is better reached by free trade in ideas—that the best test of truth is the power of the thought to get itself accepted in the competition of the market and that truth is the only ground upon which their wishes safely can be carried out. That at any rate is the theory of our constitution." Is there reason to expect truth to emerge through the self-regulating operation of a free "marketplace of ideas"? Any more than to expect the commercial marketplace always to be efficient or just? Recall from the Lochner materials that Justice Holmes would have allowed government considerable latitude to regulate the economic marketplace. Why would he tie government's hands and insist on laissez-faire when it comes to the marketplace of ideas?

A number of commentators have criticized the "marketplace" rationale on the ground that its assumptions do not fit the realities of a contemporary society in which certain political and economic interest groups wield disproportionate resources and power. See e.g., Barron, "Access to the Press—A New First Amendment Right," 80 Harv. L. Rev. 1641 (1967) (arguing that the notion of a "self-operating marketplace of ideas [has] long ceased to exist" and insisting that a "realistic view of the first amendment requires recognition that a right of expression is somewhat thin if it can be exercised only at the sufferance of the managers of mass communications"); Wellington, "On Freedom of Expression," 88 Yale L.J. 1105 (1979) ("In the long run, true ideas do tend to drive out false ones. The problem is that the short run may be very long."); Ingber, "The Marketplace of Ideas: A Legitimizing Myth," 1984 Duke L.J. 1 ("[T]he market is strongly biased in favor of positions that support entrenched ideas."); MacKinnon, Only Words (1993) ("These days, censorship occurs less through explicit state policy than through official and unofficial privileging of powerful groups and viewpoints. This is accomplished through silencing in many forms and enforced by the refusal of publishers and editors to publish [expressions] of dissent."). Note also Herbert Marcuse's assertion that, "[u]nder the rule of monopolistic media—themselves the mere instruments of economic and political power— a mentality is created for which right and wrong, true and false are predefined wherever they affect the vital interests of the society." Marcuse, "Repressive Tolerance," in Robert Wolff et al., A Critique of Pure Tolerance 95 (1965).

2. *Self-government.* Some emphasize that speech is essential to representative government. Brandeis made this argument in Whitney v. California (1927; p. 35), when he claimed that the Framers believed "that without free speech and assembly discussion would be futile; that with them, discussion affords ordinarily adequate protection against the dissemination of noxious doctrine; that the greatest menace to freedom is an inert people; that public discussion is a political duty; and that this should be a fundamental principle of the American government." Various justices have also emphasized the political function of free speech. For example, Justice Brennan, in New York Times Co. v. Sullivan (1967; p. 77), invoked "a profound national commitment to the principle that debate on public issues should be uninhibited, robust, and wide-open, and that it may well include vehement, caustic, and sometimes unpleasantly sharp attacks on government and public officials." And Justice Black, in Mills v. Alabama, 384 U.S. 214 (1966), stated that "there is practically universal agreement that a major purpose of [the First Amendment] was to protect the free discussion of governmental affairs."

Alexander Meiklejohn argued that "public" speech—speech on public issues affecting "self-government"—must be wholly immune from regulation, while "private" speech is entitled to less complete protection. See Meiklejohn, Free Speech and Its Relation to Self-Government (1948). He analogized public speech to a town meeting in which all viewpoints should be presented in order to arrive at wise public policy.

Zechariah Chafee, Jr., an important free-speech advocate who almost lost his Harvard professorship after criticizing the result in Abrams v. United States (1919; p. 20), criticized Meiklejohn's theory of public speech for taking too narrow a view of the First Amendment, finding it "shocking" that Meiklejohn would apparently omit to protect art and literature. See Chafee, "Book Review," 62 Harv. L. Rev. 891 (1949). Meiklejohn replied that art, literature, philosophy and the sciences should indeed be included in First Amendment protection, as they help "voters acquire the intelligence, integrity, sensitivity, and generous devotion to the general welfare that, in theory, casting a ballot is assumed to express." Meiklejohn, "The First Amendment Is an Absolute," 1961 Sup. Ct. Rev. 245. Judge and scholar Robert Bork (whose Supreme Court nomination was later rejected by the Senate) disagreed with Meiklejohn's concession: many activities beyond art and literature inform voting, but if there is not to be "an analogical stampede, the protection of the first amendment must be cut off when it reaches the outer limits of political speech." Bork, "Neutral Principles and Some First Amendment Problems," 47 Ind. L.J. 1 (1971). For contemporary discussion of the argument that the First Amendment is principally about political deliberation, compare Sunstein, Democracy and the Problem of Free Speech (1993); Sunstein, "Free Speech Now," 59 U. Chi. L. Rev. 255 (1992) and BeVier, "The First Amendment and Political Speech: An Inquiry Into the Substance and Limits of Principle," 30 Stan. L. Rev. 299 (1978) with Schauer, "The Boundaries of the First Amendment," 117 Harv. L. Rev. 1765 (2004) ("Theories based on self-government of democratic deliberation have a hard time explaining why . . . the doctrine now covers pornography, commercial advertising, and art, [none] of which has much to do with political deliberation or self-governance, except under such an attenuated definition of 'political' that the justification's core loses much of its power.").

Free speech in the political conception arguably serves at least four different functions. First, as Meiklejohn's town meeting analogy suggests, broad debate informs and improves the making of public policy. Second, free speech prevents government from entrenching itself indefinitely—it keeps clear the "channels of political change." Ely, Democracy and Distrust (1980). Third, free speech prevents government abuse of power. See Blasi, "The Checking Value in First Amendment Theory," 1977 A.B.F. Res. J. 521 (emphasizing "the value that free speech, a free press, and free assembly can serve in checking the abuse of power by public officials," and arguing that "the role of the ordinary citizen is not so much to contribute on a continuing basis to the formation of public policy as to retain a veto power to be employed when the decisions of officials pass certain bounds"). Fourth, free speech promotes political stability by providing a safety valve for dissent. As Justice Brandeis cautioned in his Whitney concurrence, "Those who won our independence [knew] that fear breeds repression; that repression breeds hate; that hate menaces stable government [and] that the path of safety lies in the opportunity to discuss freely supposed grievances and proposed remedies." See also Emerson, The System of Freedom of Expression (1970) (arguing that freedom of expression "provides a framework in which the conflict necessary to the progress of a society can take place without destroying the society").

If the principal purpose of speech is to further democracy, may government intervene in the marketplace of ideas in order to improve the deliberative quality of the discussion? For arguments along these lines, see Sunstein, supra; Fiss, "Free Speech and Social Structure," 71 Iowa L. Rev. 1405 (1986). Robert Post criticizes such "collectivist" political speech theories for assuming that there is some proper conception of good political discourse that stands outside of political debate itself. See Post, Constitutional Domains (1995).

While Meiklejohn's conception of free speech as facilitating democratic self-government focuses largely on the listener, and the capacity of free speech to inform and enlighten those who hear public debate, is there also a democratic benefit to the speaker? Consider the view that the speaker has an interest in participating in public debate in order to lend democratic legitimacy to the political process. See Post, "Participatory Democracy and Free Speech," 97 Va. L. Rev. 477 (2011); Weinstein, "Participatory Democracy as the Central Value of Free Speech Doctrine," 97 Va. L. Rev. 491 (2011).

3.   *Autonomy.* A third rationale for protecting speech emphasizes the values of individual liberty, autonomy, and self-fulfillment. Unlike the truth and self-government theories, which view speech as instrumental to desired social consequences, autonomy theories emphasize the intrinsic worth of speech to individual speakers and listeners. Justice Brandeis echoed this theme, too, in his Whitney concurrence, suggesting that "[t]hose who won our independence believed that the final end of the State was to make men free to develop their faculties; [they] valued liberty both as an end and as a means." In one view, this concept of individual self-realization encompasses both "development of the individual's powers and abilities—an individual 'realizes' his or her own full potential—[and] the individual's control of his or her own destiny through making life-affecting decisions—an individual 'realizes' the goals in life that he or she has set." Redish, The Value of Free Speech, 130 U. Penn. L. Rev. 591 (1982). An emphasis on individual self-

realization extends First Amendment protection beyond the political realm to art, literature and even entertainment and advertising. See id. (arguing that democratic self-government is not an end in itself but a means to "the much broader value of individual self-realization," and thus that the First Amendment is "much broader than Bork or Meiklejohn would have it").

Some autonomy-based theories of free speech emphasize the affirmative value of speech in the development of rational human capacities. See Baker, Human Liberty and Freedom of Speech (1989); Richards, "Free Speech and Obscenity Law: Toward a Moral Theory of the First Amendment," 123 U. Pa. L. Rev. 45 (1974); Baker, "Scope of the First Amendment Freedom of Speech," 25 UCLA L. Rev. 964 (1978); Emerson, Toward a General Theory of the First Amendment (1963). On this theory, freedom of expression is necessary to an individual's right to self-fulfillment through use of the "powers of imagination, insight and feeling." Others emphasize the obverse: the inconsistency of censorship with human autonomy, and the impropriety of paternalism as a ground for interference with speech. See Strauss, "Persuasion, Autonomy, and Freedom of Expression," 91 Colum. L. Rev. 334 (1991) (arguing that a central principle of the First Amendment is that government may not stop speech for reason of its power to persuade the listener, and that "[v]iolating the persuasion principle is wrong for some of the reasons that lies [are] wrong: both involve a denial of autonomy in the sense that they interfere with a person's control over her own reasoning processes"). See also Scanlon, "A Theory of Freedom of Expression," 1 Phil. & Pub. Aff. 204 (1972) (arguing that "an autonomous person cannot accept without independent consideration the judgment of others as to what he should believe or what he should do," including the judgment of the state expressed through the suppression of dissent). But see Scanlon, "Freedom of Expression and Categories of Expression," 40 U. Pitt. L. Rev. 519 (1979) (retreating from autonomy-centered view of speech).

Autonomy theories of speech have been criticized as being too broad. See Bork, supra (arguing that self-fulfillment is not a principle that can "distinguish speech from any other human activity," for "an individual may develop his faculties or derive pleasure from trading on the stock market [or] engaging in sexual activities," and there is no neutral way to rank speech ahead of these alternative forms of "personal gratification"). Consider as a potential response the argument that the First Amendment's meaning is premised on the preservation of dissent. On this idea, its purpose is "to protect the romantics—those who would break out of classical forms: the dissenters, the unorthodox, the outcasts" and to "sponsor the individualism, the rebelliousness, the antiauthoritarianism, the spirit of nonconformity within us all." Shiffrin, The First Amendment, Democracy, and Romance (1993). If the protection of autonomy serves to encourage dissent, does speech necessarily rank above other forms of autonomous human activity in its importance to achieving that goal? Is the autonomy rationale of the First Amendment then inextricably tied with notions of democracy and social contribution?

4. *Negative theories.* Some theories of speech protection focus less on the affirmative instrumental or intrinsic value of speech than on the special reasons to distrust government in the realm of speech regulation. Frederick Schauer thus defends free speech on the basis of an "argument from governmental incompetence"—an emphasis on "a distrust of the ability of government to make the necessary distinctions, a distrust of governmental

determinations of truth and falsity." Schauer, Free Speech: A Philosophical Enquiry (1982). Schauer states: "Even if there is nothing especially good about speech compared to other conduct, the state may have less ability to regulate speech than it has to regulate other forms of conduct, or the attempt to regulate speech may entail special harms or special dangers not present in regulation of other conduct. [Throughout] history the process of regulating speech has been marked with what we now see to be fairly plain errors"— including "the banning of numerous admittedly great works of art because someone thought them obscene." He adds that "acts of suppression that have been proved erroneous seem to represent a disproportionate percentage of the governmental mistakes of the past. [Experience] arguably shows that governments are particularly bad at censorship." He concludes: "Freedom of speech is based in large part on a distrust of the ability of government to make the necessary distinctions, a distrust of governmental determinations of truth and falsity, an appreciation of the fallibility of political leaders, and of somewhat deeper distrust of governmental power in a more general sense." See also Schauer, "The Second-Best First Amendment," 31 Wm. & Mary L. Rev. 1 (1989).

For a related argument that free speech protection should assume government is prone to pathological reactions to speech, see Blasi, "The Pathological Perspective and the First Amendment," 85 Colum. L. Rev. 449 (1985) (arguing that "the overriding objective at all times should be to equip the first amendment to do maximum service in those historical periods when intolerance of unorthodox ideas is most prevalent. [The] first amendment, in other words, should be targeted for the worst of times.").

Why might government regulation of speech be more suspect than governmental regulation of other activities? With respect to political speech, the answer is that the incumbent regime will be biased in its own favor against dissidents and challengers. Can this argument be broadened to reach cultural or social dissent as well? See Justice Jackson's opinion in the second flag salute case, West Virginia Board of Education v. Barnette (1943; p. 478): "If there is any fixed star in our constitutional constellation, it is that no official, high or petty, can prescribe what shall be orthodox in politics, nationalism, religion, or other matters of opinion or force citizens to confess by word or act their faith therein."

5. *Eclectic theories.* Are these varying rationales better considered jointly than separately? The Court itself often relies upon an amalgam of the above theories. Some commentators argue that any adequate protection of free speech must rely upon "several strands of theory in order to protect a rich variety of expressional modes." Tribe, American Constitutional Law 789 (2d ed. 1988). See also Bloustein, "The Origin, Validity, and Interrelationships of the Political Values Served by Freedom of Expression," 33 Rutgers L. Rev. 372 (1981); Shiffrin, "The First Amendment and Economic Regulation: Away From a General Theory of the First Amendment," 78 Nw. U. L. Rev. 1212 (1983).

———

FIRST AMENDMENT JURISPRUDENCE

Assuming that freedom of expression warrants protection because of its value to society and the individual, what is the appropriate judicial responsibility for protecting it? Should speech have a preferred position to other liberties in the Constitution, and thus receive greater protection from regulation than other activities? The Court has long shown special judicial solicitude for free speech, meaning that governmental action directed at expression must satisfy a greater burden of justification than governmental action directed at most other forms of behavior. What justifies this special protection of freedom of expression? Assuming that speech is to be specially protected, what judicial techniques best implement that protection? Should protection be absolute? If not, are exceptions to protection better made through categorization of types of speech as more or less valuable and of types of regulation as more or less permissible? Or is it better to uphold a speech regulation only by explicit balancing of speech values against countervailing governmental interests in each case? Do categories reflect implicit balancing in any event?

1. *Justifying special protection for speech.* Since the New Deal, the Court has deferred to government in the economic sphere, upholding a wide range of regulation against equal protection and substantive due process challenge. In speech cases, by contrast, the Court treats speech as enjoying strong presumptive protection, and frequently intervenes to strike down government regulation. Thus, the Court has declined to read the Fourteenth Amendment as mandating laissez-faire in economic markets. But it has read the First Amendment to require a considerable amount of laissez-faire in the marketplace of ideas. Justice Holmes himself expressed both positions: in his dissent in Lochner v. New York, 198 U.S. 45 (1905), he wrote that labor regulation is permissible because the liberty clause "does not enact Mr. Herbert Spencer's Social Statics," nor does it "embody a particular economic theory" of free trade. But in his dissent in Abrams v. United States (1919; p. 20), he argued that regulation of dissident speech is impermissible because the Free Speech Clause recognizes that "the ultimate good desired is better reached by free trade in ideas—that the best test of truth is the power of the thought to get itself accepted in the competition of the market."

What explains this asymmetrical approach? Is it a sufficient answer that the First Amendment explicitly mentions freedom of speech while the text of the Fourteenth Amendment is framed abstractly? One of the most influential statements of the modern Court's double standard occurs in footnote four in Justice Stone's opinion in United States v. Carolene Products Co., 304 U.S. 144 (1938). Stone spoke of a "narrower scope for operation of the presumption of constitutionality when legislation appears on its face to be within a specific prohibition of the Constitution, such as those of the first ten amendments, which are deemed equally specific when held to be embraced within the 14th." Are First Amendment rights truly more "specific" than, for example, the Contracts Clause and other protections of "property"? He also suggested, more tentatively, a "more exacting judicial scrutiny" of legislation restricting the "political processes," listing "restraints upon the dissemination of information" among his examples. But the Court's special solicitude has extended well beyond political speech.

Does the explanation lie instead in the difference between the practical functions of that speech and economic transactions play in the development of civil society? Justice Frankfurter—though he objected to the view that free speech was entitled to a "preferred position" and was often willing to defer to government speech regulation himself—suggested as much in explicating Holmes' asymmetrical opinions: "The ideas now governing the constitutional protection of freedom of speech derive essentially from the opinions of Mr. Justice Holmes, [who] seldom felt justified in opposing his own opinion to economic views which the legislature embodied in law. But since he also realized that the progress of civilization is to a considerable extent the displacement of error which once held sway as official truth by beliefs which in turn have yielded to other beliefs, for him the right to search for truth was of a different order than some transient economic dogma. And without freedom of expression, thought becomes checked and atrophied. Therefore, in considering what interests are so fundamental as to be enshrined in the Due Process Clause, those liberties of the individual which history has attested as the indispensable conditions of an open as against a closed society come to this Court with a momentum for respect lacking when appeal is made to liberties which derive merely from shifting economic arrangements." Kovacs v. Cooper, 336 U.S. 77 (1949) (Frankfurter, J., concurring).

Might it be argued that economic markets and the marketplace of ideas should be treated the same? Arguments for symmetry have been made from both directions. For an overview of these arguments, see Sullivan, "Free Speech and Unfree Markets," 42 UCLA L. Rev. 949 (1995). Some have suggested that constitutional guarantees should be rigorously enforced against regulation of both speech and economic markets. See, e.g., R.H. Coase, "The Economics of the First Amendment: The Market for Goods and the Market for Ideas," 64 Am. Econ. Rev. Proc. 384 (1974); Epstein, "Property, Speech, and the Politics of Distrust," 59 U. Chi. L. Rev. 41 (1992). For a reply to Epstein, see Michelman, "Liberties, Fair Values, and Constitutional Method," 59 U. Chi. L. Rev. 91 (1992). For criticism of the export of market metaphors to the area of speech, see Radin, Contested Commodities, Ch. 12 (1996).

Others have suggested a symmetrical move in the opposite direction: that there should be no more presumptive protection for speech against government regulation than for economic activities. On this view, there are imperfections in the marketplace of ideas, just as there are in the economic marketplace. If speech has negative external effects, if some persons or entities have monopoly power over speech, or if the distribution of speech is skewed by unequal speaking power, say these commentators, then regulation may be justified in the interest of speech itself just as regulation in the economic markets is sometimes justified in the interest of efficiency or distribution. For variations on such views, see Sunstein, Democracy and the Problem of Free Speech (1993); Schauer, "The Political Incidence of the Free Speech Principle," 64 U. Colo. L. Rev. 935 (1993); Balkin, "Some Realism About Pluralism: Legal Realist Approaches to the First Amendment," 1990 Duke L.J. 375. Neither of these arguments for symmetry has made headway with the contemporary Supreme Court, which continues to accord heightened protection to speech.

2. *Absolutes versus balancing.* An important debate in First Amendment adjudication in the 1960s was over whether First Amendment rights are "absolute" or subject to the "balancing" of competing interests. Justice Black was the principal advocate of the former position. Justice Black wrote, "I do not subscribe to ['the doctrine that permits constitutionally protected rights to be "balanced" away when a majority of the Court thinks that a State might have interest sufficient to justify abridgment of those freedoms'] for I believe that the First Amendment's unequivocal command that there shall be no abridgment of the rights of free speech and assembly

shows that the men who drafted our Bill of Rights did all the 'balancing' that was to be [done]. [I] fear that the creation of 'tests' by which speech is left unprotected under certain circumstances is a standing invitation to abridge [it]." Konigsberg v. State Bar of California, 366 U.S. 36 (1961) (Black, J., dissenting). See also Black, "The Bill of Rights," 35 N.Y.U. L. Rev. 865 (1960), and Black, A Constitutional Faith (1968).

Justices Frankfurter and Harlan rejected Black's approach and advocated explicit balancing instead. For example, Justice Harlan wrote for the majority in Konigsberg, supra, which upheld a denial of bar admission to an applicant who had refused to answer questions about Communist Party membership, as follows: "[W]e reject the view that freedom of speech and association [are] 'absolutes,' not only in the undoubted sense that where the constitutional protection exists it must prevail, but also in the sense that the scope of that protection must be gathered solely from a literal reading of the First Amendment. Throughout its history this Court has consistently recognized [that] constitutionally protected freedom of speech is narrower than an unlimited license to talk. [When] constitutional protections are asserted against the exercise of valid governmental powers a reconciliation must be effected, and that perforce requires an appropriate weighing of the respective interests involved." Similarly, Justice Frankfurter defended balancing: "Absolute rules would inevitably lead to absolute exceptions, and such exceptions would eventually corrode the rules. The demands of free speech in a democratic society as well as [countervailing governmental interests] are better served by candid and informed weighing of the competing interests, within the confines of the judicial process, than by announcing dogmas too inflexible for the non-Euclidean problems to be solved." Dennis v. United States, p. 40.

There may be somewhat less to the "absolutes"-"balancing" debate than meets the eye. See, e.g., Kalven, "Upon Rereading Mr. Justice Black on the First Amendment," 14 UCLA L. Rev. 428 (1967) (commenting that the "absolutes"-"balancing" controversy "seems to me on the whole to have been an unfortunate, misleading, and unnecessary one"). Justice Black, for example, did not support every freedom of expression claim. Justice Harlan's "balancing," on the other hand, was not necessarily deferential. In one of the flag burning cases, Street v. New York (1969; p. 260), for example, he wrote the majority opinion sustaining the First Amendment challenge while Justice Black dissented on the ground that the prosecution was not for "spoken words," but for speech "used as an integral part of conduct" in burning the flag in public. Similarly, in Cohen v. California (1971; p. 69), the "Fuck the Draft" case, Justice Harlan's statement for the majority was one of the most speech-protective (albeit largely "balancing" in approach), while Justice Black was once again in dissent.

The relative merits of absolute and balancing approaches were explored in an extended debate between Laurent Frantz and Wallace Mendelson. Frantz favored rules and argued that balancing would tend inevitably to be too deferential to government judgments or to the prejudices of the predominant political culture, and would provide inadequate guidance to decisionmakers. See Frantz, "The First Amendment in the Balance," 71 Yale L.J. 1424 (1962); Frantz, "Is the First Amendment Law? A Reply to Professor Mendelson," 51 Calif. L. Rev. 729 (1963). See also Ely, "Flag Desecration: A Case Study in the Roles of Categorization and Balancing in First Amendment Analysis," 88 Harv. L. Rev. 1482 (1975) ("[W]here messages are proscribed because they are dangerous, balancing tests inevitably become intertwined with the ideological predispositions of those doing the balancing—or if not that, at least with the relative confidence or paranoia of the age in which they are doing it."). Mendelson, in contrast, favored balancing: "Balancing seems to me the essence of the judicial process—the nexus between abstract law and concrete [life]. Surely the choice is simply this: shall the balancing be done 'intuitively' or rationally; covertly or out in the open?" Mendelson, "The First Amendment and the Judicial Process: A Reply to Mr. Frantz," 17 Vand. L. Rev. 479 (1964). For a discussion of "First Amendment balancing in the Harlan manner," see Gunther, "In Search of Judicial Quality on a Changing Court: The Case of Justice Powell," 24 Stan. L. Rev. 1001 (1972).

3.   *Categorization versus balancing.* Even if it is conceded that the First Amendment is *not* absolute, a pervasive question of judicial methodology remains: should any reduced protection for speech be analyzed in terms of "categorization" or of "balancing"? Categorization strives for "bright-line" rules. Categorization along a spectrum of relatively more or less "protected speech" distinguishes what kind of expression does or does not trigger the First Amendment's demands for special government justification before it may be regulated. Categorization of speech as protected or unprotected forecloses free-form balancing of interests in a particular case. It sorts cases into those presumptively won either by government or by the speaker. Balancing approaches, in contrast, could go either way depending on the particular facts and interests at issue. See generally Sullivan, "The Supreme Court—1991 Term—Foreword: The Justices of Rules and Standards," 106 Harv. L. Rev. 22 (1992); Sullivan, "Post-Liberal Judging: The Roles of Categorization and Balancing," 63 U. Colo. L. Rev. 293 (1992).

Categorization of types of speech finds certain varieties of speech unprotected on a wholesale basis because the claim simply does not belong in the First Amendment ballpark—either because some "utterances are no essential part of any exposition of ideas, and are of such slight social value as a step to truth," or because, as is often suggested implicitly, there are such powerful state interests justifying restrictions that the type of expression can be wholly excluded from "the freedom of speech." Chaplinsky v. New Hampshire (1942; p. 57). See generally, on this "two-level" theory of speech, Kalven, "The Metaphysics of the Law of Obscenity," 1960 Sup. Ct. Rev. 1. As noted in Farber, "The Categorical Approach to Protecting Speech in American Constitutional Law," 84 Ind. L.J. 917 (2009), in some cases "the categorical approach functions as a prepackaged form of strict scrutiny" that gives "clearer notice to speakers, as well as governments, about the boundaries of permissible regulation," and in others it signals a "perceived lack of First Amendment value." The balancing approach, by contrast, asserts that a very broad range of expression is presumptively within the First Amendment and may be found unprotected only after the restrictions are shown to be outweighed by the governmental interest in a particular case. A balancing approach, in short, permits judicial evaluations only on the state interest side of the balance, and would not shortcut the balancing process by encouraging judicial evaluations of the relative merit of the speech on the other side of the balance.

Categorization has the attraction of clarity and of providing guidance to judges and other government officials. Categorization is also defended as a recognition of the diversity of the types of speech, and a welcome alternative to the excessive flexibility of balancing. By avoiding the weighing of every allegedly protected speech manifestation against all relevant state interests, the argument goes, categorization curtails the manipulative, result-oriented uses of balancing and yields more uniform results across cases. Finally, by drawing sharp distinctions between protected and unprotected classes of speech, categorization might actually be speech-protective after all. A unitary theory of the First Amendment that would extend similarly strong protection to all varieties of communication might ultimately dilute First Amendment protections, because some types of speech will inevitably receive less protection, with the result that even the protection of core political speech will suffer. "It is inconceivable that we will ignore such well-established governmental concerns as safety, reputation, protection against fraud, and protection of children. [Certain] state interests are inevitably going to be recognized, and the alternatives then are diluting those tests that are valuable precisely because of their strength, or formulating new tests and categories that leave existing standards strong within their narrower range. [A] narrow but strong First Amendment, with its strong principle universally available for all speech covered by the First Amendment, has much to be said for it. First Amendment protection can be like an oil spill, thinning out as it broadens." Schauer, "Codifying the First Amendment: New York v. Ferber," 1982 Sup. Ct. Rev. 285. See also Sunstein, Democracy and the Problem of Free Speech (1993).

But categorization also may cast entire classes of speech outside the First Amendment on a wholesale basis, without adequate examination of the bases for the conclusion. It may also, in its striving for general and bright-line rules, unduly slight the distinctions among types of speech within the category and the differences in contexts (and competing state interests) that particular examples of excluded speech may in fact present. Finally, variation in the levels of protection for speech may result ultimately in a myriad, increasingly ad hoc range of First Amendment rules and an excessive codification harmful to long range protection of First Amendment values. For additional classic commentary on categorization and balancing in the context of free speech, see Scanlon, "Freedom of Expression and Categories of Expression," 40 U. Pitt. L. Rev. 519 (1979); and Ely, "Flag Desecration: A Case Study in the Roles of Categorization and Balancing in First Amendment Analysis," 88 Harv. L. Rev. 1482 (1975).

Ultimately, then, categorization and balancing may run together. Balancing can function effectively as a rule if it is given a sufficiently speech-protective form. When regulations are subject to strict judicial scrutiny, which requires both a showing of "compelling" state ends and the unavailability of less restrictive means, the government virtually always loses and the speaker virtually always wins. Strict scrutiny thus functions more like categorization than balancing. Likewise, minimum rationality review amounts in practice to a category in the government's favor. True balancing continues to operate only when the Court applies intermediate scrutiny to speech.

Conversely, categorization itself often reflects a prior or implicit balancing process. As Melville Nimmer argued, the Court's established categories of unprotected speech commonly emerge from "definitional balancing," a "third approach which avoids the all or nothing implications of absolutism versus ad hoc balancing." If the Court holds, for example, that knowingly or recklessly false and defamatory statements of fact are unprotected by the First Amendment, it must do so based on an implicit assumption that any individual's free speech interests involved in defamatory speech are trumped by the government's competing interests in suppressing the class of defamatory speech altogether. Thus, definitional balancing in the Court's earlier decisions generates per se rules or categories for future cases in which the balance is certain to come out the same way. Nimmer, "The Right to Speak from Times to Time: First Amendment Theory Applied to Libel and Misapplied to Privacy," 56 Cal. L. Rev. 935 (1968).

SECTION 2. INCITEMENT TO VIOLENCE OR SUBVERSION

Should the First Amendment protect incitement to engage in lawless or violent activities? Even to exhortations to overthrow government? Speech that advocates genocide or glorifies terrorism? Consider John Stuart Mill, the English philosopher, writing in On Liberty (1859): "No one pretends that actions should be as free as opinions. On the contrary, even opinions lose immunity, when the circumstances in which they are expressed are such as to constitute their expression a positive instigation to some mischievous act. An opinion that corn-dealers are starvers of the poor, or that private property is robbery, ought to be unmolested when simply circulated through the press, but may justly incur punishment when delivered orally to an excited mob assembled before the house of a corn-dealer, or when handed about among the same mob in the form of a placard."

The Court has grappled repeatedly with the line between "opinion" and "instigation," as illustrated first by a series of cases involving agitation against the war and the draft during World War I. Typically in these cases, the speaker presented claims at the core of First Amendment concerns: expression critical of government policies. The government asserted especially strong interests for restraining speech: protecting governmental operations, even assuring the survival of government. Moreover, the government's restrictions often resembled the traditional curbs on seditious libel.

Should subversive speech be regulated only when it presents a "clear and present danger" of severe harms such as violence? The Court developed such a test in cases reviewing prosecutions under section 3 of Title I of the 1917 Espionage Act and its 1918 amendments. The 1917 Act, while largely directed at espionage and disclosure of military secrets, also created three new offenses: "[1] Whoever, when the United States is at war, shall willfully make or convey false reports or false statements with intent to interfere with the operation or success of the military or naval forces of the United States or to promote the success of its enemies, and [2] whoever, when the United States is at war, shall willfully cause or attempt to cause insubordination, disloyalty, mutiny, or refusal of duty, in the military or naval forces of the United States, or [3] shall willfully obstruct the recruiting or enlistment service of the United States, to the injury of the service or of the United States, shall be punished by a fine of not more than $10,000 or imprisonment for not more than twenty years, or both." There were over 2,000 prosecutions and over 1,000 convictions in the lower federal courts under the 1917 and 1918 laws. Stone, "The Origins of the 'Bad Tendency' Test: Free Speech in Wartime," 2002 Sup. Ct. Rev. 411. Very few such cases reached the Supreme Court. In the following case, the Court rejected a First Amendment challenge to such a conviction, in a unanimous opinion by Justice Holmes.

Schenck v. United States

249 U.S. 47, 39 S. Ct. 247, 63 L. Ed. 470 (1919).

■ JUSTICE HOLMES delivered the opinion of the Court.

This is an indictment in three counts. The first charges a conspiracy to violate the Espionage Act of June 15, 1917, by causing and attempting to cause insubordination, & c., in the military and naval forces of the United States, and to obstruct the recruiting and enlistment service of the United States, when the United States was at war with the German Empire, to-wit, that the defendants wilfully conspired to have printed and circulated to men who had been called and accepted for military service [a document] alleged to be calculated to cause such insubordination and obstruction. [The] second count alleges a conspiracy to commit an offence against the United States, to-wit, to use the mails for the transmission of matter declared to be non-mailable by [the 1917 Espionage Act], to-wit, the above mentioned document. [The] third count charges an unlawful use of the mails for the transmission of the same matter. [The] defendants were found guilty on all the counts. They set up the First Amendment to the Constitution, [and] bringing the case here on that ground have argued some other points [also].

The document in question upon its first printed side recited the first section of the 13th Amendment, said that the idea embodied in it was violated by the Conscription Act and that a conscript is little better than a convict. In impassioned language it intimated that conscription was despotism in its worst form and a monstrous wrong against humanity in the interest of Wall Street's chosen few. It said "Do not submit to intimidation," but in form at least confined itself to peaceful measures such as a petition for the repeal of the act. The other and later printed side of the sheet was headed "Assert Your Rights." It stated reasons for alleging that any one violated the Constitution when he refused to recognize "your right to assert your opposition to the draft," and went on, "If you do not assert and support your rights, you are helping to deny or disparage rights which it is the solemn duty of all citizens and residents of the United States to retain." It described the arguments on the other side as coming from cunning politicians and a mercenary capitalist press, and even silent consent to the conscription law as helping to support an infamous conspiracy. It denied the power to send our citizens away to foreign shores to shoot up the people of other lands, and added that words could not express the condemnation such cold-blooded ruthlessness deserves, & c., & c., winding up, "You must do your share to maintain, support and uphold the rights of the people of this country." Of course the document would not have been sent unless it had been intended to have some effect, and we do not see what effect it could be expected to have upon persons subject to the draft except to influence them to obstruct the carrying of it out. The defendants do not deny that the jury might find against them on [this].

But it is said, suppose that that was the tendency of this circular, it is protected by the [First Amendment]. Two of the strongest expressions are said to be quoted respectively from well-known public men. It well may be that the prohibition of laws abridging the freedom of speech is not confined to previous restraints, although to prevent them may have been the main purpose, as intimated in Patterson v. Colorado, 205 U.S. 454 [1907]. We admit that in many places and in ordinary times the defendants in saying all that was said in the circular would have been within their constitutional rights. But the character of every act depends upon the circumstances in which it is done. The most stringent protection of free speech would not protect a man in falsely shouting fire in a theatre and causing a panic. [The] question in every case is whether the words used are used in such circumstances and are of such a nature as to create a clear and present danger that they will bring about the substantive evils that Congress has a right to prevent. It is a question of proximity and degree. When a nation is at war many things that might be said in time of peace are such a hindrance to its effort that their utterance will not be endured so long as men fight, and that no Court could regard them as protected by any constitutional right. It seems to be admitted that if an actual obstruction of the recruiting service were proved, liability for words that produced that effect might be enforced. [The 1917 law] punishes conspiracies to obstruct as well as actual obstruction. If the act (speaking, or circulating a paper), its tendency and the intent with which it is done are the same, we perceive no ground for saying that success alone warrants making the act a [crime]. Affirmed.

———

THE "CLEAR AND PRESENT DANGER" TEST

1. *Holmes's formulation.* What is the meaning of "clear and present danger" as used in Schenck? Holmes had made important contributions to the law of criminal attempt when he sat on the Massachusetts Supreme Judicial Court. See, e.g., Commonwealth v. Peaslee, 59 N.E. 55 (Mass. 1901) (Holmes, J.), which involved the attempted arson conviction of a defendant who had gathered flammable materials but had not ignited them: "The question on the evidence [is] whether the defendant's acts come near enough to the accomplishment of the substantive offense to be punishable. [It] is a question of degree. [The] degree of proximity held sufficient may vary with [circumstances]." Is the clear and present danger test simply a common law-like test for determining when speech comes close enough to causing a crime to be punished? Should mere speech ever count as preparation for crime outside the narrow case of direct solicitation of an accomplice?

2. *Early application of the test to uphold convictions.* Schenck was followed within a week by two other unanimous decisions authored by Justice Holmes, Frohwerk and Debs, which purported to follow Schenck. In **Frohwerk v. United States**, 249 U.S. 204 (1919), Justice HOLMES again spoke for the Court in affirming convictions under the 1917 Act for conspiracy and attempt to cause disloyalty, mutiny and refusal of duty in the military and naval forces of the United States—all on account of publishing and circulating twelve newspaper articles: "We think it necessary to add to what has been said in [Schenck] only that the First Amendment while prohibiting legislation against free speech as such cannot have been, and obviously was not, intended to give immunity for every possible use of language. [We] venture to believe that neither Hamilton nor Madison, nor any other competent person then or later, ever supposed that to make criminal the counseling of a murder within the jurisdiction of Congress would be an unconstitutional interference with free speech. [We] have

decided in [Schenck] that a person may be convicted of a conspiracy to obstruct recruiting by words of persuasion.

"[S]o far as the language of the articles goes there is not much to choose between expressions to be found in them and those before us in [Schenck]. The first begins by declaring it a monumental and inexcusable mistake to send our soldiers to France, says that it comes no doubt from the great trusts, and later that it appears to be outright murder without serving anything practical; speaks of the unconquerable spirit and undiminished strength of the German nation, and characterizes its own discourse as words of warning to the American people. [There] is much more to the general effect that we are in the wrong and are giving false and hypocritical reasons for our course, but the foregoing is enough to indicate the kind of matter with which we have to deal. [On] this record it is impossible to say that it might not have been found that the circulation of the paper was in quarters where a little breath would be enough to kindle a flame and that the fact was known and relied upon by those who sent the paper out."

In **Debs v. United States**, 249 U.S. 211 (1919), a companion case to Frohwerk, the defendant was Eugene V. Debs, the longtime leader and frequent presidential candidate of the Socialist Party. In 1912, Debs had gotten over 900,000 votes, nearly 6% of the total. In 1920 (while Debs was in jail because of the conviction affirmed in this case) he again received over 900,000 votes, 3.4% of the total vote. Debs did not serve the full ten-year term to which he was sentenced: in 1921, he was released, on order of President Harding. The Court considered two counts of the indictment concerning Debs's delivery of a speech at the state convention of the Ohio Socialist Party. The first alleged that, in June 1918, Debs had "caused and incited and attempted to cause and incite insubordination, disloyalty, mutiny and refusal of duty in the [armed] forces" and "with intent so to do delivered, to an assembly of people, a public speech." The second alleged that he "obstructed and attempted to obstruct the recruiting and enlistment service" of the U.S. and "to that end and with that intent delivered the same speech." In affirming the conviction, Justice HOLMES wrote:

"The main theme of the speech was socialism, its growth, and a prophecy of its ultimate success. With that we have nothing to do, but if a part or the manifest intent of the more general utterances was to encourage those present to obstruct the recruiting service and if in passages such encouragement was directly given, the immunity of the general theme may not be enough to protect the speech. The speaker began by saying that he had just returned from a visit to the workhouse in the neighborhood where three of their most loyal comrades were paying the penalty for their devotion to the working class—[persons] who had been convicted of aiding and abetting another in failing to register for the draft. He said that he had to be prudent and might not be able to say all that he thought, thus intimating to his hearers that they might infer that he meant more, but he did say that those persons were paying the penalty for standing erect and for seeking to pave the way to better conditions for all mankind. Later he added further eulogies and said that he was proud of them. [There] followed personal experiences and illustrations of the growth of socialism, a glorification of minorities, and a prophecy of the success of the international socialist crusade, with the interjection that 'you need to know that you are fit for something better than slavery and cannon fodder.' The rest of the discourse had only the indirect though not necessarily ineffective bearing on the offences alleged that is to be found in the usual contrasts between capitalists and laboring men, sneers at the advice to cultivate war gardens, attribution to plutocrats of the high price of coal, & c. [The] defendant addressed the jury himself, and while contending that his speech did not warrant the charges said 'I have been accused of obstructing the war. I admit it. Gentlemen, I abhor war. I would oppose the war if I stood alone.' The statement was not necessary to warrant the jury in finding that one purpose of the speech, whether incidental or not does not matter, was to oppose not only war in general but this war, and that the opposition was so expressed that its natural and intended effect would be to obstruct recruiting. If that was intended and if, in all the circumstances, that would be its probable effect it would not be protected by reason of its being part of a general program and expressions of a general and conscientious belief.

"[The chief defense] based upon the First Amendment [was disposed of in Schenck]. There was introduced [in evidence] an 'Anti-war Proclamation and Program' adopted at St. Louis in April, 1917, coupled with testimony that about an hour before his speech the defendant had stated that he approved of that platform in spirit and in substance. [Counsel] argued against its admissibility, at some length. This document contained the usual suggestion that capitalism was the cause of the war and that our entrance into it 'was instigated by the predatory capitalists in the United States.' [Its] first recommendation was, 'continuous, active, and public opposition to the war, through demonstrations, mass petitions, and all other means within our power.' Evidence that the defendant accepted this view and this declaration of his duties at the time that he made his speech is evidence that if in that speech he used words tending to obstruct the recruiting service he meant that they should have that effect. [We] should add that the jury were most carefully instructed that they could not find the defendant guilty for advocacy of any of his opinions unless the words used had as their natural tendency and reasonably probable effect to obstruct the recruiting service, & c., and unless the defendant had the specific intent to do so in his mind. Without going into further particulars we are of opinion that the verdict on the fourth count, for obstructing and attempting to obstruct the recruiting service of the United States, must be sustained. Therefore it is less important to consider whether that upon the third count, for causing and attempting to cause insubordination, & c., in the military and naval forces, is equally impregnable. The jury were instructed that for the purposes of the statute the persons designated by the Act of May 18, 1917, registered and enrolled under it, and thus subject to be called into the active service, were a part of the military forces of the United States. The Government presents a strong argument from the history of the statutes that the instruction was correct and in accordance with established legislative usage. We see no sufficient reason for differing from the [conclusion]."

———

Abrams v. United States
250 U.S. 616, 40 S. Ct. 17, 63 L. Ed. 1173 (1919).

[After seizing power during the Russian Revolution of 1917, the revolutionary government in the Soviet Union signed a peace treaty with Germany; the overthrown Czarist government of Russia had been an ally of the United States in the war against Germany. In 1918, the United States sent military forces to cities in the northern part of the Soviet Union. The Abrams defendants were Russian immigrants and, according to their own testimony, "revolutionists" and "anarchists." Perceiving the American military expedition as an attempt to "crush the Russian revolution," they wrote and distributed thousands of circulars on New York City streets advocating a general strike and appealing to workers in ammunitions factories to stop producing weapons to be used against the Russian revolutionaries. They were charged under the 1918 amendments to the Espionage Act for committing actions "intended to incite, provoke and encourage resistance to the United States" during World War I, and of conspiring "to urge, incite and advocate curtailment of production [of] ordnance and ammunition, necessary [to] the prosecution of the war."]

- JUSTICE CLARKE delivered the opinion of the Court.

It will not do to say [that] the only intent of these defendants was to prevent injury to the Russian cause. Men must be held to have intended, and to be accountable for, the effects which their acts were likely to produce. Even if their primary purpose and intent was to aid the cause of the Russian Revolution, the plan of action which they adopted necessarily involved, before it could be realized, defeat of the war program of the United States, for the obvious effect of this appeal, if it should become effective, as they hoped it might, would be to persuade persons of character such as those whom they regarded themselves as addressing not to aid government loans and not to work in ammunition factories where their work would produce 'bullets, bayonets, cannon' and other munitions of war, the use of which would cause the 'murder' of Germans and [Russians]. [The] interpretation we have put upon these articles circulated in the greatest port of our land, from which great numbers of soldiers were at the time taking ship daily, and in which great quantities of war supplies of every kind were at the time being manufactured for transportation overseas, is [the] fair interpretation of [them]. [The writings] sufficiently show, that while the immediate occasion for this particular outbreak of lawlessness, on the part of the defendant alien anarchists, may have been resentment caused by our Government sending troops into Russia as a strategic operation against the Germans on the eastern battle front, yet the plain purpose of their propaganda was to excite, at the supreme crisis of the war, disaffection, sedition, riots, and, as they hoped, revolution, in this country for the purpose of embarrassing and if possible defeating the military plans of the Government in Europe.

- JUSTICE HOLMES, joined by JUSTICE BRANDEIS, dissenting.

This indictment is founded wholly upon the publication of two leaflets which I shall describe in a moment. [There were four counts; the majority found sufficient evidence to justify conviction under the third and fourth.] The third count alleges a conspiracy to encourage resistance to the United States in the [war with Germany] and to attempt to effectuate the purpose by publishing the [two] leaflets. The fourth count lays a conspiracy to incite curtailment of production of things necessary to the prosecution of the war and to attempt to accomplish it by publishing the second [leaflet]. The first of these leaflets says that the President's cowardly silence about the intervention in Russia reveals the hypocrisy of the plutocratic gang in Washington. It intimates that "German militarism combined with allied capitalism to crush the Russian revolution"; goes on that the tyrants of the world fight each other until they see a common enemy—working class enlightenment, when they combine to crush it; and that now militarism and capitalism combined, though not openly, to crush the Russian revolution. It says that there is only one enemy of the workers of the world and that is capitalism; that it is a crime for workers of America, & c., to fight the workers' republic of Russia, and ends "Awake! Awake, you Workers of the World! Revolutionists." A note adds "It is absurd to call us pro-German. We hate and despise German militarism more than do you hypocritical tyrants. We have more reasons for denouncing German militarism than has the coward of the White House."

The other leaflet, headed "Workers Wake Up," with abusive language says that America together with the Allies will march for Russia to help the Czecho-Slovaks in their struggle against the Bolsheviki, and that this time the hypocrites shall not fool the Russian emigrants and friends of Russia in America. It tells the Russian emigrants that they now must spit in the face of the false military propaganda by which their sympathy and help to the prosecution of the war have been called forth and says that with the money they have lent or are going to lend "they will make bullets not only for the Germans but also for the Workers Soviets of Russia," and further, "Workers in the ammunition factories, you are producing bullets, bayonets, cannon, to murder not only the Germans, but also your dearest, best, who are in Russia and are fighting for freedom." It then appeals to the same Russian emigrants at some length not to consent to the "inquisitionary expedition to Russia," and says that the destruction of the Russian revolution is "the politics of the march to Russia." The leaflet winds up by saying "Workers, our reply to this barbaric intervention has to be a general strike!," and after a few words on the spirit of revolution, exhortations not to be afraid, and some usual tall talk ends "Woe unto those who will be in the way of progress. Let solidarity live! The Rebels."

[With regard to the fourth count] it seems too plain to be denied that the suggestion to workers in the ammunition factories that they are producing bullets to murder their dearest, and the further advocacy of a general strike, both in the second leaflet, do urge curtailment of production of things necessary to the prosecution of the war within the meaning of [the 1918 amendments of the] Act of 1917. But to make the conduct criminal that statute requires that it should be "with intent by such curtailment to cripple or hinder the United States in the prosecution of the war [with Germany]." It seems to me that no such intent is proved. I am aware of course that the word intent as vaguely used in ordinary legal discussion means no more than knowledge at the time of the act that the consequences said to be intended will ensue. Even less than that will satisfy the general principle of civil and criminal liability. But, when words are used exactly, a deed is not done with intent to produce a consequence unless that consequence is the aim of the deed. It may be obvious, and obvious to the actor, that the consequence will follow, and he may be liable for it even if he regrets it, but he does not do the act with intent to produce it unless the aim to produce it is the proximate motive of the specific act, although there may be some deeper motive behind. It seems to me that this statute must be taken to use its words in a strict and accurate sense. They would be absurd in any other. A patriot might think that we were wasting money on aeroplanes, or making more cannon of a certain kind than we needed, and might advocate curtailment with success, yet even if it turned out that the curtailment hindered and was thought by other minds to have been obviously likely to hinder the United States in the prosecution of the war, no one would hold such conduct a crime. I admit that my illustration does not answer all that might be said but it is enough to show what I think and to let me pass to a more important aspect of the case. I refer to the [First Amendment].

I never have seen any reason to doubt that the questions of law that alone were before this Court in the cases of [Schenck, Frohwerk, and Debs] were rightly decided. I do not doubt for a moment that by the same reasoning that would justify punishing persuasion to murder, the United States constitutionally may punish speech that produces or is intended to produce a clear and imminent danger that it will bring about forthwith certain substantive evils that the United States constitutionally may seek to prevent. The power undoubtedly is greater in time of war than in time of peace because war opens dangers that do not exist at other times. But as against dangers peculiar to war, as against others, the principle of the right to free speech is always the same. It is only the present danger of immediate evil or an intent to bring it about that warrants Congress in setting a limit to the expression of opinion where private rights are not concerned. Congress certainly cannot forbid all effort to change the mind of the country. Now nobody can suppose that the surreptitious publishing of a silly leaflet by an unknown man, without more, would present any immediate danger that its opinions would hinder the success of the government arms or have any appreciable tendency to do so. Publishing those opinions for the very purpose of obstructing, however, might indicate a greater danger and at any rate would have the quality of an attempt. So I assume that the second leaflet if published for the purposes alleged in the fourth count might be punishable. [But] I do not see how anyone can find the intent required by the statute in any of the defendants' words. The second leaflet is the only one that affords even a foundation for the charge, and there, without invoking the hatred of German militarism expressed in the former one, it is evident from the beginning to the end that the only object of the paper is to help Russia and stop American intervention there against the popular government—not to impede the United States in the war that it was carrying on. To say that two phrases taken literally might import a suggestion of conduct that would have interference with the war as an indirect and probably undesired effect seems to me by no means enough to show an attempt to produce that effect.

In this case sentences of twenty years imprisonment have been imposed for the publishing of two leaflets that I believe the defendants had as much right to publish as the Government has to publish the Constitution of the United States now vainly invoked by them. Even if I am technically wrong and enough can be squeezed from these poor and puny anonymities to turn the color of legal litmus paper; I will add, even if what I think the necessary intent were shown; the most nominal punishment seems to me all that possibly could be inflicted, unless the defendants are to be made to suffer not for what the indictment alleges but for the creed that they avow—a creed that I believe to be the creed of ignorance and immaturity when honestly held, as I see no reason to doubt that it was held here, but which, although made the subject of examination at the trial, no one has a right even to consider in dealing with the charges before the Court.

Persecution for the expression of opinions seems to me perfectly logical. If you have no doubt of your premises or your power and want a certain result with all your heart you naturally express your wishes in law and sweep away all opposition. To allow opposition by speech seems to indicate that you think the speech impotent, as when a man says that he has squared the circle, or that you do not care whole-heartedly for the result, or that you doubt either your power or your premises. But when men have realized that time has upset many fighting faiths, they may come to believe even more than they believe the very foundations of their own conduct that the ultimate good desired is better reached by free trade in ideas—that the best test of truth is the power of the thought to get itself accepted in the competition of the market, and that truth is the only ground upon which their wishes safely can be carried out. That at any rate is the theory of our Constitution. It is an experiment, as all life is an experiment. Every year if not every day we have to wager our salvation upon some prophecy based upon imperfect knowledge. While that experiment is part of our system I think that we should be eternally vigilant against attempts to check the expression of opinions that we loathe and believe to be fraught with death, unless they so imminently threaten immediate interference with the lawful and pressing purposes of the law that an immediate check is required to save the country. I wholly disagree with the argument of the Government that the First Amendment left the common law as to seditious libel in force. History seems to me against the notion. I had conceived that the United States through many years had shown its repentance for the Sedition Act of 1798, by repaying fines that it imposed. Only the emergency that makes it immediately dangerous to leave the correction of evil counsels to time warrants making any exception to the sweeping command, "Congress shall make no [law] abridging the freedom of speech." Of course I am speaking only of expressions of opinion and exhortations, which were all that were uttered here, but I regret that I cannot put into more impressive words my belief that in their conviction upon this indictment the defendants were deprived of their rights under the [Constitution].

————

ALTERNATIVES TO CLEAR AND PRESENT DANGER

1. *An intermediate, consequentialist approach.* The "clear and present danger" test set forth by Justice Holmes in Schenck and applied in Frohwerk, Debs, and (over Holmes's dissent) in Abrams, steers between two poles: one pole of the debate holds that restriction on speech, at least political speech, is *never* legitimate to prevent subversion, violence, or other types of law violation—that punishment must be limited to illegal action, even if the speech directly "incites" that action. Holmes rejected that "perfect immunity" for speech. At the other pole, it has been argued that "[t]here [should] be no constitutional protection for any speech advocating the violation of law." Bork, "Neutral Principles and Some First Amendment Problems," 47 Ind. L.J. 1 (1971). On this view, a democracy need not tolerate speech that would reject its own commitment to liberal toleration and peaceful electoral change. Holmes likewise rejected that approach; "clear and present danger" purports to draw the line between these poles, with special emphasis on consequences of speech. But Holmes also rejected a more restrictive intermediate solution: the "bad tendency" test widely applied by the lower courts at the time, which held that "any tendency in speech to produce bad acts, no matter how remote, would suffice to validate a repressive statute." Chafee, "Book Review," 62 Harv. L. Rev. 891 (1949).

2. *Tightening the requirements of clear and present danger.* Holmes's Schenck opinion appeared to reject the "bad tendency" test in favor of a test of "clear and present" immediacy, assuring special attention to the

immediate risk of an evil. But note the reference to "the act, [its] tendency and the intent" at the end of the opinion. What is the relevance of "intent" to immediate risk of harm? Is the "shouting fire" analogy relevant to political speech? What if the speaker believes that there is a fire? Was Holmes's approach in Frohwerk more protective of speech than the "bad tendency" test? The Frohwerk opinion refers to "language that might be taken to convey an innuendo of a different sort," and to "a little breath" that might "kindle a flame." Did Holmes persuasively demonstrate the "clear and present danger" of Debs's speech? Did he deprecate the "general theme" unduly? Did he unduly emphasize what "his hearers [might] infer"? Was a "natural tendency and reasonably probable effect" enough to send Debs to jail? Should the speech of a national candidate for President be treated the same as a cry of "fire" in a crowded theater?

The Abrams dissent emphasizes immediacy more than its predecessors. Does it concentrate adequately on immediate proximity of speech to danger? Note the comment about a "silly leaflet" that would not present "any immediate danger" *or* "have any appreciable tendency to do so." Is "tendency" enough? Note also the reference to "the present danger of immediate evil" *or* "an intent to bring it about." Should "intent" be enough? Are "tendency" and "intent" reliable indicia of immediacy of danger? Is Holmes's approach applicable only in contexts (as with the 1917 Act) where the law is mainly directed at an evil other than speech (e.g., obstruction of military recruiting), and where speech is evidence of the risk of that evil? Or is it also useful when the legislature proscribes speech directly? Does Holmes accept the legislative statement of the evil? Must speech create immediate risk of causing the legislatively determined evil—e.g., interference with recruiting? Or does the Court define the evil? Note the reference to "an immediate [check] required to save the country," in Holmes's last paragraph. Is Holmes concerned with the gravity of the evil? Do immediacy requirements vary with gravity?

3. *The evolution of Holmes's Abrams dissent.* The Abrams dissent, with its genuine immediacy requirement, arguably made the clear and present danger test more speech-protective than did Schenck-Frohwerk-Debs. Did Justice Holmes change his mind about free speech in the period between the Schenck trilogy of cases in the spring of 1919 and the Abrams dissent in the fall of that year? Some of Justice Holmes's correspondence suggests as much. Gerald Gunther concluded "that Holmes was [at the time of Schenck] quite insensitive to any claim for special judicial protection of free speech; that the Schenck standard was not truly speech-protective; and that it was not until the fall of 1919, with his famous dissent in [Abrams], that Holmes put some teeth into the clear and present danger formula, at least partly as a result of probing criticism by acquaintances such as Learned Hand." Gunther, "Learned Hand and the Origins of Modern First Amendment Doctrine: Some Fragments of History," 27 Stan. L. Rev. 719 (1975); see also Gunther, Learned Hand: the Man and the Judge 161–70 (1994). In the summer of 1918, for example, Holmes, in a letter to Hand, espoused the "natural right" to silence "the other fellow when he disagrees": free speech, he insisted, "stands no differently than freedom from vaccination"—a freedom that the state could legitimately curtail, as demonstrated in Jacobson v. Massachusetts, 197 U.S. 11 (1905), a decision consistent with Justice Holmes's generally deferential due process philosophy. In 1918, Holmes seemed impervious to Hand's arguments that the "natural right" to silence dissenters must be curbed by the law in the interests of democratic presuppositions and the search for truth.

Debs provoked criticism of Holmes both by Hand in correspondence and by Ernst Freund in an article in The New Republic. Freund wrote that "to be permitted to agitate at your own peril, subject to a jury's guessing at motive, tendency and possible effect, makes the right of free speech a precarious gift." Freund, "The Debs Case and Freedom of Speech," The New Republic, May 3, 1919, reprinted at 40 U. Chi. L. Rev. 239 (1973). And in the spring of 1919, Hand insisted to Holmes that liability for speech should not rest on guesses about the future impact of the words (but only "when the words [are] directly an incitement." Holmes wrote back, "I don't quite get your point." Hand wrote to Freund, "I have so far been unable to make [Holmes] see that he and we have any real differences." The Abrams dissent may have indicated some eventual responsiveness on Holmes's part to these criticisms. See Gunther, Learned Hand: the Man and the Judge, at 164–66. For further argument that Holmes's attitude toward free speech did shift significantly in 1919, see White, "Justice Holmes and the Modernization of Free Speech Jurisprudence: The Human Dimension," 80 Calif. L. Rev. 391 (1992).

For the contrary view that Holmes's views were consistent but that he was simply "biding his time until the Court should have before it a conviction so clearly wrong as to let him speak out his deepest thoughts about the First Amendment," see Chafee, Free Speech in the United States 86 (1941). For further argument that Holmes's views did not undergo a conversion, see Novick, Honorable Justice 473–74 (1989); Novick, "The Unrevised Holmes and Freedom of Expression," 1991 Sup. Ct. Rev. 303.

4. *An alternative approach: Learned Hand and the Masses case.* Two years before the issue reached the Court in Schenck, the problem of interpreting the Espionage Act of 1917 arose in a case before Learned Hand, then a District Judge for the Southern District of New York. Hand's opinion in Masses plainly reveals considerable solicitude for speech, but it does so without mentioning clear and present danger. Although the opinion was technically only an interpretation of the Act, Hand's private correspondence makes clear that it was designed as a carefully considered alternative to the prevalent constitutional analyses of free speech issues. See Gunther, Learned Hand: the Man and the Judge, at 151–61, 168–69. Consider the advantages and disadvantages of Hand's approach in the World War I context. How would Schenck, Debs, or Abrams have gone under that standard? Would Hand's approach have avoided some of the difficulties of the clear and present danger test?

––––––––

Masses Publishing Co. v. Patten
244 Fed. 535 (S.D.N.Y.1917).

■ LEARNED HAND, DISTRICT JUDGE.

The plaintiff applies for a preliminary injunction against the postmaster of New York to forbid his refusal to accept its magazine in the mails under the following circumstances: The plaintiff is a publishing company in the city of New York engaged in the production of a monthly revolutionary journal called "The Masses," containing both text and cartoons. [In] July, 1917, the postmaster of New York, acting upon the direction of the Postmaster General, advised the plaintiff that the August [issue] to which he had had access would be denied the mails under the Espionage Act of June 15, 1917.

[T]he defendant, while objecting generally that the whole purport of the [issue] was in violation of the law, since it tended to produce a violation of the law, to encourage the enemies of the United States, and to hamper the government in the conduct of the war, specified four cartoons and four pieces of text as especially falling within [the 1917 Act]. [In] this case there is no dispute of fact which the plaintiff can successfully challenge except the meaning of the words and pictures in the magazine.

Coming to the act itself, [I] turn directly to section 3 of title 1, which the plaintiff is said to violate. That section contains three provisions. The first is, in substance, that no one shall make any false statements with intent to interfere with the operation or success of the military or naval forces of the United States or to promote the success of its enemies. The defendant says that the cartoons and text of the magazine, constituting, as they certainly do, a virulent attack upon the war, [may] interfere with the success of the military forces of the United States. That such utterances may have the effect so ascribed to them is unhappily true. [Dissension] within a country is a high source of comfort and assistance to its [enemies]. All this, however, is beside the question whether such an attack is a willfully false statement. That phrase properly includes only a statement of fact which the utterer knows to be false, and it cannot be maintained that any of these statements are of fact, or that the plaintiff believes them to be false. They are all within the range of opinion and of criticism; they are all certainly believed to be true by the utterer. As such they fall within the scope of that right to criticise either by temperate reasoning, or by immoderate and indecent invective, which is normally the privilege of the individual in countries dependent upon the free expression of opinion as the ultimate source of authority.

The next phrase relied upon is that which forbids any one from willfully causing insubordination, disloyalty, mutiny, or refusal of duty in the military or naval forces of the United States. The defendant's position is that to arouse discontent and disaffection among the people with the prosecution of the war and with the draft tends to promote a mutinous and insubordinate temper among the troops. This, too, is true; men who become satisfied that they are engaged in an enterprise dictated by the unconscionable selfishness of the rich, and effectuated by a tyrannous disregard for the will of those who must suffer and die, will be more prone to insubordination than those who have faith in the cause and acquiesce in the means. Yet to interpret the word "cause" so broadly would, as before, involve necessarily as a consequence the suppression of all hostile criticism, and of all opinion except what encouraged and supported the existing policies, or which fell within the range of temperate argument. It would contradict the normal assumption of democratic government that the suppression of hostile criticism does not turn upon the justice of its substance or the decency and propriety of its temper.

The defendant's position, therefore, in so far as it involves the suppression of the free utterance of abuse and criticism of the existing law, or of the policies of the war, is not, in my judgment, supported by the language of the statute. Yet there has always been a recognized limit to such expressions, incident indeed to the existence of any compulsive power of the state itself. One may not counsel or advise others to violate the law as it stands. Words are not only the keys of persuasion, but the triggers of action, and those which have no purport but to counsel the violation of law cannot by any latitude of interpretation be a part of that public opinion which is the final source of government in a democratic state. To counsel or advise a man to an act is to urge upon him either that it is his interest or his duty to do it. While, of course, this may be accomplished as well by indirection as expressly, since words carry the meaning that they impart, the definition is exhaustive, I think, and I shall use it. Political agitation, by the passions it arouses or the convictions it engenders, may in fact stimulate men to the violation of law. Detestation of existing policies is easily transformed into forcible resistance of the authority which puts them in execution, and it would be folly to disregard the causal relation between the two. Yet to assimilate agitation, legitimate as such, with direct incitement to violent resistance, is to disregard the tolerance of all methods of political agitation which in normal times is a safeguard of free government. The distinction is not a scholastic subterfuge, but a hard-bought acquisition in the fight for freedom, and the purpose to disregard it must be evident when the power exists. If one stops short of urging upon others that it is their duty or their interest to resist the law, it seems to me one should not be held to have attempted to cause its violation.

It seems to me, however, quite plain that none of the language and none of the cartoons in this paper can be thought directly to counsel or advise insubordination or mutiny, without a violation of their meaning quite beyond any tolerable understanding. I come, therefore, to the third phrase of the section, which forbids any one from willfully obstructing the recruiting or enlistment service of the United States. [Here] again, [since] the question is of the expression of opinion, I construe the sentence, so far as it restrains public utterance, as I have construed the other two, and as therefore limited to the direct advocacy of resistance to the recruiting and enlistment service. If so, the inquiry is narrowed to the question whether any of the challenged matter may be said to advocate resistance to the draft, taking the meaning of the words with the utmost latitude which they can bear. As to the cartoons it seems to me quite clear that they do not fall within such a test.

The text offers more embarrassment. The poem to Emma Goldman and Alexander Berkman, at most, goes no further than to say that they are martyrs in the cause of love among nations. Such a sentiment holds them up to admiration, and hence their conduct to possible emulation. [The] paragraphs upon conscientious objectors are of the same kind. [It] is plain enough that the paper has the fullest sympathy for these people, that it admires their courage, and that it presumptively approves their conduct. [Moreover], these passages [occur] in a magazine which attacks with the utmost violence the draft and the war. That such comments have a tendency to arouse emulation in others is clear enough but that they counsel others to follow these examples is not so plain. Literally at least they do not, and while, as I have said, the words are to be taken, not literally, but according to their full import, the literal meaning is the starting point for interpretation. One may admire and approve the course of a hero without feeling any duty to follow him. There is not the least implied intimation in these words that others are under a duty to follow. The most that can be said is that, if others do follow, they will get the same admiration and the same approval. Now, there is surely an appreciable distance between esteem and emulation; and unless there is here some advocacy of such emulation, I cannot see how the passages can be said to fall within [the law]. The question before me is quite the same as what would arise upon a motion to dismiss an indictment at the close of the proof: Could any reasonable man say, not that the indirect result of the language might be to arouse a seditious disposition, for that would not be enough, but that the language directly advocated resistance to the draft? I cannot think that upon such language any verdict would [stand].

————

COMPARING THE HOLMES AND HAND APPROACHES

1. *The aftermath of Masses.* District Judge Hand's decision granting the preliminary injunction was swiftly reversed on appeal. Masses Publishing Co. v. Patten, 246 Fed. 24 (2d Cir.1917). The Circuit not only emphasized the broad administrative discretion of the Postmaster General, but also disagreed with Hand's incitement test: "This court does not agree that such is the law. If the natural and reasonable effect of what is said is to encourage resistance to a law, and the words are used in an endeavor to persuade to resistance, it is immaterial that the duty to resist is not mentioned, or the interest of the persons addressed in resistance is not suggested." As Hand wrote in one of his letters, his opinion "seemed to meet with practically no professional approval whatever." Gunther, Learned Hand: the Man and the Judge 160 (1994). He was passed over at the time for promotion to the Second Circuit. Without the ability to use the mails, The Masses could not reach its intended audience. Its editors were soon indicted and tried for Espionage Act violations, though several juries hung and failed to convict. The Masses soon went out of business.

2. *Masses and statutory construction.* Note that Hand casts his opinion in terms of statutory construction, suggesting that Congress should not be assumed to have passed a broadly speech-suppressive law without a clear statement. A reexamination of the legislative history suggests that Congress did not in fact intend to prohibit broadly all criticism of the war effort: "Although Congress's stance in enacting the Espionage Act could hardly be characterized as civil libertarian, its elimination of [a proposed] press censorship provision (over the strong objections of the President)," and its "abandonment of [proposed] 'treasonable or anarchistic' language in the 'nonmailability' provision" arguably "reflected a genuine concern for the potential impact of the legislation on the freedoms of speech and press." Stone, "Judge Learned Hand and the Espionage Act of 1917: a Mystery Unraveled," 70 U. Chi. L. Rev. 335 (2003). Does this suggest that Hand was correct that federal prosecutors were stretching the Espionage Act beyond its intended limits in pursuing publications like The Masses?

3. *The strengths and weaknesses of Hand's incitement test.* How does the Masses "incitement" standard differ from "clear and present danger"? Hand's test focused less on forecasts about the likelihood that the speech would produce danger (e.g., draft obstruction) and focused more on the speaker's words. Does the shift in focus from proximity of danger to content of speech promote greater protection of speech? How would Eugene Debs have fared under the Masses approach? Are courts more competent to use traditional judicial tools to scrutinize words for evidence of incitement than they are to assess risks and hazard guesses about the possible future impact of words in complex contexts? Or does the Masses approach underestimate the importance of context in discerning incitement? How would it deal with the indirect but purposeful incitement of Marc Anthony's oration over the body of Caesar? How would it deal with the problem of the harmless inciter, the speaker explicitly urging law violation but with little realistic hope of success? Should even express incitement sometimes be

protected? See Scanlon, "A Theory of Freedom of Expression," 1 Phil. & Pub. Aff. 204 (1972) (arguing that speech may not be restricted on the ground that it will lead listeners to believe "subsequent harmful acts [to] be worth performing").

4. ***The historical background of the Hand-Holmes contrast.*** Learned Hand's correspondence reveals that he perceived a considerable difference between his Masses approach and Holmes's clear and present danger test, even as refined in the Abrams dissent, which he welcomed. In a series of letters from 1919 to 1921 to Professor Zechariah Chafee, Jr., the period's most prominent commentator on First Amendment problems, Hand elaborated the differences between the Masses analysis and the alternatives. See Gunther, Learned Hand: the Man and the Judge 167–70 (1994). As Hand wrote to Chafee, soon after Abrams: "I do not altogether like the way Justice Holmes put the limitation. I myself think it is a little more manageable and quite adequate a distinction to say that there is an absolute and objective test to language. [I] still prefer that which I attempted to state in my first 'Masses' opinion, rather than to say that the connection between the words used and the evil aimed at should be 'immediate and direct.' " He elaborated later: "I prefer a test based upon the nature of the utterance itself. If, taken in its setting, the effect upon the hearers is only to counsel them to violate the law, it is unconditionally illegal. [As] to other utterances, it appears to me that regardless of their tendency they should be permitted."

Hand's major objection to formulations such as "clear and present danger" or "natural and reasonable tendency" was that they were too slippery in "practical administration": "I think it is precisely at those times when alone the freedom of speech becomes important as an institution, that the protection of a jury on such an issue is illusory." And, as he said in another letter, "I am not wholly in love with Holmesy's test and the reason is this. Once you admit that the matter is one of degree, [you] give to Tomdickandharry, D.J., so much latitude that the jig is at once up. [Even] the Nine Elder Statesmen have not shown themselves wholly immune from the 'herd instinct' and what seem 'immediate and direct' to-day may seem very remote next year even though the circumstances surrounding the utterance be unchanged. I own I should prefer a qualitative formula, hard, conventional, difficult to evade." See generally Gunther, "Learned Hand and the Origins of Modern First Amendment Doctrine: Some Fragments of History," 27 Stan. L. Rev. 719 (1975).

5. ***Reversion to the bad tendency test: the Red Scare cases.*** In the wake of World War I and the Russian Revolution, the United States entered the "Red Scare" era, a period of feverish anti-radicalism that lasted from the 1920s to the 1930s. In addition to mass deportations of aliens by the federal government, two-thirds of the states enacted laws prohibiting the advocacy of criminal anarchy and criminal syndicalism. Soon, such laws came before the Court in the following cases:

———

Gitlow v. New York

268 U.S. 652, 45 S. Ct. 625, 69 L. Ed. 1138 (1925).

■ JUSTICE SANFORD delivered the opinion of the Court.

Benjamin Gitlow was indicted [and convicted] for the statutory crime of criminal anarchy. New York Penal Law, §§ 160, 161.[1] [The] contention here is that the statute, by its terms and as applied in this case, is repugnant to the due process clause of the [14th Amendment]. The indictment was in two counts. The first charged that the defendant had advocated, advised and taught the duty, necessity and propriety of overthrowing and overturning organized government by force, violence and unlawful means, by certain writings therein set forth entitled "The Left Wing Manifesto"; the second that he had printed, published and knowingly circulated and distributed a certain paper called "The Revolutionary Age," containing the writings set forth in the [first count].

The defendant is a member of the Left Wing Section of the Socialist Party, a dissenting branch or faction of that party formed [in 1919] in opposition to its dominant policy of "moderate Socialism." [He] arranged for the printing [and publication of 16,000 copies of the first issue of the paper, which contained the Left Wing Manifesto]. It was admitted that the defendant signed a card subscribing to the Manifesto and Program of the [Left Wing]. There was no evidence of any effect resulting from the publication and circulation of the Manifesto. [The Manifesto] condemned the dominant "moderate Socialism" for its recognition of the necessity of the democratic parliamentary state [and] advocated [the] necessity of accomplishing the "Communist Revolution" by a militant and "revolutionary Socialism," based on "the class struggle" and mobilizing the "power of the proletariat in action," through mass industrial revolts developing into mass political strikes and "revolutionary mass action," for the purpose of conquering and destroying the parliamentary state and establishing in its place, through a "revolutionary dictatorship of the proletariat," the system of [Communist Socialism].

The court [charged] the jury, in substance, that they must determine what was the intent, purpose and fair meaning of the Manifesto; [that] a mere statement or analysis of social and economic facts and historical incidents, in the nature of an essay, accompanied by prophecy as to the future course of events, but with no teaching, advice or advocacy of action, would not constitute the advocacy, advice or teaching of a doctrine for the overthrow of government within the meaning of the statute; that a mere statement that unlawful acts might accomplish such a purpose would be insufficient, unless there was a teaching, advising and advocacy of employing

---

[1] The New York statute (enacted well before the Red Scare, in 1902, after the assassination of President McKinley) provided: "§ 160. *Criminal anarchy defined.* Criminal anarchy is the doctrine that organized government should be overthrown by force or violence, or by assassination of the executive head or of any of the executive officials of government, or by any unlawful means. The advocacy of such doctrine either by word of mouth or writing is a felony; § 161. *Advocacy of criminal anarchy.* Any person who: 1. By word of mouth or writing advocates, advises or teaches the duty, necessity or propriety of overthrowing or overturning organized government by force or violence, or by assassination of the executive head or of any of the executive officials of government, or by any unlawful means; or, 2. Prints, publishes, edits, issues or knowingly circulates, sells, distributes or publicly displays any book, paper, document, or written or printed matter in any form, containing or advocating, advising or teaching the doctrine that organized government should be overthrown by force, violence or any unlawful [means], [i]s guilty of a [felony]."

such unlawful acts for the purpose of overthrowing [government]. [The] sole contention here [is] that as there was no evidence of any concrete result flowing from the publication of the Manifesto or of circumstances showing the likelihood of such result, the statute as construed and [applied] penalizes the mere utterance, as such, of "doctrine" having no quality of incitement, without regard either to the circumstances of its utterance or to the likelihood of unlawful consequences; [and thus] contravenes [due process].

The statute does not penalize the utterance or publication of abstract "doctrine" or academic discussion having no quality of incitement to any concrete action. It is not aimed against mere historical or philosophical essays. It does not restrain the advocacy of changes in the form of government by constitutional and lawful means. What it prohibits is language advocating, advising or teaching the overthrow of organized government by unlawful means. These words imply urging to [action]. The Manifesto, plainly, is neither the statement of abstract doctrine [nor] mere prediction that industrial disturbances and revolutionary mass strikes will result spontaneously in an inevitable process of evolution in the economic system. It advocates and urges in fervent language mass action which shall progressively foment industrial disturbances and through political mass strikes and revolutionary mass action overthrow and destroy organized parliamentary government. It concludes with a call to action in these words: "The proletarian revolution and the Communist reconstruction of society—*the struggle for these*—is now indispensable. [The] Communist International calls the proletariat of the world to the final struggle!" This is not the expression of philosophical abstraction, the mere prediction of future events; it is the language of direct incitement. The means advocated for bringing about the destruction of organized parliamentary government, namely, mass industrial revolts usurping the functions of municipal government, political mass strikes directed against the parliamentary state, and revolutionary mass action for its final destruction, necessarily imply the use of force and violence, and in their essential nature are inherently unlawful in a constitutional government of law and order. That the jury were warranted in finding that the Manifesto advocated not merely the abstract doctrine of overthrowing organized government by force, violence and unlawful means, but action to that end, is clear.

For present purposes we may and do assume that freedom of speech and of the press—which are protected by the First Amendment from abridgment by Congress—are among the fundamental personal rights and "liberties" protected by the due process clause of the 14th Amendment from impairment by the States.[2] [It] is a fundamental principle, long established, that the freedom of speech and of the press which is secured by the Constitution, does not confer an absolute right to speak or publish, without responsibility, whatever one may choose. [A] State may punish utterances endangering the foundations of organized government and threatening its overthrow by unlawful means. [In] short this freedom does not deprive a State of the primary and essential right of [self preservation]. By enacting the present statute the State has determined, through its legislative body, that utterances advocating the overthrow of organized government by force, violence and unlawful means, are so inimical to the general welfare and

---

[2] This dicta was the Court's first indication that First Amendment guarantees are "incorporated" as against the States through the Due Process Clause of the Fourteenth Amendment.

involve such danger of substantive evil that they may be penalized in the exercise of its police power. That determination must be given great weight. Every presumption is to be indulged in favor of the validity of the statute. That utterances inciting to the overthrow of organized government by unlawful means, present a sufficient danger of substantive evil to bring their punishment within the range of legislative discretion, is clear. Such utterances, by their very nature, involve danger to the public peace and to the security of the State. They threaten breaches of the peace and ultimate revolution. And the immediate danger is none the less real and substantial, because the effect of a given utterance cannot be accurately foreseen. The State cannot reasonably be required to measure the danger from every such utterance in the nice balance of a jeweler's scale. A single revolutionary spark may kindle a fire that, smouldering for a time, may burst into a sweeping and destructive conflagration. It cannot be said that the State is acting arbitrarily or unreasonably when in the exercise of its judgment as to the measures necessary to protect the public peace and safety, it seeks to extinguish the spark without waiting until it has enkindled the flame or blazed into the conflagration. It cannot reasonably be required to defer the adoption of measures for its own peace and safety until the revolutionary utterances lead to actual disturbances of the public peace or imminent and immediate danger of its own destruction; but it may, in the exercise of its judgment, suppress the threatened danger in its incipiency. [We] cannot hold that the present statute is an arbitrary or unreasonable exercise of the police power of the State unwarrantably infringing the freedom of speech or press; and we must and do sustain its constitutionality.

This being so it may be applied to every utterance—not too trivial to be beneath the notice of the law—which is of such a character and used with such intent and purpose as to bring it within the prohibition of the statute. [In] other words, when the legislative body has determined generally, in the constitutional exercise of its discretion, that utterances of a certain kind involve such danger of substantive evil that they may be punished, the question whether any specific utterance coming within the prohibited class is likely, in and of itself, to bring about the substantive evil, is not open to consideration. It is sufficient that the statute itself be constitutional and that the use of the language comes within its prohibition. It is clear that the question in such cases is entirely different from that involved in those cases where the statute merely prohibits certain acts involving the danger of substantive evil, without any reference to language itself, and it is sought to apply its provisions to language used by the defendant for the purpose of bringing about the prohibited results. There, if it be contended that the statute cannot be applied to the language used by the defendant because of its protection by the freedom of speech or press, it must necessarily be found, as an original question, without any previous determination by the legislative body whether the specific language used involved such likelihood of bringing about the substantive evil as to deprive it of the constitutional protection. In such cases it has been held that the general provisions of the statute may be constitutionally applied to the specific utterance of the defendant if its natural tendency and probable effect was to bring about the substantive evil which the legislative body might prevent. [Schenck; Debs.] And the ["clear and present danger" passage in Schenck]—upon which great reliance is placed in the defendant's argument—was manifestly intended, as shown by the context, to apply only in cases of this class, and has no application to those like the present, where the legislative body itself has previously determined the danger of substantive evil arising from utterances of a specified character. [It] was not necessary, within the meaning of the statute, that the defendant should have advocated "some definite or immediate act or acts" of force, violence or unlawfulness. It was sufficient if such acts were advocated in general terms; and it was not essential that their immediate execution should have been advocated. Nor was it necessary that the language should have been "reasonably and ordinarily calculated to incite certain persons" to acts of force, violence or unlawfulness. The advocacy need not be addressed to specific persons. Thus, the publication and circulation of a newspaper article may be an encouragement or endeavor to persuade to murder, although not addressed to any person in [particular]. Affirmed.

■ JUSTICE HOLMES, dissenting.

[Justice] Brandeis and I are of opinion that this judgment should be reversed. The general principle of free speech, it seems to me, must be taken to be included in the 14th Amendment, in view of the scope that has been given to the word "liberty" as there used, although perhaps it may be accepted with a somewhat larger latitude of interpretation than is allowed to Congress by the sweeping language that governs or ought to govern the laws of the United States. If I am right, then I think that the criterion sanctioned by the full Court in [Schenck] applies. [It] is true that in my opinion this criterion was departed from in [Abrams], but the convictions that I expressed in that case are too deep for it to be possible for me as yet to believe that it [has] settled the law. If what I think the correct test is applied, it is manifest that there was no present danger of an attempt to overthrow the government by force on the part of the admittedly small minority who shared the defendant's views. It is said that this manifesto was more than a theory, that it was an incitement. Every idea is an incitement. It offers itself for belief and if believed it is acted on unless some other belief outweighs it or some failure of energy stifles the movement at its birth. The only difference between the expression of an opinion and an incitement in the narrower sense is the speaker's enthusiasm for the result. Eloquence may set fire to reason. But whatever may be thought of the redundant discourse before us it had no chance of starting a present conflagration. If in the long run the beliefs expressed in proletarian dictatorship are destined to be accepted by the dominant forces of the community, the only meaning of free speech is that they should be given their chance and have their way. If the publication of this document had been laid as an attempt to induce an uprising against government at once and not at some indefinite time in the future it would have presented a different question. The object would have been one with which the law might deal, subject to the doubt whether there was any danger that the publication could produce any result, or in other words, whether it was not futile and too remote from possible consequences. But the indictment alleges the publication and nothing more.

———

Whitney v. California

274 U.S. 357, 47 S. Ct. 641, 71 L. Ed. 1095 (1927).

[Anita Whitney was convicted under the Criminal Syndicalism Act of California, enacted in 1919.[1] The charge was that she "did [organize] and assist in organizing, and was, is, and knowingly became a member of an organization [organized] to advocate, teach, aid and abet criminal syndicalism." She had attended the 1919 national convention of the Socialist Party as a delegate from the Oakland branch. The convention split between the "radicals" and the old-line democratic Socialists. The "radicals"—including Whitney—went to another hall and formed the Communist Labor Party [CLP], adopting a platform similar to the Left Wing Manifesto involved in Gitlow. Later in 1919, she was a branch delegate to a convention called to organize a California unit of the CLP. As a member of that convention's resolutions committee, she supported a moderate resolution proposing the achievement of the CLP's goals through traditional political processes. The proposed resolution was defeated on the floor and a more militant program was adopted. Whitney remained a member of the Party and testified at the trial "that it was not her intention that the [CLP] of California should be an instrument of terrorism or violence."]

■ JUSTICE SANFORD delivered the opinion of the Court.

While it is not denied that the evidence warranted the jury in finding that the defendant became a member of and assisted in organizing the [CLP] of California, and that this was organized to [advocate] criminal syndicalism as defined by the Act, it is urged that the Act, as here construed and applied, deprived the defendant of her liberty without due process of law. [The] argument is, in effect, that the character of the state organization could not be forecast when she attended the convention; that she had no purpose of helping to create an instrument of terrorism and violence; that she "took part in formulating and presenting to the convention a resolution which, if adopted, would have committed the new organization to a legitimate policy of political reform by the use of the ballot"; that it was not until after the majority of the convention turned out to be "contrary-minded, and other less temperate policies prevailed" that the convention could have taken on the character of criminal syndicalism; and that as this was done over her protest, her mere presence in the convention, however violent the opinions expressed therein, could not thereby become a crime. This contention, while advanced in the form of a constitutional objection to the Act, is in effect nothing more than an effort to review the weight of the evidence for the purpose of showing that the defendant did not join and assist in organizing the [CLP] with a knowledge of its unlawful character and purpose. This question, which is foreclosed by the verdict of the jury, [is] one of fact merely which is not open to review in this Court, involving as it does no constitutional question [whatever].

---

[1] The pertinent provisions of the Act stated: "Section 1. The term 'criminal syndicalism' as used in this act is hereby defined as any doctrine or precept advocating, teaching or aiding and abetting the commission of crime, sabotage, [or] unlawful acts of force and violence or unlawful methods of terrorism as a means of accomplishing a change in industrial ownership or control, or effecting any political change. Sec. 2. Any person who: . . . [4.] Organizes or assists in organizing, or is or knowingly becomes a member of, any organization, society, group or assemblage of persons organized or assembled to advocate, teach or aid and abet [criminal syndicalism]; [i]s guilty of a [felony]."

[The Act] as applied in this case [is not] repugnant to the due process clause as a restraint of the rights of free speech, assembly, and association. That [a state] may punish those who abuse [freedom of speech] by utterances inimical to the public welfare, tending to incite to crime, disturb the public peace, or endanger the foundations of organized government and threaten its overthrow by unlawful means, is not open to question. [Gitlow.] [The legislative] determination must be given great weight. [The] essence of the offense [is] the combining with others in an association for the accomplishment of the desired ends through the advocacy and use of criminal and unlawful methods. It partakes of the nature of a criminal conspiracy. [That] such [united] action involves even greater danger to the public peace and security than the isolated utterances and acts of individuals, is clear. We cannot hold that, as here applied, the Act is an unreasonable or arbitrary exercise of the police power of the State, unwarrantably infringing any right of free speech, assembly or association, or that those persons are protected from punishment by [due process] who abuse such rights by joining and furthering an organization thus menacing the peace and welfare of the [State]. Affirmed.

■ JUSTICE BRANDEIS, joined by JUSTICE HOLMES, concurring.

The felony which the statute created is a crime very unlike the old felony of conspiracy or the old misdemeanor of unlawful assembly. The mere act of assisting in forming a society for teaching syndicalism, of becoming a member of it, or of assembling with others for that purpose is given the dynamic quality of crime. There is guilt although the society may not contemplate immediate promulgation of the doctrine. Thus the accused is to be punished, not for attempt, incitement or conspiracy, but for a step in preparation, which, if it threatens the public order at all, does so only remotely. The novelty in the prohibition introduced is that the statute aims, not at the practice of criminal syndicalism, nor even directly at the preaching of it, but at association with those who propose to preach it.

Despite arguments to the contrary which had seemed to me persuasive, it is settled that the due process clause of the 14th Amendment applies to matters of substantive law as well as to matters of procedure. Thus all fundamental rights comprised within the term liberty are protected by the [Constitution] from invasion by the States. The right of free speech, the right to teach and the right of assembly are, of course, fundamental rights. These may not be denied or abridged. But, although the rights of free speech and assembly are fundamental, they are not in their nature absolute. Their exercise is subject to restriction, if the particular restriction proposed is required in order to protect the State from destruction or from serious injury, political, economic or moral. That the necessity which is essential to a valid restriction does not exist unless speech would produce, or is intended to produce, a clear and imminent danger of some substantive evil which the State constitutionally may seek to prevent has been settled. See [Schenck].

It is said to be the function of the legislature to determine whether at a particular time and under the particular circumstances the formation of, or assembly with, a society organized to advocate criminal syndicalism constitutes a clear and present danger of substantive evil; and that by enacting the law here in question the legislature of California determined that question in the affirmative. Compare [Gitlow]. The legislature must obviously decide, in the first instance, whether a danger exists which calls for a particular protective measure. But where a statute is valid only in case certain conditions exist, the enactment of the statute cannot alone establish the facts which are essential to its validity. Prohibitory legislation has repeatedly been held invalid because unnecessary, where the denial of liberty involved was that of engaging in a particular business. The power of the courts to strike down an offending law is no less when the interests involved are not property rights, but the fundamental personal rights of free speech and assembly.

This Court has not yet fixed the standard by which to determine when a danger shall be deemed clear; how remote the danger may be and yet be deemed present; and what degree of evil shall be deemed sufficiently substantial to justify resort to abridgment of free speech and assembly as the means of protection. To reach sound conclusions on these matters, we must bear in mind why a State is, ordinarily, denied the power to prohibit dissemination of social, economic and political doctrine which a vast majority of its citizens believes to be false and fraught with evil consequence.

Those who won our independence believed that the final end of the State was to make men free to develop their faculties; and that in its government the deliberative forces should prevail over the arbitrary. They valued liberty both as an end and as a means. They believed liberty to be the secret of happiness and courage to be the secret of liberty. They believed that freedom to think as you will and to speak as you think are means indispensable to the discovery and spread of political truth; that without free speech and assembly discussion would be futile; that with them, discussion affords ordinarily adequate protection against the dissemination of noxious doctrine; that the greatest menace to freedom is an inert people; that public discussion is a political duty; and that this should be a fundamental principle of the American government. They recognized the risks to which all human institutions are subject. But they knew that order cannot be secured merely through fear of punishment for its infraction; that it is hazardous to discourage thought, hope and imagination; that fear breeds repression; that repression breeds hate; that hate menaces stable government; that the path of safety lies in the opportunity to discuss freely supposed grievances and proposed remedies; and that the fitting remedy for evil counsels is good ones. Believing in the power of reason as applied through public discussion, they eschewed silence coerced by law—the argument of force in its worst form. Recognizing the occasional tyrannies of governing majorities, they amended the Constitution so that free speech and assembly should be guaranteed.

Fear of serious injury cannot alone justify suppression of free speech and assembly. Men feared witches and burned women. It is the function of speech to free men from the bondage of irrational fears. To justify suppression of free speech there must be reasonable ground to fear that serious evil will result if free speech is practiced. There must be reasonable ground to believe that the danger apprehended is imminent. There must be reasonable ground to believe that the evil to be prevented is a serious one. Every denunciation of existing law tends in some measure to increase the probability that there will be violation of it. Condonation of a breach enhances the probability. Expressions of approval add to the probability. Propagation of the criminal state of mind by teaching syndicalism increases it. Advocacy of law-breaking heightens it still further. But even advocacy of violation, however reprehensible morally, is not a justification for denying free speech where the advocacy falls short of incitement and there is nothing to indicate that the advocacy would be immediately acted on. The wide difference between advocacy and incitement, between preparation and attempt, between assembling and conspiracy, must be borne in mind. In order to support a finding of clear and present danger it must be shown either that immediate serious violence was to be expected or was advocated, or that the past conduct furnished reason to believe that such advocacy was then contemplated.

Those who won our independence by revolution were not cowards. They did not fear political change. They did not exalt order at the cost of liberty. To courageous, self-reliant men, with confidence in the power of free and fearless reasoning applied through the processes of popular government, no danger flowing from speech can be deemed clear and present, unless the incidence of the evil apprehended is so imminent that it may befall before there is opportunity for full discussion. If there be time to expose through discussion the falsehood and fallacies, to avert the evil by the processes of education, the remedy to be applied is more speech, not enforced silence. Only an emergency can justify repression. Such must be the rule if authority is to be reconciled with freedom. Such, in my opinion, is the command of the Constitution. It is therefore always open to Americans to challenge a law abridging free speech and assembly by showing that there was no emergency justifying it.

Moreover, even imminent danger cannot justify resort to prohibition of these functions essential to effective democracy, unless the evil apprehended is relatively serious. Prohibition of free speech and assembly is a measure so stringent that it would be inappropriate as the means for averting a relatively trivial harm to society. A police measure may be unconstitutional merely because the remedy, although effective as a means of protection, is unduly harsh or oppressive. Thus, a State might, in the exercise of its police power, make any trespass upon the land of another a crime, regardless of the results or of the intent or purpose of the trespasser. It might, also, punish an attempt, a conspiracy, or an incitement to commit the trespass. But it is hardly conceivable that this Court would hold constitutional a statute which punished as a felony the mere voluntary assembly with a society formed to teach that pedestrians had the moral right to cross unenclosed, unposted, waste lands and to advocate their doing so, even if there was imminent danger that advocacy would lead to a trespass. The fact that speech is likely to result in some violence or in destruction of property is not enough to justify its suppression. There must be the probability of serious injury to the State. Among free men, the deterrents ordinarily to be applied to prevent crime are education and punishment for violations of the law, not abridgment of the rights of free speech and assembly.

[The California] legislative declaration [stating that the Act was "necessary to the immediate preservation of the public peace and safety," because many people were going "from place to place in this state" advocating criminal syndicalism] satisfies the requirement of the constitution of the State concerning emergency legislation. [But] it does not preclude enquiry into the question whether, at the time and under the circumstances, the conditions existed which are essential to validity under the Federal Constitution. As a statute, even if not void on its face, may be challenged because invalid as applied, the result of such an inquiry may depend upon the specific facts of the particular case. Whenever the fundamental rights of free speech and assembly are alleged to have been invaded, it must remain open to a defendant to present the issue whether there actually did exist at the time a clear danger; whether the danger, if any, was imminent; and whether the evil apprehended was one so substantial as to justify the stringent restriction interposed by the legislature. The legislative [declaration] creates merely a rebuttable presumption that these conditions have been satisfied.

Whether in 1919, when Miss Whitney did the things complained of, there was in California such clear and present danger of serious evil, might have been made the important issue in the case. She might have required that the issue be determined either by the court or the jury. She claimed below that the statute as applied to her violated the [Constitution]; but she did not claim that it was void because there was no clear and present danger of serious evil, nor did she request that the existence of these conditions of a valid measure thus restricting the rights of free speech and assembly be passed upon by the court or a jury. On the other hand, there was evidence on which the court or jury might have found that such danger existed. I am unable to assent to the suggestion in the opinion of the Court that assembling with a political party, formed to advocate the desirability of a proletarian revolution by mass action at some date necessarily far in the future, is not a right within the protection of the 14th Amendment. In the present case, however, there was other testimony which tended to establish the existence of a conspiracy, on the part of members of the International Workers of the World, to commit present serious crimes; and likewise to show that such a conspiracy would be furthered by the activity of the society of which Miss Whitney was a member. Under these circumstances the judgment of the state court cannot be disturbed. Our power of review in this case [from a state court] is limited [to] the particular claims duly made below, and denied. [We] lack here the power occasionally exercised on review of judgments of lower federal courts to correct in criminal cases vital errors, although the objection was not taken in the trial court. Because we may not enquire into the errors now alleged, I concur in affirming the judgment of the state court.

CRIMINAL ANARCHY AND SYNDICALISM LAWS

1. *Legislative presumptions of harm from speech.* In Gitlow and Whitney, unlike the Schenck trilogy and Abrams, the Court was faced with a prior legislative determination that certain classes of speech caused an intolerable risk of serious harm. Is the "clear and present danger" standard applicable in such cases? Arguably, the clear and present danger test made it inherently difficult for judges to confront and set aside a legislative judgment that a particular variety of speech is dangerous. The clear and present danger test puts great emphasis on context and guesses about future harm; to the extent that this involves an empirical judgment, judges may feel particularly incompetent to second-guess legislative judgments. Recall that, in his dissents from Court invalidations of state economic regulations on substantive due process grounds, Holmes repeatedly urged deference to legislative judgments, in cases beginning with Lochner. What explains his abandonment of such deference here? Should it matter that the Gitlow law was enacted in 1902, long before the evolution of the post-World War I radicalism that gave rise to the Gitlow prosecution? In contrast, Whitney involved prosecution for 1919 behavior under a 1919 law. On these questions, see Rogat, "Mr. Justice Holmes, Some Modern Views—The Judge as

Spectator," 31 U. Chi. L. Rev. 213 (1964), and Linde, " 'Clear and Present Danger' Reexamined: Dissonance in the Brandenburg Concerto," 22 Stan. L. Rev. 1163 (1970).

2. ***An alternative approach: the Masses test.*** Would adoption of the Masses "incitement" test have alleviated the judicial difficulty in Gitlow and Whitney? By emphasizing what speech is protected (and the speaker's words rather than guesses about future harms), would courts have been in a better position to protect speech without direct confrontations with legislative judgments that particular types of speech present a "clear and present danger" of an especially grave evil?

3. ***Comparing the Holmes and Brandeis approaches.*** Was Brandeis more successful than Holmes in confronting the Gitlow-Whitney problem? In what respects do Brandeis's justifications for the clear and present danger test differ from Holmes's? Brandeis, like Holmes, was deferential to legislative judgments underlying economic regulations during the Lochner era. Note how his Whitney concurrence sidesteps direct confrontation with the California legislature by considering Whitney's challenge to the law only "as applied." Might Brandeis have justified lessened deference to the legislature here by emphasizing that the legislators, by curtailing expressions of speech and opinions, had undercut the basis for the usual reliance on the processes of representation? Recall the Carolene Products footnote, above. Note also that Brandeis' version adds an additional variable to the "immediacy of harm" emphasis of Holmes: Brandeis also speaks of the "gravity of the evil." On the Whitney litigation and the Brandeis opinion, see Blasi, "The First Amendment and the Ideal of Civic Courage: The Brandeis Opinion in Whitney v. California," 29 Wm. & Mary L. Rev. 653 (1988). For a close reading and comparative interpretation of Holmes's and Brandeis's approaches, see Lahav, "Holmes and Brandeis: Libertarian and Republican Justifications for Free Speech," 4 J.L. & Pol. 451 (1987).

———

Dennis v. United States

341 U.S. 494, 71 S. Ct. 857, 95 L. Ed. 1137 (1951).

[After World War II, fears mounted of threats to national security posed by the Soviet Union and China, and anticommunist sentiment generated a number of restrictions on subversive speech. Former State Department official Alger Hiss was convicted of perjury in connection with a congressional inquiry into his alleged spying activities for the Soviet Union. Senator Joseph McCarthy conducted a series of hearings accusing government officials of communist activities. Against this backdrop, national leaders of the Communist Party were prosecuted under the Smith Act of 1940, a federal law quite similar to the New York criminal anarchy statute sustained in Gitlow.]

■ CHIEF JUSTICE VINSON announced the judgment of the Court and an opinion in which JUSTICES REED, BURTON and MINTON join.

Petitioners were indicted in July, 1948, for violation of the conspiracy provisions of the Smith Act[1] during the period of April, 1945, to July, 1948, [and convicted after jury trial. The] indictment charged the petitioners with willfully and knowingly conspiring (1) to organize as the Communist Party of the United States of America a society, group and assembly of persons who teach and advocate the overthrow and destruction of the Government of the United States by force and violence, and (2) knowingly and willfully to advocate and teach the duty and necessity of overthrowing and destroying the Government of the United States by force and [violence]. The trial of the case extended over nine months, [resulting] in a record of 16,000 pages. Our limited grant of the writ of certiorari has removed from our consideration any question as to the sufficiency of the [evidence]. [T]he Court of Appeals held that the record supports the following broad conclusion: [that] the Communist Party is a highly disciplined organization, adept at infiltration into strategic positions, use of aliases, and double-meaning language; that the Party is rigidly controlled; that Communists, unlike other political parties, tolerate no dissension from the policy laid down by the guiding forces; [that] the literature of the Party and the statements and activities of its leaders, petitioners here, advocate, and the general goal of the Party was, during the period in question, to achieve a successful overthrow of the existing order by force and [violence].

[No] one could conceive that it is not within the power of Congress to prohibit acts intended to overthrow the Government by force and violence. The question with which we are concerned here is not whether Congress has such *power,* but whether the *means* which it has employed conflict with [the] Constitution. [Petitioners attack] the statute on the grounds that by its terms it prohibits academic discussion of the merits of Marxism-Leninism, that it stifles ideas and is contrary to all concepts of a free speech and a free press. [The] very language of the Smith Act negates [this] interpretation. [The Act] is directed at advocacy, not discussion. Thus, the trial judge properly charged the jury that they could not convict if they found that petitioners did "no more than pursue peaceful studies and discussions or teaching and advocacy in the realm of ideas." [But the application of the Act] in this case has resulted in convictions for the teaching and advocacy of the overthrow of the Government by force and violence, which, even though coupled with the intent to accomplish that overthrow, contains an element of speech. For this reason, we must pay special heed to the demands of the First Amendment marking out the boundaries of speech.

[Although] no case subsequent to Whitney and Gitlow has expressly overruled the majority opinions in those cases, there is little doubt that subsequent opinions have inclined toward the Holmes-Brandeis rationale. [In] this case we are [therefore] squarely presented with the application of

---

[1] "Sec. 2. (a) It shall be unlawful for any person—(1) to knowingly or willfully advocate, abet, advise, or teach the duty, necessity, desirability, or propriety of overthrowing or destroying any government in the United States by force or violence, or by the assassination of any officer of any such [government]; (3) to organize or help to organize any society, group, or assembly of persons who teach, advocate, or encourage the overthrow or destruction of any government in the United States by force or violence; or to be or become a member of, or affiliate with, any such society, group, or assembly of persons, knowing the purposes [thereof]. Sec. 3. It shall be unlawful for any person to attempt to commit, or to conspire to commit, any of the acts prohibited [by] this title."

the "clear and present danger" test, and must decide what that phrase imports. [Overthrow] of the Government by force and violence is certainly a substantial enough interest for the Government to limit speech. [If], then, this interest may be protected, the literal problem which is presented is what has been meant by the use of the phrase ["clear and present danger"]. Obviously, the words cannot mean that before the Government may act, it must wait until the putsch is about to be executed, the plans have been laid and the signal is awaited. If Government is aware that a group aiming at its overthrow is attempting to indoctrinate its members and to commit them to a course whereby they will strike when the leaders feel the circumstances permit, action by the Government is required. The argument that there is no need for Government to concern itself, for Government is strong, it possesses ample powers to put down a rebellion, it may defeat the revolution with ease needs no answer. For that is not the question. Certainly an attempt to overthrow the Government by force, even though doomed from the outset because of inadequate numbers or power of the revolutionists, is a sufficient evil for Congress to prevent. The damage which such attempts create both physically and politically to a nation makes it impossible to measure the validity in terms of the probability of success, or the immediacy of a successful attempt. [We] must therefore reject the contention that success or probability of success is the criterion.

The situation with which Justices Holmes and Brandeis were concerned in Gitlow was a comparatively isolated event, bearing little relation in their minds to any substantial threat to the safety of the community. [They] were not confronted with any situation comparable to the instant one—the development of an apparatus designed and dedicated to the overthrow of the Government, in the context of world crisis after crisis. Chief Judge Learned Hand, writing for the majority [of the Second Circuit] below, interpreted the phrase as follows: "In each case [courts] must ask whether the gravity of the 'evil,' discounted by its improbability, justifies such invasion of free speech as is necessary to avoid the danger." We adopt this statement of the rule. As articulated by Chief Judge Hand, it is as succinct and inclusive as any other we might devise at this [time]. Likewise, we are in accord with the court below, which affirmed the trial court's finding that the requisite danger existed. The mere fact that from the period 1945 to 1948 petitioners' activities did not result in an attempt to overthrow the Government by force and violence is of course no answer to the fact that there was a group that was ready to make the attempt. The formation by petitioners of such a highly organized conspiracy, with rigidly disciplined members subject to call when the leaders, these petitioners, felt that the time had come for action, coupled with the inflammable nature of world conditions, similar uprisings in other countries, and the touch-and-go nature of our relations with countries with whom petitioners were in the very least ideologically attuned, convince us that their convictions were justified on this score. And this analysis disposes of the contention that a conspiracy to advocate, as distinguished from the advocacy itself, cannot be constitutionally restrained, because it comprises only the preparation. It is the existence of the conspiracy which creates the danger. [If] the ingredients of the reaction are present, we cannot bind the Government to wait until the catalyst is added.

[Petitioners] intended to overthrow the Government of the United States as speedily as the circumstances would permit. Their conspiracy to organize the Communist Party and to teach and advocate the overthrow of the [Government] by force and violence created a "clear and present danger" of an attempt to overthrow the Government by force and [violence]. Affirmed.

■ JUSTICE FRANKFURTER, concurring in affirmance of the judgment.

[The] historic antecedents of the First Amendment preclude the notion that its purpose was to give unqualified immunity to every expression that touched on matters within the range of political interest. [Absolute] rules would inevitably lead to absolute exceptions, and such exceptions would eventually corrode the rules. The demands of free speech in a democratic society as well as the interest in national security are better served by candid and informed weighing of the competing interests, within the confines of the judicial process, than by announcing dogmas too inflexible for the non-Euclidean problems to be solved. But how are competing interests to be assessed? Since they are not subject to quantitative ascertainment, the issue necessarily resolves itself into asking, who is to make the adjustments?—who is to balance[?] Full responsibility for the choice cannot be given to the courts. Courts are not representative bodies. [Their] judgment is best informed, and therefore most dependable, within narrow limits. Their essential quality is detachment, founded on independence. History teaches that the independence of the judiciary is jeopardized when courts become embroiled in the passions of the day and assume primary responsibility in choosing between competing political, economic and social pressures. Primary responsibility for adjusting the interests which compete in the situation before us of necessity belongs to the Congress. [We] are to set aside the judgment [of legislators] only if there is no reasonable basis for [it].

[These] general considerations underlie decision of the case before us. On the one hand is the interest in security. The Communist Party was not designed by these defendants as an ordinary political party. For the circumstances of its organization, its aims and methods, and the relation of the defendants to its organization and aims we are concluded by the jury's verdict. [In] finding that the defendants violated [the statute,] we may not treat as established fact that the Communist Party in this country is of significant size, well-organized, well-disciplined, conditioned to embark on unlawful activity when given the command. But in determining whether application of the statute to the defendants is within the constitutional powers of Congress, we are not limited to the facts found by the jury. We must view such a question in the light of whatever is relevant to a legislative judgment. We may take judicial notice that the Communist doctrines which these defendants have conspired to advocate are in the ascendency in powerful nations who cannot be acquitted of unfriendliness to the institutions of this country. We may take account of evidence brought forward at this trial and elsewhere, much of which has long been common knowledge. In sum, it would amply justify a legislature in concluding that recruitment of additional members for the Party would create a substantial danger to national security.

On the other hand is the interest in free speech. The right to exert all governmental powers in aid of maintaining our institutions and resisting their physical overthrow does not include intolerance of opinions and speech that cannot do harm although opposed and perhaps alien to dominant, traditional opinion. [And a] public interest is not wanting in granting freedom to speak their minds even to those who advocate the overthrow of the Government by force. For, as the evidence in this case abundantly illustrates, coupled with such advocacy is criticism of defects in our society.

[Moreover, suppressing] advocates of overthrow inevitably will also silence critics who do not advocate overthrow but fear that their criticism may be so construed. [It] is self-delusion to think that we can punish [the defendants] for their advocacy without adding to the risks run by loyal citizens who honestly believe in some of the reforms these defendants advance. It is a sobering fact that in sustaining the convictions before us we can hardly escape restriction on the interchange of [ideas].

[But it] is not for us to decide how we would adjust the clash of interests which this case presents were the primary responsibility for reconciling it ours. Congress has determined that the danger created by advocacy of overthrow justifies the ensuing restriction on freedom of speech. [To] make validity of legislation depend on judicial reading of events still in the womb of time—a forecast, that is, of the outcome of forces at best appreciated only with knowledge of the topmost secrets of nations—is to charge the judiciary with duties beyond its [equipment].

■ JUSTICE JACKSON, concurring.

[The] "clear and present danger" test was an innovation by [Justice] Holmes in [Schenck, refined] in later cases, all arising before the era of World War II revealed the subtlety and efficacy of modernized revolutionary techniques used by totalitarian parties. [I] would save it, unmodified, for application as a "rule of reason" in the kind of case for which it was devised. When the issue is criminality of a hotheaded speech on a street corner, or circulation of a few incendiary pamphlets, or parading by some zealots behind a red flag, or refusal of a handful of school children to salute our flag, it is not beyond the capacity of the judicial process to gather, comprehend, and weigh the necessary materials for decision whether it is a clear and present danger of substantive evil or a harmless letting off of steam. It is not a prophecy, for the danger in such cases has matured by the time of trial or it was never present. The test applies and has meaning where a conviction is sought to be based on a speech or writing which does not directly or explicitly advocate a crime but to which such tendency is sought to be attributed by construction or by implication from external circumstances. The formula in such cases favors freedoms that are vital to our society, and, even if sometimes applied too generously, the consequences cannot be grave.

[I] think reason is lacking for applying that test to this case. If we must decide that this Act and its application are constitutional only if we are convinced that petitioner's conduct creates a "clear and present danger" of violent overthrow, we must appraise imponderables, including international and national phenomena which baffle the best informed foreign offices and our most experienced politicians. [No] doctrine can be sound whose application requires us to make a prophecy of that sort in the guise of a legal decision. The judicial process simply is not adequate to a trial of such far-flung issues. The answers given would reflect our own political predilections and nothing more. The authors of the clear and present danger test never applied it to a case like this, nor would I. If applied as it is proposed here, it means that the Communist plotting is protected during its period of incubation; its preliminary stages of organization and preparation are immune from the law; the Government can move only after imminent action is manifest, when it would, of course, be too [late].

■ JUSTICE BLACK, dissenting.

[The] only way to affirm these convictions is to repudiate directly or indirectly the established "clear and present danger" rule. This the Court does in a way which greatly restricts the protections afforded by the First Amendment. [I] cannot agree that the First Amendment permits us to sustain laws suppressing freedom of speech and press on the basis of Congress' or our own notions of mere "reasonableness." [The] Amendment as so construed is not likely to protect any but those "safe" or orthodox views which rarely need its protection. I must also express my objection to the holding [because] it sanctions the determination of a crucial issue of fact by the judge rather than by the [jury]. Public opinion being what it now is, few will protest the conviction of these Communist petitioners. There is hope, however, that in calmer times, when present pressures, passions and fears subside, this or some later Court will restore the First Amendment liberties to the high preferred place where they belong in a free society.

■ JUSTICE DOUGLAS, dissenting.

If this were a case where those who claimed protection under the First Amendment were teaching the techniques of sabotage, the assassination of the President, the filching of documents from public files, the planting of bombs, the art of street warfare, and the like, I would have no doubts. The freedom to speak is not absolute; the teaching of methods of terror and other seditious conduct should be beyond the pale along with obscenity and immorality. This case was argued as if those were the facts. The argument imported much seditious conduct into the record. That is easy and it has popular appeal, for the activities of Communists in plotting and scheming against the free world are common knowledge. But the fact is that no such evidence was introduced at the trial. There is a statute which makes a seditious conspiracy unlawful. Petitioners, however, were not charged with a "conspiracy to overthrow" the Government. They were charged with a conspiracy to form a party and groups and assemblies of people who teach and advocate the overthrow of our Government by force or violence and with a conspiracy to advocate and teach its overthrow by force and violence. It may well be that indoctrination in the techniques of terror to destroy the Government would be indictable under either statute. But the teaching which is condemned here is of a different character.

So far as the present record is concerned, what petitioners did was to organize people to teach and themselves teach the Marxist-Leninist doctrine contained chiefly in four books: Foundations of Leninism by Stalin (1924), The Communist Manifesto by Marx and Engels (1848), State and Revolution by Lenin (1917), History of the Communist Party of the Soviet Union (B) (1939). Those books are to Soviet Communism what Mein Kampf was to Nazism. If they are understood, the ugliness of Communism is revealed, its deceit and cunning are exposed, the nature of its activities becomes apparent, and the chances of its success less likely. That is not, of course, the reason why petitioners chose these books for their classrooms. They are fervent Communists to whom these volumes are gospel. They preached the creed with the hope that some day it would be acted upon. The opinion of the Court does not outlaw these texts nor condemn them to the fire, as the Communists do literature offensive to their creed. But if the books themselves are not outlawed, if they can lawfully remain on library shelves, by what reasoning does their use in a classroom become a crime? [The] Act, as construed, requires the element of intent—that those who teach the creed believe in it. The crime then depends not on what is taught but on who the teacher is. That is to make freedom of speech turn not on *what is said*, but on the *intent* with which it is said. Once we start down that road we enter territory dangerous to the liberties of every [citizen].

There comes a time when even speech loses its constitutional immunity. Speech innocuous one year may at another time fan such destructive flames that it must be halted in the interests of the safety of the Republic. That is the meaning of the clear and present danger test. When conditions are so critical that there will be no time to avoid the evil that the speech threatens, it is time to call a halt. Otherwise, free speech which is the strength of the Nation will be the cause of its destruction. Yet free speech is the rule, not the exception. The restraint to be constitutional must be based on more than fear, on more than passionate opposition against the speech, on more than a revolted dislike for its contents. There must be some immediate injury to society that is likely if speech is [allowed].

[If] we are to take judicial notice of the threat of Communists within the nation, it should not be difficult to conclude that *as a political party* they are of little consequence. [Communism] in the world scene is no bogeyman; but Communism as a political faction or party in this country plainly is. Communism has been so thoroughly exposed in this country that it has been crippled as a political force. Free speech has destroyed it as an effective political party. [How] it can be said that there is a clear and present danger that this advocacy will succeed is, therefore, a mystery. [I]n America [Communists] are miserable merchants of unwanted ideas; their wares remain unsold. [But] the mere statement of the opposing views indicates how important it is that we know the facts before we act. Neither prejudice nor hate nor senseless fear should be the basis of this solemn act. Free speech [should] not be sacrificed on anything less than plain and objective proof of danger that the evil advocated is [imminent]. [Justice CLARK did not participate in the decision.]

"CLEAR AND PRESENT DANGER" AFTER DENNIS

1.   *The Dennis formulation.* Did Dennis ignore clear and present danger or fall prey to the inherent weaknesses of clear and present danger? What, if anything, did the Holmes standard say about the Dennis problem? What "substantive evil" was relevant? Did Dennis abandon the focus on immediacy in the Abrams dissent and the Whitney concurrence? What degree of deference to the legislative judgment was appropriate in Dennis? Should the legislative judgment have been assessed in terms of the 1940 circumstances, when the Smith Act became law or the circumstances in 1948, when the Dennis indictment was brought? See Linde, " 'Clear and Present Danger' Reexamined: Dissonance in the Brandenburg Concerto," 22 Stan. L. Rev. 1163 (1970) (arguing that, in view of the interval of more than a decade between the enactment of the Smith Act and the Dennis decision, it was effectively impossible to point to any particular "legislative judgment that would deserve deference for its assessment of the danger from revolutionary speech"). For the view that the Dennis formulation is a "powerful formula" for resolving a variety of speech issues, see Van Alstyne, "A Graphic Review of the Free Speech Clause," 70 Calif. L. Rev. 107, 128 (1982).

2. *Clear and present danger and Learned Hand.* In Dennis, the Court adopted the clear and present danger formulation set forth by Chief Judge Learned Hand in the decision of the court of appeals for the Second Circuit affirming the convictions below: "[Courts] must ask whether the gravity of the 'evil,' discounted by its improbability, justifies such invasion of free speech as is necessary to avoid the danger." How could Hand, the author of the Masses opinion, have adopted the clear and present danger test he had long criticized and interpreted it in a relatively speech-restrictive way? The answer, suggests Gerald Gunther, is that he was "a judge of a lower court who took seriously his obligation to follow Supreme Court precedents," and that his Masses test had sunk "into oblivion in the years between World War I and World War II," while the Supreme Court "had adhered to and struggled to clarify its 'clear and present danger' test." Gunther, Learned Hand: the Man and the Judge 600 (1994). Privately, Hand said at the time that he would still have preferred to rely on the Masses test, id. at 604, and that he personally would never have prosecuted the Communist leaders, for " '[t]he blood of martyrs is the seed of the church,' " id. at 603. Consider, however, how Hand transformed the clear and present danger test into a measure of gravity discounted by probability. Recall Hand's famous test for negligence liability expressed in United States v. Carroll Towing Co., 159 F.2d 169 (2d Cir. 1947) ("Possibly it serves to bring this notion into relief to state it in algebraic terms: if the probability be called P; the injury, L; and the burden, B; liability depends upon whether B is less than L multiplied by P: i.e., whether $B < PL$.") Is there a relation between these two formulations?

In his last years, Judge Hand repudiated the view that rights such as speech should receive special judicial protection, suggesting that he viewed the Bill of Rights primarily as merely "admonitory or hortatory, not definite enough to be guides on concrete occasions." Hand, The Bill of Rights (1958).

3. *Free speech theory and advocacy of totalitarian government.* Dennis, even more sharply than the earlier subversive speech cases, raises the question why the First Amendment should protect those who, were they in power, would deny free speech rights to others. Some have argued it should not: "Speech advocating violent overthrow [of government is] not 'political speech' as that term must be defined by a Madisonian system of government [because] it violates constitutional truths about processes and because it is not aimed at a new definition of political truth by a legislative majority. Violent overthrow of government breaks the premises of our system concerning the ways in which truth is defined, and yet those premises are the only reasons for protecting political speech." Bork, "Neutral Principles and Some First Amendment Problems," 47 Ind. L.J. 1 (1971).

For arguments to the contrary, finding First Amendment value in protecting radically subversive speech, see Emerson, The System of Freedom of Expression (1970) (arguing that "democratic society should tolerate opinion which attacks the fundamental institutions of democracy for much the same reasons that it tolerates other opinion," and that "suppression of any group in a society destroys the atmosphere of freedom essential to the life and progress of a healthy community. [It] is not possible for a society to practice both freedom of expression and suppression of expression at the same time."); Meiklejohn, Free Speech and Its Relation to Self-Government 48 (1948) (arguing that the First Amendment "means that certain substantive evils which, in principle, Congress has a right to prevent, must be endured if the only way of avoiding them is by the abridging of that freedom of speech upon which the entire structure of our free institutions rests"); Smith, "Radically Subversive Speech and the Authority of Law," 94 Mich. L. Rev. 348 (1995) (arguing that radically subversive speech is valuable because a democracy, unlike an authoritarian regime, requires recognition of the possibility that the existing state might be illegitimate).

4. ***Vietnam era loosening of clear and present danger.*** Issues parallel to those in the World War I Espionage Act cases arose in connection with opposition to United States policy in the Vietnam war. In **Bond v. Floyd**, 385 U.S. 116 (1966), the Court held that the First Amendment barred Georgia from refusing to seat Julian Bond, a duly elected representative, in the state legislature. The State's justification was that Bond could not conscientiously take the required oath to "support the Constitution of this State and of the United States" in light of statements he had made or subscribed to that were critical of the draft and of Vietnam policy. Bond was an official of the Student Nonviolent Coordinating Committee (SNCC), which issued a statement that "We are in sympathy with, and support, the men in this country who are unwilling to respond to a military draft." Chief Justice WARREN's opinion for a unanimous Court held that Bond could not have been constitutionally convicted for counseling, aiding, or abetting the refusal or evasion of draft registration. The SNCC statement alone "cannot be interpreted as a call to unlawful refusal to be drafted." Nor could Bond's own statement that he admired the courage of people who burned their draft cards. "No useful purpose would be served by discussing the many decisions of this Court which establish that Bond could not have been convicted for these statements consistently with the First Amendment." And Bond's position as an elected legislator did not change the situation: "[W]hile the State has an interest in requiring its legislators to swear to a belief in constitutional processes of government, surely the oath gives it no interest in limiting its legislators' capacity to discuss their views of local or national policy."

5. ***The modern incitement test and the Court's repudiation of Whitney.*** By the 1960s, the Court had become more protective of speech in connection with the civil rights movement, and the fear of domestic communism had abated politically. In a case arising from a prosecution under a state syndicalism statute much like the one upheld in Whitney, the Court overruled that decision, retaining a form of the clear and present danger test but making that test much more difficult for the government to satisfy:

———

Brandenburg v. Ohio

395 U.S. 444, 89 S. Ct. 1827, 23 L. Ed. 2d 430 (1969).

■ Per Curiam.

The appellant, a leader of a Ku Klux Klan group, was convicted under the Ohio Criminal Syndicalism statute for "advocat[ing] the duty, necessity, or propriety of crime, sabotage, violence, or unlawful methods of terrorism as a means of accomplishing industrial or political reform" and for "voluntarily assembl[ing] with any society, group, or assemblage of persons formed to teach or advocate the doctrines of criminal syndicalism." He was fined $1,000 and sentenced to one to 10 years' imprisonment.

The record shows that a man, identified at trial as the appellant, telephoned an announcer-reporter on the staff of a Cincinnati television station and invited him to come to a Ku Klux Klan "rally" to be held at a [farm]. With the cooperation of the organizers, the reporter and a cameraman attended the meeting and filmed the events. Portions of the films were later broadcast on the local station and on a national network. The prosecution's case rested on the films and on testimony identifying the appellant as the person who communicated with the reporter and who spoke at the [rally]. One film showed 12 hooded figures, some of whom carried firearms. They were gathered around a large wooden cross, which they burned. No one was present other than the participants and the newsmen who made the film. Most of the words uttered during the scene were incomprehensible when the film was projected, but scattered phrases could be understood that were derogatory of Negroes and, in one instance, of Jews.[1] Another scene on the same film showed the appellant, in Klan regalia, making a speech. The speech, in full, was as follows: "This is an organizers' meeting. We have had quite a few members here today which are—we have hundreds, hundreds of members throughout [Ohio]. I can quote from a newspaper clipping from the Columbus, Ohio Dispatch, five weeks ago Sunday morning. The Klan has more members in [Ohio] than does any other organization. We're not a revengent organization, but if our President, our Congress, our Supreme Court, continues to suppress the white, Caucasian race, it's possible that there might have to be some revengeance taken. We are marching on Congress July the Fourth, four hundred thousand strong. From there we are dividing into two groups, one group to march on St. Augustine, Florida, the other group to march into Mississippi. Thank you." The second film showed six hooded figures one of whom, later identified as the appellant, repeated a speech very similar to that recorded on the first film. The reference to the possibility of "revengeance" was omitted, and one sentence was added: "Personally, I believe the nigger should be returned to Africa, the Jew returned to Israel." Though some of the figures in the films carried weapons, the speaker did not.

The Ohio [law] was enacted in 1919. From 1917 to 1920, identical or quite similar laws were adopted by 20 States and two territories. [In 1927,] this Court sustained the constitutionality of California's Criminal Syndicalism Act, the text of which is quite similar to that of the laws of Ohio. [Whitney.] The Court upheld the statute on the ground that, without more, "advocating" violent means to effect political and economic change involves such danger to the security of the State that the State may outlaw it. But Whitney has been thoroughly discredited by later decisions. See [Dennis]. These later decisions have fashioned the principle that the constitutional guarantees of free speech and free press do not permit a State to forbid or proscribe advocacy of the use of force or of law violation except where such advocacy is directed to inciting or producing imminent lawless action and is likely to incite or produce such action. "[The] mere abstract teaching [of] the moral propriety or even moral necessity for a resort to force and violence, is not the same as preparing a group for violent action and steeling it to such

---

[1]   The significant portions that could be understood were: "How far is the nigger going to— yeah"; "This is what we are going to do to the niggers"; "A dirty nigger"; "Send the Jews back to Israel"; "Let's give them back to the dark garden"; "Save America"; "Let's go back to constitutional betterment"; "Bury the niggers"; "We intend to do our part"; "Give us our state rights"; "Freedom for the whites"; "Nigger will have to fight for every inch he gets from now on." [Footnote by the Court.]

action." A statute which fails to draw this distinction impermissibly intrudes upon the freedoms guaranteed by the First and 14th Amendments. It sweeps within its condemnation speech which our Constitution has immunized from governmental control.

Measured by this test, Ohio's [law] cannot be sustained. The Act punishes persons who "advocate or teach the duty, necessity, or propriety" of violence "as a means of accomplishing industrial or political reform"; or who publish or circulate or display any book or paper containing such advocacy; or who "justify" the commission of violent acts "with intent to exemplify, spread or advocate the propriety of the doctrines of criminal syndicalism"; or who "voluntarily assemble" with a group formed "to teach or advocate the doctrines of criminal syndicalism." Neither the indictment nor the trial judge's instructions to the jury in any way refined the statute's bald definition of the crime in terms of mere advocacy not distinguished from incitement to imminent lawless action. Accordingly, we are here confronted with a statute which, by its own words and as applied, purports to punish mere advocacy and to forbid, on pain of criminal punishment, assembly with others merely to advocate the described type of action.[2] Such a statute falls within the condemnation of the First and 14th Amendments. The contrary teaching of [Whitney] cannot be supported, and that decision is therefore overruled. Reversed.

■ JUSTICE BLACK, concurring.

I agree with [Justice Douglas] that the "clear and present danger" doctrine should have no place in the interpretation of the First Amendment. I join the Court's opinion, which, as I understand it, simply cites [Dennis] but does not indicate any agreement [with] the "clear and present danger" doctrine on which Dennis purported to rely.

■ JUSTICE DOUGLAS, concurring.

[Though] I doubt if the "clear and present danger" test is congenial to the First Amendment in time of a declared war, I am certain it is not reconcilable with the First Amendment in days of peace. [I] see no place in the regime of the First Amendment for any "clear and present danger" test, whether strict and tight as some would make it, or free-wheeling as the Court in Dennis rephrased it. When one reads the opinions closely and sees when and how the "clear and present danger" test has been applied, great misgivings are aroused. First, the threats were often loud but always puny and made serious only by judges so wedded to the status quo that critical analysis made them nervous. Second, the test was so twisted and perverted in Dennis as to make the trial of those teachers of Marxism an all-out political trial which was part and parcel of the cold war that has eroded substantial parts of the First Amendment. [The] line between what is permissible and not subject to control and what may be made impermissible and subject to regulation is the line between ideas and overt acts. The example usually given by those who would punish speech is the case of one who falsely shouts fire in a crowded theatre. This is, however, a classic case where speech is brigaded with action.

---

[2] Statutes affecting the right of assembly, like those touching on freedom of speech, must observe the established distinctions between mere advocacy and incitement to imminent lawless action, for "[the] right of peaceable assembly is a right cognate to those of free speech and free press and is equally fundamental." [Footnote by the Court.]

THE MEANING AND IMPLICATIONS OF BRANDENBURG

1. ***The best of Hand and Holmes?*** Can Brandenburg be viewed as combining Hand's incitement emphasis in Masses with the consequentialism of Holmes's clear and present danger test? Consider the following comment: "The incitement emphasis is Hand's; the reference to 'imminent' reflects a limited influence of Holmes, combined with later experience; and 'the likely to incite or produce such action' addition in the Brandenburg standard is the only reference to the need to guess about future consequences of speech, so central to the Schenck approach. Under Brandenburg, probability of harm is no longer the central criterion for speech limitations. The inciting language of the speaker—the Hand focus on 'objective' words—is the major consideration. And punishment of the harmless inciter is prevented by the Schenck-derived requirement of a likelihood of dangerous consequences." Gunther, "Learned Hand and the Origins of Modern First Amendment Doctrine," 27 Stan. L. Rev. 719 (1975).

2. ***Later applications of Brandenburg: antiwar protests, civil rights boycotts, antiabortion websites.*** The Brandenburg standard was the primary ground for reversal of a disorderly conduct conviction in **Hess v. Indiana**, 414 U.S. 105 (1973). After a campus antiwar demonstration during which there had been arrests, over 100 demonstrators blocked the street until they were moved to the curb by the police. Hess, standing off the street, said: "We'll take the fucking street later (or again)." The state court relied primarily on a finding that this statement was "intended to incite further lawless action on the part of the crowd in the vicinity of appellant and was likely to produce such action." The Court summarily reversed: "At best, [the] statement could be taken as counsel for present moderation; at worst, it amounted to nothing more than advocacy of illegal action at some indefinite future time." The Court added that "since there was no evidence, or rational inference from the import of the language, that his words were intended to produce, and likely to produce, *imminent* disorder, those words could not be punished by the State on the ground that they had 'a tendency to lead to violence.'"

In **NAACP v. Claiborne Hardware Co.**, 458 U.S. 886 (1982), the Court set aside, on First Amendment grounds, a large damages award against alleged participants in an economic boycott of white merchants by civil rights activists in a Mississippi county. The boycott sought to secure compliance with a list of demands for racial justice. One of the defendants was Charles Evers, the Field Secretary of the NAACP, who took a leading role in the boycott. One of the arguments advanced to defend the imposition of liability on Evers was that "a finding that his public speeches were likely to incite lawless action could justify holding him liable for unlawful conduct that in fact followed within a reasonable period." In one speech, Evers had stated that boycott violators would be "disciplined" by their own people. Justice STEVENS's opinion rejected the incitement rationale for imposing liability on Evers:

"While many of the comments in Evers' speeches might have contemplated 'discipline' in the permissible form of social ostracism, it cannot be denied that references [e.g.] to the possibility that necks would be [broken] implicitly conveyed a sterner message. In the passionate atmosphere in which the speeches were delivered, they might have been understood as inviting an unlawful form of discipline or, at least, as intending to create a fear of violence whether or not improper discipline was specifically intended. [This] Court has made clear, however, that mere *advocacy* of the use of force or violence does not remove speech from the protection of the First Amendment. [The] emotionally charged rhetoric of Charles Evers' speeches did not transcend the bounds of protected speech set forth in Brandenburg. The lengthy addresses generally contained an impassioned plea for black citizens to unify, to support and respect each other, and to realize the political and economic power available to them. In the course of those pleas, strong language was used. If that language had been followed by acts of violence, a substantial question would be presented whether Evers could be held liable for the consequences of that unlawful conduct. In this case, however, [almost all] acts of violence identified in 1966 occurred weeks or months after the April 1, 1966 speech; the chancellor made no finding of any violence after the challenged 1969 speech. [When an advocate's] appeals do not incite lawless action, they must be regarded as protected speech."

Does a true threat against particular individuals take speech outside any consideration of the associated political message under Brandenburg? Does the speech protection set forth in Claiborne Hardware attenuate when antiabortion activists, on a website on the Internet, display "WANTED" posters identifying physicians who perform abortions, with lines drawn through the names of those doctors who provided abortion services who had been killed or wounded by persons opposing abortion through violence? In **Planned Parenthood v. American Coalition of Life Activists**, 290 F.3d 1058 (9th Cir. 2002) (en banc), a sharply divided court of appeals upheld the application of civil liability to such speech under the Freedom of Access to Clinics Entrances Act (FACE), which provides a right of action against whoever by "threat of force [intentionally] intimidates [any] person because that person is or has been [providing] reproductive health services." 18 U.S.C. § 248(a)(1) & (c)(1)(A). The majority opinion stated that, "while advocating violence is protected, threatening a person with violence is not. [We] disagree that Claiborne is closely analogous. Claiborne, of course, did not arise under a threats statute. [As] the opinion points out, there was no context to give the speeches (including the expression 'break your neck') the implication of authorizing or directly threatening unlawful conduct. [No] specific individuals were targeted. For all that appears, 'the break your neck' comments were hyperbolic vernacular." The court held that the First Amendment did not bar submission to a jury of the question whether the "wanted" posters and similar expression constituted "true threats" under FACE. The dissenters objected that, while "the statements could reasonably be interpreted as an effort to intimidate plaintiffs into ceasing their abortion-related activities, [the] Supreme Court has told us that 'speech does not lose its protected character . . . simply because it may embarrass others or coerce them into action.' Claiborne Hardware. In other words, some forms of intimidation enjoy constitutional protection. [To] the extent Claiborne Hardware differs from our case, the difference makes ours a far weaker case for the imposition of liability." Which side had the better of the argument? For discussion of the case, see Karst, "Threats and Meanings: How the Facts Govern First Amendment Doctrine," 58 Stan. L. Rev. 1337 (2006).

3. *The scope of Brandenburg: factual data and torts.* The "incitement" and "advocacy" language of Brandenburg describes speech that

in some way *urges* people to action. Does Brandenburg apply as well to the communication of *information* that may facilitate criminal acts but does not advocate the law violation? For example, consider instructions on the chemical procedures manufacturing illegal drugs, a manual on how to be a "hit man," plans for the security system at Fort Knox, or information allegedly endangering national security because it relates to the construction of illegal (in private hands) bombs or weapons. Do the dangers involved in the dissemination of this type of information fit the Brandenburg model?

Moreover, consider whether Brandenburg should apply in the absence of any "political" component to the speech. For example, does Brandenburg have any application to speech facilitating purely private, interpersonal crimes, and lacking in any broader ideological aim or context? Consider the definition of criminal solicitation in the ALI Model Penal Code, § 5.02(1): "A person is guilty of solicitation to commit a crime if with the purpose of promoting or facilitating its commission he commands, encourages, or requests another person to engage in specific conduct which would constitute such crime or an attempt to commit such crime or which would establish his complicity in its commission or attempted commission." See also the definitions of attempt and conspiracy in Model Penal Code §§ 5.01(1)(c) and 5.03(1). See generally Greenawalt, Speech, Crime, and the Uses of Language (1989).

As the incitement cases illustrate, many instances of speech that make it easier for listeners or readers to commit crimes also have valuable uses: a manual on contract assassination may also be useful to mystery writers and executives seeking to instruct security details. Should the valuable element immunize the dangerous element? Consider the proposed rule "that crime-facilitating speech ought to be constitutionally protected unless (1) it's said to a person or a small group of people when the speaker knows these few listeners are likely to use the information for criminal purposes, (2) it's within one of the few classes of speech that has almost no noncriminal value, or (3) it can cause extraordinarily serious harm (on the order of a nuclear attack or a plague) even when it's also valuable for lawful purposes." Volokh, "Crime-Facilitating Speech," 57 Stan. L. Rev. 1095 (2005). Does such a rule adequately limit the scope of Brandenburg?

Should the First Amendment protect a mass-market trade book whose topic is crime facilitation? Would Volokh's test require as much? A suit for civil liability for wrongful death was permitted to proceed against the book Hit Man: A Technical Manual for Independent Contractors. The publisher stipulated that it knew the book would be read by would-be murderers for hire. The court of appeals reversed dismissal of the suit, stating that the publisher's "astonishing stipulations, coupled with the extraordinary comprehensiveness, detail, and clarity of Hit Man's instructions for criminal activity and murder in particular, the boldness of its palpable exhortation to murder, the alarming power and effectiveness of its peculiar form of instruction, the notable absence from its text of the kind of ideas for the protection of which the First Amendment exists, and the book's evident lack of any even arguably legitimate purpose beyond the promotion and teaching of murder, render this case unique in the law. In at least these circumstances, we are confident that the First Amendment does not erect the absolute bar to the imposition of civil liability." **Rice v. Paladin Enters.**, 128 F.3d 233 (4th Cir. 1997). Would the case have been permissible absent the publisher's stipulation?

Finally, is the incitement deemed punishable by Brandenburg limited to face-to-face encounters? Can lawless action be directed over television, radio, cable or the internet? Does use of such communications media preclude a finding of imminence? In an age of instantaneous global communication over the internet and social media, does an imminence requirement make it too difficult for government to take adequate preventive measures in the face of terrorist threats?

4. ***Brandenburg and new threats of terrorism.*** Acts of domestic and international terrorism have inspired new political efforts to curtail speech that might incite violence. For example, in the wake of the 1995 Oklahoma City bombing of a federal building and day care center, members of Congress considered amending federal law to prohibit dissemination of bombmaking information. In 1999, after extensive study by the DOJ of possible free speech objections, Congress enacted a law making it an offense "to teach or demonstrate the making or use of an explosive, a destructive device, or a weapon of mass destruction, or to distribute by any means information pertaining to, in whole or in part, the manufacture or use of an explosive, destructive device, or weapon of mass destruction" either knowing or intending "that the teaching, demonstration, or information be used for, or in furtherance of, an activity that constitutes a Federal crime of violence." Pub. L. No. 106–54, 113 Stat. 398. Does the intent requirement conform the statute to Brandenburg? Even without an imminence requirement?

The bombing of the World Trade Center and the Pentagon on September 11, 2001, and the fear of further terrorist activity by al Qaeda and other groups, have led to renewed initiatives to limit the circulation of information related to terrorist methods. "Are we entering an age where the clear and present danger will push back on the Brandenburg standard? [When] the law feels the full force of the [chemical, biological, nuclear, and radiological weapons] threat, the decision may well be made that that this test no longer fits the times we face." Donohue, "Terrorist Speech and the Future of Free Expression," 27 Cardozo L. Rev. 233 (2005). Does pure technological information stripped of any political advocacy even trigger Brandenburg at all?

In an age of proliferating terrorist incidents, should Brandenburg be relaxed to permit regulation of speech that inspires conversion to terrorist causes? Other nations do not enforce such stringent protections of speech. For example, the British Terrorism Act of 2006, passed in the wake of the July 7, 2005 bombings in London, prohibits publishing "a statement that is likely to be understood by some or all of the members of the public to whom it is published as a direct or indirect encouragement or other inducement to them to the commission, preparation or instigation of acts of terrorism." Indirect encouragement includes a statement that "glorifies the commission or preparation (whether in the past, in the future or generally) of such acts or offences; and is a statement from which those members of the public could reasonably be expected to infer that what is being glorified is being glorified as conduct that should be emulated by them in existing circumstances." 2006 Terrorism Act, Chapter 11. The Act requires intent or recklessness toward such encouragement. Would Brandenburg forbid a similar law in the United States? If so, should U.S. law be changed to emulate British law? For further consideration of Brandenburg's application to modern terrorist threats, see Healy, "Brandenburg in a Time of Terror," 84 Notre Dame L. Rev. 655 (2009).

In practice, speech in support of terrorism has been prosecuted under the so-called "material support" statute, 18 U.S.C. § 2339B. The statute criminalizes the knowing provision of "material support or resources to [an organization the entity knows to have been designated as] a foreign terrorist organization." Material support is defined as "any property, tangible or intangible, or service, including currency or monetary instruments or financial securities, financial services, lodging, training, expert advice or assistance." The Court addressed the constitutionality of this approach in Holder v. Humanitarian Law Project (2010; p. 271), in an opinion that did not mention Brandenburg at all. In that case, several U.S. citizens and organizations, including the Humanitarian Law Project, sought to facilitate the humanitarian and political activities of two groups—the Partiya Karkeran Kurdistan and the Liberation Tigers of Tamil Eelam—that had been designated by the Secretary of State as foreign terrorist organizations. HLP challenged application of the material support statute to that conduct, arguing that the prohibition was a violation of their right to freedom of speech and association under the First Amendment. HLP argued that the Government should have had to prove that plaintiffs had specific intent to further the organization's unlawful, violent activities. The Court upheld the law as applied to HLP, however, giving Congress and the executive deference in determining the types of activities that could further a terrorist threat. It held that the Government was prohibiting material support in the form of speech, but that the suppression was justified to achieve a compelling interest in preventing terrorism. Does the definition of such speech as material support render Brandenburg irrelevant for contemporary speech? Does the fact that the Court gave the Government deference on the severity of the threat posed by the communications do so? In addition to the deference argument, the Court also argued that "[m]aterial support meant to 'promot[e] peaceable, lawful conduct,' can further terrorism by [lending] legitimacy to foreign terrorist groups [which] makes it easier for those groups to persist, to recruit members, and to raise funds—all of which facilitate more terrorist attacks, [and because] money is fungible, and [may be used to support terrorist activities.]" Should the Court have required additional proof that these types of "material support" actually posed a threat? For discussion of Holder's likely impact on Brandenburg, see Cole, "The First Amendment's Borders," 6. Harv. L. & Pol'y Rev. 147 (2012) (exploring potential implications of the decision and possibilities for narrowing its application in future cases).

5. *Brandenburg in the wake of January 6th.* In the wake of the January 6, 2021 attack on the Capitol, much discussion focused on the Brandenburg standard, particularly in connection with a speech made by President Donald Trump earlier the same day on the Ellipse, near the White House. The second impeachment of President Trump charged him with "incitement of insurrection" based in part on the speech. The article stated that, in the speech, President Trump "reiterated false claims that 'we won this election, and we won it by a landslide'. He also willfully made statements that, in context, encouraged—and foreseeably resulted in—lawless action at the Capitol, such as: 'if you don't fight like hell you're not going to have a country anymore'. Thus incited by President Trump, members of the crowd he had addressed, in an attempt to, among other objectives, interfere with the Joint Session's solemn constitutional duty to certify the results of the 2020 Presidential election, unlawfully breached and vandalized the Capitol, injured and killed law enforcement personnel, menaced Members of

Congress, the Vice President, and Congressional personnel, and engaged in other violent, deadly, destructive, and seditious acts." During the impeachment trial before the Senate, the president's defense team and some senators argued that President Trump's conduct had not satisfied the Brandenburg standard and therefore did not constitute incitement. Whether the First Amendment applies in an impeachment hearing is a controversial issue beyond the scope of this Note. Few courts have (yet) addressed the issue of Brandenburg and President Trump's potential criminal liability. However, in denying a motion to dismiss for failure to state a claim, the federal district court for the District of Columbia in **Thompson v. Trump**, 2022 WL 503384 (Feb 18., 2022), wrote that "[t]he 'import' of the President's words must be viewed within the broader context in which the Speech was made and against the Speech as a whole. Before January 6th, the President and others had created an air of distrust and anger among his supporters. . . . Some of his supporters' beliefs turned to action. In the weeks after the election, some had made threats against state election officials and others clashed with police in Washington, D.C., following pro-Trump rallies. The President would have known about these events, as they were widely publicized. Against this backdrop, the President invited his followers to Washington, D.C., on January 6th. It is reasonable to infer that the President would have known that some supporters viewed his invitation as a call to action." In applying this analysis, the court stated that it did not matter if the call to violence was explicit or not. The court cited **Bible Believers v. Wayne County, Mich.**, 805 F.3d 228, 246 (6th Cir. 2015), to the effect that the first element in Brandenburg is whether "the speech explicitly or implicitly encouraged the use of violence or lawless action."

SECTION 3. FIGHTING WORDS AND HOSTILE AUDIENCES

Like the cases covered above in section 2, the cases that follow involve the problem of speech that induces violence or potential violence on the part of listeners. But here the violence is directed against the speaker rather than undertaken in sympathy with the speaker's cause. The typical claim is that a speaker's provocative message so outrages the audience that some listeners are likely to resort to violence in response. The state seeks to stop the speaker in order to promote the interest in assuring order and avoiding violence. The problem has arisen both in the context of one-on-one encounters between individuals, which has given rise to the doctrine of "fighting words," and in the context of encounters between speakers and hostile audiences, which has given rise to judicial concern over the problem of the "heckler's veto."

Does the apprehension of hostile listener reaction justify restricting the speaker? Should speakers be punished for provoking listeners to punch or want to punch them in the nose? Only if the speaker uses extremely provocative words? Even if the audience is very easily provoked? Does the First Amendment impose an obligation on the government to protect the speaker from the violent listener or the angry crowd? Or may government stop the speaker, simply by showing that his words created an immediate danger of disorder? Would recognition of that justification legitimate a "heckler's veto"? Assuming that law enforcement's capacity to prevent violent listener reaction will never be perfect, must society tolerate occasional brawls as a price of free speech?

FIGHTING WORDS

Chaplinsky v. New Hampshire
315 U.S. 568, 62 S. Ct. 766, 86 L. Ed. 1031 (1942).

[Chaplinsky, a Jehovah's Witness engaged in distributing literature on the streets of Rochester, New Hampshire, had allegedly attracted a "restless" crowd by denouncing all religion as a "racket." When a disturbance broke out, a police officer escorted Chaplinsky away. The police officer and Chaplinsky encountered the City Marshal. In the ensuing argument between Chaplinsky and the City Marshal, Chaplinsky called the Marshal a "God damned racketeer" and "a damned Fascist," adding that "the whole government of Rochester are Fascists or agents of Fascists"). Chaplinsky was subsequently convicted under a state law stating that no person "shall address any offensive, derisive or annoying word to any other person who is lawfully in any street or other public place, nor call him by any offensive or derisive name."]

■ JUSTICE MURPHY delivered the opinion of the Court.

It is now clear that "Freedom of speech and freedom of the press, which are protected by the First Amendment from infringement by Congress, are among the fundamental personal rights and liberties which are protected by the Fourteenth Amendment from invasion by state action." Allowing the broadest scope to the language and purpose of the Fourteenth Amendment, it is well understood that the right of free speech is not absolute at all times and under all circumstances. There are certain well-defined and narrowly limited classes of speech, the prevention and punishment of which have never been thought to raise any Constitutional problem. These include the lewd and obscene, the profane, the libelous, and the insulting or "fighting" words—those which by their very utterance inflict injury or tend to incite an immediate breach of the peace. It has been well observed that such utterances are no essential part of any exposition of ideas, and are of such slight social value as a step to truth that any benefit that may be derived from them is clearly outweighed by the social interest in order and morality. "Resort to epithets or personal abuse is not in any proper sense communication of information or opinion safeguarded by the Constitution, and its punishment as a criminal act would raise no question under that instrument."

The state statute here challenged comes to us authoritatively construed by the highest court of New Hampshire. On the authority of its earlier decisions, the state court declared that the statute's purpose was to preserve the public peace, no words being "forbidden except such as have a direct tendency to cause acts of violence by the person to whom, individually, the remark is addressed." It was further said: "The word 'offensive' is not to be defined in terms of what a particular addressee thinks. The test is what men of common intelligence would understand would be words likely to cause an average addressee to fight. The English language has a number of words and expressions which by general consent are 'fighting words' when said without a disarming smile. Such words, as ordinary men know, are likely to cause a fight. So are threatening, profane or obscene revilings. Derisive and annoying words can be taken as coming within the purview of the statute as heretofore interpreted only when they have this characteristic of plainly tending to excite the addressee to a breach of the peace. The statute, as construed, does no more than prohibit the face-to-face words plainly likely to cause a breach of the peace by the addressee, words whose speaking constitute a breach of the peace by the speaker—including 'classical fighting words', words in current use less 'classical' but equally likely to cause violence, and other disorderly words, including profanity, obscenity and threats."

We are unable to say that the limited scope of the statute as thus construed contravenes the constitutional right of free expression. It is a statute narrowly drawn and limited to define and punish specific conduct lying within the domain of state power, the use in a public place of words likely to cause a breach of the peace. Nor can we say that the application of the statute to the facts disclosed by the record substantially or unreasonably impinges upon the privilege of free speech. Argument is unnecessary to demonstrate that the appellations 'damn racketeer' and 'damn Fascist' are epithets likely to provoke the average person to retaliation, and thereby cause a breach of the peace.

Affirmed.

———

FIGHTING WORDS SINCE CHAPLINSKY

1. ***The Court's methodology in excluding "fighting words" from First Amendment protection.*** The Chaplinsky opinion illustrates the intersection of the categorization and balancing approaches to free speech analysis. In describing "fighting words" as one of the "classes of speech, the prevention and punishment of which have never been thought to raise any Constitutional problem," the decision categorized such speech as wholly outside of First Amendment coverage. But in reaching that categorical holding, Justice Murphy engaged in balancing: he attached a low value to the speech claiming protection ("no essential part of any exposition of ideas"; "slight social value as a step to truth"), and measured that weak variety of "speech" against the competing state interests ("any benefit that may be derived [is] clearly outweighed by the social interest in order and morality"). Such balancing took place, however, at the general, wholesale or definitional level, producing a total exclusion of a class of speech from First Amendment coverage and avoiding any more particularized inquiry.

2. ***The contemporary vitality of the "fighting words" exception.*** The Court has never overruled Chaplinsky's holding that "fighting words" are excluded from free speech protection, but it has not sustained a conviction on the basis of the fighting words doctrine since Chaplinsky. Does this mean that the fighting words doctrine is "nothing more than a quaint remnant of an earlier morality that has no place in a democratic society dedicated to the principle of free expression"? Gard, "Fighting Words as Free Speech," 58 Wash. U. L.Q. 531, 535–36 (1980). Consider the view that, especially in light of later Supreme Court decisions upholding the right to use profane language in many settings, "the entire treatment of the First Amendment in Chaplinsky is based upon some moralistic aberration in free speech jurisprudence that infects the entire fighting words thesis and deserves to be extirpated as a poisonous weed in the field of the First

Amendment." Caine, "The Trouble with 'Fighting Words': Chaplinsky v. New Hampshire Is a Threat to First Amendment Values and Should Be Overruled," 88 Marq. L. Rev. 441 (2004). For a contrary view, see Greenawalt, "Insults and Epithets, Are They Protected Speech?", 42 Rutgers L. Rev. 287 (1990) (arguing that fighting words should not be protected because they are intended to inflict harm rather than communicate ideas).

Is there any danger to freedom of speech even in a precedent that has atrophied from misuse? Does it still lie around like a loaded weapon? One comprehensive study of fighting words cases from 1996–2001 found that Chaplinsky remains an ongoing justification for state punishment of provocative speech, especially in cases involving punishment "of racial minorities for talking back to the police." Caine, supra. Should there be special reason to refrain from punishing speech directed at public officials?

3. *The limitation of the "fighting words" exception.* Justice Murphy's opinion in Chaplinsky defined fighting words as *either* those "which by their very utterance inflict injury" *or* those which "tend to incite an immediate breach of the peace." He also suggested that their suppression was justified by the social interest in "order *and* morality." Later cases, however, have focused only on the breach-of-peace and order rationales. As John Ely put it, later cases made clear that the "fighting words" exception "was no longer to be understood as a euphemism for controversial or dirty talk but was to require instead a quite unambiguous invitation to a brawl." Ely, Democracy and Distrust 114 (1980).

Supreme Court cases since Chaplinsky have repeatedly declined to find such factual support for fighting words convictions. In **Gooding v. Wilson**, 405 U.S. 518 (1972), for example, the Court reversed a conviction under a Georgia statute providing that any person "who shall, without provocation, use to or of [another], opprobrious words or abusive language, tending to cause a breach of the peace," was guilty of a misdemeanor. Antiwar picketers at an Army building refused a police request to stop blocking access to inductees. In the ensuing scuffle, appellee said to a police officer, "White son of a bitch, I'll kill you," "You son of a bitch, I'll choke you to death," and "You son of a bitch, if you ever put your hands on me again, I'll cut you all to pieces." Justice BRENNAN's majority opinion found that statute void on its face because it swept in protected speech ranging beyond the "fighting words" punishable under Chaplinsky: "We have [made] our own examination of the Georgia cases [and conclude that] Georgia appellate decisions have not construed [the statute] to be limited in application, as in Chaplinsky, to words that 'have a direct tendency to cause acts of violence by the person to whom, individually, the remark is addressed.' " See also Rosenfeld v. New Jersey, 408 U.S. 901 (1972) (vacating the conviction of a defendant who used the word "motherfucker" to describe teachers at a school board meeting, holding that in the context of such a meeting, these are not fighting words because they would not have the effect of inciting an immediate breach of the peace.)

Later cases have also tended to limit fighting words to those directed face-to-face to an individual, rather than generally at a group. See Terminiello v. Chicago (1949; p. 62), which reversed the breach-of-peace conviction of a speaker who had condemned an angry crowd outside the auditorium as "snakes," "slimy snakes," "slimy scum." For another example, in **Texas v. Johnson**, 491 U.S. 397 (1989), the Court invalidated on free speech grounds the conviction of a political protestor who burned an

American flag. The statute under which he was convicted prohibited desecration of a flag in a manner the defendant "knows will seriously offend one or more persons likely to observe or discover [such] action." The Court rejected the government's argument that Johnson's conduct fell within the exception for fighting words as defined in Chaplinsky. Justice BRENNAN wrote for the Court: "No reasonable onlooker would have regarded Johnson's generalized expression of dissatisfaction with the policies of the Federal Government as a direct personal insult or an invitation to exchange fisticuffs. We thus conclude that the State's interest in maintaining order is not implicated on these facts." For the complete holding in Texas v. Johnson, see p. 262.

Does the "fighting words" exception as narrowed to words that are invitations to breaches of the peace give too much protection to listeners who threaten to respond to provocation by fighting? Is it based on an outdated and gendered honor culture? Does it wrongly reinforce a macho code of barroom brawls? Does it give too little protection to those who respond to insulting epithets by flight rather than fight? Does it permit greater insult to be leveled at the average woman than the average man? Consider whether it would be constitutional to outlaw "street harassment," defined as occurring when a man addresses to a woman in a public place unwelcome "references to male or female genitalia or to female body parts or to sexual activities, solicitation of sex, [or] similar words that by their very utterance inflict injury or naturally tend to provoke violent resentment, even if the woman did not herself react with violence." See Bowman, "Street Harassment and the Informal Ghettoization of Women," 106 Harv. L. Rev. 517, 575 (1993).

4. *Jehovah's Witness religious persecution revisited.* Like the many Jehovah's Witnesses who were subject to religiously motivated abuse for refusing to salute the flag in the period surrounding the Court's decision in Gobitis (1940; p. 476), Chaplinsky, also a Jehovah's Witness, was subject to abuse on account of his religion. On the day of the altercation, "Walter Chaplinsky [was] surrounded by a group of men who scornfully invited him to salute the flag. While one veteran attempted to pummel Chaplinsky, the town marshal looked on, warned the [Jehovah's] Witness that things were turning ugly, but refused to arrest the assailant. After the marshal left, the assailant returned with a flag and attempted to impale Chaplinsky on the flagpole, eventually pinning him onto a car while other members of the crowd began to beat him. A police officer then arrived, not to detain or disperse members of the mob but to escort Chaplinsky to the police station. En route, the officer and others who joined the escort directed epithets at the hapless Witness. When Chaplinsky responded in kind [he was convicted of the offense at issue in the case]." Blasi & Shiffrin, The Story of W. Virginia State Bd. of Educ. v. Barnette *in* First Amendment Stories (Garnett & Koppelman eds., 2012). The Court in Chaplinsky omitted the details of the altercation leading up to the "fighting words" for which Walter Chaplinsky was convicted. Does the abuse that Chaplinsky was subjected to prior to his altercation with the police officer have any effect on whether his insults were properly considered fighting words?

HOSTILE AUDIENCES AND THE HECKLER'S VETO

The hostile audience cases that follow are similar to the fighting words cases in that they involve speech that provokes unsympathetic listeners to violence or threats of violence. But they differ in three respects. First, unlike fighting words cases, hostile audience cases need not involve speech specifically directed at the listener. Second, fighting words are treated as offensive because of the form their message takes; Chaplinsky would not likely have been convicted if he had said, "with all due respect, I find the incumbent government less than honorable." Hostile audience cases arise when an audience is provoked either by the form of the message or by the message itself. Third, and in part because it is not the form of speech that is pivotal, the hostile audience decisions have addressed the problem through balancing rather than categorization.

Do the "heckler's veto" cases that follow give adequate weight to the First Amendment interests of the abrasive speaker in the public forum, or do they give undue weight to audience reactions as justifications for curtailment of speech? Does the First Amendment impose responsibility on the state to restrain the hostile audience, or does the speaker bear the risk of having his provocative words stopped by the hecklers' response? By what standards can the competing interests best be reconciled? By what mechanisms? Subsequent punishment? Permit systems? Protective custody but not punishment of the speaker in violent situations?

EARLY HOSTILE AUDIENCES CASES

1. *Cantwell and "abusive remarks" not "directed to the person of the hearer."* Jesse Cantwell, a Jehovah's Witness, was arrested while proselytizing on the streets of New Haven, Connecticut, and convicted of the common law offense of inciting a breach of the peace. In **Cantwell v. Connecticut**, 310 U.S. 296 (1940), the Court invalidated the conviction. Justice ROBERTS wrote for the Court: "[We] must determine whether the alleged protection of the State's interest [in 'peace and good order'] has been pressed, in this instance, to a point where it has come into fatal collision with the overriding interest protected by [the First Amendment]. [No] one would have the hardihood to suggest that the principle of freedom of speech sanctions incitement to riot or that religious liberty connotes the privilege to exhort others to physical attack upon those belonging to another sect. When clear and present danger of riot, disorder, interference with traffic upon the public streets, or other immediate threat to public safety, peace, or order appears, the power of the State to prevent or punish is obvious.

"[Having] these considerations in mind, we note that Jesse Cantwell, on April 26, 1938, was upon a public street, where he had a right to be, and where he had a right peacefully to impart his views to others. There is no showing that his deportment was noisy, truculent, overbearing or offensive. [It] is not claimed that he intended to insult or affront the hearers by playing the record. It is plain that he wished only to interest them in his propaganda. The sound of the phonograph is not shown to have disturbed residents of the street, to have drawn a crowd, or to have impeded traffic.

"The record played by Cantwell embodies a general attack on all organized religious systems as instruments of Satan and injurious to man; it then singles out the Roman Catholic Church for strictures couched in terms which naturally would offend not only persons of that persuasion, but all others who respect the honestly held religious faith of their fellows. The hearers were in fact highly offended. One of them said he felt like hitting Cantwell and the other that he was tempted to throw Cantwell off the street. The one who testified he felt like hitting Cantwell said, in answer to the question 'Did you do anything else or have any other reaction?' 'No, sir, because he said he would take the victrola and he went.' The other witness testified that he told Cantwell he had better get off the street before something happened to him and that was the end of the matter as Cantwell picked up his books and walked up the street. Cantwell's conduct, in the view of the court below, considered apart from the effect of his communication upon his hearers, did not amount to a breach of the peace. One may, however, be guilty of the offense if he commit acts or make statements likely to provoke violence and disturbance of good order, even though no such eventuality be intended. [But in practically all such cases], the provocative language which was held to amount to a breach of the peace consisted of profane, indecent, or abusive remarks directed to the person of the hearer.

"We find in the instant case no assault or threatening of bodily harm, no truculent bearing, no intentional discourtesy, no personal abuse. On the contrary, we find only an effort to persuade a willing listener to buy a book or to contribute money in the interest of what Cantwell, however misguided others may think him, conceived to be true religion. [Although] the contents of the record not unnaturally aroused animosity, we think that, in the absence of a statute narrowly drawn to define and punish specific conduct as constituting a clear and present danger to a substantial interest of the State, the petitioner's communication, considered in the light of the constitutional guarantees, raised no such clear and present menace to public peace and order as to render him liable to conviction of the common law offense [in question]."

2. *Terminiello and "provocative" speech that "invites dispute."* In **Terminiello v. Chicago**, 337 U.S. 1 (1949), the Court reversed the breach of the peace conviction of an abrasive speaker, but on the basis of an improper charge to the jury and without directly reaching the "hostile audience" issue. The speaker was Father Arthur Terminiello, sometimes called "the Father Coughlin of the South," a well-known national personality whose speeches and writings warned that the United States must be saved from communists and Jews. Terminiello's speech viciously denounced various political and racial groups. Even before he spoke at an auditorium in the predominantly Jewish Chicago neighborhood of Albany Park, an angry anti-Terminiello crowd had gathered outside the auditorium. Inside, the speaker condemned the crowd as "snakes," "slimy scum," and other epithets. The crowd on the street threw bottles, stink bombs, and brickbats, breaking about twenty-eight windows in the hall. After the disturbance, Terminiello was convicted under a breach of the peace statute construed by the trial judge to include speech which "stirs the public to anger, invites dispute, brings about a condition of unrest, or creates a disturbance." Justice DOUGLAS's majority opinion found that standard unconstitutional: "[A] function of free speech under our system of government is to invite dispute. It may indeed best serve its high purpose when it induces a condition of unrest, creates dissatisfaction with conditions as they are, or even stirs people to anger. Speech is often provocative and challenging. It may strike at prejudices and preconceptions and have profound unsettling effects as it

presses for acceptance of an idea. That is why freedom of speech, though not absolute [Chaplinsky], is nevertheless protected against censorship or punishment, unless shown likely to produce a clear and present danger of a serious substantive evil that rises far above public inconvenience, annoyance, or unrest."

Writing in dissent, Justice JACKSON emphasized what he saw as a direct continuity with the struggle between Fascism and Communism in pre-World War II Europe: "As this case declares a nation-wide rule that disables local and state authorities from punishing conduct which produces conflicts of this kind, it is unrealistic not to take account of the nature, methods and objectives of the forces involved. This was not an isolated, spontaneous and unintended collision of political, racial or ideological adversaries. It was a local manifestation of a world-wide and standing conflict between two organized groups of revolutionary fanatics, each of which has imported to this country the strong-arm technique developed in the struggle by which their kind has devastated Europe. Increasingly, American cities have to cope with it. One faction organizes a mass meeting, the other organizes pickets to harass it; each organizes squads to counteract the other's pickets; parade is met with counterparade. Each of these mass demonstrations has the potentiality, and more than a few the purpose, of disorder and violence. [H]itler summed up the strategy of the mass demonstration as used by both fascism and communism: 'We should not work in secret conventicles but in mighty mass demonstrations, and it is not by dagger and poison or pistol that the road can be cleared for the movement but *by the conquest of the streets.* We must teach the Marxists that the future is National Socialism, just as it will some day be the master of the state.' (Emphasis supplied.) 1 Nazi Conspiracy & Aggression (GPO, 1946) 204, 2 id. 140, Docs. 2760–PS, 404–PS, from 'Mein Kampf.' First laughed at as an extravagant figure of speech, the battle for the streets became a tragic reality when an organized Sturmabteilung [ed. note: Storm Detachment or Brownshirts, a Nazi paramilitary force] began to give practical effect to its slogan that 'possession of the streets is the key to power in the state.' Ibid., also Doc. 2168–PS."

Justice Jackson then pointed to the apparent disparity between the Court's opinions in Terminiello and Chaplinsky: "Only recently this Court held that a state could punish as a breach of the peace use of epithets such as 'damned racketeer' and 'damned fascists,' addressed to only one person, an official, because likely to provoke the average person to retaliation. But these are mild in comparison to the epithets 'slimy scum,' 'snakes,' 'bedbugs,' and the like, which Terminiello hurled at an already inflamed mob of his adversaries. How this present decision, denying state power to punish civilly one who precipitated a public riot involving hundreds of fanatic fighters in a most violent melee, can be squared with [Chaplinsky], is incomprehensible to me. [W]e must bear in mind also that no serious outbreak of mob violence, race rioting, lynching or public disorder is likely to get going without help of some speech-making to some mass of people."

In the light of the failures of liberalism in the Weimar Republic, how seriously do you take Jackson's argument from the Nazi precedent about the need for state control of the streets? As a matter of consequentialist logic, can Terminiello be squared with Chaplinsky? Should "fighting words" doctrine be applicable to speech that provokes a mob? In September of 2012, protests broke out world-wide in response to an anti-Muslim film produced in the United States and viewable on the internet. Should insults to a religion, such as Islam, that are highly likely to provoke violence, count as fighting words?

3. ***Focus on the nature of the speech or of the audience?*** To what extent should protection of speech turn on the response of the particular audience? To what extent should it turn on the words and content of the speech? Can the Court delineate the protected area by holding that words short of "fighting words" are protected, no matter what their probable impact, or should the boundaries of protection depend on the context and environment?

———

Feiner v. New York

340 U.S. 315, 71 S. Ct. 303, 95 L. Ed. 295 (1951).

[Irving Feiner was a young veteran who had returned from three years of service in the armed forces in World War II and was attending university in Syracuse, New York, on the G.I. Bill. In March 1949, Feiner addressed a crowd of 75 to 80 persons, black and white, on a street corner in a predominantly black residential section of Syracuse. Soon after he began, two policemen, summoned by a telephone complaint, arrived to investigate and found the crowd filling the sidewalk and spreading into the street. Feiner's speech made derogatory remarks about President Truman and the Mayor of Syracuse (calling them both "bums") and about the American Legion ("a Nazi Gestapo"). He also said: "The Negroes don't have equal rights; they should rise up in arms and fight for them." Feiner's statements "stirred up a little excitement," and there was "some pushing, shoving and milling around" in the crowd. After Feiner had been speaking about 20 minutes, one of the onlookers said to the arresting policeman: "If you don't get that son of a bitch off, I will go over and get him off there myself." After Feiner ignored two police requests to stop speaking, he was arrested. The disorderly conduct charge stated the grounds as "ignoring and refusing to heed and obey reasonable police orders issued [to] regulate and control said crowd and to prevent a breach [of] the peace and to prevent injuries to pedestrians attempting to use said walk."]

■ CHIEF JUSTICE VINSON delivered the opinion of the Court.

We are not faced here with blind condonation by a state court of arbitrary police action. [The state courts] found that the officers in making the arrest were motivated solely by a proper concern for the preservation of order and protection of the general welfare, and that there was no evidence which could lend color to a claim that the acts of the police were a cover for suppression of petitioner's views and opinions. Petitioner was thus neither arrested nor convicted for the making or the content of his speech. Rather, it was the reaction which it actually engendered. [Cantwell.] [The] findings of the New York courts as to the condition of the crowd and the refusal of petitioner to obey the police requests, supported as they are by the record of this case, are persuasive that the conviction of petitioner for violation of public peace, order and authority does not exceed the bounds of proper state police action. This Court respects, as it must, the interests of the community in maintaining peace and order on its streets. [We] cannot say that the preservation of that interest here encroaches on the constitutional rights of this petitioner.

We are well aware that the ordinary murmurings and objections of a hostile audience cannot be allowed to silence a speaker, and are also mindful of the possible danger of giving overzealous police officials complete discretion to break up otherwise lawful public meetings. [But] we are not faced here with such a situation. It is one thing to say that the police cannot be used as an instrument for the suppression of unpopular views, and another to say that, when as here the speaker passes the bounds of argument or persuasion and undertakes incitement to riot, they are powerless to prevent a breach of the peace. Nor in this case can we condemn the considered judgment of three New York courts approving the means which the police, faced with a crisis, used in the exercise of their power and duty to preserve peace and order. The findings [below] as to [the] imminence of greater disorder coupled with petitioner's deliberate defiance of the police officers convince us that we should not reverse this conviction in the name of free speech.

Affirmed.

■ JUSTICE BLACK, dissenting.

The record before us convinces me that petitioner, a young college student, has been sentenced to the penitentiary for the unpopular views he expressed on matters of public interest while lawfully making a street-corner speech. [It] seems far-fetched to suggest that the "facts" show any imminent threat of riot or uncontrollable disorder. [Nor] does one isolated threat to assault the speaker forebode disorder. [Moreover], assuming that the "facts" did indicate a critical situation, I reject the implication of the Court's opinion that the police had no obligation to protect petitioner's constitutional right to talk. The police of course have power to prevent breaches of the peace. But if, in the name of preserving order, they ever can interfere with a lawful public speaker, they first must make all reasonable efforts to protect him. Here the policemen did not even pretend to try to protect petitioner. According to the officers' testimony, the crowd was restless but there is no showing of any attempt to quiet it; pedestrians were forced to walk into the street, but there was no effort to clear a path on the sidewalk; one person threatened to assault petitioner but the officers did nothing to discourage this when even a word might have sufficed. Their duty was to protect petitioner's right to talk, even to the extent of arresting the man who threatened to interfere. Instead, they shirked that duty and acted only to suppress the right to speak.

Finally, I cannot agree with the Court's statement that petitioner's disregard of the policeman's unexplained request amounted to such "deliberate defiance" as would justify an arrest or conviction for disorderly conduct. On the contrary, I think that the policeman's action was a "deliberate defiance" of ordinary official duty as well as of the constitutional right of free speech. For at least where time allows, courtesy and explanation of commands are basic elements of good official conduct in a democratic society. [Today's] holding means that as a practical matter, minority speakers can be silenced in any city.

———

DISTINGUISHING FEINER IN LATER CASES

1. ***Street demonstrations.*** Contrast the holding in Feiner with the
holdings of several later cases involving street demonstrations that attracted
hostile crowds. In **Edwards v. South Carolina**, 372 U.S. 229 (1963), the
Court reversed breach of peace convictions of 187 black student
demonstrators who had walked along the South Carolina State House
grounds to protest against racial discrimination. They carried placards with
such messages as "Down with segregation." After a large crowd of onlookers
gathered, the marchers were ordered to disperse within 15 minutes; when
they did not do so, they were arrested. The Court, in an opinion by Justice
STEWART, held that "South Carolina infringed the petitioners'
constitutionally protected rights." He added: "The 14th Amendment does not
permit a State to make criminal the peaceful expression of unpopular views.
[Terminiello.]" He noted that there had been no violence by the
demonstrators or the onlookers; that there was no evidence of "fighting
words"; and that the circumstances were "a far cry from the situation" in
Feiner. Justice CLARK's lone dissent viewed the record differently. To him,
there was a "much greater danger of riot and disorder" here than in Feiner.
"[This] was by no means the passive demonstration which this Court relates.
[It] is my belief that anyone conversant with the almost spontaneous
combustion in some Southern communities in such a situation will agree that
the City Manager's action may well have averted a major catastrophe."

Why was the protest march in Edwards held "a far cry" from Feiner?
Does the difference lie in the fact that the onlookers in Edwards in fact
remained peaceful and that ample police were at hand? Should the focus be
on the reasonable audience's reaction, or on the actual audience's response?
Would an outbreak of disorder simply show police failure to protect
"peaceful" speech?

In **Cox v. Louisiana**, 379 U.S. 536 (1965), the Court likewise
invalidated a breach of peace conviction of a civil rights demonstrator who
had attracted the attention of a hostile crowd. In December, 1961, 23
students from a black college were arrested in Baton Rouge, Louisiana, and
jailed for picketing stores that maintained segregated lunch counters. The
next day, appellant Cox, an ordained minister, led about 2,000 students in a
peaceful march toward the courthouse in order to protest the jailing. As Cox
approached the vicinity of the courthouse, he was met by the police chief,
who, according to Cox, permitted the demonstration but insisted that it must
be confined to the west side of the street, across from the courthouse. The
students lined up on the sidewalk 101 feet from the courthouse steps. About
100 to 300 whites gathered on the opposite sidewalk. About 75 policemen
were stationed on the street between the two groups. Some demonstrators
carried picket signs advocating boycotts of "unfair" stores and the group sang
songs and hymns, including "We Shall Overcome" and "God Bless America."
The jailed students, out of sight of the demonstrators, responded by singing,
and this in turn was greeted by cheers from the demonstrators. Cox gave a
speech protesting the "illegal arrest" of the jailed students and urged the
demonstrators to sit at segregated lunch counters. This evoked some
"muttering" and "grumbling" from the white onlookers across the street. The
sheriff viewed Cox's appeal to sit in at lunch counters as "inflammatory" and
ordered the demonstration "broken up immediately." When the
demonstrators did not disperse, policemen exploded tear gas shells. The

demonstrators ran away. The next day, Cox was arrested and charged with several offenses.

Justice GOLDBERG, writing for the Court, invalidated Cox's conviction for "disturbing the peace" by failing to disperse when ordered to do so by a law enforcement officer: "It is clear to us that on the facts of this case, which are strikingly similar to those present in [Edwards], Louisiana infringed appellant's rights of free speech and free assembly by convicting him under this statute. [Our] independent examination of the [record] shows no conduct which the State had a right to prohibit as a breach of the peace. [The State argues] that while the demonstrators started out to be orderly, the loud cheering and clapping by the students in response to the singing from the jail converted the peaceful assembly into a riotous one. The record, however, does not support this assertion. [The] State contends that the conviction should be sustained because of fear expressed [that] 'violence was about to erupt' because of the demonstration. [But] the students themselves were not violent and threatened no violence. [There] is no indication [that] any member of the white group threatened violence. And [the] policemen [could] have handled the crowd. This situation, like that in Edwards, is 'a far cry from the situation in [Feiner].' "

2. ***Permit requirements as an alternative approach.*** Would a prior permit scheme be a more speech-protective mechanism to deal with the hostile audience problem than the use of on-the-spot police discretion? See generally Blasi, "Prior Restraints on Demonstrations," 68 Mich. L. Rev. 1481 (1970).

In **Kunz v. New York**, 340 U.S. 290 (1951), decided the same day as Feiner, the Court reversed a conviction for violating a New York City ordinance which prohibited public worship meetings in the street "without first obtaining a permit" from the police commissioner. The ordinance also made it unlawful "to ridicule or denounce any form of religious belief" or to "expound atheism or agnosticism [in] any street." Kunz, a Baptist minister, was convicted for holding a meeting in 1948 without a permit. Two years earlier, he had obtained a permit, but that had been revoked in the same year after an administrative hearing: there had been complaints that Kunz had engaged in "scurrilous attacks on Catholics and Jews," and the revocation was based on "evidence that he had ridiculed and denounced other religious beliefs in his meetings." Kunz's application for permits in 1947 and 1948 were "disapproved," without stated reasons. Chief Justice VINSON's majority opinion condemned the permit system as involving impermissibly standardless discretion: "Disapproval of the 1948 permit application by the police commissioner was justified by the New York courts on the ground that a permit had previously been revoked 'for good reasons.' It is noteworthy that there is no mention in the ordinance of reasons for which such a permit application can be refused. [We] have here, then, an ordinance which gives an administrative official discretionary power to control in advance the right of citizens to speak on religious matters on the streets of New York. As such, the ordinance is clearly invalid as a prior restraint on the exercise of First Amendment rights."

Justice JACKSON dissented: "[I]f the Court conceives, as Feiner indicates, that upon uttering insulting, provocative or inciting words the policeman on the beat may stop the meeting, then its assurance of free speech in this decision is 'a promise to the ear to be broken to the hope,' if the patrolman on the beat happens to have prejudices of his own. [It] seems to me that this [permit] procedure better protects freedom of speech than to let everyone speak without leave, but subject to surveillance and to being ordered to stop in the discretion of the police."

3. *Permit fees.* Should it be permissible to deny a permit for a meeting or parade due to a lack of police resources to handle the anticipated hostile audience reactions? If not, may government charge demonstrators a fee based on such anticipated reactions? In **Forsyth County, Georgia v. Nationalist Movement**, 505 U.S. 123 (1992), the Court invalidated a county ordinance requiring demonstrators on public property to pay a fee of up to $1000 a day to cover any public cost that "exceeds the usual and normal cost of law enforcement." The county administrator was authorized to vary the fee depending on "the expense incident . . . to the maintenance of public order." The ordinance was passed in response to 1987 civil rights marches in Forsyth County, which had billed itself as "the whitest county in America." After a march by a group of 90 civil rights demonstrators was forced to halt by a crowd of 400 counter-demonstrators, a second march was held in which 20,000 civil rights demonstrators, including several senators and an assistant attorney general, marched successfully past a crowd of 1000 counter-demonstrators, who in turn were contained by 3000 state and local police and national guardsmen. The cost of police protection on that occasion was $670,000. This case arose when a group called the Nationalist Movement proposed to demonstrate in opposition to the federal holiday commemorating the birthday of Martin Luther King, Jr., and was assessed a $100 fee by the county.

The Court, in an opinion by Justice BLACKMUN, held the ordinance facially invalid, reasoning that it left impermissibly standardless discretion in the hands of the county administrator. "There are no articulated standards either in the ordinance or in the county's established practice. The administrator is not required to rely on any objective factors. He need not provide any explanation for his decision, and that decision is unreviewable. Nothing in the law or its application prevents the official from encouraging some views and discouraging others through the arbitrary application of fees. The First Amendment prohibits the vesting of such unbridled discretion in a government official." Justice Blackmun also noted that imposing such a fee legitimated a heckler's veto: "The fee assessed will depend on the administrator's measure of the amount of hostility likely to be created by the speech based on its content. Those wishing to express views unpopular with bottle-throwers, for example, may have to pay more for their permit. [Speech] cannot be financially burdened, any more than it can be punished or banned, simply because it might offend a hostile mob." Nor could the ordinance be saved by the $1000 fee cap, for "a tax based on the content of speech does not become more constitutional because it is a small tax." Chief Justice REHNQUIST, joined by Justices White, Scalia and Thomas, dissented.

Forsyth County suggests that the public should bear the cost of protecting a speaker who is likely to provoke a hostile audience (although it does not rule out the permissibility of a flat user fee for speech in public spaces without regard to whether the audience is likely to be hostile). Is this the proper allocation of the cost, as the public is broadly speaking the beneficiary of free speech? If so, should there be a government-funded victims compensation fund to compensate bystanders injured in a riot caused by a speaker? See generally Schauer, "Uncoupling Free Speech," 92 Colum. L. Rev. 1321 (1992).

Cohen v. California

403 U.S. 15, 91 S. Ct. 1780, 29 L. Ed. 2d 284 (1971).

■ JUSTICE HARLAN delivered the opinion of the Court.

This case may seem at first blush too inconsequential to find its way into our books, but the issue it presents is of no small constitutional significance. [Cohen] was convicted [of violating a California law] which prohibits "maliciously and willfully disturb[ing] the peace or quiet of any neighborhood or person [by] offensive conduct." He was given 30 days' imprisonment. The facts upon which his conviction rests are detailed in the opinion of the [state court] "On April 26, 1968, the defendant was observed in the Los Angeles County Courthouse in the corridor outside [of] the Municipal Court wearing a jacket bearing the words 'Fuck the Draft.' [There] were women and children present in the corridor. The defendant was arrested. The defendant testified that he wore the jacket as a means of informing the public of the depth of his feelings against the Vietnam War and the draft. The defendant did not engage in, nor threaten to engage in, nor did anyone as the result of his conduct in fact commit or threaten to commit any act of violence." In affirming the conviction the [state court] held that "offensive conduct" means "behavior which has a tendency to provoke *others* to acts of violence or to in turn disturb the peace," and that the State had proved this element because, on the facts of this case, "[i]t was certainly reasonably foreseeable that such conduct might cause others to rise up to commit a violent act against the person of the defendant or attempt to forceably remove his jacket." [We reverse.]

I.   In order to lay hands on the precise issue which this case involves, it is useful first to canvass various matters which this record does *not* present. The conviction quite clearly rests upon the asserted offensiveness of the *words* Cohen used to convey his message to the public. The only "conduct" which the State sought to punish is the fact of communication. Thus, we deal here with a conviction resting solely upon "speech," not upon any separately identifiable conduct which allegedly was intended by Cohen to be perceived by others as expressive of particular views but which, on its face, does not necessarily convey any message and hence arguably could be regulated without effectively repressing Cohen's ability to express himself. Cf. [United States v. O'Brien]. Further, the State certainly lacks power to punish Cohen for the underlying content of the message the inscription conveyed. At least so long as there is no showing of an intent to incite disobedience to or disruption of the draft, Cohen [could not] be punished for asserting the evident position on the inutility or immorality of the draft his jacket reflected. [Cohen's] conviction, then, rests squarely upon his exercise of the "freedom of speech" [and] can be justified, if at all, only as a valid regulation of the manner in which he exercised that freedom, not as a permissible prohibition on the substantive message it conveys. This does not end the inquiry, of course, for the [First Amendment has] never been thought to give absolute protection to every individual to speak whenever or wherever he pleases, or to use any form of address in any circumstances that he chooses. In this vein, too, however, we think it important to note that several issues typically associated with such problems are not presented here.

In the first place, Cohen was tried under a statute applicable throughout the entire State. Any attempt to support this conviction on the ground that the statute seeks to preserve an appropriately decorous atmosphere in the courthouse where Cohen was arrested must fail in the absence of any language in the statute that would have put appellant on notice that certain kinds of otherwise permissible speech or conduct would nevertheless [not] be tolerated in certain places. No fair reading of the phrase "offensive conduct" can be said sufficiently to inform the ordinary person that distinctions between certain locations are thereby created.

In the second place, as it comes to us, this case cannot be said to fall within those relatively few categories of instances where prior decisions have established the power of government to deal more comprehensively with certain forms of individual expression simply upon a showing that such a form was employed. This is not, for example, an obscenity case. Whatever else may be necessary to give rise to the States' broader power to prohibit obscene expression, such expression must be, in some significant way, erotic. [Roth.] It cannot plausibly be maintained that this vulgar allusion to the [draft] would conjure up such psychic stimulation in anyone likely to be confronted with Cohen's crudely defaced jacket.

This Court has also held that the States are free to ban the simple use, without a demonstration of additional justifying circumstances, of so-called "fighting words," those personally abusive epithets which, when addressed to the ordinary citizen, are, as a matter of common knowledge, inherently likely to provoke violent reaction. [Chaplinsky.] While the four-letter word displayed by Cohen in relation to the draft is not uncommonly employed in a personally provocative fashion, in this instance it was clearly not "directed to the person of the hearer." No individual actually or likely to be present could reasonably have regarded the words on appellant's jacket as a direct personal insult. Nor do we have here an instance of the exercise of the State's police power to prevent a speaker from intentionally provoking a given group to hostile reaction. There is, as noted above, no showing that anyone who saw Cohen was in fact violently aroused or that [Cohen] intended such a result.

Finally, [much] has been made of the claim that Cohen's distasteful mode of expression was thrust upon unwilling or unsuspecting viewers, and that the State might therefore legitimately act as it did in order to protect the sensitive from otherwise unavoidable exposure to appellant's crude form of protest. Of course, the mere presumed presence of unwilling listeners or viewers does not serve automatically to justify curtailing all speech capable of giving offense. While this Court has recognized that government may properly act in many situations to prohibit intrusion into the privacy of the home of unwelcome views and ideas which cannot be totally banned from the public dialogue, we have at the same time consistently stressed that "we are often 'captives' outside the sanctuary of the home and subject to objectionable speech." The ability of government, consonant with the Constitution, to shut off discourse solely to protect others from hearing it is, in other words, dependent upon a showing that substantial privacy interests are being invaded in an essentially intolerable manner. Any broader view of this authority would effectively empower a majority to silence dissidents simply as a matter of personal predilections.

In this regard, persons confronted with Cohen's jacket were in a quite different posture than, say, those subjected to the raucous emissions of sound trucks blaring outside their residences. Those in the Los Angeles courthouse could effectively avoid further bombardment of their sensibilities simply by averting their eyes. And, while it may be that one has a more substantial claim to a recognizable privacy interest when walking through a courthouse corridor than, for example, strolling through Central Park, surely it is nothing like the interest in being free from unwanted expression in the confines of one's own home. Given the subtlety and complexity of the factors involved, if Cohen's "speech" was otherwise entitled to constitutional protection, we do not think the fact that some unwilling "listeners" in a public building may have been briefly exposed to it can serve to justify this breach of the peace conviction where, as here, there was no evidence that persons powerless to avoid appellant's conduct did in fact object to it, and where [the statute] evinces no concern [with] the special plight of the captive auditor, but, instead, indiscriminately sweeps within its prohibitions all "offensive conduct" that disturbs "any neighborhood or person."

II.   Against this background, the issue flushed by this case stands out in bold relief. It is whether California can excise, as "offensive conduct," one particular scurrilous epithet from the public discourse, either upon the theory of the court below that its use is inherently likely to cause violent reaction or upon a more general assertion that the States, acting as guardians of public morality, may properly remove this offensive word from the public vocabulary. The rationale of the California court is plainly untenable. At most it reflects an "undifferentiated fear or apprehension of disturbance [which] is not enough to overcome the right to freedom of expression." We have been shown no evidence that substantial numbers of citizens are standing ready to strike out physically at whoever may assault their sensibilities with execrations like that uttered by Cohen. There may be some persons about with such lawless and violent proclivities, but that is an insufficient base upon which to erect, consistently with constitutional values, a governmental power to force persons who wish to ventilate their dissident views into avoiding particular forms of expression. The argument amounts to little more than the self-defeating proposition that to avoid physical censorship of one who has not sought to provoke such a response by a hypothetical coterie of the violent and lawless, the States may more appropriately effectuate that censorship themselves.

Admittedly, it is not so obvious that the [First Amendment] must be taken to disable the States from punishing public utterance of this unseemly expletive in order to maintain what they regard as a suitable level of discourse within the body politic. We think, however, that examination and reflection will reveal the shortcomings of a contrary viewpoint. At the outset, we cannot overemphasize that, in our judgment, most situations where the State has a justifiable interest in regulating speech will fall within one or more of the various established exceptions, discussed above but not applicable here, to the usual rule that governmental bodies may not prescribe the form or content of individual expression. Equally important to our conclusion is the constitutional backdrop against which our decision must be made. The constitutional right of free expression is powerful medicine in a society as diverse and populous as ours. It is designed and intended to remove governmental restraints from the arena of public discussion, putting the decision as to what views shall be voiced largely into the hands of each of us, in the hope that use of such freedom will ultimately produce a more capable citizenry and more perfect polity and in the belief that no other approach would comport with the premise of individual dignity and choice upon which our political system rests. See [Whitney concurrence].

To many, the immediate consequence of this freedom may often appear to be only verbal tumult, discord, and even offensive utterance. These are, however, within established limits, in truth necessary side effects of the broader enduring values which the process of open debate permits us to achieve. That the air may at times seem filled with verbal cacophony is, in this sense, not a sign of weakness but of strength. We cannot lose sight of the fact that, in what otherwise might seem a trifling and annoying instance of individual distasteful abuse of a privilege, these fundamental societal values are truly [implicated].

Against this perception of the constitutional policies involved, we discern certain more particularized considerations that peculiarly call for reversal of this conviction. First, the principle contended for by the State seems inherently boundless. How is one to distinguish this from any other offensive word? Surely the State has no right to cleanse public debate to the point where it is grammatically palatable to the most squeamish among us. Yet no readily ascertainable general principle exists for stopping short of that result were we to affirm the judgment below. For, while the particular four-letter word being litigated here is perhaps more distasteful than most others of its genre, it is nevertheless often true that one man's vulgarity is another's lyric. Indeed, we think it is largely because governmental officials cannot make principled distinctions in this area that the Constitution leaves matters of taste and style so largely to the individual.

Additionally, we cannot overlook the fact, because it is well illustrated by the episode involved here, that much linguistic expression serves a dual communicative function: it conveys not only ideas capable of relatively precise, detached explication, but otherwise inexpressible emotions as well. In fact, words are often chosen as much for their emotive as their cognitive force. We cannot sanction the view that the Constitution, while solicitous of the cognitive content of individual speech, has little or no regard for that emotive function which, practically speaking, may often be the more important element of the overall message sought to be [communicated]. Finally, and in the same vein, we cannot indulge the facile assumption that one can forbid particular words without also running a substantial risk of suppressing ideas in the process. Indeed, governments might soon seize upon the censorship of particular words as a convenient guise for banning the expression of unpopular views. [It] is, in sum, our judgment that, absent a more particularized and compelling reason for its actions, the State may not, consistently with the [First Amendment], make the simple public display here involved of this single four-letter expletive a [criminal offense]. Reversed.

■ JUSTICE BLACKMUN, with whom CHIEF JUSTICE BURGER and JUSTICE BLACK join, dissenting.

I dissent, and I do so for two reasons: Cohen's absurd and immature antic, in my view, was mainly conduct and little speech. Further, the case appears to me to be well within the sphere of [Chaplinsky]. As a consequence, this Court's agonizing over First Amendment values seems misplaced and unnecessary.

■ [JUSTICE WHITE dissented on other grounds.]

———

OFFENSIVE SPEECH

1. ***Cohen and Chaplinsky.*** The Court's decision in Cohen highlighted three limitations on the holding of Chaplinsky. First, Chaplinsky had included "the lewd" and "the profane" as categories of speech not entitled to First Amendment protection. Cohen made clear, however, that profanity was at least sometimes protected speech. Second, Cohen reiterated that the fighting words exception is limited to statements "directed to the person of the hearer," not addressed generally to the world at large. Third, Cohen undermined the notion that there is any unprotected category of "words that by their very utterance inflict injury." It emphasized the emotive power of words and suggested that preventing psychic offense was not, at least in this case, a sufficient justification for punishing speech.

2. ***Offensive words and free speech theory.*** Under which theory of the free speech protections does the Court's holding Cohen fall? Did Cohen's inflammatory choice of words serve the interests of the search for truth through discourse? Of self-government? Of personal autonomy? Or did the Court's holding defer to a skepticism of the government's competence in censoring the aesthetics of speech in the public sphere? For an argument that profanity does not contribute to the rational public discourse at the heart of the First Amendment, see Bickel, The Morality of Consent (1975); Cox, The Role of the Supreme Court in American Government (1976).

3. ***Speech thrust on the unwary.*** Justice Harlan asserted that those offended by the message on Cohen's jacket were in a public place. Should it matter that some people (jurors and defendants, for instance) may not be in the courthouse willingly, but under legal compulsion? Harlan also suggested that those in the courthouse who did not like the message could look away and avoid seeing it further. Is this a satisfactory response to speech that breaks decorum?

SECTION 4. INJURY TO REPUTATION, SENSIBILITY, DIGNITY, EQUALITY

While the previous section dealt with speech that provokes violence against the speaker, the following cases involve government regulations of speech that causes harm other than from physical violence to the subjects of his or her speech. The harm at issue in these cases may involve either direct psychological harm to the listener from hearing the hurtful speech or the more indirect harm to reputation or social relations caused by propagating harmful messages to third parties. Consider the decisions below applying the First Amendment increasingly to limit the scope of the unprotected category of libel, to impose similar limits on non-defamation torts, and to define the possible scope of new limits on speech directed at the expression of hatred or contempt toward individuals based on their racial or other group status.

———————

LIBEL

The Court in Chaplinsky (1942; p. 57) readily categorized libel—the tortious assertion as facts of defamatory statements about an individual—as a category of speech undeserving of any First Amendment protection. Over time, the Court has considered constitutional challenges to libel laws and judgments and narrowed the category of libel unprotected by the First Amendment. In more recent decades, the Court has also considered First Amendment limits on non-defamation torts such as the invasion of privacy and the intentional infliction of emotional distress.

Such cases are explored below with respect to injury to individuals, but the Court's first major libel decision after Chaplinsky, in Beauharnais, involved the context of a statute aimed not at the protection of individuals but rather directed at false and injurious statements about racial or other social groups:

———

Beauharnais v. Illinois
343 U.S. 250, 72 S. Ct. 725, 96 L. Ed. 919 (1956).

[Beauharnais, president of the White Circle League in Illinois, had organized the circulation of a leaflet setting forth a petition calling on Chicago officials "to halt the further encroachment, harassment and invasion of white people, their property, neighborhoods and persons, by the Negro." The leaflet called on Chicago's white people to unite and warned that if "persuasion and the need to prevent the white race from becoming mongrelized by the negro will not unite us, then the [aggressions], rapes, robberies, knives, guns and marijuana of the negro surely will." He was convicted under an Illinois criminal group libel law prohibiting the publishing, selling, or exhibiting in any public place of any publication which "portrays depravity, criminality, unchastity, or lack of virtue of a class of citizens, of any race, color, creed or religion, [or which] exposes the citizens of any race, color, creed or religion to contempt, derision, or obloquy, or which is productive of breach of the peace or riots." The trial court had refused to give a "clear and present danger" charge requested by petitioner.]

■ JUSTICE FRANKFURTER delivered the opinion of the Court.

The statute before us is not a catchall enactment left at large by the State court which applied it. [It] is a law specifically directed at a defined evil, its language drawing from history and practice in Illinois and in more than a score of other jurisdictions a meaning confirmed by the Supreme Court of that State in upholding this conviction.

No one will gainsay that it is libelous falsely to charge another with being a rapist, robber, carrier of knives and guns, and user of marijuana. The precise question before us, then, is whether [the 14th Amendment] prevents a State from punishing such libels—as criminal libel has been defined, limited and constitutionally recognized time out of mind—directed at designated collectivities and flagrantly disseminated. [If] an utterance directed at an individual may be the object of criminal sanctions, we cannot deny to a State power to punish the same utterance directed at a defined group, unless we can say that this is a wilful and purposeless restriction unrelated to the peace and well-being of the State.

Illinois [could conclude, from the State's own experience,] that wilful purveyors of falsehood concerning racial and religious groups promote strife and tend powerfully to obstruct the manifold adjustments required for free, ordered life in a metropolitan, polyglot community. From the murder of the abolitionist Lovejoy in 1837 to the Cicero riots of 1951, Illinois has been the scene of exacerbated tension between races, often flaring into violence and destruction. In many of these outbreaks, utterances of the character here in question, so the Illinois legislature could conclude, played a significant part. [In] the face of this history and its frequent obligato of extreme racial and religious propaganda, we would deny experience to say that the Illinois legislature was without reason in seeking ways to curb false or malicious defamation of racial and religious groups, made in public places and by means calculated to have a powerful emotional impact on those to whom it was presented. [It] may be argued, and weightily, that this legislation will not help matters. [But it] is not within our competence to confirm or deny claims of social scientists as to the dependence of the individual on the position of his racial or religious group in the community. [W]e are precluded from saying that speech concededly punishable when immediately directed at individuals cannot be outlawed if directed at groups with whose position and esteem in society the affiliated individual may be inextricably involved. [Libelous] utterances not being within the area of constitutionally protected speech, it is unnecessary, either for us or for the State courts, to consider the issues behind the phrase 'clear and present danger.' [We] find no warrant in the Constitution for denying to Illinois the power to pass the law here under attack.

■ JUSTICE BLACK, with whom JUSTICE DOUGLAS joins, dissenting.

[Reliance upon the 'group libel law'] label may make the Court's holding more palatable for those who sustain it, but the sugar-coating does not make the censorship less deadly. However tagged, the Illinois law is not that criminal libel which has been 'defined, limited and constitutionally recognized time out of mind.' For as 'constitutionally recognized' that crime has provided for punishment of false, malicious, scurrilous charges against individuals, not against huge groups. This limited scope of the law of criminal libel [has] confined state punishment of speech and expression to the narrowest of areas involving nothing more than purely private feuds. Every expansion of the law of criminal libel so as to punish discussion of matters of public concern means a corresponding invasion of the area dedicated to free expression by the First Amendment. [I] think the [First Amendment] 'absolutely' forbids such laws without any 'ifs' or 'buts' or 'whereases.' [If] there be minority groups who hail this holding as their victory, they might consider the possible relevancy of this ancient remark: 'Another such victory and I am undone.' "

■ [JUSTICES DOUGLAS, REED, and JACKSON filed separate dissents.]

THE LEGACY OF BEAUHARNAIS

1. ***Debate over Beauharnais.*** Was Beauharnais correct to subordinate "individualistic liberalism" to prevention of the social harms of group libel? See Riesman, "Democracy and Defamation: Control of Group Libel," 42 Colum. L. Rev. 727 (1942), cited by both majority and minority. Or are group libel laws, as Justice Black suggested, likely to curtail valuable discussion and hurt the very minority groups they seek to protect? See Tanenhaus, "Group Libel," 35 Cornell L.Q. 261 (1950); Beth, "Group Libel and Free Speech," 39 Minn. L. Rev. 167 (1955).

2. *The vitality of Beauharnais.* Have the First Amendment developments of recent decades drained Beauharnais of all vitality? Some of the measures adopted by Skokie, Illinois, in the late 1970s to block planned demonstrations by American neo-Nazis relied on the approach sustained in Beauharnais. As noted in the fuller treatment of the Skokie controversy at p. 105, state and lower federal courts struck down all of the ordinances designed to block the Nazi marchers, including one that prohibited the "dissemination of any materials within [Skokie] which [intentionally] promotes and incites hatred against persons by reasons of their race, national origin, or religion." Most of the judges found Beauharnais no longer controlling. The Seventh Circuit, for example, stated: "It may be questioned, after cases such as Cohen v. California, Gooding v. Wilson, and Brandenburg v. Ohio, whether the *tendency to induce violence* approach sanctioned implicitly in Beauharnais would pass constitutional muster today." Collin v. Smith, 578 F.2d 1197 (7th Cir.1978). But note Justice Blackmun's dissent, joined by Justice Rehnquist, from a denial of a stay of the Court of Appeals order: "Beauharnais has never been overruled or formally limited in any way." Smith v. Collin, 436 U.S. 953 (1978). For examples of later efforts to resuscitate and extend the reasoning of Beauharnais, see the materials at p. 105 on hate speech as well as the materials on the regulation of pornography as the subordination of women at p. 147. For an argument that state efforts to regulate group libel are not only desirable, but also might be constitutional, see Waldron, The Harm in Hate Speech (2012). Can dicta by a lower court contribute to a Supreme Court case being regarded as no longer good law? Or is Beauharnais still good law?

3. *Broader "fundamentals" of reputation.* In his Beauharnais dissent, Justice Black argued that criminal libel "has provided for punishment of false, malicious, scurrilous charges against individuals, not against huge groups. This limited scope of the law of criminal libel is of no small importance. It has confined state punishment of speech and expression to the narrowest of areas involving nothing more than purely private feuds." But is this true? Consider the view that Justice Black's claim ignores a key difference between the personal reputation concerns that animate civil libel cases and the "broader social concern for the *fundamentals* of anyone's reputation or civic dignity as a member of society in good standing" that has served as the focus of criminal libel law. See Waldron, "Dignity and Defamation: The Visibility of Hate," 123 Harv. L. Rev. 1596 (2010). According to Waldron, past cases demonstrate that criminal libel law was actually intended to address defamation on a wider scale. Does this view rehabilitate Beauharnais as a basis for regulating hate speech?

———

FIRST AMENDMENT LIMITS ON LIBEL

Chaplinsky and Beauharnais did not question that libel counted as a category of speech outside the boundaries of First Amendment protection. Subsequently, however, the Court has curtailed the boundaries of libel law to reduce the chilling effect that libel actions can have on the freedom of speech and the freedom of the press.

With some exceptions, most of the cases in this section arose as civil actions brought by private plaintiffs against defendants who then raised the freedom of speech as an affirmative defense. In these cases, the First

Amendment is implicated not when the state itself prohibits or punishes speech directly, but only when the state enforces private causes of action that have the effect of chilling speech by imposing civil damages liability.

New York Times Co. v. Sullivan

376 U.S. 254, 84 S. Ct. 710, 11 L. Ed. 2d 686 (1964).

[This libel action stemmed from a paid, full-page, fundraising advertisement in the New York Times in March 1960 by the Committee to Defend Martin Luther King and the Struggle for Freedom in the South. The ad, headed "Heed Their Rising Voices," charged the existence of "an unprecedented wave of terror" against blacks engaged in nonviolent demonstrations in the South. Sullivan, the Montgomery, Ala., police commissioner, sued the Times and several black clergymen who had signed the ad. Sullivan objected especially to the claim that "truckloads of police armed with shotguns and tear-gas ringed the Alabama State College Campus" in Montgomery and complained about inaccuracies such as the statement that Dr. King had been arrested seven times when he was only arrested four times. Sullivan's witnesses testified that they took the charges to implicate Sullivan, and that he did not participate in the events regarding Dr. King. Sullivan offered no proof that he had suffered actual pecuniary loss. He recovered a judgment for $500,000 under Alabama libel law.]

■ JUSTICE BRENNAN delivered the opinion of the Court.

We are required in this case to determine for the first time the extent to which the constitutional protections for speech and press limit a State's power to award damages in a libel action brought by a public official against critics of his official conduct. [We] hold that the rule of law applied by the Alabama courts is constitutionally deficient for failure to provide the safeguards for freedom of speech and of the press that are required by the [First Amendment] in a libel action brought by a public official against critics of his official conduct. We further hold that under the proper safeguards the evidence presented in this case is constitutionally insufficient to support the judgment." In explaining that conclusion, Justice Brennan stated:]

Under Alabama law, [a] publication is "libelous per se" if the words "tend to injure a person [in] his reputation" or to "bring [him] into public contempt." [Once] "libel per se" has been established, the defendant has no defense as to stated facts unless he can persuade the jury that they were true in all their particulars. [Unless] he can discharge the burden of proving truth, general damages are presumed, and may be awarded without proof of pecuniary injury. The question before us is whether this rule of liability, as applied to an action brought by a public official against critics of his official conduct, abridges the freedom of speech and of the [press].

Respondent [and] the Alabama courts [rely heavily] on statements of this Court to the effect that the Constitution does not protect libelous publications. Those statements do not foreclose our inquiry here. None of the cases sustained the use of libel laws to impose sanctions upon expression critical of the official conduct of public officials. [Like] insurrection, contempt, advocacy of unlawful acts, breach of the peace, obscenity, solicitation of legal business, and the various other formulae for the repression of expression that have been challenged in this Court, libel can claim no talismanic immunity from constitutional limitations. It must be measured by standards that satisfy the [First Amendment].

[W]e consider this case against the background of a profound national commitment to the principle that debate on public issues should be uninhibited, robust, and wide-open, and that it may well include vehement, caustic, and sometimes unpleasantly sharp attacks on government and public officials. The present advertisement, as an expression of grievance and protest on one of the major public issues of our time, would seem clearly to qualify for the constitutional protection. The question is whether it forfeits that protection by the falsity of some of its factual statements and by its alleged defamation of respondent. Authoritative interpretations of the First Amendment guarantees have consistently refused to recognize an exception for any test of truth—whether administered by judges, juries, or administrative officials—and especially not one that puts the burden of proving truth on the speaker. "The constitutional protection does not turn upon the truth, popularity, or social utility of the ideas and beliefs which are offered." [E]rroneous statement is inevitable in free debate and [must] be protected if the freedoms of expression are to have the "breathing space" that they "need [to] survive." [Injury] to official reputation affords no more warrant for repressing speech that would otherwise be free than does factual error. [If] judges are to be treated as "men of fortitude, able to thrive in a hardy climate," surely the same must be true of other government officials, such as elected city commissioners. Criticism of their official conduct does not lose its constitutional protection merely because it is effective criticism and hence diminishes their official reputations.

If neither factual error nor defamatory content suffices to remove the constitutional shield from criticism of official conduct, the combination of the two elements is no less inadequate. This is the lesson to be drawn from the great controversy over the Sedition Act of 1798, which first crystallized a national awareness of the central meaning of the First Amendment. [Although] the Sedition Act was never tested in this Court, the attack upon its validity has carried the day in the court of history. Fines levied in its prosecution were repaid by Act of Congress on the ground that it was unconstitutional. [President Jefferson] pardoned those who had been convicted and sentenced under the Act and remitted their fines. [Its] invalidity [has] also been assumed by Justices of this Court. [These] views reflect a broad consensus that the Act, because of the restraint it imposed upon criticism of government and public officials, was inconsistent with the [First Amendment].

What a State may not constitutionally bring about by means of a criminal statute is likewise beyond the reach of its civil law of libel. The fear of damage awards under a rule such as that invoked by the Alabama courts here may be markedly more inhibiting than the fear of prosecution under a criminal statute. [The] judgment awarded in this case—without the need for any proof of actual pecuniary loss—was [1,000] times greater than that provided by the Sedition Act. And since there is no double jeopardy limitation applicable to civil lawsuits, this is not the only judgment that may be awarded against petitioners for the same publication. Whether or not a newspaper can survive a succession of such judgments, the pall of fear and timidity imposed upon those who would give voice to public criticism is an atmosphere in which the First Amendment freedoms cannot [survive].

The state rule of law is not saved by its allowance of the defense of truth. A defense for erroneous statements honestly made is no less essential here than was the requirement of proof of guilty knowledge which [we have] held indispensable to a valid conviction of a bookseller for possessing obscene writings for sale. [A] rule compelling the critic of official conduct to guarantee the truth of all his factual assertions—and to do so on pain of libel judgments virtually unlimited in amount—leads to a comparable "self-censorship." Allowance of the defense of truth, with the burden of proving it on the defendant, does not mean that only false speech will be deterred.[1] [Under] such a rule, would-be critics of official conduct may be deterred from voicing their criticism, even though it is believed to be true and even though it is in fact true, because of doubt whether it can be proved in court or fear of the expense of having to do so. They tend to make only statements which "steer far wider of the unlawful zone." The rule thus dampens the vigor and limits the variety of public debate. It is inconsistent with the [First Amendment].

The constitutional guarantees require, we think, a federal rule that prohibits a public official from recovering damages for a defamatory falsehood relating to his official conduct unless he proves that the statement was made with "actual malice"—that is, with knowledge that it was false or with reckless disregard of whether it was false or not. [We] consider that the proof presented to show actual malice lacks the convincing clarity which the constitutional standard demands, and hence that it would not constitutionally sustain the judgment for respondent under the proper rule of law. [E.g., we] think the evidence against the Times supports at most a finding of negligence in failing to discover the misstatements, and is constitutionally insufficient to show the recklessness that is required for a finding of actual malice. We also think the evidence was constitutionally defective in another respect: it was incapable of supporting the jury's finding that the allegedly libelous statements were made "of and concerning" respondent. [There] was no reference to respondent in the advertisement, either by name or official position. [As the highest state court made clear, reliance was placed solely] on the bare fact of respondent's official position. [This] has disquieting implications for criticism of governmental conduct. [It raises] the possibility that a good-faith critic of government will be penalized for his criticism [and] strikes at the very center of the constitutionally protected area of free expression. We hold that such a proposition may not constitutionally be utilized to establish that an otherwise impersonal attack on governmental operations was a libel of an official responsible for those operations. Since it was relied on exclusively, [the] evidence was constitutionally insufficient to support a finding that the statements referred to [respondent]. Reversed and remanded.

■ JUSTICE BLACK, with whom JUSTICE DOUGLAS joins, concurring.

[I] base my vote to reverse on the belief that the First and 14th Amendments not merely "delimit" a State's power to award damages to "public officials against critics of their official conduct" but completely prohibit a State from exercising such a [power]. "Malice," even as defined by the Court, is an elusive, abstract concept, hard to prove and hard to disprove. The requirement that malice be proved provides at best an evanescent

---

[1]   Even a false statement may be deemed to make a valuable contribution to public debate, since it brings about "the clearer perception and livelier impression of truth, produced by its collision with error." Mill, On Liberty; see also Milton, Areopagitica. [Footnote by Justice Brennan.]

protection for the right critically to discuss public affairs. [Therefore], I vote to reverse exclusively on the ground that the [defendants] had an absolute, unconditional constitutional right to publish in the Times advertisement their criticisms of the Montgomery agencies and [officials].

[In another concurrence, Justice GOLDBERG, joined by Justice Douglas, stated that the Constitution afforded "an absolute, unconditional privilege to criticize official conduct" of public officials, but did not protect "defamatory statements directed against the private conduct of a public official or private citizen."]

———————

THE MEANING AND IMPLICATIONS OF NEW YORK TIMES

1. *New York Times and the civil rights movement.* By saving the New York Times and other newspapers from potentially crippling damage judgments, the New York Times decision arguably made possible important coverage of and advertisement by the civil rights movement in the South at a time of crucial activity against racial segregation. For an account of the events leading up to the decision and the stakes involved, see Lewis, Make No Law (1991).

2. *The First Amendment interest in false statements of fact.* What is the First Amendment value in the false statements of fact inherent in defamatory statements? Did New York Times overrule the Chaplinsky dictum that libel was a category of speech wholly outside First Amendment protection? Justice Brennan, relying on John Stuart Mill, suggested in New York Times that "[e]ven a false statement may be deemed to make a valuable contribution to public [debate]." But a decade later, Justice Powell wrote for the Court in Gertz v. Welch (1974; p. 86) that, although "[u]nder the First Amendment there is no such thing as a false idea, [there] is no constitutional value in false statements of fact."

Is the better view of New York Times not that it held libel intrinsically valuable, but that it held the protection of negligent libels instrumentally necessary to afford adequate "breathing room" for truth? Consider Justice Powell's acknowledgement in Gertz that "some falsehood" needs to be protected "in order to protect speech that matters." On this view, New York Times continued to treat some libel as wholly unprotected; it simply limited that category to knowingly or recklessly false statements. Consider Justice Brennan's statement soon after New York Times, in Garrison v. Louisiana, 379 U.S. 64 (1964), which extended the New York Times principle to state *criminal* libel cases: "Although honest utterance, even if inaccurate, may further the fruitful exercise of the right of free speech, it does not follow that the lie, knowingly and deliberately published about a public official, should enjoy a like immunity. [For] the use of the known lie as a tool is at once at odds with the premises of democratic government and with the orderly manner in which economic, social, or political change is to be effected. Calculated falsehood falls into that class of utterances [which are excluded under Chaplinsky]. Hence the knowingly false statement and the false statement made with reckless disregard of the truth do not enjoy constitutional protection."

Note that, despite Justice Powell's statement that "there is no such thing as a false idea," the Court has rejected the idea that the First

Amendment requires any separate threshold inquiry into whether an allegedly defamatory statement is one of fact or opinion. See Milkovich v. Lorain Journal Co., 497 U.S. 1 (1990). Writing for the Court, Chief Justice Rehnquist explained that any statement that "does not contain a provably false factual connotation will receive full constitutional protection," but that a false statement of fact gains no constitutional immunity if the speaker simply adds "the words 'I think.' "

3. *The Court's methodology in New York Times.* Soon after the New York Times decision, Harry Kalven reported that Alexander Meiklejohn viewed it as " 'an occasion for dancing in the streets.' " Kalven, "The New York Times Case: A Note on 'The Central Meaning of the First Amendment,' " 1964 Sup. Ct. Rev. 191. In their view, the "central meaning of the [First] Amendment is that seditious libel cannot be made the subject of government sanction," and New York Times got that principle "right side up for the first time." Kalven added "that the effect of the Times opinion," by effectively guaranteeing freedom to criticize the government, "is necessarily to discard or diminish in importance the clear-and-present danger test, the balancing formula, [and] the two-level speech theory of Beauharnais."

Did the Times opinion truly eschew balancing? There was no "ad hoc balancing": no resort to the view "that the court, in each case, balance the individual and social interest in freedom of expression against the social interest sought by the regulation." Emerson, "Toward a General Theory of the First Amendment," 72 Yale L.J. 877 (1963). But as Kalven himself recognized, there was, "of course, a sense in which the Court did indulge in balancing. It did not go the whole way and give an absolute privilege to the 'citizen-critic' "; it did balance "two obvious conflicting interests." As Melville Nimmer described New York Times, it was a case of "definitional balancing": the derivation, through a balancing process, of a series of categorical rules for differing problems of free speech. Nimmer, "The Right to Speak from Times to [Time]," 56 Calif. L. Rev. 935 (1968). On this view, a category of unprotected speech simply represents a per se rule for an implicit balancing that would always come out the same way if engaged in case by case. For a critical analysis of definitional balancing, see Aleinikoff, "Constitutional Law in the Age of Balancing," 96 Yale L.J. 943 (1987).

4. *Criticism of New York Times.* There have been recurrent attacks on New York Times on the ground that it gives inadequate protection to the reputation interests of defamation plaintiffs. See, e.g., Nagel, "How Useful is Judicial Review in Free Speech Cases?," 69 Cornell L. Rev. 302 (1984); Monaghan, "Of 'Liberty' and 'Property,' " 62 Cornell L. Rev. 405 (1977). For a critical analysis of the reputation interest, see Post, "The Social Foundations of Defamation Law: Reputation and the Constitution," 74 Calif. L. Rev. 691 (1986). There have also been complaints from the other side: that the actual malice test gives inadequate protection to defamation defendants because cases can still get to a jury and incur large verdicts causing litigation costs even in cases where defendants ultimately prevail on appeal. See, e.g., Anderson, "Libel and Press Self-Censorship," 53 Tex. L. Rev. 422 (1975); Lewis, "New York Times v. Sullivan [Reconsidered]," 83 Colum. L. Rev. 602 (1983); Smolla, "[The] Rejuvenation of the American Law of Libel," 132 U. Pa. L. Rev. 1 (1984).

Would any alternative approach better reconcile the competing interests in speech and reputation? Consider Justice White's argument in dissent in Dun & Bradstreet v. Greenmoss Builders (1985; p. 91), that the "necessary breathing room for speakers can be ensured by limitations on recoverable damages; it does not also require depriving many public figures of any room to vindicate their reputations sullied by false statements of fact." For the view that a return to the common law of defamation, with strict liability but relatively low damage awards, would be preferable, see Epstein, "Was New York Times v. Sullivan Wrong?," 53 U. Chi. L. Rev. 782 (1986). For the proposal that plaintiffs ought to be able to obtain a declaration of falsity (requiring no showing of fault and including no damage awards) as an alternative to libel suits, see Leval, "The No-Money, No-Fault Libel Suit: Keeping Sullivan in Its Proper Place," 101 Harv. L. Rev. 1287 (1988); and Franklin, "A Declaratory Judgment Alternative to Current Libel Law," 74 Calif. L. Rev. 809 (1986).

5. *Procedural developments after New York Times.* The Court has given plaintiffs one significant procedural victory since New York Times: In Herbert v. Lando, 441 U.S. 153 (1979), the Court rejected a television producer's claim to a broad First Amendment-based editorial privilege that would have precluded questions in pretrial discovery proceedings pertaining to his liability under the Times "actual malice" standard. Lando leaves members of the press open to wide-ranging inquiries on the issue of whether they were guilty of knowing or reckless falsity, and thus to the costs of defending against extensive discovery. Although the press vehemently criticized that ruling, none of the Justices was prepared to uphold all of the broad media claims; even Justices Marshall and Brennan were willing to grant only a limited privilege.

Most other procedural rulings in this area since New York Times, however, have benefited defendants. In Philadelphia Newspapers, Inc. v. Hepps, 475 U.S. 767 (1986), the Court held, by a 5–4 vote, that the plaintiff was required to bear the burden of proof in establishing the falsity of the allegedly defamatory statement in cases governed by New York Times, as those decisions had displaced the common law rule presuming falsity. New York Times itself required that evidence of actual malice be clear and convincing; a preponderance of evidence was not enough. Anderson v. Liberty Lobby, Inc., 477 U.S. 242 (1986), required lower courts to inquire into the convincing clarity of actual malice evidence at the summary judgment stage. And in Bose Corp. v. Consumers Union, 466 U.S. 485 (1984), the Court held that appellate courts "must exercise independent judgment and determine [de novo] whether the record establishes actual malice with convincing clarity," rather than review the judgment below only for clear error. See generally Matheson, "Procedure in Public Person Defamation Cases: The Impact of the First Amendment," 66 Tex. L. Rev. 215 (1987).

6. *Calls to reconsider the actual malice standard.* In **Berisha v. Lawson**, 141 S. Ct. 2424 (2021), the Court denied certiorari in a case applying Sullivan. Two justices filed dissents from the denial of certiorari calling for reexamination of Sullivan. Justice THOMAS wrote: "This Court's pronouncement that the First Amendment requires public figures to establish actual malice bears no relation to the text, history, or structure of the Constitution. In fact, the opposite rule historically prevailed: The common law deemed libels against public figures to be *more* serious and injurious than ordinary libels. [Our] reconsideration is all the more needed because of the doctrine's real-world effects. Public figure or private, lies impose real harm. Take, for instance, the shooting at a pizza shop rumored to be 'the home of a Satanic child sex abuse ring involving top Democrats

such as Hillary Clinton.' Or think of those who have had job opportunities withdrawn over false accusations of racism or anti-Semitism. Or read about Kathrine McKee—surely this Court should not remove a woman's right to defend her reputation in court simply because she accuses a powerful man of rape. The proliferation of falsehoods is, and always has been, a serious matter."

Justice GORSUCH wrote: "Since 1964, [our] Nation's media landscape has shifted in ways few could have foreseen. Back then, building printing presses and amassing newspaper distribution networks demanded significant investment and expertise. Broadcasting required licenses for limited airwaves and access to highly specialized equipment. Comparatively large companies dominated the press, often employing legions of investigative reporters, editors, and fact-checkers. [But] thanks to revolutions in technology, today virtually anyone in this country can publish virtually anything for immediate consumption virtually anywhere in the world. The effect of these technological changes on our Nation's media may be hard to overstate. Large numbers of newspapers and periodicals have failed. With their fall has come the rise of 24-hour cable news and online media platforms that monetize anything that garners clicks. No doubt, this new media world has many virtues—not least the access it affords those who seek information about and the opportunity to debate public affairs. At the same time, some reports suggest that our new media environment also facilitates the spread of disinformation. [The] distribution of disinformation—which costs almost nothing to generate—has become a profitable business while the economic model that supported reporters, fact-checking, and editorial oversight has deeply eroded.

"[When] the Court originally adopted the actual malice standard, it took the view that tolerating the publication of *some* false information was a necessary and acceptable cost to pay to ensure truthful statements vital to democratic self-government were not inadvertently suppressed. But over time the actual malice standard has evolved from a high bar to recovery into an effective immunity from liability. [The] bottom line? It seems that publishing *without* investigation, fact-checking, or editing has become the optimal legal strategy. [Combine] this legal incentive with the business incentives fostered by our new media world and the deck seems stacked against those with traditional (and expensive) journalistic standards—and in favor of those who can disseminate the most sensational information as efficiently as possible without any particular concern for truth. [As] Sullivan's actual malice standard has come to apply in our new world, it's hard not to ask whether it now even 'cut[s] against the very values underlying the decision.' Kagan, "A Libel Story: Sullivan Then and Now," 18 L. & Soc. Inquiry 197, 207 (1993) (reviewing A. Lewis, Make No Law: The Sullivan Case and the First Amendment (1991)). If ensuring an informed democratic debate is the goal, how well do we serve that interest with rules that no longer merely tolerate but encourage falsehoods in quantities no one could have envisioned almost 60 years ago?"

7. *False statements of fact outside the libel context.* In a case that arose outside of the libel context, the Supreme Court has found the First Amendment to forbid the criminalization of false statements of fact. The Stolen Valor Act, 18 U.S.C. § 704(b), (c), made it a crime to falsely claim receipt of military decorations or medals, and provided an enhanced penalty if the Congressional Medal of Honor was involved. After Xavier Alvarez

falsely stated at a California public hearing that he was a retired marine who had been wounded in combat and had been awarded the Congressional Medal of Honor, he was convicted under the Act. The Supreme Court reversed his conviction in **United States v. Alvarez**, 567 U.S. 709 (2012). The Court rejected the argument that false statements were completely outside First Amendment protection and held that counter-speech was sufficient to achieve the government's asserted interest in preserving the integrity and purpose of the Medal.

Writing for a plurality joined by Chief Justice Roberts and Justices Ginsburg and Sotomayor, Justice KENNEDY applied the "exacting scrutiny" he deemed appropriate to such a content-based restriction even in the context of regulating falsity, emphasizing that the Court's libel precedents had never said false statements deserve *no* protection, and explaining that "[o]ur constitutional tradition stands against the idea that we need Oceania's Ministry of Truth. [The] mere potential for the exercise of [governmental] power [to compile a list of subjects about which false statements are punishable] casts a chill, a chill the First Amendment cannot permit if free speech, thought, and discourse are to remain a foundation of our freedom. [The] remedy for speech that is false is speech that is true. [The] response to the unreasoned is the rational; to the uninformed, the enlightened; to the straightout lie, the simple truth. [See Whitney.]"

Justice BREYER, joined by Justice Kagan, concurred only in the judgment, noting that "[f]alse factual statements can serve useful human objectives, for example: in social contexts, where they may prevent embarrassment, protect privacy, shield a person from prejudice, provide the sick with comfort, or preserve a child's innocence; in public contexts, where they may stop a panic or otherwise preserve calm in the face of danger; and even in technical, philosophical, and scientific contexts, where (as Socrates' methods suggest) examination of a false statement (even if made deliberately to mislead) can promote a form of thought that ultimately helps realize the truth." The concurrence nonetheless treated regulation of false statements as undeserving of strict scrutiny, and thus, applying only potentially more deferential "intermediate scrutiny," found that the Act swept too broadly, creating "a significant risk of First Amendment harm" while the government could have served its important interests by enacting a "similar but more finely tailored statute"

Justice ALITO, in a dissent joined by Justices Scalia and Thomas, argued that the Court had "repeatedly endorsed the principle that false statements of fact do not merit First Amendment protection for their own sake," and that "the Stolen Valor Act presents no risk at all that valuable speech will be suppressed. The speech punished by the Act is not only verifiably false and entirely lacking in intrinsic value, but it also fails to serve any instrumental purpose that the First Amendment might protect."

THE SCOPE OF NEW YORK TIMES

The Court has considered three variables in deciding how far to extend New York Times' substantive limits on liability to other settings: (1) the identity of the plaintiff (public official, public figure or private figure), (2) the identity of the defendant (media or nonmedia), and (3) the nature of the issue discussed (matter of public or private concern). It has also considered whether to vary the available remedies in various settings.

1. *Public figures v. public officials.* In **Curtis Publishing Co. v. Butts** and **Associated Press v. Walker**, decided together at 388 U.S. 130 (1967), the Court applied the New York Times rule to libel actions "instituted by persons who are not public officials, but who are 'public figures' and involved in issues in which the public has a justified and important interest." Butts grew out of a Saturday Evening Post article that claimed that the University of Georgia athletic director (and former football coach) had fixed a football game. In Walker, a retired general challenged an AP report that he had led a violent crowd in opposition to the enforcement of a desegregation decree at the University of Mississippi. The Court was sharply divided in its reasoning. Four of the Justices (Harlan, Clark, Stewart and Fortas) opposed extending the New York Times rule; three (Chief Justice Warren, and Justices Brennan and White) urged application of New York Times to public figures; the remaining two (Black and Douglas) urged a broader press immunity, as they had in New York Times. But the result was that the New York Times rule was extended to "public figures" cases.

In announcing the view that became the Court position, Chief Justice WARREN stated that "differentiation between 'public figures' and 'public officials' and adoption of separate standards of proof for each have no basis in law, logic, or First Amendment policy. Increasingly in this country, the distinctions between governmental and private sectors are blurred. [It] is plain that although they are not subject to the restraints of the political process, 'public figures,' like 'public officials,' often play an influential role in ordering society. And surely as a class these 'public figures' have as ready access as 'public officials' to mass media, [both] to influence policy and to counter criticism of their views and activities. Our citizenry has a legitimate and substantial interest in the conduct of such persons, and freedom of the press to engage in uninhibited debate about their involvement in public issues and events is as crucial as it is in the case of 'public officials.' "

In announcing the position of the four Justices who opposed extension of the New York Times rule, Justice HARLAN examined the similarities and differences between "public officials" and other "public figures," agreed that "public figure" actions "cannot be left entirely to state libel laws," but insisted that "the rigorous federal requirements of New York Times are not the only appropriate accommodation of the conflicting interests at stake." He concluded: "We [would] hold that a 'public figure' who is not a public official may also recover damages for a defamatory falsehood whose substance makes substantial danger to reputation apparent, on a showing of highly unreasonable conduct constituting an extreme departure from the standards of investigation and reporting ordinarily adhered to by responsible publishers."

2. *Defining "public figures."* Despite the broad holdings in Butts and Walker, however, in other cases the Court has construed the "public figure" category quite narrowly. In the Gertz case that follows, for example, the Court found that a lawyer who had "long been active in community and professional affairs," and was "well-known in some circles," was nonetheless a private figure because "he had achieved no general fame or notoriety in the community [or] pervasive involvement in the affairs of society." In Time, Inc. v. Firestone, 424 U.S. 448 (1976), the Court held that a wealthy divorcee whose divorce was mischaracterized in Time was not a public figure because

she had not assumed "any role of especial prominence in the affairs of society, other than perhaps Palm Beach society." In Hutchinson v. Proxmire, 443 U.S. 111 (1979), the Court held that a scientist whose federally funded research on monkey behavior had been characterized by the defendant Senator as an egregious example of wasteful government spending was not a public figure, as he had not "thrust himself or his views into public controversy to influence others." And in Wolston v. Reader's Digest Ass'n, Inc., 443 U.S. 157 (1979), the Court held that Wolston's brief stint in the public eye in 1958, after a criminal contempt conviction for failure to appear before a grand jury investigating Soviet espionage, did not make him a public figure for purposes of a 1974 allegation that he was a "Soviet agent." The majority emphasized that Wolston had not "voluntarily thrust" or "injected" himself into the controversy.

3.   *Private figures.* After extending the New York Times standard to "public figures," the divided Court's balancing approach encountered new challenges when publishers claimed First Amendment defenses to defamation suits by *private* individuals. Justice Brennan's plurality opinion in **Rosenbloom v. Metromedia, Inc.**, 403 U.S. 29 (1971) extended New York Times to a "private" plaintiff's action claiming defamation in a report "about the individual's involvement in an event of public or general interest." Rosenbloom arose from a libel action by a distributor of nudist magazines, based on radio reports about police action against his allegedly obscene books, about his lawsuit, and about police interference with his business. Some of the news reports referred to "girlie book peddlers" and the "smut literature racket." Justice BRENNAN's plurality opinion, joined by Chief Justice Burger and Justice Blackmun, argued that the critical criterion should be the *subject matter* of the allegedly defamatory report rather than the status of the plaintiff. He insisted that experience since New York Times had "disclosed the artificiality, in terms of the public's interest, of a simple distinction between 'public' and 'private' individuals" and concluded: "If a matter is a subject of public or general interest, it cannot suddenly become less so merely because a private individual is involved, or because in some sense the individual did not 'voluntarily' choose to become involved. The public's primary interest is in the event; the public focus is on the conduct of the participant and the content, effect, and significance of the conduct, not the participant's prior anonymity or notoriety. [We] honor the commitment to robust debate on public issues [by] extending constitutional protection to all discussion and communication involving matters of public or general concern without regard to whether the persons involved are famous or anonymous."

Gertz v. Robert Welch, Inc.

418 U.S. 323, 94 S. Ct. 2997, 41 L. Ed. 2d 789 (1974).

[Elmer Gertz, a Chicago lawyer, initiated a libel action against the publisher of "American Opinion," an "outlet for the views of the John Birch Society." Gertz had been retained by a victim's family in a civil suit against a Chicago policeman who had been convicted of murder. The magazine charged Gertz with being an architect of the "frame-up" of the policeman in the murder trial and called Gertz, inter alia, a "Communist-fronter." Despite a jury verdict for the plaintiff, the district court entered a judgment notwithstanding the verdict on the grounds that the public nature of the case brought it within the ambit of New York Times and that Gertz had not demonstrated that the American Opinion had requisite awareness of falsity.]

■ JUSTICE POWELL delivered the opinion of the Court.

The principal issue in this case is whether a newspaper or broadcaster that publishes defamatory falsehoods about an individual who is neither a public official nor a public figure may claim a constitutional privilege against liability for the injury inflicted by those statements.

[Under] the First Amendment there is no such thing as a false idea. However pernicious an opinion may seem, we depend for its correction not on the conscience of judges and juries but on the competition of other ideas. But there is no constitutional value in false statements of fact. Neither the intentional lie nor the careless error materially advances society's interest in "uninhibited, robust, and wide-open" debate on public issues. [They] belong to that category of utterances which "are no essential part of any exposition of ideas, and are of such slight social value as a step to truth that any benefit that may be derived from them is clearly outweighed by the social interest in order and morality."

[Although] the erroneous statement of fact is not worthy of constitutional protection, it is nevertheless inevitable in free debate. [And] punishment of error runs the risk of inducing a cautious and restrictive exercise of the constitutionally guaranteed freedoms of speech and press. Our decisions recognize that a rule of strict liability that compels a publisher or broadcaster to guarantee the accuracy of his factual assertions may lead to intolerable self-censorship. [The] First Amendment requires that we protect some falsehood in order to protect speech that matters.

The need to avoid self-censorship by the news media is, however, not the only societal value at issue. If it were, this Court would have embraced long ago the view that publishers and broadcasters enjoy an unconditional and indefeasible immunity from liability for defamation. [Such] a rule would, indeed, obviate the fear that the prospect of civil liability for injurious falsehood might dissuade a timorous press from the effective exercise of First Amendment freedoms. Yet absolute protection for the communications media requires a total sacrifice of the competing value served by the law of defamation.

The legitimate state interest underlying the law of libel is the compensation of individuals for the harm inflicted on them by defamatory falsehood. We would not lightly require the State to abandon this purpose, for, as [Justice] Stewart has reminded us, the individual's right to the protection of his own good name "reflects no more than our basic concept of the essential dignity and worth of every human being—a concept at the root of any decent system of ordered liberty. The protection of private personality, like the protection of life itself, is left primarily to the individual States under the Ninth and Tenth Amendments. But this does not mean that the right is entitled to any less recognition by this Court as a basic of our constitutional system."

[Some] tension necessarily exists between the need for a vigorous and uninhibited press and the legitimate interest in redressing wrongful injury. [In] our continuing effort to define the proper accommodation between these competing concerns, we have been especially anxious to assure to the freedoms of speech and press that "breathing space" essential to their fruitful exercise. [To] that end this Court has extended a measure of strategic protection to defamatory falsehood.

The New York Times standard defines the level of constitutional protection appropriate to the context of defamation of a public person. Those who, by reason of the notoriety of their achievements or the vigor and success with which they seek the public's attention, are properly classed as public figures and those who hold governmental office may recover for injury to reputation only on clear and convincing proof that the defamatory falsehood was made with knowledge of its falsity or with reckless disregard for the truth. [Plainly] many deserving plaintiffs, including some intentionally subjected to injury, will be unable to surmount the barrier of the New York Times test. Despite this substantial abridgment of the state law right to compensation for wrongful hurt to one's reputation, the Court has concluded that the protection of the New York Times privilege should be available to publishers and broadcasters of defamatory falsehood concerning public officials and public figures. [For] the reasons stated below, we conclude that the state interest in compensating injury to the reputation of private individuals requires that a different rule should obtain with respect to them.

[We] have no difficulty in distinguishing among defamation plaintiffs. The first remedy of any victim of defamation is self-help—using available opportunities to contradict the lie or correct the error and thereby to minimize its adverse impact on reputation. Public officials and public figures usually enjoy significantly greater access to the channels of effective communication and hence have a more realistic opportunity to counteract false statements then private individuals normally enjoy. Private individuals are therefore more vulnerable to injury, and the state interest in protecting them is correspondingly greater.

More important than the likelihood that private individuals will lack effective opportunities for rebuttal, there is a compelling normative consideration underlying the distinction between public and private defamation plaintiffs. An individual who decides to seek governmental office must accept certain necessary consequences of that involvement in public affairs. He runs the risk of closer public scrutiny than might otherwise be the case. And society's interest in the officers of government is not strictly limited to the formal discharge of official duties. [Those] classed as public figures stand in a similar position. Hypothetically, it may be possible for someone to become a public figure through no purposeful action of his own, but the instances of truly involuntary public figures must be exceedingly rare. For the most part those who attain this status have assumed roles of especial prominence in the affairs of society. [More] commonly, those classed as public figures have thrust themselves to the forefront of particular public controversies in order to influence the resolution of the issues involved. In either event, they invite attention and comment.

[For] these reasons we conclude that the States should retain substantial latitude in their efforts to enforce a legal remedy for defamatory falsehood injurious to the reputation of a private individual. The extension of the New York Times test proposed by the Rosenbloom plurality would abridge this legitimate state interest to a degree that we find unacceptable. [Nor] does the Constitution require us to draw so thin a line between the drastic alternatives of the New York Times privilege and the common law of strict liability for defamatory error. The "public or general interest" test for determining the applicability of the New York Times standard to private defamation actions inadequately serves both of the competing values at stake. On the one hand, a private individual whose reputation is injured by defamatory falsehood that does concern an issue of public or general interest has no recourse unless he can meet the rigorous requirements of New York Times.

[We] hold that, so long as they do not impose liability without fault, the States may define for themselves the appropriate standard of liability for a publisher or broadcaster of defamatory falsehood injurious to a private individual. This approach provides a more equitable boundary between the competing concerns involved here. It recognizes the strength of the legitimate state interest in compensating private individuals for wrongful injury to reputation, yet shields the press and broadcast media from the rigors of strict liability for defamation.

[This] conclusion is not based on a belief that the considerations which prompted the adoption of the New York Times privilege for defamation of public officials and its extension to public figures are wholly inapplicable to the context of private individuals. Rather, we endorse this approach in recognition of the strong and legitimate state interest in compensating private individuals for injury to reputation. But this countervailing state interest extends no further than compensation for actual injury. [It] is therefore appropriate to require that state remedies for defamatory falsehood reach no farther than is necessary to protect the legitimate interest involved. It is necessary to restrict defamation plaintiffs who do not prove knowledge of falsity or reckless disregard for the truth to compensation for actual injury. We need not define 'actual injury,' as trial courts have wide experience in framing appropriate jury instructions in tort actions. Suffice it to say that actual injury is not limited to out-of-pocket loss. Indeed, the more customary types of actual harm inflicted by defamatory falsehood include impairment of reputation and standing in the community, personal humiliation, and mental anguish and suffering.

■ JUSTICE BRENNAN, dissenting.

While [the majority's] arguments are forcefully and eloquently presented, I cannot accept them, for the reasons I stated in Rosenbloom: 'The New York Times standard was applied to libel of a public official or public figure to give effect to the (First) Amendment's function to encourage ventilation of public issues, not because the public official has any less interest in protecting his reputation than an individual in private life. [In] the vast majority of libels involving public officials or public figures, the ability to respond through the media will depend on the same complex factor on which the ability of a private individual depends: the unpredictable event of the media's continuing interest in the story. Thus the unproved, and highly improbable, generalization that an as yet (not fully defined) class of "public figures" involved in matters of public concern will be better able to respond through the media than private individuals also involved in such matters seems too insubstantial a reed on which to rest a constitutional distinction.'

We recognized in [New York Times] that a rule requiring a critic of official conduct to guarantee the truth of all of his factual contentions would inevitably lead to self-censorship when publishers, fearful of being unable to prove truth or unable to bear the expense of attempting to do so, simply eschewed printing controversial articles. Adoption, by many States, of a reasonable-care standard in cases where private individuals are involved in matters of public interest—the probable result of today's decision—will likewise lead to self-censorship since publishers will be required carefully to weigh a myriad of uncertain factors before publication. [Most] hazardous, the flexibility which inheres in the reasonable-care standard will create the danger that a jury will convert it into "an instrument for the suppression of those 'vehement, caustic, and sometimes unpleasantly sharp attacks,' . . . which must be protected if the guarantees of the First and Fourteenth Amendments are to prevail."

[I] reject the argument that my Rosenbloom view improperly commits to judges the task of determining what is and what is not an issue of "general or public interest." I noted in Rosenbloom that performance of this task would not always be easy. [B]ut surely the courts, the ultimate arbiters of all disputes concerning clashes of constitutional values, would only be performing one of their traditional functions in undertaking this duty.

■ JUSTICE WHITE, dissenting.

[The] Court does not contend, and it could hardly do so, that those who wrote the First Amendment intended to prohibit the Federal Government, within its sphere of influence in the Territories and the District of Columbia, from providing the private citizen a peaceful remedy for damaging falsehood. [The] central meaning of New York Times, and for me the First Amendment as it relates to libel laws, is that seditious libel—criticism of government and public officials—falls beyond the police power of the State. [In] a democratic society such as ours, the citizen has the privilege of criticizing his government and its officials. But neither New York Times nor its progeny suggests that the First Amendment intended in all circumstances to deprive the private citizen of his historic recourse to redress published falsehoods damaging to reputation or that, contrary to history and precedent, the Amendment should now be so interpreted. Simply put, the First Amendment did not confer a "license to defame the citizen."

[It] is difficult for me to understand why the ordinary citizen should himself carry the risk of damage and suffer the injury in order to vindicate First Amendment values by protecting the press and others from liability for circulating false information. This is particularly true because such statements serve no purpose whatsoever in furthering the public interest or the search for truth but, on the contrary, may frustrate that search and at the same time inflict great injury on the defenseless individual.

[In] disagreeing with the Court on the First Amendment's reach in the area of state libel laws protecting nonpublic persons, I do not repudiate the principle that the First Amendment "rests on the assumption that the widest possible dissemination of information from diverse and antagonistic sources is essential to the welfare of the public, that a free press is a condition of a free society." [I] fail to see how the quality or quantity of public debate will be promoted by further emasculation of state libel laws for the benefit of the news media. If anything, this trend may provoke a new and radical imbalance in the communications process. [It] is not at all inconceivable that virtually unrestrained defamatory remarks about private citizens will discourage them from speaking out and concerning themselves with social problems. This would turn the First Amendment on its head.

[Freedom] and human dignity and decency are not antithetical. Indeed, they cannot survive without each other. Both exist side-by-side in precarious balance, one always threatening to over-whelm the other. Our experience as a Nation testifies to the ability of our democratic institutions to harness this dynamic tension.

DEFAMATION OF PRIVATE PARTIES AFTER GERTZ

In the years following Gertz, the constitutional limits on defamation claims for private individuals continued to divide the court. In **Dun & Bradstreet, Inc. v. Greenmoss Builders**, 472 U.S. 749 (1985), the alleged defamation involved a private credit report given by Dun & Bradstreet to a bank regarding Greenmoss, a construction contractor. The report erroneously claimed that Greenmoss had filed for voluntary bankruptcy. A Vermont jury, instructed that it need not consider "actual malice," returned a verdict for the builder and awarded $50,000 in compensatory and $300,000 in punitive damages. The Vermont Supreme Court found the Gertz standard inapplicable, holding that the operations of credit reporting agencies were not the type of activities encompassed by New York Times and its progeny. A divided Supreme Court affirmed this holding, but not on the ground that nonmedia defendants were excluded from New York Times. Rather, a majority of the Court—Justice White in concurrence plus the four dissenters—found no relevant distinction between the institutional media and other forms of communication. The plurality declined to reach any such distinction, emphasizing a different distinction between speech on matters of public and private concern.

Justice POWELL, writing for himself and Justices Rehnquist and O'Connor, began with the proposition that "not all speech is of equal First Amendment importance." He distinguished speech "on matters of public concern" from speech "on matters of purely private concern" far from the core of the First Amendment. "[In] light of the reduced constitutional value of speech involving no matters of public concern, we hold that the state interest adequately supports awards of presumed and punitive damages—even absent a showing of 'actual malice.'" Applying this approach, Justice Powell found that credit reports such as the one at issue here—involving nothing that "concerns a public matter"—were outside the Gertz principles. The credit report, he wrote, contained "speech solely in the individual interest of the speaker and its specific business audience. [Moreover,] since the credit report was made available to only five subscribers, who, under the terms of the subscription agreement, could not disseminate it further, it cannot be said that the report involves any 'strong interest in the free flow of commercial information.'"

Chief Justice BURGER and Justice WHITE separately concurred in the judgment, each urging that Gertz itself be overruled. Justice White also urged that the entire constitutionalization of the law of defamation, going back to New York Times, be reevaluated: "I remain convinced that Gertz was erroneously decided. I have also become convinced that the Court struck an improvident balance in [New York Times]. In a country like ours, [adequate] information about their government is of transcendent importance [to the people]. That flow of intelligence deserves full First Amendment protection. Criticism and assessment of the performance of public officials and of government in general are not subject to penalties imposed by law. But these First Amendment values are not at all served by circulating false statements of fact about public officials. On the contrary, erroneous information frustrates these values. They are even more disserved when the statements falsely impugn the honesty of those men and women and hence lessen the confidence in government. [It] is difficult to argue that the United States did not have a free and vigorous press before the rule in New York Times was announced."

Justice BRENNAN, joined by Justices Marshall, Blackmun and Stevens, dissented. He rejected the claim that the relevant distinction was between the media and other forms of communication. But rejecting the media/nonmedia distinction did not for the dissenters compel the conclusion reached by the Court. Rather, Justice Brennan objected to the distinction between matters of public and private concern. And even if there were such a distinction, he viewed Justice Powell's delineation as "impoverished": "[This] Court has consistently rejected the argument that speech is entitled to diminished First Amendment protection simply because it concerns economic matters. [Even] if the subject matter of credit reporting were properly considered [as] purely a matter of private discourse, this speech would fall well within the range of valuable expression for which the First Amendment demands protection. Much expression that does not directly involve public issues receives significant protection."

————

PRIVACY TORTS

States have recognized numerous torts protecting individuals from injury by speech for reasons other than defamation. Among these are various privacy torts elaborated since publication of an article on the subject by Samuel D. Warren and later Justice Brandeis, "The Right to Privacy," 4 Harv. L. Rev. 193 (1890). Four distinct types of privacy invasion have emerged: intrusion into the plaintiff's private affairs, public disclosure of non-newsworthy facts the plaintiff would have preferred to keep secret, publicity placing the plaintiff in a false light, and appropriation of the plaintiff's name or likeness. Some protection for individual privacy has been deemed necessary to preserve human dignity and individuality. Preserving privacy, however, by definition often impedes the free flow of information. Should the First Amendment be read to limit the reach of privacy torts? The Supreme Court has reached this question only with respect to "false light" invasion of privacy claims, claims against disclosure of facts already in the public record, and appropriation claims. It has yet to confront a case involving public disclosure of truly private facts.

For an argument in support of legal protections for individual privacy, see Edelman, "Free Press v. Privacy: Haunted by the Ghost of Justice Black," 68 Tex. L. Rev. 1195 (1990). For criticism of privacy torts on free speech grounds, see Kalven, "Privacy in Tort Law—Were Warren and Brandeis Wrong?," 31 Law & Contemp. Prob. 326 (1966); Zimmerman, "Requiem for a Heavyweight: a Farewell to Warren and Brandeis's Privacy Tort," 68 Cornell L. Rev. 291 (1983); Posner, "The Right to Privacy," 12 Ga. L. Rev. 393 (1978).

1.   *"False light" invasion of privacy.* In "false light" privacy cases, the claim is that the disclosure not only invaded privacy but was also false— though not necessarily injurious to reputation, the gist of defamation actions. The Supreme Court's decision in **Time, Inc. v. Hill**, 385 U.S. 374 (1967), focused primarily on "false light" privacy actions, and the decision by a

divided Court was that the New York Times standard should be applicable to such actions.

In 1952, the Hill family had been held hostage by three escaped convicts for 19 hours but was released unharmed. Three years later, a play portrayed the incident as involving considerable violence, though in fact there had been none. Life magazine's story on the play posed the actors in the original Hill home and indicated that the play accurately portrayed the actual incident. The original incident had been widely reported, but the Hills had tried to stay out of the public eye thereafter. Though the Life magazine report that was the subject of the action did not substantially damage the Hills' reputation—they were portrayed as courageous—they ultimately recovered a $30,000 judgment under New York law.

The Hill suit was based on a New York "right of privacy" statute prohibiting anyone from using "for advertising purposes, or for the purposes of trade, the name, portrait or picture of any living person without having first obtained the written consent of such person." Under the statute, truth was a defense in actions "based upon newsworthy people or events," but a "newsworthy person" could recover when he or she was the subject of a "fictitious" report—a report involving "material and substantial falsification." Justice BRENNAN's opinion for the Court concluded that "the constitutional protections for speech and press preclude the application of the New York statute to redress false reports of matters of public interest in the absence of proof that the defendant published the report with knowledge of its falsity or in reckless disregard of the truth." Justice Brennan went on to indicate, in a much-debated dictum, that "newsworthiness" would offer similar protection even in a "true" privacy action.

Does the Hill principle, announced in 1967, survive the Court's 1974 retreat in Gertz from Justice Brennan's position that the New York Times principle applies to all "newsworthy" matters? Does Hill move well beyond the seditious libel emphasis that was seen as the "central meaning" of the First Amendment in New York Times? Nimmer criticized the Court for failing to "pierce the superficial similarity between false light invasion of privacy and defamation" and urged that disclosure of nondefamatory matters interfering with privacy not be afforded First Amendment protection. He noted, for example, that, unlike "injury arising from defamation, 'more speech' is irrelevant in mitigating the injury due to an invasion of privacy." See Nimmer, "The Right to Speak From Times to Time: First Amendment Theory Applied to Libel and Misapplied to Privacy," 56 Calif. L. Rev. 935 (1968). On the other hand, is New York Times even more obviously applicable in the nondefamation setting because only true speech is involved, not false statements of fact? See Kalven, "The Reasonable Man and the First Amendment: Hill, Butts, and Walker," 1967 Sup. Ct. Rev. 267, suggesting that "the logic of New York Times and Hill taken together grants the press some measure of constitutional protection for anything the press thinks is a matter of public interest."

2. *Disclosure of rape victims' names.* In **Cox Broadcasting Corp. v. Cohn**, 420 U.S. 469 (1975), a father had sued because of the broadcasting of the fact that his daughter had been a rape victim. Barring liability, the Court relied especially on "the public interest in a vigorous press." The decision did not reach the question of whether Hill and its dictum had survived Gertz. The Court held merely that civil liability in a "true" privacy action could not be imposed upon a broadcaster for accurately

publishing information released to the public in official court records. Justice WHITE's opinion for the Court commented: "In this sphere of collision between claims of privacy and those of the free press, the interests on both sides are plainly rooted in the traditions and significant concerns of our society." But he found it unnecessary to decide "the broader question whether truthful publication may ever be subjected to civil or criminal liability," or "whether the State may ever define and protect an area of privacy free from unwanted publicity in the press." However, he recognized the "impressive credentials for a right of privacy" and claimed that earlier cases had "carefully left open the question" whether the Constitution requires "that truth be recognized as a defense in a defamation action brought by a private person," as well as "the question whether truthful publication of very private matters unrelated to public affairs could be constitutionally proscribed."

Cox Broadcasting's prohibition on the restriction of lawfully obtained truthful information, including the identities of juveniles and victims of sexual offenses, has been applied in a number of subsequent cases. In **Florida Star v. B.J.F.**, 491 U.S. 524 (1989), a newspaper published the name of a victim of a sexual offense obtained from a police report made available in the police department's press room. Justice Marshall's majority opinion overturned a judgment based on a state law barring the publication of the names of such victims. Although again declining "to hold broadly that truthful publication may never be punished consistent with the First Amendment," Justice Marshall found the law unacceptable. Justice Scalia concurred in part and in the judgment. Justice White, the author of Cox Broadcasting, dissented, joined by Chief Justice Rehnquist and Justice O'Connor, distinguishing Cox as involving judicial records. He also raised doubts about the entire line of privacy cases beginning with Time, Inc. v. Hill. Questioning whether privacy was being unduly sacrificed in all of them, he observed that "[t]oday, we have hit the bottom of the slippery slope. I would find a place to draw the line higher on the hillside: a spot high enough to protect B.J.F.'s desire for privacy and peace-of-mind in the wake of a horrible personal tragedy."

3. *Appropriation torts.* Zacchini v. Scripps-Howard Broadcasting Co., 433 U.S. 562 (1977), dealt with a suit based on the plaintiff's "right of publicity" rather than an interest in privacy per se. The Court distinguished Time and held that the First Amendment does not "immunize the media [from liability for damages] when they broadcast a performer's entire act without his consent."

Zacchini had performed a "human cannonball" act in which he was shot from a cannon into a net some 200 feet away. The defendant filmed Zacchini's performance at a county fair and showed the entire 15-second act on a television news program. In allowing recovery, Justice White distinguished this case from the 'false light' privacy claim in Hill. Hill was not a case involving 'intrusion' " or "private details" about a non-newsworthy person. And neither did Hill involve a claim of a "right of publicity" as here; this kind of claim was a "discrete kind of 'appropriation.' " Unlike "false light" cases designed to protect the interest in reputation, suits such as this one rested on the state interest "in protecting the proprietary interest of the individual in his act in part to encourage such entertainment," an interest "closely analogous to those of patent and copyright law." Moreover, a "right of publicity" case did not significantly intrude on dissemination of information to the public: "the only question is who gets to do the publishing."

Accordingly, Justice White found the performer's claim a strong one, and the media arguments weak. Justice Powell, joined by Justices Brennan and Marshall, dissented.

Issues similar to those in Zacchini are presented by the inherent tensions between copyright law and First Amendment principles. See Harper & Row v. Nation Enterprises, 471 U.S. 539 (1985), where The Nation magazine published an article containing 300 to 400 words from former President Ford's yet-to-be published memoirs. Justice O'Connor's majority opinion rejected the argument that the "fair use" defense under the copyright laws had to be interpreted in light of the First Amendment when the words of an important public figure were involved. She stated that, in view of the First Amendment protections already embodied in copyright law, and the latitude the fair use defense traditionally afforded to scholarship and comment, there was no warrant for expanding the doctrine of fair use to create what amounted to a public figure exception to copyright. Justice Brennan, joined by Justices White and Marshall, dissented.

4. *Public disclosure of illegally intercepted information.* Should the First Amendment protect the dissemination of a private conversation that is illegally obtained? Does it matter what the topic of the conversation is? Who the disseminator is? The Supreme Court addressed this issue in the following case involving a civil damages suit under a federal statute protecting the privacy of electronic communications:

Bartnicki v. Vopper

532 U.S. 514, 121 S. Ct. 1753, 149 L. Ed. 2d 787 (2001).

[Bartnicki was the chief negotiator for the Pennsylvania State Education Association, a teacher's union, during a high-profile collective-bargaining negotiation with the school board. While preparing for a possible strike, Bartnicki had a heated phone conversation regarding the school board with Kane, the president of the local union, who said, among other things, that " 'If they're not gonna move for three percent, we're gonna have to go to their, their homes. . . . To blow off their front porches, we'll have to do some work on some of those guys.' " The call was secretly intercepted and taped by an unidentified person who turned the tape over to a local citizen who opposed the union's demands, who in turn gave the tape to a local radio talk show host who then played the tape on air. The union negotiators filed complaint for damages against the radio broadcasters and their local citizen informant under 18 U.S.C. § 2511(1)(c), which provides that any person who "intentionally discloses, or endeavors to disclose, to any other person the contents of any wire, oral, or electronic communication, knowing or having reason to know that the information was obtained through the interception of a wire, oral, or electronic communication in violation of this subsection; . . . shall be punished."]

■ JUSTICE STEVENS delivered the opinion of the Court.

These cases raise an important question concerning what degree of protection, if any, the First Amendment provides to speech that discloses the contents of an illegally intercepted communication.

[The] persons who made the disclosures did not participate in the interception, but they did know—or at least had reason to know—that the interception was unlawful. Accordingly, these cases present a conflict between interests of the highest order—on the one hand, the interest in the full and free dissemination of information concerning public issues, and, on the other hand, the interest in individual privacy and, more specifically, in fostering private speech.

[We] accept respondents' submission on three factual matters that serve to distinguish most of the cases that have arisen under § 2511. First, respondents played no part in the illegal interception. Rather, they found out about the interception only after it occurred, and in fact never learned the identity of the person or persons who made the interception. Second, their access to the information on the tapes was obtained lawfully, even though the information itself was intercepted unlawfully by someone else. [Florida Star] Third, the subject matter of the conversation was a matter of public concern. If the statements about the labor negotiations had been made in a public arena—during a bargaining session, for example—they would have been newsworthy. This would also be true if a third party had inadvertently overheard Bartnicki making the same statements to Kane when the two thought they were alone.

In this suit, the basic purpose of the statute at issue is to "protec[t] the privacy of wire[, electronic,] and oral communications." [The] statute does not distinguish based on the content of the intercepted conversations, nor is it justified by reference to the content of those conversations. Rather, the communications at issue are singled out by virtue of the fact that they were illegally intercepted—by virtue of the source, rather than the subject matter. On the other hand, the naked prohibition against disclosures is fairly characterized as a regulation of pure speech.

[In the Pentagon Papers case], the Court upheld the right of the press to publish information of great public concern obtained from documents stolen by a third party. In so doing, that decision resolved a conflict between the basic rule against prior restraints on publication and the interest in preserving the secrecy of information that, if disclosed, might seriously impair the security of the Nation. [However], [we] did not resolv[e] the question "whether, in cases where information has been acquired unlawfully by a newspaper or by a source, government may ever punish not only the unlawful acquisition, but the ensuing publication as well." [Florida Star.] The question here, however, is a narrower version of that still-open question. Simply put, the issue here is this: "Where the punished publisher of information has obtained the information in question in a manner lawful in itself but from a source who has obtained it unlawfully, may the government punish the ensuing publication of that information based on the defect in a chain?"

[The] Government identifies two interests served by the statute—first, the interest in removing an incentive for parties to intercept private conversations, and second, the interest in minimizing the harm to persons whose conversations have been illegally intercepted. We assume that those interests adequately justify the prohibition in § 2511(1)(d) against the interceptor's own use of information that he or she acquired by violating § 2511(1)(a), but it by no means follows that punishing disclosures of lawfully obtained information of public interest by one not involved in the initial illegality is an acceptable means of serving those ends.

The normal method of deterring unlawful conduct is to impose an appropriate punishment on the person who engages in it. If the sanctions that presently attach to a violation of § 2511(1)(a) do not provide sufficient deterrence, perhaps those sanctions should be made more severe. But it would be quite remarkable to hold that speech by a law-abiding possessor of information can be suppressed in order to deter conduct by a non-law-abiding third party. [With] only a handful of exceptions, the violations of § 2511(1)(a) that have been described in litigated cases have been motivated by either financial gain or domestic disputes. In virtually all of those cases, the identity of the person or persons intercepting the communication has been known.

[The] Government's second argument, however, is considerably stronger. Privacy of communication is an important interest. Moreover, the fear of public disclosure of private conversations might well have a chilling effect on private speech. "In a democratic society privacy of communication is essential if citizens are to think and act creatively and constructively. Fear or suspicion that one's speech is being monitored by a stranger, even without the reality of such activity, can have a seriously inhibiting effect upon the willingness to voice critical and constructive ideas." [We] need not decide whether that interest is strong enough to justify the application of § 2511(c) to disclosures of trade secrets or domestic gossip or other information of purely private concern. [Hill.]

[The] enforcement of that provision in these cases, however, implicates the core purposes of the First Amendment because it imposes sanctions on the publication of truthful information of public concern. [Privacy] concerns give way when balanced against the interest in publishing matters of public importance. [A] stranger's illegal conduct does not suffice to remove the First Amendment shield from speech about a matter of public concern. The months of negotiations over the proper level of compensation for teachers at the Wyoming Valley West High School were unquestionably a matter of public concern, and respondents were clearly engaged in debate about that concern. That debate may be more mundane than the Communist rhetoric that inspired Justice Brandeis' classic opinion in [Whitney], but it is no less worthy of constitutional protection.

■ JUSTICE BREYER, with whom JUSTICE O'CONNOR joins, concurring.

I join the Court's opinion because I agree with its "narrow" holding, limited to the special circumstances present here: (1) the radio broadcasters acted lawfully (up to the time of final public disclosure); and (2) the information publicized involved a matter of unusual public concern, namely a threat of potential physical harm to others. I write separately to explain why, in my view, the Court's holding does not imply a significantly broader constitutional immunity for the media. As the Court recognizes, the question before us—a question of immunity from statutorily imposed civil liability— implicates competing constitutional concerns. [The] statutes directly interfere with free expression in that they prevent the media from publishing information. At the same time, they help to protect personal privacy—an interest here that includes not only the "right to be let alone," [but] also "the interest . . . in fostering private speech."

[I] would ask whether the statutes strike a reasonable balance between their speech-restricting and speech-enhancing consequences. Or do they instead impose restrictions on speech that are disproportionate when measured against their corresponding privacy and speech-related benefits, taking into account the kind, the importance, and the extent of these benefits, as well as the need for the restrictions in order to secure those benefits? What this Court has called "strict scrutiny"—with its strong presumption against constitutionality—is normally out of place where, as here, important competing constitutional interests are implicated.

[The] statutory restrictions before us directly enhance private speech. The statutes ensure the privacy of telephone conversations much as a trespass statute ensures privacy within the home. [At] the same time, these statutes restrict public speech directly, deliberately, and of necessity. [They] resemble laws that would award damages caused through publication of information obtained by theft from a private bedroom. [Rather] than broadly forbid this kind of legislative enactment, the Constitution demands legislative efforts to tailor the laws in order reasonably to reconcile media freedom with personal, speech-related privacy.

Nonetheless, looked at more specifically, the statutes, as applied in these circumstances, do not reasonably reconcile the competing constitutional objectives. Rather, they disproportionately interfere with media freedom. [The] broadcasters here engaged in no unlawful activity other than the ultimate publication of the information another had previously obtained. [The] speakers had little or no legitimate interest in maintaining the privacy of the particular conversation. [Where] publication of private information constitutes a wrongful act, the law recognizes a privilege allowing the reporting of threats to public safety. [Further], the speakers themselves, the president of a teacher's union and the union's chief negotiator, were "limited public figures," for they voluntarily engaged in a public controversy. They thereby subjected themselves to somewhat greater public scrutiny and had a lesser interest in privacy than an individual engaged in purely private affairs.

[I] emphasize the particular circumstances before us because, in my view, the Constitution permits legislatures to respond flexibly to the challenges future technology may pose to the individual's interest in basic personal privacy. Clandestine and pervasive invasions of privacy, unlike the simple theft of documents from a bedroom, are genuine possibilities as a result of continuously advancing technologies. Eavesdropping on ordinary cellular phone conversations in the street (which many callers seem to tolerate) is a very different matter from eavesdropping on encrypted cellular phone conversations or those carried on in the bedroom. But the technologies that allow the former may come to permit the latter. [For] these reasons, we should avoid adopting overly broad or rigid constitutional rules, which would unnecessarily restrict legislative flexibility.

■ CHIEF JUSTICE REHNQUIST, with whom JUSTICE SCALIA and JUSTICE THOMAS join, dissenting.

Technology now permits millions of important and confidential conversations to occur through a vast system of electronic networks. These advances, however, raise significant privacy concerns. [To] effectuate these important privacy and speech interests, Congress and the vast majority of States have proscribed the intentional interception and knowing disclosure of the contents of electronic communications.

[The] "dry-up-the-market" theory, which posits that it is possible to deter an illegal act that is difficult to police by preventing the wrongdoer from enjoying the fruits of the crime, is neither novel nor implausible. It is a time-tested theory that undergirds numerous laws, such as the prohibition of the knowing possession of stolen goods. [The] same logic applies here and demonstrates that the incidental restriction on alleged First Amendment freedoms is no greater than essential to further the interest of protecting the privacy of individual communications.

These statutes also protect the important interests of deterring clandestine invasions of privacy and preventing the involuntary broadcast of private communications. [They] further the First Amendment rights of the parties to the conversation. "At the heart of the First Amendment lies the principle that each person should decide for himself or herself the ideas and beliefs deserving of expression, consideration, and adherence." [The] chilling effect of the Court's decision upon these private conversations will surely be [great].

The Court concludes that the private conversation between Gloria Bartnicki and Anthony Kane is somehow a "debate ... worthy of constitutional protection." [The] point, however, is that Bartnicki and Kane had no intention of contributing to a public "debate" at all, and it is perverse to hold that another's unlawful interception and knowing disclosure of their conversation is speech "worthy of constitutional protection." [The] Constitution should not protect the involuntary broadcast of personal conversations. Even where the communications involve public figures or concern public matters, the conversations are nonetheless private and worthy of protection. Although public persons may have forgone the right to live their lives screened from public scrutiny in some areas, it does not and should not follow that they also have abandoned their right to have a private conversation without fear of it being intentionally intercepted and knowingly disclosed.

Surely "the interest in individual privacy," at its narrowest, must embrace the right to be free from surreptitious eavesdropping on, and involuntary broadcast of, our cellular telephone conversations. The Court subordinates that right, not to the claims of those who themselves wish to speak, but to the claims of those who wish to publish the intercepted conversations of others. Congress' effort to balance the above claim to privacy against a marginal claim to speak freely is thereby set at naught.

––––––––

INTENTIONAL INFLICTION OF EMOTIONAL DISTRESS

Another common-law non-defamation tort, the tort of intentional infliction of emotional distress, provides a private cause of action against a defendant who intentionally or recklessly causes a plaintiff severe emotional injury through extreme or outrageous conduct. Traditionally, a plaintiff can sue for civil damages even when the sole source of the distress is a speech act. A series of Supreme Court decisions, however, has suggested that the tort may be limited on First Amendment grounds for both public and private defendants.

––––––––

Hustler Magazine v. Falwell

485 U.S. 46, 108 S. Ct. 876, 99 L. Ed. 2d 41 (1988).

[In 1983, Hustler Magazine ran a "parody" of an advertisement for Campari Liqueur entitled "Jerry Falwell Talks About His First Time." The parody was modeled after actual Campari ads that included interviews with various celebrities about their "first times." Although it was clear by the end of each interview that this meant the first time they had sampled Campari, the ads clearly played on a sexual double entendre. Copying the form and layout of these Campari ads, Hustler chose Falwell, a nationally known minister and commentator on public affairs, as its featured celebrity and printed an alleged "interview" revealing that his "first time" was during a drunken incestuous rendezvous with his mother in an outhouse. The parody suggested that Falwell was a hypocrite who preached only when he was drunk. In small print at the bottom of the page, the ad contained the disclaimer, "Ad parody—not to be taken seriously." The magazine's table of contents also listed the ad as "Fiction; Ad and Personality Parody." Falwell sought damages against the magazine for invasion of privacy, libel, and intentional infliction of emotional distress. The jury found for him only on the last claim.]

■ CHIEF JUSTICE REHNQUIST delivered the opinion of the Court.

This case presents us with a novel [question]. We must decide whether a public figure may recover damages for emotional harm caused by the publication of an ad parody offensive to him, and doubtless gross and repugnant in the eyes of most. Respondent would have us find that a State's interest in protecting public figures from emotional distress is sufficient to deny First Amendment protection to speech that is patently offensive and is intended to inflict emotional injury, even when that speech could not reasonably have been interpreted as stating actual facts about the public figure involved. This we decline to do.

[The] sort of robust political debate encouraged by the First Amendment is bound to produce speech that is critical of those who hold public office or those public figures who are "intimately involved in the resolution of important public [questions]." Such criticism, inevitably, will not always be reasoned or moderate; public figures as well as public officials will be subject to "vehement, caustic, and sometimes unpleasantly sharp attacks." [In Falwell's view,] so long as the utterance was intended to inflict emotional distress, was outrageous, and did in fact inflict serious emotional distress, it is of no constitutional import whether the statement was a fact or an opinion, or whether it was true or false. It is the intent to cause injury that is the gravamen of the tort, and the State's interest in preventing emotional harm simply outweighs whatever interest a speaker may have in speech of this type.

Generally speaking the law does not regard the intent to inflict emotional distress as one which should receive much solicitude, and it is quite understandable that most if not all jurisdictions have chosen to make it civilly culpable where the conduct in question is sufficiently "outrageous." But in the world of debate about public affairs, many things done with motives that are less than admirable are protected by the First Amendment. In Garrison v. Louisiana, we held that even when a speaker or writer is motivated by hatred or ill-will his expression was protected by the First Amendment. [Thus,] while such a bad motive may be deemed controlling for purposes of tort liability in other areas of the law, we think the First Amendment prohibits such a result in the area of public debate about public figures.

Were we to hold otherwise, there can be little doubt that political cartoonists and satirists would be subjected to damages awards without any showing that their work falsely defamed its subject. [The] appeal of the political cartoon or caricature is often based on exploration of unfortunate physical traits or politically embarrassing events—an exploration often calculated to injure the feelings of the subject of the portrayal. The art of the cartoonist is often not reasoned or even-handed, but slashing and one-sided. [But from] the viewpoint of history it is clear that our political discourse would have been considerably poorer without [cartoonists]. [Falwell] contends, however, that the caricature in question here was so "outrageous" as to distinguish it from more traditional political cartoons. There is no doubt that the caricature of [Falwell] and his mother published in Hustler is at best a distant cousin of [traditional] political cartoons, [and] a rather poor relation at that. If it were possible by laying down a principled standard to separate the one from the other, public discourse would probably suffer little or no harm. But we doubt that there is any such standard, and we are quite sure that the pejorative description "outrageous" does not supply one. "Outrageousness" in the area of political and social discourse has an inherent subjectiveness about it which would allow a jury to impose liability on the basis of the jurors' tastes or views, or perhaps on the basis of their dislike of a particular expression. An "outrageousness" standard thus runs afoul of our longstanding refusal to allow damages to be awarded because the speech in question may have an adverse emotional impact on the audience. Admittedly, these oft-repeated First Amendment principles, like other principles, are subject to limitations. [But] the sort of expression involved in this case does not seem to us to be governed by any exception to the general First Amendment principles stated above.

We conclude that public figures and public officials may not recover for the tort of intentional infliction of emotional distress by reason of publications such as the one here at issue without showing in addition that the publication contains a false statement of fact which was made with "actual malice," i.e., with knowledge that the statement was false or with reckless disregard as to whether or not it was true. This is not merely a "blind application" of the New York Times standard, it reflects our considered judgment that such a standard is necessary to give adequate "breathing space" to the freedoms protected by the First Amendment.

Reversed.

■ [JUSTICE WHITE concurred, but stated that New York Times had "little to do with this case, for here the jury found that the ad contained no assertion of fact."]

Snyder v. Phelps

562 U.S. 443, 131 S. Ct. 1207, 179 L. Ed. 2d 172 (2011).

[The Westboro Baptist Church is a religious organization known for its members' public protests of homosexuality in the United States. For 20 years, Westboro members have traveled to military funerals to express their belief that God hates the United States for its tolerance of homosexuality and that God is killing American soldiers as punishment for the Nation's sinful policies. In 2006, Westboro staged a picket outside the funeral of a Marine killed in the line of duty in Iraq. The picketing was peaceful and took place on public land 1,000 feet from the funeral. A Maryland jury held Westboro liable for $2.9 million in compensatory damages and $8 million in punitive damages for the torts of intentional infliction of emotional distress, intrusion upon seclusion and civil conspiracy; the trial court remitted the punitives.]

■ CHIEF JUSTICE ROBERTS delivered the opinion of the Court.

Whether the First Amendment prohibits holding Westboro liable for its speech in this case turns largely on whether that speech is of public or private concern, as determined by all the circumstances of the case. [The] First Amendment reflects "a profound national commitment to the principle that debate on public issues should be uninhibited, robust, and wide-open." [New York Times.] However, where matters of purely private significance are at issue, First Amendment protections are often less rigorous. [See Hustler.] That is because restricting speech on purely private matters does not implicate the same constitutional concerns as limiting speech on matters of public interest.

[Speech] deals with matters of public concern when it can 'be fairly considered as relating to any matter of political, social, or other concern to the community,' or when it 'is a subject of legitimate news interest; that is, a subject of general interest and of value and concern to the public.' [Deciding] whether speech is of public or private concern requires us to examine the 'content, form, and context' of that speech, 'as revealed by the whole record.' [In] considering content, form, and context, no factor is dispositive, and it is necessary to evaluate all the circumstances of the speech, including what was said, where it was said, and how it was said.

[The] "content" of Westboro's signs plainly relates to broad issues of interest to society at large, rather than matters of "purely private concern." The placards read "God Hates the USA/Thank God for 9/11," "America is Doomed," "Don't Pray for the USA," "Thank God for IEDs," "Fag Troops," "Semper Fi Fags," "God Hates Fags," "Maryland Taliban," "Fags Doom Nations," "Not Blessed Just Cursed," "Thank God for Dead Soldiers," "Pope in Hell," "Priests Rape Boys," "You're Going to Hell," and "God Hates You." While these messages may fall short of refined social or political commentary, the issues they highlight—the political and moral conduct of the United States and its citizens, the fate of our Nation, homosexuality in the military, and scandals involving the Catholic clergy—are matters of public import. The signs certainly convey Westboro's position on those issues, in a manner designed [to] reach as broad a public audience as possible. And even if a few of the signs—such as "You're Going to Hell" and "God Hates You"—were viewed as containing messages related to Matthew Snyder or the Snyders specifically, that would not change the fact that the overall thrust and dominant theme of Westboro's demonstration spoke to broader public issues.

Apart from the content of Westboro's signs, Snyder contends that the "context" of the speech—its connection with his son's funeral—makes the speech a matter of private rather than public concern. The fact that Westboro spoke in connection with a funeral, however, cannot by itself transform the nature of Westboro's speech. Westboro's signs, displayed on public land next to a public street, [are] "fairly characterized as constituting speech on a matter of public concern," and the funeral setting does not alter that conclusion.

[Snyder] goes on to argue that Westboro's speech should be afforded less than full First Amendment protection "not only because of the words" but also because the church members exploited the funeral "as a platform to bring their message to a broader audience." There is no doubt that Westboro chose to stage its picketing at the Naval Academy, the Maryland State House, and Matthew Snyder's funeral to increase publicity for its views and because of the relation between those sites and its [views regarding homosexuality]. Westboro's choice to convey its views in conjunction with Matthew Snyder's funeral made the expression of those views particularly hurtful to many, especially to Matthew's father. The record makes clear that the applicable legal term—"emotional distress"—fails to capture fully the anguish Westboro's choice added to Mr. Snyder's already incalculable grief. But Westboro conducted its picketing peacefully on matters of public concern at a public place adjacent to a public street.

[Westboro's] choice of where and when to conduct its picketing is not beyond the Government's regulatory reach—it is "subject to reasonable time, place, or manner restrictions" that are consistent with the standards announced in this Court's precedents. Maryland now has a law imposing restrictions on funeral picketing, as do 43 other States and the Federal Government. To the extent these laws are content neutral, they raise very different questions from the tort verdict at issue in this case. [The] record confirms that any distress occasioned by Westboro's picketing turned on the content and viewpoint of the message conveyed, rather than any interference with the funeral itself. A group of parishioners standing at the very spot where Westboro stood, holding signs that said "God Bless America" and "God Loves You," would not have been subjected to liability. It was what Westboro said that exposed it to tort damages. Given that Westboro's speech was at a public place on a matter of public concern, that speech is entitled to "special protection" under the First Amendment. Such speech cannot be restricted simply because it is upsetting or arouses contempt.

The jury here was instructed that it could hold Westboro liable for intentional infliction of emotional distress based on a finding that Westboro's picketing was "outrageous." "Outrageousness," however, is a highly malleable standard with "an inherent subjectiveness about it which would allow a jury to impose liability on the basis of the jurors' tastes or views, or perhaps on the basis of their dislike of a particular expression." [Hustler] [Such] a risk is unacceptable; "in public debate [we] must tolerate insulting, and even outrageous, speech in order to provide adequate 'breathing space' to the freedoms protected by the First Amendment."

[Speech] is powerful. It can stir people to action, move them to tears of both joy and sorrow, and—as it did here—inflict great pain. On the facts before us, we cannot react to that pain by punishing the speaker. As a Nation we have chosen a different course—to protect even hurtful speech on public issues to ensure that we do not stifle public debate. That choice requires that we shield Westboro from tort liability for its picketing in this case.

■ JUSTICE BREYER, concurring.

While I agree with the Court's conclusion that the picketing addressed matters of public concern, I do not believe that our First Amendment analysis can stop at that point. A State can sometimes regulate picketing, even picketing on matters of public concern. [As] I understand the Court's opinion, it does not hold or imply that the State is always powerless to provide private individuals with necessary protection. Rather, the Court has reviewed the underlying facts in detail, as will sometimes prove necessary where First Amendment values and state-protected (say, privacy-related) interests seriously conflict. That review makes clear that Westboro's means of communicating its views consisted of picketing in a place where picketing was lawful and in compliance with all police directions. The picketing could not be seen or heard from the funeral ceremony itself. And Snyder testified that he saw no more than the tops of the picketers' signs as he drove to the funeral. To uphold the application of state law in these circumstances would punish Westboro for seeking to communicate its views on matters of public concern without proportionately advancing the State's interest in protecting its citizens against severe emotional harm.

■ JUSTICE ALITO, dissenting.

Our profound national commitment to free and open debate is not a license for the vicious verbal assault that occurred in this case.

[It] is well established that a claim for the intentional infliction of emotional distress can be satisfied by speech. [And] although this Court has not decided the question, I think it is clear that the First Amendment does not entirely preclude liability for the intentional infliction of emotional distress by means of speech. [This] Court has recognized that words may "by their very utterance inflict injury" and that the First Amendment does not shield utterances that form "no essential part of any exposition of ideas, and are of such slight social value as a step to truth that any benefit that may be derived from them is clearly outweighed by the social interest in order and morality." [Chaplinsky.] When grave injury is intentionally inflicted by means of an attack like the one at issue here, the First Amendment should not interfere with recovery.

In this case, respondents brutally attacked Matthew Snyder, and this attack, which was almost certain to inflict injury, was central to respondents' well-practiced strategy for attracting public attention. [This] strategy works because it is expected that respondents' verbal assaults will wound the family and friends of the deceased and because the media is irresistibly drawn to the sight of persons who are visibly in grief. The more outrageous the funeral protest, the more publicity the Westboro Baptist Church is able to obtain.

[It] is abundantly clear that respondents, going far beyond commentary on matters of public concern, specifically attacked Matthew Snyder because (1) he was a Catholic and (2) he was a member of the United States military. Both Matthew and petitioner were private figures, and this attack was not speech on a matter of public concern. While commentary on the Catholic Church or the United States military constitutes speech on matters of public concern, speech regarding Matthew Snyder's purely private conduct does not.

[Respondents'] outrageous conduct caused petitioner great injury, and the Court now compounds that injury by depriving petitioner of a judgment that acknowledges the wrong he suffered. In order to have a society in which public issues can be openly and vigorously debated, it is not necessary to allow the brutalization of innocent victims like petitioner. I therefore respectfully dissent.

———

Intentional infliction of emotional distress after Snyder. What facts were essential to the holding in Snyder? That the speech took place in public setting? That the speech implicated matters of public concern? Consider whether Snyder has any effect on a purely interpersonal assertion of the tort concerning statements made in a private setting, or unaffected by references to matters of public debate. What might a state or local government do after Snyder to prevent similar harms at funerals in the future? Impose "buffer zones" around funerals barring any speech within a certain time and place in relation to any funeral?

———

HATE SPEECH

While the preceding section considered First Amendment limits on traditional torts protecting individual reputation, sensibility and dignity, should the First Amendment limit efforts to curb speech perceived as harmful and offensive to racial or religious minorities or other historically disempowered groups, apart from the tendency of that speech to incite immediate violence or provoke an immediate fight? Recall that Chaplinsky included among the categories of unprotected speech those words that "by their very utterance inflict injury." And recall that Beauharnais upheld a group libel law, treating false statements about racial or other groups as categorically unprotected. Should these precedents inform challenges to new efforts to regulate abusive or denigrating words directed at racial or other groups? Should the Chaplinsky list of unprotected categories be expanded to cover a new category for such hate speech? Consider the strength of the government justifications for such regulation in the following cases:

———

Collin v. Smith

578 F.2d 1197 (7th Cir. 1978).

[In the late 1970s, the National Socialist Party of America attempted to organize a march through the town of Skokie, Illinois. The NSPA chose Skokie for their demonstration largely because the town included a large Jewish population, including thousands of survivors of the Nazi holocaust in Europe during World War II. In response, the village of Skokie enacted three ordinances to prohibit demonstrations such as the one the NSPA contemplated. The first established a comprehensive permit system for parades and public assemblies; the second prohibited the "dissemination of any materials within [Skokie] which [intentionally] promotes and incites hatred against persons by reason of their race, national origin, or religion"; the third prohibited public demonstrations by members of political parties while wearing "military-style" uniforms. The NSPA applied for a permit application for a half-hour march that would involve 30 to 50 demonstrators wearing uniforms including swastikas and carrying a party banners featuring statements such as "White Free Speech," "Free Speech for the

White Man," and "Free Speech for White America." Represented by a Jewish ACLU attorney, the NSPA and its leader at that time, Frank Collin, brought a federal court action to challenge the Skokie ordinances on First Amendment grounds.]

■ JUDGE PELL delivered the opinion of the Court.

[The] conflict underlying this litigation has commanded substantial public attention, and engendered considerable and understandable emotion. We would hopefully surprise no one by confessing personal views that NSPA's beliefs and goals are repugnant to the core values held generally by residents of this country, and, indeed, to much of what we cherish in civilization. As judges sworn to defend the Constitution, however, we cannot decide this or any case on that basis. Ideological tyranny, no matter how worthy its motivation, is forbidden as much to appointed judges as to elected legislators.

[Our] task here is to decide whether the First Amendment protects the activity in which appellees wish to engage, not to render moral judgment on their views or tactics. No authorities need be cited to establish the proposition, which the Village does not dispute, that First Amendment rights are truly precious and fundamental to our national life. Nor is this truth without relevance to the saddening historical images this case inevitably arouses. It is, after all, in part the fact that our constitutional system protects minorities unpopular at a particular time or place from governmental harassment and intimidation, that distinguishes life in this country from life under the Third Reich.

[Above] all else, the First Amendment means that government has no power to restrict expression because of its message, its ideas, its subject matter, or its content. To permit the continued building of our politics and culture, and to assure self-fulfillment for each individual, our people are guaranteed the right to express any thought, free from government censorship. [This] is not to say, of course, that content legislation is per se invalid. [But] analysis of content restrictions must begin with a healthy respect for the truth that they are the most direct threat to the vitality of First Amendment rights.

[This] ordinance cannot be sustained on the basis of some of the more obvious exceptions to the rule against content control. While some would no doubt be willing to label appellees' views and symbols obscene, the constitutional rule that obscenity is unprotected applies only to material with erotic content. Furthermore, [the] Village tells us that it does not rely on a fear of responsive violence to justify the ordinance, and does not even suggest that there will be any physical violence if the march is held. The concession also eliminates any argument based on the fighting words doctrine of Chaplinsky v. New Hampshire.

Four basic arguments are advanced by the Village to justify the content [restrictions]. First, it is said that the content criminalized by [the ordinance] is "totally lacking in social content," and that it consists of "false statements of fact" in which there is "no constitutional value." [Gertz v. Robert Welch.] To the degree that the symbols in question can be said to assert anything specific, it must be the Nazi ideology, which cannot be treated as a mere false "fact." Under the First Amendment there is no such thing as a false idea. However pernicious an opinion may seem, we depend for its correction not on the conscience of judges and juries but on the competition of other ideas.

The Village's second argument [centers] on Beauharnais v. Illinois. [It] may be questioned, after cases such as [Cohen v. California] and [Brandenburg v. Ohio], whether the tendency to induce violence approach sanctioned implicitly in Beauharnais would pass constitutional muster today. Assuming that it would, however, it does not support [the ordinance], because the Village, as we have indicated, does not assert appellees' possible violence, an audience's possible responsive violence, or possible violence against third parties by those incited by appellees, as justifications for [it].

The Village's third argument is that it has a policy of fair housing, which the dissemination of racially defamatory material could undercut. We reject this argument without extended discussion. That the effective exercise of First Amendment rights may undercut a given government's policy on some issue is, indeed, one of the purposes of those rights.

The Village's fourth argument is that the Nazi march, involving as it does the display of uniforms and swastikas, will create a substantive evil that it has a right to prohibit: the infliction of psychic trauma on resident holocaust survivors and other Jewish residents. Assuming that specific individuals could proceed in tort under this theory to recover damages provably occasioned by the proposed march, and that a First Amendment defense would not bar the action, it is nonetheless quite a different matter to criminalize protected First Amendment conduct in anticipation of such results.

It would be grossly insensitive to deny, as we do not, that the proposed demonstration would seriously disturb, emotionally and mentally, at least some, and probably many of the Village's residents. The problem with engrafting an exception on the First Amendment for such situations is that they are indistinguishable in principle from speech that "invite(s) dispute." Terminiello v. Chicago. Yet these are among the "high purposes" of the First Amendment. It is perfectly clear that a state many not "make criminal the peaceful expression of unpopular views."

[The] preparation and issuance of this opinion has not been an easy task, or one which we have relished. Recognizing the implication that often seems to follow over-protestation, we nevertheless feel compelled once again to express our repugnance at the doctrines which the appellees desire to profess publicly. [Yet] our Regret at the use appellees plan to make of their rights is not in any sense an Apology for upholding the First Amendment. The result we have reached is dictated by the fundamental proposition that if these civil rights are to remain vital for all, they must protect not only those society deems acceptable, but also those whose ideas it quite justifiably rejects and despises.

––––––––

1. *The fallout of Skokie.* Collin and the NSPA cancelled the planned demonstration three days before it was to take place. Relying on the rulings in the Skokie litigation, the Nazis had obtained a federal court order setting aside the Chicago Park District's $60,000 liability insurance requirement which had previously blocked Nazi demonstrations in city parks there. Collin explained that the aim of the Nazis' Skokie efforts had been "pure agitation to restore our right to free speech." He stated that "he had used the threat of the Skokie march to win the right to rally in [Chicago]." No serious violence occurred when about 25 Nazis held a rally in a Chicago park on July 9, 1978.

2. ***Skokie at the Supreme Court.*** The dispute over the NSPA march in Skokie reached the U.S. Supreme Court three times. The first time, the NSPA sought a stay of an injunction against the march upheld by Illinois state courts. The Supreme Court treated the stay petition as a petition for certiorari, granted the writ, and summarily reversed the highest state court's denial of the stay. In its 5–4 per curiam disposition in **National Socialist Party v. Skokie**, 432 U.S. 43 (1977), the Court emphasized the need for "strict procedural safeguards" in the First Amendment area, including immediate appellate review. The ruling led the Illinois courts to set aside the injunction.

The case reached the Supreme Court a second time following the Seventh Circuit's decision in Collin. With the Nazi demonstration scheduled for June 25, 1978, Skokie sought a Supreme Court stay of the Court of Appeals ruling, pending review. On June 12, 1978, the Supreme Court denied the stay. Justice Blackmun, joined by Justice Rehnquist, dissented from that order, stating that the Court of Appeals decision "is in some tension with this Court's decision, 25 years ago, in Beauharnais," and noting that "Beauharnais has never been overruled or formally limited in any way." Smith v. Collin, 436 U.S. 953.

The final scene in the Skokie drama took place in October 1978, when the Supreme Court declined to review the Seventh Circuit decision invalidating the Skokie ordinances. **Smith v. Collin**, 439 U.S. 916 (1978). Justice BLACKMUN, joined by Justice White, dissented, urging that certiorari be granted "in order to resolve any possible conflict that may exist between the ruling of the Seventh Circuit here and Beauharnais." He added: "I also feel that the present case affords the Court an opportunity to consider whether, in the context of the facts that this record appears to present, there is no limit whatsoever to the exercise of free speech. There indeed may be no such limit, but when citizens assert, not casually but with deep conviction, that the proposed demonstration is scheduled at a place and in a manner that is taunting and overwhelmingly offensive to the citizens of that place, that assertion, uncomfortable though it may be for judges, deserves to be examined. It just might fall into the same category as one's 'right' to cry 'fire' in a crowded theater, for 'the character of every act depends upon the circumstances in which it is done.' Schenck."

For the view that permitting the Nazi march served the value of mastering pervasive social tendencies toward intolerance, and that it makes sense to carve out free speech as an arena of "extraordinary self-restraint" in order to promote self-restraint in other arenas, see Bollinger, The Tolerant Society (1986).

3. ***Regulating racist and other discriminatory speech on campus.*** Beginning in the late 1980s, a number of colleges and universities around the nation, responding to reports of racially tense exchanges on campuses, considered or adopted regulations to curb speech expressing hatred or bias toward members of racial, religious, or other groups. These regulations provoked extensive debates on campuses, in the media, and in the academic literature about the permissibility under the First Amendment of such rules.

In April 1988, for example, the University of Michigan adopted a regulation subjecting individuals to discipline for "[any] behavior, verbal or physical, that stigmatizes or victimizes an individual on the basis of race, ethnicity, religion, sex, sexual orientation, creed, national origin, ancestry, age, marital status, handicap or Vietnam-era veteran status" which "has the purpose or reasonably foreseeable effect of interfering with an individual's academic efforts, employment, participation in University sponsored extra-curricular activities or personal safety." A federal district court held the regulation unconstitutional under the First Amendment as overbroad and impermissibly vague. Doe v. University of Mich., 721 F. Supp. 852 (E.D. Mich. 1989).

In June 1990, Stanford University added to its "fundamental standard" of conduct for members of the university community a prohibition of "discriminatory harassment": "Speech or other expression constitutes harassment by personal vilification if it: (a) is intended to insult or stigmatize an individual or small group of individuals on the basis of their sex, race, color, handicap, religion, sexual orientation, or national and ethnic origin; and (b) is addressed directly to the individual or individuals whom it insults or stigmatizes; and (c) makes use of insulting or 'fighting' words or non-verbal symbols. In [this context], insulting or 'fighting' words or non-verbal symbols are [those] 'which by their very utterance inflict injury or tend to incite to an immediate breach of the peace,' and which are commonly understood to convey direct and visceral hatred or contempt for human beings on the basis of their sex, race, color, handicap, religion, sexual orientation, or national and ethnic origin."

In 1995, a California state court struck down the Stanford standard under a California statute providing that a private university may not impose limitations on speech that would violate the First Amendment if imposed by a public university. The decision, Corry v. Stanford, No. 740309 (Cal. Super. Ct. Santa Clara Co. 1995), held that the Stanford standard was overbroad under Chaplinsky because it reached insults that did not threaten to provoke immediate violence, and was impermissibly content-discriminatory under R.A.V. v. St. Paul, which follows, because it focused on bigoted insults while leaving other insults alone. The University did not appeal. For an account of the history of the Stanford standard by its author, and an argument for its constitutionality even in the wake of R.A.V., see Grey, "How to Write a Speech Code Without Really Trying: Reflections on the Stanford Experience," 29 U.C. Davis L. Rev. 891 (1996).

R.A.V. v. City of St. Paul

505 U.S. 377, 112 S. Ct. 2538, 120 L. Ed. 2d 305 (1992).

■ JUSTICE SCALIA delivered the opinion of the Court.

In the predawn hours of June 21, 1990, petitioner and several other teenagers allegedly assembled a crudely-made cross by taping together broken chair legs. They then allegedly burned the cross inside the fenced yard of a black family that lived across the street from the house where petitioner was staying. Although this conduct could have been punished under any of a number of laws [including laws against terroristic threats, arson, and criminal damage to property], one of the two provisions under which [St. Paul] chose to charge petitioner (then a juvenile) was the St. Paul Bias-Motivated Crime Ordinance which provides:

"Whoever places on public or private property a symbol, object, appellation, characterization or graffiti, including, but not limited to, a burning cross or Nazi swastika, which one knows or has reasonable grounds to know arouses anger, alarm or resentment in others on the basis of race, color, creed, religion or gender commits disorderly conduct and shall be guilty of a misdemeanor."

Petitioner moved to dismiss this count on the ground that the St. Paul ordinance was substantially overbroad and impermissibly content-based and therefore facially invalid under the First Amendment. The trial court granted this motion, but the Minnesota Supreme Court reversed.

I.   [Assuming,] arguendo, that all of the expression reached by the ordinance is proscribable under the "fighting words" doctrine, we nonetheless conclude that the ordinance is facially unconstitutional in that it prohibits otherwise permitted speech solely on the basis of the subjects the speech addresses. The First Amendment generally prevents government from proscribing speech, or even expressive conduct, because of disapproval of the ideas expressed. Content-based regulations are presumptively invalid. From 1791 to the present, however, our society, like other free but civilized societies, has permitted restrictions upon the content of speech in a few limited areas, which are "of such slight social value as a step to truth that any benefit that may be derived from them is clearly outweighed by the social interest in order and morality." Chaplinsky. [Our] decisions since the 1960's have narrowed the scope of the traditional categorical exceptions for defamation and for obscenity, but a limited categorical approach has remained an important part of our First Amendment jurisprudence.

We have sometimes said that these categories of expression are "not within the area of constitutionally protected speech," or that the "protection of the First Amendment does not extend" to them. Such statements must be taken in context, however. [What] they mean is that these areas of speech can, consistently with the First Amendment, be regulated because of their constitutionally proscribable content (obscenity, defamation, etc.)—not that they are categories of speech entirely invisible to the Constitution, so that they may be made the vehicles for content discrimination unrelated to their distinctively proscribable content. Thus, the government may proscribe libel; but it may not make the further content discrimination of proscribing only libel critical of the government. [Nor could a] city council [enact] an ordinance prohibiting only those legally obscene works that contain criticism of the city government or, indeed, that do not include endorsement of the city government. Such a simplistic, all-or-nothing-at-all approach to First Amendment protection is at odds with common sense and with our jurisprudence as well.

The proposition that a particular instance of speech can be proscribable on the basis of one feature (e.g., obscenity) but not on the basis of another (e.g., opposition to the city government) is commonplace, and has found application in many contexts. We have long held, for example, that nonverbal expressive activity can be banned because of the action it entails, but not because of the ideas it expresses—so that burning a flag in violation of an ordinance against outdoor fires could be punishable, whereas burning a flag in violation of an ordinance against dishonoring the flag is not.

[Thus], the exclusion of "fighting words" from the scope of the First Amendment simply means that, for purposes of that Amendment, the unprotected features of the words are, despite their verbal character, essentially a "nonspeech" element of communication. Fighting words are thus analogous to a noisy sound truck: [both] can be used to convey an idea;

but neither has, in and of itself, a claim upon the First Amendment. As with the sound truck, however, so also with fighting words: The government may not regulate use based on hostility—or favoritism—towards the underlying message expressed.

The concurrences describe us as setting forth a new First Amendment principle that prohibition of constitutionally proscribable speech cannot be "underinclusive" [so that] "a government must either proscribe all speech or no speech at all." That easy target is of the concurrences' own invention. In our view, the First Amendment imposes not an "underinclusiveness" limitation but a "content discrimination" limitation upon a State's prohibition of proscribable speech. There is no problem whatever, for example, with a State's prohibiting obscenity (and other forms of proscribable expression) only in certain media or markets, for although that prohibition would be "underinclusive," it would not discriminate on the basis of content.

Even the prohibition against content discrimination that we assert the First Amendment requires is not absolute. [When] the basis for the content discrimination consists entirely of the very reason the entire class of speech at issue is proscribable, no significant danger of idea or viewpoint discrimination exists. [Thus, a state] might choose to prohibit only that obscenity which is the most patently offensive in its prurience—i.e., that which involves the most lascivious displays of sexual activity. But it may not prohibit, for example, only that obscenity which includes offensive political messages. And the Federal Government can criminalize only those threats of violence that are directed against the President, since the reasons why threats of violence are outside the First Amendment (protecting individuals from the fear of violence, from the disruption that fear engenders, and from the possibility that the threatened violence will occur) have special force when applied to the person of the President. But the Federal Government may not criminalize only those threats against the President that mention his policy on aid to inner cities. [And a state] may choose to regulate price advertising in one industry but not in others, because the risk of fraud [is] in its view greater there. But a State may not prohibit only that commercial advertising that depicts men in a demeaning fashion.

Another valid basis for according differential treatment to even a content-defined subclass of proscribable speech is that the subclass happens to be associated with particular "secondary effects" of the speech, so that the regulation is "justified without reference to the content of the . . . speech." A State could, for example, permit all obscene live performances except those involving minors. Moreover, since words can in some circumstances violate laws directed not against speech but against conduct (a law against treason, for example, is violated by telling the enemy the nation's defense secrets), a particular content-based subcategory of a proscribable class of speech can be swept up incidentally within the reach of a statute directed at conduct rather than speech. Thus, for example, sexually derogatory "fighting words," among other words, may produce a violation of Title VII's general prohibition against sexual discrimination in employment practices. Where the government does not target conduct on the basis of its expressive content, acts are not shielded from regulation merely because they express a discriminatory idea or philosophy. [Finally,] it may not even be necessary to identify any particular "neutral" basis, so long as the nature of the content discrimination is such that there is no realistic possibility that official suppression of ideas is afoot. (We cannot think of any First Amendment interest that would stand in the way of a State's prohibiting only those obscene motion pictures with blue-eyed actresses.)

II.   Applying these principles to the St. Paul ordinance, we conclude that, even as narrowly construed by the Minnesota Supreme Court [to apply only to] "fighting words," the remaining, unmodified terms make clear that the ordinance applies only to "fighting words" that insult, or provoke violence, "on the basis of race, color, creed, religion or gender." Displays containing abusive invective, no matter how vicious or severe, are permissible unless they are addressed to one of the specified disfavored topics. Those who wish to use "fighting words" in connection with other ideas—to express hostility, for example, on the basis of political affiliation, union membership, or homosexuality—are not covered. The First Amendment does not permit St. Paul to impose special prohibitions on those speakers who express views on disfavored subjects.

In its practical operation, moreover, the ordinance goes even beyond mere content discrimination, to actual viewpoint discrimination. Displays containing some words—odious racial epithets, for example—would be prohibited to proponents of all views. But "fighting words" that do not themselves invoke race, color, creed, religion, or gender—aspersions upon a person's mother, for example—would seemingly be usable ad libitum in the placards of those arguing in favor of racial, color, etc. tolerance and equality, but could not be used by that speaker's opponents. One could hold up a sign saying, for example, that all "anti-Catholic bigots" are misbegotten; but not that all "papists" are, for that would insult and provoke violence "on the basis of religion." St. Paul has no such authority to license one side of a debate to fight freestyle, while requiring the other to follow Marquis of Queensbury Rules.

[The] content-based discrimination reflected in the St. Paul ordinance comes within neither any of the specific exceptions to the First Amendment prohibition we discussed earlier, nor within a more general exception for content discrimination that does not threaten censorship of ideas. It assuredly does not fall within the exception for content discrimination based on the very reasons why the particular class of speech at issue (here, fighting words) is proscribable. [St. Paul] has not singled out an especially offensive mode of expression—it has not, for example, selected for prohibition only those fighting words that communicate ideas in a threatening (as opposed to a merely obnoxious) manner. Rather, it has proscribed fighting words of whatever manner that communicate messages of racial, gender, or religious intolerance.

Finally, St. Paul [argues] that, even if the ordinance regulates expression based on hostility towards its protected ideological content, this discrimination is nonetheless justified because it is narrowly tailored to serve compelling state interests [in protecting the] rights of members of groups that have historically been subjected to discrimination, including the right of such group members to live in peace where they wish. We do not doubt that these interests are compelling, and that the ordinance can be said to promote them. [The] dispositive question in this case, [however,] is whether content discrimination is reasonably necessary to achieve St. Paul's compelling interests; it plainly is not. An ordinance not limited to the favored topics, for example, would have precisely the same beneficial effect. In fact the only interest distinctively served by the content limitation is that of displaying the city council's special hostility towards the particular biases thus singled out. That is precisely what the First Amendment forbids. The politicians of St. Paul are entitled to express that hostility—but not through the means of imposing unique limitations upon speakers who (however benightedly) disagree.

Let there be no mistake about our belief that burning a cross in someone's front yard is reprehensible. But St. Paul has sufficient means at its disposal to prevent such behavior without adding the First Amendment to the fire. Reversed.

■ JUSTICE WHITE, with whom JUSTICES BLACKMUN and O'CONNOR join, and with whom JUSTICE STEVENS joins except as to Part I(A), concurring in the judgment.

I agree with the majority that the judgment of the Minnesota Supreme Court should be reversed. However, our agreement ends there. This case could easily be decided within the contours of established First Amendment law by holding, as petitioner argues, that the St. Paul ordinance is fatally overbroad because it criminalizes not only unprotected expression but expression protected by the First Amendment.

I. A.   This Court's decisions have plainly stated that expression falling within certain limited categories so lacks the values the First Amendment was designed to protect that the Constitution affords no protection to that expression. Chaplinsky. [Thus,] this Court has long held certain discrete categories of expression [e.g., child pornography, obscenity and most libel] to be proscribable on the basis of their content. All of these categories are content based. But the Court has held that First Amendment does not apply to them because their expressive content is worthless or of de minimis value to society. [It] is inconsistent to hold that the government may proscribe an entire category of speech because the content of that speech is evil, but that the government may not treat a subset of that category differently without violating the First Amendment; the content of the subset is by definition worthless and undeserving of constitutional protection. [A] ban on all fighting words or on a subset of the fighting words category would restrict only the social evil of hate speech, without creating the danger of driving viewpoints from the marketplace. [By] characterizing fighting words as a form of "debate," the majority legitimates hate speech as a form of public discussion.

B.   In a second break with precedent, the Court refuses to sustain the ordinance even though it would survive under the strict scrutiny applicable to other protected expression. [The] Court expressly concedes that [the government interest in ensuring the rights of members of groups that have historically been subject to discrimination] is compelling and is promoted by the ordinance, [but holds that such a law] could never pass constitutional muster if [its object] could be accomplished by banning a wider category of speech. This appears to be a general renunciation of strict scrutiny review, a fundamental tool of First Amendment analysis.

C.   The Court has patched up its argument with an apparently nonexhaustive list of ad hoc exceptions, in what can be viewed either as an attempt to confine the effects of its decision to the facts of this case, or as an effort to anticipate some of the questions that will arise from its radical revision of First Amendment law. [For example,] Title VII makes it unlawful to discriminate "because of [an] individual's race, color, religion, sex, or national origin," and the regulations covering hostile workplace claims forbid "sexual harassment," which includes "unwelcome sexual advances, requests for sexual favors, and other verbal or physical conduct of a sexual nature" which creates "an intimidating, hostile, or offensive working environment." [Hence,] the majority's second exception, which the Court indicates would insulate a Title VII hostile work environment claim from an underinclusiveness challenge because "sexually derogatory 'fighting words' . . . may produce a violation of Title VII's general prohibition against sexual discrimination in employment practices." [But if] the relationship between the broader statute and specific regulation is sufficient to bring the Title VII regulation within [this exception], then all St. Paul need do to bring its ordinance within [it] is to add some prefatory language concerning discrimination generally.

II.   Although I disagree with the Court's analysis, I do agree with its conclusion: The St. Paul ordinance is unconstitutional. However, I would decide the case on overbreadth grounds. [Although] the ordinance as construed reaches categories of speech that are constitutionally unprotected, it also criminalizes a substantial amount of expression that—however repugnant—is shielded by the First Amendment. [I] understand the [Minnesota Supreme Court] to have ruled that St. Paul may constitutionally prohibit expression that "by its very utterance" causes "anger, alarm or resentment." Our fighting words cases have made clear, however, that such generalized reactions are not sufficient to strip expression of its constitutional protection. The mere fact that expressive activity causes hurt feelings, offense, or resentment does not render the expression unprotected. The ordinance is therefore fatally overbroad and invalid on its face. [I] join the judgment, but not the folly of the opinion.

■ JUSTICE BLACKMUN, concurring in the judgment.

[I] fear that the Court has been distracted from its proper mission by the temptation to decide the issue over "politically correct speech" and "cultural diversity," neither of which is presented here. [I] see no First Amendment values that are compromised by a law that prohibits hoodlums from driving minorities out of their homes by burning crosses on their lawns, but I see great harm in preventing the people of Saint Paul from specifically punishing the race-based fighting words that so prejudice their community.

■ JUSTICE STEVENS, with whom JUSTICES WHITE and BLACKMUN join as to Part I, concurring in the judgment.

I.   [The] Court [applies] the prohibition on content-based regulation to speech that the Court had until today considered wholly "unprotected" by the First Amendment—namely, fighting words. This new absolutism in the prohibition of content-based regulations severely contorts the fabric of settled First Amendment law. Our First Amendment decisions have created a rough hierarchy in the constitutional protection of speech. Core political speech occupies the highest, most protected position; commercial speech and nonobscene, sexually explicit speech are regarded as a sort of second-class expression; obscenity and fighting words receive the least protection of all. Assuming that the Court is correct that this last class of speech is not wholly "unprotected," it certainly does not follow that fighting words and obscenity receive the same sort of protection afforded core political speech. Yet in ruling that proscribable speech cannot be regulated based on subject matter, the Court does just that.

[Perhaps] because the Court recognizes these perversities, it quickly offers some ad hoc limitations on its newly extended prohibition on content-based regulations. [For example, the Court concedes that] "the Federal Government can criminalize only those physical threats that are directed against the President." [Precisely] this same reasoning, however, compels the conclusion that St. Paul's ordinance is constitutional. Just as Congress may determine that threats against the President entail more severe consequences than other threats, so [St. Paul] may determine that threats based on the target's race, religion, or gender cause more severe harm to both the target and to society than other threats.

II.   Although I agree with much of Justice White's analysis, I do not join Part I-A of his opinion because I have reservations about the "categorical approach" to the First Amendment. Admittedly, the categorical approach to the First Amendment has some appeal: either expression is protected or it is not—the categories create safe harbors for governments and speakers alike. But this approach sacrifices subtlety for clarity and is, I am convinced, ultimately unsound. As an initial matter, the concept of "categories" fits poorly with the complex reality of expression. Few dividing lines in First Amendment law are straight and unwavering, and efforts at categorization inevitably give rise only to fuzzy boundaries. [Moreover,] the categorical approach does not take seriously the importance of context. The meaning of any expression and the legitimacy of its regulation can only be determined in context. [The] history of the categorical approach is largely the history of narrowing the categories of unprotected speech. This evolution, I believe, indicates that the categorical approach is unworkable and the quest for absolute categories of "protected" and "unprotected" speech ultimately futile.

III. As the foregoing suggests, I disagree with both the Court's and part of Justice White's analysis of the constitutionality St. Paul ordinance. Unlike the Court, I do not believe that all content-based regulations are equally infirm and presumptively invalid; unlike Justice White, I do not believe that fighting words are wholly unprotected by the First Amendment. To the contrary, I believe our decisions establish a more complex and subtle analysis, one that considers the content and context of the regulated speech, and the nature and scope of the restriction on speech. Applying this analysis and assuming arguendo (as the Court does) that the St. Paul ordinance is not overbroad, I conclude that such a selective, subject-matter regulation on proscribable speech is constitutional.

[Looking] to the content and character of the regulated activity, two things are clear. First, by hypothesis the ordinance bars only low-value speech, namely, fighting words. [Second,] the ordinance regulates "expressive conduct [rather] than . . . the written or spoken word." Looking to the context of the regulated activity, it is again significant that the statute (by hypothesis) regulates only fighting words. [By] hypothesis, then, the St. Paul ordinance restricts speech in confrontational and potentially violent situations. [The] St. Paul ordinance regulates speech not on the basis of its subject matter or the viewpoint expressed, but rather on the basis of the harm the speech causes. [Contrary] to the Court's suggestion, the ordinance regulates only a subcategory of expression that causes injuries based on "race, color, creed, religion or gender," not a subcategory that involves discussions that concern those characteristics. [Contrary] to the suggestion of the majority, the St. Paul ordinance does not regulate expression based on viewpoint. [Just] as the ordinance would prohibit a Muslim from hoisting a sign claiming that all Catholics were misbegotten, so the ordinance would bar a Catholic from hoisting a similar sign attacking Muslims. The St. Paul ordinance is evenhanded. [To] extend the Court's pugilistic metaphor, the St. Paul ordinance simply bans punches "below the belt"—by either party. It does not, therefore, favor one side of any debate.

Finally, it is noteworthy that the St. Paul ordinance is, as construed by the Court today, quite narrow. The St. Paul ordinance does not ban all "hate speech," nor does it ban, say, all cross-burnings or all swastika displays. [Petitioner] is free to burn a cross to announce a rally or to express his views about racial supremacy, he may do so on private property or public land, at day or at night, so long as the burning is not so threatening and so directed at an individual as to "by its very [execution] inflict injury." Taken together, these several considerations persuade me that the St. Paul ordinance is not an unconstitutional content-based regulation of speech. Thus, were the ordinance not overbroad, I would vote to uphold it.

———

THE MEANING AND IMPLICATIONS OF R.A.V.

1. *The hate speech debate.* Did the Supreme Court in R.A.V. wrongly discourage efforts to control hate speech? Should existing exceptions to First Amendment protection have been analogized or expanded? Recall that in Beauharnais v. Illinois (1952; p. 74), the Court found no First Amendment bar against a law prohibiting "expos[ure of] the citizens of any race, color, creed or religion to contempt, derision, or obloquy," reasoning that libel, whether individual or group, lies outside the First Amendment altogether. Beauharnais has never formally been overruled. New York Times v. Sullivan assumed libel limited to a provably false statements of fact and to speech "of and concerning" an individual, not the government in general. Does this undermine the notion that group libel is unprotected? Might it be countered that a verbal attack on a group of private individuals on the basis of their race is a far cry from seditious libel, and thus implicates lesser First Amendment concern than the verdict in New York Times? Is Beauharnais still good law under the logic of R.A.V., given the way the Illinois law was formulated?

The R.A.V. concurrences found the St. Paul ordinance overbroad if viewed as a fighting words ordinance because it encompassed non-violent responses. Could a narrower hate speech law than St. Paul's survive First Amendment review under Chaplinsky? Alternatively, should St. Paul's law (or Stanford's) have survived even as written under the forgotten branch of Chaplinsky that included words that "by their very utterance inflict injury" in addition to words that tend to incite immediate breaches of the peace? On this view, racist or other bigoted epithets should be no more protected when they cause fright or flight than when they cause fights, for in either case they are "no essential part of any exposition of ideas." For an argument that this strand of Chaplinsky is still extant or worth reviving, see Grey, "Responding to Abusive Speech on Campus: A Model Statute," Reconstruction 50, Winter 1990 (arguing against protection for any "words that would justify imposition of tort liability for intentional infliction of emotional distress"); Grey, "Civil Rights vs. Civil Liberties: The Case of Discriminatory Verbal Harassment," 8 Soc. Phil. & Pol. 81 (1991). Are the unprotected categories enumerated in Chaplinsky a nonexhaustive list that may be extended to hate speech as a new category of speech that is "of such slight social value as a step to truth" that any benefit that may be derived from them is clearly outweighed by social interests? For such arguments, see Delgado, "Words that Wound: A Tort Action for Racial Insults, Epithets, and Name-Calling," 17 Harv. C.R.-C.L. L. Rev. 133 (1982); Matsuda, "Public Response to Racist Speech: Considering the Victim's Story," 87 Mich. L. Rev. 2320 (1989); Waldron, The Harm in Hate Speech (2012).

Those opposing such initiatives object that hate speech regulation "would endanger fundamental free speech values," "violate the cardinal principles that speech restrictions must be content-and viewpoint-neutral," and go well beyond the narrow bounds the Court has imposed on the "fighting words" exception. Strossen, "Regulating Racist Speech on Campus: A Modest Proposal?", 1990 Duke L.J. 484; see also Fried, "A New First Amendment Jurisprudence: A Threat to Liberty," 59 U. Chi. L. Rev. 225 (1992) (assailing "those who promulgate these regulations [for] assign[ing] to themselves the authority to determine which ideas are false and which false ideas people may not express as they choose"); Weinstein, "A Constitutional Roadmap to the Regulation of Campus Hate Speech," 38 Wayne L. Rev. 163 (1991) (condemning as "thought control" the purpose "to combat racism by preventing its contagion from infecting the hearts and minds of a new generation of potential racists and sexists"); Lewis, Freedom for the Thought That We Hate (2007) (arguing that hate speech regulations may be overenforced, resulting in the suppression of unpopular ideas).

Other opponents suggest that such regulations are unduly paternalistic as well as misguided because articulate diatribe about racial inferiority, which is not proscribable as hate speech, might well be more hurtful to an individual and contribute more to the social construction of racism than do vulgar racial epithets, which are disfavored under conventional social norms and thus more easily discounted or ignored. See Gates, "Let Them Talk," The New Republic, Sept. 20, 1993; Karst, "Boundaries and Reasons: Freedom of Expression and the Subordination of Groups," 1990 Ill. L. Rev. 95 (arguing that "for women and for the members of racial and ethnic minorities a first amendment doctrine that offers less protection to 'low value' speech is not just unhelpful; it is dangerous" because a subordinated group's "escape from subordinate status is accomplished primarily though persuasion," and "precisely because an important part of a group's subordination consists in silencing, their emancipation requires a generously defined freedom of expression"). For an argument that grassroots organization of minority voices is preferable to top-down disciplinary solutions to racist speech, see Calleros, "Paternalism, Counterspeech, and Campus Hate-Speech [Codes]," 27 Ariz. St. L.J. 1249 (1995). For a reply to these various inefficacy arguments, see Delgado & Yun, " 'The Speech We Hate': First Amendment Totalism, The ACLU and the Principle of Dialogic Politics," 27 Ariz. St. L.J. 1281 (1995).

In Matal v. Tam (2017; p. 426), Simon Tam challenged the denial of trademark registration for his band name "The Slants." Tam argued in that by reclaiming a racial slur as the name of the rock band, he would "help to 'reclaim' the term and drain it of its denigrating force." The Court did not engage with this argument directly, but reemphasized that speech may not be banned merely because it "expressed ideas that offend," even if the government's intent is to protect marginalized groups.

2. ***Hate speech: a comparative perspective.*** Does R.A.V. make it too difficult to prosecute or regulate speech directed at expressing hatred on the basis of race or any other group characteristic that is protected against discriminatory conduct? In contrast to the U.S. approach, in which racist hate speech is protected unless it constitutes a threat (see note 6 below), nations like Great Britain, Northern Ireland, Israel and Australia regulate racist hate speech "based on the idea that hate speech that vilifies a group poses a more serious threat to the public order than insults directed at a person for his or her personal characteristics," and nations like Canada, Denmark, France, Germany, and the Netherlands have laws against racist hate speech "premised on the need to protect human dignity 'quite apart from any interest in safeguarding public order.' " Bell, "Restraining the Heartless: Racist Speech and Minority Rights," 84 Ind. L.J. 963 (2009). Note too that the International Covenant on Civil and Political Rights, Art. 20(2), provides that "any advocacy of national, racial or religious hatred that constitutes incitement to discrimination, hostility or violence shall be prohibited by law." Why might the United States be an outlier among comparable nations in its robust protection of such speech?

3. ***Distinguishing the regulation of hate speech from the regulation of hate crimes.*** One term after R.A.V., the Court confronted a First Amendment challenge to a state law enhancing the sentence for bias-motivated assault. Two state supreme courts—Wisconsin and Ohio—had reasoned that aggravating the penalty for racially motivated hate crimes violated the principle of viewpoint neutrality set forth in R.A.V. Just as government may not selectively regulate unprotected speech such as fighting words on the basis of the viewpoint of the speaker, these state courts reasoned, so government may not regulate conduct based solely on the viewpoint of an actor. For an articulation of this position, see Gellman, "Sticks and Stones Can Put You in Jail, But Can Words Increase Your Sentence?," 39 UCLA L. Rev. 333 (1991).

In **Wisconsin v. Mitchell**, 508 U.S. 476 (1993), the Supreme Court unanimously rejected that argument, drawing a sharp distinction between the regulation of speech and conduct. The effect of Mitchell was to limit the holding of R.A.V. to viewpoint-selective laws aimed expressly at otherwise unprotected words or symbols. Chief Justice REHNQUIST delivered the opinion of the Court: "On the evening of October 7, 1989, a group of young black men and boys, including Mitchell, gathered at an apartment complex in Kenosha, Wisconsin. Several members of the group discussed a scene from the motion picture 'Mississippi Burning,' in which a white man beat a young black boy who was praying. The group moved outside and Mitchell asked them: 'Do you all feel hyped up to move on some white people?' Shortly thereafter, a young white boy approached the group on the opposite side of the street where they were standing. As the boy walked by, Mitchell said: 'You all want to fuck somebody up? There goes a white boy; go get him.' Mitchell counted to three and pointed in the boy's direction. The group ran towards the boy, beat him severely, and stole his tennis shoes. The boy was rendered unconscious and remained in a coma for four days.

"[Mitchell] was convicted of aggravated battery. That offense ordinarily carries a maximum sentence of two years' imprisonment. But because the jury found that Mitchell had intentionally selected his victim because of the boy's race, the maximum sentence for Mitchell's offense was increased to seven years under [a Wisconsin] provision [that] enhances the maximum penalty for an offense whenever the defendant 'intentionally selects the person against whom the crime . . . is committed . . . because of the race, religion, color, disability, sexual orientation, national origin or ancestry of that person. . . .'

"[Mitchell] argues that the Wisconsin penalty-enhancement statute is invalid because it punishes the defendant's discriminatory motive, or reason, for acting. But [a defendant's motive for committing an offense is traditionally a factor considered by a judge at sentencing, and] motive plays the same role under the Wisconsin statute as it does under federal and state antidiscrimination laws, which we have previously upheld against constitutional challenge. Title VII, for example, makes it unlawful for an employer to discriminate against an employee 'because of such individual's race, color, religion, sex, or national origin.' [In] R.A.V. v. St. Paul, we cited Title VII [as] an example of a permissible content-neutral regulation of conduct.

"Nothing in our decision last Term in R.A.V. compels a different result here. [W]hereas the ordinance struck down in R.A.V. was explicitly directed at expression (i.e., 'speech' or 'messages'), the statute in this case is aimed at conduct unprotected by the First Amendment. Moreover, the Wisconsin statute singles out for enhancement bias-inspired conduct because this conduct is thought to inflict greater individual and societal harm. For example, according to the State and its amici, bias-motivated crimes are more likely to provoke retaliatory crimes, inflict distinct emotional harms on their victims, and incite community unrest. The State's desire to redress these perceived harms provides an adequate explanation for its penalty-enhancement provision over and above mere disagreement with offenders' beliefs or biases. As Blackstone said long ago, 'it is but reasonable that among crimes of different natures those should be most severely punished, which are the most destructive of the public safety and happiness.' 4 W. Blackstone, Commentaries *16. [Reversed.]"

4. *The role of motive in R.A.V. and Mitchell.* Mitchell permitted the state to enhance punishment for a crime motivated by the victim's race. In so doing, the Court focused heavily on the material consequences of such conduct: it assumed that such violence has greater in terrorem and incendiary effects on society than ordinary violence. What if the state instead enhanced punishment for a crime "motivated by the defendant's beliefs about race," or by "the defendant's attempt to communicate a racist message"? Such crimes might have similar effects to those described in Mitchell. But for the view that such laws might violate the First Amendment, even though Mitchell was correctly decided, see Tribe, "The Mystery of Motive, Private and [Public]," 1993 Sup. Ct. Rev. 1. To what extent was the debate between the majority and the concurring opinions in R.A.V. really about St. Paul's true motive in enacting the ordinance? As a law professor, now-Supreme Court Justice Elena Kagan argued that "half hidden beneath a swirl of doctrinal formulations," the Justices disagreed about whether the hate-crime law was "purely censorial—a simple desire to blot out ideas" or "an effort by the government, divorced from mere hostility toward ideas, to counter a severe and objectively ascertainable harm." Kagan, "Private Speech, Public Purpose: The Role of Governmental Motive in First Amendment Doctrine," 63 U. Chi. L. Rev. 413, 422 (1996). Was the law in Mitchell devoid of censorial motive?

5. ***Hostile environment sexual or racial harassment.*** Federal civil rights statutes barring employment discrimination have been construed to bar sexual or racial harassment in the workplace, including by the creation of a racially or sexually hostile environment that adversely affects working conditions. After R.A.V. and Mitchell, are such laws constitutional? For the argument that such laws raise serious First Amendment questions, see Browne, "Title VII as Censorship: Hostile-Environment Harassment and the First Amendment," 52 Ohio State L.J. 481 (1991); Volokh, "Freedom of Speech and Workplace Harassment," 39 UCLA L. Rev. 1791 (1992). For a defense based partly on the notion that employees in the workplace context are effectively a captive audience, see Fallon, "Sexual Harassment, Content-Neutrality, and the First Amendment Dog That Didn't Bark," 1994 S. Ct. Rev. 1. See also Strossen, "Regulating Workplace Sexual Harassment and Upholding the First Amendment—Avoiding a Collision," 37 Vill. L. Rev. 757 (1992).

Analogous issues arise on university campuses under Title VI's protection against a racially hostile educational environment and Title IX's protection against a hostile educational environment based on sex discrimination. See, e.g., Department of Education, Office for Civil Rights, "Racial Incidents and Harassment Against Students at Educational Institutions; Investigative Guidance," 59 Federal Register 47 (1994). Thus, in one highly publicized incident, the University of Oklahoma expelled two students who led fellow fraternity-members in a racist chant stating a commitment to exclude African-Americans from the fraternity and alluding to lynching. Some commentators deemed the expulsion unconstitutional, noting that "racist speech is constitutionally protected, just as is expression of other contemptible ideas; and universities may not discipline students based on their speech." Volokh, "No, It's Not Constitutional for the University of Oklahoma to Expel Students for Racist Speech," March 10, 2015, available at https://www.washingtonpost.com/news/volokh-conspiracy/wp/2015/03/10/no-a-public-university-may-not-expel-students-for-racist-speech/. Consider the contrary view that the students "are being expelled not for their opinions per se, but because their speech was a form of discriminatory conduct that would create a hostile educational environment for black students" because it "was literally designed to inculcate the value of racial discrimination by making pledges recite their commitment never to admit a black member to the fraternity." Feldman, "Oklahoma's Right to Expel Frat Boys," March 11, 2015, available at http://www.bloombergview.com/articles/2015-03-11/oklahoma-s-right-to-expel-frat-boys.

6. ***The problem of true threats.*** When does racist or other hateful speech escalate to a threat to cause bodily injury? In dicta in R.A.V., Justice Scalia assumed that threats are an unprotected category of speech and that threats of violence against the President are a permissibly proscribable subcategory of that category of unprotected speech. Are true threats always proscribable? Recall the discussion of threats in NAACP v. Claiborne Hardware and Planned Parenthood v. ACLA at pp. 51 and 52.

In **Watts v. United States**, 394 U.S. 705 (1969), the Court reversed, per curiam, a conviction under a 1917 law making it a felony "knowingly and willfully" to make "any threat to take the life" of the President. Petitioner had said at a public rally, "Now I have already received my draft classification as 1–A and I have got to report for my physical this Monday coming. I am not going. If they ever make me carry a rifle, the first man I want to get in my sights is L.B.J. They are not going to make me kill my black brothers." The opinion stated: "What is a threat must be distinguished from what is constitutionally protected speech. [We] do not believe that the kind of political hyperbole indulged in by petitioner fits within that statutory term. [We] agree with petitioner that his only offense [was] 'a kind of very crude offensive method of stating a political opposition to the President.' Taken in context, and regarding the expressly conditional nature of the statement and the reaction of the listeners [laughter], we do not see how it could be interpreted otherwise."

Would the cross-burning in R.A.V. have been subject to prosecution under a statute aimed at true threats generally? At threats based on race? Is a statute that focuses on cross-burning as a threat of violence more likely to satisfy the First Amendment than was the ordinance invalidated in R.A.V.? Is a ban on cross-burning intended to intimidate analogous to the ban on death threats against the President? Consider these questions in light of the following case:

Virginia v. Black

538 U.S. 343, 123 S. Ct. 1536, 155 L. Ed. 2d 535 (2003).

■ JUSTICE O'CONNOR announced the judgment of the Court and delivered the opinion of the Court with respect to Parts I, II, and III, and an opinion with respect to Parts IV and V, in which CHIEF JUSTICE REHNQUIST, and JUSTICES STEVENS and BREYER join.

In this case we consider whether the Commonwealth of Virginia's statute banning cross burning with "an intent to intimidate a person or group of persons" violates the First Amendment. Va. Code Ann. § 18.2–423 (1996). We conclude that while a State, consistent with the First Amendment, may ban cross burning carried out with the intent to intimidate, the provision in the Virginia statute treating any cross burning as prima facie evidence of intent to intimidate renders the statute unconstitutional in its current form.

I.   Respondents [were convicted] of violating Virginia's cross-burning statute, § 18.2–423. That statute provides:

"It shall be unlawful for any person or persons, with the intent of intimidating any person or group of persons, to burn, or cause to be burned, a cross on the property of another, a highway or other public place. Any person who shall violate any provision of this section shall be guilty of a Class 6 felony.

"Any such burning of a cross shall be prima facie evidence of an intent to intimidate a person or group of persons."

[Black was convicted under the statute after a jury trial in which the jury was instructed that "the burning of a cross by itself is sufficient evidence from which you may infer the required intent" to intimidate. The Supreme Court of Virginia reversed the conviction, holding that the Virginia cross-burning statute "is analytically indistinguishable from the ordinance found unconstitutional in R.A.V."]

II.   Cross burning originated in the 14th century as a means for Scottish tribes to signal each other. [Cross] burning in this country, however, long ago became unmoored from its Scottish ancestry. Burning a cross in the

United States is inextricably intertwined with the history of the Ku Klux Klan. The first Ku Klux Klan [fought] Reconstruction and the corresponding drive to allow freed blacks to participate in the political process, [imposing] "a veritable reign of terror" throughout the South. [In] response, Congress passed what is now known as the Ku Klux Klan Act. [By] the end of Reconstruction in 1877, the first Klan no longer existed. The genesis of the second Klan began in 1905. [From] the inception of the second Klan, cross burnings have been used to communicate both threats of violence and messages of shared ideology. [Often,] the Klan used cross burnings as a tool of intimidation and a threat of impending violence. [The] decision of this Court in Brown v. Board of Education, along with the civil rights movement of the 1950's and 1960's, sparked another outbreak of Klan violence. These acts of violence included bombings, beatings, shootings, stabbings, and mutilations. Members of the Klan burned crosses on the lawns of those associated with the civil rights movement, assaulted the Freedom Riders, bombed churches, and murdered blacks as well as whites whom the Klan viewed as sympathetic toward the civil rights movement.

Throughout the history of the Klan, cross burnings have also remained potent symbols of shared group identity and ideology. The burning cross became a symbol of the Klan itself and a central feature of Klan gatherings. [At] Klan gatherings across the country, cross burning became the climax of the rally or the initiation. [Throughout] the Klan's history, the Klan continued to use the burning cross in their ritual ceremonies. For its own members, the cross was a sign of celebration and ceremony. [And] cross burnings featured prominently in Klan rallies when the Klan attempted to move toward more nonviolent tactics to stop integration. In short, a burning cross has remained a symbol of Klan ideology and of Klan unity.

To this day, regardless of whether the message is a political one or whether the message is also meant to intimidate, the burning of a cross is a "symbol of hate." And while cross burning sometimes carries no intimidating message, at other times the intimidating message is the only message conveyed. For example, when a cross burning is directed at a particular person not affiliated with the Klan, the burning cross often serves as a message of intimidation, designed to inspire in the victim a fear of bodily harm. Moreover, the history of violence associated with the Klan shows that the possibility of injury or death is not just hypothetical. The person who burns a cross directed at a particular person often is making a serious threat, meant to coerce the victim to comply with the Klan's wishes unless the victim is willing to risk the wrath of the Klan. [In] sum, while a burning cross does not inevitably convey a message of intimidation, often the cross burner intends that the recipients of the message fear for their lives. And when a cross burning is used to intimidate, few if any messages are more powerful.

III. A.   [We] have long recognized that the government may regulate certain categories of expression consistent with the Constitution [such as fighting words and incitement. Chaplinsky; Brandenburg]. And the First Amendment also permits a State to ban a "true threat." Watts. "True threats" encompass those statements where the speaker means to communicate a serious expression of an intent to commit an act of unlawful violence to a particular individual or group of individuals. The speaker need not actually intend to carry out the threat. Rather, a prohibition on true threats "protect[s] individuals from the fear of violence" and "from the disruption that fear engenders," in addition to protecting people "from the possibility that the threatened violence will occur." Intimidation in the constitutionally proscribable sense of the word is a type of true threat, where a speaker directs a threat to a person or group of persons with the intent of placing the victim in fear of bodily harm or death. [Some] cross burnings fit within this meaning of intimidating speech.

B.   The Supreme Court of Virginia ruled that in light of R.A.V. v. City of St. Paul, even if it is constitutional to ban cross burning in a content-neutral manner, the Virginia cross-burning statute is unconstitutional because it discriminates on the basis of content and viewpoint. [We] disagree. [We] did not hold in R.A.V. that the First Amendment prohibits all forms of content-based discrimination within a proscribable area of speech. [Indeed,] we noted that it would be constitutional to ban only a particular type of threat [such as] "those threats of violence that are directed against the President." [Similarly,] Virginia's statute does not run afoul of the First Amendment insofar as it bans cross burning with intent to intimidate. Unlike the statute at issue in R.A.V., the Virginia statute does not single out for opprobrium only that speech directed toward "one of the specified disfavored topics." It does not matter whether an individual burns a cross with intent to intimidate because of the victim's race, gender, or religion, or because of the victim's "political affiliation, union membership, or homosexuality." Moreover, as a factual matter it is not true that cross burners direct their intimidating conduct solely to racial or religious minorities.

The First Amendment permits Virginia to outlaw cross burnings done with the intent to intimidate because burning a cross is a particularly virulent form of intimidation. Instead of prohibiting all intimidating messages, Virginia may choose to regulate this subset of intimidating messages in light of cross burning's long and pernicious history as a signal of impending violence.

IV. The Supreme Court of Virginia ruled in the alternative that Virginia's cross-burning statute was unconstitutionally overbroad due to its provision stating that "[a]ny such burning of a cross shall be prima facie evidence of an intent to intimidate a person or group of persons." [Respondents] contend that the provision is unconstitutional on its face. [The] prima facie evidence provision, as interpreted by the jury instruction [in Black's case], renders the statute unconstitutional. As construed by the jury instruction, the prima facie provision strips away the very reason why a State may ban cross burning with the intent to intimidate. The prima facie evidence provision permits a jury to convict in every cross-burning case in which defendants exercise their constitutional right not to put on a defense [and] the Commonwealth to arrest, prosecute, and convict a person based solely on the fact of cross burning itself.

It is apparent that the provision as so interpreted " 'would create an unacceptable risk of the suppression of ideas.' " The act of burning a cross may mean that a person is engaging in constitutionally proscribable intimidation. But that same act may mean only that the person is engaged in core political speech. [The] prima facie provision makes no effort to distinguish among these different types of cross burnings. [It] may be true that a cross burning, even at a political rally, arouses a sense of anger or hatred among the vast majority of citizens who see a burning cross. But this sense of anger or hatred is not sufficient to ban all cross burnings. As Gerald Gunther has stated, " 'The lesson I have drawn from my childhood in Nazi

Germany and my happier adult life in this country is the need to walk the sometimes difficult path of denouncing the bigot's hateful ideas with all my power, yet at the same time challenging any community's attempt to suppress hateful ideas by force of law.'" Casper, "Gerry," 55 Stan. L. Rev. 647, 649 (2002). The prima facie evidence provision in this case ignores all of the contextual factors that are necessary to decide whether a particular cross burning is intended to intimidate. The First Amendment does not permit such a shortcut. For these reasons, the prima facie evidence provision, as interpreted through the jury instruction and as applied in [Black's] case, is unconstitutional on its face.

■ JUSTICE STEVENS, concurring.

Cross burning with "an intent to intimidate" unquestionably qualifies as the kind of threat that is unprotected by the First Amendment. For the reasons stated in the separate opinions that Justice White and I wrote in R.A.V., that simple proposition provides a sufficient basis for upholding the basic prohibition in the Virginia statute even though it does not cover other types of threatening expressive conduct.

■ JUSTICE SCALIA, with whom JUSTICE THOMAS joins, concurring in part, concurring in the judgment in part, and dissenting in part.

I agree with the Court that, under our decision in R.A.V., a State may, without infringing the First Amendment, prohibit cross burning carried out with the intent to intimidate. [But] I believe there is no justification for the plurality's apparent decision to invalidate [the prima-facie-evidence] provision on its face.

I. ["Prima] facie evidence" [is] evidence that suffices, on its own, to establish a particular fact. But it is hornbook law that this is true only to the extent that the evidence goes unrebutted. [Presentation] of evidence that a defendant burned a cross in public view is automatically sufficient, on its own, to support an inference that the defendant intended to intimidate only until the defendant comes forward with some evidence in rebuttal.

II. The question presented, then, is whether, given this understanding of the term "prima facie evidence," the cross-burning statute is constitutional. [The] plurality is correct [that] some individuals who engage in protected speech may, because of the prima-facie-evidence provision, be subject to conviction. [But the] class of persons that the plurality contemplates could impermissibly be convicted under § 18.2–423 includes only those individuals who (1) burn a cross in public view, (2) do not intend to intimidate, (3) are nonetheless charged and prosecuted, and (4) refuse to present a defense. Conceding (quite generously, in my view) that this class of persons exists, it cannot possibly give rise to a viable facial challenge, not even with the aid of our First Amendment overbreadth doctrine. [The] notion that the set of cases identified by the plurality in which convictions might improperly be obtained is sufficiently large to render the statute substantially overbroad is fanciful.

■ JUSTICE SOUTER, with whom JUSTICE KENNEDY and JUSTICE GINSBURG join, concurring in the judgment in part and dissenting in part.

I agree with the majority that the Virginia statute makes a content-based distinction within the category of punishable intimidating or threatening expression, the very type of distinction we considered in R.A.V. I disagree that any exception should save Virginia's law from unconstitutionality under the holding in R.A.V. or any acceptable variation of it.

[R.A.V.] defines the special virulence exception to the rule barring content-based subclasses of categorically proscribable expression this way: prohibition by subcategory is nonetheless constitutional if it is made "entirely" on the "basis" of "the very reason" that "the entire class of speech at issue is proscribable" at all. The Court explained that when the subcategory is confined to the most obviously proscribable instances, "no significant danger of idea or viewpoint discrimination exists," and the explanation was rounded out with some illustrative examples. None of them, however, resembles the case before us. [This] case [does not] present any analogy to the statute prohibiting threats against the President. The content discrimination in that statute relates to the addressee of the threat and reflects the special risks and costs associated with threatening the President. Again, however, threats against the President are not generally identified by reference to the content of any message that may accompany the threat, let alone any viewpoint, and there is no obvious correlation in fact between victim and message. Millions of statements are made about the President every day on every subject and from every standpoint; threats of violence are not an integral feature of any one subject or viewpoint as distinct from others. Differential treatment of threats against the President, then, selects nothing but special risks, not special messages. A content-based proscription of cross burning, on the other hand, may be a subtle effort to ban not only the intensity of the intimidation cross burning causes when done to threaten, but also the particular message of white supremacy that is broadcast even by nonthreatening cross burning.

[No] content-based statute should survive [under] R.A.V. without a high probability that no "official suppression of ideas is afoot." I believe the prima facie evidence provision stands in the way of any finding of such a high probability here. [As] I see the likely significance of the evidence provision, its primary effect is to skew jury deliberations toward conviction in cases where the evidence of intent to intimidate is relatively weak and arguably consistent with a solely ideological reason for burning. [To] the extent the prima facie evidence provision skews prosecutions, then, it skews the statute toward suppressing ideas. [Since] no R.A.V. exception can save the statute as content based, it can only survive if narrowly tailored to serve a compelling state interest, a stringent test the statute cannot pass; a content-neutral statute banning intimidation would achieve the same object without singling out particular content.

■ JUSTICE THOMAS, dissenting.

In every culture, certain things acquire meaning well beyond what outsiders can comprehend. That goes for both the sacred and the profane. I believe that cross burning is the paradigmatic example of the latter. Although I agree with the majority's conclusion that it is constitutionally permissible to "ban . . . cross burning carried out with intent to intimidate," I believe that the majority errs in imputing an expressive component to the activity in question. [In] our culture, cross burning has almost invariably meant lawlessness and understandably instills in its victims well-grounded fear of physical violence.

Virginia's experience has been no exception. [In] the early 1950s the people of Virginia viewed cross burning as creating an intolerable atmosphere of terror. [At] the time the statute was enacted, racial segregation was not only the prevailing practice, but also the law in Virginia. [It] strains credulity to suggest that a state legislature that adopted a litany of segregationist laws self-contradictorily intended to squelch the segregationist message. Even for segregationists, violent and terroristic conduct, the Siamese twin of cross burning, was intolerable. [Accordingly], this statute prohibits only conduct, not expression. And, just as one cannot burn down someone's house to make a political point and then seek refuge in the First Amendment, those who hate cannot terrorize and intimidate to make their point. In light of my conclusion that the statute here addresses only conduct, there is no need to analyze it under any of our First Amendment tests.

———

Are apparent threats protected if posted in social media? If they emulate an artistic form like rap? In **Elonis v. United States**, 575 U.S. 723 (2015), a man who was angry that his wife had left him was convicted for posting apparently threatening statements about his former wife in rap-lyric form on Facebook (e.g., "Did you know that it's illegal for me to say I want to kill my wife? . . . It's one of the only sentences that I'm not allowed to say. . . . ") under 18 U.S.C. § 875(c), which makes it a crime to transmit in interstate commerce "any communication containing any threat . . . to injure the person of another." The Court overturned the conviction on the non-constitutional ground that the statute implicitly required a showing of purpose to make a threat or knowledge that the communication will be viewed as a threat, which had not been charged to the jury.

Justice ALITO, concurring in part and dissenting in part, would have added that a finding of recklessness was sufficient to convict. He argued that conviction on recklessness grounds would not violate the First Amendment: "It is settled that the Constitution does not protect true threats. See Virginia v. Black; R. A. V. And there are good reasons for that rule: True threats inflict great harm and have little if any social value. A threat may cause serious emotional stress for the person threatened and those who care about that person, and a threat may lead to a violent confrontation. It is true that a communication containing a threat may include other statements that have value and are entitled to protection. But that does not justify constitutional protection for the threat itself.

"Elonis argues that the First Amendment protects a threat if the person making the statement does not actually intend to cause harm. [But] whether or not the person making a threat intends to cause harm, the damage is the same. And the fact that making a threat may have a therapeutic or cathartic effect for the speaker is not sufficient to justify constitutional protection. [Elonis] also claims his threats were constitutionally protected works of art. Words like his, he contends, are shielded by the First Amendment because they are similar to words uttered by rappers and singers in public performances and recordings. To make this point, his brief includes a lengthy excerpt from the lyrics of a rap song in which a very well-compensated rapper imagines killing his ex-wife and dumping her body in a lake. If this celebrity can utter such words, Elonis pleads, amateurs like him should be able to post similar things on social media. But context matters. Taken in context, lyrics in songs that are performed for an audience or sold in recorded form are unlikely to be interpreted as a real threat to a real person. Statements on social media that are pointedly directed at their victims, by contrast, are much more likely to be taken seriously. To hold otherwise would grant a license to anyone who is clever enough to dress up a real threat in the guise of rap lyrics, a parody, or something similar."

For suppression of a threat to be permissible, does the First Amendment require subjective intent on the part of the threatener, or would an objective test pass muster? Because the Court decided the Elonis case on statutory grounds, the question remains open. Is a negligent threat any less harmful to the threatened individual than is a threat made with intent to cause harm? What about a threat made recklessly? Is Justice Alito correct that the fact that threatening communication might include other statements of value does not justify constitutional protection for the threat itself? Should it matter that the threat was made over the internet? That it was made as part of an artistic expression? Should the fact that threats have become more commonplace in new media forums and in popular music affect the analysis? For an argument that online harassment causes serious psychological and physical harm and that its trivialization, particularly in the context of threats of violence against female writers online, entrenches gender inequality, see Citron, Hate Crimes in Cyberspace (2014).

SECTION 5. SEXUALLY EXPLICIT EXPRESSION

In Chaplinsky, the Court categorized "obscenity" as expression outside of First Amendment protection, because it is "of such slight social value as a step to truth that any benefit that may be derived from [it] is outweighed by the social interest in order and morality." The Court has continued to regard obscenity as an unprotected category of speech, although it has struggled mightily with the question of how to define that category—how to delineate the area excluded from constitutional protection so that properly protected speech would not also be curtailed. The Court has added an additional category of sexually explicit speech to the Chaplinsky list by holding that child pornography is unprotected speech. If speech is sexually explicit but is not obscene and does not constitute child pornography, it is within the realm of First Amendment protection, but the Court has wrestled with the question whether it should occupy a subordinate position as "lower value" speech. A majority of the Court has never agreed with the creation of such a formal low-value category for sexually explicit speech, but the Court has nonetheless upheld a number of restrictions on such speech through balancing analysis. These developments are examined in turn in this section.

What justifications might there be for restraining sexually explicit speech? To safeguard against the violent or antisocial conduct that it might cause? Under clear and present danger or under an incitement test? To avoid the "corrupting" of individual morals and character by the "sin of obscenity"—whether or not improper behavior results? To protect the sensibilities of the audience by safeguarding against the risk of shock from offensive sexual materials? To protect children against exposure to sexual materials because of the greater susceptibility of the immature to their harmful effects? To protect society's moral standards against erosion? To preserve or improve the quality of life or the tone of the community?

Questions such as these assume that obscenity may belong in the First Amendment ballpark, thus triggering a requirement of some justification. But are sexually explicit materials properly considered a variety of "speech"? Are they more aptly described as aids to sexual arousal or sexual activity itself? Do they communicate ideas and appeal to the intellectual process, or do they simply induce a purely physical effect? Which if any of the values underlying First Amendment protection justify the imposition of First Amendment scrutiny here? The arguments from self-government and democracy seem largely directed at political speech. The arguments from the marketplace of ideas and the search for truth are broader and seem to include scientific debate as well. But do they also extend to artistic and literary communication? Note that the Court's definitions of obscenity in the cases that follow protect materials of certain "literary, artistic, political, or scientific value" and that the obscenity category typically focuses on hard-core pornography. Can such materials nevertheless claim First Amendment protection? Do they serve the autonomy rationale for protecting speech?

OBSCENITY

The Court's first direct encounter with the constitutionality of obscenity control took place fifteen years after Chaplinsky, in Roth. The Warren Court's attempt to define unprotected obscenity in Roth spawned a tortuous period of divided rulings, until a new definition of obscenity was agreed upon in 1973 by the Burger Court in Miller and Paris Adult, below. The Miller test continues to define unprotected obscenity today.

Roth v. United States; Alberts v. California

354 U.S. 476, 77 S. Ct. 1304, 1 L. Ed. 2d 1498 (1957).

[In these cases, the Court sustained the validity of federal and state obscenity laws without reaching the question of whether any particular materials to which the laws were applied were obscene. Roth, a New York publisher and seller, was convicted of mailing obscene advertising and an obscene book in violation of a federal statute barring the mailing of "obscenity." Alberts, engaged in the mail order business, was convicted under a California law for "lewdly keeping for sale obscene and indecent books" and "publishing an obscene advertisement of them."]

■ JUSTICE BRENNAN delivered the opinion of the Court.

The dispositive question is whether obscenity is utterance within the area of protected speech and press. Although this is the first time the question has been squarely presented [here], expressions found in numerous opinions indicate that this Court has always assumed that obscenity is not protected by the freedoms of speech and press. In light [of] history, it is apparent that the unconditional phrasing of the First Amendment was not intended to protect every utterance. [T]here is sufficiently contemporaneous evidence to show that obscenity [like libel, see Beauharnais] was outside the protection intended for speech and [press]. All ideas having even the slightest redeeming social importance—unorthodox ideas, controversial ideas, even ideas hateful to the prevailing climate of opinion—have the full protection of the guaranties, unless excludable because they encroach upon the limited area of more important interests. But implicit in the history of the First Amendment is the rejection of obscenity as utterly without redeeming social importance. This rejection for that reason is mirrored in the universal judgment that obscenity should be restrained, reflected in the international agreement of over 50 nations, in the obscenity laws of all of the 48 States, and in the 20 obscenity laws enacted by the Congress from 1842 to 1956. This is the same judgment expressed [in Chaplinsky]. [We] hold that obscenity is not within the area of constitutionally protected speech or press.

It is strenuously urged that these obscenity statutes offend the constitutional guaranties because they punish incitation to impure sexual *thoughts,* not shown to be related to any overt antisocial conduct which is or may be incited in the persons stimulated to such *thoughts.* [It] is insisted that the constitutional guaranties are violated because convictions may be had without proof either that obscene material will perceptibly create a clear and present danger of antisocial conduct, or will probably induce its recipients to such conduct. But, in light of our holding that obscenity is not protected speech, the complete answer to this argument is [in Beauharnais].

However, sex and obscenity are not synonymous. Obscene material is material which deals with sex in a manner appealing to prurient interest.[1] The portrayal of sex, e.g., in art, literature and scientific works, is not itself sufficient reason to deny material the constitutional protection of freedom of speech and press. Sex, a great and mysterious motive force in human life, has indisputably been a subject of absorbing interest to mankind through the ages; it is one of the vital problems of human interest and public [concern]. The fundamental freedoms of speech and press [are] indispensable to [our free society's] continued growth. [It] is therefore vital that the standards for judging obscenity safeguard the protection of freedom of speech and press for material which does not treat sex in a manner appealing to prurient interest.

The early leading standard of obscenity allowed material to be judged merely by the effect of an isolated excerpt upon particularly susceptible persons. Regina v. Hicklin, [1868] L.R. 3 Q.B. 360 [which defined obscenity as material tending "to deprave and corrupt those whose minds are open to such immoral influences"]. Some American courts adopted this standard but later decisions have rejected it and substituted this test: whether to the average person, applying contemporary community standards, the dominant theme of the material taken as a whole appeals to prurient interest. The Hicklin test, judging obscenity by the effect of isolated passages upon the most susceptible persons, might well encompass material legitimately treating with sex, and so it must be rejected as unconstitutionally restrictive of the freedoms of speech and press. On the other hand, the substituted standard provides safeguards adequate to withstand the charge of constitutional infirmity. Both trial courts below sufficiently followed the proper [standard]. [W]e hold that these statutes, applied according to the proper standard for judging obscenity, do not offend constitutional safeguards against convictions based upon protected material, or fail to give men in acting adequate notice of what is [prohibited]. Affirmed.

---

[1] I.e., material having a tendency to excite lustful thoughts. Webster's New International Dictionary (Unabridged, 2d ed., 1949) defines *prurient,* in pertinent part, as follows: "Itching; longing; uneasy with desire or longing; of persons, having itching, morbid, or lascivious longings; of desire, curiosity or propensity, lewd."

[We] perceive no significant difference between the meaning of obscenity developed in the case law and the definition of the A.L.I., Model Penal Code (Tent. Draft No. 6, 1957): "[A] thing is obscene if, considered as a whole, its predominant appeal is to prurient interest, i.e., a shameful or morbid interest in nudity, sex, or excretion, and if it goes substantially beyond customary limits of candor in description or representation of such matters." [Footnote by the Court.]

■ JUSTICE DOUGLAS, joined by JUSTICE BLACK, dissenting.

When we sustain these convictions, we make the legality of a publication turn on the purity of thought which a book or tract instills in the mind of the reader. I do not think we can approve that standard and be faithful to the command of the First Amendment. [I] reject too the implication that problems of freedom of speech and of the press are to be resolved by weighing against the values of free expression, the judgment of the Court that a particular form of that expression has 'no redeeming social importance.' I would give the broad sweep of the First Amendment full support. I have the same confidence in the ability of our people to reject noxious literature as I have in their capacity to sort out the true from the false in theology, economics, politics, or any other field.

OBSCENITY BETWEEN ROTH AND MILLER

1. ***Defining obscenity after Roth.*** The Supreme Court's holding in Roth left the Court with no consensus on the precise definition of "obscenity." As Justice Brennan's dissent in Paris Adult Theatre I v. Slaton, 413 U.S. 49, 73 (1973), aptly summarized, a decade after Roth four different approaches had emerged on the Court. "[Justices] Black and Douglas consistently maintained that government is wholly powerless to regulate any sexually oriented matter on the ground of its obscenity. [Justice] Harlan [believed] that the Federal Government [could] control the distribution of 'hard core' pornography, while the States [could ban] 'any material which, taken as a whole, has been reasonably found in state judicial proceedings to treat with sex in a fundamentally offensive manner, under rationally established criteria for judging such material.' Jacobellis v. Ohio, [378 U.S. 184 (1964)]. [Justice] Stewart regarded 'hard core' pornography as the limit of both federal and state power. See, e.g., Ginzburg v. United States, 383 U.S. 463 (1966) (dissenting opinion); [Jacobellis] (concurring opinion). [Justice Stewart's concurrence in Jacobellis said of 'hard-core pornography': 'I shall not today attempt further to define the kinds of material I understand to be embraced within that shorthand description; and perhaps I could never succeed in intelligibly doing so. But I know it when I see it, and the motion picture involved in this case is not that.']

"The view that, [in this period,] enjoyed the most, but not majority, support was an interpretation of Roth adopted by [Chief Justice Warren and Justices Fortas and Brennan] in Memoirs v. Massachusetts, 383 U.S. 413 (1966). We expressed the view that Federal or State Governments could control the distribution of material where 'three [elements] coalesce: it must be established that (a) the dominant theme of the material taken as a whole appeals to a prurient interest in sex; (b) the material is patently offensive because it affronts contemporary community standards relating to the description or representation of sexual matters; and (c) the material is utterly without redeeming social value.' Even this formulation, however, concealed differences of opinion.[1] Moreover, it did not provide a definition

----

[1]   In supporting this statement, Justice Brennan noted: "Compare Jacobellis v. Ohio, supra, at 192–195 (Brennan, J., joined by Goldberg, J.) (community standards national), with id., at 200–201 (Warren, C.J., joined by Clark, J., dissenting) (community standards local)."

covering all situations.[2] Nor, finally, did it ever command a majority of the [Court]."

As Justice Brennan noted, beginning in Redrup v. New York, 386 U.S. 767 (1967), the Court essentially treated obscenity cases as a numbers game. "The Court began the practice [of] per curiam reversals of convictions for the dissemination of materials that at least five members of the Court, applying their separate tests, deemed not to be obscene. [The] Redrup approach [resolves] cases as between the parties, but offers only the most obscure guidance to legislation, adjudication by other courts, and primary conduct. By disposing of cases through summary reversal or denial of certiorari we have deliberately and effectively obscured the rationale underlying the decisions. It comes as no surprise that judicial attempts to follow our lead conscientiously have often ended in hopeless [confusion]." "Redrupping" involved the justices in a regular practice of privately screening putatively obscene films in the Supreme Court to determine whether each of the individual justices considered them obscene according to his own standard. See Woodward & Armstrong, The Brethren (1979). How might Redrupping help explain why the Court revisited the issue of obscenity in Miller, below?

2. *Limiting portrayals of sexual immorality.* Most obscenity rulings in this period, treating obscenity as simply wholly outside the First Amendment, were conspicuously silent about the interests thought to justify control of expression pertaining to sex. One case in the post-Roth years—though not dealing directly with an "obscenity" law—spoke more explicitly about such justifications. **Kingsley Int'l Pictures Corp. v. Regents**, 360 U.S. 684 (1959), invalidated a New York motion picture licensing law. The law banned any "immoral" film, defined as a film that "portrays acts of sexual immorality [or] which expressly or impliedly presents such acts as desirable, acceptable, or proper patterns of behavior." The state denied a license to the film "Lady Chatterley's Lover" under this law because "its subject matter is adultery presented as being right and desirable for certain people under certain circumstances." The Court invalidated the State's action. Justice STEWART's opinion emphasized that "sexual immorality" under the New York scheme was "entirely different from" concepts like "obscenity" or "pornography," and that New York had not claimed that "the film would itself operate as an incitement to illegal action." He concluded that the state had prevented the exhibition of the film "because that picture advocates an idea—that adultery under certain circumstances may be proper behavior. Yet the First Amendment's basic guarantee is of freedom to advocate ideas. The State, quite simply, has thus struck at the very heart of constitutionally protected liberty. [The constitutional] guarantee is not confined to the expression of ideas that are conventional or shared by a majority. It protects advocacy of the opinion that adultery may sometimes be proper, no less than advocacy of socialism or the single tax."

3. *Possession of obscene materials.* In **Stanley v. Georgia**, 394 U.S. 557 (1969), the Court reversed a conviction for knowing "possession of obscene matter," holding that the First Amendment prohibits "making the private possession of obscene material a crime."

---

[2] In supporting this comment, Justice Brennan stated: "See Mishkin v. New York, 383 U.S. 502 (1966) (prurient appeal defined in terms of a deviant sexual group); Ginzburg v. United States, supra ('pandering' probative evidence of obscenity in close cases). See also Ginsberg v. New York, 390 U.S. 629 (1968) (obscenity for juveniles)."

In Stanley, a search of a home for bookmaking evidence had uncovered obscene films. Georgia defended its law on the basis of Roth and with the argument: "If the State can protect the body of the citizen, may it [not] protect his mind?" In striking contrast to the approach of the earlier obscenity cases, Justice MARSHALL's opinion systematically canvassed the asserted state justifications. Justice MARSHALL held: "[The constitutional] right to receive information and ideas, regardless of their social worth, [is] fundamental to our free society. Moreover, in the context of this case—a prosecution for mere possession [in] the privacy of a person's own home— that right takes on an added dimension. For also fundamental is the right to be free, except in very limited circumstances, from unwanted governmental intrusions into one's privacy. [W]e think that mere categorization of these films as 'obscene' is insufficient justification for such a drastic invasion of personal liberties guaranteed by the First and Fourteenth Amendments. Whatever may be the justifications for other statutes regulating obscenity, we do not think they reach into the privacy of one's own home. If the First Amendment means anything, it means that a State has no business telling a man, sitting alone in his own house, what books he may read or what films he may watch.

"[In] the face of these traditional notions of individual liberty, Georgia asserts the right to protect the individual's mind from the effects of obscenity. We are not certain that this argument amounts to anything more than the assertion that the State has the right to control the moral content of a person's thoughts.[3] To some, this may be a noble purpose, but it is wholly inconsistent with the philosophy of the First Amendment. [Kingsley Pictures.] Whatever the power of the state to control public dissemination of ideas inimical to the public morality, it cannot constitutionally premise legislation on the desirability of controlling a person's private thoughts. Perhaps recognizing this, Georgia asserts that exposure to obscenity may lead to deviant sexual behavior or crimes of sexual violence. [Given] the present state of knowledge, the State may no more prohibit mere possession of [obscenity] on the ground that it may lead to antisocial conduct than it may prohibit possession of chemistry books on the ground that they may lead to the manufacture of homemade spirits. It is true that in Roth this Court rejected the necessity of proving that exposure to obscene material would create a clear and present danger of antisocial [conduct]. But that case dealt with public distribution of obscene materials and such distribution is subject to different objections. For example, there is always the danger that obscene material might fall into the hands of children or that it might intrude upon the sensibilities or privacy of the general public. No such dangers are present in this case. Finally, we are faced with the argument that prohibition of possession of [obscenity] is a necessary incident to statutory schemes prohibiting distribution. That argument is based on alleged difficulties of proving an intent to distribute or in producing evidence of actual distribution. We are not convinced that such difficulties exist, but even if they did we do not think that they would justify infringement of the

---

[3] " 'Communities believe, and act on the belief, that obscenity is immoral, is wrong for the individual, and has no place in a decent society. They believe, too, that adults as well as children are corruptible in morals and character, and that obscenity is a source of corruption that should be eliminated. Obscenity is not suppressed primarily for the protection of others. Much of it is suppressed for the purity of the community and for the salvation and welfare of the "consumer." Obscenity, at bottom, is not crime. Obscenity is sin.' Henkin, Morals and the Constitution: The Sin of Obscenity, 63 Colum. L. Rev. 391, 395 (1963)." [Footnote by Justice Marshall.]

individual's right to read or observe what he pleases. Because that right is so fundamental to our scheme of individual liberty, its restriction may not be justified by the need to ease the administration of otherwise valid criminal laws."

Justice STEWART, joined by Justices Brennan and White, concurred only in the result, solely on the ground that the films were seized in violation of the Fourth Amendment. Justice Brennan later, in his Paris Adult dissent, said he was "now inclined to agree" with much of the principal Stanley opinion.

————

Miller v. California

413 U.S. 15, 93 S. Ct. 2607, 37 L. Ed. 2d 419 (1973).

[The Miller case arose from a conviction under California Penal Code § 311.2(a), for knowingly distributing obscene matter by causing five unsolicited advertising brochures for "adult" material to be sent through the mail. The State charged that the brochures consisted mostly of "pictures and drawings very explicitly depicting men and women in groups of two or more engaging in a variety of sexual activities with genitals often prominently displayed."]

■ CHIEF JUSTICE BURGER delivered the opinion of the Court.

This is one of a group of "obscenity-pornography" cases being reviewed [in] a re-examination of standards enunciated in earlier cases involving what [Justice] Harlan called "the intractable obscenity problem." [This] case involves the application of a State's criminal obscenity statute to a situation in which sexually explicit materials have been thrust by aggressive sales action upon unwilling recipients who had in no way indicated any desire to receive such materials. This Court has recognized that the States have a legitimate interest in prohibiting dissemination or exhibition of obscene material when the mode of dissemination carries with it a significant danger of offending the sensibilities of unwilling recipients or of exposure to juveniles. [Stanley.] It is in this context that we are called on to define the standards which must be used to identify obscene material that a State may regulate.

Obscene material is unprotected by the First Amendment. [Roth.] [However, state] statutes designed to regulate obscene materials must be carefully limited. As a result, we now confine the permissible scope of such regulation to works which depict or describe sexual conduct. That conduct must be specifically defined by the applicable state law, as written or authoritatively construed. [The] basic guidelines for the trier of fact must be: (a) whether "the average person, applying contemporary community standards" would find that the work, taken as a whole, appeals to the prurient interest [Roth], (b) whether the work depicts or describes, in a patently offensive way, sexual conduct specifically defined by the applicable state law, and (c) whether the work, taken as a whole, lacks serious literary, artistic, political, or scientific value. We do not adopt as a constitutional standard the "*utterly* without redeeming social value" test of [Memoirs]. If a state law that regulates obscene material is thus limited, as written or construed, [First Amendment values] are adequately protected by the ultimate power of appellate courts to conduct an independent review of constitutional claims when necessary.

We emphasize that it is not our function to propose regulatory schemes for the States. [It] is possible, however, to give a few plain examples of what a state statute could define for regulation under [part] (b) of the standard announced in this opinion: (a) Patently offensive representations or descriptions of ultimate sexual acts, normal or perverted, actual or simulated. (b) Patently offensive representations or descriptions of masturbation, excretory functions, and lewd exhibition of the genitals.

Sex and nudity may not be exploited without limit by films or pictures exhibited or sold in places of public accommodation any more than live sex and nudity can be exhibited or sold without limit in such public places. At a minimum, prurient, patently offensive depiction or description of sexual conduct must have serious literary, artistic, political, or scientific value to merit First Amendment protection. For example, medical books [necessarily] use graphic illustrations and descriptions of human anatomy. In resolving the inevitably sensitive questions of fact and law, we must continue to rely on the jury system, accompanied by the safeguards that judges, rules of evidence, presumption of innocence and other protective features provide, as we do with [other] offenses against society and its individual members.

[Justice] Brennan [has] abandoned his former position and now maintains that no formulation of this Court, the Congress, or the States can adequately distinguish obscene material unprotected by the First Amendment from protected expression. [Paris, below.] Paradoxically, [he] indicates that suppression of unprotected obscene material is permissible to avoid exposure to unconsenting adults, as in this case, and to juveniles, although he gives no indication of how the division between protected and nonprotected materials may be drawn with greater precision for these purposes than for regulation of commercial exposure to consenting adults only. Nor does he indicate where in the Constitution he finds the authority to distinguish between a willing "adult" one month past the state law age of majority and a willing "juvenile" one month younger.

Under the holdings announced today, no one will be subject to prosecution for the sale or exposure of obscene materials unless these materials depict or describe patently offensive "hard core" sexual conduct specifically defined by the regulating state law, as written or construed. We are satisfied that these specific prerequisites will provide fair notice to a dealer in such materials that his public and commercial activities may bring prosecution. If the inability to define regulated materials with ultimate, god-like precision altogether removes the power of the States or the Congress to regulate, then "hard core" pornography may be exposed without limit to the juvenile, the passerby, and the consenting adult alike, as, indeed, Mr. Justice Douglas contends. [In] this belief, however, [he] now stands alone. [Today,] for the first time since [Roth], a majority of this Court has agreed on concrete guidelines to isolate "hard core" pornography from expression protected by the First Amendment. Now we may abandon the casual practice of [Redrup] and attempt to provide positive guidance to the federal and state courts [alike].

Under a National Constitution, fundamental First Amendment limitations on the powers of the States do not vary from community to community, but this does not mean that there are, or should or can be, fixed, uniform national standards of precisely what appeals to the "prurient interest" or is "patently offensive." These are essentially questions of fact, and our nation is simply too big and too diverse for this Court to reasonably expect that such standards could be articulated for all 50 States in a single formulation, even assuming the prerequisite consensus exists. [It] is neither realistic nor constitutionally sound to read the First Amendment as requiring that the people of Maine or Mississippi accept public depiction of conduct found tolerable in Las Vegas, or New York City. [People] in different States vary in their tastes and attitudes, and this diversity is not to be strangled by the absolutism of imposed uniformity. [We] hold that the requirement that the jury evaluate the materials with reference to "contemporary standards of the State of California" [is] constitutionally adequate.

The dissenting Justices sound the alarm of repression. But, in our view, to equate the free and robust exchange of ideas and political debate with commercial exploitation of obscene material demeans the grand conception of the First Amendment and its high purposes in the historic struggle for freedom. [The] First Amendment protects works which, taken as a whole, have serious literary, artistic, political, or scientific value, regardless of whether the government or a majority of the people approve of the ideas these works represent. [But] the public portrayal of hard core sexual conduct for its own sake, and for the ensuing commercial gain, is a different matter. There is no evidence, empirical or historical, that the stern 19th century American censorship of public distribution and display of material relating to sex in any way limited or affected expression of serious literary, artistic, political, or scientific ideas. [We] do not see the harsh hand of censorship of ideas [and] "repression" of political liberty lurking in every state regulation of commercial exploitation of human interest in sex. [In] sum, we (a) reaffirm the Roth holding that obscene material is not protected by the First Amendment; (b) hold that such material can be regulated by the States, subject to the specific safeguards enunciated above, without a showing that the material is "*utterly* without redeeming social value"; and (c) hold that obscenity is to be determined by applying "contemporary community standards," [not "national standards"]. Vacated and remanded.

■ JUSTICE DOUGLAS, dissenting.

[Until] a civil proceeding has placed a tract beyond the pale, no criminal prosecution should be sustained. For no more vivid illustration of vague and uncertain laws could be designed than those we have fashioned. [If] a specific book [has] in a civil proceeding been condemned as obscene [and] thereafter a person publishes [it], then a vague law has been made specific. There would remain the underlying question whether the First Amendment allows an implied exception in the case of obscenity. I do not think it does and my views on the issue have been stated over and over again. But at least a criminal prosecution brought at that juncture would not violate [the] void-for-vagueness test. No such protective procedure has been designed by California in this case. Obscenity—which even we cannot define with precision—is a hodge-podge. To send men to jail for violating standards they cannot understand, construe, and apply is a monstrous thing to do in a Nation dedicated to fair trials and due process.

■ JUSTICE BRENNAN, with whom JUSTICES STEWART and MARSHALL join, dissenting.

In my dissent in [Paris, below], I noted that I had no occasion to consider the extent of state power to regulate the distribution of sexually oriented material to juveniles or the offensive exposure of such material to unconsenting adults. [I] need not now decide whether a statute might be drawn to impose, within the requirements of the First Amendment, criminal penalties for the precise conduct at issue here [—mailing unsolicited brochures]. For it is clear that under my dissent in [Paris], the statute [here] is unconstitutionally overbroad, and therefore invalid on its [face].

———

Paris Adult Theatre I v. Slaton

413 U.S. 49, 93 S. Ct. 2628, 37 L. Ed. 2d 446 (1973).

[This case arose from a Georgia civil proceeding to enjoin the showing of two allegedly obscene films at two "adult" theaters. At a trial before a judge, the evidence consisted primarily of the films and of photographs of the entrance to the theaters, with signs indicating that the theatres exhibit "Atlanta's Finest Mature Feature Films" and warning "Adult Theatre—You must be 21 and able to prove it. If viewing the nude body offends you, Please Do Not Enter." Two state investigators who saw the films testified that the signs did not indicate "the full nature of what was shown. In particular, nothing indicated that the films depicted—as they did—scenes of simulated fellatio, cunnilingus, and group sex intercourse." The trial judge dismissed the complaint. He held the showing of obscene films permissible where there was "requisite notice to the public" and "reasonable protection against the exposure of these films to minors." The Georgia Supreme Court reversed. The Supreme Court vacated and remanded for reconsideration in light of Miller, but noted that "nothing precludes the State of Georgia from the regulation of the allegedly obscene material exhibited in Paris Adult Theatre I provided that the applicable Georgia law, as written or authoritatively interpreted by the Georgia courts, meets the First Amendment standards set forth in Miller."]

■ CHIEF JUSTICE BURGER delivered the opinion of the Court.

We categorically disapprove the theory [that] obscene, pornographic films acquire constitutional immunity from state regulation simply because they are exhibited for consenting adults only. [Although] we have often pointedly recognized the high importance of the state interest in regulating the exposure of obscene materials to juveniles and unconsenting adults, this Court has never declared these to be the only legitimate state interests permitting regulation of obscene material. [In] particular, we hold that there are legitimate state interests at stake in stemming the tide of commercialized obscenity, even assuming it is feasible to enforce effective safeguards against exposure to juveniles and to passersby.[1] [These] include the interest of the public in the quality of life and the total community environment, the tone of commerce in the great city centers, and, possibly, the public safety itself. The Hill-Link Minority Report of the Commission on Obscenity and Pornography [1970] indicates that there is at least an

---

[1] It is conceivable that an "adult" theatre can—if it really insists—prevent the exposure of its obscene wares to juveniles. An "adult" bookstore, dealing in obscene books, magazines, and pictures, cannot realistically make this claim. [The] legitimate interest in preventing exposure of juveniles to obscene materials cannot be fully served by simply barring juveniles from the immediate physical premises of "adult" bookstores, when there is a flourishing "outside business" in these materials. [Footnote by the Court.]

arguable correlation between obscene material and crime. Quite apart from sex crimes, however, there remains one problem of large proportions aptly described by Professor Bickel: "It concerns the tone of the society, the mode, or to use terms that have perhaps greater currency, the style and quality of life, now and in the future. A man may be entitled to read an obscene book in his room, or expose himself indecently there. [We] should protect his privacy. But if he demands a right to obtain the books and pictures he wants in the market, and to foregather in public places—discreet, if you will, but accessible to all—with others who share his tastes, *then to grant him his right is to affect the world about the rest of us, and to impinge on other privacies.* Even supposing that each of us can, if he wishes, effectively avert the eye and stop the ear (which, in truth, we cannot), what is commonly read and seen and heard and done intrudes upon us all, want it or not." 22 The Public Interest 25–26 (Winter, 1971). (Emphasis added.) As [Chief] Justice Warren stated, there is a "right of the Nation and of the States to maintain a decent society" [Jacobellis dissent].

But, it is argued, there is no scientific data which conclusively demonstrate that exposure to obscene materials adversely affects men and women or their society. It is [urged] that, absent such a demonstration, any kind of state regulation is "impermissible." We reject this argument. It is not for us to resolve empirical uncertainties underlying state legislation, save in the exceptional case where that legislation plainly impinges upon rights protected by the Constitution itself. [Although] there is no conclusive proof of a connection between antisocial behavior and obscene material, the legislature of Georgia could quite reasonably determine that such a connection does or might exist. In deciding Roth, this Court implicitly accepted that a legislature could legitimately act on such a conclusion to protect *"the social interest in order and morality."*

From the beginning of civilized societies, legislators and judges have acted on various unprovable assumptions. [If] we accept the unprovable assumption that a complete education requires certain books and the well nigh universal belief that good books, plays, and art lift the spirit, improve the mind, enrich the human personality and develop character, can we then say that a state legislature may not act on the corollary assumption that commerce in obscene books, or public exhibitions focused on obscene conduct, have a tendency to exert a corrupting and debasing impact leading to antisocial behavior? [The sum of experience] affords an ample basis for legislatures to conclude that a sensitive, key relationship of human existence, central to family life, community welfare, and the development of human personality, can be debased and distorted by crass commercial exploitation of sex. Nothing in the Constitution prohibits a State from reaching such a conclusion and acting on it legislatively simply because there is no conclusive evidence or empirical [data].

It is asserted, however, that standards for evaluating state commercial regulations are inapposite in the present context, as state regulation of access by consenting adults to obscene material violates the constitutionally protected right to privacy enjoyed by petitioners' customers. [I]t is unavailing to compare a theater open to the public for a fee, with the private home of [Stanley] and the marital bedroom of [Griswold]. [Nothing] in this Court's decisions intimates that there is any "fundamental" privacy right "implicit in the concept of ordered liberty" to watch obscene movies in places of public accommodation. [The] idea of a "privacy" right and a place of public accommodation are, in this context, mutually exclusive. Conduct or depictions of conduct that the state police power can prohibit on a public street do not become automatically protected by the Constitution merely because the conduct is moved to a bar or a "live" theatre stage, any more than a "live" performance of a man and woman locked in a sexual embrace at high noon in Times Square is protected by the Constitution because they simultaneously engage in a valid political dialogue. [We also] reject the claim that [Georgia] is here attempting to control the minds or thoughts of those who patronize theaters. [Where] communication of ideas, protected by the First Amendment, is not involved, or the particular privacy of the home protected by Stanley, or any of the other "areas or zones" of constitutionally protected privacy, the mere fact that, as a consequence, some human "utterances" or "thoughts" may be incidentally affected does not bar the State from acting to protect legitimate state interests. Cf. [Roth; Beauharnais]. [Finally, for] us to say that our Constitution incorporates the proposition that conduct involving consenting adults only is always beyond state regulation, is a step we are unable to take. [W]e hold that the States have a legitimate interest in regulating commerce in obscene material and in regulating exhibition of obscene material in places of public accommodation, including so-called "adult" theaters from which minors are [excluded]. Vacated and remanded.

■ JUSTICE BRENNAN, with whom JUSTICES STEWART and MARSHALL join, dissenting.

[I] am convinced that the approach initiated 16 years ago in [Roth], and culminating in the Court's decision today, cannot bring stability to this area of the law without jeopardizing fundamental First Amendment values, and I have concluded that the time has come to make a significant departure from that approach. [The] essence of our problem in the obscenity area is that we have been unable to provide "sensitive tools" to separate obscenity from other sexually oriented but constitutionally protected speech, so that efforts to suppress the former do not spill over into the suppression of the latter. [I] am reluctantly forced to the conclusion that none of the available formulas, including the one announced today, can reduce the vagueness [of] our obscenity standards to a tolerable level. The vagueness of the standards in the obscenity area produces a number of separate problems, [including a] lack of fair notice, [a] chill on protected expression, and [a severe] stress [on] the state and federal judicial machinery. [These problems] persuade me that a significant change in direction is urgently required. I turn, therefore, to the alternatives that are now open.

1.   The approach requiring the smallest deviation from our present course would be to draw a new line between protected and unprotected speech, still permitting the States to suppress all material on the unprotected side of the line. In my view, clarity cannot be obtained pursuant to this approach except by drawing a line that resolves all doubt in favor of state [power]. We could hold, for example, that any depiction or description of human sexual organs [is] outside the protection of the First Amendment. [That] formula would [reduce the vagueness problems. But it] would be appallingly [overbroad].

2.   The alternative adopted by the Court today [embodies] a restatement of the Roth-Memoirs definition of obscenity. [In] my view, the restatement leaves unresolved the very difficulties that compel our rejection of the underlying Roth approach, while at the same time contributing

substantial difficulties of its own. [T]he Court today permits suppression if the government can prove that the materials lack "*serious* literary, artistic, political or scientific value." But [Roth] held that certain expression is obscene, and thus outside the protection of the First Amendment, precisely *because* it lacks even the slightest redeeming social value. The Court's approach necessarily assumes that some works will be deemed obscene— even though they clearly have *some* social value—because the State was able to prove that the value, measured by some unspecified standard, was not sufficiently "serious" to warrant constitutional protection. That result [is] nothing less than a rejection of the fundamental First Amendment premises and rationale of the Roth opinion and an invitation to widespread suppression of sexually oriented speech.

3.   [I] have also considered the possibility of reducing our own role, and the role of appellate courts generally, in determining whether particular matter is obscene. Thus, [we] might adopt the position that where a lower federal or state court has conscientiously applied the constitutional standard, its finding of obscenity will be no more vulnerable to reversal by this Court than any finding of fact. [But] it is implicit in [Redrup] that the First Amendment requires an independent review by appellate courts of the constitutional fact of obscenity. [In any event, while this approach would mitigate institutional stress,] it would neither offer nor produce any cure for the other vices of vagueness. [Plainly], the institutional gain would be more than offset by the unprecedented infringement of First Amendment rights.

4.   Finally, I have considered the view, urged so forcefully since 1957 by our Brothers Black and Douglas, that the First Amendment bars the suppression of any sexually oriented expression. [But that would strip] the States of power to an extent that cannot be justified by the commands of the Constitution, at least so long as there is available an alternative approach that strikes a better balance between the guarantee of free expression and the States' legitimate interests.

[Given the] inevitable side-effects of state efforts to suppress what is assumed to be *unprotected* speech, we must scrutinize with care the state interest that is asserted to justify the suppression. For in the absence of some very substantial interest in suppressing such speech, we can hardly condone the ill-effects that seem to flow inevitably from the [effort]. Because we assumed—incorrectly, as experience has proven—that obscenity could be separated from other sexually oriented expression without significant costs, [we] had no occasion in Roth to prove the asserted state interest in curtailing unprotected, sexually oriented speech. Yet, as we have increasingly come to appreciate the vagueness of the concept of obscenity, we have begun to recognize and articulate the state interests at stake. [The] opinions in Redrup and [Stanley] reflected our emerging view that the state interests in protecting children and in protecting unconsenting adults may stand on a different footing from the other asserted state interests. It may well be, as one commentator has argued, that "exposure to [erotic material] is for some persons an intense emotional experience. A communication of this nature, imposed upon a person contrary to his wishes, has all the characteristics of a physical assault. [It] constitutes an invasion of his privacy." [T. Emerson, The System of Freedom of Expression 496 (1970).] But cf. [Cohen]. Similarly, if children are "not possessed of that full capacity for individual choice which is the presupposition of First Amendment guarantees," [the] State may have a substantial interest in precluding the flow of obscene materials even to consenting juveniles. [But whatever the strength of those interests, they] cannot be asserted in defense of the holding of the Georgia Supreme Court. [The justification here] must be found [in] some independent interest in regulating the reading and viewing habits of consenting adults.

[Of course, a State need not] remain utterly indifferent to—and take no action bearing on—the morality of the community. The traditional description of state police power does embrace the regulation of morals as well as health, safety, and general welfare of the citizenry. And much legislation—compulsory public education laws, civil rights laws, even the abolition of capital punishment—is grounded, at least in part, on a concern with the morality of the community. But the State's interest in regulating morality by suppressing obscenity, while often asserted, remains essentially unfocused and ill-defined. And, since the attempt to curtail unprotected speech necessarily spills over into the area of protected speech, the effort to serve this speculative interest through the suppression of obscene material must tread heavily on rights protected by the First Amendment.

[In] short, while I cannot say that the interests of the State—apart from the question of juveniles and unconsenting adults—are trivial or nonexistent, I am compelled to conclude that these interests cannot justify the substantial damage to constitutional rights and to this Nation's judicial machinery that inevitably results from state efforts to bar the distribution even of unprotected material to consenting adults. I would hold, therefore, that at least in the absence of distribution to juveniles or obtrusive exposure to unconsenting adults, the [First Amendment prohibits governments] from attempting wholly to suppress sexually oriented materials on the basis of their allegedly "obscene" contents. Nothing in this approach precludes [governments] from taking action to serve what may be strong and legitimate interests through regulation of the manner of distribution of sexually oriented material. [I] do not pretend to have found a complete and infallible [answer]. Difficult questions must still be faced, notably in the areas of distribution to juveniles and offensive exposure to unconsenting adults. Whatever the extent of state power to regulate in those areas, it should be clear that the view I espouse today would introduce a large measure of clarity to this troubled area, would reduce the institutional pressure on this Court and the rest of the State and Federal Judiciary, and would guarantee fuller freedom of expression while leaving room for the protection of legitimate governmental [interests].

OBSCENITY LAW AFTER MILLER AND PARIS

1. *Justifications for obscenity regulation.* What government interests do the preceding cases suggest are served by suppressing obscene speech? Consider the following:

a. *Corruption.* The Hicklin test held the harm of obscenity to be the "depravity and corruption" it induced in the mind of its consumer. This frankly paternalistic rationale seeks to protect the consumer from his own worst impulses. See Henkin, "Morals and the Constitution: The Sin of Obscenity," 63 Colum. L. Rev. 391 (1963). But this rationale was undermined by Stanley, which held that the choice to consume obscene materials was up to the consumer, at least in his own home. The opinions in Miller and Paris make little reference to this rationale; Chief Justice Burger mentions the "corrupting and debasing impact" of obscenity only insofar as it leads to "antisocial behavior."

b. *Offense to unwilling onlookers.* Exposure to obscenity can be shocking to the sensibilities of many adults, who would not willingly view it. Children are presumed incapable of consenting to such exposure. All the justices appear to agree that obscenity may be regulated to prevent unwilling exposure to these audiences. Even Justice Brennan, dissenting in Paris, notes that he might uphold laws aimed at "distribution to juveniles or obtrusive exposure to unconsenting adults." Should this narrow range of state interests be the only ones tolerable in the obscenity sphere, as Justice Brennan suggested? Or do even these interests clash with the Court's approach in Cohen v. California, which read the First Amendment to require that those offended by Cohen's jacket simply avert their eyes?

c. *Inducement of criminal conduct.* Chief Justice Burger, writing for the Court in Paris, noted that there is "at least an arguable correlation between obscene material and [sex] crimes." This rationale supposes that readers and viewers of obscene materials will be induced to imitate their depictions of adultery, fornication, prostitution, sexual assault, rape, oral or anal sex, bestiality or other activities made criminal by many states. But note the absence in this reasoning of any requirement of tight causation or "clear and present danger" that these results will follow from obscenity consumption, or of intent on the part of the obscenity disseminator to bring them about. In this respect, Miller and Paris differ from Brandenburg in the incitement context.

d. *Eroding moral standards.* Chief Justice Burger in Paris notes that "crass commercial exploitation of sex" can undermine "a sensitive, key relationship of human existence, central to family life." May government suppress speech to uphold a particular moral view of sex, in particular that it is appropriately practiced only in private and in heterosexual monogamous marriages? Does Kingsley Pictures undermine this rationale for regulating obscenity by holding that speech may not be suppressed on the ground that it expresses immoral ideas? Can the interest in public morality be accepted as a justification to bar obscenity without undercutting Justice Harlan's protective approach to offensive speech in Cohen?

e. *Harming the social fabric.* Writing for the Court in Paris Adult, Chief Justice Burger notes that commercial distribution of obscenity causes harm to "the quality of life and the total community environment" even if it is consumed only by willing adults. Quoting Bickel, he takes a communitarian rather than an individualist view of speech: " 'what is commonly read and seen and heard and done intrudes upon us all, want it or not.' " On this view, the Stanleys of the world are never truly home alone consuming pornography in a purely self-regarding way. Obscenity distribution and consumption affects even non-observing bystanders. Is this view consistent with the rhetoric of the "marketplace of ideas"? Contrast this view with the highly individualistic and relativistic approach the Court took to offensive speech in Cohen and Hustler.

2. *The value of obscenity as "speech"?* Given the tensions between these government interests and other areas of First Amendment law, is the assertedly low value of sexually explicit materials doing most of the work in the Court's obscenity cases? Chaplinsky spoke of unprotected speech as that which has so little value as a step to truth that it is "clearly outweighed" by social interests. If obscenity is sufficiently low-value speech, then even vague

or problematic social interests might be sufficient to justify its regulation. What features of obscenity might render it of low value?

a.   *Nonpolitical.* Are art and literature subordinate to political speech? If so, then perhaps obscenity is unprotected because it is nonpolitical. But if that is so, "the novel, the poem, the painting, the drama, or the piece of sculpture" would likewise be unprotected. Kalven, "The Metaphysics of the Law of Obscenity," 1960 Sup. Ct. Rev. 1 The self-expression or autonomy rationale certainly brings literature and art within the First Amendment. But even Alexander Meiklejohn, a strong defender of the political conception of the First Amendment, eventually viewed literature and art as part of political discourse broadly construed: they educate voters and so give them "the knowledge, intelligence, sensitivity to human values [and] capacity for sane and objective judgment which, so far as possible, a ballot should express." Meiklejohn, "The First Amendment Is an Absolute," 1961 Sup. Ct. Rev. 245. For an exploration of the values of artistic expression, see Nahmod, "Artistic Expression and Aesthetic Theory: The Beautiful, The Sublime and the First Amendment," 1987 Wis. L. Rev. 221.

b.   *Noncognitive.* Is obscenity more like conduct than speech because it "bypasses the brain for the groin," as one court stated in an obscenity trial involving the lyrics of 2 Live Crew? Frederick Schauer, for example, argues that the First Amendment should be read to protect speech that appeals to cognitive and emotive processes. In contrast, hard-core pornography is "designed to produce a purely physical effect": "The concept fundamental to the Miller test is that material appealing to the prurient interest *is* sex, and not merely describing or advocating sex. Material that appeals to the prurient interest is material that turns you on. Period." Schauer, "Speech and 'Speech'—Obscenity and 'Obscenity': An Exercise in the Interpretation of Constitutional Language," 67 Geo. L.J. 899 (1979). See also Sunstein, "Words, Conduct, Caste," 60 U. Chi. L. Rev. 795 (1993) ("Many forms of pornography are not an appeal to the exchange of ideas, political or otherwise; they operate as masturbatory aids and do not qualify for top-tier First Amendment protection"). Might such a view undermine protection for other speech that operates in both rational and irrational ways? Is there *any* communication that is purely cognitive or purely non-cognitive? Are the categories meaningful?

c.   *Not susceptible to counterspeech.* The premise of much speech protection is that more speech is a better remedy than state suppression. Can anyone really talk back to obscene materials? Or do they act by an insidious conditioning mechanism that undermines the possibility of counterspeech? Consider Clor, Obscenity and Public Morality (1969): Obscene materials "do not make arguments which are to be met by intelligent defense," but rather have an effect upon "a delicate network of moral and aesthetic feelings, sensibilities, [and] tastes." Thus those "whose sensibilities are frequently assaulted by prurient and lurid impressions may become desensitized." Might the same argument apply to other areas of speech, such as commercial or political advertising?

3.   **Critiques of obscenity law after *Miller*.** In addition to questioning the above justifications, critics of Miller have suggested that it privileges one conception of sex over others in violation of the usual First Amendment norm of viewpoint neutrality. On this view, Miller in effect permits government to punish sexual dissent. For example, see Richards, "Free Speech and Obscenity Law: Toward a Moral Theory of the First

Amendment," 123 U. Pa. L. Rev. 45 (1974) (arguing that pornography can be seen to embody the "idea of [sexuality] as a profound and shattering ecstasy," or "a view of sensual delight in the erotic celebration of the body," in opposition to more repressive "Victorian" or "Catholic" views); Scanlon, "Freedom of Expression and Categories of Expression," 40 U. Pitt. L. Rev. 519 (1979) (describing "partisans of pornography" as seeking "a fair opportunity to influence the sexual mores of the society" through "informal politics"); Gey, "The Apologetics of Suppression: The Regulation of Pornography as Act and Idea," 86 Mich. L. Rev. 1564 (1988) (arguing that "the suppression of pornography [permits] the state [to] certify and enforce a moral code that reinforces and justifies the political status quo"); Cole, "Playing by Pornography's Rules: The Regulation of Sexual Expression," 143 U. Pa. L. Rev. 111 (1994).

If pornography is a form of sexual dissent, should its distribution be permitted only when the speaker has such a purpose, while speakers may be "forbid[den from] distributing the same material with no intent to influence people's views but merely to provide sexual stimulation"? For an argument drawing such a distinction, see Weinstein, "Democracy, Sex and the First Amendment," 31 NYU Rev. L. & Soc. Change 865 (2007); for the counterargument, see Koppelman, "Free Speech and Pornography: A Response to James Weinstein," 31 NYU Rev. L. & Soc. Change 899 (2007).

4. ***Post-Miller decisions.*** Although the number of obscenity cases decided by the Court has diminished dramatically since the 1973 rulings, the Miller-Paris standards have not wholly extricated the Court from the unwelcome task of case-by-case review in obscenity cases. In **Jenkins v. Georgia**, 418 U.S. 153 (1974), for example, the Court unanimously reversed a state conviction for showing the film "Carnal Knowledge." The state court had mistakenly assumed that, under the new standards, a jury verdict virtually precluded further review regarding most elements of obscenity. Justice REHNQUIST countered: "Even though questions of appeal to the 'prurient interest' or of patent offensiveness are 'essentially questions of fact,' it would be a serious misreading of Miller to conclude that juries have unbridled discretion in determining what is 'patently offensive.' [While the Miller illustrations] did not purport to be an exhaustive catalog of what juries might find patently offensive, [they were] certainly intended to fix substantive constitutional limitations [on] the type of material subject to such a determination." He concluded that, under Miller, "Carnal Knowledge" "could not be found to depict sexual conduct in a patently offensive way. [While] the subject matter of the picture is, in a broader sense, sex, and there are scenes in which sexual conduct including 'ultimate sexual acts' is to be understood to be taking place, the camera does not focus on the bodies of the actors at such time. There is no exhibition whatever of the actors' genitals, lewd or otherwise, during these scenes. There are occasional scenes of nudity, but nudity alone is not enough to make material legally obscene under the Miller standards." The Court relied in part on the fact that the film starred prominent actors (including Jack Nicholson) and had been nominated for Academy Awards. Jenkins thus implicitly concluded that the obscenity laws could not be easily extended to "mainstream" materials, regardless of local views. Justice BRENNAN, joined by Justices Stewart and Marshall, and Justice DOUGLAS concurred separately in the result.

5. ***Community standards.*** Whose standards are to govern in determination of "prurient interest," "patent offensiveness," and "serious

literary, artistic, political or scientific value": those of the locality, the state or the nation? Chief Justice Burger wrote in Miller that the "people of Maine or Mississippi" need not tolerate depictions that might be "tolerable in Las Vegas, or New York City." In **Hamling v. United States**, 418 U.S. 87 (1974), the Court opted for local rather than statewide or national standards in federal obscenity prosecutions and rejected the argument that application of local standards would unduly inhibit producers of materials for a national market. The Hamling ruling was again by a 5–4 vote. (In Jenkins, the Court had similarly refused to require that statewide standards be applied in state prosecutions, even though a statewide standard had been used in Miller.) And in **Smith v. United States**, 431 U.S. 291 (1977), the majority held that determination of local "community standards" in federal obscenity prosecutions was for the jury, even where the defendant had mailed the allegedly obscene materials solely intrastate, in a state which had no law prohibiting sales to adults. Justice BLACKMUN's majority opinion concluded that state law, although relevant, "is not conclusive as to the issue of contemporary community standards for appeal to the prurient interest and patent offensiveness." Justice STEVENS dissented: "The question of offensiveness to community standards, whether national or local, is not one that the average juror can be expected to answer with evenhanded consistency. [In] the final analysis, the guilt or innocence of a criminal defendant in an obscenity trial is determined primarily by individual jurors' subjective reactions to the materials in question rather than by the predictable application of rules of law. As [Justice] Harlan noted: '[It is] often true that one man's vulgarity is another's lyric [and that is why] the Constitution leaves matters of taste and style [to] the individual' [Cohen]."

Smith also made clear, however, that the "literary, artistic, political, or scientific value" factor of the Miller test was *not* to be measured by local community standards. This point was elaborated in **Pope v. Illinois**, 481 U.S. 497 (1987), where Justice WHITE's majority opinion stated: "Just as the ideas a work represents need not obtain majority approval to merit protection, neither [does] the value of the work vary from community to community based on the degree of local acceptance it has won. The proper inquiry is not whether an ordinary member of any given community would find serious [value] in allegedly obscene material, but whether a reasonable person would find such value in the material, taken as a whole." Justice SCALIA's concurrence argued that it was "quite impossible" to come to an objective assessment of (at least) literary or artistic value: "Just as there is no use arguing about taste, there is no use litigating about it." He suggested "the need for reexamination of Miller," but offered no alternative to it. Justice STEVENS's dissent, joined by Justice Marshall, attacked the majority's "reasonable person" standard, insisting that "communicative material of this sort is entitled to the protection of the First Amendment if *some reasonable persons* could consider it as having serious [value]."

Is the notion of "community standards" still meaningful in the era of the internet? It is intriguing to note that some online platforms use "community standards" as a term to describe their own rules for regulating content. With more than 2 billion users worldwide on Facebook, for example, what does it mean for the word "community" to be used in this way? Does it change the meaning of the phrase "community standards" as it relates to definitions of obscenity?

6. *Serious value.* Is "serious value" a magic bullet that allows mainstream publishers and producers to escape obscenity charges, confining the practical reach of Miller to hard-core pornography? Publishers have often called expert witnesses to testify to serious artistic value in obscenity trials. See generally de Grazia, Girls Lean Back Everywhere (1992). Similar testimony was offered in two prominent obscenity trials in the early 1990s. An art gallery and its directors were tried in Cincinnati for obscenity violations as a result of displaying an exhibit of photographs by Robert Mapplethorpe containing explicit depictions of homoerotic and sadomasochistic activities. The curator of the exhibit testified to the artistic value of the photographs. Asked repeatedly by prosecutors whether she would describe particular photographs as depicting male genitalia, she demurred, answering that she saw instead, for example, examples of "classical line and form." The Cincinnati jury found the defendants not guilty. Expert testimony on the antecedents of rap in early African-American oral traditions was less successful in averting an obscenity conviction in Broward County, Florida, for sellers of the sexually graphic lyrics in the musical recording "As Nasty As They Wanna Be" by the rap group 2 Live Crew. A federal trial judge in Fort Lauderdale found the lyrics album obscene in a civil proceeding. The judgment was reversed by the Court of Appeals. Luke Records, Inc. v. Navarro, 960 F.2d 134 (11th Cir. 1992). Does expert testimony that describes art or music in terms of its artistic value take an unduly formalist view of art, underestimating its controversial moral and political content and its emotive impact upon its audience? See Adler, Note, "Post-Modern Art and the Death of Obscenity Law," 99 Yale L.J. 1359 (1990).

7. *Pornography as a cause of antisocial conduct.* A Commission appointed by Attorney General Edwin Meese in 1986 concluded that some forms of obscenity *could* cause violent antisocial conduct. In assessing the effects of sexually explicit materials, the Commission emphasized distinctions among the content of such materials, distinguishing between (a) materials portraying sexual violence; (b) materials that contained no explicit violence but were plainly degrading, usually to women; and (c) materials, that, while sexually explicit, contained neither violence nor degradation.

With respect to sexually violent materials, the Commission concluded that the "scientific findings and ultimate conclusions of [a prior] 1970 Commission are least reliable for today, [because] material of this variety was largely absent from that Commission's inquiries. [The] research [shows] a causal relationship between exposure to [sexually violent material] and aggressive behavior towards women." The Commission relied not solely on "experimental evidence" but also on "clinical evidence" and on "less scientific evidence [as well as] our own common sense." Turning to materials containing no violence but depicting women "as existing solely for the sexual satisfaction of [men]," the Commission found the evidence "more tentative" but inclined somewhat in the same direction as with sexually violent material. But with regard to material containing neither violence nor degradation, "we are on the current state of the evidence persuaded that material of this type does not bear a causal relationship to rape or other acts of sexual violence."

With respect to the framing and enforcement of legal restraints, the Commission found that the type of material currently designated as legally obscene was properly considered outside the coverage of the First

Amendment. But its recommendations about law enforcement started with the assumption that the constitutional permissibility of regulation did not address the advisability of regulation. It rejected all proposals for expanding the scope of existing obscenity laws, recommended that enforcement of existing obscenity laws take into account as priorities the subdivisions recommended by the Commission, and urged that enforcement of existing obscenity laws against sexually violent materials be increased substantially. It divided on the issue whether there should be any enforcement at all regarding materials neither violent nor degrading. Noting that the category of sexually violent material is dominated by material "unquestionably protected by the First Amendment," the Commission nevertheless urged enforcement of existing laws with respect to the segment of that material that was legally obscene, even though such regulation "would likely address little more than the tip of the iceberg." In reaching this conclusion, the Commission emphasized that "law serves an important symbolic function [even through] strikingly underinclusive regulation. Conversely, we are aware of the message conveyed by repeal or non-enforcement of existing laws with respect to certain kinds of materials. [We] are unwilling to have the law send out the wrong signal." The Commission's report prompted immediate controversy and considerable criticism.

For further discussion of the "causation" problem, see an article by one member of the Commission. Schauer, "Causation Theory and the Causes of Sexual Violence," 1987 A.B.F.Res. J. 737. Schauer argues that "the claim of [the Report], put accurately, is that sexually violent material, some but not much of which happens to be sexually explicit and some but even less of which is legally obscene, bears a causal relationship, taken probabilistically, to the incidence of sexual violence," and that, since the causal relationship is independent of sexual explicitness, government regulation under existing First Amendment doctrine is both "strikingly underinclusive" and "a false cut at the problem." For criticism of the Commission's Report, see Hawkins & Zimring, Pornography in a Free Society (1988).

————

SEXUALLY EXPLICIT BUT NONOBSCENE EXPRESSION

The Court has considered a number of free speech challenges to laws regulating sexual expression that falls short of any of the definitions of obscenity considered above. In these cases, the Court has wrestled with the question whether such speech ought to be understood to occupy a subordinate position under the First Amendment, even if it does not comprise a wholly unprotected category of speech. Justice Stevens was a leading advocate of such a "lower value" approach: for example, in American Mini Theatres, below, he suggested that "few of us would march our sons and daughters off to war to preserve the citizen's right to see 'Specified Sexual Activities' exhibited in the theaters of our choice." In several plurality opinions, Justice Stevens supported content regulation of sexually offensive displays and speech under an approach that falls short of categorical exclusion of that type of communication from the First Amendment, but that treats such expression as less valuable than core, political speech and accordingly more readily restrainable.

By and large, however, that view has not prevailed on the Court, at least not explicitly. As the cases that follow illustrate, the Court has invalidated bans on misogynistic pornography, nudity in drive-in theaters, nude dancing, and "dial-a-porn" telephone services. In each of these decisions, the Court proceeded from the assumption that indecent or sexually explicit speech that does not amount to obscenity is protected speech and that severe restrictions or total bans of such speech will be subject to strict scrutiny.

At the same time, the Court has upheld a number of less severe restrictions on modes of disseminating sexually explicit but non-obscene expression. As one commentator put it, restrictions on sexual expression "will be permitted so long as those restrictions do not have the effect of a de facto prohibition on dissemination." Schauer, "Categories and the First Amendment," 34 Vand. L. Rev. 265 (1981). In particular, the Court has upheld zoning laws that disperse or concentrate establishments that specialize in materials of specified sexual content in order to serve goals related to property values or ancillary activities in the vicinity of such speech.

Would similar restrictions be tolerated if applied to speech of specified political content? Speech of specified political content likewise could not be channeled to another time or place merely because it was not totally banned. By deferring to content-specific regulations of sexual expression in these circumstances, has the Court implicitly, if not explicitly, treated sexually explicit speech as a subordinate species of speech?

Alternatively, can the zoning cases be explained by virtue of the secondary effects of so-called red-light districts that once occupied a prominent place in American cities, and that often featured adult movie theaters and bookstores as their anchor businesses? If so, would these cases still make sense now that the internet has reduced demand for such brick-and-mortar businesses and most have been relegated to exurban highway exits?

In examining the materials that follow, consider whether it is better to embrace openly Justice Stevens's "lower value" methodology, which treats the First Amendment as covering widely differing varieties of speech that must be aligned in a hierarchy with differing degrees of protection, or to maintain a unitary approach to the value of speech. Can the "lower value" approach be defended as enabling the Justices to deal sensibly with relatively insignificant speech without risking dilution of the protection for "political" expression at the core of the First Amendment? Or does the "lower value" approach show the weakness of judicial efforts to check majoritarian repression, by defining speech as "less valuable" in exactly those situations where it most sharply attacks majoritarian values?

REGULATING PORNOGRAPHY AS SUBORDINATION OF WOMEN

Beginning in the 1980s, opponents of sexually explicit materials advocated a novel theory for restrictive legislation that treated pornography as subject to regulation not for reason of its obscenity but rather on the ground that it constitutes sex discrimination, or the subordination of women to men. The argument was reflected in a model ordinance drafted in 1983 by two feminist theorists, Catharine MacKinnon and Andrea Dworkin, for the city of Minneapolis.

MacKinnon and Dworkin argued that pornography posed a problem not of immorality but of power: "Pornography sexualizes rape, battery, sexual harassment, prostitution, and child sexual abuse. [It] eroticizes the dominance and submission that is the dynamic common to them all." MacKinnon, "Pornography, Civil Rights, and Speech," 20 Harv. C.R.-C.L. L. Rev. 1 (1985). "Pornography, unlike obscenity, is a discrete, identifiable system of sexual exploitation that hurts women as a class by creating inequality and abuse." Dworkin, "Against the Male Flood: Censorship, Pornography, and Equality," 8 Harv. Women's L.J. 1 (1985).

The MacKinnon-Dworkin ordinance was adopted by the Minneapolis City Council at the end of 1983, but vetoed by the city's mayor on the ground that the "remedy sought [is] neither appropriate nor enforceable within our cherished tradition and constitutionally protected right of free speech." It was enacted in revised form, however, by Indianapolis in 1984. The Indianapolis ordinance was struck down by U.S. District Judge Sarah Evans Barker as overbroad, sweeping in protected speech as well as unprotected obscenity.

———

American Booksellers Ass'n v. Hudnut

771 F.2d 323 (7th Cir.1985), aff'd mem., 475 U.S. 1001 (1986).

■ EASTERBROOK, CIRCUIT JUDGE.

Indianapolis enacted an ordinance defining "pornography" as a practice that discriminates against women. [The] City's definition of "pornography" is considerably different from "obscenity," [which] is not protected by the [First Amendment].

"Pornography" under the ordinance is "the graphic sexually explicit subordination of women, whether in pictures or in words, that also includes one or more of the following: (1) Women are presented as sexual objects who enjoy pain or humiliation; or (2) Women are presented as sexual objects who experience sexual pleasure in being raped; or (3) Women are presented as sexual objects tied up or cut up or mutilated or bruised or physically hurt, or as dismembered or truncated or fragmented or severed into body parts; or (4) Women are presented as being penetrated by objects or animals; or (5) Women are presented in scenarios of degradation, injury, abasement, torture, shown as filthy or inferior, bleeding, bruised, or hurt in a context that makes these conditions sexual; or (6) Women are presented as sexual objects for domination, conquest, violation, exploitation, possession, or use, or through postures or positions of servility or submission or display."

The statute provides that the "use of men, children, or transsexuals in the place of women in [provisions] (1) through (6) above shall also constitute pornography under this section." The ordinance as passed in April 1984 defined "sexually explicit" to mean actual or simulated intercourse or the uncovered exhibition of the genitals, buttocks or anus. An amendment in June 1984 deleted this provision, leaving the term undefined.

The Indianapolis ordinance [unlike the obscenity standard] does not refer to the prurient interest, to offensiveness, or to the standards of the community. It demands attention to particular depictions, not to the work judged as a whole. It is irrelevant under the ordinance whether the work has literary, artistic, political, or scientific value. The City and many amici point to these omissions as virtues. They maintain that pornography influences attitudes, and the statute is a way to alter the socialization of men and women rather than to vindicate community standards of offensiveness. And as one of the principal drafters of the ordinance has asserted, "if a woman is subjected, why should it matter that the work has other value?" [MacKinnon, "Pornography, Civil Rights, and Speech," above.] [Those] supporting the ordinance say that it will play an important role in reducing the tendency of men to view women as sexual objects, a tendency that leads to both unacceptable attitudes and discrimination in the workplace and violence away from it. Those opposing the ordinance point out that much radical feminist literature is explicit and depicts women in ways forbidden by the ordinance and that the ordinance would reopen old battles.

[We] do not try to balance the arguments for and against [the ordinance]. The ordinance discriminates on the ground of the content of the speech. Speech treating women in the approved way—in sexual encounters "premised on equality"—is lawful no matter how sexually explicit. Speech treating women in the disapproved way—as submissive in matters sexual or as enjoying humiliation—is unlawful no matter how significant the literary, artistic, or political qualities of the work taken as a whole. The state may not ordain preferred viewpoints in this way. The Constitution forbids the state to declare one perspective right and silence opponents.

[Under] the First Amendment the government must leave to the people the evaluation of ideas. Bold or subtle, an idea is as powerful as the audience allows it to be. A belief may be pernicious—the beliefs of Nazis led to the death of millions, those of the Klan to the repression of millions. A pernicious belief may prevail. Totalitarian governments today rule much of the planet, practicing suppression of billions and spreading dogma that may enslave others. One of the things that separates our society from theirs is our absolute right to propagate opinions that the government finds wrong or even hateful. The ideas of the Klan may be propagated. [Brandenburg]. Communists may speak freely and run for office. [The] Nazi Party may march through a city with a large Jewish population. [Collin v. Smith]. People may teach religions that others despise. People may seek to repeal laws guaranteeing equal opportunity in employment or to revoke the constitutional amendments granting the vote to blacks and women. They may do this because "above all else, the First Amendment means that government has no power to restrict expression because of its message [or] its [ideas]."

Under the ordinance graphic sexually explicit speech is "pornography" or not depending on the perspective the author adopts. Speech that "subordinates" women and [even] simply presents women in "positions of servility or submission or display" is forbidden, no matter how great the literary or political value of the work taken as a whole. Speech that portrays women in positions of equality is lawful, no matter how graphic the sexual content. This is thought control. It establishes an "approved" view of women, of how they may react to sexual encounters, of how the sexes may relate to each other. Those who espouse the approved view may use sexual images; those who do not, may not.

Indianapolis justifies the ordinance on the ground that pornography affects thoughts. Men who see women depicted as subordinate are more likely to treat them so. Pornography is an aspect of dominance. It does not persuade people so much as change them. It works by socializing, by establishing the expected and the permissible. In this view pornography is not an idea; pornography is the injury. There is much to this perspective. Beliefs are also facts. People often act in accordance with the images and patterns they find around them. [People] taught from birth that black people are fit only for slavery rarely rebelled against that creed; beliefs coupled with the self-interest of the masters established a social structure that inflicted great harm while enduring for centuries. Words and images act at the level of the subconscious before they persuade at the level of the conscious. Even the truth has little chance unless a statement fits within the framework of beliefs that may never have been subjected to rational study.

Therefore we accept the premises of this legislation. Depictions of subordination tend to perpetuate subordination. The subordinate status of women in turn leads to affront and lower pay at work, insult and injury at home, battery and rape on the streets.[1] In the language of the legislature, "[p]ornography is central in creating and maintaining sex as a basis of discrimination. Pornography is a systematic practice of exploitation and subordination based on sex which differentially harms women.]"

Yet this simply demonstrates the power of pornography as speech. All of these unhappy effects depend on mental intermediation. Pornography affects how people see the world, their fellows, and social relations. If pornography is what pornography does, so is other speech. Hitler's orations affected how some Germans saw Jews. Communism is a world view, not simply a Manifesto by Marx and Engels or a set of speeches. The Alien and Sedition Acts [rested] on a sincerely held belief that disrespect for the government leads to social collapse and revolution—a belief with support in the history of many nations. Most governments of the world act on this empirical regularity, suppressing critical speech. In the United States, however, the strength of the support for this belief is irrelevant. Seditious libel is protected speech unless the danger is not only grave but also imminent.

Racial bigotry, anti-semitism, violence on television, reporters' biases— these and many more influence the culture and shape our socialization. None is directly answerable by more speech, unless that speech too finds its place in the popular culture. Yet all is protected as speech, however insidious. Any other answer leaves the government in control of all of the institutions of culture, the great censor and director of which thoughts are good for us. Sexual responses often are unthinking responses, and the association of sexual arousal with the subordination of women therefore may have a substantial effect. But almost all cultural stimuli provoke unconscious responses. Religious ceremonies condition their participants. Teachers convey messages by selecting what not to [cover]. People may be conditioned in subtle ways. If the fact that speech plays a role in a process of conditioning were enough to permit governmental regulation, that would be the end of freedom of speech.

---

[1]   [In] saying that we accept the finding that pornography as the ordinance defines it leads to unhappy consequences, we mean only that there is evidence to this effect, that this evidence is consistent with much human experience, and that as judges we must accept the legislative resolution of such disputed empirical [questions]. [Footnote by Judge Easterbrook.]

It is possible to interpret the claim that the pornography is the harm in a different way. Indianapolis emphasizes the injury that models in pornographic films and pictures may suffer. The record contains materials depicting sexual torture, penetration of women by red-hot irons and the like. These concerns have nothing to do with written materials subject to the statute, and physical injury can occur with or without the "subordination" of women. [A] state may make injury in the course of producing a film unlawful independent of the viewpoint expressed in the film. The more immediate point, however, is that the image of pain is not necessarily pain. [The film] Body Double is sexually explicit and a murder occurs—yet no one believes that the actress suffered pain or died. [No one] believes that [Jane Fonda in Barbarella] was actually tortured to make the film. In Carnal Knowledge a woman grovels to please the sexual whims of a character played by Jack Nicholson; no one believes that there was a real sexual submission, and the Supreme Court held the film protected by the First Amendment. And this works both ways. The description of women's sexual domination of men in Lysistrata was not real dominance. Depictions may affect slavery, war, or sexual roles, but a book about slavery is not itself slavery, or a book about death by poison a murder.

[Much] of Indianapolis's argument rests on the belief that when speech is "unanswerable," and the metaphor that there is a "marketplace of ideas" does not apply, the First Amendment does not apply either. The metaphor is honored; Milton's Aeropagitica and Mill's On Liberty defend freedom of speech on the ground that the truth will prevail, and many of the most important cases under the First Amendment recite this position. The Framers undoubtedly believed it. As a general matter it is true. But the Constitution does not make the dominance of truth a necessary condition of freedom of speech. To say that it does would be to confuse an outcome of free speech with a necessary condition for the application of the amendment. A power to limit speech on the ground that truth has not yet prevailed and is not likely to prevail implies the power to declare truth. At some point the government must be able to say (as Indianapolis has said): "We know what the truth is, yet a free exchange of speech has not driven out falsity, so that we must now prohibit falsity." If the government may declare the truth, why wait for the failure of speech? Under the First Amendment, however, there is no such thing as a false idea [Gertz], so the government may not restrict speech on the ground that in a free exchange truth is not yet dominant. At any time, some speech is ahead in the game; the more numerous speakers prevail. Supporters of minority candidates may be forever "excluded" from the political process because their candidates never win, because few people believe their positions. This does not mean that freedom of speech has failed.

We come, finally, to the argument that pornography is "low value" speech, that it is enough like obscenity that Indianapolis may prohibit it. Some cases hold that speech far removed from politics and other subjects at the core of the Framers' concerns may be subjected to special regulation. E.g., Chaplinsky. These cases do not sustain statutes that select among viewpoints, however. [At] all events, "pornography" is not low value speech within the meaning of these cases. Indianapolis seeks to prohibit certain speech because it believes [it] influences social relations and politics on a grand scale, that it controls attitudes at home and in the legislature. This precludes a characterization of the speech as low value. True, pornography and obscenity have sex in common. But Indianapolis left out of its definition any reference to literary, artistic, political, or scientific value. The ordinance applies to graphic sexually explicit subordination in works great and small. The Court sometimes balances the value of speech against the costs of its restriction, but it does this by category of speech and not by the content of particular works. [Indianapolis] has created an approved point of view and so loses the support of these cases.

Any rationale we could imagine in support of this ordinance could not be limited to sex discrimination. Free speech has been on balance an ally of those seeking change. Governments that want stasis start by restricting speech. [Change] in any complex system ultimately depends on the ability of outsiders to challenge accepted views and the reigning institutions. Without a strong guarantee of freedom of speech, there is no effective right to challenge what is. [The] definition of "pornography" is unconstitutional. No construction or excision of particular terms could save [it]. Affirmed.

[The Supreme Court summarily affirmed the Seventh Circuit's decision. Chief Justice Burger and Justices Rehnquist and O'Connor dissented, urging that the case be set for oral argument.]

———

HUDNUT AND THE SOCIAL HARMS OF PORNOGRAPHY

1. ***Regulating viewpoint or preventing harm?*** Is Hudnut correctly decided? For a negative answer, see Sunstein, "Pornography and the First Amendment," 1986 Duke L.J. 589 (1986), arguing that anti-pornography legislation is "directed at harm rather than at viewpoint" and that because of its "focus on harm, antipornography legislation [does] not pose the dangers associated with viewpoint-based restrictions." For a contrary view, see Tribe, American Constitutional Law 925 (2d ed. 1988): "*All* viewpoint-based regulations are targeted at some supposed harm, whether it be linked to an unsettling ideology like Communism [or] to socially shunned practices like adultery." Noting that government may outlaw incitements of sexual violence against women, as it may other incitements of crimes, Tribe adds that it is "altogether different, and far more constitutionally tenuous, for a government to outlaw [the] incitement of violence against women *only* when such incitement is caused by words or pictures that express a particular point of view: that women are meant for domination." Sunstein replies that the First Amendment permits a variety of nonneutral speech regulations to prevent serious harms: for example, banning employers during unionization periods from engaging in anti-union speech. In such cases, "the partisanship of the regulation is not apparent because there is so firm a consensus on the presence of real-world harms that the objection from neutrality does not even register." For further commentary, see Stone, "Anti-Pornography Legislation As Viewpoint Discrimination," 9 Harv. J. L. & Pub.Pol'y. 701 (1986), Kagan, "Regulation of Hate Speech and Pornography After R.A.V.," 60 U. Chi. L. Rev. 873 (1993).

2. ***Pornography and maintaining a decent society.*** Note that the MacKinnon-Dworkin argument, like Chief Justice Burger's argument for the majority in Paris Adult Theatre, views sexual speech as shaping the community rather than as merely gratifying individual consumers. But Chief Justice Burger treated obscenity as a minority practice deviating from governing norms of privacy and monogamous heterosexual marriage, while MacKinnon and Dworkin view pornography as the expression of existing majority practice.

3. *Feminist arguments against pornography regulation.* Many feminists opposed the MacKinnon-Dworkin argument: "[F]or many women (perhaps most), pornography is primarily victimizing, threatening and oppressive, [but] for others, [it] is on occasion liberating and transformative, [a] healthy attack on a stifling and oppressive societal denial of female sexuality," and a defiance of oppression by "marital, familial, productive, and reproductive values." West, "The Feminist-Conservative Anti-Pornography [Alliance]," 1987 A.B.F. Res. J. 681. "By defining sexually explicit images of women as subordinating and degrading to them, the [MacKinnon-Dworkin] ordinance reinforces the stereotypical view that 'good' women do not seek and enjoy sex [and] perpetuates a stereotype of women as helpless victims, incapable of consent, and in need of protection." Hunter & Law, "Brief Amici Curiae of Feminist Anti-Censorship Task Force," 21 U. Mich. J.L. Ref. 69 (1987–88). See also, Strossen, Defending Pornography: Free Speech, Sex, and the Fight for Women's Rights (1995); Meyer, "Sex, Sin, and Women's Liberation: Against Porn-Suppression," 72 Tex. L. Rev. 1097 (1994).

4. *Gay pornography.* Does the MacKinnon-Dworkin argument apply to pornography depicting gay sex? How can pornography subordinate women if only men are depicted or if only women are depicted? The Supreme Court of Canada has held that violent gay pornography, like violent straight pornography, constitutes sex discrimination under the Canadian Constitution. See Little Sisters Book and Art Emporium v. Canada, 2000 SCC 69. For support of this position, see also Christopher N. Kendall, Violent Gay Pornography: An Issue of Sex Discrimination (2004). For an argument that gay male pornography both liberates and helps build community among gay men and that feminist anti-pornography arguments should not apply to it, see Sherman, "Love Speech: The Social Utility of Pornography," 47 Stan. L. Rev. 661 (1995).

––––––––

NUDITY BANS

The following cases involve local attempts to regulate nudity in the entertainment industry, both in broadcast media and on the live stage. While the Court has upheld limitations on where or when adult material may be broadcast, see American Mini Theatres, below, it has consistently invalidated total bans on nudity. Consider which philosophy of free speech is implicated in these cases: can commercial nudity be defended under any cognizable theory of the First Amendment? Is the Court concerned primarily with the speaker's right to express him or herself through nudity or with the listener's right to access nudity? Do First Amendment protections for commercial nudity recognize the value of commercial nudity as speech or are they a buffer against chilling more valuable forms of expression?

––––––––

Erznoznik v. Jacksonville
422 U.S. 205, 95 S. Ct. 2268, 45 L. Ed. 2d 125 (1975).

[Erznoznik concerned a challenge to the facial validity of an ordinance prohibiting drive-in movie theaters with screens visible from public streets from showing films containing nudity. The ordinance prohibited exhibitions of "the human male or female bare buttocks, human female bare breasts, or human bare pubic areas." Concededly, the ban applied to nonobscene films. The city's major defense was that "it may protect its citizens against unwilling exposure to materials that may be offensive."]

■ JUSTICE POWELL delivered the opinion of the Court.

This Court has considered analogous issues—pitting the First Amendment rights of speakers against the privacy rights of those who may be unwilling viewers or auditors—in a variety of contexts. Such cases demand delicate balancing. [Although] each case ultimately must depend on its own specific facts, some general principles have emerged. A State or municipality may protect individual privacy by enacting reasonable time, place, and manner regulations applicable to all speech irrespective of content. But when the government, acting as censor, undertakes selectively to shield the public from some kinds of speech on the ground that they are more offensive than others, the First Amendment strictly limits its power. Such selective restrictions have been upheld only when the speaker intrudes on the privacy of the home or the degree of captivity makes it impractical for the unwilling viewer or auditor to avoid exposure. The plain, if at times disquieting, truth is that in our pluralistic society, [with] constantly proliferating new and ingenious forms of expression, "we are inescapably captive audiences for many purposes." Much that we encounter offends our esthetic, if not our political and moral, sensibilities. Nevertheless, the Constitution does not permit government to decide which types of otherwise protected speech are sufficiently offensive to require protection for the unwilling listener or viewer. Rather, absent the narrow circumstances described above, the burden normally falls upon the viewer to "avoid further bombardment of [his] sensibilities simply by averting [his] eyes." [Cohen.]

The Jacksonville ordinance discriminates among movies solely on the basis of content. Its effect is to deter drive-in theaters from showing movies containing any nudity, however innocent or even educational. This discrimination cannot be justified as a means of preventing significant intrusions on privacy. The ordinance seeks only to keep these films from being seen from public streets and places where the offended viewer readily can avert his eyes. In short, the screen of a drive-in theater is not "so obtrusive as to make it impossible for an unwilling individual to avoid exposure to it." Thus, we conclude that the limited privacy interest of persons on the public streets cannot justify this censorship of otherwise protected speech on the basis of its content.

[Appellee] attempts to support the ordinance as an exercise of the city's undoubted police power to protect children. [Assuming] the ordinance is aimed at prohibiting youths from viewing the films, the restriction is broader than permissible. The ordinance is not directed against sexually explicit nudity, nor is it otherwise limited. Rather, it sweepingly forbids display of all films containing any uncovered buttocks or breasts, irrespective of context or pervasiveness. Thus it would bar a film containing a picture of a baby's buttocks, the nude body of a war victim, or scenes from a culture in which nudity is indigenous. [Clearly] all nudity cannot be deemed obscene even as to minors. Nor can such a broad restriction be justified by any other governmental interest pertaining to minors. Speech that is neither obscene as to youths nor subject to some other legitimate proscription cannot be suppressed solely to protect the young from ideas or images that a legislative body thinks unsuitable for them.

[Appellee also] claimed that nudity on a drive-in movie screen distracts passing motorists, thus slowing the flow of traffic and increasing the likelihood of accidents. Nothing in the record or in the text of the ordinance suggests that it is aimed at traffic regulation. [By] singling out movies containing even the most fleeting and innocent glimpses of nudity the legislative classification is strikingly underinclusive. There is no reason to think that a wide variety of other scenes in the customary screen diet, ranging from soap opera to violence, would be any less distracting to the passing motorist. [Even] a traffic regulation cannot discriminate on the basis of content unless there are clear reasons for the distinctions.

[In] concluding that this ordinance is invalid we do not deprecate the legitimate interests asserted by the city of Jacksonville. We hold only that the present ordinance does not satisfy the rigorous constitutional standards that apply when government attempts to regulate expression. Where First Amendment freedoms are at stake we have repeatedly emphasized that precision of drafting and clarity of purpose are essential. These prerequisites are absent here. Accordingly the judgment below is reversed.

■ CHIEF JUSTICE BURGER, with whom JUSTICE REHNQUIST joins, dissenting.

The Court's analysis seems to begin and end with the sweeping proposition that, regardless of the circumstances, government may not regulate any form of "communicative" activity on the basis of its content. [None] of the cases upon which the Court relies remotely implies that the Court ever intended to establish inexorable limitations upon state power in this area.

[A] careful consideration of the diverse interests involved in this case illustrates, for me, the inadequacy of the Court's rigidly simplistic approach. Whatever validity the notion that passersby may protect their sensibilities by averting their eyes may have when applied to words printed on an individual's jacket, see [Cohen], it distorts reality to apply that notion to the outsize screen of a drive-in movie theater. Such screens [are] designed to [attract and hold] the attention of all observers. [It is] not unreasonable for lawmakers to believe that public nudity on a giant screen [may] have a tendency to divert attention from [the driver's] task and cause accidents. [Moreover,] those persons who legitimately desire to [view the films] are not foreclosed from doing so. [The films] may be exhibited [in] indoor theaters [and in any] drive-in movie theater [with a] screen [shielded] from public view. Thus, [the ordinance is] not a restriction on any "message." [The] First Amendment interests involved in this case are trivial at best.

[The] Jacksonville ordinance involved in this case, although no model of draftsmanship, is narrowly drawn to regulate only certain unique public exhibitions of nudity; it would be absurd to suggest that it operates to suppress expression of ideas.

NUDITY BANS AFTER ERZNOZNIK

Six years later, even after the Court upheld a zoning ordinance directed at adult theaters, see American Mini Theatres, below, **Schad v. Mount Ephraim**, 452 U.S. 61 (1981), reiterated that a total ban on displays of nudity is impermissible. The challenge was brought by the operators of a store selling "adult" materials who had added a coin-operated mechanism permitting customers to watch a live, nude dancer performing behind a glass panel. The ordinance of the Borough of Mt. Ephraim, New Jersey, described the "permitted uses" in the small community's commercial zone and barred all other uses. As construed by the state courts, the ban covered all "live entertainment." Justice WHITE's majority opinion stated: "By excluding live entertainment throughout [the] Borough, [the ordinance] prohibits a wide range of expression that has long been held to be within the protections of the [First Amendment]. Entertainment, as well as political and ideological speech, is protected. [Nor] may an entertainment program be prohibited solely because it displays the nude human figure. 'Nudity alone' does not place otherwise protected material outside the mantle of the First Amendment. [When] a zoning law infringes upon a protected liberty, it must be narrowly drawn and must further a sufficiently substantial government interest.

"[In] this case, however, Mount Ephraim has not adequately justified its substantial restriction of protected activity. [The] Borough has presented no evidence, and it is not immediately apparent as a matter of experience, that live entertainment poses problems [more] significant than those associated with various permitted uses; nor does it appear that the Borough's zoning authority has arrived at a defensible conclusion that unusual problems are presented by live entertainment. [Mount] Ephraim asserts that it could have chosen to eliminate all commercial uses within its boundaries. Yet we must assess the exclusion of live entertainment in light of the commercial uses Mount Ephraim allows, not in light of what the Borough might have done.[1] [The] Borough [contends] that live entertainment in general and nude dancing in particular are amply available in close-by areas outside the limits of the Borough. [But] there is no evidence in this record to support the proposition that the kind of entertainment appellants wish to provide is available in reasonably nearby [areas]."

Chief Justice BURGER, joined by Justice Rehnquist, dissented: "[Even] assuming that the 'expression' manifested in the nude dancing that is involved here is somehow protected speech under the First Amendment, [Mt. Ephraim] is entitled to regulate it. [The] zoning ordinance imposes a minimal intrusion on genuine rights of expression; only by contortions of logic can it be made [otherwise]. [To] invoke the First Amendment to protect the activity involved in this case trivializes and demeans that great Amendment."

————————

ZONING COMMERCIAL SEXUAL EXPRESSION

While the Court has invalidated total bans on nudity, it has indicated a willingness to allow legislatures to impose substantial regulations on where sexual commercial activity, including sexually explicit expression, may be carried out. In each of the following three cases, the Court upheld a local government's zoning regulation of adult entertainment. In doing so, the Court increasingly looked to the purported "secondary effects" of the speech in question rather than to the social value of the speech.

————————

[1] "Thus, our decision today does not establish that every unit of local government entrusted with zoning responsibilities must provide a commercial zone in which live entertainment is permitted." [Footnote by Justice White.]

Young v. American Mini Theatres

427 U.S. 50, 96 S. Ct. 2440, 49 L. Ed. 2d 310 (1976).

[A Detroit "Anti-Skid Row Ordinance" differentiated between motion picture theaters that exhibited sexually explicit "adult movies" and those that showed other fare. The Detroit ordinance required dispersal of "adult" theaters and bookstores: it stated that an "adult" theater may not be located within 1,000 feet of any two other "regulated uses" (such as bars, billiard halls, hotels and cabarets) or within 500 feet of a residential area. Theaters are classified as "adult" on the basis of the character of the motion pictures they exhibit. If a theater presented "material distinguished or characterized by emphasis on matters depicting, describing or relating to 'specified sexual activities' or 'specified anatomical areas,' "[1] it was an "adult" establishment. The impact of the classification was to channel the display of the sexually explicit (but not necessarily obscene) materials into limited portions of the city, not to ban the display from the city entirely. The ordinance was challenged by the operators of two adult motion picture theaters located within 1,000 feet of two other "regulated uses." The city argued that the ordinance was a zoning law needed because the location of several "regulated uses" in the same neighborhood tended to attract undesirable transients, adversely affected property values, and caused an increase in crime.]

■ JUSTICE STEVENS delivered the opinion of the Court.

[The following portion of Justice Stevens's opinion was joined only by Chief Justice Burger and Justices White and Rehnquist:] A remark attributed to Voltaire characterizes our zealous adherence to the principle that the Government may not tell the citizen what he may or may not say. Referring to a suggestion that the violent overthrow of tyranny might be legitimate, he said: "I disapprove of what you say, but I will defend to the death your right to say it." The essence of that comment has been repeated time after time in our decisions invalidating attempts [to] impose selective controls upon the dissemination of ideas. [Some of our statements], read literally and without regard for the facts of the case in which [they were] made, would absolutely preclude any regulation of expressive activity predicated in whole or in part on the content of the communication. [But under our decisions the] question whether speech is, or is not, protected by the First Amendment often depends on the content of the speech. [E.g., incitement, fighting words, private-figure defamation, and obscenity.] [The Detroit ordinances draw a line] on the basis of content without violating the Government's paramount obligation of neutrality in its regulation of protected communication. For the regulation of the places where sexually explicit films may be exhibited is unaffected by whatever social, political, or philosophical message the film may be intended to communicate; whether

---

[1] The ordinance defined these terms as follows: "Specified Sexual Activities" were defined as: "1. Human Genitals in a state of sexual stimulation or arousal; 2. Acts of human masturbation, sexual intercourse or sodomy; 3. Fondling or other erotic touching of human genitals, pubic region, buttock or female breast." "Specified Anatomical Areas" were defined as: "1. Less than completely and opaquely covered: (a) human genitals, pubic region, (b) buttock, and (c) female breast below a point immediately above the top of the areola; and 2. Human male genitals in a discernibly turgid state, even if completely and opaquely covered."

the motion picture ridicules or characterizes one point of view or another, the effect of the ordinances is exactly the same.

Moreover, even though we recognize that the First Amendment will not tolerate the total suppression of erotic materials that have some arguably artistic value, it is manifest that society's interest in protecting this type of expression is of a wholly different, and lesser, magnitude than the interest in untrammeled political debate that inspired Voltaire's immortal comment. Whether political oratory or philosophical discussion moves us to applaud or to despise what is said, every schoolchild can understand why our duty to defend the right to speak remains the same. But few of us would march our sons and daughters off to war to preserve the citizen's right to see "Specified Sexual Activities" exhibited in the theaters of our choice. Even though the First Amendment protects communication in this area from total suppression, we hold that the State may legitimately use the content of these materials as the basis for placing them in a different classification from other motion pictures.

The remaining question is whether the line drawn by these ordinances is justified by the city's interest in preserving the character of its neighborhoods. [The] record discloses a factual basis for the [Council's] conclusion that this kind of restriction will have the desired effect.[2] It is not our function to appraise the wisdom of its decision to require adult theaters to be separated rather than concentrated in the same areas. In either event, the city's interest in attempting to preserve the quality of urban life is one that must be accorded high respect. Moreover, the city must be allowed a reasonable opportunity to experiment with solutions to admittedly serious problems. Since what is ultimately at stake is nothing more than a limitation on the place where adult films may be exhibited,[3] even though the determination of whether a particular film fits that characterization turns on the nature of its content, we conclude that the city's interest in the present and future character of its neighborhoods adequately supports its classification of [motion pictures].

■ JUSTICE POWELL, concurring in the judgment and in portions of the opinion.

[My] approach to the resolution of this case is sufficiently different [from Justice Stevens'] to prompt me to write separately.[4] I view the case as presenting an example of innovative land-use regulation, implicating First Amendment concerns only incidentally and to a limited [extent]. [This zoning] situation is not analogous [to] any other prior case. The unique

---

[2]   The Common Council's determination was that a concentration of "adult" movie theaters causes the area to deteriorate and become a focus of crime, effects which are not attributable to theaters showing other types of films. It is this secondary effect which this zoning ordinance attempts to avoid, not the dissemination of "offensive" speech. In contrast, in Erznoznik, the justifications offered by the city rested primarily on the city's interest in protecting its citizens from exposure to unwanted, "offensive" speech. The only secondary effect relied on to support that ordinance was the impact on traffic—an effect which might be caused by a distracting open-air movie even if it did not exhibit nudity.

[3]   The situation would be quite different if the ordinance had the effect of suppressing, or greatly restricting access to, lawful speech. Here, however, the District Court [found]: 'There are myriad locations in the City of Detroit which must be over 1,000 feet from existing regulated establishments. This burden on First Amendment rights is [slight].

[4]   I do not think we need reach, nor am I inclined to agree with, the [holding] that nonobscene, erotic materials may be treated differently under First Amendment principles from other forms of protected [expression].

situation presented by this ordinance calls [for] a careful inquiry into the competing concerns of the State and the interests protected by the guaranty of free expression. Because a substantial burden rests upon the State when it would limit in any way First Amendment rights, it is necessary to identify with specificity the nature of the infringement in each [case].

The inquiry for First Amendment purposes [looks] only to the effect of this ordinance upon freedom of expression. This prompts essentially two inquiries: (i) does the ordinance impose any content limitation on the creators of adult movies or their ability to make them available to whom they desire, and (ii) does it restrict in any significant way the viewing of these movies by those who desire to see them? On the record in this case, these inquiries must be answered in the negative. At most the impact of the ordinance on these interests is incidental and minimal. [The] ordinance is addressed only to the places at which this type of expression may be presented, a restriction that does not interfere with content. Nor is there any significant overall curtailment of adult movie presentations, or the opportunity for a message to reach an audience. [In] these circumstances, it is appropriate to analyze the permissibility of Detroit's action under the four-part test of United States v. O'Brien [1968; p. 252]. Under that test, a governmental regulation is sufficiently justified, despite its incidental impact upon First Amendment interests, "if it is within the constitutional power of the Government; if it furthers an important or substantial governmental interest; if the governmental interest is unrelated to the suppression of free expression; and if the incidental restriction [on] First Amendment freedoms is no greater than is essential to the furtherance of that interest."

[There is] no question that the Ordinance was within the power of the Detroit Common Council to enact. Nor is there doubt that the interests furthered by this Ordinance are both important and substantial. The third and fourth tests of O'Brien also are met on this record. It is clear [that] Detroit has not embarked on an effort to suppress free expression. The Ordinance was already in existence, and its purposes clearly set out, for a full decade before adult establishments were brought under it. When this occurred, it is clear [that] the governmental interest prompting the inclusion in the ordinance of adult establishments was wholly unrelated to any suppression of free expression.[5] Nor is there reason to question that the degree of incidental encroachment upon such expression was the minimum necessary to further the purpose of the [ordinance].[6]

The dissent perceives support for its position in [Erznoznik]. I believe this perception is a clouded one. [T]he ordinance in Erznoznik was a misconceived attempt directly to regulate content of expression. The Detroit zoning ordinance, in contrast, affects expression only incidentally and in furtherance of governmental interests wholly unrelated to the regulation of expression. [Although] courts must be alert to the possibility of direct rather

---

[5]   [The Council] simply acted to protect the economic integrity of large areas of its city against the effects of a predictable interaction between a concentration of certain businesses and the responses of people in the area. If it had been concerned with restricting the message purveyed by adult theaters, it would have tried to close them or restrict their number rather than circumscribe their choice as to location.

[6]   In my view [the] dissent misconceives the issue in this case by insisting that it involves an impermissible time, place and manner restriction based on the content of expression. It involves nothing of the kind. We have here merely a decision by the city to treat certain movie theaters differently because they have markedly different effects upon their [surroundings].

than incidental effects of zoning on expression, and especially to the possibility of pretextual use of the power to zone as a means of suppressing expression, it is clear that this is not such a case."

■ JUSTICE STEWART, joined by JUSTICES BRENNAN, MARSHALL and BLACKMUN, dissenting.

[This] case does not involve a simple zoning ordinance, or a content-neutral time, place, and manner restriction, or a regulation of obscene expression or other speech that is entitled to less than the full protection of the First Amendment. The kind of expression at issue here is no doubt objectionable to some, but that fact does not diminish its protected status any more than did the particular content of the "offensive" expression in [Erznoznik or Cohen]. What this case does involve is the constitutional permissibility of selective interference with protected speech whose content is thought to produce distasteful effects. It is elementary that a prime function of the First Amendment is to guard against just such interference. By refusing to invalidate Detroit's ordinance the Court rides roughshod over cardinal principles of First Amendment law, which require that time, place and manner regulations that affect protected expression be content-neutral except in the limited context of a captive or juvenile audience. In place of these principles the Court invokes a concept wholly alien to the First Amendment. [The Court] stands "Voltaire's immortal comment" on its head. For if the guarantees of the First Amendment were reserved for expression that more than a "few of us" would take up arms to defend, then the right of free expression would be defined and circumscribed by current popular [opinion].

The fact that the "offensive" speech here may not address "important" topics—"ideas of social and political significance," in the Court's terminology—does not mean that it is less worthy of constitutional protection [e.g., Cohen]. Moreover, in the absence of a judicial determination of obscenity, it is by no means clear that the speech is not "important" even on the Court's terms. I can only interpret today's decision as an aberration. The Court is undoubtedly sympathetic, as am I, to the well-intentioned efforts of Detroit to "clean up" its streets and prevent the proliferation of "skid rows." But it is in those instances where protected speech grates most unpleasantly against the sensibilities that judicial vigilance must be at its height. [The] factual parallels between [Erznoznik] and this [case] are [striking]. The Court must never forget that the consequences of rigorously enforcing the guarantees of the First Amendment are frequently unpleasant. Much speech that seems to be of little or no value will enter the marketplace of ideas, threatening the quality of our social discourse and, more generally, the serenity of our lives. But that is the price to be paid for constitutional freedom.

Renton v. Playtime Theatres, Inc.
475 U.S. 41, 106 S. Ct. 925, 89 L. Ed. 2d 29 (1986).

[Unlike the Detroit ordinance at issue in Mini Theatres, the zoning ordinance at issue in Renton attempted to regulate the location of adult theaters by concentrating them rather than by dispersing them. Drawing on the findings of a zoning study conducted in the city of Seattle, the ordinance provided that such establishments "may not be located within 1,000 feet of any residential zone, single- or multiple-family dwelling, church, park, or school."]

■ JUSTICE REHNQUIST delivered the opinion of the Court.

This Court has long held that regulations enacted for the purpose of restraining speech on the basis of its content presumptively violate the First Amendment. On the other hand, so-called "content-neutral" time, place, and manner regulations are acceptable so long as they are designed to serve a substantial governmental interest and do not unreasonably limit alternative avenues of communication. [At] first glance, the Renton ordinance, like the ordinance in American Mini Theatres, does not appear to fit neatly into either the "content-based" or the "content-neutral" category. To be sure, the ordinance treats theaters that specialize in adult films differently from other kinds of theaters. Nevertheless, [the] Renton ordinance is aimed not at the *content* of the films shown at "adult motion picture theatres," but rather at the *secondary effects* of such theaters on the surrounding community. [The] District Court's finding as to "predominate" intent [is] more than adequate to establish that the city's pursuit of its zoning interests here was unrelated to the suppression of free expression. The ordinance by its terms is designed to prevent crime, protect the city's retail trade, maintain property values, and generally "protec[t] and preserv[e] the quality of [the city's] neighborhoods, commercial districts, and the quality of urban life," not to suppress the expression of unpopular views.

The appropriate inquiry in this case, then, is whether the Renton ordinance is designed to serve a substantial governmental interest and allows for reasonable alternative avenues of communication. [We] hold that Renton was entitled to rely on the experiences of Seattle and other cities, and in particular on the "detailed findings" summarized in the Washington Supreme Court's Northend Cinema opinion, in enacting its adult theater zoning ordinance. The First Amendment does not require a city, before enacting such an ordinance, to conduct new studies or produce evidence independent of that already generated by other cities, so long as whatever evidence the city relies upon is reasonably believed to be relevant to the problem that the city addresses. That was the case here.

[Finally], turning to the question whether the Renton ordinance allows for reasonable alternative avenues of communication, we note that the ordinance leaves some 520 acres, or more than five percent of the entire land area of Renton, open to use as adult theater sites. [Respondents] argue, however, that some of the land in question is already occupied by existing businesses, that "practically none" of the undeveloped land is currently for sale or lease, and that in general there are no "commercially viable" adult theater sites within the 520 acres left open by the Renton ordinance. [That] respondents must fend for themselves in the real estate market, on an equal footing with other prospective purchasers and lessees, does not give rise to a First Amendment violation. [In] our view, the First Amendment requires only that Renton refrain from effectively denying respondents a reasonable opportunity to open and operate an adult theater within the city, and the ordinance before us easily meets this requirement.

■ JUSTICE BRENNAN, joined by JUSTICE MARSHALL, dissenting.

[Renton] was interested not in controlling the "secondary effects" associated with adult businesses, but in discriminating against adult theaters based on the content of the films they exhibit. [That] some residents may be offended by the content of the films shown at adult movie theaters cannot form the basis for state regulation of speech.

[The] Court holds that Renton was entitled to rely on the experiences of cities like Detroit and Seattle, which had enacted special zoning regulations for adult entertainment businesses after studying the adverse effects caused by such establishments. However, even assuming that Renton was concerned with the same problems as Seattle and Detroit, it never actually reviewed any of the studies conducted by those cities. [The] Court's approach largely immunizes such measures from judicial scrutiny, since a municipality can readily find other municipal ordinances to rely upon, thus always retrospectively justifying special zoning regulations for adult theaters.

Even assuming that the ordinance should be treated like a content-neutral time, place, and manner restriction, I would still find it unconstitutional. [The] Renton Council was aware only that some residents had complained about adult movie theaters, and that other localities had adopted special zoning restrictions for such establishments. These are not "facts" sufficient to justify the burdens the ordinance imposed upon constitutionally protected expression.

Finally, the ordinance is invalid because it does not provide for reasonable alternative avenues of communication. The District Court found that the ordinance left 520 acres in Renton available for adult theater sites, an area comprising about five percent of the city. [Respondents] do not ask Renton to guarantee low-price sites for their businesses, but seek only a reasonable opportunity to operate adult theaters in the city. By denying them this opportunity, Renton can effectively ban a form of protected speech from its borders.

————

City of Los Angeles v. Alameda Books, Inc.

535 U.S. 425, 122 S. Ct. 1728, 152 L. Ed. 2d 670 (2002).

[In 1978, the City of Los Angeles, responding to a 1977 city study that had concluded that "concentrations of adult businesses are associated with higher rates of prostitution, robbery, assaults, and thefts in surrounding communities," enacted a law that, like the law in Young v. American Mini Theatres, imposed density limits on adult "establishments," restricting their placement near preexisting adult stores, or near schools, parks and religious institutions. Several years later, realizing that the density limits on adult "establishments" had "allow[ed] concentration of multiple adult enterprises in a single structure," and concerned that independent adult establishments could be replaced by "an adult-oriented department store," the city amended its law to also prohibit "the establishment or maintenance of more than one adult entertainment business in the same building, structure or portion thereof," defining an "Adult Entertainment Business" as an "adult arcade, bookstore, cabaret, motel, theater, or massage parlor or a place for sexual encounters." Under the amendment, any type of adult activity at an establishment was considered to "constitute a separate adult entertainment business even if operated in conjunction with another adult entertainment business at the same establishment."]

■ JUSTICE O'CONNOR announced the judgment of the Court and delivered an opinion in which CHIEF JUSTICE REHNQUIST and JUSTICES SCALIA and THOMAS join.

The central component of the 1977 study is a report on city crime patterns provided by the Los Angeles Police Department. [While] the study reveals that areas with high concentrations of adult establishments are associated with high crime rates, areas with high concentrations of adult establishments are also areas with high concentrations of adult operations, albeit each in separate establishments. It was therefore consistent with the findings of the 1977 study, and thus reasonable, for Los Angeles to suppose that a concentration of adult establishments is correlated with high crime rates because a concentration of operations in one locale draws, for example, a greater concentration of adult consumers to the neighborhood, and a high density of such consumers either attracts or generates criminal activity. [It] is rational for the city to infer that reducing the concentration of adult operations in a neighborhood, whether within separate establishments or in one large establishment, will reduce crime rates.[1]

[While] the city certainly bears the burden of providing evidence that supports a link between concentrations of adult operations and asserted secondary effects, it does not bear the burden of providing evidence that rules out every theory for the link between concentrations of adult establishments that is inconsistent with its own. [In] Renton, we specifically refused to set such a high bar, [holding instead that] a municipality may rely on any evidence that is "reasonably believed to be relevant" for demonstrating a connection between speech and a substantial, independent government interest. This is not to say that a municipality can get away with shoddy data or reasoning. The municipality's evidence must fairly support the municipality's rationale for its ordinance. If plaintiffs fail to cast direct doubt on this rationale, either by demonstrating that the municipality's evidence does not support its rationale or by furnishing evidence that disputes the municipality's factual findings, the municipality meets the standard set forth in Renton. If plaintiffs succeed in casting doubt on a municipality's rationale in either manner, the burden shifts back to the municipality to supplement the record with evidence renewing support for a theory that justifies its ordinance.

Justice Souter faults the city for relying on the 1977 study not because the study fails to support the city's theory that adult department stores, like adult minimalls, attract customers and thus crime, but because the city does not demonstrate that free-standing single-use adult establishments reduce crime. In effect, Justice Souter asks the city to demonstrate, not merely by appeal to common sense, but also with empirical data, that its ordinance will successfully lower crime. Our cases have never required that municipalities

---

[1]   The plurality left open the separate question whether Los Angeles could justify its ordinance based on another jurisdiction's finding of secondary effects where the municipality had not explicitly considered that study at the time of enacting the ordinance: "Unlike the city of Renton, the city of Los Angeles conducted its own study of adult businesses. We have concluded that the Los Angeles study provides evidence to support the city's theory that a concentration of adult operations in one locale attracts crime, and can be reasonably relied upon to demonstrate that [the ordinance] is designed to promote the city's interest in reducing crime. Therefore, the city need not present foreign studies to overcome the summary judgment against it."

make such a showing, certainly not without actual and convincing evidence from plaintiffs to the contrary.[2]

■ JUSTICE KENNEDY, concurring.

The fiction that this sort of ordinance is content neutral [is] perhaps more confusing than helpful. [These] ordinances are content based and we should call them so. Nevertheless, [the] central holding of Renton is sound: A zoning restriction that is designed to decrease secondary effects and not speech should be subject to intermediate rather than strict scrutiny. [Zoning] regulations do not automatically raise the specter of impermissible content discrimination, even if they are content based, because they have a prima facie legitimate purpose: to limit the negative externalities of land use. [The] zoning context provides a built-in legitimate rationale, which rebuts the usual presumption that content-based restrictions are unconstitutional.

[The] plurality's analysis does not address how speech will fare under the city's ordinance. As discussed, the necessary rationale for applying intermediate scrutiny is the promise that zoning ordinances like this one may reduce the costs of secondary effects without substantially reducing speech. [If] two adult businesses are under the same roof, an ordinance requiring them to separate will have one of two results: One business will either move elsewhere or close. The city's premise cannot be the latter. It is true that cutting adult speech in half would probably reduce secondary effects proportionately. But again, a promised proportional reduction does not suffice. Content-based taxes could achieve that, yet these are impermissible. The premise, therefore, must be that businesses—even those that have always been under one roof—will for the most part disperse rather than shut down." Applying this approach, Justice Kennedy found that the city's justification was credible enough to survive summary judgment: "The city may next infer—from its study and from its own experience—that two adult businesses under the same roof are no better than two next door. The city could reach the reasonable conclusion that knocking down the wall between two adult businesses does not ameliorate any undesirable secondary effects of their proximity to one another. If the city's first ordinance was justified, therefore, then the second is too. Dispersing two adult businesses under one roof is reasonably likely to cause a substantial reduction in secondary effects while reducing speech very little.

■ JUSTICE SOUTER, with whom JUSTICES STEVENS, and GINSBURG join, dissenting.

[Z]oning of businesses based on their sales of expressive adult material receives mid-level scrutiny, even though it raises a risk of content-based restriction. [Adult] speech refers not merely to sexually explicit content, but to speech reflecting a favorable view of being explicit about sex and a favorable view of the practices it depicts; a restriction on adult content is thus also a restriction turning on a particular viewpoint, of which the government may disapprove. This risk of viewpoint discrimination is subject to a relatively simple safeguard, however. If combating secondary effects of property devaluation and crime is truly the reason for the regulation, it is possible to show by empirical evidence that the effects exist, that they are

---

[2]   Justice SCALIA joined the plurality's decision, but wrote a brief concurrence reiterating his view that, "[a]s I have said elsewhere, [in] a case such as this [a] 'secondary effects' analysis [is] quite unnecessary. The Constitution does not prevent those communities that wish to do so from regulating, or indeed entirely suppressing, the business of pandering sex."

caused by the expressive activity subject to the zoning, and that the zoning can be expected either to ameliorate them or to enhance the capacity of the government to combat them, [without] suppressing the expressive activity itself. [The] weaker the demonstration of facts distinct from disapproval of the "adult" viewpoint, the greater the likelihood that nothing more than condemnation of the viewpoint drives the regulation.

[Requiring] empirical justification of claims about property value or crime is not demanding anything Herculean. [These] harms can be shown by police reports, crime statistics, and studies of market value, all of which are within a municipality's capacity or available from the distilled experiences of comparable communities. [And] precisely because this sort of evidence is readily available, reviewing courts need to be wary when the government appeals, not to evidence, but to an uncritical common sense [to] justify such a zoning restriction. [Common] sense is [not] always illegitimate in First Amendment demonstration. [But] we must be careful about substituting common assumptions for evidence, when the evidence is as readily available as public statistics and municipal property valuations, lest we find out when the evidence is gathered that the assumptions are highly debatable. [In] this case [the] government has not shown that bookstores containing viewing booths, isolated from other adult establishments, increase crime or produce other negative secondary effects in surrounding neighborhoods, and we are thus left without substantial justification for viewing the city's First Amendment restriction as [not] simply content based. By the same token, the city has failed to show any causal relationship between the breakup policy and elimination or regulation of secondary effects.

[Justice Breyer also joined the following portion of the dissent:] [The] plurality overlooks a key distinction between the zoning regulations at issue in Renton and Young [and those at issue in Los Angeles'] breakup requirement. In [Renton and Young],[the] limitations on location required no further support than the factual basis tying location to secondary effects; the zoning approved in those two cases had no effect on the way the owners of the stores carried on their adult businesses beyond controlling location. [The] Los Angeles ordinance, however, does impose a heavier burden, and one lacking any demonstrable connection to the interest in crime control. The city no longer accepts businesses as their owners choose to conduct them within their own four walls, but bars a video arcade in a bookstore, a combination shown by the record to be commercially natural, if not universal. [Since] the city presumably does not wish merely to multiply adult establishments, it makes sense to ask what offsetting gain the city may obtain from its new breakup policy. The answer may lie in the fact that two establishments in place of one will entail two business overheads in place of one: two monthly rents, two electricity bills, two payrolls. Every month business will be more expensive than it used to be, perhaps even twice as much. That sounds like a good strategy for driving out expressive adult businesses. It sounds, in other words, like a policy of content-based regulation.

ZONING LAWS AND SECONDARY EFFECTS

1. *Is sexually explicit speech different?* Is the "secondary effects" reasoning the Supreme Court embraced in Renton confined to laws

regulating sexually explicit materials? If so, is that because, as Justice Stevens insisted all along, they involve a "lower value" kind of speech? Consider the implications of the distinction between content regulation and secondary effects regulation as it might pertain to "full value" communication. May a city, in order to preserve tranquility in the park, restrict all "inflammatory" speeches, regardless of the point of view expressed? May a state, in order to prevent bodily injury, restrict all discussions of violence? May a city bar all political rallies to prevent the accumulation of litter? Are these content regulations or secondary effects regulations? Does it matter whether the effects the law aims at depend upon the listener's cognitive response or are distinct from listener response? Are not most content regulations premised ultimately on "secondary effects" of the communication in the sense of listener response? For a case limiting the "secondary effects" reasoning of Renton by declining to extend it in the context of political speech, see Boos v. Barry, p. 248.

2. *Empirical evidence of secondary effects.* What level of specificity is needed for the empirical evidence by which a government justifies its finding of adverse secondary effects resulting from adult businesses? In Alameda Books, the Court failed to reach a majority consensus on the standard for determining whether an ordinance serves a substantial government interest under Renton. Must a city provide conclusive empirical proof that crime or other social harms emanate from adult establishments? Must it prove that such harms are attributable solely to those establishments? Should legislatures be able to rely on the experiences of other similarly situated governments?

––––––––

CHILD PORNOGRAPHY

Although the Supreme Court has invalidated substantial bans on adult pornography, it has been much more deferential to legislators' attempts to regulate pornography involving minors. The Court has held that the state's unique interest in protecting children from sexual abuse justifies prohibitions against both the actual production of child pornography and the possession of it by consumers, whether or not the pornography is technically "obscene." While Chaplinsky listed a series of traditionally protected speech categories, such as libel or fighting words, child pornography stands out as a rare instance in the last several decades in which the Supreme Court has recognized a new category of unprotected speech.

––––––––

New York v. Ferber
458 U.S. 747, 102 S. Ct. 3348, 73 L. Ed. 2d 1113 (1982).

[Ferber, the owner of a bookstore specializing in sexually oriented products, was convicted under § 263.15 of the New York Penal Law for selling two films devoted almost exclusively to depicting young boys masturbating. The provision stated: "A person is guilty of promoting a sexual performance by a child when, knowing the character and content thereof, he produces, directs or promotes any performance which includes sexual conduct by a child less than sixteen years of age." Another section of the law defined "sexual conduct" as "actual or simulated sexual intercourse, deviate sexual intercourse, sexual bestiality, masturbation, sadomasochistic abuse, or lewd exhibition of the genitals." The law prohibited the distribution of material depicting children engaged in sexual conduct; it did not require that the material be legally obscene.]

■ JUSTICE WHITE delivered the opinion of the Court.

This case [constitutes] our first examination of a statute directed at and limited to depictions of sexual activity involving children.[1] We believe our inquiry should begin with the question of whether a State has somewhat more freedom in proscribing works which portray sexual acts or lewd exhibitions of genitalia by children [than in regulating obscenity].

In Chaplinsky v. New Hampshire, the Court laid the foundation for the excision of obscenity from the realm of constitutionally protected expression. [Embracing] this judgment, the Court squarely held in [Roth] that "obscenity is not within the area of constitutionally protected speech or press." Throughout this period, we recognized "the inherent dangers of undertaking to regulate any form of expression." [Miller.] The Miller standard, like its predecessors, was an accommodation between the State's interests in protecting the "sensibilities of unwilling recipients" from exposure to pornographic material and the dangers of censorship inherent in unabashedly content-based laws. Like obscenity statutes, laws directed at the dissemination of child pornography run the risk of suppressing protected expression by allowing the hand of the censor to become unduly heavy. For the following reasons, however, we are persuaded that the States are entitled to greater leeway in the regulation of pornographic depictions of children.

First. It is evident [that] a state's interest in safeguarding the physical and psychological well being of a minor" is "compelling." The prevention of sexual exploitation and abuse of children constitutes a government objective of surpassing importance. [The] legislative judgment [is] that the use of children as subjects of pornographic materials is harmful to the physiological, emotional, and mental health of the [child].

Second. The distribution of photographs and films depicting sexual activity by juveniles is intrinsically related to the sexual abuse of children in at least two ways. First, the materials produced are a permanent record of the children's participation and the harm to the child is exacerbated by their circulation. Second, the distribution network for child pornography must be closed if the production of material which requires the sexual exploitation of children is to be effectively controlled. [Ferber argues] that it is enough for the State to prohibit the distribution of materials that are legally obscene under the Miller test. While some States may find that this approach properly accommodates [their interests], it does not follow that the First Amendment prohibits a State from going further. The Miller [standard] does not reflect the State's particular and more compelling interest in prosecuting

---

[1]   Justice White had noted earlier that, "[i]n recent years, the exploitive use of children in the production of pornography has become a serious national problem." The federal government and 47 states had enacted statutes "specifically directed at the production of child pornography." At least half of these did not require "that the materials produced be legally obscene." Moreover, 35 states and Congress had passed legislation prohibiting the distribution of such materials. Twenty of these states prohibited the distribution of material depicting children engaged in sexual conduct without requiring that the material be legally obscene. New York was one of these 20 states. (The laws in the other 15 states, as well as the federal law, prohibited the dissemination of such material only if it was obscene.)

those who promote the sexual exploitation of children. [E.g.,] a work which, taken on the whole, contains serious literary, artistic, political, or scientific value may nevertheless embody the hardest core of child pornography. "It is irrelevant to the child [who has been abused] whether or not the material has a literary, artistic, political, or [social value]."

Third. The advertising and selling of child pornography provides an economic motive for and is thus an integral part of the production of such materials, an activity illegal throughout the nation. "It rarely has been suggested that the constitutional freedom for speech and press extends its immunity to speech or writing used as an integral part of conduct in violation of a valid criminal statute." We note that were the statutes outlawing the employment of children in these films and photographs fully effective, and the constitutionality of these laws have not been questioned, the First Amendment implications would be no greater than that presented by laws against distribution: enforceable production laws would leave no child pornography to be marketed.

Fourth. The value of permitting live performances and photographic reproductions of children engaged in lewd sexual conduct is exceedingly modest, if not de minimis. We consider it unlikely that visual depictions of children performing sexual acts or lewdly exhibiting their genitals would often constitute an important and necessary part of a literary performance or scientific or educational work. [If] it were necessary for literary or artistic value, a person over the statutory age who perhaps looked younger could be utilized. Simulation outside of the prohibition of the statute could provide another alternative. Nor is there any question here of censoring a particular literary theme or portrayal of sexual activity. The First Amendment interest is limited to that of rendering the portrayal somewhat more 'realistic' by utilizing or photographing children.

Fifth. Recognizing and classifying child pornography as a category of material outside the protection of the First Amendment is not incompatible with our earlier decisions. [See American Mini Theatres and, e.g., Chaplinsky; Beauharnais.] [Thus], it is not rare that a content-based classification of speech has been accepted because it may be appropriately generalized that within the confines of the given classification, the evil to be restricted so overwhelmingly outweighs the expressive interests, if any, at stake, that no process of case-by-case adjudication is [required].

There are, of course, limits on the category of child pornography which, like obscenity, is unprotected by the First Amendment. As with all legislation in this sensitive area, the conduct to be prohibited must be adequately defined by the applicable state law, as written or authoritatively construed. [The] test for child pornography is separate from the obscenity standard enunciated in Miller, but may be compared to it for purpose of clarity. The Miller formulation is adjusted in the following respects: A trier of fact need not find that the material appeals to the prurient interest of the average person; it is not required that sexual conduct portrayed be done so in a patently offensive manner; and the material at issue need not be considered as a whole.

[The law's] prohibition incorporates a definition of sexual conduct that comports with the above-stated principles. [We] hold that § 263.15 sufficiently describes a category of material the production and distribution of which is not entitled to First Amendment protection. It is therefore clear that there is nothing unconstitutionally "underinclusive" about a statute that singles out this category of material for proscription. It also follows that the State is not barred by the First Amendment from prohibiting the distribution of unprotected materials produced outside the State.

■ JUSTICE O'CONNOR, concurring.

Although I join the Court's opinion, I write separately to stress that the Court does not hold that New York must except "material with serious literary, scientific, or educational value" from its statute. The Court merely holds that, even if the First Amendment shelters such material, New York's current statute is not sufficiently overbroad to support respondent's facial attack. The compelling interests identified in today's opinion suggest that the Constitution might in fact permit New York to ban knowing distribution of works depicting minors engaged in explicit sexual conduct, regardless of the social value of the depictions. For example, a 12-year-old child photographed while masturbating surely suffers the same psychological harm whether the community labels the photograph "edifying" or "tasteless." The audience's appreciation of the depiction is simply irrelevant to New York's asserted interest in protecting children from psychological, emotional, and mental harm.

■ JUSTICE BRENNAN, joined by JUSTICE MARSHALL, concurring in the judgment.

I agree with much of what is said in the Court's opinion. [But] in my view application of § 263.15 or any similar statute to depictions of children that in themselves do have serious literary, artistic, scientific, or medical value, would violate the First Amendment. As the Court recognizes, the limited classes of speech, the suppression of which does not raise serious First Amendment concerns, have two attributes. They are of exceedingly "slight social value," and the State has a compelling interest in their regulation. See [Chaplinsky v. New Hampshire]. The First Amendment value of depictions of children that are in themselves serious contributions to art, literature, or science, is, by definition, simply not "de minimis." At the same time, the State's interest in suppression of such materials is likely to be far less compelling. For the Court's assumption of harm to the child resulting from the "permanent record" and "circulation" of the child's "participation" lacks much of its force where the depiction is a serious contribution to art or science. [In] short, it is inconceivable how a depiction of a child that is itself a serious contribution to the world of art or literature or science can be deemed "material outside the protection of the First Amendment."

■ [JUSTICE STEVENS submitted a separate opinion concurring only in the judgment and JUSTICE BLACKMUN simply noted his concurrence in the result.]

CHILD PORNOGRAPHY AS UNPROTECTED SPEECH

1. *The Court's methodology in Ferber.* On its face, the majority's analysis suggests that Ferber is a rare modern case in the tradition of the Chaplinsky exclusionary categorization approach: the majority simply casts outside the First Amendment the entire class of child pornography, even though the class concededly includes materials not "obscene." But that technique produces vastly more discussion in this case than it had in

Chaplinsky, and the Court also draws on a variety of other First Amendment techniques. In contrast to the Chaplinsky approach, the majority speaks at length not only about the limited social value of the communication involved but also, and most notably, about the state interests justifying restraint. So seen, Ferber is a core example of the "definitional balancing" technique involved in New York Times v. Sullivan. See Schauer, "Codifying the First Amendment: New York v. Ferber," 1982 Sup. Ct. Rev. 285 (noting that "Ferber can be viewed as partially relying on [a] 'covered but outweighed' path to nonprotection" and adds that defamation cases provide one of the closest parallels to the Ferber methodology). Note too that Justice White, in examining the First Amendment side of the balance, finds the value of child pornography "exceedingly modest, if not de minimis" by stating that child pornography does not constitute "an important and necessary part of a literary performance or scientific or educational work." Does that mark a departure from prior analyses? Does a work have to be "necessary" to literary expression to qualify for First Amendment protection?

2. ***Possession of child pornography.*** In **Osborne v. Ohio**, 495 U.S. 103 (1990), Stanley v. Georgia was held inapplicable to child pornography, with the effect of allowing the mere possession of child pornography to be made unlawful. Justice WHITE's majority opinion concluded that the same interests in eliminating the entire chain of distribution that justified the result in Ferber also justified eliminating the demand by criminalizing possession of child pornography. The Court also rejected Osborne's overbreadth challenge to the Ohio law. Although the law on its face barred the possession of "nude" photographs and although simple depictions of nudity cannot be proscribed, Justice White relied on the fact that the state courts had limited the reach of the law to cases in which "such nudity constitutes a lewd exhibition or involves a graphic focus on the genitals, and where the person depicted is neither the child nor the ward of the person charged." Because of the lack of instructions on lewdness at trial, however, the conviction was reversed on due process grounds and remanded for a new trial. Justice BRENNAN dissented, joined by Justices Marshall and Stevens. The dissent emphasized the statute's overbreadth and suggested that the narrowing state court construction was an insufficient guarantee that the law would not be applied to material as innocuous as the "well-known commercial advertisement for a suntan lotion show[ing] a dog pulling the bottom half of a young girl's bikini." The dissent also objected to the failure to extend Stanley to child pornography.

3. ***Virtual child pornography and proximate harm.*** In **Ashcroft v. Free Speech Coalition**, 535 U.S. 234 (2002), at p. 441 the Supreme Court clarified that the harm justifying a flat ban on child pornography is the direct harm to children in the production of pornographic materials, rather than the more attenuated harm to children from subsequent actions by consumers. The case involved a challenge to the Child Pornography Prevention Act of 1996, which extended the federal prohibition against child pornography to sexually explicit images that appear to depict minors but are produced without using any real children, either by using adults who look like minors or by using computer imaging. Justice KENNEDY's majority opinion noted that Ferber had upheld a total ban on child pornography only "[w]here the images are themselves the product of child sexual abuse. [The] production of the work, not its content, was the target of the statute. In contrast to the speech in Ferber, speech that itself is the record of sexual abuse, the CPPA prohibits speech that records no crime and creates no

victims by its production. Virtual child pornography is not 'intrinsically related' to the sexual abuse of children, as were the materials in Ferber. While the Government asserts that the images can lead to actual instances of child abuse, the causal link is contingent and indirect. The harm does not necessarily follow from the speech, but depends upon some unquantified potential for subsequent criminal acts. [Without] a significantly stronger, more direct connection, the Government may not prohibit speech on the ground that it may encourage pedophiles to engage in illegal conduct." Concurring, Justice THOMAS kept open the possibility that bans on virtual child pornography may become legitimate once advancing imaging technologies rendered virtual pornography so indistinguishable from live pornography that protected status would make it "impossible to enforce actual child pornography laws."

SECTION 6. SPEECH IN NEW MEDIA

In several key cases, the Court has addressed the special First Amendment concerns raised by successive advances in communications technology, from broadcast radio to cable to the internet. Technological advances have opened up a number of new possibilities for both self-expression and for the consumption of speech. Mass communication media like radio and television have allowed speakers to reach broader audiences than ever before. Cheap and private communication technologies, from home videos to the internet, have proliferated niche markets for expression and entertainment. Digital imaging tools have allowed artists and filmmakers to create ever more convincing simulations of reality without encountering the many legal and practical hurdles faced by traditional producers. Finally, potentially anonymous communications tools like the internet have allowed speakers to engage in increasingly controversial speech without fear of attribution or detection.

Do the new expressive possibilities of technology today require a new approach to the freedom of speech? How much weight should we attach to the unprecedented power of communications media to reach unsuspecting audiences or to harm listeners? Is there a place for something like a secondary effects doctrine for online speech? Should the Court protect community moral standards against the intrusions of new communications media or will moral standards change to accommodate the new possibilities for expression today?

INDECENT AND SEXUAL SPEECH IN NEW MEDIA

The Court has considered several restrictions on sexually explicit but not obscene communications over communications media that have vastly expanded the power of such expressions to reach broader and sometimes unwilling audiences—both minors and adults. These decisions follow a pattern similar to that in the zoning cases: outright bans are invalidated but some partial regulations are upheld. In the decisions that follow, note that Justice Stevens's theory that indecent speech should explicitly be assigned low First Amendment value again falls short of capturing a majority of the Court. What is the alternative rationale for regulation in these cases?

FCC v. Pacifica Foundation

438 U.S. 726, 98 S. Ct. 3026, 57 L. Ed. 2d 1073 (1978).

[Pacifica arose from a mid-afternoon weekday broadcast by a New York radio station of a twelve-minute monologue called "Filthy Words" by comedian George Carlin. Carlin satirized "the words you couldn't say on the public, ah, airwaves, um, the ones you definitely wouldn't say, ever," especially the "original" seven dirty words: "shit, piss, fuck, cunt, cocksucker, motherfucker, and tits." Carlin repeated these words in a variety of colloquialisms. The monologue was aired as part of a program on contemporary attitudes toward the use of language. Immediately before the broadcast, the station had advised listeners that it would include "sensitive language which might be regarded as offensive to some." The FCC received a complaint from a man who stated that he had heard the broadcast while driving with his young son. In response, the FCC issued a Declaratory Order granting the complaint and holding that Pacifica could be subject to future administrative sanctions. The FCC explained that Carlin's "patently offensive," though not obscene, language should be regulated by principles analogous to those found in the law of nuisance where the "law generally speaks to *channeling* behavior more than actually prohibiting it." Later, the FCC explained that its regulation of certain words depicting sexual and excretory activity was designed to channel them "to times of day when children most likely would not be exposed." The Court of Appeals overturned the FCC Order.

Justice STEVENS, writing for the majority, found that the governing statute's prohibition of "censorship" by the FCC did not limit the Commission's authority to impose sanctions "on licensees who engage in obscene, indecent, or profane broadcasting," found Carlin's monologue "indecent" within the meaning of the statute, and rejected Pacifica's argument that "indecent" broadcasts should be limited to those that were "obscene." He also wrote for the majority in part IV(C) of his opinion, below, noting the special problems of the broadcast medium. But in part IV(B) of his opinion, below, Justice Stevens wrote only for himself, Chief Justice Burger and Justice Rehnquist.]

IV(B).   [The] question in this case is whether a broadcast of patently offensive words dealing with sex and excretion may be regulated because of its content. [T]he fact that society may find speech offensive is not a sufficient reason for suppressing it. Indeed, if it is the speaker's opinion that gives offense, that consequence is a reason for according it constitutional protection. [If] there were any reason to believe that the Commission's characterization of the Carlin monologue as offensive could be traced to its political content—or even to the fact that it satirized contemporary attitudes about four letter words[1]—First Amendment protection might be required. But that is simply not this case. These words offend for the same reasons

---

[1]   The monologue does present a point of view; it attempts to show that the words it uses are "harmless" and that our attitudes toward them are "essentially silly." The Commission objects, not to this point of view, but to the way in which it is expressed. The belief that these words are harmless does not necessarily confer a First Amendment privilege to use them while proselytizing, just as the conviction that obscenity is harmless does not license one to communicate that conviction by the indiscriminate distribution of an obscene leaflet. [Footnote by Justice Stevens.]

that obscenity offends. Their place in the hierarchy of First Amendment values was aptly sketched by Mr. Justice Murphy [in Chaplinsky].

Although these words ordinarily lack literary, political, or scientific value, they are not entirely outside the protection of the First Amendment. Some uses of even the most offensive words are unquestionably protected. Indeed, we may assume, arguendo, that this monologue would be protected in other contexts. Nonetheless, the constitutional protection accorded to a communication containing such patently offensive sexual and excretory language need not be the same in every context. It is a characteristic of speech such as this that both its capacity to offend and its "social value" [Chaplinsky] [vary] with the circumstances. Words that are commonplace in one setting are shocking in another. To paraphrase [Justice] Harlan, one occasion's lyric is another's vulgarity. Cf. [Cohen]. In this case it is undisputed that the content of Pacifica's broadcast was "vulgar," "offensive," and "shocking." Because content of that character is not entitled to absolute constitutional protection under all circumstances, we must consider its context in order to determine whether the Commission's action was constitutionally permissible.

IV(C).   We have long recognized that each medium of expression presents special First Amendment problems. And of all forms of communication, it is broadcasting that has received the most limited First Amendment protection. [The] reasons for these distinctions are complex, but two have relevance to the present case. First, the broadcast media have established a uniquely pervasive presence in the lives of all Americans. Patently offensive, indecent material presented over the airwaves confronts the citizen, not only in public, but also in the privacy of the home, where the individual's right to be let alone plainly outweighs the First Amendment rights of an intruder. Because the broadcast audience is constantly tuning in and out, prior warnings cannot completely protect the listener or viewer from unexpected program content. To say that one may avoid further offense by turning off the radio when he hears indecent language is like saying that the remedy for an assault is to run away after the first blow. One may hang up on an indecent phone call, but that option does not give the caller a constitutional immunity or avoid a harm that has already taken place.[2]

Second, broadcasting is uniquely accessible to children, even those too young to read. Although Cohen's written message might have been incomprehensible to a first grader, Pacifica's broadcast could have enlarged a child's vocabulary in an instant. Other forms of offensive expression may be withheld from the young without restricting the expression at its source. Bookstores and motion picture theaters, for example, may be prohibited from making indecent material available to children. [Ginsberg v. New York, 390 U.S. 676 (1968)[3]]. The ease with which children may obtain access to

---

[2]   Outside the home, the balance between the offensive speaker and the unwilling audience may sometimes tip in favor of the speaker, requiring the offended listener to turn away. See [Erznoznik and Cohen]. [Footnote by Justice Stevens.]

[3]   In Ginsberg, the Court upheld against First Amendment challenge a New York statute prohibiting a person from knowingly selling to a minor material "harmful to minors" where that phrase was defined to cover any description or representation of nudity, or sexual conduct that (1) predominantly appealed to the prurient interest of minors, (2) was patently offensive to prevailing standards in the adult community as a whole with respect to what is suitable material for minors, and (3) was utterly without redeeming social importance for minors. Justice BRENNAN, writing for the Court, held that it was constitutional for a state "to accord minors under 17 a more restricted right than that assured to adults."

broadcast material, coupled with the concerns recognized in Ginsberg, amply justify special treatment of indecent broadcasting.

It is appropriate [to] emphasize the narrowness of our holding. This case does not involve a two-way radio conversation between a cab driver and a dispatcher, or a telecast of an Elizabethan comedy. We have not decided that an occasional expletive in either setting would justify any sanction or, indeed, that this broadcast would justify a criminal prosecution. The [FCC's] decision rested entirely on a nuisance rationale under which context is all-important. The concept requires consideration of a host of variables. The time of day was emphasized by the [FCC]. The content of the program in which the language is used will also affect the composition of the audience, and differences between radio, television, and perhaps closed-circuit transmissions, may also be relevant. As [Justice] Sutherland wrote, a "nuisance may be merely a right thing in the wrong place—like a pig in the parlor instead of the barnyard." Euclid v. Ambler Realty Co. We simply hold that when the Commission finds that a pig has entered the parlor, the exercise of its regulatory power does not depend on proof that the pig is obscene. Reversed.

■ [JUSTICE POWELL, joined by JUSTICE BLACKMUN, wrote a separate concurrence, declining to join part IV(B) of JUSTICE STEVENS's opinion:]

[T]he Commission sought to "channel" the monologue to hours when the fewest unsupervised children would be exposed to it. [This] consideration provides strong support for the Commission's holding. The Court has recognized society's right to "adopt more stringent controls on communicative materials available to youths than on those available to adults." [The] Commission properly held that [the] language involved in this case is as potentially degrading and harmful to children as representations of many erotic acts. In most instances, the dissemination of this kind of speech to children may be limited without also limiting willing adults' access to it. [The] difficulty is that such a physical separation of the audience cannot be accomplished in the broadcast media. During most of the broadcast hours [the] broadcaster cannot reach willing adults without also reaching children. This [is] one of the distinctions between the broadcast and other media. [The] Commission was entitled to give substantial weight to this [difference].

A second difference [is] that broadcasting [comes] directly into the home, the one place where people ordinarily have the right not to be assaulted by uninvited and offensive sights and sounds. Although the First Amendment may require unwilling adults to absorb the first blow of offensive but protected speech when they are in public before they turn away, a different order of values obtains in the home. [This] is not to say, however, that the Commission has an unrestricted license to decide what speech, protected in other media, may be banned from the airwaves in order to protect unwilling adults from momentary exposure to it in their homes. Making the sensitive judgments required in these cases is not easy. But this responsibility has been reposed initially in the Commission, and its judgment is entitled to respect. [It] is said that this ruling will have the effect of "reduc[ing] the adult population [to hearing] only what is fit for children." [Butler v. Michigan, 352 U.S. 380 (1957)]. This argument is not without force. [But the] Commission's holding does not prevent willing adults from purchasing Carlin's record, from attending his performances, or indeed, from reading the transcript reprinted as an appendix to the Court's opinion. On its face, it does not prevent respondent from broadcasting the monologue during late evening hours. [On] the facts of this case, the Commission's order did not violate respondent's First Amendment rights.

[I] do not join Part IV(B), however, because I do not subscribe to the theory that the Justices of this Court are free generally to decide on the basis of its content which speech protected by the First Amendment is most "valuable" and hence deserving of the most protection, and which is less "valuable" and hence deserving of less protection. In my view, the result in this case does not turn on whether Carlin's monologue, viewed as a whole, or the words that comprise it, have more or less "value" than a candidate's campaign speech. This is a judgment for each person to make, not one for the judges to impose upon him. The result turns instead on the unique characteristics of the broadcast media, combined with society's right to protect its children from speech generally agreed to be inappropriate for their years, and with the interest of unwilling adults in not being assaulted by such offensive speech in their homes. Moreover, I doubt whether today's decision will prevent any adult who wishes to receive Carlin's message in Carlin's own words from doing so, and from making for himself a value judgment as to the merit of the message and words.

■ JUSTICE BRENNAN, with whom JUSTICE MARSHALL joins, dissenting:

For the second time in two years, see [American Mini Theatres], the Court refuses to embrace the notion, completely antithetical to basic First Amendment values, that the degree of protection the First Amendment affords protected speech varies with the social value ascribed to that speech by five Members of this Court. [Despite] our unanimous agreement that the Carlin monologue is protected speech, a majority of the Court [finds] that, on the facts of this case, the FCC is not constitutionally barred from imposing sanctions on Pacifica for its airing of the Carlin monologue. This majority apparently believes that the FCC's disapproval of Pacifica's afternoon broadcast of Carlin's "Dirty Words" recording is a permissible time, place, and manner [regulation].

"The ability of government, consonant with the Constitution, to shut off discourse solely to protect others from hearing it [is] dependent upon a showing that substantial privacy interests are being invaded in an essentially intolerable manner." [Cohen.] [But an] individual's actions in switching on and listening to communications transmitted over the public airways and directed to the public at large do not implicate fundamental privacy interests, even when engaged in within the home. Instead, [these] actions are more properly viewed as a decision to take part, if only as a listener, in an ongoing public discourse [through] communication he voluntarily admits into his home. [Moreover,] the very fact that those interests are threatened only by a radio broadcast precludes any intolerable invasion of privacy; for unlike other intrusive modes of communication, such as sound trucks, "[t]he radio can be turned off"—and with a minimum of effort. Whatever the minimal discomfort suffered by a listener who inadvertently tunes into a program he finds offensive during the brief interval before he can simply extend his arm and switch stations, [it] is surely worth the candle to preserve the broadcaster's right to send, and the right of those interested to receive, a message entitled to full First Amendment protection. To reach a contrary balance [is] clearly, to follow [Justice] Stevens' reliance on animal metaphors, "to burn the house to roast the pig."

[The] government unquestionably has a special interest in the well-being of children. [But here] the Court, for the first time, allows the government to prevent minors from gaining access to materials that are not obscene, and are therefore protected, as to them. [This] result violates [the] principle of Butler v. Michigan [that government may not] "reduce the adult population [to] reading only what is fit for children." [Taken] to their logical extreme, the [majority's] rationales would support the cleansing of public radio of any "four-letter words" whatsoever, regardless of their context. The rationales could justify the banning from radio of a myriad of literary works, novels, poems, and plays by the likes of Shakespeare, Joyce, Hemingway, Ben Jonson, Henry Fielding, Robert Burns, and Chaucer; they could support the suppression of a good deal of political speech, such as the Nixon tapes; and they could even provide the basis for imposing sanctions for the broadcast of certain portions of the Bible. [I] would place the responsibility and the right to weed worthless and offensive communications from the public airways where it belongs and where, until today, it resided: in a public free to choose those communications worthy of its attention from a marketplace unsullied by the censor's hand.

[It is no answer to suggest that] "[t]here are few, if any, thoughts that cannot be expressed by the use of less offensive language." [For a] given word may have a unique capacity to capsule an idea, evoke an emotion, or conjure up an image. Cohen. [Nor is it sufficient to suggest alternatives to hearing the broadcast, such as buying Carlin's record, for] in many cases, the medium may well be the message. [There] runs throughout the opinions of my Brothers Powell and Stevens [a] depressing inability to appreciate that in our land of cultural pluralism, there are many who think, act, and talk differently from the Members of this Court, and who do not share their fragile sensibilities. [Today's] decision will thus have its greatest impact [on] persons who do not share the Court's view as to which words or expressions are acceptable and who, for a variety of reasons, including a conscious desire to flout majoritarian conventions, express themselves using words that may be regarded as offensive by those from different socio-economic backgrounds. [The Court] confirm[s] Carlin's prescience as a social commentator by the result it reaches today.

―――――――

THE LIMITS OF PACIFICA

1. *Pacifica and "fleeting expletives."* How important to the free speech ruling in Pacifica was the fact that Carlin's monologue made deliberate, repeated, and pervasive use of sexual and excretory terms? Should the First Amendment protect the use, even in the broadcasting context, of isolated utterances of "the F- and S-words" where those words are not repeated? After U2 leader Bono used the F-word at the Golden Globe awards as an intensifier to say how "brilliant" he found his award, the FCC issued an order stating that any prior interpretations exempting the use of fleeting expletives from its indecency regulations were "no longer good law." After celebrities Cher and Nicole Richie used the F- and S-words on other live broadcasts, the FCC issued sanction orders finding those utterances indecent. The Commission reasoned that any "dichotomy between 'expletives' and 'descriptions or depictions of sexual or excretory functions' is artificial," and that "granting an automatic exemption for 'isolated or

fleeting' expletives unfairly forces viewers (including children)" to take " 'the first blow.' "

In **Federal Communications Commission v. Fox Television Stations, Inc.**, 556 U.S. 502 (2009), the Supreme Court, without reaching the question of whether such an application of the statutory ban on indecent broadcasts was constitutional under the Free Speech Clause, found by a vote of 5–4 that the FCC had not acted arbitrarily or capriciously in violation of the Administrative Procedure Act by changing its policy to extend to fleeting expletives. Justice SCALIA wrote the opinion of the Court, finding the FCC's policy change neither arbitrary nor capricious despite its exemptions for some uses of fleeting expletives such as those in the broadcast movie Saving Private Ryan. The majority opinion declined to rule on the constitutionality of the FCC's orders but noted that "any chilled references to excretory and sexual material 'surely lie at the periphery of First Amendment concern.' Pacifica."

Justice THOMAS filed a concurrence joining the Court's opinion but noting "the questionable viability" of Pacifica in light of "technological advances" that had undermined its factual assumptions: "[T]raditional broadcast television and radio are no longer the 'uniquely pervasive' media forms they once were. For most consumers, traditional broadcast media programming is now bundled with cable or satellite services. Broadcast and other video programming is also widely available over the Internet. And like radio and television broadcasts, Internet access is now often freely available over the airwaves and can be accessed by portable computer, cell phones, and other wireless devices." Justice Thomas stated that he was "open to reconsideration" of Pacifica in a future case.

Justices Stevens and Ginsburg filed dissents and Justice Breyer filed a dissent joined by Justices Stevens, Souter and Ginsburg. Justice STEVENS, the author of Pacifica, denied that Pacifica "permits the FCC to punish the broadcast of *any* expletive that has a sexual or excretory origin. [There] is a critical distinction between the use of an expletive to describe a sexual or excretory function and the use of such a word for an entirely different purpose, such as to express an emotion. [Those] words may not be polite, but that does not mean they are necessarily 'indecent.' " Justice GINSBURG wrote that "there is no way to hide the long shadow the First Amendment casts over what the Commission has done," and emphasized that "the unscripted fleeting expletives at issue here," unlike the " 'verbal shock treatment' " in the Carlin monologue in Pacifica, "are neither deliberate nor relentlessly repetitive." Justice BREYER would have found the FCC's change of policy arbitrary and capricious, and in particular faulted the FCC for failing to take into account the significant risk that local broadcasters would reduce live coverage because they were unable to afford "bleeping" technology or other costly means of complying with the FCC's new policy.

2. *Captive audiences: Pacifica's privacy invasion rationale.* Recall that in Cohen v. California (1971; p. 69 above), Justice Harlan's opinion rejected any "captive audience" rationale for restricting Cohen's speech, reasoning that government may not shield listeners from offensive speech in the public square—they must simply avert their eyes and ears. But, as Pacifica illustrates, the Court *has* allowed government to rely upon such "captive audience" rationales when applied to the home. Pacifica relied upon prior decisions including **Rowan v. U.S. Post Office Department**, 397 U.S. 728 (1970), which upheld against First Amendment challenge a

federal law permitting recipients of a "pandering advertisement" that offered for sale "matter which the addressee in his sole discretion believes to be erotically arousing or sexually provocative" to request a post office order requiring the mailer to remove his or her name from his mailing list and to stop all future mailings. The law was enacted in response to concern "with use of mail facilities to distribute unsolicited advertisements that recipients found to be offensive because of their lewd and salacious character." A mail order business claimed that the federal law violated its right to communicate.

Chief Justice BURGER's opinion found the constitutional challenge unpersuasive: "[T]he right of every person 'to be let alone' must be placed in the scales with the right of others to communicate. In today's complex society we are inescapably captive audiences for many purposes, but a sufficient measure of individual autonomy must survive to permit every householder to exercise control over unwanted mail. [Weighing] the highly important right to communicate [against] the very basic right to be free from sights, sounds and tangible matter we do not want, it seems to us that a mailer's right to communicate must stop at the mailbox of an unreceptive addressee. [In] effect the power of a householder under the statute is unlimited; he may prohibit the mailing of a dry goods catalog because he objects to the contents—or indeed the text of the language touting the merchandise. Congress provided the sweeping power not only to protect privacy but to avoid possible constitutional questions that might arise from vesting the power to make any discretionary evaluation of the material in a governmental official." Chief Justice Burger added: "If this prohibition operates to impede the flow of even valid ideas, the answer is that no one has a right to press even 'good' ideas on an unwilling recipient. That we are often 'captives' outside the sanctuary of the home and subject to objectionable speech and other sound does not mean we must be captives everywhere."

Does it matter who controls the right to opt out: government or the householder? Consider the development of the so-called "V-chip" for television. Such a device would enable parents to block selected channels or shows based on their violent content. Would a law mandating that television sets contain V-chips provide a closer analogy to Rowan than did the law in Pacifica? What if the V-chip screened out only programs rated excessively violent by a government official?

Does the "captive audience" rationale for broadcasting or cable restrictions extend beyond sexually explicit speech? Could government ban, on grounds of offensiveness or harm to children, the broadcast of political advertisements for an anti-abortion candidate that contained photographs of aborted fetuses? See Levi, "The FCC, Indecency, and Anti-Abortion Political Advertising," 3 Villanova Sports & Ent. L.J. 85 (1996).

The Court limited Rowan's "captive audience" rationale in Consolidated Edison [Con Ed.] v. Public Service Comm'n [PSC], 447 U.S. 530 (1980), which invalidated an order of the New York PSC prohibiting the inclusion in monthly electric bills of inserts that discussed controversial issues of public policy. The PSC order had barred "utilities from using bill inserts to discuss political matters, including the desirability of future development of nuclear power." The highest state court had sustained the order as protecting the privacy of the utility's customers, reasoning that they "have no choice whether to receive the insert and the views expressed in the insert may inflame their sensibilities." The Court reversed. Justice POWELL's majority opinion explained: "Even if a short exposure to Consolidated Edison's views may offend the sensibilities of some consumers, [they may] escape exposure to objectionable material simply by transferring the bill insert from envelope to wastebasket." Justice STEVENS concurred in the judgment, reiterating his "lower value speech" theory of American Mini Theatres and Pacifica, but limiting it to cases of offensiveness that is "independent[ ] of the message the speaker intends to convey."

Does the Con Ed. principle apply only to political speech? Or does it extend to sexual materials? In **Bolger v. Youngs Drug Products Corp.**, 463 U.S. 60 (1983), the Court invalidated a federal law barring the mailing of unsolicited advertisements for contraceptive products, especially condoms. One of the proffered justifications was to protect recipients from offense. The Court rejected that argument. Writing for the Court, Justice MARSHALL observed: "[We] have never held that [government] can shut off the flow of mailings to protect those recipients who might potentially be offended. The First Amendment 'does not permit the government to prohibit speech as intrusive unless the "captive" audience cannot avoid objectionable speech.' [The] 'short, regular, journey from mail box to trash can [is] an acceptable burden [so] far as the Constitution is concerned.' " Any interest in protecting children's sensibilities, he suggested, could be adequately served by parental self-help: "We can reasonably assume that parents already exercise substantial control over the disposition of mail once it enters their mailbox. [And parents] must already cope with a multitude of external stimuli that color their children's perception of sensitive subjects." The advertisements were "entirely suitable for adults. [The] level of discourse reaching a mailbox cannot be limited to that which would be suitable for a sandbox." Pacifica was distinguished on the ground that the receipt of mail is "far less intrusive and uncontrollable" than are radio and television broadcasts.

Justice REHNQUIST, joined by Justice O'Connor, concurred in the judgment. He noted the substantial governmental interest in preventing intrusion into the home, but argued that the statute here imposed an unduly large restriction in view of the extent of the intrusion. Justice STEVENS, also concurring in the judgment, took issue with the majority's "virtually complete rejection of offensiveness as a possibly legitimate justification for the suppression of speech." But he found the statute nonetheless objectionable because it prohibits "ideas, not style": by limiting information about contraception but not conception, it excluded "one advocate from a forum to which adversaries have unlimited access."

Sable Communications, Inc. v. FCC

492 U.S. 115, 117, 109 S. Ct. 2829, 2832, 106 L. Ed. 2d 93 (1989).

[Sable involved a challenge to congressional control of "sexually-oriented pre-recorded telephone messages" ("dial-a-porn" services), available on a pay-per-message basis by a telephone call initiated by the listener. In 1988, Congress amended the Communications Act of 1934 to target such services, criminally prohibiting telephone messages that were either obscene or indecent.]

■ JUSTICE WHITE delivered the opinion of the Court.

The District Court upheld the prohibition against obscene interstate telephone communications for commercial purposes, but enjoined the enforcement of the statute insofar as it applied to indecent messages. We affirm the District Court in both respects.

[Sexual] expression which is indecent but not obscene is protected by the First Amendment; and the federal parties do not submit that the sale of such materials to adults could be criminalized solely because they are indecent. The Government may, however, regulate the content of constitutionally protected speech in order to promote a compelling interest if it chooses the least restrictive means to further the articulated interest. We have recognized that there is a compelling interest in protecting the physical and psychological well-being of minors.

[In] attempting to justify the complete ban and criminalization of the indecent commercial telephone communications with adults as well as minors, the federal parties rely on FCC v. Pacifica. [Pacifica] is readily distinguishable from these cases, most obviously because it did not involve a total ban on broadcasting indecent material. [Pacifica] also relied on the "unique" attributes of broadcasting, noting that broadcasting is "uniquely pervasive," can intrude on the privacy of the home without prior warning as to program content, and is "uniquely accessible to children, even those too young to read." The private commercial telephone communications at issue here are substantially different from the public radio broadcast at issue in Pacifica. In contrast to public displays, unsolicited mailings and other means of expression which the recipient has no meaningful opportunity to avoid, the dial-it medium requires the listener to take affirmative steps to receive the communication. There is no "captive audience" problem here; callers will generally not be unwilling listeners. The context of dial-in services, where a caller seeks and is willing to pay for the communication, is manifestly different from a situation in which a listener does not want the received message. Placing a telephone call is not the same as turning on a radio and being taken by surprise by an indecent message. Unlike an unexpected outburst on a radio broadcast, the message received by one who places a call to a dial-a-porn service is not so invasive or surprising that it prevents an unwilling listener from avoiding exposure to it.

[The] federal parties nevertheless argue that the total ban on indecent commercial telephone communications is justified because nothing less could prevent children from gaining access to such messages. We find the argument quite unpersuasive. The FCC, after lengthy proceedings, determined that its credit card, access code, and scrambling rules were a satisfactory solution to the problem of keeping indecent dial-a-porn messages out of the reach of minors. [For] all we know from this record, the FCC's technological approach to restricting dial-a-porn messages to adults who seek them would be extremely effective, and only a few of the most enterprising and disobedient young people would manage to secure access to such messages.

Under our precedents, § 223(b), in its present form, has the invalid effect of limiting the content of adult telephone conversations to that which is suitable for children to hear. [Because] the statute's denial of adult access to telephone messages which are indecent but not obscene far exceeds that which is necessary to limit the access of minors to such messages, we hold that the ban does not survive constitutional scrutiny.

■ JUSTICE SCALIA, concurring.

I join the Court's opinion because I think it correct that a wholesale prohibition upon adult access to indecent speech cannot be adopted merely because the FCC's alternate proposal could be circumvented by as few children as the evidence suggests. But where a reasonable person draws the line in this balancing process—that is, how few children render the risk unacceptable—depends in part upon what mere "indecency" (as opposed to "obscenity") includes. The more narrow the understanding of what is "obscene," and hence the more pornographic what is embraced within the residual category of "indecency," the more reasonable it becomes to insist upon greater assurance of insulation from minors. [Finally,] I note that while we hold the Constitution prevents Congress from banning indecent speech in this fashion, we do not hold that the Constitution requires public utilities to carry it.

■ JUSTICE BRENNAN, with whom JUSTICES MARSHALL and STEVENS join, concurring in part and dissenting in part.

[I] have long been convinced that the exaction of criminal penalties for the distribution of obscene materials to consenting adults is constitutionally intolerable. [The] very evidence the Court adduces to show that denying adults access to all indecent commercial messages "far exceeds that which is necessary to limit the access of minors to such messages," also demonstrates that forbidding the transmission of all obscene messages is unduly heavyhanded. Because this criminal statute curtails freedom of speech far more radically than the Government's interest in preventing harm to minors could possibly license on the record before us, I would [strike] down the statute on its face.

––––––

TOTAL BANS ON INDECENT SPEECH ON CABLE AND ONLINE

1. *Indecent sexual speech and cable programming.* In light of Sable, Congress could not simply ban sexually explicit but non-obscene programming on cable television. But in **Denver Area Educational Telecommunications Consortium v. FCC**, 518 U.S. 727 (1996), the Court, in an opinion by Justice BREYER, held it lawful for the federal government, under the Cable Television Consumer Protection and Competition Act of 1992, to authorize "a cable operator to enforce prospectively a written and published policy of prohibiting programming that the cable operator reasonably believes describes or depicts sexual or excretory activities or organs in a patently offensive manner as measured by contemporary community standards." Justice Breyer reasoned that the importance of the interest in "protecting children from exposure to patently offensive depictions of sex" and "the similarity of the problem and its solution to those at issue in Pacifica" justified such a grant of discretion to cable operators. Like broadcasting, he suggested, cable programs are highly accessible to children, pervasive, and likely to confront citizens in the privacy of their homes without prior warning. Justice Breyer also distinguished Sable: "The ban at issue in Sable [was] not only a total governmentally imposed ban on a category of communications, but also involved a communications medium, telephone service, that was significantly less likely to expose children to the banned material, was less intrusive, and allowed for significantly more control over what comes into the home than either

broadcasting or the cable transmission system before us." (This portion of Justice Breyer's plurality opinion was joined by Justices Stevens, Souter, and O'Connor plus Chief Justice Rehnquist and Justices Scalia and Thomas writing separately.) In other portions of Denver Area, however, the Court invalidated provisions of the Cable Act that gave cable operators discretion over indecent programming on "leased access channels," which federal law requires cable operators to reserve for commercial use by cable programmers who are unaffiliated with the operator, and "public access channels," which federal law permits municipalities to reserve for their own public, educational, or governmental use.

    2.   *Distinguishing cable from broadcasting.* Did Denver Area mean that cable would be treated like broadcasting in subsequent cases? A negative answer to that question issued in **United States v. Playboy Entertainment Group**, 529 U.S. 803 (2000), where the Court for the first time struck down, under strict scrutiny, a law that regulated indecency on a non-broadcast medium even while falling short of a total ban. By a vote of 5–4, the Court invalidated provisions of a federal telecommunications law that required cable operators either to fully scramble sexually explicit programming or, if they were unable to do so because of "signal bleed," to confine such programming to late-night hours when children were unlikely to view it. Writing for the Court, Justice KENNEDY, joined by Justices Stevens, Souter, Thomas and Ginsburg, held the law subject to strict scrutiny on the grounds that it was content-based, and that its time-channeling requirement significantly restricted cable operators' speech even though it did not impose a complete prohibition: "The distinction between laws burdening and laws banning speech is but a matter of degree. The Government's content-based burdens must satisfy the same rigorous scrutiny as its content-based bans." He distinguished zoning cases as "irrelevant," writing that "the lesser scrutiny afforded regulations targeting the secondary effects of crime or declining property values has no application to content-based regulations targeting the primary effects of protected speech." He likewise distinguished broadcasting cases, reasoning that cable systems, unlike broadcasters, "have the capacity to block unwanted channels on a household-by-household basis," and that "targeted blocking is less restrictive than banning."

    Applying strict scrutiny, Justice Kennedy wrote: "When a plausible, less restrictive alternative is offered to a content-based speech restriction, it is the Government's obligation to prove that the alternative will be ineffective to achieve its goals. The Government has not met that burden here." He found such an alternative in a different provision of the law requiring cable operators to block undesired channels at individual households upon request, and rejected, at least without a better record, a variety of government arguments as to why such voluntary blocking might be ineffective.

    Justice THOMAS concurred separately to express the view that the government might regulate much sexual cable programming as obscene under the Miller test, but that its attempt to regulate merely indecent sexual speech on cable was not defensible. Justice SCALIA dissented on the ground that lesser scrutiny should apply to regulation of commercial trafficking in sexual speech, a proposition that Justice STEVENS disputed in a separate concurrence. Justice BREYER dissented, joined by Chief Justice Rehnquist and Justices O'Connor and Scalia. He concluded that the voluntary opt-out provision was not a *"similarly* practical and *effective* way to accomplish [the time channeling provision's] child-protecting objective," and argued for applying a First Amendment narrow tailoring standard that would afford "a degree of leeway [for] the legislature when it chooses among possible alternatives in light of predicted comparative effects."

3. ***Sexually explicit speech and the internet.*** The decisions allowing regulation of sexual speech on the broadcast media relied heavily on the assumption that television and radio broadcast technology invade privacy and repose, "pushing" unwanted sounds or images upon unwitting audiences. What is the implication of such decisions for the new medium of the internet, in which text, sounds, and images are "pulled" from their sources through the volition of the user rather than broadcast en masse? What latitude does government have to seek to prevent children from having too-ready access to sexually explicit material over the internet?

Reno v. American Civil Liberties Union
521 U.S. 844, 117 S. Ct. 2329, 138 L. Ed. 2d 874 (1997).

■ JUSTICE STEVENS delivered the opinion of the Court.

At issue is the constitutionality of two statutory provisions enacted to protect minors from "indecent" and "patently offensive" communications on the Internet. Notwithstanding the legitimacy and importance of the congressional goal of protecting children from harmful materials, we [agree] that the statute abridges "the freedom of speech" protected by the First Amendment.

[Two provisions of] the "Communications Decency Act of 1996" (CDA) [are] challenged in this case. [The "indecent transmission" provision, 47 U.S.C. § 223(a),] prohibits the knowing transmission of obscene or indecent messages to any recipient under 18 years of age. It provides in pertinent part: "(a) Whoever (1) in interstate or foreign communications . . . (B) by means of a telecommunications device knowingly (i) makes, creates, or solicits, and (ii) initiates the transmission of, any comment, request, suggestion, proposal, image, or other communication which is obscene or indecent, knowing that the recipient of the communication is under 18 years of age, regardless of whether the maker of such communication placed the call or initiated the communication; . . . [or] (2) knowingly permits any telecommunications facility under his control to be used for any activity prohibited by paragraph (1) with the intent that it be used for such activity, shall be fined [or] imprisoned not more than two years, or both."

The ["patently offensive display" provision, 47 U.S.C. § 223(d),] prohibits the knowing sending or displaying of patently offensive messages in a manner that is available to a person under 18 years of age. It provides: "(d) Whoever (1) in interstate or foreign communications knowingly (A) uses an interactive computer service to send to a specific person or persons under 18 years of age, or (B) uses any interactive computer service to display in a manner available to a person under 18 years of age, any comment, request, suggestion, proposal, image, or other communication that, in context, depicts or describes, in terms patently offensive as measured by contemporary community standards, sexual or excretory activities or organs, regardless of whether the user of such service placed the call or initiated the communication; or (2) knowingly permits any telecommunications facility under such person's control to be used for an activity prohibited by paragraph (1) with the intent that it be used for such activity, shall be fined [or] imprisoned not more than two years, or both." The breadth of these prohibitions is qualified by two affirmative defenses.[1]

The judgment of the District Court enjoins the Government from enforcing the prohibitions in § 223(a)(1)(B) insofar as they relate to "indecent" communications, but expressly preserves the Government's right to investigate and prosecute the obscenity or child pornography activities prohibited therein. The injunction against enforcement of §§ 223(d)(1) and (2) is unqualified because those provisions contain no separate reference to obscenity or child pornography. [We] conclude that the judgment should be affirmed.

In arguing for reversal, the Government [relies upon] Ginsberg v. New York, 390 U.S. 629 (1968); Pacifica; Renton. A close look at these cases, however, raises—rather than relieves—doubts concerning the constitutionality of the CDA. In Ginsberg, we upheld the constitutionality of a New York statute that prohibited selling to minors under 17 years of age material that was considered obscene as to them even if not obscene as to adults. [But] the statute upheld in Ginsberg was narrower than the CDA. First, we noted in Ginsberg that "the prohibition against sales to minors does not bar parents who so desire from purchasing the magazines for their children." Under the CDA, by contrast, neither the parents' consent—nor even their participation—in the communication would avoid the application of the statute. Second, the New York statute applied only to commercial transactions, whereas the CDA contains no such limitation. Third, the New York statute cabined its definition of material that is harmful to minors with the requirement that it be "utterly without redeeming social importance for minors." The CDA fails to provide us with any definition of the term "indecent" [and] omits any requirement that the "patently offensive" material covered by § 223(d) lack serious literary, artistic, political, or scientific value. Fourth, the New York statute defined a minor as a person under the age of 17, whereas the CDA, in applying to all those under 18 years, includes an additional year of those nearest majority.

[There] are significant differences between the order upheld in Pacifica and the CDA. First, the order in Pacifica, issued by an agency that had been regulating radio stations for decades, targeted a specific broadcast that represented a rather dramatic departure from traditional program content in order to designate when—rather than whether—it would be permissible to air such a program in that particular medium. The CDA's broad categorical prohibitions are not limited to particular times and are not dependent on any evaluation by an agency familiar with the unique characteristics of the Internet. Second, unlike the CDA, the Commission's declaratory order was not punitive; we expressly refused to decide whether

---

[1]   [47 U.S.C.] § 223(e)(5) provides: (5) It is a defense to a prosecution under subsection (a)(1)(B) or (d) of this section, or under subsection (a)(2) of this section with respect to the use of a facility for an activity under subsection (a)(1)(B) of this section that a person (A) has taken, in good faith, reasonable, effective, and appropriate actions under the circumstances to restrict or prevent access by minors to a communication specified in such subsections, which may involve any appropriate measures to restrict minors from such communications, including any method which is feasible under available technology; or (B) has restricted access to such communication by requiring use of a verified credit card, debit account, adult access code, or adult personal identification number. [Footnote by Justice Stevens.]

the indecent broadcast "would justify a criminal prosecution." Finally, the Commission's order applied to a medium which as a matter of history had "received the most limited First Amendment protection," in large part because warnings could not adequately protect the listener from unexpected program content. The Internet, however, has no comparable history. Moreover, the District Court found that the risk of encountering indecent material by accident is remote because a series of affirmative steps is required to access specific material.

In Renton, we upheld a zoning ordinance that kept adult movie theatres out of residential neighborhoods. The ordinance was aimed, not at the content of the films shown in the theaters, but rather at the "secondary effects"—such as crime and deteriorating property values—that these theaters fostered. [According] to the Government, the CDA is constitutional because it constitutes a sort of "cyberzoning" on the Internet. But the CDA applies broadly to the entire universe of cyberspace. And the purpose of the CDA is to protect children from the primary effects of "indecent" and "patently offensive" speech, rather than any "secondary" effect of such speech. Thus, the CDA is a content-based blanket restriction on speech, and, as such, cannot be "properly analyzed as a form of time, place, and manner regulation." These precedents, then, surely do not require us to uphold the CDA and are fully consistent with the application of the most stringent review of its provisions.

[Some] of our cases have recognized special justifications for regulation of the broadcast media that are not applicable to other speakers, see Red Lion Broadcasting Co. v. FCC [1969; Chapter 3]; Pacifica. In these cases, the Court relied on the history of extensive government regulation of the broadcast medium; the scarcity of available frequencies at its inception; and its "invasive" nature, see Sable. Those factors are not present in cyberspace. Neither before nor after the enactment of the CDA have the vast democratic fora of the Internet been subject to the type of government supervision and regulation that has attended the broadcast industry. Moreover, the Internet is not as "invasive" as radio or television. The District Court specifically found that "communications over the Internet do not 'invade' an individual's home or appear on one's computer screen unbidden. Users seldom encounter content 'by accident.' " It also found that "almost all sexually explicit images are preceded by warnings as to the content." We distinguished Pacifica in Sable on just this basis, [explaining that the "dial-a-porn medium] requires the listener to take affirmative steps to receive the communication."

[Finally,] unlike the conditions that prevailed when Congress first authorized regulation of the broadcast spectrum, the Internet can hardly be considered a "scarce" expressive commodity. It provides relatively unlimited, low-cost capacity for communication of all kinds, [including] not only traditional print and news services, but also audio, video, and still images, as well as interactive, real-time dialogue. Through the use of chat rooms, any person with a phone line can become a town crier with a voice that resonates farther than it could from any soapbox. Through the use of Web pages, mail exploders, and newsgroups, the same individual can become a pamphleteer. As the District Court found, "the content on the Internet is as diverse as human thought." We agree with its conclusion that our cases provide no basis for qualifying the level of First Amendment scrutiny that should be applied to this medium.

[The] Government argues that the statute is no more vague than the obscenity standard this Court established in Miller v. California. But that is not so. [The] Miller test [contains] a critical requirement that is omitted from the CDA: that the proscribed ["patently offensive"] material be "specifically defined by the applicable state law." [Moreover,] the Miller definition is limited to "sexual conduct," whereas the CDA extends also to include "excretory activities" as well as "organs" of both a sexual and excretory nature. [Each] of Miller's additional two prongs—that, taken as a whole, the material appeal to the "prurient" interest, and that it "lack serious literary, artistic, political, or scientific value"—critically limits the uncertain sweep of the obscenity definition. The [latter] requirement is particularly important because, unlike the "patently offensive" and "prurient interest" criteria, it is not judged by contemporary community standards. This "societal value" requirement, absent in the CDA, allows appellate courts to impose some limitations and regularity on the definition by setting, as a matter of law, a national floor for socially redeeming value. [In] contrast to Miller and our other previous cases, the CDA thus presents a greater threat of censoring speech that, in fact, falls outside the statute's scope. [That] danger provides further reason for insisting that the statute not be overly broad.

We are persuaded that the CDA lacks the precision that the First Amendment requires when a statute regulates the content of speech. In order to deny minors access to potentially harmful speech, the CDA effectively suppresses a large amount of speech that adults have a constitutional right to receive and to address to one another. That burden on adult speech is unacceptable if less restrictive alternatives would be at least as effective in achieving the legitimate purpose that the statute was enacted to serve.

[It] is true that we have repeatedly recognized the governmental interest in protecting children from harmful materials. But that interest does not justify an unnecessarily broad suppression of speech addressed to adults. [In] arguing that the CDA does not so diminish adult communication, the Government relies on the incorrect factual premise that prohibiting a transmission whenever it is known that one of its recipients is a minor would not interfere with adult-to-adult communication. The findings of the District Court make clear that this premise is untenable. Given the size of the potential audience for most messages, in the absence of a viable age verification process, the sender must be charged with knowing that one or more minors will likely view it.

[The] District Court found that at the time of trial existing technology did not include any effective method for a sender to prevent minors from obtaining access to its communications on the Internet without also denying access to adults. The Court found no effective way to determine the age of a user who is accessing material through e-mail, mail exploders, newsgroups, or chat rooms. As a practical matter, the Court also found that it would be prohibitively expensive for noncommercial—as well as some commercial—speakers who have Web sites to verify that their users are adults. These limitations must inevitably curtail a significant amount of adult communication on the Internet. By contrast, the District Court found that "despite its limitations, currently available user-based software suggests that a reasonably effective method by which parents can prevent their children from accessing sexually explicit and other material which parents may believe is inappropriate for their children will soon be widely available."

The breadth of the CDA's coverage is wholly unprecedented. [It] is not limited to commercial speech or commercial entities. Its open-ended prohibitions embrace all nonprofit entities and individuals posting indecent messages or displaying them on their own computers in the presence of minors. The general, undefined terms "indecent" and "patently offensive" cover large amounts of nonpornographic material with serious educational or other value. Moreover, the "community standards" criterion as applied to the Internet means that any communication available to a nation-wide audience will be judged by the standards of the community most likely to be offended by the message. [The] breadth of this content-based restriction of speech imposes an especially heavy burden on the Government to explain why a less restrictive provision would not be as effective as the CDA. It has not done so. The arguments in this Court have referred to possible alternatives such as requiring that indecent material be "tagged" in a way that facilitates parental control of material coming into their homes, making exceptions for messages with artistic or educational value, providing some tolerance for parental choice, and regulating some portions of the Internet—such as commercial web sites—differently than others, such as chat rooms. Particularly in the light of the absence of any detailed findings by the Congress, or even hearings addressing the special problems of the CDA, we are persuaded that the CDA is not narrowly tailored if that requirement has any meaning at all.

[We] agree with the District Court's conclusion that the CDA places an unacceptably heavy burden on protected speech, and that the defenses do not constitute the sort of "narrow tailoring" that will save an otherwise patently invalid unconstitutional provision. In Sable, we remarked that the speech restriction at issue there amounted to " 'burning the house to roast the pig.' " The CDA, casting a far darker shadow over free speech, threatens to torch a large segment of the Internet community.

[Finally,] the Government [argues that an] interest in fostering the growth of the Internet provides an independent basis for upholding the constitutionality of the CDA. The Government apparently assumes that the unregulated availability of "indecent" and "patently offensive" material on the Internet is driving countless citizens away from the medium because of the risk of exposing themselves or their children to harmful material. We find this argument singularly unpersuasive. [The] record demonstrates that the growth of the Internet has been and continues to be phenomenal. As a matter of constitutional tradition, in the absence of evidence to the contrary, we presume that governmental regulation of the content of speech is more likely to interfere with the free exchange of ideas than to encourage it. The interest in encouraging freedom of expression in a democratic society outweighs any theoretical but unproven benefit of censorship. [Affirmed.]

■ JUSTICE O'CONNOR, with whom CHIEF JUSTICE REHNQUIST joins, concurring in the judgment in part and dissenting in part.

I write separately to explain why I view the CDA as little more than an attempt by Congress to create "adult zones" on the Internet. [The] creation of "adult zones" is by no means a novel concept. States have long denied minors access to certain establishments frequented by adults. States have also denied minors access to speech deemed to be "harmful to minors." The Court has previously sustained such zoning laws, but only if they [succeed] in preserving adults' access while denying minors' access to the regulated speech. [The] Court has previously only considered laws that operated in the physical world, a world that with two characteristics that make it possible to create "adult zones": geography and identity. See Lessig, Reading the Constitution in Cyberspace, 45 Emory L. J. 869, 886 (1996). A minor can see an adult dance show only if he enters an establishment that provides such entertainment. And should he attempt to do so, the minor will not be able to conceal completely his identity (or, consequently, his age). Thus, the twin characteristics of geography and identity enable the establishment's proprietor to prevent children from entering the establishment, but to let adults inside.

The electronic world is fundamentally different. Because it is no more than the interconnection of electronic pathways, cyberspace allows speakers and listeners to mask their identities. [Cyberspace is also] malleable. Thus, it is possible to construct barriers in cyberspace and use them to screen for identity, making cyberspace more like the physical world and, consequently, more amenable to zoning laws. This transformation of cyberspace is already underway. Internet speakers (users who post material on the Internet) have begun to zone cyberspace itself through the use of "gateway" technology. Such technology requires Internet users to enter information about themselves—perhaps an adult identification number or a credit card number—before they can access certain areas of cyberspace, much like a bouncer checks a person's driver's license before admitting him to a nightclub. Internet users who access information have not attempted to zone cyberspace itself, but have tried to limit their own power to access information in cyberspace, much as a parent controls what her children watch on television by installing a lock box. This user-based zoning is accomplished through the use of screening software [or] browsers with screening capabilities, both of which search addresses and text for keywords that are associated with "adult" sites and, if the user wishes, blocks access to such sites. [Despite] this progress, the transformation of cyberspace is not complete. [Gateway] technology is not ubiquitous in cyberspace, and because without it "there is no means of age verification," cyberspace still remains largely unzoned—and unzoneable. User-based zoning is also in its infancy. Although the prospects for the eventual zoning of the Internet appear promising, [given] the present state of cyberspace, I agree with the Court that the "display" provision cannot pass muster. Until gateway technology is available throughout cyberspace, [a] speaker cannot be reasonably assured that the speech he displays will reach only adults because it is impossible to confine speech to an "adult zone." Thus, the only way for a speaker to avoid liability under the CDA is to refrain completely from using indecent speech. But this forced silence impinges on the First Amendment right of adults to make and obtain this speech and, for all intents and purposes, "reduces the adult population [on the internet] to reading only what is fit for children." [I thus] agree with the Court that the provisions are overbroad in that they cover any and all communications between adults and minors, regardless of how many adults might be part of the audience to the communication. [But I would] therefore sustain the "indecency transmission" and "specific person" provisions to the extent they apply to the transmission of Internet communications where the party initiating the communication knows that all of the recipients are minors.

————

ONLINE REGULATIONS AFTER RENO

1. ***Child Online Protection Act.*** In response to the Court's invalidation of the CDA, Congress made a second attempt to protect children from sexually explicit internet speech by enacting the Child Online Protection Act of 1998 ("COPA"), 112 Stat. 2681–736, codified at 47 U.S.C. § 231. COPA prohibits any person from "knowingly and with knowledge of the character of the material, in interstate or foreign commerce by means of the World Wide Web, mak[ing] any communication for commercial purposes that is available to any minor and that includes any material that is harmful to minors," which in turn is defined in § 231(a)(1) as:

> "any communication, picture, image, graphic image file, article, recording, writing, or other matter of any kind that is obscene or that (A) the average person, applying contemporary community standards, would find, taking the material as a whole and with respect to minors, is designed to appeal to, or is designed to pander to, the prurient interest; (B) depicts, describes, or represents, in a manner patently offensive with respect to minors, an actual or simulated sexual act or sexual contact, an actual or simulated normal or perverted sexual act, or a lewd exhibition of the genitals or post-pubescent female breast; and (C) taken as a whole, lacks serious literary, artistic, political, or scientific value for minors."

The statute also provides affirmative defenses: one may escape conviction by demonstrating that he "has restricted access by minors to material that is harmful to minors (A) by requiring use of a credit card, debit account, adult access code, or adult personal identification number; (B) by accepting a digital certificate that verifies age, or (C) by any other reasonable measures that are feasible under available technology." § 231(c)(1).

2. ***Ashcroft v. American Civil Liberties Union I.*** In **Ashcroft v. American Civil Liberties Union**, 535 U.S. 564 (2002), the Court rejected the argument that COPA was unconstitutional on its face simply by virtue of its use of "community standards" to identify "material that is harmful to minors." The challengers claimed that COPA's "community standards" component would effectively force all speakers on the Web to abide by the "most puritan" community's standards. Justice THOMAS wrote for a plurality of the Court, joined by Chief Justice Rehnquist, Justice Scalia and in part by Justice O'Connor. He stated that, even though Web publishers cannot control the geographic scope of the recipients of their communications, the use of "community standards" did not *by itself* "render[ ] COPA's reliance on community standards constitutionally infirm. [It] is sufficient to note that community standards need not be defined by reference to a precise geographic area. [Absent] geographic specification, a juror applying community standards will inevitably draw upon personal 'knowledge of the community or vicinage from which he comes.' [When] the scope of an obscenity statute's coverage is sufficiently narrowed by a 'serious value' prong and a 'prurient interest' prong, we have held that requiring a speaker disseminating material to a national audience to observe varying community standards does not violate the First Amendment. [Sable.] [We] do not believe that the [internet's] 'unique characteristics' justify adopting a different approach than that set forth in Hamling and Sable. If a publisher chooses to send its material into a particular community, [then] it is the publisher's responsibility to abide by that community's standards. [If] a publisher wishes for its material to be judged only by the standards of

particular communities, then it need only take the simple step of utilizing a medium that enables it to target the release of its material into those communities."

Justice O'CONNOR, concurred in part and in the judgment, stating that, given "Internet speakers' inability to control the geographic location of their audience, [adoption] of a national standard is necessary in my view for any reasonable regulation of Internet obscenity." Justice BREYER concurred in part and in the judgment, suggesting that "Congress intended the statutory word 'community' to refer to the Nation's adult community taken as a whole, not to geographically separate local areas. [To] read the statute as adopting the community standards of every locality in the United States would provide the most puritan of communities with a heckler's Internet veto affecting the rest of the Nation." Justice KENNEDY, joined by Justices Souter and Ginsburg, concurred only in the judgment: "[The] economics and technology of Internet communication differ in important ways from those of telephones and mail. Paradoxically, [it] is easy and cheap to reach a worldwide audience on the Internet, but expensive if not impossible to reach a geographic subset. A Web publisher in a community where avant garde culture is the norm may have no desire to reach a national market; he may wish only to speak to his neighbors; nevertheless, if an eavesdropper in a more traditional, rural community chooses to listen in, there is nothing the publisher can do. As a practical matter, COPA makes the eavesdropper the arbiter of propriety on the Web. [The] national variation in community standards constitutes a particular burden on Internet speech. [But] this observation '*by itself*' [does not suffice] to enjoin the Act."

Justice STEVENS dissented: "[In] its original form, the community standard provided a shield for communications that are offensive only to the least tolerant members of society. [In] the context of the Internet, however, community standards become a sword, rather than a shield. If a prurient appeal is offensive in a puritan village, it may be a crime to post it on the World Wide Web. [By] approving the use of community standards in this context, [the majority] endorses a construction of COPA that has 'the intolerable consequence of denying some sections of the country access to material, there deemed acceptable, which in others might be considered offensive to prevailing community standards of decency.' [If] the material were forwarded through the mails, as in Hamling, or over the telephone, as in Sable, the sender could avoid destinations with the most restrictive standards. [A] provider who posts material on the Internet cannot prevent it from entering any geographic community. [In] light of this fundamental difference in technologies, the rules applicable to the mass mailing of an obscene montage or to obscene dial-a-porn should not be used to judge the legality of messages on the World Wide Web."

3.   *Ashcroft v. American Civil Liberties Union II.* On remand in the case, the court of appeals affirmed on the merits the district court's previous issuance of a preliminary injunction barring enforcement of COPA pending trial on grounds of likely invalidity under the First Amendment.

This time, a 5–4 majority of the Supreme Court affirmed. In **Ashcroft v. American Civil Liberties Union**, 542 U.S. 656 (2004), Justice KENNEDY, joined by Justices Stevens, Souter, Thomas, and Ginsburg, wrote for the Court: "As the Government bears the burden of proof on the ultimate question of COPA's constitutionality, respondents must be deemed likely to prevail unless the Government has shown that respondents' proposed less restrictive alternatives are less effective than COPA. Applying that analysis, the District Court concluded that respondents were likely to prevail. That conclusion was not an abuse of discretion, because on this record there are a number of plausible, less restrictive alternatives to the statute.

"The primary alternative considered by the District Court was blocking and filtering software. Blocking and filtering software is an alternative that is less restrictive than COPA, and, in addition, likely more effective as a means of restricting children's access to materials harmful to them. [Filters] impose selective restrictions on speech at the receiving end, not universal restrictions at the source. Under a filtering regime, adults without children may gain access to speech they have a right to see without having to identify themselves or provide their credit card information. Even adults with children may obtain access to the same speech on the same terms simply by turning off the filter on their home computers. Above all, promoting the use of filters does not condemn as criminal any category of speech, and so the potential chilling effect is eliminated, or at least much diminished.

"[Filters] also may well be more effective than COPA. First, a filter can prevent minors from seeing all pornography, not just pornography posted to the Web from [the U.S.] COPA does not prevent minors from having access to [foreign] materials. [In] addition, [verification] systems may be subject to evasion and circumvention, for example by minors who have their own credit cards. Finally, filters also may be more effective because they can be applied to all forms of Internet communication, including e-mail, not just communications available via the World Wide Web. [Filtering] software, of course, is not a perfect solution to the problem of children gaining access to harmful-to-minors materials. It may block some materials that are not harmful to minors and fail to catch some that are. Whatever the deficiencies of filters, however, the Government failed to introduce specific evidence proving that existing technologies are less effective than the restrictions in COPA. In the absence of a showing as to the relative effectiveness of COPA and the alternatives proposed by respondents, it was not an abuse of discretion for the District Court to grant the preliminary injunction.

"The closest precedent on the general point is our decision in Playboy Entertainment Group, [which,] like this case, involved a content-based restriction designed to protect minors from viewing harmful materials. The choice was between a blanket speech restriction and a more specific technological solution that was available to parents who chose to implement it. Absent a showing that the proposed less restrictive alternative would not be as effective, we concluded, the more restrictive option preferred by Congress could not survive strict scrutiny. [Here] too, the Government has failed to show, at this point, that the proposed less restrictive alternative will be less effective."

Justice BREYER, joined by Chief Justice Rehnquist and Justice O'Connor, dissented, arguing that, even if strict scrutiny applied, the government had satisfied its burden of showing that no less restrictive means was available to serve the concededly compelling interest in preventing child access to sexually explicit speech on the internet: "Conceptually speaking, the presence of filtering software is not an alternative legislative approach to the problem of protecting children from exposure to commercial pornography. Rather, it is part of the status quo, i.e., the backdrop against which Congress enacted the present statute. It is always true, by definition, that the status quo is less restrictive than a new regulatory law. It is always less restrictive to do nothing than to do something. But 'doing nothing' does not address the problem Congress sought to address—namely that, despite the availability of filtering software, children were still being exposed to harmful material on the Internet.

"[Given] the existence of filtering software, does the problem Congress identified remain significant? Does the Act help to address it? [The] answers to [these] questions are clear: Filtering software, as presently available, does not solve the 'child protection' problem. It suffers from four serious inadequacies that prompted Congress to pass legislation instead of relying on its voluntary use. First, its filtering is faulty, allowing some pornographic material to pass through without hindrance. [Second,] filtering software costs money. Not every family has the $40 or so necessary to install it. Third, filtering software depends upon parents willing to decide where their children will surf the Web and able to enforce that decision. As to millions of American families, that is not a reasonable possibility. [Fourth,] software blocking lacks precision, with the result that those who wish to use it to screen out pornography find that it blocks a great deal of material that is valuable. [Thus,] Congress could reasonably conclude that a system that relies entirely upon the use of such software is not an effective system. And a law that adds to that system an age-verification screen requirement significantly increases the system's efficacy. [It thus] significantly helps to achieve a compelling congressional goal, protecting children from exposure to commercial pornography. There is no serious, practically available 'less restrictive' way similarly to further this compelling interest." Justice Scalia filed a separate dissent reiterating his view that regulation of commercial pornography ought not be subjected to strict scrutiny.

4. ***Child pornography and digital simulation of reality.*** Digital imaging technology today allows speakers to create ever more realistic depictions of fictional characters, scenes, and events. These technological tools can mitigate the risks involved in more traditional forms of speech, for example by avoiding the harms of producing violent, sexual, or otherwise graphic content. Yet they may also create greater harms in the reception of speech, by proliferating previously impractical levels of graphic expression. Consider how digital simulation affects the permissible scope of regulation of child pornography in the following case:

———————

Ashcroft v. Free Speech Coalition

535 U.S. 234, 122 S. Ct. 1389, 152 L. Ed. 2d 403 (2002).

[The Child Pornography Prevention Act of 1996 (CPPA), 18 U.S.C. § 2251, extended the federal prohibition against child pornography to sexually explicit images that appear to depict minors but are produced without using any real children, either by using adults who look like minors or by using computer imaging. Section § 2256(8)(B) prohibited "any visual depiction, including any photograph, film, video, picture, or computer or computer-generated image or picture' that 'is, or appears to be, of a minor engaging in sexually explicit conduct." Section 2256(8)(D) prohibited possession of films containing no child pornography, "if they had, at any time anywhere in the chain of distribution, been promoted or sold in a manner erroneously suggesting the presence of child pornography." The government argued that the consumption and use of even simulated child pornography could increase the incidence of sexual abuse of children.]

■ JUSTICE KENNEDY delivered the opinion of the Court.

By prohibiting child pornography that does not depict an actual child, the [CPPA] goes beyond Ferber, which distinguished child pornography from other sexually explicit speech because of the State's interest in protecting the children exploited by the production process. The CPPA [prohibits] "any visual depiction, including any photograph, film, video, picture, or computer or computer-generated image or picture," that "is, or appears to be, of a minor engaging in sexually explicit conduct." The section captures a range of depictions, sometimes called "virtual child pornography," which include computer-generated images, as well as images produced by more traditional means.

[These] images do not involve, let alone harm, any children in the production process; but Congress decided the materials threaten children in other, less direct, ways. Pedophiles might use the materials to encourage children to participate in sexual activity. [Furthermore], pedophiles might "whet their own sexual appetites" with the pornographic images, "thereby increasing the creation and distribution of child pornography and the sexual abuse and exploitation of actual children." [The] sexual abuse of a child is a most serious crime and an act repugnant to the moral instincts of a decent people. The prospect of crime, however, by itself does not justify laws suppressing protected speech. It is also well established that speech may not be prohibited because it concerns subjects offending our sensibilities. See [FCC v. Pacifica].

The CPPA prohibits speech despite its serious literary, artistic, political, or scientific value. The statute proscribes the visual depiction of an idea— that of teenagers engaging in sexual activity—that is a fact of modern society and has been a theme in art and literature throughout the ages. [William] Shakespeare created the most famous pair of teenage lovers, one of whom is just 13 years of age. See Romeo and Juliet. [Contemporary] movies pursue similar themes. [If] these films, or hundreds of others of lesser note that explore those subjects, contain a single graphic depiction of sexual activity within the statutory definition, the possessor of the film would be subject to severe punishment without inquiry into the work's redeeming value. This is inconsistent with an essential First Amendment rule: The artistic merit of a work does not depend on the presence of a single explicit scene.

Where the images are themselves the product of child sexual abuse, Ferber recognized that the State had an interest in stamping it out without regard to any judgment about its content. The production of the work, not its content, was the target of the statute. In contrast to the speech in Ferber, speech that itself is the record of sexual abuse, the CPPA prohibits speech that records no crime and creates no victims by its production. [While] the Government asserts that the images can lead to actual instances of child abuse, the causal link is contingent and indirect. The harm does not necessarily follow from the speech, but depends upon some unquantified potential for subsequent criminal acts.

[The Government] argues that the CPPA is necessary because pedophiles may use virtual child pornography to seduce children. The Government, of course, may punish adults who provide unsuitable materials to children, and it may enforce criminal penalties for unlawful solicitation. The precedents establish, however, that speech within the rights of adults to hear may not be silenced completely in an attempt to shield children from it. [The] Government cannot ban speech fit for adults simply because it may fall into the hands of children.

The Government submits further that virtual child pornography whets the appetites of pedophiles and encourages them to engage in illegal conduct. This rationale cannot sustain the provision in question. [The] government "cannot constitutionally premise legislation on the desirability of controlling a person's private thoughts." [Without] a significantly stronger, more direct connection, the Government may not prohibit speech on the ground that it may encourage pedophiles to engage in illegal conduct.

The Government next argues that its objective of eliminating the market for pornography produced using real children necessitates a prohibition on virtual images as well. [The] hypothesis is somewhat implausible. If virtual images were identical to illegal child pornography, the illegal images would be driven from the market by the indistinguishable substitutes. Few pornographers would risk prosecution by abusing real children if fictional, computerized images would suffice.

Finally, the Government says that the possibility of producing images by using computer imaging makes it very difficult for it to prosecute those who produce pornography by using real children. Experts, we are told, may have difficulty in saying whether the pictures were made by using real children or by using computer imaging. [The] argument, in essence, is that protected speech may be banned as a means to ban unprotected speech. This analysis turns the First Amendment upside down. The Government may not suppress lawful speech as the means to suppress unlawful speech. [The] Constitution requires the reverse.

[The] Government relies on an affirmative defense under the statute, which allows a defendant to avoid conviction for nonpossession offenses by showing that the materials were produced using only adults and were not otherwise distributed in a manner conveying the impression that they depicted real children. The Government raises serious constitutional difficulties by seeking to impose on the defendant the burden of proving his speech is not unlawful.

Respondents challenge § 2256(8)(D) as well. This provision bans depictions of sexually explicit conduct that are "advertised, promoted, presented, described, or distributed in such a manner that conveys the impression that the material is or contains a visual depiction of a minor engaging in sexually explicit conduct." [Even] if a film contains no sexually explicit scenes involving minors, it could be treated as child pornography if the title and trailers convey the impression that the scenes would be found in the movie. [The] Court has recognized that pandering may be relevant, as an evidentiary matter, to the question whether particular materials are obscene. Section 2256(8)(D), however, prohibits a substantial amount of speech that falls outside [the Court's previously recognized] rationale. Materials falling within the proscription are tainted and unlawful in the hands of all who receive it, though they bear no responsibility for how it was marketed, sold, or described. [Possession] is a crime even when the possessor knows the movie was mislabeled. The First Amendment requires a more precise restriction.

■ JUSTICE THOMAS, concurring in the judgment.

In my view, the Government's most persuasive [justification for CPPA] is the prosecution rationale—that persons who possess and disseminate pornographic images of real children may escape conviction by claiming that the images are computer-generated, thereby raising a reasonable doubt as to their guilt. At this time, however, the Government['s assertion of the problem is not supported by any examples of defendants] acquitted [in this fashion]. [Technology] may evolve to the point where it becomes impossible to enforce actual child pornography laws because the Government cannot prove that certain pornographic images are of real children. In the event this occurs, the Government should not be foreclosed from enacting a regulation of virtual child pornography that contains an appropriate affirmative defense or some other narrowly drawn restriction.

■ CHIEF JUSTICE REHNQUIST, joined by JUSTICE SCALIA, dissenting.

Congress has a compelling interest in ensuring the ability to enforce prohibitions of actual child pornography, and we should defer to its findings that rapidly advancing technology soon will make it all but impossible to do so. [I agree] that serious First Amendment concerns would arise were the Government ever to prosecute someone for simple distribution or possession of a film with literary or artistic value. [But the CPPA] need not be construed to reach such materials. [The statute's definition of] "sexually explicit conduct" [only] reaches "visual depictions" of: "actual or simulated . . . sexual intercourse, including genital-genital, oral-genital, anal-genital, or oral-anal, whether between persons of the same or opposite sex; . . . bestiality; . . . masturbation; . . . sadistic or masochistic abuse; . . . or lascivious exhibition of the genitals or pubic area of any person." [I] think the definition reaches only the sort of "hard core of child pornography" that we found without protection in Ferber.

---

5. ***Deep fakes.*** Since Ashcroft, new technology for creating "deep fakes" has come into existence. Such technology allows a virtually seamless merger of images of one person's face and another person's body to be created and distributed on the internet. It also allows for the manipulation of moving images so that a person can be shown to say words he or she did not in fact say. What does this suggest for the future of pornography regulation going forward? What about regulation of faked moving images, regardless of sexual content?

6. ***Social media bans.*** In **Packingham v. North Carolina**, 582 U.S. ___, 137 S. Ct. 1730 (2017), the Court considered a state law that made it a felony for a registered sex offender "to access a commercial social networking Web site where the sex offender knows that the site permits minor children to become members or to create or maintain personal Web pages." North Carolina had prosecuted over 1,000 people for violating this law, including petitioner, who was indicted after posting a statement on his personal Facebook profile about a positive experience in traffic court. Finding the law invalid on its face, Justice KENNEDY, joined by Justices Ginsburg, Breyer, Sotomayor, and Kagan, wrote: "A fundamental principle of the First Amendment is that all persons have access to places where they can speak and listen, and then, after reflection, speak and listen once more. The Court has sought to protect the right to speak in this spatial context. A basic rule, for example, is that a street or a park is a quintessential forum

for the exercise of First Amendment rights. Even in the modern era, these places are still essential venues for public gatherings to celebrate some views, to protest others, or simply to learn and inquire. While in the past there may have been difficulty in identifying the most important places (in a spatial sense) for the exchange of views, today the answer is clear. It is cyberspace—the 'vast democratic forums of the Internet' in general, Reno v. American Civil Liberties Union, and social media in particular. Seven in ten American adults use at least one Internet social networking service. One of the most popular of these sites is Facebook, the site used by petitioner leading to his conviction in this case. According to sources cited to the Court in this case, Facebook has 1.79 billion active users. This is about three times the population of North America. Social media offers relatively unlimited, low-cost capacity for communication of all kinds. On Facebook, for example, users can debate religion and politics with their friends and neighbors or share vacation photos. On LinkedIn, users can look for work, advertise for employees, or review tips on entrepreneurship. And on Twitter, users can petition their elected representatives and otherwise engage with them in a direct manner. Indeed, Governors in all 50 States and almost every Member of Congress have set up accounts for this purpose. In short, social media users employ these websites to engage in a wide array of protected First Amendment activity on topics as diverse as human thought. [The] forces and directions of the Internet are so new, so protean, and so far reaching that courts must be conscious that what they say today might be obsolete tomorrow.

"[This] case is one of the first this Court has taken to address the relationship between the First Amendment and the modern Internet. As a result, the Court must exercise extreme caution before suggesting that the First Amendment provides scant protection for access to vast networks in that medium. [Even] making the assumption that the statute is content neutral and thus subject to intermediate scrutiny, the provision cannot stand. [For] centuries now, inventions heralded as advances in human progress have been exploited by the criminal mind. [So] it will be with the Internet and social media. [The] statute here enacts a prohibition unprecedented in the scope of First Amendment speech it burdens. [By] prohibiting sex offenders from using those websites, North Carolina with one broad stroke bars access to what for many are the principal sources for knowing current events, checking ads for employment, speaking and listening in the modern public square, and otherwise exploring the vast realms of human thought and knowledge. These websites can provide perhaps the most powerful mechanisms available to a private citizen to make his or her voice heard. [It] is unsettling to suggest that only a limited set of websites can be used even by persons who have completed their sentences. Even convicted criminals—and in some instances especially convicted criminals—might receive legitimate benefits from these means for access to the world of ideas, in particular if they seek to reform and to pursue lawful and rewarding lives."

Justice ALITO, joined by Chief Justice Roberts and Justice Thomas, concurred only in the judgment: "[I] agree with the Court that [the law] violates the Free Speech Clause of the First Amendment. I cannot join the opinion of the Court, however, because of its undisciplined dicta. The Court is unable to resist musings that seem to equate the entirety of the internet with public streets and parks. And this language is bound to be interpreted by some to mean that the States are largely powerless to restrict even the most dangerous sexual predators from visiting any internet sites, including, for example, teenage dating sites and sites designed to permit minors to discuss personal problems with their peers. [The] State's interest in protecting children from recidivist sex offenders plainly applies to internet use. [It] is not enough, however, that the law before us is designed to serve a compelling state interest; it also must not 'burden substantially more speech than is necessary to further the government's legitimate interests.' The North Carolina law fails this requirement." Justice Gorsuch did not participate.

7. *Newer media*. Further questions are raised by the emergence of highly-regulated social media platforms. Does the existence of private content regulation reduce the need for government regulation? Is it all the more necessary for the government to not regulate alternative platforms? In general, how does the advent of social media, also called Internet 3.0, change your understanding of the First Amendment? Does the more active regulation by European states, which tends to require platforms to respect privacy to a greater degree, influence that understanding?

A doctrinal problem not yet resolved involves private users blocking others from accessing social media accounts or channels they control. In **Knight First Amendment Inst. at Columbia Univ. v. Trump**, 302 F. Supp. 3d 541 (S.D.N.Y. 2018), Judge Buchwald ruled that President Donald Trump's blocking of Twitter users from his feed violated the First Amendment. Buchwald held that the Twitter feed constituted a designated public forum because it was an " 'interactive space' where users may directly engage with the content of the President's tweets." Blocking users because their tweets disagreed with or criticized the president thus "constitute[d] viewpoint discrimination that violates the First Amendment." The question of whether Twitter is a limited public forum is discussed further at p. 345.

Further issues arise with regard to a private media platform's regulation of its own user base. Following the "Unite the Right" rally that took place in August 2017, Twitter banned a number of high-profile white-supremacist accounts from the platform. One such banned user sued Twitter, raising a free speech claim, among others. See Johnson v. Twitter, Inc., No. 18CECG00078 (Cal. Super. Ct. June 6, 2018). In Johnson, the district court granted Twitter's motion to dismiss. As a private sector company, the court reasoned, Twitter's "choice not to allow certain speech is a right protected by the First Amendment." [Note that the issue of compelled access to other's private property for speech purposes is discussed at p. 488.]

In **Sandvig v. Sessions**, 315 F. Supp. 3d 1 (D.D.C. 2018), the D.C. District Court considered whether researchers can be prosecuted under the Computer Fraud and Abuse Act (CFAA) for violating a platform's terms of service when the researchers test whether the platform discriminates based on various legally-protected traits. While dismissing plaintiffs claims that the statute was facially overbroad or impermissibly vague, the court held the plaintiffs had stated a valid First Amendment claim against the law as applied to them. The court viewed receiving information from the websites and as well as publishing the results as protected First Amendment activity.

VIOLENT SPEECH IN NEW MEDIA

The proliferation of cheap and private communications technology has led to the rise of increasingly specialized, clandestine markets for speech. Many of these markets involve violence, cruelty, or other behavior considered offensive by more mainstream audiences. The Court has not designated any category of speech "unprotected" since Ferber placed child pornography outside the reach of the First Amendment in 1982. Are there other categories of speech so presumptively injurious and lacking in social value that they may be deemed similarly unprotected?

———

United States v. Stevens

559 U.S. 460, 130 S. Ct. 1577, 176 L. Ed. 2d 435 (2010).

[18 U.S.C. § 48 criminalized the commercial creation, sale, or possession of any visual or auditory depiction "in which a living animal is intentionally maimed, mutilated, tortured, wounded, or killed," if that conduct violates federal or state law where "the creation, sale, or possession takes place," unless the depiction has "serious religious, political, scientific, educational, journalistic, historical, or artistic value." While the legislative history focused primarily on "crush videos," which show torture and killing of helpless animals to appeal to a sexual fetish, the statute's text was not limited to such videos. Stevens challenged his indictment for distributing videos of dogfighting, which is unlawful in all 50 States and the District of Columbia.]

■ CHIEF JUSTICE ROBERTS delivered the opinion of the Court.

From 1791 to the present, [this Court has recognized several] "well-defined and narrowly limited classes of speech, the prevention and punishment of which have never been thought to raise any Constitutional problem." Chaplinsky.

The Government argues that "depictions of animal cruelty" should be added to the list. [We] are unaware of any [tradition] excluding depictions of animal cruelty from "the freedom of speech" codified in the First Amendment, and the Government points us to none. The Government contends [that] categories of speech may be exempted from the First Amendment's protection without any long-settled tradition of subjecting that speech to regulation. [The] Government thus proposes that a claim of categorical exclusion should be considered under a simple balancing test: "Whether a given category of speech enjoys First Amendment protection depends upon a categorical balancing of the value of the speech against its societal costs."

As a free-floating test for First Amendment coverage, that sentence is startling and dangerous. The First Amendment's guarantee of free speech does not extend only to categories of speech that survive an ad hoc balancing of relative social costs and benefits. The First Amendment itself reflects a judgment by the American people that the benefits of its restrictions on the Government outweigh the costs.

In Ferber, for example, we [noted] that the State of New York had a compelling interest in protecting children from abuse, and that the value of using children in these works (as opposed to simulated conduct or adult actors) was de minimis. But our decision did not rest on this "balance of competing interests" alone. We made clear that Ferber presented a special case: The market for child pornography was "intrinsically related" to the underlying abuse, and was therefore "an integral part of the production of such materials, an activity illegal throughout the Nation." [Our] decisions in Ferber and other cases cannot be taken as establishing a freewheeling authority to declare new categories of speech outside the scope of the First Amendment.

[The] Government makes no effort to defend the constitutionality of § 48 as applied beyond crush videos and depictions of animal fighting. It argues that those particular depictions are intrinsically related to criminal conduct or are analogous to obscenity (if not themselves obscene), and that the ban on such speech is narrowly tailored to reinforce restrictions on the underlying conduct, prevent additional crime arising from the depictions, or safeguard public mores. [Nor] does the Government seriously contest that the presumptively impermissible applications of § 48 (properly construed) far outnumber any permissible ones. However "growing" and "lucrative" the markets for crush videos and dogfighting depictions might be, they are dwarfed by the market for other depictions, such as hunting magazines and videos, that we have determined to be within the scope of § 48. We therefore need not and do not decide whether a statute limited to crush videos or other depictions of extreme animal cruelty would be constitutional. We hold only that § 48 is not so limited but is instead substantially overbroad, and therefore invalid under the First Amendment.

■ JUSTICE ALITO, dissenting.

The First Amendment protects freedom of speech, but it most certainly does not protect violent criminal conduct, even if engaged in for expressive purposes. Crush videos [record] the commission of violent criminal acts, and it appears that these crimes are committed for the sole purpose of creating the videos. [Congress] was presented with compelling evidence that the only way of preventing these crimes was to target the sale of the videos. Under these circumstances, I cannot believe that the First Amendment commands Congress to step aside and allow the underlying crimes to continue. [The] most relevant of our prior decisions is Ferber. [The] Court there held that child pornography is not protected speech, and I believe that Ferber's reasoning dictates a similar conclusion here.

[The core characteristics of Ferber] are shared by § 48, as applied to crush videos. First, the conduct depicted in crush videos is criminal in every State and the District of Columbia. Thus, any crush video made in this country records the actual commission of a criminal act that inflicts severe physical injury and excruciating pain and ultimately results in death. [Second], the criminal acts shown in crush videos cannot be prevented without targeting the conduct prohibited by § 48—the creation, sale, and possession for sale of depictions of animal torture with the intention of realizing a commercial profit. [Finally], the harm caused by the underlying crimes vastly outweighs any minimal value that the depictions might conceivably be thought to possess.

REGULATING VIOLENT SPEECH IN NEW MEDIA AFTER STEVENS

1. ***Subcultures and online speech.*** Is there a way in which advancing communications technologies might actually limit the expressive possibilities of underground cultures? In Ashcroft v. American Civil Liberties Union I, p. 189, a plurality of the Court insisted that communications on the internet may constitutionally be judged for obscenity under the "community standards" of any audience those communications reach. Yet four Justices countered that submitting online speech to the community standards of any potential audience, rather than its *intended* audience, might impermissibly chill communications among fringe subcultures. Concurring only in the judgment, Justice Kennedy, joined by Justices Souter and Ginsburg, wrote: "[The] economics and technology of Internet communication differ in important ways from those of telephones and mail. [A] Web publisher in a community where avant garde culture is the norm may have no desire to reach a national market; he may wish only to speak to his neighbors; nevertheless, if an eavesdropper in a more traditional, rural community chooses to listen in, there is nothing the publisher can do. [The plurality's holding] makes the eavesdropper the arbiter of propriety on the Web." Justice Stevens noted: "[In] its original form, the community standard provided a shield for communications that are offensive only to the least tolerant members of society. [In] the context of the Internet, however, community standards become a sword, rather than a shield. If a prurient appeal is offensive in a puritan village, it may be a crime to post it on the World Wide Web. [By] approving the use of community standards in this context, [the plurality] endorses a construction of COPA that has 'the intolerable consequence of denying some sections of the country access to material, there deemed acceptable, which in others might be considered offensive to prevailing community standards of decency.' "

2. ***Violent video games.*** Do the Court's decisions on sexually explicit speech in new media leave any latitude to regulate speech embodying violent activities? Even if the protection is directed specifically at minors? The Court considered these issues in the following case:

Brown v. Entertainment Merchants Ass'n

564 U.S. 786, 131 S. Ct. 2729, 180 L. Ed. 2d 708 (2011).

[A California statute prohibited the sale or rental to minors of violent video games, defined as any games "in which the range of options available to a player includes killing, maiming, dismembering, or sexually assaulting an image of a human being" in a depiction that "appeals to a deviant or morbid interest of minors," is "patently offensive to prevailing standards in the community as to what is suitable for minors," and "causes the game, as a whole, to lack serious literary, artistic, political, or scientific value for minors."]

■ JUSTICE SCALIA delivered the opinion of the Court.

California correctly acknowledges that video games qualify for First Amendment protection. The Free Speech Clause exists principally to protect discourse on public matters, but we have long recognized that it is difficult to distinguish politics from entertainment, and dangerous to try. Like the protected books, plays, and movies that preceded them, video games communicate ideas—and even social messages—through many familiar literary devices (such as characters, dialogue, plot, and music) and through features distinctive to the medium (such as the player's interaction with the virtual world). That suffices to confer First Amendment protection.

[Last Term], in Stevens, we held that new categories of unprotected speech may not be added to the list by a legislature that concludes certain speech is too harmful to be tolerated. [That] holding controls this case. As in Stevens, California has tried to make violent-speech regulation look like obscenity regulation by appending a saving clause required for the latter. That does not suffice. Our cases have been clear that the obscenity exception to the First Amendment does not cover whatever a legislature finds shocking, but only depictions of "sexual conduct," Miller.

California does not argue that it is empowered to prohibit selling offensively violent works to adults—and it is wise not to, since that is but a hair's breadth from the argument rejected in Stevens. Instead, it wishes to create a wholly new category of content-based regulation that is permissible only for speech directed at children.

That is unprecedented and mistaken. "[M]inors are entitled to a significant measure of First Amendment protection, and only in relatively narrow and well-defined circumstances may government bar public dissemination of protected materials to them." Erznoznik v. Jacksonville. No doubt a State possesses legitimate power to protect children from harm, but that does not include a free-floating power to restrict the ideas to which children may be exposed.

California's argument would fare better if there were a longstanding tradition in this country of specially restricting children's access to depictions of violence, but there is none. Certainly the books we give children to read—or read to them when they are younger—contain no shortage of gore. Grimm's Fairy Tales, for example, are grim indeed. As her just deserts for trying to poison Snow White, the wicked queen is made to dance in red hot slippers "till she fell dead on the floor, a sad example of envy and jealousy." Cinderella's evil stepsisters have their eyes pecked out by doves. And Hansel and Gretel (children!) kill their captor by baking her in an oven.

Because the Act imposes a restriction on the content of protected speech, it is invalid unless California can demonstrate that it passes strict scrutiny—that is, unless it is justified by a compelling government interest and is narrowly drawn to serve that interest. [California] cannot meet that standard. [It] acknowledges that it cannot show a direct causal link between violent video games and harm to minors. [California's studies] do not prove that violent video games cause minors to act aggressively. [And] California has (wisely) declined to restrict Saturday morning cartoons, the sale of games rated for young children, or the distribution of pictures of guns. The consequence is that its regulation is wildly underinclusive when judged against its asserted justification, which in our view is alone enough to defeat it. Underinclusiveness raises serious doubts about whether the government is in fact pursuing the interest it invokes, rather than disfavoring a particular speaker or viewpoint. [Moreover,] California cannot show that the Act's restrictions meet a substantial need of parents who wish to restrict their children's access to violent video games but cannot do so. The video-game industry has in place a voluntary rating system designed to inform consumers about the content of games. [And] finally, the Act's purported aid to parental authority is vastly overinclusive. Not all of the children who are forbidden to purchase violent video games on their own have parents who care whether they purchase violent video games. [This] is not the narrow tailoring to 'assisting parents' that restriction of First Amendment rights requires.

California's effort to regulate violent video games is the latest episode in a long series of failed attempts to censor violent entertainment for minors. While we have pointed out above that some of the evidence brought forward to support the harmfulness of video games is unpersuasive, we do not mean to demean or disparage the concerns that underlie the attempt to regulate them—concerns that may and doubtless do prompt a good deal of parental oversight. [But e]ven where the protection of children is the object, the constitutional limits on governmental action apply.

■ JUSTICE ALITO, with whom CHIEF JUSTICE ROBERTS joins, concurring in the judgment.

Respondents in this case, representing the video-game industry, ask us to strike down the California law on [the] narrower ground that the law's definition of "violent video game" is impermissibly vague. [I] agree with the latter argument[.] [The] California violent video game law fails to provide the fair notice that the Constitution requires. And I would go no further.

[In resolving the First Amendment claim], the Court is far too quick to dismiss the possibility that the experience of playing video games (and the effects on minors of playing violent video games) may be very different from anything that we have seen before. [Today's] most advanced video games create realistic alternative worlds in which millions of players immerse themselves for hours on end. These games feature visual imagery and sounds that are strikingly realistic, and in the near future video-game graphics may be virtually indistinguishable from actual video footage. Many of the games already on the market can produce high definition images, and it is predicted that it will not be long before video-game images will be seen in three dimensions. [Some] amici who support respondents foresee the day when " 'virtual-reality shoot-'em-ups' " will allow children to " 'actually feel the splatting blood from the blown-off head' " of a victim.

[In] some of these games, the violence is astounding. Victims by the dozens are killed with every imaginable implement, including machine guns, shotguns, clubs, hammers, axes, swords, and chainsaws. [The] objective of one game is to rape a mother and her daughters; in another, the goal is to rape Native American women. There is a game in which players engage in "ethnic cleansing" and can choose to gun down African-Americans, Latinos, or Jews. In still another game, players attempt to fire a rifle shot into the head of President Kennedy as his motorcade passes by the Texas School Book Depository.

If the technological characteristics of the sophisticated games that are likely to be available in the near future are combined with the characteristics of the most violent games already marketed, the result will be games that allow troubled teens to experience in an extraordinarily personal and vivid way what it would be like to carry out unspeakable acts of violence. [When] all of the characteristics of video games are taken into account, there is certainly a reasonable basis for thinking that the experience of playing a video game may be quite different from the experience of reading a book, listening to a radio broadcast, or viewing a movie. And if this is so, then for at least some minors, the effects of playing violent video games may also be quite different. The Court acts prematurely in dismissing this possibility out of hand.

■ JUSTICE THOMAS, dissenting.

The practices and beliefs of the founding generation establish that "the freedom of speech," as originally understood, does not include a right to speak to minors (or a right of minors to access speech) without going through the minors' parents or guardians. [T]he founding generation understood parents to have a right and duty to govern their children's growth. Parents were expected to direct the development and education of their children and ensure that bad habits did not take root. [In] light of this history, the Framers could not possibly have understood 'the freedom of speech' to include an unqualified right to speak to minors.

■ JUSTICE BREYER, dissenting.

California's law imposes no more than a modest restriction on expression. The statute prevents no one from playing a video game, it prevents no adult from buying a video game, and it prevents no child or adolescent from obtaining a game provided a parent is willing to help. [There] is considerable evidence that California's statute significantly furthers [a] compelling interest. Unlike the majority, I would find sufficient grounds in [the state's psychological] studies and expert opinions for this Court to defer to an elected legislature's conclusion that the video games in question are particularly likely to harm children. This Court has always thought it owed an elected legislature some degree of deference in respect to legislative facts of this kind, particularly when they involve technical matters that are beyond our competence, and even in First Amendment cases.

———

3. *The role of history in categories of unprotected or less protected speech.* In Stevens, the Court asserted that historical evidence of a "long-settled tradition of subjecting [certain categories of] speech to regulation" is required for those categories to receive an exemption from First Amendment protection. This holding was reiterated in Entertainment Merchants. Is history the proper basis upon which to determine the value of a category of speech? One scholar has argued that even the categories of speech traditionally recognized as having always been excepted from the First Amendment—obscenity, libel, profanity, and fighting words—have in fact only been treated this way since the New Deal. Lakier, "Inventing Low-Value Speech," 128 Harv. L. Rev. 2166 (2015). If this analysis is correct, is there good reason for history to serve as a limit to regulation of new types of speech?

SECTION 7. COMMERCIAL SPEECH

This section considers one last category of speech—commercial advertising, or speech that merely proposes a commercial transaction—that, because of its content, was once treated as wholly outside the First Amendment. Since 1976, commercial speech has been held to be protected, but not fully protected speech. It thus operates as a category of "lower value" speech not entitled to the high degree of protection afforded to "core" speech. A number of justices have questioned this categorization approach, urging that commercial speech instead be protected just like other speech unless it poses distinctively commercial harms, such as the danger of deception or overreaching. Their approach would substitute balancing for categorization. But they have not yet commanded a majority of the Court. Thus, commercial speech continues to stand as the lone formal exception to the two-level approach to speech set forth in Chaplinsky: unlike incitement, fighting words, malicious libel, obscenity, or child pornography, it enjoys First Amendment protection, but not as much First Amendment protection as other speech.

Before 1976, the Court assumed that most types of commercial speech fell wholly outside the First Amendment. In **Valentine v. Chrestensen**, 316 U.S. 52 (1942), the Court stated that the First Amendment imposed no "restraint on government as respects purely commercial advertising." Valentine sustained a ban on distribution of a handbill advertisement soliciting customers to pay admission to tour a privately owned submarine. The entrepreneur in Valentine printed his advertising message on one side of the circular; on the other side, he published a protest against the city's denial of permission to use a municipal pier for his exhibit. The Court viewed the ban as a regulation of business activity rather than protected political speech and considered the political protest merely an attempt to evade the city regulation forbidding distribution of advertisements in the streets.

The Valentine approach did not mean that First Amendment protection was denied simply because the speaker had a commercial motive. Recall that New York Times v. Sullivan rejected the argument that the First Amendment did not apply to a "paid 'commercial' advertisement": "That the Times was paid for publishing the advertisement is as immaterial [as] is the fact that newspapers and books are sold." In similar fashion, movies have long enjoyed First Amendment protections even though they are produced and distributed for profit.

Virginia Pharmacy Board v. Virginia Citizens Consumer Council

425 U.S. 748, 96 S. Ct. 1817, 48 L. Ed. 2d 346 (1976).

[A Virginia law provided that pharmacists were guilty of "unprofessional conduct" if they advertised the prices of prescription drugs. Since only pharmacists were authorized to dispense such drugs, the law effectively prevented the dissemination of prescription drug price information in the State. About 95% of all prescription drugs were prepared by pharmaceutical manufacturers rather than by the pharmacists themselves. A lower court invalidated the law on First Amendment grounds.]

■ JUSTICE BLACKMUN delivered the opinion of the Court.

[Justice Blackmun began by noting that the challenge to the law came not from a pharmacist but from prescription drug consumers who claimed that the First Amendment entitled them to drug price information, but found that the audience for drug price information could assert a First Amendment interest: "[W]here a speaker exists [as here], the protection afforded [by the First Amendment] is to the communication, to its source and to its recipients both. [If] there is a right to advertise, there is a reciprocal right to receive the advertising, and it may be asserted by [the consumers here].")

IV. The appellants contend that the advertisement of prescription drug prices is outside the protection of the First Amendment because it is "commercial speech." There can be no question that in past decisions the Court has given some indication that commercial speech is unprotected. [Last] Term, in Bigelow v. Virginia, 421 U.S. 809 (1975), the notion of unprotected "commercial speech" all but passed from the scene. We reversed a conviction for violation of a Virginia statute that made the circulation of any publication to encourage or promote the processing of an abortion in Virginia a misdemeanor. The defendant had published in his newspaper the availability of abortions in New York. We rejected the contention that the publication was unprotected because it was commercial. [We] noted that [the] advertisement "did more than simply propose a commercial transaction. It contained factual material of clear 'public interest.' " [Here,] in contrast, the question whether there is a First Amendment exception for "commercial speech" is squarely before us. Our pharmacist does not wish to editorialize on any subject, cultural, philosophical, or political. He does not wish to report any particularly newsworthy fact, or to make generalized observations even about commercial matters. The "idea" he wishes to communicate is simply this: "I will sell you the X prescription drug at the Y price." Our question, then, is whether this communication is wholly outside the protection of the First Amendment.

V. [It] is clear [that] speech does not lose its First Amendment protection because money is spent to project it, as in a paid [advertisement]. [E.g., New York Times.] [Our] question is whether speech which does "no more than propose a commercial transaction" is so removed from any "exposition of ideas" [Chaplinsky] and from "truth, science, morality, and arts in general, in its diffusion of liberal sentiments on the administration of Government" [Roth] that it lacks all protection. Our answer is that it is not. Focusing first on the individual parties to the transaction that is proposed in the commercial advertisement, we may assume that the advertiser's interest is a purely economic one. That hardly disqualifies him for protection under the First Amendment. The interests of the contestants in a labor dispute are primarily economic, but it has long been settled that both the employee and the employer are protected by the First Amendment where they express themselves on the merits of the dispute in order to influence its outcome. [As] to the particular consumer's interest in the free flow of commercial information, that interest may be as keen, if not keener by far, than his interest in the day's most urgent political debate. [Those] whom the suppression of prescription drug price information hits the hardest are the poor, the sick, and particularly the aged. [When] drug prices vary as strikingly as they do, information as to who is charging what becomes more than a convenience. It could mean the alleviation of physical pain or the enjoyment of basic necessities.

Advertising, however tasteless and excessive it sometimes may seem, is nonetheless dissemination of information as to who is producing and selling what product, for what reason, and at what price. So long as we preserve a predominantly free enterprise economy, the allocation of our resources in large measure will be made through numerous private economic decisions. It is a matter of public interest that those decisions, in the aggregate, be intelligent and well informed. To this end, the free flow of commercial information is indispensable. And if it is indispensable to the proper allocation of resources in a free enterprise system, it is also indispensable to the formation of intelligent opinions as to how that system ought to be regulated or altered. Therefore, even if the First Amendment were thought to be primarily an instrument to enlighten public decisionmaking in a democracy, we could not say that the free flow of information does not serve that goal.

Arrayed against these substantial individual and societal interests are a number of justifications for the advertising ban. These have to do principally with maintaining a high degree of professionalism on the part of licensed pharmacists. Indisputably, the State has a strong interest in maintaining that professionalism. [Price] advertising, it is argued, will place in jeopardy the pharmacist's expertise and, with it, the customer's health. It is claimed that the aggressive price competition that will result from unlimited advertising will make it impossible for the pharmacist to supply professional services in the compounding, handling, and dispensing of prescription drugs. [The] strength of these proffered justifications is greatly undermined by the fact that high professional standards, to a substantial extent, are guaranteed by the close regulation to which pharmacists in Virginia are subject. [At] the same time, we cannot discount the Board's justifications entirely. The Court regarded justifications of this type sufficient to sustain [such advertising bans] on due process and equal protection grounds.

The challenge now made, however, is based on the First Amendment. This casts the Board's justifications in a different light, for on close inspection it is seen that the State's protectiveness of its citizens rests in large measure on the advantages of their being kept in ignorance. The advertising ban does not directly affect professional standards one way or the other. It affects them only through the reactions it is assumed people will have to the free flow of drug price information. [It] appears to be feared that if the pharmacist who wishes to provide low cost, and assertedly low quality, services is permitted to advertise, he will be taken up on his offer by too many unwitting customers. They will choose the low-cost, low-quality service and drive the "professional" pharmacist out of business. They will [destroy] the pharmacist-customer relationship. [There] is, of course, an alternative to this highly paternalistic approach. That alternative is to assume that this information is not in itself harmful, that people will perceive their own best interests if only they are well enough informed, and that the best means to that end is to open the channels of communication rather than to close them. [It] is precisely this kind of choice, between the dangers of suppressing information, and the dangers of its misuse if it is freely available, that the First Amendment makes for us. Virginia is free to require whatever professional standards it wishes of its pharmacists. [But] it may not do so by keeping the public in ignorance of the entirely lawful terms that competing pharmacists are [offering].

VI. In concluding that commercial speech, like other varieties, is protected, we of course do not hold that it can never be regulated in any way. Some forms of commercial speech regulation are surely permissible. [There] is no claim, for example, that the prohibition on prescription drug price advertising is a mere time, place, and manner restriction. We have often approved restrictions of that kind provided that they are justified without reference to the content of the regulated speech, that they serve a significant governmental interest, and that in so doing they leave open ample alternative channels for communication of the information. [But this law] singles out speech of a particular content and seeks to prevent its dissemination completely. Nor is there any claim that prescription drug price advertisements are forbidden because they are false or misleading in any way. Untruthful speech, commercial or otherwise, has never been protected for its own sake. [E.g., Gertz.] Obviously, much commercial speech is not provably false, or even wholly false, but only deceptive or misleading. We foresee no obstacle to a State's dealing effectively with this problem.[1] The First Amendment, as we construe it today, does not prohibit the State from insuring that the stream of commercial information flows cleanly as well as freely. Also, there is no claim that the transactions proposed in the forbidden advertisements are themselves illegal in any way. [Cf., e.g., Pittsburgh Press.] Finally, the special problems of the electronic broadcast media are likewise not in this case. What is at issue is whether a State may completely suppress the dissemination of concededly truthful information about entirely lawful activity, fearful of that information's effect upon its disseminators and its recipients. Reserving other questions, we conclude that the answer to this one is in the negative. Affirmed.

■ JUSTICE REHNQUIST, dissenting.

The logical consequences of the Court's decision in this case, a decision which elevates commercial intercourse between a seller hawking his wares and a buyer seeking to strike a bargain to the same plane as has been previously reserved for the free marketplace of ideas, are far reaching indeed. Under the Court's opinion the way will be open not only for dissemination of price information but for active promotion of prescription drugs, liquor, cigarettes and other products the use of which it has previously been thought desirable to discourage.

The Court speaks of the consumer's interest in the free flow of commercial [information]. [It] speaks of the importance in a "predominantly free enterprise economy" of intelligent and well-informed decisions as to allocation of resources. While there is again much to be said for [this] as a matter of desirable public policy, there is certainly nothing in the [Constitution] which requires [Virginia] to hew to the teachings of Adam Smith in its legislative decisions regulating the pharmacy profession. [I]f the sole limitation on permissible state proscription of advertising is that it may

---

[1] In concluding that commercial speech enjoys First Amendment protection, we have not held that it is wholly undifferentiable from other forms. There are commonsense differences between speech that does "no more than propose a commercial transaction" and other varieties. Even if the differences do not justify the conclusion that commercial speech is valueless, and thus subject to complete suppression by the State, they nonetheless suggest that a different degree of protection is necessary to insure that the flow of truthful and legitimate commercial information is unimpaired. The truth of commercial speech, for example, may be more easily verifiable by its disseminator than, let us say, news reporting or political commentary, in that ordinarily the advertiser seeks to disseminate information about a specific product or service that he himself provides and presumably knows more about than anyone else. Also, commercial speech may be more durable than other kinds. Since advertising is the sine qua non of commercial profits, there is little likelihood of its being chilled by proper regulation and foregone entirely.

Attributes such as these, the greater objectivity and hardiness of commercial speech, may make it less necessary to tolerate inaccurate statements for fear of silencing the speaker. They may also make it appropriate to require that a commercial message appear in such a form, or include such additional information, warnings and disclaimers as are necessary to prevent its being deceptive. They also make inapplicable the prohibition against [prior restraints]. [Footnote by Justice Blackmun.]

not be false or misleading, surely the difference between pharmacists' advertising and lawyers' and doctors' advertising can be only one of degree and not of [kind].

The Court insists that the rule it lays down is consistent even with the view that the First Amendment is "primarily an instrument to enlighten public decisionmaking in a democracy." I had understood this view to relate to public decisionmaking as to political, social, and other public issues, rather than the decision of a particular individual as to whether to purchase one or another kind of shampoo. It is undoubtedly arguable that many people in the country regard the choice of shampoo as just as important as who may be elected to local, state, or national political office, but that does not automatically bring information about competing shampoos within the protection of the First Amendment. [It] is one thing to say that the line between strictly ideological and political commentaries and other kinds of commentary is difficult to [draw]. But it is another thing to say that because that line is difficult to draw, we will stand at the other end of the [spectrum].

In the case of "our" hypothetical pharmacist, he may now presumably advertise not only the prices of prescription drugs, but may attempt to energetically promote their sale so long as he does so truthfully. But such a line simply makes no allowance whatever for what appears to have been a considered legislative judgment in most States that while prescription drugs are a necessary and vital part of medical care and treatment, there are sufficient dangers attending their widespread use that they simply may not be promoted in the same manner as hair creams, deodorants, and toothpaste. The very real dangers that general advertising for such drugs might create in terms of encouraging, even though not sanctioning, illicit use of them by individuals for whom they have not been prescribed, or by generating patient pressure upon physicians to prescribe them, are simply not dealt with in the Court's [opinion].

I do not believe that the First Amendment mandates the Court's "open door policy" toward such commercial advertising.

———

COMMERCIAL SPEECH AND FIRST AMENDMENT THEORY

1. *Advertising as "speech."* Is commercial speech "speech" or merely an aspect of the conduct of commercial sales? For an argument that advertising is merely a first step in contracts or exchanges that are fully regulable, see Farber, "Commercial Speech and First Amendment Theory," 74 Nw. U. L. Rev. 372 (1979). See also Posner, "Free Speech in an Economic Perspective," 20 Suffolk L. Rev. 1 (1986) (suggesting that unlike most speech, which will be underproduced because speakers cannot fully capture its benefits once it is disseminated, the benefits of commercial speech "are more readily captured by its producer through sale of the underlying product," reducing the need for free speech protection); Cass, "Commercial Speech, Constitutionalism, Collective Choice," 56 U. Cin. L. Rev. 1317 (1988).

2. *Advertising and the rationales for freedom of speech.* Recall the varying rationales for protecting expression under the First Amendment discussed at pp. 5–10 above. Does speech that does "no more than propose a commercial transaction" warrant protection under any of these rationales? Does commercial advertising contribute to better decisionmaking in a

representative form of government (recall the Meiklejohn rationale)? Is it a part of the free marketplace of ideas (recall the Holmes rationale)? Is protection of advertising justifiable only under an individual self-realization, autonomy rationale? If the primary purpose of commercial advertising is to contribute to a more efficient operation of the free *economic* market, is that a quality relevant to First Amendment theory? Can protection of the economic market under the First Amendment be reconciled with the modern Court's "hands-off" attitude in economic regulation cases? For a general discussion of these questions, see Collins, Shiffrin, Chemerinsky & Sullivan, "Symposium: Thoughts On Commercial Speech: A Roundtable Discussion," 41 Loy. L.A. L. Rev. 333 (2007); Brudney, "The First Amendment and Commercial Speech," 53 B.C. L. Rev. 1153 (2012).

In light of Virginia Board, consider the following possible defenses and critiques of the proposition that commercial speech should be protected under the First Amendment:

a. *Self-government.* Justice Rehnquist dissented from Virginia Pharmacy and progeny on the ground that "in a democracy, the economic is subordinate to the political." Central Hudson, (1980; p. 214). On this view, advertising is subordinate to expressions of political ideology and dissent, for it does not inform public deliberation or contribute to representative government. For elaborations of this critique of protection for commercial speech, see Jackson & Jeffries, "Commercial Speech: Economic Due Process and the First Amendment," 65 Va. L. Rev. 1 (1979); Sunstein, Democracy and the Problem of Free Speech 130–44 (1993).

In Virginia Pharmacy, Justice Blackmun answers such arguments by suggesting that "public decisionmaking" should be viewed broadly, and that the free flow of commercial information contributes to that process by making the "numerous private economic decisions" that drive our "free enterprise economy" more "intelligent and well informed." Jackson & Jeffries reply: this is "a non sequitur. [In] terms of relevance to political decisionmaking, advertising is neither more nor less significant than a host of other market activities that legislatures concededly may regulate." For a contrary view, see Shiffrin, "The First Amendment and Economic Regulation: Away from a General Theory of the First Amendment," 78 Nw. U. L. Rev. 1212 (1983). For discussion of the relationship between commercial speech and democratic values and the proper limits of commercial speech protection in a democracy, see Post, "The Constitutional Status of Commercial Speech," 48 UCLA L. Rev. 1 (2000).

b. *Truth.* The Millian notion that the unregulated clash of individual expression will produce truth in the long run might seem unrelated to pitches for sales for short-run profit. But Justice Blackmun's opinion likens the clash between advertisers to other clashes of opinion: if the discount drug retailer advertises his low prices, "nothing prevents the 'professional' pharmacist from marketing his own assertedly superior product." Individuals, he suggests, may be relied on to choose between them. See Coase, "Advertising and Free Speech," 6 J. Legal Studies 1 (1977) (arguing for parallel treatment of markets and the marketplace of ideas). Jackson & Jeffries, supra, argue that this argument confuses economic values—"the opportunity of the individual producer or consumer to maximize his own economic utility" and "the aggregate economic efficiency of a free market economy"—with free speech values, effectively resurrecting Lochner under the guise of the First Amendment.

c.   *Autonomy*. Some proponents of autonomy as a central value underlying the Free Speech Clause reject protection for commercial speech because it is generally engaged in by corporations, which lack a human personality or capacity for self-fulfillment. See Jackson & Jeffries, supra ("[w]hatever else it may mean, the concept of a first amendment right of speaker autonomy in matters of belief and expression stops short of a seller hawking his wares"); Baker, Human Liberty and Freedom of Speech 194–224 (1989); Baker, "Commercial [Speech]," 62 Iowa L. Rev. 1 (1976) ("commercial speech is not a manifestation of individual freedom or choice," and "lacks the crucial connections with individual liberty and self-realization which exist for speech generally").

Justice Blackmun's opinion suggests, however, that it is not the speaker's but rather the *listener*'s autonomy that matters here: the alternative to "paternalistic" speech regulation is to assume that *consumers* "will perceive their own best interests if only they are well enough informed." For the view that such listener autonomy is a central free speech value that helps justify protection of commercial speech, see Strauss, "Persuasion, Autonomy and Freedom of Expression," 91 Colum. L. Rev. 334 (1991); Neuborne, "The First Amendment and Government Regulation of Capital Markets," 55 Brooklyn L. Rev. 5 (1989); Redish, "The First Amendment in the Marketplace: Commercial Speech and the Values of Free Expression," 39 Geo. Wash. L. Rev. 429 (1971) (choosing among "the relative merits of competing products" promotes "the intangible goal of rational self-fulfillment"). But are consumers truly choosing freely when they respond to advertising? Is not a goal of advertising to create demands and alter tastes? Might the listener's autonomy be impaired by lack of relevant information or by addiction to a product? See Fallon, "Two Senses of Autonomy," 46 Stan. L. Rev. 875 (1994); Law, "Addiction, Autonomy and Advertising," 77 Iowa L. Rev. 909 (1992) (arguing that advertising for psychoactive products that cause physiological dependence may be regulated).

d.   *Negative First Amendment theory*. Some theories rely less on the affirmative values of free speech than on the premise that there is special reason to distrust government when it regulates speech. For example, incumbents have an incentive to suppress challengers and dissidents. But is there any reason to fear that government will suppress commercial speech for ideologically partisan reasons? See Scanlon, "Freedom of Expression and Categories of Expression," 40 U. Pitt. L. Rev. 519 (1979) (arguing that commercial speech should not get full protection because government is less partisan in the competition between firms than in the struggle between political views). What if government is captured by powerful private interest groups, such as the pharmacy profession in Virginia Pharmacy? If bias against a competitor of such a group justifies First Amendment protection of the competitor's advertising, should it also justify protection of the competitor's production and sales under the Equal Protection or Due Process Clauses? See Jackson & Jeffries, supra ("Exactly the same values that are impaired by Virginia's ban against drug price advertising are also invaded by [most] other instances of governmental regulation of the economy.").

3.   *"Commonsense differences" between commercial and other speech.* In dicta in Virginia Pharmacy, the Court set forth three important limitations on protection for commercial speech: First, free speech protection does not extend to advertisements for illegal transactions. Second, free speech protection does not extend to factually false or misleading

advertisements. Third, commercial speech does not enjoy the special procedural protections other speech does against the ban on prior restraint or the presumption against laws that are overbroad, even if aimed at an unprotected category. Justice Blackmun explained this "different degree of protection" by reference to two "commonsense differences": that commercial speech is hardier than other speech because profit-driven, and more objectively verifiable than other speech. Are these distinctions persuasive? Consider the following comments:

a.   *Hardiness.* "It might just as easily be said that we need not fear that commercial magazines and newspapers will cease publication for fear of governmental regulation, because they are in business for profit." Redish, "The Value of Free Speech," 130 U. Pa. L. Rev. 591 (1982). "[O]ther interests can be just as strong as economics, sometimes stronger. [Speech] backed by religious feeling can persist in extraordinarily hostile climates; [a]rtistic impulses can also cause expression to persist in the face of hostile government regulation." Kozinski & Banner, "Who's Afraid of Commercial Speech?," 76 Va. L. Rev. 627 (1990).

b.   *Verifiability.* "[T]he seller can check his facts more easily than can a third party. However so can certain politicians who make false and deceptive political statements regarding facts within their knowledge." Alexander, "Speech in the Local [Marketplace]," 14 San Diego L. Rev. 357 (1977). "It is certainly easier to determine the truth of the claim 'Cucumbers cost sixty-nine cents' than the claim 'Republicans will govern more effectively.' But not all commercial speech is so objective. What about the statement 'America is turning 7-Up'?" Kozinski & Banner, supra. "[M]uch scientific speech can easily be labeled true or false, but we would be shocked at the suggestion that it is therefore entitled to a lesser degree of protection." Id.

4.   ***Defining commercial speech.*** Virginia Board defined commercial speech as that which "does no more than propose a commercial transaction," and made clear that it did *not* include all speech produced for profit. Later in Central Hudson, below, the Court referred to commercial speech as "expression related solely to the economic interests of the speaker and its audience." Justice Stevens, in concurrence, objected that such a definition "is unquestionably too broad." Later decisions would appear to agree with him. It is settled that corporate speech can amount to political or other fully protected speech, even when engaged in out of commercial self-interest. The fact of economic motivation does not automatically ratchet down the level of scrutiny. Thus the definition of commercial speech would appear to be the narrower one set forth in Virginia Board.

What if an advertisement contains a mixture of promotional and informational content? In **Bolger v. Youngs Drug Products Corp.**, 463 U.S. 60 (1983), the Court invalidated a federal statute prohibiting the mailing of unsolicited advertisements for contraceptives. At issue were a "drug store flyer" as well as two informational pamphlets, "Condoms and Human Sexuality" and "Plain Talk about Venereal Disease." Justice MARSHALL's opinion for the Court reasoned that the materials amounted to commercial rather than fully protected speech: "The mailings constitute commercial speech notwithstanding the fact that they contain discussions of important public issues such as venereal disease and family planning. A company has the full panoply of protections available [for] its direct comments on public issues, so there is no reason for providing similar constitutional protection when such statements are made in the context of commercial transactions."

———

COMMERCIAL SPEECH AFTER VIRGINIA PHARMACY

1. *Real estate "For Sale" signs as protected speech.* In **Linmark Associates, Inc. v. Town of Willingboro**, 431 U.S. 85 (1977), the Court relied in part on Virginia Pharmacy to strike down an ordinance prohibiting the posting of real estate "For Sale" and "Sold" signs. The town's objective was to stem the flight of white homeowners from a racially integrated community through "panic selling." Justice MARSHALL wrote for the Court: "The [town here, like the State in Virginia Pharmacy,] acted to prevent its residents from obtaining certain information. That information [is] of vital interest to Willingboro residents, since it may bear on one of the most important decisions they have a right to make: where to live and raise their families. The [town] has sought to restrict the free flow of this data because it fears that otherwise, homeowners will make decisions inimical to what the [town] views as the homeowners' self-interest and the corporate interest of the township: they will choose to leave town. The [town's] concern, then, was not with any commercial aspect of 'For Sale' signs—with offerors communicating offers to offerees—but with the substance of the information communicated to Willingboro citizens. If dissemination of this information can be restricted, then every locality in the country can suppress any facts that reflect poorly on the locality, so long as a plausible claim can be made that disclosure would cause the recipients of the information to act 'irrationally.' Virginia Pharmacy denies government such sweeping powers [to deny its citizens] information that is neither false nor misleading."

2. *Contraceptive advertising.* The Court relied on Virginia Pharmacy in **Carey v. Population Services, International**, 431 U.S. 678 (1977), which invalidated a New York ban on the advertising or display of nonprescription contraceptives. Justice Brennan noted that here, as in Virginia Pharmacy, there were "substantial individual and societal interests in the free flow of commercial information," and, as in Bigelow, the information suppressed "related to activity with which, at least in some respects, the State could not interfere."

3. *Regulating lawyer advertising.* Virginia Pharmacy had left some doubt about whether it would apply to commercial communications by lawyers. But the Court soon made it clear that the Virginia Pharmacy principles would apply to lawyers' advertising as well. The course of decisions began with the 5–4 ruling in **Bates v. State Bar of Arizona**, 433 U.S. 350 (1977), holding that states could not prohibit lawyers from price advertising of "routine legal services." Justice BLACKMUN's majority opinion rejected a variety of justifications for the restraint, including "adverse effect on professionalism" and the claim that attorney advertising was "inherently misleading."

A year later, two cases involving lawyers' solicitation of clients came to the Court. In these cases, the distinction between commercial and noncommercial speech proved critical. In **Ohralik v. Ohio State Bar Association**, 436 U.S. 447 (1978), involving "classic examples of 'ambulance chasing,'" the Court sustained a lawyer's suspension from law practice for violating anti-solicitation rules. Justice POWELL's majority opinion stated that "the State may proscribe in-person solicitation for pecuniary gain under circumstances likely to result in adverse consequences" without a showing of actual harm and with some leeway for prophylactic rules. But in **In re Primus**, 436 U.S. 412 (1978), the Court set aside disciplinary action in a case involving an attorney who did volunteer work for the ACLU. She had been reprimanded for writing a letter asking a woman who had been sterilized whether she wanted to become a plaintiff in a lawsuit against a doctor who had allegedly participated in a program of sterilizing pregnant mothers as a condition of continued receipt of Medicaid benefits. Justice Powell's majority opinion there emphasized that the attorney's letter fell within "the generous zone of First Amendment protection reserved for associational freedoms" and concluded that a state may not punish a lawyer "who, seeking to further political and ideological goals through associational activity, including litigation, advises a lay person of her legal rights and discloses in a subsequent letter that free legal assistance is available from a nonprofit organization." Bates and its progeny were explored and applied in a number of cases over the ensuing decade. In **Zauderer v. Office of Disciplinary Counsel**, 471 U.S. 626 (1985), an Ohio attorney had been reprimanded for advertising his availability to represent women who had suffered injuries in connection with the use of the Dalkon Shield intrauterine device. The ad contained a line drawing of the device and stated: "If there is no recovery, no legal fees are owed by our clients." The State objected in part because the ad solicited clients with respect to a specific legal problem and contained an illustration. Justice WHITE's opinion for the Court struck down the restriction on illustrations: "[W]e are unsure that the State's desire that attorneys maintain their dignity in their communications with the public is an interest substantial enough to justify the abridgment of their First Amendment rights."

The Zauderer ruling in turn provided a major basis for the Court's decision in **Shapero v. Kentucky Bar Ass'n**, 486 U.S. 466 (1988), striking down a flat ban on direct-mail solicitation by lawyers that was "targeted" to specific recipients known to need legal services of a particular kind. Kentucky claimed that it was needed to prevent potential clients from feeling "overwhelmed." Justice BRENNAN's majority opinion distinguished Ohralik as dealing with the special dangers of face-to-face solicitation and found the flat ban too broad a remedy for a mere possibility of abuse: "The State can regulate [any] abuses and minimize mistakes through far less restrictive and more precise means."

Two years later, **Peel v. Attorney Registration and Disciplinary Comm'n of Ill.**, 496 U.S. 91 (1990), followed both Zauderer and Shapero in invalidating a disciplinary sanction for an attorney's representation on his letterhead that he was "certified as a civil trial specialist by the National Board of Trial Advocacy." Justice STEVENS' plurality opinion concluded that truthful representation of certification by a legitimate organization with "rigorous requirements" could not be deemed misleading under the First Amendment just because some readers might think the organization was governmentally affiliated.

The Court, however, remains willing to uphold some restrictions on lawyer advertising. In **Florida Bar v. Went For It, Inc.**, 515 U.S. 618 (1995), the Court upheld, by a vote of 5–4, a Florida Bar rule prohibiting personal injury lawyers from sending targeted direct-mail solicitations to victims and their relatives for 30 days following an accident or disaster, and from receiving referrals from anyone who made such a contact. Justice O'CONNOR, writing for the Court, held that the bar rule served substantial state interests in "protecting the privacy and tranquility of personal injury victims and their loved ones against intrusive, unsolicited contact by lawyers," and in "protecting the flagging reputations of Florida lawyers by preventing them from engaging in conduct that, the Bar maintains, 'is universally regarded as deplorable and beneath common decency because of its intrusion upon the special vulnerability and private grief of victims or their families.'" Justice KENNEDY wrote a pointed dissent, joined by Justices Stevens, Souter and Ginsburg: "I take it to be uncontroverted that when an accident results in death or injury, it is often urgent at once to investigate the occurrence, identify witnesses, and preserve evidence."

Justice Kennedy rejected the state's arguments "that victims or their families will be offended by receiving a solicitation during their grief and trauma. [We] do not allow restrictions on speech to be justified on the ground that the expression might offend the listener."

————

Central Hudson Gas v. Public Service Comm'n
447 U.S. 557, 100 S. Ct. 2343, 65 L. Ed. 2d 341 (1980).

[The New York Public Service Commission (PSC) prohibited electrical utilities from engaging in promotional advertising designed to stimulate demand for electricity. The ban continued a policy begun at a time of severe fuel shortage, even though the shortage had eased. The PSC permitted "institutional and informational" advertising not intended to promote sales. The Court invalidated the promotional advertising restriction.]

■ JUSTICE POWELL delivered the opinion of the Court.

The Commission's order restricts only commercial speech, that is, expression related solely to the economic interests of the speaker and its audience. [In previous] commercial speech cases, a four-part analysis has developed. At the outset, we must determine whether the expression is protected by the First Amendment. For commercial speech to come within that provision, it at least must concern lawful activity and not be misleading. Next, we ask whether the asserted governmental interest is substantial. If both inquiries yield positive answers, we must determine whether the regulation directly advances the governmental interest asserted, and whether it is not more extensive than is necessary to serve that interest.

[The] Commission does not claim that the expression at issue either is inaccurate or relates to unlawful activity. [The] Commission [argues that] the State's interest in conserving energy is sufficient to support suppression of advertising designed to increase consumption of electricity. In view of our country's dependence on energy resources beyond our control, no one can doubt the importance of energy conservation. Plainly, therefore, the state interest asserted is substantial. [Moreover,] the State's interest in energy conservation is directly advanced by the Commission order at issue here. There is an immediate connection between advertising and demand for electricity. Central Hudson would not contest the advertising ban unless it believed that promotion would increase its sales. Thus, we find a direct link between the state interest in conservation and the Commission's order.

[The] critical inquiry in this case [is] whether the Commission's complete suppression of speech ordinarily protected by the First Amendment is no more extensive than necessary to further the State's interest in energy conservation. The Commission's order reaches all promotional advertising, regardless of the impact of the touted service on overall energy use. [The] Commission's order prevents appellant from promoting electric services [such as the "heat pump" and the use of electric heat as a "backup" to solar and other heat sources] that would reduce energy use by diverting demand from less efficient sources, or that would consume roughly the same amount of energy as do alternative sources. In neither situation would the utility's advertising endanger conservation or mislead the public. To the extent that the Commission's order suppresses speech that in no way impairs the State's interest in energy conservation, the Commission's order violates the [First Amendment]. The Commission also has not demonstrated that its interest in conservation cannot be protected adequately by more limited regulation of appellant's commercial expression. To further its policy of conservation, the Commission could attempt to restrict the format and content of Central Hudson's advertising. It might, for example, require that the advertisements include information about the relative efficiency and expense of the offered service. In the absence of a showing that more limited speech regulation would be ineffective, we cannot approve the complete suppression of Central Hudson's [advertising]. Reversed.

■ JUSTICE BLACKMUN, with whom JUSTICE BRENNAN joins, concurring.

[I] concur only in the Court's judgment, [because] I believe the test now evolved and applied by the Court is not consistent with our prior cases and does not provide adequate protection for truthful, nonmisleading, noncoercive commercial speech. I agree with the Court that [its] level of intermediate scrutiny is appropriate for a restraint on commercial speech designed to protect consumers from misleading or coercive speech, or a regulation related to the time, place, or manner of commercial speech. I do not agree, however, that the Court's four-part test is the proper one to be applied when a State seeks to suppress information about a product in order to manipulate a private economic decision that the State cannot or has not regulated or outlawed directly. [I] disagree with the Court [when] it says that suppression of speech may be a permissible means to achieve [energy conservation]. [I] seriously doubt whether suppression of information concerning the availability and price of a legally offered product is ever a permissible way for the State to "dampen" demand for or use of the product. Even though "commercial" speech is involved, such a regulatory measure strikes at the heart of the First Amendment. This is because it is a covert attempt by the State to manipulate the choices of its citizens, not by persuasion or direct regulation, but by depriving the public of the information needed to make a free choice.

■ JUSTICE STEVENS, with whom JUSTICE BRENNAN joins, concurring in the judgment.

This case involves a governmental regulation that completely bans promotional advertising by an electric utility. This ban encompasses a great deal more than mere proposals to engage in certain kinds of commercial transactions. It prohibits all advocacy of the immediate or future use of electricity. It curtails expression by an informed and interested group of persons of their point of view on questions relating to the production and consumption of electrical energy—questions frequently discussed and debated by our political leaders. [I] concur in the result because I do not consider this to be a "commercial speech" case. Accordingly, I see no need to decide whether the Court's four-part analysis adequately protects commercial speech—as properly defined—in the face of a blanket ban of the sort involved in this case.

■ JUSTICE REHNQUIST, dissenting.

The Court's analysis [is] wrong in several respects. Initially, I disagree with the Court's conclusion that the speech of a state-created monopoly, which is the subject of a comprehensive regulatory scheme, is entitled to protection under the First Amendment. [The] extensive regulations governing decisionmaking by public utilities suggest that for purposes of First Amendment analysis, a utility is far closer to a state-controlled enterprise than is an ordinary corporation. Accordingly, I think a State has broad discretion in determining the statements that a utility may make in that such statements emanate from the entity created by the State to provide important and unique public services. [I] also think New York's ban on such advertising falls within the scope of permissible state regulation of an economic activity by an entity that could not exist in corporate form, say nothing of enjoy monopoly status, were it not for the laws of New York.

[The] Court's decision today fails to give due deference to [the] subordinate position of commercial speech. [The] test adopted by the [Court] elevates the protection accorded commercial speech that falls within the scope of the First Amendment to a level that is virtually indistinguishable from that of noncommercial speech. I think [that] by labeling economic regulation of business conduct as a restraint on "free speech," [the Court has] gone far to resurrect the discredited doctrine of cases such as [Lochner]. [Identification] of speech that falls within [the First Amendment's] protection is not aided by the metaphorical reference to a "marketplace of ideas." There is no reason for believing that the marketplace of ideas is free from market imperfections any more than there is to believe that the invisible hand will always lead to optimum economic decisions in the commercial market. [Even] if I were to agree that commercial speech is entitled to some First Amendment protection, I would hold here that the State's decision to ban promotional advertising, in light of the substantial state interest at stake, [is] constitutionally [permissible].

The plethora of opinions filed in this case highlights the doctrinal difficulties that emerge from this Court's decisions granting First Amendment protection to commercial speech. [I] remain of the view that the Court unleashed a Pandora's box when it "elevated" commercial speech to the level of traditional political speech by according it First Amendment protection. [The] notion that more speech is the remedy to expose falsehood and fallacies is wholly out of place in the commercial [bazaar]. [In] a democracy, the economic is subordinate to the [political].

[The] final part of the Court's [test] leaves room for so many hypothetical "better" ways that any ingenious lawyer will surely seize on one of them to secure the invalidation of what the state agency actually did. [It] is in my view inappropriate for the Court to invalidate the State's ban on commercial advertising here based on its speculation that in some cases the advertising may result in a net savings in electrical energy [use].

———

COMMERCIAL SPEECH REGULATION AFTER CENTRAL HUDSON

1. *Commercial speech and "least restrictive alternative" analysis.* Central Hudson stated that commercial speech regulations must be "no more extensive than necessary" to serve a substantial government interest. In **Board of Trustees, State Univ. of New York v. Fox**, 492 U.S. 469 (1989), the Court explicitly clarified that this did *not* mean that government must employ the "least restrictive alternative." The case involved a regulation by the University restricting the operation of commercial enterprises on its campuses. The effect of the regulation was to bar a company from selling its housewares in dormitories through the use of "Tupperware parties." Justice SCALIA's majority opinion rejected the constitutional challenge. He first concluded that the speech involved was commercial, and that the Central Hudson analysis was applicable. Turning to that analysis, he noted that the speech proposed a lawful transaction and was not misleading. He found, however, that the state interests in promoting an educational rather than a commercial atmosphere on campuses, insuring the security of students, and preventing their exploitation were sufficiently substantial to satisfy that prong of the Central Hudson test.

Justice Scalia acknowledged that the Court's own prior statements in Central Hudson and in cases such as Zauderer, above, supported the impression that the use of the word "necessary" in Central Hudson could be read as incorporating a "least restrictive alternative" requirement. Nevertheless, he rejected that interpretation, concluding: "[O]ur decisions require [a] 'fit between the legislature's ends and the means chosen to accomplish those ends,'—a fit that is not necessarily perfect, but reasonable; that represents not necessarily the single best disposition but one whose scope is 'in proportion to the interest served'; that employs not necessarily the least restrictive means but [a] means narrowly tailored to achieve the desired objective. Within those bounds we leave it to governmental decisionmakers to judge what manner of regulation may best be employed."

2. *Differential treatment of commercial speech.* In **Metromedia, Inc. v. San Diego**, 453 U.S. 490 (1981), the Court struck down an ordinance regulating the placement of *non*commercial billboards, but made clear that portions of the ordinance banning offsite commercial billboards would be permissible. Applying the Central Hudson test, Justice WHITE's plurality opinion found that the ban on offsite commercial billboards satisfied its first, second, and fourth criteria, but found more problematic the question of whether such a ban "directly advanced" the acknowledged governmental interests "in traffic safety and the appearance of the city." Finding no ulterior motives, the plurality reviewed deferentially the determinations made by San Diego, especially those relating to traffic safety, and suggested that the ban on commercial billboards satisfied all aspects of the Central Hudson test. Because the dissenting opinions of Chief Justice Burger and Justices Rehnquist and Stevens would have upheld the restriction in its entirety, a majority of the Court agreed that restrictions on *commercial* billboards for both aesthetic and traffic safety reasons satisfy the Central Hudson standard.

In **City of Cincinnati v. Discovery Network, Inc.**, 507 U.S. 410 (1993), however, the Court held that commercial speech may not be treated differently from noncommercial speech for aesthetic or safety purposes in the absence of some distinctive harm from commercial speech. Cincinnati barred respondents from placing 62 newsracks on public property to dispense free advertisements for adult education classes and real estate sales, treating such materials as "commercial handbills" whose distribution on public property was prohibited. But the city permitted the placement on public property of between 1500 and 2000 newsracks distributing general circulation newspapers. The city defended the selective commercial newsrack ban as "motivated by its interest in the safety and attractive appearance of its streets and sidewalks" and as justified by the lower value of commercial speech. The Court invalidated the ban.

Justice STEVENS, writing for the Court, noted: "[In] this case, the distinction bears no relationship whatsoever to the particular interests that the city has asserted. [The] city has asserted an interest in esthetics, but respondent publishers' newsracks are no greater an eyesore than the newsracks permitted to remain on Cincinnati's sidewalks. Each newsrack, whether containing 'newspapers' or 'commercial handbills,' is equally unattractive. [The] city's primary concern [is] with the aggregate number of newsracks on its streets. On that score, however, all newsracks, regardless of whether they contain commercial or noncommercial publications, are equally at fault. [Cincinnati] has not asserted an interest in preventing commercial harms by regulating the information distributed by respondent publishers' newsracks. [In] the absence of some basis for distinguishing between 'newspapers' and 'commercial handbills' that is relevant to an interest asserted by the city, we are unwilling to recognize Cincinnati's bare assertion that the 'low value' of commercial speech is a sufficient justification for its selective and categorical ban on newsracks dispensing 'commercial handbills.' "

In a later decision, the Court declined to find a First Amendment violation in the differential treatment of speech intended to be used for commercial purposes. In **Los Angeles Police Department v. United Reporting**, 528 U.S. 32 (1999), the Court rejected a facial attack on a state law that permitted arrest records to be disclosed for "scholarly, journalistic, political, or governmental" purposes, but not in order "to sell a product or service." The opinion of the Court by Chief Justice REHNQUIST found that "the section in question is not an abridgment of anyone's right to engage in speech, be it commercial or otherwise, but simply a law regulating access to information in the hands of the police department."

3. *The rise and fall of the "vice" exception.* Virginia Board and Central Hudson made clear that the limited protection of commercial advertising does not extend to advertising of illegal activity. But what of restrictions on the advertising of products or services that are legal but are widely viewed as harmful, such as cigarettes, alcohol, and gambling? Virginia Board suggested that paternalism is an invalid basis for speech regulation. But Central Hudson suggested that advertising restrictions are directly related to suppressing demand. Assuming that suppressing demand for vice is a substantial government end, should suppression of advertisements for vice-related activities always be upheld, even if paternalistic?

In **Posadas de Puerto Rico Assocs. v. Tourism Company of Puerto Rico**, 478 U.S. 328 (1986), the Court upheld, by a vote of 5–4, a Puerto Rico law prohibiting gambling casinos from advertising their facilities to residents of Puerto Rico. Justice REHNQUIST's majority opinion stated: "The particular kind of commercial speech at issue here [concerns] a lawful activity and is not misleading or fraudulent, at least in the abstract. We must therefore proceed to the three remaining steps of the Central Hudson analysis. [The] first [involves] an assessment of the strength of the government's interest in restricting the speech. The interest at stake in this case [is] the reduction of demand for casino gambling by the residents of Puerto Rico." Justice Rehnquist found that the legislative determination that excess gambling would impair the health, safety, and welfare of Puerto Rico residents, "some of the very same concerns [that] have motivated the vast majority of the 50 States to prohibit casino gambling," were sufficient to qualify as a "substantial" governmental interest. Turning to the remaining steps of the Central Hudson analysis, Justice Rehnquist noted that the law directly advanced the government's asserted interest: "[Puerto Rico] obviously believed [that] advertising of casino gambling aimed at [its residents] would serve to increase the demand for the product advertised. We think the legislature's belief is [reasonable]." Finally, he found the law "no more extensive than necessary to serve the government's interest," noting that the law had been construed to permit advertising of casino gambling aimed at tourists, and rejecting the challengers' argument that Puerto Rico ought employ "a 'counterspeech' policy" as a less restrictive means.

The Court's deferential approach to the regulation of gambling advertising in Posadas led many observers to conclude that there was an implicit "vice" exception to the protection of commercial speech. The Court reinforced such an impression in **United States v. Edge Broadcasting Co.**, 509 U.S. 418 (1993), which upheld a federal statute prohibiting the broadcast of lottery advertisements except by stations licensed to states that conduct lotteries. Edge Broadcasting operated a radio station in North Carolina, a nonlottery state, but over 90% of its listeners were in neighboring Virginia, a lottery state. North Carolina listeners could also hear a number of Virginia radio stations that broadcast lottery ads. The Court rejected Edge's claim that it had a First Amendment right to broadcast advertisements for the Virginia lottery. Justice WHITE wrote the opinion for the Court. Upholding the law both on its face and as applied to Edge, he wrote: "We have no doubt that the statutes directly advanced the governmental interest at stake in this case. [Instead] of favoring either the lottery or the nonlottery State, Congress opted to support the antigambling policy of a State like North Carolina by forbidding stations in such a State from airing lottery advertising. At the same time it sought not to unduly interfere with the policy of a lottery sponsoring State such as Virginia. [This] congressional policy of balancing the interests of lottery and nonlottery States is the substantial governmental interest that satisfies Central Hudson. [It] is also the interest that is directly served by applying the statutory restriction to all stations in North Carolina." He noted that here, "as in Posadas de Puerto Rico, the Government obviously legislated on the premise that the advertising of gambling serves to increase the demand for the advertised product. See also Central Hudson. Congress clearly was entitled to determine that broadcast of promotional advertising of lotteries undermines North Carolina's policy against gambling, even if the North Carolina audience is not wholly unaware of the lottery's existence."

But in **Rubin v. Coors Brewing Co.**, 514 U.S. 476 (1995), and 44 Liquormart, Inc. v. Rhode Island, which follows, the Court decisively rejected any notion that there is a "vice" exception to the protection of commercial speech. In Coors, the Court unanimously invalidated a provision of the federal Alcohol Administration Act that prohibited beer labels from displaying alcohol content. The government defended the provision as necessary to preventing "strength wars" among brewers who would seek to compete in the marketplace based on the potency of their beer. Writing for the Court, Justice THOMAS rejected the government's suggestion "that legislatures have broader latitude to regulate speech that promotes socially harmful activities, such as alcohol consumption, than they have to regulate other types of speech." Rather, the Central Hudson test applied to commercial advertising of vice and other activities alike. Applying that test, he found that the government had asserted "a significant interest in protecting the health, safety, and welfare of its citizens by preventing brewers from competing on the basis of alcohol strength, which could lead to greater alcoholism and its attendant social costs."

Justice Thomas found, however, that the provision did not directly advance that interest, "given the overall irrationality of the Government's regulatory scheme." Furthermore, Justice Thomas concluded that the ban was "more extensive than necessary" because the government had alternative options, "such as directly limiting the alcohol content of beers, prohibiting marketing efforts emphasizing high alcohol strength (which is apparently the policy in some other Western nations), or limiting the labeling ban only to malt liquors, [all] of which could advance the Government's asserted interest in a manner less intrusive to respondent's First Amendment rights."

---

44 Liquormart, Inc. v. Rhode Island
517 U.S. 484, 116 S. Ct. 1495, 134 L. Ed. 2d 711 (1996).

[Rhode Island law prohibited advertisement of the price of alcoholic beverages "in any manner whatsoever," except by tags or signs inside liquor stores. The state courts had several times upheld the law against First Amendment challenge, finding that the law reasonably served the state goal of promoting "temperance." Two high-volume discount liquor retailers challenged the law under the Free Speech Clause in federal court. The Rhode Island Liquor Stores Association intervened on behalf of the state. The district court invalidated the law, finding "that Rhode Island's off-premises liquor price advertising ban has no significant impact on levels of alcohol consumption in Rhode Island." The court of appeals reversed, finding "inherent merit" in Rhode Island's argument that competitive price advertising would lower prices and that lower prices would produce more sales, increasing the consumption of alcohol.

[The Supreme Court unanimously reversed, invalidating the Rhode Island law. But it divided into several camps on the reasoning. Justice Stevens announced the judgment of the Court and wrote a plurality opinion joined at different points by Justices Kennedy, Souter, Thomas and Ginsburg. Joined by Justices Kennedy and Ginsburg only, he wrote that bars against "dissemination of truthful, nonmisleading commercial messages for reasons unrelated to the preservation of a fair bargaining process" should receive strict scrutiny, which the Rhode Island law failed. In the alternative, Justice Stevens wrote, joined on this point by Justices Kennedy, Souter and Ginsburg, the Rhode Island law in any event failed the Central Hudson test. Justice Thomas concurred but would have held that a ban on truthful price information is per se illegitimate. Justice O'Connor, joined by Chief Justice Rehnquist and Justices Souter and Breyer, concurred in the judgment, reasoning simply that the Rhode Island law failed the Central Hudson test. Justice Scalia concurred in the judgment.]

■ JUSTICE STEVENS [joined by JUSTICES KENNEDY and GINSBURG].

[Not] all commercial speech regulations are subject to a similar form of constitutional review. [When] a State regulates commercial messages to protect consumers from misleading, deceptive, or aggressive sales practices, or requires the disclosure of beneficial consumer information, the purpose of its regulation is consistent with the reasons for according [less than full] constitutional protection to commercial speech and therefore justifies less than strict review. However, when a State entirely prohibits the dissemination of truthful, nonmisleading commercial messages for reasons unrelated to the preservation of a fair bargaining process, there is far less reason to depart from the rigorous review that the First Amendment generally demands. [Complete] speech bans, unlike content-neutral restrictions on the time, place, or manner of expression, are particularly dangerous because they all but foreclose alternative means of disseminating certain information.

[The] special dangers that attend complete bans on truthful, nonmisleading commercial speech cannot be explained away by appeals to the "commonsense distinctions" that exist between commercial and noncommercial speech. [It] is the State's interest in protecting consumers from "commercial harms" [such as deception and overreaching] that provides "the typical reason why commercial speech can be subject to greater governmental regulation than noncommercial speech." Discovery Network. Yet bans that target truthful, nonmisleading commercial messages rarely protect consumers from such harms. Instead, [bans] against truthful, nonmisleading commercial speech [usually] rest solely on the offensive assumption that the public will respond "irrationally" to the truth. Linmark. The First Amendment directs us to be especially skeptical of regulations that seek to keep people in the dark for what the government perceives to be their own good. That teaching applies equally to state attempts to deprive consumers of accurate information about their chosen products.

■ JUSTICE STEVENS [joined by JUSTICES KENNEDY, SOUTER and GINSBURG].

The State argues that the price advertising prohibition should [be] upheld because it directly advances the State's substantial interest in promoting temperance, and because it is no more extensive than necessary. Central Hudson. [The] State bears the burden of showing not merely that its regulation will advance its interest, but also that it will do so "to a material degree." Edenfield. We can agree that common sense supports the conclusion that a prohibition against price advertising [will] tend to mitigate competition and maintain prices at a higher level than would prevail in a completely free market. [We] can even agree [that] demand, and hence consumption throughout the market, is somewhat lower whenever a higher, noncompetitive price level prevails. However, [we] cannot agree [that] the price advertising ban will significantly advance the State's interest in promoting temperance. [The] State has presented no evidence to suggest that its speech prohibition will significantly reduce market-wide consumption. Indeed, the District Court's considered and uncontradicted finding on this point is directly to the contrary. [In] addition, [the] State has not identified what price level would lead to a significant reduction in alcohol consumption, nor has it identified the amount that it believes prices would decrease without the ban. Thus, [any] connection between the ban and a significant change in alcohol consumption would be purely fortuitous. [Any] conclusion that elimination of the ban would significantly increase alcohol consumption would [rest on] "speculation or conjecture."

[The] State also cannot satisfy the requirement that its restriction on speech be no more extensive than necessary. It is perfectly obvious that alternative forms of regulation that would not involve any restriction on speech would be more likely to achieve the State's goal of promoting temperance. [Higher] prices can be maintained either by direct regulation or by increased taxation. Per capita purchases could be limited as is the case with prescription drugs. Even educational campaigns focused on the problems of excessive, or even moderate, drinking might prove to be more effective. As a result, even under the less than strict standard that generally applies in commercial speech cases, the State has failed to establish a "reasonable fit" between its abridgment of speech and its temperance goal. Fox, Coors, Linmark. It necessarily follows that the price advertising ban cannot survive the more stringent constitutional review that Central Hudson itself concluded was appropriate for the complete suppression of truthful, nonmisleading commercial speech.

■ JUSTICE STEVENS [joined by JUSTICES KENNEDY, THOMAS, and GINSBURG].

[Relying] on the Central Hudson analysis set forth in Posadas and Edge Broadcasting, Rhode Island [argues] that, because expert opinions as to the effectiveness of the price advertising ban "go both ways," the Court of Appeals correctly concluded that the ban constituted a "reasonable choice" by the legislature. [The] reasoning in Posadas does support the State's argument, but, on reflection, we are now persuaded that Posadas [clearly] erred in concluding that it was "up to the legislature" to choose suppression over a less speech-restrictive policy. The Posadas majority's conclusion on that point cannot be reconciled with the unbroken line of prior cases striking down similarly broad regulations on truthful, nonmisleading advertising when non-speech-related alternatives were available. [We] also cannot accept the State's [contention that it may ban liquor price advertising because it may ban the sale of alcoholic beverages outright. Such] "greater-includes-the-lesser" reasoning, [which was] endorsed toward the end of the majority's opinion in Posadas, [is] inconsistent with both logic and well-settled doctrine. [Contrary] to the assumption made in Posadas, we think it quite clear that banning speech may sometimes prove far more intrusive than banning conduct. [Finally,] we find unpersuasive the State's contention that, under Posadas and Edge, the price advertising ban should be upheld because it targets commercial speech that pertains to a "vice" activity. [Our] decision last Term striking down an alcohol-related advertising restriction effectively rejected the very contention respondents now make. See Coors Brewing. Moreover, the scope of any "vice" exception to the protection afforded by the First Amendment would be difficult, if not impossible, to define.

■ JUSTICE SCALIA, concurring in part and concurring in the judgment.

[The] briefs and arguments of the parties in the present case provide no illumination on [state legislative practices toward advertising regulation at the time the First and Fourteenth Amendments were adopted.] [Since] I do not believe we have before us the wherewithal to declare Central Hudson wrong—or at least the wherewithal to say what ought to replace it—I must resolve this case in accord with our existing jurisprudence, which all except Justice Thomas agree would prohibit the challenged regulation. I am not disposed to develop new law, or reinforce old, on this issue, and accordingly I merely concur in the judgment of the Court.

■ JUSTICE THOMAS, concurring in part and concurring in the judgment.

In cases such as this, in which the government's asserted interest is to keep legal users of a product or service ignorant in order to manipulate their choices in the marketplace, the balancing test adopted in Central Hudson should not be applied, in my view. Rather, such an "interest" is per se illegitimate and can no more justify regulation of "commercial" speech than it can justify regulation of "noncommercial" speech. [Where,] as here, the asserted interest is one that is to be achieved through keeping would-be recipients of the speech in the dark, [a]pplication of the advancement-of-state-interest prong of Central Hudson makes little sense. [Faulting] the State for failing to show that its price advertising ban decreases alcohol consumption "significantly," as Justice Stevens does, seems to imply that if the State had been more successful at keeping consumers ignorant and thereby decreasing their consumption, then the restriction might have been upheld. This contradicts Virginia Pharmacy Board's rationale for protecting "commercial" speech in the first instance.

[In] their application of [Central Hudson,] both Justice Stevens and Justice O'Connor hold that because the State can ban the sale of lower priced alcohol altogether by instituting minimum prices or levying taxes, it cannot ban advertising regarding lower priced liquor. [Their] opinions would appear to commit the courts to striking down restrictions on speech whenever a direct regulation (i.e., a regulation involving no restriction on speech regarding lawful activity at all) would be an equally effective method of dampening demand by legal users. But it would seem that directly banning a product (or rationing it, taxing it, controlling its price, or otherwise restricting its sale in specific ways) would virtually always be at least as effective in discouraging consumption as merely restricting advertising regarding the product would be, and thus virtually all restrictions with such a purpose would fail the fourth prong of the Central Hudson test. [I] welcome this outcome; but, rather than "applying" the fourth prong of Central Hudson to reach the inevitable result that all or most such advertising restrictions must be struck down, I would adhere to the doctrine adopted in Virginia Pharmacy Board, and in Justice Blackmun's Central Hudson concurrence, that all attempts to dissuade legal choices by citizens by keeping them ignorant are impermissible.

■ JUSTICE O'CONNOR, with whom CHIEF JUSTICE REHNQUIST and JUSTICES SOUTER and BREYER join, concurring in the judgment.

[I] agree with the Court that Rhode Island's price-advertising ban is invalid. I would resolve this case more narrowly, however, by applying our established Central Hudson test to determine whether this commercial-speech regulation survives First Amendment scrutiny. Under that test, [our] conclusion is plain: Rhode Island's regulation fails First Amendment scrutiny. Both parties agree that the first two prongs of the Central Hudson test are met. Even if we assume arguendo that Rhode Island's regulation also satisfies the requirement that it directly advance the governmental interest, Rhode Island's regulation fails the final prong; that is, its ban is more extensive than necessary to serve the State's interest.

Rhode Island offers [one] justification for its ban on price advertising: [to] keep alcohol prices high as a way to keep consumption low. By preventing sellers from informing customers of prices, the regulation prevents competition from driving prices down and requires consumers to spend more time to find the best price for alcohol. The higher cost of obtaining alcohol, Rhode Island argues, will lead to reduced consumption. The fit between Rhode Island's method and this particular goal is not reasonable. [The] State has other methods at its disposal [that] would more directly accomplish this stated goal without intruding on sellers' ability to provide truthful, nonmisleading information to customers. [A sales] tax, for example, is not normally very difficult to administer and would have a far more certain and direct effect on prices, without any restriction on speech. The principal opinion suggests further alternatives, such as limiting per capita purchases or conducting an educational campaign about the dangers of alcohol consumption. The ready availability of such alternatives—at least some of which would far more effectively achieve Rhode Island's only professed goal, at comparatively small additional administrative cost—demonstrates that the fit between ends and means is not narrowly tailored. [Because] Rhode Island's regulation fails even the less stringent standard set out in Central Hudson, nothing here requires adoption of a new analysis for the evaluation of commercial speech regulation.

––––––––

COMMERCIAL SPEECH REGULATION AFTER LIQUORMART

1. *What standard of scrutiny?* Central Hudson clearly set forth a standard of intermediate scrutiny for review of regulations of commercial speech, even where content-based. A number of justices have advocated full strict scrutiny for at least some regulations of commercial speech: Justices Brennan, Marshall, Blackmun and Stevens did so in pre-Liquormart concurrences or dissents, and Justices Stevens, Kennedy, Ginsburg and Thomas did so in Liquormart. But never have five of them sat on the Court at the same time or on the same case. Thus, even after Liquormart, Central Hudson remains the governing test for reviewing commercial speech regulations.

But what does Central Hudson mean after Liquormart? Arguably, the stringency of a standard of review depends more on its application than its verbal formulation: it is a function of the factors that must be examined, the strength of the state justifications required, and the rigor with which an appellate court will in fact examine legislative or lower court determinations with respect to those justifications. Does Liquormart subject the Rhode Island regulation to the practical equivalent of strict scrutiny? Is its emphasis on the availability of less restrictive regulatory alternatives such as price floors and taxes consistent with the holding in Fox that the government need not employ the least restrictive alternative? Is Justice Thomas correct to predict that, after Liquormart, no ban on truthful price advertising may be upheld? Even if that is so, does the stringent application of Central Hudson in Liquormart have any application beyond the context of a total ban on truthful price data? For discussion of such questions, see Sullivan, "Cheap Spirits, Cigarettes and Free Speech," 1996 Sup. Ct. Rev. 123.

In **Lorillard Tobacco Co. v. Reilly**, 533 U.S. 525 (2001), the Court found the Central Hudson test "an adequate basis for decision" for striking down a set of tobacco advertising regulations. Massachusetts, seeking to protect children from seeing tobacco advertising, had sought to prohibit outdoor advertising of cigarettes, smokeless tobacco, and cigars within 1,000 feet of a school or playground, and to require that indoor point-of-sale advertising of such products be placed no lower than five feet from the floor. A 6–3 majority of the Court found these regulations as to cigarettes preempted by the Federal Cigarette Labeling and Advertising Act, which requires specific warning labels on cigarette packages and expressly prohibits state regulations requiring different labels and any other state law "with respect to the advertising or promotion of any cigarettes" whose packages do bear the specified labels. That ruling left for consideration whether the same regulations with respect to smokeless tobacco and cigars violated the First Amendment.

A majority found that they did, with Justice O'CONNOR writing the opinion of the Court. Neither of the first two parts of the Central Hudson test was in issue: the State had conceded for purposes of litigation that the advertising was not unlawful or misleading, and the tobacco advertisers did not contest that the government had an important interest in preventing tobacco use by minors. Six justices—Justice O'Connor, joined in this part of her opinion by Chief Justice Rehnquist and Justices Stevens, Souter, Ginsburg and Breyer—concluded that the outdoor advertising regulations would have satisfied the third part of the Central Hudson test by directly and materially advancing the state interest in preventing harms from underage use of smokeless tobacco or cigars that they believed the state had adequately empirically documented.

But a different 5–4 majority—Justice O'Connor, joined in this part of her opinion by Chief Justice Rehnquist and Justices Scalia, Kennedy and Thomas—found that the outdoor advertising regulations were not sufficiently narrowly tailored to satisfy the fourth part of Central Hudson: "In some geographical areas, these regulations would constitute nearly a complete ban on the communication of truthful information about smokeless tobacco and cigars to adult consumers. [The] uniformly broad sweep of the geographical limitation demonstrates a lack of tailoring. [In] addition, the range of communications restricted seems unduly broad. For instance, [a] ban on all signs of any size seems ill suited to target the problem of highly visible billboards, as opposed to smaller signs. [The] State's interest in preventing underage tobacco use is substantial, and even compelling, but it is no less true that the sale and use of tobacco products by adults is a legal activity. We must consider that tobacco retailers and manufacturers have an interest in conveying truthful information about their products to adults, and adults have a corresponding interest in receiving truthful information about tobacco products. In a case involving indecent speech on the Internet we explained that 'the governmental interest in protecting children from harmful materials . . . does not justify an unnecessarily broad suppression of speech addressed to adults.' Reno v. ACLU." The same five justices picked up a sixth vote from Justice Souter in concluding that the indoor advertising height regulations failed both the third and fourth steps of Central Hudson analysis: "Not all children are less than 5 feet tall, and those who are certainly have the ability to look up and take in their surroundings."

Justices KENNEDY, joined by Justice Scalia, and Justice THOMAS each wrote separate concurrences in part and in the judgment that raised questions about the adequacy of the Central Hudson test. Justice Kennedy stated his "continuing concerns that the test gives insufficient protection to truthful, nonmisleading commercial speech," and Justice Thomas restated his view that "when the government seeks to restrict truthful speech in order to suppress the ideas it conveys, strict scrutiny is appropriate, whether or not the speech in question may be characterized as 'commercial.' " Justice STEVENS, joined by Justices Ginsburg, Breyer and Souter, would have remanded for further factfinding on whether the 1000-foot outdoor advertising ban was narrowly tailored to the important state interest in preventing underage tobacco use, and joined by Justices Ginsburg and Breyer only, would have upheld the sales display regulations as a mere adjunct to the regulation of conduct.

Note that in 2009, Congress passed the Family Smoking Prevention and Tobacco Control Act, which included several significant restrictions on tobacco advertising. Tobacco manufacturers challenged the restrictions on First Amendment grounds. Applying the Central Hudson test, the Sixth Circuit upheld a majority of the regulations, finding that the government had significant interest in preventing juvenile smoking, and that the bans on free samples, non-tobacco merchandise, and event sponsorship were sufficiently tailored to achieving that interest. See Discount Tobacco City & Lottery, Inc. v. U.S., 674 F.3d 509 (2012). The panel held, however, that the Act's ban on distribution of free gifts with tobacco purchases was insufficiently tailored to achieving a substantial governmental interest and thus violated the First Amendment. It also rejected a ban on color imagery in tobacco advertising. The Supreme Court denied certiorari.

Another case in which the Supreme Court applied the Central Hudson test was **Thompson v. Western States Medical Center**, 535 U.S. 357 (2002). There, the Court struck down a provision of the Food and Drug Modernization Act of 1997 that conditioned an exemption from FDA approval requirements for makers of "compounded drugs" on their not "advertis[ing] or promot[ing] the compounding of any particular drug, class of drug, or type of drug." The Act did, however, allow providers to advertise and promote the compounding *service* without losing their exemption. Writing for the Court, Justice O'CONNOR found the government's ends important but its means insufficiently narrowly tailored to them: "Preserving the effectiveness and integrity of the FDCA's new drug approval process is clearly an important governmental interest, and the Government has every reason to want as many drugs as possible to be subject to that approval process. The Government also has an important interest [in] permitting the continuation of the practice of compounding so that patients with particular needs may obtain medications suited to those needs.

"[But] the Government has failed to demonstrate that the speech restrictions are 'not more extensive than is necessary to serve [those] interest[s].' [Several] non-speech-related means of drawing a line between compounding and large-scale manufacturing might be possible here. [Even] if the Government had argued that the [speech-related] restrictions were motivated by a fear that advertising compounded drugs would put people who do not need such drugs at risk by causing them to convince their doctors to prescribe the drugs anyway, [this] concern amounts to a fear that people would make bad decisions if given truthful information about compounded drugs. [We] have previously rejected the notion that the Government has an interest in preventing the dissemination of truthful commercial information in order to prevent members of the public from making bad decisions with the information. [Virginia Board.]"

Justice BREYER dissented, joined by Chief Justice Rehnquist and Justices Stevens and Ginsburg: "[The] Court seriously undervalues the importance of the Government's interest in protecting the health and safety of the American public." Endorsing a "lenient" interpretation of the First Amendment in the commercial speech context, he concluded: "[An] overly rigid 'commercial speech' doctrine will transform what ought to be a legislative or regulatory decision about the best way to protect the health and safety of the American public into a constitutional decision prohibiting the legislature from enacting necessary protections. As history in respect to the Due Process Clause shows, any such transformation would involve a tragic constitutional misunderstanding."

2. *Paternalism and commercial speech.* The opinions of Justices Stevens and Thomas in Liquormart emphasized the illegitimacy of any government interest in keeping consumers ignorant of truthful and nonmisleading commercial information. Tracking the reasoning of Virginia Pharmacy, they suggested that government may not suppress truthful price data out of fear that consumers will act on it in ways that are harmful to their self-interest. How far does this anti-paternalism rationale extend? May the state ban tobacco ads that depict smokers as rugged and healthy or as socially and financially successful, on the ground that such positive images of smoking will induce consumers to act against their own self-interest in health? For an argument that such regulation should be permissible, see Blasi & Monaghan, "The First Amendment and Cigarette Advertising," 250 JAMA 502 (1986). For an argument that such regulation is unconstitutional, see Redish, "Tobacco Advertising and the First Amendment," 81 Iowa L. Rev. 589 (1996).

3. *Commercial speech fault lines on the Roberts Court.* May a State restrict the sale, disclosure, and use of pharmacy records for the purpose of revealing to pharmaceutical manufacturers the prescribing practices of individual doctors? In **Sorrell v. IMS Health Co.**, 564 U.S. 552 (2011), the Court considered a free speech challenge to § 4631(d) of Vermont's Prescription Confidentiality Law, which attempted to limit the practice of pharmaceutical "detailing" by providing that, unless the prescriber consents, health insurers and pharmacies "shall not sell, license, or exchange for value regulated records containing prescriber-identifiable information, nor permit the use of regulated records containing prescriber-identifiable information for marketing or promoting a prescription drug" and that "[p]harmaceutical manufacturers and pharmaceutical marketers shall not use prescriber-identifiable information for marketing or promoting a prescription drug." The law contained exceptions allowing sale of the same information to other users, such as private or academic researchers. By a vote of 6–3 in which the Justices diverged sharply into two camps on commercial speech methodology, the Court ruled that Vermont's law violated the First Amendment even if reviewed under the heightened scrutiny applicable to commercial speech rather than the strict scrutiny applicable to other content-and speaker-based restrictions.

Justice KENNEDY wrote for the Court, joined by Chief Justice Roberts and Justices Scalia, Thomas, Alito, and Sotomayor: "Vermont's law enacts content-and speaker-based restrictions on the sale, disclosure, and use of prescriber-identifying information. [As] a result of these content-and speaker-based rules, detailers cannot obtain prescriber-identifying information, even though the information may be purchased or acquired by other speakers with diverse purposes and viewpoints. Detailers are likewise barred from using the information for marketing, even though the information may be used by a wide range of other speakers. [The] law on its face burdens disfavored speech by disfavored speakers." Justice Kennedy observed that the law even discriminated on the basis of viewpoint because it sought to restrict promotional efforts for brand-name drugs at the expense of generic drugs favored by state policy.

Justice Kennedy continued: "It follows that heightened judicial scrutiny is warranted. Commercial speech is no exception. A 'consumer's concern for the free flow of commercial speech often may be far keener than his concern for urgent political dialogue.' That reality has great relevance in the fields of medicine and public health, where information can save lives." The majority opinion rejected the State's arguments that "heightened judicial scrutiny is unwarranted because its law is a mere commercial regulation" or "because sales, transfer, and use of prescriber-identifying information are conduct, not speech." To the contrary, Justice Kennedy wrote, "the creation and dissemination of information are speech within the meaning of the First Amendment." Turning to the standard of scrutiny, he continued: "In the ordinary case it is all but dispositive to conclude that a law is content-based and, in practice, viewpoint-discriminatory. [The] outcome is the same whether a special commercial speech inquiry or a stricter form of judicial scrutiny is applied.

"[The] State seeks to achieve its policy objectives through the indirect means of restraining certain speech by certain speakers—that is, by diminishing detailers' ability to influence prescription decisions. Those who seek to censor or burden free expression often assert that disfavored speech has adverse effects. But the 'fear that people would make bad decisions if given truthful information' cannot justify content-based burdens on speech. Thompson; Virginia Bd. of Pharmacy; 44 Liquormart."

Justice BREYER filed a dissent, joined by Justices Ginsburg and Kagan. He argued that the Court should have applied a "more lenient" standard of scrutiny than Central Hudson because Vermont's law was part of a broader scheme of "ordinary commercial or regulatory legislation that affects speech in less direct ways" than a simple ban on advertising. Echoing then-Justice Rehnquist's dissent in Central Hudson, he suggested that the majority's approach portended a " 'retur[n] to the bygone era of Lochner v. New York, in which it was common practice for this Court to strike down economic regulations adopted by a State based on the Court's own notions of the most appropriate means for the State to implement its considered policies.' " Because the Vermont statute's "requirements form part of a traditional, comprehensive regulatory regime" to ensure that pharmaceutical products are both safe and effective, and because "Vermont's statute is directed toward information that exists only by virtue of government regulation," the dissenters would have applied the mere rational-basis review applicable to ordinary economic regulations. Even under Central Hudson, however, Justice Breyer concluded, the Vermont anti-detailing law should have been upheld as narrowly tailored to a substantial state interest in protecting public health by ensuring more "fair and balanced" prescribing practices by physicians.

In Matal v. Tam (2017; p. 426), the Court focused its attention on government speech doctrine but also noted that, even if the commercial speech doctrine applied, the Lanham Act's disparagement clause "cannot withstand even Central Hudson review." Justice Alito delivered the opinion of the Court in Part IV, which the Chief Justice, Justice Thomas, and Justice Breyer joined:

"It is claimed that the disparagement clause serves two interests. The first is [that] Government has an interest in preventing speech expressing ideas that offend. [That] idea strikes at the heart of the First Amendment. Speech that demeans on the basis of race, ethnicity, gender, religion, age, disability, or any other similar ground is hateful; but the proudest boast of our free speech jurisprudence is that we protect the freedom to express 'the thought that we hate.'

The second interest asserted is protecting the orderly flow of commerce. [A] simple answer [is] that the disparagement clause is not 'narrowly drawn' to drive out trademarks that support invidious discrimination. [It] applies to trademarks like the following: 'Down with racists,' 'Down with sexists,' 'Down with homophobes.' It is not an anti-discrimination clause; it is a happy-talk clause.

[There] is also a deeper problem with the argument that commercial speech may be cleansed of any expression likely to cause offense. The commercial market is well stocked with merchandise that disparages prominent figures and groups, and the line between commercial and non-commercial speech is not always clear. [If] affixing the commercial label permits the suppression of any speech that may lead to political or social 'volatility,' free speech would be endangered."

FREEDOM OF SPEECH—MODES OF REGULATION AND STANDARDS OF REVIEW

Chapter 1 explored the distinction between protected and unprotected or less protected forms of expression. In Chapter 2, the focus shifts from the nature of the speech involved to the nature of the government regulation involved. Section 1 of this chapter examines a key distinction: that between regulations that aim at the content of speech and regulations that aim at some other, content-neutral interest, such as peace and quiet, the orderly movement of crowds, the aesthetic attractiveness of public spaces, or the economic competitiveness of an industry. Outside the area of unprotected categories of speech, the Court has scrutinized content-based distinctions more carefully than those it considers content-neutral, although it still subjects most content-neutral regulations of speech or symbolic conduct to heightened rather than minimum rationality review. Section 2 turns to the problem of speech-restrictive laws that the government enacts or enforces in its capacity as proprietor, educator, employer, or patron. The discussion there begins with the law governing public forums and ends with the problem of unconstitutional conditions on government subsidies. Finally, Section 3 turns to a set of special procedural restrictions on how government regulates speech—the strong presumptions against overbreadth, vagueness and prior restraint—that seek to prevent government from restricting speech too broadly, too unclearly or too soon, even if it could restrict the very same speech under a law that was written or applied in a different way.

SECTION 1. CONTENT-BASED AND CONTENT-NEUTRAL REGULATIONS

Does it matter for First Amendment purposes if a law is written with reference to the ideas, message or communicative impact of expression? If the effect is the suppression of speech, why should it matter how government accomplishes that suppression? The Court has paid close attention to the distinction between content-based and content-neutral laws. Why might that be so?

To introduce the problem, suppose that a municipality enacted laws prohibiting the construction or maintenance, even on private property, of:

1.   any billboard

2.   any political billboard

3.   any billboard supporting a Republican candidate

4.   any billboard tending to arouse political anger or hostility

5.   any message on a billboard during the three weeks preceding a general election

6.   any billboard in any area zoned for residential use

7.   any billboard larger than 12 by 40 feet

Every one of these laws would alike prohibit a Republican proprietor from erecting, in a residential neighborhood, a 20- by 50-foot billboard urging election of a Republican candidate in a close race in the weeks just before the election. Yet while each of these laws would have the identical effect on such proposed speech, the Court would scrutinize them differently. Which of these laws appear content-neutral? Which ones appear content-based? Which ones, if any, do not appear to aim at speech at all? Which, if any, of these laws more troubling than others under First Amendment principles? Why? The Supreme Court has addressed this issue most prominently in the following case, Reed v. Town of Gilbert, 576 U.S. 155 (2015).

———

THE DISTINCTION BETWEEN CONTENT-BASED AND CONTENT-NEUTRAL LAWS

For some time, the Court treated the distinction between content-based and content-neutral regulations as crucial in First Amendment law. In Reed, the Court drew a bright line. See Genevieve Lakier, "Reed v. Town of Gilbert, Arizona, and the Rise of the Anticlassificatory First Amendment," 2016 Sup. Ct. Rev. 223 (2016).

———

Reed v. Town of Gilbert
576 U.S. 155, 135 S. Ct. 2218, 192 L. Ed. 2d 236 (2015).

■ JUSTICE THOMAS delivered the opinion of the Court.

The town of Gilbert, Arizona, has adopted a comprehensive code governing the manner in which people may display outdoor signs. [The] Sign Code prohibits the display of outdoor signs anywhere within the Town without a permit, but it then exempts 23 categories of signs from that requirement. These exemptions include everything from bazaar signs to flying banners. Three categories of exempt signs are particularly relevant here.

The first is "Ideological Sign[s]." This category includes any "sign communicating a message or ideas for noncommercial purposes that is not a Construction Sign, Directional Sign, Temporary Directional Sign Relating to a Qualifying Event, Political Sign, Garage Sale Sign, or a sign owned or required by a governmental agency." Of the three categories discussed here, the Code treats ideological signs most favorably, allowing them to be up to 20 square feet in area and to be placed in all "zoning districts" without time limits.

The second category is "Political Sign[s]." This includes any "temporary sign designed to influence the outcome of an election called by a public body." The Code treats these signs less favorably than ideological signs. The Code allows the placement of political signs up to 16 square feet on residential property and up to 32 square feet on nonresidential property, undeveloped municipal property, and "rights-of-way." These signs may be displayed up to

60 days before a primary election and up to 15 days following a general election.

The third category is "Temporary Directional Signs Relating to a Qualifying Event." This includes any "Temporary Sign intended to direct pedestrians, motorists, and other passersby to a 'qualifying event.'" A "qualifying event" is defined as any "assembly, gathering, activity, or meeting sponsored, arranged, or promoted by a religious, charitable, community service, educational, or other similar non-profit organization." The Code treats temporary directional signs even less favorably than political signs. Temporary directional signs may be no larger than six square feet. They may be placed on private property or on a public right-of-way, but no more than four signs may be placed on a single property at any time. And, they may be displayed no more than 12 hours before the "qualifying event" and no more than 1 hour afterward.

Petitioners Good News Community Church (Church) and its pastor, Clyde Reed, wish to advertise the time and location of their Sunday church services. The Church is a small, cash-strapped entity that owns no building, so it holds its services at elementary schools or other locations in or near the Town. In order to inform the public about its services, which are held in a variety of different locations, the Church began placing 15 to 20 temporary signs around the Town, frequently in the public right-of-way abutting the street. The signs typically displayed the Church's name, along with the time and location of the upcoming service. Church members would post the signs early in the day on Saturday and then remove them around midday on Sunday.

[This] practice caught the attention of the Town's Sign Code compliance manager, who twice cited the Church for violating the Code.

[Content-based] laws—those that target speech based on its communicative content—are presumptively unconstitutional and may be justified only if the government proves that they are narrowly tailored to serve compelling state interests. Government regulation of speech is content based if a law applies to particular speech because of the topic discussed or the idea or message expressed.

[The] Town's Sign Code is content based on its face. [The] restrictions in the Sign Code that apply to any given sign [depend] entirely on the communicative content of the sign. If a sign informs its reader of the time and place a book club will discuss John Locke's Two Treatises of Government, that sign will be treated differently from a sign expressing the view that one should vote for one of Locke's followers in an upcoming election, and both signs will be treated differently from a sign expressing an ideological view rooted in Locke's theory of government. More to the point, the Church's signs inviting people to attend its worship services are treated differently from signs conveying other types of ideas. [A] law that is content based on its face is subject to strict scrutiny regardless of the government's benign motive, content-neutral justification, or lack of animus toward the ideas contained in the regulated speech.

[The] Court of Appeals [reasoned] that the Sign Code was content neutral because it "does not mention any idea or viewpoint, let alone single one out for differential treatment." This analysis conflates two distinct but related limitations that the First Amendment places on government regulation of speech. [A] speech regulation targeted at specific subject matter is content based even if it does not discriminate among viewpoints within that subject matter. For example, a law banning the use of sound trucks for political speech—and only political speech—would be a content-based regulation, even if it imposed no limits on the political viewpoints that could be expressed. The Town's Sign Code likewise singles out specific subject matter for differential treatment, even if it does not target viewpoints within that subject matter. [That] is a paradigmatic example of content-based discrimination.

[The] Sign Code's distinctions are [also] not speaker based. The restrictions for political, ideological, and temporary event signs apply equally no matter who sponsors them. [But] the fact that a distinction is speaker based does not [automatically] render the distinction content neutral. [A] law limiting the content of newspapers, but only newspapers, could not evade strict scrutiny simply because it could be characterized as speaker based.

Nor do the Sign Code's distinctions hinge on whether and when an event is occurring. The Code does not permit citizens to post signs on any topic whatsoever within a set period leading up to an election, for example. Instead, come election time, it requires Town officials to determine whether a sign is "designed to influence the outcome of an election" (and thus "political") or merely "communicating a message or ideas for noncommercial purposes" (and thus "ideological"). That obvious content-based inquiry does not evade strict scrutiny review simply because an event (*i.e.*, an election) is involved.

[It] is the Town's burden to demonstrate that the Code's differentiation between temporary directional signs and other types of signs [furthers] a compelling governmental interest and is narrowly tailored to that end.

The Town [has] offered only two governmental interests in support of the distinctions the Sign Code draws: preserving the Town's aesthetic appeal and traffic safety. Assuming for the sake of argument that those are compelling governmental interests, the Code's distinctions fail as hopelessly underinclusive. [The] Town cannot claim that placing strict limits on temporary directional signs is necessary to beautify the Town while at the same time allowing unlimited numbers of other types of signs that create the same problem.

The Town similarly has not shown that limiting temporary directional signs is necessary to eliminate threats to traffic safety, but that limiting other types of signs is not.

The Town has ample content-neutral options available to resolve problems with safety and aesthetics.

[At] the same time, the presence of certain signs may be essential, both for vehicles and pedestrians, to guide traffic or to identify hazards and ensure safety. A sign ordinance narrowly tailored to the challenges of protecting the safety of pedestrians, drivers, and passengers—such as warning signs marking hazards on private property, signs directing traffic, or street numbers associated with private houses—well might survive strict scrutiny.

■ JUSTICE ALITO, with whom JUSTICE KENNEDY and JUSTICE SOTOMAYOR join, concurring.

[As] the Court shows, the regulations at issue in this case are replete with content-based distinctions, and as a result they must satisfy strict scrutiny. This does not mean, however, that municipalities are powerless to enact and enforce reasonable sign regulations. I will not attempt to provide anything like a comprehensive list, but here are some rules that would not be content based:

Rules regulating the size of signs. These rules may distinguish among signs based on any content-neutral criteria, including any relevant criteria listed below.

Rules regulating the locations in which signs may be placed. These rules may distinguish between free-standing signs and those attached to buildings.

Rules distinguishing between lighted and unlighted signs.

Rules distinguishing between signs with fixed messages and electronic signs with messages that change.

Rules that distinguish between the placement of signs on private and public property.

Rules distinguishing between the placement of signs on commercial and residential property.

Rules distinguishing between on-premises and off-premises signs.

Rules restricting the total number of signs allowed per mile of roadway.

Rules imposing time restrictions on signs advertising a one-time event. Rules of this nature do not discriminate based on topic or subject and are akin to rules restricting the times within which oral speech or music is allowed.

Properly understood, today's decision will not prevent cities from regulating signs in a way that fully protects public safety and serves legitimate esthetic objectives.

■ JUSTICE KAGAN, with whom JUSTICE GINSBURG and JUSTICE BREYER join, concurring in the judgment.

Countless cities and towns across America have adopted ordinances regulating the posting of signs, while exempting certain categories of signs based on their subject matter.

[Given] the Court's analysis, many sign ordinances of that kind are now in jeopardy. [On] the majority's view, courts would have to determine that a town has a compelling interest in informing passersby where George Washington slept. [The] consequence—unless courts water down strict scrutiny to something unrecognizable—is that our communities will find themselves in an unenviable bind: They will have to either repeal the exemptions that allow for helpful signs on streets and sidewalks, or else lift their sign restrictions altogether and resign themselves to the resulting clutter.

Although the majority insists that applying strict scrutiny to all such ordinances is "essential" to protecting First Amendment freedoms, I find it challenging to understand why that is so. [We] apply strict scrutiny to facially content-based regulations of speech [when] there is any realistic possibility that official suppression of ideas is afoot. That is always the case when the regulation facially differentiates on the basis of viewpoint.

[Subject-matter] regulation [may] have the intent or effect of favoring some ideas over others. When that is realistically possible [we] insist that the law pass the most demanding constitutional test. But when that is not realistically possible, we may do well to relax our guard so that "entirely reasonable" laws imperiled by strict scrutiny can survive.

[The] Town of Gilbert's defense of its sign ordinance—most notably, the law's distinctions between directional signs and others—does not pass strict scrutiny, or intermediate scrutiny, or even the laugh test. [Accordingly,] there is no need to decide in this case whether strict scrutiny applies to every sign ordinance in every town across this country containing a subject-matter exemption

---

1. *Viewpoint restrictions.* Well before the Supreme Court squarely ruled that content-based restrictions always invoke strict scrutiny, the Court used discrimination against certain ideas or viewpoints as its archetypal model for triggering strict scrutiny. Several of the decisions already explored in Chapter 1 are illustrative. For example, Kingsley International Pictures Corp. v. Regents (1959; p. 131) held that a state may not deny a license to a film "because that picture advocates an idea—that adultery under certain circumstances may be proper behavior. [The] First Amendment's basic guarantee is of freedom to advocate ideas." Brandenburg v. Ohio (1969; p. 48) made clear that, in the absence of incitement to imminent lawless action, the "mere advocacy" of violent overthrow of democracy or capitalism could not be made a crime. Justice Scalia's opinion for the Court in R.A.V. v. St. Paul (1992; p. 109), suggested that the St. Paul ordinance prohibiting symbols that tend to arouse racial anger or alarm was invalid in part as "viewpoint discrimination" because it prohibited fighting words by bigots but not against them: "St. Paul has no [authority] to license one side of a debate to fight freestyle, while requiring the other to follow Marquis of Queensbury rules." And Judge Easterbrook's decision in American Booksellers Ass'n v. Hudnut (1985; p. 148) invalidated a feminist-inspired anti-pornography ordinance as "thought control" because "speech that 'subordinates' women [is] forbidden" while speech "that portrays women in positions of equality is lawful, no matter how graphic the sexual content."

After Reed v. Gilbert, the emphasis on viewpoint discrimination may well have become secondary, because every case of viewpoint discrimination necessarily appears to involve content-based discrimination. (Can you think of any exceptions?) In 2021, the Court considered a case that raised essentially the same issues addressed in Reed, presumably to offer some clarification of the meaning of "content-based." Did the Court succeed?

City of Austin, Texas v. Reagan National Advertising of Austin

597 U.S. ___, 142 S. Ct. 1464, 212 L. Ed. 2d 418 (2022).

■ JUSTICE SOTOMAYOR delivered the opinion of the Court.

Like thousands of jurisdictions around the country, the City of Austin, Texas, [regulates] signs that advertise things that are not located on the same premises as the sign, as well as signs that direct people to offsite locations. These are known as off-premises signs, and they include, most notably, billboards. The question presented is whether, under this Court's precedents interpreting the Free Speech Clause of the First Amendment, the City's regulation is subject to strict scrutiny. We hold that it is not.

[The] Court of Appeals interpreted Reed to mean that if "a reader must ask: who is the speaker and what is the speaker saying" to apply a regulation, then the regulation is automatically content based. This rule, which holds that a regulation cannot be content neutral if it requires reading the sign at issue, is too extreme an interpretation of this Court's precedent. Unlike the regulations at issue in Reed, the City's off-premises distinction requires an examination of speech only in service of drawing neutral, location-based lines. It is agnostic as to content. Thus, absent a content-based purpose or justification, the City's distinction is content neutral and does not warrant the application of strict scrutiny.

[Unlike] the sign code at issue in Reed, [the] City's provisions at issue here do not single out any topic or subject matter for differential treatment. A sign's substantive message itself is irrelevant to the application of the provisions. [Rather], the City's provisions distinguish based on location: A given sign is treated differently based solely on whether it is located on the same premises as the thing being discussed or not. [The] on-/off-premises distinction is therefore similar to ordinary time, place, or manner restrictions. Reed does not require the application of strict scrutiny to this kind of location-based regulation.

[This] Court's First Amendment precedents and doctrines have consistently recognized that restrictions on speech may require some evaluation of the speech and nonetheless remain content neutral. [The] First Amendment allows for regulations of solicitation. [To] identify whether speech entails solicitation, one must read or hear it first. Even so, the Court has reasoned that restrictions on solicitation are not content based and do not inherently present the potential for becoming a means of suppressing a particular point of view, so long as they do not discriminate based on topic, subject matter, or viewpoint.

[The] Court has previously understood distinctions between on-premises and off-premises signs, like the one at issue in this case, to be content neutral. [Underlying] these cases and others is a rejection of the view that *any* examination of speech or expression inherently triggers heightened First Amendment concern. Rather, it is regulations that discriminate based on the topic discussed or the idea or message expressed that are content based.

The principle the Reed Court articulated is [that while] overt subject-matter discrimination is facially content based (for example, Ideological Signs, defined as those communicating a message or ideas for noncommercial purposes), so, too, are subtler forms of discrimination that achieve identical results based on function or purpose (for example, Political Signs, defined as those designed to influence the outcome of an election). In other words, a regulation of speech cannot escape classification as facially content based simply by swapping an obvious subject-matter distinction for a "function or purpose" proxy that achieves the same result. That does not mean that any classification that considers function or purpose is *always* content based. Such a reading of "function or purpose" would contravene numerous precedents. [Reed] did not purport to cast doubt on these cases. Nor did Reed cast doubt on the Nation's history of regulating off-premises signs.

[We] do not nullify Reed's protections, resuscitate a decision that we do not cite, or fashion a novel "specificity test" simply by quoting the standard repeatedly enunciated in Reed. We merely [reach] the commonsense result that a location-based and content-agnostic on-/off-premises distinction does not, on its face, single out specific subject matter for differential treatment. [The] dissent would hold that tens of thousands of jurisdictions have presumptively violated the First Amendment, some for more than half a century, and that they have done so by use of an on-/off-premises distinction this Court has repeatedly reviewed and never previously questioned. [The]Constitution does not require that bizarre result.

This Court's determination that the City's ordinance is facially content neutral does not end the First Amendment inquiry. If there is evidence that an impermissible purpose or justification underpins a facially content-neutral restriction, for instance, that restriction may be content based. Moreover, to survive intermediate scrutiny, a restriction on speech or expression must be narrowly tailored to serve a significant governmental interest. [Because] the Court of Appeals did not address these issues, the Court leaves them for remand and expresses no view on the matters.

■ JUSTICE BREYER, concurring.

Given [Reed], I join the majority's opinion. I write separately because I continue to believe that the Court's reasoning in Reed was wrong. [The] First Amendment is not the Tax Code. Its purposes are often better served when judge-made categories (like "content discrimination") are treated, not as bright-line rules, but instead as rules of thumb. And, where strict scrutiny's harsh presumption of unconstitutionality is at issue, it is particularly important to avoid jumping to such presumptive conclusions without first considering whether the regulation at issue works harm to First Amendment interests that is disproportionate in light of the relevant regulatory objectives.

If Reed is taken as setting forth a formal rule that courts must strictly scrutinize regulations simply because they refer to particular content, we have good reason to fear [that] courts will strike down entirely reasonable regulations that reflect the will of the people. If so, the Court's content-based line-drawing will substitute judicial for democratic decisionmaking and threaten the ability of the people to translate their ideas into policy. A second possibility is that courts instead will (perhaps unconsciously) dilute the stringent strict scrutiny standard in an effort to avoid striking down reasonable regulations. Doing so would weaken the First Amendment's protection in instances where strict scrutiny should apply in full force. A third possibility is that courts will develop a matrix of formal subsidiary rules and exceptions that seek to distinguish between reasonable and unreasonable content-based regulations. Such a patchwork, however, may prove overly complex, unwieldy, or unworkable. And it may make it more difficult for ordinary Americans to understand the importance of First Amendment values and to live their lives in accord with those values.

■ JUSTICE ALITO, concurring in the judgment in part and dissenting in part.

[The] Court of Appeals did not apply the tests that must be met before a law is held to be facially unconstitutional [and] it is doubtful that they can be met. Many (and possibly the great majority) of the situations in which the relevant provisions may apply involve commercial speech, and under our precedents, regulations of commercial speech are analyzed differently. [On] remand, the lower courts should determine whether those provisions are unconstitutional as applied to each of the billboards at issue.

Today's decision, however, goes further and holds flatly that "the sign code provisions challenged here do not discriminate on the basis of the topic discussed or the idea or message expressed," and that categorical statement is incorrect. The provisions defining on- and off-premises signs clearly discriminate on those grounds, and at least as applied in some situations, strict scrutiny should be required. [Under] the provisions in effect when petitioner's applications were denied, a sign was considered to be off-premises if it advertised among other things, a "person, activity, or service not located on the site where the sign is installed" or if it "directed persons to any location not on that site." Consider what this definition would mean as applied to signs posted in the front window of a commercial establishment, say, a little coffee shop. If the owner put up a sign advertising a new coffee drink, the sign would be classified as on-premises, but suppose the owner instead mounted a sign in the same location saying: "Contribute to X's legal defense fund" or "Free COVID tests available at Y pharmacy" or "Attend City Council meeting to speak up about Z." All those signs would appear to fall within the definition of an off-premises sign and would thus be disallowed. Providing disparate treatment for the sign about a new drink and the signs about social and political matters constitutes discrimination on the basis of topic or subject matter.

■ JUSTICE THOMAS, with whom JUSTICE GORSUCH and JUSTICE BARRETT join, dissenting.

[Per Reed], all that matters is that the regulation draws distinctions based on a sign's communicative content, which the off-premises restriction plainly does. This conclusion is not undermined because the off-premises sign restriction depends in part on a content-neutral element: the location of the sign. Much like in Reed, that an Austin official applying the sign code must know *where* the sign is does not negate the fact that he also must know *what* the sign says. Take, for instance, a sign outside a Catholic bookstore. If the sign says, "Visit the Holy Land," it is likely an off-premises sign because it conveys a message directing people elsewhere (unless the name of the bookstore is "Holy Land Books"). But if the sign instead says, "Buy More Books," it is likely a permissible on-premises sign (unless the sign also contains the address of another bookstore across town). Finally, suppose the sign says, "Go to Confession." After examining the sign's message, an official would need to inquire whether a priest ever hears confessions at that location. If one does, the sign could convey a permissible "on-premises" message. If not, the sign conveys an impermissible off-premises message. [In] sum, the off-premises rule is content based and thus invalid unless Austin can satisfy strict scrutiny.

To reach the opposite result, the majority implicitly rewrites Reed's bright-line rule for content-based restrictions. [The] upshot of the majority's reasoning appears to be that a regulation based on a sufficiently general or broad category of communicative content is not actually content based. [Tellingly], the only decision that even remotely supports the majority's rule is one it does not cite: Hill v. Colorado. There, the Court held that an undeniably content-based law was nonetheless content neutral because it discriminated against an extremely broad category of communications, supposedly without regard to subject matter. The majority's decision today is erroneous for the same reasons that Hill is an aberration in our case law.

Ultimately, the majority's only "historical" support is that regulations like Austin's proliferated following the enactment of the Highway Beautification Act of 1965. The majority's suggestion that the First Amendment should yield to a speech restriction that "proliferated"—under pressure from the Federal Government—some two centuries after the founding is both startling and dangerous. This Court has never hinted that the government can, with a few decades of regulation, subject "new categories of speech" to less exacting First Amendment scrutiny.

Regardless, even if this allegedly "unbroken tradition" did not fall short by a century or two, the majority offers no explanation why historical regulation is relevant to the question whether the off-premises restriction is content based under *Reed* and our modern content-neutrality jurisprudence. If Austin had met its burden of identifying a historical tradition of analogous regulation—as can be done, say, for obscenity or defamation—that would not make the off-premises rule content neutral. It might simply mean that the off-premises rule is a constitutional form of content-based discrimination. But content neutrality under Reed is an empirical question, not a historical one. Thus, the majority's historical argument is not only meritless but misguided.

———

1. *City of Austin's version of Reed.* Justice Sotomayor's majority opinion "reject[ed] the view that any examination of speech or expression inherently triggers heightened First Amendment concern" in favor of the view that "rather, it is regulations that discriminate based on the topic discussed or the idea or message expressed that are content based." Justice Thomas, who wrote Reed, disagreed with this reading of his opinion, endorsing the view that if you must read the sign, to apply the regulation, the regulation is content-based and merits strict scrutiny. In his view, the Court rewrote the "bright-line" rule of Reed.

2. *Content neutrality after City of Austin.* According to the Court's City of Austin opinion, a "distinction" that "requires an examination of speech only in service of drawing neutral, location-based lines" is content neutral because "[it] is agnostic as to content." The court also held that "absent a content-based purpose or justification, the City's distinction is content neutral." What does this mean for defining content neutrality? Is the test whether the challenged regulation focuses on a substantive "topic, idea, or message"? If so, is Reed now limited to the situation in which, as the City of Austin court put it, the government regulation is "swapping an obvious subject-matter distinction for a 'function or purpose' proxy that achieves the same result"? If that is the new rule, is Justice Thomas correct that Reed has been rewritten?

3. *Subject matter restrictions.* Is content discrimination suspect in the absence of viewpoint discrimination? What if government eliminates expression on an entire topic? The Court has generally scrutinized subject matter restrictions strictly. Recall that Justice Scalia's opinion for the Court subjected the St. Paul ordinance in R.A.V. to strict scrutiny not only because it involved viewpoint discrimination but also because it forbade only those fighting words that were "addressed to one of the specified disfavored topics" of race, color, creed, religion or gender. Recall too the Court's invalidation of a ban on the display of all nudity on drive-in theater screens in Erznoznik v.

Jacksonville (1975; p. 153). Consider the following cases involving other restrictions on the subject matter of speech.

In **Police Department v. Mosley**, 408 U.S. 92 (1972), the Court invalidated a Chicago disorderly conduct ordinance which barred picketing within 150 feet of a school while the school was in session, but exempted "peaceful picketing of any school involved in a labor dispute." Mosley had conducted a solitary picket outside a Chicago high school, carrying a sign saying "Jones High School practices black discrimination." Justice MARSHALL's opinion for the Court found the law's "selective exclusion [of speech] from a public place" unconstitutional. He stated: "The central problem with Chicago's ordinance is that it describes the permissible picketing in terms of its subject matter. [The] operative distinction is the message on a picket sign. [Above] all else, the First Amendment means that government has no power to restrict expression because of its message, its ideas, its subject matter, or its content. To permit the continued building of our politics and culture, and to assure self-fulfillment for each individual, our people are guaranteed the right to express any thought, free from government censorship. The essence of this forbidden censorship is content control. [Necessarily], then, under [equal protection], not to mention the First Amendment itself, government may not grant the use of a forum to people whose views it finds acceptable, but deny use to those wishing to express less favored or more controversial views. And it may not select which issues are worth discussing or debating in public facilities. There is an 'equality of status in the field of ideas,' and government must afford all points of view an equal opportunity to be heard."

Justice Marshall noted that "reasonable 'time, place, and manner'" regulations of picketing may be necessary to further significant governmental interests." But this was not a time, place, and manner regulation, as it defined the prohibited speech "in terms of subject matter," which was "never permitted." He rejected the argument that preventing school disruption justified the ordinance: "If peaceful labor picketing is permitted, there is no justification for prohibiting all nonlabor picketing, both peaceful and nonpeaceful. 'Peaceful' nonlabor picketing [is] obviously no more disruptive than 'peaceful' labor picketing. But Chicago's ordinance permits the latter and prohibits the former." Moreover, he rejected the argument that a city could prohibit all nonlabor picketing "because, as a class, nonlabor picketing is more prone to produce violence than labor picketing": "Predictions about imminent disruption from picketing involve judgments appropriately made on an individualized basis, not by means of broad classifications, especially those based on subject matter."

Technically, Justice Marshall rested the Mosley judgment on the Equal Protection Clause of the Fourteenth Amendment. But he noted: "Of course, the equal protection claim in this case is closely intertwined with First Amendment interests: the Chicago ordinance affects picketing, which is expressive conduct; moreover, it does so by classifications formulated in terms of the subject of the picketing." Later cases have assimilated the Mosley holding into First Amendment analysis.

In **Carey v. Brown**, 447 U.S. 455 (1980), the Court found another picketing restriction unconstitutional under Mosley. The case involved a peaceful picket outside the mayor's home advocating racial integration of the schools through busing. The picketers were convicted under a state law that generally barred picketing outside residences or dwellings, but exempted "the peaceful picketing of a place of employment involved in a labor dispute." Justice BRENNAN, writing for the majority, held that the law impermissibly "accords preferential treatment to the expression of views on one particular subject; information about labor disputes may be freely disseminated, but discussion of all other issues is restricted." It was thus "constitutionally indistinguishable" from Mosley. Justice REHNQUIST, joined by Chief Justice Burger and Justice Blackmun, dissented, arguing that the basis for distinction in the law was "not content, [but] rather the character of the residence sought to be picketed."

Simon & Schuster, Inc. v. Members of New York State Crime Victims Board, 502 U.S. 105 (1991), involved a challenge to New York's "Son of Sam" law, enacted to prevent a serial murderer and other criminals from profiting at the expense of their victims from books about their crimes. The law required payment to the Crime Victims Board of any proceeds due to a person accused of, convicted of, or admitting to a crime, for the production of a book or other work describing the crime. The Board was to place these funds in escrow for five years so that they would be available to satisfy any damage judgments that victims of the defendant's crimes might obtain. The law was challenged by the publisher of a book entitled "Wiseguy: Life in a Mafia Family." A principal source for the book was a former organized crime operative, Henry Hill, who, in exchange for compensation, had recounted his participation in various robberies, extortions, drug dealing and frauds. New York sought payment from the publisher and the publisher challenged the statute under the First Amendment. The Court unanimously invalidated the statute. Justice O'CONNOR, writing for the Court, stated: "[T]he Government's ability to impose content-based burdens on speech raises the specter that the Government may effectively drive certain ideas or viewpoints from the marketplace. The Son of Sam law is a such a content-based statute. It singles out income derived from expressive activity for a burden the State places on no other income, and it is directed only at works with a specified content. Whether the First Amendment 'speaker' is considered to be Henry Hill, whose income the statute places in escrow because of the story he has told, or Simon & Schuster, which can publish books about crime with the assistance of only those criminals willing to forgo remuneration for at least five years, the statute plainly imposes a financial disincentive only on speech of a particular content."

Because the statute was content-based, Justice O'Connor subjected it to strict scrutiny, and found it not narrowly tailored to the state's "undisputed compelling interest in ensuring that criminals do not profit from their crimes." She found that the State had not shown "any greater interest in compensating victims from the proceeds of such 'storytelling' than from any of the criminal's other assets." She also found the law "significantly overinclusive" as it would potentially sweep in "such works as The Autobiography of Malcolm X, which describes crimes committed by the civil rights leader before he became a public figure; Civil Disobedience, in which Thoreau acknowledges his refusal to pay taxes and recalls his experience in jail; and even the Confessions of Saint Augustine, in which the author laments 'my past foulness and the carnal corruptions of my soul,' one instance of which involved the theft of pears from a neighboring vineyard." Justice KENNEDY, concurring in the judgment, would not have applied strict scrutiny but would have found the law invalid per se: "Here a law is directed to speech alone where the speech in question is not obscene, not defamatory, not words tantamount to an act otherwise criminal, not an impairment of some other constitutional right, not an incitement to lawless action, and not calculated or likely to bring about imminent harm the State has the substantive power to prevent. No further inquiry is necessary to reject the State's argument that the statute should be upheld. [The] New York statute amounts to raw censorship based on content. [That] ought to end the matter."

Could the defect of the laws struck down in Mosley and Carey be cured by an ordinance barring *all* picketing outside a school or home? Would such a law be less restrictive of speech? How? Could New York pass a new law requiring the escrow of *all* proceeds from crime and apply it to Henry Hill's book proceeds? What is the difference between that law and the law struck down in Simon & Schuster? The above cases indicate that the Court will accord subject matter restrictions strict scrutiny, which is almost always fatal. But as the next case suggests, there might be occasional exceptions.

In **Burson v. Freeman**, 504 U.S. 191 (1992), the Court upheld against a First Amendment challenge a state law prohibiting the solicitation of votes, the display of political posters or signs, and the distribution of political campaign materials within 100 feet of the entrance to a polling place. Justice BLACKMUN announced the judgment of the Court and wrote for a plurality joined by Chief Justice Rehnquist and Justices White and Kennedy: "This Court has held that the First Amendment's hostility to content-based regulation extends not only to a restriction on a particular viewpoint, but also to a prohibition of public discussion of an entire topic. [As] a facially content-based restriction on political speech in a public forum, [the ban on campaign materials] must be subjected to exacting scrutiny. Tennessee asserts [that] its regulation protect[s] the right of its citizens to vote freely for the candidates of their choice [and] protects the right to vote in an election conducted with integrity and reliability. [These interests] obviously are compelling ones. [To] survive strict scrutiny, however, a State must do more than assert a compelling state interest—it must demonstrate that its law is necessary to serve the asserted interest. [An] examination of the evolution of election reform, both in this country and abroad, demonstrates the necessity of restricted areas in or around polling places. [That history] reveals a persistent battle against two evils: voter intimidation and election fraud. After an unsuccessful experiment with an unofficial ballot system, all 50 States, together with numerous other Western democracies, settled on the same solution: a secret ballot secured in part by a restricted zone around the voting compartments. [It] is the rare case in which we have held that a law survives strict scrutiny. This, however, is such a rare case. [The] State [has] asserted that the exercise of free speech rights conflicts with another fundamental right, the right to cast a ballot in an election free from the taint of intimidation and fraud. A long history, a substantial consensus, and simple common sense show that some restricted zone around polling places is necessary to protect that fundamental right. Given the conflict between these two rights, we hold that requiring solicitors to stand 100 feet from the entrances to polling places does not constitute an unconstitutional compromise."

Justice KENNEDY wrote a separate concurrence, stating that, despite the preference he expressed in Simon & Schuster for a per se rule against content discrimination rather than case-by-case strict scrutiny, "there is a narrow area in which the First Amendment permits freedom of expression to yield to the extent necessary for the accommodation of another constitutional right. That principle can apply here without danger that the general rule permitting no content restriction will be engulfed by the analysis." Justice Scalia concurred in the judgment, finding that the vicinity of the polling place was not a traditional public forum and therefore that viewpoint neutrality was all that was required. Justice STEVENS dissented, joined by Justices O'Connor and Souter: "Tennessee's statutory 'campaign-free zone' raises constitutional concerns of the first magnitude. The statute directly regulates political expression and thus implicates a core concern of the First Amendment. Moreover, it targets only a specific subject matter (campaign speech) and a defined class of speakers (campaign workers) and thus regulates expression based on its content. [Within] the zone, [the law] silences all campaign-related expression, but allows expression on any other subject: religious, artistic, commercial speech, even political debate and solicitation concerning issues or candidates not on the day's ballot. [This] discriminatory feature of the statute severely undercuts the credibility of its purported law-and-order justification. Tennessee's content-based discrimination is particularly problematic because such a regulation will inevitably favor certain groups of candidates. [Candidates] with fewer resources, candidates for lower visibility offices, and 'grassroots' candidates benefit disproportionately from last-minute campaigning near the polling place." Accordingly, the dissenters concluded, the law could not survive the applicable strict scrutiny.

In another election context, that of *judicial* elections, the Court by contrast struck down as impermissibly content-based a restriction on the subject matter of speech, this time by judicial candidates. In **Republican Party of Minnesota v. White**, 536 U.S. 765 (2002), the Court invalidated by a vote of 5–4 a provision of the Minnesota code of judicial conduct that stated that a "candidate for a judicial office, including an incumbent judge," shall not "announce his or her views on disputed legal or political issues." The provision—known as the "announce clause"—was challenged by a candidate who sought to distribute literature criticizing Minnesota Supreme Court decisions on crime, welfare, and abortion. In his opinion for the Court, Justice SCALIA wrote: "[The] announce clause both prohibits speech on the basis of its content and burdens a category of speech that is 'at the core of our First Amendment freedoms'—speech about the qualifications of candidates for public office. [The] proper test to be applied to determine the constitutionality of such a restriction is what our cases have called strict scrutiny. [Under] the strict-scrutiny test, respondents have the burden to prove that the announce clause is (1) narrowly tailored, to serve (2) a compelling state interest. In order for respondents to show that the announce clause is narrowly tailored, they must demonstrate that it does not 'unnecessarily circumscribe protected expression.' "

Justice Scalia rejected the state's arguments that its interests in preserving the impartiality or the appearance of the impartiality of the state judiciary were sufficiently compelling to justify the announce clause: "One meaning of 'impartiality' in the judicial context—and of course its root meaning—is the lack of bias for or against either *party* to the proceeding. Impartiality in this sense assures equal application of the law. [We] think it plain that the announce clause is not narrowly tailored to serve impartiality (or the appearance of impartiality) in this sense. Indeed, the clause is barely tailored to serve that interest *at all*, inasmuch as it does not restrict speech for or against particular *parties*, but rather speech for or against particular *issues*. [It] is perhaps possible to use the term 'impartiality' in the judicial context [to] mean lack of preconception in favor of or against a particular *legal view*. [Impartiality] in this sense may well be an interest served by the announce clause, but it is not a *compelling* state interest, as strict scrutiny requires. [Even] if it were possible to select judges who did not have preconceived views on legal issues, it would hardly be desirable to do so. 'Proof that a Justice's mind at the time he joined the Court was a complete *tabula rasa* in the area of constitutional adjudication would be evidence of lack of qualification, not lack of bias.' [A] third possible meaning of 'impartiality' [might] be described as open-mindedness. [It] may well be that impartiality in this sense, and the appearance of it, are desirable in the judiciary, but we need not pursue that inquiry, since we do not believe the Minnesota Supreme Court adopted the announce clause for that purpose. [In] Minnesota, a candidate for judicial office may not say 'I think it is constitutional for the legislature to prohibit same-sex marriages.' He may say the very same thing, however, up until the very day before he declares himself a candidate, and may say it repeatedly (until litigation is pending) after he is elected. As a means of pursuing the objective of open-mindedness that respondents now articulate, the announce clause is so woefully underinclusive as to render belief in that purpose a challenge to the credulous."

Justice Scalia likewise rejected the suggestion that elected judges might feel special compulsion in later cases to adhere to views they had announced during an election, putting at risk due process for litigants: "[E]lected judges—regardless of whether they have announced any views beforehand—*always* face the pressure of an electorate who might disagree with their rulings and therefore vote them off the bench. [If] it violates due process for a judge to sit in a case in which ruling one way rather than another increases his prospects for reelection, then [the] practice of electing judges is itself a violation of due process." He also downplayed the difference between judicial and legislative elections, noting that "[n]ot only do state-court judges possess the power to 'make' common law, but they have the immense power to shape the States' constitutions as well. Which is precisely why the election of state judges became popular." He concluded that opposition to judicial elections "may be well taken (it certainly had the support of the Founders of the Federal Government), but the First Amendment does not permit it to achieve its goal by leaving the principle of elections in place while preventing candidates from discussing what the elections are about."

Justice O'Connor concurred but wrote separately to express concern that judicial elections undermine the actual and perceived impartiality of state judges. Justice KENNEDY also concurred to argue that "content-based speech restrictions that do not fall within any traditional exception" should be held invalid per se without undergoing the compelling interest and narrow tailoring inquiries required by strict scrutiny. Justice STEVENS dissented, joined by Justices Souter, Ginsburg, and Breyer: "There is a critical difference between the work of the judge and the work of other public officials. In a democracy, issues of policy are properly decided by majority vote; it is the business of legislators and executives to be popular. But in litigation, issues of law or fact should not be determined by popular vote; it is the business of judges to be indifferent to unpopularity." Justice GINSBURG also dissented, joined by Justices Stevens, Souter, and Breyer: "I would differentiate elections for political offices, in which the First Amendment holds full sway, from elections designed to select those whose office it is to administer justice without respect to persons. [Judges] are not political actors. [Thus], the rationale underlying unconstrained speech in elections for political office—that representative government depends on the public's ability to choose agents who will act at its behest—does not carry over to campaigns for the bench."

The Court's cases since White have reaffirmed that strict scrutiny attaches to content-based distinctions on speech. See, for example, the plurality opinion in United States v. Alvarez (2012; p. 105). Recall, however, that this stringent standard of review applies only where the relevant category of speech is protected; where speech falls within an unprotected category, a content-based distinction is permissible if it "reflect[s] the distinction and rationale for the initial nonprotection." Schauer, "Intentions, Conventions, and the First Amendment: The Case of Cross-Burning," 2003 Sup. Ct. Rev. 197 (citing Virginia v. Black (2003; p. 121)). Can these two disparate standards for content-based distinctions be squared?

In **Williams-Yulee v. Florida Bar**, 575 U.S. 433 (2015), the Court revisited judicial speech in connection with state elections. Chief Justice ROBERTS's opinion upheld the application of Florida's Canon 7C(1), which governs fundraising in judicial elections, to impose sanctions on a judicial candidate's personal solicitation of campaign contributions The Canon, based on a provision in the American Bar Association's Model Code of Judicial Conduct, provides: " 'A candidate, including an incumbent judge, for a judicial office that is filled by public election between competing candidates shall not personally solicit campaign funds, or solicit attorneys for publicly stated support, but may establish committees of responsible persons to secure and manage the expenditure of funds for the candidate's campaign and to obtain public statements of support for his or her candidacy. Such committees are not prohibited from soliciting campaign contributions and public support from any person or corporation authorized by law.' " Most other States, like Florida, prohibit judicial candidates from soliciting campaign funds personally, but allow them to raise money through committees.

The Chief Justice, writing only for a plurality, applied strict scrutiny to Florida's action, asserting that "we hold today what we assumed in Republican Party of Minn. v. White: A State may restrict the speech of a judicial candidate only if the restriction is narrowly tailored to serve a compelling interest." He then continued for a majority of the Court to find that the Florida law was narrowly tailored: "We have emphasized that it is the rare case in which a State demonstrates that a speech restriction is narrowly tailored to serve a compelling interest. But those cases do arise. See Holder v. Humanitarian Law Project (2010; p. 271 below). [The] Florida Supreme Court adopted Canon 7C(1) to promote the State's interests in 'protecting the integrity of the judiciary' and 'maintaining the public's confidence in an impartial judiciary.' [Judges], charged with exercising strict neutrality and independence, cannot supplicate campaign donors without diminishing public confidence in judicial integrity."

Expressly contrasting the judicial elections case to the mainstream of campaign finance cases (see Chapter 3, Section 3 below), the Chief Justice went on: "A State's interest in preserving public confidence in the integrity of its judiciary extends beyond its interest in preventing the appearance of corruption in legislative and executive elections. [The] role of judges differs from the role of politicians. [The] same is not true of judges. In deciding cases, a judge is not to follow the preferences of his supporters, or provide any special consideration to his campaign donors. [As] in White, therefore, our precedents applying the First Amendment to political elections have little bearing on the issues here."

Rejecting a claim of underinclusivity, Chief Justice Roberts wrote that "[a] State need not address all aspects of a problem in one fell swoop; policymakers may focus on their most pressing concerns. [The] solicitation ban aims squarely at the conduct most likely to undermine public confidence in the integrity of the judiciary: personal requests for money by judges and judicial candidates. [And the] Canon contains zero exceptions to its ban on personal solicitation."

On narrow tailoring, Chief Justice Roberts wrote: "Canon 7C(1) leaves judicial candidates free to discuss any issue with any person at any time. Candidates can write letters, give speeches, and put up billboards. They can contact potential supporters in person, on the phone, or online. They can promote their campaigns on radio, television, or other media. [The] First Amendment requires that Canon 7C(1) be narrowly tailored, not that it be perfectly tailored. The impossibility of perfect tailoring is especially apparent when the State's compelling interest is as intangible as public confidence in the integrity of the judiciary. [The] desirability of judicial elections is a question that has sparked disagreement for more than 200 years. [It] is not our place to resolve this enduring debate."

Justice GINSBURG concurred but did not join the plurality in applying strict scrutiny: "As explained in my dissenting opinion in Republican Party of Minnesota v. White, I would not apply exacting scrutiny to a State's endeavor sensibly to differentiate elections for political offices . . . , from elections designed to select those whose office it is to administer justice without respect to persons."

Justice SCALIA dissented, maintaining that "the Court flattens one settled First Amendment principle after another. [One] need not equate judges with politicians to see that the electoral setting calls for all the more vigilance in ensuring observance of the First Amendment. When a candidate asks someone for a campaign contribution, he tends [also] to talk about his qualifications for office and his views on public issues. This expression lies at the heart of what the First Amendment is meant to protect. In addition, banning candidates from asking for money personally favors some candidates over others—incumbent judges (who benefit from their current status) over non-judicial candidates, the well-to-do (who may not need to raise any money at all) over lower-income candidates, and the well-connected (who have an army of potential fundraisers) over outsiders. This danger of legislated (or judicially imposed) favoritism is the very reason the First Amendment exists. [Among] its other functions, the First Amendment is a kind of Equal Protection Clause for ideas. [The] Court's decision disregards these principles.

"[The court's underinclusiveness] analysis elides the distinction between selectivity on the basis of content and selectivity on other grounds. Because the First Amendment does not prohibit underinclusiveness as such, lawmakers may target a problem only at certain times or in certain places. [The] First Amendment is not abridged for the benefit of the Brotherhood of the Robe."

Justice KENNEDY dissented "to underscore the irony in the Court's having concluded that the very First Amendment protections judges must enforce should be lessened when a judicial candidate's own speech is at issue."

4. ***Speaker restrictions.*** Would Mosley and Carey have come out any differently if the law had limited the antipicketing exception to "unions" rather than speech concerning a labor dispute? Would the "Son of Sam" law have fared better if it had escrowed all proceeds of "memoirs by criminal defendants"? A speaker's identity can sometimes function as a proxy for viewpoint or subject matter. When it does, the Court typically applies the same strict scrutiny to speaker-based restrictions as it applies to other content restrictions.

Speaker restrictions, however, are not always considered the practical equivalent of content restrictions, so long as the ground on which speakers are classified can be described as related to some aspect of their status independent of their beliefs or points of view. For example, the Court declined to find speaker identity a proxy for viewpoint when the government: gave a tax benefit to veterans' groups and not other lobbyists, see Regan v. Taxation with Representation (1983; p. 406 below) (relating the distinction to veterans' service to the nation); required cable operators to carry the programs of over-the-air broadcasters, but not other video programmers, see Turner Broadcasting v. FCC (1994; p. 492 below) (relating the distinction to cable's technological chokehold monopoly); enjoined protesters outside abortion clinics but not other entities, see Madsen v. Women's Health Center (1994; p. 315 below) (relating the distinction to the protesters' past actions that gave rise to the injunction); permitted charitable organizations but not advocacy organizations to solicit funds from federal office workers, see Cornelius v. NAACP (1985; p. 336 below) (relating the distinction to the function of charitable services); and granted access to public teachers' in-school mailboxes to the incumbent teachers' union but not to its rival, see Perry Education Ass'n v. Perry Local Educators' Ass'n (1983; p. 333 below) (relating the distinction to service as a collective bargaining representative).

5. ***Communicative impact on the audience.*** Laws barring speech that is deemed likely to cause a certain response in the audience based on its content are typically viewed as skeptically as direct content restrictions. Recall, for example, Forsyth Co. v. Nationalist Movement (1992; p. 68), which invalidated a scheme calibrating the price of a parade permit to the expected hostility of the audience response. Likewise, Cohen v. California (1971; p. 69) held that a breach-of-peace law could not be applied in order to prevent audience offense. And R.A.V. v. St. Paul (1992; p. 109) found a ban on symbols that caused racial anger or alarm to be impermissibly content-based. Might it be argued that all content-based laws are in a sense aimed at the communicative impact of expression, and presumptively invalid for that reason? If so, laws aimed at audience response are just examples of the general category. See Ely, "Flag Desecration: A Case Study in the Roles of Categorization and Balancing in First Amendment Analysis," 88 Harv. L. Rev. 1482 (1975).

6. ***Content-neutral laws.*** Two types of content-neutral laws have come before the Court on free speech challenge. One type aims at conduct, not speech, but may have the effect of suppressing speech when applied to a "symbolic" or "expressive" version of such conduct. This issue arises in such decisions as United States v. O'Brien (1968; p. 252 below) (draft-card burning); Arcara v. Cloud Books (1986; p. 258 below) (abating as a nuisance a brothel in a bookstore); Clark v. Community for Creative Non-Violence

(1984; p. 307 below) (applying a ban on sleeping in the park to a demonstration against homelessness); and Cohen v. Cowles Media (1991; p. 630 below) (applying promissory estoppel to a press breach of promise). A pervasive problem in the symbolic conduct cases is when to find the First Amendment triggered at all. Even speakers must obey generally applicable laws; a newscaster is not exempt from the speeding laws merely because she is late for a newscast, nor may she trespass or burgle in pursuit of a hot story. But do speakers sometime merit a constitutionally compelled exemption from content-neutral regulations of conduct? In O'Brien, the Court held that they do, and thus that government may criminally convict a Vietnam War-era draftee who burned his draft card in public in protest, but only because the law barring draft card destruction was closely tailored to serve a "substantial" or "significant" governmental interest and thus met heightened (or intermediate) scrutiny. See p. 252 below.

A second type of content-neutral law aims at expression, but for reasons unrelated to its content. "Time, place, and manner" regulations of speech in the public forum represent the most common example of this type of content-neutral law. For example, a parade permit requirement, a law limiting the decibel level of amplified sound, and an injunction keeping protestors a certain distance from an abortion clinic entrance all aim at interests in public order, aesthetics, or tranquility and repose—interests that have nothing to do with the content or communicative impact of the speech. The governing standard of review for this type of content-neutral regulation is the same as that for O'Brien-type symbolic conduct regulations: a form of intermediate scrutiny that requires that a law be narrowly tailored or closely related to serving a significant or substantial government interest. Note that, under this test—unlike under the strict scrutiny applied to content-based regulations—the government interest need not be compelling, and the means/ends fit need not be perfect; the state is not obliged to exhaust less restrictive alternatives before it may enact or enforce a content-neutral law.

The Court has used somewhat different language in setting forth the standards of scrutiny applicable to restrictions on symbolic conduct on the one hand and time, place, and manner regulations of speech on the other. In the time, place, and manner context, for example, it has set forth a seemingly additional requirement that a law leave open "ample alternative channels of communication." But the Court has clarified that review in both settings is materially the same—that is, that the O'Brien test "is little if any, different from the standard applied to time, place, and manner restrictions." Clark v. Community for Creative Non-Violence, 468 U.S. 288 (1984; p. 307 below). Is such consolidation of different kinds of speech restrictions under a single standard of scrutiny appropriate? For one study arguing against such use of intermediate scrutiny as a "default standard" for disparate kinds of speech regulations, see Bhagwat, "The Test that Ate Everything: Intermediate Scrutiny in First Amendment Jurisprudence," 2007 U. Ill. L. Rev. 783.

7. **Reasons for treating content-based and content-neutral laws differently.** What First Amendment considerations warrant requiring high standards of justification for content-based regulations, yet less intensive scrutiny of content-neutral ones?

Consider the following possibilities:

a. *Purpose.* Are content-based laws more likely than content-neutral laws to reflect governmental disapproval of the ideas expressed? Government bias in favor of its own viewpoint? Government paternalism toward the listener? Are these improper motivations for a law? For an argument that such concerns with illicit motivation partially explain special scrutiny of content-based laws, see Stone, "Content Regulation and the First Amendment," 25 Wm. & Mary L. Rev. 189 (1983).

If the content-based form of a law is merely the best evidence of the true problem of content-based purpose, then should even content-neutral laws be invalidated whenever such a content-based purpose can be smoked out? Conversely, might some laws that are content-based in form be treated as content-neutral in purpose? Recall that, in Renton v. Playtime Theaters (1986; p. 160), the Court upheld the regulation of sexually explicit speech, even though explicitly drawn by reference to content, because its purpose was found to be prevention of negative "secondary effects" on the surrounding community. For one study suggesting that purpose is the touchstone of the Court's analysis of speech restrictions, and that the Court frequently "designat[es] as content-neutral" speech regulations that "make content distinctions on their face," see McDonald, "Speech and Distrust: Rethinking the Content Approach to Protecting the Freedom of Expression," 81 Notre Dame L. Rev. 1347 (2006).

b.   *Effect.* Are content-based laws more likely than content-neutral laws to distort the dialogue that would otherwise take place? Stone, supra, argues as much: "Any law that substantially prevents the communication of a particular idea, viewpoint, or item of information violates the first amendment except, perhaps, in the most extraordinary of circumstances.

Stone's assertion stands not because such a law restricts 'a lot' of speech, but because by effectively excising a specific message from public debate, it mutilates 'the thinking process of the community.' " Do all content-based laws cause such distortion? A law that bars political billboards, for example, has no effect on political leaflets. And yet the presumption against content-based laws extends even to such partial regulations. Should the Court give more consideration to the extent of a content-based law? Moreover, what is the status quo from which "distortion" should be measured? See Baker, "Turner Broadcasting: Content-Based Regulation of Persons and Presses," 1994 Sup. Ct. Rev. 57 ("There is no 'natural' version of public dialogue that the First Amendment could prohibit the government from distorting," given government's existing role in shaping the debate); Sunstein, Democracy and the Problem of Free Speech (1993).

If effect on speech is the problem, might not a content-neutral law do more substantial damage than a content-based law to the permissible quantity, and effective exercise, of speech? For example, judicial invalidation of content-based restrictions might create an incentive for flat bans rather than partial prohibitions, despite their greater impact on the total quantity and diversity of speech. See Redish, "The Content Distinction in First Amendment Analysis," 34 Stan. L. Rev. 113 (1981) ("While governmental attempts to regulate the content of expression undoubtedly deserve strict judicial review, it does not logically follow that equally serious threats to first amendment freedoms cannot derive from restrictions imposed to regulate expression in a manner unrelated to content. [Whatever] rationale one adopts for the constitutional protection of speech, the goals behind that rationale are undermined by *any* limitation on expression, content-based or not.").

c.   *Political safeguards.* Are content-neutral laws less likely to require judicial intervention because the political process itself will help protect unpopular speakers against such laws? Consider the case of Lady Godiva, who allegedly rode naked on horseback to Coventry Market to protest an excessive tax. A law prohibiting "nude tax protests" is likely to evince hostility to Lady Godiva's ideas. A law prohibiting "public nudity" generally, in contrast, is less likely to have been passed out of similar hostility. Lady Godiva need not fight passage of such a law by herself; nude sunbathers and commercial purveyors of nude entertainment will be her political allies. Might the impact of this type of content-neutral law on nonspeech interests make it less likely that they will be passed at all? Would the same argument apply to a content-neutral time, place, or manner regulation of speech?

8. *Total medium bans.* Is a government ban on the use of a particular medium or format of expression more like a content-based or a content-neutral law? Such laws involve discrimination on neither the basis of viewpoint nor subject matter, yet do single out for special treatment activities of First Amendment concern. Consider the following pairs of regulations: a prohibition on all bookstores in a certain area and a prohibition on all commercial establishments in a certain area, implicitly including bookstores; a prohibition on parades designed to prevent obstruction of traffic and a prohibition on obstructing traffic, including by trucks that take too long to make a delivery and to organizers of parades; a prohibition on soundtrucks designed to prevent excess noise and a prohibition on making excess noise, applied both to jackhammers and soundtrucks; and a prohibition on billboards and a prohibition on all structures higher than a certain height, including billboards. Is the first example in each of these pairs more troublesome than the second? Why? Because the first example singles out speech? Because there is greater reason to trust the political process that generated the second than the first regulation in each pair? Because the regulators are less likely in the second examples to be aiming at unpopular ideas?

Total medium bans have posed difficult questions for the Court that are explored in a number of cases below. The Court struck down various total medium bans in cases of the 1930s and 1940s, focusing on their negative effects on the distribution of speech. See, for example, the invalidation of a total ban on handbills in Schneider v. New Jersey (1939; p. 290 below); and the invalidation of a ban on door-to-door canvassing in Martin v. City of Struthers (1943; p. 291 below). These cases in effect treated medium bans as just as suspect under the First Amendment as discrimination against particular ideas. Why? Because a ban on a particular format might have a major effect on the quantity of communication? Because restriction of an entire format might discriminate in effect against those groups who are financially unable to resort to more conventional (and more expensive) means of communication, such as newspapers and the broadcasting media? Modern cases have tended to emphasize the theme of discrimination rather than distribution. Is it tenable to see discrimination as the First Amendment's *only* concern? The Court made clear that it will still invalidate some total medium bans on the ground that they suppress too much speech, without regard to whether they do so selectively. See, for example, City of Ladue v. Gilleo (1994; p. 294 below), which involved a ban on residential signs.

———

CONTENT-NEUTRAL REGULATION AND SYMBOLIC CONDUCT

What if critics of public policies seek to express their views through symbolic *behavior* rather than words: e.g., by burning a draft card or by mutilating or burning the flag? May such critics claim as much protection as would be afforded if their criticism manifested in spoken or printed word? As is clear from R.A.V. v. St. Paul (1992; p. 109), the Court recognizes symbolic conduct as constitutionally protected "speech." Indeed, as early as Stromberg v. California, 283 U.S. 359 (1931), the Court held a state prohibition on displaying a red flag "as a sign, symbol, or emblem of opposition to organized government" unconstitutional on grounds that the law curtailed "the opportunity for free political discussion." In West Virginia Board of Education v. Barnette (1943; p. 478 below), the Court held that public school children could not be compelled to salute the flag. As made clear in the prevailing opinion in Brown v. Louisiana (1966; p. 323 below), protecting a public library sit-in, First Amendment rights "are not confined to verbal expression" and "embrace appropriate types of action." See also Tinker v. Des Moines Sch. (1969; p. 369 below) (holding black armbands as symbolic war protest).

Why should symbolic conduct ever be treated as "speech" within the meaning of the First Amendment? For the argument that treating symbolic expression as speech makes originalist sense "because Framing-era English and American political culture was rich with symbolic expression, used interchangeably with words," including burning effigies, wearing cockaded hats, and raising "liberty poles," see Volokh, "Symbolic Expression and the Original Meaning of the First Amendment," 97 Geo. L.J. 1057 (2009).

In cases such as Stromberg and R.A.V., the challenged law was aimed expressly at symbolic conduct for reason of its symbolism and communicative impact. Such laws are deemed content-based. May a critic also claim First Amendment immunity from a governmental restraint that is not so aimed but that happens to hit his "speech"? The following cases raise the question whether an assertedly content-neutral law that has the effect of prohibiting symbolic conduct should be treated as content-neutral in fact, and even if so, whether a person engaged in symbolic conduct in violation of that law should nonetheless be exempted from it.

United States v. O'Brien

391 U.S. 367, 88 S. Ct. 1673, 20 L. Ed. 2d 672 (1968).

■ CHIEF JUSTICE WARREN delivered the opinion of the Court.

On the morning of March 31, 1966, David Paul O'Brien and three companions burned their Selective Service registration certificates on the steps of the South Boston Courthouse. A sizable crowd, including several [FBI agents], witnessed the event. Immediately after the burning, [O'Brien] stated [that] he had burned his registration certificate because of his beliefs, knowing that he was violating federal law. [For this act, O'Brien was convicted. He stated] to the jury that he burned the certificate publicly to influence others to adopt his antiwar beliefs, as he put it, "so that other people would reevaluate their positions with Selective Service, with the armed forces, and reevaluate their place in the culture of today, to hopefully consider my position."

The indictment upon which he was tried charged that he "willfully and knowingly did mutilate, destroy, and change by burning [his] Registration Certificate" in violation of [§ 462(b)(3) of the Universal Military Training and Service Act (UMTSA) of 1948], amended by Congress in 1965 (adding the words italicized below), so that at the time O'Brien burned his certificate an offense was committed by any person "who forges, alters, *knowingly destroys, knowingly mutilates,* or in any manner changes any such certificate." (Italics supplied.) [The Court of Appeals] held the 1965 Amendment unconstitutional as a law abridging freedom of speech. At the time the Amendment was enacted, a regulation of the Selective Service System required registrants to keep their registration certificates in their "personal possession at all times." Willful violations of regulations promulgated pursuant to [UMTSA] were made criminal by statute. The Court of Appeals, therefore, was of the opinion that conduct punishable under the 1965 Amendment was already punishable under the nonpossession regulation, and consequently that the Amendment served no valid purpose; further, that in light of the prior regulation, the Amendment must have been "directed at public as distinguished from private destruction." On this basis, the court concluded that the 1965 Amendment ran afoul of the First Amendment by singling out persons engaged in protests for special treatment. [We] hold that the 1965 Amendment is constitutional both as enacted and [as applied].

When a male reaches the age of 18, he is required by the [Act] to register with a local draft board. He is assigned a Selective Service number, and within five days he is issued a registration certificate. Subsequently, [he] is assigned a classification denoting his eligibility for induction. [Both] the registration and classification certificates bear notices that the registrant must notify his local board [of] every change in address, physical condition, [etc.]. [The] 1965 Amendment plainly does not abridge free speech on its face. [On its face, it] deals with conduct having no connection with speech. [It] does not distinguish between public and private destruction,[1] and it does not punish only destruction engaged in for the purpose of expressing views. [Cf. Stromberg.] A law prohibiting destruction of Selective Service certificates no more abridges free speech on its face than a motor vehicle law prohibiting the destruction of drivers' licenses, or a tax law prohibiting the destruction of books and records.

[O'Brien nonetheless] first argues that the 1965 Amendment is unconstitutional as applied to him because his act of burning his registration certificate was protected "symbolic speech" within the First Amendment. His argument is that the freedom of expression which the First Amendment guarantees includes all modes of "communication of ideas by conduct," and that his conduct is within this definition because he did it in "demonstration against the war and against the draft." We cannot accept the view that an apparently limitless variety of conduct can be labeled "speech" whenever the person engaging in the conduct intends thereby to express an idea. However, even on the assumption that the alleged communicative element in O'Brien's

---

[1] Compare the comment in the opinion of the Court of Appeals, 376 F.2d at 541: "We would be closing our eyes [if] we did not see on the face of the amendment that it was precisely directed at public as distinguished from private destruction. [In] singling out persons engaging in protest for special treatment the amendment strikes at the very core of what the First Amendment protects."

conduct is sufficient to bring into play the First Amendment, it does not necessarily follow that the destruction of a registration certificate is constitutionally protected activity. This Court has held that when "speech" and "non-speech" elements are combined in the same course of conduct, a sufficiently important governmental interest in regulating the nonspeech element can justify incidental limitations on First Amendment freedoms. To characterize the quality of the governmental interest which must appear, the Court has employed a variety of descriptive terms: compelling; substantial; subordinating; paramount; cogent; strong. [We] think it clear that a government regulation is sufficiently justified if it is within the constitutional power of the Government; if it furthers an important or substantial governmental interest; if the governmental interest is unrelated to the suppression of free expression; and if the incidental restriction on alleged First Amendment freedoms is no greater than is essential to the furtherance of that interest.

We find that the 1965 Amendment [meets] all of these requirements, and consequently that O'Brien can be constitutionally convicted for violating it. [Pursuant to its power] to classify and conscript manpower for military service, [Congress] may establish a system of registration [and] may require such individuals within reason to cooperate in the registration system. The issuance of certificates indicating the registration and eligibility classification of individuals is a legitimate and substantial administrative aid in the functioning of this system. And legislation to insure the continuing availability of issued certificates serves a legitimate and substantial purpose in the system's administration.

O'Brien's argument to the contrary is necessarily premised upon his unrealistic characterization of Selective Service certificates. He essentially adopts the position that such certificates are so many pieces of paper designed to notify registrants of their registration or classification, to be retained or tossed in the wastebasket according to the convenience or taste of the registrant. [However, the registration and classification certificates serve] purposes in addition to initial notification. Many of these purposes would be defeated by the certificates' destruction or mutilation. Among these are [proving that the individual has registered for the draft, facilitating communication between registrants and local boards, demonstrating availability for induction in times of national crisis, and reminding registrants to notify local boards of changes in status]. The many functions performed by Selective Service certificates establish beyond doubt that Congress has a legitimate and substantial interest in preventing their wanton and unrestrained destruction and assuring their continuing availability by punishing people who knowingly and wilfully destroy or mutilate them. And we are unpersuaded that the pre-existence of the nonpossession regulations in any way negates this interest. In the absence of a question as to multiple punishment, it has never been suggested that there is anything improper in Congress' providing alternative statutory avenues of prosecution to assure the effective protection of one and the same [interest].

Equally important, a comparison of the regulations with the 1965 Amendment indicates that they protect overlapping but not identical governmental interests, and that they reach somewhat different classes of wrongdoers. The gravamen of the offense defined by the statute is the deliberate rendering of certificates unavailable for the various purposes which they may serve. Whether registrants keep their certificates in their personal possession at all times, as required by the regulations, is of no particular concern under the 1965 Amendment, as long as they do not mutilate or destroy the certificates so as to render them unavailable. [And] the 1965 Amendment [is] concerned with abuses involving *any* issued Selective Service certificates, not only with the registrant's own certificates. [We] think it apparent that the continuing availability to each registrant of his Selective Service certificates substantially furthers the smooth and proper functioning of the system that Congress has established to raise [armies].

It is equally clear that the 1965 Amendment specifically protects this substantial governmental interest. We perceive no alternative means that would more precisely and narrowly assure the continuing availability of issued Selective Service certificates than a law which prohibits their wilful mutilation or destruction. [Moreover,] both the governmental interest and the operation of the 1965 Amendment are limited to the noncommunicative aspect of O'Brien's conduct. The governmental interest and the scope of the 1965 Amendment are limited to preventing harm to the smooth and efficient functioning of the Selective Service System. When O'Brien deliberately rendered unavailable his registration certificate, he wilfully frustrated this governmental interest. For this noncommunicative impact of his conduct, and for nothing else, he was convicted. The case [is] therefore unlike one where the alleged governmental interest in regulating conduct arises in some measure because the communication allegedly integral to the conduct is itself thought to be harmful. In Stromberg [the "red flag" case], for example, the statute was aimed at suppressing communication [and therefore] could not be sustained as a regulation of noncommunicative conduct. [We] find that because of the Government's substantial interest in assuring the continuing availability of issued Selective Service certificates, because amended § 462(b) is an appropriately narrow means of protecting this interest and condemns only the independent noncommunicative impact of conduct within its reach, and because the noncommunicative impact of O'Brien's act of burning his registration certificate frustrated the Government's interest, a sufficient governmental interest has been shown to justify O'Brien's conviction.

O'Brien finally argues that the 1965 Amendment is unconstitutional as enacted because what he calls the "purpose" of Congress was "to suppress freedom of speech." We reject this argument because under settled principles the purpose of Congress, as O'Brien uses that term, is not a basis for declaring this legislation unconstitutional. It is a familiar principle of constitutional law that this Court will not strike down an otherwise constitutional statute on the basis of an alleged illicit legislative motive. [Inquiries] into congressional motives or purposes are a hazardous matter. When the issue is simply the interpretation of legislation, the Court will look to statements by legislators for guidance as to the purpose of the legislature, because the benefit to sound decision-making in this circumstance is thought sufficient to risk the possibility of misreading Congress' purpose. It is entirely a different matter when we are asked to void a statute that is, under well-settled criteria, constitutional on its face, on the basis of what fewer than a handful of Congressmen said about it. What motivates one legislator to make a speech about a statute is not necessarily what motivates scores of others to enact it, and the stakes are sufficiently high for us to eschew guesswork. We decline to void essentially on the ground that it is unwise legislation which Congress has the undoubted power to enact and which could be reenacted in its exact form if the same or another legislator made a "wiser" speech about it. Reversed.[2]

THE SIGNIFICANCE OF O'BRIEN

1. *Expression and action.* Chief Justice Warren assumed arguendo that O'Brien's act was symbolic conduct without deciding as much. In so doing, he cautioned that conduct does not become speech "whenever the person engaging in the conduct intends thereby to express an idea." Was he too cavalier toward O'Brien's symbolic speech claim? See Alfange, "Free Speech and Symbolic Conduct: The Draft-Card Burning Case," 1968 Sup. Ct. Rev. 1. Warren feared that an "apparently limitless variety of conduct" might be labeled "speech." Is that fear of such a "slippery slope" justified, or are there principled ways of distinguishing action from speech? See Emerson, The System of Freedom of Expression (1970) ("To some extent expression and action are always mingled; [the] guiding principle must be to determine which element is predominant. [It] seems quite clear that the predominant element in [the burning of a draft card] is expression (opposition to the draft) rather than action (destruction of a piece of cardboard.")). But see Ely, "Flag Desecration: A Case Study in the Roles of Categorization and Balancing in First Amendment Analysis," 88 Harv. L. Rev. 1482 (1975) ("[B]urning a draft card to express opposition to the draft is an undifferentiated whole, 100% action and 100% expression. [Attempts] to determine which element 'predominates' will therefore inevitably degenerate into question-begging judgments about whether the activity should be protected."); Henkin, "Foreword: On Drawing Lines," 82 Harv. L. Rev. 63 (1968) ("A constitutional distinction between speech and conduct is specious. [I]f it is intended as expression, if in fact it communicates, especially if it becomes a common comprehensible form of expression, it is 'speech.' "). See also Velvel, "Freedom of Speech and the Draft Card Burning Cases," 16 U. Kan. L. Rev. 149 (1968) (arguing that draft-card burning was an especially effective means of protesting the war because it attracted media attention); Nimmer, "The Meaning of Symbolic Speech Under the First Amendment," 21 UCLA L. Rev. 29 (1973) (suggesting that symbolic conduct requires an audience— i.e., both a "communicator and a communicatee"); Baker, "Scope of the First Amendment Freedom of Speech," 25 UCLA L. Rev. 964 (1978).

2. *The O'Brien test and the content-based/content-neutral distinction.* O'Brien set forth a test that has since become canonical in the review of content-neutral laws: they must "further an important or substantial governmental interest" and involve an "incidental restriction on alleged First Amendment freedoms [that] is no greater than is essential to

----

[2] A concurrence by Justice HARLAN stated: "I wish to make explicit my understanding that [the Court's criteria do] not foreclose consideration of First Amendment claims in those rare instances when an 'incidental' restriction upon expression, imposed by a regulation which furthers an 'important or substantial' governmental interest and satisfies the Court's other criteria, in practice has the effect of entirely preventing a 'speaker' from reaching a significant audience with whom he could not otherwise lawfully communicate. This is not such a case, since O'Brien manifestly could have conveyed his message in many ways other than by burning his draft card." Justice DOUGLAS dissented, urging reargument on "the question of the constitutionality of a peacetime draft"; the next year in Brandenburg v. Ohio (p. 48), he asserted that O'Brien's conviction was inconsistent with the First Amendment.

the furtherance of that interest." The latter part of the test has been modified in later cases to make clear that, while a content-neutral law must be closely tailored to its ends, the government need *not* employ the least restrictive alternative. See Ward v. Rock Against Racism (1989; p. 312 below). O'Brien also set forth an influential definition for distinguishing content-based from content-neutral laws: for a law to be treated as content-neutral, the governmental interest behind the law must be "unrelated to the suppression of free expression." Thus the third of the four factors listed in the O'Brien test on p. 252 actually performs a critical switching function at the threshold: in situations where the state interest *is* "related to the suppression of free expression," strict scrutiny is required *unless* the speech is in an unprotected category; but where the state interest is *unrelated* to the suppression of free expression, balancing is the appropriate response. See Ely, "Flag Desecration: A Case Study in the Roles of Categorization and Balancing in First Amendment Analysis," 88 Harv. L. Rev. 1482 (1975).

How can a court tell whether a law is or is not "related to the suppression of free expression"? As Ely explains, "restrictions on free expression are seldom defended on the ground that the state simply didn't like what the defendant was saying: reference will generally be made to some danger beyond the message, such as the danger of riot, unlawful action, or violent overthrow of the government. The constitutional reference must therefore be not to the ultimate interest to which the state points, for that will always be unrelated to expression, but rather to the causal connection the state asserts. If, for example, the state asserts an interest in discouraging riots, the Court should ask why that interest is implicated in the case at bar. If the answer is, as in such cases it will likely have to be, that the danger of riot was created by what the defendant was saying, the state's interest is not unrelated to the suppression of free expression, and the inhibition should be upheld only in the event the expression falls within one of the few unprotected categories." Ely, supra.

How speech-protective was the application of the O'Brien test in O'Brien itself? Ely suggests that the supposedly "substantial" governmental interests identified by the Court were in fact merely "plausible but little more." And the "no greater restriction than essential" criterion was weakly applied: the Court essentially deferred to the government without serious inquiry whether alternative means would serve the government's interest nearly as efficiently at much less cost to speech. See Ely, supra.

3. *Legislative motivation.* Should the Court have gone the other way in O'Brien because "the 'purpose' of Congress was 'to suppress freedom of speech' "? See Alfange, supra (suggesting that the legislative history of the 1965 amendment shows with "indisputable clarity" that "the intent of [members of Congress] was purely and simply to put a stop to this particular form of antiwar protest, which they deemed extraordinarily contemptible and vicious—even treasonous—at a time when American troops were engaged in combat"). Chief Justice Warren rejected summarily any inquiry into congressional motive, and noted that statements by members of Congress expressing hostility to draft resisters were offset by the more authoritative committee reports: while the reports "make clear a concern with the 'defiant' destruction [of draft cards] and with 'open' encouragement to others to destroy their cards, both reports also indicate that this concern stems from an apprehension that unrestrained destruction of cards would disrupt the smooth functioning of the Selective Service System."

Clearly, the Court frequently does inquire into the motivation of executive and administrative decisions. In the equal protection context, see, for example, Arlington Heights v. Metropolitan Housing Corp., 429 U.S. 252 (1977); and Yick Wo v. Hopkins, 118 U.S. 356 (1886). In other contexts, such as the religion context, the Court is not shy about looking into even legislative history as a source of possibly impermissible motivation. See, e.g., Church of the Lukumi Babalu Aye v. City of Hialeah, 508 U.S. 520 (1993; p. 662 below), and Edwards v. Aguillard, 482 U.S. 578 (1987; p. 754 below). Why then, in O'Brien, was the Court reluctant to inquire into legislative motivation? Are the reasons ones of institutional competence, such as the difficulty of ascertaining any single "real" motivation in a multi-member body where each representative might be voting for different reasons, the inappropriateness of questioning the integrity of a coordinate branch, and the futility of striking down a law that could be reenacted after an assertion of legitimate motives? Doesn't the distinction between content-based and content-neutral laws require some inquiry into legislative ends? Or is the Court suggesting that such an inquiry may take place, so long as it focuses on the objective purpose of the law rather than the subjective motive of particular legislators? On the problem of motivation inquiries, see generally Ely, "Legislative and Administrative Motivation in Constitutional Law," 79 Yale L.J. 1205 (1970); and Brest, "Palmer v. Thompson: An Approach to the Problem of Unconstitutional Legislative Motive," 1971 Sup. Ct. Rev. 95.

4. *"Incidental" restrictions on expression.* In O'Brien, the Court employed less-than-strict scrutiny to deal with what it called "incidental limitations on First Amendment freedoms." Was the effect of the law on O'Brien's speech merely "incidental"? Or did the law forbid precisely the action O'Brien engaged in as speech? Should the central question be what was aimed at, as O'Brien suggests, or rather what was hit? See generally Stone, "Content-Neutral Restrictions," 54 U. Chi. L. Rev. 46 (1987).

Should all "incidental" restrictions on speech receive the heightened First Amendment scrutiny required by the O'Brien test? Do some laws have an impact on speech only as a mere byproduct or side effect? A "no parking" zone might preclude one from using a car covered with bumper stickers as a mobile billboard parked before a desired audience. A "no speeding" law might prevent a newscaster from reaching the studio in time to announce the news. Should such laws be subject to more exacting First Amendment review when applied in such circumstances, or need they only satisfy the requirements of minimum rationality?

Consider **Arcara v. Cloud Books, Inc.**, 478 U.S. 697 (1986), which involved a New York law defining places of prostitution, assignation, and lewdness as public health nuisances and providing for the closure of any building found to be such a nuisance. In Arcara, an investigation of an "adult" bookstore found that sexual acts and solicitations to perform sexual acts were occurring on the premises. As a result, the store was ordered closed as a nuisance. The bookstore claimed that this had the effect of preventing the sale of books and other materials that were presumptively protected by the First Amendment. The highest state court, applying the O'Brien test, found that the closure order incidentally burdened speech and that it was unnecessarily broad to achieve its purpose, since an injunction against the illegal activity could achieve the same effect.

The Court reversed that judgment, upholding the closure remedy and holding that it did not warrant even the intermediate scrutiny of the O'Brien standard. Chief Justice BURGER's majority opinion explained that, "unlike the symbolic draft card burning in O'Brien, the sexual activity carried on [here] manifests absolutely no element of protected expression." He continued: "Nor does the distinction drawn by the [law] inevitably single out bookstores or others engaged in First Amendment protected activities for the imposition of its burden. [If] the city imposed closure penalties for demonstrated Fire Code violations or health hazards from inadequate sewage treatment, the First Amendment would not aid the owner of premises who had knowingly allowed such violations to persist." Nor was Chief Justice Burger impressed by the argument that the closure burdened bookselling activities: "The severity of this burden is dubious at best, and is mitigated by the fact that respondents remain free to sell the same materials at another location. In any event, this argument proves too much, since every civil and criminal remedy imposes some conceivable burden on First Amendment protected activities." He added: "[W]e have not traditionally subjected every criminal or civil sanction [to] 'least restrictive means' scrutiny simply because each particular remedy will have some effect [on] First Amendment activities. [Rather,] we have subjected such restrictions to scrutiny only where it was conduct with a significant expressive element that drew the legal remedy in the first place, as in O'Brien, or where a statute based on a nonexpressive activity has the inevitable effect of singling out those engaged in expressive activity, as in Minneapolis Star [(1983; p. 623 below)]. This case involves neither situation, and we conclude the First Amendment is not implicated by the enforcement of the public health regulation of general application against the physical premises in which respondents happen to sell books." Justice O'Connor's concurrence, joined by Justice Stevens, emphasized that there had been no evidence that the use of a generally applicable regulatory statute was merely a "pretext" for closing down a bookstore.

Justice BLACKMUN, joined by Justices Brennan and Marshall, dissented, arguing: "Until today, this Court has never suggested that a State may suppress speech as much as it likes, without justification, so long as it does so through generally applicable regulations that have 'nothing to do with any expressive conduct.' [When] a State directly and substantially impairs First Amendment activities, such as by shutting down a bookstore, I believe that the state must show, at a minimum, that it has chosen the least restrictive means of pursuing its legitimate objectives. [Petitioner] has not demonstrated that a less restrictive remedy would be inadequate to abate the nuisance. [Because the law] is not narrowly tailored to further the asserted governmental interest, it is unconstitutional as applied."

Was the majority's refusal to apply any First Amendment scrutiny in Arcara justifiable under O'Brien or under general First Amendment principles? Would the opposite result have extended the First Amendment to virtually every law? See Alexander, "Trouble on Track Two: Incidental Regulations of Speech and Free Speech Theory," 44 Hastings L.J. 921 (1993) (arguing that virtually every law, even a marginal tax rate, may be said to have some "incidental" effect on speech, and thus questioning First Amendment review of content-neutral regulation); see also Dorf, "Incidental Burdens on Fundamental Rights," 109 Harv. L. Rev. 1175 (1996).

————

FLAG DESECRATION

May government bar the burning, mutilation, or physical misuse of the United States flag? The Court considered a series of challenges to efforts to curb such symbolic protests beginning in 1969, but did not squarely reach the central constitutional issue until the flag-burning cases of 1989 and 1990. Is flag desecration "speech" entitled to strong First Amendment protection? What state interests underlie the efforts to protect the flag? Can any of them be described as content-neutral? If not, can any of them be described as compelling?

In **Street v. New York**, 394 U.S. 576 (1969), the Court, in a 5–4 decision, overturned a conviction under a New York law that made it a crime "publicly [to] mutilate, deface, defile, or defy, trample upon, or cast contempt upon either by words or act [any flag of the United States]." Street had burned a flag on a street corner after hearing that civil rights leader James Meredith had been shot by a sniper in Mississippi. He had said to the crowd that gathered, "We don't need no damn flag," and when a police officer stopped and confronted him, he had replied: "Yes, that is my flag; I burned it. If they let that happen to Meredith we don't need an American flag." The Court did not reach the question whether it was constitutional to ban flag burning as a means of political protest, finding instead that, on the record below, the law had been unconstitutionally applied to permit punishment of Street "merely for speaking defiant or contemptuous words about the American flag." Justice HARLAN's majority opinion noted that Street's words had not constituted incitement or fighting words, reiterated that "public expression of ideas may not be prohibited merely because the ideas are themselves offensive to some of their hearers," and held that the conviction could not be justified "on the theory that by making [his] remarks about the flag appellant failed to show the respect for our national symbol which may properly be demanded of every citizen," for the flag-salute cases (see p. 476 below) had established "the freedom to express publicly one's opinions about our flag, including those opinions which are defiant or contemptuous." Chief Justice Warren and Justices Black, White, and Fortas dissented, each arguing that Street had been punished for his act, not his words, and that the state had constitutional authority to protect the flag from acts of desecration.

In **Smith v. Goguen**, 415 U.S. 566 (1974), the Court, in a 6–3 decision, reversed a appellee's conviction, under a Massachusetts law making it a crime to "publicly mutilate, trample upon, deface or treat contemptuously the flag of the United States," for wearing a small United States flag sewn to the seat of his trousers. Justice POWELL's majority opinion found it unnecessary to reach a variety of First Amendment claims and rested instead on "the due process doctrine of vagueness." Though appellee's behavior seemed to reflect "immaturity" and "silly conduct," Justice Powell observed that "casual treatment of the flag in many contexts has become a widespread contemporary phenomenon." Here, the statutory language "fails to draw reasonably clear lines between the kinds of nonceremonial treatment (of the flag) that are criminal and those that are not." Fair notice standards were not met, given "today's tendencies to treat the flag unceremoniously." Justice Powell emphasized: "Statutory language of such standardless sweep allows policemen, prosecutors, and juries to pursue their personal predilections." Justice WHITE disagreed with the majority's reasoning, though not its result. He defended the constitutionality of flag mutilation

laws, but objected that the conviction here "punish[ed] for communicating ideas about the flag unacceptable to the controlling majority." Justice REHNQUIST, joined by Chief Justice Burger, dissented at length, describing the flag as a "unique physical object" and emphasizing the strong state interest in protecting "the physical integrity of a unique national symbol." There was also a dissent by Justice Blackmun, joined by Chief Justice Burger.

And in **Spence v. Washington**, 418 U.S. 405 (1974), the Court, per curiam, overturned a conviction under a Washington statute prohibiting "improper use" of the flag, including the display of any flag to which a "word, figure, mark, picture, design, drawing or advertisement" had been attached. Spence had displayed a United States flag, which he owned, outside the window of his apartment with a large peace symbol made of removable tape affixed to both sides. He testified that he had done so as a protest against the invasion of Cambodia and the killings at Kent State University. The Court found Spence's "pointed expression of anguish [about] the then current domestic and foreign affairs of his government" to be speech within the meaning of the First Amendment and set forth the still-governing test for whether conduct is protected by the First Amendment: "An intent to convey a particularized message was present, and in the surrounding circumstances the likelihood was great that the message would be understood by those who viewed it."

The Court was willing to assume arguendo that the state's asserted interest in "preserving the national flag as an unalloyed symbol of our country" was valid even though it noted that such an interest was "directly related to expression." But it nonetheless found the statute "unconstitutional as applied to appellant's activity. There was no risk that appellant's acts would mislead viewers into assuming that the Government endorsed his viewpoint. To the contrary, he was plainly and peacefully protesting the fact that it did not." Justice REHNQUIST, joined by Chief Justice Burger and Justice White, dissented, arguing that the state's interest in "preserving the flag as 'an important symbol of nationhood and unity' " was a legitimate one.

Does Spence helpfully delineate the contours of protected symbolic conduct? Note the Court's emphasis on two factors: the speaker's intent; and the context indicating that the message would be understood by the audience. Is that a useful approach? Is it adequate? Does it risk the slippery slope Chief Justice Warren feared in O'Brien? What about conduct more ambiguous than that in Spence? For criticism of the Spence standard, see Post, "Recuperating First Amendment Doctrine," 47 Stan. L. Rev. 1249 (1995).

Is there any governmental interest in the flag that is "unrelated to the suppression of free expression" within the meaning of O'Brien? See Ely, "Flag Desecration: A Case Study in the Roles of Categorization and Balancing in First Amendment Analysis," 88 Harv. L. Rev. 1482 (1975) (suggesting that flag misuse laws "do not single out certain messages for proscription," but "*do* single out one set of messages, namely the set of messages conveyed by the American flag, for protection," and that "[o]rthodoxy of thought can be fostered not simply by placing unusual restrictions on 'deviant' expression but also by granting unusual protection to expression that is officially acceptable"). Consider the flag-burning cases of 1989 and 1990, which follow.

———

Texas v. Johnson

491 U.S. 397, 109 S. Ct. 2533, 105 L. Ed. 2d 342 (1989).

■ JUSTICE BRENNAN delivered the opinion of the Court.

After publicly burning an American flag as a means of political protest, Gregory Lee Johnson was convicted of desecrating a flag in violation of Texas law. This case presents the question whether his conviction is consistent with the First Amendment. We hold that it is not.

I.   While the Republican National Convention was taking place in Dallas in 1984, [Johnson] participated in a political demonstration dubbed the "Republican War Chest Tour." [The] purpose of this event was to protest the policies of the Reagan administration and of certain Dallas-based corporations. The demonstrators marched through the Dallas streets, chanting political slogans and stopping at several corporate locations to stage "die-ins" intended to dramatize the consequences of nuclear war. On several occasions they spray-painted the walls of buildings and overturned potted plants, but Johnson himself took no part in such activities. He did, however, accept an American flag handed to him by a fellow protestor who had taken it from a flag pole outside one of the targeted buildings. The demonstration ended in front of Dallas City Hall, where Johnson unfurled the American flag, doused it with kerosene, and set it on fire. While the flag burned, the protestors chanted, "America, the red, white, and blue, we spit on you." After the demonstrators dispersed, a witness to the flag-burning collected the flag's remains and buried them in his backyard. No one was physically injured or threatened with injury, though several witnesses testified that they had been seriously offended by the flag-burning. Of the approximately 100 demonstrators, Johnson alone was charged with a crime. The only criminal offense with which he was charged was the desecration of a venerated object.[1] [He] was convicted, sentenced to one year in prison, and fined $2,000. [The] Texas Court of Criminal Appeals [overturned the conviction.] We affirm.

II.   Johnson was convicted of flag desecration for burning the flag rather than for uttering insulting words. This fact somewhat complicates our consideration of his conviction under the First Amendment. We must first determine whether Johnson's burning of the flag constituted expressive conduct, permitting him to invoke the [First Amendment]. [Spence.] If his conduct was expressive, we next decide whether the State's regulation is related to the suppression of free expression. [O'Brien.] If the State's regulation is not related to expression, then the less stringent standard we announced in [O'Brien] for regulations of noncommunicative conduct controls. If it is, then we are outside of O'Brien's test, and we must ask whether this interest justifies Johnson's conviction under a more demanding standard.[2] [Spence.] A third possibility is that the State's asserted interest

---

[1]   Tex. Penal Code Ann. section 42.09 (1989) [provided]: "Section 42.09. Desecration of Venerated Object. (a) A person commits an offense if he intentionally or knowingly desecrates: (1) a public monument; (2) a place of worship or burial; or (3) a state or national flag. (b) For purposes of this section, 'desecrate' means deface, damage, or otherwise physically mistreat in a way that the actor knows will seriously offend one or more persons likely to observe or discover his action." [Footnote by Justice Brennan.]

[2]   Although Johnson has raised a facial challenge to [the law], we choose to resolve this case on the basis of his ["as-applied" claim]. Because the prosecution of a person who had not engaged in expressive conduct would pose a different case, and because we are capable of disposing of this case on narrower grounds, we address only Johnson's claim that [the law] as

is simply not implicated on these facts, and in that event the interest drops out of the picture.

The First Amendment literally forbids the abridgement only of "speech," but we have long recognized that its protection does not end at the spoken or written word. [In] deciding whether particular conduct possesses sufficient communicative elements to bring the First Amendment into play, we have asked whether "[a]n intent to convey a particularized message was present, and (whether) the likelihood was great that the message would be understood by those who viewed it." [Spence.] [Especially] pertinent to this case are our decisions recognizing the communicative nature of conduct relating to flags. Attaching a peace sign to the flag, Spence; saluting the flag [Barnette (1943; p. 478 below)]; and displaying a red flag, Stromberg, we have held, all may find shelter under the First Amendment. That we have had little difficulty identifying an expressive element in conduct relating to flags should not be surprising. The very purpose of a national flag is to serve as a symbol of our country. [Pregnant] with expressive content, the flag as readily signifies this Nation as does the combination of letters found in "America." [Texas] conceded for purposes of its oral argument in this case that Johnson's conduct was expressive conduct. [Johnson] burned an American flag as part—indeed, as the culmination—of a political demonstration that coincided with the convening of the Republican Party and its renomination of Ronald Reagan for President. The expressive, overtly political nature of this conduct was both intentional and overwhelmingly apparent [and thus implicates] the First Amendment.

III. The Government generally has a freer hand in restricting expressive conduct than it has in restricting the written or spoken word. It may not, however, proscribe particular conduct because it has expressive elements. [It] is [not] simply the verbal or nonverbal nature of the expression, but the governmental interest at stake, that helps to determine whether a restriction on that expression is valid. Thus, [we] have limited the applicability of O'Brien's relatively lenient standard to those cases in which "the governmental interest is unrelated to the suppression of free expression." [In] order to decide whether O'Brien's test applies here, therefore, we must decide whether Texas has asserted an interest in support of Johnson's conviction that is unrelated to the suppression of expression. If we find that an interest asserted by the State is simply not implicated on the facts before us, we need not ask whether O'Brien's test applies. The State offers two separate interests to justify this conviction: preventing breaches of the peace, and preserving the flag as a symbol of nationhood and national unity. We hold that the first interest is not implicated on this record and that the second is related to the suppression of expression.

A.   Texas claims that its interest in preventing breaches of the peace justifies Johnson's conviction for flag desecration. However, no disturbance of the peace actually occurred or threatened to occur because of Johnson's burning of the flag. [The] only evidence offered [at trial] to show the reaction to Johnson's actions was the testimony of several persons who had been seriously offended by the flag-burning. The State's position, therefore, amounts to a claim that an audience that takes serious offense at particular expression is necessarily likely to disturb the peace and that the expression may be prohibited on this basis. Our precedents do not countenance such a

---

applied to political expression like his violates the First Amendment. [Footnote by Justice Brennan.]

presumption. On the contrary, they recognize that a principal "function of free speech under our system of government is to invite [dispute]." [Terminiello.] [We] have not permitted the Government to assume that every expression of a provocative idea will incite a riot, but have instead required careful consideration of the actual circumstances surrounding such [expression]. [Brandenburg.] To accept Texas' arguments that it need only demonstrate "the potential for a breach of the peace," and that every flag-burning necessarily possesses that potential, would be to eviscerate our holding in Brandenburg. This we decline to do.

[Nor] does Johnson's expressive conduct fall within that small class of "fighting words" that are "likely to provoke the average person to retaliation, and thereby cause a breach of the peace." [Chaplinsky.] No reasonable onlooker would have regarded Johnson's generalized expression of dissatisfaction with the policies of the Federal Government as a direct personal insult or an invitation to exchange fisticuffs. We thus conclude that the State's interest in maintaining order is not implicated on these [facts].

B.   The State also asserts an interest in preserving the flag as a symbol of nationhood and national unity. [We are persuaded, as we were in Spence,] that this interest is related to expression in the case of Johnson's burning of the flag. The State, apparently, is concerned that such conduct will lead people to believe either that the flag does not stand for nationhood and national unity, but instead reflects other, less positive concepts, or that the concepts reflected in the flag do not in fact exist, that is, we do not enjoy unity as a Nation. These concerns blossom only when a person's treatment of the flag communicates some message, and thus are related "to the suppression of free expression" within the meaning of O'Brien. We are thus outside of O'Brien's test altogether.

IV.   It remains to consider whether the State's interest in preserving the flag as a symbol of nationhood and national unity justifies Johnson's conviction. [Johnson] was not [prosecuted] for the expression of just any idea; he was prosecuted for his expression of dissatisfaction with the policies of this country, expression situated at the core of our First Amendment values. Moreover, Johnson was prosecuted because he knew that his politically charged expression would cause "serious offense." If he had burned the flag as a means of disposing of it because it was dirty or torn, he would not have been convicted of flag desecration under this Texas law: federal law designates burning as the preferred means of disposition of a flag "when it is in such condition that it is no longer a fitting emblem for display," and Texas has no quarrel with this means of disposal. The Texas law is thus not aimed at protecting the physical integrity of the flag in all circumstances, but is designed instead to protect it only against impairments that would cause serious offense to others. Texas concedes as [much]. Whether Johnson's treatment of the flag violated Texas law thus depended on the likely communicative impact of his expressive conduct. [This] restriction on Johnson's expression is content-based. [Johnson's] political expression was restricted because of the content of the message he conveyed. We must therefore subject the State's asserted interest in preserving the special symbolic character of the flag to "the most exacting scrutiny." [Boos.]

Texas argues that its interest in preserving the flag as a symbol of nationhood and national unity survives this close analysis. [The] State's argument is not that it has an interest simply in maintaining the flag as a symbol of *something,* no matter what it symbolizes. [Rather,] the State's claim is that it has an interest in preserving the flag as a symbol of *nationhood* and *national unity,* a symbol with a determinate range of meanings. According to Texas, if one physically treats the flag in a way that would tend to cast doubt on either the idea that nationhood and national unity are the flag's referents or that national unity actually exists, the message conveyed thereby is a harmful one and therefore may be prohibited.

If there is a bedrock principle underlying the First Amendment, it is that the Government may not prohibit the expression of an idea simply because society finds the idea itself offensive or disagreeable. [We] have not recognized an exception to this principle even where our flag has been involved. [Street; Spence.] [Nothing] in our precedents suggests that a State may foster its own view of the flag by prohibiting expressive conduct relating to it. To bring its argument outside our precedents, Texas attempts to convince us that even if its interest in preserving the flag's symbolic role does not allow it to prohibit words or some expressive conduct critical of the flag, it does permit it to forbid the outright destruction of the flag. [Texas's] focus on the precise nature of Johnson's expression [misses] the point of our prior decisions: their enduring lesson, that the Government may not prohibit expression simply because it disagrees with its message, is not dependent on the particular mode in which one chooses to express an idea. If we were to hold that a State may forbid flag-burning wherever it is likely to endanger the flag's symbolic role, but allow it wherever burning a flag promotes that role—as where, for example, a person ceremoniously burns a dirty flag—we would be saying that when it comes to impairing the flag's physical integrity, the flag itself may be used as a symbol [only] in one direction. We would be permitting a State to "prescribe what shall be orthodox" by saying that one may burn the flag to convey one's attitude toward it and its referents only if one does not endanger the flag's representation of nationhood and national unity.

We never before have held that the Government may ensure that a symbol be used to express only one view of that symbol or its referents. Indeed, in Schacht v. United States [398 U.S. 58 (1970)], we invalidated a federal statute permitting an actor portraying a member of one of our armed forces to " 'wear the uniform of that armed force if the portrayal does not tend to discredit that armed force.' " This proviso, we held, "which leaves Americans free to praise the war in Vietnam but can send persons like Schacht to prison for opposing it, cannot survive in a country which has the First Amendment." We perceive no basis on which to hold that the principle underlying our decision in Schacht does not apply to this case. To conclude that the Government may permit designated symbols to be used to communicate only a limited set of messages would be to enter territory having no discernible or defensible boundaries. Could the Government, on this theory, prohibit the burning of state flags? Of copies of the Presidential seal? Of the Constitution? In evaluating these choices under the First Amendment, how would we decide which symbols were sufficiently special to warrant this unique status? To do so, we would be forced to consult our own political preferences, and impose them on the citizenry, in the very way that the First Amendment forbids us to do.

There is, moreover, no indication—either in the text of the Constitution or in our cases interpreting it—that a separate juridical category exists for the American flag alone. [The] First Amendment does not guarantee that other concepts virtually sacred to our Nation as a whole—such as the principle that discrimination on the basis of race [is] odious and destructive—will go unquestioned in the marketplace of ideas. [Brandenburg.] We decline, therefore, to create for the flag an exception to the joust of principles protected by the First Amendment. It is not the State's ends, but its means, to which we object. It cannot be gainsaid that there is a special place reserved for the flag in this Nation, and thus we do not doubt that the Government has a legitimate interest in making efforts to "preserv[e] the national flag as an unalloyed symbol of our country." [Spence.] [To] say that the Government has an interest in encouraging proper treatment of the flag, however, is not to say that it may criminally punish a person for burning a flag as a means of political protest.

[We] are fortified in today's conclusion by our conviction that forbidding criminal punishment for conduct such as Johnson's will not endanger the special role played by our flag or the feelings it inspires. To paraphrase Justice Holmes, we submit that nobody can suppose that this one gesture of an unknown man will change our Nation's attitude towards its flag. [Abrams.] [We] are tempted to say, in fact, that the flag's deservedly cherished place in our community will be strengthened, not weakened, by our holding today. Our decision is a reaffirmation of the principles of freedom and inclusiveness that the flag best reflects, and of the conviction that our toleration of criticism such as Johnson's is a sign and source of our strength. [It] is the Nation's resilience, not its rigidity, that Texas sees reflected in the flag—and it is that resilience that we reassert today. The way to preserve the flag's special role is not to punish those who feel differently about these matters. It is to persuade them that they are wrong. [Precisely] because it is our flag that is involved, one's response to the flag-burner may exploit the uniquely persuasive power of the flag itself. We can imagine no more appropriate response to burning a flag than waving one's own, no better way to counter a flag-burner's message than by saluting the flag that burns, no surer means of preserving the dignity even of the flag that burned than by— as one witness here did—according its remains a respectful burial. We do not consecrate the flag by punishing its desecration, for in doing so we dilute the freedom that this cherished emblem represents. [Affirmed.][3]

■ CHIEF JUSTICE REHNQUIST, with whom JUSTICES WHITE and O'CONNOR join, dissenting.

In holding this Texas statute unconstitutional, the Court ignores Justice Holmes' familiar aphorism that "a page of history is worth a volume of logic." For more than 200 years, the American flag has occupied a unique position as the symbol of our Nation, a uniqueness that justifies a governmental prohibition against flag burning in the way [Johnson] did here.[4]

---

[3] Justice KENNEDY, who joined Justice Brennan's opinion to make the 5–4 majority here, added a concurrence noting: "Sometimes we must make decisions we do not like. We make them because they are right, right in the sense that the law and the Constitution [compel] the result." He added: "I do not believe the Constitution gives us the right to rule as the [dissenters] urge, however painful this judgment is to announce. [It] is poignant but fundamental that the flag protects those who hold it in contempt. [Johnson's] acts were speech. [So] I agree with the Court that he must go free."

[4] At this point, Chief Justice Rehnquist devoted a substantial number of pages to a review of the importance of the flag in American history and literature. He quoted from the poetry of Ralph Waldo Emerson and from Francis Scott Key's "Star-Bangled Banner." Moreover, he printed the full text of John Greenleaf Whittier's "Barbara Fritchie" (including the line " 'Shoot if you must, This old grey head, But spare your country's flag,' She said").

[The] American flag, [throughout] more than 200 years of our history, has come to be the visible symbol embodying our Nation. It does not represent the views of any particular political party, and it does not represent any particular political philosophy. The flag is not simply another "idea" or "point of view" competing for recognition in the marketplace of ideas. Millions [of] Americans regard it with an almost mystical reverence regardless of what sort of social, political, or philosophical beliefs they may have. I cannot agree that the First Amendment invalidates the Act of Congress, and the laws of 48 of the 50 States, which make criminal the public burning of the flag.

[But] the Court insists that the [Texas law infringes on] Johnson's freedom of expression. Such freedom, of course, is not absolute. [Here] it may [well] be said that the public burning of the American flag by Johnson was no essential part of any exposition of ideas[, Chaplinsky], and at the same time it had a tendency to incite a breach of the peace. [The] Court could not, and did not, say that Chaplinsky's utterances were not expressive phrases—they clearly and succinctly conveyed an extremely low opinion of the addressee. The same may be said of Johnson's public burning of the flag in this case; it obviously did convey Johnson's bitter dislike of his country. But his act, like Chaplinsky's provocative words, conveyed nothing that could not have been [conveyed] just as forcefully in a dozen different ways. As with "fighting words," so with flag burning, for purposes of the [First Amendment].

[Flag burning] is the equivalent of an inarticulate grunt or roar that [is] most likely to be indulged in not to express any particular idea, but to antagonize others. [The] Texas statute deprived Johnson of only one rather inarticulate symbolic form of protest—a form of protest that was profoundly offensive to many—and left him with a full panoply of other symbols and every conceivable form of verbal expression to express his deep disapproval of national policy. Thus, in no way can it be said that Texas is punishing him because his hearers [were] profoundly opposed to the message that he sought to convey. Such opposition is no proper basis for restricting speech or expression under the First Amendment. It was Johnson's use of this particular symbol, and not the idea that he sought to [convey], for which he was punished. Our prior cases dealing with flag desecration statutes have left open the question that the Court resolves today. [E.g., Street; Spence.]

The Court concludes its opinion with a regrettably patronizing civics lecture, presumably addressed [in part] to the Members of both Houses of Congress [and] the members of the 48 state legislatures that enacted prohibitions against flag burning. [The] Court's role as the final expositor of the Constitution is well established, but its role as a platonic guardian admonishing those responsible to public opinion as if they were truant school children has no similar place in our system of government. [Surely] one of the high purposes of a democratic society is to legislate against conduct that is regarded as evil and profoundly offensive to the majority of people—whether it be murder, embezzlement, pollution, or flag burning. [Uncritical] extension of constitutional protection to the burning of the flag risks the frustration of the very purpose for which organized governments are instituted. The Court decides that the American flag is just another symbol, about which not only must opinions pro and con be tolerated, but for which the most minimal public respect may not be enjoined. The government may conscript men into the Armed Forces where they [may] die for the flag, but the government may not prohibit the public burning of the banner under which they fight. I would uphold the Texas statute as applied in this case.

■ JUSTICE STEVENS, dissenting.

[A] country's flag is a symbol of more than "nationhood and national unity." [It is also] a symbol of freedom, of equal opportunity, of religious tolerance, and of goodwill for other peoples who share our aspirations. [The] value of the flag as a symbol cannot be measured. Even so, I have no doubt that the interest in preserving that value for the future is both significant and legitimate. [The] content of respondent's message has no relevance whatsoever to the case. [Moreover, the] case has nothing to do with "disagreeable ideas." It involves disagreeable conduct that, in my opinion, diminishes the value of an important national asset. The Court is therefore quite wrong in blandly asserting that respondent "was prosecuted for his expression of dissatisfaction with the policies of this [country]." Respondent was prosecuted because of the method he chose to express his dissatisfaction with those policies. Had he chosen to spray paint [his] message of dissatisfaction on the facade of the Lincoln Memorial, there would be no question about the power of the Government to prohibit his means of expression. [Though] the asset at stake in this case is intangible, given its unique value, the same interest supports a prohibition on the desecration of the American flag.[5]

TEXAS V. JOHNSON AND ITS AFTERMATH

1. *The history of the flag as an American symbol.* Justice Rehnquist predicates his dissent on the argument that "[f]or more than 200 years, the American flag has occupied a unique position as the symbol of our Nation, a uniqueness that justifies a governmental prohibition against flag burning." But the American veneration of the flag has not been consistent throughout U.S. history: "before the Civil War the flag was not widely displayed and played only a minor role in the nation's patriotic oratory and iconography." By the outbreak of the war, the flag had become an important enough national symbol that "President James Buchanan's treasury secretary, John Dix, telegraphed to a clerk in New Orleans, 'If anyone attempts to haul down the American flag, shoot him on the spot.'" Such drastic punishment for flag-desecration was carried out at least once during the Civil War, when Union-occupied New Orleans resident William Mumford "was hung for treason [after] a military court found him guilty of pulling

---

[5] The Court suggests that a prohibition against flag desecration is not content-neutral because this form of symbolic speech is only used by persons who are critical of the flag or the ideas it represents. In making this suggestion the Court does not pause to consider the far-reaching consequences of its introduction of disparate impact analysis into our First Amendment jurisprudence. It seems obvious that a prohibition against the desecration of a gravesite is content-neutral even if it denies some protesters the right to make a symbolic statement by extinguishing the flame in Arlington Cemetery where John F. Kennedy is buried while permitting others to salute the flame by bowing their heads. Few would doubt that a protester who extinguishes the flame has desecrated the gravesite, regardless of whether he prefaces that act with a speech explaining that his purpose is to express deep admiration or unmitigated scorn for the late President. Likewise, few would claim that the protester who bows his head has desecrated the gravesite, even if he makes clear that his purpose is to show disrespect. In such a case, as in a flag burning case, the prohibition against desecration has absolutely nothing to do with the content of the message that the symbolic speech is intended to convey. [Footnote by Justice Stevens.]

down, dragging in the mud, and tearing to shreds an American flag that had been hoisted over the New Orleans mint amid federal reoccupation of the city." The modern flag protection movement arose out of these Civil War-era American nationalist forces. Goldstein, Flag Burning and Free Speech 1–6 (2000).

2. *Congressional response to Johnson.* The decision in Johnson elicited considerable public criticism. Soon after the decision, and after outraged floor speeches, the House and Senate passed, by overwhelming votes, resolutions disagreeing with the ruling and pledging to seek means to restore penalties for "such reprehensible conduct." In short order, the battle lines were drawn between those in Congress who wanted the Constitution amended to permit restraints on flag desecration and those who supported new legislation rather than a constitutional amendment. President George H. W. Bush strongly supported the amendment approach, and many of those who agreed with him believed that any new federal law would meet the same fate in the Court as did the Texas law in Johnson. But others (including many liberal Democrats) believed that a carefully drawn statute might be upheld, and that this would forestall the pressure for a constitutional amendment. Several constitutional scholars, including Laurence Tribe, Rex Lee and Geoffrey Stone, testified before Congress that a flag-burning statute might be drafted so as to pass constitutional muster. For a summary of these arguments, see Stone, "Flag Burning and the Constitution," 75 Iowa L. Rev. 111 (1989). The statutory strategy prevailed, and the Flag Protection Act of 1989 was adopted by overwhelming majorities in each House. The bill became law without the President's signature. The Act provided in relevant part: "(a)(1) Whoever knowingly mutilates, defaces, physically defiles, burns, maintains on the floor or ground, or tramples upon any flag of the United States shall be [fined] or imprisoned for not more than one year or both. (2) This subsection does not prohibit any conduct consisting of the disposal of the flag when it has become worn or soiled."

The new law was immediately and publicly violated in order to challenge its constitutionality. In **United States v. Eichman**, 496 U.S. 310 (1990), the Court struck down the 1989 federal law, once again in a 5–4 decision. The Eichman case stemmed from two prosecutions, one in Washington, D.C. and the other in Seattle. In each case, the trial courts dismissed the charges on the ground that the Act was unconstitutional. The Government conceded in Eichman that the flag burning here constituted expressive conduct, but asked the Court to reconsider its rejection in Johnson of the claim that flag burning, like obscenity or "fighting words," was not protected by the First Amendment. Justice BRENNAN's majority opinion replied: "This we decline to do." That left only the question of whether the Flag Protection Act was "sufficiently distinct" from the Texas law in Johnson to be enforceable here. The Government argued that, unlike the law in Johnson, the new federal law did not "target expressive conduct on the basis of the content of its message," that the federal law was designed to safeguard "the physical integrity of the flag under all circumstances," and that it proscribed "conduct (other than disposal) that damages or mistreats a flag, without regard to the actor's motive, his intended message, or the likely effects of his conduct on onlookers." In rejecting that effort, Justice Brennan emphasized that while the Act "contains no explicit content-based limitation, [it] is nevertheless clear that the Government's asserted *interest* is 'related to the suppression of free expression,' Johnson, and concerned with the content of such expression."

He continued: "Although Congress cast the Flag Protection Act in somewhat broader terms than the Texas statute at issue in Johnson, the Act still suffers from the same fundamental flaw: it suppresses expression out of concern for its likely communicative impact. Despite the Act's wider scope, its restriction on expression cannot be 'justified without reference to the content of the regulated speech.' The Act therefore must be subjected to 'the most exacting scrutiny,' and for the reasons stated in Johnson, the Government's interest cannot justify its infringement on First Amendment rights. We decline the Government's invitation to reassess this conclusion in light of Congress' recent recognition of a purported 'national consensus' favoring a prohibition on flag-burning. Even assuming such a consensus exists, any suggestion that the Government's interest in suppressing speech becomes more weighty as popular opposition to that speech grows is foreign to the First Amendment.

"Government may create national symbols, promote them, and encourage their respectful treatment. But the [Act] goes well beyond this by criminally proscribing expressive conduct because of its likely communicative impact. We are aware that desecration of the flag is deeply offensive to many. But the same might be said, for example, of virulent ethnic and religious epithets, see [Terminiello], vulgar repudiations of the draft, see [Cohen], and scurrilous caricatures, see [Hustler]. 'If there is a bedrock principle underlying the First Amendment, it is that the Government may not prohibit the expression of an idea simply because society finds the idea itself offensive or disagreeable.' Johnson. Punishing desecration of the flag dilutes the very freedom that makes this emblem so revered, and worth revering."

Justice STEVENS's dissent, joined by Chief Justice Rehnquist and Justices White and O'Connor, developed the argument in his Johnson dissent: "[C]ertain methods of expression may be prohibited if (a) the prohibition is supported by a legitimate societal interest that is unrelated to suppression of the ideas the speaker desires to express; (b) the prohibition does not entail any interference with the speaker's freedom to express these ideas by other means; and (c) the interest in allowing the speaker complete freedom of choice of alternative methods of expression is less important than the societal interest supporting the prohibition." He thought that all of these criteria were satisfied here. He emphasized that the Government may "protect the symbolic value of this flag without regard to the specific content of the flag burners' speech. The prosecution in this case does not depend upon the object of the defendants' protest."

3. *Statute vs. amendment.* Which would have had more effect on free speech law: the Flag Protection Act if it had been upheld, or a constitutional amendment providing that "Congress and the States shall have power to prohibit the physical desecration of the flag of the United States"? The assumption of many of the reluctant backers of the Flag Protection Act in Congress was that the constitutional amendment would be by far the greater evil. Such an amendment would, for the first time, have amended an original provision of the Bill of Rights. It would also have been only the fifth constitutional amendment to overrule a decision of the Supreme Court. For the contrary argument that a constitutional amendment would have done *less* harm to the fabric of First Amendment doctrine than would a new flag desecration law upheld by the Court, see Michelman,

"Saving Old Glory: On Constitutional Iconography," 42 Stan. L. Rev. 1337 (1990).

The decision in Eichman spurred a renewed campaign for a constitutional amendment, but the proposed amendment that reached the floor of both Houses in 1990 fell 34 votes short of the required two-thirds majority in the House and 9 votes short in the Senate. A 1995 version of the proposed amendment fared better, passing by a vote of 312–120 in the House but falling three votes short in the Senate, which voted for the amendment 63–46. Renewed proposals for a flag desecration amendment have continued to circulate in later sessions of Congress.

Consider the application of O'Brien, Texas v. Johnson, and the flag desecration cases in the important War on Terror case below, which involved a statute arguably directed generally at conduct but with provisions that applied to speech.

Holder v. Humanitarian Law Project
561 U.S. 1, 130 S. Ct. 2705, 177 L. Ed. 2d 355 (2010).

■ CHIEF JUSTICE ROBERTS delivered the opinion of the Court.

[The] plaintiffs in this litigation seek to provide support to two [groups designated as foreign terrorist organizations]. Plaintiffs claim that they seek to facilitate only the lawful, nonviolent purposes of those groups, and that applying the material-support law to prevent them from doing so violates the Constitution. In particular, they claim that the statute is too vague, in violation of the Fifth Amendment, and that it infringes their rights to freedom of speech and association, in violation of the First Amendment. We conclude that the material-support statute is constitutional as applied to the particular activities plaintiffs have told us they wish to pursue. We do not, however, address the resolution of more difficult cases that may arise under the statute in the future.

I.   This litigation concerns 18 U.S.C. § 2339B, which makes it a federal crime to "knowingly provid[e] material support or resources to a foreign terrorist organization."[1] [The definition of "material support or resources" in the statute is:] "any property, tangible or intangible, or service, including currency or monetary instruments or financial securities, financial services, lodging, training, expert advice or assistance, safehouses, false documentation or identification, communications equipment, facilities, weapons, lethal substances, explosives, personnel (1 or more individuals who may be or include oneself), and transportation, except medicine or religious materials."

The authority to designate an entity a "foreign terrorist organization" rests with the Secretary of State. [In] 1997, [she] designated 30 groups as

---

[1] In full, 18 U.S.C. § 2339B(a)(1) provides: "UNLAWFUL CONDUCT.—Whoever knowingly provides material support or resources to a foreign terrorist organization, or attempts or conspires to do so, shall be fined under this title or imprisoned not more than 15 years, or both, and, if the death of any person results, shall be imprisoned for any term of years or for life. To violate this paragraph, a person must have knowledge that the organization is a designated terrorist organization . . . , that the organization has engaged or engages in terrorist activity . . . , or that the organization has engaged or engages in terrorism. . . ." [Footnote by Chief Justice Roberts.]

foreign terrorist organizations. Two of those groups are the Kurdistan Workers' Party (also known as the Partiya Karkeran Kurdistan, or PKK) and the Liberation Tigers of Tamil Eelam (LTTE). The PKK is an organization founded in 1974 with the aim of establishing an independent Kurdish state in southeastern Turkey. The LTTE is an organization founded in 1976 for the purpose of creating an independent Tamil state in Sri Lanka.

[Plaintiffs] in this litigation are two U.S. citizens and six domestic organizations. [In] 1998, plaintiffs filed suit in federal court challenging the constitutionality of the material-support statute. [Plaintiffs] claimed that they wished to provide support for the humanitarian and political activities of the PKK and the LTTE in the form of monetary contributions, other tangible aid, legal training, and political advocacy, but that they could not do so for fear of prosecution under § 2339B.[2] [As] relevant here, plaintiffs claimed that the material-support statute was unconstitutional [because] it violated their freedom of speech and freedom of association under the First Amendment [by] criminaliz[ing] their provision of material support to the PKK and the LTTE, without requiring the Government to prove that plaintiffs had a specific intent to further the unlawful ends of those organizations. [Plaintiffs also argued that the statute was unconstitutionally vague.]

V. A. We next consider whether the material-support statute, as applied to plaintiffs, violates the freedom of speech guaranteed by the First Amendment. Both plaintiffs and the Government take extreme positions on this question. Plaintiffs claim that Congress has banned their "pure political speech." It has not. Under the material-support statute, plaintiffs may say anything they wish on any topic. They may speak and write freely about the PKK and LTTE, the governments of Turkey and Sri Lanka, human rights, and international law. They may advocate before the United Nations. As the Government states: "The statute does not prohibit independent advocacy or expression of any kind." Section 2339B also "does not prevent [plaintiffs] from becoming members of the PKK and LTTE or impose any sanction on them for doing so." Congress has not, therefore, sought to suppress ideas or opinions in the form of "pure political speech." Rather, Congress has prohibited "material support," which most often does not take the form of speech at all. And when it does, the statute is carefully drawn to cover only a narrow category of speech to, under the direction of, or in coordination with foreign groups that the speaker knows to be terrorist organizations.

For its part, the Government takes the foregoing too far, claiming that the only thing truly at issue in this litigation is conduct, not speech. Section 2339B is directed at the fact of plaintiffs' interaction with the PKK and LTTE, the Government contends, and only incidentally burdens their expression. The Government argues that the proper standard of review is therefore the one set out in [O'Brien]. In that case, [we] applied what we have since called "intermediate scrutiny," under which a "content-neutral regulation will be sustained under the First Amendment if it advances important governmental interests unrelated to the suppression of free

---

    [2]   At the time plaintiffs first filed suit, [the statute] provided: "Whoever, within the United States or subject to the jurisdiction of the United States, knowingly provides material support or resources to a foreign terrorist organization, or attempts or conspires to do so, shall be fined under this title or imprisoned not more than 10 years, or both." [Footnote by Chief Justice Roberts.]

speech and does not burden substantially more speech than necessary to further those interests."

The Government is wrong that the only thing actually at issue in this litigation is conduct, and therefore wrong to argue that O'Brien provides the correct standard of review. O'Brien does not provide the applicable standard for reviewing a content-based regulation of speech, [see R.A.V.,] and § 2339B regulates speech on the basis of its content. Plaintiffs want to speak to the PKK and the LTTE, and whether they may do so under § 2339B depends on what they say. [The] Government argues that § 2339B should nonetheless receive intermediate scrutiny because it *generally* functions as a regulation of conduct. That argument runs headlong into a number of our precedents, most prominently [Cohen v. California]. Cohen also involved a generally applicable regulation of conduct, barring breaches of the peace. But when Cohen was convicted for wearing a jacket bearing an epithet, we did not apply O'Brien. Instead, we recognized that the generally applicable law was directed at Cohen because of what his speech communicated—he violated the breach of the peace statute because of the offensive content of his particular message. We accordingly applied more rigorous scrutiny and reversed his conviction.

This suit falls into the same category. The law here may be described as directed at conduct, as the law in Cohen was directed at breaches of the peace, but as applied to plaintiffs the conduct triggering coverage under the statute consists of communicating a message. As we explained in Texas v. Johnson: "If the [Government's] regulation is not related to expression, then the less stringent standard we announced in [O'Brien] for regulations of noncommunicative conduct controls. If it is, then we are outside of O'Brien's test, and we must [apply] a more demanding standard."

B.   The First Amendment issue before us is more refined than either plaintiffs or the Government would have it. It is not whether the Government may prohibit pure political speech, or may prohibit material support in the form of conduct. It is instead whether the Government may prohibit what plaintiffs want to do—provide material support to the PKK and LTTE in the form of speech.

Everyone agrees that the Government's interest in combating terrorism is an urgent objective of the highest order. Plaintiffs' complaint is that the ban on material support, applied to what they wish to do, is not "necessary to further that interest." The objective of combating terrorism does not justify prohibiting their speech, plaintiffs argue, because their support will advance only the legitimate activities of the designated terrorist organizations, not their terrorism.

Whether foreign terrorist organizations meaningfully segregate support of their legitimate activities from support of terrorism is an empirical question. When it enacted § 2339B in 1996, Congress made specific findings regarding the serious threat posed by international terrorism. One of those findings explicitly rejects plaintiffs' contention that their support would not further the terrorist activities of the PKK and LTTE: "[F]oreign organizations that engage in terrorist activity are so tainted by their criminal conduct that any contribution to such an organization facilitates that conduct."

Plaintiffs argue that the reference to "any contribution" in this finding meant only monetary support. There is no reason to read the finding to be so limited, particularly because Congress expressly prohibited so much more than monetary support in § 2339B. Congress's use of the term "contribution" is best read to reflect a determination that any form of material support furnished "to" a foreign terrorist organization should be barred, which is precisely what the material-support statute does. [We] are convinced that Congress was justified in rejecting [the view that ostensibly peaceful aid has no harmful effects]. The PKK and the LTTE are deadly groups. "The PKK's insurgency has claimed more than 22,000 lives." The LTTE has engaged in extensive suicide bombings and political assassinations, including killings of the Sri Lankan President, Security Minister, and Deputy Defense Minister. "On January 31, 1996, the LTTE exploded a truck bomb filled with an estimated 1,000 pounds of explosives at the Central Bank in Colombo, killing 100 people and injuring more than 1,400. This bombing was the most deadly terrorist incident in the world in 1996." It is not difficult to conclude as Congress did that the "tain[t]" of such violent activities is so great that working in coordination with or at the command of the PKK and LTTE serves to legitimize and further their terrorist means.

Material support meant to "promot[e] peaceable, lawful conduct," can further terrorism by foreign groups in multiple ways. "Material support" is a valuable resource by definition. Such support frees up other resources within the organization that may be put to violent ends. It also importantly helps lend legitimacy to foreign terrorist groups—legitimacy that makes it easier for those groups to persist, to recruit members, and to raise funds— all of which facilitate more terrorist attacks. "Terrorist organizations do not maintain organizational 'firewalls' that would prevent or deter . . . sharing and commingling of support and benefits." [Money] is fungible, and "[w]hen foreign terrorist organizations that have a dual structure raise funds, they highlight the civilian and humanitarian ends to which such moneys could be put." But "there is reason to believe that foreign terrorist organizations do not maintain legitimate financial firewalls between those funds raised for civil, nonviolent activities, and those ultimately used to support violent, terrorist operations." [There] is evidence that the PKK and the LTTE, in particular, have not "respected the line between humanitarian and violent activities."

The dissent argues that there is "no natural stopping place" for the proposition that aiding a foreign terrorist organization's lawful activity promotes the terrorist organization as a whole. But Congress has settled on just such a natural stopping place: The statute reaches only material support coordinated with or under the direction of a designated foreign terrorist organization. Independent advocacy that might be viewed as promoting the group's legitimacy is not covered.[3]

Providing foreign terrorist groups with material support in any form also furthers terrorism by straining the United States' relationships with its allies and undermining cooperative efforts between nations to prevent terrorist attacks. We see no reason to question Congress's finding that "international cooperation is required for an effective response to terrorism,

---

[3]   The dissent also contends that the particular sort of material support plaintiffs seek to provide cannot be diverted to terrorist activities, in the same direct way as funds or goods. This contention misses the point. Both common sense and the evidence submitted by the Government make clear that material support of a terrorist group's lawful activities facilitates the group's ability to attract "funds," "financing," and "goods" that will further its terrorist acts. [Footnote by Chief Justice Roberts.]

as demonstrated by the numerous multilateral conventions in force providing universal prosecutive jurisdiction over persons involved in a variety of terrorist acts, including hostage taking, murder of an internationally protected person, and aircraft piracy and sabotage." The material-support statute furthers this international effort by prohibiting aid for foreign terrorist groups that harm the United States' partners abroad.

C. In analyzing whether it is possible in practice to distinguish material support for a foreign terrorist group's violent activities and its nonviolent activities, we do not rely exclusively on our own inferences drawn from the record evidence. [The] State Department informs us that "[t]he experience and analysis of the U.S. government agencies charged with combating terrorism strongly suppor[t]" Congress's finding that all contributions to foreign terrorist organizations further their terrorism. [That] evaluation of the facts by the Executive, like Congress's assessment, is entitled to deference. This litigation implicates sensitive and weighty interests of national security and foreign affairs. [It] is vital in this context "not to substitute . . . our own evaluation of evidence for a reasonable evaluation by the Legislative Branch."

Our precedents, old and new, make clear that concerns of national security and foreign relations do not warrant abdication of the judicial role. We do not defer to the Government's reading of the First Amendment, even when such interests are at stake. [But] when it comes to collecting evidence and drawing factual inferences in this area, "the lack of competence on the part of the courts is marked," and respect for the Government's conclusions is appropriate. [The] Government, when seeking to prevent imminent harms in the context of international affairs and national security, is not required to conclusively link all the pieces in the puzzle before we grant weight to its empirical conclusions.

This context is different from that in decisions like Cohen. In that case, the application of the statute turned on the offensiveness of the speech at issue. Observing that "one man's vulgarity is another's lyric," we invalidated Cohen's conviction in part because we concluded that "governmental officials cannot make principled distinctions in this area." In this litigation, by contrast, Congress and the Executive are uniquely positioned to make principled distinctions between activities that will further terrorist conduct and undermine United States foreign policy, and those that will not.

[We] turn to the particular speech plaintiffs propose to undertake. First, plaintiffs propose to "train members of [the] PKK on how to use humanitarian and international law to peacefully resolve disputes." Congress can, consistent with the First Amendment, prohibit this direct training. It is wholly foreseeable that the PKK could use the "specific skill[s]" that plaintiffs propose to impart as part of a broader strategy to promote terrorism. The PKK could, for example, pursue peaceful negotiation as a means of buying time to recover from short-term setbacks, lulling opponents into complacency, and ultimately preparing for renewed attacks. [Second,] plaintiffs propose to "teach PKK members how to petition various representative bodies such as the United Nations for relief." The Government acts within First Amendment strictures in banning this proposed speech because it teaches the organization how to acquire "relief," which plaintiffs never define with any specificity, and which could readily include monetary aid. [Finally,] plaintiffs propose to "engage in political advocacy on behalf of Kurds who live in Turkey," and "engage in political advocacy on behalf of Tamils who live in Sri Lanka." [These] proposals are phrased at such a high level of generality that they cannot prevail in this preenforcement challenge.

VI. [The] Preamble to the Constitution proclaims that the people of the United States ordained and established that charter of government in part to "provide for the common defence." As Madison explained, "[s]ecurity against foreign danger is . . . an avowed and essential object of the American Union." [The Federalist No. 41.] We hold that, in regulating the particular forms of support that plaintiffs seek to provide to foreign terrorist organizations, Congress has pursued that objective consistent with the limitations of the First and Fifth Amendments.

■ JUSTICE BREYER, with whom JUSTICES GINSBURG and SOTOMAYOR join, dissenting.

[I] cannot agree with the Court's conclusion that the Constitution permits the Government to prosecute the plaintiffs criminally for engaging in coordinated teaching and advocacy furthering the designated organizations' lawful political objectives. [In] my view, the Government has not made the strong showing necessary to justify under the First Amendment the criminal prosecution of those who engage in these activities. All the activities involve the communication and advocacy of political ideas and lawful means of achieving political ends. [That] this speech and association for political purposes is the *kind* of activity to which the First Amendment ordinarily offers its strongest protection is elementary. [Although] in the Court's view the statute applies only where the PKK helps to coordinate a defendant's activities, the simple fact of "coordination" alone cannot readily remove protection that the First Amendment would otherwise grant.

["Coordination"] with a group that engages in unlawful activity also does not deprive the plaintiffs of the First Amendment's protection under any traditional "categorical" exception to its protection. The plaintiffs do not propose to solicit a crime. They will not engage in fraud or defamation or circulate obscenity. And the First Amendment protects advocacy even of unlawful action so long as that advocacy is not "directed to inciting or producing imminent lawless action and . . . likely to incite or produce such action." [Brandenburg.] Here the plaintiffs seek to advocate peaceful, lawful action to secure political ends; and they seek to teach others how to do the same. No one contends that the plaintiffs' speech to these organizations can be prohibited as incitement under Brandenburg.

[It] is not surprising that the majority, in determining the constitutionality of criminally prohibiting the plaintiffs' proposed activities, would apply, not the kind of intermediate First Amendment standard that applies to conduct, but "a more demanding standard." Indeed, where, as here, a statute applies criminal penalties and at least arguably does so on the basis of content-based distinctions, I should think we would scrutinize the statute and justifications "strictly"—to determine whether the prohibition is justified by a "compelling" need that cannot be "less restrictively" accommodated. [But,] even if we assume for argument's sake that "strict scrutiny" does not apply, [I] doubt that the statute, as the Government would interpret it, can survive any reasonably applicable First Amendment standard. [The] Government does identify a compelling countervailing interest, namely, the interest in protecting the security of the United States and its nationals from the threats that foreign terrorist organizations pose by denying those organizations financial and other fungible resources. I do not dispute the importance of this interest. But I do dispute whether the interest can justify the statute's criminal prohibition. To put the matter more specifically, precisely how does application of the statute to the protected activities before us *help achieve* that important security-related end?

The Government makes two efforts to answer this question. First, the Government says that the plaintiffs' support for these organizations is "fungible" in the same sense as other forms of banned support. [The] proposition that the two very different kinds of "support" are "fungible," however, is not obviously true. There is no obvious way in which undertaking advocacy for political change through peaceful means or teaching the PKK and LTTE, say, how to petition the United Nations for political change is fungible with other resources that might be put to more sinister ends in the way that donations of money, food, or computer training are fungible. [Second,] the Government says that the plaintiffs' proposed activities will "bolste[r] a terrorist organization's efficacy and strength in a community" and "undermin[e] this nation's efforts to delegitimize and weaken those groups." In the Court's view, too, the Constitution permits application of the statute to activities of the kind at issue in part because those activities could provide a group that engages in terrorism with "legitimacy." [But] this "legitimacy" justification cannot by itself warrant suppression of political speech, advocacy, and association. Speech, association, and related activities on behalf of a group will often, perhaps always, help to legitimate that group. Thus, were the law to accept a "legitimating" effect, in and of itself and without qualification, as providing sufficient grounds for imposing such a ban, the First Amendment battle would be lost in untold instances where it should be won. Once one accepts this argument, there is no natural stopping place.

[Nor] can the Government overcome these considerations simply by narrowing the covered activities to those that involve coordinated, rather than independent, advocacy. Conversations, discussions, or logistical arrangements might well prove necessary to carry out the speech-related activities here at issue (just as conversations and discussions are a necessary part of membership in any organization). The Government does not distinguish this kind of "coordination" from any other. I am not aware of any form of words that might be used to describe "coordination" that would not, at a minimum, seriously chill not only the kind of activities the plaintiffs raise before us, but also the "independent advocacy" the Government purports to permit. And, as for the Government's willingness to distinguish independent advocacy from coordinated advocacy, the former is more likely, not less likely, to confer legitimacy than the latter. Thus, other things being equal, the distinction "coordination" makes is arbitrary in respect to furthering the statute's purposes. And a rule of law that finds the "legitimacy" argument adequate in respect to the latter would have a hard time distinguishing a statute that sought to attack the former.

[What] is one to say about [the Government's] arguments—arguments that would deny First Amendment protection to the peaceful teaching of international human rights law on the ground that a little knowledge about "the international legal system" is too dangerous a thing; that an opponent's subsequent willingness to negotiate might be faked, so let's not teach him how to try? What might be said of these claims by those who live, as we do, in a Nation committed to the resolution of disputes through "deliberative forces"? [Whitney.]

[I] believe application of the statute as the Government interprets it would gravely and without adequate justification injure interests of the kind the First Amendment protects. [I] would read the statute as criminalizing First-Amendment-protected pure speech and association only when the defendant knows or intends that those activities will assist the organization's unlawful terrorist actions. [This] reading of the statute protects those who engage in pure speech and association ordinarily protected by the First Amendment. But it does not protect that activity where a defendant purposefully intends it to help terrorism or where a defendant knows (or willfully blinds himself to the fact) that the activity is significantly likely to assist terrorism. Where the activity fits into these categories of purposefully or knowingly supporting terrorist ends, the act of providing material support to a known terrorist organization bears a close enough relation to terrorist acts that, in my view, it likely can be prohibited notwithstanding any First Amendment interest. Cf. [Brandenburg.]

THE IMPLICATIONS OF HUMANITARIAN LAW PROJECT

1. *The standard of review.* The majority opinion in Humanitarian Law Project (HLP) purports to apply a distinct standard—"more rigorous scrutiny"—for laws that are generally directed at conduct but are triggered in the particular case by the communication of a message. Was that the standard of review applied by the Court in Cohen v. California (1971; p. 69), or referred to in Texas v. Johnson (1989; p. 262)? Is it relevant that in Cohen, the government interest in proscribing speech did not outweigh the First Amendment considerations, whereas in HLP it did? Or was Chief Justice Roberts's heightened standard just strict scrutiny in disguise? The Supreme Court has itself characterized HLP as applying strict scrutiny (albeit only parenthetically), as have several courts of appeals. See McCullen v. Coakley (2014; p. 320 below); see also United States v. Baumgartner, 581 F. App'x 522, 530 (6th Cir. 2014); Al Haramain Islamic Found., Inc. v. U.S. Dep't of Treasury, 686 F.3d 965, 996 (9th Cir. 2012). If HLP indeed applied strict scrutiny, was its application not highly deferential to the government? As a more basic matter, was the material support statute in HLP generally directed at conduct, as Chief Justice Roberts suggests? Should it matter that the statute specifically refers to "advice" as a form of material support?

2. *Prohibitions on counseling.* What other types of part-conduct, part-speech regulation might be subject to HLP's heightened standard? Several states have passed statutes prohibiting licensed mental health professionals from offering minors the controversial "sexual orientation change efforts" (SOCE) therapy. Since HLP, two federal courts of appeal have upheld such prohibitions, but the courts have disagreed on whether HLP's "more rigorous scrutiny" or O'Brien's "intermediate scrutiny" should apply. Compare King v. Governor of State of N.J., 767 F.3d 216 (3d Cir. 2014) (finding SOCE therapy was "speech" subject to HLP's heightened scrutiny), with Pickup v. Brown, 740 F.3d 1208 (9th Cir. 2013) (holding SOCE therapy is "conduct" subject to O'Brien standard).

3. *"Material support" and Brandenburg.* Can the Court's holding in HLP be squared with its decision in Brandenburg v. Ohio (1969; p. 48)?

Recall that in Brandenburg, the Court held that speech that is not "directed to inciting or producing imminent lawless action and [likely] to incite or produce such action" is protected under the First Amendment. Isn't Chief Justice Roberts's failure even to mention Brandenburg puzzling? Roberts's opinion places great weight on the distinction between "independent" and "coordinated" advocacy; is that difference helpful here?

For his part, Justice Breyer stated in his dissent that the plaintiffs' speech could not be barred as incitement under Brandenburg. The plaintiffs here sought to advocate merely "peaceful, *lawful* action," and Brandenburg protects advocacy of even unlawful behavior, provided it does not amount to incitement. Given this apparent irreconcilability, why does Justice Breyer not state that HLP overrules Brandenburg?

4. ***Deference to congressional findings?*** Whether offering otherwise lawful advice to a terrorist organization constitutes the conduct of material support depends, the Court suggested, on the "empirical question" whether terrorist organizations sequester or separate their lawful from their unlawful activities. On this point, the Court appeared to defer to Congress. Can this approach be reconciled with Justice Brandeis's dissent in Whitney v. California (1927; p. 35), where he maintained that the judiciary must not defer to legislative findings of the dangerousness of political speech?

5. ***Material support and the War on Terror.*** After HLP, is there any reason for law enforcement ever to invoke incitement laws to punish speakers who support terrorism? Wouldn't it be easier to charge such speakers with material support of terrorism and then try to show that their speech was not uncoordinated advocacy but intended to support the organization? Consider the defendants in Brandenburg: they were members of the Ku Klux Klan, which certainly acted as a terrorist organization in some (perhaps most) periods of its history. Could their speech have been punished under a properly framed material support statute? If so, then does the Brandenburg tradition of protection for unpopular speech even by members of groups advocating violence still exist in the post-September 11 era?

6. ***Support for domestic organizations.*** The HLP majority was careful to note that its holding was limited to the statute's prohibition on material support for *foreign* terrorist organizations: "We [do] not suggest that Congress could extend the same prohibition on material support at issue here to domestic organizations." Are there compelling reasons to scrutinize the constitutionality of statutes regulating contributions to domestic terrorist groups more carefully? At least one court of appeals thinks so: In **Al Haramin Islamic Foundation, Inc. v. U.S. Department of Treasury**, 686 F.3d 965 (9th Cir. 2011), the Ninth Circuit held that the government could not constitutionally prohibit an Oregon-based community group, MCASO, from advocating on behalf of a domestic foundation designated by executive order as tied to an international terrorist organization. While the court did not treat the foreign-domestic distinction as dispositive, it was persuaded that the foundation's domestic status undermined the government's interest in prohibiting MCASO's advocacy on its behalf; the court found "little evidence that the pure-speech activities proposed by MCASO on behalf of the domestic branch will aid the larger international organization's sinister purposes." The court thus held that applying the executive's designation to bar MCASO's advocacy did not meet the strict scrutiny required by HLP.

NUDE DANCING

Recall that the Court invalidated a citywide ban on nude entertainment in Schad v. Mt. Ephraim (1981; p. 155) but upheld zoning regulations concentrating or dispersing adult entertainment establishments in Young v. American Mini Theatres (1976; p. 157) and Renton v. Playtime Theatres (1986; p. 160). A 1991 challenge to a ban on public nudity as applied to nude dancing elicited sharp disagreement among the Justices over the applicable standard of review: the plurality found the law content-neutral and reviewed its application under the O'Brien test; Justice Scalia found it content-neutral but subject to more deferential review; and the dissent found it content-based because it aimed at communicative impact.

Barnes v. Glen Theatre, Inc.

501 U.S. 560, 111 S. Ct. 2456, 115 L. Ed. 2d 504 (1991).

■ CHIEF JUSTICE REHNQUIST delivered the opinion of the Court.

Respondents [Kitty Kat Lounge and Glen Theatre] are two establishments in South Bend, Indiana that wish to provide totally nude dancing as entertainment, and individual dancers who are employed at these establishments. The Kitty Kat Lounge, Inc. [ ] sells alcoholic beverages and presents "go-go dancing." Its proprietor desires to present "totally nude dancing," but an applicable Indiana statute regulating public nudity requires that the dancers wear "pasties" and "G-strings" when the dance. Glen Theatre, Inc., suppl[ies] so-called adult entertainment through written and printed materials, movie showings, and live entertainment at an enclosed "bookstore." The live entertainment at the "bookstore" consists of nude and seminude performances and showings of the female body through glass panels. Customers sit in a booth and insert coins into a timing mechanism that permits them to observe the live nude and seminude dancers for a period of time.

[Respondents object to] enforcement of a public indecency statute [providing that] "[a] person who knowingly or intentionally, in a public place, [appears] in a state of nudity [commits] public indecency, a [misdemeanor] and [defining nudity as] showing of the human male or female genitals, pubic area, or buttocks with less than a fully opaque covering [or] the showing of the female breast with less than a fully opaque covering of any part of the nipple." Respondents assert[ed] that [Indiana's] prohibition against complete nudity in public places violated the First Amendment.

[N]ude dancing of the kind sought to be performed here is expressive conduct within the outer perimeters of the First Amendment, though we view it as only marginally so. Indiana, of course, has not banned nude dancing as such, but has proscribed public nudity across the board. Applying the four-part O'Brien test, [we] find that Indiana's public indecency statute is justified despite its incidental limitations on some expressive activity. The public indecency statute is clearly within the constitutional power of the State and furthers substantial governmental interests. It is impossible to discern, other than from the text of the statute, exactly what governmental interest the Indiana legislators had in mind when they enacted this statute, for Indiana does not record legislative history, and the State's highest court has not shed additional light on the statute's purpose. Nonetheless, the statute's purpose of protecting societal order and morality is clear from its text and history. Public indecency statutes of this sort are of ancient origin and presently exist in at least 47 States. Public indecency, including nudity, was a criminal offense at common law. [Public] nudity was considered an act malum in se. Public indecency statutes such as the one before us reflect moral disapproval of people appearing in the nude among strangers in public places. [This] and other public indecency statutes were designed to protect morals and public order. The traditional police power of the States is defined as the authority to provide for the public health, safety, and morals, and we have upheld such a basis for legislation. [Paris Adult; Hardwick.]

[This] interest is unrelated to the suppression of free expression. Some may view restricting nudity on moral grounds as necessarily related to expression. We disagree. It can be argued, of course, that almost limitless types of conduct—including appearing in the nude in public—are "expressive," and in one sense of the word this is true. People who go about in the nude in public may be expressing something about themselves by so doing. But the court rejected this expansive notion of 'expressive conduct' in O'Brien, saying: "We cannot accept the view that an apparently limitless variety of conduct can be labeled 'speech' whenever the person engaging in the conduct intends thereby to express an idea."

■ JUSTICE SCALIA, concurring.

I agree that the judgment of the Court of Appeals must be reversed. In my view, however, the challenged regulation must be upheld, not because it survives some lower level of First Amendment scrutiny, but because, as a general law regulating conduct and not specifically directed at expression, it is not subject to First Amendment scrutiny at all. [Indiana's] statute is in the line of a long tradition of laws against public nudity, which have never been thought to run afoul of traditional understanding of 'the freedom of speech.' Public indecency—including public nudity—has long been an offense at common law. Indiana's first public nudity statute predated by many years the appearance of nude barroom dancing. It was general in scope, directed all public nudity, and not just at public nude expression; and all succeeding statutes, down to the present one, have been the same. Were it the case that Indiana in practice targeted only expressive nudity, while turning a blind eye to nude beaches and unclothed purveyors of hot dogs and machine tools, it might be said that what posed as a regulation of conduct in general was in reality a regulation of only communicative conduct. Respondents have adduced no evidence of that. Indiana officials have brought many public indecency prosecutions for activities having no communicative element.

[The] dissent confidently asserts that the purpose of restricting nudity in public places in general is to protect nonconsenting parties from offense; and argues that since only consenting, admission-paying patrons see respondents dance, that purpose cannot apply and the only remaining purpose must relate to the communicative elements of the performance. Perhaps the dissenters believe that 'offense to others' ought to be the only reason for restricting nudity in public places generally, but there is no basis for thinking that our society has ever shared that Thoreauvian 'you-may-do-what-you-like-so-long-as-it-does-not-injure-someone-else' beau ideal—much less for thinking that it was written into the Constitution. The purpose of

Indiana's nudity law would be violated, I think, if 60,000 fully consenting adults crowded into the Hoosier Dome to display their genitals to one another, even if there were not an offended innocent in the crowd. Our society prohibits, and all human societies have prohibited, certain activities not because they harm others but because they are considered, in the traditional phrase, 'contra bonos mores,' i.e., immoral. In American society, such prohibitions have included, for example, sadomasochism, cockfighting, bestiality, suicide, drug use, prostitution, and sodomy. [The] Constitution does not prohibit [such laws] simply because they regulate 'morality.' [See Hardwick; Paris Adult.] The purpose of the Indiana statute, as both its text and the manner of its enforcement demonstrate, is to enforce the traditional moral belief that people should not expose their private parts indiscriminately, regardless of whether those who see them are disedified. Since that is so, the dissent has no basis for positing that, where only thoroughly edified adults are present, the purpose must be repression of communication.

Since the Indiana regulation is a general law not specifically targeted at expressive conduct, its application to such conduct does not in my view implicate the First Amendment. [Virtually] every law restricts conduct, and virtually any prohibited conduct can be performed for an expressive purpose—if only expressive of the fact that the actor disagrees with the prohibition. It cannot reasonably be demanded, therefore, that every restriction of expression incidentally produced by a general law regulating conduct pass normal First Amendment scrutiny, or even [the O'Brien test.] Nor do our holdings require such justification: We have never invalidated the application of a general law simply because the conduct that it reached was being engaged in for expressive purposes and the government could not demonstrate a sufficiently important state interest.

■ JUSTICE SOUTER, concurring.

[The state] assert[s] that the statute is applied to nude dancing because such dancing 'encourages prostitution, increases sexual assaults, and attracts other criminal activity.' This asserted justification for the statute may not be ignored merely because it is unclear to what extent this purpose motivated the Indiana Legislature in enacting the statute. Our appropriate focus is not an empirical enquiry into the actual intent of the enacting legislature, but rather the existence or not of a current governmental interest in the service of which the challenged application of the statute may be constitutional. [In] my view, the interest asserted by petitioners [is] sufficient under O'Brien to justify the State's enforcement of the statute against the type of adult entertainment at issue here.

[This] interest [is] 'unrelated to the suppression of free expression.' [To] say that pernicious secondary effects are associated with nude dancing establishments is not necessarily to say that such effects result from the persuasive effect of the expression inherent in nude dancing. It is to say, rather, only that the effects are correlated with the existence of establishments offering such dancing, without deciding what the precise causes of the correlation actually are.

■ JUSTICE WHITE, dissenting.

The purpose of forbidding people from appearing nude in parks, beaches, hot dog stands, and like public places is to protect others from offense. But that could not possibly be the purpose of preventing nude dancing in theaters and barrooms since the viewers are exclusively consenting adults who pay money to see these dances. The purpose of the proscription in these contexts is to protect the viewers from what the State believes is the harmful message that nude dancing communicates. [The] emotional or erotic impact of the dance is intensified by the nudity of the performers. [The] sight of a fully clothed, or even a partially clothed, dancer generally will have a far different impact on a spectator than that of a nude dancer, even if the same dance is performed. The nudity is itself an expressive component of the dance, not merely incidental 'conduct.'

[This] being the case, it cannot be that the statutory prohibition is unrelated to expressive conduct. Since the State permits the dancers to perform if they wear pasties and G-strings but forbids nude dancing, it is precisely because of the distinctive, expressive content of the nude dancing performances at issue in this case that the State seeks to apply the statutory prohibition. It is only because nude dancing performances may generate emotions and feelings of eroticism and sensuality among the spectators that the State seeks to regulate such expressive activity, apparently on the assumption that creating or emphasizing such thoughts and ideas in the minds of the spectators may lead to increased prostitution and the degradation of women. But generating thoughts, ideas, and emotions is the essence of communication. [Thus] the level of First Amendment protection to be accorded the performances at issue here [should be the] 'exacting scrutiny' [required in Texas v. Johnson.] [Our] cases require us to affirm absent a compelling state interest supporting the statute. [Even] if there were compelling interests, the Indiana statute is not narrowly drawn.

———

APPLYING BARNES

The Court revisiting the constitutionality of public nudity bans as applied to nude dancing in **City of Erie v. Pap's A.M.**, 529 U.S. 277 (2000). The Pennsylvania Supreme Court, finding no clear precedent in the fragmented Barnes opinions, had employed strict scrutiny to invalidate a municipal nudity ban as applied to the right of an establishment called Kandyland to feature totally nude erotic dancing by women. The state court reasoned that a law was not content-neutral but had sought to "impact negatively on the erotic message of the dance." Reversing, the United States Supreme Court again fragmented in its reasoning, as it had in Barnes. Justice O'CONNOR, writing for the Court in a plurality opinion joined by Chief Justice Rehnquist and Justices Kennedy and Breyer, found that government restrictions on public nudity should be evaluated under the O'Brien test as content-neutral restrictions on symbolic conduct. She rejected any reading of the Erie ordinance as content-based, finding it instead aimed at "combat[ing] the negative secondary effects associated with nude dancing establishments," such as the promotion of "violence, public intoxication, prostitution, and other serious criminal activity." Justice O'Connor found this justification sufficient to satisfy O'Brien, even in the absence of a specific evidentiary record of such secondary effects.

Justice SCALIA, joined by Justice Thomas, concurred in the judgment, reiterating his view in Barnes that a public nudity law such as Erie's is a "general law regulating conduct and not specifically directed at expression," and thus subject to no First Amendment scrutiny at all. He continued:

"[E]ven if one hypothesizes that the city's object was to suppress only nude dancing, that would not establish an intent to suppress what (if anything) nude dancing communicates. I do not feel the need, as the Court does, to identify some 'secondary effects' associated with nude dancing that the city could properly seek to eliminate. (I am highly skeptical, to tell the truth, that the addition of pasties and g-strings will at all reduce the tendency of establishments such as Kandyland to attract crime and prostitution, and hence to foster sexually transmitted disease.) The traditional power of government to foster good morals (bonos mores), and the acceptability of the traditional judgment (if Erie wishes to endorse it) that nude public dancing itself is immoral, have not been repealed by the First Amendment."

Justice SOUTER filed an opinion concurring in part and dissenting in part. He agreed that O'Brien was the right test, but insisted that "intermediate scrutiny requires a regulating government to make some demonstration of an evidentiary basis for the harm it claims to flow from the expressive activity, and for the alleviation expected from the restriction imposed." He found the evidentiary record in the case "deficient" under this standard, finding not facts but "emotionalism" in the statements made by city council members. In requiring a better empirical justification for the law in order to satisfy the O'Brien standard, Justice Souter took the unusual step of confessing error about his own prior opinion in Barnes: "Careful readers, and not just those on the Erie City Council, will of course realize that my partial dissent rests on a demand for an evidentiary basis that I failed to make when I concurred in Barnes. I should have demanded the evidence then, too, and my mistake calls to mind Justice Jackson's foolproof explanation of a lapse of his own, when he quoted Samuel Johnson, 'Ignorance, sir, ignorance.' "

Justice STEVENS, joined by Justice Ginsburg, dissented, opposing the plurality's extension of the "secondary effects" test from zoning cases to what he characterized as a "total ban" on a medium of expression. He also criticized the plurality's lenient application of that test: "To believe that the mandatory addition of pasties and a G-string will have any kind of noticeable impact on secondary effects requires nothing short of a titanic surrender to the implausible." He would have found that the Erie ordinance was impermissibly aimed at nude dancing rather than nudity in general, and invalidated it.

Note that, by converging on the secondary effects rationale in Pap's, the Court abandoned as an apparent isolated anomaly the plurality's view in Barnes that morality alone was a good enough content-neutral reason to uphold a regulation of speech under O'Brien review. While the Court once held that morality was a good enough reason to prohibit sex (but recall that Bowers v. Hardwick was later overruled in Lawrence v. Texas), it had never otherwise held that morality alone was a sufficient ground for regulating protected speech. But note how thin an empirical record of harm from secondary effects was sufficient for the plurality here to uphold the nudity ban—a point emphasized by Justice Souter in his partial dissent. For criticism of the secondary effects doctrine as it has been applied to prohibitions on nude dancing, see Adler, "Girls! Girls! Girls!: The Supreme Court Confronts the G-String," 80 N.Y.U. L. Rev. 1108 (2005).

For further exploration of the issues in Barnes, see the opinions of Judges Posner (concurring) and Easterbrook (dissenting) in the decision of the Court of Appeals for the Seventh Circuit holding the application of the law unconstitutional below. Miller v. Civil City of South Bend, 904 F.2d 1081 (1990) (en banc). See also Blasi, "Six Conservatives in Search of the First Amendment: The Revealing Case of Nude Dancing," 33 Wm. & Mary L. Rev. 611 (1992).

———

SPEECH VERSUS CONDUCT IN PRICING

In **Expressions Hair Design v. Schneiderman**, 581 U.S. ___, 137 S. Ct. 1144 (2017), the Court considered a free-speech challenge to New York State law that prohibited merchants from telling customers that they must pay a surcharge on credit-card transactions. In an opinion by Chief Justice ROBERTS, the Court held that the law regulated speech, not conduct, as the Second Circuit had held: "[A] typical price regulation[—for] example, a law requiring all New York delis to charge $10 for their sandwiches—would simply regulate the amount that a store could collect. In other words, it would regulate the sandwich seller's conduct. To be sure, in order to actually collect that money, a store would likely have to put '$10' on its menus or have its employees tell customers that price. Those written or oral communications would be speech, and the law—by determining the amount charged—would indirectly dictate the content of that speech. But the law's effect on speech would be only incidental to its primary effect on conduct. [This law] is different. The law tells merchants nothing about the amount they are allowed to collect from a cash or credit card payer. Sellers are free to charge $10 for cash and $9.70, $10, $10.30, or any other amount for credit. What the law does regulate is how sellers may communicate their prices. A merchant who wants to charge $10 for cash and $10.30 for credit may not convey that price any way he pleases. He is not free to say '$10, with a 3% credit card surcharge' or '$10, plus $0.30 for credit' because both of those displays identify a single sticker price—$10—that is less than the amount credit card users will be charged. Instead, if the merchant wishes to post a single sticker price, he must display $10.30 as his sticker price. Accordingly, [we] cannot accept [the] conclusion that [the law] is nothing more than a mine-run price regulation. In regulating the communication of prices rather than prices themselves, [the law] regulates speech. [The] parties dispute whether [the law] is a valid commercial speech regulation under Central Hudson Gas & Elec. Corp. v. Public Serv. Comm'n of N. Y., and whether the law can be upheld as a valid disclosure requirement under Zauderer v. Office of Disciplinary Counsel of Supreme Court of Ohio. [We] decline to consider those questions in the first instance. Instead, we remand for the Court of Appeals to analyze [the law] as a speech regulation." Does Chief Justice Roberts's opinion telegraph an answer to the question whether the credit-card regulation is commercial speech? And if so, whether the regulation is valid?

SECTION 2. GOVERNMENT POWER TO LIMIT SPEECH IN CONFERRAL OF BENEFITS AS REGULATOR AND EMPLOYER

———

PUBLIC FORUMS AND PUBLIC PROPERTY

To what extent may government regulate those who want to march in city streets or speak in parks to publicize their views? To what extent does concern with such values as order, quiet, traffic control, and audience sensibilities justify curbs on expression in these contexts? Restraints on speech in public places in the interest of local tranquility did not reach the Court until the late 1930s. Since then, these problems have regularly produced litigation as speakers and demonstrators have sought to use streets, parks, and other public places to publicize their causes, change views and win adherents. Many early cases were stimulated by the "robust evangelism" of the Jehovah's Witnesses. During the fifties, as Harry Kalven remarked, "the story of the streets became a bit quaint." But by the sixties, with the rise of the civil rights and anti-war movements, it became clear "that the story [was] not over." Kalven, "The Concept of the Public Forum: Cox v. Louisiana," 1965 Sup. Ct. Rev. 1. In this era, the proselytizing of the single evangelist selling magazines, ringing doorbells, and speaking at street corners, gave way to a different kind of public speech: sizeable parades in streets, vigils in parks, and protest meetings outside public buildings.

What legal analyses are appropriate in evaluating the claims of those who seek access to public places to air their views? Does the First Amendment guarantee speakers access to the public forum or merely assure them equal access if public spaces are opened to speech at all? May government prohibit noisy parades in residential areas late at night or mass gatherings on heavily traveled streets during rush hour? How far may it go in advancing interests in public safety and order, aesthetic attractiveness, or tranquility, privacy, and repose? Furthermore, should speech in all public places be treated alike? The streets and parks have been treated as the quintessential public forum. Might some other public places—the Senate gallery? courtrooms? libraries? jails? airports?—be so specialized in their function as to justify total exclusion of public speakers? These questions are explored in the cases that follow.

———

EARLY PUBLIC FORUM CASES

1. *The First Amendment "right" to a public forum.* Is government free to exclude any speech it wishes from public places because it "owns" them? Is government in this context equivalent to a private proprietor? This was the view articulated by Justice Holmes when he was a state court judge. In Massachusetts v. Davis, 39 N.E. 113 (Mass. 1895), aff'd, 167 U.S. 43 (1897), the Massachusetts Supreme Judicial Court upheld the conviction of a preacher for speaking on Boston Common without a required permit from the mayor. Justice Oliver Wendell Holmes Jr., then on the Massachusetts court, wrote: "As representative of the public, [the legislature] may and does exercise control over the use which the public may make of such places. [For]

the legislature absolutely or conditionally to forbid public speaking in a highway or public park is no more an infringement of the rights of a member of the public than for the owner of a private house to forbid it in his house." The U.S. Supreme Court affirmed, reasoning—at a time before the First Amendment had been held to apply against the states—that "the right to absolutely exclude all right to use, necessarily includes the authority to determine under what circumstances such use may be availed of, as the greater power contains the lesser."

The later Court has not embraced that view. Since the 1930s, the Court has imposed limits on the restrictions government may impose on speech in the "public forum." The origin of the right to speak in a public forum is often traced to a dictum in Justice ROBERTS's opinion in **Hague v. CIO**, 307 U.S. 496 (1939): "Wherever the title of streets and parks may rest they have immemorially been held in trust for the use of the public and, time out of mind, have been used for purposes of assembly, communicating thoughts between citizens, and discussing public questions. Such use of the streets and public places has, from ancient times, been a part of the privileges, immunities, rights and liberties of citizens. The privilege [to] use the streets and parks for communication of views on national questions may be regulated in the interest of all; [but] it must not, in the guise of regulation, be abridged or denied." In answer to Justice Holmes's suggestion that a city is the equivalent of a private proprietor possessing a right to exclude, Justice Roberts suggested that the public has "a kind of First-Amendment easement" of access to the streets and parks for purposes of speech. Kalven, "The Concept of the Public Forum: Cox v. Louisiana," 1965 Sup. Ct. Rev. 1.

2. *Guaranteed access vs. equal access: is the issue distribution or discrimination?* Does the First Amendment mandate some guaranteed minimum access to the public forum? Or does it merely require that, if the public forum is opened to speech, it is opened on an evenhanded basis? Both answers appear in different strands of the early cases concerning public forums. One strand suggests that government *must* make some public places available for the expression of ideas. This strand treats the streets and parks as important to the distribution of speech. Just as handbilling is the "poor man's printing press," so too streets and parks have special importance for those who cannot afford to resort to other means of communication. On this view, access to the public forum operates as a compelled subsidy for speech that otherwise might not be heard. Another strand in the early public forum cases focuses on discrimination rather than distribution. On this view, government's obligation is merely to provide *equal* access to public places if it permits access for speech at all. On this view, the danger is not that there will be too little speech, but that the government will pick and choose among speakers in a biased way. Might the two different approaches point to different outcomes in some cases? How would each approach treat a law banning "radical demonstrations in the park"? How would each approach treat a law banning "all demonstrations in the park"?

For an endorsement of the broader, guaranteed-access view, see Kalven, "The Concept of the Public Forum: Cox v. Louisiana," 1965 Sup. Ct. Rev. 1 ("[I]n an open democratic society the streets, the parks, and other public places are an important facility for public discussion and political process. They are in brief a public forum that the citizen can commandeer."). For a critical reexamination of Kalven's position, see Post, "Between Governance and Management: The History and Theory of the Public Forum," 34 UCLA

L. Rev. 1713 (1987) (suggesting that government is subject to greater First Amendment restraints when it acts to govern the general public than when it acts in a "managerial" capacity toward its own institutions). For further discussion of the public forum, see Stone, "Fora Americana: Speech in Public Places," 1974 Sup. Ct. Rev. 233; Cass, "First Amendment Access to Government Facilities," 65 Va. L. Rev. 1287 (1979); Goldberger, "Judicial Scrutiny in Public Forum Cases: Misplaced Trust in the Judgment of Public Officials," 32 Buffalo L. Rev. 175 (1983); and Farber & Nowak, "The Misleading Nature of Public Forum Analysis: Content and Context in First Amendment Adjudication," 70 Va. L. Rev. 1219 (1984).

3. *Early cases: standardless licensing and the problem of discrimination.* Several of the Court's early public forum decisions invalidated standardless licensing schemes for conferring too much discretion on public officials to discriminate on the basis of content in regulating access to the public forum. These cases give more support to the equal-access than the guaranteed-access approach. For example, in Lovell v. Griffin (1938; p. 453 below), the Court invalidated a conviction for leafleting without a license from the city manager on the ground that the licensing scheme vested unfettered discretion in the city manager. Hague v. CIO, the 1939 case containing Justice Roberts's famous dictum, relied on Lovell in holding a Jersey City, New Jersey, ordinance "void upon its face" because access to streets and parks required a permit, and the standards of the ordinance governing issuance of the permit did not adequately curb the possible use of discretion. Thus, a permit could be refused on the "mere opinion [of the head of the police] that such refusal will prevent 'riots, disturbances or disorderly assemblage.' It can thus [be] made the instrument of arbitrary suppression of free expression of views on [national affairs]." That risked "uncontrolled official suppression." Similarly, in Cantwell v. Connecticut (1940; p. 61), the Court invalidated a law requiring official approval for the solicitation of contributions to "religious causes."

And in **Saia v. New York**, 334 U.S. 558 (1948), the Court's 5–4 decision held invalid a Lockport, New York, ordinance prohibiting the use of amplification devices without the permission of the police chief. Relying on Lovell, Hague, and Cantwell, Justice DOUGLAS's majority opinion found the ordinance unconstitutional "on its face" for establishing a standardless "previous restraint" on free speech. He stated: "Loud-speakers are today indispensable instruments of effective public speech. The sound truck has become an accepted method of political campaigning. It is the way people are reached. [This] ordinance would be a dangerous weapon if it were allowed to get a hold on our public life. [When] a city allows an official to ban them in his uncontrolled discretion, it sanctions a device for suppression of free communication of ideas. In this case a permit is denied because some persons were said to have found the sound annoying. In the next one a permit may be denied because some people find the ideas annoying. Annoyance at ideas can be cloaked in annoyance at sound. The power of censorship inherent in this type of ordinance reveals its vice." Justice FRANKFURTER dissented, joined by Justices Reed and Burton, arguing that "no arbitrary action or discrimination" had been shown, and that loudspeakers were instruments of "aural aggression" that could intrude into "cherished privacy: [Surely] there is not a constitutional right to force unwilling people to listen." Justice Jackson also dissented.

For later analogues to these early cases emphasizing the dangers of abuse of official discretion over speech, and thus the equal-access rather than the guaranteed-access approach, see, e.g., **Staub v. Baxley**, 355 U.S. 313 (1958) (striking down on its face an ordinance prohibiting the solicitation of membership in dues-paying organizations without a permit from city officials, and holding that First Amendment freedoms may not be made "contingent upon the uncontrolled will of an official"); **Hynes v. Mayor of Oradell**, 425 U.S. 610 (1976) (invalidating as vague an ordinance requiring advance notice to police in writing by "any person desiring to canvass, solicit or call from house to house [for] a recognized charitable [or] political campaign or cause," holding that such an ordinance suffered "from the vice condemned in [Lovell, Cantwell, and Staub]"); **Lakewood v. Plain Dealer Publishing Co.**, 486 U.S. 750 (1988) (invalidating a city ordinance requiring a permit from the mayor in order to place newsracks on public property, holding that it conferred impermissibly "unbridled discretion").

In contrast to these standardless licensing schemes, permit requirements for speech in the public forum have been upheld when they contain some objective criteria that curtail the possibility of discrimination against disfavored content. In **Cox v. New Hampshire**, 312 U.S. 569 (1941), a unanimous Court affirmed the convictions of several Jehovah's Witnesses for violating a state law prohibiting a "parade or procession" upon a public street without first obtaining a permit from local authorities and paying a license fee of not more than three hundred dollars a day. The defendants had marched on busy city sidewalks carrying signs bearing such slogans as "Religion is a Snare and a Racket" and "Serve God and Christ the King." They did not apply for a permit and none was issued.

Writing for the Court, Chief Justice HUGHES stated: "The authority of a municipality to impose regulations in order to assure the safety and convenience of the people in the use of public highways has never been regarded as inconsistent with civil liberties. [The] control of travel on the streets of cities is the most familiar illustration of this recognition of social need. Where a restriction of the use of highways in that relation is designed to promote the public convenience in the interest of all, it cannot be disregarded by the attempted exercise of some civil right which in other circumstances would be entitled to protection. One would not be justified in ignoring the familiar red traffic light because he thought it his religious duty to disobey the municipal [command]. As regulation of the use of the streets for parades and processions is a traditional exercise of control by local government, the question in a particular case is whether that control is exerted so as not to deny or unwarrantedly abridge the right of assembly and the opportunities for the communication of thought and the discussion of public questions immemorially associated with resort to public places.

"In the instant case, we are aided by the opinion of the Supreme Court of the State, [which] defined the limitations of the authority conferred for the granting of licenses. [T]he state court considered and defined the duty of the licensing authority and the rights of the appellants to a license for their parade, with regard only to considerations of time, place and manner so as to conserve the public convenience. The obvious advantage of requiring application for a permit [was] giving the public authorities notice in advance so as to afford opportunity for proper policing. [Moreover,] the license served 'to prevent confusion by overlapping parades, [to] secure convenient use of the streets by other travelers, and to minimize the risk of disorder.' [If] a municipality has authority to control the use of its public streets for parades or processions, as it undoubtedly has, it cannot be denied authority to give consideration, without unfair discrimination, to time, place and manner in relation to the other proper uses of the streets. We find it impossible to say that the limited authority conferred by the licensing provisions of the statute in question as thus construed by the state court contravened any constitutional right.[1] [There] is no evidence that the statute has been administered otherwise than in the fair and non-discriminatory manner which the state court has construed it to [require]."

Consider the following comment: "Of course, Cox v. New Hampshire did no more than to give a general standard for accommodation of the conflicting interests. It did not tell whether certain congested areas or certain times of the day might not always be held unavailable for parading, nor whether the size of some crowds might always be too large. But it seems [to] symbolize the ideal of Robert's Rules of Order for use of the public forum of the streets." Kalven, "The Concept of the Public Forum: Cox v. Louisiana," 1965 Sup. Ct. Rev. 1. But see Baker, "Unreasoned Reasonableness: Mandatory Parade Permits and Time, Place, and Manner Restrictions," 32 Hastings L.J. 711 (1981) (emphasizing the harms of licensing schemes: the loss of " 'spontaneous' demonstrations," the requirement that protestors "bow to the very authorities" they may be criticizing, and the creation of opportunities for subtle official "harassment").

4. *Early cases: total medium bans and the problem of distribution.* May government deny access to the public forum for an entire medium of speech, so long as it does so evenhandedly? Is such a total medium ban an impermissible interference with free speech even when the risks of abuse of discretion are absent? In **Schneider v. New Jersey**, 308 U.S. 147 (1939), and consolidated cases from other states, the Court invalidated local ordinances forbidding distribution of leaflets. The cities' central defense was that flat bans were necessary to prevent littering. Justice ROBERTS, writing for the Court, replied: "Municipal authorities [have] a duty to keep their communities' streets open for movement of people and [property]. So long as legislation to this end does not abridge the constitutional liberty of one rightfully upon the street to import information through speech or the distribution of literature, it may lawfully regulate the conduct of those using the streets. For example, [the] guarantee of freedom of speech or of the press [does not] deprive a municipality of power to enact regulations against throwing literature broadcast in the streets. [But this] Court has characterized the freedom of speech and freedom of press as fundamental personal rights and liberties. [Mere] legislative preferences or beliefs

---

[1]   The Court also sustained the license fee requirement, noting that it was "not a revenue tax, but one to meet the expense incident to the administration of the Act," and thus constitutional. Should municipalities be permitted to impose fees—even very large fees—so long as they are designed to defray the cost of policing? Could such a scheme be attacked as imposing an undue financial burden on the exercise of a constitutional right? See generally Blasi, "Prior Restraints on Demonstrations," 68 Mich. L. Rev. 1481 (1970). See also Goldberger, "A Reconsideration of Cox v. New Hampshire: Can Demonstrators be Required to Pay the Costs of Using America's Public Forums?," 62 Tex. L. Rev. 403 (1983) (arguing that a "proper distribution of costs" would allocate "the costs generated by speech activities to the society as a whole"); Neisser, "Charging for Free Speech: User Fees and Insurance in the Marketplace of Ideas," 74 Geo. L.J. 257 (1985). The Court has never invalidated a content-neutral user fee. Recall, however, the Court's invalidation in Forsyth Co. v. Nationalist Movement (1992; p. 67) of a user fee to be calculated according to the anticipated hostility of the audience. Are other advance payment conditions—e.g., insurance requirements—vulnerable to a First Amendment attack?

respecting matters of public convenience may well support regulation directed at other personal activities, but be insufficient to justify such as diminishes the exercise of rights so vital to the maintenance of democratic institutions. And so, as cases arise, the delicate and difficult task falls upon the courts to weigh the circumstances and to appraise the substantiality of the reasons advanced in support of the regulation of the free enjoyment of the rights.

"[Although] the alleged offenders were not charged with themselves scattering paper in the streets, their convictions were sustained upon the theory that distribution by them encouraged or resulted in such littering. We are of opinion that the purpose to keep the streets clean [is] insufficient to justify an ordinance which prohibits a person rightfully on a public street from handing literature to one willing to receive it. Any burden imposed upon the city authorities in cleaning and caring for the streets as an indirect consequence of such distribution results from the constitutional protection of the freedom of speech and press."

Note that Schneider accepted that a city's interest in preventing littering and keeping its streets clean is a legitimate and content-neutral local interest, and that distributing leaflets creates a risk of littering. Yet the Court struck down the ban, by applying a variety of strict scrutiny. Invalidating the leaflet ban might impose greater cost on the city in cleaning the streets; yet that was a cost that had to be borne because of the First Amendment. And antilitter laws were available as a less restrictive means. As Kalven stated in "The Concept of the Public Forum," supra: "Leaflet distribution in public places [is] a method of communication that carries as an inextricable and expected consequence substantial littering of the [streets]. It is also a method of communication of some annoyance to a majority of people so [addressed]. Yet the constitutional balance in Schneider was struck emphatically in favor of keeping the public forum open for this mode of communication. [The] operative theory of the Court, at least for the leaflet situation, is that, although it is a method of communication that interferes with the public use of the streets, the right to the streets as a public forum is such that leaflet distribution cannot be prohibited and can be regulated only for weighty reasons." Kalven concluded that Schneider strengthened the case for an assured minimum access right to the streets as a public forum.

Like the decision in Schneider invalidating a flat ban on leafleting, the decision in **Martin v. City of Struthers**, 319 U.S. 141 (1943), invalidated an ordinance prohibiting a medium of communication: here, the distribution of handbills to residences by ringing doorbells or otherwise summoning residents to the door. The City of Struthers, an Ohio industrial community, argued that the law was necessary to protect residents from annoyance and crime; and it emphasized that many of the residents worked night shifts and slept days, making them especially vulnerable to "casual bell pushers" disrupting their sleep. The ordinance was challenged by a Jehovah's Witness who had gone door-to-door to distribute leaflets advertising a religious meeting. In an opinion by Justice BLACK, the Court struck down the ordinance: "While door to door distributors of literature may be either a nuisance or a blind for criminal activities, they may also be useful members of society engaged in the dissemination of ideas in accordance with the best tradition of free discussion. The widespread use of this method of communication by many groups espousing various causes attests its major importance. [Door-to-door] distribution of circulars is essential to the poorly financed causes of little people. Freedom to distribute information to every citizen whenever he desires to receive it is so clearly vital to the preservation of a free society that, putting aside reasonable police and health regulations of time and manner of distribution, it must be fully preserved." Justice Black noted that it would be permissible to make it an offense "for any person to ring the bell of a householder who has appropriately indicated that he is unwilling to be disturbed. [Because the] dangers of distribution [such as annoyance and crime] can so easily be controlled by traditional legal methods, leaving to each householder the full right to decide whether he will receive strangers as visitors, [the] stringent prohibition [here] can serve no purpose but that forbidden by the Constitution, the naked restriction of the dissemination of ideas."

Compare with the decisions in Schneider and Martin the decision in **Kovacs v. Cooper**, 336 U.S. 77 (1949), which upheld a Trenton, New Jersey, ordinance designed to regulate loudspeakers. Kovacs was convicted of violating the ordinance, which banned "any device known as a sound truck, loud speaker or sound amplifier [which] emits therefrom loud and raucous noises and is attached to and upon any vehicle operated or standing [upon] streets or public places." Justice REED's plurality opinion was joined only by Chief Justice Vinson and Justice Burton. He indicated that absolute prohibition of loudspeakers would probably be unconstitutional but found that the ordinance was valid because, as construed by the state court, it applied only to loudspeakers emitting "loud and raucous" noises. He explained: "City streets are recognized as a normal place for the exchange of ideas by speech or paper. But this does not mean the freedom is beyond all control. We think it is a permissible exercise of legislative discretion to bar sound trucks with broadcasts of public interest, amplified to a loud and raucous volume, from the public ways of municipalities. On the business streets, [such] distractions would be dangerous to traffic at all hours useful for the dissemination of information, and in the residential thoroughfares the quiet and tranquility so desirable for city dwellers would likewise be at the mercy of advocates of particular religious, social or political persuasions. We cannot believe that rights of free speech compel a municipality to allow such mechanical voice amplification on any of its streets."

Justice JACKSON concurred in the result even though, unlike Justice Reed, he viewed the ordinance as a flat ban on loudspeakers. He thought the prohibition was justified because loudspeakers conflict "with quiet enjoyment of home and park": loudspeaker regulations were permissible so long as they did not seek "to censor the contents." He agreed with the dissenters that the plurality opinion repudiated Saia. Saia, he noted, "struck down a more moderate exercise of the state's police power" than the one sustained here. In another opinion concurring in the result, Justice FRANKFURTER also voted to sustain the ordinance as a flat ban, in accordance with his Saia dissent. He emphasized that, so long as a city does not seek to censor or discriminate among ideas, "it is not for us to supervise the limits the legislature may impose in safeguarding the steadily narrowing opportunities for serenity and reflection."

Justice BLACK, joined by Justices Douglas and Rutledge, dissented: "The appellant was neither charged with nor convicted of operating a sound truck that emitted 'loud and raucous noises.' The charge [was] that he violated the city ordinance 'in that he [used] a device known as a sound truck.' [This] ordinance wholly bars the use of all loud speakers mounted upon any vehicle in any of the city's public streets. In my view this repudiation of [Saia] makes a dangerous and unjustifiable breach in the constitutional barriers designed to insure freedom of expression. Ideas and beliefs are today chiefly disseminated to the masses of people through the press, radio, moving pictures, and public address systems. [The] basic premise of the First Amendment is that all present instruments of communication, as well as others that inventive genius may bring into being, shall be free from governmental censorship or prohibition. Laws which hamper the free use of some instruments of communication thereby favor competing channels. [Thus,] laws like [this] can give an overpowering influence to views of owners of legally favored instruments of communication.

"There are many people who have ideas that they wish to disseminate but who do not have enough money to own or control publishing plants, newspapers, radios, moving picture studios, or chains of show places. Yet everybody knows the vast reaches of these powerful channels of communication which from the very nature of our economic system must be under the control and guidance of comparatively few people. [It] is no reflection on the value of preserving freedom for dissemination of the ideas of publishers of newspapers [etc.] to believe that transmission of ideas through public speaking is also essential. [Criticism] of governmental action [should] not be limited to criticisms by press, radio, and moving pictures. [And] it is an obvious fact that public speaking today without sound amplifiers is a wholly inadequate way to reach the people on a large scale. Consequently, to tip the scales against transmission of ideas through public speaking [is] to deprive the people of a large part of the basic advantages of the receipt of ideas that the First Amendment was designed to protect." Justice Murphy also dissented.

Would a flat ban on all sound trucks be constitutional? Should it be? Did the various opinions in Kovacs settle the issue? Are the access claims of loudspeaker users entitled to special weight because of the importance of sound trucks (like leaflets) as a form of "poor man's printing press"? Is a ban on loudspeakers justifiable because of a legislative judgment that the particular method of communication is obnoxious? Would a specific ban on all speeches or marches in residential neighborhoods be similarly supportable on grounds of deference to legislative judgment? A ban on all street demonstrations? Would it depend on the available alternative communication channels?

In the decades following these cases, the Court extended the antidiscrimination principle in Schneider, Martin and the Kovacs dissents to invalidate nearly every content-based regulation in the public forum. But the Court upheld several regulations that challengers sought to characterize as total medium bans, characterizing them instead as "time, place, and manner" regulations that were to be upheld so long as the government could show they were closely tailored to a significant governmental interest. The distributive strand of the Schneider line of cases stayed partially alive in the Court's admonition that time, place, and manner laws must also leave open "ample alternative channels of communication." But such a requirement was less protective of speakers than Justice Roberts's approach in Schneider, which had suggested that "one is not to have the exercise of his liberty of expression in appropriate places abridged on the plea that it may be exercised in some other place."

Schneider and its progeny were never overruled, however, and in 1994, the Rehnquist Court resurrected them in a decision demonstrating that the presumption against total medium bans is, at least in some circumstances, still alive. In **City of Ladue v. Gilleo**, 512 U.S. 43 (1994), the Court unanimously invalidated an ordinance of the City of Ladue, a residential suburb of St. Louis, Missouri, that banned the posting of most signs in order to minimize visual clutter. The ordinance provided for ten exceptions, including signs identifying a home or business, for-sale signs, and on-site signs advertising gasoline. Gilleo challenged the ordinance because it barred her from placing an 8.5- by 11-inch sign in the second story window of her home stating, "For Peace in the Gulf." The district court and the court of appeals invalidated the ordinance on the ground that the selective exemptions rendered it impermissibly content-based. Justice STEVENS wrote for the Court affirming the judgment, but on an expressly different ground. He held that, even assuming that the ordinance and the exemptions were content-neutral, the ordinance banned "too much" speech: "In examining the propriety of Ladue's near-total prohibition of residential signs, we will assume, arguendo, the validity of the City's submission that the various exemptions are free of impermissible content or viewpoint discrimination [because the distinctions are drawn to distinguish signs that are likely to cause more visual clutter from those that are not. Nevertheless,] Ladue has almost completely foreclosed a venerable means of communication that is both unique and important. [Often] placed on lawns or in windows, residential signs play an important part in political campaigns, during which they are displayed to signal the resident's support for particular candidates, parties, or causes. [Our] prior decisions have voiced particular concern with laws that foreclose an entire medium of expression. [Lovell; Martin; Schneider.] Although prohibitions foreclosing entire media may be completely free of content or viewpoint discrimination, the danger they pose to the freedom of speech is readily apparent—by eliminating a common means of speaking, such measures can suppress too much speech.

"Ladue contends, however, that its ordinance is a mere regulation of the 'time, place, or manner' of speech because residents remain free to convey their desired messages by other means, such as hand-held signs, 'letters, handbills, flyers, telephone calls, newspaper advertisements, bumper stickers, speeches, and neighborhood or community meetings.' [We] are not persuaded that adequate substitutes exist for the important medium of speech that Ladue has closed off. Displaying a sign from one's own residence often carries a message quite distinct from placing the same sign someplace else, or conveying the same text or picture by other means. Precisely because of their location, such signs provide information about the identity of the 'speaker.' [Residential] signs are an unusually cheap and convenient form of communication. Especially for persons of modest means or limited mobility, a yard or window sign may have no practical substitute.

"[A] special respect for individual liberty in the home has long been part of our culture and our law; that principle has special resonance when the government seeks to constrain a person's ability to speak there. Most Americans would be understandably dismayed, given that tradition, to learn that it was illegal to display from their window an 8- by 11-inch sign expressing their political views. Whereas the government's need to mediate among various competing uses, including expressive ones, for public streets and facilities is constant and unavoidable, see [Cox v. New Hampshire], its need to regulate temperate speech from the home is surely much less pressing. Our decision that Ladue's ban on almost all residential signs violates the First Amendment by no means leaves the City powerless to address the ills that may be associated with residential signs. We are confident that more temperate measures could in large part satisfy Ladue's stated regulatory needs without harm to the First Amendment rights of its citizens." Justice O'Connor wrote a separate concurrence suggesting that the Court should have decided first whether the ordinance was content-based.

Did the sign ban struck down in Ladue differ in any material respect from the medium bans at issue in Schneider, Martin and Kovacs? How important was it to the holding in Ladue that the ban regulated the use of one's own private home? Should it have mattered whether or not Gilleo herself was advancing "the poorly financed causes of little people"? For pre-Ladue background, see Stone, "Content-Neutral Restrictions," 54 U. Chi. L. Rev. 46 (1987).

Drawing heavily upon early leafleting cases such as Schneider and Martin, the Court in **Watchtower Bible & Tract Society v. Stratton**, 536 U.S. 150 (2002), by a vote of 8–1, invalidated a municipal ordinance's permit requirement for door-to-door activity, reasoning that even though the ordinance was nondiscriminatory, and even though it did not amount to a total medium ban, it inhibited too much speech. The ordinance provided: "The practice of going in and upon private property and/or the private residence of Village residents in the Village by canvassers, solicitors, peddlers, hawkers, itinerant merchants or transient vendors of merchandise or services, not having been invited to do so by the owners or occupants of such private property or residences, and not having first obtained a permit, [for] the purpose of advertising, promoting, selling and/or explaining any product, service, organization or cause, or for the purpose of soliciting orders for the sale of goods, wares, merchandise or services, is hereby declared to be a nuisance and is prohibited."

Justice STEVENS wrote for the Court: "For over 50 years, the Court has invalidated restrictions on door-to-door canvassing and pamphleteering. It is more than historical accident that most of these cases involved First Amendment challenges brought by Jehovah's Witnesses, because door-to-door canvassing is mandated by their religion. [The] Jehovah's Witnesses ['take] literally the mandate of the Scriptures, "Go ye into all the world, and preach the gospel to every creature." Mark 16:15.' Moreover, because they lack significant financial resources, the ability of the Witnesses to proselytize is seriously diminished by regulations that burden their efforts to canvass door-to-door." Justice Stevens noted that cases like Schneider and Martin had established "the historical importance of door-to-door canvassing and pamphleteering as vehicles for the dissemination of ideas." He also noted that dicta in those cases had acknowledged "the interests a town may have in some form of regulation, particularly when the solicitation of money is involved, in preventing the use of door-to-door canvassing as a shield for fraud or crime."

Justice Stevens declined to choose a particular standard of review in assessing the constitutionality of the ordinance: "We find it unnecessary [to] resolve that dispute because the breadth of speech affected by the ordinance and the nature of the regulation make it clear that the Court of Appeals erred in upholding it. [Had the ordinance] been construed to apply only to commercial activities and the solicitation of funds, arguably the ordinance would have been tailored to the Village's interest in protecting the privacy of its residents and preventing fraud. Yet [the] provisions apply to a significant number of noncommercial 'canvassers' promoting a wide variety of 'causes.' [The] ordinance unquestionably applies, not only to religious causes, but to political activity as well. It would seem to extend to 'residents casually soliciting the votes of neighbors,' or ringing doorbells to enlist support for employing a more efficient garbage collector. The mere fact that the ordinance covers so much speech raises constitutional concerns. It is offensive—not only to the values protected by the First Amendment, but to the very notion of a free society—that in the context of everyday public discourse a citizen must first inform the government of her desire to speak to her neighbors and then obtain a permit to do so." In particular, Justice Stevens noted, the permit requirement inhibited both anonymous and spontaneous speech.

But, he continued, "[t]he breadth and unprecedented nature of this regulation does not alone render the ordinance invalid. Also central to our conclusion that the ordinance does not pass First Amendment scrutiny is that it is not tailored to the Village's stated interests. Even if the interest in preventing fraud could adequately support the ordinance insofar as it applies to commercial transactions and the solicitation of funds, that interest provides no support for its application to petitioners, to political campaigns, or to enlisting support for unpopular causes. The Village, however, argues that the ordinance is nonetheless valid because it serves the two additional interests of protecting the privacy of the resident and the prevention of crime. With respect to the former, it seems clear that [a provision allowing] posting of 'No Solicitation' signs, [coupled] with the resident's unquestioned right to refuse to engage in conversation with unwelcome visitors, provides ample protection for the unwilling listener. The annoyance caused by an uninvited knock on the front door is the same whether or not the visitor is armed with a permit. With respect to the latter, it seems unlikely that the absence of a permit would preclude criminals from knocking on doors and engaging in conversations not covered by the ordinance. They might, for example, ask for directions or permission to use the telephone, or pose as surveyors or census takers." Justice BREYER, joined by Justices Souter and Ginsburg, concurred separately to emphasize that an interest in crime prevention could not justify the ordinance because it had not been the village's actual purpose at the time of enactment, and "in the intermediate scrutiny context, the Court ordinarily does not supply reasons the legislative body has not given." Justice Scalia, joined by Justice Thomas, submitted a brief concurrence in the judgment.

Chief Justice REHNQUIST was the lone dissenter: "More than half a century ago we recognized that canvassers, 'whether selling pots or distributing leaflets, may lessen the peaceful enjoyment of a home,' and that 'burglars frequently pose as canvassers, either in order that they may have a pretense to discover whether a house is empty and hence ripe for burglary, or for the purpose of spying out the premises in order that they may return later.' [Martin v. City of Struthers.] These problems continue to be associated with door-to-door canvassing, as are even graver ones. A recent double murder in Hanover, New Hampshire, [of two Dartmouth professors by two teenagers posing as canvassers] illustrates these dangers. [For] over 60 years, we have categorically stated that a permit requirement for door-to-door canvassers, which gives no discretion to the issuing authority, is constitutional. [The] Court today, however, abruptly changes course and invalidates [the] Stratton ordinance [even though it] suffers from none of the defects deemed fatal in [earlier] decisions. The ordinance does not prohibit door-to-door canvassing; it merely requires that canvassers fill out a form and receive a permit. Cf. Martin. The mayor does not exercise any discretion in deciding who receives a permit; approval of the permit is automatic upon proper completion of the form. Cf. Cantwell.

"Just as troubling as the Court's ignoring over 60 years of precedent is the difficulty of discerning from the Court's opinion what exactly it is about the Stratton ordinance that renders it unconstitutional. It is not clear what test the Court is applying, or under which part of that indeterminate test the ordinance fails. [There] is no support in our case law for applying anything more stringent than intermediate scrutiny to the ordinance. The ordinance is content neutral and does not bar anyone from going door-to-door in Stratton. It merely regulates the manner in which one must canvass. [It] is aimed at three significant governmental interests: the prevention of fraud, the prevention of crime, and the protection of privacy. [And it] leave[s] open ample alternatives for expression. [Most] obviously, canvassers are free to go door-to-door after filling out the permit application. And those without permits may communicate on public sidewalks, on street corners, through the mail, or through the telephone. Intermediate scrutiny analysis thus confirms what our cases have long said: A discretionless permit requirement for canvassers does not violate the First Amendment."

THE "TIME, PLACE AND MANNER" TEST

Recall that in Cox v. New Hampshire, (1941; p. 289) Chief Justice Hughes wrote that a government faced with public access claims by speakers is entitled to "give consideration, without unfair discrimination, to time, place and manner in relation to the other proper uses of the streets." What government interests justify such time, place, and manner regulations in the traditional public forum of the streets and parks? How closely must such regulations fit those asserted interests? Should courts defer to legislative and executive judgments on the management of public forums? Or should they scrutinize them independently to make sure government has not, "in the guise of regulation," suppressed too much speech? Should the Court's only concern be content neutrality, or does an emphasis on discrimination or the lack of it obscure underlying problems with the degree of access speakers enjoy? Consider the following decisions elaborating the standard of review for time, place and manner regulations, organized by reference to the asserted government interest.

PUBLIC ORDER AND SAFETY

In **Cox v. Louisiana**, 379 U.S. 536 (1965), the Court invalidated a breach of peace conviction arising from a civil rights demonstration near a courthouse. In the same decision, the Court also overturned Cox's conviction under a Louisiana law prohibiting the obstruction of "the free, convenient and normal use of any public sidewalk, street, [or] other passageway [by] impeding, hindering, stifling, retarding or restraining traffic or passage thereon." Justice GOLDBERG wrote for the Court: "The rights of free speech and assembly, while fundamental in our democratic society, still do not mean that everyone with opinions or beliefs to express may address a group at any public place and at any time. The constitutional guarantee of liberty implies the existence of an organized society maintaining public order, without which liberty itself would be lost in the excesses of anarchy. The control of travel on the streets is a clear example of governmental responsibility to insure this necessary order. A restriction in that relation, designed to promote the public convenience in the interest of all, and not susceptible to abuses of discriminatory application, cannot be disregarded by the attempted exercise of some civil right which, in other circumstances, would be entitled to protection. One would not be justified in ignoring the familiar red light because this was thought to be a means of social protest. Nor could one, contrary to traffic regulations, insist upon a street meeting in the middle of Times Square at the rush hour as a form of freedom of [speech]. Governmental authorities have the duty and responsibility to keep their streets open and available for movement.

"[But we] have no occasion in this case to consider the constitutionality of the uniform, consistent, and nondiscriminatory application of a statute forbidding all access to streets and other public facilities for parades and meetings. Although the statute here involved on its face precludes all street assemblies and parades, it has not been so [applied]. City officials [indicated] that certain meetings and parades are permitted in Baton Rouge, even though they have the effect of obstructing traffic, provided prior approval is obtained. [The] statute itself provides no standards for the determination of local officials as to which assemblies to permit or which to prohibit. [It] appears that the authorities in Baton Rouge permit or prohibit parades or street meetings in their completely uncontrolled discretion. [The] pervasive restraint on freedom of discussion by the practice of the authorities under the statute is not any less effective than a statute expressly permitting such selective [enforcement]. [Such] broad discretion in a public official [permits] the official to act as a censor."

Compare the Court's decision upholding—as a permissible time, place, and manner regulation—the "booth rule" restricting literature distribution and solicitation of funds at the Minnesota State Fair in **Heffron v. International Society for Krishna Consciousness (ISKCON)**, 452 U.S. 640 (1981). Minnesota State Fair Rule 6.05 prohibited the sale or distribution of any merchandise, including printed or written material, except from booths rented to all applicants in a nondiscriminatory manner on a first-come, first-served basis. The rule was challenged by ISKCON, a religious society espousing the views of the Krishna religion. ISKCON asserted that the Rule suppressed the practice of Sankirtan, a religious ritual that enjoins its members to go into public places to distribute or sell religious literature and to solicit donations for the support of the Krishna religion. The highest state court struck down the rule, but Justice WHITE's majority opinion found the restriction permissible. He explained: "[The] First Amendment does not guarantee the right to communicate one's views at all times and places or in any manner that may be desired. [See Cox v. Louisiana.] [T]he activities of ISKCON, like those of others protected by the First Amendment, are subject to reasonable time, place, and manner restrictions. [Cox v. New Hampshire.] We have often approved restrictions of that kind provided that they are justified without reference to the content of the regulated speech, that they serve a significant governmental interest, and that in doing so they leave open ample alternative channels for communication of the information." Under that standard, the Court held the booth rule valid.

Justice White found Rule 6.05 clearly content-neutral, for it applied "evenhandedly to all who wish to distribute and sell written materials or to solicit funds. [Nor] does Rule 6.05 suffer from the more covert forms of discrimination that may result when arbitrary discretion is vested in some governmental authority. The method of allocating space is a straightforward first-come, first-served system." Moreover, it served a "significant governmental interest"—"the need to maintain the orderly movement of the crowd given the large number of exhibitors and persons attending the Fair." (The Fair had an average daily attendance of over 100,000.) "[I]t is clear that a State's interest in protecting the 'safety and convenience' of persons using a public forum is a valid governmental objective. [And the] flow of the crowd and demands of safety are more pressing in the context of the Fair [than in the typical city street or park]." In response to the state court's reasoning that an exemption for the Hare Krishna devotees alone would not defeat the state's interest, Justice White said: "[The] justification for the Rule should not be measured by the disorder that would result from granting an exemption solely to ISKCON. [If the Rule cannot be applied to ISKCON], it is no more valid with respect to the [other] organizations that have rented booths at the Fair. [Intercepting] fair patrons as they move about, [as ISKCON wishes to do], and if success is achieved, stopping them momentarily or for longer periods as money is given or exchanged for literature [could lead to] widespread disorder at the fairgrounds.

Justice White found as well that "alternative forums for the expression [exist] despite the effects of the Rule": "[The] Rule does not prevent ISKCON from practicing Sankirtan anywhere outside the fairgrounds. [It] does not exclude ISKCON from the fairgrounds, nor does it deny that organization the right to conduct any desired activity at some point within the forum. Its members may mingle with the crowd and orally propagate their views [and] may also arrange for a booth and distribute and sell literature and solicit funds from that location on the fairgrounds itself. [Considering] the limited functions of the Fair and the [confined] area within which it operates, we are unwilling to say that [the Rule] does not provide ISKCON and other organizations with an adequate means to sell and solicit on the fairgrounds."

Four Justices were in partial dissent. Justice BRENNAN, joined by Justices Marshall and Stevens, agreed that the limitation of literature sales and funds solicitation to fixed booths was justified, not as a crowd control measure but as an "antifraud measure." But they found the ban on distribution of literature outside of booths "an overly intrusive means of achieving the State's interest in crowd control." Justice Brennan stated his general approach as follows:

"[Once] a governmental regulation is shown to impinge upon basic First Amendment rights, the burden falls on the government to show the validity of its asserted interest and the absence of less intrusive alternatives. See, e.g., [Schneider]. The challenged 'regulation must be narrowly tailored to further the State's legitimate interest.' [The Rule] does not meet this test. [Significantly], each and every fairgoer, whether political candidate, concerned citizen, or member of a religious group, is free to give speeches, engage in face-to-face advocacy, campaign, or proselytize. No restrictions are placed on any fairgoer's right to speak at any time, at any place, or to any person. [Because of the Rule], however, as soon as a proselytizing member of ISKCON hands out a free copy of the Bhagavad-Gita to an interested listener, or a political candidate distributes his campaign brochure to a potential voter, he becomes subject to arrest and removal from the fairgrounds. This constitutes a significant restriction on First Amendment rights.

"In support of its crowd control justification, the State contends that if fairgoers are permitted to distribute literature, large crowds will gather, blocking traffic lanes and causing safety problems. [But] the State has failed to provide any support for these assertions. Relying on a general, speculative fear of disorder, the [State] has placed a significant restriction on respondents' ability to exercise core First Amendment rights. This restriction is not narrowly drawn to advance the State's interests, and for that reason is unconstitutional. [If] the State had a reasonable concern that distribution in certain parts of the fairgrounds—for example, entrances and exits—would cause disorder, it could have drafted its rule to prohibit distribution of literature at those points. If the State felt it necessary to limit the number of persons distributing an organization's literature, it could, within reason, have done that as well. It had no right, however, to ban all distribution of literature outside the booths." Justice Blackmun also concurred in part and dissented in part, favoring the same result as Justice Brennan.

Should the booth rule have been viewed as a total medium ban akin to the bans on distributing literature struck down in Schneider and Martin, rather than as a permissible time, place, or manner regulation? Distribution was prohibited in the open thoroughfares of the fair and confined to the "private" space of rented booths. Should there have been any concern that the rule would have content-differential effects, disadvantaging unpopular speakers who need to approach their audience because their audience is unlikely to come to them? ISKCON ventured such an argument, but Justice White replied in a footnote: "The argument is interesting but has little force. [A preference for listener-initiated exchanges over those originating with the speaker] is inherent in the determination to confine exhibitors to fixed locations, it applies to all exhibitors alike, and it does not invalidate the Rule as a reasonable time, place, and manner regulation."

―――――――

AESTHETICS

May government limit speech in order to protect the attractive appearance or ambience of its public spaces, even without regard to concerns of public safety? May it prevent visual or aural "pollution"? Is securing beautiful or tranquil surroundings enough of a reason to limit speech? Is there a danger that assertion of such amorphous, intangible interests might conceal improper hostility to the regulated speech? The Court has recognized government aesthetic interests as substantial or significant in a number of cases.

In **Metromedia, Inc. v. San Diego**, 453 U.S. 490 (1981), for example, the Court reviewed a free speech challenge to a San Diego ordinance regulating billboard displays in order "to eliminate hazards to pedestrians and motorists brought about by distracting sign displays" and "to preserve and improve the appearance of the City." Recall that the Court upheld part of the ordinance restricting commercial billboard displays, see p. 217. While the Court struck down the part of a San Diego ordinance restricting noncommercial billboard displays, the opinions of a majority of the Court— the four members of the plurality plus the three dissenters—indicated considerable general willingness to defer to the government's aesthetic interests.

The plurality opinion of Justice WHITE, joined by Justices Stewart, Marshall, and Powell, acknowledged the problems billboards pose "for land-use planning and development," but found San Diego's ordinance impermissibly content-based because it provided a number of exceptions, including exceptions for on-site commercial signs, government signs, temporary political campaign signs, for-sale and for-lease signs, religious symbols, signs telling the time and temperature, historical commemorative plaques, and signs within shopping malls: "[Billboards] combine communicative and noncommunicative aspects. [The] government has legitimate interests in controlling the noncommunicative aspects of the medium, but [the First Amendment forecloses] a similar interest in controlling the communicative aspects." The plurality found that the exceptions unconstitutionally distinguished among subject matters. The exceptions for commercial billboards inverted the usual First Amendment hierarchy "by affording a greater degree of protection to commercial than to noncommercial speech." And "[w]ith respect to noncommercial speech, the city may not choose the appropriate subjects for public discourse. Because some noncommercial messages may be conveyed on billboards throughout the commercial and industrial zones, San Diego must similarly allow billboards conveying other noncommercial messages throughout those zones."

Justice BRENNAN, joined by Justice Blackmun, concurred in the judgment, focusing not on any discrimination in the ordinance but rather on its distributive aspects. Justice Brennan argued that "the *practical* effect of the San Diego ordinance is to eliminate the billboard as an effective medium of communication. [Instead] of relying on the exceptions to the ban to invalidate the ordinance, I would apply the tests [developed] to analyze content-neutral prohibitions of particular media of communication. [Schad; Schneider; Martin.]" Under such a standard, he argued, the city must show "that a sufficiently substantial governmental interest is directly furthered by the total ban, and that any more narrowly drawn restriction, i.e., anything less than a total ban, would promote less well the achievement of that goal." He found the ban unjustified under that standard. He found the evidentiary support for the traffic safety claims weak, and he was especially skeptical of the asserted aesthetic interests: "[B]efore deferring to a city's judgment, a court must be convinced that the city is seriously and comprehensively addressing aesthetic concerns with respect to its environment." (In comparing Justice White's and Justice Brennan's opinions, recall the discussion at p. 287 of the discrimination and distribution—or equal-access and guaranteed-access—strands in the early public forum cases.)

Chief Justice BURGER, Justice REHNQUIST, and Justice STEVENS each filed a separate dissent. Chief Justice Burger chided the plurality for undervaluing the importance of local control over local problems. Because ample alternative channels of communications were available, he would not hold the First Amendment to bar San Diego's justifiable and reasonable effort to do something about "what it perceives—and what it has a right to perceive—as ugly and dangerous eyesores thrust upon its citizens." Justice Stevens's dissent disagreed that completely effective alternative channels of communication were available. But he did not see the diminution of communications opportunities as fatal: "The essential concern embodied in the First Amendment is that government not impose its viewpoint on the public or select the topics on which public debate is permissible," and no viewpoint discrimination was presented. Justice Stevens emphasized that a government interest "in securing beautiful surroundings" may sometimes outweigh interests in "uninhibited expression by means of words and pictures in public places." Justice Rehnquist largely agreed with the other dissents.

The Court in Metromedia did not reach the question of the permissibility of a total, content-neutral prohibition of billboards. But the various opinions alluded to such a flat ban in dicta. Justice White, the author of the Metromedia plurality opinion, observed several years later: "A majority of this Court found [in Metromedia] that [aesthetic] considerations *would* be sufficient to justify a content-neutral ban on all outdoor advertising signs, notwithstanding the extent to which such signs convey First Amendment protected messages." Lakewood v. Plain Dealer Publishing Co., 486 U.S. 750, 783 (1988) (White, J., dissenting) (citing the plurality opinion and the dissenting opinions of Burger, C.J., and Rehnquist and Stevens, JJ.) (emphasis added).

Consider in light of Metromedia the following cases involving a ban on the placement of political signs on utility poles and crosswires, and a ban on overnight camping in a public park as applied to anti-homelessness demonstrators. The political sign case arose when Taxpayers for Vincent, a group of supporters of Roland Vincent, a candidate for the Los Angeles City Council, arranged for the production and posting of signs with Vincent's name on them. They attached the signs to utility poles at various locations in Los Angeles by draping them over the cross-arms which support the poles and stapling the cardboard together at the bottom. The signs read: "Roland Vincent—City Council." Acting under a city ordinance, city employees removed all posters attached to utility poles. Most of the signs that were removed were commercial ones, but 48 out of more than 1200 signs removed from public property during the first week of March were "Vincent" signs. This suit challenged the constitutionality of the ordinance. The trial court dismissed the case, but the Court of Appeals reversed. After rejecting an overbreadth challenge, the Supreme Court also rejected Taxpayers' as-applied challenge:

Members of City Council v. Taxpayers for Vincent
466 U.S. 789, 104 S. Ct. 2118, 80 L. Ed. 2d 772 (1984).

■ JUSTICE STEVENS delivered the opinion of the Court.

Section 28.04 of the Los Angeles Municipal Code prohibits the posting of signs on public property. The question presented is whether that prohibition abridges appellees' freedom of speech within the meaning of the First Amendment. The ordinance prohibits appellees from communicating with the public in a certain manner, and presumably diminishes the total quantity of their communication in the City. [But it] has been clear since this

Court's earliest decisions [that] the state may sometimes curtail speech when necessary to advance a significant and legitimate state interest. [The] First Amendment forbids the government from regulating speech in ways that favor some viewpoints or ideas at the expense of [others]. That general rule has no application to this case. For there is not even a hint of bias or censorship in the City's enactment or enforcement of this ordinance.

In [O'Brien] the Court set forth the appropriate [four-step] framework for reviewing a viewpoint neutral regulation of this kind. [In] this case, [Taxpayers] do not dispute that it is within the constitutional power of the City to attempt to improve its appearance, or that this interest is basically unrelated to the suppression of ideas. Therefore the critical inquiries are whether that interest is sufficiently substantial to justify the effect of the ordinance on appellees' expression, and whether that effect is no greater than necessary to accomplish the City's purpose.

[Metromedia] dealt with San Diego's prohibition of certain forms of outdoor billboards. There the Court considered the city's interest in avoiding visual clutter, and seven Justices explicitly concluded that this interest was sufficient to justify a prohibition of billboards. [We] reaffirm the conclusion of the majority in Metromedia. The problem addressed by this ordinance— the visual assault on the citizens of Los Angeles presented by an accumulation of signs posted on public property—constitutes a significant substantive evil within the City's power to prohibit. We turn to the question whether the scope of the restriction on appellees' expressive activity is substantially broader than necessary to protect the City's interest in eliminating visual clutter. The incidental restriction on expression which results from the City's attempt to accomplish such a purpose is considered justified as a reasonable regulation of the time, place, or manner of expression if it is narrowly tailored to serve that interest. [By] banning these signs, the City did no more than eliminate the exact source of the evil it sought to remedy.

It is true that the esthetic interest in preventing the kind of litter that may result from the distribution of leaflets on the public streets and sidewalks cannot support a prophylactic prohibition against the citizens' exercise of that method of expressing his views. In Schneider v. State, the Court held that ordinances that absolutely prohibited handbilling on the streets were invalid. The Court explained that cities could adequately protect the esthetic interest in avoiding litter without abridging protected expression merely by penalizing those who actually litter. Taxpayers contend that their interest in supporting Vincent's political campaign, which affords them a constitutional right to distribute [leaflets] on the public streets of Los Angeles, provides equal support for their asserted right to post temporary signs on objects adjacent to the streets and sidewalks. They argue that the mere fact that their temporary signs "add somewhat" to the city's visual clutter is entitled to no more weight than the temporary unsightliness of discarded handbills and the additional street cleaning burden that were insufficient to justify the ordinances reviewed in Schneider.

The rationale of Schneider is inapposite in the context of the instant case. There, individual citizens were actively exercising their right to communicate directly with potential recipients of their message. The conduct continued only while the speakers or distributors remained on the scene. In this case, appellees posted dozens of temporary signs throughout an area where they would remain unattended until removed. As the Court expressly noted in Schneider, the First Amendment does not "deprive a municipality of power to enact regulations against throwing literature broadcast in the [streets]." A distributor of leaflets has no right simply to scatter his pamphlets in the air—or to toss large quantities of paper from the window of a tall building or a low flying airplane. Characterizing such an activity as a separate means of communication does not diminish the state's power to condemn it as a public nuisance. [With] respect to signs posted by appellees, [it] is the tangible medium of expressing the message that has the adverse impact on the appearance of the landscape. In Schneider, an anti-littering statute could have addressed the substantive evil without prohibiting expressive activity, whereas application of the prophylactic rule actually employed gratuitously infringed upon the right of an individual to communicate directly with a willing listener. Here, the substantive evil— visual blight—is not merely a possible by-product of the activity, but is created by the medium of expression itself. In contrast to Schneider, therefore, the application of [the] ordinance in this case responds precisely to the substantive problem which legitimately concerns the City. The ordinance curtails no more speech than is necessary to accomplish its purpose.

[The challengers argue] that a prohibition against the [posting of signs on public property] cannot be justified on esthetic grounds if it fails to apply to all equally unattractive signs [including those on private property.] [But the] private citizen's interest in controlling the use of his own property justifies the disparate treatment. Moreover, by not extending the ban to all locations, a significant opportunity to communicate by means of temporary signs is preserved, and private property owners' esthetic concerns will keep the posting of signs on their property within reasonable bounds. Even if some visual blight remains, a partial, content-neutral ban may nevertheless enhance the City's appearance.

[A] restriction on expressive activity may be invalid if the remaining modes of communication are inadequate. [E.g., Heffron.] The Los Angeles ordinance does not affect any individual's freedom to exercise the right to speak and to distribute literature in the same place where the posting of signs on public property is prohibited. To the extent that the posting of signs on public property has advantages over these forms of expression, there is no reason to believe that these same advantages cannot be obtained through other means. To the contrary, the findings [indicate] that there are ample alternative modes of communication in Los Angeles. Notwithstanding appellees' general assertions [concerning] the utility of political posters, nothing in the findings indicates that the posting of political posters on public property is a uniquely valuable or important mode of communication, or that appellees' ability to communicate effectively is threatened by ever-increasing restrictions on expression.

Appellees suggest that the public property covered by the ordinance is [a] "public forum." [Appellees'] reliance on the public forum doctrine is misplaced. They fail to demonstrate the existence of a traditional right of access respecting such items as utility poles for purposes of their communication comparable to that recognized for public streets and parks, and it is clear that "the First Amendment does not guarantee access to government property simply because it is owned or controlled by the government." Rather, the "existence of a right of access to public property and the standard by which limitations upon such a right must be evaluated differ depending on the character of the property at issue." Lampposts can of course be used as signposts, but the mere fact that government property can be used as a vehicle for communication does not mean that the Constitution requires such uses to be permitted.[1] Public property which is not by tradition or designation a forum for public communication may be reserved by the state "for its intended purposes, communicative or otherwise, as long as the regulation on speech is reasonable and not an effort to suppress expression merely because public officials oppose the speaker's view." [Perry.] Given our analysis of the legitimate interest served by the ordinance, its viewpoint neutrality, and the availability of alternative channels of communication, the ordinance is certainly constitutional as applied to appellees under this standard.

Finally, [Taxpayers] argue that Los Angeles could have written an ordinance that would have had a less severe effect on expressive activity such as theirs, by permitting the posting of any kind of sign at any time on some types of public property, or by making a variety of other more specific exceptions to the ordinance: for signs carrying certain types of messages (such as political campaign signs), for signs posted during specific time periods (perhaps during political campaigns), for particular locations (perhaps for areas already cluttered by an excessive number of signs on adjacent private property), or for signs meeting design specifications (such as size or color). Plausible public policy arguments might well be made in support of any such exception, but it by no means follows that it is therefore constitutionally mandated, nor is it clear that some of the suggested exceptions would even be constitutionally permissible. [An] assertion that "Jesus Saves," that "Abortion is Murder," that every woman has the "Right to Choose," or that "Alcohol Kills," may have a claim to a constitutional exemption from the ordinance that is just as strong as "[Roland] Vincent— City Council." To create an exception for appellees' political speech and not these other types of speech might create a risk of engaging in constitutionally forbidden content discrimination. [Carey; Mosley.] Moreover, the volume of permissible postings under such a mandated exemption might so limit the ordinance's effect as to defeat its aim of combatting visual blight. Any constitutionally mandated exception to the City's total prohibition against temporary signs on public property would necessarily rest on a judicial determination [that] the City's interests in esthetics are not sufficiently important to justify the prohibition in that category. But [there is] no basis for questioning the substantiality of the esthetic interest [or] for believing that a uniquely important form of communication has been abridged for the categories of expression engaged in by [the challengers].

Therefore, we accept the City's position that it may decide that the esthetic interest in avoiding "visual clutter" justifies a removal of signs creating or increasing that clutter. [We] hold that on this record [the] interests are sufficiently substantial to justify this content neutral, impartially administered [prohibition]. [Reversed.]

---

[1] Any tangible property owned by the government could be used to communicate— bumper stickers may be placed on official automobiles—and yet appellees could not seriously claim the right to attach "Taxpayer for Vincent" bumper stickers to City-owned automobiles. At some point, the government's relationship to things under its dominion and control is virtually identical to a private owner's property interest in the same kinds of things, and in such circumstances, the State, "no less than a private owner of property, has power to preserve the property under its control for the use to which it is lawfully dedicated." [Footnote by Justice Stevens.]

■ JUSTICE BRENNAN, with whom JUSTICES MARSHALL and BLACKMUN join, dissenting.

[Because] the Court's lenient approach towards the restriction of speech for reasons of aesthetics [here and in Metromedia] threatens seriously to undermine the protections of the First Amendment, I dissent. [In my view, Los Angeles] has not shown that its interest in eliminating "visual clutter" justifies its restriction of appellees' ability to communicate with the local electorate. [In] deciding this First Amendment question, the critical importance of the posting of signs as a means of communication must not be overlooked. Use of this medium of communication is particularly valuable in part because it entails a relatively small expense in reaching a wide audience, allows flexibility in accommodating various formats, typographies, and graphics, and conveys its message in a manner that is easily read and understood by its reader or viewer. There may be alternative channels of communication, but the prevalence of a large number of signs in Los Angeles is a strong indication that, for many speakers, those alternatives are far less satisfactory. [There] is no proof [e.g.,] that a sufficient number of private parties would allow the posting of signs on their property. A speaker with a message that is generally unpopular or simply unpopular among property owners is hardly likely to get his message across if forced to rely on this medium. [Similarly], the adequacy of distributing handbills is dubious, [for] a message on a sign will typically reach far more people than one on a handbill. [Because] the City has completely banned the use of this particular medium of communication, and because, given the circumstances, there are no equivalent alternative media that provide an adequate substitute, the Court must examine with particular care the justifications that the City proffers for its ban.

[If a] restriction is content-neutral, the court's task is to determine (1) whether the governmental objective advanced by the restriction is substantial, and (2) whether the restriction imposed on speech is no greater than is essential to further that objective. Unless both conditions are met the restriction must be invalidated. [I suggested] in Metromedia [that] courts should exercise special care in addressing these questions when a purely aesthetic objective is asserted to justify a restriction of speech. [I] adhere to that view. [A]esthetic interests are easy for a city to assert and difficult for a court to evaluate. [The] source of those difficulties is the unavoidable subjectivity of aesthetic judgments. As a consequence, [laws] defended on aesthetic grounds raise problems for judicial review that are not presented by laws defended on more objective grounds—such as national security, public health, or public safety. [E.g.,] a reviewing court faces substantial difficulties determining whether the actual objective is related to the suppression of speech. The asserted interest in aesthetics may be only a facade for content-based suppression. [Thus, the real] objective might simply be the elimination of the messages typically carried by the signs. [The] City might easily mask [such an] objective [by] declaring that signs constitute visual clutter.

[Similarly,] when a total ban is justified solely in terms of aesthetics, the means inquiry necessary to evaluate the constitutionality of the ban may be impeded by deliberate or unintended government manipulation. [Once] the government has identified a substantial aesthetic objective and has selected a preferred means of achieving its objective, it will be possible for the government to correct any mismatch between means and ends by redefining the ends to conform with the means. [When] a court reviews a restriction of speech imposed in order to promote an aesthetic objective, there is a significant possibility that the court will be able to do little more than pay lip service to the First Amendment inquiry into the availability of less restrictive alternatives.

The fact that there are difficulties inherent in judicial review of aesthetics-based restrictions of speech does not imply that government may not engage in such activities. [But] because the implementation of these functions creates special dangers to our First Amendment freedoms, there is a need for more stringent judicial scrutiny than the Court seems willing to exercise. In cases like this, where a total ban is imposed on a particularly valuable method of communication, a court should require the government to provide tangible proof of the legitimacy and substantiality of its aesthetic objective. [Statements] of aesthetic objectives should be accepted as substantial and unrelated to the suppression of speech only if the government demonstrates that it is pursuing an identified objective seriously and comprehensively and in ways that are unrelated to the restriction of speech. [In] this case, however, there is no indication that the City has addressed its visual clutter problem in any way other than by prohibiting the posting of signs—throughout the City and without regard to the density of their presence. Therefore, I would hold that the prohibition violates appellees' First Amendment rights.

[A] more limited approach to the visual clutter problem, however, might well pass constitutional muster. I have no doubt, [for example,] that signs posted on public property in certain areas—including, perhaps, parts of Los Angeles—could contribute to the type of eyesore that a city would genuinely have a substantial interest in eliminating. These areas might include parts of the City that are particularly pristine, reserved for certain uses, designated to reflect certain themes, or so blighted that broad gauged renovation is necessary. Presumably, in these types of areas the City would also regulate the aesthetic environment in ways other than the banning of temporary signs. [Similarly,] Los Angeles might be able to attack its visual clutter problem in more areas of the City by reducing the stringency of the ban, perhaps by regulating the density of temporary signs, and coupling that approach with additional measures designed to reduce other forms of visual clutter. In [this] case, I believe that Los Angeles' total ban sweeps so broadly and trenches so completely on appellees' use of an important medium of political expression that it must be struck down as violative of the [First Amendment].

Clark v. Community for Creative Non-Violence

468 U.S. 288, 104 S. Ct. 3065, 82 L. Ed. 2d 221 (1984).

■ JUSTICE WHITE delivered the opinion of the Court.

The issue in this case is whether a National Park Service regulation prohibiting camping in certain parks violates the First Amendment when applied to prohibit demonstrators from sleeping in Lafayette Park and the Mall in connection with a demonstration intended to call attention to the plight of the homeless. We hold that it does [not].

I.   The Interior Department, through the National Park Service, is charged with responsibility for the [management] of the National Parks and is authorized to promulgate rules and regulations for the use of the parks in accordance with the purposes for which they were established. The network of National Parks includes the National Memorial-core parks [Lafayette Park and the Mall].[1] Under the regulations involved in this case, camping in National Parks is permitted only in campgrounds designated for that purpose. No such campgrounds have ever been designated in Lafayette Park or the Mall.[2] [Demonstrations] for the airing of views or grievances are permitted in the Memorial-core parks, but for the most part only by Park Service permits. Temporary structures may be erected for demonstration purposes but may not be used for camping.[3]

In 1982, the Park Service issued a renewable permit to respondent Community for Creative Non-Violence (CCNV) to conduct a wintertime demonstration in Lafayette Park and the Mall for the purpose of demonstrating the plight of the homeless. The permit authorized the erection of two symbolic tent [cities]. The Park Service, however, [denied] CCNV's request that demonstrators be permitted to sleep in the symbolic tents. CCNV and several individuals then filed an action to prevent the application of the anti-camping regulations to the proposed [demonstration].[4]

II.   We need not differ with the view of the Court of Appeals that overnight sleeping in connection with the demonstration is expressive conduct protected to some extent by the First Amendment. We assume for present purposes, but do not decide, that such is the case, cf. [O'Brien], but this assumption only begins the inquiry. Expression, whether oral or written or symbolized by conduct, is subject to reasonable time, place, and manner restrictions. We have often noted that restrictions of this kind are valid provided that they are justified without reference to the content of the regulated speech, that they are narrowly tailored to serve a significant governmental interest, and that they leave open ample alternative channels for communication of the information. It is also true that a message may be delivered by conduct that is intended to be communicative and that, in context, would reasonably be understood by the viewer to be communicative. [Spence.] Symbolic expression of this kind may be forbidden or regulated if the conduct itself may constitutionally be regulated, if the regulation is narrowly drawn to further a substantial governmental interest, and if the interest is unrelated to the suppression of free speech. [O'Brien.]

---

[1]   Lafayette Park is a seven-acre square located across Pennsylvania Avenue from the White House. The Mall is a stretch of land running westward from the Capitol to the Lincoln Memorial some two miles away; it includes the Washington Monument as well as a series of pools, trees, lawns, and other greenery. Both park areas are visited by "vast numbers of visitors."

[2]   The regulation defined "camping" as "the use of park land for living accommodation purposes such as sleeping activities, or making preparations to sleep." Under the regulations, these activities "constitute camping when it reasonably appears [that] the participants [are] in fact using the area as a living accommodation regardless of the intent of the participants or the nature of any other activities in which they may also be engaging."

[3]   The regulations state: "In connection with permitted demonstrations or special events, temporary structures may be erected for the purpose of symbolizing a message or meeting logistical needs such as [first aid facilities]. Temporary structures may not be used outside designated camping areas for [camping activities]."

[4]   The District Court had granted summary judgment for the Park Service. The Court of Appeals had reversed by a vote of 6–5 in an en banc decision, finding the regulations invalid as applied. (The eleven judges produced six opinions. See 703 F.2d 586).

The United States submits [that] the regulation forbidding sleeping is defensible either as a time, place, or manner restriction or as a regulation of symbolic conduct. We [agree]. [The regulations,] including the ban on sleeping, are clearly limitations on the manner in which the demonstration could be carried out. That sleeping, like the symbolic tents themselves, may be expressive and part of the message delivered by the demonstration does not make the ban any less a limitation on the manner of demonstrating, for reasonable time, place, and manner regulations normally have the purpose and direct effect of limiting expression but are nevertheless valid. Neither does the fact that sleeping, arguendo, may be expressive conduct, rather than oral or written expression, render the sleeping prohibition any less a time, place, or manner regulation. [We] have very little trouble concluding that the Park Service may prohibit overnight sleeping in the parks involved here.

The requirement that the regulation be content neutral is clearly satisfied. [It] is not disputed here that the prohibition on camping, and on sleeping specifically, is content neutral and is not being applied because of disagreement with the message presented. Neither was the regulation faulted, nor could it be, on the ground that without overnight sleeping the plight of the homeless could not be communicated in other ways. The regulation otherwise left the demonstration intact, with its symbolic city, signs, and the presence of those who were willing to take their turns in a day-and-night vigil. Respondents do not suggest that there was, or is, any barrier to delivering to the media, or to the public by other means, the intended message concerning the plight of the homeless. It is also apparent to us that the regulation narrowly focuses on the Government's substantial interest in maintaining the parks in the heart of our capital in an attractive and intact condition, readily available to the millions of people who wish to [enjoy them]. To permit camping [would] be totally inimical to these [purposes].

[It] is evident from our cases that the validity of this regulation need not be judged solely by reference to the demonstration at hand. [Heffron.] Absent the prohibition on sleeping, there would be other groups who would demand permission to deliver an asserted message by camping in Lafayette Park. Some of them would surely have as credible a claim in this regard as does CCNV, and the denial of permits to still others would present difficult problems for the Park Service. With the prohibition, however, [at] least some around-the-clock demonstrations lasting for days on end will not materialize, others will be limited in size and duration, and the purposes of the regulation will thus be materially served. Perhaps these purposes would be more effectively and not so clumsily achieved by preventing tents and 24-hour vigils entirely in the core areas. But the Park Service's decision to permit non-sleeping demonstrations does not, in our view, impugn the camping prohibition as a valuable, but perhaps imperfect, protection to the parks. If the Government has a legitimate interest in ensuring that the National Parks are adequately protected, which we think it has, and if the parks would be more exposed to harm without the sleeping prohibition than with it, the ban is safe from invalidation under the First Amendment as a reasonable regulation on the manner in which a demonstration may be carried out. As in [Taxpayers for Vincent], the regulation "responds precisely to the substantive problems which legitimately concern the [Government]."

[The] foregoing analysis demonstrates that the Park Service regulation is sustainable under the four-factor standard of [O'Brien] for validating a regulation of expressive conduct, which, in the last analysis is little, if any, different from the standard applied to time, place, and manner restrictions.[5] No one contends that aside from its impact on speech a rule against camping or overnight sleeping in public parks is beyond the constitutional power of the Government to enforce. And [there] is a substantial government interest in conserving park property, an interest that is plainly served by, and requires for its implementation, measures such as the proscription of sleeping that are designed to limit the wear and tear on park properties. That interest is unrelated to suppression of expression.

We are unmoved by [view] that the challenged regulation is unnecessary, and hence invalid, because there are less speech-restrictive alternatives that could have satisfied the government interest in preserving park lands. There is no gainsaying that preventing overnight sleeping will avoid a measure of actual or threatened damage to Lafayette Park and the Mall. The Court of Appeals' suggestions that the Park Service minimize the possible injury by reducing the size, duration, or frequency of demonstrations would still curtail the total allowable expression in which demonstrators could engage, whether by sleeping or otherwise, and these suggestions represent no more than a disagreement with the Park Service over how much protection the core parks require or how an acceptable level of preservation is to be attained. We do not believe, however, that either [O'Brien] or the time, place, and manner decisions assign to the judiciary the authority to replace the Park Service as the manager of the Nation's parks or endow the judiciary with the competence to judge how much protection of park lands is wise and how that level of conservation is to be attained. [Reversed.] [Chief Justice Burger filed a separate concurrence suggesting that the activity here was more "conduct" than speech.]

■ JUSTICE MARSHALL, with whom JUSTICE BRENNAN joins, dissenting.

[The] proper starting point for analysis [is] a recognition that the activity in which respondents seek to engage [is] symbolic speech protected by the First Amendment. The majority [so] assumes, without deciding. [Here] respondents clearly intended to protest the reality of homelessness by sleeping outdoors in the winter in the near vicinity of the [White House]. Nor can there be any doubt that in the surrounding circumstances the likelihood was great that the political significance of sleeping in the parks would be understood by those who viewed it. [This] likelihood stems from the remarkably apt fit between the activity in which respondents seek to engage and the social problems they seek to highlight. [It] is true that we all go to sleep as part of our daily regimen and that, for the most part, sleep represents a physical necessity and not a vehicle for expression. But these characteristics need not prevent an activity that is normally devoid of expressive purpose from being used as a novel mode of communication.

---

[5]   Reasonable time, place, and manner restrictions are valid even though they directly limit oral or written expression. It would be odd to insist on a higher standard for limitations aimed at regulable conduct and having only an incidental impact on speech. Thus, if the time, place, and manner restriction on expressive sleeping, if that is what is involved in this case, sufficiently and narrowly serves a substantial enough governmental interest to escape First Amendment condemnation, it is untenable to invalidate it under O'Brien on the ground that the governmental interest is insufficient to warrant the intrusion on First Amendment concerns or that there is an inadequate nexus between the regulation and the interest sought to be served. We note that only recently, in a case dealing with the regulation of signs, the Court framed the issue under O'Brien and then based a crucial part of its analysis on the time, place, and manner cases. [Taxpayers for Vincent.] [Footnote by Justice White.]

[Although] sleep in the context of this case is symbolic speech protected by the First Amendment, it is nonetheless subject to reasonable time, place, and manner restrictions. I agree with the standard enunciated by the majority.[6] [I] conclude, however, that the regulations at issue [here], as applied to respondents, fail to satisfy this standard. [The] majority cites no evidence indicating that sleeping engaged in as symbolic speech will cause *substantial* wear and tear on park property. Furthermore, the Government's application of the sleeping ban in the circumstances of this case is strikingly underinclusive. The majority acknowledges that a proper time, place, and manner restriction must be "narrowly tailored." Here, however, the tailoring requirement is virtually forsaken inasmuch as the Government offers no justification for applying its absolute ban on sleeping yet is willing to allow respondents to engage in activities—such as feigned sleeping—that is no less burdensome.

[By] limiting its concern to whether a given regulation creates a content-based distinction, the Court has seemingly overlooked the fact that content-neutral restrictions are also capable of unnecessarily restricting protected expressive activity. The Court [has] transformed the ban against content-distinctions from a floor that offers all persons at least equal liberty under the First Amendment into a ceiling that restricts persons to the protection of First Amendment equality—but nothing more.[7] [The] Court evidently assumes that the balance struck by officials is deserving of deference so long as it does not appear to be tainted by content discrimination. What the Court fails to recognize is that public officials have strong incentives to overregulate even in the absence of an intent to censor particular views. This incentive stems from the fact that of the two groups whose interests officials must accommodate—on the one hand, the interests of the general public and on the other, the interests of those who seek to use a particular forum for First Amendment activity—the political power of the former is likely to be far greater than that of the latter. [In light of government officials' greater] sensitivity to regulatory as opposed to First Amendment interests, [facial] viewpoint-neutrality is no shield against unnecessary restrictions on unpopular ideas or modes of expression, and [here] the Court [should have] subject[ed] the Government's restrictive policy to something more than minimal [scrutiny].

---

[6] I also agree with the majority that no substantial difference distinguishes the test applicable to time, place, and manner restrictions and the test articulated in United States v. O'Brien. [Footnote by Justice Marshall.]

[7] Furthermore, a content-neutral regulation does not necessarily fall with random or equal force upon different groups or different points of view. A content-neutral regulation that restricts an inexpensive mode of communication will fall most heavily upon relatively poor speakers and the points of view that such speakers typically espouse. This sort of latent inequality is very much in evidence in this case, for respondents lack the financial means necessary to buy access to more conventional modes of persuasion. A disquieting feature about the disposition of this case is that it lends credence to the charge that judicial administration of the First Amendment, in conjunction with a social order marked by large disparities in wealth and other sources of power, tends systematically to discriminate against efforts by the relatively disadvantaged to convey their political ideas. In the past, this Court has taken such considerations into account in adjudicating the First Amendment rights of those among us who are financially deprived. See, e.g., [Martin v. Struthers.] [Footnote by Justice Marshall.]

TRANQUILITY, PRIVACY AND REPOSE

1.   ***Noise regulations.*** Recall that, in Kovacs v. Cooper (1949; p. 292), the Court upheld a ban on "loud and raucous" sound trucks. In **Ward v. Rock Against Racism**, 491 U.S. 781 (1989), the Court rejected a First Amendment challenge to New York City's regulation mandating the use of city-provided sound systems and technicians to control the volume of concerts at the bandshell in Central Park. The regulation was challenged by a group that claimed that the inability to use its own equipment and technicians in a concert in a public forum interfered with its free expression rights. There was a consensus on the Court that the case involved a "public forum," that the City's interest in limiting excessive noise was substantial, and that the regulation was "content-neutral." The dispute turned on how strictly to interpret the "narrowly tailored means" requirement. Recall that O'Brien had suggested that content-neutral restrictions are valid "if the incidental restriction on alleged First Amendment freedoms is no greater than is essential to the furtherance of that interest." The court of appeals in Ward had read O'Brien to require the "least intrusive means" and found that the city had not shown that it lacked other, less restrictive means of regulating concert volume.

Justice KENNEDY, writing for the Court, explicitly repudiated this view: "[T]he Court of Appeals erred in requiring the city to prove that this regulation was the least intrusive means. [Our] cases quite clearly hold that restrictions on the time, place, or manner of protected speech are not invalid 'simply because there is some imaginable alternative that might be less burdensome on speech. [Lest] any confusion on the point remain, we reaffirm today that a regulation of the time, place, or manner of protected speech must be narrowly tailored to serve the government's legitimate content-neutral interests but that it need not be the least-restrictive or least-intrusive means of doing so. Rather, [narrow] tailoring is satisfied 'so long as [the] regulation promotes a substantial government interest that would be achieved less effectively absent the regulation.' [To] be sure, this standard does not mean that a time, place, or manner regulation may burden substantially more speech than is necessary to further the government's legitimate interests. [So] long as the means chosen are not substantially broader than necessary to achieve the government's interest, however, the regulation will not be invalid simply because a court concludes that the government's interest could be adequately served by some less-speech-restrictive alternative." Applying this deferential standard, and finding that the regulation left open "ample alternative channels of communication," he concluded that it was "a reasonable regulation of the place and manner of expression."

Justice MARSHALL, joined by Justices Brennan and Stevens, dissented, contending that a "least-restrictive-alternative" analysis was built into the "narrowly tailored" requirement. To hold otherwise, he said, was a "serious distortion of the narrow tailoring requirement. [By] holding that the guidelines are valid time, place, and manner restrictions, notwithstanding the availability of less intrusive but effective means of controlling volume, the majority deprives the narrow tailoring requirement of all meaning. [The] majority replaces constitutional scrutiny with mandatory deference. [Under] the majority's view, it will be enough] that the challenged regulation advances the government's interest only in the slightest, for any differential burden on speech that results does not enter the calculus. [After] today's decision, a city could claim that bans on handbill distribution or on door-to-door solicitation are the most effective means of avoiding littering and [fraud]."

2. **Protecting "captive audiences."** Recall that in Cohen v. California (1971; p. 69), the Court held that audiences must simply avert their eyes and ears when they encounter speech that offends them in open public spaces; government may not protect them in advance. The Court likewise held in Consolidated Edison Co. v. PSC (1980; p. 178) and Bolger v. Youngs Drug Products (1983; p. 211), that audiences offended by mail they receive must simply make the "short, regular, journey from mail box to trash can." But the Court held in Rowan v. Post Office (1970; p. 177) that an offended recipient may request that his or her name be removed from mailing lists, and held in FCC v. Pacifica (1978; p. 172) that the federal government may bar indecent radio broadcasts during daytime hours to prevent assault on unwilling listeners who are "captive" in their homes. Are there other contexts in which the Court will permit government to protect the sensibilities of a "captive audience," even from speech upon the public streets and sidewalks? Consider the following cases, which involved targeted residential picketing and abortion clinic protests.

a. *Targeted residential picketing.* Recall that in Carey v. Brown (1980; p. 241), the Court invalidated a law banning all residential picketing except labor picketing, but did not reach the question of the validity of a law "barring all residential picketing regardless of its subject matter." Justice Brennan's majority opinion stated: "We are not to be understood to imply [that] residential picketing is beyond the reach of uniform and nondiscriminatory regulation. For the right to communicate is not limitless. [The] State's interest in protecting the well-being, tranquility, and privacy of the home is certainly of the highest order in a free and civilized society." In **Frisby v. Schultz**, 487 U.S. 474 (1988), the Court narrowly construed and sustained a flat ban on what it called "focused picketing" of a particular residence. A group ranging from 11 to over 40 people picketed, on six occasions within one month, the residence of a doctor who performed abortions. The picketing was orderly and peaceful. Thereafter, the town (a residential suburb of Milwaukee with a population of about 4,300) enacted a flat ban on all residential picketing, barring picketing "on or about the residence [of] any individual." The lower courts enjoined the ordinance, but the Court upheld it. As construed by the Court, the ordinance did not prohibit all residential picketing but only residential picketing that focused on and took place in front of a particular residence.

Justice O'CONNOR's majority opinion in the 6–3 ruling noted that "a public street does not lose its status as a traditional public forum simply because it runs through a residential neighborhood," but nevertheless concluded that the ordinance was valid because it was content-neutral, was "narrowly tailored to serve a significant government interest," and left open "ample alternative channels of communication." Justice O'Connor found the latter requirement "readily" satisfied here, in light of the narrow construction she invoked: the ordinance left protesters free to march through the neighborhood, so long as they did not focus on a particular residence; moreover, they were left free to proselytize door-to-door, and to distribute literature. In addition, there was a "significant government interest": "the protection of residential privacy." She noted that earlier decisions had held that "individuals are not required to welcome unwanted speech into their own homes," citing Pacifica and Kovacs, and added: "There simply is no right to force speech into the home of an unwilling listener."

Turning to the means/end fit, Justice O'Connor found the ordinance "narrowly tailored to protect only unwilling recipients of the communications. [A] complete ban can be narrowly tailored, but only if each activity within the proscription's scope is an appropriately targeted evil. [Taxpayers for Vincent]." She elaborated: "The type of focused picketing [here] is fundamentally different from more generally directed means of communication, that may not be completely banned in residential areas. See, e.g., [Schneider; Martin.] [Here the] picketing is narrowly directed at the household, not the public. The type of picketers banned by the [ordinance] generally do not seek to disseminate a message to the general public, but to intrude upon the targeted resident, and to do so in an especially offensive way. Moreover, even if some such picketers have a broader communicative purpose, their activity nonetheless inherently and offensively intrudes on residential privacy. The devastating effect of targeted picketing on the quiet enjoyment of the home is beyond doubt." She thus rejected the facial challenge to the ordinance.

Justice BRENNAN's dissent, joined by Justice Marshall, accepted that the majority had set forth the appropriate legal test, but argued that the ordinance banned "significantly more speech than is necessary to achieve the government's substantial and legitimate goal." In explaining why the ordinance was not "narrowly tailored," he acknowledged that there were clearly "many aspects of residential picketing that, if unregulated, might easily become intrusive or unduly coercive." Some of these aspects were illustrated here: the trial court had found that the protesters had, for example, warned young children not to go near the house because the physician was a "baby killer," had repeatedly trespassed on his property, and had at least once blocked the exits to his home. Such "intrusive and coercive abuses" could clearly be regulated: "Thus, for example, the government could constitutionally regulate the number of residential picketers, the hours during which a residential picket may take place, or the noise level of such a picket, [to] neutralize the intrusive or unduly coercive aspects of picketing around the home. But to say that picketing may be substantially regulated is not to say that it may be prohibited in its entirety. Once size, time, volume, and the like have been controlled to ensure that the picket is no longer intrusive or coercive, only the speech itself remains, conveyed perhaps by a lone, silent individual, walking back and forth with a sign. Such speech, which no longer implicates the heightened governmental interest in residential privacy, is nevertheless banned by [the ordinance]. Therefore, [it] is not narrowly tailored."

In a separate dissent, Justice STEVENS stated: "[Under this ordinance,] it is unlawful for a fifth-grader to carry [a sign saying 'Get Well Charlie—our Team Needs You'] in front of a residence for the period of time necessary to convey its friendly message to its intended audience. [My] hunch is that the town will probably not enforce its ban against friendly, innocuous, or even brief unfriendly picketing, and that the Court may be right in concluding that its legitimate sweep makes its overbreadth insubstantial. But [the] scope of the ordinance gives the town officials far too much discretion in making enforcement decisions; while [we] await further developments, potential picketers must act at their peril."

b. *Abortion clinic protests.* In **Madsen v. Women's Health Center,
Inc.**, 512 U.S. 753 (1994), the Court in part upheld and in part struck down
a Florida state court injunction that limited the activities of antiabortion
protestors on the public streets outside an abortion clinic. The injunction was
aimed largely at protecting the privacy and repose of women seeking to enter
and use the abortion clinic's facilities. Chief Justice REHNQUIST, writing
for the Court, first found that the injunction was not content-or viewpoint-
based simply because it restricted only the speech of antiabortion protesters:
"To accept petitioners' claim would be to classify virtually every injunction
as content or viewpoint based. An injunction, by its very nature, applies only
to a particular group (or individuals) and regulates the activities, and
perhaps the speech, of that group." The injunction had been issued because
the protestors had violated a previous, narrower injunction against blocking
clinic access. "[In] determining content neutrality [we] look to governmental
purpose as the primary consideration. Here, the state court imposed
restrictions on petitioners [because] they repeatedly violated the court's
original order. That petitioners all share the same viewpoint regarding
abortion does not in itself demonstrate that some invidious content-or
viewpoint-based purpose motivated the issuance of the order. It suggests
only that those in the group whose conduct violated the court's order happen
to share the same opinion regarding abortions being performed at the clinic."

Having found the injunction content-neutral, Chief Justice Rehnquist
nonetheless held that the Ward time, place, and manner test must be applied
with special stringency in the context of an injunction, as opposed to a
general statute, because "[i]njunctions [carry] greater risks of censorship and
discriminatory application than do general ordinances. [When] evaluating a
content-neutral injunction, we [must ask] whether the challenged provisions
of the injunction burden no more speech than necessary to serve a significant
government interest." The majority opinion agreed with the Florida Supreme
Court that the injunction served a number of "significant government
interests": interests "[in] protecting a woman's freedom to seek lawful
medical or counseling services in connection with her pregnancy, [in]
ensuring the public safety and order, in promoting the free flow of traffic on
public streets and sidewalks, [in] protecting the property rights of all its
citizens, [and in vindicating] the State's strong interest in residential
privacy, [Frisby], applied by analogy to medical privacy. The [state] court
observed that while targeted picketing of the home threatens the
psychological well-being of the 'captive' resident, targeted picketing of a
hospital or clinic threatens not only the psychological, but the physical well-
being of the patient held 'captive' by medical circumstance. We agree [that]
the combination of these governmental interests is quite sufficient to justify
an appropriately tailored injunction to protect them."

Chief Justice Rehnquist then considered whether each challenged
provision of the injunction met the heightened narrow tailoring requirement
he had set forth. He upheld the injunction's requirement of a "36-foot buffer
zone" around the front of the clinic in which the protestors were barred from
"congregating, picketing, patrolling, [or] demonstrating." He emphasized the
need for "some deference" to the state court's findings "even under our
heightened review": "The state court seems to have had few other options to
protect access given the narrow confines around the clinic. The state court
was convinced that allowing the petitioners to remain on the clinic's sidewalk
and driveway was not a viable option in view of the failure of the first
injunction to protect access. And allowing the petitioners to stand in the

middle of [the adjacent street] would obviously block vehicular traffic. [Protesters] standing across the narrow street from the clinic can still be seen and heard from the clinic parking lots. On balance, we hold that the 36-foot buffer zone around the clinic entrances and driveway burdens no more speech than necessary to accomplish the governmental interest at stake." He held, however, that the 36-foot buffer zone was invalid as applied to the private property along the side and back of the clinic, as there had been no showing that such speech interfered with clinic access.

He next turned to a portion of the injunction restraining the petitioners from "singing, chanting, whistling, shouting, yelling, use of bullhorns, auto horns, sound amplification equipment or other sounds or images observable to or within earshot of the patients inside the clinic" during the hours of 7:30 a.m. through noon on Mondays through Saturdays. He upheld the provision restricting high noise levels, noting that "[n]oise control is particularly important around hospitals and medical facilities during surgery and recovery periods." But, he held, "[t]he same cannot be said for the 'images observable' provision." Chief Justice Rehnquist reasoned that this restriction burdened "more speech than necessary to achieve the purpose of limiting threats to clinic patients or their families," since it is much easier for the clinic to pull its curtains than for a patient to stop up her ears, and no more is required to avoid seeing placards through the windows of the clinic."

Chief Justice Rehnquist's majority opinion next invalidated a provision of the state court order requiring that the protestors "refrain from physically approaching any person seeking services of the clinic 'unless such person indicates a desire to communicate' in an area within 300 feet of the clinic. The state court was attempting to prevent clinic patients and staff from being 'stalked' or 'shadowed' by the petitioners as they approached the clinic. But it is difficult, indeed, to justify a prohibition on all uninvited approaches of persons seeking the services of the clinic, regardless of how peaceful the contact may be, without burdening more speech than necessary to prevent intimidation and to ensure access to the clinic. Absent evidence that the protesters' speech is independently proscribable (i.e., 'fighting words' or threats), or is so infused with violence as to be indistinguishable from a threat of physical harm, this provision cannot stand."

Finally, the Court invalidated the injunction's prohibition against picketing, demonstrating, or using sound amplification equipment within 300 feet of the residences of clinic staff: "[T]he 300-foot zone around the residences in this case is much larger than the zone provided for in the ordinance which we approved in Frisby. The ordinance at issue there [was] limited to 'focused picketing taking place solely in front of a particular residence.' By contrast, the 300-foot zone would ban 'general marching through residential neighborhoods, or even walking a route in front of an entire block of houses.' [Frisby.] The record before us does not contain sufficient justification for this broad a ban on picketing; it appears that a limitation on the time, duration of picketing, and number of pickets outside a smaller zone could have accomplished the desired result.

"[In] sum, we uphold the noise restrictions and the 36-foot buffer zone around the clinic entrances and driveway because they burden no more speech than necessary to eliminate the unlawful conduct targeted by the state court's injunction. We strike down as unconstitutional the 36-foot buffer zone as applied to the private property to the north and west of the clinic, the 'images observable' provision, the 300-foot no-approach zone around the clinic, and the 300-foot buffer zone around the residences, because these provisions sweep more broadly than necessary to accomplish the permissible goals of the injunction."

Justice STEVENS concurred in part and dissented in part. Unlike the majority, he would have subjected the injunction to more deferential scrutiny, not more stringent scrutiny, than a comparable statute, because an injunction is limited "solely to an individual or a limited group of individuals, who, by engaging in illegal conduct, have been judicially deprived of some liberty." Under that more lenient standard, he would have upheld the 300-foot no-approach zone around the clinic, but would not have reached the question whether the other restrictions were permissible time, place, or manner regulations. Justice Souter also wrote a separate concurrence.

Justice SCALIA, joined by Justices Kennedy and Thomas, concurred in the portions of the majority opinion striking down portions of the injunction, but dissented sharply from the portions upholding the 36-foot buffer zone and the noise prohibition: "[The majority's] appearance of moderation and Solomonic wisdom [is] deceptive." Describing at length a videotape from the record, he concluded that it showed "that a great many forms of expression and conduct occurred in the vicinity of the clinic. [What] the videotape, the rest of the record, and the trial court's findings do not contain is any suggestion of violence near the clinic, nor do they establish any attempt to prevent entry or exit."

Justice Scalia disagreed with the majority's standard of review. He derided the new standard of "intermediate-intermediate scrutiny" as manufactured "for this abortion-related case." He argued instead that restrictions upon speech imposed by injunction generally are "at least as deserving of strict scrutiny as a statutory, content-based restriction," because injunctions likewise lend themselves "to the targeted suppression of particular ideas." He also argued that the particular injunction here was content-based, because it reached all those "acting in concert or participation" with the protestors rather than merely those who had violated the previous order; it thus was, in his view, "tailored to restrain persons distinguished, not by proscribable conduct, but by proscribable views." He found that all the provisions of the injunction failed strict scrutiny, and even failed the majority's test, given the lack of tailoring between the injunction under review and any violation by all of the protestors of the previous injunction or other Florida law. He concluded that "petitioners have a right, not merely to demonstrate and protest at some reasonably effective place, but to demonstrate and protest where they want to and where all other Floridians can, namely, right there on the public sidewalk in front of the clinic. 'One is not to have the exercise of his liberty of expression in appropriate places abridged on the plea that it may be exercised in some other place.' [Schneider.] [What] we have decided seems to be, and will be reported by the media as, an abortion case. But it will go down in the lawbooks, it will be cited, as a free-speech injunction case—and the damage its novel principles produce will be considerable."

In **Schenck v. Pro-Choice Network of Western New York**, 519 U.S. 357 (1997), the Court again reviewed a First Amendment challenge to an injunction against protestors outside an abortion clinic. The injunction, issued by a federal district court after a series of large-scale protests and blockades, banned "demonstrating within fifteen feet from either side or edge of, or in front of, doorways or doorway entrances, parking lot entrances, driveways and driveway entrances of" clinic facilities, or "within fifteen feet of any person or vehicle seeking access to or leaving such facilities." Antiabortion counselors could approach persons entering or exiting clinics in order to make "non-threatening" conversation with them, but if requested to "cease and desist," they had to retreat 15 feet from the people they had been counseling. As construed by the Court, the injunction thus created two kinds of buffer zones: "fixed buffer zones" and "floating buffer zones." Applying the standard set forth in Madsen, Chief Justice REHNQUIST, writing for the Court, struck down the floating buffer zones but upheld the fixed buffer zones:

"We strike down the floating buffer zones around people entering and leaving the clinics because they burden more speech than is necessary to serve the relevant governmental interests. The floating buffer zones prevent defendants—except for two sidewalk counselors, while they are tolerated by the targeted individual—from communicating a message from a normal conversational distance or handing leaflets to people entering or leaving the clinics who are walking on the public sidewalks. [Since] the buffer zone floats, protesters on the public sidewalks who wish (i) to communicate their message to an incoming or outgoing patient or clinic employee and (ii) to remain as close as possible (while maintaining an acceptable conversational distance) to this individual, must move as the individual moves, maintaining 15 feet of separation. But this would be difficult to accomplish [without stepping into the street or into other persons' floating buffer zones]."

In contrast, the Court upheld the fixed buffer zones around clinic doorways, driveways, and driveway entrances, reasoning that such buffer zones were necessary to ensure that people and vehicles trying to enter or exit the clinic property or clinic parking lots could do so. Chief Justice Rehnquist wrote: "As in Madsen, the record shows that protesters purposefully or effectively blocked or hindered people from entering and exiting the clinic doorways, from driving up to and away from clinic entrances, and from driving in and out of clinic parking lots. Based on this conduct [the] District Court was entitled to conclude that the only way to ensure access was to move back the demonstrations away from the driveways and parking lot entrances. [Although] one might quibble about whether 15 feet is too great or too small a distance if the goal is to ensure access, we defer to the District Court's reasonable assessment of the number of feet necessary to keep the entrances clear."

Justice SCALIA, joined by Justices Kennedy and Thomas, dissented from the decision insofar as it upheld fixed buffer zones. He argued that the majority opinion had mischaracterized the zones as intended to preserve unimpeded clinic access, when they were in fact grounded at least in part on the impermissible purpose of protecting listeners from having to hear "unwanted" speech. Justice BREYER dissented from the decision insofar as it struck down the floating buffer zones, arguing that "the preliminary injunction's language does not necessarily create the kind of 'floating bubble' that leads the Court to find the injunction unconstitutionally broad."

In **Hill v. Colorado**, 530 U.S. 703 (2000), the Court reviewed a statute, as opposed to an injunction, challenged for limiting the speech of abortion protestors outside abortion clinics, and upheld it by a vote of 6–3. The statute makes it unlawful within the vicinity of a health care facility for anyone to "knowingly approach" within eight feet of another person, without that person's consent, "for the purpose of passing a leaflet or handbill to, displaying a sign to, or engaging in oral protest, education, or counseling with such other person." Justice STEVENS delivered the opinion of the Court, joined by Chief Justice Rehnquist and Justices O'Connor, Souter, Ginsburg, and Breyer. He found the statute a valid, content-neutral time, place, and manner regulation under the Ward test. It was content-neutral, he wrote, because it regulated not speech but "the places where some speech may occur," it was not adopted because of disagreement with a message, and it was justified by interests in access and privacy that were unrelated to ideas. He declined to find a content basis in the distinction between approaches for "protest, education or counseling" and for other purposes, such as "pure social or random conversation." He concluded that the statute "applies to all 'protest,' to all 'counseling,' and to all demonstrators whether or not the demonstration concerns abortion, and whether they oppose or support the woman who has made an abortion decision. That is the level of neutrality that the Constitution demands." He went on to hold the statute narrowly tailored to important interests in privacy and access and left protestors adequate alternative means of getting their message across. Justice SOUTER filed a concurrence, joined by Justices O'Connor, Ginsburg, and Breyer, emphasizing that the statute addressed "not the content of speech but the circumstances of its delivery," and thus was properly evaluated as content-neutral.

Dissents were filed by Justice SCALIA, joined by Justice Thomas, and by Justice KENNEDY. Justice Scalia argued that the floating buffer zone around oral communication was "obviously and undeniably content-based," because "[w]hether a speaker must obtain permission before approaching within eight feet—and whether he will be sent to prison for failing to do so—depends entirely on what he intends to say when he gets there." He would have applied strict scrutiny, which the statute could not survive: "Suffice it to say that if protecting people from unwelcome communications (the governmental interest the Court posits) is a compelling state interest, the First Amendment is a dead letter. And if forbidding peaceful, nonthreatening, but uninvited speech from a distance closer than eight feet is a 'narrowly tailored' means of preventing the obstruction of entrance to medical facilities (the governmental interest the State asserts) narrow tailoring must refer not to the standards of Versace, but to those of Omar the tentmaker." He accused the Court of distorting First Amendment law in order to "sustain this restriction upon the free speech of abortion opponents": "Does the deck seem stacked? You bet." Justice Kennedy likewise would have found the law content-based, as restrictive of particular topics, and denied that "citizens have a right to avoid unpopular speech in a public forum." He added that the statute interfered with an important First Amendment interest in "immediacy": "Here the citizens who claim First Amendment protection seek it for speech which, if it is to be effective, must take place at the very time and place a grievous moral wrong, in their view, is about to occur. The Court tears away from the protesters the guarantees of the First Amendment when they most need it."

Was Hill unusual in permitting a listener preclearance requirement for speech in the public forum? Note that in cases such as Cohen v. California (1971; p. 69), the Court ruled that, in the public forum, speakers may take what initiative they wish toward listeners while offended listeners must simply turn the other cheek. Do Madsen, Schenck, and Hill together establish an exception to that principle for the curtilage of a health facility? Does the law in Hill, by requiring listeners affirmatively to consent to speech, have the likely effect of discriminating in favor of popular or widely accepted messages and against those that are unorthodox or unpopular, where the speaker must initiate contact because the listener will not? Note that, in Heffron v. ISKCON (1981; p. 298), the Court rejected a similar argument against a rule requiring literature distribution and solicitation of funds to be confined to a fixed rented booth at a state fair, noting that the argument that "the regulation is not content-neutral in that it prefers listener-initiated exchanges to those originating with the speaker [is] interesting but has little force." Did Justice Scalia's dissent in Hill find new force in such an argument?

In **McCullen v. Coakley**, 573 U.S. 464 (2014), the Court considered a 2007 Massachusetts statute that went beyond the law in Hill and created a 35-foot buffer zone around abortion-providing facilities during business hours that categorically excluded anyone except persons entering or leaving, facility employees in the scope of their duties, emergency personnel like police and firefighters, and people passing by. The court struck down the law in an opinion by Chief Justice ROBERTS that was joined by Justices Ginsburg, Breyer, Kagan, and Sotomayor. The Court said the law was content-neutral because it "does not draw content-based distinctions on its face. It is true, of course, that by limiting the buffer zones to abortion clinics, the Act has the 'inevitable effect' of restricting abortion-related speech more than speech on other subjects. But a facially neutral law does not become content based simply because it may disproportionately affect speech on certain topics." The Court then held the law to be viewpoint-neutral as well. "There is nothing inherently suspect about providing some kind of exemption to allow individuals who work at the clinics to enter or remain within the buffer zones. In particular, the exemption cannot be regarded as simply a carve-out for the clinic escorts; it also covers employees such as the maintenance worker shoveling a snowy sidewalk or the security guard patrolling a clinic entrance."

Having held that strict scrutiny was unnecessary, Chief Justice Roberts then applied ordinary intermediate scrutiny and found that the law was not narrowly tailored because it burdened "substantially more speech than necessary to further the government's legitimate interests." In particular, the law limited "one-on-one communication" between pro-life activists and women who might be seeking abortions. "Petitioners are not protestors," Chief Justice Roberts wrote. "They seek not merely to express their opposition to abortion, but to inform women of various alternatives and to provide help in pursuing them. Petitioners believe that they can accomplish this objective only through personal, caring, consensual conversations. And for good reason: It is easier to ignore a strained voice or a waving hand than a direct greeting or an outstretched arm." The Court's opinion never directly addressed the status of Hill v. Colorado.

Justice SCALIA, joined by Justices Thomas and Kennedy, concurred only in the judgment and would have found the law to discriminate on the basis of content. He rejected the Court's reliance on facial neutrality. "Every objective indication shows that the provision's primary purpose is to restrict speech that opposes abortion." He also objected to the Court reaching the issue of content neutrality when its decisions truck down the law. Justice Scalia addressed the status of Colorado v. Hill directly: "The provision at issue here was indisputably meant to serve the same interest [as the law in Hill] in protecting citizens' supposed right to avoid speech that they would rather not hear. For that reason, we granted a second question for review in this case (though one would not know that from the Court's opinion, which fails to mention it): whether Hill should be cut back or cast aside. The majority avoids that question by declaring the Act content neutral on other (entirely unpersuasive) grounds. In concluding that the statute is content based and therefore subject to strict scrutiny, I necessarily conclude that Hill should be overruled. [Protecting] people from speech they do not want to hear is not a function that the First Amendment allows the government to undertake in the public streets and sidewalks. One final thought regarding Hill: It can be argued, and it should be argued in the next case, that by stating that 'the Act would not be content neutral if it were concerned with undesirable effects that arise from . . . [l]isteners' reactions to speech,' and then holding the Act unconstitutional for being insufficiently tailored to safety and access concerns, the Court itself has sub silentio (and perhaps inadvertently) overruled Hill. The unavoidable implication of that holding is that protection against unwelcome speech cannot justify restrictions on the use of public streets and sidewalks."

Justice ALITO concurred only in the judgment and wrote to say that the law was not viewpoint-neutral. "Consider this entirely realistic situation. A woman enters a buffer zone and heads haltingly toward the entrance. A sidewalk counselor, such as petitioners, enters the buffer zone, approaches the woman and says, 'If you have doubts about an abortion, let me try to answer any questions you may have. The clinic will not give you good information.' At the same time, a clinic employee, as instructed by the management, approaches the same woman and says, 'Come inside and we will give you honest answers to all your questions.' The sidewalk counselor and the clinic employee expressed opposing viewpoints, but only the first violated the statute."

Was the decision a victory for pro-life or pro-choice activists? What, if anything, does the voting line-up tell you about this question?

INVALID TIME, PLACE, OR MANNER REGULATION

Is time, place, and manner review heightened in theory but toothless in fact? The preceding cases suggest that the Court has generally deferred to government when applying time, place, and manner review. The Court's implementation of the requirement that a regulation be "narrowly drawn to further a substantial governmental interest"—a requirement common to both symbolic expression claims and time, place, and manner challenges— does not involve strict scrutiny, nor serious inquiry into the availability of "less restrictive means" to implement the governmental interest.

As evidence that time, place, and manner review, even under the relatively deferential Ward/CCNV standard, remains more speech-protective than rationality review, consider the different burdens of justification each standard places on the government. Minimal rationality review does not require a showing of actual purpose or empirically sound means/end fit, but rather may be satisfied entirely by conjectural justifications. Rationality review thus permits the government to win dismissal on the pleadings so long as the government can hypothesize a rational relationship to a conceivable government interest. Time, place, and manner review, by contrast, requires government to make an evidentiary showing of substantial ends and means closely tailored to those ends. Arguably, by requiring governments to adduce some empirical evidence that the harms they seek to avoid are material, and that the means they have chosen are superior to obvious alternatives, the test continues to serve a protective First Amendment purpose: even if the government rarely loses a litigated case, it might well avoid enacting or enforcing regulation that could not withstand an evidentiary hearing. On this view, intermediate scrutiny operates as a powerful deterrent even if it is a rarely wielded club.

Moreover, the Supreme Court does occasionally invalidate a challenged time, place, or manner restriction. A leading example is **United States v. Grace**, 461 U.S. 171 (1983). In Grace, the challengers attacked a provision of 40 U.S.C. § 13k that prohibited the "display [of] any flag, banner, or device designed or adapted to bring into public notice any party, organization, or movement" in the U.S. Supreme Court building and on its grounds. One of the challengers sought to distribute to passers-by on the sidewalk leaflets concerning the removal of unfit judges from the bench. The other, Mary Grace, sought to display on the sidewalk a two-and-a-half by four-foot sign on which was inscribed verbatim the text of the First Amendment. The Court held the prohibition invalid as applied to the public sidewalks surrounding the Court building.

Justice WHITE stated: "The sidewalks comprising the outer boundaries of the Court grounds are indistinguishable from any other sidewalks in Washington, D.C., and we can discern no reason why they should be treated any differently. Sidewalks, of course, are among those areas of public property that traditionally have been held open to the public for expressive activities and are clearly within those areas of public property that may be considered, generally without further inquiry, to be public forum property. [There is] no separation, no fence, and no indication whatever to persons stepping from the street to the curb and sidewalks that serve as the perimeter of the Court grounds that they have entered some special type of enclave. [Traditional] public forum property occupies a special position in terms of First Amendment protection and will not lose its historically recognized character for the reason that it abuts government property that has been dedicated to a use other than as a forum for public expression."

Justice White rejected the Government's argument that the ban could be justified as "a reasonable time, place, and manner restriction" on public forum property. He found no sufficient connection with any of the asserted state interests to warrant the restriction. He questioned whether the ban substantially served the purpose of maintaining proper order and decorum within the Court grounds. He also rejected the Government's claim that the restraint was needed lest it "*appear* to the public that the Supreme Court is subject to outside influence or that picketing or marching, singly or in groups, is an acceptable or proper way of appealing to or influencing the Supreme Court": "[We] seriously doubt that the public would draw a different inference from a lone picketer carrying a sign on the sidewalks around the building than it would from a similar picket on the sidewalks across the street." In a separate opinion, Justice MARSHALL argued that the ban should be found "unconstitutional on its face": "[Since] the continuing existence of the statute will inevitably have a chilling effect on freedom of expression, there is no virtue in deciding its constitutionality on a piecemeal basis."

SPEAKER ACCESS TO PUBLIC PLACES OTHER THAN TRADITIONAL PUBLIC FORUMS

In Hague v. CIO (1939; p. 287), Justice Roberts, in speaking of public places which have "immemorially" and "time out of mind" been used for "discussing public questions," mentioned only "streets and parks." And most of the preceding materials involved access to and regulation of streets and parks. What of other public places? In a series of cases, the Court has confronted claims of speakers seeking access to such nontraditional forums as public libraries, jail environs, buses, military installations, mailboxes and federal charitable campaigns. Should an assured minimum-access claim be recognized in these contexts as well? At least an equal-access claim?

The cases that follow consider two different approaches to these questions. One approach, typical in earlier cases such as Brown, Adderley, and Grayned, asks with respect to any public property whether the proposed speech is compatible or not with its other principal uses. On this approach, speech restrictions might theoretically be invalidated in any public space, depending on its particular characteristics. See Stone, "Fora Americana: Speech in Public Places," 1974 Sup. Ct. Rev. 233 (noting that the incompatibility approach turns on functional considerations that bring "streets, parks, public libraries, and other publicly owned places [all] under the same roof"). The second approach, typical of later cases and summarized below in Perry Education Ass'n v. Perry Local Educators' Ass'n, instead uses the characteristics of public property as a ground to classify it in advance as a "public forum," a "designated public forum," or a "nonpublic forum," with different rules applying to each category.

As you read the following materials, consider which approach seems more helpful. How do the governing criteria vary between these approaches? What is the role of tradition or custom in each approach? What is the role of the contemporary function of the property in each approach? What is the role of the compatibility of expressive activities with other uses of the property in each approach? The availability to the First Amendment claimant of alternative forums for expression? The relationship between the subject matter of the protest and the nontraditional forum of protest?

LIBRARIES, JAILS AND SCHOOLS

1. *Libraries.* **Brown v. Louisiana**, 383 U.S. 131 (1966), arose from events at a segregated regional public library in Louisiana in 1964. Five young black men entered the reading room and one of them, Brown, asked branch assistant Reeves for a book. Reeves told Brown that she did not have the book but would request it from the state library and would notify him upon receipt. When Reeves asked the young black men to leave, they refused. Instead, Brown, in protest against the library's "whites only" policy, sat down and the others stood near him. There was no noise or boisterous talking. After about 10 minutes, the sheriff arrived and asked the men to leave; when they did not, he arrested them. Brown and his companions were convicted under Louisiana's breach of the peace statute.

The sharply divided 5–4 decision reversed the convictions. Justice FORTAS's plurality opinion, joined only by Chief Justice Warren and Justice Douglas, stated at the outset that there was no evidence that petitioners had violated the law—"no disorder, no intent to provoke a breach of the peace and no circumstances indicating that a breach might be occasioned by petitioners' actions." But he did not rest exclusively on this due process ground. He added: "We are here dealing with an aspect of a basic constitutional right—the right [of] speech and of assembly, and freedom to petition the Government for a redress of grievances. [These] rights are not confined to verbal expression. They embrace appropriate types of action which certainly include the right in a peaceable and orderly manner to protest by silent and reproachful presence, in a place where the protestant has every right to be, the unconstitutional segregation of public facilities. Accordingly, even if the accused action were within the scope of the [law], [we] would have to hold that the statute cannot constitutionally be applied to punish petitioners' actions in the circumstances of this case. The statute was deliberately and purposefully applied solely to terminate the reasonable, orderly, and limited exercise of the right to protest the unconstitutional segregation of a public facility. Interference with this right, so exercised, by state action is intolerable under our Constitution. [Fortunately], the circumstances here were such that no claim can be made that use of the library by others was disturbed by the demonstration. [Were] it otherwise, a factor not present in this case would have to be considered." Justices Brennan and WHITE each concurred in the judgment. Justice White found that petitioners' actions did not "depart significantly from what normal library use would contemplate."

Justice BLACK dissented, joined by Justices Clark, Harlan and Stewart: "[I]t is incomprehensible to me that a State must measure disturbances in its libraries and on the streets with identical standards. [A] tiny parish branch library, staffed by two women, is not a department store [nor] a bus terminal [nor] a public thoroughfare as in Edwards and Cox v. Louisiana." He continued: "[The plurality's] conclusion that the statute was unconstitutionally applied because it interfered with the petitioners' so-called protest establishes a completely new constitutional doctrine. [The First Amendment] does not guarantee to any person the right to use someone else's property, even that owned by government and dedicated to other purposes, as a stage to express dissident ideas. The novel constitutional doctrine of the prevailing opinion [exalts] the power of private nongovernmental groups to determine what use shall be made of governmental property over the power of the elected governmental officials."

Consider the comment in Kalven, "Upon Rereading Mr. Justice Black on the First Amendment," 14 UCLA L. Rev. 428 (1967): "[I]t remains something of a puzzle how Justice Black, who has been so sympathetic to the 'poor man's printing press' and so tolerant of noise in Kovacs, the intrusion in [Martin v. City of Struthers], the anonymity in [Talley v. California], can be so impatient with this kind of communication. It is as though his strategy of protecting all speech just because it was something other than conduct traps him when he is confronted by conduct which is symbolic."

2. *Jails.* In **Adderley v. Florida**, 385 U.S. 39 (1966), in contrast, the Court upheld the convictions of 32 students at Florida A. & M. University in Tallahassee for "trespass with a malicious and mischievous intent" upon the premises of the county jail. They had gone to the jail to protest the arrests of other students the day before and to demonstrate against racial segregation. They did not leave at the county sheriff's request. They did move back from the jail entrance but remained in a driveway normally used by the sheriff's

department to transport prisoners to and from the courts several blocks away and by commercial vehicles.

Justice BLACK, writing for the Court, rejected the students' claim that their convictions violated their First Amendment rights. "The sheriff, as jail custodian, had power [to] direct that this large crowd of people get off the grounds. There is not a shred of evidence in this record that this power was exercised [because] the sheriff objected to what was being sung or said by the demonstrators or because he disagreed with the objectives of their protest. The record reveals that he objected only to their presence on that part of the jail grounds reserved for jail uses. There is no evidence at all that on any other occasion had similarly large groups of the public been permitted to gather on this portion of the jail grounds for any purpose. Nothing in the [Constitution] prevents Florida from even-handed enforcement of its general trespass statute against those refusing to obey the sheriff's order to remove themselves from what amounted to the curtilage of the jailhouse. The State, no less than a private owner of property, has power to preserve the property under its control for the use to which it is lawfully dedicated. [The Constitution] does not forbid a State to control the use of its own property for its own lawful nondiscriminatory purpose."

Justice DOUGLAS dissented, joined by Chief Justice Warren and Justices Brennan and Fortas: "[T]he Court errs in treating the case as if it were an ordinary trespass case or an ordinary picketing case. The jailhouse, like an executive mansion, a legislative chamber, a courthouse, or the statehouse itself [Edwards], is one of the seats of government, whether it be the Tower of London, the Bastille, or a small county jail. And when it houses political prisoners or those whom many think are unjustly held, it is an obvious center for protest. The right to petition for the redress of grievances has an ancient history and is not limited to writing a letter or sending a telegram to a congressman; it is not confined to appearing before the local city council, or writing letters to the President or Governor or Mayor. Conventional methods of petitioning may be, and often have been, shut off to large groups of our citizens. Legislators may turn deaf ears; formal complaints may be routed endlessly through a bureaucratic maze; courts may let the wheels of justice grind very slowly. Those who do not control television and radio, those who cannot afford to advertise in newspapers or circulate elaborate pamphlets may have only a more limited type of access to public officials. Their methods should not be condemned as tactics of obstruction and harassment as long as the assembly and petition are peaceable, as these were.

"There is no question that petitioners had as their purpose a protest against the arrest of Florida A. & M. students for trying to integrate public theatres. [There] was no violence; no threat of violence; no attempted jail break; no storming of a prison; no plan or plot to do anything but protest. The evidence is uncontradicted that the petitioners' conduct did not upset the jailhouse routine. [There] was no shoving, no pushing, no disorder or threat of riot. It is said that some of the group blocked part of the driveway leading to the jail entrance. [But] whenever the students were requested to move they did so. If there was congestion, the solution was a further request to move to lawns or parking areas, not complete ejection and arrest."

Does Justice Black in Adderley retreat all the way to Justice Holmes's analogy between the state and the private property owner in Massachusetts v. Davis (1895; p. 286)? Would Justice Black sustain a blanket prohibition of the use of streets and parks for meetings and parades? Or are his broad comments applicable only to such nontraditional forums as jailhouse driveways? Does the holding in Adderley reject any assured access claim beyond the traditional public forum of the streets and parks? Or is there access to nontraditional forums so long as there is no showing of substantial disruption of or interference with the functioning of their primary uses? Is that the message of the Brown case? Can a claim to a nontraditional public forum be adequately analyzed without inquiries as to the availability of adequate alternative forums in which the speaker may reach the desired audience? Should the public forum claimant be required to demonstrate his special interest in the particular location? Was there special justification for the protest near the jailhouse in Adderley? As much as with the library protest in Brown?

3. **Schools.** In **Grayned v. Rockford**, 408 U.S. 104 (1972), the Court upheld an ordinance barring a demonstration near a school. Grayned had participated in a demonstration in front of a high school protesting black underrepresentation in activities at the school. The Court affirmed a conviction under an "antinoise" ordinance stating that no person on grounds "adjacent to any [school] building" in which a class is in session "shall willfully make or assist in the making of any noise or diversion which disturbs or tends to disturb the peace or good order of such school session." Justice MARSHALL's majority opinion emphasized that it was "the nature of a place, 'the pattern of its normal activities,' " that determines the reasonableness of time, place, and manner restrictions: "The crucial question is whether the manner of expression is basically incompatible with the normal activity of a particular place at a particular time."

Here, he found the restraint appropriate to the school environment: "Although a silent vigil may not unduly interfere with a public library [Brown], making a speech in the reading room almost certainly would. That same speech should be perfectly appropriate in a park. [Our] cases make clear that in assessing the reasonableness of a regulation, we must weigh heavily the fact that communication is involved [Schneider; Hague]; the regulation must be narrowly tailored to further the State's legitimate interest. Access to the 'streets, sidewalks, parks, and other similar public places [for] the purpose of exercising [First Amendment rights] cannot constitutionally be denied broadly.' In light of these general principles, we do not think that Rockford's ordinance is an unconstitutional regulation of activity around a school. [The] public sidewalk adjacent to school grounds may not be declared off-limits for expressive activity by members of the public. [But] expressive activity may be prohibited if it 'materially disrupts classwork or involves substantial disorder or invasion of the rights of others.' [Tinker (p. 369 below).] We would be ignoring reality if we did not recognize that the public schools [are] often the focus of significant grievances. [But] schools could hardly tolerate boisterous demonstrators who drown out classroom conversation, make studying impossible, block entrances, or incite children to leave the schoolhouse. [The ordinance] is narrowly tailored to further Rockford's compelling interest in having an undisrupted school session conducive to the students' learning, and does not unnecessarily interfere with First Amendment rights."

———

BUSES, THEATERS AND MILITARY BASES

Several decisions in the mid-1970s began to foreshadow the Court's later categorizing approach to public property. In these decisions, the nature of the property at issue begins to be more of a focal point than the functional compatibility of speech with its environment:

1. *Public transportation.* In **Lehman v. Shaker Heights**, 418 U.S. 298 (1974), the Court upheld a city rule against political advertising on city-owned buses. The city allowed commercial advertising on the buses. A candidate for state assembly who sought unsuccessfully to buy space for campaign advertisements challenged the rule. The Court rejected the challenge in a 5–4 decision. Justice BLACKMUN wrote a plurality opinion joined by Chief Justice Burger and Justices White and Rehnquist: "[It] is urged that the car cards here constitute a public forum protected by the First Amendment, and that there is a guarantee of nondiscriminatory access to such publicly owned and controlled areas of communication 'regardless of the primary purpose for which the area is dedicated.' We disagree. [This situation is] different from the traditional settings where First Amendment values inalterably prevail. Although [our cases have] been jealous to preserve access to public places for purposes of free speech, the nature of the forum and the conflicting interests involved have remained important in determining the degree of protection afforded. [In] much the same way that a newspaper or periodical, or even a radio or television station, need not accept every proffer of advertising from the general public, a city transit system has discretion to develop and make reasonable choices concerning the type of advertising that may be displayed in its [vehicles]."

Justice Blackmun found that the city's distinction between commercial and political advertising was not "arbitrary, capricious, or invidious": "Here, the city has decided that '[p]urveyors of goods and services saleable in commerce may purchase advertising space on an equal basis, whether they be house builders or butchers.' This decision is little different from deciding to impose a 10-, 25-, or 35-cent fare, or from changing schedules or the location of bus stops. Revenue earned from long-term commercial advertising could be jeopardized by a requirement that short-term candidacy or issue-oriented advertisements be displayed on car cards. Users would be subjected to the blare of political propaganda. There could be lurking doubts about favoritism, and sticky administrative problems might arise in parceling out limited space to eager politicians. In these circumstances, the managerial decision to limit car card space to innocuous and less controversial commercial and service oriented advertising does not rise to the dignity of a First Amendment violation."

Justice DOUGLAS, whose vote was needed to forge a majority, concurred in the judgment, emphasizing that transit users were a "captive audience" whom the city could constitutionally protect: "[A] streetcar or bus is plainly not a park or sidewalk or other meeting place for discussion. [It] is only a way to get to work or back home. The fact that it is owned and operated by the city does not without more make it a forum. [If] we are to turn a bus or street car into either a newspaper or a park, we take great liberties with people who because of necessity become commuters and at the same time captive viewers or listeners."

Justice BRENNAN dissented, joined by Justices Stewart, Marshall, and Powell: "[The] city created a forum for the dissemination of information and expression of ideas when it accepted and displayed commercial and public service advertisements on its rapid transit vehicles. Having opened a forum for communication, the city is barred by the [First Amendment] from discriminating among forum users solely on the basis of message content."

Some public transit authorities allow political advertisements generally but maintain rules allowing the exclusion of advertisements that they deem offensive (for example, ads that "demean or disparage" a certain group). Does Lehman's reasoning extend to allow these types of exclusions? Several courts of appeal have struck them down, holding that the respective transit authorities—through accepting political advertising in the first place—had created designated public fora and thus could not exclude advertisements based on their content. See, e.g., United Food & Commercial Workers Union, Local 1099 v. Sw. Ohio Reg'l Transit Auth., 163 F.3d 341 (6th Cir. 1998); N.Y. Magazine v. Metro. Transp. Auth., 136 F.3d 123 (2d Cir. 1998); Planned Parenthood Ass'n/Chi. Area v. Chi. Transit Auth., 767 F.2d 1225 (7th Cir. 1985). But the First and Ninth Circuits have held that accepting some political advertising, even if that advertising features controversial issues, does not transform public-transit advertising space into a designated public forum. See Am. Freedom Defense Initiative v. Mass. Bay Transp. Auth., 781 F.3d 571 (1st Cir. 2015); Seattle Mideast Awareness Campaign v. King County, 781 F.3d 489 (9th Cir. 2015). Those cases allowed the exclusion of controversial advertisements so long as the exclusion was not viewpoint discriminatory, and both courts held that the exclusions at issue were viewpoint-neutral.

What if a transit system excludes *all* advertising, commercial as well as noncommercial? Is a city bus an "anomalous" place for messages? Note that the government property involved here (bus advertising) and in the next note (municipal theater) is property designed for communicative purposes, in contrast to the primary *non*communicative purposes of the public property involved in such contexts as jails. Should that make a difference in the analysis? Even assuming the city could bar all messages on city buses, why could it discriminate against political speech? Doesn't such a subject matter distinction run afoul of Mosley? Is an exception to the Mosley principle justified because the city is running the bus as a business? See generally Wells & Hellerstein, "The Governmental-Proprietary Distinction in Constitutional Law," 66 Va. L. Rev. 1073 (1980) (suggesting that government's "quasi-business interest may adequately support regulation that a court might strike down if applied to the public at large"). Finally, should members of the "captive audience" on the bus have been required, like Cohen's audience, simply to avert their eyes?

2. *Municipal theaters.* Contrast Justice BLACKMUN's reluctance to recognize a public forum claim in Lehman with his majority opinion less than a year later in **Southeastern Promotions, Ltd. v. Conrad**, 420 U.S. 546 (1975). There, the Court found that the challenger's First Amendment rights were violated when the municipal board managing city theaters in Chattanooga refused permission to present "the controversial rock musical 'Hair.'" The refusal was based on the ground that the production would not be "in the best interest of the community." Although the alleged obscenity of "Hair" had been the major issue in the lower courts, Justice Blackmun did not reach that question, but rather found that the refusal constituted a prior restraint imposed without sufficient procedural safeguards.

In the course of reaching that conclusion, Justice Blackmun commented that the municipal theaters were "public forums designed for and dedicated to expressive activities. [Petitioner] was not seeking to use a facility primarily serving a competing use. [E.g., Adderley; Brown.] Nor was rejection of the application based on any regulation of time, place, or manner related to the nature of the facility or applications from other users. [E.g., Cox v. New Hampshire.] No rights of individuals in surrounding areas were violated by noise or any other aspect of the production. [Kovacs v. Cooper.] There was no captive audience. See [Lehman; Pollak]. Whether the petitioner might have used some other, privately owned, theater in the city for the production is of no consequence. [That] alone would not justify an otherwise impermissible prior restraint. [Schneider.]"

Justice DOUGLAS, in a concurring opinion, thought the majority's holding did not go far enough: in his view, no prior screening process of any sort was permissible. And he added: "A municipal theater is no less a forum for the expression of ideas than is a public park, or a sidewalk." A dissent by Justice WHITE, joined by Chief Justice Burger, concluded that, whether or not "Hair" was obscene, the city "could constitutionally forbid exhibition of the musical for children" and could "reserve its auditorium for productions suitable for exhibition to all the citizens of the city, adults and children alike." Another dissent, by Justice REHNQUIST, argued that a public auditorium should not be equated with public streets and parks. He feared that the majority had given "no constitutionally permissible role in the way of selection to the municipal authorities" and asked: "May a municipal theater devote an entire season to Shakespeare, or is it required to book any potential producer on a first-come, first-served basis?" He concluded that a city policy not to show attractions "of the kind that would offend any substantial number of potential theater goers" was not "arbitrary or unreasonable."

3. ***Military bases.*** To what extent may a First Amendment claimant gain access to a military base that has been opened up to the general public for some purposes? The per curiam decision in Flower v. United States, 407 U.S. 197 (1972), suggested that military bases might be treated as nontraditional public forums. There, the 7–2 decision reversed a conviction for distributing peace leaflets on a street within the boundaries of an Army base in San Antonio: "Whatever power the authorities may have to restrict general access to a military facility, here the fort commander chose not to exclude the public from the street where petitioner was arrested." But when the Court confronted the issue more fully four years later, in **Greer v. Spock**, 424 U.S. 828 (1976), the majority interpreted Flower narrowly.

The Spock decision upheld two regulations at Fort Dix, a large Army post in rural New Jersey, that barred political activities on the base: the first prohibited, inter alia, speeches and demonstrations of a partisan political nature; the second, distribution of literature without prior approval of the base commander. Justice STEWART's majority opinion emphasized that the business of a base such as Fort Dix was "to train soldiers, not to provide a public forum," and rejected any claim to a generalized constitutional right to "make political speeches or distribute leaflets" there. He observed that in Spock, unlike in Flower, the military authorities had never "abandoned any claim of special interest" in regulating political activities. Noting "the special constitutional function of the military in our national life," he stated: "The notion that federal military reservations, like municipal streets and parks, have traditionally served as a place for free public assembly and communication of thoughts by private citizens [is] historically and constitutionally false." After using these broad grounds to reject the facial challenges, the majority turned down the as-applied attacks with similar deference to the military. With respect to the ban on speeches and demonstrations, Justice Stewart noted that the regulation had been applied evenhandedly rather than discriminatorily, in accordance with a policy of "keeping official military activities there wholly free of entanglement with partisan political campaigns of any kind"—a policy "wholly consistent with the American constitutional tradition of a politically neutral military establishment under civilian control."

Justice POWELL's concurrence emphasized that access was sought to an "enclave of [the military] system that stands apart from and outside of many of the rules that govern ordinary civilian life in our country." In that context, "our inquiry is not limited to claims that the exercise of First Amendment rights is disruptive of base activity. We also must consider functional and symbolic incompatibility with the 'specialized society separate from civilian society' that has its home on the base." The requirement of prior approval to distribute literature, in his view, was justified not by the public interest in military neutrality, but rather by "the unique need of the military to 'insist upon a respect for duty and a discipline without counterpart in civilian life.' "

Justice BRENNAN's dissent, joined by Justice Marshall, argued that the challengers should be permitted to speak at Fort Dix even if the military installation was not a "public forum." "[The] determination that a locale is a 'public forum' has never been erected as an absolute prerequisite to all forms of demonstrative First Amendment activity. [Because] the permissibility of a certain form of public expression at a given locale may differ depending on whether it is asked if the locale is a public forum or if the form of expression is compatible with the activities occurring at the locale, it becomes apparent that there is need for a flexible approach. Otherwise, with the rigid characterization of a given locale as not a public forum, there is the danger that certain forms of public speech at the locale may be suppressed, even though they are basically compatible with the activities otherwise occurring at the locale." Applying his more flexible test, Justice Brennan concluded that leaflet distribution should be permitted "in those streets and lots unrestricted to civilian traffic," since those areas did not "differ in their nature and use from city streets and lots where open speech long has been protected." Political rallies posed more difficulty because of the "potential for disruption even in unrestricted areas," but not so much as "significantly to impair training or defense, thereby requiring its prohibition." Justice Brennan further argued that the ban was not necessary for military neutrality because no one would associate the speakers' causes with the military, and that allowing speech in unrestricted areas might even enhance neutrality because the military itself is "highly susceptible to politicization," and its isolated members would benefit from "the moderating influence of other ideas."

The Court reaffirmed its view of the special nature of military bases in **United States v. Albertini**, 472 U.S. 675 (1985). That case upheld the exclusion of an individual from Hickam Air Force Base in Hawaii after he had previously been barred for prior unlawful conduct. He sought to enter the base in order to engage in peaceful expressive activity during Hickam's annual open house, when the general public was allowed to enter. Justice O'Connor's majority opinion emphasized that Hickam had not become a public forum merely because the general public had been invited on that day and relied in part on O'Brien in sustaining Albertini's conviction for reentering the base after he had been barred. See also Brown v. Glines, 444 U.S. 348 (1980) (upholding Air Force regulations requiring service members to obtain approval from commanders before circulating petitions on bases). Are these military base cases explainable on the basis of the Court's typical extraordinary deference to military judgments in a range of constitutional contexts? Recall, for example, Rostker v. Goldberg, 453 U.S. 57 (1981) (finding no sex discrimination in exclusion of women from registration in anticipation of the draft); see also Goldman v. Weinberger (1986; p. 679 below) (finding no freedom of religion violation in applying an Air Force headgear regulation to bar wearing of yarmulke).

PUBLIC AND NONPUBLIC FORUMS

1.   *The types of forums.* At one time, commentators assumed that the Court categorized spaces into "traditional, quintessential" public forums, "designated" public forums, and "nonpublic" forums. In traditional public forums, such as streets and parks, content-based exclusions of speech must be necessary to serve a compelling state interest and narrowly drawn to achieve that end. Designated public forums are where the government opens public property for expressive activity. Since the government opens up these forums for expression, only reasonable time, place, and manner restrictions are permissible and content-based restrictions must be narrowly tailored to meet a compelling state interest. Nonpublic forums, like airport terminals, household mailboxes, and open areas in a military base, are public property which is not by tradition or designation a forum for public communication. See Perry Education Ass'n v. Perry Local Educators' Ass'n (1983; below p. 333).

There was considerable criticism of this classification scheme. See, e.g., Farber & Nowak, "The Misleading Nature of Public Forum Analysis: Content and Context in First Amendment Adjudication," 70 Va. L. Rev. 1219 (1984) ("Classification of public places as various types of forums has only confused judicial opinions by diverting attention from the real First Amendment [issues]—the First Amendment values and governmental interests involved in the case."); Tribe, Constitutional Choices (1985) (criticizing Perry as avoiding "a rigorous analysis of the viewpoint discrimination issue by focusing on the public forum analysis"). For the contrary view, see BeVier, "Rehabilitating Public Forum Doctrine: In Defense of Categories," 1993 Sup. Ct. Rev. 79 (arguing that the central function of the First Amendment is to prevent government distortion of public dialogue, not to enhance the amount of speech, and that "[t]he role of categorical analysis in public forum jurisprudence is to generalize about the kinds of places where denials of access tend systematically to trigger well-founded concerns about deliberate governmental abuse and distortion").

Since then, things have gotten considerably more complicated. First, the Court has been faced with applying forum analysis for non-physical institutional arrangements like the student activities fund in Rosenberger and access to student organization status as in Christian Legal Society v.

Martinez (2010; below p. 354) and cyberspace as in Packingham v. North Carolina (2017; p. 345). Second, the categories of forum appear to have shifted from "traditional," "designated," and "nonpublic" forum to something else. In Perry Education Ass'n v. Perry Local Educators' Ass'n (1983; below p. 333), first laying out the three part scheme, Justice White seemed to imply in a footnote that the limited public forum was a type of designated forum. But in a footnote to Christian Legal Society, Justice Ginsburg for the Court distinguished traditional public forum, designated public forum, and limited public forum analysis. Nonpublic forum went unmentioned.

Has the limited public forum been gradually added as a separate category to the original list of three? In Walker v. Texas Division, Sons of Confederate Veterans, (2015; below p. 347), the Court hinted at the existence of four forum categories. The Walker Court held that words or symbols on specialty license plates were government speech. Justice Breyer, writing for the majority, found that the specialty plates were not a "forum for private speech" and rejected the applicability of traditional, designated, limited, and nonpublic forums. Has the Court displaced the designated public forum, as some commentators have believed based on Justice White's original introduction of the view in Perry? See, e.g., Rohr, "First Amendment Fora Revisited: How Many Categories Are There?", 41 Nova L. Rev. 221, 226 (2017). Or does the Court now use the terms nonpublic forum and limited public forum synonymously, describing a setting governed by the requirement that the government regulation be reasonable and viewpoint neutral? Christian Legal Society suggests the latter: "[T]he Court has permitted restrictions on access to a limited public forum, [w]ith this key caveat: Any access barrier must be reasonable and viewpoint neutral." This description is essentially identical to Justice O'Connor's account of the nonpublic forum in Cornelius, where she wrote that "[c]ontrol over access to a nonpublic forum can be based on subject matter and speaker identity so long as the distinctions drawn are reasonable in light of the purpose served by the forum and are viewpoint neutral." This schema was endorsed in Justice Thomas's dissent in the denial of certiorari in Am. Freedom Def. Initiative v. King Cty., 577 U.S. 1202, 1202 (2016), where he wrote that a "limited public forum, [is] also called a nonpublic forum."

Thus, the Court increasingly seems not to speak of the nonpublic forum, and its legal treatment now seems to be the same as the limited public forum. Yet, lower courts continue to struggle to determine "what distinction, if any, exists between a 'designated public forum' and a 'limited public forum.'" Bowman v. White, 444 F.3d 967, 975 (8th Cir. 2006).

2. *Mailboxes.* In **U.S. Postal Service v. Council of Greenburgh Civic Ass'ns**, 453 U.S. 114 (1981), the Court rejected a First Amendment challenge to 18 U.S.C. § 1725, which prohibited the deposit of unstamped "mailable matter" in home letter boxes approved by the Postal Service. The statute was challenged by a group of civic associations who asserted that the ban on their delivering messages to local residents by placing unstamped notices and pamphlets in the letter boxes of private homes unduly inhibited their communications with the residents. Justice REHNQUIST, writing for the Court, found the First Amendment challenge without merit. Finding that a letter box "is not traditionally [a] 'public forum,'" he found it unnecessary to apply the principles governing time, place, and manner restrictions on the use of public forums: "property owned or controlled by the government which is *not* a public forum may be subject to a prohibition of speech, leafleting,

picketing, or other forms of communication without running afoul of the First Amendment [so long as the government] act[s] reasonably in imposing such restrictions, and the prohibition [is] content-neutral. § 1725 is both a reasonable and content-neutral regulation."

In rejecting the public-forum claim, Justice Rehnquist noted that a "letterbox provided by a postal customer which meets the Postal Service's specifications [becomes] part of the [Service's] nationwide system for the receipt and delivery of mail. [In] effect, the postal customer, although he pays for the physical components of the 'authorized depository,' agrees to abide by the Postal Service's regulations in exchange for the Postal Service agreeing to deliver and pick up his mail. [A] letter box, once designated an 'authorized depository,' does not [undergo] a transformation into a 'public forum' of some limited nature to which the First Amendment guarantees access to all comers." Justice Rehnquist contended that his opinion was consistent with Greer, Adderly, and Shaker Heights, which each "recognized that the First Amendment does not guarantee access to property simply because it is owned or controlled by the government."

Justice BRENNAN, concurring in the judgment, insisted that a letter box *is* a public forum because "the mails and the letter box are specifically used for the communication of information and ideas." But although he disagreed with the majority's mode of analysis, he would have nevertheless held that the law was a reasonable time, place and manner regulation. He noted that the restraint was "content-neutral" and that it advanced "a significant governmental interest—preventing loss of mail revenues." Moreover, there were "ample alternative channels for communication"—for example, placing circulars under doors or attaching them to doorknobs.

Justice MARSHALL dissented. He argued that "[e]ven if the Postal Service were not a public forum, [the] statute advanced in its aid is a law challenged as an abridgment of free expression. [The] question, then, is whether this statute burdens any First Amendment rights enjoyed by appellees. If so, it must be determined whether this burden is justified by a significant governmental interest substantially advanced by the statute." The Postal Service could not meet this standard, he argued, because "the statute's asserted purposes easily could be advanced by less intrusive alternatives, such as a nondiscriminatory permit requirement for depositing unstamped circulars in letter boxes." In any event, he argued, given "its pervasive and traditional use as purveyor of written communication, the Postal Service [may] properly be viewed as a [public forum]. For the Postal Service's very purpose is to facilitate communication, which surely differentiates it from the military bases, jails, and mass transportation discussed in cases relied on by the Court." Justice STEVENS, in a separate dissent, agreed with Justice Marshall's result, but on the different ground that letter boxes are private property and the law "interferes with the owner's receipt of information that he may want to receive" without adequate justification.

3. *Teachers' mailboxes.* In **Perry Education Ass'n v. Perry Local Educators' Ass'n**, 460 U.S. 37 (1983), the Court upheld a provision of a collective bargaining contract giving the incumbent teacher's union, the Perry Education Association (PEA), access to the local interschool mail system and teacher mailboxes, but denying that same access to rival groups, including the Perry Local Educators' Association (PLEA). The Court rejected PLEA's First Amendment challenge. Justice WHITE, writing for the Court,

acknowledged that the policy implicated the First Amendment. But, he wrote, "[t]he existence of a right of access to public property and the standard by which limitations upon such a right must be evaluated differ depending on the character of the property at issue." He explained:

"In places which by long tradition or by government fiat have been devoted to assembly and debate, the rights of the state to limit expressive activity are sharply circumscribed. At one end of the spectrum are [streets and parks. Hague v. CIO.] In these quintessential public forums, the government may not prohibit all communicative activity. For the state to enforce a content-based exclusion it must show that its regulation is necessary to serve a compelling state interest and that it is narrowly drawn to achieve that end. The state may also enforce regulations of the time, place, and manner of expression which are content-neutral, are narrowly tailored to serve a significant government interest, and leave open ample alternative channels of communication.

"A second category consists of public property which the state has opened for use by the public as a place for expressive activity. The Constitution forbids a state to enforce certain exclusions from a forum generally open to the public even if it was not required to create the forum in the first place. [E.g., Southeastern Promotions.][1] Although a state is not required to indefinitely retain the open character of the facility, as long as it does so it is bound by the same standards as apply to the traditional public forum.

"Public property which is not by tradition or designation a forum for public communication is governed by different standards. [Greenburgh.] [In] addition to time, place, and manner regulations, the state may reserve the forum for its intended purposes, communicative or otherwise, as long as the regulation on speech is reasonable and not an effort to suppress expression merely because public officials oppose the speaker's view. '[The] State, no less than a private owner of property, has power to preserve the property under its control for the use to which it is lawfully dedicated.' [Greenburgh; Greer; Adderley.]

"The school mail facilities at issue here fall within this third category [of nonpublic forums]. [The] interschool mail system is not a traditional public forum. [On] this point the parties agree. [The] internal mail system [is] not held open to the general public. It is instead PLEA's position that the school mail facilities have become a 'limited public forum' from which it may not be excluded because of the periodic use of the system by private non-school connected groups, and PLEA's own unrestricted access to the system prior to PEA's certification as exclusive representative. Neither of these arguments is persuasive. [The] schools do allow some outside organizations such as the YMCA, Cub Scouts, and other civic and church organizations to use the facilities. This type of selective access does not transform government property into a public forum. [Greer; Lehman.] Moreover, even if we assume that by granting access to [some groups], the school district has created a 'limited' public forum, the constitutional right of access would in any event extend only to other entities of similar character. While the school mail facilities thus might be a forum generally open for use [by] other organizations that engage in activities of interest and educational relevance

---

[1]   A public forum may be created for a limited purpose such as use by certain groups [e.g., student groups], or for the discussion of certain subjects [e.g., school board business]. [Footnote by Justice White.]

to students, they would not as a consequence be open to an organization such as PLEA, which is concerned with the terms and conditions of teacher employment.

"[Nor does the] access policy adopted by the Perry schools favor[ ] a particular viewpoint, that of the PEA, on labor relations, [in which case it would] be strictly scrutinized regardless of whether a public forum is involved. There is [no] indication that the school board intended to discourage one viewpoint and advance another. We believe it is more accurate to characterize the access policy as based on the *status* of the respective unions rather than their views. Implicit in the concept of the nonpublic forum is the right to make distinctions in access on the basis of subject matter and speaker identity.

"The differential access provided PEA and PLEA is reasonable because it is wholly consistent with the district's legitimate interest in 'preserv[ing] the property [for] the use to which it is lawfully dedicated.' [Greenburgh.] Use of school mail facilities enables PEA to perform effectively its obligations as exclusive representative of *all* Perry Township teachers. Conversely, PLEA does not have any official responsibility in connection with the school district and need not be entitled to the same rights of access to school mailboxes. [Moreover], exclusion of the rival union may reasonably be considered a means of insuring labor-peace within the [schools]. Finally, the reasonableness of the limitations on PLEA's access to the school mail system is also supported by the substantial alternative channels that remain open for union-teacher communication to take place. These means range from bulletin boards to meeting facilities to the United States mail. During election periods, PLEA is assured of equal access to all modes of communication. [On] government property that has not been made a public forum, not all speech is equally situated, and the state may draw distinctions which relate to the special purpose for which the property is used. [For] a school mail facility, the difference in status between the exclusive bargaining representative and its rival is such a distinction."

Justice BRENNAN dissented, joined by Justices Marshall, Powell, and Stevens: "[Because] the exclusive access provision in the collective bargaining agreement amounts to viewpoint discrimination that infringes the respondents' First Amendment rights and fails to advance any substantial state interest, I dissent. [According] to the Court, the petitioner's status as the exclusive bargaining representative provides a reasonable basis for the exclusive access policy. The Court fundamentally misperceives the essence of the respondents' claims. [This] case does not involve an 'absolute access' claim. It involves an 'equal access' claim. As such it does not turn on whether the internal school mail system is a 'public forum.' In focusing on the public forum issue, the Court disregards the First Amendment's central proscription against censorship, in the form of viewpoint discrimination, in any forum, public or nonpublic. [Addressing] the question of viewpoint discrimination directly, free of the Court's irrelevant public forum analysis, it is clear that the exclusive access policy discriminates on the basis of viewpoint. [The] only reason for [PEA] to seek an exclusive access policy is to deny its rivals access to an effective channel of communication. No other group is explicitly denied access to the mail system. In fact, [many] other groups have been granted access to the system. [The] board has agreed to amplify the speech of [PEA], while repressing the speech of [PLEA] based on [PLEA's] point of view. This sort of discrimination amounts to censorship and infringes the First Amendment rights of the respondents [without] further[ing] any substantial state interest."

Notice that, in a footnote describing the concept of the designated public forum, Justice White wrote that "[a] public forum may be created for a limited purpose such as use by certain groups, or for the discussion of certain subjects." This footnote inaugurated the confusing terminological relation between the "designated public forum" and the "limited public forum." Because it is described in a brief footnote, the limited public forum might seem to be a subset of the designated public forum or interchangeable with it; indeed, several subsequent commentators have treated the two as identical. See, e.g., Laycock, "Theology Scholarships, the Pledge of Allegiance, and Religious Liberty: Avoiding the Extremes but Missing the Liberty," 118 Harv. L. Rev. 155 (2004). Yet Justice White in Perry held that, in a designated public forum, the government "is bound by the same standards as apply to the traditional public forum" which seems discordant with his footnote statement that, in a limited public forum, the government may restrict speech according to subject matter. Perhaps as a result of this discord, the Court has recently described the designated public forum and the limited public forum as distinct and separate categories. See Christian Legal Soc'y v. Martinez (2010; p. 354 below).

4. *Charitable campaigns in federal offices.* **Cornelius v. NAACP Legal Defense & Ed. Fund**, 473 U.S. 788 (1985), was a 4–3 decision (Justices Marshall and Powell did not participate) that upheld the exclusion of political and advocacy groups from the Combined Federal Campaign (CFC), an annual charitable fundraising drive conducted in federal offices during working hours mainly through the voluntary efforts of federal employees. The Executive Order at issue limited the organizations that could participate in CFC to voluntary, tax-exempt, nonprofit charitable agencies that provide direct health and welfare services to individuals; the Order expressly excluded legal defense and political advocacy groups. Justice O'CONNOR's plurality opinion, following the tripartite classification of forums articulated in Perry, found the CFC (not the federal workplace generally) the relevant forum and held that it was a "nonpublic forum," not a "traditional" public forum or a "public forum created by government designation": "[The] government does not create a public forum by inaction or by permitting limited discourse, but only by intentionally opening a non-traditional forum for public discourse. [Perry.] Accordingly, the Court has looked to the policy and practice of the government to ascertain whether it intended to designate a place not traditionally open to assembly and debate as a public forum. The Court has also examined the nature of the property and its compatibility with expressive activity to discern the government's intent. [Not] every instrumentality used for communication, however, is a traditional public forum or a public forum by designation. [Greenburgh.] [We] will not find that a public forum has been created in the face of clear evidence of a contrary intent, nor will we infer that the government intended to create a public forum when the nature of the property is inconsistent with expressive activity."

Here, Justice O'Connor was not persuaded that the CFC was a "designated" public forum: "The government's consistent policy has been to limit participation in the CFC to 'appropriate' voluntary agencies. [Such] selective access, unsupported by evidence of a purposeful designation for public use, does not create a public forum. [Greer v. Spock.] Nor does the history of the CFC support a finding that the Government was motivated by an affirmative desire to provide an open forum for charitable solicitation in the federal workplace. [It] follows that the Government has the right to exercise control over access to the federal workplace in order to avoid interruptions to the performance of the duties of its employees."

Having determined that the CFC was a "nonpublic forum," Justice O'Connor held the exclusion only to a standard of reasonableness: "Control over access to a nonpublic forum can be based on subject matter and speaker identity so long as the distinctions drawn are reasonable in light of the purpose served by the forum and are viewpoint neutral. [Perry.] Although a speaker may be excluded from a nonpublic forum if he wishes to address a topic not encompassed within the purpose of the forum [Lehman] or if he is not a member of the class of speakers for whose especial benefit the forum was created [Perry], the government violates the First Amendment when it denies access to a speaker solely to suppress the point of view he espouses on an otherwise includible subject." She emphasized: "The Government's decision to restrict access to a nonpublic forum need only be *reasonable;* it need not be the most reasonable or the only reasonable limitation. In contrast to a public forum, a finding of strict incompatibility between the nature of the speech or the identity of the speaker and the functioning of the nonpublic forum is not mandated. [Cf. Perry; Lehman.] [Nor] is there a requirement that the restriction be narrowly tailored or that the Government's interest be compelling. The First Amendment does not demand unrestricted access to a nonpublic forum merely because use of that forum may be the most efficient means of delivering the speaker's message [Greenburgh.]"

Justice BLACKMUN dissented, joined by Justice Brennan. He objected to the majority's holding that, "when the Government acts as the holder of public property other than streets, parks, and similar places, the Government may do whatever it reasonably intends to do, so long as it does not intend to suppress a particular viewpoint." He argued that the CFC was a limited public forum, and that the government's exclusion of "speech that would be compatible with the intended uses of the property" triggered a demand for a "compelling governmental interest." Applying this analysis, he concluded that the asserted justifications "neither reserve the CFC for expressive activity compatible with the property nor serve any other compelling governmental interest." Moreover, he argued that the challenged exclusions were "blatantly viewpoint-based" because "Government employees may hear only from those charities that think that charitable goals can best be achieved within the confines of existing social policy and the status quo." Justice Stevens also submitted a dissent, arguing that the case could be disposed of without using "multitiered analysis" to label the forum, simply on the ground that it discriminated based on viewpoint.

Notice that in Cornelius, Justice O'Connor held that the CFC was a nonpublic forum, while Justice Blackmun would have held that it was a "limited public forum."

5. *Post office sidewalks.* Usually, streets and sidewalks are public forums on which speech restrictions demand a strong justification. But **United States v. Kokinda**, 497 U.S. 720 (1990), indicated that use of an area that *appears* to be a sidewalk does not necessarily assure the most careful scrutiny. The Court upheld a Postal Service prohibition of "soliciting" contributions on postal premises. The regulation was applied to soliciting by

volunteers for the National Democratic Policy Committee who had set up a table on the sidewalk near the entrance of the Bowie, Maryland, post office in order to collect contributions. As described by the lower court, the post office was a "freestanding" building, with its own sidewalk and parking lot. It was located on a major highway. "A sidewalk runs along the edge of the highway, separating the post office property from the street. To enter the post office, cars enter a driveway that traverses the public sidewalk and enter a parking lot that surrounds the post office building. Another sidewalk runs adjacent to the building itself, separating the parking lot from the building. Postal patrons must use [this] sidewalk to enter the post office. The sidewalk belongs to the post office and is used for no other purpose."

Justice O'CONNOR's plurality opinion, joined by Chief Justice Rehnquist and Justices White and Scalia, began by concluding that the postal "sidewalk" was not the kind of sidewalk that constituted a traditional public forum. Instead, she found that the postal sidewalk was a nonpublic forum and that the postal regulation was constitutional because viewpoint-neutral and reasonable as applied: "Respondents contend that although the sidewalk is on postal service property, because it is not distinguishable from the municipal sidewalk across the parking lot from the post office's entrance, it must be a traditional public forum and therefore subject to strict scrutiny. This argument is unpersuasive. [The] postal sidewalk at issue does not have the characteristics of public sidewalks traditionally open to expressive activity. The municipal sidewalk that runs parallel to the road in this case is a public passageway. The Postal Service's sidewalk is not such a thoroughfare. Rather, it leads only from the parking area to the front door of the post office." Although the postal entryways are open to the public, "that fact alone does not establish that such areas must be treated as traditional public fora." She noted that the Postal Service had not "expressly dedicated its sidewalks to any expressive activity." Instead, the sidewalk was "expressly dedicated to only one means of free communication: the posting of public notices on designated bulletin boards. [To] be sure, individuals and groups have been permitted to leaflet, speak, and picket on postal premises, [but] a practice of allowing some speech activities on public postal property [does] not add up to the dedication of postal property to speech activities. [Cornelius.]"

In finding the restriction "reasonable," Justice O'Connor emphasized what she called "a long-settled principle" that "governmental actions are subject to a lower level of First Amendment scrutiny" when the government is not acting "as lawmaker [but] rather as proprietor." She emphasized that Congress had wanted the Postal Service "to be run more like a business" than had its predecessor, the Post Office Department. Noting that regulation must merely be "reasonable" when Government acts in a proprietary capacity [Lehman], she found that "it is reasonable to restrict access [to] solicitation, because solicitation is inherently disruptive of the Postal Service's business." The plurality also found no impermissible content discrimination in singling out solicitation for special treatment.

Significantly, however, the "reasonableness" standard did not receive support from a majority of the Court. Justice KENNEDY, who had joined the Court after Cornelius, concurred only in the judgment and specifically distanced himself from the plurality's approach. He suggested that the walkway surrounding a post office "may be an appropriate place for the exercise of vital rights of expression. As society becomes more insular in character, it becomes essential to protect public places where traditional modes of speech [can] take place." However, he found it unnecessary to determine whether the sidewalk was a public or nonpublic forum, because in his view "the postal regulation [meets] the traditional standards we have applied to time, place, and manner restrictions of protected expression," citing Clark and Ward. "Given the Postal Service's past experience with expressive activity on its property, I cannot reject its judgment that in-person solicitation deserves different treatment from alternative forms of solicitation and expression."

Justice BRENNAN, joined by Justices Marshall and Stevens and in part by Justice Blackmun, dissented, criticizing the plurality's distinction between types of sidewalks: "[The plurality] insists, with logic that is both strained and formalistic, that the specific sidewalk at issue is not a public forum. This conclusion is unsupportable. [It] is only common sense that a public sidewalk adjacent to a public building to which citizens are freely admitted is a natural location for speech to occur. [It] is irrelevant that [this] sidewalk [may] have been constructed only to provide access to the [post office]. Public sidewalks, parks, and streets have been reserved for public use as forums for speech even though government has not constructed them for expressive purposes. Parks are usually constructed to beautify a city and to provide opportunities for recreation, rather than to afford a forum for soapbox orators or leafleteers; streets are built to facilitate transportation, not to enable protestors to conduct marches; and sidewalks are created with pedestrians in mind, not solicitors. [That] the walkway at issue is a sidewalk open and accessible to the general public is alone sufficient to identify it as a public forum. [Whatever] the proper application of public forum doctrine to novel situations [such as those in Cornelius and Perry], we ought not unreflectively transfer principles [developed] in those specialized and difficult contexts to traditional forums such as streets, sidewalks, and parks."

Justice Brennan added: "Even if I did not believe that the postal sidewalk is a 'traditional' public forum, I would find that it is a 'limited-purpose' forum from which respondents may not be excluded absent a showing of a compelling interest to which any exclusion is narrowly tailored." He insisted that the regulation could not pass muster under that requirement or the standard applicable to time, place, and manner regulations. He added: "Even if I did not believe that [this] sidewalk was a public forum, I nevertheless could not agree [that] the postal regulation [is] reasonable. [The] Postal Service does not subject to the same categorical prohibition many other types of speech presenting the same risk of disruption as solicitation, such as soapbox oratory, pamphleteering, [or] even flag-burning. [This] inconsistent treatment renders the prohibition on solicitation unreasonable."

6. *Airport terminals.* Shifting majorities in **International Society for Krishna Consciousness, Inc. (ISKCON) v. Lee**, 505 U.S. 672 (1992) and its companion case, **Lee v. ISKCON**, 505 U.S. 830 (1992), upheld a ban on the solicitation of money in a public airport terminal, but struck down a ban on the sale or distribution of literature there. The Port Authority operates the three major airports in the New York metropolitan area. It had promulgated rules restricting solicitation and leafleting activities to sidewalks outside the airports' terminals. The Court considered a challenge

by ISKCON to these rules. The multiple opinions produced three holdings by different configurations of Justices:

First, by a vote of 5–4, the Court found airport terminals to be *nonpublic forums*. Chief Justice REHNQUIST, writing for the Court on this point, stated that, "given the lateness with which the modern air terminal has made its appearance, it hardly qualifies for the description of having 'immemorially . . . time out of mind' been held in the public trust and used for purposes of expressive activity. [Hague.] [Nor] can we say that [airport] terminals generally have been intentionally opened by their operators to [expressive] activity; the frequent and continuing litigation evidencing the operators' objections belies any such claim. [Airports] are commercial establishments funded by users fees and designed to make a regulated profit," and their purpose is "the facilitation of passenger air travel, not the promotion of expression." Accordingly, "[t]he restrictions here challenged [need] only satisfy a requirement of reasonableness. [Kokinda, Cornelius.]"

Justice KENNEDY's partial concurrence disagreed that airports were nonpublic forums, and was joined on this point by Justices Blackmun, Stevens and Souter: "Our public forum doctrine ought not to be a jurisprudence of categories rather than ideas or convert what was once an analysis protective of expression into one which grants the government authority to restrict speech by fiat." Justice Kennedy's opinion noted the importance of public forums to democracy: "At the heart of our jurisprudence lies the principle that in a free nation citizens must have the right to gather and speak with other persons in public places." He also objected to the majority's deference to the airport authorities' managerial role: "The Court [reintroduces] today into our First Amendment law a strict doctrinal line between the proprietary and regulatory functions of government which I thought had been abandoned long ago. [Compare Davis with Hague; Schneider; Grayned.] [But a] fundamental tenet of our Constitution is that the government is subject to constraints which private persons are not." Finally, he charged that "[t]he Court's analysis rests on an inaccurate view of history. The notion that traditional public forums are property which have public discourse as their principal purpose is a most doubtful fiction. The types of property that we have recognized as the quintessential public forums are streets, parks, and sidewalks. It would seem apparent that the principal purpose of streets and sidewalks, like airports, is to facilitate transportation, not public discourse. [Similarly], the purpose for the creation of public parks may be as much for beauty and open space as for discourse. Thus under the Court's analysis, even the quintessential public forums would appear to lack the necessary elements of what the Court defines as a public forum."

Justice Kennedy urged an alternative approach: "In my view the policies underlying the doctrine cannot be given effect unless we recognize that open, public spaces and thoroughfares which are suitable for discourse may be public forums, whatever their historical pedigree and without concern for a precise classification of the property. [Without] this recognition our forum doctrine retains no relevance in times of fast-changing technology and increasing insularity. In a country where most citizens travel by automobile, and parks all too often become locales for crime rather than social intercourse, our failure to recognize the possibility that new types of government property may be appropriate forums for speech will lead to a serious curtailment of our expressive activity. One of the places left in our mobile society that is suitable for discourse is a metropolitan airport. [If] the objective, physical characteristics of the property at issue and the actual public access and uses which have been permitted by the government indicate that expressive activity would be appropriate and compatible with those uses, the property is a public forum.

"[Under] this analysis, it is evident that the public spaces of the Port Authority's airports are public forums. [First, there are] physical similarities between the Port Authority's airports and public streets. [Airports have] broad, public thoroughfares full of people and lined with stores and other commercial activities. [Second,] the airport areas involved here are open to the public without restriction. [Third,] and perhaps most important, [when] adequate time, place, and manner regulations are in place, expressive activity is quite compatible with the uses of major airports."

Justice SOUTER, joined by Justices Blackmun and Stevens, filed a separate partial concurrence and partial dissent agreeing with Justice Kennedy that airport terminals should be analyzed as public forums: "To treat the class of such forums as closed by their description as 'traditional,' taking that word merely as a charter for examining the history of the particular public property claimed as a forum, has no warrant in a Constitution whose values are not to be left behind in the city streets that are no longer the only focus of our community life. If that were the line of our direction, we might as well abandon the public forum doctrine altogether."

In a second holding, the Court upheld the *solicitation ban* by a vote of 6–3. Chief Justice REHNQUIST again wrote for the Court on this point: "We have on many prior occasions noted the disruptive effect that solicitation may have on business. 'Solicitation requires action by those who would respond: The individual solicited must decide whether or not to contribute (which itself might involve reading the solicitor's literature or hearing his pitch), and then, having decided to do so, reach for a wallet, search it for money, write a check, or produce a credit card.' [Kokinda; see Heffron.] Passengers who wish to avoid the solicitor may have to alter their path, slowing both themselves and those around them. The result is that the normal flow of traffic is impeded. This is especially so in an airport, where [delays] may be particularly costly. [In] addition, face-to-face solicitation presents risks of duress that are an appropriate target of regulation. The skillful, and unprincipled, solicitor can target the most vulnerable, including those accompanying children or those suffering physical impairment and who cannot easily avoid the solicitation. The unsavory solicitor can also commit fraud through concealment of his affiliation or through deliberate efforts to shortchange those who agree to purchase. Compounding this problem is the fact that, in an airport, the targets of such activity frequently are on tight schedules. This in turn makes such visitors unlikely to stop and formally complain to airport authorities. As a result, the airport faces considerable difficulty in achieving its legitimate interest in monitoring solicitation activity to assure that travelers are not interfered with unduly." Noting that "[t]he Port Authority has concluded that its interest in monitoring the activities can best be accomplished by limiting solicitation and distribution to the sidewalk areas outside the terminals," Justice Rehnquist concluded "that the solicitation ban is reasonable."

Justice O'CONNOR, who had joined the majority in finding airports to be nonpublic forums, concurred in the holding that the solicitation ban was constitutional, but wrote separately to emphasize that the fact that "airports are not public fora [does] not mean that the government can restrict speech in whatever way it likes." In her view, some inquiry into a nonpublic forum's "characteristic nature and function" was still required. Even taking into account that an airport is "multipurpose," operating more like "a shopping mall" than like a jail, mailbox, or post office sidewalk, however, she found that "the ban on solicitation is reasonable. Face-to-face solicitation is incompatible with the airport's functioning in a way that the other, permitted activities are not. '[As] residents of metropolitan areas know from daily experience, confrontation by a person asking for money disrupts passage and is more intrusive and intimidating than an encounter with a person giving out information.' [Kokinda.] The record in this case confirms that the problems of congestion and fraud that we have identified with solicitation in other contexts have also proved true in the airports' experience."

Justice KENNEDY provided a sixth vote to uphold the solicitation ban, finding that, even though in his view an airport was a public forum, the solicitation ban satisfied the appropriately heightened scrutiny: "The regulation may be upheld as either a reasonable time, place, and manner restriction, or as a regulation directed at the nonspeech element of expressive conduct. The two standards have considerable overlap in a case like this one. [Solicitation] is a form of protected speech. If the Port Authority's solicitation regulation prohibited all speech which requested the contribution of funds, I would conclude that it was a direct, content-based restriction of speech in clear violation of the First Amendment. The Authority's regulation does not prohibit all solicitation, however; it prohibits the 'solicitation and receipt of funds.' I do not understand this regulation to prohibit all speech that solicits funds. [The] regulation permits expression that solicits funds, but limits the manner of that expression to forms other than the immediate receipt of money.

"So viewed, [the] Port Authority's rule survives our test for speech restrictions in the public forum. In-person solicitation of funds, when combined with immediate receipt of that money, creates a risk of fraud and duress which is well recognized, and which is different in kind from other forms of expression or conduct. [Because] the Port Authority's solicitation ban is directed at these abusive practices and not at any particular message, idea, or form of speech, the regulation is a content-neutral rule serving a significant government interest. [The] regulation does not burden any broader category of speech or expressive conduct than is the source of the evil sought to be avoided. [And] the Port Authority has left open ample alternative channels for the communication of the message which is an aspect of solicitation."

Justice SOUTER, joined by Justices Blackmun and Stevens, dissented from the judgment upholding the solicitation ban, finding the ban not narrowly tailored to preventing coercion because, "[w]hile a solicitor can be insistent, a pedestrian on the street or airport concourse can simply walk away or walk on," and finding it not narrowly tailored to preventing fraud because the Port Authority had available less restrictive alternatives such as prohibiting fraudulent misrepresentations directly and imposing disclosure requirements on solicitors.

In its third holding, by a vote of 5–4, the Court invalidated the *ban on sale or distribution of literature* in the airport terminals. Justice KENNEDY concurred in the judgment on this issue, joined by Justices Blackmun, Stevens, and Souter: "[A] grant of plenary power allows the government to tilt the dialogue heard by the public, to exclude many, more marginal voices. [We] have long recognized that the right to distribute flyers and literature lies at the heart of the liberties guaranteed by the Speech and Press Clauses of the First Amendment. [Schneider.] The Port Authority's rule, which prohibits almost all such activity, is among the most restrictive possible of those liberties. [I] have no difficulty deciding the regulation cannot survive the [stringent] rules applicable to regulations in public forums. The regulation is not drawn in narrow terms and it does not leave open ample alternative channels for communication. The Port Authority's concerns with the problem of congestion can be addressed through narrow restrictions on the time and place of expressive activity." Justice O'CONNOR, concurring in the judgment, provided the fifth vote to invalidate the distribution ban. She stated that the distribution ban was impermissible even under the lenient "reasonableness" test she and the majority viewed as applicable to nonpublic forums: "While the difficulties posed by solicitation in a nonpublic forum are sufficiently obvious that its regulation may 'ring of common-sense,' the same is not necessarily true of leafletting. '[The] distribution of literature does not require that the recipient stop in order to receive the message the speaker wishes to convey; instead the recipient is free to read the message at a later time.'"

Chief Justice REHNQUIST, joined by Justices White, Scalia, and Thomas, dissented from the judgment invalidating the distribution ban: "Leafletting presents risks of congestion similar to those posed by solicitation. The weary, harried, or hurried traveler may have no less desire and need to avoid the delays generated by having literature foisted upon him than he does to avoid delays from a financial solicitation. [Moreover,] those who accept material may often simply drop it on the floor once out of the leafletter's range, creating an eyesore, a safety hazard, and additional clean-up work for airport staff." Thus, he concluded that "the distribution ban, no less than the solicitation ban, is reasonable."

7. *Non-physical limited public forums.* In Rosenberger v. Rector (1995; p. 410 below), the University of Virginia maintained a student activities fund (SAF), funded by mandatory payments of $14 per semester by all students. Qualified student organizations engaged in activities "related to the educational purpose of the University of Virginia" were authorized to submit expenses to the fund for payment. Among these organizations were "student news, information, opinion, entertainment, or academic communications media groups." The SAF was not available to support "religious activities, philanthropic contributions and activities, political activities, activities that would jeopardize the University's tax-exempt status, those which involve payment of honoraria or similar fees, or social entertainment or related expenses." A student group that published a magazine called "Wide Awake," dedicated to advancing "the Christian perspective," claimed that the SAF challenged the exclusion of religious activities as viewpoint discrimination.

In granting their claim, Justice KENNEDY addressed the question of the limited public forum: "The necessities of confining a forum to the limited and legitimate purposes for which it was created may justify the State in reserving it for certain groups or for the discussion of certain topics. Once it has opened a limited forum, however, the State must respect the lawful boundaries it has itself set. The State may not exclude speech where its distinction is not 'reasonable in light of the purpose served by the forum,' nor may it discriminate against speech on the basis of its viewpoint. Thus, in determining whether the State is acting to preserve the limits of the forum it has created so that the exclusion of a class of speech is legitimate, we have observed a distinction between, on the one hand, content discrimination, which may be permissible if it preserves the purposes of that limited forum, and, on the other hand, viewpoint discrimination, which is presumed impermissible when directed against speech otherwise within the forum's limitations.

"The SAF is a forum more in a metaphysical than in a spatial or geographic sense, but the same principles are applicable. See, e.g., Perry (forum analysis of a school mail system); Cornelius, (forum analysis of charitable contribution program). The most recent and most apposite case is our decision in Lamb's Chapel [1993; p. 361 below]. There, a school district had opened school facilities for use after school hours by community groups for a wide variety of social, civic, and recreational purposes. The district, however, had enacted a formal policy against opening facilities to groups for religious purposes. Invoking its policy, the district rejected a request from a group desiring to show a film series addressing various child-rearing questions from a 'Christian perspective.' There was no indication in the record in Lamb's Chapel that the request to use the school facilities was 'denied, for any reason other than the fact that the presentation would have been from a religious perspective.' "

In both Perry and Cornelius, the Court analyzed non-physical forums and held that the speech restrictions were permissible and not viewpoint discrimination. In Rosenberger, the Court for the first time held that there was viewpoint discrimination in what Justice Kennedy called a "metaphysical" forum. The Court analogized the non-physical forum to physical space in a school that had been opened "for a wide variety of social, civic, and recreational purposes."

This analogy applies to the internet. The Court first tackled the regulation of online speech in **Reno v. American Civil Liberties Union**, 521 U.S. 844 (1991). Without squarely addressing the traditional forum dichotomy, the Court unanimously held that a provision of the Communications Decency Act prohibiting anyone from knowingly sending minors materials that "depicts or describes, in terms patently offensive as measured by contemporary community standards, sexual or excretory activities or organs" violated the First Amendment. Justice Stevens, writing for the Court, stated that the court was "persuaded that the CDA lacks the precision that the First Amendment requires when a statute regulates the content of speech." He continued: "In order to deny minors access to potentially harmful speech, the CDA effectively suppresses a large amount of speech that adults have a constitutional right to receive and to address to one another. That burden on adult speech is unacceptable if less restrictive alternatives would be at least as effective in achieving the legitimate purpose that the statute was enacted to serve. . . . It is true that we have repeatedly recognized the governmental interest in protecting children from harmful materials. But that interest does not justify an unnecessarily broad suppression of speech addressed to adults. As we have explained, the Government may not reduce the adult population to only what is fit for children. Regardless of the strength of the government's interest in protecting children, the level of discourse reaching a mailbox simply cannot be limited to that which would be suitable for a sandbox."

In **Packingham v. North Carolina**, 582 U.S. ___, 137 S. Ct. 1730 (2017), the Court inched closer to answering whether the internet is a public forum. The Court struck down a North Carolina law prohibiting registered sex offenders from accessing social media sites. Justice Kennedy, writing for the majority, traced the mechanics of the forum doctrine: "A fundamental principle of the First Amendment is that all persons have access to places where they can speak and listen, and then, after reflection, speak and listen once more. The Court has sought to protect the right to speak in this spatial context. A basic rule, for example, is that a street or a park is a quintessential forum for the exercise of First Amendment Rights. Even in the modern era, these places are still essential venues for public gatherings to celebrate some views, to protest others, or simply to learn and inquire. While in the past there may have been difficulty in identifying the important places (in a spatial sense) for the exchange of views, today the answer is clear. It is cyberspace—the vast democratic forums of the Internet in general, and social media in particular." He emphasized that social media facilitates low-cost communication to debate, seek employment, and participate in politics. Yet he cautioned that "While we now may be coming to the realization that the Cyber Age is a revolution of historic proportions, we cannot appreciate yet its full dimensions and vast potential to alter how we think, express ourselves, and define who we want to be. The forces and directions of the Internet are so new, so protean, and so far reaching that courts must be conscious that what they say today might be obsolete tomorrow." Declining to define the internet squarely as a public forum in the analytical sense, Justice Kennedy simply described social media as "the modern public square" that remains a "principal source[ ] for knowing current events, checking ads for employment, speaking and listening."

The remaining ambiguity is evident in Justice Alito's concurrence. " Agreeing with the majority that the North Carolina statute "ha[d] a very broad reach and cover[ed] websites that are ill suited for use in stalking or abusing children," he cautioned that "if the entirety of the internet or even just social media sites are the 21st century equivalent of public streets and parks, then States may have little ability to restrict the sites that may be visited by even the most dangerous sex offenders."

Reno and Packingham represent two of the few instances the Supreme Court has addressed the constitutionality of restrictions on internet speech. Lower courts more routinely examine such cases. In **Knight First Amendment Institute v. Trump**, 302 F. Supp. 3d 541 (S.D.N.Y. 2018), a group of Twitter users blocked by President Trump's personal Twitter account sued that blocking access to the page constituted a violation under the First Amendment. Judge Buchwald held that parts of President Trump's personal Twitter page, specifically the content of the tweets, timeline of the account's tweets, and interactive space of each tweet, were a designated public forum. Judge Buchwald first assessed whether Twitter is amenable to forum analysis. "To potentially qualify as a forum, the space in question must be owned or controlled by the government" and whether the forum analysis is consistent with "the purpose, structure, and intended use" of the space. Finding both in the affirmative, Judge Buchwald then proceeded to classify the Twitter page as a designated public forum. She found that the "interactive space of a tweet" sent by President Trump was not a traditional public forum, given the lack of historical practice of the space being used for public expression. Referring to the Court's decisions in Reno and Packingham, Judge Buchwald noted that while the Court had analogized the internet to "essential venues of public gatherings of streets and parks, the lack of historical practice is dispositive." Judge Buchwald considered the interactive Twitter space to be a designated public forum, as the account is generally accessible to the public at large such that any person can view his tweets and anyone who wants to follow the account can do so unless the person has been blocked. Finally, Judge Buchwald found that the blocking constituted impermissible viewpoint discrimination.

The Second Circuit upheld the district court. After Donald Trump was no longer president, the Supreme Court in **Biden v. Knight First Amendment Institute**, 141 S. Ct. 1220 (2021), granted certiorari, vacated the Second Circuit's judgment and sent the case back to it with instructions to dismiss it as moot.

Justice THOMAS concurred to offer his own views on the issues: "[Applying] old doctrines to new digital platforms is rarely straightforward. [Some] aspects of Mr. Trump's account resemble a constitutionally protected public forum. But it seems rather odd to say that something is a government forum when a private company has unrestricted authority to do away with it. The disparity between Twitter's control and Mr. Trump's control is stark, to say the least. Mr. Trump blocked several people from interacting with his messages. Twitter barred Mr. Trump not only from interacting with a few users, but removed him from the entire platform, thus barring *all* Twitter users from interacting with his messages. Under its terms of service, Twitter can remove any person from the platform—including the President of the United States—at any time for any or no reason.

"[Today's] digital platforms provide avenues for historically unprecedented amounts of speech, including speech by government actors. Also unprecedented, however, is the concentrated control of so much speech in the hands of a few private parties. We will soon have no choice but to address how our legal doctrines apply to highly concentrated, privately owned information infrastructure such as digital platforms. [If] part of the problem is private, concentrated control over online content and platforms available to the public, then part of the solution may be found in doctrines that limit the right of a private company to exclude. Historically, at least two legal doctrines limited a company's right to exclude. First, our legal system and its British predecessor have long subjected certain businesses, known as common carriers, to special regulations, including a general requirement to serve all comers. [In] exchange for regulating transportation and communication industries, governments—both State and Federal—have sometimes given common carriers special government favors. For example, governments have tied restrictions on a carrier's ability to reject clients to immunity from certain types of suits or to regulations that make it more difficult for other companies to compete with the carrier (such as franchise licenses). By giving these companies special privileges, governments place them into a category distinct from other companies and closer to some functions, like the postal service, that the State has traditionally undertaken. Second, governments have limited a company's right to exclude when that company is a public accommodation. This concept—related to common-carrier law—applies to companies that hold themselves out to the public but do not carry freight, passengers, or communications. It also applies regardless of the company's market power. Internet platforms of course have their own First Amendment interests, but regulations that might affect speech are valid if they would have been permissible at the time of the founding. The long history in this country and in England of restricting the exclusion right of common carriers and places of public accommodation may save similar regulations today from triggering heightened scrutiny— especially where a restriction would not prohibit the company from speaking or force the company to endorse the speech."

8. *License plates.* In **Walker v. Texas Division, Sons of Confederate Veterans, Inc.**, 576 U.S. 200 (2015), the Court considered a Texas automotive license plate scheme that gave organizations or individuals the chance to design a particular "specialty plate" by proposing a plate design comprising a slogan, a graphic, or (most commonly) both. If the Texas Department of Motor Vehicles Board approved the design, the State would make it available for display on vehicles registered in Texas. The Texas Division of the Sons of Confederate Veterans proposed a specialty license plate design featuring a Confederate battle flag. The Board rejected the proposal, and the Sons of Confederate Veterans challenged the decision as viewpoint discrimination in a limited public forum.

The Court upheld the State's decision by a vote of 5–4. Justice BREYER wrote for the Court: "When government speaks, it is not barred by the Free Speech Clause from determining the content of what it says. [In] our view, specialty license plates issued pursuant to Texas's statutory scheme convey government speech. Our reasoning rests primarily on our analysis in Pleasant Grove v. Summum [(2009); p. 364 below]. [First], the history of license plates shows that, insofar as license plates have conveyed more than state names and vehicle identification numbers, they long have communicated messages from the States. [Second], Texas license plate designs are often closely identified in the public mind with the state. Each Texas license plate is a government article serving the governmental purposes of vehicle registration and identification. The governmental nature of the plates is clear from their faces: The State places the name 'TEXAS' in large letters at the top of every plate. [Texas] license plates are, essentially, government IDs. And issuers of ID 'typically do not permit' the placement on their IDs of 'message[s] with which they do not wish to be associated.'

"Indeed, a person who displays a message on a Texas license plate likely intends to convey to the public that the State has endorsed that message. If not, the individual could simply display the message in question in larger letters on a bumper sticker right next to the plate. But the individual prefers a license plate design to the purely private speech expressed through bumper stickers. That may well be because Texas's license plate designs convey government agreement with the message displayed.

"Third, Texas maintains direct control over the messages conveyed on its specialty plates. [The] State has rejected at least a dozen proposed designs. [This] final approval authority allows Texas to choose how to present itself and its constituency. Thus, Texas offers plates celebrating the many educational institutions attended by its citizens. But it need not issue plates deriding schooling. Texas offers plates that pay tribute to the Texas citrus industry. But it need not issue plates praising Florida's oranges as far better. And Texas offers plates that say 'Fight Terrorism.' But it need not issue plates promoting al Qaeda.

"[We] have previously used what we have called forum analysis to evaluate government restrictions on purely private speech that occurs on government property. But forum analysis is misplaced here. Because the

State is speaking on its own behalf, the First Amendment strictures that attend the various types of government-established forums do not apply.

"[We] conclude that Texas's specialty license plates are not a nonpublic forum which exists where the government is acting as a proprietor, managing its internal operations. With respect to specialty license plate designs, Texas is not simply managing government property, but instead is engaging in expressive conduct. [The] fact that private parties take part in the design and propagation of a message does not extinguish the governmental nature of the message or transform the government's role into that of a mere forum-provider. [Additionally], the fact that Texas vehicle owners pay annual fees in order to display specialty license plates does not imply that the plate designs are merely a forum for private speech."

Justice ALITO dissented, joined by Chief Justice Roberts and Justices Scalia and Kennedy. He would have found the State to have created a limited public forum in which it could not discriminate based on viewpoint. "Here is a test," he wrote. "Suppose you sat by the side of a Texas highway and studied the license plates on the vehicles passing by. You would see, in addition to the standard Texas plates, an impressive array of specialty plates. (There are now more than 350 varieties.) You would likely observe plates that honor numerous colleges and universities. You might see plates bearing the name of a high school, a fraternity or sorority, the Masons, the Knights of Columbus, the Daughters of the American Revolution, a realty company, a favorite soft drink, a favorite burger restaurant, and a favorite NASCAR driver.

"As you sat there watching these plates speed by, would you really think that the sentiments reflected in these specialty plates are the views of the State of Texas and not those of the owners of the cars?

"[While] all license plates unquestionably contain *some* government speech, [the] State of Texas has converted the remaining space on its specialty plates into little mobile billboards on which motorists can display their own messages. And what Texas did here was to reject one of the messages that members of a private group wanted to post on some of these little billboards because the State thought that many of its citizens would find the message offensive. That is blatant viewpoint discrimination.

"[The] Court badly misunderstands Summum. [Governments] have long used monuments as a means of expressing a government message. [There] is no history of landowners allowing their property to be used by third parties as the site of large permanent monuments that do not express messages that the landowners wish to convey. [And] spatial limitations played a prominent part in our analysis. [These] characteristics [are] not present in Texas's specialty plate program.

"[The] Confederate battle flag is a controversial symbol. [The] Board rejected the plate design because it concluded that many Texans would find the flag symbol offensive. That was pure viewpoint discrimination. [Many] other specialty plates have the potential to irritate and perhaps even infuriate those who see them. Texas allows a plate with the words 'Choose Life,' but the State of New York rejected such a plate because the message '[is] so incredibly divisive.' [Allowing] States to reject specialty plates based on their potential to offend is viewpoint discrimination."

Notice that Justice Thomas joined the Court's majority without explanation. Why? Might his vote be connected to his opinion in Virginia v. Black (2003; p. 121)?

9. *The special problem of solicitation.* Is solicitation of funds speech protected by the First Amendment? The Court has held as much in invalidating various restrictions on solicitation. See, e.g., Murdock v. Pennsylvania, 319 U.S. 105 (1943) (flat tax); Hynes v. Mayor of Oradell, 425 U.S. 610 (1976) (licensing requirement); Schaumburg v. Citizens for a Better Environment, 444 U.S. 620 (1980) (overhead limit). In Schaumburg, the Court stated that "charitable appeals for funds [involve] a variety of speech interests—communication of information, the dissemination and propagation of views and ideas, and the advocacy of causes—that are within the protection of the First Amendment." But in Kokinda and ISKCON, the Court readily deferred to government bans on solicitation on public property, suggesting that solicitation causes unique harms. These cases emphasize that solicitation poses greater risk to crowd control than other modes of expression because those solicited must stop and reach for money. They also suggest that solicitation raises a danger of fraud that will be difficult to police except by a prophylactic ban.

Are these problems unique to the settings of "nonpublic forums" such as airports and post office sidewalks? Could a city ban solicitation on all streets and sidewalks? Recall that the Court upheld a solicitation ban throughout the open thoroughfares of the Minnesota State Fair in Heffron v. ISKCON (1981; p. 298), relying on conventional time, place, and manner analysis. Is the solicitation ban in Heffron distinguishable from a citywide solicitation ban because a fair is more enclosed than city streets? Because a citywide ban is broader? Or do the special problems of solicitation emphasized by the Justices in Heffron, Kokinda, and ISKCON suggest that even a citywide ban on in-person solicitation on the streets might be upheld?

Consider in light of these questions the issue of whether begging in public places implicates the First Amendment. Does begging communicate information or advocate a cause? Is it distinguishable for First Amendment purposes from commercial sales? On commercial solicitation, see Breard v. Alexandria, 341 U.S. 622 (1951) (upholding an ordinance barring door-to-door solicitation for magazine subscriptions without the prior consent of the homeowners). Even if it is protected expression, does begging trigger government interests similar to those found sufficient in Kokinda and ISKCON? For the view that begging is protected speech and that most restrictions on it are unconstitutional, see Hershkoff & Cohen, "Begging to Differ: The First Amendment and the Right to Beg," 104 Harv. L. Rev. 896 (1991). For an argument for government leeway to regulate the public location of begging, see Ellickson, "Controlling Chronic Misconduct in City Spaces: Of Panhandlers, Skid Rows, and Public Space Zoning," 105 Yale L.J. 1165 (1996).

Note that ISKCON, while upholding the airport solicitation ban, invalidated a ban on the *sale* or distribution of literature at airports. Is the sale of literature more like the distribution of leaflets or the solicitation of funds? If sales of charitable literature are allowed in a public place, must sales of other items be granted equal access? What about sales of other expressive items, such as commemorative key rings or message-bearing T-shirts? Would a ban on all peddling in public streets implicate the First Amendment as applied to such sales? Can government draw any lines short of a flat ban without discriminating impermissibly on the basis of the expressive content of the merchandise? Justice Kennedy, who along with Justice O'Connor was one of only two justices to vote for both results in ISKCON, stated in his partial concurrence: "Much of what I have said about the solicitation of funds may seem to apply to the sale of literature, but the differences between the two activities are of sufficient significance to require they be distinguished for constitutional purposes. [The] danger of a fraud arising from such sales is much more limited than from pure solicitation, because in the case of a sale the nature of the exchange tends to be clearer to both parties. [And] the flat ban on sales of literature leaves open fewer alternative channels of communication [as] sales of literature must be completed in one transaction to be workable."

10. *Candidate debate on public television.* In **Arkansas Educational Television Commission (AETC) v. Forbes**, 523 U.S. 666 (1998), the Court rejected a free speech challenge to the exclusion of a candidate from a candidate debate televised by a public broadcasting station. The challenge was brought by Ralph Forbes, who had gained enough signatures to run on the ballot as an independent for Arkansas's third congressional district seat, but was regarded by the debate producers as lacking enough popular support to warrant inclusion in the debate along with the Democratic and Republican candidates. Justice KENNEDY, writing the 6–3 decision of the Court, upheld the exclusion, finding that "the candidate debate was subject to constitutional constraints applicable to nonpublic fora under our forum precedents," but that "the broadcaster's decision to exclude the candidate was a reasonable, viewpoint-neutral exercise of journalistic discretion" that satisfied the First Amendment.

Justice Kennedy cautioned that, "having first arisen in the context of streets and parks, the public forum doctrine should not be extended in a mechanical way to the very different context of public television broadcasting," where "broad rights of access for outside speakers would be antithetical, as a general rule, to the discretion that stations and their editorial staff must exercise to fulfill their journalistic purpose and statutory obligations." Thus First Amendment obligations might not apply at all to most public television programming. But the First Amendment does apply in the limited context of publicly televised candidate debates, he wrote, because they are "by design a forum for political speech by the candidates" and have "exceptional significance in the electoral process."

The issue then was whether Forbes's exclusion from the debate was subject to the stricter standards applicable to a designated public forum or the more deferential standards applicable to a nonpublic forum, and Justice Kennedy concluded that nonpublic forum rules applied here: "Under our precedents, the AETC debate was not a designated public forum. To create a forum of this type, the government must intend to make the property 'generally available' to a class of speakers. [Widmar.] [The] government does not create a designated public forum when it does no more than reserve eligibility for access to the forum to a particular class of speakers, whose members must then, as individuals, 'obtain permission,' to use it. [Perry, Cornelius.]" Under this test, he reasoned, "the debate was a nonpublic forum": "Here, the debate did not have an open-microphone format. [AETC] did not make its debate generally available to candidates for Arkansas' Third Congressional District seat. Instead, [AETC] reserved eligibility for participation in the debate to candidates for the Third Congressional District seat (as opposed to some other seat). At that point, [AETC] made candidate-by-candidate determinations as to which of the eligible candidates would participate in the debate." Justice Kennedy suggested that this "distinction between general and selective access furthers First Amendment interests. By recognizing the distinction, we encourage the government to open its property to some expressive activity in cases where, if faced with an all-or-nothing choice, it might not open the property at all." Under the standards applicable to nonpublic forums, the majority found Forbes's exclusion reasonable and viewpoint-neutral: "There is no substance to Forbes' suggestion that he was excluded because his views were unpopular or out of the mainstream. His own objective lack of support, not his platform, was the criterion."

Justice STEVENS dissented, joined by Justices Souter and Ginsburg: "[T]he First Amendment will not tolerate arbitrary definitions of the scope of the forum. [The] dispositive issue in this case [is] not whether AETC created a designated public forum or a nonpublic forum, as the Court concludes, but whether AETC defined the contours of the debate forum with sufficient specificity to justify the exclusion of a ballot-qualified candidate." Justice Stevens analogized AETC's decision to exclude Forbes to the exercise of impermissibly standardless discretion to exclude speakers from the public forum: "No written criteria cabined the discretion of the AETC staff. Their subjective judgment about a candidate's 'viability' or 'newsworthiness' allowed them wide latitude either to permit or to exclude a third participant in any debate. [The] importance of avoiding arbitrary or viewpoint-based exclusions from political debates militates strongly in favor of requiring the controlling state agency to use (and adhere to) pre-established, objective criteria to determine who among qualified candidates may participate."

11. *Public libraries.* In **United States v. American Library Ass'n**, 539 U.S. 194 (2003), the Court upheld by a vote of 6–3 the Children's Internet Protection Act (CIPA), under which a public library receiving federal subsidies is required to install filtering software blocking internet access to obscenity, child pornography, or indecent material harmful to minors. In so doing, the Court first rejected the attempted analogy of a public library to a public forum or designated public forum, in a plurality opinion written by Chief Justice Rehnquist and joined by Justices O'Connor, Scalia, and Thomas. (For a different portion of the decision also rejecting a challenge to CIPA as an unconstitutional condition on public funding, see p. 419 below.)

Chief Justice REHNQUIST wrote: "Public libraries pursue the worthy missions of facilitating learning and cultural enrichment. [To] fulfill their traditional missions, public libraries must have broad discretion to decide what material to provide to their patrons. Although they seek to provide a wide array of information, their goal has never been to provide 'universal coverage.' Instead, public libraries seek to provide materials 'that would be of the greatest direct benefit or interest to the community.' To this end, libraries collect only those materials deemed to have 'requisite and appropriate quality.'

"We have held in two analogous contexts that the government has broad discretion to make content-based judgments in deciding what private speech to make available to the public. In AETC v. Forbes, we held that public forum principles do not generally apply to a public television station's editorial judgments regarding the private speech it presents to its viewers. [The] principles underlying Forbes also apply to a public library's exercise of judgment in selecting the material it provides to its patrons. Just as forum analysis and heightened judicial scrutiny are incompatible with the role of public television stations and the role of the NEA, they are also incompatible with the discretion that public libraries must have to fulfill their traditional missions. Public library staffs necessarily consider content in making collection decisions and enjoy broad discretion in making them.

"[Public] forum principles [are] out of place in the context of this case. Internet access in public libraries is neither a 'traditional' nor a 'designated' public forum. [A] public library does not acquire Internet terminals in order to create a public forum for Web publishers to express themselves, any more than it collects books in order to provide a public forum for the authors of books to speak. It provides Internet access, not to 'encourage a diversity of views from private speakers,' but for the same reasons it offers other library resources: to facilitate research, learning, and recreational pursuits by furnishing materials of requisite and appropriate quality. [The fact that a library] does not review every Web site that it makes available [is not] constitutionally relevant. A library's failure to make quality-based judgments about all the material it furnishes from the Web does not somehow taint the judgments it does make. A library's need to exercise judgment in making collection decisions depends on its traditional role in identifying suitable and worthwhile material; it is no less entitled to play that role when it collects material from the Internet than when it collects material from any other source. Most libraries already exclude pornography from their print collections because they deem it inappropriate for inclusion. We do not subject these decisions to heightened scrutiny; it would make little sense to treat libraries' judgments to block online pornography any differently, when these judgments are made for just the same reason. Moreover, because of the vast quantity of material on the Internet and the rapid pace at which it changes, libraries cannot possibly segregate, item by item, all the Internet material that is appropriate for inclusion from all that is not. While a library could limit its Internet collection to just those sites it found worthwhile, it could do so only at the cost of excluding an enormous amount of valuable information that it lacks the capacity to review. Given that tradeoff, it is entirely reasonable for public libraries to reject that approach and instead exclude certain categories of content, without making individualized judgments that everything they do make available has requisite and appropriate quality.

"[Assuming] the tendency of filtering software to 'overblock' [presents] constitutional difficulties, any such concerns are dispelled by the ease with which patrons may have the filtering software disabled. When a patron encounters a blocked site, he need only ask a librarian to unblock it or (at least in the case of adults) disable the filter. [The] Constitution does not guarantee the right to acquire information at a public library without any risk of embarrassment."

Justices Kennedy and Breyer concurred in the judgment. Justice BREYER wrote: "In ascertaining whether the statutory provisions are constitutional, I would apply a form of heightened scrutiny, examining the statutory requirements in question with special care. The Act directly restricts the public's receipt of information. And it does so through limitations imposed by outside bodies (here Congress) upon two critically important sources of information—the Internet as accessed via public libraries. For that reason, we should not examine the statute's constitutionality as if it raised no special First Amendment concern—as if, like tax or economic regulation, the First Amendment demanded only a 'rational basis' for imposing a restriction. [At] the same time, in my view, the First Amendment does not here demand application of the most limiting constitutional approach—that of 'strict scrutiny.' The statutory restriction in question is, in essence, a kind of 'selection' restriction (a kind of editing). It affects the kinds and amount of materials that the library can present to its patrons. And libraries often properly engage in the selection of materials, either as a matter of necessity (i.e., due to the scarcity of resources) or by design (i.e., in accordance with collection development policies). [To] apply 'strict scrutiny' to the 'selection' of a library's collection (whether carried out by public libraries themselves or by other community bodies with a traditional legal right to engage in that function) would unreasonably interfere with the discretion necessary to create, maintain, or select a library's 'collection' (broadly defined to include all the information the library makes available)."

Under such intermediate scrutiny, in Justice Breyer's view, the law was valid: it "seeks to restrict access to obscenity, child pornography, and, in respect to access by minors, material that is comparably harmful. These objectives are 'legitimate,' and indeed often 'compelling.' " Moreover, he concluded, "software filters 'provide a relatively cheap and effective' means of furthering these goals," and are narrowly tailored because an exception "allows libraries to permit any adult patron access to an 'overblocked' Web site; the adult patron need only ask a librarian to unblock the specific Web site or, alternatively, ask the librarian, 'Please disable the entire filter.' The Act does impose upon the patron the burden of making this request. But it is difficult to see how that burden [could] prove more onerous than traditional library practices associated with segregating library materials in, say, closed stacks, or with interlibrary lending practices that require patrons to make requests that are not anonymous and to wait while the librarian obtains the desired materials from elsewhere. [Given] the comparatively small burden that the Act imposes upon the library patron seeking legitimate Internet, I cannot say that any speech-related harm that the Act may cause is disproportionate when considered in relation to the Act's legitimate objectives."

Justice Stevens and Justice Souter, the latter joined by Justice Ginsburg, dissented, emphasizing the crudeness of filtering software and its likely tendency to "overblock" materials protected by the First Amendment. Justice SOUTER also questioned the assumption made by the plurality and the concurrences that internet filtering software is simply an example of standard selectivity in acquisitions by a library: "The question [is] whether a local library could itself constitutionally impose these restrictions on the content otherwise available to an adult patron through an Internet connection, at a library terminal provided for public use. The answer is no. A library that chose to block an adult's Internet access to material harmful to children (and whatever else the undiscriminating filter might interrupt) would be imposing a content-based restriction on communication of material in the library's control that an adult could otherwise lawfully see. This would simply be censorship. [As] to those who did not qualify for discretionary unblocking, the censorship would be complete and, like all censorship by an agency of the Government, presumptively invalid owing to strict scrutiny in implementing the Free Speech Clause of the First Amendment.

"[The] Court's plurality does not treat blocking affecting adults as censorship, but chooses to describe a library's act in filtering content as simply an instance of the kind of selection from available material that every library [must] perform. Public libraries are indeed selective in what they acquire to place in their stacks, as they must be. There is only so much money and so much shelf space, and the necessity to choose some material and reject the rest justifies the effort to be selective with an eye to demand, quality, and the object of maintaining the library as a place of civilized enquiry by widely different sorts of people. Selectivity is thus necessary and complex, and these two characteristics explain why review of a library's selection decisions must be limited: the decisions are made all the time, and only in extreme cases could one expect particular choices to reveal impermissible reasons (reasons even the plurality would consider to be illegitimate), like excluding books because their authors are Democrats or their critiques of organized Christianity are unsympathetic.

"[But] the Internet blocking here defies comparison to the process of acquisition. Whereas traditional scarcity of money and space require a library to make choices about what to acquire, and the choice to be made is whether or not to spend the money to acquire something, blocking is the subject of a choice made after the money for Internet access has been spent or committed. Since it makes no difference to the cost of Internet access whether an adult calls up material harmful for children or the Articles of Confederation, blocking (on facts like these) is not necessitated by scarcity of either money or space. In the instance of the Internet, what the library acquires is electronic access, and the choice to block is a choice to limit access that has already been acquired. [The] proper analogy therefore is not to passing up a book that might have been bought; it is either to buying a book and then keeping it from adults lacking an acceptable 'purpose,' or to buying an encyclopedia and then cutting out pages with anything thought to be unsuitable for all adults."

12. ***Student organization membership at a public law school.*** Do "limited public forum" principles extend to the setting of membership in public university student organizations? In **Christian Legal Society Chapter of the University of California Hastings College of Law v. Martinez**, 561 U.S. 661 (2010), a public law school established a "Registered Student Organization (RSO)" program that conferred the use of school funds, facilities, and the law school's name and logo on condition that RSOs allow "all comers" to participate, become members, or seek leadership positions, regardless of their status or beliefs. The parties jointly stipulated in the lower courts that the policy was universally applied to all groups: " 'Hastings requires that registered student organizations allow *any* student to participate, become a member, or seek leadership positions in the organization, regardless of [her] status or beliefs. Thus, for example, the Hastings Democratic Caucus cannot bar students holding Republican political beliefs from becoming members or seeking leadership positions in the organization.' " Under this policy, Hastings declined to grant RSO status to a chapter of the Christian Legal Society (CLS) on the ground that, by requiring members and officers to sign onto a "Statement of Faith" and renounce "unrepentant homosexual conduct," it excluded students based on religion and sexual orientation in violation of the all-comers policy. CLS challenged this denial, claiming that application of the all-comers policy violated its rights to freedom of speech and association.

The Supreme Court rejected the First Amendment challenge by a closely divided 5–4 vote. Justice GINSBURG wrote for the majority, joined by Justices Stevens, Kennedy, Breyer, and Sotomayor. Crucial to her decision was the premise that "Hastings, through its RSO program, [had] established a limited public forum." She explained: "In diverse contexts, our decisions have distinguished between policies that require action and those that withhold benefits. Application of the less-restrictive limited public forum analysis better accounts for the fact that Hastings, through its RSO program, is dangling the carrot of subsidy, not wielding the stick of prohibition." And she found limited public forum principles equally dispositive of CLS's free speech and expressive-association claims.

In a footnote, Justice Ginsburg laid out an account of public forum doctrine and applicable standards of review: "In conducting forum analysis, our decisions have sorted government property into three categories. First, in traditional public forums, such as public streets and parks, 'any restriction based on the content of . . . speech must satisfy strict scrutiny, that is, the restriction must be narrowly tailored to serve a compelling government interest.' Summum. Second, governmental entities create designated public forums when 'government property that has not traditionally been regarded as a public forum is intentionally opened up for that purpose'; speech restrictions in such a forum 'are subject to the same strict scrutiny as restrictions in a traditional public forum.' Id. Third, governmental entities establish limited public forums by opening property 'limited to use by certain groups or dedicated solely to the discussion of certain subjects.' Ibid. As noted in [Summum], '[i]n such a forum, a governmental entity may impose restrictions on speech that are reasonable and viewpoint-neutral.' "

Justice Ginsburg reiterated the standard of scrutiny governing a limited public forum: "Recognizing a State's right to preserve the property under its control for the use to which it is lawfully dedicated, the Court has permitted restrictions on access to a limited public forum, like the RSO program here, with this key caveat: Any access barrier must be reasonable and viewpoint neutral." Applying that standard, she first considered "whether Hastings' policy is reasonable taking into account the RSO forum's function and 'all the surrounding circumstances,' " and answered that question in the affirmative: "[A] college's commission—and its concomitant license to choose among pedagogical approaches—is not confined to the classroom, for extracurricular programs are, today, essential parts of the educational process. [First,] the open-access policy 'ensures that the leadership, educational, and social opportunities afforded by [RSOs] are available to all students.' [Second,] the all-comers requirement helps Hastings police the written terms of its Nondiscrimination Policy without inquiring into an RSO's motivation for membership restrictions. [Third,] the Law School reasonably adheres to the view that an all-comers policy, to the extent it brings together individuals with diverse backgrounds and beliefs, 'encourages tolerance, cooperation, and learning among students.' [These] several justifications [are] surely reasonable in light of the RSO forum's purposes."

Justice Ginsburg next "consider[ed] whether Hastings' all-comers policy is viewpoint neutral," and again answered affirmatively: "In contrast to [Widmar and Rosenberger], in which universities singled out organizations for disfavored treatment because of their points of view, Hastings' all-comers requirement draws no distinction between groups based on their message or perspective. An all-comers condition on access to RSO status, in short, is textbook viewpoint neutral." The majority opinion rejected CLS's argument that the policy is viewpoint-discriminatory in effect because " 'it systematically and predictably burdens most heavily those groups whose viewpoints are out of favor with the campus mainstream,' " finding that such a "differential impact" did not render the policy nonneutral. Justice Ginsburg concluded: "Finding Hastings' open-access condition on RSO status reasonable and viewpoint neutral, we reject CLS' free-speech and expressive-association claims."

Justice STEVENS, joined by Justice Kennedy, concurred to emphasize that "[i]t is critical, in evaluating CLS's challenge [to] keep in mind that an RSO program is a limited forum—the boundaries of which may be delimited by the proprietor. When a religious association, or a secular association, operates in a wholly public setting, it must be allowed broad freedom to control its membership and its message, even if its decisions cause offense to outsiders. [But] the CLS chapter that brought this lawsuit does not want to be just a Christian group; it aspires to be a recognized student organization. The Hastings College of Law is not a legislature. And no state actor has demanded that anyone do anything outside the confines of a discrete, voluntary academic program. [The] RSO forum is [not] an open commons that Hastings happens to maintain. It is a mechanism through which Hastings confers certain benefits and pursues certain aspects of its educational mission. [CLS] excludes students who will not sign its Statement of Faith or who engage in 'unrepentant homosexual conduct.' Other groups may exclude or mistreat Jews, blacks, and women—or those who do not share their contempt for Jews, blacks, and women. A free society must tolerate such groups. It need not subsidize them, give them its official imprimatur, or grant them equal access to law school facilities."

Justice KENNEDY filed a concurrence emphasizing the case's differences from Rosenberger v. Rector (1995; p. 410 below): "[H]ere the school policy in question is not content based either in its formulation or evident purpose; and were it shown to be otherwise, the case likely should have a different outcome. Here, the policy applies equally to all groups and views. And, given the stipulation of the parties, there is no basis for an allegation that the design or purpose of the rule was, by subterfuge, to discriminate based on viewpoint."

Justice ALITO dissented, joined by Chief Justice Roberts and Justices Scalia and Thomas. The dissent began by vigorously disputing that the stipulation setting forth the all-comers policy truly captured the policy Hastings had applied, arguing that the policy was a pretextual substitute for a prior Nondiscrimination Policy that in practice discriminated against student groups organized around religious viewpoints. The dissent next argued that the case should have been controlled by Healy v. James, 408 U.S. 169 (1972), which invalidated a public college's refusal to recognize a student chapter of Students for a Democratic Society (SDS) because it would not renounce violence.

Reaching the limited public forum principles central to the majority opinion, Justice Alito argued that Hastings' application of its policy is impermissible even if the stipulated all-comers policy were deemed the operative policy and the RSO program were deemed a limited public forum: "Taken as a whole, the regulations plainly contemplate the creation of a forum within which Hastings students are free to form and obtain registration of essentially the same broad range of private groups that nonstudents may form off campus. [The] way in which the RSO forum actually developed corroborates this design. [Hastings] had more than 60 RSOs in 2004–2005, each with its own independently devised purpose. Some addressed serious social issues; others—for example, the wine appreciation and ultimate Frisbee clubs—were simply recreational. Some organizations focused on a subject but did not claim to promote a particular viewpoint on that subject (for example, the Association of Communications, Sports & Entertainment Law); others were defined, not by subject, but by viewpoint. The forum did not have a single Party Politics Club; rather, it featured both the Hastings Democratic Caucus and the Hastings Republicans. There was no Reproductive Issues Club; the forum included separate pro-choice and pro-life organizations. Students did not see fit to create a Monotheistic Religions Club, but they have formed the Hastings Jewish Law Students Association and the Hastings Association of Muslim Law Students. In short, the RSO forum, true to its design, has allowed Hastings students to replicate on campus a broad array of private, independent, noncommercial organizations that is very similar to those that nonstudents have formed in the outside world. The accept-all-comers policy is antithetical to the design of the RSO forum for the same reason that a state-imposed accept-all-comers policy would violate the First Amendment rights of private groups if applied off campus."

13. *Rights of access to private property.* Do the principles of the above cases aid in developing claims of access to *private* property? Is there a "private forum" counterpart to the public forum? In Marsh v. Alabama, 326 U.S. 501 (1946), the Court held that Jehovah's Witnesses could claim a constitutional right of access to distribute religious literature in a company-owned town since such a town served a "public function" creating state action. Does such a principle extend to shopping centers? Are shopping centers the modern functional equivalent of the public square?

The 5–4 decision in **Amalgamated Food Employees v. Logan Valley Plaza, Inc.**, 391 U.S. 308 (1968), relied in part on Marsh to hold that a state trespass law could not be applied to enjoin peaceful union picketing of a supermarket in a privately owned shopping center. Justice MARSHALL's majority opinion found that the ban on picketing could not be justified on the ground that picketing constituted an unconsented invasion of private property rights: "The shopping center here is clearly the functional equivalent of the business district of Chickasaw involved in Marsh. [We] see no reason why access to a business district in a company town for the purpose of exercising First Amendment rights should be constitutionally required, while access for the same purpose to property functioning as a business district should be limited simply because the property surrounding the 'business district' is not under the same ownership." Accordingly, Justice Marshall applied public forum principles and found that the state could not "delegate the power, through the use of its trespass laws, wholly to exclude those members of the public wishing to exercise their First Amendment rights on the premises in a manner and for a purpose generally consonant with the use to which the property is actually put."

Logan Valley was "distinguished" in the 5–4 decision in **Lloyd Corp. v. Tanner**, 407 U.S. 551 (1972). In Lloyd, the lower federal courts had relied on Marsh and Logan Valley in holding unconstitutional the application to anti-war leafleteers of a shopping center's ban on the distribution of handbills. The Court reversed, finding the facts in its earlier cases "significantly different." Justice POWELL emphasized that in Logan Valley the First Amendment activity—union picketing of a store—"was related to the shopping center's operations" and the store was "in the center of a large private enclave with the consequence that no other reasonable opportunities" to convey the picketers' message existed. Here, by contrast, the handbilling "had no relation to any purpose for which the center was built and being used" and alternative means of communication were available. He noted, moreover, that "[a]lthough accommodations between [speech and property values] are sometimes necessary, and the courts properly have shown a special solicitude for the [First Amendment], this Court has never held that a trespasser or an uninvited guest may exercise general rights of free speech on property privately owned." Justice MARSHALL's dissent, joined by Justices Douglas, Brennan, and Stewart, objected to the majority's departure from Logan Valley and emphasized the "tremendous need" of the handbillers to have access to the private shopping center.

Even though Lloyd had purported to distinguish Logan Valley, **Hudgens v. NLRB**, 424 U.S. 507 (1976), announced that Lloyd had in effect overruled Logan Valley. Hudgens involved labor picketing of a store in a private shopping center. The picketers were employees of a warehouse maintained by the store owner at a location outside of the shopping center. Justice STEWART's majority opinion concluded that "the constitutional guarantee of free expression has no part to play in a case such as this. [If] the respondent in the Lloyd case did not have a First Amendment right to enter that shopping center to distribute handbills concerning Vietnam, then the respondents in the present case did not have a First Amendment right to enter this shopping center for the purpose of advertising their strike." Justices Marshall and Brennan dissented. On labor speech and the First Amendment generally, see Pope, "The Three-Systems Ladder of First Amendment Values: Two Rungs and a Black Hole," 11 Hast. Const. L.Q. 189 (1984).

14. *Polling place.* In **Minnesota Voters Alliance v. Mansky**, 585 U.S. ___, 138 S. Ct. 1876 (2018), the Court struck down a Minnesota law prohibiting individuals from wearing a "political badge, political button, or other political insignia" inside a polling place on Election Day. Chief Justice ROBERTS wrote for the 7–2 Court: "Today, all 50 States and the District of Columbia have laws curbing various forms of speech in and around polling places on Election Day. [The Minnesota] ban applies only in a specific location: the interior of a polling place. [A] polling place in Minnesota qualifies as a nonpublic forum. It is, at least on Election Day, government-controlled property set aside for the sole purpose of voting. [The] question accordingly is whether Minnesota's ban on political apparel is reasonable in light of the purpose served by the forum: voting. [In] light of the special purpose of the polling place itself, Minnesota may choose to prohibit certain apparel there because of the message it conveys, so that voters may focus on the important decisions immediately at hand. [Although] there is no requirement of narrow tailoring in a nonpublic forum, the State must be able to articulate some sensible basis for distinguishing what may come in from what must stay out. Here, the unmoored use of the term 'political' in the Minnesota law, combined with haphazard interpretations the State has provided in official guidance and representations to this Court, cause Minnesota's restriction to fail even this forgiving test.

"[The] State interprets the ban to proscribe 'only words and symbols that an objectively reasonable observer would perceive as conveying a message about the electoral choices at issue in [the] polling place.' At the same time, the State argues that the category of 'political' apparel is *not* limited to campaign apparel. [Far] from clarifying the indeterminate scope of the political apparel provision, the State's 'electoral choices' construction introduces confusing line-drawing problems. [The] State points to the 2010 Election Day Policy—which it continues to hold out as authoritative guidance regarding implementation of the statute. The first three examples in the Policy are clear enough: items displaying the name of a political party, items displaying the name of a candidate, and items demonstrating 'support of or opposition to a ballot question.' But the next example—'[i]ssue oriented material designed to influence or impact voting,'—raises more questions than it answers. What qualifies as an 'issue'? The answer, as far as we can tell from the State's briefing and argument, is any subject on which a political candidate or party has taken a stance. For instance, the Election Day Policy specifically notes that the 'Please I.D. Me' buttons are prohibited. But a voter identification requirement was not on the ballot in 2010, so a Minnesotan would have had no explicit 'electoral choice' to make in that respect. The buttons were nonetheless covered, the State tells us, because the Republican candidates for Governor and Secretary of State had staked out positions on whether photo identification should be required.

"A rule whose fair enforcement requires an election judge to maintain a mental index of the platforms and positions of every candidate and party on the ballot is not reasonable. Candidates for statewide and federal office and major political parties can be expected to take positions on a wide array of subjects of local and national import. [The] next broad category in the Election Day Policy—any item 'promoting a group with recognizable political views,'—makes matters worse. [The] American Civil Liberties Union, the AARP, the World Wildlife Fund, and Ben & Jerry's all have stated positions on matters of public concern.

"[That] is not to say that Minnesota has set upon an impossible task. Other States have laws proscribing displays (including apparel) in more lucid terms. We do not suggest that such provisions set the outer limit of what a State may proscribe, and do not pass on the constitutionality of laws that are not before us. But we do hold that if a State wishes to set its polling places apart as areas free of partisan discord, it must employ a more discernible approach than the one Minnesota has offered here."

In dissent, Justice SOTOMAYOR, joined by Justice Breyer, wrote that she would have certified the case to the Minnesota Supreme Court for a definitive interpretation of the political apparel ban, likely obviating "the hypothetical line-drawing problems that form the basis of the Court's decision today."

Note that the Court applied the most lenient level of forum analysis—the deferential scrutiny applicable to a nonpublic forum—but still struck down the law as an unconstitutional restriction of speech. What accounts for that decision? In another polling place speech case, Burson v. Freeman (1992; p. 243), the plurality applied strict scrutiny to a signage ban outside the polling place but still upheld the law. Can the decisions be reconciled?

———

RELIGIOUS SPEECH ON PUBLIC PROPERTY

The exclusion of religious expression from public spaces would appear to be content discrimination that would normally be impermissible in a traditional or designated public forum, or viewpoint discrimination that would be impermissible even in a nonpublic forum. But is such exclusion dictated by the countervailing constitutional command of the Establishment Clause of the First Amendment? The establishment principles governing these cases are discussed below in Chapter 4. The Establishment Clause has been held to prohibit government from establishing religion not only through coercion but also through symbolic endorsement or financial support. Government bodies have sometimes read the clause to require it to exclude religious speech from forums it has otherwise opened to expression. When these cases have come before the Court, it has consistently held that the Free Speech Clause forbids such discrimination, and that the Establishment Clause does not require it. Consider the following decisions:

In **Widmar v. Vincent**, 454 U.S. 263 (1981), the Court exercised the strict scrutiny it typically applies to content-based exclusions from public places. It held that a state university that makes its facilities generally available for the activities of registered student groups may not constitutionally bar a group desiring to use the facilities for religious worship and discussion. The case arose when the University of Missouri at Kansas City, relying on its policy of prohibiting the use of its facilities "for purposes of religious worship or religious teaching," barred a student religious group from meeting anywhere on its grounds. The Court rejected the University's argument that its interest in promoting the separation of church and state was adequate to survive strict scrutiny.

In explaining the application of free speech principles, Justice POWELL's majority opinion stated: "Through its policy of accommodating their meetings, the University has created a forum generally open for use by student groups. Having done so, the University has assumed an obligation to justify its discriminations and exclusions under applicable constitutional norms. The Constitution forbids a State to enforce certain exclusions from a forum generally open to the public, even if it was not required to create the forum in the first place. The University's institutional mission, which it describes as providing a 'secular education' to its students, does not exempt its actions from constitutional scrutiny. With respect to persons entitled to be there, our cases leave no doubt that the First Amendment rights of speech and association extend to the campuses of state universities. Here the [University] has discriminated against student groups and speakers based on their desire to use a generally open forum to engage in religious worship and discussion. These are forms of speech and association protected by the First Amendment. In order to justify discriminatory exclusion from a public forum based on the religious content of a group's intended speech, the University must therefore satisfy the standard of review appropriate to content-based exclusions. It must show that its regulation is necessary to serve a compelling state interest and that it is narrowly drawn to achieve that end. See [Carey.]" Finding that there would be no establishment violation if the university granted access to religious student groups, Justice Powell found no compelling state interest in their exclusion.

In an opinion concurring only in the judgment, Justice STEVENS took issue with the majority's approach: "In my opinion, the use of the terms 'compelling state interest' and 'public forum' to analyze the question presented in this case may needlessly undermine the academic freedom of public universities." He elaborated: "Because every university's resources are limited, an educational institution must routinely make decisions concerning the use of the time and space that is available for extracurricular activities. In my judgment, it is both necessary and appropriate for those decisions to evaluate the content of a proposed student activity. I should think it obvious, for example, that if two groups of 25 students requested the use of a room at a particular time—one to view Mickey Mouse cartoons and the other to rehearse an amateur performance of Hamlet—the First Amendment would not require that the room be reserved for the group that submitted its application first. [Judgments] of this kind should be made by academicians, not by federal judges, and their standards for decision should not be encumbered with ambiguous phrases like 'compelling state interest.' Thus, I do not subscribe to the view that a public university has no greater interest in the content of student activities than the police chief has in the content of a soap box oration on Capitol Hill. A university legitimately may regard some subjects as more relevant to its educational mission than others.

"But the university, like the police officer, may not allow its agreement or disagreement with the viewpoint of a particular speaker to determine whether access to a forum will be granted. If a state university is to deny recognition to a student organization—or is to give it a lesser right to use school facilities than other student groups—it must have a valid reason for doing so." Despite his different approach, Justice Stevens found the University decision unjustified. He explained: "It seems apparent that the policy under attack would allow groups of young philosophers to meet to discuss their skepticism that a Supreme Being exists, or a group of political scientists to meet to debate the accuracy of the view that religion is the 'opium of the people.' If school facilities may be used to discuss anti-clerical doctrine, it seems to me that comparable use by a group desiring to express a belief in God must also be permitted. The fact that their expression of faith includes ceremonial conduct is not, in my opinion, a sufficient reason for suppressing their discussion entirely."

Justice WHITE, the sole dissenter, disagreed with the majority's Establishment Clause and free speech analysis. He objected to the argument that, "because religious worship uses speech, it is protected by the Free Speech Clause of the First Amendment." He added: "This case involves religious worship only; the fact that that worship is accomplished through speech does not add anything to [the challengers'] argument. That argument must rely upon the claim that the state's action impermissibly interferes with the free exercise of respondents' religious practices. Although this is a close question, I conclude that it does not."

In **Lamb's Chapel v. Center Moriches Union Free School District**, 508 U.S. 384 (1993), the Court considered a free speech challenge to a local school district policy that permitted public school facilities to be used after school hours for social, civic, and recreational purposes and by political organizations, but provided that "the school premises shall not be used by any group for religious purposes." The school district twice denied permission to Lamb's Chapel, a local evangelical organization, to show a six-part film series featuring a psychologist who would argue in favor of "Christian family values instilled at an early stage." The district gave as its reason that the series appeared "church related."

The Court unanimously held the district's rule unconstitutional as applied to the Lamb's Chapel film series. Justice WHITE wrote for the Court: "There is no question that the District, like the private owner of property, may legally preserve the property under its control for the use to which it is dedicated. It is also common ground that the District need not have permitted after-hours use of its property for any [expressive] uses." The Church had argued that the schools had been opened after hours to such a wide variety of speech that the district's program should be analyzed as a designated public forum. Justice White declined to reach that issue, holding that, even assuming that the after-hours program was *not* a traditional or designated public forum, the exclusion of the Lamb's Chapel series amounted to impermissible viewpoint discrimination:

"That all religions and all uses for religious purposes are treated alike under [the rule] does not answer the critical question whether it discriminates on the basis of viewpoint to permit school property to be used for the presentation of all views about family issues and child-rearing except those dealing with the subject matter from a religious standpoint. There is no suggestion [that] a lecture or film about child-rearing and family values would not be a use for social or civic purposes otherwise permitted. [Nor] is there any indication [that] the application to exhibit the particular film involved here [would] have been denied for any reason other than [its] religious perspective. In our view, denial on that basis was plainly invalid under [Cornelius:] 'although a speaker may be excluded from a nonpublic forum if he wishes to address a topic not encompassed within the purpose of the forum . . . or if he is not a member of the class of speakers for whose special benefit the forum was created . . . the government violates the First Amendment when it denies access to a speaker solely to suppress the point of view he espouses on an otherwise includible subject.' " As in Widmar, the Court rejected the government's Establishment Clause defense.

Should the reasoning of Lamb's Chapel extend to afterschool use of public school facilities by an evangelical club seeking to engage in prayer and worship as part of its activities? The Court held that it did in **Good News Club v. Milford Central School**, 533 U.S. 98 (2001). The case involved a challenge to a New York local school district's refusal to allow the Good News Club, a private Christian organization, to hold weekly afterschool meetings for elementary school students in order to sing religious songs, hold Bible lessons and memorize scripture. School policy, consistent with Lamb's Chapel, would have allowed speech at afterschool meetings from a religious perspective, but excluded Good News as involving instead "religious instruction."

By a vote of 6–3, the Court held the exclusion unconstitutional under the Free Speech Clause, and rejected the school's establishment defense. Justice THOMAS wrote for the Court, joined by Chief Justice Rehnquist and Justices O'Connor, Scalia, and Kennedy and in part by Justice Breyer. As in Lamb's Chapel, the Court assumed without deciding that the school's afterschool meetings program did not constitute a traditional or designated public forum, but held nonetheless that the exclusion was invalid: "[W]e hold that the exclusion constitutes viewpoint discrimination. Like the church in Lamb's Chapel, the Club seeks to address a subject otherwise permitted under the rule, the teaching of morals and character, from a religious standpoint. [The] only apparent difference between the activity of Lamb's Chapel and the activities of the Good News Club is that the Club chooses to teach moral lessons from a Christian perspective through live storytelling and prayer, whereas Lamb's Chapel taught lessons through films. This distinction is inconsequential."

Justices Stevens filed a dissent, as did Justice Souter joined by Justice Ginsburg. Both dissents argued that the school should have been free to exclude religious uses from the scope of the limited public forum they defined. Justice STEVENS wrote: "Speech for 'religious purposes' may [encompass] religious speech that is simply speech about a particular topic from a religious point of view, [religious] speech that amounts to worship, [or] an intermediate category that is aimed principally at proselytizing or inculcating belief in a particular religious faith. The novel question that this case presents [is] whether a school can, consistently with the First Amendment, create a limited public forum that admits the first type of religious speech without allowing the other two. [As] long as this is done in an even handed manner, I see no constitutional violation in such an effort."

Quoting extensively from the record, Justice SOUTER wrote: "It is beyond question that Good News intends to use the public school premises not for the mere discussion of a subject from a particular, Christian point of view, but for an evangelical service of worship calling children to commit themselves in an act of Christian conversion. The majority avoids this reality only by resorting to the bland and general characterization of Good News's activity as 'teaching of morals and character, from a religious standpoint.' If the majority's statement ignores reality, as it surely does, then today's holding may be understood only in equally generic terms. Otherwise, indeed, this case would stand for the remarkable proposition that any public school opened for civic meetings must be opened for use as a church, synagogue, or mosque."

Should the reasoning in Lamb's Chapel and Good News apply to restrictions on the use of government resources for religious *services*? In **Bronx Household of Faith v. Board of Education of New York City**, 650 F.3d 30 (2d Cir. 2011), the Second Circuit upheld as viewpoint-neutral a school board's prohibition on the after-school use of facilities for "religious worship services." Judge LEVAL distinguished the prohibitions struck down in Lamb's Chapel and Good News because they "categorically excluded *expressions* of religious content," whereas the board's exclusion dealt only with "the conduct of a certain type of *activity*—the conduct of worship services" (emphasis added). And because the Second Circuit had previously found that the facilities were a limited public forum, the viewpoint-neutral prohibition on religious services needed only to be "reasonable in light of the purposes served by the forum." (The court found the prohibition reasonable because the board could have reasonably concluded that allowing religious services in its facilities would run afoul of another First Amendment proscription: the Establishment Clause, a subject taken up in Chapter 4 below.)

In **Capitol Square Review Board v. Pinette**, 515 U.S. 753 (1995), the Court invalidated the denial of permission to the Ku Klux Klan to erect a large Latin cross on Capitol Square, a 10-acre, state-owned plaza surrounding the Statehouse in Columbus, Ohio. The Square was designated a public forum by state law, and several unattended displays had been permitted there. The Court assumed that the Board had denied permission solely on the ground of the cross's religious content and that such a ground for exclusion would violate the Free Speech Clause unless required by the

Establishment Clause, which the Court held it was not (see p. 773 below). Justice SCALIA's plurality opinion stated: "Respondents' religious display in Capitol Square was private expression. Our precedent establishes that private religious speech, far from being a First Amendment orphan, is as fully protected under the Free Speech Clause as secular private expression. Indeed, in Anglo-American history, at least, government suppression of speech has so commonly been directed precisely at religious speech that a free-speech clause without religion would be Hamlet without the prince. [Heffron, Widmar.] It is undeniable, of course, that speech which is constitutionally protected against state suppression is not thereby accorded a guaranteed forum on all property owned by the State. [But] Capitol Square [is] a traditional public forum. Petitioners do not claim that their denial of respondents' application was based upon a content-neutral time, place, or manner restriction. To the contrary, they concede—indeed it is the essence of their case—that the Board rejected the display precisely because its content was religious." The rest of the plurality and the concurring opinions went on to reject the argument that this exclusion was required by the Establishment Clause.

This series of victories for those seeking to engage in religious speech or symbolism on public property came to an end in **Pleasant Grove City v. Summum**, 555 U.S. 460 (2009). A Utah city displayed permanently in a public park various privately donated symbols, including a Ten Commandments monument donated by the Fraternal Order of Eagles. The city, however, denied permission to a religious organization to erect a monument containing the "Seven Aphorisms of Summum." The city explained to the Summum group that monuments in the park were limited to those related to the city's history or donated by groups with longstanding community ties. The Supreme Court unanimously rejected Summum's free speech challenge and upheld the exclusion, holding that, even though a park is undoubtedly a public forum, the display of permanent monuments is "government speech" to which public forum principles are inapplicable.

Justice ALITO wrote the opinion of the Court: "[A]lthough a park is a traditional public forum for speeches and other transitory expressive acts, the display of a permanent monument in a public park is not a form of expression to which forum analysis applies. Instead, the placement of a permanent monument in a public park is best viewed as a form of government speech and is therefore not subject to scrutiny under the Free Speech Clause. [The] Free Speech Clause restricts government regulation of private speech; it does not regulate government speech. Indeed, it is not easy to imagine how government could function if it lacked this freedom. [A] government entity may exercise this same freedom to express its views when it receives assistance from private sources for the purpose of delivering a government-controlled message.

"[There] may be situations in which it is difficult to tell whether a government entity is speaking on its own behalf or is providing a forum for private speech, but this case does not present such a situation. Permanent monuments displayed on public property typically represent government speech. Governments have long used monuments to speak to the public. Since ancient times, kings, emperors, and other rulers have erected statues of themselves to remind their subjects of their authority and power. Triumphal arches, columns, and other monuments have been built to commemorate military victories and sacrifices and other events of civic importance. A monument, by definition, is a structure that is designed as a means of expression. When a government entity arranges for the construction of a monument, it does so because it wishes to convey some thought or instill some feeling in those who see the structure.

"[Just] as government-commissioned and government-financed monuments speak for the government, so do privately financed and donated monuments that the government accepts and displays to the public on government land. It certainly is not common for property owners to open up their property for the installation of permanent monuments that convey a message with which they do not wish to be associated. And because property owners typically do not permit the construction of such monuments on their land, persons who observe donated monuments routinely—and reasonably— interpret them as conveying some message on the property owner's behalf. [While] government entities regularly accept privately funded or donated monuments, they have exercised selectivity. [Government] decisionmakers select the monuments that portray what they view as appropriate for the place in question, taking into account such content-based factors as esthetics, history, and local culture. The monuments that are accepted, therefore, are meant to convey and have the effect of conveying a government message, and they thus constitute government speech.

"In this case, it is clear that the monuments in Pleasant Grove's [park] represent government speech. Although many of the monuments were not designed or built by the City and were donated in completed form by private entities, the City decided to accept those donations and to display them in the Park. [The] City has selected those monuments that it wants to display for the purpose of presenting the image of the City that it wishes to project to all who frequent the Park; it has taken ownership of most of the monuments in the Park, [and] the City has now expressly set forth the criteria it will use in making future selections."

Justice Alito rejected the argument that a monument must have a single meaning, embraced by the government, in order to constitute government speech, noting that the "Imagine" monument to John Lennon in New York City's Central Park or a "Peace" monument may have different meanings for different observers: "[I]t frequently is not possible to identify a single 'message' that is conveyed by an object or structure, and consequently, the thoughts or sentiments expressed by a government entity that accepts and displays such object may be quite different from those of either its creator or its donor. [By] accepting such a monument, a government entity does not necessarily endorse the specific meaning that any particular donor sees in the monument."

Justice Alito also rejected Summum's proposed analogy of "the installation of permanent monuments in a public park to the delivery of speeches and the holding of marches and demonstrations" in a traditional public forum, noting that "a park can accommodate many speakers and, over time, many parades and demonstrations," but "public parks can accommodate only a limited number of permanent monuments. [Speakers], no matter how long-winded, eventually come to the end of their remarks; persons distributing leaflets and carrying signs at some point tire and go home; monuments, however, endure. They monopolize the use of the land on which they stand and interfere permanently with other uses of public space."

Finally, Justice Alito rejected Summum's proposed analogy to Capital Square v. Pinnette: "[T]hat case involved a very different situation—a request by a private group, the Ku Klux Klan, to erect a cross for a period of 16 days on public property that had been opened up for similar temporary displays, including a Christmas tree and a menorah. Although some public parks can accommodate and may be made generally available for temporary private displays, the same is rarely true for permanent monuments."

The Court did not reach the question whether, if the displays in the park are government speech, the Ten Commandments monument might violate the Establishment Clause. Justice Stevens filed a concurrence, joined by Justice Ginsburg, noting that the city's actions might nonetheless be constrained by the Establishment Clause. Disputing that view, Justice SCALIA filed a concurrence, joined by Justice Thomas, stating: "The city ought not fear that today's victory has propelled it from the Free Speech Clause frying pan into the Establishment Clause fire." Justice BREYER filed a concurrence cautioning that he joined the opinion "on the understanding that the 'government speech' doctrine is a rule of thumb, not a rigid category. Were the City to discriminate in the selection of permanent monuments on grounds unrelated to the display's theme, say solely on political grounds, its action might well violate the First Amendment." And Justice SOUTER concurred only in the judgment, cautioning that, if a monument "has some religious character, the specter of violating the Establishment Clause will behoove [a city] to take care to avoid the appearance of a flat-out establishment of religion, in the sense of the government's adoption of the tenets expressed or symbolized. In such an instance, there will be safety in numbers, and it will be in the interest of a careful government to accept other monuments to stand nearby, to dilute the appearance of adopting whatever particular religious position the single example alone might stand for."

By treating the erection of monuments in the park as a form of government speech, Summum curtailed the possibility that the public park would be treated as a public forum with respect to monuments. Government speech doctrine thus had the effect of avoiding practical problems that might exist if a limited public forum were found. That in turn raises the thorny question of when government speech doctrine may be invoked. The Court set out to answer that question in the case that follows, which also concerned religious speech on government property:

Shurtleff v. City of Boston, Massachusetts

596 U.S. ___, 142 S. Ct. 1583, 212 L. Ed. 2d 621 (2022).

■ JUSTICE BREYER delivered the opinion of the Court.

[This] case concerns a flagpole outside Boston City Hall. For years, Boston has allowed private groups to request use of the flagpole to raise flags of their choosing. As part of this program, Boston approved hundreds of requests to raise dozens of different flags. The city did not deny a single request to raise a flag until, in 2017, Harold Shurtleff, the director of a group called Camp Constitution, asked to fly a Christian flag. Boston refused. At that time, Boston admits, it had no written policy limiting use of the flagpole based on the content of a flag.

The first and basic question we must answer is whether Boston's flag-raising program constitutes government speech. [When the government wishes to state an opinion, to speak for the community, to formulate policies, or to implement programs, it naturally chooses what to say and what not to say. That must be true for government to work. Boston could not easily congratulate the Red Sox on a victory were the city powerless to decline to simultaneously transmit the views of disappointed Yankees fans. [We] conduct a holistic inquiry designed to determine whether the government intends to speak for itself or to regulate private expression. Our review is not mechanical; it is driven by a case's context rather than the rote application of rigid factors. Our past cases have looked to [the] history of the expression at issue; the public's likely perception as to who (the government or a private person) is speaking; and the extent to which the government has actively shaped or controlled the expression.

[Flags] on Boston's City Hall Plaza usually convey the city's messages. [The] question remains whether, on the 20 or so times a year when Boston allowed private groups to raise their own flags, those flags, too, expressed the city's message. Next, then, we consider whether the public would tend to view the speech at issue as the government's. In this case, the circumstantial evidence does not tip the scale. [Finally], we look at the extent to which Boston actively controlled these flag raisings and shaped the messages the flags sent. The answer, it seems, is not at all. And that is the most salient feature of this case.

[We] do not settle this dispute by counting noses—or, rather, counting flags. [Boston] told the public that it sought "to accommodate all applicants" who wished to hold events at Boston's "public forums," including on City Hall Plaza. The application form asked only for contact information and a brief description of the event, with proposed dates and times. The city employee who handled applications testified by deposition that he had previously "never requested to review a flag or requested changes to a flag in connection with approval"; nor did he even see flags before the events. The city's practice was to approve flag raisings, without exception. It has no record of denying a request until Shurtleff's.

[In] Summum, we emphasized that Pleasant Grove City always selected which monuments it would place in its park (whether or not the government funded those monuments), and it typically took ownership over them. In Walker, a state board maintained direct control over license plate designs by actively reviewing every proposal and rejecting at least a dozen.

The facts of this case are much closer to Matal v. Tam. There, we held that trademarks were not government speech because the Patent and Trademark Office registered all manner of marks and normally did not consider their viewpoint, except occasionally to turn away marks it deemed "offensive." [Boston] could easily have done more to make clear it wished to speak for itself by raising flags. [Nothing] prevents Boston from changing its policies going forward.

■ JUSTICE ALITO, with whom JUSTICE THOMAS and JUSTICE GORSUCH join, concurring in the judgment.

[I] cannot go along with the Court's decision to analyze this case in terms of the triad of factors—history, the public's perception of who is speaking, and the extent to which the government has exercised control over speech— that our decision in Walker derived from Summum. [Treating] those factors as a test obscures the real question in government-speech cases: whether the government is *speaking* instead of regulating private expression.

[To] prevent the government-speech doctrine from being used as a cover for censorship, courts must focus on the identity of the speaker. The ultimate question is whether the government is actually expressing its own views or the real speaker is a private party and the government is surreptitiously engaged in the regulation of private speech. [Government] speech occurs if—but only if—a government purposefully expresses a message of its own through persons authorized to speak on its behalf, and in doing so, does not rely on a means that abridges private speech. [For] "speech" to be spoken by the government, the relevant act of communication must be government action. [And] because "speech" requires the purposeful communication of the speaker's own message, the message expressed must have been formulated by a person with the power to determine what messages the government will communicate. In short, the government must set the overall message to be communicated through official action.

[The] government-speech doctrine is not based on the view—which we have neither accepted nor rejected—that governmental entities have First Amendment rights. Instead, the doctrine is based on the notion that governmental communication—and the exercise of control over those charged by law with implementing a government's communicative agenda—do not normally restrict the activities of persons acting as private individuals.

[To] establish that expression constitutes government speech exempt from First Amendment attack, the government must satisfy two conditions. First, it must show that the challenged activity constitutes government speech in the literal sense—purposeful communication of a governmentally determined message by a person acting within the scope of a power to speak for the government. Second, the government must establish it did not rely on a means that abridges the speech of persons acting in a private capacity.

Our precedents recognize two ways in which a government can speak using private assistance. First, the government can prospectively enlist private entities to convey its own message by deputizing private persons as its agents. In that kind of situation, private persons assume a public or quasi-public capacity that empowers them to speak on behalf of the government. So long as this responsibility is voluntarily assumed, speech by a private party within the scope of his power to speak for the government constitutes government speech.

Second, the government can adopt a medium of expression created by a private party and use it to express a government message. In that circumstance, private parties are not deputized by the government; instead a private person generates a medium of expression and transfers it to the government. For the adopted expression to qualify as the government's, the private party must alienate control over the medium of expression to the government. And government actors must put the medium to use to intentionally express a government message. Otherwise, the government is simply providing a forum for private parties to submit their own productions and usual First Amendment principles apply. And to avoid running afoul of the prohibition on compelled speech, that alienation must be voluntary.

[Facilitating] speech by private persons cannot constitute government speech unless the government assigns a power to speak to those persons or appropriates the products of their expressive activity to express its own message. [For] analogous reasons, private-party expression in any type of forum recognized by our precedents does not constitute government speech.

A forum, by definition, is a space for private parties to express their own views.

The government can of course speak as a participant in a forum, but the creation of a space for private discourse does not involve expressing a governmental message, deputizing private parties to express it, or adopting a private party's contribution as a vehicle of government speech. So when examination of the government's policy and practice indicates that the government has intentionally opened a nontraditional forum for public discourse, a court may immediately infer that private-party expression in the forum is not government speech. There is no need to consider history, public perception, or control in the abstract.

———

SPHERES OF GOVERNMENT CONTROL: GOVERNMENT AS EDUCATOR, EMPLOYER AND PATRON

How may government regulate speech when acting as educator, employer, and dispenser of public benefits? In these settings, does government enjoy some of the characteristics of private actors, such that it has greater latitude to control speech? Is the speech of students, employees, and grantees likely to be attributed to government in such settings? Should government be able to regulate or edit its own "message"? The cases below explore this question.

———

STUDENT SPEECH IN PUBLIC SCHOOLS

Unlike streets and parks and other public "forums," public education is a context in which speech is highly controlled. The classroom is a place of structured dialogue bounded by teacher authority and rules of decorum, and the curriculum itself prescribes which ideas are to be studied and discussed. Yet not every aspect of school is curricular, even inside the classroom. Students socialize outside of class, in the hallways, cafeterias or playing fields. Teachers sometimes share their personal views with students. And students might engage in silent demonstrative conduct even while in class. Does the First Amendment protect student speech in these noncurricular contexts? What should the standard of review be for a restriction on student speech? Should school authorities be given more authority to curtail disruption, or nip it in the bud, than the police enjoy with respect to speakers in the public square? Only in curricular settings or in noncurricular settings too? The following cases explore these questions.

1. ***Black armbands as nondisruptive symbolic conduct.*** In **Tinker v. Des Moines Independent Community School District**, 393 U.S. 503 (1969), the Court held that a public school could not discipline two high school students and one junior high school student for wearing black armbands to school to publicize their objections to the Vietnam War. They were asked to remove their armbands and refused. In accordance with a school policy adopted two days earlier in anticipation of such a protest, the students were suspended until they were ready to return without the armbands. The lower federal court refused to enjoin the disciplinary action.

In reversing, Justice FORTAS's majority opinion stated that "First Amendment rights, applied in light of the special characteristics of the school environment, are available to teachers and students. It can hardly be argued that either students or teachers shed their constitutional rights to freedom of speech or expression at the schoolhouse gate. [The] problem here involves direct, primary First Amendment rights akin to 'pure speech.' The school officials banned and sought to punish petitioners for a silent, passive expression of opinion, unaccompanied by any disorder or disturbance on the part of petitioners. There is here no evidence whatever of petitioners' interference, actual or nascent, with the schools' work or of collision with the rights of other students to be secure and to be let alone. Accordingly, this case does not concern speech or action that intrudes upon the work of the schools or the rights of other students.

"[In] our system, undifferentiated fear or apprehension of disturbance is not enough to overcome the right to freedom of expression. [In] order for the State [to] justify prohibition of a particular expression of opinion, it must be able to show that its action was caused by something more than a mere desire to avoid the discomfort and unpleasantness that always accompany an unpopular viewpoint. [Here, there was no] evidence that the school authorities had reason to anticipate that the wearing of the armbands would substantially interfere with the work of the school or impinge upon the rights of other students. On the contrary, the action of the school authorities appears to have been based upon an urgent wish to avoid the controversy which might result from the expression, even by the silent symbol of armbands, of opposition to this Nation's part in the conflagration in Vietnam.

"It is also relevant that the school authorities did not purport to prohibit the wearing of all symbols of political or controversial significance. The record shows that students in some of the schools wore buttons relating to national political campaigns, and some even wore the Iron Cross, traditionally a symbol of Nazism. The order prohibiting the wearing of armbands did not extend to these. Instead, a particular symbol [was] singled out for prohibition. [In] our system, state-operated schools may not be enclaves of totalitarianism. School officials do not possess absolute authority over their students. Students in school as well as out of school [are] possessed of fundamental rights which the State must respect, just as they themselves must respect their obligations to the State. In our system, students may not be regarded as closed-circuit recipients of only that which the State chooses to communicate. They may not be confined to the expression of those sentiments that are officially approved.

"[This] principle [is] not confined to the supervised and ordained discussion which takes place in the classroom. The principal use to which the schools are dedicated is to accommodate students during prescribed hours for the purpose of certain types of activities. Among those activities is personal intercommunication among the students. [A] student's rights, therefore, do not embrace merely the classroom hours. When he is in the cafeteria, or on the playing field, or on the campus during the authorized hours, he may express his opinions, even on controversial subjects like the conflict in Vietnam, if he does so without 'materially and substantially interfer[ing] with the requirements of appropriate discipline in the operation of the school' and without colliding with the rights of others. [This standard was quoted from Burnside v. Byars, 363 F.2d 744 (5th Cir. 1966) (holding school could not ban "freedom buttons").] But conduct by the student, in class or out of it, which for any reason—whether it stems from time, place, or type of behavior—materially disrupts classwork or involves substantial disorder or invasion of the rights of others is, of course, not immunized by the constitutional guarantee of freedom of speech."

Justice BLACK's dissent charged the majority with taking over from school officials "the power to control pupils." He objected to any view that "students and teachers may use the schools at their whim as a platform for the exercise of free speech—'symbolic' or 'pure.' [I] have never believed that any person has a right to give speeches or engage in demonstrations where he pleases and when he pleases." He argued, moreover, that "the record overwhelmingly shows that the [wearing of the] armbands did exactly what [the school officials] foresaw it would, that is, took the students' minds off their classwork and diverted them to thoughts about the highly emotional subject of the Vietnam War. [One] does not need to be a prophet or the son of a prophet to know that after the Court's holding today some students [will] be ready, able, and willing to defy their teachers on practically all orders. This is the more unfortunate for the schools since groups of students all over the land are already running loose, conducting break-ins, sit-ins, lie-ins, and smash-ins." Justice Harlan also dissented, conceding that the First Amendment applied in school but arguing that impermissible viewpoint discrimination had not been demonstrated.

After Tinker, could a public school prohibit students from wearing all buttons or insignia on their clothing? All "political" buttons or insignia? Could it require students to wear prescribed uniforms? Could it ban the wearing of "gang colors" to prevent outbreaks of violence? Could it stop male students from wearing T-shirts bearing sexist slogans in order to boost female students' self-esteem and academic performance? Could it bar *teachers* from wearing black armbands?

2. *Coercion in the school setting: the example of the Tinker case.* Might the vulnerability of minors in the school setting justify special speech protections? Consider the facts of the plaintiffs' Vietnam War protest in Tinker: "Christopher Eckhart [one of the high school student-plaintiffs in Tinker] [was] 'fearful and trembling' as he got out of the car [arriving] at school about eight o'clock went to his locker, and removed his winter coat. [After refusing the principal's request that he remove the armband, Eckhardt was told that] he was 'too young to have opinions' and that 'colleges didn't accept protesters.' [At] this point, [Eckhardt] recalls that [the principal] told him that the 'senior boys were not going to like what [he] was doing' and then he asked him if he 'was looking for a busted nose.' " Johnson, The Struggle for Student Rights 16–17 (1997).

3. *Book removal from public school libraries.* In **Board of Education v. Pico**, 457 U.S. 853 (1982), the Court confronted the problem of school authorities' removal of books from school libraries. Members of the school board of Island Trees, New York, obtained from a conservative parents' organization a list of books described as "objectionable" or "improper fare for school students." They found nine of these books in the high school library, and the board ordered all but one of the books to be removed and condemned them as "anti-American, anti-Christian, anti-Semitic, and just plain filthy." They disregarded the recommendation of a staff/parent committee that several more of the books should be retained. The Court held that summary judgment should not have been granted below to the school board, because there remained a genuine issue of material fact: namely,

whether the book removal was ideologically or pedagogically motivated. Justice BRENNAN, writing for a plurality including Justices Marshall, Stevens, and (in large part) Blackmun, wrote "Because we are concerned in this case with the suppression of ideas, our holding today affects only the discretion to *remove* books. In brief, we hold that local school boards may not remove books from school library shelves simply because they dislike the ideas contained in those books and seek by their removal to 'prescribe what shall be orthodox in politics, nationalism, religion, or other matters of opinion.' [Barnette (p. 478 below).] Such purposes stand inescapably condemned by our precedents." Because the key question of intent was disputed in the record, the Court remanded for trial. (The case was abandoned after remand and there was no further hearing on the merits.)." Justice BLACKMUN, concurring in part and concurring in the judgment, disagreed with the plurality's emphasis on the right to receive information: "[T]he principle involved here is both narrower and more basic than the 'right to receive information' identified by the plurality. I do not suggest that the State has any affirmative obligation to provide students with information or ideas, something that may well be associated with a 'right to receive.' " Justice WHITE, casting the crucial fifth vote, concurred only in the judgment, expressing no view on the constitutional merits. He suggested that the case should have been decided narrowly under routine summary judgment law, thus avoiding "a dissertation on the extent to which the First Amendment limits the discretion of the school board to remove books from the school library."

Chief Justice BURGER dissented, joined by Justices Powell, Rehnquist, and O'Connor. He argued that the schools' role in inculcating fundamental values necessitated "content-based decisions about the appropriateness of retaining materials in the school library and curriculum." Such decisions "express the views of their community; they may err, of course, and the voters may remove them."

Justice REHNQUIST also dissented, joined by Chief Justice Burger and Justice Powell. He urged that the Court "candidly recogniz[e] that the role of government as sovereign is subject to more stringent limitations than is the role of government as employer, property owner, or [educator]": "[Had] petitioners been the members of a town council, I suppose all would agree that [ordinarily] they could not have prohibited the sale of these books by private booksellers within the municipality. But we have also recognized that the government may act in other capacities than as sovereign, and when it does the First Amendment may speak with a different voice. When it acts as an educator, at least at the elementary and secondary school level, the government is engaged in inculcating social values and knowledge in relatively impressionable young people." He continued: "[In] the very course of administering the many-faceted operations of a school district, the mere decision to purchase some books will necessarily preclude the possibility of purchasing others. The decision to teach a particular subject may preclude the possibility of teaching another subject. A decision to replace a teacher because of ineffectiveness may by implication be seen as a disparagement of the subject matter taught. In each of these instances, however, the book or the exposure to the subject matter may be acquired elsewhere. The managers of the school district are not proscribing it as to the citizenry in general, but are simply determining that it will not be included in the curriculum or school library. In short, actions by the government as educator do not raise the same First Amendment concerns as actions by the government as sovereign."

"[Despite] Justice Brennan's suggestion to the contrary, this Court has never held that the First Amendment grants junior high school and high school students a right of access to certain information in school. It is true that the Court has recognized a limited version of that right in other settings, [but] not one of these cases concerned or even purported to discuss elementary or secondary educational institutions. [The] idea [that] students have a right of access, *in the school,* to information other than that thought by their educators to be necessary is contrary to the very nature of an inculcative education." Education consists of the selective presentation and explanation of ideas. The effective acquisition of knowledge depends upon an orderly exposure to relevant information. [Determining] what information *not* to present to the students is often as important as identifying relevant material. [The] libraries of such schools serve as supplements to this inculcative role. Unlike university or public libraries, elementary and secondary school libraries are not designed for free-wheeling inquiry; they are tailored, as the public school curriculum is tailored, to the teaching of basic skills and ideas. [Finally,] the most obvious reason that petitioners' removal of the books did not violate respondents' right to receive information is the ready availability of the books [elsewhere]. The government as educator does not seek to reach beyond the confines of the school. Indeed, following the removal from the school library of the books at issue in this case, the local public library put all nine books on display [and they were] fully accessible to any inquisitive student."

Justice Rehnquist concluded by suggesting that Justice Brennan's distinctions between book acquisition and removal and between good and bad motives were incoherent in relation to the asserted right to receive ideas: "[If] Justice Brennan truly has found a 'right to receive ideas, [the] distinction between acquisition and removal makes little sense. The failure of a library to acquire a book denies access to its contents just as effectively as does the removal of the book from the library's shelf. [If] 'suppression of ideas' is to be the talisman, one would think that a school board's public announcement of its refusal to acquire certain books would have every bit as much impact on public attention as would an equally publicized decision to remove the books. And yet only the latter action would violate the First Amendment under Justice Brennan's analysis. [Moreover,] bad motives and good motives alike deny access to the books removed. If [there truly is] a constitutional right to receive information, it is difficult to see why the reason for the denial makes any difference. Of course Justice Brennan's view is that intent matters because the First Amendment does not tolerate an officially prescribed orthodoxy. But this reasoning mixes First Amendment apples and oranges. The right to receive information differs from the right to be free from an officially prescribed orthodoxy. Not every educational denial of access to information casts a pall of orthodoxy over the [classroom]." He accordingly found the school board's decision "sufficiently related to 'educational suitability' to pass muster under the First Amendment." Justices Powell and O'Connor also filed separate dissents.

Parent-initiated book removal from school curricula and libraries continues to be a frequently litigated issue in the lower courts. Does Pico give adequate guidance? Consider the following comment: "[I]f school boards know that the courts will sometimes get involved, even if only in extreme cases, and [therefore] restrain themselves accordingly, Pico may serve as an effective constitutional limit, even if that limit is poorly defined and mostly symbolic and self-enforced." Yudof, "Library Book Selection and the Public Schools: The Quest for the Archimedean Point," 59 Ind. L.J. 527 (1984).

Pico identified a school library as lying somewhere between the prescribed curriculum, in which student speech may be controlled, and the realm protected by Tinker in which students are free, as public citizens, to engage in voluntary expression and inquiry. Do First Amendment interests attenuate, and government interests increase, as student speech moves closer to the curriculum? Consider the following cases involving speech at a mandatory school assembly and production of a school newspaper in connection with a journalism class.

4. *Sexual innuendo at a student assembly.* In **Bethel School District No. 403 v. Fraser**, 478 U.S. 675 (1986), the Court held that the First Amendment did not prevent a school district "from disciplining a high school student for giving a lewd speech at a [school] assembly." Fraser, in nominating a fellow student for student elective office before a high school assembly of approximately 600 students, delivered a speech containing sexual innuendo.[1] During the speech, some students hooted, yelled, and made gestures simulating the sexual activities alluded to in the speech; others appeared bewildered and embarrassed. The school disciplined Fraser under its disruptive-conduct rule by suspending him for two days. He brought an action claiming a violation of his First Amendment rights. The District Court sustained his claim and the Court of Appeals, relying upon Tinker, affirmed. The Court reversed by a vote of 7–2.

Chief Justice BURGER's majority opinion chastised the lower court for ignoring the "marked distinction between the political 'message' of the armbands in Tinker and the sexual content of [Fraser's] speech" here and pointed out that Tinker had emphasized that the armbands worn there did not intrude upon the work of the schools. He pointed out that the "undoubted freedom to advocate unpopular and controversial views in schools and classrooms must be balanced against the society's countervailing interest in teaching students the boundaries of socially appropriate behavior." He added that the inculcation of fundamental societal values was truly the "work of the schools." Accordingly, the school district had acted legitimately in "imposing sanctions upon Fraser in response to his offensively lewd and indecent speech": "Unlike the sanctions imposed [in] Tinker, the penalties imposed [here] were unrelated to any political viewpoint. The First Amendment does not prevent the school officials from determining that to permit a vulgar and lewd speech such as [Fraser's] would undermine the school's basic educational mission. A high school assembly [is] no place for a sexually explicit monologue directed towards an unsuspecting audience of teenage students. Accordingly, it was perfectly appropriate for the school to disassociate itself to make the point to the pupils that vulgar speech and lewd conduct is wholly inconsistent with the 'fundamental values' of public school education."

---

[1] Fraser's speech had included the following passage: "I know a man who is firm—he's firm in his pants, he's firm in his shirt, his character is firm—but most [of] all, his belief in you, the students of Bethel, is firm. Jeff Kuhlman is a man who takes his point and pounds it in. If necessary, he'll take an issue and nail it to the wall. He doesn't attack things in spurts—he drives hard, pushing and pushing until finally—he succeeds. Jeff is a man who will go to the very end—even the climax, for each and every one of you."

In an opinion concurring in the judgment, Justice BRENNAN agreed that the school officials' action was not unconstitutional "under the circumstances of this case," but emphasized that Fraser would have been protected had he given the same speech outside of the school environment and might well even have been protected "had he given it in school but under different circumstances, where the school's legitimate interests in teaching and maintaining civil public discourse were less weighty." Justice MARSHALL agreed with Justice Brennan's principles but dissented, relying on the fact that the school board "had not demonstrated any disruption of the educational process." Justice STEVENS also submitted a dissent, arguing that Fraser did not have adequate "reason to anticipate punitive consequences" from his speeches.

5. *Articles on pregnancy and divorce in a school newspaper.*
Hazelwood School District v. Kuhlmeier, 484 U.S. 260 (1988), examined the extent to which educators may exercise editorial control over the contents of a high school newspaper produced as part of a school journalism class and funded by the school. The 5–3 decision upheld a high school principal's deletion of two stories from the school newspaper. One story described three students' experiences with pregnancy; the other discussed the impact of parents' divorce on students at the school. At the outset, Justice WHITE's majority opinion found that the newspaper was not a public forum, either traditionally or by "designation." "Accordingly, school officials were entitled to regulate the contents of [the newspaper] in any reasonable manner. It is this standard, rather than our decision in Tinker, that governs this case." He proceeded:

"The question whether the First Amendment requires a school to tolerate particular student speech—the question that we addressed in Tinker—is different from the question whether the First Amendment requires a school affirmatively to promote particular student speech. The former question addresses educators' ability to silence a student's personal expression that happens to occur on the school premises. The latter question concerns educators' authority over school-sponsored publications, theatrical productions, and other expressive activities that students, parents, and members of the public might reasonably perceive to bear the imprimatur of the school. These activities may fairly be characterized as part of the school curriculum, whether or not they occur in a traditional classroom setting, so long as they are supervised by faculty members and designed to impart particular knowledge or skills to student participants and audiences.

"Educators are entitled to exercise greater control over this second form of student expression to assure that participants learn whatever lessons the activity is designed to teach, that readers or listeners are not exposed to material that may be inappropriate for their level of maturity, and that the views of the individual speaker are not erroneously attributed to the school. Hence, a school may in its capacity as publisher of a school newspaper or producer of a school play 'disassociate itself,' Fraser, [from] speech that is, for example, ungrammatical, poorly written, inadequately researched, biased or prejudiced, vulgar or profane, or unsuitable for immature audiences. A school must be able to set high standards for the student speech that is disseminated under its auspices [and] may refuse to disseminate student speech that does not meet those standards. In addition, a school must be able to take into account the emotional maturity of the intended audience in determining whether to disseminate student speech on potentially sensitive [topics].

"[Accordingly,] we conclude that the standard articulated in Tinker for determining when a school may punish student expression need not also be the standard for determining when a school may refuse to lend its name and resources to the dissemination of student expression. Instead, we hold that educators do not offend the First Amendment by exercising editorial control over the style and content of student speech in school-sponsored expressive activities so long as their actions are reasonably related to legitimate pedagogical concerns. This standard is consistent with our oft-expressed view that the education of the Nation's youth is primarily the responsibility of parents, teachers, and state and local school officials, and not of federal judges. It is only when the decision to censor a school-sponsored publication, theatrical production, or other vehicle of student expression has no valid educational purpose that the First Amendment [requires] judicial intervention to protect students' constitutional rights."

Applying this standard, Justice White held that the principal's deletion of the pregnancy story was "reasonable" because, even though the students mentioned had consented and fictitious names had been used, it was possible that "the students' anonymity was not adequately protected," so that there was a reasonable fear that "the article violated whatever pledge of anonymity had been given to the pregnant students." Moreover, since the article contained discussion of sexual histories and students' use of birth control, it was not unreasonable "for the principal to have concluded that such frank talk was inappropriate in a school-sponsored publication distributed to 14-year-old freshmen and presumably taken home to be read by students' even younger brothers and sisters." Similarly, the deletion of the divorce story was reasonable because a student quoted by name in the article made comments sharply critical of her father, so that the principal could have concluded "that an individual publicly identified as an inattentive parent [was] entitled to an opportunity to defend himself as a matter of journalistic fairness."

Justice BRENNAN's dissent, joined by Justices Marshall and Blackmun, argued that Tinker was controlling and that, under Tinker's standard, there was no valid basis for deleting the stories. In his view, the principal had "violated the First Amendment's prohibitions against censorship of any student expression that neither disrupts classwork nor invades the rights of others, and against any censorship that is not narrowly tailored to serve its purpose." He elaborated: "If mere incompatibility with the school's pedagogical message were a constitutionally sufficient justification for the suppression of student speech, school officials [could convert] our public schools into 'enclaves of totalitarianism' that 'strangle the free mind at its source.' The First Amendment permits no such blanket censorship authority." The Tinker test, he insisted, was adequate to resolve the issue here. After applying it in Fraser, the Court had avoided it here by distinguishing between personal and school-sponsored speech, a distinction unsupported by the precedents. The Court's opinion, he concluded, "denudes high school students of much of the First Amendment protection that Tinker itself prescribed. [The] young men and women of Hazelwood East expected a civics lesson, but not the one the Court teaches them today."

After Hazelwood, could the school restrain publication of the same stories if printed in an "underground" student newspaper funded through private advertisements and sales? Even if distributed on school property? Do

Fraser and Hazelwood have any application to a public university setting? For commentary, see Hafen, "Hazelwood School District and the Role of First Amendment Institutions," 1988 Duke L.J. 685 (arguing that Hazelwood indicates that Fraser was "an important transitional case that signaled the Court's [recognition] that broad interpretations of Tinker [had] reduced schools' institutional authority in ways that undermined their educational effectiveness"); and Diamond, "The First Amendment and Public Schools: the Case Against Judicial Intervention," 59 Tex. L. Rev. 477 (1981).

Note that Fraser and Hazelwood emphasize the government's interest in removing its apparent imprimatur of approval from lewd or controversial speech by students in school-sponsored activities. Does this interest in disassociation suggest that government, not the student, will be perceived as the speaker here? Implicit in this view is that government *as speaker* is not constrained by the First Amendment in the same way as it is constrained as sovereign. Do these suggestions in Fraser and Hazelwood vindicate Justice Rehnquist's dissent in Pico? Consider the view that, because "school-sponsored activities are intrinsically and pervasively expressive," such activities should be treated as the equivalent of a "nonforum," in which "government control of student speech [is] shielded from free speech scrutiny." See Brownstein, "The Nonforum as a First Amendment Category: Bringing Order Out of the Chaos of Free Speech Cases Involving School-Sponsored Activities," 42 U.C. Davis L. Rev. 717 (2009). Is it desirable to immunize government from free speech scrutiny altogether when government is "speaking"? Might government distort public dialogue even in its role as speaker or editor?

6. ***Drug-related student speech at a school-sponsored event.*** Under Tinker, Fraser, and Hazelwood, may a public school discipline a student for displaying a 14-foot banner saying "BONG HiTS 4 JESUS" at a school-sponsored event? When the Olympic torch passed through Juneau, Alaska, the local high school principal allowed students to go outside the school to watch. The outing was treated as a school-approved class trip under teacher supervision. When high school senior Joseph Frederick unfurled his banner before the other students (and television cameras), the principal, Deborah Morse, interpreted it as drug-related speech, confiscated it and disciplined Frederick. Juneau school board policy specifically prohibited "any assembly or public expression [that] advocates the use of substances that are illegal to minors." In **Morse v. Frederick**, 551 U.S. 393 (2007), by a vote of 6–3, the Court rejected Frederick's claim that his free speech rights had been violated. Chief Justice ROBERTS wrote for the Court:

"At the outset, we reject Frederick's argument that this is not a school speech. [The] event occurred during normal school hours. It was sanctioned by Principal Morse 'as an approved social event or class trip.' Teachers and administrators were interspersed among the students and charged with supervising them. The high school band and cheerleaders performed. Frederick, standing among other [Juneau] students across the street from the school, directed his banner toward the school, making it plainly visible to most students. Under these circumstances, we agree with the superintendent that Frederick cannot 'stand in the midst of his fellow students, during school hours, at a school-sanctioned activity and claim he is not at school.'

"The message on Frederick's banner is cryptic. It is no doubt offensive to some, perhaps amusing to others. To still others, it probably means nothing at all. Frederick himself claimed 'that the words were just nonsense meant to attract television cameras.' But Principal Morse thought the banner would be interpreted by those viewing it as promoting illegal drug use, and that interpretation is plainly a reasonable one. [The] phrase could be interpreted as an imperative: '[Take] bong hits.' [Alternatively,] the phrase could be viewed as celebrating drug use—'bong hits [are a good thing],' or '[we take] bong hits.' [Frederick does not argue] that the banner conveys any sort of political or religious message. [This] is plainly not a case about political debate over the criminalization of drug use or possession.

"[Our cases] recognize that deterring drug use by schoolchildren is an 'important—indeed, perhaps compelling' interest. Drug abuse can cause severe and permanent damage to the health and well-being of young people. [Student] speech celebrating illegal drug use at a school event, in the presence of school administrators and teachers, thus poses a particular challenge for school officials working to protect those entrusted to their care from the dangers of drug abuse. [The] 'special characteristics of the school environment,' Tinker, and the governmental interest in stopping student drug abuse, [allow] schools to restrict student expression that they reasonably regard as promoting illegal drug use. Tinker warned that schools may not prohibit student speech because of 'undifferentiated fear or apprehension of disturbance' or 'a mere desire to avoid the discomfort and unpleasantness that always accompany an unpopular viewpoint.' The danger here is far more serious and palpable. The particular concern to prevent student drug abuse at issue here, embodied in established school policy, extends well beyond an abstract desire to avoid controversy.

"Petitioners urge us to adopt the broader rule that Frederick's speech is proscribable because it is plainly 'offensive' as that term is used in Fraser. We think this stretches Fraser too far; that case should not be read to encompass any speech that could fit under some definition of 'offensive.' After all, much political and religious speech might be perceived as offensive to some. The concern here is not that Frederick's speech was offensive, but that it was reasonably viewed as promoting illegal drug use. [Reversed.]"

Justice THOMAS concurred, stating his view that there is no constitutional basis to find any free speech rights whatever for students in school. Schools act "*in loco parentis*," Justice Thomas noted, and this doctrine at common law allowed schools to regulate student speech virtually completely: "As originally understood, the Constitution does not afford students a right to free speech in public schools. [Early] public schools gave total control to teachers, who expected obedience and respect from students. And courts routinely deferred to schools' authority to make rules and to discipline students for violating those rules. [I] join the Court's opinion because it erodes Tinker's hold in the realm of student speech, even though it does so by adding to the patchwork of exceptions to the Tinker standard. I think the better approach is to dispense with Tinker altogether, and given the opportunity, I would do so."

Justice ALITO also concurred separately, joined by Justice Kennedy. He emphasized that the majority opinion was narrowly limited to restriction of speech advocating drug use, and "provides no support for any restriction of speech that can plausibly be interpreted as commenting on any political or social issue, including speech on issues such as 'the wisdom of the war on drugs or of legalizing marijuana for medicinal use.'" He also emphasized that the opinion of the Court "does not endorse the broad argument advanced by petitioners and the United States that the First Amendment permits public school officials to censor any student speech that interferes with a school's 'educational mission.' This argument can easily be manipulated in dangerous ways, and I would reject it before such abuse occurs. The 'educational mission' of the public schools is defined by the elected and appointed public officials with authority over the schools and by the school administrators and faculty. As a result, some public schools have defined their educational missions as including the inculcation of whatever political and social views are held by the members of these groups. [The] 'educational mission' argument would give public school authorities a license to suppress speech on political and social issues based on disagreement with the viewpoint expressed. The argument, therefore, strikes at the very heart of the First Amendment." Justice Alito also suggested that, in light of the confined and mandatory environment to which students are subject, schools may regulate speech to nip violence in the bud; by analogy, he suggested, it may regulate speech to prevent drug use, which is also a safety threat to students.

Justice STEVENS dissented, joined by Justices Souter and Ginsburg: "In my judgment, the First Amendment protects student speech if the message itself neither violates a permissible rule nor expressly advocates conduct that is illegal and harmful to students. This nonsense banner does neither, and the Court does serious violence to the First Amendment in [upholding] a school's decision to punish Frederick for expressing a view with which it disagreed. [The] Court's test invites stark viewpoint discrimination. In this case, [the] principal has unabashedly acknowledged that she disciplined Frederick because she disagreed with the pro-drug viewpoint she ascribed to the message on the banner. [And] 'promoting illegal drug use 'comes nowhere close to proscribable 'incitement to imminent lawless action.' Brandenburg. [No] one seriously maintains that drug advocacy (much less Frederick's ridiculous sign) comes within the vanishingly small category of speech that can be prohibited because of its feared consequences.

"Given that the relationship between schools and students 'is custodial and tutelary,' [it] might well be appropriate to tolerate some targeted viewpoint discrimination in this unique setting. And while conventional speech may be restricted only when likely to 'incite imminent lawless action,' it is possible that our rigid imminence requirement ought to be relaxed at schools. But it is one thing to restrict speech that *advocates* drug use. It is another thing entirely to prohibit an obscure message with a drug theme that a third party subjectively—and not very reasonably—thinks is tantamount to express advocacy. Cf. Masses (Hand, J.). [Just] as we insisted in Tinker that the school establish some likely connection between the armbands and their feared consequences, so too [Juneau] must show that Frederick's supposed advocacy stands a meaningful chance of making otherwise-abstemious students try marijuana. [This] is a nonsense message, not advocacy. [Admittedly,] some high school students (including those who use drugs) are dumb. Most students, however, do not shed their brains at the schoolhouse gate, and most students know dumb advocacy when they see it. The notion that the message on this banner would actually persuade either the average student or even the dumbest one to change his or her behavior is most implausible. That the Court believes such a silly message can be proscribed as advocacy underscores the novelty of its position, and suggests that the principle it articulates has no stopping point." Justice Breyer concurred in part and dissented in part, suggesting that the First

Amendment question need not be reached as the Court could reverse simply
by granting the principal qualified immunity for reasonably thinking the
speech was constitutionally proscribable.

Does Morse v. Frederick develop a new exception to Tinker? Note that
the majority opinion does not purport to rest the ruling on the Fraser
exception for inappropriately vulgar speech in a school setting. Nor does it
rest on the Hazelwood exception for speech that is educationally unsuitable
and might be wrongly attributed to the school. Indeed, Chief Justice Roberts
wrote that "[Hazelwood] does not control this case because no one would
reasonably believe that Frederick's banner bore the school's imprimatur."
Finally, the ruling does not rest on a categorical exception for *all* drug-
related speech; both the majority and Justice Alito's concurrence seem to
concede that student discussion of drug reform in civics class would receive
Tinker protection. So what is the theory of the decision? Recall that Tinker
itself allowed prevention of material disruption of the educational mission.
Is drug abuse such a material disruption? Is it a stretch to equate the need
to prevent drug use with the need to avert schoolyard violence before it
occurs? If so, is the harm sufficiently imminent? Is peer pressure from a sign
the equivalent of taunts that provoke a brawl? Does the decision implicitly
embrace but water down Tinker's holding that preventing harm to student
safety justifies limiting even protected speech? Or is the implicit theory that
advocacy of drug use is so worthless in the school context that little
justification is required? Finally, was the banner in question "cryptic," as the
Court suggested, or "nonsensical," as Justice Stevens had it? Can you make
the case that the banner was straightforwardly parodic?

7. *Public schools and technology.* To what extent should school
officials be able to regulate off-campus speech in an increasingly digital age?
The Supreme Court has yet to address the issue, but consider two high-
profile Third Circuit en banc decisions, J.S. ex rel. Snyder v. Blue Mountain
School District, 650 F.3d 915 (3d Cir. 2011); and Layshock ex rel. Layshock
v. Hermitage School District, 650 F.3d 205 (3d Cir. 2011). Both Snyder and
Layshock involved students who created fake online profiles of school
officials. The Third Circuit found in favor of the students, holding that school
officials could not punish students for off-campus expression absent a
reasonable forecast that the expression would cause substantial disruption
to the school's operation. By contrast, the Ninth Circuit held that a public
high school could expel a student for sending instant messages to his
classmates "that could be interpreted as a plan to attack the school"; under
Tinker, the violent messages "made it reasonable for school officials to
forecast a substantial disruption of school activities." Wynar v. Douglas
County School Dist., 728 F.3d 1062 (9th Cir. 2013). Should school officials
have any authority to regulate students' off-campus speech? If so, how should
that authority be cabined? The Supreme Court finally considered the issue
in the following case:

———

Mahanoy Area School District v. B.L., a Minor

___ U.S. ___, 141 S. Ct. 2038, 210 L. Ed. 2d 403 (2021).

■ JUSTICE BREYER delivered the opinion of the Court.

B. L. [was] a student at Mahanoy Area High School, a public school in Mahanoy City, Pennsylvania. At the end of her freshman year, B. L. tried out for a position on the school's varsity cheerleading squad and for right fielder on a private softball team. She did not make the varsity cheerleading team or get her preferred softball position, but she was offered a spot on the cheerleading squad's junior varsity team. [That] weekend, B. L. used her smartphone to post two photos on Snapchat, a social media application that allows users to post photos and videos that disappear after a set period of time. [The] first image B. L. posted showed B. L. and a friend with middle fingers raised; it bore the caption: "Fuck school fuck softball fuck cheer fuck everything." The second image was blank but for a caption, which read: "Love how me and [another student] get told we need a year of jv before we make varsity but tha[t] doesn't matter to anyone else?" The caption also contained an upside-down smiley-face emoji. [At] least one of [B. L.'s Snapchat friends] took pictures of B. L.'s posts and shared them with other members of the cheerleading squad. One of the students who received these photos showed them to her mother (who was a cheerleading squad coach), and the images spread. That week, several cheerleaders and other students approached the cheerleading coaches "visibly upset" about B. L.'s posts. Questions about the posts persisted during an Algebra class taught by one of the two coaches. After discussing the matter with the school principal, the coaches decided that because the posts used profanity in connection with a school extracurricular activity, they violated team and school rules. As a result, the coaches suspended B. L. from the junior varsity cheerleading squad for the upcoming year.

[We] do not believe the special characteristics that give schools [license] to regulate student speech always disappear when a school regulates speech that takes place off campus. The school's regulatory interests remain significant in some off-campus circumstances. [Several] types of off-campus behavior [may] call for school regulation. These include serious or severe bullying or harassment targeting particular individuals; threats aimed at teachers or other students; the failure to follow rules concerning lessons, the writing of papers, the use of computers, or participation in other online school activities; and breaches of school security devices, including material maintained within school computers.

[Particularly] given the advent of computer-based learning, we hesitate to determine precisely which of many school-related off-campus activities belong on such a list. Neither do we now know how such a list might vary, depending upon a student's age, the nature of the school's off-campus activity, or the impact upon the school itself. Thus, we do not now set forth a broad, highly general First Amendment rule stating just what counts as "off campus" speech and whether or how ordinary First Amendment standards must give way off campus to a school's special need to prevent, *e.g.*, substantial disruption of learning-related activities or the protection of those who make up a school community.

We can, however, mention three features of off-campus speech that often, even if not always, distinguish schools' efforts to regulate that speech from their efforts to regulate on-campus speech. Those features diminish the strength of the unique educational characteristics that might call for special First Amendment leeway.

First, a school, in relation to off-campus speech, will rarely stand *in loco parentis*. [Geographically] speaking, off-campus speech will normally fall within the zone of parental, rather than school-related, responsibility.

Second, from the student speaker's perspective, regulations of off-campus speech, when coupled with regulations of on-campus speech, include all the speech a student utters during the full 24-hour day. That means courts must be more skeptical of a school's efforts to regulate off-campus speech, for doing so may mean the student cannot engage in that kind of speech at all. When it comes to political or religious speech that occurs outside school or a school program or activity, the school will have a heavy burden to justify intervention.

Third, the school itself has an interest in protecting a student's unpopular expression, especially when the expression takes place off campus. America's public schools are the nurseries of democracy. Our representative democracy only works if we protect the marketplace of ideas. This free exchange facilitates an informed public opinion, which, when transmitted to lawmakers, helps produce laws that reflect the People's will. That protection must include the protection of unpopular ideas, for popular ideas have less need for protection. Thus, schools have a strong interest in ensuring that future generations understand the workings in practice of the well-known aphorism, "I disapprove of what you say, but I will defend to the death your right to say it." (Although this quote is often attributed to Voltaire, it was likely coined by an English writer, Evelyn Beatrice Hall.)

[Taken] together, these three features of much off-campus speech mean that the leeway the First Amendment grants to schools in light of their special characteristics is diminished. We leave for future cases to decide where, when, and how these features mean the speaker's off-campus location will make the critical difference. This case can, however, provide one example.

Consider B. L.'s speech. Putting aside the vulgar language, the listener would hear criticism, of the team, the team's coaches, and the school—in a word or two, criticism of the rules of a community of which B. L. forms a part. This criticism did not involve features that would place it outside the First Amendment's ordinary protection. B. L.'s posts, while crude, did not amount to fighting words. Chaplinsky. And while B. L. used vulgarity, her speech was not obscene as this Court has understood that term. Cohen.

[Consider] too when, where, and how B. L. spoke. Her posts appeared outside of school hours from a location outside the school. She did not identify the school in her posts or target any member of the school community with vulgar or abusive language. B. L. also transmitted her speech through a personal cellphone, to an audience consisting of her private circle of Snapchat friends. These features of her speech, while risking transmission to the school itself, nonetheless [diminish] the school's interest in punishing B. L.'s utterance.

But what about the school's interest, here primarily an interest in prohibiting students from using vulgar language to criticize a school team or its coaches—at least when that criticism might well be transmitted to other students, team members, coaches, and faculty? We can break that general interest into three parts.

[The] strength of this anti-vulgarity interest is weakened considerably by the fact that B. L. spoke outside the school on her own time. B. L. spoke under circumstances where the school did not stand *in loco parentis*. [Moreover,] the vulgarity in B. L.'s posts encompassed a message. [The] school has presented no evidence of any general effort to prevent students from using vulgarity outside the classroom.

[We] can find no evidence in the record of the sort of "substantial disruption" of a school activity or a threatened harm to the rights of others that might justify the school's action. [When] one of B. L.'s coaches was asked directly if she had "any reason to think that this particular incident would disrupt class or school activities other than the fact that kids kept asking . . . about it," she responded simply, "No." [The] alleged disturbance here does not meet Tinker's demanding standard.

[One] of the coaches testified that the school decided to suspend B. L. "[based] on the fact that there was negativity put out there that could impact students in the school." There is little else, however, that suggests any serious decline in team morale—to the point where it could create a substantial interference in, or disruption of, the school's efforts to maintain team cohesion.

It might be tempting to dismiss B. L.'s words as unworthy of the robust First Amendment protections discussed herein. But sometimes it is necessary to protect the superfluous in order to preserve the necessary.

■ JUSTICE ALITO, with whom JUSTICE GORSUCH joins, concurring.

Why should enrollment in a public school result in the diminution of a student's free-speech rights? [Parents] are treated as having relinquished the measure of authority that the schools must be able to exercise in order to carry out their state-mandated educational mission, as well as the authority to perform any other functions to which parents expressly or implicitly agree. [It] is reasonable to infer that this authority extends to periods when students are in school but are not in class, for example, when they are walking in a hall, eating lunch, congregating outside before the school day starts, or waiting for a bus after school. [A] public school's regulation of off-premises student speech is a different matter. [Parents] do not implicitly relinquish all that authority when they send their children to a public school.

[Between the] two extremes [of] off-premises speech that is tantamount to on-campus speech and general statements made off premises on matters of public concern [lie] the categories of off-premises student speech that appear to have given rise to the most litigation. [One] group of cases involves perceived threats to school administrators, teachers, other staff members, or students. [Another] common category involves speech that criticizes or derides school administrators, teachers, or other staff members. [Parents] surely do not relinquish their children's ability to complain in an appropriate manner about wrongdoing, dereliction, or even plain incompetence. [Perhaps] the most difficult category involves criticism or hurtful remarks about other students.

Bullying and severe harassment are serious (and age-old) problems, but these concepts are not easy to define with the precision required for a regulation of speech.

■ JUSTICE THOMAS, dissenting.

I would begin the assessment of the scope of free-speech rights incorporated against the States by looking to what ordinary citizens at the time of the Fourteenth Amendment's ratification would have understood the right to encompass. Cases and treatises from that era reveal that public schools retained substantial authority to discipline students. [And,] although schools had less authority after a student returned home, it was well settled that they still could discipline students for off-campus speech or conduct that had a proximate tendency to harm the school environment.

Perhaps the most familiar example applying this rule is a case where a student, after returning home from school, used "disrespectful language" against a teacher—he called the teacher "old"—"in presence of the [teacher] and of some of his fellow pupils." The Vermont Supreme Court held that the teacher could discipline a student for this speech because the speech had "a direct and immediate tendency to injure the school, to subvert the master's authority, and to beget disorder and insubordination." Lander v. Seaver, 32 Vt. 114 (1859). [So] widespread was this rule that it served not only as the basis for schools to discipline disrespectful speech but also to regulate truancy. Although modern doctrine draws a clear line between speech and conduct, cases in the 19th century did not. [Some] courts made statements that, if read in isolation, could suggest that schools had no authority at all to regulate off-campus speech. But, these courts made it clear that the rule against regulating off-campus speech applied only when that speech was "nowise connected with the management or successful operation of the school."

If there is a good constitutional reason to depart from this historical rule, the majority and the parties fail to identify it.

––––––––

SPEECH AND ASSOCIATION BY PUBLIC EMPLOYEES AND CONTRACTORS

To what extent does the First Amendment limit governmental power to regulate the behavior of its employees or contractors? Does the government's status as employer or contractor justify regulations and disqualifications because of political expression or association? Is ideological conformity sometimes a bona fide occupational qualification? Does it matter if the expression or association takes place on or off the job?

These would not have been viewed as substantial constitutional questions if Justice HOLMES's views as a state court judge had prevailed. In 1892, he said: "The petitioner may have a constitutional right to talk politics, but he has no constitutional right to be a policeman. There are few employments for hire in which the servant does not agree to suspend his constitutional right of free speech, as well of idleness, by the implied terms of his contract. The servant cannot complain, as he takes the employment on the terms which are offered him." **McAuliffe v. Mayor of New Bedford**, 155 Mass. 216, 29 N.E. 517 (1892). But the Holmes position has not prevailed: it has long been recognized that, even though there is no "right" to public employment or to a contract, some constitutional restrictions apply when government attempts to discharge employees or contractors for reason of their exercise of constitutionally protected liberties.

The decisions that follow first explore the question of whether government may discharge or otherwise sanction an employee for statements or other expressive activity. Note the Court's distinction between two categories: where the public employer restricts an employee's First Amendment speech rights *as a citizen* on matters of public concern, and where the restriction applies the public employee's free speech rights *as an employee*. The focus next shifts to the question whether hiring and firing decisions may be based on party affiliation—that is, whether a patronage system violates employee rights of political association. Finally, the materials consider whether rights of speech or association enjoyed by public employees should also extend to independent contractors with the government.

PUBLIC EMPLOYEE SPEECH

In **Pickering v. Board of Education**, 391 U.S. 563 (1968), the Court held that a public school teacher could not constitutionally be dismissed from his job for writing a letter to a newspaper criticizing the school board's handling of revenue measures for the schools and its allocation of financial resources between the schools' educational and athletic programs. Justice MARSHALL's majority opinion "unequivocally" rejected the proposition that "teachers may constitutionally be compelled to relinquish the First Amendment rights they would otherwise enjoy as citizens to comment on matters of public interest in connection with the operation of the public schools in which they work." He relied heavily on decisions from the 1950s and 1960s invalidating efforts to require public employees, especially teachers, to disclose their associations and swear loyalty oaths to the state. (See Chapter 3 below.) But he also noted that "the State has interests as an employer in regulating the speech of its employees that differ significantly from those it possesses in connection with regulation of the speech of the citizenry in general. The problem in any case is to arrive at a balance between the interests of the teacher, as a citizen, in commenting upon matters of public concern and the interest of the State, as an employer, in promoting the efficiency of the public services it performs through its employees."

In the circumstances of the case, Justice Marshall found that the government interests did not outweigh Pickering's speech rights: "[T]he question whether a school system requires additional funds is a matter of legitimate public concern on which the judgment of the school administration, including the School Board, cannot, in a society that leaves such questions to popular vote, be taken as conclusive. On such a question free and open debate is vital to informed decision-making by the electorate. Teachers are, as a class, the members of a community most likely to have informed and definite opinions as to how funds allotted to the operation of the schools should be spent. Accordingly, it is essential that they be able to speak out freely on such questions without fear of retaliatory dismissal. [Pickering's statements were] critical of his ultimate employer but [had not been shown] to have in any way either impeded the teacher's proper performance of his daily duties in the classroom or to have interfered with the regular operation of the schools generally. In these circumstances we conclude that the interest of the school administration in limiting teachers' opportunities to contribute to public debate is not significantly greater than its interest in limiting a similar contribution by any member of the general public." Accordingly, absent any malicious libel of the school board actionable under the New York Times standard, Pickering could not be dismissed.

Givhan v. Western Line Consolidated School District, 439 U.S. 410 (1979), extended the Pickering principle to hold unconstitutional a teacher's dismissal for statements criticizing the school's allegedly racially discriminatory policies in a series of *private* encounters with a school principal. For commentary, see Schauer, " 'Private' Speech and the 'Private' Forum," 1979 Sup. Ct. Rev. 217.

Contrast with Pickering and Givhan the Court's decision in the following case, involving speech by an assistant district attorney critical of her supervisors. The case arose when Sheila Myers, an assistant district attorney in New Orleans, was informed by her boss, longtime New Orleans District Attorney Harry Connick, Sr., that she would be transferred to prosecute cases in a different section of the criminal court. Myers opposed the transfer and expressed her view to several supervisors, including Connick. When one supervisor told her that her concerns were not shared by others in the office, she told him she would do some research and prepared a questionnaire soliciting the views of her fellow staff members concerning office transfer policy, office morale, the need for a grievance committee, the level of confidence in supervisors, and whether employees felt pressured to work in political campaigns. She distributed the questionnaire to 15 assistant district attorneys. One of Connick's first assistants told Connick that Myers was creating a "mini-insurrection" within the office. Connick terminated Myers because of her refusal to accept the transfer and because he found her distribution of the questionnaire an act of insubordination. Myers claimed that her termination violated the Free Speech Clause, and the district court and court of appeals agreed, relying on Pickering. The Court reversed by a vote of 5–4:

Connick v. Myers
461 U.S. 138, 103 S. Ct. 1684, 75 L. Ed. 2d 708 (1983).

■ JUSTICE WHITE delivered the opinion of the Court.

[It has long] been settled that a state cannot condition public employment on a basis that infringes the employee's constitutionally protected interest in freedom of expression. [Pickering.] [But the lower courts misapplied Pickering] in striking the balance for respondent. [Connick] contends at the outset that no balancing of interests is required in this case because Myers' questionnaire concerned only internal office matters and that such speech is not upon a matter of "public concern," as the term was used in Pickering. Although we do not agree that Myers' communication in this case was wholly without First Amendment protection, there is much force to Connick's submission. The repeated emphasis in Pickering on the right of a public employee "as a citizen, in commenting upon matters of public concern," was not accidental. This language [reflects] both the historical evolvement of the rights of public employees, and the common sense realization that government offices could not function if every employment decision became a constitutional matter. [Pickering], its antecedents and progeny, lead us to conclude that if Myers' questionnaire cannot be fairly characterized as constituting speech on a matter of public concern, it is unnecessary for us to scrutinize the reasons for her discharge. When employee expression cannot be fairly considered as relating to any matter of political, social, or other concern to the community, government officials should enjoy wide latitude in managing their offices, without intrusive oversight by the judiciary in the name of the [First Amendment].

We do not suggest, however, that Myers' speech, even if not touching upon a matter of public concern, is totally beyond the protection of the First Amendment. [We] in no sense suggest that speech on private matters falls into one of the narrow and well-defined classes of expression which carries so little social value, such as obscenity, that the state can prohibit and punish such expression by all persons in its jurisdiction. For example, an employee's false criticism of his employer on grounds not of public concern may be cause for his discharge but would be entitled to the same protection in a libel action accorded an identical statement made by a man on the street. We hold only that when a public employee speaks not as a citizen upon matters of public concern, but instead as an employee upon matters only of personal interest, absent the most unusual circumstances, a federal court is not the appropriate forum in which to review the wisdom of a personnel decision taken by a public agency allegedly in reaction to the employee's behavior. Our responsibility is to ensure that citizens are not deprived of fundamental rights by virtue of working for the government; this does not require a grant of immunity for employee grievances not afforded by the First Amendment to those who do not work for the state.

Whether an employee's speech addresses a matter of public concern must be determined by the content, form, and context of a given statement, as revealed by the whole record. In this case, with but one exception, the questions posed by Myers to her coworkers do not fall under the rubric of matters of "public concern." We view the questions pertaining to the confidence and trust that Myers' coworkers possess in various supervisors, the level of office morale, and the need for a grievance committee as mere extensions of Myers' dispute over her transfer to another section of the criminal court. Unlike the dissent, we do not believe these questions are of public import in evaluating the performance of the District Attorney as an elected official. Myers did not seek to inform the public that the District Attorney's office was not discharging its governmental responsibilities in the investigation and prosecution of criminal cases. Nor did Myers seek to bring to light [wrongdoing] or breach of public trust on the part of Connick and others. Indeed, the questionnaire, if released to the public, would convey no information at all other than the fact that a single employee is upset with the status quo. While discipline and morale in the workplace are related to an agency's efficient performance of its duties, the focus of Myers' questions is not to evaluate the performance of the office but rather to gather ammunition for another round of controversy with her superiors. These questions reflect one employee's dissatisfaction with a transfer and an attempt to turn that displeasure into a cause célèbre. To presume that all matters which transpire within a government office are of public concern would mean that virtually every remark—and certainly every criticism directed at a public official—would plant the seed of a constitutional case. [The] First Amendment does not require a public office to be run as a roundtable for employee complaints over internal office affairs.

One question in Myers' questionnaire, however, does touch upon a matter of public concern. Question 11 inquires if assistant district attorneys "ever feel pressured to work in political campaigns on behalf of office supported candidates." We have recently noted that official pressure upon employees to work for political candidates not of the worker's own choice constitutes a coercion of belief in violation of fundamental constitutional rights. [see Branti; Elrod, p. 399 below.] In addition, there is a demonstrated interest in this country that government service should depend upon meritorious performance rather than political service. Given this history, we believe it apparent that the issue of whether assistant district attorneys are pressured to work in political campaigns is a matter of interest to the community upon which it is essential that public employees be able to speak out freely without fear of retaliatory dismissal.

Because one of the questions in Myers' survey touched upon a matter of public concern, and contributed to her discharge, we must determine whether Connick was justified in discharging Myers. Here the District Court again erred in imposing an unduly onerous burden on the state to justify Myers' discharge. The District Court viewed the issue of whether Myers' speech was upon a matter of "public concern" as a threshold inquiry, after which it became the government's burden to "clearly demonstrate" that the speech involved "substantially interfered" with official responsibilities. Yet Pickering unmistakably states [that] the state's burden in justifying a particular discharge varies depending upon the nature of the employee's expression. Although such particularized balancing is difficult, the courts must reach the most appropriate possible balance of the competing interests.

The Pickering balance requires full consideration of the government's interest in the effective and efficient fulfillment of its responsibilities to the public. [Connick's] judgment [was] that Myers' questionnaire was an act of insubordination which interfered with working relationships. When close working relationships are essential to fulfilling public responsibilities, a wide degree of deference to the employer's judgment is appropriate. Furthermore, we do not see the necessity for an employer to allow events to unfold to the extent that the disruption of the office and the destruction of working relationships is manifest before taking action. We caution that a stronger showing may be necessary if the employee's speech more substantially involved matters of public concern. [Also] relevant is the manner, time, and place in which the questionnaire was distributed. [The] fact that Myers, unlike Pickering, exercised her rights to speech at the office supports Connick's fears that the functioning of his office was endangered.

Finally, the context in which the dispute arose is also significant. This is not a case where an employee, out of purely academic interest, circulated a questionnaire so as to obtain useful research. [When] employee speech concerning office policy arises from an employment dispute concerning the very application of that policy to the speaker, additional weight must be given to the supervisor's view that the employee has threatened the authority of the employer to run the office. Although we accept the District Court's factual finding that Myers' reluctance to accede to the transfer order was not a sufficient cause in itself for her dismissal, [this] does not render irrelevant the fact that the questionnaire emerged after a persistent dispute between Myers and Connick and his deputies over office transfer policy.

Myers' questionnaire touched upon matters of public concern in only a most limited sense; her survey, in our view, is most accurately characterized as an employee grievance concerning internal office policy. The limited First Amendment interest involved here does not require that Connick tolerate action which he reasonably believed would disrupt the office, undermine his authority, and destroy close working relationships. Myers' discharge therefore did not offend the First Amendment. [Although] today the balance is struck for the government, this is no defeat for the First Amendment. For it would indeed be a Pyrrhic victory for the great principles of free expression if the Amendment's safeguarding of a public employee's right, as a citizen, to participate in discussions concerning public affairs were confused with the attempt to constitutionalize the employee grievance that we see presented [here]. [Reversed.]

■ JUSTICE BRENNAN, with whom JUSTICE MARSHALL, BLACKMUN, and STEVENS join, dissenting.

[The] Court distorts the balancing analysis required under Pickering by suggesting that one factor, the context in which a statement is made, is to be weighed *twice*—first in determining whether an employee's speech addresses a matter of public concern and then in deciding whether the statement adversely affected the government's interest as an employer. [Moreover,] in concluding that the effect of respondent's personnel policies on employee morale and the work performance of the District Attorney's Office is not a matter of public concern, the Court impermissibly narrows the class of subjects on which public employees may speak out without fear of retaliatory dismissal.

[The Court] suggests that there are two classes of speech of public concern: statements "of public import" because of their content, form and context, and statements that, by virtue of their subject matter, are "inherently of public concern." In my view, however, whether a particular statement by a public employee is addressed to a subject of public concern does not depend on where it was said or why. The First Amendment affords special protection to speech that may inform public debate about how our society is to be governed—regardless of whether it actually becomes the subject of a public controversy. [The] Court misapplies the Pickering test and holds—against our previous authorities—that a public employer's mere apprehension that speech will be disruptive justifies suppression of that speech when all the objective evidence suggests that those fears are essentially [unfounded]. Such extreme deference to the employer's judgment is not appropriate when public employees voice critical views concerning the operations of the agency for which they work. [In] order to protect public employees' First Amendment right to voice critical views on issues of public importance, the courts must make their own appraisal of the effects of the speech.

The Court's decision today inevitably will deter public employees from making critical statements about the manner in which government agencies are operated for fear that doing so will provoke their dismissal. As a result, the public will be deprived of valuable information with which to evaluate the performance of elected officials.

———

PICKERING AND CONNICK COMPARED

1. *Public employee political hyperbole.* In **Rankin v. McPherson**, 483 U.S. 378 (1987), the Court held by a vote of 5–4 that a clerical employee in a county constable's office could not be discharged for remarking, after hearing of the attempted assassination of President Reagan in 1981, "If they go for him again, I hope they get him." Justice MARSHALL's majority opinion held that, even after Connick, the remark constituted speech on a matter of public concern and that the firing violated the First Amendment. He noted that the remark was made in the course of a conversation addressing the policies of the Reagan Administration and added that the "inappropriate or controversial character of a statement is irrelevant to the question whether it deals with a matter of public concern." Having determined that the remark in the context in which it was made did involve a matter of public concern, Justice Marshall balanced the employee's speech interest against the State's interest in the "effective functioning" of government under the Pickering test. He noted that the State "bears a burden of justifying the discharge on legitimate grounds" and commented that the State's interest in content-related sanctions was minimal where the employee "serves no confidential, policymaking, or public contact role." He concluded that there had been no showing that McPherson's statement had interfered with the effective functioning of the office, nor that it was made in a context where it could bring discredit upon the office, and thus that her discharge violated the First Amendment. Justice POWELL concurred, emphasizing that this case involved only "a single, offhand comment" directed to "a co-worker who happened also to be her boyfriend" in a private conversation that was unforeseeably overheard by another co-worker.

Justice SCALIA, joined by Chief Justice Rehnquist and Justices White and O'Connor, dissented. He insisted that "no law enforcement agency is required by the First Amendment to permit one of its employees to 'ride with the cops and cheer for the robbers.' " After disagreeing with the majority's conclusion that this was speech on a matter of public concern, he argued that the employee's statement was, because of the unprotected nature of actual threats, "so near the category of completely unprotected speech" that it could not "fairly be viewed as lying within the 'heart' of the First Amendment's protection." Finding the State's interest in not having such statements made by its employees quite reasonable, he also objected to the Court's distinction between policymaking and nonpolicymaking employees: "Nonpolicymaking employees [can] hurt working relationships and undermine public confidence in an organization every bit as much as policymaking employees. I, for one, do not look forward to the new First Amendment world the Court creates, in which nonpolicymaking employees of the [EEOC] must be permitted to make remarks on the job approving of racial discrimination, nonpolicymaking employees of the Selective Service System to advocate noncompliance with the draft laws, [and] nonpolicymaking constable's deputies to express approval for the assassination of the President."

2. *Who determines public vs. private concern?* After Connick, who is to determine whether an employee's speech is on a matter of public or private concern if there is a factual dispute about what was actually said? In **Waters v. Churchill**, 511 U.S. 661 (1994), a nurse sued her public hospital employer for firing her based on a conversation with a co-worker. She claimed the remark was a legitimate complaint about training that could harm patients, but her employer thought was disruptive speech critical of

her bosses and unprotected under Connick. A plurality opinion by Justice O'Connor ruled that a public employer does not violate the First Amendment if it fires an employee for what the employer reasonably believed was speech on a matter of private concern. Justice Scalia concurred but would have been even more protective of the employer: he argued that the employer ought not be liable unless it had intentionally—not merely negligently—retaliated against an employee for speech on a matter of public concern. Justice Stevens's dissent argued that an employer ought be absolutely liable if the speech for which the employee was fired was actually on a matter of public concern as objectively determined by a court, regardless of the employer's subjective state of mind.

3. *The scope of speech on matters of public concern.* Connick left intact Pickering's broad protection for public employee speech on matters of "public concern." But it left unclear whether an employee had to make any affirmative showing of public interest or importance. Is such speech limited to criticism of governmental policy, as was involved in the letter to the editor in Pickering or in the political hyperbole in McPherson? Or was "matters of public concern" a residual catch-all that included any matter that wasn't an internal employee grievance (that is, a matter of private concern)?

The Court took a broad view of "matters of public concern" in **United States v. National Treasury Employees Union (NTEU)**, 513 U.S. 454 (1995). The case involved a challenge to § 501(b) of the Ethics in Government Act, as amended in 1989 and 1991 to bar a wide range of officers and employees of the federal government from receiving payment of any honorarium "for an appearance, speech or article (including a series of appearances, speeches, or articles if the subject matter is directly related to the individual's official duties or the payment is made because of the individual's status with the Government)." The honorarium ban was challenged by a class of executive branch employees below federal salary grade GS-16. Among the class were a mail handler who had given lectures on the Quaker religion, an aerospace engineer who had lectured on black history, a microbiologist at the Food and Drug Administration who had reviewed dance performances, and a tax examiner who wrote articles about the environment.

Justice STEVENS wrote for the Court, holding the honorarium ban invalid: "Federal employees who write for publication in their spare time have made significant contributions to the marketplace of ideas. They include literary giants like Nathaniel Hawthorne and Herman Melville, who were employed by the Customs Service; Walt Whitman, who worked for the Departments of Justice and Interior; and Bret Harte, an employee of the mint. Respondents have yet to make comparable contributions to American culture, but they share with these great artists important characteristics that are relevant to the issue we confront." Justice Stevens found the case governed by Pickering rather than Connick: "Respondents' expressive activities in this case fall within the protected category of citizen comment on matters of public concern rather than employee comment on matters related to personal status in the workplace. The speeches and articles for which they received compensation in the past were addressed to a public audience, were made outside the workplace, and involved content largely unrelated to their government employment." And he found that the government's "prohibition on compensation unquestionably imposes a significant burden on expressive activity. See [Simon & Schuster.][1]"

Turning to the government's asserted justifications, Justice Stevens stated: "The Government's underlying concern is that federal officers not misuse or appear to misuse power by accepting compensation for their unofficial and nonpolitical writing and speaking activities. This interest is undeniably powerful, but the Government cites no evidence of misconduct related to honoraria in the vast rank and file of federal employees below grade GS-16. [Congress] reasonably could assume that payments of honoraria to [its own Members,] judges or high-ranking officials in the Executive Branch might generate [an] appearance of improper influence. Congress could not, however, reasonably extend that assumption to all federal employees below Grade GS-16, an immense class of workers with negligible power to confer favors on those who might pay to hear them speak or to read their articles."

Justice Stevens also found that the necessity of the total ban to "operational efficiency" was called into "serious doubt" by the fact that honoraria were banned for "a *series* of appearances, speeches, or articles" only if "the subject matter is directly related to the individual's official duties or the payment is made because of the individual's status with the Government." He explained: "Congress' decision to provide a total exemption for all unrelated series of speeches undermines application of the ban to individual speeches and articles with no nexus to Government employment. Absent such a nexus, no corrupt bargain or even appearance of impropriety appears likely. The Government's only argument against a general nexus limitation is that a wholesale prophylactic rule is easier to enforce than one that requires individual nexus determinations. The nexus limitation for series, however, unambiguously reflects a congressional judgment that agency ethics officials [can] enforce the statute when it includes a nexus test. A blanket burden on the speech of nearly 1.7 million federal employees requires a much stronger justification than the Government's dubious claim of administrative convenience. [Such] anomalies in the text of the statute and regulations underscore our conclusion: the speculative benefits the honoraria ban may provide the Government are not sufficient to justify this crudely crafted burden on respondents' freedom to engage in expressive activities."

Justice Stevens, for the Court, held that the appropriate remedy was facial invalidation of the statutory provision. Justice O'Connor concurred in the judgment in part and dissented in part, arguing that facial invalidation was excessive and that the Court should have invalidated the provision only to the extent it was applied without a nexus provision.

Chief Justice REHNQUIST, joined by Justices Scalia and Thomas, dissented: "The ban neither prohibits anyone from speaking or writing, nor does it penalize anyone who speaks or writes; the only stricture effected by the statute is a denial of compensation. [Unlike] the law at issue in Simon & Schuster, the honoraria ban is neither content nor viewpoint based. As a result, the ban does not raise the specter of Government control over the marketplace of ideas. To the extent that the honoraria ban implicates First Amendment concerns, the proper standard of review is found in our cases

---

[1]   This proposition is self-evident even to those who do not fully accept Samuel Johnson's cynical comment: " 'No man but a blockhead ever wrote, except for money.' " J. Boswell, Life of Samuel Johnson LL.D. 302 (R. Hutchins ed. 1952). [Footnote by Justice Stevens.]

dealing with the Government's ability to regulate the First Amendment activities of its employees.

"[Applying] these standards to the honoraria ban, I cannot say that the balance that Congress has struck between its interests and the interests of its employees to receive compensation for their First Amendment expression is unreasonable. The Court largely ignores the Government's foremost interest—prevention of impropriety and the appearance of impropriety—by focusing solely on the burdens of the statute as applied to several carefully selected Executive Branch employees whose situations present the application of the statute where the Government's interests are at their lowest ebb [but who] by no means represent the breadth of the class. [Nor is it necessarily true that] federal employees below grade GS-16 have negligible power to confer favors on those who might pay to hear them speak or to read their articles. [Tax] examiners, bank examiners, enforcement officials, or any number of federal employees have substantial power to confer favors even though their compensation level is below Grade GS-16. [The] Government's related concern regarding the difficulties that would attach in administering a case-by-case analysis of the propriety of particular honoraria also supports the honoraria ban's validity. [Congress] reasonably determined that the prior ethics regime, which required these case-by-case determinations, was inadequate.

"[Unlike] our prototypical application of Pickering which normally involves a response to the content of employee speech, the honoraria ban prohibits no speech and is unrelated to the message or the viewpoint expressed by the government employee. Because there is only a limited burden on respondents' First Amendment rights, Congress reasonably could have determined that its paramount interests in preventing impropriety and the appearance of impropriety in its work force justified the honoraria ban." Chief Justice Rehnquist also objected to the remedy: "One would expect the Court to hold the statute inapplicable on First Amendment grounds to persons such as the postal worker who lectures on the Quaker religion, and others of similar ilk. But the Court, [in] what may fairly be described as an O. Henry ending, holds the statute inapplicable to the entire class before the Court."

In contrast to the broad approach taken in NTEU, however, the Court's per curiam decision in **City of San Diego v. Roe**, 543 U.S. 77 (2004), made clear that there are limits to the scope of matters of public concern on which public employees may make commentary in their capacity as citizens. The case involved a San Diego police officer who made videos of himself stripping off a police uniform and masturbating, including while issuing a traffic ticket, and sold them online on eBay, listing himself in his user profile as in the field of law enforcement. He was terminated from the police force, and alleged that the termination violated his right to free speech. The Court reversed a court of appeals opinion that had deemed his off-duty, off-premises speech protected under Pickering and NTEU: "The Court of Appeals' reliance on NTEU was seriously misplaced. Although Roe's activities took place outside the workplace and purported to be about subjects not related to his employment, the [police department] demonstrated legitimate and substantial interests of its own that were compromised by his speech. Far from confining his activities to speech unrelated to his employment, Roe took deliberate steps to link his videos [to] his police work, all in a way injurious to his employer. [The] present case falls outside the protection afforded in NTEU."

The Court went on to clarify that not all public employee speech that is unrelated to internal workplace grievances under Connick is automatically entitled to Pickering review: "Pickering did not hold that any and all statements by a public employee are entitled to balancing. [In] order to merit Pickering balancing, a public employee's speech must touch on a matter of 'public concern.' [P]ublic concern is something that is a subject of legitimate news interest, that is, a subject of general interest and of value and concern to the public at the time of publication. [Applying] these principles to the instant case, there is no difficulty in concluding that Roe's expression does not qualify as a matter of public concern under any view of the public concern test. He fails the threshold test and Pickering balancing does not come into play."

Garcetti v. Ceballos, 543 U.S. 1186 (2006), further clarified the limited scope of public employee speech on matters of public concern. The case arose in the context of a Los Angeles deputy district attorney who wrote his supervisors a memo stating that an affidavit police had used to obtain a critical search warrant contained serious misrepresentations. He recommended dismissal of a prosecution based on that affidavit. The case was reargued after Justice Alito was confirmed to Justice O'Connor's seat. Writing for a narrowly divided court, Justice KENNEDY, joined by Chief Justice Roberts and Justices Scalia, Thomas, and Alito, rejected the argument that the County's allegedly retaliatory employment actions in the wake of the memo violated the First Amendment: "When a citizen enters government service, the citizen by necessity must accept certain limitations on his or her freedom. [At] the same time, the Court has recognized that a citizen who works for the government is nonetheless a citizen. [The Court's decisions] have sought both to promote the individual and societal interests that are served when employees speak as citizens on matters of public concern and to respect the needs of government employers attempting to perform their important public functions.

"That Ceballos expressed his views inside his office, rather than publicly, is not dispositive. Employees in some cases may receive First Amendment protection for expressions made at work. [The] memo concerned the subject matter of Ceballos' employment, but this, too, is nondispositive. The First Amendment protects some expressions related to the speaker's job. The controlling factor in Ceballos' case is that his expressions were made pursuant to his duties as a calendar deputy. That consideration—the fact that Ceballos spoke as a prosecutor fulfilling a responsibility to advise his supervisor about how best to proceed with a pending case—distinguishes Ceballos' case from those in which the First Amendment provides protection against discipline.

"We hold that when public employees make statements pursuant to their official duties, the employees are not speaking as citizens for First Amendment purposes, and the Constitution does not insulate their communications from employer discipline. [Restricting] speech that owes its existence to a public employee's professional responsibilities does not infringe any liberties the employee might have enjoyed as a private citizen. It simply reflects the exercise of employer control over what the employer itself has commissioned or created. Contrast, for example, the expressions made by the speaker in Pickering, whose letter to the newspaper had no official significance and bore similarities to letters submitted by numerous citizens every day. [Ceballos'] proposed contrary rule [would] commit state and federal courts to a new, permanent, and intrusive role, mandating judicial oversight of communications between and among government employees and their superiors in the course of official business. This displacement of managerial discretion by judicial supervision finds no support in our precedents."

Justice STEVENS filed a dissent arguing that "public employees are still citizens while they are in the office. [It] is senseless to let constitutional protection for exactly the same words hinge on whether they fall within a job description." Justice SOUTER, joined by Justices Stevens and Ginsburg, also dissented, stating: "There is no adequate justification for the majority's line categorically denying Pickering protection to any speech uttered 'pursuant to . . . official duties.' [The] need for a balance hardly disappears when an employee speaks on matters his job requires him to address; rather, it seems obvious that the individual and public value of such speech is no less, and may well be greater, when the employee speaks pursuant to his duties in addressing a subject he knows intimately for the very reason that it falls within his duties. [The] majority is rightly concerned that the employee who speaks out on matters subject to comment in doing his own work has the greater leverage to create office uproars and fracture the government's authority to set policy to be carried out coherently through the ranks. [But] why do the majority's concerns, which we all share, require categorical exclusion of First Amendment protection against any official retaliation for things said on the job?" Justice Souter rejected as a "fallacy" the view that "any statement made within the scope of public employment is [the] government's own speech." He also rejected the view that state and federal statutory protections for "whistleblowers" were sufficient to satisfy the First Amendment.

Justice BREYER filed a separate dissent that, like Justice Souter's, advocated use of the Pickering balancing test in the case, but emphasized "two special circumstances that together justify First Amendment review. First, the speech at issue is professional speech—the speech of a lawyer. Such speech is subject to independent regulation by canons of the profession. Those canons provide an obligation to speak in certain instances. [Second,] the Constitution itself here imposes speech obligations upon the government's professional employee. A prosecutor has a constitutional obligation to learn of, to preserve, and to communicate with the defense about exculpatory and impeachment evidence in the government's possession. [Where] professional and special constitutional obligations are both present, the need to protect the employee's speech is augmented, the need for broad government authority to control that speech is likely diminished, and administrable standards are quite likely available. Hence, I would find that the Constitution mandates special protection of employee speech in such circumstances."

In **Lane v. Franks**, 573 U.S. 228 (2014), the Court applied Pickering and distinguished Garcetti, holding that a government employee's truthful testimony in court outside the scope of his job duties necessarily counts as protected citizen speech. The facts involved an employee of a state community college who fired a no-show employee, then gave testimony at grand jury and trial that led to the fraud conviction of the no-show. Lane, the original employee, was fired in apparent retaliation. Justice SOTOMAYOR wrote for a unanimous Court: "Sworn testimony in judicial proceedings is a quintessential example of speech as a citizen for a simple reason: Anyone who testifies in court bears an obligation, to the court and society at large, to tell the truth. When the person testifying is a public employee, he may bear separate obligations to his employer—for example, an obligation not to show up to court dressed in an unprofessional manner. But any such obligations as an employee are distinct and independent from the obligation, as a citizen, to speak the truth. That independent obligation renders sworn testimony speech as a citizen and sets it apart from speech made purely in the capacity of an employee. [Garcetti] said nothing about speech that simply relates to public employment or concerns information learned in the course of public employment. [The] mere fact that a citizen's speech concerns information acquired by virtue of his public employment does not transform that speech into employee—rather than citizen—speech. The critical question under Garcetti is whether the speech at issue is itself ordinarily within the scope of an employee's duties, not whether it merely concerns those duties."

Justice THOMAS, joined by Justices Scalia and Alito, concurred to observe that the Court had "no occasion to address the quite different question whether a public employee speaks 'as a citizen' when he testifies in the course of his ordinary job responsibilities. For some public employees—such as police officers, crime scene technicians, and laboratory analysts—testifying is a routine and critical part of their employment duties. Others may be called to testify in the context of particular litigation as the designated representatives of their employers."

4.   *Pickering, Connick and school athletic associations.* Connick and follow-on cases like Ceballos make clear that public employees do not enjoy presumptive protection of speech that interferes with the efficiency of the public entity's internal operations. Does the same principle extend beyond public employees to those who voluntarily join other kinds of public entities or associations? May a school athletic association sanction the speech of a member private school that interferes with the efficient pursuit of its mission? In **Tennessee Secondary School Athletic Ass'n v. Brentwood Academy**, 551 U.S. 291 (2007), the Court gave an affirmative answer to that question. Recall that the Court deemed the Tennessee Secondary School Athletic Association (TSSAA)—a not-for-profit membership corporation organized to regulate interscholastic sports—a "state actor" by virtue of its "entwinement" with the 290 public schools that were among its membership. TSSAA also had 55 private high schools as members, including Brentwood Academy. Since the early 1950's, TSSAA has prohibited high schools from using "undue influence" in recruiting middle school students for their athletic programs. In April 1997, Brentwood's football coach sent a letter to a group of eighth-grade boys inviting them to attend spring practice sessions. That invitation violated TSSAA's antirecruiting rule and the association sanctioned Brentwood. Brentwood claimed the sanction violated its right to speak to prospective recruits.

Justice STEVENS wrote for the Court, which was unanimous in its judgment that TSSAA had not violated Brentwood's free speech rights. He analogized to the public employee line of cases: "Brentwood made a voluntary decision to join TSSAA and to abide by its antirecruiting rule. Just as the government's interest in running an effective workplace can in some circumstances outweigh employee speech rights, see Connick, so too can an athletic league's interest in enforcing its rules sometimes warrant curtailing the speech of its voluntary participants. See Pickering; Umbehr [(1996; p. 403 below)]. This is not to say that TSSAA has unbounded authority to condition membership on the relinquishment of any and all constitutional rights. As we recently emphasized in the employment context, 'so long as employees are speaking as citizens about matters of public concern, they must face only those speech restrictions that are necessary for their employers to operate efficiently and effectively.' Ceballos. Assuming, without deciding, that the coach in this case was 'speaking as [a] citizen about matters of public concern,' TSSAA can similarly impose only those conditions on such speech that are necessary to managing an efficient and effective state-sponsored high school athletic league.

"That necessity is obviously present here. We need no empirical data to credit TSSAA's common-sense conclusion that hard-sell tactics directed at middle school students could lead to exploitation, distort competition between high school teams, and foster an environment in which athletics are prized more highly than academics. TSSAA's rule discourages precisely the sort of conduct that might lead to those harms, any one of which would detract from a high school sports league's ability to operate 'efficiently and effectively.' For that reason, the First Amendment does not excuse Brentwood from abiding by the same anti-recruiting rule that governs the conduct of its sister schools. To hold otherwise would undermine the principle, succinctly articulated by the dissenting judge at the court of appeals, that 'high school football is a game. Games have rules.' It is only fair that Brentwood follow them."

Justice THOMAS concurred in the judgment, noting that it was "bizarre" to stretch the Pickering line of public employee speech cases to "speech by a private school that is a member of a private athletic association," but that this stretch "was occasioned by the Court when it held that TSSAA, a private organization, was a state actor," a decision he would overrule as erroneous. Was Justice Thomas right? Did Justice Stevens faithfully apply the Connick test here? Does Connick require proof of "necessity" to the efficient operation of the public entity? Was Justice Stevens's application of such "necessity" test in any event quite deferential?

5. *Targeting error and intent.* In **Heffernan v. City of Paterson,** 578 U.S. 266 (2016), the Court addressed a situation in which the government employer targeted an employee's speech based on a mistake of fact. A police officer was targeted for supporting a mayoral candidate, but in fact he was not supporting the candidate and had merely picked up one of the candidate's signs for his mother. Justice BREYER wrote the opinion for the Court, holding that the First Amendment covered the situation: "In this case a government official demoted an employee because the official believed, but *incorrectly* believed, that the employee had supported a particular candidate for mayor. [When] an employer demotes an employee out of a desire to prevent the employee from engaging in political activity that the First Amendment protects, the employee is entitled to challenge that unlawful action under the First Amendment—[even] if, as here, the employer makes a factual mistake about the employee's behavior. [A] rule of law finding liability in these circumstances tracks the language of the First Amendment more closely than would a contrary rule. Unlike, say, the Fourth Amendment, which begins by speaking of the 'right of the people to be secure in their persons, houses, papers, and effects,' the First Amendment begins by focusing upon the activity of the Government. [We] also consider relevant

the constitutional implications of a rule that imposes liability. The constitutional harm at issue in the ordinary case consists in large part of discouraging employees—both the employee discharged (or demoted) and his or her colleagues—from engaging in protected activities. The discharge of one tells the others that they engage in protected activity at their peril. [The] employer's factual mistake does not diminish the risk of causing precisely that same harm."

Justice THOMAS, joined by Justice Alito, dissented, reasoning that Section 1983 "does not provide a cause of action to plaintiffs whose constitutional rights have not been violated."

———

PUBLIC EMPLOYEE POLITICAL PARTY AFFILIATION

Since the rise of political parties in the early days of the republic, elected officials have engaged in the practice of political patronage: rewarding one's political friends with jobs in or contracts with the government, and declining to so reward one's political enemies. Various statutory devices have been employed over time to check this "spoils system," including state and federal bribery and extortion laws, and the use of merit examinations and civil service protection for rank-and-file government employees. Another device is the federal Hatch Act and the state "mini-Hatch acts," which prohibit active political campaigning by public employees. The decisions that follow rejected challenges to these laws brought by public employees who claimed that they had a free speech right to electioneer. The decisions noted after the Hatch Act challenges review First Amendment challenges by public employees from the other side of the patronage coin: claims by discharged or demoted public officials that they have been turned out by the victorious party solely because of their party affiliation in violation of their rights of free political association.

1. *The Hatch Act cases.* In United Public Workers v. Mitchell, 330 U.S. 75 (1947), the Court sustained the constitutionality of § 9(a) of the Hatch Act of 1940, which prohibited federal employees in the executive branch from taking "any active part in political management or in political campaigns." The Court held that "Congress may regulate the political conduct of government employees 'within reasonable limits,' even though the regulation trenches to some extent upon unfettered political action." Justice Black dissented: "It would hardly seem to be imperative to muzzle millions of citizens because some of them, if left their constitutional freedoms, might corrupt the political process." He suggested that the law actually harmed "the body politic" by "depriving it of the political participation and interest of such a large segment of our citizens."

A Hatch Act challenge likewise failed in **United States Civil Service Commission v. National Ass'n of Letter Carriers**, 413 U.S. 548 (1973). There, the Court rejected a facial overbreadth challenge to § 9(a) and "unhesitatingly reaffirm[ed]" Mitchell: "Neither the right to associate nor the right to participate in political activities is absolute. [P]lainly identifiable acts of political management and political campaigning may constitutionally be prohibited on the part of federal employees." Justice WHITE's majority opinion deferred to the congressional judgment that "partisan political activities by federal employees must be limited if the Government is to operate effectively and fairly, elections are to play their proper part in representative government, and employees themselves are to be sufficiently free from improper influences." He noted that the restrictions were "not aimed at particular parties, groups or points of view, but apply equally to all [covered] partisan activities. [Nor] do they seek to control political opinions or beliefs, or to interfere with or influence anyone's vote at the polls." Applying the Pickering balancing test, he found three government interests substantial enough to outweigh the free speech claims of public employees: ensuring that employees "administer the law in accordance with the will of Congress, rather than [with the] will of a political party," preventing the use of government workers "to build a powerful, invincible, and perhaps corrupt political machine," and ensuring "that Government employees [are] free from pressure [to] vote in a certain way or perform political chores in order to curry favor with their superiors rather than to act out of their own beliefs." Justice DOUGLAS, joined by Justices Brennan and Marshall, dissented: "[No] one could object if employees were barred from using office time to engage in outside activities whether political or otherwise. But it is of no concern of Government what an employee does in his spare time, [unless] what he does impairs efficiency or other facets of the merits of his job."

2. *Patronage dismissals of public employees.* In several decisions, the Court has curtailed governmental power to penalize public employees on party allegiance grounds. This development began with **Elrod v. Burns**, 427 U.S. 347 (1976), a 5–3 decision holding that the newly elected Democratic Sheriff of Cook County, Illinois, could not discharge several Republican employees—three process servers, and a juvenile court bailiff and security guard. Justice BRENNAN's plurality opinion, joined by Justices White and Marshall, held that "[t]he cost of the practice of patronage is the restraint it places on freedoms of belief and association. [An] individual who is a member of the out-party maintains affiliation with his own party at the risk of losing his job." He went on to reject three government interests asserted in defense of patronage practices. He doubted that they served "the need to insure effective government and the efficiency of public employees," which could be safeguarded by discharge for good cause, and argued that the lack of an efficiency justification distinguished the case from Mitchell and Letter Carriers. He also denied that wholesale patronage is necessary "for political loyalty" and implementation of the electorate's policy choices; this interest, he argued, could be served by "[l]imiting patronage dismissals to policymaking positions." And he found that patronage was not necessary to the "preservation of the two-party system," which had already survived the inroads made by civil service merit systems. Justice STEWART's concurrence, joined by Justice Blackmun, concluded more narrowly that "a nonpolicymaking, nonconfidential government employee [cannot be discharged] from a job that he is satisfactorily performing upon the sole ground of his political beliefs."

Justice POWELL, joined by Chief Justice Burger and Justice Rehnquist, dissented, finding strong government interests served by patronage: "[Patronage] hiring practices have contributed to American democracy by stimulating political activity and by strengthening parties. [Patronage] hiring practices also enable party organizations to persist and function at the local level. [In] the dull periods between elections, [precinct] organizations must be maintained; new voters registered; and minor political 'chores' performed for citizens. [It] is naive to think that these types of political activities are motivated at these levels by some academic interest in 'democracy.' [As] every politician knows, the hope of some reward generates a major portion of the local political activity supporting parties." The dissenters found these state interests sufficient to outweigh the limited First Amendment interest in avoiding "the coercion on associational choices that may be created by one's desire [to] obtain [government] employment."

In **Branti v. Finkel**, 445 U.S. 507 (1980), the Court reconsidered patronage systems and expanded the immunity of public employees from patronage dismissals, but left the contours of the broadened constitutional protections somewhat unclear. The new governing rule in Branti invoked criteria differing from Elrod: "the ultimate inquiry is not whether the label 'policymaker' or 'confidential' fits a particular position; rather, the question is whether the hiring authority can demonstrate that party affiliation is an appropriate requirement for the effective performance of the public office involved."

In Branti, two Republican assistant county public defenders successfully challenged their dismissal by the newly named Democratic head of the public defender's office. Justice STEVENS's majority opinion concluded, under his newly formulated standard, that "it is manifest that the continued employment of an assistant public defender cannot properly be conditioned upon his allegiance to the political party in control of the county government." He noted that any policymaking in a public defender's office related to the needs of individual clients, not to any partisan political interests, and that the assistant public defenders' access to confidential information arising out of attorney-client relationships had no bearing on partisan concerns. Accordingly, "it would undermine, rather than promote, the effective performance of an assistant public defender's office to make his tenure dependent on his allegiance to the dominant political party." He conceded that "party affiliation may be an acceptable requirement for some types of government employment," but insisted that the "policymaking or confidential position" criterion did not adequately delineate the proper use of party considerations. He explained: "Under some circumstances, a position may be appropriately considered political even though it is neither confidential nor policymaking in character." (He gave as an example the use of local election judges of different parties to supervise elections at the precinct level.) He added: "It is equally clear that party affiliation is not necessarily relevant to every policymaking or confidential position." (He noted that, for example, a "policymaking" football coach could not be discharged on party affiliation grounds, but that the position of a speechwriting assistant to a governor could properly involve party allegiance if it was to be performed "effectively.") Justice Stevens expressly declined to decide whether a prosecutor, like a public defender, was protected from dismissal on grounds of political party affiliation or loyalty.

Justice POWELL, in the lengthy dissent, objected to the majority's new, "substantially expanded standard for determining which governmental employees may be retained or dismissed on the basis of political affiliation," which he feared would create "vast uncertainty." He noted, for example, that "it would be difficult to say [under the new standard] that 'partisan' concerns properly are relevant to the performance of the duties of a United States Attorney." As in his Elrod dissent, he emphasized that patronage appointments "helped build stable political parties" and that political parties served "a variety of substantial governmental interests." They helped candidates "to muster donations of time and money necessary to capture the attention of the electorate" and thus contribute to the democratic process;

moreover, they "aid effective governance after election campaigns end." The majority's approach, he argued, imposed "unnecessary constraints upon the ability of responsible officials to govern effectively and to carry out new policies." Moreover, the "breakdown of party discipline that handicaps elected officials also limits the ability of the electorate to choose wisely among candidates." He concluded: "In sum, the effect of the Court's decision will be to decrease the accountability and denigrate the role of our national political parties."

3. ***Patronage sanctions short of dismissal.*** In Elrod and Branti, then, the First Amendment was held to prohibit patronage dismissals of public employees unless the government could demonstrate that party affiliation was an appropriate requirement for the position involved. Ten years after Branti, the Court confronted the question whether the First Amendment also barred patronage practices other than dismissals. In **Rutan v. Republican Party of Illinois**, 497 U.S. 62 (1990), a divided Court extended Elrod and Branti to decisions about hiring, promotion, transfer, and recalls after layoffs. The case arose from Illinois Republican Governor James Thompson's institution of a hiring freeze, exceptions to which depended on permissions from his office. The challengers claimed that his office operated as a "patronage machine," and that they were denied promotions, transfers, and recalls because they lacked Republican credentials. Justice BRENNAN's majority opinion held that none of these decisions could constitutionally be based on party affiliation and support. Even without being discharged, he found, "[e]mployees who find themselves in dead-end positions due to their political backgrounds [will] feel a significant obligation to support political positions held by their superiors, and to refrain from acting on the political views they actually hold." He held that employees need not show that their treatment amounts to a constructive discharge in order to prevail in their First Amendment claims. Patronage practices even short of dismissal or its equivalent, he held, must be "narrowly tailored to further vital government interests." Justice Stevens concurred separately.

Justice SCALIA dissented, joined by Chief Justice Rehnquist and Justice Kennedy, and in part by Justice O'Connor. Justice Scalia insisted that "Elrod and Branti should be overruled, rather than merely not extended." In his extensive attack on Elrod and Branti, he emphasized the difference in the constitutional restrictions "upon the government in its capacity as lawmaker, i.e., as the regulator of private conduct" and "the restrictions [upon] the government in its capacity as employer." Thus, private citizens "cannot be punished for speech of merely private concern, but government employees can be fired without reason" [Connick], and private citizens "cannot be punished for partisan political activity, but [public] employees can be dismissed and otherwise punished for that reason" [Mitchell; Letter Carriers]. He added, in a section of the dissent not joined by Justice O'Connor: "The provisions of the Bill of Rights were designed to restrain transient majorities from impairing long-recognized personal liberties. They did not create by implication novel individual rights overturning accepted political norms. Thus, when a practice not expressly prohibited by the text of the Bill of Rights bears the endorsement of a long tradition of open, widespread, and unchallenged use that dates back to the beginning of the Republic, we have no proper basis for striking it down. Such a venerable and accepted tradition is not to be laid on the examining table and scrutinized for its conformity to some abstract principle of First Amendment adjudication devised by this Court."

Justice Scalia further objected to the majority's use of a "strict-scrutiny standard." Reiterating that speech restrictions on public employees "are not judged by the test applicable to similar restrictions on speech by non-employees," he noted that the Mitchell case had applied a lenient test of whether the practice could be "reasonably deemed" to further a legitimate goal. He argued that patronage practices satisfied even a less deferential "general 'balancing' test: can the governmental advantages of this employment practice reasonably be deemed to outweigh its 'coercive' effects?" Reiterating Justice Powell's arguments in defense of patronage in his Elrod dissent, Justice Scalia noted that "patronage stabilizes political parties and prevents excessive political fragmentation," both strong governmental interests. He added to Justice Powell's list an additional interest served by patronage: "Patronage, moreover, has been a powerful means of achieving the social and political integration of excluded groups. ['Every] ethnic group that has achieved political power in American cities has used the bureaucracy to provide jobs in return for political support.' " He conceded that "the patronage system entails some constraint upon the expression of views [and] considerable constraint upon the employee's right to associate with the other party." But he denied that patronage really involved "coercion" at all and insisted it did not represent "a significant impairment of free speech or free association."

4. *The expressive values served in the patronage cases.* In Elrod, Branti, and Rutan, there arguably were speech interests on both sides. If the out-party employees' free speech and association claims are rejected, they are given an incentive to tailor their views and allegiance to the other party against their true beliefs. If their claims are sustained, however, the expressive and associational rights of members of the in-party are arguably diminished. Moreover, constraints on patronage might even diminish the quantity of political speech on the whole by inhibiting party activism. Did the Court undervalue the interests of the in-party in these cases? Did it undervalue the contributions of patronage to political expression?

Note that the standard of scrutiny in the patronage cases is stricter than the Pickering balancing test. Pickering permits the government to win if it can demonstrate an interest in efficiency in a particular case. Elrod, Branti, and Rutan, in contrast, presume as a general matter that party affiliation is not a justifiable basis for government employment decisions unless the government can demonstrate narrow tailoring to vital "interests." Is it odd to give less constitutional protection in this context to speech, which is an enumerated right, than to association, which is not? Is there a possibility for confusion in applying the two standards if a fact situation involves retaliation for a mixture of both speech and party affiliation?

5. *Patronage and independent contractors.* Should the protections granted to public employees in the Pickering and Elrod lines of cases extend to independent contractors with government? On the one hand, contractors might appear less vulnerable than public employees to government coercion of belief and association, as they are less dependent on government work and more likely as a practical matter to support both parties in order to obtain jobs. On the other hand, treating contractors differently from employees might encourage government simply to manipulate job titles and work arrangements so as to increase its power to

enforce ideological and partisan fealty. The issue divided the lower courts until settled by two cases decided on the same day.

In **Board of County Commissioners v. Umbehr**, 518 U.S. 668 (1996), a case involving an outspoken trash hauler, the Court extended to independent contractors the protections of the Pickering line of cases. Umbehr had a contract to haul trash for Wabuansee County, Kansas. While under contract, he vocally criticized the three-member governing body of the County. He spoke at the Board's meetings and wrote critical letters and editorials in local newspapers regarding the County's landfill user rates, the Board's meeting practices, and the County's alleged mismanagement of taxpayers' money. The county terminated his contract and Umbehr filed a First Amendment complaint. The Court, by a vote of 7–2, affirmed the court of appeals' reversal of summary judgment for the county.

Justice O'CONNOR wrote for the Court. She reviewed the possible distinctions between public employees and contractors and found them no basis for a departure from the Pickering balancing test: "[I]ndependent contractors work at a greater remove from government officials than do most government employees. [The] Board argues that the lack of day-to-day control accentuates the government's need to have the work done by someone it trusts. [Umbehr,] on the other hand, argues that the government interests in maintaining harmonious working environments and relationships recognized in our government employee cases are attenuated where the contractor does not work at the government's workplace and does not interact daily with government officers and employees. He also points out that to the extent that he is publicly perceived as an independent contractor, any government concern that his political statements will be confused with the government's political positions is mitigated. The Board [retorts] that the cost of fending off litigation, and the potential for government contracting practices to ossify into prophylactic rules to avoid potential litigation and liability, outweigh the interests of independent contractors, who are typically less financially dependent on their government contracts than are government employees. Each of these arguments for and against the imposition of liability has some force. But all of them can be accommodated by applying our existing framework for government employee cases to independent contracts. We [see] no reason to believe that proper application of the Pickering balancing test cannot accommodate the differences between employees and independent contractors." She emphasized that because the case applied only to a terminations, "we need not address the possibility of suits by bidders or applicants for new government contracts."

In **O'Hare Truck Service, Inc. v. City of Northlake**, 518 U.S. 712 (1996), the Court extended to independent contractors the protections of the Elrod line of cases. O'Hare, a tow truck operator who had been on the city's list of available towers, was removed from the list after its owner, John Gratzianna, refused political support and campaign contributions to the mayor and supported the mayor's opponent in the election. Without deciding the case on the merits, the Court held that O'Hare had stated a First Amendment claim. Justice KENNEDY wrote for the Court, which again voted 7–2: "There is no doubt that if Gratzianna had been a public employee whose job was to perform tow truck operations, the city could not have discharged him for refusing to contribute to [the mayor's] campaign or for supporting his opponent. [We] cannot accept the proposition [that] those who perform the government's work outside the formal employment relationship are subject to what we conclude is the direct and specific abridgment of First Amendment rights described in this complaint. [We] see no reason [why] the constitutional claim here should turn on the distinction [between employees and contractors,] which is, in the main, a creature of the common law of agency and torts. Recognizing the distinction in these circumstances would invite manipulation by government, which could avoid constitutional liability simply by attaching different labels to particular jobs."

Justice Kennedy was not convinced that patronage practices are less coercive of independent contractors than employees: "[Perhaps] some contractors are so independent from government support that the threat of losing business would be ineffective to coerce them to abandon political activities. The same might be true of certain public employees, however; they, too, might find work elsewhere if they lose their government jobs. If results were to turn on these sorts of distinctions, courts would have to inquire into the extent to which the government dominates various job markets as employer or as contractor. We have been, and we remain, unwilling to send courts down that path. [Nor are we willing to assume that most independent contractors are] 'political hermaphrodites,' who find it in their self-interest to stay on good terms with both major political parties and so are not at great risk of retaliation for political association." He concluded: "The absolute right to enforce a patronage scheme, insisted upon by respondents as a means of retaining control over independent contractors, [has] not been shown to be a necessary part of a legitimate political system in all instances. [We] decline to draw a line excluding independent contractors from the First Amendment safeguards of political association afforded to employees."

Justice SCALIA, joined by Justice Thomas, dissented from both Umbehr and O'Hare. He first expressed surprise that in O'Hare, despite the addition to the Court of Justice Thomas (who opposes the Elrod line of cases) and the fact that all four Rutan dissenters remained on the Court, the Court had not only declined to overrule Elrod and Branti, but had "extended [them] far beyond Rutan to the massive field of all government contracting." He reiterated that patronage is a longstanding American tradition, and, noting elaborate state and federal laws governing procurement practices, suggested that any answer to the disadvantages of patronage in the contracting context must come from the political process and not the Court. He insisted that political favoritism is an inevitable feature of government: "Government favors those who agree with its political views, and disfavors those who disagree, every day—in where it builds its public works, in the kinds of taxes it imposes and collects, in its regulatory prescriptions, in the design of its grant and benefit programs—in a million ways, including the letting of contracts for government business." And he argued that, even if Elrod and Branti had made any sense, there was no reason to extend them to contractors: "If it is to be possible to dig in our cleats at some point on this [slippery] slope—before we end up holding that the First Amendment requires the City of Chicago to have as few potholes in Republican wards (if any) as in Democratic ones—would not the most defensible point of termination for this indefensible exercise be public employment? A public employee is always an individual, and a public employee below the highest political level (which is exempt from Elrod) is virtually always an individual who is not rich; the termination or denial of a public job is the termination or denial of a livelihood. A public contractor, on the other hand, is usually a corporation; and the contract it loses is rarely its entire business, or even an indispensable part of its entire business."

How far do these cases go in protecting public contractor speech? Suppose that a government contracts out the job of providing security services at a public housing project, and later finds out that the contractor is affiliated with a party that preaches racial supremacy. After O'Hare, may the government terminate the contract?

––––––––––

SPEECH-RESTRICTIVE CONDITIONS ON PUBLIC FUNDS

1. *Unconstitutional conditions.* The principle that governmental benefits may not be conditioned on the surrender of First Amendment rights has not been limited to employment. In **Speiser v. Randall**, 357 U.S. 513 (1958), for example, the Court overturned a California requirement that property tax exemptions for veterans would be available only to those who declared that they did not advocate the forcible overthrow of the government. Rejecting California's claim that it could condition the award of a mere "privilege" or "bounty," Justice Brennan's opinion for the Court noted that "to deny an exemption to claimants who engage in certain forms of speech is in effect to penalize them for such speech." The principle has been extended to a variety of government benefits, including both tax benefits and direct grants.

Why should government be constrained not to make speech or silence a condition of a benefit, when it is free not to confer the benefit at all? After all, government is not constitutionally required affirmatively to subsidize the exercise of constitutional rights. This is the conundrum of all so-called "unconstitutional conditions" cases. Unconstitutional conditions problems arise when government offers a benefit on condition that the recipient perform or forego an activity that is generally constitutionally protected from government interference. Such problems have given rise to voluminous commentary. See, e.g., Hale, "Unconstitutional Conditions and Constitutional Rights," 35 Colum. L. Rev. 321 (1935); Van Alstyne, "The Demise of the Right-Privilege Distinction in Constitutional Law," 81 Harv. L. Rev. 1439 (1968); Kreimer, "Allocational Sanctions: the Problem of Negative Rights in a Positive State," 132 U. Pa. L. Rev. 1293 (1984); Epstein, "Foreword: Unconstitutional Conditions, State Power, and the Limits of Consent," 102 Harv. L. Rev. 4 (1988); Sullivan, "Unconstitutional Conditions," 102 Harv. L. Rev. 1413 (1989).

2. *Penalties vs. nonsubsidies.* In the speech context, the Court has attempted to resolve the conundrum by distinguishing denials of benefits that operate as "penalties" on speech from those that operate as mere "nonsubsidies." Under this distinction, government may not use the leverage of a subsidy to induce recipients to refrain from speech they would otherwise engage in with their own resources, but it may refrain from paying for speech with which it disagrees. This distinction is structurally parallel to the distinctions the Court has drawn in the preceding contexts of public space, public education, and public employment. In those contexts, the Court similarly distinguished public forums from nonpublic forums, noncurricular from curricular aspects of public schools, and public employee speech as a citizen on matters of public concern from employee speech on internal matters of labor grievance. In the first category of each pair, the Court views

the government as constrained by the First Amendment in much the same manner as if it were regulating the general citizenry, and employs strict or intermediate scrutiny. In the second category of each pair, the Court defers to government with only minimal scrutiny, viewing it as having far more constitutional leeway in its capacity as manager, educator, or boss than it does in its capacity as sovereign regulator. The following pair of cases illustrates the distinction between nonsubsidies and funding penalties on speech.

In **Regan v. Taxation With Representation of Washington (TWR)**, 461 U.S. 540 (1983), the Court unanimously upheld against First Amendment challenge a provision of the Internal Revenue Code (IRC) barring a nonprofit organization that engages in lobbying from receiving tax-deductible contributions. There is no doubt that lobbying, or attempting to influence legislation, is a protected First Amendment activity. The issue in the case was whether lobbying organizations were entitled to the same tax benefits as nonprofit organizations that do not lobby. The Code provides for tax exemptions to two kinds of nonprofit organizations. Nonprofits organized under IRC § 501(c)(3) may not lobby, but taxpayers who contribute to them are permitted to deduct the amount of their contributions on their federal income tax returns. Nonprofits organized under IRC § 501(c)(4) are free to lobby, but contributions to § 501(c)(4) organizations are not tax-deductible to the contributor. Taxation With Representation (TWR) challenged the prohibition against substantial lobbying in § 501(c)(3) because it wanted to use tax-deductible contributions to support its substantial lobbying activities.

Justice REHNQUIST, writing for the Court, accepted that tax-deductibility of contributions to contributors represented a substantial benefit to TWR: "Both tax exemptions and tax deductibility are a form of subsidy that is administered through the tax system. A tax exemption has much the same effect as a cash grant to the organization of the amount of tax it would have to pay on its income. Deductible contributions are similar to cash grants of the amount of a portion of the individual's contributions. The system Congress has enacted provides this kind of subsidy [in the form of tax exemptions] to nonprofit civic welfare organizations generally, and an additional subsidy [in the form of tax deductibility to contributors] to those charitable organizations that do not engage in substantial lobbying. In short, Congress chose not to subsidize lobbying as extensively as it chose to subsidize other activities that nonprofit organizations undertake to promote the public welfare." But Justice Rehnquist rejected the argument that denial of the benefit of tax deductibility violated TWR's First Amendment rights: "TWR is certainly correct when it states that we have held that the government may not deny a benefit to a person because he exercises a constitutional right. But TWR is just as certainly incorrect when it claims that this case fits the [Speiser] model. The Code does not deny TWR the right to receive deductible contributions to support its nonlobbying activity, nor does it deny TWR any independent benefit on account of its intention to lobby. Congress has merely refused to pay for the lobbying out of public moneys. This Court has never held that Congress must grant a benefit such as TWR claims here to a person who wishes to exercise a constitutional right. [Congress] is not required by the First Amendment to subsidize lobbying."

Justice Rehnquist, quoting Speiser, noted that "[t]he case would be different if Congress were to discriminate invidiously in its subsidies in such a way as to '[aim] at the suppression of dangerous ideas.' 'But he held that an exception allowing veterans' organizations to receive tax-deductible contributions even if they lobbied did not constitute content discrimination in violation of this principle. He pointed out that the exemption was based on status, not content: "Veterans have 'been obliged to drop their own affairs to take up the burdens of the nation,' [and our] country has a longstanding policy of compensating veterans for their past contributions by providing them with numerous advantages." In the absence of any viewpoint discrimination, Justice Rehnquist held applicable only a minimal standard of review: "It is not irrational for Congress to decide that tax-exempt charities such as TWR should not further benefit at the expense of taxpayers at large by obtaining a further subsidy for lobbying."

Justice BLACKMUN, joined by Justices Brennan and Marshall, concurred but emphasized that "[t]he constitutional defect that would inhere in 501(c)(3) alone is avoided by § 501(c)(4)," for TWR could simply use its existing § 501(c)(3) organization for its nonlobbying activities while establishing a § 501(c)(4) affiliate to pursue its goals through lobbying. Thus, in the concurring justices' view, "[a] § 501(c)(3) organization's right to speak is not infringed, because it is free to make known its views on legislation through its § 501(c)(4) affiliate without losing tax benefits for its nonlobbying activities."

Contrast with TWR the Court's holding in **FCC v. League of Women Voters**, 468 U.S. 364 (1984). The Public Broadcasting Act of 1967 established the nonprofit Corporation for Public Broadcasting (CPB) to disburse federal funds to noncommercial television and radio stations in support of station operations and educational programming. In League of Women Voters, the Court invalidated, by a vote of 5–4, a provision of the Act forbidding any "noncommercial educational broadcasting station which receives a grant from the Corporation" to "engage in editorializing." Justice BRENNAN, writing for the majority, found the no-editorializing condition to be a penalty on public broadcasters' protected speech, not a mere nonsubsidy of speech as in TWR: "In this case, [unlike] the situation faced by the charitable organization in [TWR], a noncommercial educational station that receives only 1% of its overall income from CPB grants is barred absolutely from all editorializing. Therefore, in contrast to the appellee in Taxation With Representation, such a station is not able to segregate its activities according to the source of its funding. The station has no way of limiting the use of its federal funds to all noneditorializing activities, and, more importantly, it is barred from using even wholly private funds to finance its editorial activity." He noted that the case would be different if Congress permitted "public broadcasting stations, [like] the charitable organization in [TWR, which could lobby through a § 501(c)(4) affiliate], to make known its views on matters of public importance through [a] nonfederally funded, editorializing affiliate without losing federal grants for its noneditorializing broadcast activities."

Having found the editorial ban a penalty on public broadcasters' speech, he also found it impermissibly content-based, even under the less stringent review applicable to broadcasters than other speakers: "Because broadcast regulation involves unique considerations [such as spectrum scarcity], our cases have not followed precisely the same approach that we have applied to other media and have never gone so far as to demand that such regulations serve 'compelling' governmental interests. [But], as our cases attest, [restrictions on broadcaster speech] have been upheld only when we were satisfied that the restriction is narrowly tailored to further a substantial governmental interest, such as ensuring adequate and balanced coverage of public issues." [See Red Lion v. FCC (p. 634 below).] Under this intermediate standard of scrutiny, he found the government's justifications for the editorial ban inadequate: it was not closely tailored to the goal of protecting public broadcasters from "being coerced, as a result of federal financing, into becoming vehicles for Government propagandizing or the objects of governmental influence," and was far too broad to serve any goal of preventing public broadcasting stations "from becoming convenient targets for capture by private interest groups wishing to express their own partisan viewpoints."

Justice REHNQUIST, joined by Chief Justice Burger and Justice White, wrote a dissent arguing that TWR ought to have been controlling and that the restriction was a permissible nonsubsidy of speech. He wrote that the majority had presented "a scenario in which the Government appears as the 'Big Bad Wolf,' and appellee Pacifica as 'Little Red Riding Hood.' In the Court's scenario, the Big Bad Wolf cruelly forbids Little Red Riding Hood to take to her grandmother some of the food that she is carrying in her basket. [A] truer picture of the litigants, [would show] that some of the food in the basket was given to Little Red Riding Hood by the Big Bad Wolf himself, and that the Big Bad Wolf had told Little Red Riding Hood in advance that if she accepted his food she would have to abide by his conditions. Congress, in enacting [the editorial ban], has simply determined that public funds shall not be used to subsidize noncommercial, educational broadcasting stations which engage in 'editorializing.' " Nor did Justice Rehnquist find any problem in the ban's extension to private as well as public sources of funds: "Given the impossibility of compartmentalizing programming expenses in any meaningful way, it seems clear to me that the only effective means for preventing the use of public moneys to subsidize the airing of management's views is for Congress to ban a subsidized station from all on-the-air editorializing." He therefore rejected the majority's application of intermediate scrutiny: "[W]hen the Government is simply exercising its power to allocate its own public funds, we need only find that the condition imposed has a rational relationship to Congress' purpose in providing the subsidy and that it is not primarily 'aimed at the suppression of dangerous ideas.' " Here, he found, the condition was both rational and viewpoint-neutral: "[I]t is plainly rational for Congress to have determined that taxpayer moneys should not be used to subsidize management's views. [Furthermore,] Congress' prohibition is strictly neutral. In no sense can it be said that Congress has prohibited only editorial views of one particular ideological bent." Justice STEVENS also dissented, finding the ban viewpoint-neutral and justified by "the overriding interest in forestalling the creation of propaganda organs for the Government."

3. ***Abortion-related conditions on family planning subsidies.*** In **Rust v. Sullivan**, 500 U.S. 173 (1991), the Court found a speech-restrictive condition on funds more analogous to the one upheld in TWR than the one struck down in League of Women Voters. In Rust, the Court upheld Health and Human Services Department (HHS) regulations forbidding projects receiving federal family planning funds under Title X of the Public Health Service Act from counseling or referring women for abortion and from encouraging, promoting, or advocating abortion. If the funding recipient engaged in either of these activities, they had to be "physically and

financially separate" from the recipient's Title X project. The regulations
permitted Title X projects to provide pregnant women with information
about childbirth and prenatal care, but advised them to tell any pregnant
woman who inquired about abortion that the project does not consider
abortion an "appropriate method of family planning." Doctors and Title X
grantees did not succeed in their challenge to the regulations under the First
Amendment.

The challengers argued that the regulations impermissibly
discriminated on the basis of viewpoint because they prohibited discussion
of abortion while requiring doctors or counselors to provide information
about continuing a pregnancy to term. They relied on the Court's previous
statements that, even in the provision of subsidies, government may not "aim
at the suppression of dangerous ideas." Chief Justice REHNQUIST, writing
for the majority in the 5–4 decision, rejected this argument: "The
Government can, without violating the Constitution, selectively fund a
program to encourage certain activities it believes to be in the public interest,
without at the same time funding an alternative program which seeks to deal
with the problem in another way. In so doing, the Government has not
discriminated on the basis of viewpoint; it has merely chosen to fund one
activity to the exclusion of the other. [This] is not a case of the Government
'suppressing a dangerous idea,' but of a prohibition on a project grantee or
its employees from engaging in activities outside of the project's scope. To
hold that the Government unconstitutionally discriminates on the basis of
viewpoint when it chooses to fund a program dedicated to advance certain
permissible goals, because the program in advancing those goals necessarily
discourages alternative goals, would render numerous Government
programs constitutionally suspect. [When] Congress established a National
Endowment for Democracy to encourage other countries to adopt democratic
principles, it was not constitutionally required to fund a program to
encourage competing lines of political philosophy such as communism and
fascism. [Within] far broader limits than petitioners are willing to concede,
when the government appropriates public funds to establish a program it is
entitled to define the limits of that program."

The challengers also argued that the regulations impermissibly
conditioned the receipt of Title X funding on the relinquishment of their right
to engage in abortion advocacy and counseling with their own funds. Chief
Justice Rehnquist rejected this argument too: "[H]ere the Government is not
denying a benefit to anyone, but is instead simply insisting that public funds
be spent for the purposes for which they were authorized. The Secretary's
regulations do not force the Title X grantee to give up abortion-related
speech; they merely require that the grantee keep such activities separate
and distinct from Title X activities. Title X expressly distinguishes between
a Title X grantee and a Title X project. The grantee, which normally is a
health care organization, may receive funds from a variety of sources for a
variety of purposes. The grantee receives Title X funds, however, for the
specific and limited purpose of establishing and operating a Title X project.
The regulations govern the scope of the Title X project's activities, and leave
the grantee unfettered in its other activities. [In] contrast, our
'unconstitutional conditions' cases involve situations in which the
Government has placed a condition on the recipient of the subsidy rather
than on a particular program or service, thus effectively prohibiting the
recipient from engaging in the protected conduct outside the scope of the
federally funded program. [See League of Women Voters.]" He found it

irrelevant that Title X required all Title X projects to raise private matching funds, and that the abortion counseling and advocacy restrictions extended to those funds: "The recipient is in no way compelled to operate a Title X project; to avoid the force of the regulations, it can simply decline the subsidy. [Potential] grant recipients can choose between accepting Title X funds— subject to the Government's conditions that they provide matching funds and forgo abortion counseling and referral in the Title X project—or declining the subsidy and financing their own unsubsidized program. We have never held that the Government violates the First Amendment simply by offering that choice."

Chief Justice Rehnquist cautioned that "[t]his is not to suggest that funding by the Government, even when coupled with the freedom of the fund recipients to speak outside the scope of the Government-funded project, is invariably sufficient to justify Government control over the content of expression." He cited as examples cases upholding speech rights in traditional public forums and academic freedom at public universities. But he found no infringement of any analogous traditional doctor-patient relationship: "Nothing in [the regulations] requires a doctor to represent as his own any opinion that he does not in fact hold. Nor is the doctor-patient relationship established by the Title X program sufficiently all encompassing so as to justify an expectation on the part of the patient of comprehensive medical advice."

Justice BLACKMUN dissented, joined by Justices Marshall and Stevens: "Until today, the Court never has upheld viewpoint-based suppression of speech simply because that suppression was a condition upon the acceptance of public funds. Whatever may be the Government's power to condition the receipt of its largess upon the relinquishment of constitutional rights, it surely does not extend to a condition that suppresses the recipient's cherished freedom of speech based solely upon the content or viewpoint of that speech. [Speiser.] It cannot seriously be disputed that the counseling and referral provisions at issue in the present cases constitute content-based regulation of speech. Title X grantees may provide counseling and referral regarding any of a wide range of family planning and other topics, save abortion. The regulations are also clearly viewpoint based. While suppressing speech favorable to abortion with one hand, the Secretary compels antiabortion speech with the other." Justice Blackmun contended that this viewpoint discrimination distinguished the regulations from those upheld in TWR. He also disagreed with Chief Justice Rehnquist that they constituted mere earmarking of funds to the limited purpose of preconception family planning advice: "[The] majority's claim that the regulations merely limit a Title X project's speech to preventive or preconceptional services rings hollow in light of the broad range of nonpreventive services that the regulations authorize Title X projects to provide [including referral for prenatal or adoption services, physical examinations, and treatment of gynecological problems and sexually transmitted diseases]." He concluded that the regulations should be struck down under strict scrutiny. Justice O'Connor also dissented, but solely on the ground that the regulations exceeded HHS's statutory authority.

4. *Religion-related conditions on student activity funds.* The TWR and Rust decisions both stated in dictum that subsidies may not be made selectively so as to "aim at the suppression of dangerous ideas." In **Rosenberger v. Rector & Visitors of University of Virginia**, 515 U.S.

819 (1995), the Court invalidated a funding limitation as viewpoint discrimination. The case arose from a program at the University of Virginia in which mandatory student fees were used to pay the costs of extracurricular activities, including the costs of printing various student-edited publications. The University refused to pay the printing costs of "Wide Awake," a publication of a student group dedicated to advancing "the Christian perspective," under guidelines prohibiting the use of the activities fees for any "religious activity," defined as any activity that "primarily promotes or manifests a particular belief in or about a deity or an ultimate reality." Leaders of the student group claimed that this denial of funding violated their right of free speech. The University argued that it was a permissible nonsubsidy. The Court held, by a vote of 5–4, that Wide Awake's exclusion was forbidden by the Free Speech Clause and was not required by the Establishment Clause. (For the portion of the opinion discussing the Establishment Clause, see p. 653 below.)

Justice KENNEDY, writing for the Court, found the funding restriction to constitute discrimination on the basis of viewpoint, not subject matter. He analogized the University's action to the school district's exclusion of a religious film series from after-hours use of public school facilities that was invalidated by the Court in Lamb's Chapel (p. 361): "[W]e have observed a distinction between, on the one hand, content discrimination, which may be permissible if it preserves the purposes of [a] limited forum, and, on the other hand, viewpoint discrimination, which is presumed impermissible when directed against speech otherwise within the forum's limitations. The [Student Activities Fund (SAF)] is a forum more in a metaphysical than in a spatial or geographic sense, but the same principles are applicable. [It] is [something] of an understatement to speak of religious thought and discussion as just a viewpoint, as distinct from a comprehensive body of thought. The nature of our origins and destiny and their dependence upon the existence of a divine being have been subjects of philosophic inquiry throughout human history. We conclude, nonetheless, that here, as in Lamb's Chapel, viewpoint discrimination is the proper way to interpret the University's objections to Wide Awake. By the very terms of the SAF prohibition, the University does not exclude religion as a subject matter but selects for disfavored treatment those student journalistic efforts with religious editorial viewpoints. Religion may be a vast area of inquiry, but it also provides, as it did here, a specific premise, a perspective, a standpoint from which a variety of subjects may be discussed and considered. The prohibited perspective, not the general subject matter, resulted in the refusal to make third-party payments, for the subjects discussed were otherwise within the approved category of publications."

The University, relying on TWR and Rust, argued that "content-based funding decisions are both inevitable and lawful." Justice Kennedy found TWR inapposite because it involved no viewpoint discrimination, and Rust inapposite because it, in effect, involved government speech: "[In Rust,] the government did not create a program to encourage private speech but instead used private speakers to transmit specific information pertaining to its own program. We recognized that when the government appropriates public funds to promote a particular policy of its own it is entitled to say what it wishes. When the government disburses public funds to private entities to convey a governmental message, it may take legitimate and appropriate steps to ensure that its message is neither garbled nor distorted by the grantee. It does not follow, however, [that] viewpoint-based restrictions are proper when the University does not itself speak or subsidize transmittal of a message it favors but instead expends funds to encourage a diversity of views from private speakers. [The] distinction between the University's own favored message and the private speech of students is evident in the case before us. [The] University declares that the student groups eligible for SAF support are not the University's agents, are not subject to its control, and are not its responsibility. Having offered to pay the third-party contractors on behalf of private speakers who convey their own messages, the University may not silence the expression of selected viewpoints."

Justice SOUTER dissented, joined by Justices Stevens, Ginsburg, and Breyer: "There is no viewpoint discrimination in the University's application of its Guidelines to deny funding to Wide Awake. [If] the Guidelines were written or applied so as to limit only [Christian] advocacy and no other evangelical efforts that might compete with it, the discrimination would be based on viewpoint. But that is not what the regulation authorizes; it applies to Muslim and Jewish and Buddhist advocacy as well as to Christian. And since it limits funding to activities promoting or manifesting a particular belief not only 'in' but 'about' a deity or ultimate reality, it applies to agnostics and atheists as well as it does to deists and theists. The Guidelines, and their application to Wide Awake, thus do not skew debate by funding one position but not its competitors. As understood by their application to Wide Awake, they simply deny funding for hortatory speech that 'primarily promotes or manifests' any view on the merits of religion; they deny funding for the entire subject matter of religious apologetics." He distinguished Lamb's Chapel as a case in which antireligious perspectives were permitted and only religious perspectives were excluded.

After Rust and Rosenberger, could the government constitutionally condition disbursement of federal Medicaid or Medicare funds to doctors upon their agreement to refrain from prescribing certain especially expensive drugs or courses of treatment? Could it condition federal grants for medical research on researchers' agreement not to publish any results not precleared by the government?

Note that, while Rust v. Sullivan did not make such a distinction, Justice Kennedy in Rosenberger characterized and distinguished Rust as a case about government speech. Rust itself suggested that barring the use of government family funds for abortion counseling did not constitute viewpoint discrimination but rather was a form of subject matter limitation or earmarking. Did he mean to suggest that, when government is speaking through a private recipient of government funds, even viewpoint discrimination is allowed? When government is itself the speaker, it might be argued, viewpoint discrimination is inevitable, and the government has a special interest in not having attributed to it views that are contrary to its preferred policies. A government-sponsored drug treatment program, for example, need not give equal time to a campaign to legalize marijuana. But if government gave out grants for private research "on optimal drug policy," could it rescind the money from a researcher whose data led him to conclude that marijuana should be legalized?

For more commentary on these questions, see Cole, "Beyond Unconstitutional Conditions: Charting Spheres of Neutrality in Government-Funded Speech," 67 N.Y.U. L. Rev. 675 (1992); Fiss, "State Activism and State Censorship," 100 Yale L.J. 2087 (1991); Post, "Subsidized Speech," 106 Yale L.J. 151 (1996); Redish & Kessler, "Government Subsidies and Free Expression," 80 Minn. L. Rev. 543 (1995); Roberts, "Rust v. Sullivan and the Control of Knowledge," 61 Geo. Wash. L. Rev. 587 (1993).

5. *Conditions on arts funding.* What leeway does government have to restrict the content of art produced with the support of public subsidies? After a long and heated political debate that began in 1989 with public controversy over the federally subsidized exhibition of homoerotic photographs by Robert Mapplethorpe and religiously controversial photographs by Andres Serrano, this question finally reached the Court in **National Endowment for the Arts (NEA) v. Finley**, 524 U.S. 569 (1998). The case arose from a facial challenge by four individual performance artists and an artists' organization to a 1990 congressional amendment, codified at 20 U.S.C. § 954(d)(1), requiring the Chairperson of the NEA to ensure that "artistic excellence and artistic merit are the criteria by which [grant] applications are judged, taking into consideration general standards of decency and respect for the diverse beliefs and values of the American public." By a vote of 8–1, the Court held the law constitutional on its face. Justice O'CONNOR wrote the opinion of the Court: "Respondents argue that the provision is a paradigmatic example of viewpoint discrimination because it rejects any artistic speech that either fails to respect mainstream values or offends standards of decency. The premise of respondents' claim is that § 954(d)(1) constrains the agency's ability to fund certain categories of artistic expression. The NEA, however, reads the provision as merely hortatory, and contends that it stops well short of an absolute restriction. [It] is clear [that] the text of § 954(d)(1) imposes no categorical requirement. [The] criteria in § 954(d)(1) inform the assessment of artistic merit, but Congress declined to disallow any particular viewpoints. [That] § 954(d)(1) admonishes the NEA merely to take 'decency and respect' into consideration [undercuts] respondents' argument that the provision inevitably will be utilized as a tool for invidious viewpoint discrimination. In cases where we have struck down legislation as facially unconstitutional, the dangers were both more evident and more substantial. [See, e.g., R.A.V. v. City of St. Paul (1992; p. 109).] [Given] the varied interpretations of the criteria [of decency and respect] and the vague exhortation to 'take them into consideration,' it seems unlikely that this provision will introduce any greater element of selectivity than the determination of 'artistic excellence' itself.

"[Any] content-based considerations that may be taken into account in the grant-making process are a consequence of the nature of arts funding. The NEA has limited resources and it must deny the majority of the grant applications that it receives, including many that propose 'artistically excellent' projects. The agency may decide to fund particular projects for a wide variety of reasons, 'such as the technical proficiency of the artist, the creativity of the work, the anticipated public interest in or appreciation of the work, the work's contemporary relevance, its educational value, its suitability for or appeal to special audiences (such as children or the disabled), its service to a rural or isolated community, or even simply that the work could increase public knowledge of an art form.' [It] would be 'impossible to have a highly selective grant program without denying money to a large amount of constitutionally protected expression.' The 'very assumption' of the NEA is that grants will be awarded according to the 'artistic worth of competing applications,' and absolute neutrality is simply 'inconceivable.'

"Respondent's reliance on our decision in Rosenberger is therefore misplaced. In Rosenberger, a public university declined to authorize disbursements from its Student Activities Fund to finance the printing of a Christian student newspaper. We held that by subsidizing the Student Activities Fund, the University had created a limited public forum, from which it impermissibly excluded all publications with religious editorial viewpoints. Although the scarcity of NEA funding does not distinguish this case from Rosenberger, the competitive process according to which the grants are allocated does. In the context of arts funding, in contrast to many other subsidies, the Government does not indiscriminately 'encourage a diversity of views from private speakers.' The NEA's mandate is to make aesthetic judgments, and the inherently content-based 'excellence' threshold for NEA support sets it apart from the subsidy at issue in Rosenberger— which was available to all student organizations that were 'related to the educational purpose of the University,'—and from comparably objective decisions on allocating public benefits, such as access to a school auditorium or a municipal theater [see Lamb's Chapel; Conrad (p. 361)]."

While rejecting the facial challenge to the decency and respect provision, Justice O'Connor held out the possibility that particular applications of such criteria might violate the Free Speech Clause: "Respondents do not allege discrimination in any particular funding decision. [Thus,] we have no occasion here to address an as-applied challenge in a situation where the denial of a grant may be shown to be the product of invidious viewpoint discrimination. If the NEA were to leverage its power to award subsidies on the basis of subjective criteria into a penalty on disfavored viewpoints, then we would confront a different case. We have stated that, even in the provision of subsidies, the Government may not 'aim at the suppression of dangerous ideas,' and if a subsidy were 'manipulated' to have a 'coercive effect,' then relief could be appropriate. [Likewise,] a more pressing constitutional question would arise if government funding resulted in the imposition of a disproportionate burden calculated to drive 'certain ideas or viewpoints from the marketplace.' Unless and until § 954(d)(1) is applied in a manner that raises concern about the suppression of disfavored viewpoints, however, we uphold the constitutionality of the provision."

Justice SCALIA, joined by Justice Thomas, concurred only in the judgment, arguing that there was no need to read § 954(d)(1) as merely hortatory because it was constitutional even if mandatory and clearly viewpoint-based: " 'The operation was a success, but the patient died.' What such a procedure is to medicine, the Court's opinion in this case is to law. It sustains the constitutionality of § 954(d)(1) by gutting it. [By] its terms, [§ 954(d)(1)] establishes content- and viewpoint-based criteria upon which grant applications are to be evaluated. And that is perfectly constitutional.

"[It] is entirely, 100% clear that decency and respect are to be taken into account in evaluating applications. This is so apparent that I am at a loss to understand what the Court has in mind [when] it speculates that the statute is merely 'advisory.' [This] does not mean that those factors must always be dispositive, but it does mean that they must always be considered. [Such] factors need not be conclusive to be discriminatory. To the extent a particular applicant exhibits disrespect for the diverse beliefs and values of the American public or fails to comport with general standards of decency, the likelihood that he will receive a grant diminishes. [The] decisionmaker, all else being equal, will favor applications that display decency and respect, and disfavor applications that do not. This unquestionably constitutes viewpoint discrimination. [If] viewpoint discrimination in this context is unconstitutional, the law is invalid unless there are some situations in which the decency and respect factors do not constitute viewpoint discrimination. And there is none. The applicant who displays 'decency,' that is, 'conformity to prevailing standards of propriety or modesty,' and the applicant who displays 'respect,' that is, 'deferential regard,' for the diverse beliefs and values of the American people, will always have an edge over an applicant who displays the opposite.

"The Court devotes so much of its opinion to explaining why this statute means something other than what it says that it neglects to cite the constitutional text governing our analysis. The First Amendment reads: 'Congress shall make no law . . . abridging the freedom of speech.' To abridge is 'to contract, to diminish; to deprive of.' With the enactment of § 954(d)(1), Congress did not abridge the speech of those who disdain the beliefs and values of the American public, nor did it abridge indecent speech. Those who wish to create indecent and disrespectful art are as unconstrained now as they were before the enactment of this statute. Avant-garde artistes such as respondents remain entirely free to epater les bourgeois;[1] they are merely deprived of the additional satisfaction of having the bourgeoisie taxed to pay for it. It is preposterous to equate the denial of taxpayer subsidy with measures 'aimed at the suppression of dangerous ideas.' One might contend, I suppose, that a threat of rejection by the only available source of free money would constitute coercion and hence 'abridgment' within the meaning of the First Amendment. I would not agree with such a contention, which would make the NEA the mandatory patron of all art too indecent, too disrespectful, or even too kitsch to attract private support. But even if one accepts the contention, it would have no application here. The NEA is far from the sole source of funding for art—even indecent, disrespectful, or just plain bad art. Accordingly, the Government may earmark NEA funds for projects it deems to be in the public interest without thereby abridging speech.

"Respondents, relying on Rosenberger, argue that viewpoint-based discrimination is impermissible unless the government is the speaker or the government is 'disbursing public funds to private entities to convey a governmental message.' It is impossible to imagine why that should be so; one would think that directly involving the government itself in the viewpoint discrimination (if it is unconstitutional) would make the situation even worse. Respondents are mistaken. It is the very business of government to favor and disfavor points of view on (in modern times, at least) innumerable subjects—which is the main reason we have decided to elect those who run the government, rather than save money by making their

---

[1] "Which they do quite well. The oeuvres d'art for which the four individual plaintiffs in this case sought funding have been described as follows: Finley's controversial show, 'We Keep Our Victims Ready,' contains three segments. In the second segment, Finley visually recounts a sexual assault by stripping to the waist and smearing chocolate on her breasts and by using profanity to describe the assault. Holly Hughes' monologue 'World Without End' is a somewhat graphic recollection of the artist's realization of her lesbianism and reminiscence of her mother's sexuality. John Fleck, in his stage performance 'Blessed Are All the Little Fishes,' confronts alcoholism and Catholicism. During the course of the performance, Fleck appears dressed as a mermaid, urinates on the stage and creates an altar out of a toilet bowl by putting a photograph of Jesus Christ on the lid. Tim Miller derives his performance 'Some Golden States' from childhood experiences, from his life as a homosexual, and from the constant threat of AIDS. Miller uses vegetables in his performances to represent sexual symbols." [Footnote by Justice Scalia.]

posts hereditary. And it makes not a bit of difference, insofar as either common sense or the Constitution is concerned, whether these officials further their (and, in a democracy, our) favored point of view by achieving it directly (having government-employed artists paint pictures, for example, or government-employed doctors perform abortions); or by advocating it officially (establishing an Office of Art Appreciation, for example, or an Office of Voluntary Population Control); or by giving money to others who achieve or advocate it (funding private art classes, for example, or Planned Parenthood). None of this has anything to do with abridging anyone's speech. Rosenberger found the viewpoint discrimination unconstitutional, not because funding of 'private' speech was involved, but because the government had established a limited public forum—to which the NEA's granting of highly selective (if not highly discriminating) awards bears no resemblance. The nub of the difference between me and the Court is that I regard the distinction between 'abridging' speech and funding it as a fundamental divide, on this side of which the First Amendment is inapplicable."

Justice SOUTER alone dissented: "The decency and respect proviso mandates viewpoint-based decisions in the disbursement of government subsidies, and the Government has wholly failed to explain why the statute should be afforded an exemption from the fundamental rule of the First Amendment that viewpoint discrimination in the exercise of public authority over expressive activity is unconstitutional. [Because] 'the normal definition of "indecent" . . . refers to nonconformance with accepted standards of morality' [Pacifica], restrictions turning on decency, especially those couched in terms of 'general standards of decency,' are quintessentially viewpoint based: they require discrimination on the basis of conformity with mainstream mores. [Just] as self-evidently, a statute disfavoring speech that fails to respect America's 'diverse beliefs and values' is the very model of viewpoint discrimination; it penalizes any view disrespectful to [the] ideology, opinions, or convictions of a significant segment of the American public. [It does not matter that § 954(d)(1)] admonishes the NEA merely to take 'decency and respect' into consideration, not to make funding decisions specifically on those grounds. [What] if the statute required a panel to apply criteria 'taking into consideration the centrality of Christianity to the American cultural experience,' or 'taking into consideration whether the artist is a communist,' or 'taking into consideration the political message conveyed by the art,' or even 'taking into consideration the superiority of the white race'? Would the Court hold these considerations facially constitutional, merely because the statute had no requirement to give them any particular, much less controlling, weight? I assume not.

"[The] Government calls attention to the roles of government-as-speaker and government-as-buyer, in which the government is of course entitled to engage in viewpoint discrimination: if the Food and Drug Administration launches an advertising campaign on the subject of smoking, it may condemn the habit without also having to show a cowboy taking a puff on the opposite page; and if the Secretary of Defense wishes to buy a portrait to decorate the Pentagon, he is free to prefer George Washington over George the Third. The Government freely admits, however, that it neither speaks through the expression subsidized by the NEA, nor buys anything for itself with its NEA grants. [When] the Government acts as a patron, financially underwriting the production of art by private artists and impresarios for independent consumption, [this] patronage falls embarrassingly on the wrong side of the line between government-as-buyer or-speaker and government-as-regulator-of-private-speech. [Thus,] Rosenberger [controls] here. The NEA, like the student activities fund in Rosenberger, is a subsidy scheme created to encourage expression of a diversity of views from private speakers. [Given] this congressional choice to sustain freedom of expression, Rosenberger teaches that the First Amendment forbids decisions based on viewpoint popularity. So long as Congress chooses to subsidize expressive endeavors at large, it has no business requiring the NEA to turn down funding applications of artists and exhibitors who [defy] our tastes, our beliefs, or our values."

6. *Conditions on legal aid funding.* In **Legal Services Corporation v. Velazquez**, 531 U.S. 533 (2001), the Court, by a vote of 5–4, held invalid as an impermissible viewpoint-based restriction a federal appropriations law barring Legal Services Corporation (LSC) funding of any organization that represented indigent clients in "an effort to amend or otherwise challenge existing" welfare law. The majority, however, declined to address other related federal prohibitions on legal service grantees "participat[ing] [in] litigation, lobbying, or rulemaking, involving an effort to reform a Federal or State welfare system," which the court of appeals had upheld as "prohibit[ing] the type of activity named regardless of viewpoint."

Writing for the Court, Justice KENNEDY, joined by Justices Stevens, Souter, Ginsburg, and Breyer, explained: "[V]iewpoint-based funding decisions can be sustained in instances in which the government is itself the speaker, or instances, like Rust, in which the government 'used private speakers to transmit information pertaining to its own program.' Rosenberger. [Neither] the latitude for government speech nor its rationale applies to subsidies for private speech in every instance, however. [Like] the program in Rosenberger, the LSC program was designed to facilitate private speech, not to promote a governmental message. [The] Government has designed this program to use the legal profession and the established Judiciary of the States and the Federal Government to accomplish its end of assisting welfare claimants in determination or receipt of their benefits. The advice from the attorney to the client and the advocacy by the attorney to the courts cannot be classified as governmental speech even under a generous understanding of the concept. In this vital respect this suit is distinguishable from Rust."

"[The] Government seeks to use an existing medium of expression and to control it, in a class of cases, in ways which distort its usual functioning. [Restricting] LSC attorneys in advising their clients and in presenting arguments and analyses to the courts distorts the legal system by altering the traditional role of the attorneys [and] threatens severe impairment of the judicial function.

"[Moreover,] with respect to the litigation services Congress has funded, there is no alternative channel for expression of the advocacy Congress seeks to restrict. This is in stark contrast to Rust. There, a patient could receive the approved Title X family planning counseling funded by the Government and later could consult an affiliate or independent organization to receive abortion counseling. Unlike indigent clients who seek LSC representation, the patient in Rust was not required to forfeit the Government-funded advice when she also received abortion counseling through alternative channels. Because LSC attorneys must withdraw whenever a question of a welfare statute's validity arises, an individual could not obtain joint representation so that the constitutional challenge would be presented by a non-LSC attorney, and other, permitted, arguments advanced by LSC counsel.

"[Nor is the restriction] necessary to define the scope and contours of the federal program. [Congress] cannot recast a condition on funding as a mere definition of its program in every case, lest the First Amendment be reduced to a simple semantic exercise. Here, notwithstanding Congress' purpose to confine and limit its program, the restriction operates to insulate current welfare laws from constitutional scrutiny and certain other legal challenges. [Arguments] by indigent clients that a welfare statute is unlawful or unconstitutional cannot be expressed in this Government-funded program for petitioning the courts, even though the program was created for litigation involving welfare benefits, and even though the ordinary course of litigation involves the expression of theories and postulates on both, or multiple, sides of an issue. [In] the context of this statute there is no programmatic message of the kind recognized in Rust and which sufficed there to allow the Government to specify the advice deemed necessary for its legitimate objectives. This serves to distinguish [the LSC provision] from any of the Title X program restrictions upheld in Rust, and to place it beyond any congressional funding condition approved in the past by this Court.

"[The] attempted restriction is designed to insulate the Government's interpretation of the Constitution from judicial challenge. The Constitution does not permit the Government to confine litigants and their attorneys in this manner. We must be vigilant when Congress imposes rules and conditions which in effect insulate its own laws from legitimate judicial challenge. Where private speech is involved, even Congress' antecedent funding decision cannot be aimed at the suppression of ideas thought inimical to the Government's own interest. TWR."

Justice SCALIA dissented, joined by Chief Justice Rehnquist and Justices O'Connor and Thomas, taking the view that the LSC measure "defines the scope of a federal spending program. It does not directly regulate speech, and it neither establishes a public forum nor discriminates on the basis of viewpoint. Accordingly, the dissenters would have found the case controlled by Rust: "The LSC Act, like the scheme in Rust, does not create a public forum. Far from encouraging a diversity of views, it has always, 'placed restrictions on its use of funds,' Nor does [the act] discriminate on the basis of viewpoint, since it funds neither challenges to nor defenses of existing welfare law. The provision simply declines to subsidize a certain class of litigation, and under Rust that decision 'does not infringe the right' to bring such litigation. [No] litigant who, in the absence of LSC funding, would bring a suit challenging existing welfare law is deterred from doing so. [Rust] thus controls these cases and compels the conclusion that [the act] is constitutional."

Justice Scalia's dissent further challenged the proposition that "Rust is different because the program at issue subsidized government speech, while the LSC funds private speech": "If the private doctors' confidential advice to their patients at issue in Rust constituted 'government speech,' it is hard to imagine what subsidized speech would *not* be government speech. Moreover, the majority's contention that the subsidized speech in these cases is not government speech because the lawyers have a professional obligation to represent the interests of their clients founders on the reality that the doctors in Rust had a professional obligation to serve the interests of their patients." He concluded by suggesting that the majority had displayed "an improper special solicitude for our own profession."

7. *Conditions on public library internet access.* In **United States v. American Library Ass'n**, 539 U.S. 194 (2003), the Court upheld by a vote of 6–3 the Children's Internet Protection Act (CIPA), under which a public library receiving federal subsidies is required to install filtering software blocking internet access to obscenity, child pornography, or indecent material harmful to minors. Writing for a plurality, Chief Justice REHNQUIST, joined by Justices O'Connor, Scalia, and Thomas, first rejected arguments that public library computer terminals are akin to public forums or designated public forums, as libraries are inherently selective in their acquisition of material. (For this portion of the opinion, see p. 351.)

Going on to reject an additional challenge that the restriction was an unconstitutional condition on government funding, Chief Justice Rehnquist stated: "Appellees argue that CIPA imposes an unconstitutional condition on libraries that receive [federal] subsidies by requiring them, as a condition on their receipt of federal funds, to surrender their First Amendment right to provide the public with access to constitutionally protected speech. The Government counters that this claim fails because Government entities do not have First Amendment rights. We need not decide this question because, even assuming that appellees may assert an 'unconstitutional conditions' claim, this claim would fail on the merits. Within broad limits, 'when the Government appropriates public funds to establish a program it is entitled to define the limits of that program.' [Rust.] The same is true here. The [federal subsidy] programs were intended to help public libraries fulfill their traditional role of obtaining material of requisite and appropriate quality for educational and informational purposes. Congress may certainly insist that these 'public funds be spent for the purposes for which they were authorized.' Especially because public libraries have traditionally excluded pornographic material from their other collections, Congress could reasonably impose a parallel limitation on its Internet assistance programs. As the use of filtering software helps to carry out these programs, it is a permissible condition under Rust.

"Appellees mistakenly contend, in reliance on LSC v. Velazquez, that CIPA's filtering conditions '[d]istor[t] the [u]sual [f]unctioning of [p]ublic [l]ibraries.' In Velazquez, the Court concluded that a Government program of furnishing legal aid to the indigent differed from the program in Rust '[i]n th[e] vital respect' that the role of lawyers who represent clients in welfare disputes is to advocate *against* the Government, and there was thus an assumption that counsel would be free of state control. The Court concluded that the restriction on advocacy in such welfare disputes would distort the usual functioning of the legal profession and the federal and state courts before which the lawyers appeared. Public libraries, by contrast, have no comparable role that pits them against the Government, and there is no comparable assumption that they must be free of any conditions that their benefactors might attach to the use of donated funds or other assistance."

In dissent, Justice STEVENS argued: "A federal statute penalizing a library for failing to install filtering software on every one of its Internet-accessible computers would unquestionably violate [the First] Amendment. I think it equally clear that the First Amendment protects libraries from being denied funds for refusing to comply with an identical rule. An abridgment of speech by means of a threatened denial of benefits can be just as pernicious as an abridgment by means of a threatened penalty. [In] an analogous situation, we specifically held that when 'the Government seeks to use an existing medium of expression and to control it, in a class of cases, in ways which distort its usual functioning,' the distorting restriction must be struck down under the First Amendment. [Velazquez.]."

Justice Stevens's dissent distinguished Rust and Finley: "The plurality argues that the controversial decision in [Rust] requires rejection of appellees' unconstitutional conditions claim. But, as subsequent cases have explained, Rust only involved and only applies to instances of governmental speech—that is, situations in which the government seeks to communicate a specific message. The discounts under the [federal subsidy programs] involved in this case do not subsidize any message favored by the Government. As Congress made clear, these programs were designed '[t]o help public libraries provide their patrons with Internet access,' which in turn 'provide[s] patrons with a vast amount of valuable information.' These programs thus are designed to provide access, particularly for individuals in low-income communities, to a vast amount and wide variety of private speech. They are not designed to foster or transmit any particular governmental message.

"[The] plurality's reliance on [Finley] is also misplaced. [Unlike] Finley, the Government does not merely seek to control a library's discretion with respect to computers purchased with Government funds or those computers with Government-discounted Internet access. CIPA requires libraries to install filtering software on *every* computer with Internet access if the library receives *any* discount from the [federal subsidy programs.] This Court should not permit federal funds to be used to enforce this kind of broad restriction of First Amendment rights, particularly when such a restriction is unnecessary to accomplish Congress' stated goal. The abridgment of speech is equally obnoxious whether a rule like this one is enforced by a threat of penalties or by a threat to withhold a benefit." Justice Souter, joined by Justice Ginsburg, filed a separate dissent.

———

Agency for International Development v. Alliance for Open Society International, Inc.

570 U.S. 205, 133 S. Ct. 2321, 186 L. Ed. 2d 398 (2013).

■ CHIEF JUSTICE ROBERTS delivered the opinion of the Court.

Congress passed the United States Leadership Against HIV/AIDS Act in 2003 after finding that HIV/AIDS had "assumed pandemic proportions, spreading from the most severely affected regions, sub-Saharan Africa and the Caribbean, to all corners of the world, and leaving an unprecedented path of death and devastation." [The] Act "make[s] the reduction of HIV/AIDS behavioral risks a priority of all prevention efforts." [The] President's strategy for addressing such risks must, for example, promote abstinence, encourage monogamy, increase the availability of condoms, promote voluntary counseling and treatment for drug users, and, as relevant here, "educat[e] men and boys about the risks of procuring sex commercially" as well as "promote alternative livelihoods, safety, and social reintegration strategies for commercial sex workers." Congress found that the "sex industry, the trafficking of individuals into such industry, and sexual

violence" were factors in the spread of the HIV/AIDS epidemic, and
determined that "it should be the policy of the United States to eradicate"
prostitution and "other sexual victimization." The United States has enlisted
the assistance of nongovernmental organizations to help achieve the many
goals of the program. Such organizations "with experience in health care and
HIV/AIDS counseling," Congress found, "have proven effective in combating
the HIV/AIDS pandemic and can be a resource in . . . provid[ing] treatment
and care for individuals infected with HIV/AIDS." Since 2003, Congress has
authorized the appropriation of billions of dollars for funding these
organizations' fight against HIV/AIDS around the world. Those funds,
however, come with two conditions: First, no funds made available to carry
out the Leadership Act "may be used to promote or advocate the legalization
or practice of prostitution or sex trafficking." [22 U.S.C.] § 7631(e). Second,
no funds made available may "provide assistance to any group or
organization that does not have a policy explicitly opposing prostitution and
sex trafficking, except . . . to the Global Fund to Fight AIDS, Tuberculosis
and Malaria, the World Health Organization, the International AIDS
Vaccine Initiative or to any United Nations agency." § 7631(f). It is this
second condition—the Policy Requirement—that is at issue here.

The Department of Health and Human Services (HHS) and the United
States Agency for International Development (USAID) are the federal
agencies primarily responsible for overseeing implementation of the
Leadership Act. To enforce the Policy Requirement, the agencies have
directed that the recipient of any funding under the Act agree in the award
document that it is opposed to "prostitution and sex trafficking because of
the psychological and physical risks they pose for women, men, and
children."

[Respondents] are a group of domestic organizations engaged in
combating HIV/AIDS overseas. [They] fear that adopting a policy explicitly
opposing prostitution may alienate certain host governments, and may
diminish the effectiveness of some of their programs by making it more
difficult to work with prostitutes in the fight against HIV/AIDS. They are
also concerned that the Policy Requirement may require them to censor their
privately funded discussions in publications, at conferences, and in other
forums about how best to prevent the spread of HIV/AIDS among prostitutes.
[Respondents] sought a preliminary injunction barring the Government from
cutting off their funding under the Act for the duration of the litigation, from
unilaterally terminating their cooperative agreements with the United
States, or from otherwise taking action solely on the basis of respondents'
own privately funded speech. The District Court granted such a preliminary
injunction, and the Government appealed. While the appeal was pending,
HHS and USAID issued guidelines on how recipients of Leadership Act
funds could retain funding while working with affiliated organizations not
bound by the Policy Requirement. The guidelines permit funding recipients
to work with affiliated organizations that "engage [ ] in activities
inconsistent with the recipient's opposition to the practices of prostitution
and sex trafficking" as long as the recipients retain "objective integrity and
independence from any affiliated organization." Whether sufficient
separation exists is determined by the totality of the circumstances,
including "but not . . . limited to" (1) whether the organizations are legally
separate; (2) whether they have separate personnel; (3) whether they keep
separate accounting records; (4) the degree of separation in the
organizations' facilities; and (5) the extent to which signs and other forms of

identification distinguish the organizations. The Court of Appeals summarily remanded the case to the District Court to consider whether the preliminary injunction was still appropriate in light of the new guidelines. On remand, the District Court issued a new preliminary injunction along the same lines as the first, and the Government renewed its appeal.

[The] Policy Requirement mandates that recipients of Leadership Act funds explicitly agree with the Government's policy to oppose prostitution and sex trafficking. It is, however, a basic First Amendment principle that "freedom of speech prohibits the government from telling people what they must say." Were it enacted as a direct regulation of speech, the Policy Requirement would plainly violate the First Amendment. The question is whether the Government may nonetheless impose that requirement as a condition on the receipt of federal funds.

A. [As] a general matter, if a party objects to a condition on the receipt of federal funding, its recourse is to decline the funds. This remains true when the objection is that a condition may affect the recipient's exercise of its First Amendment rights. At the same time, however, we have held that the Government "may not deny a benefit to a person on a basis that infringes his constitutionally protected . . . freedom of speech even if he has no entitlement to that benefit." In some cases, a funding condition can result in an unconstitutional burden on First Amendment rights.

[In] the present context, the relevant distinction that has emerged from our cases is between conditions that define the limits of the government spending program—those that specify the activities Congress wants to subsidize—and conditions that seek to leverage funding to regulate speech outside the contours of the program itself. The line is hardly clear, in part because the definition of a particular program can always be manipulated to subsume the challenged condition. We have held, however, that "Congress cannot recast a condition on funding as a mere definition of its program in every case, lest the First Amendment be reduced to a simple semantic exercise." Velazquez. [Our] decision in Rust v. Sullivan elaborated on the approach reflected in Regan and League of Women Voters. [The] Court stressed that "Title X expressly distinguishes between a Title X *grantee* and a Title X *project*." The regulations governed only the scope of the grantee's Title X projects, leaving it "unfettered in its other activities." "The Title X *grantee* can continue to . . . engage in abortion advocacy; it simply is required to conduct those activities through programs that are separate and independent from the project that receives Title X funds." Because the regulations did not "prohibit[ ] the recipient from engaging in the protected conduct outside the scope of the federally funded program," they did not run afoul of the First Amendment.

B. [Here], we are confident that the Policy Requirement falls on the unconstitutional side of the line. [The] Leadership Act has two conditions relevant here. The first—unchallenged in this litigation—prohibits Leadership Act funds from being used "to promote or advocate the legalization or practice of prostitution or sex trafficking." The Government concedes that § 7631(e) by itself ensures that federal funds will not be used for the prohibited purposes. The Policy Requirement therefore must be doing something more—and it is. [The] Policy Requirement is an ongoing condition on recipients' speech and activities, a ground for terminating a grant after selection is complete. In any event, as the Government acknowledges, it is not simply seeking organizations that oppose prostitution. Rather, it explains, "Congress has expressed its purpose 'to eradicate' prostitution and sex trafficking, and it wants recipients *to adopt* a similar stance." This case is not about the Government's ability to enlist the assistance of those with whom it already agrees. It is about compelling a grant recipient to adopt a particular belief as a condition of funding. By demanding that funding recipients adopt—as their own—the Government's view on an issue of public concern, the condition by its very nature affects "protected conduct outside the scope of the federally funded program." Rust. A recipient cannot avow the belief dictated by the Policy Requirement when spending Leadership Act funds, and then turn around and assert a contrary belief, or claim neutrality, when participating in activities on its own time and dime. By requiring recipients to profess a specific belief, the Policy Requirement goes beyond defining the limits of the federally funded program to defining the recipient.

[The] Government suggests the guidelines alleviate any unconstitutional burden on the respondents' First Amendment rights by allowing them to either: (1) accept Leadership Act funding and comply with Policy Requirement, but establish affiliates to communicate contrary views on prostitution; or (2) decline funding themselves (thus remaining free to express their own views or remain neutral), while creating affiliates whose sole purpose is to receive and administer Leadership Act funds, thereby "cabin[ing] the effects" of the Policy Requirement within the scope of the federal program. Neither approach is sufficient. When we have noted the importance of affiliates in this context, it has been because they allow an organization bound by a funding condition to exercise its First Amendment rights outside the scope of the federal program. See Rust. Affiliates cannot serve that purpose when the condition is that a funding recipient espouse a specific belief as its own. If the affiliate is distinct from the recipient, the arrangement does not afford a means for the *recipient* to express *its* beliefs. If the affiliate is more clearly identified with the recipient, the recipient can express those beliefs only at the price of evident hypocrisy. [The] Government cites but one case to support that argument, Holder v. Humanitarian Law Project. That case concerned the quite different context of a ban on providing material support to terrorist organizations, where the record indicated that support for those organizations' nonviolent operations was funneled to support their violent activities.

[The] Policy Requirement goes beyond preventing recipients from using private funds in a way that would undermine the federal program. It requires them to pledge allegiance to the Government's policy of eradicating prostitution. As to that, we cannot improve upon what Justice Jackson wrote for the Court 70 years ago: "If there is any fixed star in our constitutional constellation, it is that no official, high or petty, can prescribe what shall be orthodox in politics, nationalism, religion, or other matters of opinion or force citizens to confess by word or act their faith therein." Barnette [p. 478 below].

■ KAGAN, J., took no part in the consideration or decision of this case.

■ JUSTICE SCALIA, with whom JUSTICE THOMAS joins, dissenting.

The Leadership Act provides that "any group or organization that does not have a policy explicitly opposing prostitution and sex trafficking" may not receive funds appropriated under the Act. This Policy Requirement is nothing more than a means of selecting suitable agents to implement the Government's chosen strategy to eradicate HIV/AIDS. That is perfectly permissible under the Constitution. The First Amendment does not mandate a viewpoint-neutral government. Government must choose between rival ideas and adopt some as its own: competition over cartels, solar energy over coal, weapon development over disarmament, and so forth. Moreover, the government may enlist the assistance of those who believe in its ideas to carry them to fruition; and it need not enlist for that purpose those who oppose or do not support the ideas. That seems to me a matter of the most common common sense. For example: One of the purposes of America's foreign-aid programs is the fostering of good will towards this country. If the organization Hamas—reputed to have an efficient system for delivering welfare—were excluded from a program for the distribution of U.S. food assistance, no one could reasonably object. And that would remain true if Hamas were an organization of United States citizens entitled to the protection of the Constitution. So long as the unfunded organization remains free to engage in its activities (including anti-American propaganda) "without federal assistance," refusing to make use of its assistance for an enterprise to which it is opposed does not abridge its speech. And the same is true when the rejected organization is not affirmatively opposed to, but merely unsupportive of, the object of the federal program, which appears to be the case here. (Respondents do not promote prostitution, but neither do they wish to oppose it.) A federal program to encourage healthy eating habits need not be administered by the American Gourmet Society, which has nothing against healthy food but does not insist upon it.

The argument is that this commonsense principle will enable the government to discriminate against, and injure, points of view to which it is opposed. Of course the Constitution does not prohibit government spending that discriminates against, and injures, points of view to which the government is opposed; every government program which takes a position on a controversial issue does that. Anti-smoking programs injure cigar aficionados, programs encouraging sexual abstinence injure free-love advocates, etc. The constitutional prohibition at issue here is not a prohibition against discriminating against or injuring opposing points of view, but the First Amendment's prohibition against the coercing of speech. I am frankly dubious that a condition for eligibility to participate in a minor federal program such as this one runs afoul of that prohibition even when the condition is irrelevant to the goals of the program. Not every disadvantage is a coercion.

But that is not the issue before us here. Here the views that the Government demands an applicant forswear—or that the Government insists an applicant favor—are relevant to the program in question. The program is valid only if the Government is entitled to disfavor the opposing view (here, advocacy of or toleration of prostitution). And if the program can disfavor it, so can the selection of those who are to administer the program. There is no risk that this principle will enable the Government to discriminate arbitrarily against positions it disfavors. It would not, for example, permit the Government to exclude from bidding on defense contracts anyone who refuses to abjure prostitution. But here a central part of the Government's HIV/AIDS strategy is the suppression of prostitution, by which HIV is transmitted. It is entirely reasonable to admit to participation in the program only those who believe in that goal.

According to the Court, however, this transgresses a constitutional line between conditions that operate *inside* a spending program and those that control speech *outside* of it. I am at a loss to explain what this central pillar of the Court's opinion [has] to do with the First Amendment. The distinction was alluded to, to be sure, in Rust, but not as (what the Court now makes it) an invariable requirement for First Amendment validity. That the pro-abortion speech prohibition was limited to "inside the program" speech was relevant in Rust because the program itself was not an anti-abortion program. The Government remained neutral on that controversial issue, but did not wish abortion to be promoted within its family-planning-services program. The statutory objective could not be impaired, in other words, by "outside the program" pro-abortion speech. The purpose of the limitation was to prevent Government funding from providing the *means* of pro-abortion propaganda, which the Government did not wish (and had no constitutional obligation) to provide. The situation here is vastly different. Elimination of prostitution *is* an objective of the HIV/AIDS program, and *any* promotion of prostitution—whether made inside or outside the program—*does* harm the program.

Of course the most obvious manner in which the admission to a program of an ideological opponent can frustrate the purpose of the program is by freeing up the opponent's funds for use in its ideological opposition. To use the Hamas example again: Subsidizing that organization's provision of social services enables the money that it would otherwise use for that purpose to be used, instead, for anti-American propaganda. Perhaps that problem does not exist in this case since the respondents do not affirmatively promote prostitution. But the Court's analysis categorically rejects that justification for ideological requirements in *all* cases, demanding "record indica[tion]" that "federal funding will simply supplant private funding, rather than pay for new programs." This seems to me quite naive. Money is fungible. The economic reality is that when NGOs can conduct their AIDS work on the Government's dime, they can expend greater resources on policies that undercut the Leadership Act. The Government need not establish by record evidence that this will happen. To make it a valid consideration in determining participation in federal programs, it suffices that this is a real and obvious risk.

[The] Court makes a head-fake at the unconstitutional conditions doctrine, but that doctrine is of no help. There is no case of ours in which a condition that is relevant to a statute's valid purpose and that is not in itself unconstitutional (e.g., a religious-affiliation condition that violates the Establishment Clause) has been held to violate the doctrine.

[The] majority cannot credibly say that this speech condition is coercive, so it does not. It pussyfoots around the lack of coercion by invalidating the Leadership Act for "*requiring* recipients to profess a specific belief" and "*demanding* that funding recipients adopt—as their own—the Government's view on an issue of public concern." But like King Cnut's commanding of the tides, here the Government's "requiring" and "demanding" have no coercive effect. In the end, and in the circumstances of this case, "compell[ing] *as a condition* of federal funding the affirmation of a belief," is no compulsion at all. It is the reasonable price of admission to a limited government-spending program that each organization remains free to accept or reject. Section 7631(f) "defin[es] the recipient" only to the extent he decides that it is in his interest to be so defined.

Ideological-commitment requirements such as the one here are quite rare; but making the choice between competing applicants on relevant ideological grounds is undoubtedly quite common. As far as the Constitution is concerned, it is quite impossible to distinguish between the two. If the government cannot demand a relevant ideological commitment as a condition of application, neither can it distinguish between applicants on a relevant ideological ground. And that is the real evil of today's opinion. One can expect, in the future, frequent challenges to the denial of government funding for relevant ideological reasons.

———

In **Agency for International Development v. Alliance for Open Society International Inc.**, 591 U.S. ___, 140 S. Ct. 2082 (2020), the Court upheld the same law at issue in AOSII as applied to foreign affiliates of U.S.-based organizations. Justice KAVANAUGH wrote for the Court that the foreign affiliates had no First Amendment rights because "foreign citizens outside U. S. territory do not possess rights under the U.S. Constitution" and "separately incorporated organizations are separate legal units with distinct legal rights and obligations" as a matter of corporate law.

Justice BREYER dissented, joined by Justices Ginsburg and Sotomayor (Justice Kagan was recused). He wrote: "This case is not about the First Amendment rights of foreign organizations [but rather] about the First Amendment rights of American organizations. [Respondents] and their affiliates receive federal funding to fight HIV/AIDS *overseas*. What has been at stake in this case from the beginning, then, is protected speech often aimed at audiences abroad. Our decision in AOSII shielded respondents' global message from government-compelled distortion in the eyes of those foreign audiences, as well as listeners here at home. Yet in the wake of our ruling, respondents have continued to suffer that exact same First Amendment harm. True, respondents' international mission sometimes requires that they convey their message through affiliates incorporated in far-off countries, rather than registered here at home. But so what? Audiences everywhere attribute speech based on whom they perceive to be speaking, not on corporate paperwork they will never see. [The] idea that foreign citizens abroad *never* have constitutional rights is not a 'bedrock' legal principle. [This] Court has studiously avoided establishing an absolute rule that forecloses that protection in all circumstances. [The] exhaustive review of our precedents that we conducted in Boumediene pointed to the opposite conclusion. [And] our First Amendment precedents (including AOSII) refute any suggestion that a workaday principle of corporate law somehow resolves the constitutional issue here in dispute."

———

8. *Viewpoint and trademark.*

———

Matal v. Tam

581 U.S. ___, 137 S. Ct. 1744, 198 L. Ed. 2d 366 (2017).

■ JUSTICE ALITO announced the judgment of the Court and delivered the opinion of the Court with respect to Parts I, II, and III-A, and an opinion with respect to Parts III-B, III-C, and IV, in which THE CHIEF JUSTICE, JUSTICE THOMAS, and JUSTICE BREYER join.

[Simon Tam, lead singer of dance-rock band called "The Slants," chose the name to "reclaim" the anti-Asian slur. The members of the ban are Asian-

Americans. Tam sought federal registration of the mark "THE SLANTS" from the Patent and Trademark Office (PTO), which denied the application under a Lanham Act provision prohibiting the registration of trademarks that may "disparage . . . or bring . . . into contemp[t] or disrepute" any "persons, living or dead." 15 U.S.C. § 1052(a).]

[We] now hold that this provision violates the Free Speech Clause of the First Amendment. It offends a bedrock First Amendment principle: Speech may not be banned on the ground that it expresses ideas that offend.

I. [Federal] law does not create trademarks. Trademarks and their precursors have ancient origins, and trademarks were protected at common law and in equity at the time of the founding. [For] most of the 19th century, trademark protection was the province of the States. [Under] the Lanham Act, [there] are now more than two million marks that have active federal certificates of registration. [Without] federal registration, a valid trademark may still be used in commerce. And an unregistered trademark can be enforced against would-be infringers in several ways. Most important, even if a trademark is not federally registered, it may still be enforceable under § 43(a) of the Lanham Act, which creates a federal cause of action for trademark infringement. And an unregistered trademark can be enforced under state common law, or if it has been registered in a State, under that State's registration system. Federal registration, however, [(1) serves] as constructive notice of the registrant's claim of ownership of the mark; (2) is prima facie evidence of the validity of the registered mark and of the registration of the mark, of the owner's ownership of the mark, and of the owner's exclusive right to use the registered mark in commerce on or in connection with the goods or services specified in the certificate; and (3) can make a mark incontestable once a mark has been registered for five years.

[At] issue in this case is [what] we will call "the disparagement clause." [When] deciding whether a trademark is disparaging, an examiner at the PTO generally applies a two-part test. The examiner first considers the likely meaning of the matter in question. ["If] that meaning is found to refer to identifiable persons, institutions, beliefs or national symbols," the examiner moves to the second step, asking "whether that meaning may be disparaging to a substantial composite of the referenced group." If the examiner finds that a "substantial composite, although not necessarily a majority, of the referenced group would find the proposed mark . . . to be disparaging in the context of contemporary attitudes," a prima facie case of disparagement is made out, and the burden shifts to the applicant to prove that the trademark is not disparaging. What is more, the PTO has specified that "[t]he fact that an applicant may be a member of that group or has good intentions underlying its use of a term does not obviate the fact that a substantial composite of the referenced group would find the term objectionable."

II. [Before] reaching the question whether the disparagement clause violates the First Amendment, we consider Tam's argument that the clause does not reach marks that disparage racial or ethnic groups [because] racial and ethnic groups are neither natural nor "juristic" persons. Tam's argument is refuted by the plain terms of the disparagement clause. [A] mark that disparages a "substantial" percentage of the members of a racial or ethnic group necessarily disparages many "persons," namely, members of that group.

III. [At] the outset, we must consider three arguments that would either eliminate any First Amendment protection or result in highly permissive rational-basis review. Specifically, the Government contends (1) that trademarks are government speech, not private speech, (2) that trademarks are a form of government subsidy, and (3) that the constitutionality of the disparagement clause should be tested under a new "government-program" doctrine.

A. [Our] cases recognize that "the Free Speech Clause . . . does not regulate government speech." Pleasant Grove City v. Summum. [But] while the government-speech doctrine is important—indeed, essential—it is a doctrine that is susceptible to dangerous misuse. If private speech could be passed off as government speech by simply affixing a government seal of approval, government could silence or muffle the expression of disfavored.

[At] issue here is the content of trademarks that are registered by the PTO. [The] Federal Government does not dream up these marks, and it does not edit marks submitted for registration. Except as required by the statute involved here, an examiner may not reject a mark based on the viewpoint that it appears to express. Thus, unless that section is thought to apply, [registration] is mandatory. [If] an examiner finds that a mark is eligible for placement on the principal register, that decision is not reviewed by any higher official unless the registration is challenged. Moreover, once a mark is registered, the PTO is not authorized to remove it from the register. [In] light of all this, it is far-fetched to suggest that the content of a registered mark is government speech. If the federal registration of a trademark makes the mark government speech, the Federal Government is babbling prodigiously and incoherently.

[The] case on which the Government relies most heavily, Walker, [likely] marks the outer bounds of the government-speech doctrine. Holding that the messages on Texas specialty license plates are government speech, the Walker Court cited three factors distilled from Summum. First, license plates have long been used by the States to convey state messages. Second, license plates "are often closely identified in the public mind" with the State, since they are manufactured and owned by the State, generally designed by the State, and serve as a form of "government ID." Third, Texas "maintain[ed] direct control over the messages conveyed on its specialty plates." [None] of these factors are present in this case.

[If] the registration of trademarks constituted government speech, other systems of government registration could easily be characterized in the same way. [If] federal registration makes a trademark government speech and thus eliminates all First Amendment protection, would the registration of the copyright for a book produce a similar transformation? The Government attempts to distinguish copyright on the ground that it is "the engine of free expression," but as this case illustrates, trademarks often have an expressive content. Trademarks are private, not government, speech.

B. We next address the Government's argument that this case is governed by cases in which this Court has upheld the constitutionality of government programs that subsidized speech expressing a particular viewpoint. These cases implicate a notoriously tricky question of constitutional law. [Unlike] the present case, the decisions on which the Government relies all involved cash subsidies or their equivalent. In Rust v. Sullivan, a federal law provided funds to private parties for family planning services. In National Endowment for Arts v. Finley, cash grants were awarded to artists. And federal funding for public libraries was at issue in United States v. American Library Assn., Inc. [Th]e federal registration of a trademark is nothing like the programs at issue in these cases. The PTO does not pay money to parties seeking registration of a mark.

C.   [Finally,] the Government urges us to sustain the disparagement clause under a new doctrine that would apply to "government-program" cases. [But] those cases occupy a special area of First Amendment case law, and they are far removed from the registration of trademarks.

[Potentially] more analogous are cases in which a unit of government creates a limited public forum for private speech. When government creates such a forum, in either a literal or "metaphysical" sense, see *Rosenberger*, some content- and speaker-based restrictions may be allowed. However, even in such cases, what we have termed "viewpoint discrimination" is forbidden.

Our cases use the term "viewpoint" discrimination in a broad sense, and in that sense, the disparagement clause discriminates on the bases of "viewpoint." To be sure, the clause evenhandedly prohibits disparagement of all groups. It applies equally to marks that damn Democrats and Republicans, capitalists and socialists, and those arrayed on both sides of every possible issue. It denies registration to any mark that is offensive to a substantial percentage of the members of any group. But in the sense relevant here, that is viewpoint discrimination: Giving offense is a viewpoint.

IV.   [The parties dispute] whether trademarks are commercial speech and are thus subject to the relaxed scrutiny outlined in Central Hudson. We need not resolve this debate [because] the disparagement clause cannot withstand even *Central Hudson* review.

It is claimed that the disparagement clause serves two interests. The first is [that] Government has an interest in preventing speech expressing ideas that offend. [That] idea strikes at the heart of the First Amendment. Speech that demeans on the basis of race, ethnicity, gender, religion, age, disability, or any other similar ground is hateful; but the proudest boast of our free speech jurisprudence is that we protect the freedom to express "the thought that we hate."

The second interest asserted is protecting the orderly flow of commerce. [A] simple answer [is] that the disparagement clause is not "narrowly drawn" to drive out trademarks that support invidious discrimination. [It] applies to trademarks like the following: "Down with racists," "Down with sexists," "Down with homophobes." It is not an anti-discrimination clause; it is a happy-talk clause.

[There] is also a deeper problem with the argument that commercial speech may be cleansed of any expression likely to cause offense. The commercial market is well stocked with merchandise that disparages prominent figures and groups, and the line between commercial and non-commercial speech is not always clear. [If] affixing the commercial label permits the suppression of any speech that may lead to political or social "volatility," free speech would be endangered.

■ JUSTICE KENNEDY, with whom JUSTICE GINSBURG, JUSTICE SOTOMAYOR, and JUSTICE KAGAN join, concurring in part and concurring in the judgment.

[This] separate writing explains in greater detail why the First Amendment's protections against viewpoint discrimination apply to the trademark here. It submits further that the viewpoint discrimination rationale renders unnecessary any extended treatment of other questions raised by the parties.

[In] the instant case, the disparagement clause [identifies] the relevant subject as "persons, living or dead, institutions, beliefs, or national symbols." 15 U.S.C. § 1052(a). Within that category, an applicant may register a positive or benign mark but not a derogatory one. The law thus reflects the Government's disapproval of a subset of messages it finds offensive. This is the essence of viewpoint discrimination.

[To] prohibit all sides from criticizing their opponents makes a law more viewpoint based, not less so. The logic of the Government's rule is that a law would be viewpoint neutral even if it provided that public officials could be praised but not condemned. The First Amendment's viewpoint neutrality principle protects more than the right to identify with a particular side. It protects the right to create and present arguments for particular positions in particular ways, as the speaker chooses. By mandating positivity, the law here might silence dissent and distort the marketplace of ideas.

[The] Court has suggested that viewpoint discrimination occurs when the government intends to suppress a speaker's beliefs, but viewpoint discrimination need not take that form in every instance. The danger of viewpoint discrimination is that the government is attempting to remove certain ideas or perspectives from a broader debate. That danger is all the greater if the ideas or perspectives are ones a particular audience might think offensive, at least at first hearing. An initial reaction may prompt further reflection, leading to a more reasoned, more tolerant position.

[To] the extent trademarks qualify as commercial speech, they are an example of why that term or category does not serve as a blanket exemption from the First Amendment's requirement of viewpoint neutrality. Justice Holmes' reference to the "free trade in ideas" and the "power of . . . thought to get itself accepted in the competition of the market," Abrams v. United States, (dissenting opinion), was a metaphor. In the realm of trademarks, the metaphorical marketplace of ideas becomes a tangible, powerful reality. Here that real marketplace exists as a matter of state law and our common-law tradition, quite without regard to the Federal Government. These marks make up part of the expression of everyday life. [To] permit viewpoint discrimination in this context is to permit Government censorship.

––––––––

Iancu v. Brunetti, 588 U.S. ___, 139 S. Ct. 2294 (2019), raised an issue similar to that in Matal v. Tam: Could the Patent and Trademark Office refuse registration to a mark that it found "scandalous" or "immoral" under the Lanham Act? At issue was a clothing line seeking to register its brand name, "FUCT." Writing for the Court, Justice KAGAN found Tam controlling: "[The] mark (which functions as the clothing's brand name) is pronounced as four letters, one after the other: F-U-C-T. But you might read it differently and, if so, you would hardly be alone. [To] determine whether a mark [is scandalous or immoral under the Lanham Act], the PTO asks whether a 'substantial composite of the general public' would find the mark 'shocking to the sense of truth, decency, or propriety'; 'giving offense to the conscience or moral feelings'; 'calling out for condemnation'; 'disgraceful'; 'offensive'; 'disreputable'; or 'vulgar.' [The] Board stated that the mark was 'highly offensive' and 'vulgar,' and that it had 'decidedly negative sexual connotations.' " Under Tam, Justice Kagan held, "the key question becomes: Is the 'immoral or scandalous' criterion in the Lanham Act viewpoint-neutral or viewpoint-based? It is viewpoint-based. [The] Lanham Act allows registration of marks when their messages accord with, but not when their messages defy, society's sense of decency or propriety. Put the pair of overlapping terms together and the statute, on its face, distinguishes between two opposed sets of ideas: those aligned with conventional moral standards and those hostile to them. [Here] are some samples. The PTO rejected marks conveying approval of drug use (YOU CAN'T SPELL HEALTHCARE WITHOUT THC for pain-relief medication, MARIJUANA COLA and KO KANE for beverages) because it is scandalous to 'inappropriately glamorize drug abuse.' But at the same time, the PTO registered marks with such sayings as D.A.R.E. TO RESIST DRUGS AND VIOLENCE and SAY NO TO DRUGS—REALITY IS THE BEST TRIP IN LIFE. Similarly, the PTO disapproved registration for the mark BONG HITS 4 JESUS because it "suggests that people should engage in an illegal activity in connection with worship" and because 'Christians would be morally outraged by a statement that connects Jesus Christ with illegal drug use.' [But] the PTO approved marks—PRAISE THE LORD for a game and JESUS DIED FOR YOU on clothing—whose message suggested religious faith rather than blasphemy or irreverence. [The] Government basically asks us to treat decisions like those described above as PTO examiners' mistakes. [The] Government's idea, abstractly phrased, is to narrow the statutory bar to 'marks that are offensive [or] shocking to a substantial segment of the public because of their *mode* of expression, independent of any views that they may express.' More concretely, the Government explains that this reinterpretation would mostly restrict the PTO to refusing marks that are 'vulgar'—meaning 'lewd,' 'sexually explicit or profane.' A reconfigured bar, the Government says, would not turn on viewpoint, and so we could uphold it.

[Even] assuming the Government's reading would eliminate First Amendment problems, we may adopt it only if we can see it in the statutory language. And we cannot. [The] statute as written does not draw the line at lewd, sexually explicit, or profane marks."

Justice ALITO concurred, offering a recommendation to Congress: "[In] many countries with constitutions or legal traditions that claim to protect freedom of speech, serious viewpoint discrimination is now tolerated, and such discrimination has become increasingly prevalent in this country. At a time when free speech is under attack, it is especially important for this Court to remain firm on the principle that the First Amendment does not tolerate viewpoint discrimination. [Our] decision does not prevent Congress from adopting a more carefully focused statute that precludes the registration of marks containing vulgar terms that play no real part in the expression of ideas. The particular mark in question in this case could be denied registration under such a statute. The term suggested by that mark is not needed to express any idea and, in fact, as commonly used today, generally signifies nothing except emotion and a severely limited vocabulary. The registration of such marks serves only to further coarsen our popular culture. But we are not legislators and cannot substitute a new statute for the one now in force."

Chief Justice ROBERTS concurred in part and dissented in part, suggesting a compromise between the majority and dissent: "I agree with the majority that the 'immoral' portion of the provision is not susceptible of a narrowing construction that would eliminate its viewpoint bias. [However,] the 'scandalous' portion of the provision is susceptible of such a narrowing construction. Standing alone, the term 'scandalous' need not be understood to reach marks that offend because of the ideas they convey; it can be read more narrowly to bar only marks that offend because of their mode of expression—marks that are obscene, vulgar, or profane. That is how the PTO now understands the term, in light of our decision in Tam. I agree with Justice Sotomayor that such a narrowing construction is appropriate in this context. [Refusing] registration to obscene, vulgar, or profane marks does not offend the First Amendment. Whether such marks can be registered does not affect the extent to which their owners may use them in commerce to identify goods. No speech is being restricted; no one is being punished. The owners of such marks are merely denied certain additional benefits associated with federal trademark registration. The Government, meanwhile, has an interest in not associating itself with trademarks whose content is obscene, vulgar, or profane. The First Amendment protects the freedom of speech; it does not require the Government to give aid and comfort to those using obscene, vulgar, and profane modes of expression."

Justice BREYER, concurred in part and dissented in part, suggesting a proportionality approach as he did in Reed v. Gilbert: "I would place less emphasis on trying to decide whether the statute at issue should be categorized as an example of 'viewpoint discrimination,' 'content discrimination,' 'commercial speech,' 'government speech,' or the like. [I] believe we would do better to treat this Court's speech-related categories not as outcome-determinative rules, but instead as rules of thumb. After all, these rules are not absolute. The First Amendment is not the Tax Code. Indeed, even when we consider a regulation that is ostensibly viewpoint discriminatory or that is subject to strict scrutiny, we sometimes find the regulation to be constitutional after weighing the competing interests involved. Unfortunately, the Court has sometimes applied these rules—especially the category of 'content discrimination'—too rigidly. [This] case illustrates the limits of relying on rigid First Amendment categories, for the statute at issue does not fit easily into any of these categories. [The] trademark statute does not clearly fit within any of the existing outcome-determinative categories. Why, then, should we rigidly adhere to these categories? Rather than puzzling over categorization, I believe we should focus on the interests the First Amendment protects and ask a more basic proportionality question: Does the regulation at issue work harm to First Amendment interests that is disproportionate in light of the relevant regulatory objectives? Based on this proportionality analysis, I would conclude that the statute at issue here, as interpreted by Justice Sotomayor, does not violate the First Amendment.

Justice SOTOMAYOR, joined by Justice Breyer, concurred in part and dissented in part: "The Court's decision today will beget unfortunate results. With the Lanham Act's scandalous-marks provision struck down as unconstitutional viewpoint discrimination, the Government will have no statutory basis to refuse (and thus no choice but to begin) registering marks containing the most vulgar, profane, or obscene words and images imaginable.

"The coming rush to register such trademarks—and the Government's immediate powerlessness to say no—is eminently avoidable. Rather than read the relevant text as the majority does, it is equally possible to read that provision's bar on the registration of 'scandalous' marks to address only obscenity, vulgarity, and profanity. Such a narrowing construction would save that duly enacted legislative text by rendering it a reasonable, viewpoint-neutral restriction on speech that is permissible in the context of a beneficial governmental initiative like the trademark-registration system. I would apply that narrowing construction to the term 'scandalous' and accordingly reject petitioner Erik Brunetti's facial challenge.

"[As] for the word 'immoral,' I agree with the majority that there is no tenable way to read it that would ameliorate the problem. [It] is with regard to the word 'scandalous' that I part ways with the majority. Unquestionably, 'scandalous' can mean something similar to 'immoral' and thus favor some viewpoints over others. But it does not have to be read that way. To say that a word or image is 'scandalous' can instead mean that it is simply indecent, shocking, or generally offensive. [Here,] Congress used not only the word 'scandalous,' but also the words 'immoral' and 'disparage, in the same block of statutory text—each as a separate feature that could render a mark unregistrable. [What] work did Congress intend for 'scandalous' to do? A logical answer is that Congress meant for 'scandalous' to target a third and distinct type of offensiveness: offensiveness in the mode of communication rather than the idea. [The] most obvious ways—indeed, perhaps the only conceivable ways—in which a trademark can be expressed in a shocking or offensive manner are when the speaker employs obscenity, vulgarity, or profanity. Obscenity has long been defined by this Court's decision in Miller v. California. As for what constitutes 'scandalous' vulgarity or profanity, I do not offer a list, but I do interpret the term to allow the PTO to restrict (and potentially promulgate guidance to clarify) the small group of lewd words or 'swear' words that cause a visceral reaction, that are not commonly used around children, and that are prohibited in comparable settings. [If] a word, though not exactly polite, cannot be said to be 'scandalous'—*e.g.*, 'shocking' or 'extremely offensive,' 8 Century Dictionary 5374—it is clearly not the kind of vulgarity or profanity that Congress intended to target. Everyone can think of a small number of words (including the apparent homonym of Brunetti's mark) that would, however, plainly qualify. [Properly] narrowed, 'scandalous' is a viewpoint-neutral form of content discrimination that is permissible in the kind of discretionary governmental program or limited forum typified by the trademark-registration system." Justice Sotomayor then sought to distinguish Cohen v. California:

"Cohen arose in the criminal context: Cohen had been arrested and imprisoned under a California criminal statute targeting disturbances of the peace because he was wearing a jacket bearing the words 'F[***] the Draft.' The Court held that applying that statute to Cohen because of his jacket violated the First Amendment. But the Court did not suggest that the State had targeted Cohen to suppress his view itself (*i.e.*, his sharp distaste for the draft), such that it would have accepted an equally colorful statement of praise for the draft (or hostility toward war protesters). Rather, the Court suggested that the State had simply engaged in what later courts would more precisely call viewpoint-neutral content discrimination—it had regulated the form or content of individual expression. Cohen also famously recognized that 'words are often chosen as much for their emotive as their cognitive force,' and that 'one man's vulgarity is another's lyric.' That is all consistent with observing that a plain, blanket restriction on profanity (regardless of the idea to which it is attached) is a viewpoint-neutral form of content discrimination. The essence of Cohen's discussion is that profanity can serve to tweak (or amplify) the viewpoint that a message expresses, such that it can be hard to disentangle the profanity from the underlying message—

without the profanity, the message is not quite the same. But those statements merely reinforce that profanity is still properly understood as protected First Amendment content. Cohen's discussion does not also go further to declare [that] a provision that treats all instances of profanity equally is nevertheless by nature an instance of the government targeting particular views taken by speakers on a subject. To be sure, such a restriction could have the incidental effect of tamping down the overall volume of debate on all sides. But differential effects alone [do] not render a restriction viewpoint (or even content) discriminatory. [Yes,] Brunetti has been, as Cohen was, subject to content discrimination, but that content discrimination is properly understood as viewpoint neutral. And whereas even viewpoint-neutral content discrimination is (in all but the most compelling cases, such as threats) impermissible in the context of a criminal prosecution like the one that Cohen faced, Brunetti is subject to such regulation only in the context of the federal trademark-registration system."

VIEWPOINT DISCRIMINATION

The majority opinion in Iancu is the Court's latest word on what constitutes viewpoint discrimination, and, along with the opinion in Matal v. Tam, represents a broad expansion of what is considered viewpoint discrimination. Writing for the Matal majority, Justice Alito wrote "Our cases use the term 'viewpoint' discrimination in a broad sense, and in that sense, the disparagement clause discriminates on the bases of 'viewpoint.' [ ] To be sure, the clause evenhandedly prohibits disparagement of all groups. It applies equally to marks that damn Democrats and Republicans, capitalists and socialists, and those arrayed on both sides of every possible issue. It denies registration to any mark that is offensive to a substantial percentage of the members of any group. But in the sense relevant here, that is viewpoint discrimination: Giving offense is a viewpoint." See Ned Snow, Denying Trademark for Scandalous Speech, 51 U.C. Davis L. Rev. 2331 (2018); Maura Douglas, *Finding Viewpoint Neutrality in Our Constitutional Constellation*, 20 U. Pa. J. Const. L. 727 (2018).

SECTION 3. OVERBREADTH, VAGUENESS AND PRIOR RESTRAINT

This section turns to a last set of doctrines limiting how government may regulate speech: the doctrines of overbreadth, vagueness, and prior restraint. The flaw in laws invalidated on these grounds is procedural: government went about things the wrong way even if the speaker might constitutionally be restricted if government went about it in a different way. An overbroad law sweeps in too much speech, a vague law is unclear about what speech it sweeps in, and a prior restraint is premature even if publication might be subsequently punished. These doctrines are accordingly of particular usefulness to a speaker whose own speech might not be protected under the First Amendment under a differently drawn law.

OVERBREADTH

Even if speech is proscribable by a properly drawn law, a speaker may be able to invalidate a law that is overly broad. For example, recall the case of Gooding v. Wilson (1972; p. 59), in which the Court invalidated a conviction of an anti-war demonstrator at an induction center who in a scuffle with police said such things as "White son of a bitch, I'll kill you." He was convicted under a Georgia statute prohibiting the use of "opprobrious words or abusive language, tending to cause a breach of the peace." The Court, per Justice Brennan, held that the law swept in too much protected speech along with fighting words proscribable under Chaplinsky: "[It] matters not that the words appellee used might have been constitutionally prohibited under a narrowly and precisely drawn statute. At least when statutes regulate or proscribe speech and when 'no readily apparent construction suggests itself as a vehicle for rehabilitating the statutes in a single prosecution,' [the] transcendent value to all society of constitutionally protected expression is deemed to justify allowing 'attacks on overly broad statutes with no requirement that the person making the attack demonstrate that his own conduct could not be regulated by a statute drawn with the requisite narrow specificity.' [Dombrowski v. Pfister, 380 U.S. 479 (1965).]" Unlike the New Hampshire courts in Chaplinsky, Justice Brennan found, the Georgia courts in Gooding had failed to narrowly construe the opprobrious-words statute to limit its reach to fighting words. Accordingly, the Court voided the statute on its face.

For an example of similar overbreadth reasoning, recall Justice White's concurrence in R.A.V. v. City of St. Paul (1992; p. 109), finding that a law barring racist symbols causing anger or alarm was overbroad because not limited to fighting words. For other examples of overbreadth determinations covered in earlier sections, see Erznoznik v. Jacksonville (1975; p. 153) (ban on nudity in drive-in movies); Schad v. Mt. Ephraim (1981; p. 155) (ban on live entertainment).

1. *The distinctive features of overbreadth.* Overbreadth analysis is an exception to two traditional rules of constitutional litigation. First, it results in the invalidation of a law "on its face" rather than "as applied" to a particular speaker. Ordinarily, a particular litigant claims that a statute is unconstitutional as applied to him or her; if the litigant prevails, the courts carve away the unconstitutional aspects of the law by invalidating its improper applications on a case-by-case basis. If a law restricting speech is invalidated as applied to a protected speaker, it is held inapplicable to that speaker, and thus, in effect, judicially trimmed down. Overbreadth analysis, in contrast, does not reach the question whether the *challenger's* speech is constitutionally protected; instead it strikes down the statute entirely, because it might be applied to others not before the Court whose activities are constitutionally protected. When invalidated for overbreadth, a law is not narrowed, but rather becomes wholly unenforceable until a legislature rewrites it or a properly authorized court construes it more narrowly.

Second, overbreadth is an exception to the usual rules of standing. Ordinarily, challengers to a law are not permitted to raise the rights of third parties and can only assert their own interests. See generally Note, "Standing to Assert Constitutional Jus Tertii," 88 Harv. L. Rev. 423 (1974). In overbreadth analysis, challengers *are* in effect permitted to raise the rights of third parties. But see Monaghan, "Overbreadth," 1981 Sup. Ct. Rev. 1 (arguing that overbreadth involves first-party, not third-party standing, because the litigant's own conduct may only be regulated by a valid rule of law); Monaghan, "Third-Party Standing," 84 Colum. L. Rev. 277 (1984).

The factor that motivates courts to depart from these normal rules of adjudication is the concern with the deterrent or "chilling" effect of the overbroad statute on third parties not courageous enough to bring suit. The Court assumes that an overbroad law's very existence may cause others not before the court to refrain from constitutionally protected speech or expression. An overbreadth ruling is designed to remove that deterrent effect on the speech of those third parties. As Justice Brennan wrote in Gooding, invalidation for overbreadth is "necessary because persons whose expression is constitutionally protected may well refrain from exercising their rights for fear of criminal sanctions provided by a statute susceptible of application to protected expression." See generally Note, "The First Amendment Overbreadth Doctrine," 83 Harv. L. Rev. 844 (1970); Redish, "The Warren Court, the Burger Court, and the First Amendment Overbreadth Doctrine," 78 Nw. U. L. Rev. 1031 (1983); Fallon, "Making Sense of Overbreadth," 100 Yale L.J. 853 (1991). An additional reason to contain overbroad statutes, like vague statutes, is to curb "their potential for selective enforcement" at the discretion of law enforcement officials. See Karst, "Equality as a Central Principle in the First Amendment," 43 U. Chi. L. Rev. 20 (1975).

2. **_The attractiveness of overbreadth analysis._** Overbreadth analysis has been especially attractive to some Justices because it gives the appearance of judicial modesty. Rather than rewriting a law, it purports to leave alternatives open to the legislature. By holding out the prospect that narrower means may be available to achieve legislative objectives, it conveys the appearance of intervening in legislative policy choices far more marginally than outright "balancing" would. See, e.g., **United States v. Robel**, 387 U.S. 939 (1967), which invalidated as overbroad a federal law making it a crime for members of Communist organizations to be employed in a defense facility, because it swept in passive and active members alike. Chief Justice WARREN's opinion disavowed any substantive "balancing": "[We] have confined our analysis to whether Congress has adopted a constitutional means in achieving its concededly legitimate [goal]. In making this determination we have found it necessary to measure the validity of the means [against] both the goal [and] the First Amendment. But we have in no way 'balanced' those respective interests. We have ruled only that the Constitution requires that the conflict between congressional power and individual rights be accommodated by legislation drawn more narrowly to avoid the conflict."

Is this appearance of judicial modesty deceptive? For an argument that Robel engaged in implicit balancing despite its disavowal, see Gunther, "Reflections on Robel: It's Not What the Court Did but the Way that It Did It," 20 Stan. L. Rev. 1140 (1968). Arguably, overbreadth analysis cannot altogether avoid substantive judgments. In order to decide that a law sweeps in protected as well as unprotected expression, a judgment of overbreadth necessarily must delineate some contours of protected expression. To strike down an excessively broad "means" because it impinges on an "area of protected freedom" presupposes, after all, at least an implicit judgment about what the contours of that "area" are.

A second attraction of overbreadth analysis in the context of state laws is an apparent respect for the values of federalism. In the case of state legislation, only the state courts have authority to construe the statute; the federal courts, including the Supreme Court, may construe federal statutes but must abide by state court construction of state laws. Thus a federal court lacks authority to issue a narrowing construction of an overbroad state law. For a federal court in effect to rewrite a state statute by narrowing it arguably would amount to a quasi-legislative intrusion upon state policymaking prerogatives, whereas a judgment of facial invalidation of an overbroad state statute appears to defer to the state's policymaking role. But is facial invalidation truly a less intrusive exercise of federal judicial power than a narrowing construction would be?

3. *Criticisms of overbreadth analysis.* Overbreadth analysis has elicited a number of criticisms, beginning in the Warren Court era. One set of criticisms relates to its departure from usual case and controversy requirements. First, it has been criticized for allowing the Court to act "as if it had a roving commission" to cure unconstitutional provisions. Cox, The Warren Court (1968); see Younger v. Harris, 401 U.S. 37 (1971) (Black, J.) (noting that the federal judicial power to resolve "concrete disputes [does] not amount to an unlimited power to survey the statute books and pass judgment on laws before the courts are called upon to enforce them"). Second, it has been criticized for permitting decisions outside of concrete factual settings and in sterile, abstract contexts. See Bickel, The Least Dangerous Branch (1962). Third, it has been criticized as too speculative. It allows a court to invalidate a law so long as it can hypothesize some impermissible application in circumstances not before it. See, e.g., Gooding v. Wilson, supra (Burger, C.J., dissenting) (criticizing overbreadth for resting on "some insubstantial or imagined potential for occasional and isolated applications that go beyond constitutional bounds"); Younger, supra ("[T]he existence of a 'chilling effect' even in the area of First Amendment rights has never been considered a sufficient basis, in and of itself, for prohibiting state action.").

A second set of criticisms of overbreadth relates to its consequences. Typically, overbreadth analysis assumes that the challenger's behavior is not protected by the First Amendment and is reachable by the state under a more "narrowly drawn" law. Thus the doctrine permits an individual whose own First Amendment rights have not been violated to enjoy a free ride unless and until the appropriate legislature or court redraws the statute. This may well undermine important state interest in the meantime. And there may be various practical obstacles to prompt redrafting by the relevant policymaking bodies. Moreover, it may appear perverse for an unprotected speaker to wield a more powerful weapon against a law than a protected speaker can, since the protected speaker is more likely to be confined to an "as applied" analysis.

4. *Limits on overbreadth analysis: the requirement of "substantial" overbreadth.* The above criticisms bore fruit in 1973, when the Court required that overbreadth must be "substantial" before facial invalidation is appropriate and suggested that overbreadth analysis was less applicable when the challenged statute affected "conduct" rather than "speech." In **Broadrick v. Oklahoma**, 413 U.S. 601 (1973), Justice White— who had dissented from some earlier overbreadth invalidations—wrote for the majority, and Justice Brennan—who had written some of the major overbreadth opinions of the Warren era—wrote for most of the dissenters. Broadrick arose from a challenge to § 818 of Oklahoma's Merit System Act restricting political activities by classified civil servants. Among the challenged provisions of this mini-Hatch Act was one prohibiting employees from "tak[ing] part in the management or affairs of any political party or in any political campaign, except to exercise his right as a citizen privately to

express his opinion and to cast his vote." Other provisions more specifically prohibited soliciting for campaign contributions. Appellants, who had campaigned for a superior, challenged § 818 on vagueness and overbreadth grounds. The Court's 5–4 decision rejected those challenges. Justice WHITE's majority opinion devoted most of its focus to overbreadth:

"Appellants assert that § 818 has been construed as applying to such allegedly protected political expression as the wearing of political buttons or the displaying of bumper stickers. But appellants did not engage in any such activity. They are charged with actively engaging in partisan political activities—including the solicitation of money—among their co-workers for the benefit of their superior. Appellants concede [that] § 818 would be constitutional as applied to this type of conduct. [See the Hatch Act cases, p. 398.] They nevertheless maintain that the statute is overbroad and purports to reach protected, as well as unprotected conduct, and must therefore be struck down on its face and held to be incapable of any constitutional application. We do not believe that the overbreadth doctrine may appropriately be invoked in this manner here."

Justice White then proceeded to justify and delineate a "substantial overbreadth" approach: "Embedded in the traditional rules governing constitutional adjudication is the principle that a person to whom a statute may constitutionally be applied will not be heard to challenge that statute on the ground that it may conceivably be applied unconstitutionally to others, in other situations not before the Court. [This principle reflects] the conviction [that] our constitutional courts are not roving commissions assigned to pass judgment on the validity of the Nation's laws. [In] the past, the Court has recognized some limited exceptions to these principles, but only because of the most 'weighty countervailing policies.' [One such exception] has been carved out in the area of the First Amendment. It has long been recognized that the First Amendment needs breathing space and that statutes attempting to restrict or burden the exercise of First Amendment rights must be narrowly drawn and represent a considered legislative judgment that a particular mode of expression has to give way to other compelling needs of society. As a corollary, the Court has altered its traditional rules of standing to permit [litigants] in the First Amendment area to challenge a statute not because their own rights of free expression are violated, but because of a judicial prediction or assumption that the statute's very existence may cause others not before the court to refrain from constitutionally protected speech or expression.

"Such claims of facial overbreadth have been entertained in cases involving statutes which, by their terms, seek to regulate 'only spoken words.' [Gooding v. Wilson.] In such cases, it has been the judgment of this Court that the possible harm to society in permitting some unprotected speech to go unpunished is outweighed by the possibility that protected speech of others may be muted and perceived grievances left to fester because of the possible inhibitory effects of overly broad statutes. Overbreadth attacks have also been allowed where the Court thought rights of association were ensnared in statutes which, by their broad sweep, might result in burdening innocent associations. Robel.

"[The] consequence of our departure from traditional rules of standing in the First Amendment area is that any enforcement of a statute thus placed at issue is totally forbidden until and unless a limiting construction or partial invalidation so narrows it as to remove the seeming threat or deterrence to constitutionally protected expression. Application of the overbreadth doctrine in this manner is, manifestly, strong medicine. It has been employed by the Court sparingly and only as a last resort. Facial overbreadth has not been invoked when a limiting construction has been or could be placed on the challenged statute. [See, e.g., Cox v. New Hampshire]. Equally important, overbreadth claims, if entertained at all, have been curtailed when invoked against ordinary criminal laws that are sought to be applied to protected conduct.

"It remains a 'matter of no little difficulty' to determine when a law may properly be held void on its face and when 'such summary action' is inappropriate. [But] the plain import of our cases is, at the very least, that facial overbreadth adjudication is an exception to our traditional rules of practice and that its function, a limited one at the outset, attenuates as the otherwise unprotected behavior that it forbids the State to sanction moves from 'pure speech' towards conduct and that conduct—even if expressive— falls within the scope of otherwise valid criminal [laws]. Although such laws, if too broadly worded, may deter protected speech to some unknown extent, there comes a point where that effect—at best a prediction—cannot, with confidence, justify invalidating a statute on its face and so prohibiting a State from enforcing the statute against conduct that is admittedly within its power to proscribe. [To] put the matter another way, particularly where conduct and not merely speech is involved, we believe that the overbreadth of a statute must not only be real, but substantial as well, judged in relation to the statute's plainly legitimate sweep. It is our view that § 818 is not substantially overbroad and that whatever overbreadth may exist should be cured through case-by-case analysis of the fact situations to which its sanctions, assertedly, may not be applied.

"Unlike ordinary breach-of-the-peace statutes or other broad regulatory acts, § 818 is directed, by its terms, at political expression which if engaged in by private persons would plainly be protected by the [First Amendment]. But at the same time, § 818 is not a censorial statute, directed at particular groups or viewpoints. The statute, rather, seeks to regulate political activity in an even-handed and neutral manner. As indicated, such statutes have in the past been subject to a less exacting overbreadth scrutiny. Moreover, the fact remains that § 818 regulates a substantial spectrum of conduct that is as manifestly subject to state regulation as the public peace or criminal trespass. Without question, the conduct appellants have been charged with falls squarely within those proscriptions. Appellants assert that § 818 goes much farther. [They point to] interpretive rules purporting to restrict such allegedly protected activities as the wearing of political buttons or the use of bumper stickers. It may be that such restrictions are impermissible and that § 818 may be susceptible of some other improper applications. But, as presently construed, we do not believe that § 818 must be discarded in toto because some persons' arguably protected conduct may or may not be caught or chilled by the statute. Section 818 is not substantially overbroad and is not, therefore, unconstitutional on its face."

The major dissent was by Justice BRENNAN, joined by Justices Stewart and Marshall. Justice Brennan thought the decision a "wholly unjustified retreat from fundamental and previously well-established" principles. The majority had conceded the possibility of some "improper applications," and "that assumption requires a finding that the statute is unconstitutional on its face."

Justice Brennan objected to the majority's "substantial overbreadth" approach: "In the first place, the Court makes no effort to define what it means by 'substantial overbreadth.' We have never held that a statute should be held invalid on its face merely because it is possible to conceive of a single impermissible application, and in that sense a requirement of substantial overbreadth is already implicit in the doctrine. [Whether] the Court means to require some different or greater showing of substantiality is left obscure by today's opinion, in large part because the Court makes no effort to explain why the overbreadth of the Oklahoma Act, while real, is somehow not quite substantial. [More] fundamentally, the Court offers no rationale to explain its conclusion that, for purposes of overbreadth analysis, deterrence of conduct should be viewed differently from deterrence of speech, even where both are equally protected by the [First Amendment]. At this stage, it is obviously difficult to estimate the probable impact of today's decision. If the requirement of 'substantial' overbreadth is construed to mean only that facial review is inappropriate where the likelihood of an impermissible application of the statute is too small to generate a 'chilling effect' on protected speech or conduct, then the impact is likely to be small. On the other hand, if today's decision necessitates the drawing of artificial distinctions between protected speech and protected conduct, and if the 'chill' on protected conduct is rarely, if ever, found sufficient to require the facial invalidation of an overbroad statute, then the effect could be very grave indeed." Justice Douglas dissented separately.

What is the definition of "substantial" overbreadth? How great a ratio of protected to unprotected speech must be covered to qualify? In City Council v. Taxpayers for Vincent (1984; p. 302), Justice Stevens's majority opinion stated: "The concept of 'substantial overbreadth' is not readily reduced to an exact definition. It is clear, however, that the mere fact that one can conceive of some impermissible applications of a statute is not sufficient to render it susceptible to an overbreadth challenge. On the contrary, [there] must be a realistic danger that the statute itself will significantly compromise recognized First Amendment protections of parties not before the Court for it to be facially challenged on overbreadth grounds." For discussion, see Fallon, supra.

Applying Broadrick, the Court found no substantial overbreadth in the New York child pornography law at issue in **New York v. Ferber**, 458 U.S. 747 (1982) (see p. 166). The claim there was that the New York law was "unconstitutionally overbroad because it would forbid the distribution of material with serious literary, scientific or educational value or material which does not threaten the harms sought to be combatted by the State." Justice WHITE wrote for the Court: "We consider this the paradigmatic case of a state statute whose legitimate reach dwarfs its arguably impermissible applications. [While] the reach of the statute is directed at the hard core of child pornography, the [highest New York court] was understandably concerned that some protected expression, ranging from medical textbooks to pictorials in National Geographic, would fall prey to the statute. How often, if ever, it may be necessary to employ children to engage in conduct clearly within the reach of the [law] in order to produce educational, medical or artistic works cannot be known with certainty. Yet we seriously doubt [that] these arguably impermissible applications of the statute amount to more than a tiny fraction of the materials within the statute's reach. [Under] these circumstances, [the law] is 'not substantially overbroad and whatever overbreadth exists should be cured through case-by-case analysis of the fact situations to which its sanctions, assertedly, may not be applied.' [Broadrick.]"

In an opinion concurring in the judgment, Justice STEVENS objected to the majority's quantitative approach. He stated: "My reasons for avoiding overbreadth analysis in this case are more qualitative than quantitative. When we follow our traditional practice of adjudicating difficult and novel constitutional questions only in concrete factual situations, the adjudications tend to be crafted with greater wisdom. Hypothetical rulings are inherently treacherous and prone to lead us into unforeseen errors; they are qualitatively less reliable than the products of case-by-case adjudication. [Moreover,] generally marginal speech does not warrant the extraordinary protection afforded by the overbreadth doctrine."

In contrast, in **Ashcroft v. Free Speech Coalition**, 535 U.S. 234 (2002), the Court found that the Child Pornography Prevention Act of 1996 (CPPA) was unconstitutional for substantial overbreadth. The CPPA had prohibited depictions appearing to portray children engaged in sexual acts, but with no actual children involved in the production process as would make such depictions proscribable under Ferber. (For other portions of the opinion, see p. 192.) Speaking for the Court, Justice KENNEDY applied the overbreadth doctrine to reject the government's argument that the ban on virtual child pornography was justified as a means to enforce the ban on real child pornography: "[T]he Government says that the possibility of producing images by using computer imaging makes it very difficult for it to prosecute those who produce pornography by using real children. [The] argument, in essence, is that protected speech may be banned as a means to ban unprotected speech. This analysis turns the First Amendment upside down."

Dissenting from this part of the Court's decision, Justice O'CONNOR considered the overbreadth too unproven to invalidate the law in its entirety. While she agreed with the Court that "the CPPA's ban on youthful-adult pornography is overbroad," so that films using adult actors to simulate child sexual conduct could not be banned, she found that the challengers had not made out an overbreadth claim against "virtual-child pornography" made with computer-generated images of children: "[Respondents] provide no examples of films or other materials that are wholly computer-generated and contain images that 'appea[r] to be . . . of minors' engaging in indecent conduct, but that have serious value or do not facilitate child abuse. Their overbreadth challenge therefore fails."

Chief Justice REHNQUIST's dissent, joined by Justice Scalia, proposed a narrowing interpretation of the statute that would eliminate the overbreadth problem: "[We] normally do not strike down a statute on First Amendment grounds 'when a limiting instruction has been or could be placed on the challenged statute.' [Broadrick]. [The] CPPA can be limited so as not to reach any material that was not already unprotected before the CPPA. The CPPA's definition of 'sexually explicit conduct'[1] [should be read to reach] only the sort of 'hard core of child pornography' that we found without protection in Ferber. So construed, the CPPA bans visual depictions of youthful looking adult actors engaged in actual sexual activity; mere

---

[1]   Here, Chief Justice Rehnquist quoted CPPA's definition of "sexually explicit conduct" as "visual depictions" of: "actual or simulated . . . sexual intercourse, including genital-genital, oral-genital, anal-genital, or oral-anal, whether between persons of the same or opposite sex; . . . bestiality; . . . masturbation; . . . sadistic or masochistic abuse; . . . or lascivious exhibition of the genitals or pubic area of any person."

suggestions of sexual activity, such as youthful looking adult actors squirming under a blanket, are more akin to written descriptions than visual depictions, and thus fall outside the purview of the statute. [While] potentially impermissible applications of the CPPA may exist, I doubt that they would be 'substantial . . . in relation to the statute's plainly legitimate sweep.' [Broadrick]. The aim of ensuring the enforceability of our Nation's child pornography laws is a compelling one. The CPPA is targeted to this aim by extending the definition of child pornography to reach computer-generated images that are virtually indistinguishable from real children engaged in sexually explicit conduct. The statute need not be read to do any more than precisely this, which is not offensive to the First Amendment."

In **Virginia v. Hicks**, 539 U.S. 113 (2003), the Court unanimously rejected a First Amendment challenge to a public housing development's policy controlling entry to its premises. Aimed at social order and crime control, the policy authorized the Richmond police to serve notice on any person lacking "a legitimate business or social purpose" for being on the premises and to arrest for trespassing any person who returned after having been so notified. Hicks, who was not a resident of the development and who had been charged with damaging property there, returned after being given written notice not to enter, and was charged and convicted of trespass. Although Hicks was not seeking entry in order to engage in any speech, the Virginia Supreme Court found the policy facially void for overbreadth, reasoning that the policy carried with it an "unwritten" rule giving the development manager unfettered discretion to pick and choose which persons might enter the development in order to leaflet or demonstrate. Justice SCALIA wrote for all the Justices, reversing:

"[We] have insisted that a law's application to protected speech be 'substantial,' not only in an absolute sense, but also relative to the scope of the law's plainly legitimate applications, before applying the 'strong medicine' of overbreadth invalidation. [Hicks] has not made such a showing. [Both] the notice-barment rule and the 'legitimate business or social purpose' rule apply to all persons who enter the streets of [the development], not just to those who seek to engage in expression. The rules apply to strollers, loiterers, drug dealers, roller skaters, bird watchers, soccer players, and others not engaged in constitutionally protected conduct—a group that would seemingly far outnumber First Amendment speakers. Even assuming invalidity of the 'unwritten' rule that requires leafleters and demonstrators to obtain advance permission from [the development manager], Hicks has not shown, based on the record in this case, that the [housing authority's] trespass policy as a whole prohibits a 'substantial' amount of protected speech in relation to its many legitimate applications. [Rarely,] if ever, will an overbreadth challenge succeed against a law or regulation that is not specifically addressed to speech or to conduct necessarily associated with speech (such as picketing or demonstrating)."

5. ***Limits on overbreadth analysis: incapable of a narrowing construction.*** In **Brockett v. Spokane Arcades, Inc.**, 472 U.S. 491 (1985), the Court held that appeals to the "prurient interest" under the Miller test for obscenity (see p. 133) did not encompass "material that provoked only normal, healthy sexual desires," but was limited to materials appealing to a "shameful or morbid interest" in sex. It thus held a Washington obscenity law unconstitutional because it defined "prurient interest" as "that which incites lasciviousness or lust," a definition broad enough to encompass

"normal" as well as "shameful" sexual responses. But despite this apparent overbreadth finding, the Court declined to permit an individual whose own rights were violated under the statute to invalidate the law on its face, limiting the challenger to an "as-applied" challenge. Justice WHITE, writing for a 6–2 majority, explained: "[An] individual whose own speech [may] validly be prohibited [is] permitted to challenge a statute on its face because it also threatens others not before the court. [But where, as here,] the parties challenging the statute are those who desire to engage in protected speech that the overbroad statute purports to punish, [there is] no want of a proper party to challenge the [law and it] may forthwith be declared invalid to the extent it reaches too far, but otherwise left intact." Justice BRENNAN, joined by Justice Marshall, dissented, insisting that the law was "substantially overbroad and therefore invalid on its face."

When is such partial validation appropriate? In Brockett, the U.S. Supreme Court could not issue a narrowing construction of the state statute; only the state courts could. But the Court in effect decided that a narrowing construction was readily available to the state courts, as the improper portion of the obscenity definition was easily severable from the rest. Its invalidation of the law as applied in effect cued the state courts as to how to rewrite the law. On the relationship between overbreadth and severability, see Dorf, "Facial Challenges to State and Federal Statutes," 46 Stan. L. Rev. 235 (1994).

In Brockett, the state's otherwise constitutional obscenity statute could be "trimmed of unconstitutional branches," but the Court continues to employ facial invalidation when a statute is "rotten at its very root." Tribe, American Constitutional Law 1029 (2d ed. 1988). For example, the Court has invalidated facially several laws designed to limit charitable solicitation to organizations with low overhead expenses. The 8–1 decision in **Schaumburg v. Citizens for Better Environment**, 444 U.S. 620 (1980), struck down as overbroad an ordinance barring door-to-door and on-street solicitations of contributions by charitable organizations that did not use at least 75% of their receipts for "charitable purposes." "Charitable purposes" were defined to exclude solicitation expenses. Because of that 75% rule, Citizens for a Better Environment (CBE), an environmental group, was denied permission to solicit contributions in Schaumburg, a suburb of Chicago. CBE challenged the law as a free speech violation.

Justice WHITE's majority opinion found that CBE was entitled to a "judgment of facial invalidity if the ordinance purported to prohibit canvassing by a substantial category of charities to which the 75-percent limitation could not be applied consistently with the [First Amendment], even if there was no demonstration that CBE itself was one of these organizations." The organizations to whom the 75% rule could not be applied were found to be those whose "primary purpose is not to provide money or services for the poor, the needy or other worthy objects of charity, but to gather and disseminate information about and advocate positions on matters of public concern." Typically, these organizations use paid employees not only to solicit funds, but also to gather information and advocate positions and thus "would necessarily spend more than 25% of their budgets on salaries and administrative expenses [but] would be completely barred from solicitation in [Schaumburg]." As to such organizations, the ordinance constituted "a direct and substantial limitation of protected activity that cannot be sustained unless it serves a sufficiently strong, subordinating interest that the Village is entitled to protect." Here, Justice White concluded, "the Village's proffered justifications are inadequate."

The Court found that the asserted interests "in protecting the public from fraud, crime and undue annoyance" were "indeed substantial," but were "only peripherally promoted by the 75-percent requirement and could be sufficiently served by measures less destructive of First Amendment interests." With respect to the prevention of fraud, the Court found the 75% rule not a justifiable device for distinguishing charitable from commercial enterprises: organizations primarily engaged in research, advocacy, or publication that use their own paid staffs to carry out these functions could not be labeled as presumptively "fraudulent" or as using the "charitable" label as a cloak for profit making. Under the First Amendment, Schaumburg had to employ more precise measures to separate genuine charitable organizations from profitmaking ones—for example, by prohibiting fraudulent misrepresentations or by requiring financial disclosures. Nor was the Court able to "perceive any substantial relationship" between the 75% rule and the interests in the protection of safety and residential privacy. Organizations devoting more than 25% of their funds to administrative expenses were no more likely "to employ solicitors who would be a threat to public safety than are other charitable organizations." And "householders are equally disturbed by solicitation on behalf of organizations satisfying the 75-percent requirement as they are by solicitation on behalf of other organizations. The 75-percent requirement protects privacy only by reducing the total number of solicitors." Moreover, "[other] provisions of the ordinance, [such as those] permitting homeowners to bar solicitors from their property by posting signs, [suggest] the availability of less intrusive and more effective measures to protect privacy. See [Rowan; Martin]."

In short, the flaw in the statute in Schaumburg was "not simply that it includes within its sweep some impermissible applications, but that in all its applications it operates on a fundamentally mistaken premise that high solicitation costs are an accurate measure of fraud." There was no obvious way for such a statute to be narrowed to a "core of easily identifiable and constitutionally proscribable conduct." In the absence of any conceivable available narrowing construction, facial invalidation was the chosen remedy. In this setting, unlike Brockett, partial invalidation was not an available option.

In **Secretary of State v. Joseph H. Munson Co.**, 467 U.S. 947 (1984), the Court extended Schaumburg to strike down a similar restriction on charitable solicitations despite its provision for a waiver if a charitable organization could demonstrate that the overhead limit "would effectively prevent [it] from raising contributions." The law was challenged by a professional fundraiser who claimed primarily the First Amendment rights of his customers, who were not parties to the action. But the Court, in an opinion by Justice BLACKMUN, found these factors insufficient to distinguish Schaumburg, as the possibility of gaining an exemption was inadequate to prevent the inhibition of protected solicitation.

In Munson, Justice Blackmun distinguished the claim at issue from the type of overbreadth claim in which the challenger's own conduct is unprotected, but the challenge is permitted in order to protect the First Amendment rights of third parties not before the Court. In Schaumburg, he suggested, the term " 'overbreadth' [was] used to describe a challenge to a statute that in *all its applications* directly restricts protected First

Amendment activity and does not employ means narrowly tailored to serve a compelling governmental interest" (emphasis added).

Is the latter type of case truly an "overbreadth" case? In Justice Blackmun's interpretation of Schaumburg in Munson, the overhead limit was void "in all its applications" because it drew the wrong sort of line—it used high overhead as a proxy for fraud when such a financial structure might have indicated instead the organization's devotion to education and advocacy. Thus there was no issue whether the overbreadth was substantial or insubstantial in Broadrick's terms; the ratio of impermissible to permissible applications was infinite. Are Schaumburg and Munson simply determinations on the merits that the law amounted to impermissible speaker-based discrimination with content-differential effects? See Monaghan, supra ("[O]verbreadth determinations are simply determinations on the merits of the litigant's substantive constitutional claim."). Recall that the Court frequently invalidates speech-restrictive statutes on their face without any consideration of their overbreadth. See, for instance, Justice Scalia's majority opinion (as opposed to Justice White's concurrence) in R.A.V. v. St. Paul (1992; p. 109). Is overbreadth analysis better reserved for laws that have some constitutional applications?

In Riley v. National Federation of the Blind, 487 U.S. 781 (1988), the Court continued the Schaumburg and Munson line of cases by striking down a state law defining a "reasonable fee" that a professional fundraiser may charge as a percentage of the gross revenues solicited; requiring professional fundraisers to disclose to potential donors the gross percentage of revenues retained in prior charitable solicitations; and requiring professional fundraisers to obtain a license before engaging in solicitation. Justice Brennan's prevailing opinion found this regulatory scheme insufficiently different from those at issue in Schaumburg and Munson to survive First Amendment scrutiny. Justices Scalia and Stevens concurred in part; Chief Justice Rehnquist, joined by Justice O'Connor, dissented, reasoning that the activities of large-scale professional fundraisers were "a far cry indeed" from the grass-roots charitable solicitation protected in cases like Lovell, Martin, and Schneider, and that a limitation of such fundraisers to forego unreasonable fees was not an excessive burden on their speech.

In **Illinois v. Telemarketing Associates, Inc.**, 538 U.S. 600 (2003), the Court clarified the limits of the Schaumburg, Munson, Riley line of cases, holding that these precedents did not preclude enforcement of state antifraud laws against charitable solicitors who make misleading statements about the percentage of funds raised from donors that will go to charitable purposes. The case involved a telemarketing firm retained by a nonprofit organization seeking to raise funds for Vietnam veterans. Their contract provided that the telemarketers would retain 85% of proceeds from donors in Illinois, with the veteran beneficiaries receiving 15%. The Illinois Attorney General charged the telemarketers with fraud for having allegedly made a series of particular false representations to donors that a significant amount of each dollar donated would be paid over to the veterans' organization for its charitable purposes. The Illinois courts dismissed the complaint, holding it precluded by the First Amendment under Schaumburg, Munson, and Riley. Reading those decisions differently, the Supreme Court reversed and allowed the case to proceed. Justice GINSBURG wrote for a unanimous Court:

"The First Amendment protects the right to engage in charitable solicitation. But the First Amendment does not shield fraud. Like other forms of public deception, fraudulent charitable solicitation is unprotected speech. [The] Court's opinions in Schaumburg, Munson, and Riley took care to leave a corridor open for fraud actions to guard the public against false or misleading charitable solicitations. As those decisions recognized, there are differences critical to First Amendment concerns between fraud actions trained on representations made in individual cases and statutes that categorically ban solicitations when fundraising costs run high. Simply labeling an action one for 'fraud,' of course, will not carry the day. [Had] the complaint against Telemarketers charged fraud based solely on the percentage of donations the fundraisers would retain, or their failure to alert potential donors to their fee arrangements at the start of each telephone call, [our precedents] would support swift dismissal. [But fraud actions] targeting misleading affirmative representations about how donations will be used are plainly distinguishable from the measures invalidated in Schaumburg, Munson and Riley. So long as the emphasis is on what the fundraisers misleadingly convey, and not on percentage limitations on solicitors' fees per se, such actions need not impermissibly chill protected speech. [The] gravamen of the fraud action in this case is not high costs or fees, it is particular representations made with intent to mislead."

6. *Overbreadth and due process.* What is the effect of a narrowing change in the challenged state law after an overbreadth lawsuit is brought? Ordinarily, an authoritative narrowing construction of an overbroad statute can blunt the effectiveness of an overbreadth attack. The effect of subsequent changes in state law came before the Court in two cases, in 1989 and 1990. The net result of the cases was that a legislative change after the lawsuit was brought could not eliminate an overbreadth challenge, but a *judicial* narrowing of an otherwise overbroad law was effective to eliminate the overbreadth concern.

In **Massachusetts v. Oakes**, 491 U.S. 576 (1989), a law that prohibited the taking of nude and similar photographs of those under the age of 18 was challenged by a man who had been convicted for taking "sexually provocative" photographs of "his partially nude and physically mature 14-year-old stepdaughter." After the highest state court had struck down the law as substantially overbroad, the legislature amended the law to add a "lascivious intent" requirement. As a result, four Justices (Justice O'Connor, joined by Chief Justice Rehnquist and Justices White and Kennedy) refused to reach the overbreadth challenge, insisting that the overbreadth doctrine did not apply to laws no longer in force: "Because it has been repealed, the former version of [the law] cannot chill protected expression in the future." A majority, however, disagreed: Justice SCALIA, joined on this issue by Justices Blackmun, Brennan, Marshall, and Stevens, rejected the argument that an amendment could foreclose an overbreadth challenge. He explained: "It seems to me strange judicial theory that a conviction initially invalid can be resuscitated by postconviction alteration of the statute under which it was obtained. The overbreadth doctrine serves to protect constitutionally legitimate speech not merely ex post, but also ex ante, that is, when the legislature is contemplating what sort of statute to enact. If the promulgation of overbroad laws was cost free, as the plurality's new doctrine would make it—that is, if no conviction of constitutionally proscribable conduct would be lost, so long as the offending statute was narrowed before the final appeal—then legislatures would have significantly reduced incentive to stay within constitutional bounds in the first place. [In consequence,] a substantial amount of legitimate speech would be 'chilled' as a consequence of the rule the plurality would adopt." (Justice Scalia, joined by Justice Blackmun, found the law not substantially overbroad; only Justice Brennan, joined by Justices Marshall and Stevens, would have struck it down on overbreadth grounds.)

In **Osborne v. Ohio**, 495 U.S. 103 (1990), another child pornography case, Justice WHITE's majority opinion found that a *judicial* narrowing of an otherwise overbroad law *did* end the overbreadth concern. He explained: "Legislators who know they can cure their own mistakes by amendment without significant cost may not be as careful to avoid drafting overbroad statutes as they might otherwise be. But a similar effect will not be likely if a judicial construction of a statute to eliminate overbreadth is allowed to be applied in the case before the Court. This is so primarily because the legislatures cannot be sure that the statute, when examined by a court, will be saved by a narrowing construction rather than invalidated for overbreadth." Accordingly, the statute as construed could be applied "to conduct occurring prior to the construction, provided such application affords fair warning for the defendant." Here, the Court found such "fair warning" yet nevertheless held the conviction a violation of due process because the jury had not been instructed in accordance with the highest state court's subsequent narrowing construction. Do the differing results in these two cases make sense?

7. ***The Court's continued reliance on overbreadth invalidation.*** Later cases made clear that overbreadth analysis survived Broadrick and sometimes offered an attractive alternative to as-applied analysis. In **Houston v. Hill**, 482 U.S. 451 (1987), for example, overbreadth analysis enabled the Court to achieve some degree of agreement where the particular facts were substantially more problematic under the First Amendment than was the statute involved. The case arose from an incident in which Hill, a founding member of the Gay Political Caucus, observed a friend intentionally stopping traffic on a busy street, evidently to enable a vehicle to enter traffic. Two Houston police officers, one of them named Kelley, approached the friend and began speaking with him. Soon after, Hill began shouting to the officers "in an admitted attempt to divert Kelley's attention from [the friend]. Hill first shouted 'why don't you pick on somebody your own size?' After [Officer Kelley] responded '[A]re you interrupting me in my official capacity of a Houston police officer?' Hill then shouted 'Yes, why don't you pick on somebody my size?' " Hill was arrested under a section of the municipal code for "wilfully or intentionally interrupt[ing] a city policeman [by] verbal challenge during an investigation." After Hill was acquitted in a local court, he brought suit to challenge the law, under which he had been arrested several times and which he was likely to encounter again. The text of the section provided that it was "unlawful for any person to assault, strike or in any manner oppose, molest, abuse or interrupt any policeman in the execution of his duty, or any person summoned to aid in making the arrest."

Justice BRENNAN's majority opinion found the provision overbroad under the Broadrick line of cases. Noting that the provisions dealing with assaulting and striking had been preempted by state law, he found that "the enforceable portion of the ordinance deals not with core criminal conduct, but with speech." He stated that the freedom "verbally to oppose or challenge police action without thereby risking arrest is one of the principal characteristics by which we distinguish a free nation from a police state" and found the ordinance "not narrowly tailored to prohibit only disorderly conduct or fighting words." He added: "Although we appreciate the difficulties of drafting precise laws, we have repeatedly invalidated laws that provide the police with unfettered discretion to arrest individuals for words or conduct that annoy or offend them. The Constitution does not allow such speech to be made a crime." A partial concurrence by Justice POWELL, joined by Justices O'Connor and Scalia, agreed with the overbreadth judgment, but not with its reasoning. He insisted that the view "that the ordinance 'deals not with core criminal conduct, but with speech' [draws] a distinction where none exists." He emphasized, moreover, that there was "no doubt that a municipality constitutionally may punish an individual who chooses to stand near a police officer and persistently attempts to engage the officer in conversation while the officer is directing traffic at a busy intersection." Nevertheless, he concluded that, in the absence of an authoritative limiting construction of the ordinance, it vested excessive discretion in police officers to act against protected speech and was thus unconstitutional.

Overbreadth was also the tool for fashioning agreement in **Board of Airport Commissioners v. Jews for Jesus**, 482 U.S. 569 (1987). At issue was the Board's resolution providing that "if any individual and/or entity seeks to engage in First Amendment activities within the Central Terminal Area at Los Angeles International Airport, said individual and/or entity shall be deemed to be acting in contravention of the stated policy" of the Board. Respondents, who were prevented from distributing religious literature on a pedestrian walkway in the airport, brought an action challenging the resolution. Justice O'CONNOR's opinion relied exclusively on the spectacular overbreadth of the resolution and thus was able to avoid the difficult issues of the constitutionally protected nature of the respondents' behavior and of the then-unsettled "public forum status" of an airport terminal. Speaking for a unanimous Court, she concluded that the resolution was overbroad and hence facially void: "On its face, the resolution [reaches] the universe of expressive activity [and prohibits] *all* protected expression." She noted that it reached "even talking and reading, or the wearing of campaign buttons or symbolic clothing. Under such a sweeping ban, virtually every individual who enters [the airport] may be found to violate the resolution by engaging in some 'First Amendment activit[y].' We think it obvious that such a ban cannot be justified [because] no conceivable governmental interest would justify such an absolute prohibition on speech."

In **United States v. Stevens**, 559 U.S. 460 (2010), the Court facially invalidated as overbroad 18 U.S.C. § 48, which criminalizes the commercial creation, sale, or possession of any visual or auditory depiction "in which a living animal is intentionally maimed, mutilated, tortured, wounded, or killed," if that conduct violates federal or state law where "the creation, sale, or possession takes place," unless the depiction has "serious religious, political, scientific, educational, journalistic, historical, or artistic value." Without deciding whether depictions of extreme animal cruelty might be categorically prohibited by a narrower law, the Court, in a 8–1 opinion by Chief Justice ROBERTS, held the statute invalid as overbroad because " 'a substantial number of its applications are unconstitutional, judged in relation to the statute's plainly legitimate sweep.' " (For the aspects of the decision discussing the speech in relation to other unprotected categories of speech, see p. 198).

In explicating the overbreadth basis for the ruling, the Chief Justice wrote: "We read § 48 to create a criminal prohibition of alarming breadth. [The] text of the statute's ban on a 'depiction of animal cruelty' nowhere requires that the depicted conduct be cruel. [What] is more, the application of § 48 to depictions of illegal conduct extends to conduct that is illegal in only a single jurisdiction. [Views] about cruelty to animals and regulations having no connection to cruelty vary widely from place to place. In the District of Columbia, for example, all hunting is unlawful. Other jurisdictions permit or encourage hunting, and there is an enormous national market for hunting-related depictions in which a living animal is intentionally killed." The Chief Justice rejected the government's argument that the statute was sufficiently narrowed by its exemption for "any depiction that has serious religious, political, scientific, educational, journalistic, historical, or artistic value. And he denied that Miller v. California, on which the "serious value" exception was modeled, had held "that serious value could be used as a general precondition to protecting other types of speech."

Noting that "the markets for crush videos and dogfighting depictions [are] dwarfed by the market for other depictions, such as hunting magazines and videos," covered by § 48, the Chief Justice concluded that "the presumptively impermissible applications of § 48 (properly construed) far outnumber any permissible ones," and thus that the statute was facially invalid for overbreadth.

The sole dissenter, Justice ALITO, disputed the Court's conclusion that § 48 bans a substantial quantity of protected speech. Noting that overbreadth analysis should focus on "a statute's application to real-world conduct, not fanciful hypotheticals," he denied that § 48 even applies to the depictions of hunting on which the majority focused, as hunting is generally legal in all 50 states and any exceptions are not based on the prevention of animal cruelty. He also found the scope of other possible protected speech reached by the statute too trivial to warrant invalidation for substantial overbreadth, noting that "nothing in the record suggests that any one has ever created, sold, or possessed for sale a depiction of the slaughter of food animals or of the docking of the tails of dairy cows that would not easily qualify under the exception" for depictions with serious value.

For portions of the decision declining to denominate depictions of animal cruelty a new, unprotected category of speech, see p. 198.

8. *"Less restrictive means" analysis and its relation to overbreadth.* Overbreadth cases typically emphasize the availability of more carefully tailored, narrower means to achieve legislative ends. "Less restrictive means" analysis, however, is not limited to the overbreadth context. For example, the strict scrutiny applied to content-based laws requires carefully tailored means to "compelling" ends. Does this suggest that overbreadth is simply one application of strict scrutiny? See Monaghan, supra.

————

VAGUENESS

An "overbreadth" challenge should not be confused with one based on "vagueness," though a challenger will often assert both grounds of invalidity.

An unconstitutionally vague statute, like an overbroad one, creates risks of a "chilling effect" upon protected speech and produces rulings of facial invalidity. But a statute can be quite specific—that is, *not* "vague"—and yet be overbroad. Consider a law forbidding "the display of a nude human body on a motion picture screen." A statute can also be vague but not overbroad. Consider a law forbidding "all unprotected speech."

1. *Vagueness and due process.* The concept of vagueness under the First Amendment draws on the procedural due process requirement of adequate notice, under which a law must convey "sufficiently definite warning as to the proscribed conduct when measured by common understanding and practices." Jordan v. De George, 341 U.S. 223 (1951). A law will be void on its face for vagueness if persons "of common intelligence must necessarily guess at its meaning and differ as to its application." Connally v. General Constr. Co., 269 U.S. 385 (1926). One of the purposes of this requirement is to ensure fair notice to the defendant. But the ban on vagueness protects not only liberty, but also equality and the separation of executive from legislative power through the prevention of selective enforcement. See Smith v. Goguen (1974; p. 260) ("[We] have recognized [that] the more important aspect of the vagueness doctrine 'is not actual notice,' but the other principal element of the doctrine—the requirement that 'legislatures [set] reasonably clear guidelines for law enforcement officials and triers of fact in order to prevent arbitrary and discriminatory enforcement.' "); see also Kolender v. Lawson, 461 U.S. 352 (1983) (striking down on vagueness grounds a California law "that requires persons who loiter or wander on the streets to provide a 'credible and reliable' identification and to account for their presence when requested by a peace officer"); Papachristou v. Jacksonville, 405 U.S. 156 (1972) (unanimously invalidating as vague a vagrancy ordinance directed at "rogues and vagabonds, or dissolute persons who go about begging," "common drunkards," "common night walkers," "habitual loafers," and "persons wandering or strolling around from place to place without any lawful purpose or object"). See generally Amsterdam, "The Void-for-Vagueness Doctrine in the Supreme Court," 109 U. Pa. L. Rev. 67 (1960); Jeffries, "Legality, Vagueness, and the Construction of Statutes," 71 Va. L. Rev. 189 (1985).

But a finding of First Amendment vagueness has greater bite than a finding of due process vagueness. Like overbreadth challenges, vagueness challenges in the First Amendment context typically produce facial invalidations, while statutes found vague as a matter of due process typically are invalidated "as applied" to a particular defendant. Why might this be? Does it follow from a special concern about the "chilling effect" of vague statutes on protected speech? As Justice Powell wrote in Smith v. Goguen, "Where a statute's literal scope, unaided by a narrowing state court interpretation, is capable of reaching expression sheltered by the First Amendment, the [vagueness] doctrine demands a greater degree of specificity than in other contexts." And as the Court stated in Baggett v. Bullitt, 377 U.S. 360 (1964), which invalidated a loyalty oath for teachers, vague statutes cause citizens to " 'steer far wider of the unlawful zone' [than] if the boundaries of the forbidden areas were clearly marked," causing them to "restrict[ ] their conduct to that which is unquestionably safe. Free speech may not be so inhibited."

2. *First Amendment vagueness.* For an example of a decision finding a law impermissibly vague as well as overbroad, consider **Coates v.**

Cincinnati, 402 U.S. 611 (1971): An ordinance made it illegal for "three or more persons to assemble [on] any of the sidewalks [and] there conduct themselves in a manner annoying to persons passing by." Justice STEWART's opinion found the ordinance "unconstitutionally vague because it subjects the exercise of the right of assembly to an unascertainable standard, and unconstitutionally broad because it authorizes the punishment of constitutionally protected conduct." On the vagueness point, he stated that the "annoying" criterion meant that "no standard of conduct is specified at all." With respect to overbreadth, he emphasized that the right of assembly could not be restricted "simply because its exercise may be 'annoying' to some people." Such a prohibition "contains an obvious invitation to discriminatory enforcement against those whose association together is 'annoying' because their ideas, their lifestyle or their physical appearance is resented by the majority of their fellow citizens." The majority analyzed the ordinance in Coates "on the face" rather than "as applied." It was able to state all of the facts known to the Court in a portion of a single sentence: the record "tells us no more than that [Coates] was a student involved in a demonstration and the other appellants were pickets involved in a labor dispute." To the four dissenters, that lack of record data was a major factor counseling against a ruling of unconstitutionality. Justice White's dissent argued the law was not vague on its face and added: "Even accepting the overbreadth doctrine with respect to statutes clearly reaching speech, the Cincinnati ordinance does not purport to bar or regulate speech as such."

For an example of a decision rejecting a First Amendment vagueness challenge, recall Grayned v. Rockford (1972; p. 326), where Justice Marshall's opinion found an antinoise ordinance applicable to places adjacent to school buildings not vague because the state courts were likely to interpret the law "to prohibit only actual or imminent interference with the 'peace or good order' of the school." Justice Marshall argued that the ordinance was distinguishable from the ordinance in Coates or general breach of the peace ordinances because it was "written specifically for the school context, where the prohibited disturbances are easily measured by their impact on the normal activities of the school."

3. ***Vagueness and third-party standing.*** Does vagueness, like overbreadth, permit a speaker third-party standing to represent the rights of others not before the Court? It is clear that a litigant may invalidate a law on its face if it is vague in all its possible applications. For example, the Court held in Coates that "no standard of conduct is specified at all." Such a statute has no core of proscribable speech to which it might constitutionally be applied. But what if a litigant's own conduct was unquestionably within the core of the statute's permissible application, and he or she seeks to invalidate the law because it might be vague to others? See Smith v. Goguen (White, J., concurring) (arguing that anyone of "reasonable comprehension" should have "realize[d] that sewing a flag on the seat of his pants is contemptuous of the flag"); Young v. Am. Mini Theatres (1976; p. 157) (rejecting a vagueness challenge because zoning law was "unquestionably applicable" to the challengers' speech and the Court was "not persuaded" that the law would have a significant chilling effect on other protected speakers).

4. ***Vagueness and subsidies.*** Does the First Amendment prohibition on vagueness extend to vague conditions on public subsidies for speech? In **National Endowment for the Arts v. Finley**, 524 U.S. 569 (1998), the

Court unanimously answered that question no. The decision upheld against
facial challenge a 1990 amendment to the statutes authorizing arts grants
by the National Endowment for the Arts (NEA) that required the
Chairperson of the NEA to ensure that "artistic excellence and artistic merit
are the criteria by which [grant] applications are judged, taking into
consideration general standards of decency and respect for the diverse beliefs
and values of the American public." Writing for the Court, Justice
O'CONNOR stated: "Under the First and Fifth Amendments, speakers are
protected from arbitrary and discriminatory enforcement of vague
standards. The terms of the [NEA] provision are undeniably opaque, and if
they appeared in a criminal statute or regulatory scheme, they could raise
substantial vagueness concerns. It is unlikely, however, that speakers will
be compelled to steer too far clear of any 'forbidden area' in the context of
grants of this nature. We recognize, as a practical matter, that artists may
conform their speech to what they believe to be the decision-making criteria
in order to acquire funding. But when the Government is acting as patron
rather than as sovereign, the consequences of imprecision are not
constitutionally severe." While filing a lone dissent arguing that the
provision amounted to unconstitutional viewpoint discrimination, Justice
SOUTER agreed that the provision was not unconstitutionally vague: "The
necessary imprecision of artistic-merit-based criteria justifies tolerating a
degree of vagueness that might be intolerable when applying the First
Amendment to attempts to regulate political discussion."

PRIOR RESTRAINT

The Court has frequently reiterated that prior restraint is especially
disfavored under the First Amendment: "Any system of prior restraints of
expression comes to this Court bearing a heavy presumption against its
constitutional validity." Bantam Books, Inc. v. Sullivan, 372 U.S. 58 (1963).
That theme has strong historical roots. As noted above in Chapter 1, the
licensing system for English presses against which Milton protested played
a central role in the development of free speech theories. Blackstone, indeed,
argued that prior restraint was the *only* evil to be guarded against, and that
subsequent punishment was permissible; and Holmes initially embraced
that idea and abandoned it only grudgingly in Schenck. But the question
whether there is contemporary justification for greater suspicion of prior
restraint than of subsequent punishment is more controversial. The prior
restraint concept, like the overbreadth and vagueness doctrines, focuses on
the constitutional *means* of restricting speech. Thus, a prior restraint may
be struck down even though the particular expression involved could validly
be restricted through subsequent criminal punishment or civil liability. In
examining these materials, consider especially whether the special hostility
to prior restraint is justified, either as a theoretical or a practical matter.

LICENSING

1. *The concern with administrative discretion.* What's wrong
with licensing? What are the evils of a system that requires preclearance of
speech by an official censor? Recall the cases involving standardless licensing

of speech in the public forum. Those cases found standardless licensing schemes to confer excessive discretion on public officials, creating the risk of selective and content-discriminatory enforcement. Because of concern with the risks of abuse of discretionary authority, laws granting excessive discretion have been invalidated on their face, apart from any showing that, as applied, the discretion was in fact unconstitutionally abused and without any showing by the challenger that specific protected speech was curtailed.

In **Lovell v. Griffin**, 303 U.S. 444 (1938), the Court invalidated a conviction under an ordinance of the city of Griffin, Georgia, prohibiting the distribution of "circulars, handbooks, advertising, or literature of any kind" within the city "without first obtaining written permission from the City Manager." A Jehovah's Witness distributed religious tracts without applying for a permit. She challenged her conviction on free press and free exercise of religion grounds. Chief Justice HUGHES's opinion for a unanimous Court, in reversing her conviction, stated: "The ordinance is not limited to 'literature' that is obscene or offensive to public morals or that advocates unlawful conduct. [It] embraces 'literature' in the widest sense. The ordinance is comprehensive with respect to the method of distribution. There is thus no restriction in its application with respect to time or place. It is not limited to ways which might be regarded as inconsistent with the maintenance of public order or as involving disorderly conduct, the molestation of the inhabitants, or the misuse or littering of the streets. The ordinance prohibits the distribution of literature of any kind at any time, at any place, and in any manner without a permit from the City Manager.

"We think that the ordinance is invalid on its face. Whatever the motive which induced its adoption, its character is such that it strikes at the very foundation of the freedom of the press by subjecting it to license and censorship. The struggle for the freedom of the press was primarily directed against the power of the licensor. [The] liberty of the press became initially a right to publish '*without* a license what formerly could be published only *with* one.' While this freedom from previous restraint upon publication cannot be regarded as exhausting the guaranty of liberty, the prevention of that restraint was a leading purpose in the adoption of the [First Amendment]. As the ordinance is void on its face, it was not necessary for appellant to seek a permit under it. She was entitled to contest its validity in answer to the charge against [her]."

The reasons for *facially* invalidating licensing laws that grant excessive administrative discretion, as opposed to allowing licensees to challenge abuses of discretion case by case, were elaborated in the 4–3 decision (Chief Justice Rehnquist and Justice Kennedy did not participate) in **Lakewood v. Plain Dealer Publishing Co.**, 486 U.S. 750 (1988). At issue was a local ordinance restricting the placement of newspaper vending racks on public property. Newsracks could be placed on public property only upon an application for and receipt of an annual permit that could be denied for a number of specified reasons including "other terms and conditions deemed necessary and reasonable by the Mayor." Justice BRENNAN's opinion for the Court allowed a facial challenge to the ordinance: "[W]e have [identified] two major First Amendment risks associated with unbridled licensing schemes: self-censorship by speakers in order to avoid being denied a license to speak; and the difficulty of effectively detecting, reviewing, and correcting content-based censorship 'as applied' without standards by which to measure the licensor's action. It is when statutes threaten these risks to a significant degree that courts must entertain an immediate facial attack on the law. Therefore, a facial challenge lies whenever a licensing law gives a government official or agency substantial power to discriminate based on the content or viewpoint of speech by suppressing disfavored speech or disliked speakers."

The Court went on to find these criteria for facial challenges satisfied here: "[The City's scheme is] the sort of system in which an individual must apply for multiple licenses over time, or periodically renew a license. [In addition,] the licensing system [is directed] narrowly and specifically at expression or conduct commonly associated with expression: the circulation of newspapers. Such a framework [establishes] an official charged particularly with reviewing speech, or conduct commonly associated with it, breeding an 'expertise' tending to favor censorship over speech. [Because] of these features in the regulatory system [here], we think that a facial challenge is appropriate, and that standards controlling the Mayor's discretion must be required. Of course, the City may require periodic licensing, and may even have special licensing procedures for conduct commonly associated with expression; but the Constitution requires that [it] establish neutral criteria to insure that the licensing decision is not based on the content or viewpoint of the speech being considered."

Having decided to entertain the facial challenge, the Court had little difficulty in holding the standardless ordinance unconstitutional: "The City asks us to presume that the Mayor will deny a permit application only for reasons related to the health, safety, or welfare of Lakewood [citizens]. This presumes the Mayor will act in good faith and adhere to standards absent from the statute's face. But this is the very presumption that the doctrine forbidding unbridled discretion disallows. The doctrine requires that the limits that the City claims are implicit in its law be made explicit by textual incorporation, binding judicial or administrative construction, or well-established practice. This Court will not write nonbinding limits into a silent state statute."

Justice WHITE, joined by Justices Stevens and O'Connor, dissented. He viewed facial challenges as the exception and not the rule, and an exception that in past cases had been allowed only in those circumstances in which the relevant conduct could not have been prohibited entirely. But where there is no such absolute right to engage in the relevant conduct, he argued, a scheme allowing that conduct under some circumstances but not others should be actionable only if and when it is actually applied in an unconstitutional manner: "[T]he [Lovell] lines of cases would be applicable here if the [City] sought to license the distribution of all newspapers in the City, or if it required licenses for all stores which sold newspapers. These are obviously newspaper circulation activities which a municipality cannot prohibit and therefore, any licensing scheme of this scope would have to pass muster under the [Lovell] doctrine. But—and this is critical—Lakewood has not cast so wide a net. Instead, it has sought to license only the placement of newsracks [on] City property. As I read our precedents, the [Lovell] line of cases is applicable here only if the Plain Dealer has a constitutional right to distribute its papers by means of dispensing devices or newsboxes, affixed to the public sidewalks. I am not convinced that this is the case. [Where] an activity that could be forbidden altogether (without running afoul of the First Amendment) is subjected to a local license requirement, the mere presence of administrative discretion in the licensing scheme will not render it invalid per se. In such a case—which does not involve the exercise of First Amendment protected freedoms—the [Lovell] doctrine does not apply, and our usual rules concerning the permissibility of discretionary local licensing laws (and facial challenges to those laws) must prevail. [The] Court mentions the risk of censorship, the ever-present danger of censorship, and the power of prior restraint to justify the result. Yet these fears and concerns have little to do with this case, which involves the efforts of Ohio's largest newspaper to place a handful of newsboxes in a few locations in a small suburban community. [It] is hard to see how the Court's concerns have any applicability here."

2. *Procedural safeguards.* The flaws of a licensing scheme may be corrected as a substantive matter by the provision of objective standards for the licensor to administer. Should procedural safeguards also be required to check abuses of administrative discretion? Some decades ago, the Court's special suspicion of excessive discretion by administrators had especially frequent airings in the context of motion picture licensing, under censorship schemes then widely in use. Beginning with Joseph Burstyn, Inc. v. Wilson, 343 U.S. 495 (1952), the Court scrutinized the statutory standards in film licensing schemes with special care, to avoid abuse of administrative discretion. The Court declined to impose a ban on all prior restraints of films, see Times Film Corp. v. Chicago, 365 U.S. 43 (1961), but repeatedly invalidated particular laws because they lacked adequate specificity, see, e.g., Burstyn (invalidating a ban on a movie as "sacrilegious"). But in the Freedman case in 1965, the Court announced "procedural safeguards designed to obviate the dangers of a censorship system"—safeguards which have proven important in the protection of First Amendment interests in contexts well beyond the obscenity area. On special procedural safeguards in the First Amendment context generally, see Monaghan, "First Amendment 'Due Process,' " 83 Harv. L. Rev. 518 (1970); and Bogen, "First Amendment Ancillary Doctrines," 37 Md. L. Rev. 679 (1978).

Freedman v. Maryland, 380 U.S. 51 (1965), was a successful constitutional challenge to the procedural aspects of a Maryland motion picture censorship law. The challenger exhibited a movie without first submitting the picture to the state censorship board. He was convicted for failure to submit the film for licensing (even though the State conceded that the movie would have been licensed if it had been properly submitted). He argued that the censorship scheme was an invalid prior restraint. He focused particularly on the procedure for an initial decision by the censorship board which, without any judicial participation, effectively barred exhibition of any disapproved film unless and until the exhibitor undertook a time-consuming appeal to the state courts in order to get the censorship agency's decision reversed. The statute did not impose a time limit for completion of judicial review.

The Court, in an opinion by Justice BRENNAN, found the statutory procedure, especially its long time delays for the review process, unconstitutional. Noting that "[risk] of delay is built into the Maryland procedure," Justice Brennan stressed the "heavy presumption" against the validity of prior restraints, noted that a state "is not free to adopt whatever procedures it pleases for dealing with obscenity [without] regard to the possible consequences for constitutionally protected speech," and added: "The administration of a censorship system for motion pictures presents peculiar dangers to constitutionally protected speech. Unlike a prosecution for obscenity, a censorship proceeding puts the initial burden on the exhibitor or distributor. Because the censor's business is to censor, there inheres the danger that he may well be less responsive than a court [to] the constitutionally protected interests in free expression. And if it is made unduly onerous, by reason of delay or otherwise, to seek judicial review, the censor's determination may in practice be final."

The Court proceeded to identify several constitutionally mandated safeguards: "[W]e hold that a noncriminal process which requires the prior submission of a film to a censor avoids constitutional infirmity only if it takes place under procedural safeguards designed to obviate the dangers of a censorship system. First, the burden of proving that the film is unprotected expression must rest on the censor. As we said in Speiser v. Randall, 'Where the transcendent value of speech is involved, due process certainly requires [that] the State bear the burden of persuasion to show that the appellants engaged in criminal speech.' Second, while the State may require advance submission of all films, in order to proceed effectively to bar all showings of unprotected films, the requirement cannot be administered in a manner which would lend an effect of finality to the censor's determination whether a film constitutes protected expression. [Because] only a judicial determination in an adversary proceeding ensures the necessary sensitivity to freedom of expression, only a procedure requiring a judicial determination suffices to impose a valid final restraint. To this end, the exhibitor must be assured [that] the censor will, within a specified brief period, either issue a license or go to court to restrain showing the film. Any restraint imposed in advance of a final judicial determination on the merits must similarly be limited to preservation of the status quo for the shortest fixed period compatible with sound judicial resolution. Moreover, we are well aware that, even after expiration of a temporary restraint, an administrative refusal to license [may] have a discouraging effect on the exhibitor. Therefore, the procedure must also assure a prompt final judicial decision, to minimize the deterrent effect of an interim and possibly erroneous denial of a license. It is readily apparent that the Maryland procedural scheme does not satisfy these criteria [and it therefore constitutes] an invalid previous restraint." A concurrence by Justice DOUGLAS, joined by Justice Black, stated: "I do not believe any form of censorship—no matter how speedy or prolonged it may be—is permissible."

The Freedman standards were relied on in Justice O'Connor's plurality opinion in **FW/PBS, Inc. v. Dallas**, 493 U.S. 215 (1990). The case held that an ordinance requiring the licensing of sexually oriented businesses was an unconstitutional prior restraint in violation of Freedman because there was no "effective limitation on the time within which the licensor's decision must be made" and because the ordinance failed to provide "an avenue for a prompt judicial review." But Justice O'Connor also held that Freedman's requirement that the licensor bear the burden of going to court and the burden of proof was inapplicable where there was no "direct censorship of particular expressive material." Since the licensing board evaluated the business and not each film or book, it was not "passing judgment on the content of any protected speech" and thus a truncated version of the Freedman requirements was sufficient. Justice White (joined by Chief Justice Rehnquist) and Justice Scalia would have upheld the scheme without applying any of the Freedman requirements.

In **Thomas v. Chicago Park District**, 534 U.S. 316 (2002), Justice SCALIA, speaking for a unanimous Court, held that Freedman's procedural requirements did not apply to "a municipal park ordinance requiring individuals to obtain a permit before conducting large-scale events." The ordinance at issue required permits for any " 'public assembly, parade, picnic, or other event involving more than fifty individuals,' " and for any activity featuring amplified sound. Permit applications were to be processed in order of receipt, and the Park District was required to render decisions on applications within 14 days, with the option to extend the decision period by one additional 14-day term. The ordinance enumerated specific grounds for denying an application, and required the District to notify applicants in writing of the reason for denial and suggest alternative times and places if the denial was because of scheduling conflicts for use of the requested venue. Denials were appealable to the Park District superintendent, and applicants could also seek judicial review in state court by common law certiorari.

Justice Scalia wrote: "Freedman is inapposite because the licensing scheme at issue here is not subject-matter censorship but content-neutral time, place, and manner regulation of the use of a public forum. The Park District's ordinance does not authorize a licensor to pass judgment on the content of speech: None of the grounds for denying a permit has anything to do with what a speaker might say. Indeed, the ordinance (unlike the classic censorship scheme) is not even directed to communicative activity as such, but rather to *all* activity conducted in a public park. The picnicker and soccer-player, no less than the political activist or parade marshal, must apply for a permit if the 50-person limit is to be exceeded. And the object of the permit system [is] not to exclude communication of a particular content, but to coordinate multiple uses of limited space, to assure preservation of the park facilities, to prevent uses that are dangerous, unlawful, or impermissible under the Park District's rules, and to assure financial accountability for damage caused by the event.

"We have never required that a content-neutral permit scheme regulating speech in a public forum adhere to the procedural requirements set forth in Freedman. [Such] a traditional exercise of authority does not raise the censorship concerns that prompted us to impose the extraordinary procedural safeguards on the film licensing process in Freedman." Although the specific requirements of Freedman did not apply, the Court recognized the possibility that content-neutral time, place, and manner restrictions might be applied in a discriminatory manner. "Where the licensing official enjoys unduly broad discretion in determining whether to grant or deny a permit, there is a risk that he will favor or disfavor speech based on its content. See Forsyth County [(1992; p. 68)]. We have thus required that a time, place, and manner regulation contain adequate standards to guide the official's decision and render it subject to effective judicial review."

The Park District ordinance passed that test: "[Under the ordinance,] the Park District may deny a permit only for one or more of the reasons set forth in the ordinance. [These] grounds are reasonably specific and objective, and do not leave the decision 'to the whim of the administrator.' They provide 'narrowly drawn, reasonable and definite standards' to guide the licensor's determination. And they are enforceable on review—first by appeal to the General Superintendent of the Park District, and then by writ of common-law certiorari in the Illinois courts."

Although the law specified only that the District "may" deny permits on the specified grounds, rather than requiring denial in every instance of violation, the Court did not consider this grant of discretion to be a flaw: "[Granting] waivers to favored speakers (or, more precisely, denying them to disfavored speakers) would of course be unconstitutional, but we think that this abuse must be dealt with if and when a pattern of unlawful favoritism appears, rather than by insisting upon a degree of rigidity that is found in few legal arrangements. [The] prophylaxis achieved by insisting upon a rigid, no-waiver application of the ordinance requirements would be far outweighed [by] the accompanying senseless prohibition of speech (and of other activity in the park) by organizations that fail to meet the technical requirements of the ordinance but for one reason or another pose no risk of the evils that those requirements are designed to avoid."

3. *Standing to challenge licensing schemes.* The Court allowed both Lovell and Freedman to challenge the licensing scheme at issue on its face, without their having applied for and been refused a license. As the Court explained in Lovell: "As the ordinance is void on its face, it was not necessary for appellant to seek a permit under it. She was entitled to contest its validity in answer to the charge against [her]." See also Shuttlesworth v. Birmingham, 394 U.S. 147 (1969) (invalidating on its face, as conferring "virtually unbridled and absolute power," a parade permit ordinance authorizing the city commission to deny a permit if "in its judgment the public welfare, peace, safety, health, decency, good order, morals, or convenience require" as much, at the behest of a civil rights marcher who had not sought or obtained a permit).

Thus speakers need not challenge the denial of permission in advance— or even to seek permission—where the claim is that the law is unconstitutional *on its face.* But if the challenge is that a valid permit law is unconstitutionally *applied,* the challengers may not go ahead and hold their meeting or parade if they want to preserve their constitutional defenses. In **Poulos v. New Hampshire**, 345 U.S. 395 (1953), for example, a conviction for holding a meeting in a park without a required permit was sustained without considering the argument that the denial had been arbitrary, because the speakers had not gone to court to challenge the denial of the permission. In Poulos, unlike Lovell, the law requiring a permit was valid on its face; it was the administrative denial of the permit that was claimed to be unconstitutional. Justice REED was unpersuaded by the defendant's objection that "his right to preach may be postponed until a case, possibly after years, reaches this Court for final adjudication of constitutional rights": "Delay is unfortunate, but the expense and annoyance of litigation is a price citizens must pay for life in an orderly society where the rights of the First Amendment have a real and abiding meaning." Has such delay been curtailed as a result of the "careful procedural provisions"—including time requirements—required by Freedman?

4. *What distinction between prior restraint and subsequent punishment?* Consider the following arguments that prior restraints are worse than subsequent punishments: (1) It is easier for an official to restrict speech "by a simple stroke of the pen" than by the more cumbersome apparatus of subsequent punishment and thus prior restraint is likely to restrict more speech. (2) Censors will have a professional bias in favor of censorship, and thus will systematically overvalue government interests and undervalue speech. (3) Censors operate more informally than judges and so

afford less procedural safeguards to speakers. (4) Speech suppressed in advance never reaches the marketplace of ideas at all. (5) When speech is suppressed in advance, there is no empirical evidence from which to measure its alleged likely harms; subsequent punishment will thus afford more protection to speech whose bark is worse than its bite. See Emerson, "The Doctrine of Prior Restraint," 20 Law & Contemp. Probs. 648 (1955).

Some of these asserted justifications go to the timing of the restraint. Are such justifications coherent? Doesn't the threat of subsequent punishment, if it is effective, have an equally deterrent effect on speech? Consider the following comment: "The doctrine of prior restraint focuses on the largely irrelevant *timing* of the restraint, to the detriment of attention to those flaws that are the actual source of the objection. It is the identity and discretion of the restrainers and not the timing of the restraint that is important." Schauer, Free Speech: A Philosophical Enquiry 152 (1982). Other justifications above concern the institutional features of administrative licensing schemes. Are such problems cured by the substantive safeguards of objective standards and the procedural safeguards of Freedman? Do they exist at all when the prior restraint is issued not by an executive official but by a judge? Consider the following comment: the only legitimate basis for hostility to interim prior restraints is that "they authorize abridgment of expression prior to a full and fair determination of the constitutionally protected nature of the expression by an independent judicial forum." Redish, "The Proper Role of the Prior Restraint Doctrine in First Amendment Theory," 70 Va. L. Rev. 53 (1984).

In **Kingsley Books, Inc. v. Brown**, 354 U.S. 436 (1957), the Court itself suggested that prior restraints—at least in a scheme with clear standards and speedy judicial hearings—are *not* inevitably more harmful to speech than subsequent punishments. That 5–4 decision sustained a New York procedure, § 22–a, which authorized an injunction to prevent the sale and distribution of allegedly obscene printed matter pending an expedited trial. Kingsley consented to a preliminary injunction and, after trial, his books were found obscene, their further distribution was enjoined, and they were ordered destroyed. Kingsley did not challenge the finding of obscenity, but objected to the injunction as a prior restraint. In sustaining the procedure, Justice FRANKFURTER's opinion stated:

"The phrase 'prior restraint' is not a self-wielding sword. Nor can it serve as a talismanic test. [One] would be bold to assert that the in terrorem effect of [criminal sanctions] less restrains booksellers in the period before the law strikes than does § 22–a. Instead of requiring the bookseller to dread that the offer for sale of a book may, without prior warning, subject him to a criminal prosecution, [the] civil procedure assures him that such consequences cannot follow unless he ignores a court order specifically directed to him for a prompt and carefully circumscribed determination of the issue of obscenity. Until then, he may keep the book for sale and sell it on his own judgment rather than steer 'nervously among the treacherous shoals.'

"[Criminal] enforcement and the proceeding under § 22–a interfere with a book's solicitation of the public precisely at the same stage. In each situation the law moves after publication; the book need not in either case have yet passed into the hands of the public. [In] each case the bookseller is put on notice by the complaint that sale of the publication charged with obscenity in the period before trial may subject him to penal consequences.

In the one case he may suffer fine and imprisonment for violation of the criminal statute, in the other, for disobedience of the temporary injunction. The bookseller may of course stand his ground and confidently believe that in any judicial proceeding the book could not be condemned as obscene, but both modes of procedure provide an effective deterrent against distribution prior to adjudication of the book's content—the threat of subsequent penalization."

For further commentary on the distinction between prior restraints and subsequent punishments, see Blasi, "Prior Restraints on Demonstrations," 68 Mich. L. Rev. 1481 (1970); Barnett, "The Puzzle of Prior Restraint," 29 Stan. L. Rev. 539 (1977); Fiss, The Civil Rights Injunction (1978); Blasi, "Toward a Theory of Prior Restraint: The Central Linkage," 66 Minn. L. Rev. 11 (1981); Mayton, "Toward a Theory of First Amendment Process: Injunctions of Speech, Subsequent Punishment, and the Costs of the Prior Restraint Doctrine," 67 Cornell L. Rev. 245 (1982); Jeffries, "Rethinking Prior Restraint," 92 Yale L.J. 409 (1983); and Scordato, "Distinction Without a Difference: A Reappraisal of the Doctrine of Prior Restraint," 68 N.C. L. Rev. 1 (1989).

––––––––

INJUNCTIONS

Licensing schemes were the paradigmatic prior restraint against which the First Amendment was directed. The institutional weaknesses of a licensing scheme include the fact that an executive official charged with protecting the public from dangerous speech may have excessive zeal for censorship and little incentive to protect speech. But aren't the structural incentives different when a judge is asked to restrain speech? Is not the judge a neutral magistrate who will consider speech interests in the balance? Why, then, extend the doctrine against prior restraints to judicial injunctions restricting speech?

That prior restraints are presumptively forbidden even to judges was made clear in the following case, Near v. Minnesota. A Minnesota law authorized abatement, as a public nuisance, of a "malicious, scandalous and defamatory newspaper, or other periodical." A prosecutor sought to abate publication of "The Saturday Press." The Press had published articles charging in substance "that a Jewish gangster was in control of gambling, bootlegging and racketeering in Minneapolis, and that law enforcing officers and agencies were not energetically performing their duties." The Press especially targeted the chief of police, who was charged with several loosely defined offenses, e.g., "illicit relations with gangsters [and] participation in graft." A state court order "abated" the Press and perpetually enjoined the defendants from publishing or circulating "any publication whatsoever which is a malicious, scandalous or defamatory newspaper." The Supreme Court set aside this state injunction:

––––––––

Near v. Minnesota ex rel. Olson

283 U.S. 697, 51 S. Ct. 625, 75 L. Ed. 1357 (1931).

■ CHIEF JUSTICE HUGHES delivered the opinion of the Court.

[The] object of the [nuisance abatement] statute is not punishment, in the ordinary sense, but suppression of the offending newspaper. [The] reason for the enactment [is] that prosecutions to enforce penal statutes for libel do not result in "efficient repression or suppression of the evils of scandal." [The] operation and effect of the statute [is] that public authorities may bring the owner or publisher of a newspaper or periodical before a judge upon a charge of conducting a business of publishing scandalous and defamatory matter [and] unless the owner or publisher is able [to prove] that the charges are true and are published with good motives and for justifiable ends, his newspaper or periodical is suppressed and further publication is made punishable as a contempt. This is of the essence of censorship.

The question is whether a statute authorizing such proceedings [is] consistent with the conception of the liberty of the press as historically conceived and guaranteed. In determining the extent of the constitutional protection, it has been generally, if not universally, considered that it is the chief purpose of the guaranty to prevent previous restraints upon publication. The struggle in England, directed against the legislative power of the licenser, resulted in renunciation of the censorship of the press. The liberty deemed to be established was thus described by Blackstone: "The liberty of the press is indeed essential to the nature of a free state; but this consists in laying no *previous* restraints upon publications, and not in freedom from censure for criminal matter when [published]." [The] criticism upon Blackstone's statement has not been because immunity from previous restraint upon publication has not been regarded as deserving of special emphasis, but chiefly because that immunity cannot be deemed to exhaust the conception of the liberty guaranteed by state and federal [constitutions].

[The] protection even as to previous restraint is not absolutely unlimited. But the limitation has been recognized only in exceptional cases. [No] one would question but that a government might prevent actual obstruction to its recruiting service or the publication of the sailing dates of transports or the number and location of troops. On similar grounds, the primary requirements of decency may be enforced against obscene publications. The security of the community life may be protected against incitements to acts of violence and the overthrow by force of orderly government. These limitations are not applicable [here].

The fact that for approximately [150] years there has been almost an entire absence of attempts to impose previous restraints upon publications relating to the malfeasance of public officers is significant of the deep-seated conviction that such restraints would violate constitutional right. Public officers, whose character and conduct remain open to debate and free discussion in the press, find their remedies for false accusations in actions under libel laws providing for redress and punishment, and not in proceedings to restrain the publication of newspapers and periodicals. [The] fact that the liberty of the press may be abused by miscreant purveyors of scandal does not make any the less necessary the immunity of the press from previous restraint in dealing with official misconduct. Subsequent punishment for such abuses as may exist is the appropriate remedy, consistent with constitutional privilege.

The statute in question cannot be justified by reason of the fact that the publisher is permitted to show, before injunction issues, that the matter published is true and is published with good motives and for justifiable ends. If such a statute [is] valid, it would be equally permissible for the legislature to provide that at any time the publisher of any newspaper could be brought before a court, or even an administrative officer, and required to produce proof of the truth of his publication, or of what he intended to publish and of his motives, or stand enjoined. If this can be done, the legislature may provide the machinery for determining in the complete exercise of its discretion what are justifiable ends and restrain publication accordingly. And it would be but a step to a complete system of censorship. [We] hold the statute, so far as it authorized the proceedings in this action, [to] be an infringement of the liberty of the press guaranteed by the [14th Amendment]. [Reversed.]

■ JUSTICE BUTLER joined by JUSTICES VAN DEVANTER, MCREYNOLDS, and SUTHERLAND, dissenting.

[T]he *previous restraint* referred to by [Blackstone] subjected the press to the arbitrary will of an administrative officer. [The] Minnesota statute does not operate as a *previous* restraint on publication within the proper meaning of that phrase. It does not authorize administrative control in advance such as was formerly exercised by the licensers and censors but prescribes a remedy to be enforced by a suit in equity. In this case there was previous publication made in the course of the business of regularly producing malicious, scandalous and defamatory periodicals. The business and publications unquestionably constitute an abuse of the right of free press. [There] is no question of the power of the State to denounce such transgressions. The restraint authorized is only in respect of continuing to do what has been duly adjudged to constitute a nuisance. [It] is fanciful to suggest similarity between the granting or enforcement of the decree authorized by this statute to prevent *further* publication of malicious, scandalous and defamatory articles and the *previous restraint* upon the press by licensers as referred to by Blackstone and described in the history of the times to which he [alludes]. It is well known [that] existing libel laws are inadequate effectively to suppress evils resulting from the kind of [publications] that are shown in this case. The doctrine [of this ruling] exposes the peace and good order of every community and the business and private affairs of every individual to the constant and protracted false and malicious assaults of any insolvent publisher who may have purpose and sufficient capacity to contrive and put into effect a scheme or program for oppression, blackmail or extortion.[1]

———

1. *Judges and prior restraint.* Why should an injunction ever be considered a prior restraint? A judicial determination lacks the institutional features that make administrative censorship particularly suspect: it is formal rather than informal, a judge is not in the business of censorship, and it requires some consideration of evidence rather than a mere stroke of the pen. See Redish, "The Proper Role of the Prior Restraint Doctrine in First Amendment Theory," 70 Va. L. Rev. 53 (1984) (suggesting that permanent injunctions issued after trial are far less problematic than nonjudicial

---

[1] For the history of Near v. Minnesota, see Friendly, Minnesota Rag: The Dramatic Story of the Landmark Supreme Court Case That Gave New Meaning to Freedom of the Press (1981).

administrative licensing schemes, with preliminary injunctions and temporary restraining orders falling in between). Yet the Court in Near and later cases has extended the presumption against prior restraint in the licensing context to judicial restraints as well. For the view that Near was not really about the procedural problem of prior restraint, but rather the substantive problem of seditious libel, see Jeffries, "Rethinking Prior Restraint," 92 Yale L.J. 409 (1983).

2. *The "collateral bar" rule.* A frequent explanation for the extension of prior restraint doctrine to injunctions stems from the "collateral bar rule": the rule that an injunction must be obeyed until lifted, and that if it is violated, its unconstitutionality is no defense to a finding of contempt. Perhaps the most famous application of the rule arose in connection with a Good Friday civil rights protest march in Birmingham in 1963, led by several black ministers, including the Rev. Martin Luther King, Jr. The marchers challenged a Birmingham parade permit ordinance that was ultimately found to be unconstitutional. They marched in the face of an ex parte injunction directing compliance with the ordinance without challenging the injunction in court before marching. Indeed, they openly flouted the injunction because they considered it "raw tyranny."

In **Walker v. Birmingham**, 388 U.S. 307 (1967), the Court held, by a vote of 5–4, that the marchers could not defend against contempt charges by asserting the unconstitutionality of the ordinance or the injunction. Justice STEWART, writing for the Court, concluded: "This Court cannot hold that the petitioners were constitutionally free to ignore all the procedures of the law and carry their battle to the streets." The Alabama courts had justifiably relied on the general rule that court orders must be obeyed until "reversed for error by orderly review." Justice BRENNAN's dissent, joined by Chief Justice Warren and Justices Douglas and Fortas, insisted that the Court had elevated a "rule of judicial administration above the right of free expression."

Note that the Court in Walker suggested that the case might have come out differently if the injunction had been "transparently invalid." Does this afford some greater latitude to disobey injunctions? Recall that Lovell, Freedman, and Shuttlesworth were permitted to disobey permit schemes found by the Court to be facially unconstitutional. Why should those bound by an injunction be more restricted? See generally Blasi, "Prior Restraints on Demonstrations," 68 Mich. L. Rev. 1481 (1970).

Moreover, the Court has mitigated the effect of Walker by imposing procedural safeguards limiting the power of courts to issue speech-restrictive injunctions. For example, in **Carroll v. President & Commissioners of Princess Anne**, 393 U.S. 175 (1968), the Court found unconstitutional the ex parte procedure followed in issuing a 10-day temporary restraining order against holding a public rally. Petitioners had held a meeting at which they made "aggressively and militantly racist" speeches to a crowd of both whites and blacks. They announced that they would resume the rally the following night. Before then, local officials obtained the order restraining petitioners and their "white supremacist" National States Rights Party from holding meetings "which will tend to disturb and endanger the citizens of the County." There was no notice to petitioners prior to the issuance of the order. The rally was cancelled and petitioners (rather than ignoring the injunction as in Walker) challenged the injunction in court. Justice FORTAS's opinion for the Court found no adequate justification for the ex parte nature of the proceedings. In the rare situations where prior restraints were permissible, "the Court has insisted upon careful procedural provisions. [Freedman.] [There] is a place in our jurisprudence for ex parte issuance, without notice, of temporary restraining orders of short duration; but there is no place within the area of basic freedoms guaranteed by the First Amendment for such orders where no showing is made that it is impossible to serve or to notify the opposing parties and to give them an opportunity to participate." Here, procedural care was even more important than in the obscenity context of Freedman: "The present case involves a rally and 'political' speech in which the element of timeliness may be important." Without an adversary hearing, there was "insufficient assurance of the balanced analysis and careful conclusions which are essential in the area of First Amendment adjudication."

PRIOR RESTRAINT AND NATIONAL SECURITY

Recall that in Near, the Court cautioned that the presumption against prior restraint is not absolute: "No one would question but that a government might prevent actual obstruction to its recruiting service or the publication of the sailing dates of transports or the number and location of troops." When, if ever, are concerns of national security sufficient to justify a prior restraint? The following cases explore this question:

New York Times Co. v. United States
[The Pentagon Papers Case]
403 U.S. 713, 91 S. Ct. 2140, 29 L. Ed. 2d 822 (1971).

■ PER CURIAM.

We granted certiorari in these cases in which the United States seeks to enjoin the New York Times and the Washington Post from publishing the contents of a classified study entitled "History of U.S. Decision-Making Process on Viet Nam Policy."[1]

"Any system of prior restraints of expression comes to this Court bearing a heavy presumption against its constitutional validity." [Bantam Books; see Near.] The Government "thus carries a heavy burden of showing justification

---

[1] Portions of that secret Defense Department study (popularly known as the "Pentagon Papers") were published by The New York Times (beginning June 13, 1971) and the Washington Post (on June 18, 1971). The top-secret study reviewed in considerable detail the formulation of American policy toward Indochina, including military operations and diplomatic negotiations. The newspapers obtained this study from Daniel Ellsberg, a former Pentagon official. The government actions to restrain further publication made their way through two district courts and two courts of appeals between June 15 and June 23. The Government claimed that publication would interfere with national security and would undermine the ability to conduct diplomatic negotiations, produce the death of military personnel, and prolong the war. On June 25, the Supreme Court granted certiorari in the Times and Post cases. The cases were argued on June 26 and the decision was issued on June 30, 1971. Restraining orders remained in effect while the decision was pending. (Four Justices—Black, Douglas, Brennan, and Marshall—dissented from the decision to grant certiorari and urged summary action instead, stating that they "would not continue the restraint" on the newspapers.) For insight into the history of the litigation, see Oakes, "The Doctrine of Prior Restraint Since the Pentagon Papers," 15 U. Mich. J.L. Reform 497 (1982).

for the enforcement of such a restraint." The [District Court] in the New York Times case and the [District Court] and the [Court of Appeals] in the Washington Post case held that the Government had not met that burden. We agree. [The] stays entered June 25, 1971, by the [Second Circuit] are vacated.

■ JUSTICE BLACK, with whom JUSTICE DOUGLAS joins, concurring.

[I] believe that every moment's continuance of the injunctions against these newspapers amounts to a flagrant, indefensible, and continuing violation of the First Amendment. Furthermore, after oral arguments, I agree completely [with] my Brothers Douglas and Brennan. In my view it is unfortunate that some of my Brethren are apparently willing to hold that the publication of news may sometimes be enjoined. Such a holding would make a shambles of the First Amendment. [The] press was protected [by the First Amendment] so that it could bare the secrets of government and inform the people. Only a free and unrestrained press can effectively expose deception in government. [To] find that the President has "inherent power" to halt the publication of news by resort to the courts would wipe out the First Amendment. [The] word "security" is a broad, vague generality whose contours should not be invoked to abrogate the fundamental law embodied in the [First Amendment].

■ JUSTICE DOUGLAS, with whom JUSTICE BLACK joins, concurring.

[The First Amendment] leaves [no] room for governmental restraint on the press. There is, moreover, no statute barring the publication by the press of the material which the Times and Post seek to use. [18 U.S.C. § 793(e), prohibiting "communication" of information relating to the national defense that could be used to the injury of the United States, does not apply to publication.] [I]t is apparent that Congress was capable of and did distinguish between publishing and communication in the various sections of the Espionage Act.[2] So any power that the Government possesses must come from its "inherent power." The power to wage war is "the power to wage war successfully." But the war power stems from a declaration of war. The Constitution by Article I, § 8, gives Congress, not the President, power "to declare War." Nowhere are presidential wars authorized.

[These] disclosures[3] may have a serious impact. But that is no basis for sanctioning a previous restraint on the press. [Near.] [The] Government says that it has inherent powers to go into court and obtain an injunction to protect [national] security. [Near] repudiated that expansive doctrine in no uncertain terms. The dominant purpose of the First Amendment was to prohibit the widespread practice of governmental suppression of embarrassing information. [A] debate of large proportions goes on in the Nation over our posture in Vietnam. The debate antedated the disclosure of

---

[2]   Justice Douglas added: "The other evidence that § 793 does not apply to the press is a rejected version of § 793. That version read: 'During any national emergency, [the] President may [prohibit] the publishing or communicating of [any] information relating to the national defense which, in his judgment, is of such character that it is or might be useful to the enemy.' During the [1917] debates in the Senate the First Amendment was specifically cited and that provision was defeated."

[3]   There are numerous sets of this material in existence and they apparently are not under any controlled custody. Moreover, the President has sent a set to the Congress. We start then with a case where there already is rather wide distribution of the material that is destined for publicity, not secrecy. I have gone over the material listed in the in camera brief of the United States. It is all history, not future events. None of it is more recent than 1968. [Footnote by Justice Douglas.]

the contents of the present documents. The latter are highly relevant to the debate in progress. Secrecy in government is fundamentally anti-democratic, perpetuating bureaucratic errors. Open debate and discussion of public issues are vital to our national health. [The] stays in these cases that have been in effect for more than a week constitute a flouting of the principles of the [First Amendment].

■ JUSTICE BRENNAN, concurring.

The error that has pervaded these cases from the outset was the granting of any injunctive relief whatsoever, interim or otherwise. The entire thrust of the Government's claim throughout these cases has been that publication of the material sought to be enjoined "could," or "might," or "may" prejudice the national interest in various ways. But the First Amendment tolerates absolutely no prior judicial restraints of the press predicated upon surmise or conjecture that untoward consequences may result.[4] Our cases, it is true, have indicated that there is a single, extremely narrow class of cases in which the First Amendment's ban on prior judicial restraint may be overridden. Our cases have thus far indicated that such cases may arise only when the Nation "is at war" [Schenck], during which times "no one would question but that a government might prevent actual obstruction to its recruiting service or the publication of the sailing dates of transports or the number and location of troops." [Near.] Even if the present world situation were assumed to be tantamount to a time of war, or if the power of presently available armaments would justify even in peacetime the suppression of information that would set in motion a nuclear holocaust, in neither of these actions has the Government presented or even alleged that publication of items from or based upon the material at issue would cause the happening of an event of that nature. "The chief purpose of [the First Amendment's] guarantee [is] to prevent previous restraints upon publication." [Near.] Thus, only governmental allegation and proof that publication must inevitably, directly and immediately cause the occurrence of an event kindred to imperiling the safety of a transport already at sea can support even the issuance of an interim restraining order. [Unless] and until the Government has clearly made out its case, the First Amendment commands that no injunction may issue.

■ JUSTICE STEWART, with whom JUSTICE WHITE joins, concurring.

[The] only effective restraint upon executive policy and power in the areas of national defense and international affairs may lie in an enlightened citizenry. [For] this reason, it is perhaps here that a press that is alert, aware, and free most vitally serves the basic purpose of the First Amendment. [Yet] it is elementary that the successful conduct of international diplomacy and the maintenance of an effective national defense require both confidentiality and secrecy. [I] think there can be but one answer to this dilemma, if dilemma it be. The responsibility must be where the power is. [The] Executive must have the largely unshared duty to determine and preserve the degree of internal security necessary to exercise [its] power successfully. [It] is the constitutional duty of the Executive—as a

---

[4] Freedman v. Maryland and similar cases regarding temporary restraints of allegedly obscene materials are not in point. For those cases rest upon the proposition that "obscenity is not protected by the freedoms of speech and press." Here there is no question but that the material sought to be suppressed is within the protection of the First Amendment; the only question is whether, notwithstanding that fact, its publication may be enjoined for a time because of the presence of an overwhelming [national interest]. [Footnote by Justice Brennan.]

matter of sovereign prerogative and not as a matter of law as the courts know law—through the promulgation and enforcement of executive regulations to protect the confidentiality necessary to carry out its responsibilities in the fields of international relations and national defense. This is not to say that Congress and the courts have no role to play. Undoubtedly Congress has the power to enact specific and appropriate criminal laws to protect government property and preserve government secrets. [But] in the cases before us we are asked neither to construe specific regulations nor to apply specific laws. We are asked, instead, to perform a function that the Constitution gave to the Executive, not the Judiciary. We are asked, quite simply, to prevent the publication by two newspapers of material that the Executive Branch insists should not, in the national interest, be published. I am convinced that the Executive is correct with respect to some of the documents involved. But I cannot say that disclosure of any of them will surely result in direct, immediate, and irreparable damage to our Nation or its people. That being so, there can under the First Amendment be but one judicial resolution of the issues before us. I join the judgments of the Court.

■ JUSTICE WHITE, with whom JUSTICE STEWART joins, concurring.

I concur in today's judgments, but only because of the concededly extraordinary protection against prior restraints enjoyed by the press under our constitutional system. I do not say that in no circumstances would the First Amendment permit an injunction against publishing information about government plans or operations. Nor, after examining the materials the Government characterizes as the most sensitive and destructive, can I deny that revelation of these documents will do substantial damage to public interests. Indeed, I am confident that their disclosure will have that result. But I nevertheless agree that the United States has not satisfied the very heavy burden which it must meet to warrant an injunction against publication in these cases, at least in the absence of express and appropriately limited congressional authorization for prior restraints in circumstances such as these.

The Government's position is simply stated: The responsibility of the Executive for the conduct of the foreign affairs and for the security of the Nation is so basic that the President is entitled to an injunction against publication of a newspaper story whenever he can convince a court that the information to be revealed threatens "grave and irreparable" injury to the public interest; and the injunction should issue whether or not the material to be published is classified, whether or not publication would be lawful under relevant criminal statutes enacted by Congress and regardless of the circumstances by which the newspaper came into possession of the information. At least in the absence of legislation by Congress, based on its own investigations and findings, I am quite unable to agree that the inherent powers of the Executive and the courts reach so far as to authorize remedies having such sweeping potential for inhibiting publications by the press. [To] sustain the Government in these cases would start the courts down a long and hazardous road that I am not willing to travel, at least without congressional guidance and direction.

[Prior] restraints require an unusually heavy justification under the First Amendment; but failure by the Government to justify prior restraints does not measure its constitutional entitlement to a conviction for criminal publication. That the Government mistakenly chose to proceed by injunction does not mean that it could not successfully proceed in another way. [Justice

White discussed a number of "potentially relevant" criminal provisions.] It is thus clear that Congress has addressed itself to the problems of protecting the security of the country and the national defense from unauthorized disclosure of potentially damaging information. Youngstown Sheet & Tube Co. v. Sawyer, 343 U.S. 579 (1952) (the Steel Seizure Case). It has not, however, authorized the injunctive remedy against threatened publication. It has apparently been satisfied to rely on criminal sanctions and their deterrent effect on the responsible as well as the irresponsible press. I am not, of course, saying that either of these newspapers has yet committed a crime or that either would commit a crime if they published all the material now in their possession. That matter must await resolution in the context of a criminal proceeding if one is [instituted].[5]

■ JUSTICE MARSHALL, concurring.

[I] believe the ultimate issue in this case [is] whether this Court or the Congress has the power to make law. [I]n some situations it may be that under whatever inherent powers the [Executive may have], there is a basis for the invocation of the equity jurisdiction of this Court as an aid to prevent the publication of material damaging to "national security," however that term may be defined. It would, however, be utterly inconsistent with the concept of separation of powers for this Court to use its power of contempt to prevent behavior that Congress has specifically declined to prohibit. There would be a similar damage to the basic concept of these co-equal branches of Government if when the [executive] had adequate authority granted by Congress to protect "national security" it can choose instead to invoke the contempt power of a court to enjoin the threatened conduct. [In] these cases we are not faced with a situation where Congress has failed to provide the Executive with broad power to protect the Nation from disclosure of damaging state secrets. [See the power to "classify" secret materials in 18 U.S.C. Chapter 37, Espionage and Censorship.] [It] is plain that Congress has specifically refused to grant the authority the Government seeks from this Court. [It] is not for this Court to fling itself into every breach perceived by some Government [official].

■ JUSTICE HARLAN, with whom CHIEF JUSTICE BURGER and JUSTICE BLACKMUN join, dissenting.

[It] is plain to me that the scope of the judicial function in passing upon the activities of the Executive Branch of the Government in the field of foreign affairs is very narrowly restricted. This view is, I think, dictated by the concept of separation of powers upon which our constitutional system rests. [I] agree that, in performance of its duty to protect the values of the First Amendment against political pressures, the judiciary must review the initial Executive determination to the point of satisfying itself that the subject matter of the dispute does lie within the proper compass of the President's foreign relations power. [Moreover], the judiciary may properly

---

[5] On July 1, 1971—the day after the decision in this case—Attorney General Mitchell commented that the Justice Department "will prosecute all those who have violated federal criminal laws in connection with this matter" and added: "A review of the Court's opinions indicates that there is nothing in them to affect the situation." Daniel Ellsberg and Anthony Russo (the government officials accused of leaking the Pentagon Papers) were subsequently indicted by a grand jury under provisions of federal espionage, theft, and conspiracy laws. Another federal grand jury investigated the involvement of newspapers and reporters. On May 11, 1973, District Judge Matthew Byrne dismissed the Ellsberg-Russo indictment and granted a mistrial based on prosecutorial misconduct, namely that the government had illegally wiretapped the men and lost files pertaining to the taps.

insist that the determination that disclosure of the subject matter would irreparably impair the national security be made by the head of the Executive Department concerned [after] actual personal consideration by that officer. [But] in my judgment the judiciary may not properly go beyond these two inquiries and redetermine for itself the probable impact of disclosure on the national security.

[Even] if there is some room for the judiciary to override the executive determination, it is plain that the scope of review must be exceedingly narrow. I can see no indication in the opinions of [the lower courts] in the Post litigation that the conclusions of the Executive were given even the deference owing to an administrative agency, much less that owing to a co-equal branch of the Government operating within the field of its constitutional prerogative. [Pending] further hearings in each case conducted under the appropriate ground rules, I would continue the restraints on publication. I cannot believe that the doctrine prohibiting prior restraints reaches to the point of preventing courts from maintaining the status quo long enough to act responsibly in matters of such national importance as those involved here.

■ JUSTICE BLACKMUN, dissenting.

I join Justice Harlan in his dissent. [The] First Amendment, after all, is only one part of an entire Constitution. First Amendment absolutism has never commanded a majority of this Court. [E.g., Near; Schenck.] What is needed here is a weighing, upon properly developed standards, of the broad right of the press to print and of the very narrow right of the Government to prevent. Such standards are not yet developed. The parties here are in disagreement as to what those standards should be. But even the newspapers concede that there are situations where restraint is in order and is constitutional. [I] therefore would remand [for the orderly presentation of evidence]. I hope that damage has not already been done. If, however, damage has been done, and if, with the Court's action today, these newspapers proceed to publish the critical documents and there results therefrom "the death of soldiers, the destruction of alliances, the greatly increased difficulty of negotiation with our enemies, the inability of our diplomats to negotiate," to which list I might add the factors of prolongation of the war and of further delay in the freeing of United States prisoners, then the Nation's people will know where the responsibility for these sad consequences rests.

[Chief Justice BURGER's dissent stated that he agreed "generally" with Justices Harlan and Blackmun, but that he was "not prepared to reach the merits." He urged that the temporary restraining orders be extended pending a full trial on the merits. He commented that the cases had been "conducted in unseemly haste" and that "we literally do not know what we are acting on."]

————

THE SCOPE AND LIMITS OF PENTAGON PAPERS

1. *Bombmaking instructions.* Were the principles of Near and the Pentagon Papers case properly applied in **United States v. Progressive, Inc.**, 467 F. Supp. 990 (W.D. Wis. 1979)? There, the district court issued an order enjoining The Progressive, a monthly magazine, from publishing

technical material on hydrogen bomb design in an article entitled "The H-Bomb Secret: How We Got It, Why We're Telling It." The author and publisher claimed that the article merely synthesized information available in public documents, insisting that the article would contribute to informed opinion about nuclear weapons and would benefit the nation by demonstrating that open debate was preferable to "an oppressive and ineffective system of secrecy and classification." In issuing the temporary injunction, the district judge distinguished the Pentagon Papers case on three grounds: (1) the documents there had contained only "historical data"; (2) the Government there had not proved that publication affected the national security; and (3) the Government there had failed to establish a statutory basis for injunctive relief.[1]

Although the Government conceded that at least some of the information in the article had been declassified or was in the public domain, it argued that the interest in "national security" permitted it to bar publication of information "originating in the public domain, if when drawn together, synthesized and collated, such information acquires the character of presenting immediate, direct and irreparable harm to the interests of the United States." It submitted affidavits from Cabinet members asserting that publication would increase the risk of thermonuclear proliferation. The district judge accepted the Government's key claims. He noted that the article "contains concepts that are not found in the public realm, concepts that are vital to the operation of the bomb." Moreover, despite the prior declassification of some of the materials in the article, he found that "the danger lies in the exposition of certain concepts never heretofore disclosed in conjunction with one another." Although the district judge conceded that the article probably did not "provide a 'do-it-yourself' guide for the hydrogen bomb," he noted that the article "could possibly provide sufficient information to allow a medium size nation to move faster in developing a hydrogen weapon."

In justifying "the first instance of prior restraint against a publication in this fashion in the history of this country," the district judge explained: "A mistake in ruling against The Progressive [will] curtail defendants' First Amendment rights in a drastic and substantial fashion. [But a] mistake in ruling against the United States could pave the way for thermonuclear annihilation for us all. In that event, our right to life is extinguished and the right to publish becomes moot." He concluded: "Because of this 'disparity of risk,' because the government has met its heavy burden of showing justification for the imposition of a prior restraint, [and] because the Court is unconvinced that suppression of the objected-to technical portions of the [article] would in any plausible fashion impede the defendants in their laudable crusade to stimulate public knowledge of nuclear armament and bring about enlightened debate on national policy questions, the Court finds that the objected-to portions of the article fall within the narrow area recognized by the Court in Near v. Minnesota in which a prior restraint on

---

[1] For statutory support, the district court relied primarily upon the Atomic Energy Act of 1954, which imposes sanctions on anyone who "communicates, transmits, or discloses [restricted data] with reason to believe such data will be utilized to injure the United States or to secure an advantage to any foreign nation." 42 U.S.C. § 2274(b). The Act also authorizes the Government to seek injunctive relief. 42 U.S.C. § 2280. The trial court ruled that the statute and its definition of "restricted data"—including "all data concerning design, manufacture, or utilization of atomic weapons"—were neither vague nor overbroad "[a]s applied to this case" and that the prohibition against one who "communicates" extended to publication in a magazine.

publication is appropriate."[2] He added: "In view of the showing of harm made by the United States, a preliminary injunction would be warranted even in the absence of statutory authorization because of the existence of the likelihood of direct, immediate and irreparable injury to our nation and its people. New York Times (Justice Stewart)."[3]

2.   *Alternative sanctions.* Even if it may not restrain the press, may the government seek civil and criminal remedies against former employees who publish secret information? Dicta in the Pentagon Papers case suggested as much. May the government impose employment sanctions as well? Obviously it may fire or demote an employee who divulges secrets. The question of further remedies against a former government employee who had agreed not to disclose confidential government information without authorization came before the Court in **Snepp v. United States**, 444 U.S. 507 (1980). Snepp, a former CIA employee, had agreed not to divulge classified information without authorization and not to publish any information relating to the Agency without prepublication clearance. Without submitting his manuscript for clearance, he published a book about CIA activities in Vietnam. (The Government did not claim that the book contained classified data.) The Court of Appeals held that Snepp could be subjected to punitive damages, but refused to impress a constructive trust on his profits from the book. The Supreme Court's per curiam reversal, decided without oral argument, held that punitive damages were an inappropriate and inadequate remedy and instead imposed a constructive trust on Snepp's profits. The majority's only mention of the First Amendment came in a footnote insisting that "this Court's cases make clear that—even in the absence of an express agreement—the CIA could have acted to protect substantial government interests by imposing reasonable restrictions on employee activities that in other contexts might be protected by the First Amendment. The Government has a compelling interest in protecting both the secrecy of information important to our national security and the appearance of confidentiality so essential to the effective operation of our foreign intelligence service. The agreement that Snepp signed is a reasonable means for protecting this vital interest." A dissent by Justice STEVENS, joined by Justices Brennan and Marshall, objected not only to the Court's extraordinary procedure (deciding without argument an issue raised only in the Government's conditional cross-petition for certiorari, filed to bring the entire case up in the event the Court granted Snepp's certiorari petition), but also to the Court's fashioning of a "drastic new remedy [to] enforce a species of prior restraint on a citizen's right to criticize his government."

For commentary on Pentagon Papers and related problems, see, for example, Symposium, "National Security and the First Amendment," 26 Wm. & Mary L. Rev. 715 (1985); and Cox, "Foreword—Freedom of

---

[2]   In arguing that the Near exception applied, the district judge pointed to the "troop movements" reference there and added: "Times have changed significantly since 1931 when Near was decided. Now war by foot soldiers has been replaced in large part by war by machines and bombs. No longer need there be any advance warning or any preparation time before a nuclear war could be commenced. In light of these factors, this court concludes that publication of the technical information of the hydrogen bomb contained in the article is analogous to publication of troop movements or locations in time of war and falls within the extremely narrow exception to the rule against prior restraint."

[3]   The Government's proceedings against The Progressive were abandoned before full appellate proceedings and a hearing regarding a permanent injunction could take place, because similar information pertaining to nuclear weapons was published independently by others while the litigation was under way.

Expression in the Burger Court," 94 Harv. L. Rev. 1 (1980). For commentary
on Snepp, see Easterbrook, "Insider Trading, Secret Agents, Evidentiary
Privileges, and the Production of Information," 1981 Sup. Ct. Rev. 309;
Medow, "The First Amendment and the Secrecy State," 130 U. Pa. L. Rev.
775 (1982); and Sunstein, "Government Control of Information," 74 Calif. L.
Rev. 889 (1986).

3. *Prior restraint and WikiLeaks.* How should Pentagon Papers
inform modern-day challenges to government efforts to curb speech on
national security grounds? In 2010 and 2011, WikiLeaks—a self-described
"not-for profit media organization"—made several high-profile disclosures of
classified U.S. materials, including military footage, confidential diplomatic
cables, and other sensitive government documents. Predictably, the
disclosures precipitated swift and harsh responses from the media and
political figures, many of whom sought to distinguish WikiLeaks from the
Pentagon Papers.

Does the rationale of the Pentagon Papers case extend to WikiLeaks?
Should a prior restraint on expression by such groups be barred only when,
as Justice Stewart stated, disclosure would "surely result in direct,
immediate, and irreparable damage to our Nation and its people"? Or do the
unique circumstances of the WikiLeaks disclosures warrant a different
approach? For opposing perspectives, see Benkler, "A Free Irresponsible
Press: Wikileaks and the Battle Over the Soul of the Networked Fourth
Estate," 46 Harv. C.R.-C.L. L. Rev. 311 (2011) and Bellia, "WikiLeaks and
the Institutional Framework for National Security Disclosures," 121 Yale
L.J. 1448 (2012). Note that in April 2019, the Department of Justice revealed
that it had charged Julien Assange, founder of WikiLeaks, with conspiracy
to commit computer intrusion.

PRIOR RESTRAINT AND FAIR TRIAL

In **Nebraska Press Ass'n v. Stuart**, 427 U.S. 539 (1976), the Court
considered the permissibility of a prior restraint on the press imposed in the
interest of protecting a criminal defendant's right to a fair trial before an
impartial jury. The Court reemphasized the high constitutional barriers to
prior restraints and held the challenged pretrial restraint unconstitutional.

The state court "gag order," issued in anticipation of a trial in a widely
publicized mass murder case, prohibited publication or broadcasting of the
accused's confessions or admissions, and of any other facts "strongly
implicative" of the accused. In his majority opinion, Chief Justice BURGER
found that "the showing before the state court" did not justify the order.
Though Chief Justice Burger rejected the priority, "in all circumstances," of
the "right to publish" over the "right of an accused," he found a common
thread in the prior decisions such as Near and Pentagon Papers: "[P]rior
restraints [are] the most serious and least tolerable infringement on First
Amendment rights. A criminal penalty or [a defamation judgment] is subject
to the whole panoply of protections afforded by deferring the impact of the
judgment until all avenues of appellate review have been exhausted. [A]
prior restraint [has] an immediate and irreversible sanction. If it can be said
that a threat of criminal or civil sanctions after publication 'chills' speech,
prior restraint 'freezes' it at least for the time." Moreover, "the protection

against prior restraints should have particular force as applied to reporting of criminal proceedings."

Chief Justice Burger noted that, although the trial judge could reasonably conclude, "based on common human experience, that publicity might impair" the defendant's rights by affecting prospective jurors, that conclusion "was of necessity speculative." Moreover, alternative measures to curb the impact of media publicity might well have been effective: for example, change of venue; postponement of the trial; careful questioning of jurors; jury instructions; sequestration of jurors; and curbing statements by the contending lawyers, the police, and witnesses. Chief Justice Burger also questioned the efficacy of any restraint of the media, in view of the likelihood of rumors in a sensational case. Turning to the terms of the order, he especially objected to the ban on reporting "implicative" information as "too vague and too broad." He concluded that, though there was no doubt about "the gravity of the evil pretrial publicity can work, [the] probability that it would do so here was not demonstrated with the degree of certainty our cases on prior restraint require."

Justices POWELL and WHITE, while joining the majority opinion, each submitted brief concurring statements. Justice Powell emphasized "the unique burden" on a proponent of prior restraint on pretrial publicity. Justice White indicated his "grave doubt [whether] orders with respect to the press such as were entered in this case would ever be justifiable."

In an opinion concurring only in the judgment, Justice BRENNAN, joined by Justices Stewart and Marshall, urged an absolute ban on prior restraints issued in the interest of a fair trial: "I would hold [that] resort to prior restraints on the freedom of the press is a constitutionally impermissible method for enforcing [the right to a fair trial]; judges have at their disposal a broad spectrum of devices for ensuring that fundamental fairness is accorded the accused without necessitating so drastic an incursion on the equally fundamental and salutary constitutional mandate that discussion of public affairs in a free society cannot depend on the preliminary grade of judicial censors." He emphasized that "[c]ommentary and reporting on the criminal justice system is at the core of First Amendment values." Though he recognized pretrial publicity could "destroy the fairness of a criminal trial," he viewed the bar on prior restraints on the press as applicable "no matter how shabby the means by which the information is obtained." He added in a footnote that this did "not necessarily immunize [the press] from civil liability for libel or invasion of privacy or from criminal liability for transgressions of general criminal laws during the course of obtaining that information."

Justice Brennan stressed that, under Near and its progeny, exceptions to the ban on prior restraints were confined to "exceptional cases." He insisted that the narrow national security exception recognized in dicta in Near and Pentagon Papers did not mean, as the highest state court had assumed in this case, "that prior restraints can be justified on an ad hoc balancing approach that concludes that the 'presumption' must be overcome in light of some perceived 'justification.'" Rather, "prior restraints even within a recognized exception to the rule against prior restraints will be extremely difficult to justify; but as an initial matter, the purpose for which a prior restraint is sought to be imposed 'must fit within one of the narrowly defined exceptions to the prohibition against prior restraints.'" And there was no justification here for creating "a new, potentially pervasive exception [for fair trial purposes] to this settled rule of virtually blanket prohibition of prior restraints." He added that "speculative deprivation of an accused's Sixth Amendment right to an impartial jury [is not] comparable to the damage to the Nation or its people that Near and [Pentagon Papers] would have found sufficient to justify a prior restraint on reporting."

In another separate opinion concurring in the judgment, Justice STEVENS stated that he subscribed to "most" of Justice Brennan's opinion, but pointed out some problems he was not yet ready to resolve: "Whether the same absolute protection would apply no matter how shabby or illegal the means by which the information is obtained, no matter how serious an intrusion on privacy might be involved, no matter how demonstrably false the information might be, no matter how prejudicial it might be to the interests of innocent persons, and no matter how perverse the motivation for publishing it, is a question I would not answer without further argument."

Does the Court's special hostility to prior restraint in Nebraska Press underestimate the damage that might be done by other methods of restricting pretrial reporting? Does that emphasis implicitly open the door to other sanctions that may threaten free speech and press to a similar degree, such as subsequent punishment of reporters and orders excluding the press and public from hearings?

CHAPTER 3

BEYOND SPEAKING— COMPELLED SPEECH, ASSOCIATION, MONEY AND THE MEDIA

The Supreme Court has interpreted the right of free speech to entail several associated rights: the right *not* to speak, the right to associate with others for expressive purposes (and *not* to associate), and the right to facilitate speech through the expenditure of money in connection with political campaigns. None of these rights is separately enumerated in the First Amendment, except to the extent that the right of association derives in part from "the right of the people peaceably to assemble, and to petition the Government for a redress of grievances." The right to "freedom of the press," in contrast, is separately enumerated.

These rights are examined in this chapter in turn. Section 1 examines claims that the government may not force one to speak or to serve as a mouthpiece or platform for the speech of others. Section 2 considers what regulations restricting group activities or compelling disclosure about them might violate the First Amendment right of association, or the right against compelled association. Section 3 deals with efforts to regulate the use of money in political campaigns. The "speech" involved here is manifested in funds directed to the support of candidates and causes. Section 4 surveys a series of problems involving the institutional media, considers whether the media are entitled to special protection because "the press" is separately mentioned in the text of the First Amendment, and examines the Court's different treatment of the print and broadcasting media as well as its treatment of cable and the Internet.

SECTION 1. COMPELLED SPEECH: THE RIGHT *NOT* TO SPEAK

Does the right to speak free of government interference entail a right to be free of government compulsion to speak? May government use citizens as mouthpieces for official orthodoxy? May government compel citizens to serve as vehicles for favored expression even if the speech so favored does not express the government's point of view? Any particular point of view? May government compel citizens to provide access to their property for the speech of others? Does it matter whether that property ordinarily has an expressive function? Does it matter why government has sought to compel such access? Does it matter to whom bystanders are likely to attribute the content of the required speech? The following cases examine these questions.

COMPELLED INDIVIDUAL SPEECH

1. *Citizens as mouthpieces.* In several cases in the 1940s, members of Jehovah's Witnesses attacked public school regulations requiring students to salute the flag and recite the pledge of allegiance. The challengers claimed that their participation in the exercises amounted to the worship of "graven images" in a manner "forbidden by command of scripture," and thus that the state's requirements violated their rights to the free exercise of religion and to freedom of speech. In the first case, **Minersville School Dist. v. Gobitis**, 310 U.S. 586 (1940), the Court sustained the flag salute requirement by a vote of 8–1. Justice FRANKFURTER found no grounds for a free exercise exemption, then added in his opinion the Court: "[Nor] does the freedom of speech assured by Due Process move in a more absolute circle of immunity than that enjoyed by religious freedom. Even if it were assumed that freedom of speech goes beyond the historic concept of full opportunity to utter and to disseminate views, however heretical or offensive to dominant opinion, and includes freedom from conveying what may be deemed an implied but rejected affirmation, the question remains whether school children [must] be excused from conduct required of all the other children in the promotion of national cohesion. We are dealing with an interest inferior to none in the hierarchy of legal values. National unity is the basis of national security. To deny the legislature the right to select appropriate means for its attainment presents a totally different order of problem from that of the propriety of subordinating the possible ugliness of littered streets to the free expression of opinion through distribution of handbills. [The] case before us must be viewed as though the legislature of Pennsylvania had itself formally directed the flag-salute for the children of Minersville; had made no exemption for children whose parents were possessed of conscientious scruples like those of the Gobitis family; and had indicated its belief in the desirable ends to be secured by having its public school children share a common experience at those periods of development when their minds are supposedly receptive to its assimilation. The precise issue, then, for us to decide is whether the legislatures of the various states and the authorities in a thousand counties and school districts of this country are barred from determining the appropriateness of various means to evoke that unifying sentiment without which there can ultimately be no liberties, civil or religious. To stigmatize legislative judgment in providing for this universal gesture of respect for the symbol of our national life in the setting of the common school as a lawless inroad on that freedom of conscience which the Constitution protects, would amount to no less than the pronouncement of pedagogical and psychological dogma in a field where courts possess no marked and certainly no controlling competence. For ourselves, we might be tempted to say that the deepest patriotism is best engendered by giving unfettered scope to the most crotchety beliefs. But the courtroom is not the arena for debating issues of educational policy. So to hold would in effect make us the school board for the country. That authority has not been given to this Court, nor should we assume it. Except where the transgression of constitutional liberty is too plain for argument, personal freedom is best maintained—so long as the remedial channels of the democratic process remain open and unobstructed—when it is ingrained in a people's habits and not enforced against popular policy by the coercion of adjudicated law. A society which is dedicated to the preservation of these ultimate values of civilization may in self-protection utilize the educational process for inculcating those almost unconscious feelings which bind men together in a comprehending loyalty,

whatever may be their lesser differences and difficulties. That is to say, the process may be utilized so long as men's right to believe as they please, to win others to their way of belief, and their right to assemble in their chosen places of worship for the devotional ceremonies of their faith, are all fully respected. Judicial review, itself a limitation on popular government, is a fundamental part of our constitutional scheme. But to the legislature no less than to courts is committed the guardianship of deeply-cherished liberties."

In his solo dissent, Justice STONE wrote: "The law which is thus sustained is unique in the history of Anglo-American legislation. It does more than suppress freedom of speech and more than prohibit the free exercise of religion, which concededly are forbidden by the First Amendment and are violations of the liberty guaranteed by the Fourteenth. For by this law the state seeks to coerce these children to express a sentiment which, as they interpret it, they do not entertain, and which violates their deepest religious convictions. The guaranties of civil liberty are but guaranties of freedom of the human mind and spirit and of reasonable freedom and opportunity to express them. They presuppose the right of the individual to hold such opinions as he will and to give them reasonably free expression, and his freedom, and that of the state as well, to teach and persuade others by the communication of ideas. The very essence of the liberty which they guaranty is the freedom of the individual from compulsion as to what he shall think and what he shall say, at least where the compulsion is to bear false witness to his religion. If these guaranties are to have any meaning they must, I think, be deemed to withhold from the state any authority to compel belief or the expression of it where that expression violates religious convictions, whatever may be the legislative view of the desirability of such compulsion. We have previously pointed to the importance of a searching judicial inquiry into the legislative judgment in situations where prejudice against discrete and insular minorities may tend to curtail the operation of those political processes ordinarily to be relied on to protect minorities. See United States v. Carolene Products Co., 304 U.S. 144, 152, note 4."

In the aftermath of the Court's holding in Gobitis, Jehovah's Witnesses were targeted for a wave of abuse throughout the country. The ruling "was handed down June 3, 1940, as routed French and British troops [fighting in World War II] were desperately being evacuated from Dunkirk. Many Americans regarded the Witnesses' refusal to recite the pledge as evidence of disloyalty and of their sympathy and even collaboration with the Nazi regime. [For example, in] Richmond, West Virginia, a group of American Legion vigilantes, led by a sheriff's deputy, forced several witnesses to drink large quantities of castor oil, roped them together, then paraded them through the town. Over five hundred taunting citizens followed the procession, which at one point was halted for an impromptu flag salute ceremony . . . the [Jehovah's] Witnesses were [then] marched to the edge of town, where they found their automobiles painted with swastikas and graffiti accusing them of being 'Hitler's spies' and a 'Fifth Column.' Hundreds of other similar events occurred throughout the country. One Deep-South sheriff explained his refusal to intervene when a mob began throwing pieces of wood and rubble at a procession of Jehovah's Witnesses by remarking of the Witnesses that "[t]hey're traitors—the Supreme Court says so. Ain't you heard?" Blasi & Shiffrin, The Story of W. Virginia State Bd. of Educ. v. Barnette 109–11 *in* First Amendment Stories (Garnett & Koppelman eds., 2012).

It was in the backdrop of this religiously motivated violence that the Court would revisit the pledge of allegiance issue in **West Virginia State Bd. of Educ. v. Barnette**, 319 U.S. 624 (1943). Justice JACKSON, who had not been on the Court that decided Gobitis, wrote for the Court in Barnette. Analyzing the issue in terms of free speech rather than free exercise, he held that the state was precluded from making the flag salute and pledge compulsory: "[T]he compulsory flag salute and pledge requires affirmation of a belief and an attitude of mind. It is not clear whether the regulation contemplates that pupils forego any contrary convictions of their own and become unwilling converts to the prescribed ceremony or whether it will be acceptable if they simulate assent by words without belief and by a gesture barren of meaning. [Either way,] the power of compulsion is invoked without any allegation that remaining passive during a flag salute ritual creates a clear and present danger that would justify an effort even to muffle expression. To sustain the compulsory flag salute we are required to say that a Bill of Rights which guards the individual's right to speak his own mind, left it open to public authorities to compel him to utter what is not in his mind."

Having found that the compulsory flag salute implicated freedom of speech, Justice Jackson rejected the argument, relied upon in Gobitis, that the matter should be left to the legislature: "The very purpose of the Bill of Rights was to withdraw certain subjects from the vicissitudes of political controversy, to place them beyond the reach of majorities and officials and to establish them as legal principles to be applied by the courts. One's right to life, liberty, and property, to free speech, a free press, freedom of worship and assembly, and other fundamental rights may not be submitted to vote; they depend on the outcome of no elections. [First Amendment rights] are susceptible of restriction only to prevent grave and immediate danger to interests which the State may lawfully protect."

Finally, he rejected the adequacy of the state's justification that the flag salute promoted national unity: "National unity as an end which officials may foster by persuasion and example is not in question. The problem is whether under our Constitution compulsion as here employed is a permissible means for its achievement. Struggles to coerce uniformity of sentiment in support of some end thought essential to their time and country have been waged by many good as well as by evil men. [Ultimate] futility of such attempts to compel coherence is the lesson of every such effort from the Roman drive to stamp out Christianity as a disturber of its pagan unity, the Inquisition, as a means to religious and dynastic unity, the Siberian exiles as a means to Russian unity, down to the fast failing efforts of our present totalitarian enemies. Those who begin coercive elimination of dissent soon find themselves exterminating dissenters. Compulsory unification of opinion achieves only the unanimity of the graveyard. It seems trite but necessary to say that the First Amendment to our Constitution was designed to avoid these ends by avoiding these beginnings."

He concluded: "[W]e apply the limitations of the Constitution with no fear that freedom to be intellectually and spiritually diverse or even contrary will disintegrate the social organization. To believe that patriotism will not flourish if patriotic ceremonies are voluntary and spontaneous instead of a compulsory routine is to make an unflattering estimate of the appeal of our institutions to free minds. We can have intellectual individualism and the rich cultural diversities that we owe to exceptional minds only at the price of occasional eccentricity and abnormal attitudes. When they are so harmless to others or to the State as those we deal with here, the price is not too great. But freedom to differ is not limited to things that do not matter much. That would be a mere shadow of freedom. The test of its substance is the right to differ as to things that touch the heart of the existing order. If there is any fixed star in our constitutional constellation, it is that no official, high or petty, can prescribe what shall be orthodox in politics, nationalism, religion, or other matters of opinion or force citizens to confess by word or act their faith therein."

Justice BLACK, joined by Justice Douglas, submitted a "statement of reasons for our change of view" since Gobitis. Despite the private urgings of Justice Murphy that he avoid bringing personal matters into his opinion, Justice FRANKFURTER wrote a lengthy dissent, which began: "One who belongs to the most vilified and persecuted minority in history is not likely to be insensible to the freedoms guaranteed by our Constitution. Were my purely personal attitude relevant I should whole-heartedly associate myself with the general libertarian views in the Court's opinion, representing as they do the thought and action of a lifetime. But as judges we are neither Jew nor Gentile, neither Catholic nor agnostic. We owe equal attachment to the Constitution and are equally bound by our judicial obligations whether we derive our citizenship from the earliest or the latest immigrants to these shores. As a member of this Court I am not justified in writing my private notions of policy into the Constitution, no matter how deeply I may cherish them or how mischievous I may deem their disregard. [I]t can never be emphasized too much that one's own opinion about the wisdom or evil of a law should be excluded altogether when one is doing one's duty on the bench. [Of course] patriotism cannot be enforced by the flag salute. But neither can the liberal spirit be enforced by judicial invalidation of illiberal legislation." Justices Roberts and Reed joined Justice Frankfurter in adhering to Gobitis.

Gobitis and Barnette were factually identical cases. Why then did the Court treat Gobitis primarily as a free exercise of religion case, and Barnette primarily as a freedom of speech case? Is there any political or doctrinal significance in the decision to use one framework rather than the other?

2.   *Citizens as mobile billboards.* The Court relied heavily on Barnette in **Wooley v. Maynard**, 430 U.S. 705 (1977). The case involved a New Hampshire law requiring most automobiles to bear license plates carrying the state motto, "Live Free or Die." Challengers were a married couple, members of Jehovah's Witnesses, who found the motto repugnant to their moral, religious and political beliefs and who covered up the motto on their license plate, a misdemeanor. Chief Justice BURGER's majority opinion stated: "Here, as in Barnette, we are faced with a state measure which forces an individual as part of his daily life—indeed constantly while his automobile is in public view—to be an instrument for fostering public adherence to an ideological point of view he finds unacceptable. In doing so, the State 'invades the sphere of intellect and spirit which it is the purpose of the First Amendment [to] reserve from all official control.' [Barnette.] New Hampshire's statute in effect requires that appellees use their private property as a 'mobile billboard' for the State's ideological message—or suffer a penalty," and this burden was not justified by any sufficiently weighty state interest. Chief Justice Burger emphasized that First Amendment freedom of thought "includes both the right to speak freely and the right to refrain from

speaking at all"; both rights are "complementary components of a broader concept of 'individual freedom of mind.' "

Was the Court correct to analogize the license plate in Wooley to the flag salute in Barnette? Was there a comparable degree of government ventriloquy involved? To whom would passing motorists likely attribute the license plate motto: Maynard or New Hampshire? What is the remedy here: allowing Maynard to cover up the motto? To request a mottoless license plate? Do such remedies themselves involve compelled speech? Consider the following view: "By holding that individuals have a right to refuse this state slogan on their plates while letting the state keep distributing plates bearing the slogan, the Court was forcing those who are most offended by the slogan to come out of the closet. No longer able to just blend in as law abiding citizens whose views nobody could guess from their license plates, now those keeping the 'Live Free or Die' slogan would be marked as having no objection to the sentiment it expressed, while those replacing it would be marked as having affirmatively rejected the slogan." Tribe, "Disentangling Symmetries: Speech, Association, Parenthood," 28 Pepp. L. Rev. 641, 643–44 (2001).

3. *Compelled disclosure of speaker identity.* In **Talley v. California**, 362 U.S. 60 (1960), the Court, by a vote of 6–3, invalidated a Los Angeles ordinance that prohibited the distribution of any handbill in the city unless it had printed on it the name and address of the person who prepared, distributed, or sponsored it. The ordinance was challenged by distributors of unsigned handbills urging readers to boycott certain Los Angeles merchants who were allegedly engaging in racially discriminatory employment practices. Holding the ordinance "void on its face," the Court noted that the identification requirement would tend to restrict freedom of expression. Writing for the Court, Justice Black noted that "persecuted groups and sects from time to time throughout history have been able to criticize oppressive practices and laws either anonymously or not at all." The Court rejected the argument that the law was a justifiable "way to identify those responsible for fraud, false advertising and libel," stating that "the ordinance is in no manner so limited."

In **McIntyre v. Ohio Elections Commission**, 514 U.S. 334 (1995), the Court, by a vote of 7–2, invalidated an Ohio election law that, like the law of virtually every state, prohibited the circulation of anonymous leaflets in connection with political campaigns. The law provided: "No person shall write, print, post, or distribute [any] general publication [designed] to promote the nomination or election or defeat of a candidate, or to promote the adoption or defeat of any issue [unless] there appears on such [publication] in a conspicuous place [the] name and residence or business address of [the] person who issues [it]." Margaret McIntyre was fined $100 by the Commission for circulating leaflets opposing a school tax referendum that were either unsigned or signed only "Concerned Parents and Taxpayers."

Justice STEVENS, writing for the Court, reaffirmed Talley and held that "an author's decision to remain anonymous, like other decisions concerning omissions or additions to the content of a publication, is an aspect of the freedom of speech protected by the First Amendment." He noted that "[g]reat works of literature have frequently been produced by authors writing under assumed names," including those written under such pseudonyms as Mark Twain, O. Henry, Voltaire, George Sand, and George Eliot. He noted further that "the Court's reasoning [in Talley] embraced a respected tradition of anonymity in the advocacy of political causes," including the Federalist Papers, written under the pseudonym "Publius," and the papers of the Anti-Federalists, written under such pseudonyms as "Cato," "Brutus," and "the Federal Farmer."

Justice Stevens held the Ohio anonymity requirement invalid even though it was narrower than the blanket ban on anonymous handbilling struck down in Talley. First, he held strict scrutiny to be the appropriate standard: "When a law burdens core political speech, we apply 'exacting scrutiny,' and we uphold the restriction only if it is narrowly tailored to serve an overriding state interest." Next, he found Ohio's proffered interests in increasing voter information and preventing fraud insufficient to satisfy such scrutiny: "[Ohio's] interest in providing voters with additional relevant information does not justify a state requirement that a writer make statements or disclosures she would otherwise omit." And while the state had an undoubtedly legitimate interest in preventing the dissemination of false factual statements in election campaigns, he wrote, "we are not persuaded that they justify [the anonymity ban's] extremely broad prohibition," which "encompasses documents that are not even arguably false or misleading." He suggested that Ohio's direct regulation of falsity in other detailed provisions of its election code was a less restrictive alternative. Finally, he distinguished mandatory disclosure of contributions to political candidates, which the Court had upheld, as "a far cry from compelled self-identification on all election-related writings. A written election-related document—particularly a leaflet—is often a personally crafted statement of a political viewpoint [and] identification of the author against her will is particularly intrusive [because] it reveals unmistakably the content of her thoughts on a controversial issue."

Justice Stevens concluded: "Under our Constitution, anonymous pamphleteering is not a pernicious, fraudulent practice, but an honorable tradition of advocacy and of dissent. Anonymity is a shield from the tyranny of the majority. [Mill, On Liberty.] It thus exemplifies the purpose behind [the] First Amendment: [to] protect unpopular individuals from retaliation—and their ideas from suppression—at the hand of an intolerant society." Justice GINSBURG concurred separately, emphasizing that, in another setting, "a State's interest in protecting an election process 'might justify a more limited identification requirement.' "

Justice THOMAS concurred in the judgment, but argued that the interpretation of the Free Speech and Press Clauses should be determined by reference to "their original meaning," not by the broader principles employed by the majority. Under such an originalist approach, he found McIntyre's leaflets protected by the First Amendment: "There is little doubt that the Framers engaged in anonymous political writing. The essays in the Federalist Papers, published under the pseudonym of 'Publius,' are only the most famous example of the outpouring of anonymous political writing that occurred during the ratification of the Constitution. Of course, the simple fact that the Framers engaged in certain conduct does not necessarily prove that they forbade its prohibition by the government. In this case, however, the historical evidence indicates that Founding-era Americans opposed attempts to require that anonymous authors reveal their identities on the ground that forced disclosure violated the 'freedom of the press.' For example, the earliest and most famous American experience with freedom of the press, the 1735 Zenger trial, [involved] a printer, John Peter Zenger, who refused to reveal the anonymous authors of published attacks on the Crown governor of New York. When the governor and his council could not discover the identity of the authors, they prosecuted Zenger himself for seditious libel. Although the case set the colonies afire for its example of a jury refusing to convict a defendant of seditious libel against Crown authorities, it also signified at an early moment the extent to which anonymity and the freedom of the press were intertwined in the early American mind." He cited as another example the successful Anti-Federalist attack on Federalist editors' policy of refusing to publish anonymous works, which in his view indicated that "both Anti-Federalists and Federalists believed that the freedom of the press included the right to publish without revealing the author's name." He concluded: "While [I] am loath to overturn a century of practice shared by almost all of the States, I believe the historical evidence from the framing outweighs recent tradition."

Justice SCALIA dissented, arguing that, to the contrary, the nearly uniform tradition among the states over the last century trumped the ambiguous textual and historical claims for anonymous leafletting. He objected that the majority had invalidated "a species of protection for the election process that exists, in a variety of forms, in every State except California, and that has a pedigree dating back to the end of the 19th century. Preferring the views of the English utilitarian philosopher John Stuart Mill to the considered judgment of the American people's elected representatives from coast to coast, the Court discovers a hitherto unknown right-to-be-unknown while engaging in electoral politics." He disagreed with Justice Thomas about the inference to be drawn from the history of anonymous pamphleteering: "to prove that anonymous electioneering was used frequently is not to establish that it is a constitutional right." He would have deferred therefore, to the states' longstanding tradition disfavoring anonymity in connection with elections: "Where the meaning of a constitutional text (such as 'the freedom of speech') is unclear, the widespread and long-accepted practices of the American people are the best indication of what fundamental beliefs it was intended to enshrine." Justice Scalia also viewed anonymity more skeptically than the majority, noting that it might well "facilitate[ ] wrong by eliminating accountability." He would have recognized an "exemption from otherwise valid disclosure requirements," if at all, only "on the part of someone who could show a 'reasonable probability' that the compelled disclosure would result in 'threats, harassment, or reprisals from either Government officials or private parties.' "

If the First Amendment as interpreted in McIntyre v. Ohio Elections Commission protects the right to leaflet anonymously, may one who signs a petition to place a referendum on the ballot also claim a right to anonymity? In **Doe v. Reed**, 561 U.S. 186 (2010), the Supreme Court rebuffed such a claim, upholding against First Amendment challenge a requirement of Washington's Public Records Act (PRA) that the names and addresses of those who sign referendum ballot petitions be publicly disclosed. The challenge was brought by supporters of a petition challenging a state law extending certain benefits to same-sex couples.

Writing for an 8–1 majority joined by all but Justice Thomas, Chief Justice ROBERTS explained: "The compelled disclosure of signatory information on referendum petitions is subject to review under the First Amendment. An individual expresses a view on a political matter when he signs a petition under Washington's referendum procedure. In most cases, the individual's signature will express the view that the law subject to the petition should be overturned. [But] that is not to say that the electoral context is irrelevant to the nature of our First Amendment review. [First] Amendment challenges to disclosure requirements in the electoral context [are subject to] 'exacting scrutiny,' which 'requires a "substantial relation" between the disclosure requirement and a "sufficiently important" governmental interest.' " Under that standard, the Chief Justice found disclosure of petition information substantially related to an important interest in "preserving the integrity of the electoral process by combating fraud, detecting invalid signatures, and fostering government transparency and accountability." He accordingly did not reach or resolve the question whether the State had a constitutionally sufficient interest in "providing information to the electorate about who supports the petition."

As the Chief Justice noted, the challengers objected that, "once on the Internet, the petition signers' names and addresses 'can be combined with publicly available phone numbers and maps,' in what will effectively become a blueprint for harassment and intimidation. To support their claim that they will be subject to reprisals, plaintiffs cite examples from the history of a similar proposition in California [i.e., Proposition 8, overturning a decision of the California Supreme Court upholding a constitutional right to gay marriage]." But stating that "typical referendum petitions 'concern tax policy, revenue, budget, or other state law issues,' " he found "no reason to assume that any burdens imposed by disclosure of typical referendum petitions would be remotely like the burdens plaintiffs fear in this case." He concluded: "[W]e must reject plaintiffs' broad challenge to the PRA. In doing so, we note [that] upholding the law against a broad-based challenge does not foreclose a litigant's success in a narrower one" if disclosure could be shown to pose a specific danger of threats, reprisal or harassment.

Justice ALITO concurred, emphasizing the need for potential petition signators to be able to obtain such as-applied exemptions "quickly and well in advance of speaking" and "without clearing a high evidentiary hurdle." He suggested that the petitioners in this case would have a strong argument for an as-applied exemption on remand, given evidence of "widespread harassment and intimidation suffered by supporters of California's Proposition 8." He suggested that any "informational" interest in disclosure attenuates upon proof of risk of harassment, and expressed skepticism about the need for disclosure to prevent electoral fraud, noting that California, which "has had more initiatives on the ballot than any other State save Oregon, [explicitly] protects the privacy of initiative and referendum signatories."

Justice SOTOMAYOR, joined by Justices Stevens and Ginsburg, filed a concurrence emphasizing that the State has strong interests in the integrity of the ballot process and that "the burden of public disclosure on speech and associational rights [is] minimal in this context [as] the process of legislating by referendum is inherently public." She suggested that "any party attempting to challenge particular applications of the State's regulations will bear a heavy burden," and that as-applied exceptions should be available only "when a State selectively applies a facially neutral petition disclosure rule in a manner that discriminates based on the content of referenda or the viewpoint of petition signers, or in the rare circumstance in which disclosure poses a reasonable probability of serious and widespread harassment that the State is unwilling or unable to control."

Justice STEVENS, joined by Justice Breyer, concurred in part and in the judgment, stating that this was "not a hard case" and emphasizing that, unlike in McIntyre, the PRA does not "require that any person signing a petition disclose or say anything." Like Justice Sotomayor, he suggested that as-applied challenges to petition disclosure requirements should be sparingly granted: "For an as-applied challenge to a law such as the PRA to succeed, there would have to be a significant threat of harassment directed at those who sign the petition that cannot be mitigated by law enforcement measures. [Debates] about tax policy and regulation of private property can become just as heated as debates about domestic partnerships. And as a general matter, it is very difficult to show that by later disclosing the names of petition signatories, individuals will be less willing to sign petitions. [I] would demand strong evidence before concluding that an indirect and speculative chain of events imposes a substantial burden on speech."

Justice SCALIA concurred only in the judgment, expressing "doubt whether signing a petition that has the effect of suspending a law fits within 'the freedom of speech' at all" and arguing that "[w]e should not repeat and extend the mistake of McIntyre v. Ohio Elections Comm'n." He would forego "judicial interest-balancing" in this context and hold that "[o]ur Nation's longstanding traditions of legislating and voting in public refute the claim that the First Amendment accords a right to anonymity in the performance of an act with governmental effect." He continued: "When a Washington voter signs a referendum petition subject to the PRA, he is acting as a legislator. [The] exercise of lawmaking power in the United States has traditionally been public. [Voting] was public until 1888 when the States began to adopt the Australian secret ballot. [The] long history of public legislating and voting contradicts plaintiffs' claim that disclosure of petition signatures having legislative effect violates the First Amendment." As to the petitioners' claimed fears of harassment, Justice Scalia replied: "There are laws against threats and intimidation; and harsh criticism, short of unlawful action, is a price our people have traditionally been willing to pay for self-governance. Requiring people to stand up in public for their political acts fosters civic courage, without which democracy is doomed."

Justice THOMAS filed the lone dissent. He would have found the PRA's compelled disclosure requirement unconstitutional because it "severely burdens [and] chills citizen participation in the referendum process" and "there will always be a less restrictive means by which Washington can vindicate its stated interest in preserving the integrity of its referendum process." He explained: "[U]nlike the Court, I read our precedents to require application of strict scrutiny to laws that compel disclosure of protected First Amendment association," meaning that "a disclosure requirement passes constitutional muster only if it is [the] least restrictive means to serve a compelling state interest." Even if the State has a compelling interest in electoral integrity, he argued, it does not need to use the "blunderbuss" approach of public disclosure of referendum signers' names and addresses: it "could put the names and addresses of referendum signers into [an] electronic database that state employees could search without subjecting the name and address of each signer to wholesale public disclosure," "could create a Web site, linked to the electronic referendum database, where a voter concerned that his name had been fraudulently signed could conduct a search using his unique identifier to ensure that his name was absent from the database," or could otherwise enforce existing laws against fraud. And, citing McIntyre, he found constitutionally insufficient any state " 'interest in providing the electorate with relevant information.' " Finding as-applied challenges too time-consuming and cumbersome to protect the speech interests at stake, he would have invalidated the PRA's disclosure requirement on its face.

4. ***Compelled disclosure by providers of professional services.*** The cases above related to the compelled disclosure of citizens in their capacity as general members of the population. Should the analysis of compelled disclosure requirements change when the requirements regulate the speech of professionals? If so, how possible is it to draw a principled scope for who counts as a professional? If not, are all disclosure requirements, even those that relate to professional conduct or food and product safety subject to strict First Amendment scrutiny? Consider these questions in the context of case below.

National Institute of Family and Life Advocates v. Becerra

585 U.S. ___, 138 S. Ct. 2361, 201 L. Ed. 2d 835 (2018).

[The California Reproductive Freedom, Accountability, Comprehensive Care, and Transparency Act (FACT Act) required licensed clinics that primarily serve pregnant women to notify patients that California provides free or low-cost services, including abortions, and to give them a phone number to call. The law also required unlicensed clinics to notify patients that California had not licensed the clinics to provide medical services. Both parts of the law—the licensed and unlicensed notices—were challenged by "crisis pregnancy centers" that aimed to discourage pregnant women from obtaining abortions.]

■ JUSTICE THOMAS delivered the opinion of the Court.

[The] licensed notice is a content-based regulation of speech. By compelling individuals to speak a particular message, such notices alter the content of their speech. Here, for example, licensed clinics must provide a government-drafted script about the availability of state-sponsored services, as well as contact information for how to obtain them. One of those services is abortion—the very practice that petitioners are devoted to opposing.

[Our] precedents have applied more deferential review to some laws that require professionals to disclose factual, noncontroversial information in their "commercial speech." See, e.g., Zauderer v. Office of Disciplinary Counsel of Supreme Court of Ohio [1985; p. 213]. [And under] our precedents, States may regulate professional conduct, even though that conduct incidentally involves speech. Planned Parenthood of Southeastern Pennsylvania v. Casey [1992]. But neither line of precedents is implicated here. [The] licensed notice at issue here is not an informed-consent requirement or any other regulation of professional conduct. The notice does not facilitate informed consent to a medical procedure. [The] licensed notice regulates speech as speech. Outside of the two contexts discussed above, [this] Court's precedents have long protected the First Amendment rights of professionals. [As] with other kinds of speech, regulating the content of professionals' speech "poses the inherent risk that the Government seeks not to advance a legitimate regulatory goal, but to suppress unpopular ideas or information." ["Professional speech"] is also a difficult category to define with precision. As defined by the courts of appeals, the professional-speech doctrine would cover a wide array of individuals—doctors, lawyers, nurses, physical therapists, truck drivers, bartenders, barbers, and many others. [But] that gives the States unfettered power to reduce a group's First Amendment rights by simply imposing a licensing requirement.

[California has not] identified a persuasive reason for treating professional speech as a unique category that is exempt from ordinary First Amendment principles. We do not foreclose the possibility that some such reason exists. We need not do so because the licensed notice cannot survive even intermediate scrutiny. California asserts a single interest to justify the licensed notice: providing low-income women with information about state-sponsored services. Assuming that this is a substantial state interest, the licensed notice is not sufficiently drawn to achieve it.

If California's goal is to educate low-income women about the services it provides, then the licensed notice is wildly underinclusive. The notice applies only to clinics that have a "primary purpose" of "providing family planning or pregnancy-related services" and that provide two of six categories of specific services. [Such] underinclusiveness raises serious doubts about whether the government is in fact pursuing the interest it invokes, rather than disfavoring a particular speaker or viewpoint. The FACT Act also excludes, without explanation, federal clinics and Family PACT providers from the licensed-notice requirement. [Further,] California could inform low-income women about its services [with] a public-information campaign.

[The] FACT Act unduly burdens protected speech. The unlicensed notice imposes a government-scripted, speaker-based disclosure requirement that is wholly disconnected from California's informational interest. [The] application of the unlicensed notice to advertisements demonstrates just how burdensome it is. [As] California conceded at oral argument, a billboard for an unlicensed facility that says "Choose Life" would have to surround that two-word statement with a 29-word statement from the government, in as many as 13 different languages. In this way, the unlicensed notice drowns out the facility's own message.

[We] express no view on the legality of a similar disclosure requirement that is better supported or less burdensome.

■ JUSTICE KENNEDY, with whom the CHIEF JUSTICE, JUSTICE ALITO, and JUSTICE GORSUCH join, concurring.

[This] separate writing seeks to underscore that the apparent viewpoint discrimination here is a matter of serious constitutional concern. [This] law is a paradigmatic example of the serious threat presented when government seeks to impose its own message in the place of individual speech, thought, and expression. For here the State requires primarily pro-life pregnancy centers to promote the State's own preferred message advertising abortions. This compels individuals to contradict their most deeply held beliefs, beliefs grounded in basic philosophical, ethical, or religious precepts, or all of these. And the history of the Act's passage and its underinclusive application suggest a real possibility that these individuals were targeted because of their beliefs.

■ JUSTICE BREYER, with whom JUSTICE GINSBURG, JUSTICE SOTOMAYOR, and JUSTICE KAGAN join, dissenting.

[The] majority says it applies [heightened] scrutiny to the Act because the Act, in its view, is content based. [This] constitutional approach threatens to create serious problems. Because much, perhaps most, human behavior takes place through speech and because much, perhaps most, law regulates that speech in terms of its content, the majority's approach at the least threatens considerable litigation over the constitutional validity of much, perhaps most, government regulation. Virtually every disclosure law could be considered "content based," for virtually every disclosure law requires individuals "to speak a particular message." Thus, the majority's view, if taken literally, could radically change prior law, perhaps placing much securities law or consumer protection law at constitutional risk, depending on how broadly its exceptions are interpreted.

[The] majority, [perhaps] recognizing this problem, [says] that it does not "question the legality of health and safety warnings long considered permissible, or purely factual and uncontroversial disclosures about commercial products." But this generally phrased disclaimer would seem more likely to invite litigation than to provide needed limitation and clarification. The majority, for example, does not explain why the Act here, which is justified in part by health and safety considerations, does not fall within its "health" category.

[Precedent] does not require a test such as the majority's. [Historically,] the Court has been wary of claims that regulation of business activity, particularly health-related activity, violates the Constitution. Ever since this Court departed from the approach it set forth in Lochner v. New York [1905], ordinary economic and social legislation has been thought to raise little constitutional concern. [The] Court has taken this same respectful approach to economic and social legislation when a First Amendment claim like the claim present here is at issue. Even during the Lochner era, when this Court struck down numerous economic regulations concerning industry, this Court was careful to defer to state legislative judgments concerning the medical profession. [In] the name of the First Amendment, the majority today treads into territory where the pre-New Deal, as well as the post-New Deal, Court refused to go.

In Casey [1992], the Court [considered] a state law that required doctors to provide information to a woman deciding whether to proceed with an abortion. [The Court held that] the statute was constitutional. The joint opinion stated that the statutory requirements amounted to "reasonable measures to ensure an informed choice, one which might cause the woman to choose childbirth over abortion." [The] joint opinion specifically [concluded] that the statute did not violate the First Amendment. [If] a State can lawfully require a doctor to tell a woman seeking an abortion about adoption services, why should it not be able, as here, to require a medical counselor to tell a woman seeking prenatal care or other reproductive healthcare about childbirth and abortion services? As the question suggests, there is no convincing reason to distinguish between information about adoption and information about abortion in this context.

[With respect to the unlicensed clinics, there] is no basis for finding the State's interest "hypothetical." The legislature heard that information-related delays in qualified healthcare negatively affect women seeking to terminate their pregnancies as well as women carrying their pregnancies to term, with delays in qualified prenatal care causing life-long health problems for infants. [The] majority suggests that the Act is suspect because it covers some speakers but not others. [There] is no cause for such concern here. The Act does not, on its face, distinguish between facilities that favor pro-life and those that favor pro-choice points of view. Nor is there any convincing evidence before us or in the courts below that discrimination was the purpose or the effect of the statute. [Finally,] the majority concludes that the Act is overly burdensome. [But] these and similar claims are claims that the statute could be applied unconstitutionally, not that it is unconstitutional on its face.

————

STATE COMPELLED ACCESS TO PRIVATE FORUMS

1. *Compelled rights of reply.* May government compel the press to furnish free coverage of replies by those it has attacked? Two decisions came to opposite answers for the electronic and print media. In **Red Lion Broadcasting Co. v. FCC**, 395 U.S. 367 (1969), discussed further at p. 634, the Court upheld against First Amendment challenge the FCC's "fairness doctrine," which required broadcast stations to provide free reply time for individuals subjected to personal attack on the air. The Court relied heavily on the scarcity of the broadcast spectrum as a justification for imposing forced access rights on unwilling media.

In contrast, in **Miami Herald Pub. Co. v. Tornillo**, 418 U.S. 241 (1974), the Court held unconstitutional Florida's "right of reply" law, which granted political candidates a right to equal space to reply to criticism and attacks on their record by a newspaper. The state court had sustained the law because it furthered the "broad societal interest in the free flow of information." Chief Justice BURGER's opinion concluded, however, that the law violated the First Amendment rights of the newspaper by forcing it to publish undesired speech: "[Government] compulsion to publish that which '[newspaper editors believe] should not be published' is unconstitutional. A responsible press is an undoubtedly desirable goal, but press responsibility is not mandated by the Constitution and like many other virtues it cannot be legislated." The fact that the newspaper was not being prevented from giving its own views did not help the defenders of the law: "The Florida statute exacts a penalty on the basis of the content of a newspaper. [Faced] with the penalties that would accrue to any newspaper that published news or commentary arguably within the reach of the right-of-access statute, editors might well conclude that the safe course is to avoid controversy. [Government]-enforced right of access inescapably 'dampens the vigor and limits the variety of public debate.'" And even if there were no such consequences to the law, it would nevertheless be invalid "because of its intrusion into the function of editors": "A newspaper is more than a passive receptacle or conduit for news, comment, and advertising. The choice of material to go into a newspaper, and the decisions made as to limitations on the size and content of the paper, and treatment of public issues and public officials—whether fair or unfair—constitute the exercise of editorial control and judgment."

2. *Compelled access by speakers to private property.* In **PruneYard Shopping Center v. Robins**, 447 U.S. 74 (1980), a shopping center, in accordance with its nondiscriminatory policy of barring all

expressive activity not directly related to its commercial purposes, had excluded several high school students who sought to solicit signatures for a petition protesting a UN resolution against Zionism. California's highest court interpreted its *state* constitution to guarantee such speakers access to a privately owned shopping center, even though the Supreme Court had rejected such an access right as a matter of federal First Amendment law. PruneYard argued that that interpretation violated its own federal free speech rights. The Court unanimously rejected that argument.

Justice REHNQUIST's opinion for the Court concluded that "state constitutional provisions which permit individuals to exercise free speech and petition rights on the property of a privately owned shopping center to which the public is invited" do not violate the shopping center owner's "First Amendment right not to be forced by the State to use his property as a forum for the speech of others." Although there might be circumstances in which a State could not require an individual "to participate in the dissemination of an ideological message by displaying it on his private property," this was not such a case. Since PruneYard was open to the public, the views expressed in passing out pamphlets or seeking signatures "will not likely be identified with those of the owner." Moreover, "no specific message is dictated by the State to be displayed," so that there was "no danger of governmental discrimination for or against a particular message." And PruneYard could "expressly disavow any connection with a message by simply posting signs in the area where the speakers or handbillers stand." The majority opinion thus found both Wooley and Barnette distinguishable.

Justice POWELL's partial concurrence, joined by Justice White, cautioned that the decision did not constitute "blanket approval for state efforts to transform privately owned commercial property into public forums." He explained that, "even when no particular message is mandated by the State, First Amendment interests are affected by state action that forces a property owner to admit third-party speakers." He noted that "customers might well conclude that the messages reflect the view of the proprietor." Moreover, there might be valid First Amendment objections when speakers sought use of the premises "as a platform for views that [the owner] finds morally repugnant": "To require the owner to specify the particular ideas he finds objectionable enough to compel a response would force him to relinquish his 'freedom to maintain his own beliefs without public disclosure.' Thus, the right to control one's own speech may be burdened impermissibly even when listeners will not assume that the messages expressed on private property are those of the owner." But he found that, "[o]n the record before us, I cannot say that customers of this vast center would be likely to assume that appellees' limited speech activity expressed the views of the PruneYard or of its owner," nor that the owner had any strong ideological disagreement with anything the students or other groups were likely to say. Justices White, Marshall and Blackmun also submitted separate concurrences.

Decided in 1980, PruneYard has gained renewed significance in the era of social media. In lawsuits filed in California state courts, white supremacist and right-wing Twitter users challenged the platform's ban on their accounts. At least one of these users, see **Johnson v. Twitter, Inc.**, No. 18CECG00078 (Cal. Super. Ct. June 6, 2018), argued that platforms like Twitter are analogous to the shopping center in PruneYard, such that the banning of his account violated California's state constitutional guarantee.

The superior court in California dismissed the suit as a SLAPP (strategic lawsuits against public participation), stating that Twitter has a "First Amendment right to exercise independent editorial control over the content on its platform."

Can Twitter, for the purposes of First Amendment analysis, be compared to the PruneYard shopping center? Do the nature of the two spaces differ? What about their missions or purposes? Perhaps more fundamentally, is the PruneYard doctrine still vital at all given the following cases that succeeded that 1980 decision?

3. *Compelled inclusion of third-party speech in private publications.* After PruneYard, the issue of compelled access again came before the Court in **Pacific Gas & Elec. Co. [PG & E] v. Public Util. Comm'n [PUC]**, 475 U.S. 1 (1986). In upholding a First Amendment claim against state-compelled access, the Court relied on Tornillo and distinguished PruneYard. The case involved a newsletter distributed by PG & E to its customers in the monthly billing envelope. The Commission found that the "extra space" in billing envelopes (i.e., the difference between the maximum weight mailable with a postage stamp and the weight of the monthly bill and any required legal notices) belonged to the ratepayers. The PUC held that PG & E had to allow a private advocacy group called Toward Utility Rate Normalization (TURN), which was typically opposed to PG & E in ratemaking proceedings and elsewhere, to use the extra space four times a year to communicate with PG & E customers. PG & E, a privately owned utility, claimed that requiring it "to include in its billing envelope speech of a third party with which the utility disagrees" violated its First Amendment rights.

The Court sustained this First Amendment claim. Justice POWELL's plurality opinion, joined only by Chief Justice Burger and Justices Brennan and O'Connor, relied heavily on Tornillo in overturning this state-imposed access: "Compelled access like that ordered in this case both penalizes the expression of particular points of view and forces speakers to alter their speech to conform with an agenda they do not set. These impermissible effects are not remedied by the Commission's definition of the relevant property rights. [The] concerns that caused us to invalidate the compelled access rule in Tornillo apply to appellant as well as to the institutional press. [Just] as the State is not free to 'tell a newspaper in advance what it can print and what it cannot,' [the] State is not free either to restrict appellant's speech to certain topics or views or to force appellant to respond to views that others may hold. [Under] Tornillo a forced access rule that would accomplish these purposes indirectly is similarly forbidden. [PruneYard] is not to the contrary. [Notably] absent [there] was any concern that access to this area might affect the shopping center owner's exercise of his own right to speak: the owner did not even allege that he objected to the content of the pamphlets; nor was the access right content-based. PruneYard thus does not undercut the proposition that forced associations that burden protected speech are impermissible."

Justice Powell emphasized that the Commission's order did not "simply award access to the public at large; rather, it discriminates on the basis of the viewpoints of the selected speakers." Among the acknowledged purposes of the access order was the aim "to assist groups [that] challenged [PG & E] in the Commission's ratemaking proceedings in raising funds. [Access] to the envelopes thus is not content-neutral. [Because] access is awarded only to those who disagree with [PG & E's] views and who are hostile to [its] interests, [PG & E] must contend with the fact that whenever it speaks out on a given issue, it may be forced [to] help disseminate hostile views. [PG & E] 'might well conclude' that, under these circumstances, 'the safe course is to avoid controversy,' thereby reducing the free flow of information and ideas that the First Amendment seeks to promote. Appellant does not [have] the right to be free from vigorous debate. But it *does* have the right to be free from government restrictions that abridge its own rights in order to 'enhance the relative voice' of its opponents. [In addition to constituting an impermissible content regulation by favoring some groups rather than others, the] Commission's access order also impermissibly requires appellant to associate with speech with which appellant may disagree. [For] corporations as for individuals, the choice to speak includes within it the choice of what not to say. [Were] the government freely able to compel corporate speakers to propound political messages with which they disagree, this protection [of corporate speech] would be empty, for the government could require speakers to affirm in one breath that which they deny in the next."

Justice MARSHALL concurred only in the judgment, emphasizing two distinctions between this case and PruneYard: PG & E had "issued no invitation to the general public to use its billing envelope for speech or for any other purpose," and the state here had deprived PG & E of control over "the space in [its billing] envelope that [it] would otherwise use for its own speech." Chief Justice Burger, while joining Justice Powell's opinion, submitted a separate concurrence as well.

Justice REHNQUIST, joined by Justices White and Stevens, dissented, emphasizing PG & E's status as a corporation and regulated public utility: "This Court has recognized that natural persons enjoy negative free speech rights because of their interest in self-expression; an individual's right not to speak or to associate with the speech of others is a component of the broader constitutional interest of natural persons in freedom of conscience. [Extension] of the individual freedom of conscience decisions to business corporations strains the rationale of those cases beyond the breaking point. To ascribe to such artificial entities an 'intellect' or 'mind' for freedom of conscience purposes is to confuse metaphor with reality." Even if such a right extended to the institutional media, he argued, it ought not extend to other businesses: "Corporations generally have not played the historic role of newspapers as conveyers of individual ideas and opinion." The dissenters also distinguished Tornillo on the ground that the likelihood of deterrence of speech by PG & E was minimal.

Justice STEVENS added in a separate dissent: "I assume that the plurality would not object to a utility commission rule dictating the format of the bill, even as to required warnings and the type size of various provisos and disclaimers [and] would permit the Commission to require the utility to disseminate legal notices of public hearings and ratemaking proceedings written by it. [Given] that the Commission can require the utility to make certain statements and to carry the Commission's own messages to its customers, it seems but a small step to acknowledge that the Commission can also require the utility to act as the conduit for a public interest group's message that bears a close relationship to the purpose of the billing envelope. An analog to this requirement appears in securities law: the Securities and Exchange Commission requires the incumbent board of directors to transmit proposals of dissident shareholders which it opposes. Presumably the plurality does not doubt the constitutionality of the SEC's requirement under the First Amendment." Justice Blackmun did not participate in the case.

In **Turner Broadcasting System, Inc. v. FCC**, 512 U.S. 622 (1994) (Turner I), the Court considered a claim that compelled access for broadcasters to cable television transmission violates the First Amendment. In Turner, the Court rejected cable operators' argument that sections 4 and 5 of the Cable Television Consumer Protection and Competition Act of 1992, which require cable operators to carry the signals of a specified number of local broadcast television stations, were subject to strict scrutiny under the Court's compelled-speech precedents. Congress enacted the "must-carry" provisions out of concern that "the physical characteristics of cable transmission, compounded by the increasing concentration of economic power in the cable industry, are endangering the ability of over-the-air broadcast television stations to compete for a viewing audience and thus for necessary operating revenues." Cable operators, relying upon Tornillo and PG & E, argued that the must-carry rules interfered with their editorial discretion and forced them to carry unwanted speech in violation of their First Amendment rights.

Justice KENNEDY, writing for the Court, began by acknowledging that "[a]t the heart of the First Amendment lies the principle that each person should decide for him or herself the ideas and beliefs deserving of expression, consideration, and adherence," and that "[g]overnment action [that] requires the utterance of a particular message favored by the Government contravenes this essential right." But he found that the must-carry rules did not fall within this line of precedent because they were content-neutral rather than content-based: "the must-carry rules, on their face, impose burdens and confer benefits without reference to the content of speech. Although the provisions interfere with cable operators' editorial discretion by compelling them to offer carriage to a certain minimum number of broadcast stations, [the] number of channels a cable operator must set aside depends only on the operator's channel capacity, [not] the programming it offers to subscribers." He also rejected the cable operators' argument that "Congress' purpose in enacting [must-carry] was to promote speech of a favored content": "Our review of the Act and its various findings persuades us that Congress' overriding objective in enacting must-carry was not to favor programming of a particular subject matter, viewpoint, or format, but rather to preserve access to free television programming for the 40 percent of Americans without cable. [This] overriding congressional purpose is unrelated to the content of expression disseminated by cable and broadcast speakers." Thus, Justice Kennedy concluded, the must-carry rules, unlike those at issue in Tornillo and PG & E, involved no content-based trigger or penalty. Also unlike the rules in Tornillo and PG & E, must-carry would not "force cable operators to alter their own messages to respond to the broadcast programming they are required to carry. Given cable's long history of serving as a conduit for broadcast signals, there appears little risk that cable viewers would assume that the broadcast stations carried on a cable system convey ideas or messages endorsed by the cable operator."

Having found the compelled access here content-neutral, Justice Kennedy concluded that the appropriate standard of scrutiny was not strict scrutiny as in Tornillo or PG & E, but rather the intermediate scrutiny set forth in United States v. O'Brien and Ward v. Rock Against Racism. He concluded that the must-carry provisions served three important interests unrelated to the suppression of free expression: "(1) preserving the benefits of free, over-the-air local broadcast television, (2) promoting the widespread dissemination of information from a multiplicity of sources, and (3) promoting fair competition in the market for television programming." But, joined on this point only by Chief Justice Rehnquist and Justices Blackmun and Souter, he found the congressional record and the record on summary judgment below insufficient to show must-carry to be narrowly tailored to those interests, and concluded that the case should be remanded. Justice STEVENS provided a fifth vote for remand, even though he stated in a partial concurrence that he would have preferred to affirm the summary judgment for the government: "[a]n industry need not be in its death throes before Congress may act to protect it from economic harm threatened by a monopoly." Justice Blackmun also filed a concurrence.

Justice O'CONNOR, joined by Justices Scalia and Ginsburg and in part by Justice Thomas, dissented in part, arguing that the must-carry rules amounted to impermissibly content-based compulsion of speech: "[L]ooking at the statute at issue, I cannot avoid the conclusion that its preference for broadcasters over cable programmers is justified with reference to content"— for example, by Congress's advertence to the desirable diversity and local affairs focus of broadcast programming. She continued: "[M]y conclusion that the must-carry rules are content based leads me to conclude that they are an impermissible restraint on the cable operators' editorial discretion as well as on the cable programmers' speech. For reasons related to the content of speech, the rules restrict the ability of cable operators to put on the programming they prefer, and require them to include programming they would rather avoid. This, it seems to me, puts this case squarely within the rule of [PG & E and Tornillo.]" Justice GINSBURG also filed a separate partial dissent agreeing that the must-carry rules reflected a content preference and thus required strict scrutiny.

The remand in Turner I led to 18 months of additional factfinding, after which the district court granted summary judgment for the Government and other appellees, concluding that the expanded record contained substantial evidence supporting Congress's predictive judgment that the must-carry provisions furthered important governmental interests in preserving cable carriage of local broadcast stations, and were narrowly tailored to promote those interests. In **Turner Broadcasting System, Inc. v. FCC**, 520 U.S. 180 (1997) (Turner II), the Court affirmed by a vote of 5–4. Justice Kennedy again wrote for the Court. Reiterating the standard of intermediate scrutiny set forth in Turner I, he emphasized the need for deference to Congress: "This is not a case in which we are called upon to give our best judgment as to the likely economic consequences of certain financial arrangements or business structures, or to assess competing economic theories and predictive judgments, as we would in a case arising, say, under the antitrust laws. [The] issue before us is whether, given conflicting views of the probable development of the television industry, Congress had substantial evidence for making the judgment that it did. [We] cannot displace Congress' judgment respecting content-neutral regulations with our own, so long as its policy is grounded on reasonable factual findings supported by evidence that is substantial for a legislative determination."

Under this approach, Justice KENNEDY found that the must-carry requirements were substantially related to important government interests in competition and diversity in video programming. Justice Blackmun had voted with the majority in Turner I, and Justice BREYER, who succeeded him, also joined the majority but concurred separately to note the presence of "important First Amendment interests on both sides of the equation," and to say that he found persuasive the diversity rationale but not the competition rationale. Justice O'CONNOR wrote an extended dissent, joined by all the other dissenters in Turner I. She criticized the majority for applying an "inappropriately lenient level of scrutiny" and "exhibiting an extraordinary and unwarranted deference for congressional judgments," and found even on the new record that "the statute is not narrowly tailored to serve a substantial interest in preventing anticompetitive conduct." For other aspects of Turner see p. 630.

———

COMPELLED SPEECH, COMMERCIAL SPEECH AND ECONOMIC REGULATION

Federal and state regulatory schemes compel a great deal of speech. Recall Justice Stevens's example, in dissent in PG & E (1986; p. 490), of the SEC requirement that certain materials, including dissident stockholders' proposals, be included in the proxy statements of publicly traded corporations. Consider also the requirement that the Surgeon General's official warnings on the dangers of tobacco be affixed to cigarette packages, and the Food and Drug Administration's many requirements that food content or drug warnings be disclosed on food and drug labels. Most of these regulatory requirements have never been the subject of any serious First Amendment challenge. Consider this traditional deference in the light of Justice Breyer's concern in his National Institute of Family and Life Advocates v. Becerra ("NIFLA") dissent (2018; p. 485) that the Court's reasoning threatened to pull the rug out from under the vast array of economic disclosure regulations. Is it still justified?

What should the limits of this deference to compelled speech in the regulatory context? In **R.J. Reynolds Tobacco Co. v. FDA**, 696 F.3d 1205 (2012), the D.C. Circuit applied intermediate scrutiny and struck down an FDA regulation requiring tobacco companies to display large, graphic warnings on cigarette packaging. Recall that in Virginia Board of Pharmacy (1976; p. 204), the Court suggested that it may be "appropriate to require that a commercial message appear in such a form, or include such additional information, warnings and disclaimers as are necessary to prevent its being deceptive." Are such regulations best understood as infringing speech rights, but justified nonetheless by the government's compelling interest in protecting health and safety?

May the government compel producers to contribute fees to finance generic advertising of their products, even if they object to the advertising? This issue has now reached the Court three times in connection with various agricultural marketing programs, with inconsistent results.

1. *Compulsory funding for advertising.* In **Glickman v. Wileman Bros.**, 521 U.S. 457 (1997), by a vote of 5–4, the Court upheld against First Amendment challenge agricultural marketing orders assessing from California fruit growers the costs of generic advertising of California nectarines, plums, and peaches. The court of appeals had invalidated the assessments, holding that such compelled commercial speech did not satisfy

the Central Hudson test (1980; p. 214) because collective generic advertising had not been shown more effective than individual advertising. The Supreme Court reversed.

Justice STEVENS, writing for the Court, found that the assessments did not raise a First Amendment issue at all, but rather "simply a question of economic policy for Congress and the Executive to resolve." He reasoned: "Three characteristics of the regulatory scheme at issue distinguish it from laws that we have found to abridge the freedom of speech protected by the First Amendment. First, the marketing orders impose no restraint on the freedom of any producer to communicate any message to any audience. Second, they do not compel any person to engage in any actual or symbolic speech. Third, they do not compel the producers to endorse or to finance any political or ideological views. Indeed, since all of the respondents are engaged in the business of marketing California nectarines, plums, and peaches, it is fair to presume that they agree with the central message of the speech that is generated by the generic program."

Justice Stevens found that these features distinguished the regulations from those held to have unconstitutionally compelled speech in earlier cases: "The use of assessments to pay for advertising does not require respondents to repeat an objectionable message out of their own mouths, Barnette, require them to use their own property to convey an antagonistic ideological message, Wooley; PG & E v. PUC, force them to respond to a hostile message when they 'would prefer to remain silent,' or require them to be publicly identified or associated with another's message, PruneYard. Respondents are not required themselves to speak, but are merely required to make contributions for advertising. With trivial exceptions [none] of the generic advertising conveys any message with which respondents disagree. Furthermore, the advertising is attributed not to them, but to the California Tree Fruit Agreement."

Justice Stevens concluded that under appropriately deferential scrutiny the assessments were clearly constitutional: "Generic advertising is intended to stimulate consumer demand for an agricultural product in a regulated market. That purpose is legitimate and consistent with the regulatory goals of the overall statutory scheme. [Whether] the benefits from the advertising justify its cost is a question that [involves] the exercise of policy judgments that are better made by producers and administrators than by judges."

Justice SOUTER dissented, joined by Chief Justice Rehnquist and Justice Scalia and in part by Justice Thomas. He would have affirmed the court of appeals, finding that the marketing assessments implicated commercial speech, not mere economic conduct; that they were thus subject to the Central Hudson test generally applicable to commercial speech; and that, under that test, the government's justifications were inadequate. He further argued that the fruit growers' apparent lack of disagreement with the advertising could not be a reason for denying the First Amendment's protection: "[Another ground for] the Court's conclusion that the First Amendment is not implicated here is its assumption that respondents do not disagree with the advertisements they object to subsidizing. But this assumption is doubtful and would be beside the point even if true. [Respondents] do claim to disagree with the messages of some promotions they are being forced to fund: some of the ads promote specific varieties of plums, peaches, and nectarines marketed by respondents' competitors but not by respondents; other ads characterize California tree fruits as a generic and thus fungible commodity, whereas respondents believe that their produce is superior to most grown in California. [In] any event, the requirement of disagreement finds no legal warrant in our compelled-speech cases. [Requiring] a profession of disagreement is [at] odds with our holding [in Hurley] that no articulable message is necessary for expression to be protected. [What] counts here [is] not whether respondents fail to disagree with the generalized message of the generic ads that California fruit is good, but that they do indeed deny that the general message is as valuable and worthy of their support as more particular claims about the merits of their own brands." Justice Thomas also dissented.

2.   *Comprehensive regulation.* In **United States v. United Foods, Inc.**, 533 U.S. 405 (2001), by contrast, the Court, by a vote of 6–3, found invalid under the First Amendment a federal law mandating that fresh mushroom handlers pay assessments used primarily to fund advertisements promoting mushroom sales. A large mushroom grower objected to being compelled to support generic mushroom advertisements, preferring to be free to convey the message that its brand of mushrooms was superior to those grown by other producers. Writing for the Court, Justice KENNEDY, joined by Chief Justice Rehnquist, and Justices Stevens, Scalia, Souter, and Thomas, sustained the challenge, distinguishing the stone fruit advertising assessment upheld in Glickman on the ground that it involved a comprehensive program of cooperative marketing: "The program sustained in Glickman differs from the one under review in a most fundamental respect. In Glickman the mandated assessments for speech were ancillary to a more comprehensive program restricting marketing autonomy. Here, for all practical purposes, the advertising itself, far from being ancillary, is the principal object of the regulatory scheme. [Here] the statute does not require group action, save to generate the very speech to which some handlers object. [We] have not upheld compelled subsidies for speech in the context of a program where the principal object is speech itself. [The] cooperative marketing structure relied upon by a majority of the Court in Glickman to sustain an ancillary assessment finds no corollary here; the expression respondent is required to support is not germane to a purpose related to an association independent from the speech itself. [For] these and other reasons we have set forth, the assessments are not permitted under the First Amendment."

Justice BREYER dissented, joined by Justice Ginsburg and in part by Justice O'Connor, finding "[t]his case, although it involves mushrooms rather than fruit, [identical] in [all] critical respects" to Glickman: "The Court sees an important difference in what it says is the fact that [Glickman's] fruit producers were subject to regulation (presumably price and supply regulation) that 'displaced competition,' [but] it is difficult to understand why the presence or absence of price and output regulations could make a critical First Amendment difference. [The] advertising here relates directly, not in an incidental or subsidiary manner, to the regulatory program's underlying goal of 'maintaining and expanding existing markets and uses for mushrooms.' [And] compelled payment may be needed to produce those benefits where, otherwise, some producers would take a free ride on the expenditures of others. [Compared] with traditional 'command and control,' price, or output regulation, this kind of regulation—which relies upon self-regulation through industry trade associations and upon the dissemination of information—is more consistent, not less consistent, with producer choice. It is difficult to see why a Constitution that seeks to protect individual freedom would consider the absence of 'heavy regulation,' to amount to a special, determinative reason for refusing to permit this less intrusive program." Justice Breyer found the compelled expression here, like that in Glickman and unlike that in Barnette and Wooley, "incapable of 'engendering any crisis of conscience.' " He found the producers' objections therefore " 'trivial.' "

Justices Breyer, joined on this point only by Justice Ginsburg, would have treated the mushroom regulation as a mere " 'species of economic regulation' " warranting no special First Amendment scrutiny whatsoever: "First, the program does not significantly interfere with protected speech interests. It does not compel speech itself; it compels the payment of money. Money and speech are not identical. [Second], this program furthers, rather than hinders, the basic First Amendment 'commercial speech' objective [by] promot[ing] the dissemination of truthful information to consumers. [Third], there is no special risk of [significant] harm to an individual's conscience [nor] censor[ship of] producer views unrelated to its basic regulatory justification. And there is little risk of harming any 'discrete, little noticed group' [since the] Act excludes small producers, unlike respondent, a large, influential corporation." Justice Breyer cautioned that the Court, "in applying stricter First Amendment standards and finding them violated, sets an unfortunate precedent. That precedent suggests, perhaps requires, striking down any similar program that, for example, would require tobacco companies to contribute to an industry fund for advertising the harms of smoking or would use a portion of museum entry charges for a citywide campaign to promote the value of art." In a final portion of the dissent joined by both Justices O'Connor and Ginsburg, Justice Breyer concluded that, even if the compulsory fee program were subject to First Amendment review under Central Hudson, it should be upheld as serving a substantial government interest in agricultural promotion by means "necessary and proportionate to the legitimate promotional goals that it seeks."

3. ***Compelled speech or compelled subsidy?*** A third free speech challenge to advertising exactions under federal agricultural marketing orders, this time to those used for beef promotion including the slogan "Beef—It's What's for Dinner," made its way to the Court in **Johanns v. Livestock Marketing Association**, 544 U.S. 550 (2005). This time the decision, like that in Glickman and unlike that in United Foods, came down in favor of the government. But the Court expressly disclaimed reliance on Glickman, noting that, while Glickman had found that "compelled support for generic advertising was legitimately part of the Government's 'collectivist' centralization of the market for tree fruit," here, as in United Foods, "there is no broader regulatory system in place that collectivizes aspects of the beef market unrelated to speech, so Glickman is not controlling." Instead, the Court rested its rejection of the free speech challenge on the notion that the beef exaction, like taxation, supported *government* speech. Justice SCALIA wrote the opinion of the Court, which was joined by Chief Justice Rehnquist and Justices O'Connor, Thomas and Breyer: "In all of the cases invalidating exactions to subsidize speech, the speech was, or was presumed to be, that of an entity other than the government itself. Keller, Abood, United Foods, Southworth. Our compelled-subsidy cases have consistently respected the principle that 'compelled support of a private association is fundamentally different from compelled support of government.' 'Compelled support of government'—even those programs of government one does not approve—is of course perfectly

constitutional, as every taxpayer must attest. [We] have generally assumed, though not yet squarely held, that compelled funding of government speech does not alone raise First Amendment concerns."

Applying these principles, Justice Scalia concluded that the beef exactions supported the speech of the government, not of the Beef Board, a nongovernmental entity that was delegated some responsibility over the advertising: "The message of the promotional campaigns is effectively controlled by the Federal Government itself. The message set out in the beef promotions is from beginning to end the message established by the Federal Government. [Congress] and the Secretary have set out the overarching message [and] the Secretary exercises final approval authority over every word used in every promotional campaign." Justice Scalia also rejected the cattle growers' contention "that the beef program does not qualify as 'government speech' because it is funded by a targeted assessment on beef producers, rather than by general revenues": "The compelled-*subsidy* analysis is altogether unaffected by whether the funds for the promotions are raised by general taxes or through a targeted assessment. [The] First Amendment does not confer a right to pay one's taxes into the general fund, because the injury of compelled funding [does] not stem from the Government's mode of accounting. [Here,] the beef advertisements are subject to political safeguards more than adequate to set them apart from private messages." The majority declined to reach the cattle growers' additional argument that "crediting the advertising to 'America's Beef Producers' impermissibly uses not only their money but also their seeming endorsement to promote a message with which they do not agree," reasoning that this compelled-speech as opposed to compelled-subsidy argument was not appropriate on a facial challenge, "[s]ince neither the Beef Act nor the Beef Order *requires* attribution." The opinion noted that such an argument might form the basis for an as-applied challenge if it were established that individual advertisements were attributed to the challengers.

Justice THOMAS concurred, reiterating that he would hold compelled advertising exactions subject to strict First Amendment scrutiny but recognized "that this principle must be qualified where the regulation compels the funding of speech that is the government's own." Justice BREYER filed a concurrence stating that the beef program was analytically indistinguishable from the mushroom program struck down in United Foods, and reiterated his position in dissent from United Foods that the challenged assessments in both cases "involved a form of economic regulation, not speech." Justice GINSBURG concurred only in the judgment: "I resist ranking the promotional messages funded under the [Beef Act], but not attributed to the Government, as government speech, given the message the Government conveys in its own name [urging the American public to limit intake of fatty foods]. I remain persuaded, however, that the assessments in these cases, as in [United Foods and Glickman] qualify as permissible economic regulation."

Justice SOUTER dissented, joined by Justices Stevens and Kennedy: "The ranchers' complaint is on all fours with the objection of the mushroom growers in United Foods, where a similar statutory exaction was struck down as a compelled subsidy of speech prohibited by the First Amendment absent a comprehensive regulatory scheme to which the speech was incidental. [The] Court accepts the [government-speech] defense unwisely. [I] take the view that if government relies on the government-speech doctrine to compel specific groups to fund speech with targeted taxes, it must make itself politically accountable by indicating that the content actually is a government message, not just the statement of one self-interested group the government is currently willing to invest with power. [Because] the Beef Act fails to require the Government to show its hand, I would [hold] the Act unconstitutional. [The] ads are not required to show any sign of being speech by the Government, and [the] tag line, 'funded by America's Beef Producers,' [all] but ensures that no one reading them will suspect that the message comes from the National Government [rather than] the beef producers who stand to profit when beef is on the table. No one hearing a commercial for Pepsi or Levi's thinks Uncle Sam is the man talking behind the curtain. Why would a person reading a beef ad think Uncle Sam was trying to make him eat more steak? [It] means nothing that Government officials control the message if that fact is never required to be made apparent to those who get the message, let alone if it is affirmatively concealed from them." Justice Kennedy also filed a dissent.

4. ***Reconciling Glickman, United Foods and Johanns.*** Can this trilogy of cases be reconciled? All three involved compelled exactions to fund advertising that some producers found unacceptable in content, and all three involved the danger that the reasonable observer would inaccurately associate all producers of the advertised goods with the offending ads. Justice Scalia suggests in Johanns that any objection is eliminated when "government speech" is at stake. But if what's wrong with compelled subsidization of speech is that it violates autonomy, then does forced subsidy of the government's ads differ from forced subsidy of the beef association's ads? For discussion, see Sullivan & Post, "Symposium: Commercial Speech: Past, Present & Future: It's What's For Lunch: Nectarines, Mushrooms, And Beef—The First Amendment And Compelled Commercial Speech," 41 Loy. L. Rev. 359 (2007). Should it matter whether the objecting farmers assert economic self-interest or ideological objection as the basis for their objection to the compelled exactions? For discussion of whether it would make any difference if "these objectors were small organic farmers objecting to the undifferentiated product descriptions, not because they wanted to differentiate their product as such for self-interested purposes" but rather because they "farm organically for moral and political reasons, from concern for the environment, the health of consumers, or the humane treatment of animals," see Shiffrin, "Symposium: Commercial Speech: Past, Present & Future: Compelled Association, Morality, and Market Dynamics," 41 Loy. L. Rev. 317 (2007).

Consider the following possible rationalization of the government speech exception in Johanns, based on the view that the central value of free speech is participation in public discourse: "Because the state always speaks for the community as a whole, and never for the personal views of private citizens, the state can never become the personal spokesperson of a citizen, no matter how much money she donates to it. [It] follows that restrictions on donations to the state do not compromise the ability of persons to participate in public discourse. [The] fundamental constitutional question posed by the government speech exception in Johanns is whether the Beef Board advertisements [should] be understood as 'speaking for' the private and particular views of the beef industry, which represents the perspective of one group in the community, or instead as 'speaking for' the official views of the state, which represents the outlook of the whole community." Post,

"Compelled Subsidization of Speech: Johanns v. Livestock Marketing Association," 2005 Sup. Ct. Rev. 195.

What other values are at stake in the disagreement over government speech in Johanns? If regulations of the type at issue in Glickman, United Foods, and Johanns are seen as violative of the First Amendment, does this expansion threaten the ability of the government to engage in other types of economic regulation as Justice Breyer's concurrence in Johanns suggests? For the argument that the First Amendment can be used as a resuscitation of Lochner-era economic due process, see Jackson & Jeffries, "Commercial Speech: Economic Due Process and the First Amendment," 65 Va. L. Rev. 1 (1979).

———

COMPELLED SPEECH AND PRIVATE DISCRIMINATION

———

Hurley v. Irish-American Gay, Lesbian and Bisexual Group of Boston [GLIB]

515 U.S. 557, 115 S. Ct. 2338, 132 L. Ed. 2d 487 (1995).

[Hurley addressed whether the private organizers of a St. Patrick's Day parade could be required to include a self-proclaimed gay contingent among the parade's marchers. Massachusetts state antidiscrimination law forbids discrimination on the basis of, inter alia, sexual orientation in the admission or treatment of any person in a place of public accommodation. The state courts found the annual Boston St. Patrick's Day parade to be a public accommodation, found GLIB's exclusion from the parade to be based on sexual orientation, and ordered GLIB admitted to the parade. John J. "Wacko" Hurley and other members of the South Boston Allied War Veterans Council, the private organization that customarily organized the parade, protested this forced inclusion as a violation of their First Amendment rights, and the Court sustained their claim.]

■ JUSTICE SOUTER delivered the opinion for a unanimous Court:

The issue in this case is whether Massachusetts may require private citizens who organize a parade to include among the marchers a group imparting a message the organizers do not wish to convey. We hold that such a mandate violates the First Amendment. [We] use the word "parade" to indicate marchers who are making some sort of collective point, not just to each other but to bystanders along the way. [Parades] are [a] form of expression, not just motion. [The] protected expression that inheres in a parade is not limited to its banners and songs, [but extends to its] "symbolism." [A] narrow, succinctly articulable message is not a condition of constitutional protection, which if confined to expressions conveying a "particularized message," would never reach the unquestionably shielded painting of Jackson Pollock, music of Arnold Schonberg, or Jabberwocky verse of Lewis Carroll. [The] South Boston celebration is [expressive:] Spectators line the streets; people march in costumes and uniforms, carrying flags and banners with all sorts of messages (e.g., "England get out of Ireland," "Say no to drugs"); marching bands and pipers play, floats are

pulled along, and the whole show is broadcast over Boston television. To be sure, [the Council] is rather lenient in admitting participants. But a private speaker does not forfeit constitutional protection simply by combining multifarious voices, or by failing to edit their themes to isolate an exact message as the exclusive subject matter of the speech. [The] presentation of an edited compilation of speech generated by other persons is a staple of most newspapers' opinion pages, which, of course, fall squarely within the core of First Amendment security [Tornillo], [and the] selection of contingents to make a parade is entitled to similar protection.

Respondents' participation as a unit in the parade was equally expressive. GLIB was formed for the very purpose of marching in it, as the trial court found, in order to celebrate its members' identity as openly gay, lesbian, and bisexual descendants of the Irish immigrants, to show that there are such individuals in the community, and to support the like men and women who sought to march in the New York [St. Patrick's Day] parade. [M]embers of GLIB [the previous year] marched behind a shamrock-strewn banner with the simple inscription "Irish American Gay, Lesbian and Bisexual Group of Boston." GLIB understandably seeks to communicate its ideas as part of the existing parade, rather than staging one of its own.

[Hurley and the Council] disclaim any intent to exclude homosexuals as such, and no individual member of GLIB claims to have been excluded from parading as a member of any group that the Council has approved to march. Instead, the disagreement goes to the admission of GLIB as its own parade unit carrying its own banner. Since every participating unit affects the message conveyed by the private organizers, the state courts' application of the statute produced an order essentially requiring petitioners to alter the expressive content of their parade. [The] state courts' application of the statute had the effect of declaring the sponsors' speech itself to be the public accommodation. Under this approach any contingent of protected individuals with a message would have the right to participate in petitioners' speech, so that the communication produced by the private organizers would be shaped by all those protected by the law who wished to join in with some expressive demonstration of their own. But this use of the State's power violates the fundamental rule of protection under the First Amendment, that a speaker has the autonomy to choose the content of his own message.

[The Council's] claim to the benefit of this principle of autonomy to control one's own speech is as sound as the South Boston parade is expressive. [The] Council clearly decided to exclude a message it did not like from the communication it chose to make, and that is enough to invoke its right as a private speaker to shape its expression by speaking on one subject while remaining silent on another. The message it disfavored is not difficult to identify. Although GLIB's point (like the Council's) is not wholly articulate, a contingent marching behind the organization's banner would at least bear witness to the fact that some Irish are gay, lesbian, or bisexual, and the presence of the organized marchers would suggest their view that people of their sexual orientations have as much claim to unqualified social acceptance as heterosexuals and indeed as members of parade units organized around other identifying characteristics. The parade's organizers may not believe these facts about Irish sexuality to be so, or they may object to unqualified social acceptance of gays and lesbians or have some other reason for wishing to keep GLIB's message out of the parade. But whatever the reason, it boils down to the choice of a speaker not to propound a particular point of view, and that choice is presumed to lie beyond the government's power to control. [Considering] that GLIB presumably would have had a fair shot (under neutral criteria developed by the city) at obtaining a parade permit of its own, respondents have not shown that petitioners enjoy the capacity to "silence the voice of competing speakers."

———————

HURLEY'S REACH

1. *Public and private forums compared.* Suppose the parade had been run by the city of Boston rather than the South Boston Allied War Veterans Council. Would GLIB's exclusion have been forbidden by the First Amendment? Would such a parade have amounted to a public forum? A limited public forum? Or not a public forum at all? If the federal government sponsored a parade for military veterans, would it be obliged to include a contingent of avowedly gay former service members? Even if it maintained a policy of excluding homosexuals from the military?

2. *The limits of Hurley.* In **Rumsfeld v. Forum for Academic and Institutional Rights (FAIR)**, 547 U.S. 47 (2006), the Court reviewed a First Amendment challenge to the Solomon Amendment, a statute denying federal funding to any institution of higher education that "has a policy or practice [that] either prohibits, or in effect prevents" the military "from gaining access to campuses, or access to students [on] campuses, for purposes of military recruiting in a manner that is at least equal in quality and scope to the access to campuses and to students that is provided to any other employer." A group of law faculties objected to this condition on the ground that the military's "Don't Ask, Don't Tell" policy discriminated on the basis of sexual orientation in violation of the nondiscrimination policies their law schools apply to employers who recruit on campus. Their challenge on free speech, compelled speech, and compelled association grounds was unsuccessful. (For portions of the opinion rejecting FAIR's compelled association claim, see p. 541.)

Writing for a unanimous Court, Chief Justice ROBERTS found that the Solomon Amendment did not amount to an infringement or compulsion of speech and thus required no heightened First Amendment scrutiny: "The Solomon Amendment neither limits what law schools may say nor requires them to say anything. Law schools remain free under the statute to express whatever views they may have on the military's congressionally mandated employment policy, all the while retaining eligibility for federal funds. As a general matter, the Solomon Amendment regulates conduct, not speech. It affects what law schools must *do*—afford equal access to military recruiters—not what they may or may not *say*. [Recruiting] assistance provided by the schools often includes elements of speech. For example, schools may send e-mails or post notices on bulletin boards on an employer's behalf. [This] sort of recruiting assistance, however, is a far cry from the compelled speech in Barnette and Wooley. The Solomon Amendment, unlike the laws at issue in those cases, does not dictate the content of the speech at all, which is only 'compelled' if, and to the extent, the school provides such speech for other recruiters. There is nothing in this case approaching a Government-mandated pledge or motto that the school must endorse."

Having distinguished Barnette and Wooley, the Chief Justice likewise distinguished Hurley and Tornillo: "[A]ccommodating the military's message does not affect the law schools' speech, because the schools are not speaking when they host interviews and recruiting receptions. Unlike a parade organizer's choice of parade contingents, a law school's decision to allow recruiters on campus is not inherently expressive. Law schools facilitate recruiting to assist their students in obtaining jobs. A law school's recruiting services lack the expressive quality of a parade, a newsletter, or the editorial page of a newspaper; its accommodation of a military recruiter's message is not compelled speech because the accommodation does not sufficiently interfere with any message of the school." He also opined that here, as in PruneYard, there was little danger that the military recruiters' speech would be erroneously attributed to the law schools: "Nothing about recruiting suggests that law schools agree with any speech by recruiters, and nothing in the Solomon Amendment restricts what the law schools may say about the military's policies."

3. *Antidiscrimination law and private commercial transactions.* Parallel issues were raised in Masterpiece Cakeshop v. Colorado Civil Rights Commission, 584 U.S. ___, 138 S. Ct. 1719 (2018), discussed at p. 667. Although the baker raised compelled speech and association claims, the Court resolved the case on the grounds of animus under Lukumi, thereby avoiding the primary claims. If the Court had resolved the case on those grounds, how should the case have been decided? Under the Chief Justice's logic in FAIR, should the compelled baking of a wedding cake for a gay couple be characterized as a mere regulation of conduct? Or should Hurley apply, such that a baker's decision to provide an otherwise available service to a gay couple be seen as "inherently expressive"?

4. *What standard of scrutiny applies in compelled speech cases?* Note that the question whether government has compelled a speaker to utter or to be associated with undesired speech is a threshold question. If a law does not compel speech, as the Court found the California constitutional provision upheld in PruneYard did not, then no special First Amendment scrutiny is required; rationality review is sufficient. If a law *does* compel speech, then it is analyzed just as a law forbidding speech would be analyzed. Thus, if a law compels speech of a particular content, as did the laws in Barnette, Wooley, and McIntyre, or compels counterspeech in response to speech of particular content, as did the laws in Tornillo and PG & E, it is treated as content-based and receives strict scrutiny. But if a law compels speech for reasons unrelated to content, as did the must-carry rules in Turner as the majority read them, then, at most, intermediate scrutiny under O'Brien and Ward is required.

What are the other factors that are driving the Court's analysis of compelled speech? In addition to the content neutrality of the provision, the Court has considered the risk of identifying the compelled message with the speaker in PruneYard, the scarcity of available media in Red Lion, and the speaker's ability to convey its own message despite the compelled speech in PG & E. Which of these is most important in the Court's analysis? Which of these factors should be the most important? Consider how these factors reflect underlying free speech values. Should it matter whether disclaimers are available as a practical matter? Justice Souter contrasted Hurley with PruneYard by noting that a shopkeeper can easily disavow leafletters' message but that "disclaimers would be quite curious in a moving parade."

5.   *Compulsion of speech and First Amendment theory.* Why does compulsion of speech offend free speech values? Because government should not reach into the minds and bodies of speakers and treat them like puppets? Because of concern about enforced adherence to government messages as a form of civic orthodoxy? Note that such justifications cover only cases like Barnette and Wooley, and not cases where government does not script the speaker. What is the core free speech concern in the other cases above? Autonomy from government paternalism?

Note that many of the challengers in the above compelled speech cases are corporations. If the principal value served by the protection from compelled speech is human autonomy, and if corporations lack souls and consciences and thus a capacity for autonomy comparable to that of individuals, then what theory of free speech calls for their protection here? Should corporations like PG & E have a right against compelled speech? A right of free speech at all? Justice Rehnquist's dissent in PG & E notwithstanding, the Court has held that they do. See First National Bank v. Bellotti (1978; p. 564). What alternative rationale might protect corporate rights to speak or not to speak? Might corporate speech be instrumentally valuable in enhancing the free flow of ideas and information to the public, even if it is not intrinsically valuable to any human agent? While such a systemic view might argue against prohibitions of corporate speech, how can it argue against compulsion of corporate speech, which increases the information available to the public? For critical assessments of corporate speech rights, see Bezanson, "Institutional Speech," 80 Iowa L. Rev. 735 (1995); Baker, "Turner Broadcasting: Content-Based Regulation of Persons and Presses," 1994 Sup. Ct. Rev. 57.

If the First Amendment protects a right not to speak, does it also protect a right not to listen? Should objecting listeners be able to exempt themselves from mandatory abortion counseling or mandatory diversity training? For exploration of such a possible right, see Corbin, "The First Amendment Right Against Compelled Listening," 89 Bos. U. L. Rev. 939 (2009).

SECTION 2. FREEDOM OF EXPRESSIVE ASSOCIATION

As early as De Jonge v. Oregon, 299 U.S. 353 (1937), the Court relied on the First Amendment reference to "the right of the people peaceably to assemble" in invalidating a conviction. In NAACP v. Alabama, the 1958 decision that follows, the Court identified an independent constitutional "right of association." The right to associate reflects the notion that individual rights of expression can be made more effectual by collective action. As the Court later summarized in Roberts v. United States Jaycees (1984; p. 536): "An individual's freedom to speak, worship, and to petition the Government for the redress of grievances could not be vigorously protected from interference by the State unless a correlative freedom to engage in group effort toward those ends were not also guaranteed." The Court has tended to view the right of association as dependent on underlying individual rights of expression; there is no right of association in the abstract. See Dallas v. Stanglin, 490 U.S. 19 (1989) (rejecting a freedom of association claim against a Dallas ordinance barring social dancing between teenagers and adults, stating "we do not think the Constitution recognizes a generalized right of 'social association' that includes chance encounters in dance halls").

The Court has reviewed several types of government infringement of the right of expressive association protected by the First Amendment. Most directly, government might simply outlaw an organization or membership in it. The Court has limited such direct restrictions in cases discussed earlier. Recall that the Court in Brandenburg v. Ohio, overruling Whitney, held that one may not be punished simply for assembling with an organization that advocates violent political or industrial reform.

The materials that follow explore several additional government techniques sometimes held to infringe associational liberty. First, government might seek to monitor or intimidate an association by requiring either that the group or an individual member of a group disclose information about group membership in violation of what the Court in NAACP v. Alabama called the right to "privacy in group association." Second, government might restrict activities centrally linked to the purpose of an association, such as meetings or litigation or boycott activities. Third, government might deny governmental benefits or privileges to members of certain associations. Recall that in the Elrod line of cases (p. 399), the Court held that most public jobs may not be conditioned on membership in the victorious political party.

The Court has also held that the right to associate entails a right not to associate, comparable to the right not to speak. It has therefore, for example, invalidated certain compulsory fees exacted from unwilling group members and reviewed laws requiring groups to include unwanted members. These various techniques of interference with associational freedom are examined in turn in the materials that follow.

COMPELLED DISCLOSURE OF MEMBERSHIP

A series of cases in the late 1950s and early 1960s reviewed efforts to inhibit the activities of the National Association for the Advancement of Colored People (NAACP) by requiring disclosure of its membership lists in various contexts. In addition to the cases that follow, see Bates v. Little Rock, 361 U.S. 516 (1960), invalidating a requirement that membership lists be disclosed in connection with an occupational license tax, and Louisiana ex rel. Gremillion v. NAACP, 366 U.S. 293 (1961), restraining enforcement of a statute requiring nonprofit organizations to file membership lists. On these and related cases generally, see Kalven, The Negro and the First Amendment (1965).

NAACP v. Alabama

357 U.S. 449, 78 S. Ct. 1163, 2 L. Ed. 2d 1488 (1958).

[In NAACP v. Alabama, which follows, the Court held unconstitutional Alabama's demand that the NAACP reveal the names and addresses of all of its Alabama members and agents. The State's demand was made in the course of an injunction action brought in 1956 to stop the NAACP from conducting activities in Alabama, on the ground that it had failed to comply with the requirement that foreign corporations qualify before "doing business" in the State. The NAACP, a New York membership corporation, operated in Alabama largely through local affiliates that were unincorporated associations. It considered itself exempt from the State's foreign corporation registration law. While the injunction action was pending, the State moved for the production of a large number of the NAACP's records. The NAACP produced substantially all the data called for, but not its membership lists, as to which it contended that Alabama could not constitutionally compel disclosure. The trial court adjudged the NAACP in contempt and imposed a $100,000 fine. The Supreme Court reversed.]

■ JUSTICE HARLAN delivered the opinion of the Court:

Effective advocacy of both public and private points of view, particularly controversial ones, is undeniably enhanced by group association, as this Court has [recognized] by remarking upon the close nexus between the freedoms of speech and assembly. It is beyond debate that freedom to engage in association for the advancement of beliefs and ideas is an inseparable aspect of the "liberty" assured by the Due Process Clause of the 14th Amendment, which embraces freedom of speech. Of course, it is immaterial whether the beliefs sought to be advanced by association pertain to political, economic, religious or cultural matters, and state action which may have the effect of curtailing the freedom to associate is subject to the closest scrutiny. The fact that Alabama [has] taken no direct action [to] restrict the right of petitioner's members to associate freely does not end inquiry into the effect of the production order. [I]n the domain of these indispensable liberties, whether of speech, press, or association, the decisions of this Court recognize that abridgment of such rights, even though unintended, may inevitably follow from varied forms of governmental [action]. It is hardly a novel perception that compelled disclosure of affiliation with groups engaged in advocacy may constitute [an effective] restraint on freedom of association. [There is a] vital relationship between freedom to associate and privacy in one's associations. [Inviolability] of privacy in group association may in many circumstances be indispensable to preservation of freedom of association, particularly where a group espouses dissident [beliefs].

We think that the production order [must] be regarded as entailing the likelihood of a substantial restraint upon the exercise by petitioner's members of their right to freedom of association. Petitioner has made an uncontroverted showing that on past occasions revelation of the identity of its rank-and-file members has exposed these members to economic reprisal, loss of employment, threat of physical coercion, and other manifestations of public hostility. Under these circumstances, we think it apparent that compelled disclosure of petitioner's Alabama membership is likely to affect adversely the ability of petitioner and its members to pursue their collective effort to foster beliefs which they admittedly have the right to advocate, in that it may induce members to withdraw from the Association and dissuade others from joining it because of fear of exposure of their beliefs shown through their associations and of the consequences of this [exposure].

We turn to the [question] whether Alabama has demonstrated an interest in obtaining the disclosures it seeks from petitioner which is sufficient to justify the deterrent effect which we have concluded these disclosures may well have on the free exercise [of] constitutionally protected right of association. [Such a] "subordinating interest of the State must be compelling." It is important to bear in mind that petitioner asserts no right to absolute immunity from state investigation. [Petitioner] has not objected to divulging the identity of its members who are employed by or hold official positions with it. It has urged the rights solely of its ordinary rank-and-file [members]. Whether there was "justification" in this instance turns solely on the substantiality of Alabama's interest in obtaining the membership lists. [The] exclusive purpose [claimed] was to determine whether petitioner was conducting intrastate business in violation of the Alabama foreign corporation registration statute. [W]e are unable to perceive that the disclosure of the names of petitioner's rank-and-file members has a substantial bearing on the state interest. [W]hatever interest the State may have in obtaining names of ordinary members has not been shown to be sufficient to overcome petitioner's constitutional objections to the production order.[1] [W]e conclude that Alabama has fallen short of showing a controlling justification for the deterrent effect on the free enjoyment of the right to associate which disclosure of membership lists is likely to [have]. Reversed.

COMPELLED DISCLOSURE IN THE CIVIL RIGHTS ERA

1. *Compelled disclosure and public employment.* In **Shelton v. Tucker**, 364 U.S. 479 (1960), the Court held unconstitutional an Arkansas statute—Act 10—which required every teacher, as a condition of employment in a state-supported school or college, to file "annually an affidavit listing without limitation every organization to which he has belonged or regularly contributed within the preceding five years." Shelton, who had taught in the Little Rock schools for 25 years, refused to file an affidavit, and his contract was not renewed. In the trial court, the evidence showed that he was not a member of any organization advocating the overthrow of the Government but that he was a member of the NAACP.

Justice STEWART delivered the opinion of the Court: "It is urged [that] Act 10 deprives teachers in Arkansas of their rights to personal, associational, and academic liberty. [I]n considering this contention, we deal with two basic postulates. *First.* There can be no doubt of the right of a state to investigate the competence and fitness of those whom it hires to teach in its schools. [*Second*]. [To] compel a teacher to disclose his every associational tie is to impair that teacher's right of free association. [Such] interference with personal freedom is conspicuously accented when the teacher serves at the absolute will of those to whom the disclosure must be made. [The] statute does not provide that the information it requires be kept confidential. [The] record contains evidence to indicate that fear of public disclosure is neither theoretical nor groundless. Even if there were no disclosure to the general public, the pressure upon a teacher to avoid any ties which might displease those who control his professional destiny would be constant and heavy. [The] vigilant protection of constitutional freedoms is nowhere more vital than in the community of American [schools].

The question to be decided here is not whether the State [can] ask certain of its teachers about all their organizational relationships. It is not

---

[1] Justice Harlan distinguished Bryant v. Zimmerman, 278 U.S. 63 (1928), where the Court had upheld a New York law requiring disclosure of membership lists of any organization requiring an oath as a condition of membership. That law had been challenged by a member of the Ku Klux Klan. One of the distinctions noted by Justice Harlan was that Bryant had rested on "the peculiar character of the Klan's activities, involving acts of unlawful intimidation and violence." Moreover, the KKK, unlike the NAACP here, had refused to give the state "*any* information as to its local activities."

whether the State can ask all of its teachers about certain of their associational ties. It is not whether teachers can be asked how many organizations they belong to, or how much time they spend in organizational activity. The question is whether the State can ask every one of its teachers to disclose every single organization with which he has been associated over a five-year period. The scope of the inquiry required by Act 10 is completely unlimited. [The Act] requires a teacher [to] list, without number, every conceivable kind of associational tie—social, professional, political, avocational, or religious. Many such relationships could have no possible bearing upon the teacher's occupational competence or fitness. [This] Court has held that, even though the governmental purpose be legitimate and substantial, that purpose cannot be pursued by means that broadly stifle fundamental personal liberties when the end can be more narrowly achieved. The breadth of legislative abridgment must be viewed in the light of less drastic means for achieving the same basic purpose. [The] unlimited and indiscriminate sweep of the statute now before us brings it within the ban of our prior cases. The statute's comprehensive interference with associational freedom goes far beyond what might be justified in the exercise of the State's legitimate inquiry into the fitness and competency of its teachers. Reversed."

Justice FRANKFURTER dissented: "[The] Court strikes down [the law] on the ground that 'many such relationships could have no possible bearing upon the teacher's occupational competence or fitness.' [The selection of teachers] is an intricate affair [and] if it is to be informed, it must be based upon a comprehensive range of information. I am unable to say [that] Arkansas could not reasonably find that the information which the statute requires [is] germane to that selection. [Of course,] if the information gathered [is] used to further a scheme of terminating the employment of teachers solely because of their membership in unpopular organizations, that use will run afoul of the Fourteenth Amendment. It will be time enough, if such use is made, to hold the application of the [law] unconstitutional."

2. *Compelled disclosure and legislative investigations.* In **Gibson v. Florida Legislative Investigation Comm.**, 372 U.S. 539 (1963), the Court held that the imprisonment of an NAACP official for failure to comply with a legislative committee's request for a membership list violated the First Amendment. In 1957, an earlier legislative committee had sought the entire membership list of the local NAACP branch. Florida's highest court barred that request but stated that the committee could compel the custodian of the records to bring them to committee hearings and to refer to them to determine whether specific individuals, identified as or suspected of being Communists, were NAACP members. The committee in Gibson was established in 1959 to resume the investigation. Gibson, the President of the Miami branch, was ordered to bring the records pertaining to the identity of members of and contributors to the Miami and state NAACP organizations. Gibson, relying on the First Amendment, did not bring the records but told the Committee that he would answer questions concerning membership in the NAACP on the basis of his personal knowledge. He was given the names and shown photographs of 14 persons previously identified as being involved in Communist or Communist-front affairs. Gibson said that he could associate none of them with the NAACP. For his failure to produce the records, a state court found him in contempt and sentenced him to six months' imprisonment and a $1200 fine.

Writing for the Court, Justice GOLDBERG struck down the conviction, reasoning that "it is an essential prerequisite to the validity of an investigation which intrudes into the area of constitutionally protected rights of speech, press, association and petition that the State convincingly show a substantial relation between the information sought and a subject of overriding and compelling state interest. Absent such a ['nexus'], the Committee has not 'demonstrated so cogent an interest in obtaining and making public' the membership information sought [as] to 'justify the substantial abridgment of associational freedom which such disclosures will effect.'

[The] record in this case is insufficient to show a substantial connection between the Miami branch of the NAACP and Communist *activities* which [is] an essential prerequisite to demonstrating the immediate, substantial, and subordinating state interest necessary to sustain its right of inquiry into the membership lists. [There] is here merely indirect, less than unequivocal, and mostly hearsay testimony that in years past some 14 people who were asserted to be, or to have been, Communists or members of Communist front or 'affiliated organizations' attended occasional meetings of the Miami branch of the NAACP 'and/or' were members of that branch, which had a total membership of about 1,000. [The] strong associational interest in maintaining the privacy of membership lists of groups engaged in the constitutionally protected free trade in ideas and beliefs may not be substantially infringed upon such a slender showing. [While,] of course, all legitimate organizations are the beneficiaries of these protections, they are all the more essential here, where the challenged privacy is that of persons espousing beliefs already unpopular with their neighbors and the deterrent and 'chilling' effect on the free exercise of constitutionally enshrined rights of free speech, expression, and association is consequently the more immediate and substantial. Reversed."

Justice HARLAN dissented: "[Until] today, I had never supposed that any of our decisions [could] possibly be taken as suggesting any difference in the degree [of] investigatory interest as between Communist infiltration *of* organizations and Communist activity *by* organizations. [The 'nexus' here was sufficient] unless 'nexus' requires an investigating agency to prove in advance the very things it is trying to find out. [I] also find it difficult to see how this case really presents any serious question as to interference with freedom of association. Given the willingness of the petitioner to testify from recollection as to individual memberships in the local branch of the NAACP, the germaneness of the membership records to the subject matter of the Committee's investigation, and the limited purpose for which their use was sought—as an aid to refreshing the witness' recollection, involving their divulgence only to the petitioner himself—this case of course bears no resemblance whatever to [NAACP v. Alabama] or [Bates], [where] the State had sought general divulgence of local NAACP membership lists without any showing of a justifying state interest."

Americans for Prosperity Foundation v. Bonta

___ U.S. ___, 141 S. Ct. 2373, 210 L. Ed. 2d 716 (2021).

■ CHIEF JUSTICE ROBERTS delivered the opinion of the Court, except as to Part II-B-1.

To solicit contributions in California, charitable organizations must disclose to the state Attorney General's Office the identities of their major donors. The State contends that having this information on hand makes it easier to police misconduct by charities. We must decide whether California's disclosure requirement violates the First Amendment right to free association.

I. [In] order to operate and raise funds in California, charities generally must register with the Attorney General and renew their registrations annually. Over 100,000 charities are currently registered in the State, and roughly 60,000 renew their registrations each year. [The] Attorney General requires charities renewing their registrations to file copies of their Internal Revenue Service Form 990, along with any attachments and schedules. [Schedule B] to Form 990—the document that gives rise to the present dispute—requires organizations to disclose the names and addresses of donors who have contributed more than $5,000 in a particular tax year (or, in some cases, who have given more than 2 percent of an organization's total contributions).The petitioners are tax-exempt charities that solicit contributions in California and are subject to the Attorney General's registration and renewal requirements. [Since] 2001, each petitioner has renewed its registration and has filed a copy of its Form 990 with the Attorney General [but they] have declined to file their Schedule Bs. [When] they continued to resist disclosing their contributors' identities, the Attorney General threatened to suspend their registrations and fine their directors and officers.

II. A. [This] Court has "long understood as implicit in the right to engage in activities protected by the First Amendment a corresponding right to associate with others." [We] have also noted that "[compelled] disclosure of affiliation with groups engaged in advocacy may constitute as effective a restraint on freedom of association as [other] forms of governmental action." NAACP v. Alabama [p. 505].

B.1. NAACP v. Alabama did not phrase in precise terms the standard of review that applies to First Amendment challenges to compelled disclosure. We have since settled on a standard referred to as "exacting scrutiny."

2. [While] exacting scrutiny does not require that disclosure regimes be the least restrictive means of achieving their ends, it does require that they be narrowly tailored to the government's asserted interest. [A] substantial relation to an important interest is not enough to save a disclosure regime that is insufficiently tailored. [Narrow] tailoring is crucial where First Amendment activity is chilled—even if indirectly—"[b]ecause First Amendment freedoms need breathing space to survive."

III. For the reasons below, we conclude that California's blanket demand for Schedule Bs is facially unconstitutional.

A. [We] do not doubt that California has an important interest in preventing wrongdoing by charitable organizations. [There] is a dramatic mismatch, however, between the interest that the Attorney General seeks to promote and the disclosure regime that he has implemented in service of that end. [The] record amply supports the District Court's finding that there was not "a single, concrete instance in which pre-investigation collection of a Schedule B did anything to advance the Attorney General's investigative, regulatory or enforcement efforts." [The] Attorney General and the dissent contend that alternative means of obtaining Schedule B information—such as a subpoena or audit letter—are inefficient and ineffective compared to up-front collection. It became clear at trial, however, that the Office had not even considered alternatives to the current disclosure requirement. [The] upshot is that California casts a dragnet for sensitive donor information from tens of thousands of charities each year, even though that information will become relevant in only a small number of cases involving filed complaints. [The] need for up-front collection is particularly dubious given that California—one of only three States to impose such a requirement—did not rigorously enforce the disclosure obligation until 2010.

B. [The] foregoing discussion also makes clear why a facial challenge is appropriate in these cases. [In] the First Amendment context, [we] have recognized [that] "a law may be invalidated as overbroad if a substantial number of its applications are unconstitutional, judged in relation to the statute's plainly legitimate sweep." We have no trouble concluding here that the Attorney General's disclosure requirement is overbroad. The lack of tailoring to the State's investigative goals is categorical—present in every case—as is the weakness of the State's interest in administrative convenience. Every demand that might chill association therefore fails exacting scrutiny.

The Attorney General tries to downplay the burden on donors, arguing that "California's Schedule B requirement is confidential." [We] are unpersuaded. Our cases have said that disclosure requirements can chill association "[e]ven if there [is] no disclosure to the general public." [While] assurances of confidentiality may reduce the burden of disclosure to the State, they do not eliminate it.

[The] gravity of the privacy concerns in this context is further underscored by the filings of hundreds of organizations as *amici curiae* in support of the petitioners. Far from representing uniquely sensitive causes, these organizations span the ideological spectrum, and indeed the full range of human endeavors: from the American Civil Liberties Union to the Proposition 8 Legal Defense Fund; from the Council on American-Islamic Relations to the Zionist Organization of America; from Feeding America—Eastern Wisconsin to PBS Reno. The deterrent effect feared by these organizations is real and pervasive.

[We] are left to conclude that the Attorney General's disclosure requirement imposes a widespread burden on donors' associational rights. And this burden cannot be justified on the ground that the regime is narrowly tailored to investigating charitable wrongdoing. [We] therefore hold that the up-front collection of Schedule Bs is facially unconstitutional.

■ JUSTICE THOMAS, concurring in Parts I, II-A, II-B-2, and III-A, and concurring in the judgment.

The Court correctly holds that California's disclosure requirement violates the First Amendment. [But] I would approach three issues differently.

First, [the] text and history of the Assembly Clause suggest that the right to assemble includes the right to associate anonymously. [Laws] directly burdening the right to associate anonymously, including compelled disclosure laws, should be subject to the same [strict] scrutiny as laws directly burdening other First Amendment rights. [Second], I continue to have "doubts about [the] origins and application" of our "overbreadth doctrine." Third, and relatedly, [a] declaration that the law is "facially" unconstitutional "seems to me no more than an advisory opinion—which a federal court should never issue at all." Despite the Court's use of the term "facially unconstitutional," I join Part III-A, which finds that California's law fails exacting scrutiny, because the Court does not say that it is "provid[ing] relief beyond the parties to the case.

■ JUSTICE ALITO, with whom JUSTICE GORSUCH joins, concurring in Parts I, II-A, II-B-2, and III, and concurring in the judgment.

[I] agree that the exacting scrutiny standard [has] real teeth. It requires both narrow tailoring and consideration of alternative means of obtaining the sought-after information. [California's] blunderbuss approach to charitable disclosures fails exacting scrutiny and is facially unconstitutional. The question is not even close. [But] because the choice between exacting and strict scrutiny has no effect on the decision in these cases, I see no need to decide which standard should be applied here or whether the same level of scrutiny should apply in all cases in which the compelled disclosure of associations is challenged under the First Amendment.

■ JUSTICE SOTOMAYOR, with whom JUSTICES BREYER and KAGAN join, dissenting.

[Today,] the Court holds that reporting and disclosure requirements must be narrowly tailored even if a plaintiff demonstrates no burden. [In] so holding, the Court discards its decades-long requirement that, to establish a cognizable burden on their associational rights, plaintiffs must plead and prove that disclosure will likely expose them to objective harms, such as threats, harassment, or reprisals. [Instead,] it presumes (contrary to the evidence, precedent, and common sense) that all disclosure requirements impose associational burdens.

[All] this would be less troubling if the Court still required means-end tailoring commensurate to the actual burden imposed. [Exacting scrutiny] incorporates a degree of flexibility into the means-end analysis. The more serious the burden on First Amendment rights, the more compelling the government's interest must be, and the tighter must be the fit between that interest and the government's means of pursuing it. By contrast, a less substantial interest and looser fit will suffice where the burden on First Amendment rights is weaker (or nonexistent). In other words, to decide how closely tailored a disclosure requirement must be, courts must ask an antecedent question: How much does the disclosure requirement actually burden the freedom to associate?

[Under] a First Amendment analysis that is faithful to this Court's precedents, California's Schedule B requirement is constitutional. Begin with the burden it imposes on associational rights. Petitioners have unquestionably provided evidence that their donors face a reasonable probability of threats, harassment, and reprisals if their affiliations are made public. California's Schedule B regulation, however, is a nonpublic reporting requirement, and California has implemented security measures to ensure that Schedule B information remains confidential. Nor have petitioners shown that their donors, or any organization's donors, will face threats, harassment, or reprisals if their names remain in the hands of a few California state officials. [Given] the modesty of the First Amendment burden, California may justify its Schedule B requirement with a correspondingly modest showing that the means achieve its ends. California easily meets this standard. [The] Schedule B reporting requirement is properly tailored to further California's efforts to police charitable fraud. [Schedule B] and other parts of Form 990 help attorneys in the Charitable Trusts Section of the California Department of Justice uncover whether an officer or director of a charity is engaged in self-dealing, or whether a charity has diverted donors' charitable contributions for improper use. [That] is more than enough to satisfy the First Amendment here. [In] a final coup de grâce, the Court concludes that California's reporting requirement is unconstitutional not just as applied to petitioners, but on its very face. [The] Court points to not a single piece of record evidence showing that California's reporting requirement will chill "a substantial number" of top donors from giving to their charities of choice. Yet it strikes the requirement down in every application. [Of] course, it is always possible that an organization is inherently controversial or for an apparently innocuous organization to explode into controversy. The answer, however, is to ensure that confidentiality measures are sound or, in the case of public disclosures, to require a procedure for governments to address requests for exemptions in a timely manner. It is not to hamper all government law enforcement efforts by forbidding confidential disclosures en masse. [If] the Court had simply granted as-applied relief to petitioners based on its reading of the facts, I would be sympathetic, although my own views diverge. But the Court's decision is not nearly so narrow or modest. [With] respect, I dissent.

COMPELLED DISCLOSURE OF POLITICAL CAMPAIGN CONTRIBUTIONS

In **Buckley v. Valeo**, 424 U.S. 1 (1976), discussed in full at p. 550, the Court rejected challenges to the disclosure provisions of the Federal Election Campaign Act. The Act required that every political candidate and "political committee" maintain records of the name and address of every person contributing more than $10 in a calendar year and his or her occupation and principal place of business if his contribution exceeded $100, to make such records available for inspection by the Federal Election Commission (FEC), and to file quarterly reports with the FEC disclosing the source of every contribution exceeding $100.

The per curiam opinion stated: "We long have recognized that significant encroachments on First Amendment rights of the sort that compelled disclosure imposes cannot be justified by a mere showing of some legitimate governmental interest. Since [NAACP v. Alabama] we have required that the subordinating interests of the State must survive exacting scrutiny. We also have insisted that there be a 'substantial relation' [Gibson] between the governmental interest and the information required to be disclosed. This type of scrutiny is necessary even if any deterrent effect on the exercise of First Amendment rights arises, not through direct government action, but indirectly as an unintended but inevitable result of the government's conduct in requiring disclosure. [NAACP v. Alabama.]

"Appellees argue that the disclosure requirements of the Act differ significantly from those at issue in Alabama and its progeny because the Act only requires disclosure of the names of contributors and does not compel political organizations to submit the names of their members. [T]he invasion of privacy of belief may be as great when the information sought concerns the giving and spending of money as when it concerns the joining of [organizations]. The strict test established by Alabama is necessary because compelled disclosure has the potential for substantially infringing the exercise of First Amendment rights. But we have acknowledged that there are governmental interests sufficiently important to outweigh the possibility of infringement.

"[The] governmental interests sought to be vindicated by the disclosure requirements are of this magnitude. They fall into three categories. First, disclosure provides the electorate with information 'as to where political campaign money comes [from]' in order to aid the voters in evaluating those who seek Federal office. [Second], disclosure requirements deter actual corruption and avoid the appearance of corruption by exposing large [contributions] to the light of publicity. [Third, such] requirements are an essential means of gathering the data necessary to detect violations of the contribution limitations. [Thus, the] disclosure requirements [directly] serve substantial governmental interests. [It] is undoubtedly true that public disclosure of contributions [will] deter some individuals who otherwise might contribute. In some instances, disclosure may even expose contributors to harassment or retaliation. These are not insignificant burdens on individual rights, and they must be weighed carefully against the interests which Congress has sought to promote by this legislation. [But we agree] that disclosure requirements—certainly in most applications—appear to be the least restrictive means of curbing the evils of campaign ignorance and corruption that Congress found to exist."

The Court also rejected the claim that the disclosure requirements were invalid as applied to minor parties: "[NAACP v. Alabama] is inapposite where, as here, any serious infringement on First Amendment rights brought about by the compelled disclosure of contributors is highly speculative. It is true that the governmental interest in disclosure is diminished when the contribution in question is made to a minor party with little chance of winning an election. [We] are not unmindful that the damage done by disclosure to [the] minor parties [could] be significant. [In] some instances fears of reprisal may deter contributions to the point where the movement cannot survive. [There] could well be a case [where] the threat to the exercise of First Amendment rights is so serious and the state interest furthered by disclosure so insubstantial that the Act's requirements cannot be constitutionally applied. But no appellant in this case has tendered record evidence of [that] sort. [On] this record, the substantial public interest in disclosure identified by the legislative history of this Act outweighs the harm generally alleged. [In any particular case,] [m]inor parties must be allowed sufficient flexibility in the proof of injury to assure a fair consideration of their claim. The evidence offered need show only a reasonable probability that the compelled disclosure of a party's contributors' names will subject them to threats, harassment or reprisals from either government officials or private parties."

Chief Justice BURGER dissented from this portion of Buckley: "[Secrecy] and privacy as to political preferences and convictions are fundamental in a free society. [I] suggest the Court has failed to give the traditional standing to some of the First Amendment values at stake here. Specifically, it has failed to confine the particular exercise of governmental power within limits reasonably required. [Shelton v. Tucker.] [It] seems to me that the threshold limits fixed at $10 and $100 for anonymous contributions are constitutionally impermissible on their face. [To] argue that a 1976 contribution of $10 or $100 entails a risk of corruption or its appearance is simply too extravagant to be maintained. [There] is, in short, no relation whatever between the means used and the legitimate goal of ventilating possible undue influence. Congress has used a shotgun to kill wrens as well as hawks.

"In saying that the lines drawn by Congress are 'not wholly without rationality,' the Court [makes an] abrupt departure from traditional standards; [surely] a greater burden rests on Congress than merely to avoid 'irrationality' when regulating in the core area of the First Amendment. Even taking the Court at its word, the particular dollar amounts fixed by Congress that must be reported to the Commission fall short of meeting the test of rationality when measured by the goals sought to be achieved. Finally, no legitimate public interest has been shown in forcing the disclosure of modest contributions that are the prime support of new, unpopular or unfashionable political causes. There is no realistic possibility that such modest donations will have a corrupting influence, especially on parties that enjoy only 'minor' status. Major parties would not notice them; minor parties need [them]. Flushing out the names of supporters of minority parties will plainly have a deterrent effect on potential [contributors]."

The possibility held out by Buckley—that certain minor parties might, on a proper showing, obtain exemptions from compelled disclosures—was realized in **Brown v. Socialist Workers '74 Campaign Committee**, 459 U.S. 87 (1982). In an opinion by Justice MARSHALL, the Court held, unanimously on this point, that the Socialist Workers Party in Ohio had made a sufficient showing of a "reasonable probability of threats, harassment, or reprisals" so that it could not constitutionally be compelled to disclose information concerning campaign contributions. The Court noted that the Party was "a minor political party which historically has been the object of harassment by government officials and private parties." (The Court also held, over the dissents of Justices O'Connor, Rehnquist, and Stevens, that the same showing also exempted the Party from compelled disclosure of campaign *disbursements*.)

In **McConnell v. Federal Election Comm'n**, 540 U.S. 93 (2003), discussed in full at p. 569, the Court upheld against free speech challenge various new provisions of the Bipartisan Campaign Reform Act of 2002 (BCRA), including disclosure provisions. BCRA extended the disclosure requirements upheld in Buckley from hard-money contributions to candidates to expenditures for so-called "electioneering communications," defined as broadcast ads that specifically identify any candidate for federal office within 60 days before an election or 30 days before a primary election. The majority, in an opinion by Justices STEVENS and O'CONNOR, upheld this requirement as closely tailored to the important state interests Buckley had identified in deterring actual or apparent corruption and keeping voters informed. Dissenting from this aspect of the ruling, Justice THOMAS cited his McIntyre concurrence to conclude that "the established right to anonymous speech" may not be abridged in order merely to provide information to voters.

BCRA's disclosure provisions were the only disputed provisions to survive First Amendment challenge in **Citizens United v. Federal Election Commission**, 558 U.S. 310 (2010). By a vote of 5–4, the Court invalidated BCRA's limitations on corporate expenditures for advocacy in electoral campaigns (see p. 583), but, by a vote of 8–1, the Court upheld BCRA's disclaimer and disclosure requirements as applied to *Hillary*, a documentary critical of then-Senator Clinton during her campaign for the presidency, and advertisements for the film. Justice KENNEDY wrote for the Court: "Under BCRA § 311, televised electioneering communications funded by anyone other than a candidate must include a disclaimer that '_____ is responsible for the content of this advertising.' The required statement must be made in a 'clearly spoken manner,' and displayed on the screen in a 'clearly readable manner' for at least four seconds. It must state that the communication 'is not authorized by any candidate or candidate's committee; it must also display the name and address (or Web site address) of the person or group that funded the advertisement. Under BCRA § 201, any person who spends more than $10,000 on electioneering communications within a calendar year must file a disclosure statement with the FEC. That statement must identify the person making the expenditure, the amount of the expenditure, the election to which the communication was directed, and the names of certain contributors.

"[We] find the statute valid as applied to the ads for the movie and to the movie itself. [Disclosure] is a less restrictive alternative to more comprehensive regulations of speech. [The] public has an interest in knowing who is speaking about a candidate shortly before an election. [Citizens United] argues that disclosure requirements can chill donations to an organization by exposing donors to retaliation. In McConnell [v. FEC (2003; p. 569)], the Court recognized that § 201 would be unconstitutional as applied to an organization if there were a reasonable probability that the group's members would face threats, harassment, or reprisals if their names were disclosed. [Citizens United,] however, has offered no evidence that its members may face similar threats or reprisals.

"[A] campaign finance system that pairs corporate independent expenditures with effective disclosure has not existed before today. [With] the advent of the Internet, prompt disclosure of expenditures can provide shareholders and citizens with the information needed to hold corporations and elected officials accountable for their positions and supporters. Shareholders can determine whether their corporation's political speech advances the corporation's interest in making profits, and citizens can see whether elected officials are ' "in the pocket" of so-called moneyed interests.' [This] transparency enables the electorate to make informed decisions and give proper weight to different speakers and messages."

Only Justice THOMAS dissented from this portion of the decision, stating: "The disclosure, disclaimer, and reporting requirements in BCRA §§ 201 and 311 [are] unconstitutional. Congress may not abridge the 'right to anonymous speech' based on the 'simple interest in providing voters with additional relevant information.' " He noted that, after California voters passed Proposition 8, a 2008 state ballot proposition that amended California's constitution to overrule a state supreme court decision upholding a right to gay marriage, opponents of Proposition 8 had used information posted on the Internet under California's mandatory disclosure rules to "create[ ] Web sites with maps showing the locations of homes or businesses of Proposition 8 supporters. Many supporters (or their customers) suffered property damage, or threats of physical violence or death, as a result. [The] success of such intimidation tactics has apparently spawned a cottage industry that uses forcibly disclosed donor information to pre-empt citizens' exercise of their First Amendment rights. [These] instances of retaliation sufficiently demonstrate why this Court should invalidate mandatory disclosure and reporting requirements."

Does such anecdotal evidence justify a broader presumption in favor of anonymous political contributions? Who should bear the burden of overcoming the presumption—those who would show good cause for identifying contributors, or those who would show good cause for keeping contributors' identities hidden? Are these contemporary cases consistent with NAACP v. Alabama? Or has the pendulum swung in the opposite direction, rendering NAACP v. Alabama a relic of the Civil Rights Era? Is it possible that disclosure requirements are not only potentially pernicious, as the Civil Rights Era cases demonstrate, but also insufficient to deal with contemporary problems posed by campaign finance regulation?

RESTRICTIONS ON ORGANIZATIONAL ACTIVITY

The Court has also invalidated various direct restraints on characteristic associational activity. For example, in Healy v. James, 408 U.S. 169 (1972), the Court invalidated efforts by Central Connecticut State College to prevent a local chapter of Students for a Democratic Society (SDS), a radical student organization that advocated participatory democracy, racial equality, and antiwar messages, from holding meetings or otherwise organizing on campus, at least in the absence of any demonstrated actual misconduct. More controversial has been the constitutionality of restrictions on such organizational activity as conducting political litigation or boycotts.

How have restraints on association varied across time? Do contemporary politics raise the same potential for government restraint on association that occurred as a result of the Communist Scare in the 1950s? Or the Civil Rights and Antiwar Movements of the 1960s and 1970s? Consider the following historical cases.

NAACP v. Button

371 U.S. 415, 83 S. Ct. 328, 9 L. Ed. 2d 405 (1963).

[The Virginia Conference of the NAACP financed litigation aimed at ending racial segregation of the Virginia public schools. NAACP cases were typically not initiated by aggrieved persons applying to the Conference for assistance. Instead, a local NAACP branch usually invited a member of the Conference legal staff to explain to a meeting of parents and children the legal steps necessary to achieve desegregation. The staff member would bring printed forms authorizing NAACP attorneys, rather than any particular lawyer, to represent the signers in desegregation suits.

Virginia prohibited "the improper solicitation of any legal or professional business" and had long banned the solicitation of legal business in the form of "running" or "capping." Before 1956, there was no attempt to apply those regulations to curb the NAACP's activities in sponsoring litigation directed at racial segregation. But in 1956, the laws were amended by adding a Chapter 33 to include, in the definition of "runner" or "capper," an agent for any organization which "employs, retains or compensates" any lawyer "in connection with any judicial proceeding in which it has no pecuniary right or liability." Virginia's highest court held that the NAACP's Virginia activities violated Chapter 33. The Supreme Court reversed and held that the Virginia law was unconstitutional as applied to the NAACP.]

■ JUSTICE BRENNAN delivered the opinion of the Court:

[We] hold that the activities of the NAACP, its affiliates and legal staff shown on this record are modes of expression and association protected by the [First Amendment] which Virginia may not prohibit [as] improper solicitation of legal business. [We reject] the contention that "solicitation" is wholly outside the area of freedoms protected by the First Amendment. [Abstract] discussion is not the only species of communication which the Constitution protects; the First Amendment also protects vigorous advocacy, certainly of lawful ends, against governmental intrusion. [In] the context of NAACP objectives, litigation is not a technique of resolving private differences; it is a means for [achieving] equality of treatment for the members of the Negro community. [It] is thus a form of political expression. Groups which find themselves unable to achieve their objectives through the ballot frequently turn to the courts. [And] litigation may well be the sole practicable avenue open to a minority to petition for redress of grievances. [There] is no longer any doubt that the [First Amendment protects] certain forms of orderly group activity. Thus we have affirmed the right "to engage in association for the advancement of beliefs and ideas." NAACP v. Alabama. [The] NAACP is not a conventional political party, but [for the group] it assists, [association] for litigation may be the most effective form of [political association].

[Under Chapter 33,] a person who advises another that his legal rights have been infringed and refers him to a particular attorney or group of attorneys [for] assistance has committed a [crime]. There thus inheres in the statute the gravest danger of smothering all discussion looking to the eventual institution of litigation on behalf of the rights of members of an unpopular minority. [Such] a vague and broad statute lends itself to selective enforcement against unpopular causes. We cannot close our eyes to the fact that the militant Negro civil rights movement has engendered the intense resentment and opposition of the politically dominant white community of Virginia; litigation assisted by the NAACP has been bitterly fought. In such circumstances a statute broadly curtailing group activity leading to litigation may easily become a weapon of oppression, however evenhanded its terms appear. Its mere existence could well freeze out of existence all such activity on behalf of the civil rights of Negro citizens. [We] have consistently held that only a compelling state interest in the regulation of a subject within [a state's power] can justify limiting First Amendment freedoms. [However] valid may be Virginia's interest in regulating the traditionally illegal practices of barratry, maintenance and champerty, that interest does not justify the prohibition of the NAACP activities disclosed by this record.

■ JUSTICE HARLAN, with whom JUSTICES CLARK and STEWART join, dissenting.

[Litigation,] whether or not associated with the attempt to vindicate constitutional rights, is *conduct*. It is speech *plus*. Although the State surely may not broadly prohibit individuals with a common interest from joining together to petition a court for redress of their grievances, it is equally certain that the State may impose reasonable regulations limiting the permissible form of litigation and the manner of legal representation within its borders.

The interest which Virginia has here asserted is that of maintaining high professional standards among those who practice law within its borders. [A] State's felt need for regulation of professional conduct may reasonably extend beyond mere "ambulance chasing." [Running] perhaps even deeper is the desire of the profession, of courts, and of legislatures to prevent any interference with the uniquely personal relationship between lawyer and client and to maintain untrammeled by outside influences the responsibility which the lawyer owes to the courts he serves. [The] important function of organizations like petitioner in vindicating constitutional rights [is] not substantially impaired by this statute. [This enactment], contrary to the majority's suggestion, [does not] prevent petitioner from recommending the services of attorneys who are not subject to its directions and control. [It] prevents only the solicitation of business for attorneys subject to petitioner's control, and as so limited, should be sustained.

THE MEANING AND IMPLICATIONS OF NAACP V. BUTTON

1. *Non-constitutional litigation.* A year after Button, in **Brotherhood of Railroad Trainmen v. Virginia**, 377 U.S. 1 (1964), the Court extended its holding outside the area of litigation involving constitutional rights. The union advised its members to obtain legal advice before making settlements of their personal injury claims, and recommended particular attorneys. The result of its plan was "to channel legal employment to the particular lawyers approved by the Brotherhood." A Virginia court issued an injunction against the union for solicitation and unauthorized practice of law. Justice BLACK's majority opinion concluded that the injunction violated the First Amendment: "The State can no more keep these workers from using their cooperative plan to advise one another than it could use more direct means to bar them from resorting to the courts to vindicate their legal rights." As in the Button case, "the State again has failed to show any appreciable public interest in preventing the Brotherhood from carrying out its plan to recommend the lawyers it selects to represent injured workers. [The] Constitution protects the associational rights of the members of the union precisely as it does those of the NAACP." Justice CLARK's dissent, joined by Justice Harlan, objected that "[p]ersonal injury litigation is not a form of political expression, but rather a procedure for the settlement of damage claims," and thus that Button was distinguishable.

2. *Group legal services.* The Button and Trainmen cases in turn provided the basis for setting aside a state order against another variety of allegedly unauthorized practice of law by a union in **United Mine Workers v. Illinois State Bar Ass'n**, 389 U.S. 217 (1967). The union had employed a salaried attorney to assist its members with workmen's compensation

claims. Justice BLACK's majority opinion concluded that the state order "substantially impairs the associational rights of the Mine Workers and is not needed to protect the State's interest in high standards of legal ethics." Justice HARLAN dissented. And the Court relied on the Button, Trainmen, and United Mine Workers cases in **United Transportation Union v. State Bar of Michigan**, 401 U.S. 576 (1971), setting aside a broad state court injunction against a union's plan purportedly designed to protect union members from excessive fees by incompetent attorneys in actions under the Federal Employers' Liability Act. Justice BLACK, writing for the Court, emphasized "the basic right to group legal action, a right first asserted in this Court by an association of Negroes seeking the protection of freedoms guaranteed by the Constitution." He added: "The common thread running through our decisions in NAACP v. Button, Trainmen, and United Mine Workers is that collective activity undertaken to obtain meaningful access to the courts is a fundamental right within the protection of the First Amendment. [That] right would be a hollow promise if courts could deny associations of workers or others the means of enabling their members to meet the costs of legal representation." Justices Harlan, White and Blackmun dissented in part.

Were the associational rights concerns protected in the NAACP context of Button equally applicable in the union cases that followed? Would a distinction between "personal injury litigation" and "civil rights litigation" itself have been constitutional? Recall that in Ohralik (1978; p. 212), the right of commercial free speech did not bar regulation of in-person solicitation of clients; but in Primus, the companion case, the Court relied on the Button legacy to protect an ACLU lawyer against solicitation charges for seeking a client to bring a suit against alleged compulsory sterilization. Should the Court have inquired further into (and explicitly relied upon) the State's motives in Button? May reluctance to identify improper motives in cases such as Button have led the Court to give inadequate weight in other cases to "purer" state concerns regarding professional ethics and conflicts of interest?

3.   *Boycotts.* Does the right of expressive association extend beyond litigation to collective efforts to induce employers or merchants to change their policies through more direct action? Does it extend to picketing or other forms of boycott? The Court has reviewed a number of disputes over labor picketing. In Thornhill v. Alabama, 310 U.S. 88 (1940), the Court held unconstitutional a statute that had been applied to ban all picketing. In Giboney v. Empire Storage & Ice Co., 336 U.S. 490 (1949), however, the Court upheld an injunction barring, as a conspiracy in restraint of trade, a union picket against a wholesale dealer to induce it to refrain from selling to nonunion peddlers. The Court unanimously rejected the argument that the injunction was "an unconstitutional abridgement of free speech because the picketers were attempting peacefully to publicize truthful facts about a labor dispute." Later decisions "established a broad field in which a State, in enforcing some public policy, [could] constitutionally enjoin peaceful picketing in preventing effectuation of that policy." International Brotherhood of Teamsters v. Vogt, Inc., 354 U.S. 284 (1957).

Does the state's power to regulate economic boycotts extend to a boycott motivated by political purposes? This question came before the Court in **NAACP v. Claiborne Hardware Co.**, 458 U.S. 886 (1982). The case (other aspects of which are discussed at p. 51) involved an NAACP boycott of white merchants by black citizens in Claiborne County, Mississippi. The boycott, begun in 1966, sought to induce white civic and business leaders to comply with a long list of black citizens' demands for equality and racial justice. The boycott was conducted by largely peaceful means, but it included some incidents of violence as well. In a civil action brought by some of the merchants to recover economic losses allegedly caused by the boycott, a state trial court imposed a judgment for over $1,250,000 on a large group of defendants (including the NAACP). The Mississippi Supreme Court, although not accepting all of the lower court's theories, upheld the judgment of liability on the basis of the common law tort of malicious interference with plaintiffs' businesses. The court found the boycott unlawful because, in its view, the defendants had agreed to use and did use force, violence, and intimidation to coerce nonparticipating blacks to join the boycott, and remanded for a recomputation of damages.

Without dissent (Justice Rehnquist concurred only in the result and Justice Marshall did not participate), the Court reversed, holding "that the nonviolent elements of petitioners' activities are entitled to the protection of the First Amendment" and that, "[w]hile the State legitimately may impose damages for the consequences of violent conduct, it may not award compensation for the consequences of nonviolent, protected activity."

Justice STEVENS, writing for the Court, began by explaining why "the nonviolent elements of petitioners' activities" were entitled to First Amendment protection. He noted that the boycott "took many forms": "The boycott was supported by speeches and nonviolent picketing. Participants repeatedly encouraged others to join in its cause. Each of these elements of the boycott is a form of speech or conduct that is ordinarily entitled to protection under the [First] Amendment. [In] addition, [the names] of boycott violators were read aloud at meetings [and] published in a local black newspaper. Petitioners admittedly sought to persuade others to join the boycott through social pressure and the 'threat' of social ostracism. Speech does not lose its protected character, however, simply because it may embarrass others or coerce them into action." He also noted that "[t]he right to associate does not lose all constitutional protection merely because some members of the group may have participated in conduct or advocated doctrine that itself is not protected."

True, the "presence of protected activity [did] not end the relevant constitutional inquiry": "Governmental regulation that has an incidental effect on First Amendment freedoms may be justified in certain narrowly defined instances. [O'Brien.] A nonviolent and totally voluntary boycott may have a disruptive effect on local economic conditions. This Court has recognized the strong governmental interest in certain forms of economic regulation, even though such regulation may have an incidental effect on rights of speech and association. The right of business entities to 'associate' to suppress competition may be curtailed. Unfair trade practices may be restricted. Secondary boycotts and picketing by labor unions may be prohibited." But, Justice Stevens added, "[w]hile States have broad power to regulate economic activity, we do not find a comparable right to prohibit peaceful political activity such as that found in the boycott in this case. This Court has recognized that expression on public issues 'has always rested on the highest rung of the hierarchy of First Amendment values.'"

Applying these principles, Justice Stevens suggested that the purpose of affecting governmental action was protected by the First Amendment even if there was also an anticompetitive effect: "[A] major purpose of the boycott in this case was to influence governmental action. [The] petitioners certainly foresaw—and directly intended—that the merchants would sustain economic injury as a result of their campaign. [However], the purpose of petitioners' campaign was not to destroy legitimate competition. [The] right of the State to regulate economic activity could not justify a complete prohibition against a nonviolent, politically-motivated boycott designed to force governmental and economic change and to effectuate rights guaranteed by the Constitution itself."

He continued: "[The] fact that such activity is constitutionally protected [imposes] a special obligation on this Court to examine critically the basis on which liability was imposed." Clearly, there were unprotected aspects of the boycott: "The First Amendment does not protect violence. [There] is no question that acts of violence occurred. No federal rule of law restricts a State from imposing tort liability for business losses that are caused by violence and by threats of violence. When such conduct occurs in the context of a constitutionally protected activity, however, 'precision of regulation' is demanded. [NAACP v. Button.] Specifically, the presence of activity protected by the First Amendment imposes restraints on the grounds that may give rise to damage liability and on the persons who may be held accountable for those damages." One such restraint was that petitioners could not be held liable for *all* damages "resulting from the boycott"; "[o]nly those losses proximately caused by unlawful conduct may be recovered."

A second restraint concerned who may be named as a defendant: "The First Amendment [restricts] the ability of the State to impose liability on an individual solely because of his association with another. Civil liability may not be imposed merely because an individual belonged to a group, some members of which committed acts of violence. For liability to be imposed by reason of association alone, it is necessary to establish that the group itself possessed unlawful goals and that the individual held a specific intent to further those illegal aims. 'In this sensitive field, the State may not employ 'means that broadly stifle fundamental personal liberties when the end can be more narrowly achieved.' Shelton v. Tucker." With respect to most of the petitioners, the record failed to show an adequate basis to sustain the judgments against them. Mere participation in the local meetings of the NAACP was "an insufficient predicate on which to impose liability." That would "not even constitute 'guilt by association,' since there is no evidence that the association possessed unlawful aims. Rather, liability could only be imposed on a 'guilt *for* association' theory. Neither is permissible under the First Amendment." Nor could NAACP liability be predicated on any allegedly unlawful conduct by NAACP leader and boycott organizer Charles Evers: "To impose liability without a finding that the NAACP authorized— either actually or apparently—or ratified unlawful conduct would impermissibly burden the rights of political association that are protected by the First Amendment."

Justice Stevens concluded: "The taint of violence colored the conduct of some of the petitioners. They, of course, may be held liable for the consequences of their violent deeds. The burden of demonstrating that it colored the entire collective effort, however, is not satisfied by evidence that violence occurred or even that violence contributed to the success of the boycott. A massive and prolonged effort to change the social, political, and economic structure of a local environment cannot be characterized as a violent conspiracy simply by reference to the ephemeral consequences of relatively few violent acts. Such a characterization must be supported by findings that adequately disclose the evidentiary basis for concluding that specific parties agreed to use unlawful means, that carefully identify the impact of such unlawful conduct, and that recognize the importance of avoiding the imposition of punishment for constitutionally protected activity. The burden of demonstrating that fear rather than protected conduct was the dominant force in the movement is heavy. [The] findings of [the trial court] are constitutionally insufficient to support the judgment that all petitioners are liable for all losses resulting from the boycott."

Does NAACP v. Claiborne Hardware have any application to an economically motivated boycott? In **International Longshoremen's Ass'n v. Allied International, Inc.**, 456 U.S. 212 (1982), decided shortly before Claiborne, the Court rejected a First Amendment claim by a union that refused to unload cargoes shipped from the Soviet Union, as a protest against the Soviet invasion of Afghanistan. The unanimous Court found the protest to be an illegal secondary boycott under federal labor law and rejected the claim that the boycott "was not a labor dispute [but] a political dispute." The Court noted that "conduct designed not to communicate but to coerce merits [little] consideration under the First Amendment." Does Claiborne overrule Longshoremen's? If not, is the distinction between "political" and "economic" purposes justifiable under the First Amendment? For later rulings declining to apply NAACP v. Claiborne Hardware to boycotts stemming from economic rather than political purposes, see Allied Tube & Conduit Corp. v. Indian Head, Inc., 486 U.S. 492 (1988), and FTC v. Superior Court Trial Lawyers Ass'n, 493 U.S. 411 (1990).

4. *Material support and terrorism.* The government's increasing focus on terrorism in recent decades raises novel problems related to the freedom of association. May the government restrict individuals from associating with terrorists even if those individuals do not themselves engage in any violence? Is associating with terrorists different from belonging to a Communist organization? In **Holder v. Humanitarian Law Project**, 561 U.S. 1 (2010), (p. 271), the Court addressed a First Amendment challenge on freedom of speech and association grounds to a federal criminal provision which made it unlawful to "knowingly provid[e] material support or resources to a foreign terrorist organization."

Chief Justice ROBERTS delivered the opinion of the Court. "[The] plaintiffs in this litigation seek to provide support to two [organizations that engage in terrorist activity]. Plaintiffs claim that they seek to facilitate only the lawful, nonviolent purposes of those groups, and that applying the material-support law to prevent them from doing so violates the Constitution.

[Plaintiffs] in this litigation are two U.S. citizens and six domestic organizations. [In] 1998, plaintiffs filed suit in federal court challenging the constitutionality of the material-support statute. [Plaintiffs] claimed that they wished to provide support for the humanitarian and political activities of the [Kurdistan Workers' Party (PKK)] and the [Liberation Tigers of Tamil Eelam (LTTE)] in the form of monetary contributions, other tangible aid, legal training, and political advocacy, but that they could not do so for fear of prosecution under § 2339B."

After rejecting the plaintiffs' free speech claim, Chief Justice Roberts turned to the plaintiffs' freedom of association claim: "Plaintiffs' final claim is that the material-support statute violates their freedom of association under the First Amendment. Plaintiffs argue that the statute criminalizes the mere fact of their associating with the PKK and the LTTE, thereby running afoul of decisions like [De Jonge and Keyishian].

The Court of Appeals correctly rejected this claim because the statute does not penalize mere association with a foreign terrorist organization. As the Ninth Circuit put it: 'The statute does not prohibit being a member of one of the designated groups or vigorously promoting and supporting the political goals of the group. . . . What [§ 2339B] prohibits is the act of giving material support. . . . ' Plaintiffs want to do the latter. Our decisions scrutinizing penalties on simple association or assembly are therefore inapposite.

Plaintiffs also argue that the material-support statute burdens their freedom of association because it prevents them from providing support to designated foreign terrorist organizations, but not to other groups. [Any] burden on plaintiffs' freedom of association in this regard is justified for the same reasons that we have denied plaintiffs' free speech challenge. It would be strange if the Constitution permitted Congress to prohibit certain forms of speech that constitute material support, but did not permit Congress to prohibit that support only to particularly dangerous and lawless foreign organizations. Congress is not required to ban material support to every group or none at all."

Justice BREYER, joined by Justices Ginsburg and Sotomayor, dissented: "The plaintiffs, all United States citizens or associations, now seek an injunction and declaration providing that, without violating the statute, they can [train on issues of humanitarian and international for peaceful dispute resolution; engage in political advocacy; and teach organization PKK members how to petition representative bodies.] All these activities are of a kind that the First Amendment ordinarily protects.

[That] this speech and association for political purposes is the kind of activity to which the First Amendment ordinarily offers its strongest protection is elementary. [Although] in the Court's view the statute applies only where the PKK helps to coordinate a defendant's activities, [the] simple fact of 'coordination' alone cannot readily remove protection that the First Amendment would otherwise grant. That amendment, after all, also protects the freedom of association. [See NAACP v. Claiborne Hardware Co. and Dejonge]. 'Coordination' with a political group, like membership, involves association.

[The] Government says that the plaintiffs' proposed activities will 'bolste[r] a terrorist organization's efficacy and strength in a community' and 'undermin[e] this nation's efforts to delegitimize and weaken those groups.' In the Court's view, too, the Constitution permits application of the statute to activities of the kind at issue in part because those activities could provide a group that engages in terrorism with 'legitimacy.'

[But] this 'legitimacy' justification cannot by itself warrant suppression of political speech, advocacy, and association. Speech, association, and related activities on behalf of a group will often, perhaps always, help to legitimate that group. Thus, were the law to accept a 'legitimating' effect, in and of itself and without qualification, as providing sufficient grounds for imposing such a ban, the First Amendment battle would be lost in untold instances where it should be won.

[The] 'legitimacy' justification itself is inconsistent with critically important First Amendment case law. Consider the cases involving the protection the First Amendment offered those who joined the Communist Party intending only to further its peaceful activities. In those cases, this Court took account of congressional findings that the Communist Party not only advocated theoretically but also sought to put into practice the overthrow of our Government through force and violence. The Court had previously accepted Congress' determinations that the American Communist Party was a 'Communist action organization.' [Nonetheless,] the Court held that the First Amendment protected an American's right to belong to that party—despite whatever 'legitimating' effect membership might have had— as long as the person did not share the party's unlawful purposes. [See, e.g., Dejonge and Keyishian]. As I have pointed out, those cases draw further support from other cases permitting pure advocacy of even the most unlawful activity-as long as that advocacy is not 'directed to inciting or producing imminent lawless action and . . . likely to incite or produce such action.' [Brandenburg] The Government's 'legitimating' theory would seem to apply to these cases with equal justifying force; and, if recognized, it would have led this Court to conclusions other than those it reached.

[For] the reasons I have set forth, I believe application of the statute as the Government interprets it would gravely and without adequate justification injure interests of the kind the First Amendment protects."

Does Justice Stevens's admonition in NAACP v. Claiborne Hardware Co. that "[t]he right to associate does not lose all constitutional protection merely because some members of the group may have participated in conduct or advocated doctrine that itself is not protected" still hold true for individuals who associate with terrorist organizations? Perhaps Humanitarian Law Project demonstrates that each national security scare adopts new technologies to address the potential threat of civil liberties.

DENIAL OF GOVERNMENT BENEFITS BECAUSE OF ASSOCIATION

Even if government may not outlaw an association, force disclosure of its membership, or restrict its central activities, may it nonetheless use associational ties as a ground for disqualification from government benefits such as jobs and licenses? May government condition such benefits on oaths of loyalty or disavowal of disfavored associations?

The Court has several times relied upon the prohibition on bills of attainder to hold that associational ties may not be the basis for denying a position of public trust. Soon after the Civil War, the Court struck down, as bills of attainder, loyalty oaths directed at former supporters of the Confederacy. See Cummings v. Missouri, 4 Wall. (71 U.S.) 277 (1867) (invalidating denial of the right to preach to those who did not disavow Confederate sympathy), and Ex parte Garland, 4 Wall. (71 U.S.) 333 (1867) (invalidating denial of the right to practice law in federal courts to those who did not disavow Confederate sympathy). The Court has relied on the bill of attainder ban in only one modern case: United States v. Brown, 381 U.S. 437 (1965), holding unconstitutional a federal law making it a crime for a member of the Communist Party to serve as an officer or an employee of a labor union. Chief Justice Warren's majority opinion emphasized that it was not necessary that a bill of attainder name the parties to be punished. He viewed the prohibition "as an implementation of the separation of powers, a general safeguard against legislative exercise of the judicial function, or more simply—trial by legislature."

More commonly, the issue has arisen in connection with First Amendment claims. Such claims typically assert either that membership in an organization is not in itself a sufficient ground to deny a public privilege, or that refusal to discuss or disavow membership is not such a ground. During the Cold War era that followed World War II, for example, loyalty requirements proliferated at all levels of government employment. These programs aimed to prevent Communists and other "subversives" from occupying sensitive government or industrial positions. The Court initially sustained various loyalty programs against constitutional challenge. For example, Adler v. Board of Education, 342 U.S. 485 (1952), upheld a New York law barring from a position as a public school teacher anyone who knowingly became a member of any organization that advocated the violent overthrow of government. In Garner v. Los Angeles Bd. of Public Works, 341 U.S. 716 (1951), the Court upheld a requirement that each city employee take an oath that, within the past five years, he or she had not advocated the overthrow of government by force or violence or belonged to any organization advocating such overthrow, and that the employee disclose whether he or she was or ever had been a Communist Party member. Such requirements were deemed relevant to fitness for the job. The only limitation the Court imposed was a requirement of *knowing* membership. In Wieman v. Updegraff, 344 U.S. 183 (1952), a unanimous Court struck down, on due process grounds, an Oklahoma loyalty oath requiring employees to state that they were not and had not for five years been affiliated with any organization that had been deemed a "Communist front or subversive organization." The Court distinguished Garner and Adler on the ground that, under the Oklahoma law, it did not matter "whether association existed innocently or knowingly."

During these years, the Court also considered a number of cases involving refusals to answer subversion-related questions in the course of bar admission proceedings. In its first encounters with the problem, the Court held on due process grounds that a state could not refuse to admit applicants to the bar on the basis of mere membership in the Communist party. Schware v. Board of Bar Examiners, 353 U.S. 232 (1957); Konigsberg v. State Bar, 353 U.S. 252 (1957). But when the Konigsberg case returned to the Court four years later, the Court upheld the denial of admission on the ground that the applicant had refused, on First Amendment grounds, to answer questions about his political associations and beliefs. **Konigsberg v. State Bar of California [Konigsberg II]**, 366 U.S. 36 (1961). Justice HARLAN, writing for the 5–4 majority, emphasized the distinction between refusals to answer relevant questions and substantive grounds for denials of a license. Thus, a state could deny admission for refusing to answer even if affirmative answers would not by themselves have justified exclusion. In response to Konigsberg's claim that questions about his Communist Party membership "unconstitutionally impinged upon rights of free speech and association," Justice Harlan replied: "[We] regard the State's interest in having lawyers who are devoted to the law in its broader sense, [including] its procedures for orderly change, as clearly sufficient to outweigh the minimal effect upon free association occasioned by compulsory disclosure in the circumstances here presented."

In the 1960s, the Warren Court struck down several state-imposed loyalty oaths on "void-for-vagueness" grounds. In **Cramp v. Board of Public Instruction**, 368 U.S. 278 (1961), the Court invalidated a Florida law requiring public employees to swear that they had never "knowingly lent their aid, support, advice, counsel or influence to the Communist Party." Even though the state court had construed the law to include "the element of scienter," Justice STEWART emphasized its "extraordinary ambiguity" and found it "completely lacking [in] terms susceptible of objective measurement." He added that the "vice of unconstitutional vagueness [was] further aggravated [because the law] operates to inhibit the exercise of individual freedoms affirmatively protected by the Constitution." Similarly, in **Baggett v. Bullitt**, 377 U.S. 360 (1964), the Court, in partial reliance on Cramp, invalidated two state loyalty oath requirements, including one obligating state employees to swear that they were not members of a "subversive organization." The majority found the requirements "invalid on their face because their language is unduly vague, uncertain and broad."

In **Elfbrandt v. Russell**, 384 U.S. 11 (1966), the Court finally invalidated a loyalty oath as an infringement of expressive association. Justice DOUGLAS wrote for the Court, holding that Arizona could not impose on an unwilling employee an oath of loyalty to the state and federal constitutions on threat of perjury and discharge if the employee "knowingly and wilfully becomes or remains a member" of subversive organizations. His opinion rested on the danger of guilt by association: "One who subscribes to this Arizona oath and who is, or thereafter becomes, a knowing member of an organization which has as 'one of its purposes' the violent overthrow of the government, is subject to immediate discharge and criminal penalties. Nothing in the oath, the statutory gloss, or the construction of the oath and statutes given by the Arizona Supreme Court purports to exclude association by one who does not subscribe to the organization's unlawful ends. [Thus,] the 'hazard of being prosecuted for knowing but guiltless behavior' is a reality. People often label as 'communist' ideas which they oppose; and they make up our juries."

"[Those] who join an organization but do not share its unlawful purposes and who do not participate in its unlawful activities surely pose no threat, either as citizens or as public employees. Laws such as this which are not restricted in scope to those who join with the "specific intent" to further illegal action impose, in effect, a conclusive presumption that the member shares the unlawful aims of the organization. [This] Act threatens the cherished freedom of association protected by the First Amendment. [A] statute touching those protected rights must be "narrowly drawn." [Legitimate] legislative goals "cannot be pursued by means that broadly stifle fundamental personal liberties when the end can be more narrowly achieved." [Shelton v. Tucker.] [A] law which applies to membership without the "specific intent" to further the illegal aims of the organization infringes unnecessarily on protected freedoms. It rests on the doctrine of "guilt by association" which has no place here. Such a law cannot stand."

Justice WHITE, dissented, joined by Justices Clark, Harlan and Stewart: "[If] the State is entitled to condition employment on the absence of knowing membership, and if an employee obtains employment by falsifying his present qualifications, there is no sound constitutional reason for denying the State the power to treat such false swearing as perjury."

And in **Keyishian v. Board of Regents**, 385 U.S. 589 (1967), the Court again cited the freedom of expressive association as a ground for invalidating a loyalty oath required as a condition of public employment, this time for state university faculty members. Writing for the Court, Justice BRENNAN stated: "[Mere] Party membership, even with knowledge of the Party's unlawful goals, can not suffice to justify criminal punishment. [Legislation that] sanctions membership unaccompanied by specific intent to further the unlawful goals of the organization or which is not active membership violates constitutional limitations. Measured against this standard, [these provisions] sweep overbroadly into association which may not be proscribed. The presumption of disqualification arising from proof of mere membership [cannot be rebutted by] proof of nonactive membership or a showing of the absence of intent to further unlawful aims. [Thus, the provisions] suffer from impermissible 'overbreadth.' They seek to bar employment both for association which legitimately may be proscribed and for association which may not be proscribed consistently with First Amendment rights. Where statutes have an overbroad sweep, just as where they are vague, 'the hazard of loss of substantial impairment of those precious rights may be critical,' [since] those covered by the statute are bound to limit their behavior to that which is unquestionably safe. [Shelton v. Tucker.] We therefore hold [the relevant provisions] invalid insofar as they proscribe mere knowing membership without any showing of specific intent to further the unlawful aims of the [Communist Party]." The Elfbrandt dissenters repeated their dissenting views here.

These decisions did not mean that all oaths of public office were unconstitutional. In **Cole v. Richardson**, 405 U.S. 676 (1972), the Court, by a vote of 4–3, upheld a two-part loyalty oath required of all Massachusetts public employees. The first part required a promise to "uphold and defend the federal and state constitutions"; the second required a promise to "oppose the overthrow of the [government] by force, violence or by any illegal or unconstitutional method." The Court read the "oppose the overthrow" clause as imposing no significantly greater obligation than the "uphold and defend" provision and accordingly concluded that both parts of the oath were constitutional.

And in a trilogy of 5–4 decisions involving challenges to oaths for admission to the bar, Court held that a state may not deny admission to the bar based on the applicant's refusal to answer the question whether she had ever been a member of the Communist Party or any organization "that advocates overthrow of the United States Government by force or violence," see **Baird v. State Bar of Arizona**, 401 U.S. 1 (1971) ("[A] State may not inquire about a man's views or associations solely for the purpose of withholding a right or benefit because of what he believes."); that a state may not refuse bar admission to an applicant for refusing to answer questions about membership in "any organization which advocates the overthrow of the government of the United States by force," and about all other organizations of which he had been a member, see **Application of Stolar**, 401 U.S. 23 (1971) (holding requests for general lists of organizational memberships "impermissible in light of the First Amendment [under Shelton v. Tucker]"); but that a state *could* employ a screening system that asked first, whether the applicant had been a member of any organization he or she knew advocated the overthrow of government by force or violence, and second, if the first answer was affirmative, whether the applicant had the "specific intent to further the aims of such organization," see **Law Students**

Civil Rights Research Council v. Wadmond, 401 U.S. 154 (1971) ("[We] are not persuaded that careful administration of such a system as New York's need result in chilling effects upon the exercise of constitutional freedoms."). Is the upshot of these three cases that bar authorities may inquire into an applicant's knowing membership in the Communist Party with the specific intent to advance its ends, and refuse bar admission to one who refuses to cooperate with such a properly narrowed inquiry, but may not refuse admission to one who refuses to answer a question that may disadvantage him or her on the basis of organizational affiliation alone? On the speech implications of moral character requirements for bar admission generally, see Rhode, "Moral Character as a Professional Credential," 94 Yale L.J. 491 (1985).

COMPELLED ASSOCIATION: THE RIGHT NOT TO ASSOCIATE

1. *Compulsory fees to unions.* After NAACP v. Alabama clarified that the "right of association" under the First Amendment could not be infringed, claims were made that there was a similar right *not* to associate. Initially, such compelled association claims were brought by individuals who objected to compulsory contributions to organizations—e.g., employees subject to mandatory dues under union shop agreements and lawyers attacking mandatory dues requirements under integrated bar systems.

These cases coincide with an extended period of gradual decline in the power and membership of labor unions. Unions like the American Federation of Labor (AFL) were key to securing workers' rights, like the 40-hour work week, workers' compensation systems, and important labor statutes like the National Labor Relations Act, in the late part of the nineteenth and early twentieth centuries. Today, however, the proper role of unions in American society has become a contentious issue. In particular, public employee unions have come under attack as opponents of unions have sought to curtail their collective bargaining rights and bolster the freedom of non-union employees. Union advocates claim that strong collective bargaining rights, which might entail incidental infringements on the associational rights of employees, are necessary to preserve the gains made on behalf of workers. Opponents argue that these infringements are antithetical to their First Amendment rights of speech and association. Consider the cases that follow in light of this debate.

In **Abood v. Detroit Board of Educ.**, 431 U.S. 209 (1977), the Court confronted a compelled association claim in the context of public employees' unions. Many states allow public-sector unions to negotiate agency-shop agreements that entitle a union to levy fees on employees who are not union members but whom the union represents in collective bargaining. Abood involved public sector employees who were subject to such an agency-shop agreement adopted by a school board and a union pursuant to state law. Under the agreement, every nonunion employee was required to pay to the union "a service fee equal in amount to union dues" as a condition of employment. That scheme was challenged by dissenting employees who objected to having to pay fees for (1) "collective bargaining in the public sector" and (2) "ideological union expenditures not directly related to collective bargaining."

Justice STEWART's majority opinion recognized a right to "refus[e] to associate" and rejected the first challenge but sustained the second. In upholding the exaction of compulsory fees for collective bargaining expenses, Justice Stewart relied in part on earlier cases that had upheld, largely on statutory grounds, the exaction of compulsory dues in the private sector. He found that in the public sector, as in the private sector, the interests in the operation of a collective bargaining system, in assuring labor peace, and in avoiding the risk of "free riders" overcame the objectors' First Amendment interests "in not being compelled to contribute to the costs of exclusive union representation." Justice Stewart concluded, however, that the First Amendment barred requiring dissidents to contribute financially to the support of an ideological cause they found objectionable, and thus a public employee may not be required "to contribute to the support of an ideological cause he may oppose as a condition of holding a job as a public school teacher." The union was free to advance "ideological causes not germane to its duties as collective-bargaining representative," but it had to finance such expenditures with dues only from "employees who do not object to advancing those ideas and who are not coerced into doing so against their will by the threat of loss of governmental employment." He accordingly remanded for development of remedies to prevent "compulsory subsidization of ideological activities by employees who object thereto without restricting the union's ability to require every employee to contribute to the cost of collective-bargaining activities."

Justice POWELL, joined by Chief Justice Burger and Justice Blackmun, concurred in the judgment, arguing that "compelling a government employee to give financial support to a union in the public sector—regardless of the uses to which the union puts the contribution—impinges seriously upon interests in free speech and association protected by the First Amendment," and that the burden should have rested with the State to come forward and demonstrate, as to each union expenditure for which it would exact support from minority employees, that the "compelled contribution is necessary to serve overriding governmental objectives." He objected to the majority's placement of the burden on the dissenting employee to come forward and identify his disagreement in order to obtain a rebate from the union.

Abood appeared to strike a compromise with regard to the constitutionality of union fee charges. Some thirty years later however, the Court began incrementally to weaken the ability of unions to collect such fees in a series of cases that undercut Abood. First, in **Davenport v. Washington Education Ass'n**, 551 U.S. 177 (2007), the Court held that a state law mandating that a union obtain a nonmember's affirmative authorization before using their fees for election-related purposes was constitutional, and that such a requirement was not a violation of the union's own expressive or associational rights. The ruling effectively allowed states to shift the burden of enforcing Abood rights from a dissenting employee to the union.

The Court next decided **Knox v. Serv. Employees Int'l Union (SEIU)**, 567 U.S. 298 (2012), which involved a special assessment on public employees to create a fund for the union's political activities. While the union had sent out a notice for a regular assessment, it failed to send out a new notice for an increase in political expenditures that would have given employees an opportunity to opt out of those fees. Justice ALITO's opinion for the Court held that the special fee assessment violated the First Amendment. In language signaling that Abood's rationale was under attack, he wrote: "The First Amendment creates 'an open marketplace' in which differing ideas about political, economic, and social issues can compete freely for public acceptance without improper government interference. The government may not prohibit the dissemination of ideas that it disfavors, nor compel the endorsement of ideas that it approves. [R.A.V.; Brandenburg; Barnette; Wooley].

[By] allowing unions to collect any fees from nonmembers and by permitting unions to use opt-out rather than opt-in schemes when annual dues are billed, our cases have substantially impinged upon the First Amendment rights of nonmembers. In the new situation presented here, we see no justification for any further impingement. The general rule— individuals should not be compelled to subsidize private groups or private speech—should prevail."

In **Harris v. Quinn**, 573 U.S. 616 (2014), the Court next declined to extend Abood to what it called "partial public employees," home healthcare personal assistants who belonged to an Illinois union that contracted with the state but were individually answerable to their patient-customers. In a 5–4 opinion for the Court, Justice ALITO did not directly overrule Abood, but nevertheless indicated that it was not long for this world. Calling its analysis "questionable on several grounds," he wrote: "Abood failed to appreciate the conceptual difficulty of distinguishing in public-sector cases between union expenditures that are made for collective-bargaining purposes and those that are made to achieve political ends. In the private sector, the line is easier to see. Collective bargaining concerns the union's dealings with the employer; political advocacy and lobbying are directed at the government. But in the public sector, both collective-bargaining and political advocacy and lobbying are directed at the government. [Abood] likewise did not foresee the practical problems that would face objecting nonmembers. Employees who suspect that a union has improperly put certain expenses in the "germane" category must bear a heavy burden if they wish to challenge the union's actions. [Finally,] a critical pillar of the Abood Court's analysis rests on an unsupported empirical assumption, namely, that the principle of exclusive representation in the public sector is dependent on a union or agency shop."

Justice Alito then applied strict scrutiny and dismissed the union's claims as failing to present a compelling state interest. "A union's status as exclusive bargaining agent and the right to collect an agency fee from non-members are not inextricably linked. For example, employees in some federal agencies may choose a union to serve as the exclusive bargaining agent for the unit, but no employee is required to join the union or to pay any union fee. [Any] threat to labor peace is diminished because the personal assistants do not work together in a common state facility but instead spend all their time in private homes, either the customers' or their own. [The] State is not like the closed-fisted employer that is bent on minimizing employee wages and benefits and that yields only grudgingly under intense union pressure. [A] host of organizations advocate on behalf of the interests of persons falling within an occupational group, and many of these groups are quite successful even though they are dependent on voluntary contributions."

In dissent, Justice KAGAN, joined by Justices Ginsburg, Breyer, and Sotomayor, took the view that the collective bargaining agreements in the case "fall squarely within Abood's holding." Abood, she wrote, is not an anomaly. "Our decisions have long afforded government entities broad latitude to manage their workforces, even when that affects speech they could not regulate in other contexts. Abood is of a piece with all those decisions: While protecting an employee's most significant expression, that decision also enables the government to advance its interests in operating effectively—by bargaining, if it so chooses, with a single employee representative and preventing free riding on that union's efforts." Furthermore, Justice Kagan wrote, "The Abood rule is deeply entrenched, and is the foundation for not tens or hundreds, but thousands of contracts between unions and governments across the Nation. Our precedent about precedent, fairly understood and applied, makes it impossible for this Court to reverse that decision."

Then in **Janus v. American Federation of State, County, and Municipal Employees, Council 31**, 585 U.S. ___, 138 S. Ct. 974 (2018), the Court in a 5–4 decision reversed the part of Abood that allowed collection of agency fees. Justice ALITO again wrote the opinion, joined by Chief Justice Roberts and Justices Kennedy, Thomas and Gorsuch: "Under Illinois law, public employees are forced to subsidize a union, even if they choose not to join and strongly object to the positions the union takes in collective bargaining and related activities. We conclude that this arrangement violates the free speech rights of nonmembers by compelling them to subsidize private speech on matters of substantial public concern.

"[Petitioner] in the present case contends that the Illinois law at issue should be subjected to strict scrutiny. The dissent, on the other hand, proposes that we apply what amounts to rational-basis review. [This] form of minimal scrutiny is foreign to our free-speech jurisprudence, and we reject it here. At the same time, we again find it unnecessary to decide the issue of strict scrutiny because the Illinois scheme cannot survive under even the more permissive standard applied in Knox and Harris.

"In Abood, the main defense of the agency-fee arrangement was that it served the State's interest in 'labor peace.' [We] assume that 'labor peace' [is] a compelling state interest, but Abood cited no evidence that the pandemonium it imagined would result if agency fees were not allowed.

"[The] federal employment experience is illustrative. Under federal law, a union chosen by majority vote is designated as the exclusive representative of all the employees, but federal law does not permit agency fees. Nevertheless, nearly a million federal employees—about 27% of the federal work force—are union members. [Likewise,] millions of public employees in the 28 States that have laws generally prohibiting agency fees are represented by unions that serve as the exclusive representatives of all the employees. Whatever may have been the case 41 years ago when Abood was handed down, it is now undeniable that 'labor peace' can readily be achieved through means significantly less restrictive of associational freedoms than the assessment of agency fees.

"In addition, [Abood] cited the risk of 'free riders' as justification for agency fees. [Petitioner] argues that he is not a free rider on a bus headed for a destination that he wishes to reach but is more like a person shanghaied for an unwanted voyage. [Avoiding] free riders is not a compelling interest. [Many] private groups speak out with the objective of obtaining government action that will have the effect of benefiting nonmembers. May all those who are thought to benefit from such efforts be compelled to subsidize this speech?

"[Those] supporting agency fees contend that the situation here is different because unions are statutorily required to represent the interests of all public employees in the unit, whether or not they are union members. Why might this matter? [It] is simply not true that unions will refuse to serve as the exclusive representative of all employees in the unit if they are not given agency fees. As noted, unions represent millions of public employees in jurisdictions that do not permit agency fees. No union is ever compelled to seek that designation. On the contrary, designation as exclusive representative is avidly sought.

"[There] remains the question whether *stare decisis* nonetheless counsels against overruling Abood. It does not. [*Stare decisis*] applies with perhaps least force of all to decisions that wrongly denied First Amendment rights. Our cases identify factors that should be taken into account in deciding whether to overrule a past decision. [An] important factor in determining whether a precedent should be overruled is the quality of its reasoning. [Abood] was poorly reasoned. [Abood] failed to appreciate the conceptual difficulty of distinguishing in public-sector cases between union expenditures that are made for collective-bargaining purposes and those that are made to achieve political ends. [Abood's] line between chargeable and nonchargeable union expenditures has proved to be impossible to draw with precision. [Objecting] employees also face a daunting and expensive task if they wish to challenge union chargeability determinations. [Developments] since Abood, both factual and legal, have also eroded the decision's underpinnings and left it an outlier among our First Amendment cases. Abood pinned its result on the unsupported empirical assumption that the principle of exclusive representation in the public sector is dependent on a union or agency shop. But [experience] has shown otherwise. It is also significant that the Court decided Abood against a very different legal and economic backdrop. Public-sector unionism was a relatively new phenomenon in 1977. [Since] then, public-sector union membership has come to surpass private-sector union membership, even though there are nearly four times as many total private-sector employees as public-sector employees. This ascendance of public-sector unions has been marked by a parallel increase in public spending. [Not] all that increase can be attributed to public-sector unions, of course, but the mounting costs of public-employee wages, benefits, and pensions undoubtedly played a substantial role. [Unsustainable] collective-bargaining agreements have also been blamed for multiple municipal bankruptcies. These developments, and the political debate over public spending and debt they have spurred, have given collective-bargaining issues a political valence that Abood did not fully appreciate. Abood is also an anomaly in our First Amendment jurisprudence [when] viewed against our cases holding that public employees generally may not be required to support a political party. [Reliance also] does not carry decisive weight. [It] would be unconscionable to permit free speech rights to be abridged in perpetuity in order to preserve contract provisions that will expire on their own in a few years' time. [Abood also] does not provide a clear or easily applicable standard, so arguments for reliance based on its clarity are misplaced. This is especially so because public-sector unions have been on notice for years regarding this Court's misgivings about Abood."

Justice KAGAN dissented, joined by Justices Ginsburg, Breyer, and Sotomayor: "For over 40 years, Abood struck a stable balance between public employees' First Amendment rights and government entities' interests in running their workforces as they thought proper. [The] Court's decisions have long made plain that government entities have substantial latitude to regulate their employees' speech—especially about terms of employment—in the interest of operating their workplaces effectively. [The] Abood regime was a paradigmatic example of how the government can regulate speech in its capacity as an employer. [The] decision will have large-scale consequences. Public employee unions will lose a secure source of financial support. State and local governments that thought fair-share provisions furthered their interests will need to find new ways of managing their workforces. Across the country, the relationships of public employees and employers will alter in both predictable and wholly unexpected ways. Rarely if ever has the Court overruled a decision [with] so little regard for the usual principles of *stare decisis*. [More] than 20 States have statutory schemes built on the decision. [Reliance] interests do not come any stronger. [And] likewise, judicial disruption does not get any greater.

"[The majority avoids] the key question, which is whether unions without agency fees will be *able to* (not whether they will *want to*) carry on as an effective exclusive representative. And as to that question, the majority again fails to reckon with how economically rational actors behave—in public as well as private workplaces. Without a fair-share agreement, the class of union non-members spirals upward. Employees (including those who love the union) realize that they can get the same benefits even if they let their memberships expire. And as more and more stop paying dues, those left must take up the financial slack (and anyway, begin to feel like suckers)—so they too quit the union. And when the vicious cycle finally ends, chances are that the union will lack the resources to effectively perform the responsibilities of an exclusive representative—or, in the worst case, to perform them at all. The result is to frustrate the interests of every government entity that thinks a strong exclusive-representation scheme will promote stable labor relations.

"In many cases over many decades, this Court has addressed how the First Amendment applies when the government, acting not as sovereign but as employer, limits its workers' speech. [It] must be able, much as a private employer is, to manage its workforce as it thinks fit. A public employee thus must submit to certain limitations on his or her freedom. Garcetti. [When] the government imposes speech restrictions relating to workplace operations, of the kind a private employer also would, the Court reliably upholds them. See, e.g., Connick. Like Pickering, Abood drew the constitutional line by analyzing the connection between the government's managerial interests and different kinds of expression.

"[But] the worse part of today's opinion is where the majority subverts all known principles of *stare decisis*. [Abood] is not just any precedent: It is embedded in the law (not to mention [in] the world) in a way not many decisions are. [Abood is not an outlier because it] coheres with the Pickering approach to reviewing regulation of public employees' speech. [The] majority is likewise wrong to invoke 'workability' as a reason for overruling Abood. [As] exercises of constitutional linedrawing go, Abood stands well above average. In the 40 years since Abood, this Court has had to resolve only a handful of cases raising questions about the distinction.

"[One] *stare decisis* factor—reliance—dominates all others here. [The] Court today wreaks havoc on entrenched legislative and contractual arrangements. Over 20 States have by now enacted statutes authorizing fair-share provisions. [Thousands] of current contracts covering millions of workers provide for agency fees. [There] is no sugarcoating today's opinion.

[The majority] prevents the American people [from] making important choices about workplace governance. And it does so by weaponizing the First Amendment, in a way that unleashes judges, now and in the future, to intervene in economic and regulatory policy.

[The majority] has overruled Abood because it wanted to. Because, that is, it wanted to pick the winning side in what should be—and until now, has been—an energetic policy debate. [And] maybe most alarming, the majority has chosen the winners by turning the First Amendment into a sword, and using it against workaday economic and regulatory policy. [Speech] is everywhere—a part of every human activity (employment, health care, securities trading, you name it). For that reason, almost all economic and regulatory policy affects or touches speech. So the majority's road runs long. And at every stop are black-robed rulers overriding citizens' choices. The First Amendment was meant for better things."

2.   *Compulsory fees to public universities.* Should students at a public university have an Abood right to a rebate of the amount of their compulsory student activities fee used to finance student organizations engaging in political or ideological speech to which they object? In **Board of Regents of The University of Wisconsin v. Southworth**, 529 U.S. 217 (2000), the Court held that they do not, and largely rejected a First Amendment challenge to a public university's requirement that students contribute to a student activity fund used in part to support controversial student advocacy organizations. Distinguishing Abood and Keller, Justice KENNEDY wrote for a unanimous Court: "In Abood and Keller the constitutional rule took the form of limiting the required subsidy to speech germane to the purposes of the union or bar association. [But] the standard of germane speech as applied to student speech at a university is unworkable. [The] speech the University seeks to encourage in the program before us is distinguished not by discernable limits but by its vast, unexplored bounds. To insist upon asking what speech is germane would be contrary to the very goal the University seeks to pursue. It is not for the Court to say what is or is not germane to the ideas to be pursued in an institution of higher learning." He cautioned, though, that "the University must provide some protection to its students' First Amendment interests. [The] proper measure, and the principal standard of protection for objecting students, we conclude, is the requirement of viewpoint neutrality in the allocation of funding support." While upholding the fee program in most respects, he remanded for the lower courts' determination the question whether the University's referendum system for activity funding was adequately viewpoint-neutral. Justice SOUTER, joined by Justices Stevens and Breyer, concurred only in the judgment, cautioning that too rigid an approach to viewpoint neutrality in the university setting might ultimately conflict with principles of academic freedom.

3.   *Compulsory fees for advertising.* In Glickman (p. 494), writing for the majority, Justice SCALIA analyzed the compulsory fees in the context of compelled association and found the compelled funding for advertising distinct from that involved in the Abood line of cases: "Abood, and the cases that follow it, did not announce a broad First Amendment right not to be compelled to provide financial support for any organization that conducts expressive activities. Rather, Abood merely recognized a First Amendment interest in not being compelled to contribute to an organization whose expressive activities conflict with one's 'freedom of belief.' [In Abood we]

found that compelled contributions for political purposes unrelated to collective bargaining implicated First Amendment interests because they interfere with the values lying at the 'heart of the First Amendment.' Here, however, requiring respondents to pay the assessments cannot be said to engender any crisis of conscience. None of the advertising in this record promotes any particular message other than encouraging consumers to buy California tree fruit. Neither the fact that respondents may prefer to foster that message independently in order to promote and distinguish their own products, nor the fact that they think more or less money should be spent fostering it, makes this case comparable to those in which an objection rested on political or ideological disagreement with the content of the message." Moreover, he noted that nothing in the Abood line of cases barred the assessment of fees for nonideological purposes that are " 'germane' to the purpose for which compelled association was justified." Here, he noted, "the generic advertising of California peaches and nectarines is unquestionably germane to the purposes of the marketing orders [and] the assessments are not used to fund ideological activities." Does Glickman limit Abood's holding to organizations with a political message? If so, does this conflict with First Amendment principles of content and viewpoint neutrality? Note that United Foods and Johanns, discussed at p. 496, focused primarily on the compelled speech aspects of the cases.

4. *Compulsory inclusion in membership.* In **Roberts v. United States Jaycees**, 468 U.S. 609 (1984), the Court rejected an all-male organization's claim that a state antidiscrimination law infringed its freedom of association by requiring it to admit women. At issue was a Minnesota statute prohibiting sex discrimination in a "place of public accommodation." The law had been applied to the Jaycees, or Junior Chamber of Commerce, a national civic organization which restricted full voting membership to men between the ages of 18 and 35. The Jaycees argued that this restriction on their membership policies interfered with their members' freedom of association.

Justice BRENNAN's opinion for the Court first rejected any claim on the Jaycees' part to a right of intimate association rooted in the liberty clause of the Fourteenth Amendment, given its large and relatively unselective composition. He then proceeded to consider the Jaycees' claim to a right of association protected by the First Amendment. Because the Jaycees engaged in various civic, educational, and related activities, the Court found expressive associational rights "plainly implicated in this case": "There can be no clearer example of an intrusion into the internal structure or affairs of an association than a regulation that forces the group to accept members it does not desire. Such a regulation may impair the ability of the original members to express only those views that brought them together. Freedom of association therefore plainly presupposes a freedom not to associate. Abood." But Justice Brennan did not find that right dispositive here: "The right to associate for expressive purposes is [not] absolute. Infringements on that right may be justified by regulations adopted to serve compelling state interests, unrelated to the suppression of ideas, that cannot be achieved through means significantly less restrictive of associational freedoms." Justice Brennan found this standard satisfied here: "We are persuaded that Minnesota's compelling interest in eradicating discrimination against its female citizens justifies the impact that application of the statute to the Jaycees may have on the male members' associational freedoms."

Crucially, Justice Brennan found the state antidiscrimination law content-neutral both on its face and as applied: "[T]he Minnesota Act does not aim at the suppression of speech, does not distinguish between prohibited and permitted activity on the basis of viewpoint, and does not license enforcement authorities to administer the statute on the basis of such constitutionally impermissible criteria, [nor was it] applied in this case for the purpose of hampering the organization's ability to express its views." Any restriction on associational liberty was merely incidental to Minnesota's interest in preventing sex discrimination. Nor was there any indication that the law imposed "any serious burden on the male members' freedom of expressive association": "The Act requires no change in the Jaycees' creed of promoting the interests of young men, and it imposes no restrictions on the organization's ability to exclude individuals with ideologies or philosophies different from those of its existing members. [Because] Jaycees already invites women to share the group's views and philosophy and to participate in much of its training and community activities, [any] claim that admission of women as full voting members will impair a symbolic message conveyed by the very fact that women are not permitted to vote is attenuated at best." In the absence of a showing far more substantial than that attempted here, "we decline to indulge in the sexual stereotyping that underlies appellee's contention that, by allowing women to vote, application of the Minnesota Act will change the content or impact of an organization's speech."

Justice O'CONNOR's concurring opinion drew a distinction between rights of commercial association and rights of expressive association. As to the former, state regulation should be "readily permit[ted]," but there remained "the ideal of complete protection for purely expressive association." Because the Jaycees, in her view, were primarily commercial, she concurred in rejecting the associational challenge. Justice Rehnquist concurred only in the judgment.

The Court unanimously followed Roberts in **Board of Directors of Rotary International v. Rotary Club**, 481 U.S. 537 (1987). The Court held that application of a California antidiscrimination law that barred exclusion of women from local Rotary clubs did not deny either freedom of intimate, private association or freedom of expressive association. (In a footnote, however, the Court noted that "we have no occasion [to] consider the extent to which the First Amendment protects the right of individuals to associate in the many clubs and other entities with selective membership that are found throughout the country. Whether the 'zone of privacy' established by the First Amendment extends to a particular [club] requires a careful inquiry into the objective characteristics of the particular relationships at issue.") A year later, in **New York State Club Ass'n v. City of New York**, 487 U.S. 1 (1988), the Court unanimously upheld against facial First Amendment challenge a law prohibiting racial, religious, or sex discrimination in any institution, club, or place of accommodation that has more than 400 members, provides regular meal service, and "regularly receives payment from [nonmembers] for facilities and services for the furtherance of trade or business." Justice WHITE's opinion stated that it was "conceivable [that] an association might be able to show that it is organized for specific expressive purposes and that it will not be able to advocate its desired viewpoints nearly as effectively if it cannot confine its membership. [Here,] however, it seems sensible enough to believe that many of the large clubs covered by the [law] are not of this kind." Note also the cursory rejection of a law firm's freedom of association claim in a Title VII sex discrimination case, in Hishon v. King & Spalding, 467 U.S. 69 (1984).

What principle underlies the freedom from compelled association asserted (and rejected) in Jaycees? Under the principles set forth in Jaycees, may a self-styled Male Supremacist Society exclude women? May a self-styled Feminist Separatist Organization exclude men? May the Ku Klux Klan exclude black members? May the NAACP exclude members of the Ku Klux Klan? To what extent must an organization set forth an exclusionary principle publicly in advance in order to maintain a First Amendment right against compulsory inclusion of unwanted members, and how central must such a principle be to its mission? May the exclusion be based upon a fact or status about a person or must it be based upon speech or symbolic conduct that person is likely to engage in? Is there a constitutionally relevant difference between organizations that seek to inculcate values in their members and organizations that serve a more social or commercial purpose? Are courts capable of drawing such lines objectively, or should subjective declarations by the organization be unreviewable? Ex post or only ex ante the exclusion?

Boy Scouts of America v. Dale

530 U.S. 640, 120 S. Ct. 2446, 147 L. Ed. 2d 554 (2000).

[A closely divided Court upheld the First Amendment expressive association right of the Boy Scouts to exclude an otherwise qualified scoutmaster, James Dale, on the ground that he had publicly disclosed his homosexuality. In a 5–4 decision, the Court held that New Jersey may not constitutionally apply its public accommodations law, which bars discrimination on the basis of sexual orientation, to require the Boy Scouts to admit Dale.]

■ CHIEF JUSTICE REHNQUIST delivered the opinion of the Court, in which JUSTICES O'CONNOR, SCALIA, KENNEDY, and THOMAS, joined.

The forced inclusion of an unwanted person in a group infringes the group's freedom of expressive association if the presence of that person affects in a significant way the group's ability to advocate public or private viewpoints. [To] determine whether a group is protected by the First Amendment's expressive associational right, we must determine whether the group engages in "expressive association."

[The] Boy Scouts is a private, nonprofit organization. According to its mission statement: "It is the mission of the Boy Scouts of America to serve others by helping to instill values in young people and, in other ways, to prepare them to make ethical choices over their lifetime in achieving their full potential. The values we strive to instill are based on those found in the Scout Oath—'On my honor I will do my best to do my duty to God and my country and to obey the Scout Law; To help other people at all times; To keep myself physically strong, mentally awake, and morally straight'—and Scout Law—'A Scout is: Trustworthy, Loyal, Friendly, Courteous, Helpful, Kind, Obedient, Cheerful, Thrifty, Brave, Clean, [and] Reverent.' " Thus, the general mission of the Boy Scouts is clear: "[T]o instill values in young people." The Boy Scouts seeks to instill these values by having its adult leaders spend time with the youth members, instructing and engaging them in activities like camping, archery, and fishing. During the time spent with the youth members, the scoutmasters and assistant scoutmasters inculcate them with the Boy Scouts' values—both expressly and by example. It seems indisputable that an association that seeks to transmit such a system of values engages in expressive activity.

Given that the Boy Scouts engages in expressive activity, we must determine whether the forced inclusion of Dale as an assistant scoutmaster would significantly affect the Boy Scouts' ability to advocate public or private viewpoints. This inquiry necessarily requires us first to explore, to a limited extent, the nature of the Boy Scouts' view of homosexuality. The values the Boy Scouts seeks to instill are "based on" those listed in the Scout Oath and Law. Boy Scouts explains that the Scout Oath and Law provide "a positive moral code for living; they are a list of 'do's' rather than 'don'ts.' " The Boy Scouts asserts that homosexual conduct is inconsistent with the values embodied in the Scout Oath and Law, particularly with the values represented by the terms "morally straight" and "clean." Obviously, the Scout Oath and Law do not expressly mention sexuality or sexual orientation. And the terms "morally straight" and "clean" are by no means self-defining. Different people would attribute to those terms very different meanings. For example, some people may believe that engaging in homosexual conduct is not at odds with being "morally straight" and "clean." And others may believe that engaging in homosexual conduct is contrary to being "morally straight" and "clean." The Boy Scouts says it falls within the latter category.

The New Jersey Supreme Court analyzed the Boy Scouts' beliefs and found that the "exclusion of members solely on the basis of their sexual orientation is inconsistent with Boy Scouts' commitment to a diverse and 'representative' membership . . . [and] contradicts Boy Scouts' overarching objective to reach 'all eligible youth.' " But our cases reject this sort of inquiry; it is not the role of the courts to reject a group's expressed values because they disagree with those values or find them internally inconsistent. The Boy Scouts asserts that it "teach[es] that homosexual conduct is not morally straight," and that it does "not want to promote homosexual conduct as a legitimate form of behavior." We accept the Boy Scouts' assertion.

We must then determine whether Dale's presence as an assistant scoutmaster would significantly burden the Boy Scouts' desire to not "promote homosexual conduct as a legitimate form of behavior." As we give deference to an association's assertions regarding the nature of its expression, we must also give deference to an association's view of what would impair its expression. That is not to say that an expressive association can erect a shield against antidiscrimination laws simply by asserting that mere acceptance of a member from a particular group would impair its message. But here Dale, by his own admission, is one of a group of gay Scouts who have "become leaders in their community and are open and honest about their sexual orientation." Dale was the copresident of a gay and lesbian organization at college and remains a gay rights activist. Dale's presence in the Boy Scouts would, at the very least, force the organization to send a message, both to the youth members and the world, that the Boy Scouts accepts homosexual conduct as a legitimate form of behavior.

Hurley v. GLIB is illustrative on this point. There we considered whether the application of Massachusetts' public accommodations law to require the organizers of a private St. Patrick's Day parade to include among the marchers an Irish—American gay, lesbian, and bisexual group, GLIB, violated the parade organizers' First Amendment rights. We noted that the parade organizers did not wish to exclude the GLIB members because of their sexual orientations, but because they wanted to march behind a GLIB banner. [Here], we have found that the Boy Scouts believes that homosexual conduct is inconsistent with the values it seeks to instill in its youth members. [As] the presence of GLIB in Boston's St. Patrick's Day parade would have interfered with the parade organizers' choice not to propound a particular point of view, the presence of Dale as an assistant scoutmaster would just as surely interfere with the Boy Scout's choice not to propound a point of view contrary to its beliefs.

[Having] determined that the Boy Scouts is an expressive association and that the forced inclusion of Dale would significantly affect its expression, we inquire whether the application of New Jersey's public accommodations law to require that the Boy Scouts accept Dale as an assistant scoutmaster runs afoul of the Scouts' freedom of expressive association. We conclude that it does. [We] recognized in cases such as Roberts that States have a compelling interest in eliminating discrimination against women in public accommodations. But [we] went on to conclude that the enforcement of these statutes would not materially interfere with the ideas that the organization sought to express. [We] have already concluded that a state requirement that the Boy Scouts retain Dale as an assistant scoutmaster would significantly burden the organization's right to oppose or disfavor homosexual conduct. The state interests embodied in New Jersey's public accommodations law do not justify such a severe intrusion on the Boy Scouts' rights to freedom of expressive association. That being the case, we hold that the First Amendment prohibits the State from imposing such a requirement through the application of its public accommodations law.

[That] homosexuality has gained greater societal acceptance [is] scarcely an argument for denying First Amendment protection to those who refuse to accept these views. We are not, as we must not be, guided by our views of whether the Boy Scouts' teachings with respect to homosexual conduct are right or wrong; public or judicial disapproval of a tenet of an organization's expression does not justify the State's effort to compel the organization to accept members where such acceptance would derogate from the organization's expressive message. The judgment of the New Jersey Supreme Court is reversed.

■ JUSTICE STEVENS dissented.

It is plain as the light of day that neither [of the] principles—"morally straight" and "clean"—says the slightest thing about homosexuality. [A] State's antidiscrimination law does not impose a "serious burden" or a "substantial restraint" upon the group's "shared goals" if the group itself is unable to identify its own stance with any clarity. [Dale's] inclusion in the Boy Scouts is nothing like the case in Hurley. His participation sends no cognizable message to the Scouts or to the world. Unlike GLIB, Dale did not carry a banner or a sign; he did not distribute any fact sheet; and he expressed no intent to send any message. If there is any kind of message being sent, then, it is by the mere act of joining the Boy Scouts. Such an act does not constitute an instance of symbolic speech under the First Amendment. [The] only apparent explanation for the majority's holding, then, is that homosexuals are simply so different from the rest of society that their presence alone—unlike any other individual's—should be singled out for special First Amendment treatment. [The harm done by such] atavistic [anti-gay opinions should not] be aggravated by the creation of a constitutional shield for a policy that is itself the product of a habitual way of thinking about strangers.

DALE AND COMPELLED SPEECH AND ASSOCIATION

1. ***Free speech theory and Dale.*** What theory of freedom of speech and association might support the result in Dale? Is the problem that compelled inclusion of Scoutmaster Dale will distort the message that the Boy Scouts will be able to communicate to the outside world as an amplification device for its members? Or is the problem instead that the government is seeking to homogenize all groups in society and assimilate them to shared public values, whereas private expressive associations "provide sites in which the thoughts and ideas of members are formed and in which the content of their expressions is generated and germinated," a function important to a system of expression free from government control? Shiffrin, "What Is Really Wrong With Compelled Association?," 99 Nw. U. L. Rev. 839 (2005).

2. ***Compelled speech and on-campus recruiting.*** Does it follow from Dale that law school faculties should be able to exclude from their on-campus recruiting programs employers they deem to be in violation of their schools' antidiscrimination policies?

In a unanimous decision, the Court rejected such compelled association claims. (For the Court's rejection of related compelled speech claims, see p. 502.) The so-called "Solomon Amendment" (see p. 502) requires equal access for military recruiting on campus as a condition of universities' receiving federal funds. A group of law faculties objected that unwilling association with an employer that discriminates against gay students in violation of their nondiscrimination policies burdened their First Amendment rights, just as the unwanted membership of a gay scoutmaster in a Boy Scout troop did in Dale. Writing for the Court in **Rumsfeld v. Forum for Academic and Institutional Rights (FAIR)**, 547 U.S. 47 (2006), Chief Justice ROBERTS distinguished Dale and found that the Solomon Amendment did not infringe any associational rights belonging to law school faculties: "To comply with the statute, law schools must allow military recruiters on campus and assist them in whatever way the school chooses to assist other employers. Law schools therefore 'associate' with military recruiters in the sense that they interact with them. But recruiters are not part of the law school. Recruiters are, by definition, outsiders who come onto campus for the limited purpose of trying to hire students—not to become members of the school's expressive association. This distinction is critical. Unlike the public accommodations law in Dale, the Solomon Amendment does not force a law school 'to accept members it does not desire.' [A] military recruiter's mere presence on campus does not violate a law school's right to associate, regardless of how repugnant the law school considers the recruiter's message."

Why did the Court not accord deference to FAIR members' own self-defined account of their associational mission, as it did in Dale? For the view that the Court should have accorded greater deference to law school faculties' self-identified mission in the case, see Horwitz, "Three Faces of Deference,"

83 Notre Dame L. Rev. 3 (2008) (arguing that the cases either both should have denied deference because "the Boy Scouts do not rise to the level of an occult mystery," or both should have accorded deference because "law school are in a better position than the Court to understand what they do and what would impair them").

———————

FREEDOM OF ASSOCIATION AND POLITICAL PARTY PROCEDURES

1. *Ballot access.* The Court has relied upon the First Amendment freedom of association to limit the states' authority to curtail access to ballots by independent candidates and third parties. In **Williams v. Rhodes**, 393 U.S. 23 (1968), the Court held that Ohio's election laws created unduly burdensome obstacles to third-party candidates seeking a place on presidential ballots. Under the Ohio laws, major parties retained their positions on the ballot simply by obtaining 10% of the votes in the last gubernatorial election, while parties newly seeking access to the presidential election had to conduct primaries and to obtain 15%. Justice BLACK's majority opinion stated that these requirements unconstitutionally placed "unequal burdens" on "the right of individuals to associate for the advancement of political beliefs, and the right of qualified voters [to] cast their votes effectively." He concluded that the state had "failed to show any 'compelling interest' which justifie[d] imposing such heavy burdens" on such "precious freedoms." There were dissents by Justices Stewart and White and by Chief Justice Warren. A concurrence by Justice HARLAN stated that he would rest "entirely" on First Amendment associational rights, not equal protection.

Three years later, a unanimous Court distinguished Williams in rejecting challenges to Georgia's nominating procedures in **Jenness v. Fortson**, 403 U.S. 431 (1971). Unlike Ohio, Georgia permitted write-in votes and allowed independent candidates to appear on the ballots without third-party endorsement if they had filed nominating petitions signed by at least 5% of those eligible to vote in the last election for the office, without any need for an elaborate primary election machinery. Justice STEWART found the scheme more justifiable than that in Williams: "There is surely an important state interest in requiring some preliminary showing of a significant modicum of support before printing the name of a political organization and its candidates on the ballot—the interest, if no other, in avoiding confusion, deception, and even frustration of the democratic [process]." In **Storer v. Brown**, 415 U.S. 724 (1974), and **American Party of Texas v. White**, 415 U.S. 767 (1974), the Court found a set of ballot access barriers to independent candidates and small political parties to be of a magnitude somewhere between Williams and Jenness, and rejected most of the challenges. The majority acknowledged that strict scrutiny was applicable. In Storer, the Court sustained a California provision denying a ballot position to an independent candidate if he or she had registered with a political party within a year prior to the immediately preceding primary election or had voted in that election. In the Texas case, the Court sustained most of that state's provisions regarding independents and minor parties, but invalidated a provision under which only names of major parties were included on absentee ballots.

This line of cases continued to develop in new kinds of equal protection challenges. In **Bullock v. Carter**, 405 U.S. 134 (1972), and **Lubin v. Panish**, 415 U.S. 709 (1974), a unanimous Court invalidated filing fee requirements for candidates. Chief Justice BURGER, writing the prevailing opinion in each case, concluded that the state had not established the "requisite justification" either in its concern about regulating the size of the ballot or in its interest in financing the election, and held "that in the absence of reasonable alternative means of valid access, a State may not, consistently with constitutional standards, require from an indigent candidate filing fees he cannot pay." But in **Clements v. Fashing**, 457 U.S. 957 (1982), Justice Rehnquist's plurality opinion announced that "[n]ot all ballot access restrictions require 'heightened' equal protection scrutiny," and sustained under rationality review two Texas constitutional provisions limiting an incumbent public official's ability to become a candidate for another public office.

Eventually, the Court came to decide ballot access cases entirely on First Amendment, not equal protection grounds. At issue in **Anderson v. Celebrezze**, 460 U.S. 780 (1983), was an Ohio statute that required independent candidates, but not party nominees, to file their nominating petitions by late March in order to be on the November ballot. John Anderson, independent candidate for President in 1980, challenged the statute, claiming that the early filing deadline excessively restricted access to the ballot and impermissibly discriminated against independent candidates. Justice STEVENS's majority opinion upheld Anderson's claim, finding that Ohio's asserted interests in voter education, equal treatment for partisan and independent candidates, and political stability were either illegitimate or too remotely related to the early filing deadline to justify such a substantial barrier to independent candidates. Stating that the ruling rested solely on First Amendment, not equal protection grounds, he set forth the following test: "[A] court [must] first consider the character and magnitude of the asserted injury to the [First Amendment rights]. It then must identify and evaluate the precise interests put forward by the State as justifications for the burden imposed. [Only] after weighing all these factors is the reviewing court in a position to decide whether the challenged provision is unconstitutional."

In **New York State Board of Elections v. Lopez Torres**, 552 U.S. 196 (2008), the Supreme Court rendered a unanimous judgment rejecting a challenge to a New York election law that required parties to select nominees to state trial court judgeships by a convention composed of delegates elected by party members. The challengers sought to compel primary elections for these seats. Justice SCALIA, writing for the Court, found nothing in the First Amendment that would entitle a challenger to so alter a party's selection process: "Respondents' real complaint is [that] the convention process that follows the delegate election does not give them a realistic chance to secure the party's nomination. The party leadership, they say, inevitably garners more votes for its slate of delegates (delegates uncommitted to any judicial nominee) than the unsupported candidate can amass for himself. And thus the leadership effectively determines the nominees. But this says nothing more than that the party leadership has more widespread support than a candidate not supported by the leadership. No New York law compels election of the leadership's slate—or, for that matter, compels the delegates elected on the leadership's slate to vote the way the leadership desires. And no state law prohibits an unsupported candidate from attending the convention and seeking to persuade the delegates to support her.

"Our cases invalidating ballot-access requirements have focused on the requirements themselves, and not on the manner in which political actors function under those requirements. See, e.g., Bullock v. Carter, Williams v. Rhodes, Anderson v. Celebrezze. Here respondents complain not of the state law, but of the voters' (and their elected delegates') preference for the choices of the party leadership." Justices Stevens and Kennedy each concurred separately, expressing doubts about the wisdom of the State's policy.

2. *Write-in voting.* In **Burdick v. Takushi**, 504 U.S. 428 (1992), the Court, applying Anderson's flexible standard of review, rejected First Amendment associational claims in upholding Hawaii's prohibition on write-in voting. Justice WHITE's opinion for the Court rejected the idea that all restrictions on the right to vote were subject to strict scrutiny: "[Instead, a] more flexible standard applies. [Anderson]. [Under] this standard, the rigorousness of our inquiry into the propriety of a state election law depends upon the extent to which a challenged regulation burdens First and Fourteenth Amendment rights. [When] those rights are subject to 'severe' restrictions, the regulation must be 'narrowly drawn to advance a state interest of compelling importance.' But when a state election law provision imposes only 'reasonable, nondiscriminatory restrictions' upon the First and Fourteenth Amendment rights of voters, 'the State's important regulatory interests are generally sufficient to justify' the restrictions." Applying this standard, Justice White found the prohibition on write-in voting constitutionally permissible: "[When] a State's ballot access laws pass constitutional muster, [a] prohibition on write-in voting will be presumptively valid. [In] such situations, the objection [amounts] to nothing more than the insistence that the State record, count, and publish individual protests against the election system or the choices presented on the ballot through the efforts of those who actively participate in the system." Justice KENNEDY, joined by Justices Blackmun and Stevens, dissented, arguing that because "Democratic candidates often run unopposed," a ban on write-in candidates gave dissidents "no way to cast a meaningful vote."

3. *Fusion tickets.* In **Timmons v. Twin Cities Area New Party**, 520 U.S. 351 (1997), the Court, by a vote of 6–3, rejected a claim that a state ban on multiparty or "fusion" candidacies violated a party's or candidate's associational rights under the First and Fourteenth Amendments. Chief Justice REHNQUIST, writing for the Court, rejected the argument that such a ban was a "severe burden" on ballot access triggering strict scrutiny: "That a particular individual may not appear on the ballot as a particular party's candidate does not severely burden that party's association rights. [The fusion ticket] ban, which applies to major and minor parties alike, simply precludes one party's candidate from appearing on the ballot, as that party's candidate, if already nominated by another party. Respondent is free to try to convince [a candidate] to be [its], not [another party's], candidate." Nor did the ban prevent a minor party such as respondent "from developing consensual political alliances and thus broadening the base of public participation in and support for its activities." The majority was "unpersuaded [by] the Party's contention that it has a right to use the ballot itself to send a particularized message, to its candidate and to the voters, about the nature of its support for the candidate. Ballots serve primarily to elect candidates, not as fora for political expression."

Accordingly, Chief Justice Rehnquist viewed the fusion ban as among the "lesser burdens" or " 'reasonable, nondiscriminatory restrictions' " that, under Anderson and Burdick, "trigger less exacting review." Under this deferential standard, he concluded that "the burdens Minnesota's fusion ban imposes on the New Party's associational rights are justified by 'correspondingly weighty' valid state interests in ballot integrity and political stability." Specifically, fusion tickets might be used detrimentally to associate party or candidate names with popular slogans and catchphrases, to allow minor parties to hijack another party's popularity to their own use, or to cause "the destabilizing effects of party-splintering and excessive factionalism."

Justice STEVENS dissented, joined by Justice Ginsburg and for the most part by Justice Souter. He found the burden imposed by the fusion ban "significant" rather than minor: "[The] members of a recognized political party unquestionably have a constitutional right to select their nominees for public office and to communicate the identity of their nominees to the voting public. [The] Minnesota statutes place a significant burden on both of those rights. [In] this case [the] burden [is] imposed upon the members of a minor party, but its potential impact is much broader. Fiorello LaGuardia, Earl Warren, Ronald Reagan, and Franklin D. Roosevelt, are names that come readily to mind as candidates whose reputations and political careers were enhanced because they appeared on election ballots as fusion candidates. A statute that denied a political party the right to nominate any of those individuals for high office simply because he had already been nominated by another party would, in my opinion, place an intolerable burden on political expression and association." Nor was Justice Stevens convinced that the fusion ban actually served asserted state interests in "avoiding voter confusion, preventing ballot clutter and manipulation, encouraging candidate competition, and minimizing intraparty factionalism."

4. *Political party primaries.* The Court has increasingly found First Amendment freedom of association a limit on state intrusions into political party primary elections. In **Tashjian v. Republican Party**, 479 U.S. 208 (1986), the Court struck down a Connecticut law requiring that the voters in any party primary be registered members of that party. The challenger was the state's Republican Party, which had adopted a party rule permitting independents to vote in its primary. Justice MARSHALL's majority opinion held that the law unconstitutionally interfered with the associational rights of party members to decide for themselves who could vote in their primaries: "The Party's determination of the boundaries of its own association, and of the structure which best allows it to pursue its political goals, is protected by the Constitution." Three years later, in **EU v. San Francisco County Democratic Central Committee**, 489 U.S. 214 (1989), a unanimous Court relied on Tashjian in striking down provisions of California's election law barring political parties from endorsing, supporting or opposing "any candidate for nomination by that party for partisan office in the direct primary election." Justice MARSHALL's opinion applied strict scrutiny and held that the bar on candidate endorsements burdened both the speech and associational rights of the parties, and that California's asserted interest in preserving party stability was not "compelling."

What if the parties prefer to restrict access to their primary elections, rather than to make such access open as in Tashjian? In **California Democratic Party v. Jones**, 530 U.S. 567 (2000), the Court held that the same associational principles dictate deference to the party's choice either way. By a vote of 7–2, the Court struck down a California initiative, Proposition 198, which had changed California's partisan primary election from a closed primary to a blanket primary. Under the new system, any voter could vote for any candidate regardless of party affiliation or registration, and the candidate of each party winning the largest number of votes became the party's nominee. The blanket primary was challenged by the California Democratic Party, the California Republican Party, the Libertarian Party of California, and the Peace and Freedom Party, each of which sought to restrict to its own members primary voting for its candidates.

Writing for the Court, Justice SCALIA rejected the argument that primaries "are wholly public affairs that States may regulate freely," and invalidated the blanket primary system as a violation of parties' right of expressive association under the First Amendment: "Representative democracy in any populous unit of governance is unimaginable without the ability of citizens to band together in promoting among the electorate candidates who espouse their political views. The formation of national political parties was almost concurrent with the formation of the Republic itself. [A] corollary of the right to associate is the right not to associate. [In] no area is the political association's right to exclude more important than in the process of selecting its nominee. [Proposition 198] forces political parties to associate with—to have their nominees, and hence their positions, determined by—those who, at best, have refused to affiliate with the party, and, at worst, have expressly affiliated with a rival.

"[The] evidence in this case demonstrates that under California's blanket primary system, the prospect of having a party's nominee determined by adherents of an opposing party [through cross-over voting] is far from remote—indeed, it is a clear and present danger. [The] record also supports the obvious proposition that these substantial numbers of voters who help select the nominees of parties they have chosen not to join often have policy views that diverge from those of the party faithful. [Even] when the person favored by a majority of the party members prevails, he will have prevailed by taking somewhat different positions—and, should he be elected, will continue to take somewhat different positions in order to be renominated. [After all], the whole purpose of Proposition 198 was to favor nominees with 'moderate' positions. [In] sum, Proposition 198 forces petitioners to adulterate their candidate-selection process—the 'basic function of a political party'—by opening it up to persons wholly unaffiliated with the party. Such forced association has the likely outcome—indeed, in this case the intended outcome—of changing the parties' message. We can think of no heavier burden on a political party's associational freedom. Proposition 198 is therefore unconstitutional unless it is narrowly tailored to serve a compelling state interest."

Applying that standard, Justice Scalia found the state's proffered justifications wanting. He rejected as "inadmissible" any interest in "producing elected officials who better represent the electorate and expanding candidate debate beyond the scope of partisan concerns," or in drawing in "disenfranchised" voters, suggesting that such interests "reduce to nothing more than a stark repudiation of freedom of political association." And he found constitutionally inadequate any supposed government interest in promoting fairness, affording voters greater choice, increasing voter participation, or protecting privacy, by means of the blanket primary device.

Even if such interests were compelling, he noted, the state could further them less restrictively by operating a nonpartisan blanket primary, in which voters could pick nominees regardless of party affiliation so long as those nominees did not advance to the general election as any party's nominees.

Justice STEVENS, joined by Justice Ginsburg, dissented, suggesting that "[a] State's power to determine how its officials are to be elected is a quintessential attribute of sovereignty," and that accordingly, "the associational rights of political parties are neither absolute nor as comprehensive as the rights enjoyed by wholly private associations." He insisted that the right not to associate "is simply inapplicable to participation in a [state-run and state-financed primary] election." He also would have given more deference to the state's proffered interests, ranking them "substantial, indeed compelling."

In a later decision concerning political party primaries, the Court ruled, by a vote of 6–3, that Oklahoma's semiclosed primary law did not violate the freedom of political association. The system provided that a political party may invite only its own party members and voters registered as Independents to vote in the party's primary. Under that system, the Libertarian Party of Oklahoma (LPO) was prevented from inviting Republicans and Democrats as well as registered Independents from voting in its primary elections. Writing for the Court in **Clingman v. Beaver**, 544 U.S. 581 (2005), Justice THOMAS upheld this barrier, writing for the Court in an opinion joined by Chief Justice Rehnquist and Justices Scalia, and Kennedy, and in relevant party by Justices O'Connor and Breyer. He distinguished Tashjian as involving more severe burdens on political association: "Connecticut's closed primary limited citizens' freedom of political association [by requiring] Independent voters to affiliate publicly with a party to vote in its primary. That is not true in this case. At issue here are voters who have *already* affiliated publicly with one of Oklahoma's political parties. [These] minor barriers between voter and party do not compel strict scrutiny." Applying a more deferential standard of review, Justice Thomas found reasonable and politically neutral Oklahoma's regulatory interests in preserving the identity of political parties and aiding their efforts at electioneering and party-building.

Justice STEVENS dissented, joined by Justices Souter and Ginsburg: "The Court's decision today diminishes the value of two important rights protected by the First Amendment: the individual citizen's right to vote for the candidate of her choice and a political party's right to define its own mission. No one would contend that a citizen's membership in either the Republican or the Democratic Party could disqualify her from attending political functions sponsored by another party, or from voting for a third party's candidate in a general election. If a third party invites her to participate in its primary election, her right to support the candidate of her choice merits constitutional protection, whether she elects to make a speech, to donate funds, or to cast a ballot. The importance of vindicating that individual right far outweighs any public interest in punishing registered Republicans or Democrats for acts of disloyalty." He would have found the associational interests at stake "virtually identical" to those in Tashjian, and found the state interests so "speculative or simply protectionist" of the parties in power that, "[n]o matter what the standard, they simply do not outweigh the interests of the LPO and its voters."

Eight years after deciding California Democratic Party v. Jones, the Supreme Court reached the opposite result in **Washington State Grange v. Washington State Republican Party**, 552 U.S. 442 (2008). This decision upheld against facial First Amendment challenge a Washington state law (I-872), enacted by voter initiative, providing that candidates must be identified on the primary ballot by their self-designated party preference, that voters may vote for any candidate, and that the two top vote-getters for each office advance to the general election regardless of a party's preference.

Writing for the 7–2 majority, Justice THOMAS, joined by Chief Justice Roberts and Justices Stevens, Souter, Ginsburg, Breyer, and Alito, explained why Jones was not controlling: "[U]nlike the California primary, the I-872 primary does not, by its terms, choose parties' nominees. The essence of nomination—the choice of a party representative—does not occur under I-872. The law never refers to the candidates as nominees of any party, nor does it treat them as such. To the contrary, the election regulations specifically provide that the primary 'does not serve to determine the nominees of a political party but serves to winnow the number of candidates to a final list of two for the general election.' The top two candidates from the primary election proceed to the general election regardless of their party preferences. Whether parties nominate their own candidates outside the state-run primary is simply irrelevant.

"At bottom, respondents' objection to I-872 is that voters will be confused by candidates' party-preference designations. [They] argue that even if voters do not assume that candidates on the general election ballot are the nominees of their parties, they will at least assume that the parties associate with, and approve of, them. This, they say, compels them to associate with candidates they do not endorse, alters the messages they wish to convey, and forces them to engage in counterspeech to disassociate themselves from the candidates and their positions on the issues. We reject each of these contentions for the same reason: They all depend, not on any facial requirement of I-872, but on the possibility that voters will be confused as to the meaning of the party-preference designation. But respondents' assertion that voters will misinterpret the party-preference designation is sheer speculation. [Of course,] it is *possible* that voters will misinterpret the candidates' party-preference designations as reflecting endorsement by the parties. But these cases involve a facial challenge, and we cannot strike down I-872 on its face based on the mere possibility of voter confusion." Finding no heavy burden on party or voter associational rights, the Court found no need for a compelling state interest, and found that, on appropriately deferential review, Washington's "asserted interest in providing voters with relevant information about the candidates on the ballot is easily sufficient to sustain I-872."

Justice SCALIA, joined by Justice Kennedy, dissented, finding Jones materially indistinguishable: "The Court makes much of the fact that the party names shown on the Washington ballot may be billed as mere statements of candidate 'preference.' To be sure, the party is not *itself* forced to display favor for someone it does not wish to associate with, as the Boy Scouts were arguably forced to do by employing the homosexual scoutmaster in Dale, and as the political parties were arguably forced to do by lending their ballot-endorsement as party nominee in Jones. But thrusting an unwelcome, self-proclaimed association upon the party on the election ballot itself is amply destructive of the party's associational rights. An individual's endorsement of a party shapes the voter's view of what the party stands for, no less than the party's endorsement of an individual shapes the voter's view of what the individual stands for. Not only is the party's message distorted, but its goodwill is hijacked. [There] is therefore 'no set of circumstances' under which Washington's law would not severely burden political parties."

Justice Scalia's dissent would have found Washington's law incapable of withstanding the strict scrutiny he thus deemed appropriate: "Even if I were to assume, [that] Washington has a legitimate interest in telling voters on the ballot (above all other things) that a candidate *says* he favors a particular political party, and even if I were further to assume *(per impossibile)* that that interest was a compelling one, Washington would still have to 'narrowly tailor' its law to protect that interest with minimal intrusion upon the parties' associational rights. There has been no attempt to do that here. Washington could, for example, have permitted parties to disclaim on the general-election ballot the asserted association or to designate on the ballot their true nominees. The course the State has chosen makes sense only as an effort to use its monopoly power over the ballot to undermine the expressive activities of the political parties."

5. ***Political gerrymandering.*** In **Vieth v. Jubelirer**, 541 U.S. 267 (2004), Justice KENNEDY suggested that political gerrymandering plaintiffs seek recourse under the First Amendment: "The First Amendment may be the more relevant constitutional provision in future cases that allege unconstitutional partisan gerrymandering. After all, these allegations involve the First Amendment interest of not burdening or penalizing citizens because of their participation in the electoral process, their voting history, their association with a political party, or their expression of political views." In **Gill v. Whitford**, 585 U.S. ___, 138 S. Ct. 1916 (2018), Justice KAGAN endorsed this argument, introducing an "associational theory" of harm to show how "partisan gerrymanders may infringe the First Amendment rights of association held by parties, other political organizations, and their members." Such an associational claim, she wrote, "would occasion a different standing inquiry" because "the gerrymander has burdened the ability of like-minded people across the State to affiliate in a political party and carry out that organization's activities and objects." However, when the Court in Rucho v. Common Cause held that partisan gerrymandering poses a political question not justiciable by Article III courts, the majority opinion by Chief Justice Roberts expressly rejected the idea that a First Amendment analysis would give rise to judicially manageable standards.

SECTION 3. MONEY AND POLITICAL CAMPAIGNS

For a generation since the 1972 Watergate burglary of Democratic campaign headquarters by Republican operatives and the comprehensive federal election campaign regulation that ensued, the Supreme Court has grappled with the question of what First Amendment limits might apply to Congress's and the states' efforts to restrict the flow of money into political campaigns. American elections are expensive because states and congressional districts are relatively large and dispersed, television and radio broadcast advertisements are crucial to reach the electorate in those districts, and the broadcast media are privately owned and charge steeply for such advertisements. The Court's first decision in the area, Buckley v. Valeo, which follows, held that free speech constraints apply with greater force to expenditure limits than to contribution limits, in effect refashioning the statutory scheme that Congress had devised, and setting the template for later cases:

Buckley v. Valeo

424 U.S. 1, 96 S. Ct. 612, 46 L. Ed. 2d 659 (1976).

■ PER CURIAM.

These appeals present constitutional challenges to the key provisions of the Federal Election Campaign Act of 1971 [FECA] and related provisions [as] amended in 1974. [The challenged laws] in broad terms [provide]: (a) individual political contributions are limited to $1,000 to any single candidate per election with an overall annual limitation of $25,000 by any contributor; independent expenditures by individuals and groups "relative to a clearly identified candidate" are limited to $1,000 a year; campaign spending by candidates for various federal offices and spending for national conventions by political parties are subject to prescribed limits; (b) contributions and expenditures above certain threshold levels must [be] publicly disclosed; (c) a system for public funding of Presidential campaign activities is established; [and] (d) a Federal Election Commission is established to administer [the Act].

I. *Contribution and Expenditure Limitations.*

[A.] *General Principles.* The Act's contribution and expenditure limitations operate in an area of the most fundamental First Amendment activities. Discussion of public issues and debate on the qualifications of candidates are integral to the operation of the system of government established by our Constitution. [In] upholding the constitutional validity of the Act's contribution and expenditure provisions on the ground that those provisions should be viewed as regulating conduct not speech, the Court of Appeals relied upon United States v. O'Brien. [We] cannot share the view that the present Act's contribution and expenditure limitations are comparable to the restrictions on conduct upheld in O'Brien. The expenditure of money simply cannot be equated with such conduct as destruction of a draft card. Some forms of communication made possible by the giving and spending of money involve speech alone, some involve conduct primarily, and some involve a combination of the two. Yet, this Court has never suggested that the dependence of a communication on the expenditure of money operates itself to introduce a nonspeech element or to reduce the exacting scrutiny required by the [First Amendment].

Even if the categorization of the expenditure of money as conduct were accepted, the limitations challenged here would not meet the O'Brien test because the governmental interests advanced in support of the Act involve "suppressing communication." The interests served by the Act include restricting the voices of people and interest groups who have money to spend and reducing the overall scope of federal election campaigns. Although the Act does not focus on the ideas expressed by persons or groups subjected to its regulations, it is aimed in part at equalizing the relative ability of all voters to affect electoral outcomes by placing a ceiling on expenditures for political expression by citizens and groups. Unlike [the situation in O'Brien], it is beyond dispute that the interest in regulating the alleged "conduct" of giving or spending money "arises in some measure because the communication allegedly integral to the conduct is itself thought to be harmful." Nor can the Act's contribution and expenditure limitations be sustained [by] reference to the constitutional principles reflected in such decisions as [Kovacs v. Cooper.] [The] critical difference between this case and those time, place and manner cases is that the present Act's contribution and expenditure limitations impose direct quantity restrictions on political communication and association [in] addition to any reasonable time, place, and manner regulations otherwise imposed.[1]

A restriction on the amount of money a person or group can spend on political communication during a campaign necessarily reduces the quantity of expression by restricting the number of issues discussed, the depth of their exploration, and the size of the audience reached.[2] This is because virtually every means of communicating ideas in today's mass society requires the expenditure of money. [The] expenditure limitations contained in the Act represent substantial rather than merely theoretical restraints on the quantity and diversity of political speech. [E.g., the] $1,000 ceiling on spending "relative to a clearly identified candidate" would appear to exclude all citizens and groups except candidates, political parties and the institutional press from any significant use of the most effective means of [communication].

By contrast with a limitation upon expenditures for political expression, a limitation upon the amount that any one person or group may contribute [entails] only a marginal restriction upon the contributor's ability to engage in free communication. A contribution serves as a general expression of support for the candidate and his views, but does not communicate the underlying basis for the support. [At most,] the size of the contribution provides a very rough index of the intensity of the contributor's support for the candidate. A limitation on [contributions] thus involves little direct restraint [on] political communication, for it permits the symbolic expression of support evidenced by a contribution but does not in any way infringe the contributor's freedom to discuss candidates and issues. While contributions may result in political expression if spent by a candidate or an association to present views to the voters, the transformation of contributions into political debate involves speech by someone other than the contributor.

Given the important role of contributions in financing political campaigns, contribution restrictions could have a severe impact on political dialogue if the limitations prevented candidates and political committees from amassing the resources necessary for effective advocacy. There is no indication, however, that the contribution limitations imposed by the Act would have any dramatic adverse effect on the funding of campaigns and political associations. The overall effect of the Act's contribution ceilings is merely to require candidates and political committees to raise funds from a greater number of persons and to compel people who would otherwise

---

[1] The nongovernmental appellees argue that just as the decibels emitted by a sound truck can be regulated consistent with the First Amendment, Kovacs, the Act may restrict the volume of dollars in political campaigns without impermissibly restricting freedom of speech. This comparison underscores a fundamental misconception. The decibel restriction upheld in Kovacs limited the *manner* of operating a sound truck but not the *extent* of its proper use. By contrast, the Act's dollar ceilings restrict the extent of the reasonable use of virtually every means of communicating information. [Footnote by the Court.]

[2] Being free to engage in unlimited political expression subject to a ceiling on expenditures is like being free to drive an automobile as far and as often as one desires on a single tank of gasoline. [Footnote by the Court.]

contribute amounts greater than the statutory limits to expend such funds on direct political expression, rather than to reduce the total amount of money potentially available to promote political expression. The Act's contribution and expenditure limitations also impinge on protected associational freedoms. [In] sum, although the Act's contribution and expenditure limitations both implicate fundamental First Amendment interests, its expenditure ceilings impose significantly more severe restrictions on protected freedoms of political expression and association than do its limitations on financial contributions.

B. *Contribution Limitations.* [T]he primary First Amendment problem raised by the Act's contribution limitations is their restriction of one aspect of the contributor's freedom of political association. [G]overnmental "action which may have the effect of curtailing the freedom to associate is subject to the closest scrutiny." [NAACP v. Alabama.] Yet, [e]ven a " 'significant interference' with protected rights of political association" may be sustained if the State demonstrates a sufficiently important interest and employs means closely drawn to avoid unnecessary abridgment of associational [freedoms].

It is unnecessary to look beyond the Act's primary purpose—to limit the actuality and appearance of corruption resulting from large individual financial contributions—in order to find a constitutionally sufficient justification for the $1,000 contribution limitation. [To] the extent that large contributions are given to secure political quid pro quos from current and potential officeholders, the integrity of our system of representative democracy is undermined. [The] deeply disturbing examples surfacing after the 1972 election demonstrate that the problem is not an illusory one. [Of] almost equal concern [is] the impact of the appearance of corruption stemming from public awareness of the opportunities for abuse inherent in a regime of large individual financial contributions. [Appellants] contend that the contribution limitations must be invalidated because bribery laws and narrowly-drawn disclosure requirements constitute a less restrictive means of dealing with "proven and suspected quid pro quo arrangements." But laws making criminal the giving and taking of bribes deal with only the most blatant and specific attempts of those with money to influence governmental action. And [Congress] was surely entitled to conclude that disclosure was only a partial measure, and that contribution ceilings were a necessary legislative concomitant to deal with the reality or appearance of [corruption].

[The Court also rejected similar challenges to the $5000 limit on contributions to candidates by "political committees," the limits on volunteers' incidental expenses, and the $25,000 limit on total contributions by an individual during a calendar year.]

C. *Expenditure Limitations.* The Act's expenditure ceilings impose direct and substantial restraints on the quantity of political speech. [It] is clear that a primary effect of these expenditure limitations is to restrict the quantity of campaign [speech]. [While neutral] as to the ideas expressed, [the restrictions] limit political expression "at the core of our electoral process and of the First Amendment [freedoms]."

1. *The $1,000 limitation on expenditures "relative to a clearly identified candidate."* Section 608(e)(1) provides that "[n]o person may make any expenditure [relative] to a clearly identified candidate during a calendar year [which] exceeds $1,000." [Appellants claim] that the provision is

unconstitutionally vague. [Unconstitutional vagueness] can be avoided only by reading § 608(e)(1) as limited to communications that include explicit words of advocacy of election or defeat of a candidate.

[We] turn then to the basic First Amendment question—whether § 608(e)(1), even as thus narrowly and explicitly construed, impermissibly burdens the constitutional right of free expression. [T]he constitutionality of § 608(e)(1) turns on whether the governmental interests advanced in its support satisfy the exacting scrutiny applicable to limitations on core First Amendment rights of political expression.

We find that the governmental interest in preventing corruption and the appearance of corruption is inadequate to justify § 608(e)(1)'s ceiling on independent expenditures. First, [the section] prevents only some large expenditures. So long as persons and groups eschew expenditures that in express terms advocate the election or defeat of a clearly identified candidate, they are free to spend as much as they want to promote the candidate and his views. [It] would naively underestimate the ingenuity and resourcefulness of persons and groups desiring to buy influence to believe that they would have much difficulty devising expenditures that skirted the restriction on express advocacy of election or defeat but nevertheless benefited the candidate's campaign. [Second, the] parties defending § 608(e)(1) contend that it is necessary to prevent would-be contributors from avoiding the contribution limitations by the simple expedient of paying directly for media advertisements or for other portions of the candidate's campaign activities. [But] controlled or coordinated expenditures are treated as contributions rather than expenditures under the Act [and are restricted by the valid § 608(b)]. By contrast, § 608(e)(1) limits expenditures for express advocacy of candidates made totally independently of the candidate and his campaign. Unlike contributions, such independent expenditures may well provide little assistance to the candidate's campaign and indeed may prove counterproductive. The absence of prearrangement and coordination of an expenditure with the candidate or his agent not only undermines the value of the expenditure to the candidate, but also alleviates the danger that expenditures will be given as a quid pro quo for improper commitments from the candidate. [While] the independent expenditure ceiling thus fails to serve any substantial governmental interest in stemming the reality or appearance of corruption in the electoral process, it heavily burdens core First Amendment expression.

It is argued, however, that the ancillary governmental interest in equalizing the relative ability of individuals and groups to influence the outcome of elections serves to justify [this expenditure limitation]. But the concept that government may restrict the speech of some elements of our society in order to enhance the relative voice of others is wholly foreign to the First Amendment, which was designed "to secure 'the widest possible dissemination of information from diverse and antagonistic sources,' " and " 'to assure unfettered interchange of ideas.' " [The] First Amendment's protection against governmental abridgment of free expression cannot properly be made to depend on a person's financial ability to engage in public discussion. [We] conclude that § 608(e)(1)'s independent expenditure limitation is unconstitutional under the First Amendment.

2.   *Limitation on expenditures by candidates from personal or family resources.* The Act also sets limits on expenditures by a candidate "from his personal funds, or the personal funds of his immediate family, in connection

with his campaigns during any calendar year." § 608(a)(1). [The] ceiling on personal expenditures by a candidate in furtherance of his own [candidacy] clearly and directly interferes with constitutionally protected freedoms. [The] interest in equalizing the relative financial resources of candidates competing for elective office [is] clearly not sufficient to justify the provision's infringement of fundamental First Amendment rights. First, the limitation may fail to promote financial equality among candidates. A candidate who spends less of his personal resources on his campaign may nonetheless outspend his rival as a result of more successful fundraising efforts. Indeed, a candidate's personal wealth may impede his efforts to persuade others that he needs their financial contributions or volunteer efforts to conduct an effective campaign. Second, and more fundamentally, the First Amendment simply cannot tolerate § 608(a)'s restriction upon the freedom of a candidate to speak [on] behalf of his own [candidacy].

3. *Limitations on campaign expenditures.* Section 608(c) of the Act places limitations on overall campaign expenditures by candidates seeking nomination for election and election to federal office. [Presidential] candidates may spend $10,000,000 in seeking nomination for office and an additional $20,000,000 in the general election campaign. [Senate campaign expenditures are limited to] the greater of eight cents multiplied by the voting-age population or $100,000 [in the primary], and in the general election the limit is increased to 12 cents multiplied by the voting-age population or $150,000. The Act imposes blanket $70,000 limitations on both primary campaigns and general election campaigns for the House of Representatives. [These limits are subject to adjustments for inflation.]

[No] governmental interest that has been suggested is sufficient to justify [these restrictions] on the quantity of political expression. [The] interest in alleviating the corrupting influence of large contributions is served by [the] contributions limitations and disclosure provisions. [The] interest in equalizing the financial resources of candidates [is not a convincing justification] for restricting the scope of federal election campaigns. [The] campaign expenditure ceilings appear to be designed primarily to serve the governmental interests in reducing the allegedly skyrocketing costs of political campaigns. [But the] First Amendment denies government the power to determine that spending to promote one's political views is wasteful, excessive, or unwise. In the free society ordained by our Constitution it is not the government but the people—individually as citizens and candidates and collectively as associations and political committees—who must retain control over the quantity and range of debate on public issues in a political campaign. [W]e hold that § 608(c) is constitutionally invalid.

In sum, the [contribution limits] are constitutionally valid. These limitations along with the disclosure provisions, constitute the Act's primary weapons against the reality or appearance of improper influence stemming from the dependence of candidates on large campaign contributions. The contribution ceilings thus serve the basic governmental interest in safeguarding the integrity of the electoral process without directly impinging upon the rights of individual citizens and candidates to engage in political debate and discussion. By contrast, the First Amendment requires the invalidation of the Act's independent expenditure ceiling, its limitation on a candidate's expenditures from his own personal funds, and its ceilings on overall campaign expenditures. These provisions place substantial and direct restrictions on the ability of [candidates] to engage in protected political expression, restrictions that the First Amendment cannot [tolerate].

III. *Public Financing of Presidential Election Campaigns*

[Portions of the Act codified at Subtitle H of the Internal Revenue Code provided for a Presidential Election Campaign Fund, financed by taxpayer checkoff on tax returns, that would provide for up to $20 million (indexed for inflation) to finance presidential campaigns by major parties (those that had received more than 25 per cent of the popular vote in the preceding presidential election). It also provided for funding for minor-party campaigns (those receiving 5 to 25 per cent of the vote in the previous election) and new-party campaigns (those receiving less than 5 per cent in the current election) proportional to their share of the vote. Public subsidies for party nominating conventions and matching funds for primary campaigns were also provided. As a condition of receiving a public subsidy, major-party candidates were required to limit their campaign expenditures to the amount of the subsidy and to forego all private contributions except to the extent that the fund was insufficient to provide the full entitlement. Minor-party candidates similarly had to limit their campaign expenditures to the amount of the major-party entitlement and forego private contributions except to the extent needed to make up the difference between that amount and their public funding grant. The Court rejected Spending Clause and equal protection challenges to the funding provisions. In response to the First Amendment challenge, it held:]

Subtitle H is a congressional effort, not to abridge, restrict, or censor speech, but rather to use public money to facilitate and enlarge public discussion and participation in the electoral process, goals vital to a self-governing people. Thus, Subtitle H furthers, not abridges, pertinent First Amendment values.

[In a footnote earlier in the opinion, the Court summarized its holding on the public funding conditions as follows: "For the reasons discussed in Part III, Congress may engage in public financing of election campaigns and may condition acceptance of public funds on an agreement by the candidate to abide by specified expenditure limitations. Just as a candidate may voluntarily limit the size of the contributions he chooses to accept, he may decide to forego private fundraising and accept public funding."]

Affirmed in part and reversed in part.

■ CHIEF JUSTICE BURGER, concurring in part and dissenting [in part].

Contribution and expenditure limits. I agree fully with that part of the Court's opinion that holds unconstitutional the limitations the Act puts on campaign expenditures. [Yet] when it approves similarly stringent limitations on contributions, the Court ignores the reasons it finds so persuasive in the context of expenditures. For me contributions and expenditures are two sides of the same First Amendment [coin]. [Limiting] contributions, as a practical matter, will limit expenditures and will put an effective ceiling on the amount of political activity [that] Government will permit to take place. [The] Court's attempt to distinguish the communication inherent in political *contributions* from the speech aspects of political *expenditures* simply will not wash. We do little but engage in word games unless we recognize that people—candidates and contributors—spend money on political activity because they wish to communicate ideas, and their constitutional interest in doing so is precisely the same whether they or someone else utter the words. [It] is not simply speculation to think that the limitations on contributions will foreclose some candidacies. The limitations will also alter the nature of some electoral contests drastically. At any rate, the contribution limits are a far more severe restriction on First Amendment activity than the sort of "chilling" legislation for which the Court has shown such extraordinary concern in the past. If such restraints can be justified at all, they must be justified by the very strongest of [state interests].

■ JUSTICE WHITE, concurring in part and dissenting [in part].

I dissent [from] the Court's view that the expenditure limitations [violate] the First Amendment. [The Court] accepts the congressional judgment that the evils of unlimited contributions are sufficiently threatening to warrant restriction regardless of the impact of the limits on the contributor's opportunity for effective speech and in turn on the total volume of the candidate's political communications by reason of his inability to accept large sums from those willing to give. The congressional judgment, which I would also accept, was that other steps must be taken to counter the corrosive effects of money in federal election campaigns. One of these steps is § 608(e) [the expenditure limits]. [It] would make little sense to me, and apparently made none to Congress, to limit the amounts an individual may give to a candidate or spend with his approval but fail to limit the amounts that could be spent on his behalf. Yet the Court permits the former while striking down the latter [limitation]. I would take the word of those who know—that limiting independent expenditures is essential to prevent transparent and widespread evasion of the contribution limits.

[The] Court also rejects Congress' judgment manifested in § 608(c) that the federal interest in limiting total campaign expenditures by individual candidates justifies the incidental effect on their opportunity for effective political speech. [There] is no sound basis for invalidating the expenditure limitations, so long as the purposes they serve are legitimate and sufficiently substantial, which in my view they are. [Expenditure] ceilings reinforce the contribution limits and help eradicate the hazard of corruption. [Moreover,] the corrupt use of money by candidates is as much to be feared as the corrosive influence of large contributions. [I] have little doubt in addition that limiting the total that can be spent will ease the candidate's understandable obsession with fundraising, and so free him and his staff to communicate in more places and ways unconnected with the fundraising function. [It] is also important to restore and maintain public confidence in federal elections. It is critical to obviate or dispel the impression that federal elections are purely and simply a function of money, that federal offices are bought and sold or that political races are reserved for those who have the facility—and the stomach—for doing whatever it takes to bring together those interests, groups, and individuals that can raise or contribute large fortunes in order to prevail at the polls. The ceiling on candidate expenditures represents the considered judgment of Congress that elections are to be decided among candidates none of whom has an overpowering advantage by reason of a huge campaign war chest. [This] seems an acceptable purpose and the means chosen a common sense way to achieve [it].

I also disagree with the Court's judgment that § 608(a), which limits the amount of money that a candidate or his family may spend on his campaign, violates the Constitution. [By] limiting the importance of personal wealth, § 608(a) helps to assure that only individuals with a modicum of support from others will be viable candidates. This in turn would tend to discourage any notion that the outcome of elections is primarily a function of money. Similarly, § 608(a) tends to equalize access to the political arena, encouraging the less wealthy [to] run for political office. As with the campaign expenditure limits, Congress was entitled to determine that personal wealth ought to play a less important role in political campaigns than it has in the past. Nothing in the First Amendment stands in the way of that [determination].

[In a separate opinion, Justice BLACKMUN dissented from the portion of the decision upholding the contribution restrictions. He found no "principled constitutional distinction" between limits on contributions and limits on expenditures.]

[In another separate opinion, Justice MARSHALL dissented from the invalidation of the limits on the amount a candidate may spend from his own funds. He emphasized the governmental interest "in promoting the reality and appearance of equal access to the political arena," insisting that, even if the wealthy candidate's initial advantage can be overcome, "the perception that personal wealth wins elections may not only discourage potential candidates without significant personal wealth [but] also undermine public confidence in the integrity of the electoral process."]

[Finally, Chief Justice BURGER and Justice REHNQUIST dissented from the portion of the decision upholding the public financing provisions. Justice Rehnquist argued that Congress had "enshrined the Republican and Democratic parties in a permanently preferred position."]

―――――――――

BUCKLEY'S APPROACH AND AFTERMATH

1. *The level of scrutiny in Buckley: the contribution/ expenditure distinction.* The Court assumed that FECA implicated the First Amendment. What was the speech involved? Is writing a check speech? Is a donor's writing a check speech because it facilitates the candidate's speech? Would price ceilings on book sales implicate the First Amendment? What level of scrutiny did the Court apply in Buckley? Why was any heightened scrutiny appropriate? Because the Act covered political speech at the core of the First Amendment? Because the Act decreased the quantity of speech? Don't all content-neutral regulations decrease the quantity of speech? Why should the quantity restriction here receive stricter scrutiny?

Note that the Court in effect applied less stringent scrutiny to the contribution limits than to the expenditure limits? Why? Do contributions implicate a lesser First Amendment interest than independent expenditures? Do congressional judgments warrant greater deference with respect to contribution limits than to expenditure limits? For commentary on these questions, see Polsby, "Buckley v. Valeo: The Special Nature of Political Speech," 1976 Sup. Ct. Rev. 1; and Sullivan, "Political Money and Freedom of Speech," 30 U.C. Davis L. Rev. 663 (1997).

The Court continued after Buckley to adhere to the distinction between expenditure and contribution limits, reviewing the former more strictly than the latter. From the outset, this distinction was controversial; note that, in Buckley, Justice White would have upheld both types of restriction and Chief Justice Burger and Justice Blackmun would have struck both down as "two sides of the same [coin]." In later decisions, a number of justices likewise argued that the distinction should be eliminated, with some arguing both types of restriction should be invalidated and others suggesting that both should be upheld. Nonetheless, the contribution/expenditure distinction has remained central to the Court's decisions in this area, and over time the Court increasingly formalized the two-tier review applicable to contribution limits on the one hand and expenditure limits on the other.

In **Nixon v. Shrink Missouri Government PAC**, 528 U.S. 377 (2000), for example, the Court reiterated that contribution limits are subject to greater deference than expenditure limits in rejecting a challenge to Missouri's limits on contributions to candidates for state office, brought by a candidate for state auditor who said that a $1075 limit on individual contributions for that office was too low, even if Buckley had upheld a $1000 federal contribution limit, because inflation had since eroded the real value of such a sum. Writing for the 6–3 majority, Justice SOUTER, joined by Chief Justice Rehnquist and Justices Stevens, O'Connor, Ginsburg and Breyer, reiterated that contribution limits need not satisfy strict scrutiny, but will survive if "closely drawn" to a "sufficiently important interest" such as prevention of corruption and the appearance of corruption. He also rejected the challengers' argument that the state must adduce strong empirical evidence of such corruption or its appearance: "The quantum of empirical evidence needed to satisfy heightened judicial scrutiny of legislative judgments will vary up or down with the novelty and plausibility of the justification raised. Buckley demonstrates that the dangers of large, corrupt contributions and the suspicion that large contributions are corrupt are neither novel nor implausible." Justice Souter also rejected the argument that the $1075 was too low in terms of real purchasing power to be constitutional under Buckley: "In Buckley, we specifically rejected the contention that $1,000, or any other amount, was a constitutional minimum below which legislatures could not regulate. [We] asked [instead] whether the contribution limitation was so radical in effect as to render political association ineffective." Justices Stevens and Breyer filed separate concurrences.

Justice KENNEDY dissented, emphasizing that Buckley's "wooden" distinction between contributions and expenditures had led to "adverse, unintended consequences"—specifically, it "has forced a substantial amount of political speech underground, as contributors and candidates devise ever more elaborate methods of avoiding contribution limits, limits which take no account of rising campaign costs. [Soft] money may be contributed to political parties in unlimited amounts, and is used often to fund so-called issue advocacy, advertisements that promote or attack a candidate's positions without specifically urging his or her election or defeat. [Thus] has the Court's decision given us covert speech. This mocks the First Amendment. The current system would be unfortunate, and suspect under the First Amendment, had it evolved from a deliberate legislative choice; but its unhappy origins are in our earlier decree in Buckley, which by accepting half of what Congress did (limiting contributions) but rejecting the other (limiting expenditures) created a misshapen system, one which distorts the meaning of speech." He concluded: "I would overrule Buckley and then free Congress or state legislatures to attempt some new reform, if, based upon their own considered view of the First Amendment, it is possible to do so. Until any reexamination takes place, however, the existing distortion of speech caused by the half-way house we created in Buckley ought to be eliminated. The

First Amendment ought to be allowed to take its own course without further obstruction from the artificial system we have imposed. It suffices here to say that the law in question does not come even close to passing any serious scrutiny."

Justice THOMAS likewise dissented, joined by Justice Scalia. He described as a "curious anomaly" the majority's willingness to give less protection to campaign contributions than to other forms of speech (like nude dancing) less central to the political process. He questioned Buckley's contribution/expenditure distinction, stating that "the Constitution leaves it entirely up to citizens and candidates to determine who shall speak, the means they will use, and the amount of speech sufficient to inform and persuade." Finally, he criticized the majority for applying a lower standard of scrutiny to contribution regulations, suggesting that it had "permit[ted] vague and unenumerated harms to suffice as a compelling reason for the government to smother political speech," and argued that the Missouri law should have been subject to strict scrutiny, which it could not survive.

Note the substitution effects described by Justice Kennedy, whereby limitations on political contributions drive political money away from candidates who are accountable at the polls and toward political parties and independent advocacy organizations that are not. Congress later took the view that "soft money" expenditures by parties and "issue ads" by private organizations constitute "loopholes" in the federal election campaign laws and sought to control them by amendments to FECA. These amendments gave rise to constitutional challenges discussed at p. 568. For discussion of these substitution effects, see Sullivan, "Against Campaign Finance Reform," 1998 Utah L. Rev. 311 (1998); and Issacharoff & Karlan, "The Hydraulics of Campaign Finance Reform," 77 Tex. L. Rev. 1705 (1999).

In **Randall v. Sorrell**, 548 U.S. 230 (2006), the Court again reiterated the contribution/expenditure distinction, but for the first time found a contribution limit so low that it could not satisfy Buckley's avoidance-of-corruption rationale. Announcing the judgment of the Court, Justice BREYER, joined by Chief Justice Roberts, invalidated Vermont's expenditure limits under Buckley's strict scrutiny, and, joined by Justice Alito, also rejected Vermont's proposed new justification for expenditure limits, namely "that expenditure limits are necessary in order to reduce the amount of time candidates must spend raising money. [In] our view, it is highly unlikely that fuller consideration of this time protection rationale would have changed Buckley's result."

The same three-justice plurality held invalid Vermont's unusually low contribution limits, which allowed any individual to contribute only $400 to a governor's race, $300 to a state senator's race, and $200 to a state representative's race in each election cycle. Justice Breyer wrote: "Since Buckley, the Court has consistently upheld contribution limits in other statutes. [Nonetheless,] as Buckley acknowledged, we must recognize the existence of some lower bound. At some point the constitutional risks to the democratic electoral process become too great. [Contribution] limits that are too low can harm the electoral process by preventing challengers from mounting effective campaigns against incumbent officeholders, thereby reducing democratic accountability. [We] find those danger signs present here. [Vermont's] contribution limits are the lowest in the Nation [and] well below the lowest limit this Court has previously upheld, the limit of $1,075 per election [in Shrink]. [Such] contribution limits are too restrictive.

[Taken] together, [Vermont's] substantial restrictions on the ability of candidates to raise the funds necessary to run a competitive election, on the ability of political parties to help their candidates get elected, and on the ability of individual citizens to volunteer their time to campaigns show that the Act is not closely drawn to meet its objectives."

Justice KENNEDY concurred only in the judgment, as did Justice THOMAS in an opinion, joined by Justice Scalia, stating "I continue to believe that Buckley provides insufficient protection to political speech, the core of the First Amendment." Justices Scalia and Thomas would have overruled Buckley insofar as it upheld contribution limits. Justices STEVENS filed a dissent stating that he too would overrule Buckley but in the opposite direction: "I am convinced that holding on expenditure limits is wrong, and that the time has come to overrule it. [I] am firmly persuaded that the Framers would have been appalled by the impact of modern fundraising practices on the ability of elected officials to perform their public responsibilities [and] they surely would not have expected judges to interfere with the enforcement of expenditure limits that merely require candidates to budget their activities without imposing any restrictions whatsoever on what they may say in their speeches, debates, and interviews." Justice SOUTER likewise filed a dissent, joined by Justice Ginsburg and in part by Justice Stevens, stating that he would have upheld Vermont's contribution limits under Buckley and Shrink, and allowed further evidentiary proceedings on whether Vermont's expenditure limits might be justified.

2. *Government justifications for campaign finance restrictions: the corruption/equalization distinction.* Buckley found the government interest in avoidance of corruption or the appearance of corruption sufficient to justify contribution limits. What did the Court mean by "corruption"? Not literal bribery, which was already illegal. Disproportionate influence by some over others with respect to legislative decision-making? The Court found the corruption rationale irrelevant to expenditure limits, and rejected as an illegitimate justification for those limits the asserted governmental interest "in equalizing the relative ability of individuals and groups to influence the outcome of elections," finding such an interest "wholly foreign to the First Amendment." Did the Court give adequate weight to the interest in equality as a justification for expenditure limits? Consider the following comments:

a.   "We do not think of 'one person one vote' as an example of reducing the speech of some to enhance the relative speech of others. [Why should] superior spending power [be] rightfully mine [if] superior voting power is not [?]" Strauss, "Corruption, Equality, and Campaign Finance," 94 Colum. L. Rev. 1369 (1994).

b.   "[In the political process,] ideas and candidates [should] prevail because of their inherent worth, not because [one or the other] side puts on a more elaborate show of support." Wright, "Politics and the Constitution: Is Money Speech?," 85 Yale L.J. 1001 (1976). See also Wright, "Money and the Pollution of Politics: Is the First Amendment an Obstacle to Political Equality?," 82 Colum. L. Rev. 609 (1982).

c.   "[Buckley, like Lochner, rests on] a decision to take the market status quo as just and prepolitical, and to use that decision to invalidate democratic efforts at reform." Sunstein, "Free Speech Now," 59 U. Chi. L. Rev. 255 (1992).

d. "[W]hen wealth is unfairly distributed and money dominates politics, then, though individual citizens may be equal in their vote and their freedom to hear the candidates they wish to hear, they are not equal in their own ability to command the attention of others for their own candidates, interests, and convictions. [But] democracy [supposes] that citizens are equals not only as judges but as participants as well." Dworkin, "The Curse of American Politics," N.Y. Rev. of Books, Oct. 17, 1996.

e. "[In a fair constitutional democracy,] each eligible voter should receive the same amount of financial resources for the purpose of participating in electoral politics." Foley, "Equal-Dollars-Per-Voter: A Constitutional Principle of Campaign Finance," 94 Colum. L. Rev. 1204 (1994).

How effectively could campaign finance restrictions advance the goal of equality among speakers in political campaigns, if such a goal were permissible? Is wealth only one basis for political inequality? Would finance reform leave untouched inequality among candidates and their campaigns based on fame, incumbency, and experience in the political arena? Based on the time their supporters were willing to donate to their campaigns? See BeVier, "Campaign Finance Reform: Specious Arguments, Intractable Dilemmas," 94 Colum. L. Rev. 1258 (1994).

Are there any other government interests that might suffice to justify campaign finance restrictions? Might expenditure limits be justified as reducing the diversion of candidates' time to fundraising? (Note that such a justification was rejected in Randall v. Sorrell.) Might they be justified as increasing the responsiveness of elected officials to their constituencies rather than "special interests," or improve the quality of debate by shifting candidates' energies away from expensive but uninformative ads? For commentary on government interests beyond corruption and equalization, see Blasi, "Free Speech and the Widening Gyre of Fund-Raising: Why Campaign Spending Limits May Not Violate the First Amendment After All," 94 Colum. L. Rev. 1281 (1994); Sorauf, "Politics, Experience, and the First Amendment: The Case of American Campaign Finance," 94 Colum. L. Rev. 1348 (1994).

3. *Public funding of political campaigns.* Buckley upheld public subsidies for presidential elections, conditioned on the candidates' agreement not to spend above a certain ceiling. Note that such expenditure limits would be unconstitutional if imposed directly. Why wasn't it an unconstitutional condition on the receipt of public funds to impose this ceiling indirectly? The Court gave virtually no discussion to this question in Buckley. Could Congress make any subsidy scheme mandatory rather than voluntary? Would a mandatory public funding scheme violate the First Amendment? Suppose that government offered subsidies in kind, for example by mandating free air time for candidates on the broadcast media. Would such a subsidy violate broadcasters' First Amendment rights, or could such free air time in turn be exacted from broadcasters as a condition of their receipt of a public benefit in the form of a license to a portion of the airwaves? For arguments in favor of public funding, see Raskin & Bonifaz, "The Constitutional Imperative and Practical Superiority of Democratically Financed Elections," 94 Colum. L. Rev. 1160 (1994); see also Powe, "Mass Speech and the Newer First Amendment," 1982 Sup. Ct. Rev. 243.

PARTIES, CORPORATIONS, PACS, SUPER PACS AND POLITICAL MONEY

1. ***Campaign-related expenditures by political parties.*** May
political parties expend funds freely in support of or opposition to candidates,
so long as they do so independently of a candidate's own campaign?
Colorado Republican Federal Campaign Committee v. FEC, 518 U.S.
604 (1996) ("Colorado I"), the Court invalidated a provision of FECA
imposing dollar limits upon political party "expenditures in connection with
the general election campaign of a [congressional] candidate." Justice
BREYER, joined in a plurality opinion by Justices O'Connor and Souter,
wrote that "the First Amendment prohibits the application of this provision
to the kind of expenditure at issue here—an expenditure that the political
party has made independently, without coordination with any candidate."
He reasoned that "independent expression of a political party's views is 'core'
First Amendment activity no less than is the independent expression of
individuals, candidates, or other political committees. [We] therefore believe
that this Court's prior case law controls the outcome here. We do not see how
a Constitution that grants to individuals, candidates, and ordinary political
committees the right to make unlimited independent expenditures could
deny the same right to political parties." The plurality rejected the
government's view that party expenditures on behalf of a candidate's election
should be conclusively presumed to be coordinated with the candidate's
campaign and thus treated as "contributions" that could be regulated
permissibly under Buckley. But in light of its finding that the ads in this case
had in fact been independent of any candidate's campaign, the plurality
declined to reach the question whether the First Amendment forbids
congressional efforts to limit expenditures that were in fact coordinated
rather than independent.

Justice KENNEDY, joined by Chief Justice Rehnquist and Justice
Scalia, concurred in the judgment and dissented in part. He would have
invalidated the party expenditure limits on their face, whether applied to
independent or coordinated expenditures. Justice THOMAS, joined by Chief
Justice Rehnquist and Justice Scalia in a concurrence in the judgment and
partial dissent, also would have invalidated the party spending limits in
their entirety on the ground that the anticorruption rationale set forth in
Buckley has no application here: "What could it mean for a party to 'corrupt'
its candidate or to exercise 'coercive' influence over him? The very aim of a
political party is to influence its candidate's stance on issues and, if the
candidate takes office or is reelected, his votes. When political parties
achieve that aim, [that] is not corruption; that is successful advocacy of ideas
in the political marketplace and representative government in a party
system." Justice STEVENS, joined by Justice Ginsburg, dissented, arguing
that the party expenditure limits were constitutional as to both independent
and coordinated expenditures because they served important interests both
in avoiding corruption and in "leveling the electoral playing field by
constraining the cost of federal campaigns."

The 1996 Colorado Republican decision left open the constitutionality of
limits on expenditures by political parties that are coordinated with a
candidate's campaign. That question was resolved, in the government's
favor, in a second appeal in the same case after remand. In **FEC v. Colorado
Republican Federal Campaign Committee**, 533 U.S. 431 (2001)
("Colorado II"), the plurality and the dissenters in Colorado I united to hold,

in a 5–4 opinion for the Court by Justice SOUTER, that limits on a party's coordinated expenditures are facially constitutional: "[Parties] are [necessarily] the instruments of some contributors whose object is not to support the party's message or to elect party candidates across the board, but rather [to] use parties as conduits for contributions meant to place candidates under obligation. [A] party is [therefore] in the same position as some individuals and PACs, as to whom coordinated spending limits have already been held valid, Buckley. [We] accordingly apply to a party's coordinated spending limitation the same scrutiny we have applied to the other political actors, that is, scrutiny appropriate for a contribution limit, enquiring whether the restriction is 'closely drawn' to match what we have recognized as the 'sufficiently important' government interest in combating political corruption. Shrink."

Under that standard of intermediate scrutiny, Justice Souter found the limits justified "on the theory that unlimited coordinated spending by a party raises the risk of corruption (and its appearance) through circumvention of valid contribution limits. [Despite] years of enforcement of the challenged limits, substantial evidence demonstrates how candidates, donors, and parties test the limits of the current law, and it shows beyond serious doubt how contribution limits would be eroded if inducement to circumvent them were enhanced by declaring parties' coordinated spending wide open. [Therefore] the choice here is not, as in Buckley and Colorado I, between a limit on pure contributions and pure expenditures. The choice is between limiting contributions and limiting expenditures whose special value as expenditures is also the source of their power to corrupt. Congress is entitled to its choice."

Justice THOMAS dissented, joined by Justices Scalia and Kennedy and in part by Chief Justice Rehnquist. All but the Chief agreed they would overrule Buckley too and apply strict scrutiny to contribution limits. The Chief joined the other three dissenters in concluding that burdens on coordinated expenditures by parties would fail even the intermediate scrutiny applicable to individual contribution limits. Justice Thomas explained: "[T]he Government [has] presented no evidence at all of corruption or the perception of corruption. [The] Court's [alternative] theory [that] the Party Expenditure Provision helps combat circumvention of the limits on individual donors' contributions [is] weak speculation ungrounded in any evidence. [Even] if the Government had presented evidence that the Party Expenditure Provision affects corruption, [there] are better tailored alternatives for addressing the corruption. In addition to bribery laws and disclosure laws, the Government could [treat] contributions that [were 'earmarked] or otherwise directed through an intermediary or conduit to [a] candidate' [as] contributions to the candidate."

2. ***Expenditures by corporations for political speech.*** Should corporations have free speech rights to spend money in political campaigns? In favor of referenda and initiative propositions? In favor of or opposition to candidates? From their own treasuries or only through separate political action committees? Federal election law has long prohibited corporations (since 1907) and labor unions (since 1947) from making contributions from their own treasuries directly to candidates' political campaigns, while allowing them to establish separate, segregated political action committees or "PACs" to support candidates during federal elections.

But in **First National Bank of Boston v. Bellotti**, 435 U.S. 765 (1978), the Court held that the First Amendment prohibits a restriction on corporate expenditures for political speech from their own treasuries to express corporate points of view in state referenda campaigns. By a vote of 5–4, Bellotti invalidated a Massachusetts statute barring any corporation from making contributions or expenditures "for the purpose [of] influencing or affecting the vote on any questions submitted to the voters, other than one materially affecting any of the property, business or assets of the corporation." The law further specified that "[n]o question submitted to the voters solely concerning the taxation of the income, property, or transactions of individuals shall be deemed materially to affect the property, business or assets of the corporation." The challengers in this case (banks and business corporations) were prevented from spending money to oppose a proposed state constitutional amendment to authorize a graduated individual income tax. The state court upheld the statute, holding that the First Amendment rights of a corporation were limited to issues that materially affect its business, property, or assets.

The Supreme Court reversed, with Justice POWELL writing the majority opinion. To begin inquiry with the extent of corporate free speech rights (as the state court had done), he wrote, was to pose "the wrong question": "The proper question [is] not whether corporations 'have' First Amendment rights and, if so, whether they are coextensive with those of natural persons. Instead, the question must be whether [the law] abridges expression that the First Amendment was meant to protect. We hold that it does." In explaining why substantial First Amendment interests were implicated, Justice Powell noted that the expression the challengers wanted to engage in—publicizing their views on a proposed constitutional amendment—lay "at the heart of the First Amendment's protection": "It is the type of speech indispensable to decisionmaking in a democracy. [The] inherent worth of the speech in terms of its capacity for informing the public does not depend on the identity of its [source]." The Constitution and the case law accordingly did not support "the proposition that speech that otherwise would be within the protection of the First Amendment loses that protection simply because its source is a corporation that cannot prove, to the satisfaction of a court, a material effect on its business or property."

Having found the First Amendment implicated, Justice Powell found that the law was content-based and thus required strict scrutiny: "In the realm of protected speech, the legislature is constitutionally disqualified from dictating the subjects about which persons may speak and the speakers who may address a public issue. [Mosley.] If a legislature may direct business corporations to 'stick to business,' it also may limit other corporations—religious, charitable, or civic—to their respective 'business' when addressing the public. Such power in government to channel the expression of views is unacceptable under the First Amendment. Especially where, as here, the legislature's suppression of speech suggests an attempt to give one side of a debatable public question an advantage in expressing its views to the people, the First Amendment is plainly offended."

Under strict scrutiny, Justice Powell found, the law could not survive because it prohibited "protected speech in a manner unjustified by a compelling state interest." The state asserted, first, an interest "in sustaining the active role of the individual citizen in the electoral process and thereby preventing diminution of the citizen's confidence in government." Justice Powell did not find this interest "implicated in this case": he concluded that "there had been no showing that the relative voice of corporations has been overwhelming or even significant in influencing referenda in Massachusetts, or that there has been any threat to the confidence of the citizenry in government." Moreover, he found that the risk of actual or apparent corruption recognized in cases involving candidate elections "simply is not present in a popular vote on a public issue." The "State's paternalism evidenced by this statute" was inconsistent with the First Amendment's emphasis on the people's right to hear.

The state also asserted a second interest in "protecting the rights of shareholders whose views differ from those expressed by management on behalf of the corporation." Justice Powell also rejected this justification, finding that the statute poorly fit it: the statute was underinclusive in that it permitted corporations to lobby for legislation and contribute to candidates, and overinclusive in that it forbade them from spending on referenda even if the shareholders unanimously agreed on their position. Moreover, "The fact that a particular kind of ballot question has been singled out for special treatment undermines the likelihood of a genuine state interest in protecting shareholders. It suggests instead that the legislature may have been concerned with silencing corporations on a particular subject." Justice Powell also questioned the strength of the state interest in protecting shareholders from compulsory support of objectionable causes, noting that "no shareholder has been 'compelled' to contribute anything, [for] the shareholder invests in a corporation of his own volition and is free to withdraw his investment at any time and for any reason."

In a lengthy dissent, Justice WHITE, joined by Justices Brennan and Marshall, wrote that the majority's "fundamental error" was "its failure to realize that the state regulatory interests [are] themselves derived from the First Amendment"—primarily, the value of promoting the free marketplace of ideas by preventing corporate domination. Although Justice White conceded that corporate speech was within the First Amendment, he insisted that corporate speech was "subject to restrictions which individual expression is not." He noted that corporate communications do not further a "principal function of the First Amendment, the use of communication as a means of self-expression, self-realization and self-fulfillment." He added: "Ideas which are not a product of individual choice are entitled to less First Amendment protection." Moreover, "the restriction of corporate speech concerned with political matters impinges much less severely upon the availability of ideas to the general public than do restrictions upon individual speech."

Justice White argued further that the "governmental interest in regulating corporate political communications [raises] considerations which differ significantly from those governing the regulation of individual speech. [T]he special status of corporations has placed them in a position to control vast amounts of economic power which may, if not regulated, dominate not only the economy but also the very heart of our democracy, the electoral process. Although [Buckley] provides support for the position that the desire to equalize the financial resources available to candidates does not justify the limitation upon the expression of support which a restriction upon individual contributions entails, the interest of [the states] which have restricted corporate political activity is quite different. It is not one of equalizing the resources of opposing candidates or opposing positions but rather of preventing institutions which have been permitted to amass wealth as a result of special advantages extended by the State for certain economic purposes from using that wealth to acquire an unfair advantage in the political process. [The] State need not permit its own creation to consume it." Moreover, Justice White found compelling the state's additional interest in "assuring that shareholders are not compelled to support and financially further beliefs with which they disagree."

A separate dissent by Justice REHNQUIST concluded "that the 14th Amendment does not require a State to endow a business corporation with the power of political speech." He emphasized that corporations were created by the state and were limited to rights explicitly or implicitly guaranteed as part of the state-granted charter. He insisted that it could not be readily concluded that "the right of political expression is [necessary] to carry out the functions of a corporation organized for commercial purposes." He explained: "[The] States might reasonably feel that the corporation would use its economic power to obtain further benefits beyond those already bestowed." And he emphasized: "I can see no basis for concluding that the liberty of a corporation to engage in political activity with regard to matters having no material effect on its business is necessarily incidental to the purposes for which the Commonwealth permitted these corporations to be organized." Accordingly, the Massachusetts law provided "at least as much protection as the 14th Amendment requires." He noted that he would uphold the law even if the legislature's actual motive had been to "muzzle corporations on [the tax] issue" in order to increase the chances that the referendum would pass.

3. ***Segregated spending by PACs.*** While barring corporations from contributing directly to candidate campaigns, the federal election laws and the laws of many states have allowed corporations to operate separate, segregated "political action committees" or "PACs" in order to express support for or opposition to political candidates. Might the requirement of operating a separate fund itself burden free speech rights in violation of the First Amendment? In **FEC v. Massachusetts Citizens For Life, Inc. [MCFL]**, 479 U.S. 238 (1986), the Court held that certain nonprofit ideological corporations like MCFL, a grass-roots antiabortion organization, must be permitted to make independent campaign expenditures from their own corporate treasuries. Justice BRENNAN's opinion for the Court held that, as applied to MCFL, a financial segregation requirement is, "while [not] an absolute restriction on speech, a substantial one" that triggers strict scrutiny, and cannot be justified by any interest in preventing corruption (since the expenditures are independent) or by any interest in protecting contributors from the diversion of their funds to causes they do not support (since "individuals who contribute to [MCFL] are fully aware of its political purposes, and in fact contribute precisely because they support those purposes"). Chief Justice REHNQUIST, joined by Justices White, Blackmun, and Stevens, dissented.

Did the MCFL exception from segregated funding requirements apply to any entities beyond nonprofit ideological corporations? The Court rejected an extension of MCFL to an entity serving the interests of for-profit corporations in **Austin v. Michigan Chamber of Commerce**, 494 U.S. 652 (1990). Austin upheld a Michigan restriction that barred corporations from making independent expenditures from general treasury funds on behalf of candidates in political campaigns, even though the restriction was materially identical to the federal restriction invalidated as applied in MCFL.

Justice MARSHALL's majority opinion emphasized the "unique legal and economic characteristics of corporations" that enable them "to use 'resources amassed in the economic marketplace' to obtain 'an unfair advantage in the political marketplace.'" He elaborated: "the political advantage of corporations is unfair because '[t]he resources in the treasury of a business corporation [are] not an indication of popular support for the corporation's political ideas. They reflect instead the economically motivated decisions of investors and customers. The availability of these resources may make a corporation a formidable political presence, even though the power of the corporation may be no reflection of the power of its ideas.'" He held that the state had "articulated a sufficiently compelling rationale" for its restrictions on spending since the law was designed to deal with "the corrosive and distorting effects of immense aggregations of wealth that are accumulated with the help of the corporate form and that have little or no correlation to the public's support for the corporation's political ideas." Justice Marshall held the restriction permissibly applied to the Michigan Chamber of Commerce, reasoning that, unlike MCFL, the Michigan group "was involved in a wide range of activities other than political activity" and "had a large number of members many of whom might not share the Chamber's political goals."

Justice SCALIA dissented, rejecting the majority's view that the corporate form conferred advantages so different in kind from other state benefits as to justify a restriction on political speech and viewing the majority opinion as an attempt to overrule Buckley's rejection of restrictions on political activity in order to equalize speaking power. In another dissent, Justice KENNEDY, joined by Justices O'Connor and Scalia, objected that the majority had upheld "a direct restriction on the independent expenditure of funds for political speech for the first time in the Court's history." He argued that the Court's own distinction between the Michigan Chamber and MCFL was itself a "value-laden, content-based speech suppression that permits some nonprofit corporate groups but not others to engage in political speech." He would have found the Michigan law unable to survive "exacting First Amendment scrutiny": "[In] Buckley and Bellotti, [we] rejected the argument that the expenditure of money to increase the quantity of political speech somehow fosters corruption. The key to the majority's reasoning appears to be that because some corporate speakers are well-supported, [government] may ban all corporate speech to ensure that it will not dominate political debate. The argument is flawed in at least two respects. First, the statute is overinclusive because it covers all groups which use the corporate form, including all nonprofit corporations. Second, it assumes that the government has a legitimate interest in equalizing the relative influence of speakers. [Similar arguments were] rejected in Bellotti."

Was there any way to reconcile Austin with Buckley or Bellotti? Note that Justice Marshall sought to distinguish Austin as implicating an interest in avoiding the distortion of individual speakers' views rather than an interest in equalizing relative speaking power—the interest deemed illegitimate in Buckley. And Austin arose in the context of expenditures on behalf of candidates, not issues in a referendum campaign, as in Bellotti. But if a corporation may make unlimited expenditures on referendum campaigns under Bellotti, why may it not make unlimited independent expenditures in support of political candidates? The tension between Austin on the one hand and Buckley and Bellotti on the other eventually proved too much to sustain, and in Citizens United v. FEC, 558 U.S. 310 (2010), the Court expressly overruled Austin. For the Citizens United decision, see p. 583.

ENACTMENT OF AND CONSTITUTIONAL CHALLENGES TO BCRA

By upholding contribution limits but invalidating expenditure limits, Buckley in effect held that the First Amendment permitted restrictions on the supply of political money, but forbade restrictions on demand. Predictably, as Justice Kennedy noted in Shrink, p. 558, political money found other outlets. Federal election campaigns witnessed a rise in the expenditure of "soft money" by political parties and private interest group "issue advertisements" referencing candidates. Critics called these substitution effects "loopholes" in need of closure, prompting Congress to enact new campaign finance legislation in the Bipartisan Campaign Reform Act of 2002 (BCRA)—commonly called the "McCain-Feingold" law based on its two lead Senate sponsors, Republican John McCain and Democrat Russ Feingold.

1. ***"Soft money."*** Under the Federal Election Campaign Act of 1971 ("FECA") as amended and upheld in Buckley, contributions to federal election campaigns had to be made in limited amounts, had to be fully disclosed, and could not be made directly by certain entities such as unions and corporations. Donations made solely for the purpose of influencing state or local elections, however, were not governed by these disclosure requirements or source and amount limitations. Thus corporations and unions, as well as individuals who had contributed the maximum amounts to federal candidates, could contribute unlimited amounts of what came to be known as "soft money" (as opposed to so-called "hard money" that went directly to candidates) to political parties for activities intended to influence state or local elections. A series of FEC rulings allowed political parties to fund with soft money some mixed state/federal election activities, such as get-out-the-vote drives and generic party advertising. The amount of soft money used in federal campaigns increased each election cycle, accounting for 5% ($21.6 million) in 1984, 11% ($45 million) in 1988, 16% ($80 million) in 1992, 30% ($272 million) in 1996, and 42% ($498 million) in 2000. Advocates of campaign finance restrictions argued that the solicitation of soft money by the national parties for transfer and use by the state parties for de facto federal campaign activity amounted to circumvention of FECA's limitations.

2. ***"Issue advertising."*** In Buckley, the Court construed FECA's disclosure requirements and expenditure limitations "to reach only funds used for communications that expressly advocate the election or defeat of a clearly identified candidate" like "Elect Smith" or "Defeat Doe"—which could be understood as de facto contributions. The use or omission of such so-called "magic words" came to be viewed as determinative of a bright-line test separating regulable "express advocacy," which could be financed using only hard money subject to FECA's source and amount limits, from nonregulable "issue advocacy," which could be funded with soft money donated to the parties or paid for directly by advocacy organizations, corporations, and unions, and aired without disclosing its sponsor. Federal elections

increasingly witnessed a proliferation of issue ads eschewing the use of the magic words and thus in amounts and from sources unregulated by FECA.

3. *Enactment of the Bipartisan Campaign Reform Act of 2002 (BCRA).* In response to these trends, Congress enacted BCRA, which amended FECA, the Communications Act of 1934, and other portions of federal law. The law imposed new restrictions on soft money and issue ads that were designed, said its sponsors, to "close loopholes" in existing campaign finance regulation. Portions of the law were challenged immediately on First Amendment grounds by an array of plaintiffs from Republican Senator Mitch McConnell, a leading opponent of the law, to the National Rifle Association, the National Right to Life Committee, the Republican National Committee, the California Democratic Committee and the ACLU. In the 2003 decision in McConnell v. FEC, which follows, the Court upheld both the "soft money" and the "electioneering communications" provisions of BCRA against facial constitutional challenge, but in the 2007 decision in Wisconsin Right to Life, which follows after McConnell, the Court found that the electioneering communications provisions violate the First Amendment as applied to most issue ads:

McConnell v. Federal Election Commission

540 U.S. 93, 124 S. Ct. 619, 157 L. Ed. 2d 491 (2003).

■ JUSTICE STEVENS and JUSTICE O'CONNOR delivered the opinion of the Court with respect to BCRA Titles I and II. [JUSTICES SOUTER, GINSBURG, and BREYER joined this opinion in its entirety.]

III. [Title I] is Congress' effort to plug the soft-money loophole. The cornerstone of Title I is new FECA § 323(a), which prohibits national party committees and their agents from soliciting, receiving, directing, or spending any soft money. [The] remaining provisions of new FECA § 323 largely reinforce the restrictions in § 323(a). New FECA § 323(b) prevents the wholesale shift of soft-money influence from national to state party committees by prohibiting state and local party committees from using such funds for activities that affect federal elections. [New] FECA § 323(d) reinforces these soft-money restrictions by prohibiting political parties from soliciting and donating funds to tax-exempt organizations that engage in electioneering activities. New FECA § 323(e) restricts federal candidates and officeholders from receiving, spending, or soliciting soft money in connection with federal elections and limits their ability to do so in connection with state and local elections. Finally, new FECA § 323(f) prevents circumvention of the restrictions on national, state, and local party committees by prohibiting state and local candidates from raising and spending soft money to fund advertisements and other public communications that promote or attack federal candidates.

[Like] the contribution limits we upheld in Buckley, § 323's restrictions have only a marginal impact on the ability of contributors, candidates, officeholders, and parties to engage in effective political speech. [For example,] while § 323(a) prohibits national parties from receiving or spending nonfederal money, and § 323(b) prohibits state party committees from spending nonfederal money on federal election activities, neither provision in any way limits the total amount of money parties can spend.

Rather, they simply limit the source and individual amount of donations. [Similarly,] the solicitation provisions of § 323(a) and § 323(e), [leave] open ample opportunities for soliciting federal funds on behalf of entities subject to FECA's source and amount restrictions. [The] fact that party committees and federal candidates and officeholders must now ask only for limited dollar amounts or request that a corporation or union contribute money through its PAC in no way alters or impairs the political message "intertwined" with the solicitation.

[With] these principles in mind, we apply the less rigorous scrutiny applicable to contribution limits to evaluate the constitutionality of new FECA § 323. [New FECA § 323(a)'s restrictions on national party committees] simply effect[] a return to the scheme that was approved in Buckley and that was subverted by the creation of the FEC's allocation regime, which permitted the political parties to fund federal electioneering efforts with a combination of hard and soft money. [The] question for present purposes is whether large soft-money contributions to national party committees have a corrupting influence or give rise to the appearance of corruption. Both common sense and the ample record in these cases confirm Congress' belief that they do. [It] is not only plausible, but likely, that candidates would feel grateful for such donations and that donors would seek to exploit that gratitude. The evidence in the record shows that candidates and donors alike have in fact exploited the soft-money loophole, the former to increase their prospects of election and the latter to create debt on the part of officeholders, with the national parties serving as willing intermediaries.

[Our] cases have firmly established that Congress' legitimate interest extends beyond preventing simple cash-for-votes corruption to curbing "undue influence on an officeholder's judgment, and the appearance of such influence." [The] record in the present case is replete [with] examples of national party committees peddling access to federal candidates and officeholders in exchange for large soft-money donations. [Just] as troubling to a functioning democracy as classic quid pro quo corruption is the danger that officeholders will decide issues not on the merits or the desires of their constituencies, but according to the wishes of those who have made large financial contributions valued by the officeholder. [The] best means of prevention is to identify and to remove the temptation. [Accordingly,] we reject the plaintiffs' First Amendment challenge to new FECA § 323(a).

[The Court also upheld Sections 323(b), (d), (e) and (f) as measures that served to prevent circumvention of 323(a) by foreclosing parties from diverting soft money to other conduits and surrogates "and thereby eviscerating FECA." In so doing, the Court applied "substantial deference to the predictive judgments of Congress."]

IV. [Title II] of BCRA [regulates] "Electioneering Communications" and "Independent and Coordinated Expenditures." [Section] 201 comprehensively coins a new term, "electioneering communication," [which] is defined to encompass any "broadcast, cable, or satellite communication" that "(I) refers to a clearly identified candidate for Federal office; (II) is made within (aa) 60 days before a general, special, or runoff election for the office sought by the candidate; or (bb) 30 days before a primary or preference election, or a convention or caucus of a political party that has authority to nominate a candidate, for the office sought by the candidate; and (III) in the case of a communication which refers to a candidate other than President or Vice President, is targeted to the relevant electorate."

[BCRA's] amendments [restrict] corporations' and labor unions' funding of electioneering communications. Plaintiffs challenge the constitutionality of the new term, [arguing] that Buckley drew a constitutionally mandated line between express advocacy and so-called issue advocacy, and that speakers possess an inviolable First Amendment right to engage in the latter category of speech. [That] position misapprehends our prior decisions, for the express advocacy restriction was an endpoint of statutory interpretation, not a first principle of constitutional law. [In] narrowly reading the FECA provisions in Buckley to avoid problems of vagueness and overbreadth, we nowhere suggested that a statute that was neither vague nor overbroad would be required to toe the same express advocacy line. [Nor] are we persuaded, independent of our precedents, that the First Amendment erects a rigid barrier between express advocacy and so-called issue advocacy. [Buckley's] magic-words requirement is functionally meaningless. Not only can advertisers easily evade the line by eschewing the use of magic words, but they would seldom choose to use such words even if permitted. And although the resulting advertisements do not urge the viewer to vote for or against a candidate in so many words, they are no less clearly intended to influence the election.

[Since] our decision in Buckley, Congress' power to prohibit corporations and unions from using funds in their treasuries to finance advertisements expressly advocating the election or defeat of candidates in federal elections has been firmly embedded in our law. The ability to form and administer separate segregated funds [has] provided corporations and unions with a constitutionally sufficient opportunity to engage in express advocacy. [Section] 203 of BCRA [extends] this rule, which previously applied only to express advocacy, to all "electioneering communications." [Because] corporations can still fund electioneering communications with PAC money, it is "simply wrong" to view the provision as a "complete ban" on expression rather than a regulation.

[Plaintiffs] do not contest that the Government has a compelling interest in regulating advertisements that expressly advocate the election or defeat of a candidate for federal office. [Rather,] plaintiffs argue that the justifications that adequately support the regulation of express advocacy do not apply to significant quantities of speech encompassed by the definition of electioneering communications. This argument fails to the extent that the issue ads broadcast during the 30- and 60-day periods preceding federal primary and general elections are the functional equivalent of express advocacy. [The] precise percentage of issue ads that clearly identified a candidate and were aired during those relatively brief preelection time spans but had no electioneering purpose is a matter of dispute between the parties. [Nevertheless,] the vast majority of ads clearly had such a purpose. Moreover, whatever the precise percentage may have been in the past, in the future corporations and unions may finance genuine issue ads during those time frames by simply avoiding any specific reference to federal candidates [or] paying for the ad from a segregated fund. We are therefore not persuaded that plaintiffs have carried their heavy burden of proving that [this section] is [substantially] overbroad.

[Section] 213 of BCRA [forces a political] party that wishes to spend more than $5,000 in coordination with its nominee [to] forgo independent expenditures that make use of magic words[—a] valuable statutory benefit that has been available to parties for many years. To survive constitutional scrutiny, a provision that has such consequences must be supported by a meaningful governmental interest. The interest in requiring political parties to avoid the use of magic words is not such an interest. [Any] claim that a restriction on independent express advocacy serves a strong Government interest is belied by the overwhelming evidence that the line between express advocacy and other types of election-influencing expression is, for Congress' purposes, functionally meaningless. [The] portion of the judgment of the District Court invalidating BCRA § 213 is affirmed.

V.   [We] are under no illusion that BCRA will be the last congressional statement on the matter. Money, like water, will always find an outlet. What problems will arise, and how Congress will respond, are concerns for another day. [Affirmed in part and reversed in part.]

Chief Justice REHNQUIST delivered the opinion of the Court with respect to BCRA Titles III and IV. [Justices O'Connor, Scalia, Kennedy, and Souter joined this opinion in its entirety.]

■ CHIEF JUSTICE REHNQUIST, dissenting with respect to BCRA Titles I and V. [JUSTICES SCALIA and KENNEDY joined this dissent in its entirety].

[The] issue presented by Title I is not, as the Court implies, whether Congress can permissibly regulate campaign contributions to candidates, de facto or otherwise, or seek to eliminate corruption in the political process. Rather, the issue is whether Congress can permissibly regulate much speech that has no plausible connection to candidate contributions or corruption to achieve those goals. [Section] 323(a) does not regulate only donations given to influence a particular federal election; it regulates all donations to national political committees, no matter the use to which the funds are put. The Court attempts to sidestep the unprecedented breadth of this regulation by stating that the "close relationship between federal officeholders and the national parties" makes all donations to the national parties "suspect." But a close association with others, especially in the realm of political speech, is not a surrogate for corruption; it is one of our most treasured First Amendment rights. [Under] any definition of "exacting scrutiny," the means chosen by Congress, restricting all donations to national parties no matter the purpose for which they are given or are used, are not "closely drawn to avoid unnecessary abridgment of associational freedoms."

[All] political speech that is not sifted through federal regulation circumvents the regulatory scheme to some degree or another, and thus by the Court's standard would be a "loophole" in the current system.[1] Unless the Court would uphold federal regulation of all funding of political speech, a rationale dependent on circumvention alone will not do. JUSTICE SCALIA, concurring with respect to BCRA Titles III and IV, dissenting with respect to BCRA Titles I and V, and concurring in the judgment in part and dissenting in part with respect to BCRA Title II.

[It] was said by congressional proponents of this legislation, with support from the law reviews, that since this legislation regulates nothing but the expenditure of money for speech, as opposed to speech itself, the

---

[1]   BCRA does not even close all of the "loopholes" that currently exist. Nonprofit organizations are currently able to accept, without disclosing, unlimited donations for voter registration, voter identification, and get-out-the-vote activities, and the record indicates that such organizations already receive large donations, sometimes in the millions of dollars, for these activities. [And] who knows what the next "loophole" will be. [Footnote by Chief Justice Rehnquist.]

burden it imposes is not subject to full First Amendment scrutiny. [But in] any economy operated on even the most rudimentary principles of division of labor, effective public communication requires the speaker to make use of the services of others. An author may write a novel, but he will seldom publish and distribute it himself. [To] a government bent on suppressing speech, this mode of organization presents opportunities: [License] printers, and it matters little whether authors are still free to write. Restrict the sale of books, and it matters little who prints them. [What] good is the right to print books without a right to buy works from authors? Or the right to publish newspapers without the right to pay deliverymen? The right to speak would be largely ineffective if it did not include the right to engage in financial transactions that are the incidents of its exercise. [Where] the government singles out money used to fund speech as its legislative object, it is acting against speech as such, no less than if it had targeted the paper on which a book was printed or the trucks that deliver it to the bookstore.

Another proposition which could explain at least some of the results of today's opinion is that the First Amendment right to spend money for speech does not include the right to combine with others in spending money for speech. [But the] freedom to associate with others for the dissemination of ideas—not just by singing or speaking in unison, but by pooling financial resources for expressive purposes—is part of the freedom of speech. [If] it were otherwise, Congress would be empowered to enact legislation requiring newspapers to be sole proprietorships, banning their use of partnership or corporate form.

[The] last proposition that might explain at least some of today's casual abridgment of free-speech rights is [that] the particular form of association known as a corporation does not enjoy full First Amendment protection. Of course the text of the First Amendment does not limit its application in this fashion, even though "[b]y the end of the eighteenth century the corporation was a familiar figure in American economic life." Nor is there any basis in reason why First Amendment rights should not attach to corporate associations—and we have said so. [Bellotti; Button.] People who associate— who pool their financial resources—for purposes of economic enterprise overwhelmingly do so in the corporate form; and with increasing frequency, incorporation is chosen by those who associate to defend and promote particular ideas—such as the American Civil Liberties Union and the National Rifle Association, parties to these cases. [A] candidate should not be insulated from the most effective speech that the major participants in the economy and major incorporated interest groups can generate. But what about the danger to the political system posed by "amassed wealth"? The most direct threat from that source comes in the form of undisclosed favors and payoffs to elected officials—which have already been criminalized, and will be rendered no more discoverable by the legislation at issue here. The use of corporate wealth (like individual wealth) to speak to the electorate is unlikely to "distort" elections—especially if disclosure requirements tell the people where the speech is coming from. The premise of the First Amendment is that the American people are neither sheep nor fools, and hence fully capable of considering both the substance of the speech presented to them and its proximate and ultimate source.

But, it is argued, quite apart from its effect upon the electorate, corporate speech in the form of contributions to the candidate's campaign, or even in the form of independent expenditures supporting the candidate, engenders an obligation which is later paid in the form of greater access to the officeholder, or indeed in the form of votes on particular bills. [If] the Bill of Rights had intended an exception to the freedom of speech in order to combat this malign proclivity of the officeholder to agree with those who agree with him, and to speak more with his supporters than his opponents, it would surely have said so. It did not do so, I think, because the juice is not worth the squeeze. Evil corporate (and private affluent) influences are well enough checked (so long as adequate campaign-expenditure disclosure rules exist) by the politician's fear of being portrayed as "in the pocket" of so-called moneyed interests. The incremental benefit obtained by muzzling corporate speech is more than offset by loss of the information and persuasion that corporate speech can contain.

■ JUSTICE THOMAS, concurring with respect to BCRA Titles III and IV, concurring in the judgment in part and dissenting in part with respect to BCRA Title II, and dissenting with respect to BCRA Titles I and V. [JUSTICE SCALIA joins Parts I, II-A, and II-B of this opinion.]

[Today's] holding continues a disturbing trend: the steady decrease in the level of scrutiny applied to restrictions on core political speech [including] limitations on independent expenditures. A. [BCRA § 214] captures expenditures with "no constitutional difference" from "a purely independent one" [and is thus unconstitutional.] B. As for §§ 203 and 204, the Court rests its decision on another vast expansion of the First Amendment framework described in Buckley, this time of the Court's, rather than Congress', own making. In Austin [the] Court recognized a "different type of corruption" from the " 'financial quid pro quo' ": the "corrosive and distorting effects of immense aggregations of wealth that are accumulated with the help of the corporate form and that have little or no correlation to the public's support for the corporation's political ideas." The only effect, however, that the "immense aggregations" of wealth will have (in the context of independent expenditures) on an election is that they might be used to fund communications to convince voters to select certain candidates over others. Apparently, winning in the marketplace of ideas is no longer a sign that "the ultimate good" has been "reached by free trade in ideas." [It] is now evidence of "corruption." This conclusion is antithetical to everything for which the First Amendment stands. Because Austin's definition of "corruption" is incompatible with the First Amendment, I would overturn Austin and hold that the potential for corporations and unions to influence voters, via independent expenditures aimed at convincing these voters to adopt particular views, is not a form of corruption justifying any state regulation or suppression.

■ JUSTICE KENNEDY, concurring in the judgment in part and dissenting in part with respect to BCRA Titles I and II. [CHIEF JUSTICE REHNQUIST joined this opinion in its entirety, and JUSTICES SCALIA and THOMAS in part; they disagreed, inter alia, that § 323(e) was constitutional.]

The First Amendment guarantees our citizens the right to judge for themselves the most effective means for the expression of political views and to decide for themselves which entities to trust as reliable speakers. [The] majority permits a new and serious intrusion on speech when it upholds § 203, the key provision in Title II that prohibits corporations and labor unions from using money from their general treasury to fund electioneering communications. [The] Government and the majority are right about one thing: The express-advocacy requirement, with its list of magic words, is easy to circumvent. The Government seizes on this observation to defend BCRA § 203, arguing it will prevent what it calls "sham issue ads" that are really to the same effect as their more express counterparts. What the Court and the Government call sham, however, are the ads speakers find most effective. [That] the Government would regulate it for this reason goes only to prove the illegitimacy of the Government's purpose. [We] are now told that "the government also has a compelling interest in insulating federal elections from the type of corruption arising from the real or apparent creation of political debts." [This] rationale has no limiting principle. Were we to accept it, Congress would have the authority to outlaw even pure issue ads, because they, too, could endear their sponsors to candidates who adopt the favored positions. [Section] 203 should be held unconstitutional.

[The] hostility toward corporations and unions that infuses the majority opinion is inconsistent with the viewpoint neutrality the First Amendment demands. [Corporations,] after all, are the engines of our modern economy. They facilitate complex operations on which the Nation's prosperity depends. To say these entities cannot alert the public to pending political issues that may threaten the country's economic interests is unprecedented. Unions are also an established part of the national economic system. They, too, have their own unique insights to contribute to the political debate, but the law's impact on them is just as severe. [The] Court is quite incorrect to suggest that the mainstream press is a sufficient palliative for the novel and severe constraints this law imposes on the political process. The Court should appreciate the dynamic contribution diverse groups and associations make to the intellectual and cultural life of the Nation. It should not permit Congress to foreclose or restrict those groups from participating in the political process by constraints not applicable to the established press.

Federal Election Comm'n v. Wisconsin Right to Life

551 U.S. 449, 127 S. Ct. 2652, 168 L. Ed. 2d 329 (2007).

■ CHIEF JUSTICE ROBERTS announced the judgment of the Court and delivered the opinion of the Court with respect to Parts I and II, and an opinion with respect to Parts III and IV, in which JUSTICE ALITO joins.

Section 203 of the Bipartisan Campaign Reform Act of 2002 (BCRA), makes it a federal crime for any corporation to broadcast, shortly before an election, any communication that names a federal candidate for elected office and is targeted to the electorate. In McConnell v. Federal Election Comm'n, this Court considered whether § 203 was facially overbroad under the First Amendment because it captured within its reach not only campaign speech, or "express advocacy," but also speech about public issues more generally, or "issue advocacy," that mentions a candidate for federal office. The Court concluded that there was no overbreadth concern to the extent the speech in question was the "functional equivalent" of express campaign speech. On the other hand, the Court "assumed" that the interests it had found to "justify the regulation of campaign speech might not apply to the regulation of genuine issue ads." The Court nonetheless determined that § 203 was not facially overbroad. [In] upholding § 203 against a facial challenge, we did not purport to resolve future as-applied challenges. We now confront such an as-applied challenge.

[WRTL is a nonprofit advocacy organization incorporated under § 501(c)(4) that ran several broadcast ads urging constituents to "call Senator Feingold" to protest the Senate's filibuster of judicial nominees and sought a declaratory judgment permitting broadcast of similar ads during the 2004 blackout period.]

III. [Because] BCRA § 203 burdens political speech, it is subject to strict scrutiny. This Court has already ruled that BCRA survives strict scrutiny to the extent it regulates express advocacy or its functional equivalent. So to the extent the ads in these cases fit this description, the FEC's burden is not onerous; all it need do is point to McConnell and explain why it applies here. If, on the other hand, WRTL's ads are *not* express advocacy or its equivalent, the Government [must] then demonstrate that banning such ads during the blackout periods is narrowly tailored to serve a compelling interest. No precedent of this Court has yet reached that conclusion.

The FEC [contends] that McConnell already established the constitutional test for determining if an ad is the functional equivalent of express advocacy: whether the ad is intended to influence elections and has that effect. WRTL and the District Court majority, on the other hand, claim that McConnell did not adopt any test as the standard for future as-applied challenges. We agree. McConnell's analysis was grounded in the evidentiary record before the Court. [The] Court did not explain that it was adopting a particular test for determining what constituted the "functional equivalent" of express advocacy.

[We] decline to adopt a test for as-applied challenges turning on the speaker's intent to affect an election. The test to distinguish constitutionally protected political speech from speech that BCRA may proscribe should provide a safe harbor for those who wish to exercise First Amendment rights. The test should also "reflect our 'profound national commitment to the principle that debate on public issues should be uninhibited, robust, and wide-open.'" A test turning on the intent of the speaker does not remotely fit the bill.

[The] proper standard for an as-applied challenge to BCRA § 203 must be objective, focusing on the substance of the communication rather than amorphous considerations of intent and effect. It must entail minimal if any discovery, to allow parties to resolve disputes quickly without chilling speech through the threat of burdensome litigation. And it must eschew "the open-ended rough-and-tumble of factors," which "invites complex argument in a trial court and a virtually inevitable appeal." In short, it must give the benefit of any doubt to protecting rather than stifling speech.

In light of these considerations, a court should find that an ad is the functional equivalent of express advocacy only if the ad is susceptible of no reasonable interpretation other than as an appeal to vote for or against a specific candidate. Under this test, WRTL's three ads are plainly not the functional equivalent of express advocacy. First, their content is consistent with that of a genuine issue ad: The ads focus on a legislative issue, take a position on the issue, exhort the public to adopt that position, and urge the public to contact public officials with respect to the matter. Second, their content lacks indicia of express advocacy: The ads do not mention an election, candidacy, political party, or challenger; and they do not take a position on a candidate's character, qualifications, or fitness for office.

Looking beyond the content of WRTL's ads, the FEC argue[s] that several "contextual" factors prove that the ads are the equivalent of express advocacy. [For example,] the ads were to be aired near elections but not near actual Senate votes on judicial nominees, [the] ads were run shortly after the Senate had recessed, [and the ads referred to a website that] stated both Wisconsin Senators' positions on judicial filibusters, and allowed visitors to sign up for "e-alerts," some of which contained exhortations to vote against Senator Feingold. [Given] the standard we have adopted for determining whether an ad is the "functional equivalent" of express advocacy, contextual factors of [this] sort should seldom play a significant role in the inquiry.

[Because] WRTL's ads may reasonably be interpreted as something other than as an appeal to vote for or against a specific candidate, we hold they are not the functional equivalent of express advocacy, and therefore fall outside the scope of McConnell's holding.

IV. BCRA § 203 can be constitutionally applied to WRTL's ads only if it is narrowly tailored to further a compelling interest. [That] a compelling interest justifies restrictions on express advocacy tells us little about whether a compelling interest justifies restrictions on issue advocacy. [This] Court has long recognized "the governmental interest in preventing corruption and the appearance of corruption" in election campaigns. McConnell arguably applied this interest—which this Court had only assumed could justify regulation of express advocacy—to ads that were the "functional equivalent" of express advocacy. But to justify regulation of WRTL's ads, this interest must be stretched yet another step to ads that are *not* the functional equivalent of express advocacy. Enough is enough. Issue ads like WRTL's are by no means equivalent to contributions, and the *quid-pro-quo* corruption interest cannot justify regulating them. To equate WRTL's ads with contributions is to ignore their value as political speech.

[One] possible compelling interest recognized by this Court lies in addressing a "different type of corruption in the political arena: the corrosive and distorting effects of immense aggregations of wealth that are accumulated with the help of the corporate form and that have little or no correlation to the public's support for the corporation's political ideas." Austin invoked this interest to uphold a state statute making it a felony for corporations to use treasury funds for independent expenditures on express election advocacy. McConnell relied on this interest in upholding regulation not just of express advocacy, but also its "functional equivalent." These cases did not suggest, however, that the interest in combating "a different type of corruption" extended beyond campaign speech. Quite the contrary. [Accepting] the notion that a ban on campaign speech could also embrace issue advocacy would call into question our holding in Bellotti that the corporate identity of a speaker does not strip corporations of all free speech rights. We hold that the interest recognized in Austin as justifying regulation of corporate campaign speech and extended in McConnell to the functional equivalent of such speech has no application to issue advocacy of the sort engaged in by WRTL.

[Because] WRTL's ads are not express advocacy or its functional equivalent, and because appellants identify no interest sufficiently compelling to justify burdening WRTL's speech, we hold that BCRA § 203 is unconstitutional as applied to WRTL's [ads]. when it comes to defining what speech qualifies as the functional equivalent of express advocacy subject to such a ban [we] give the benefit of the doubt to speech, not censorship.

■ JUSTICE SCALIA, with whom JUSTICES KENNEDY and THOMAS join, concurring in part and concurring in the judgment.[1]

[Austin] was a significant departure from ancient First Amendment principles. In my view, it was wrongly decided. [But] at least Austin was limited to express advocacy, and *nonexpress* advocacy was presumed to remain protected under Buckley and Bellotti, even when engaged in by corporations. [I] recognize the practical reality that corporations can evade the express-advocacy standard. I share the instinct that "what separates issue advocacy and political advocacy is a line in the sand drawn on a windy day." But the way to indulge that instinct consistently with the First Amendment is either to eliminate restrictions on independent expenditures altogether or to *confine* them to one side of the *traditional* line—the express-advocacy line, set in concrete on a calm day by *Buckley*, several decades ago. Section 203's line is bright, but it bans vast amounts of political advocacy indistinguishable from hitherto protected speech.

The foregoing analysis shows that McConnell was mistaken in its belief that as-applied challenges could eliminate the unconstitutional applications of § 203. They can do so only if a test is adopted which contradicts the holding of McConnell—that § 203 is facially valid because the vast majority of pre-election issue ads can constitutionally be proscribed. In light of the weakness in Austin's rationale, and in light of the longstanding acceptance of the clarity of Buckley's express-advocacy line, it was adventurous for McConnell to extend Austin beyond corporate speech constituting express advocacy. Today's cases make it apparent that the adventure is a flop, and that McConnell's holding concerning § 203 was wrong. "*Stare decisis* is not an inexorable command." Overruling a constitutional case decided just a few years earlier is far from unprecedented (citing numerous cases).

■ JUSTICE SOUTER, with whom JUSTICES STEVENS, GINSBURG, and BREYER join, dissenting.

[McConnell's holding] declaring the facial validity of [BCRA's § 203] is effectively, and unjustifiably, overruled today.

[A] century-long tradition of legislation and judicial precedent rests on facing undeniable facts and testifies to an equally undeniable value. Campaign finance reform has been a series of reactions to documented threats to electoral integrity obvious to any voter, posed by large sums of money from corporate or union treasuries, with no redolence of "grassroots" about them. Neither Congress's decisions nor our own have understood the corrupting influence of money in politics as being limited to outright bribery or discrete *quid pro quo;* campaign finance reform has instead consistently focused on the more pervasive distortion of electoral institutions by concentrated wealth, on the special access and guaranteed favor that sap the representative integrity of American government and defy public confidence in its institutions. From early in the 20th century through the decision in McConnell, we have acknowledged that the value of democratic integrity justifies a realistic response when corporations and labor organizations commit the concentrated moneys in their treasuries to electioneering.

[Any] Wisconsin voter who paid attention would have known that Democratic Senator Feingold supported filibusters against Republican presidential judicial nominees, that the propriety of the filibusters was a

---

[1] Justice Alito concurred separately to note that the Court might be asked to reconsider McConnell if the principal opinion's as-applied standard is found to chill political speech.

major issue in the senatorial campaign, and that WRTL along with the Senator's Republican challengers opposed his reelection because of his position on filibusters. Any alert voters who heard or saw WRTL's ads would have understood that WRTL was telling them that the Senator's position on the filibusters should be grounds to vote against him. Given these facts, it is beyond all reasonable debate that the ads are constitutionally subject to regulation under McConnell. [By refusing] to see and hear what any listener to WRTL's ads would actually consider, [the Chief Justice] thus effectively reinstates the same toothless "magic words" criterion of regulable electioneering that led Congress to enact BCRA in the first place.

McCONNELL COMPARED WITH WRTL

1. *Stare decisis.* Note that Chief Justice Roberts went to considerable lengths in WRTL to distinguish rather than overrule McConnell's holding that the broadcast electioneering provision was facially constitutional. He emphasized that WRTL was an as-applied challenge, and rested on a different factual record. The concurring justices would have overruled McConnell outright on this point, and the dissenting justices lamented that this is the effective result of the decision. Was Chief Justice Roberts's opinion an exercise in judicial moderation? Or was Justice Scalia correct to charge in a footnote that this was "faux judicial modesty" that causes "judicial obfuscation"?

2. *Regulation or ban?* The FEC argued that § 203 was narrowly tailored since it left open various alternative means by which an organization like WRTL could have avoided sanction for alleged electioneering. Justice Souter summarized these ostensible alternatives in his dissent: "WRTL could have run a newspaper ad, could have paid for the broadcast ads through its PAC, could have established itself as an MCFL organization free of corporate money, and could have said 'call your Senators' instead of naming Senator Feingold in its ads broadcasted just before the election." Are these alternatives adequate substitutes for the broadcast ads WRTL sought to run?

3. *For-profit vs. nonprofit corporations.* All the opinions in WRTL declined to distinguish between for-profit and nonprofit corporations. The decision turns on the nature of the speech rather than the identity of the speaker. But is there greater reason to fear the distorting effect of speech from the corporate treasury of IBM or Google than from the corporate treasury of the National Rifle Association or the ACLU? Would an alternative route to a judgment for WRTL have been to require an exception to the electioneering provision only for nonprofit corporations? An original provision of BCRA proffered by Senators Snowe and Jeffords had taken this approach, but it was superseded by an amendment proposed by the late Senator Wellstone. Did the Court go too far in freeing issue ads by all corporations rather than those engaged in nonprofit advocacy? Is the concern about amassed wealth, gathered for other purposes, greater as to the former than the latter?

4. *Challenge to BCRA's "Millionaire's Amendment."* Can expenditures of a wealthy candidate's own money trigger government interest sufficient to justify regulation? In **Davis v. Federal Election Comm'n**, 554 U.S. 724 (2008), the Court invalidated § 319(a) of the

Bipartisan Campaign Reform Act of 2002 (BCRA), the so-called
"Millionaire's Amendment," which provided that, when a candidate's
expenditure of personal funds exceeded $350,000, he would remain subject
to normal contribution limits but his opponent would be permitted to receive
individual contributions at treble the normal limit and unlimited
coordinated party expenditures. The Court found the law barred by the First
Amendment in an opinion by Justice ALITO, joined by Chief Justice Roberts
and Justices Scalia, Kennedy and Thomas. Justice Alito wrote:

"If § 319(a) simply raised the contribution limits for all
candidates, Davis' argument would plainly fail. [There is] no
constitutional basis for attacking contribution limits on the ground
that they are too high. [Section 319(a),] however, does not raise the
contribution limits across the board. Rather, it raises the limits
only for the non-self-financing candidate and does so only when the
self-financing candidate's expenditure of personal funds causes the
[$350,000] threshold to be exceeded. We have never upheld the
constitutionality of a law that imposes different contribution limits
for candidates who are competing against each other, and we agree
with Davis that this scheme impermissibly burdens his First
Amendment right to spend his own money for campaign speech.

"[Section 319(a)] requires a candidate to choose between the
First Amendment right to engage in unfettered political speech and
subjection to discriminatory fundraising limitations. Many
candidates who can afford to make large personal expenditures to
support their campaigns may choose to do so despite § 319(a), but
they must shoulder a special and potentially significant burden if
they make that choice. Under § 319(a), the vigorous exercise of the
right to use personal funds to finance campaign speech produces
fundraising advantages for opponents in the competitive context of
electoral politics. [Because] § 319(a) imposes a substantial burden
on the exercise of the First Amendment right to use personal funds
for campaign speech, that provision cannot stand unless it is
'justified by a compelling state interest.' No such justification is
present here.

"The burden imposed by § 319(a) on the expenditure of
personal funds is not justified by any governmental interest in
eliminating corruption or the perception of corruption. [Buckley]
reasoned that reliance on personal funds *reduces* the threat of
corruption, and therefore § 319(a), by discouraging use of personal
funds, disserves the anticorruption interest. [The Government also]
maintains that § 319(a)'s asymmetrical limits are justified because
they 'level electoral opportunities for candidates of different
personal wealth.' Our prior decisions, however, provide no support
for the proposition that this is a legitimate government objective.
[The] argument that a candidate's speech may be restricted in order
to " 'level electoral opportunities' has ominous implications because
it would permit Congress to arrogate the voters' authority to
evaluate the strengths of candidates competing for office." The
majority likewise invalidated the disclosure provisions of Section
319(a) as excessively burdening self-financed candidates' First
Amendment rights.

A dissent by Justice STEVENS, joined by Justices, Souter, Ginsburg and Breyer, disagreed with the majority's First Amendment reasoning: "[T]he Millionaire's Amendment represents a modest, sensible, and plainly constitutional attempt by Congress to minimize the advantages enjoyed by wealthy candidates vis-a-vis those who must rely on the support of others to fund their pursuit of public office. [It] cannot be gainsaid that the twin rationales at the heart of the Millionaire's Amendment—reducing the importance of wealth as a criterion for public office and countering the perception that seats in the United States Congress are available for purchase by the wealthiest bidder—are important Government interests. It is also evident that Congress, in enacting the provision, crafted a solution that was carefully tailored to those concerns. [Enhancing] the speech of the millionaire's opponent, far from contravening the First Amendment, actually advances its core principles. If only one candidate can make himself heard, the voter's ability to make an informed choice is impaired." In a portion of Justice Stevens's dissent in which he spoke only for himself, he expressed the view that Justice White's dissent in Buckley had proved correct, and that expenditure limits in general should no longer be subject to strict scrutiny.

In **Arizona Free Enterprise Club's Freedom Club PAC v. Bennett**, 564 U.S. 721 (2011), the Court applied Davis to invalidate, by a vote of 5–4, provisions of the Arizona Citizens Clean Elections Act that allowed candidates for state office who participated in state public financing for elections additional matching funds if expenditures by a privately financed candidate, plus independent expenditures by his supporters, exceeded the publicly financed candidate's initial allotment of public funds. Finding that "[t]he logic of Davis largely controls our approach to this case," Chief Justice ROBERTS wrote for the Court, joined by Justices Scalia, Kennedy, Thomas and Alito, holding that the Arizona scheme burdened a privately financed candidate's speech because "each personal dollar spent by the privately financed candidate results in an award of almost one additional dollar to his opponent." Indeed, the majority found the burden heavier than in Davis because "the benefit to the publicly financed candidate is the direct and automatic release of public money" rather than the mere relaxation of contribution limits, because of the "multiplier effect" on the private candidate if he faced more than one publicly financed opponent, and because "any spending by independent expenditure groups to promote the privately financed candidate's election—regardless whether such support was welcome or helpful—could trigger matching funds." The majority noted that the scheme likewise burdened the speech of groups seeking to make independent expenditures in support of or opposition to candidates.

The majority rejected the State's argument "that the matching funds provision actually results in more speech by 'increas[ing] debate about issues of public concern' in Arizona elections" and that "this promotion of First Amendment ideals offsets any burden the law might impose on some speakers": "[E]ven if the matching funds provision did result in more speech by publicly financed candidates and more speech in general, it would do so at the expense of impermissibly burdening (and thus reducing) the speech of privately financed candidates and independent expenditure groups. This sort of 'beggar thy neighbor' approach to free speech—'restrict[ing] the speech of some elements of our society in order to enhance the relative voice of others'—is 'wholly foreign to the First Amendment.' " The majority also rejected the argument of the United States as amicus in support of Arizona that " '[p]roviding additional funds to petitioners' opponents does not make petitioners' own speech any less effective' and thus does not substantially burden speech": "All else being equal, an advertisement supporting the election of a candidate that goes without a response is often more effective than an advertisement that is directly controverted. And even if the publicly funded candidate decides to use his new money to address a different issue altogether, the end goal of that spending is to claim electoral victory over the opponent that triggered the additional state funding."

Turning to whether the Arizona law could be justified by a compelling state interest, Chief Justice Roberts rejected as illegitimate any state interest in " 'leveling the playing field' in terms of candidate resources": " 'Leveling the playing field' can sound like a good thing. But in a democracy, campaigning for office is not a game. It is a critically important form of speech. The First Amendment embodies our choice as a Nation that, when it comes to such speech, the guiding principle is freedom—the 'unfettered interchange of ideas'—not whatever the State may view as fair." The majority likewise found the burdens imposed by the matching funds provision unjustified "even if [its] ultimate objective [is] to combat corruption," because neither a candidate's expenditure of his own money nor independent expenditures in his support give rise to a threat of corruption or its appearance. Accordingly, the majority concluded, "Arizona's matching funds provision substantially burdens the speech of privately financed candidates and independent expenditure groups without serving a compelling state interest."

Justice KAGAN strongly disagreed in a dissent joined by Justices Ginsburg, Breyer and Sotomayor: "The First Amendment's core purpose is to foster a healthy, vibrant political system full of robust discussion and debate. Nothing in [the] Arizona Citizens Clean Elections Act violates this constitutional protection. To the contrary, the Act promotes the values underlying both the First Amendment and our entire Constitution by enhancing the 'opportunity for free political discussion to the end that government may be responsive to the will of the people.' "

The dissent disagreed with both steps of the majority's analysis. First, Justice Kagan disagreed that the Arizona law burdened speech: "The law has quite the opposite effect: It subsidizes and so produces *more* political speech. [Except] in a world gone topsy-turvy, additional campaign speech and electoral competition is not a First Amendment injury." Noting that the Court has often "distinguished between speech restrictions and speech subsidies" and upheld viewpoint-neutral subsidy schemes, Justice Kagan argued that, because it was viewpoint-neutral, "Arizona's subsidy statute should easily survive First Amendment scrutiny." She continued: "This suit, in fact, may merit less attention than any challenge to a speech subsidy ever seen in this Court. In the usual First Amendment subsidy case, a person complains that the government declined to finance his speech, while bankrolling someone else's. [But] the candidates bringing this challenge [were] never denied a subsidy. Arizona [offers] to support any person running for state office. Petitioners here *refused* that assistance [but argue] that Arizona violated *their* First Amendment rights by disbursing funds to *other* speakers even though they could have received (but chose to spurn) the same financial assistance. Some people might call that *chutzpah*."

Justice Kagan likewise rejected the majority's analogy to the burden on speech struck down in Davis: "In Davis, the candidate's expenditure triggered a discriminatory speech restriction, which Congress could not otherwise have imposed consistent with the First Amendment; by contrast, in this case, the candidate's expenditure triggers a non-discriminatory speech subsidy, which all parties agree Arizona could have provided in the first instance. [Two] great fault lines run through our First Amendment doctrine: one, between speech restrictions and speech subsidies, and the other, between discriminatory and neutral government action. The Millionaire's Amendment fell on the disfavored side of both divides."

The dissent argued, second, that, even if the Arizona law did trigger First Amendment review, it served a compelling interest in preventing corruption or the appearance of corruption in the State's political system. Finding that interest evident from the title of and findings in the statute, and rejecting as unsupported any inference that the State's goal was instead to level the playing field, Justice Kagan concluded that "that interest justifies the matching funds provision at issue because it is [the] thing that makes the whole Clean Elections Act work. [Public] financing has an Achilles heel—the difficulty of setting the subsidy at the right amount. Too small, and the grant will not attract candidates to the program; and with no participating candidates, the program can hardly decrease corruption. Too large, and the system becomes unsustainable, or at the least an unnecessary drain on public resources. But finding the sweet-spot is near impossible because of variation, across districts and over time, in the political system. Enter the matching funds provision, which takes an ordinary lump-sum amount, divides it into thirds, and disburses the last two of these (to the extent necessary) via a self-calibrating mechanism. [If] public financing furthers a compelling interest [then] so too does the disbursement formula that Arizona uses to make public financing effective." Finally, referring to the majority's assertion that "campaigning for office is not a game," Justice Kagan responded, "Truly, democracy is not a game. I respectfully dissent."

5. *Corporate expenditures and the overruling of Austin.* After WRTL and Davis, it was unclear what vitality was left to the rationale used in Austin v. Michigan Chamber of Commerce (1990; p. 566) to uphold a requirement that a corporation make independent political expenditures only from a separate, segregated fund or PAC rather than from its own corporate treasury. The majority decision in WRTL sidestepped this issue by holding that Austin did not apply to WRTL's own expenditures. In the case that follows, the Court expressly confronted and overruled Austin, invalidating BCRA's limitations on independent corporate expenditures from corporate treasuries in political campaigns:

Citizens United v. Federal Election Commission
558 U.S. 310, 130 S. Ct. 876, 175 L. Ed. 2d 753 (2010).

■ JUSTICE KENNEDY delivered the opinion of the Court.

[Citizens United] is a nonprofit corporation [with] an annual budget of about $12 million. Most of its funds are from donations by individuals; but, in addition, it accepts a small portion of its funds from for-profit corporations. In January 2008, Citizens United released [a] 90-minute documentary [called "Hillary"] about then-Senator Hillary Clinton, who was a candidate in the Democratic Party's 2008 Presidential primary elections. Hillary mentions Senator Clinton by name and depicts interviews with political commentators and other persons, most of them quite critical of Senator Clinton. Hillary was released in theaters and on DVD, but Citizens United wanted to increase distribution by making it available through video-on-demand. [To] promote the film, it produced two 10-second ads and one 30-second ad for Hillary. Each ad includes a short (and, in our view, pejorative) statement about Senator Clinton, followed by the name of the movie and the movie's Website address. Citizens United desired to promote the video-on-demand offering by running advertisements on broadcast and cable television. [Under] the approach taken in WRTL, Hillary is equivalent to express advocacy. The movie, in essence, is a feature-length negative advertisement that urges viewers to vote against Senator Clinton for President.

[Section 441b] makes it a felony for all corporations—including nonprofit advocacy corporations—either to expressly advocate the election or defeat of candidates or to broadcast electioneering communications within 30 days of a primary election and 60 days of a general election. [Section 441b] is a ban on corporate speech notwithstanding the fact that a PAC created by a corporation can still speak. A PAC is a separate association from the corporation. So the PAC exemption from § 441b's expenditure ban does not allow corporations to speak. Even if a PAC could somehow allow a corporation to speak—and it does not—the option to form PACs does not alleviate the First Amendment problems with § 441b. PACs are burdensome alternatives; they are expensive to administer and subject to extensive regulations. [This] might explain why fewer than 2,000 of the millions of corporations in this country have PACs.

[We] find no basis for the proposition that, in the context of political speech, the Government may impose restrictions on certain disfavored speakers. [The] Court has recognized that First Amendment protection extends to corporations. This protection has been extended by explicit holdings to the context of political speech. [At] least since the latter part of the 19th century, the laws of some States and of the United States imposed a ban on corporate direct contributions to candidates. Yet not until 1947 did Congress first prohibit independent expenditures by corporations and labor unions. [Buckley] did not consider [the] separate ban on corporate and union independent expenditures. [Had that ban] been challenged in the wake of Buckley, however, it could not have been squared with the reasoning and analysis of that precedent. Notwithstanding this precedent, Congress recodified [the] corporate and union expenditure ban [as] § 441b four months after Buckley was decided. Less than two years after Buckley, Bellotti struck down a state-law prohibition on corporate independent expenditures related to referenda issues. [Bellotti] did not address the constitutionality of the State's ban on corporate independent expenditures to support candidates. In our view, however, that restriction would have been unconstitutional under Bellotti's central principle: that the First Amendment does not allow political speech restrictions based on a speaker's corporate identity.

Thus the law stood until Austin [v. Michigan Chamber of Commerce (1990); p. 566]. [To] bypass Buckley and Bellotti, [Austin] identified a new [compelling] governmental interest in preventing "the corrosive and distorting effects of immense aggregations of wealth that are accumulated with the help of the corporate form and that have little or no correlation to the public's support for the corporation's political ideas." [The] Government does little to defend [Austin's antidistortion rationale]. And with good reason, for the rationale cannot support § 441b. [If] the antidistortion rationale were to be accepted, [it] would permit Government to ban political speech simply because the speaker is an association that has taken on the corporate form. [If] Austin were correct, the Government could prohibit a corporation from expressing political views in media beyond those presented here, such as by printing books. [Austin's] antidistortion rationale [also] would produce the dangerous, and unacceptable, consequence that Congress could ban political speech of media corporations. Media corporations are now exempt from § 441b's ban on corporate expenditures. Yet media corporations accumulate wealth with the help of the corporate form, [and] the views expressed by media corporations often "have little or no correlation to the public's support" for those views. [The] law's exception for media corporations is, on its own terms, all but an admission of the invalidity of the antidistortion rationale. And the exemption results in a further, separate reason for finding this law invalid.

Austin [permits] the Government to ban the political speech of millions of associations of citizens. Most of these are small corporations without large amounts of wealth. (96% of the 3 million businesses that belong to the U.S. Chamber of Commerce have fewer than 100 employees [and] more than 75% of corporations whose income is taxed under federal law have less than $1 million in receipts per year). This fact belies the Government's argument that the statute is justified on the ground that it prevents the "distorting effects of immense aggregations of wealth." It is not even aimed at amassed wealth.

[The] Government falls back on the argument that corporate political speech can be banned in order to prevent corruption or its appearance. [The] anticorruption interest is not sufficient to displace the speech here in question. Indeed, 26 States do not restrict independent expenditures by for-profit corporations. The Government does not claim that these expenditures have corrupted the political process in those States. [We] now conclude that independent expenditures, including those made by corporations, do not give rise to corruption or the appearance of corruption. [When] Buckley identified a sufficiently important governmental interest in preventing corruption or the appearance of corruption, that interest was limited to quid pro quo corruption. [Independent] expenditures do not lead to, or create the appearance of, quid pro quo corruption. In fact, there is only scant evidence that independent expenditures even ingratiate. Ingratiation and access, in any event, are not corruption. [Here] Congress has created categorical bans on speech that are asymmetrical to preventing quid pro quo corruption.

[The] Government contends further that corporate independent expenditures can be limited because of its interest in protecting dissenting shareholders from being compelled to fund corporate political speech. This asserted interest, like Austin's antidistortion rationale, would allow the Government to ban the political speech even of media corporations. [The] First Amendment does not allow that power. There is, furthermore, little evidence of abuse that cannot be corrected by shareholders "through the procedures of corporate democracy." Bellotti. [Moreover,] the statute is both underinclusive and overinclusive. [If] Congress had been seeking to protect dissenting shareholders, it would not have banned corporate speech in only certain media within 30 or 60 days before an election. A dissenting shareholder's interests would be implicated by speech in any media at any time. [And] the statute is overinclusive because it covers all corporations, including nonprofit corporations and for-profit corporations with only single shareholders.

Our precedent is to be respected unless the most convincing of reasons demonstrates that adherence to it puts us on a course that is sure error. "Beyond workability, the relevant factors in deciding whether to adhere to the principle of stare decisis include the antiquity of the precedent, the reliance interests at stake, and of course whether the decision was well reasoned." We have also examined whether "experience has pointed up the precedent's shortcomings." [These] considerations counsel in favor of rejecting Austin, which itself contravened this Court's earlier precedents in Buckley and Bellotti. [Austin] was not well reasoned. [Austin is also] undermined by experience since its announcement. Political speech is so ingrained in our culture that speakers find ways to circumvent campaign finance laws. [Corporations,] like individuals, do not have monolithic views. On certain topics corporations may possess valuable expertise, leaving them the best equipped to point out errors or fallacies in speech of all sorts, including the speech of candidates and elected officials. Rapid changes in technology—and the creative dynamic inherent in the concept of free expression—counsel against upholding a law that restricts political speech in certain media or by certain speakers. No serious reliance interests are at stake.

Due consideration leads to this conclusion: Austin should be and now is overruled. We return to the principle established in Buckley and Bellotti that the Government may not suppress political speech on the basis of the speaker's corporate identity. No sufficient governmental interest justifies limits on the political speech of nonprofit or for-profit corporations. [Given] our conclusion we are further required to overrule the part of McConnell that upheld BCRA § 203's extension of § 441b's restrictions on corporate independent expenditures.

■ JUSTICE SCALIA, with whom JUSTICES ALITO and THOMAS join, concurring.[1]

[The dissent] purports to show that today's decision is not supported by the original understanding of the First Amendment, [embarking] on a detailed exploration of the Framers' views about the "role of corporations in society." The Framers didn't like corporations, the dissent concludes, and therefore it follows (as night the day) that corporations had no rights of free speech. [Despite] the corporation-hating quotations the dissent has dredged up, it is far from clear that by the end of the 18th century corporations were despised. If so, how came there to be so many of them? [Even] if we agreed that the Founders disliked founding-era corporations; modern corporations might not qualify for exclusion. Most of the Founders' resentment towards corporations was directed at the state-granted monopoly privileges that individually chartered corporations enjoyed. [Moreover,] at the time of the founding, religious, educational, and literary corporations were incorporated under general incorporation statutes, much as business corporations are today. There were also small unincorporated business associations, which some have argued were the " 'true progenitors' " of today's business

---

[1]   Justice Thomas dissented from the opinion of the Court insofar as it upheld BCRA's disclaimer and disclosure requirements as applied to the Hillary film and advertisements, see p. 516. Chief Justice Roberts, joined by Justice Alito, filed a separate concurrence explaining why they agreed the case warranted a departure from stare decisis.

corporations. Were all of these silently excluded from the protections of the First Amendment?

[The] dissent says that when the Framers "constitutionalized the right to free speech in the First Amendment, it was the free speech of individual Americans that they had in mind." That is no doubt true. All the provisions of the Bill of Rights set forth the rights of individual men and women—not, for example, of trees or polar bears. But the individual person's right to speak includes the right to speak *in association with other individual persons.* Surely the dissent does not believe that speech by the Republican Party or the Democratic Party can be censored because it is not the speech of "an individual American." [The] association of individuals in a business corporation is no different—or at least it cannot be denied the right to speak on the simplistic ground that it is not "an individual American."

[The First] Amendment is written in terms of "speech," not speakers. Its text offers no foothold for excluding any category of speaker, from single individuals to partnerships of individuals, to unincorporated associations of individuals, to incorporated associations of individuals. [To] exclude or impede corporate speech is to muzzle the principal agents of the modern free economy. We should celebrate rather than condemn the addition of this speech to the public debate.

■ JUSTICE STEVENS, with whom JUSTICES GINSBURG, BREYER, and SOTOMAYOR join, dissenting.[2]

[In] the context of election to public office, the distinction between corporate and human speakers is significant. Although they make enormous contributions to our society, corporations are not actually members of it. They cannot vote or run for office. [The] financial resources, legal structure, and instrumental orientation of corporations raise legitimate concerns about their role in the electoral process. Our lawmakers have a compelling constitutional basis, if not also a democratic duty, to take measures designed to guard against the potentially deleterious effects of corporate spending in local and national races.

The majority's approach to corporate electioneering marks a dramatic break from our past. Congress has placed special limitations on campaign spending by corporations ever since the passage of the Tillman Act in 1907. [The] Court today rejects a century of history when it treats the distinction between corporate and individual campaign spending as an invidious novelty born of Austin. [I] am not an absolutist when it comes to *stare decisis*, in the campaign finance area or in any other. No one is. But if this principle is to do any meaningful work in supporting the rule of law, it must at least demand a significant justification, beyond the preferences of five Justices, for overturning settled doctrine. [No] such justification exists in this case. [The] only relevant thing that has changed since Austin and McConnell is the composition of this Court.

[Pervading] the Court's analysis is the ominous image of a "categorical ba[n]" on corporate speech. [This] characterization is highly misleading. [The] statutes upheld in Austin and McConnell [provide] exemptions for PACs, separate segregated funds established by a corporation for political purposes. [A] significant and growing number of corporations avail

---

[2]   The dissenters concurred in part in the opinion of the Court insofar as it upheld BCRA's disclaimer and disclosure requirements as applied to the Hillary film and advertisements, see p. 516.

themselves of this option; during the most recent election cycle, corporate and union PACs raised nearly a billion dollars. [And like] all other natural persons, every shareholder of every corporation remains entirely free under Austin and McConnell to do however much electioneering she pleases outside of the corporate form. The owners of a "mom & pop" store can simply place ads in their own names, rather than the store's. If ideologically aligned individuals wish to make unlimited expenditures through the corporate form, they may utilize an MCFL organization that has policies in place to avoid becoming a conduit for business or union interests. [Moreover,] § 203 functions [like] a time, place, and manner restriction. It applies in a viewpoint-neutral fashion to a narrow subset of advocacy messages about clearly identified candidates for federal office, made during discrete time periods through discrete channels. [The] majority's incessant talk of a "ban" aims at a straw man.

[The] second pillar of the Court's opinion is its assertion that "the Government cannot restrict political speech based on the speaker's . . . identity." [Bellotti.] But the holding in [Bellotti] was far narrower than the Court implies. [Our] First Amendment doctrine has "frowned on" certain identity-based distinctions, particularly those that may reflect invidious discrimination or preferential treatment of a politically powerful group. But it is simply incorrect to suggest that we have prohibited all legislative distinctions based on identity or content. [Campaign] finance distinctions based on corporate identity tend to be less worrisome [because] the "speakers" are not natural persons, much less members of our political community, and the governmental interests are of the highest order. Furthermore, when corporations, as a class, are distinguished from noncorporations, as a class, there is a lesser risk that regulatory distinctions will reflect invidious discrimination or political favoritism.

[A] third fulcrum of the Court's opinion is the idea that Austin and McConnell are radical outliers, "aberration[s]," in our First Amendment tradition. The Court has it exactly backwards. It is today's holding that is the radical departure from what had been settled First Amendment law. [To] the extent that the Framers' views are discernible and relevant to the disposition of this case, they would appear to cut strongly against the majority's position. This is not only because the Framers and their contemporaries conceived of speech more narrowly than we now think of it, but also because they held very different views about the nature of the *First Amendment* right and the role of corporations in society.

Those few corporations that existed at the founding were authorized by grant of a special legislative charter. Corporate sponsors would petition the legislature, and the legislature, if amenable, would issue a charter that specified the corporation's powers and purposes and "authoritatively fixed the scope and content of corporate organization," including "the internal structure of the corporation." Corporations were created, supervised, and conceptualized as quasi-public entities, "designed to serve a social function for the state." [The] individualized charter mode of incorporation reflected the "cloud of disfavor under which corporations labored" in the early years of this Nation. Thomas Jefferson famously fretted that corporations would subvert the Republic. General incorporation statutes, and widespread acceptance of business corporations as socially useful actors, did not emerge until the 1800's. [The] Framers thus took it as a given that corporations could be comprehensively regulated in the service of the public welfare. Unlike our colleagues, they had little trouble distinguishing corporations from human beings, and when they constitutionalized the right to free speech in the *First Amendment*, it was the free speech of individual Americans that they had in mind. While individuals might join together to exercise their speech rights, business corporations, at least, were plainly not seen as facilitating such associational or expressive ends. Even "the notion that business corporations could invoke the First Amendment would probably have been quite a novelty," given that "at the time, the legitimacy of every corporate activity was thought to rest entirely in a concession of the sovereign." In light of these background practices and understandings, it seems to me implausible that the Framers believed "the freedom of speech" would extend equally to all corporate speakers, much less that it would preclude legislatures from taking limited measures to guard against corporate capture of elections.

[The] majority emphasizes Buckley's statement that " '[t]he concept that government may restrict the speech of some elements of our society in order to enhance the relative voice of others is wholly foreign to the First Amendment.' " But this elegant phrase cannot bear the weight that our colleagues have placed on it. [We] made it clear in Austin that a restriction on the way corporations spend their money is no mere exercise in disfavoring the voice of some elements of our society in preference to others. Indeed, we expressly ruled that the compelling interest supporting Michigan's statute was not one of " 'equaliz[ing] the relative influence of speakers on elections,' " but rather the need to confront the distinctive corrupting potential of corporate electoral advocacy financed by general treasury dollars.

[The majority also claims] that Bellotti's holding forbade distinctions between corporate and individual expenditures like the one at issue here. [But Bellotti distinguished] between general corporate speech and campaign speech intended to promote or prevent the election of specific candidates for office. [The] anticorruption interests that animate regulations of corporate participation in candidate elections [do] not apply equally to regulations of corporate participation in referenda. A referendum cannot owe a political debt to a corporation, seek to curry favor with a corporation, or fear the corporation's retaliation. [Bellotti also] involved a *viewpoint-discriminatory* statute, created to effect a particular policy outcome, [and] the law at issue did not make any allowance for corporations to spend money through PACs. [Austin and McConnell,] then, sit perfectly well with Bellotti.

[Having] explained why this is not an appropriate case in which to revisit Austin and McConnell, [I] come at last to the interests that are at stake. [The] majority recognizes that Austin and McConnell may be defended on anticorruption, antidistortion, and shareholder protection rationales. It badly errs both in explaining the nature of these rationales, which overlap and complement each other, and in applying them to the case at hand.

[Corruption] can take many forms. Bribery may be the paradigm case. But the difference between selling a vote and selling access is a matter of degree, not kind. And selling access is not qualitatively different from giving special preference to those who spent money on one's behalf. Corruption operates along a spectrum, and the majority's apparent belief that *quid pro quo* arrangements can be neatly demarcated from other improper influences does not accord with the theory or reality of politics. It certainly does not accord with the record Congress developed in passing BCRA, a record that stands as a remarkable testament to the energy and ingenuity with which corporations, unions, lobbyists, and politicians may go about scratching each other's backs—and which amply supported Congress' determination to target a limited set of especially destructive practices. [When] private interests are seen to exert outsized control over officeholders solely on account of the money spent on (or withheld from) their campaigns, the result can depart so thoroughly "from what is pure or correct" in the conduct of Government, that it amounts to a "subversion . . . of the electoral process." At stake in the legislative efforts to address this threat is therefore not only the legitimacy and quality of Government but also the public's faith therein. [We] have ample evidence to suggest that [the Framers] would have been appalled by the evidence of corruption that Congress unearthed in developing BCRA and that the Court today discounts to irrelevance. It is fair to say that "[t]he Framers were obsessed with corruption," which they understood to encompass the dependency of public officeholders on private interests.

[Even] under the majority's "crabbed view of corruption," the Government should not lose this case. [*Quid pro quo* debts need not] take the form of outright vote buying or bribes, which have long been distinct crimes. Rather, they encompass the myriad ways in which outside parties may induce an officeholder to confer a legislative benefit in direct response to, or anticipation of, some outlay of money the parties have made or will make on behalf of the officeholder. [The] legislative and judicial proceedings relating to BCRA generated a substantial body of evidence suggesting that, as corporations grew more and more adept at crafting "issue ads" to help or harm a particular candidate, these nominally independent expenditures began to corrupt the political process in a very direct sense. The sponsors of these ads were routinely granted special access after the campaign was over; "candidates and officials knew who their friends were."

[The] majority fails to appreciate that Austin's antidistortion rationale is itself an anticorruption rationale, tied to the special concerns raised by corporations. [Corporations] are different from human beings. [Unlike] natural persons, corporations have "limited liability" for their owners and managers, "perpetual life," separation of ownership and control, "and favorable treatment of the accumulation and distribution of assets . . . that enhance their ability to attract capital and to deploy their resources in ways that maximize the return on their shareholders' investments." [Corporations also] have no consciences, no beliefs, no feelings, no thoughts, no desires. Corporations help structure and facilitate the activities of human beings, to be sure, and their "personhood" often serves as a useful legal fiction. But they are not themselves members of "We the People" by whom and for whom our Constitution was established. These basic points help explain why corporate electioneering is not only more likely to impair compelling governmental interests, but also why restrictions on that electioneering are less likely to encroach upon First Amendment freedoms. [The] majority's unwillingness to distinguish between corporations and humans similarly blinds it to the possibility that corporations' "war chests" and their special "advantages" in the legal realm, may translate into special advantages in the market for legislation.

[Interwoven] with Austin's concern to protect the integrity of the electoral process is a concern to protect the rights of shareholders from a kind of coerced speech: electioneering expenditures that do not "reflec[t] [their] support." When corporations use general treasury funds to praise or attack a particular candidate for office, it is the shareholders, as the residual claimants, who are effectively footing the bill. Those shareholders who disagree with the corporation's electoral message may find their financial investments being used to undermine their political convictions. The PAC mechanism, by contrast, helps assure that those who pay for an electioneering communication actually support its content and that managers do not use general treasuries to advance personal agendas.

[In] a democratic society, the longstanding consensus on the need to limit corporate campaign spending should outweigh the wooden application of judge-made rules. The majority's rejection of this principle "elevate[s] corporations to a level of deference which has not been seen at least since the days when substantive due process was regularly used to invalidate regulatory legislation thought to unfairly impinge upon established economic interests." At bottom, the Court's opinion is thus a rejection of the common sense of the American people, who have recognized a need to prevent corporations from undermining self-government since the founding, and who have fought against the distinctive corrupting potential of corporate electioneering since the days of Theodore Roosevelt. It is a strange time to repudiate that common sense.

AFTER CITIZENS UNITED

1. *The role of corporate speech in politics.* Citizens United allows unlimited independent political expenditures from corporate treasuries for the support or defeat of political candidates—even if they fund what would be classified as "express advocacy" under the definition in WRTL. The dissent—like many commentators critical of the decision—suggests that corporations should not be as free as individual speakers to speak in support of or opposition to political campaigns and that a "distinctive threat to democratic integrity" is posed "by corporate domination of politics." What is the basis for such arguments? Do the majority and the dissent have competing views of freedom of speech, with the majority favoring a libertarian conception and the dissent favoring an egalitarian conception? For discussion of this possibility, see Sullivan, "The Supreme Court—2009 Term—Comment: Two Concepts of Freedom of Speech," 124 Harv. L. Rev. 143 (2010).

Or do the majority and the dissent divide on whether corporations share relevant characteristics with natural persons? Does the dissent's view depend on the fact that corporations are fictional persons that do not vote? That corporations can use state-conferred powers to amass resources that do not reflect popular support for the speech they engage in? Consider the countervailing view that "restricting corporate speech may impose social costs by reducing the quantity and balance of information made available to voters," and that "restricting corporate political activity could cause laws to be inefficient by permitting noncorporate groups to dominate the political process." Ribstein, "Corporate Political Speech," 49 Wash. & Lee L. Rev. 109 (1992).

Is the dissent's concern rather that shareholders lack sufficient power under existing corporate law to protect themselves from managers who will use corporate money to express views the shareholders disagree with? Shareholders can sell their shares, or try to unseat directors who allow such spending in board elections. Are such methods practical? Consider the view that they are not, and that instead "[t]he answer is to mandate that corporations let stockholders vote annually on whether they want the company to exercise the rights that Citizens United gave them to get into political races. Managers who seek stockholder approval of political activity would explain the actions they intend to take, how those actions would be in stockholders' interests and what the cost will be. If they don't make the case their spending will be voted down." Gilson & Klausner, "That's My Money You're Using," Forbes, Mar. 29, 2010. Would such a mandate itself violate the First Amendment by singling out corporate speakers for special burdens? Does this proposed mandate differ from the notice and opt-in requirements placed on unions in Knox (2012; p. 530)? Is such a mandate necessary given shareholders' wide array of contractual choices? Consider the view that "[e]ven the rare shareholder who cares about corporate speech could choose to invest only in firms that did not engage in political activities or in mutual funds that monitor the political correctness of the corporations in which they invest." Ribstein, supra.

In the wake of Citizens United, are for-profit corporations likely to increase their direct spending on political campaign advocacy? Will the incentives to make money to stay in business or to channel profit to executive compensation or other self-interested ends operate as de facto constraints on the level of corporate political investments? Is there reason to expect that corporate treasury money will instead be pooled in less visible form in the treasuries of trade associations and other advocacy organizations?

Or perhaps corporate managers will engage in an altogether different sort of advocacy. One scholar, drawing on empirical analysis of Supreme Court and appellate decisions, has found that corporations "have increasingly displaced individuals as direct beneficiaries of First Amendment rights." Today, almost half of First Amendment legal challenges benefit business corporations and trade groups. Consider the view that such cases represent a corrosive form of rent seeking: "the use of legal tools by business managers in specific cases to entrench reregulation in their personal interests at the expense of shareholders, consumers, and employees." In addition to the risks to democratic integrity underscored by most critics of Citizens United, as American businesses invest in legal innovation rather than technological innovation this form of corruption could also threaten the productivity of the U.S. economy. Coates, "Corporate Speech and the First Amendment: History, Data, and Implications," 30 Const. Comment. 223 (2015).

2. ***Lower court interpretations of Citizens United.*** In **SpeechNow.org v. Federal Election Comm'n**, 599 F.3d 686 (D.C. Cir. 2010), the D.C. Circuit sitting en banc addressed the question whether FECA's limits on individual contributions to political committees (so-called 527s, named for the provision in Internal Revenue Code) were consistent with the First Amendment. Writing for a unanimous court, Chief Judge SENTELLE assessed the claim of SpeechNow, a First Amendment advocacy organization, that alleged that the FECA restrictions violated the First Amendment: "SpeechNow is an unincorporated nonprofit association registered as a 'political organization' under § 527 of the Internal Revenue Code. [SpeechNow] intends to acquire funds solely through donations by individuals. SpeechNow further intends to operate exclusively through 'independent expenditures.' FECA defines 'independent expenditures' as expenditures 'expressly advocating the election or defeat of a clearly

identified candidate' that are 'not made in concert or cooperation with or at the request or suggestion of such candidate, the candidate's authorized political committee, or their agents, or a political party committee or its agents.'

"[In addition to the donations of its five members] as of August 2008, seventy-five other individuals had indicated on SpeechNow's website that they were interested in making donations. As for expenditures, SpeechNow planned ads for the 2008 election cycle against two incumbent candidates for federal office who, in the opinion of SpeechNow, did not sufficiently support First Amendment rights. These ads would have cost around $12,000 to produce. [SpeechNow] intended to place the ads so that the target audience would view the ads at least ten times, which would have cost around $400,000.

"[Under] FECA, a political committee is 'any committee, club, association, or other group of persons' that receives contributions of more than $1000 in a year or makes expenditures of more than $1000 in a year. 2 U.S.C. § 431(4). Once a group is so designated, contributions to the committee are restricted by 2 U.S.C. § 441a(a)(1)(C) and 441a(a)(3). The first provision limits an individual's contribution to a political committee to $5000 per calendar year; the second limits an individual's total contributions to all political committees to $69,900 biennially.

"[The] First Amendment mandates that 'Congress shall make no law . . . abridging the freedom of speech.' [The] Supreme Court has recognized only one interest sufficiently important to outweigh the First Amendment interests implicated by contributions for political speech: preventing corruption or the appearance of corruption. [The] Court has rejected each of the few other interests the government has, at one point or another, suggested as a justification for contribution or expenditure limits. Equalization of differing viewpoints is not a legitimate government objective. [An] informational interest in 'identifying the sources of support for and opposition to' a political position or candidate is not enough to justify the First Amendment burden. [And] though this rationale would not affect an unincorporated association such as SpeechNow, the Court has also refused to find a sufficiently compelling governmental interest in preventing 'the corrosive and distorting effects of immense aggregations of wealth that are accumulated with the help of the corporate form.' [Citizens United].

"Given this precedent, the only interest we may evaluate to determine whether the government can justify contribution limits as applied to SpeechNow is the government's anticorruption interest. Because of the Supreme Court's recent decision in Citizens United v. FEC, the analysis is straightforward. There, the Court held that the government has no anti-corruption interest in limiting independent expenditures.

"[In Citizens United, the] Court stated, '[W]e now conclude that independent expenditures, including those made by corporations, do not give rise to corruption or the appearance of corruption.' The Court came to this conclusion by looking to the definition of corruption and the appearance of corruption. For several decades after Buckley, the Court's analysis of the government's anti-corruption interest revolved largely around the 'hallmark of corruption,' 'financial quid pro quo: dollars for political favors,' However, in a series of cases culminating in McConnell, the Court expanded the definition to include 'the appearance of undue influence' created by large donations given for the purpose of 'buying access.' [The] Citizens United

Court retracted this view of the government's interest, saying that '[t]he fact that speakers may have influence over or access to elected officials does not mean that these officials are corrupt.' The Court returned to its older definition of corruption that focused on quid pro quo, saying that '[i]ngratiation and access ... are not corruption.' Therefore, without any evidence that independent expenditures 'lead to, or create the appearance of, quid pro quo corruption,' and only 'scant evidence' that they even ingratiate, the Court concluded that independent expenditures do not corrupt or create the appearance of corruption.

"In its briefs in this case, the FEC relied heavily on McConnell, arguing that independent expenditures by groups like SpeechNow benefit candidates and that those candidates are accordingly grateful to the groups and to their donors. [Whatever] the merits of those arguments before Citizens United, they plainly have no merit after Citizens United.

"In light of the Court's holding as a matter of law that independent expenditures do not corrupt or create the appearance of quid pro quo corruption, contributions to groups that make only independent expenditures also cannot corrupt or create the appearance of corruption. The Court has effectively held that there is no corrupting 'quid' for which a candidate might in exchange offer a corrupt 'quo.'

"Given this analysis from Citizens United, we must conclude that the government has no anti-corruption interest in limiting contributions to an independent expenditure group such as SpeechNow. This simplifies the task of weighing the First Amendment interests implicated by contributions to SpeechNow against the government's interest in limiting such contributions. [All] that matters is that the First Amendment cannot be encroached upon for naught." The court also upheld FECA's organizational and reporting requirements.

What is the combined effect of Citizens United and SpeechNow? First, under Citizens United, unions and corporations may spend unlimited amounts on independent expenditures. SpeechNow added individuals to this list. (Is it surprising that SpeechNow added individuals? Note that the Office of the Solicitor General declined to seek Supreme Court review of the D.C. Circuit's decision.) Second, Citizens United dealt with *spending* by corporations and unions, while SpeechNow addresses *fundraising* by independent expenditure groups. Taken together, these cases affirm both the First Amendment rights of individuals, unions, and corporations to spend unlimited amounts on independent expenditures and the First Amendment rights of independent expenditure groups to fundraise unlimited amounts from each of these parties.

3. *Citizens United in state courts.* In **Western Tradition Partnership v. Montana**, 271 P.3d 1 (Mont. 2011), the Montana Supreme Court upheld portions of the Montana Corrupt Practices Act that prohibited independent expenditures by corporations to political campaigns. Attempting to justify why the state law still passed constitutional muster under Citizens United, the court characterized Citizens United as having "applied the long-standing rule that restrictions upon speech are not per se unlawful, but rather may be upheld if the government demonstrates a sufficiently strong interest."

In seeking to prove this sufficiently strong interest, the court then discussed at length the specific history of corporate domination and political contestation in Montana during the early twentieth century. Specifically, this history told the story of how "mining and industrial enterprises controlled by foreign trusts or corporations" dominated the political process, including by engaging in quid pro quo transactions with the Montana Governor and Legislature. To the court, the fact that the state campaign finance law was enacted to counteract these evils helped prove that there was a sufficiently compelling reason for the law, thereby distinguishing Citizens United.

Yet in **American Tradition Partnership, Inc. v. Bullock**, 567 U.S. 516 (2012), the Supreme Court overruled the state court. The short per curiam decision stated plainly that "[t]here can be no serious doubt" that Citizens United applied, such that the Montana state law violates the First Amendment.

Should the Montana Supreme Court have been permitted to take into account the unique political and historical context underlying a state law when calibrating the degree of a compelling state interest? If a state court disagrees with the federal Supreme Court's pronouncements on a constitutional issue, what avenues does it have to express dissent? Imagine that the Montana Supreme Court had first upheld the law as constitutional under the state's free speech provisions, and provided a reasoned explanation for this conclusion Would such an analysis have held any discursive value, even if the court held in the same opinion that it was bound by Citizens United to strike down the law on the basis of the federal constitution? For a discussion of the role that state courts can play in dissenting to federal court pronouncements, and the perspective of California Supreme Court Justice Goodwin Liu, see Liu, "State Constitutions and the Protection of Individual Rights: A Reappraisal," 92 N.Y.U. L. Rev. 1307 (2017).

4. *Political response to Citizens United.* In the wake of Citizens United, President Obama criticized the decision and invited a legislative response in his State of the Union address, and members of Congress introduced a variety of bills designed to check its impact. Would any of the following proposals be constitutional in light of the Court's decision in Citizens United: A ban on independent political expenditures by corporations more than twenty percent owned by foreign residents? A ban on independent political expenditures by corporations that receive government contracts? A ban on the use of federal bailout money to fund corporate political advertisements? A requirement that CEOs personally appear on camera to say they support a corporate-funded ad? A requirement that publicly traded companies disclose all political expenditures to shareholders and the SEC? After Bennett, discussed at p. 581, certain public financing programs are no longer a viable option.

Some critics of Citizens United suggest that such proposed responses do not go far enough; Professor Lawrence Lessig, for example, has urged Congress to consider a proposed constitutional amendment that would provide: "Nothing in this Constitution shall be construed to restrict the power to limit, though not to ban, campaign expenditures of non-citizens of the United States during the last 60 days before an election." Would such an amendment be desirable? If corporations are deemed non-citizens for this purpose, should they also be deemed non-"persons" for purposes of equal protection, due process, and other constitutional guarantees that now apply to them?

Should post-Citizens United elections dampen or stoke the ire around the impact of Citizens United? The 2012 election was the most expensive in history with $6 billion spent over the course of the cycle. Of this, so-called Super PACs spent $546.5 million in the 2012 election, though some reports suggest that Super PAC spending exceeded $858 million. As noted above, President Obama originally decried Citizens United, but he eventually deployed campaign supporters to raise money for pro-Obama Super PACs in his 2012 reelection bid. Confessore, "Result Won't Limit Campaign Money Any More than Ruling Did," N.Y. Times, Nov. 11, 2012. But compare the amount spent by Super PACs to the amount spent by each of the campaigns: $553 million by President Obama's campaign and $360 million spent by Mitt Romney's campaign. Does this suggest that Super PACs are only part of the story of the astronomical increase in campaign spending? Reports also suggest that both candidates spent significant time fundraising, with President Obama holding twice as many fundraising events as campaign rallies and Mitt Romney having only one single public event a day because of a packed fundraising schedule. See Confessore, supra. Does this make the argument that voters are getting more information about the candidates more or less convincing?

5.   *Are some contribution limits invalid?* In Citizens United, the Court narrowly defined the permissible scope of the government's anti-corruption interest in regulating campaign finance: combating quid pro quo corruption. Although Citizens United dealt exclusively with independent corporate expenditures, might its reasoning be applied to other features of Congress' regulatory scheme? In the case that follows, the Court turned its attention to contribution limits that limited the aggregate amounts that a donor can contribute during an election cycle:

McCutcheon v. F.E.C.
572 U.S. 185, 134 S. Ct. 1434, 188 L. Ed. 2d 468 (2014).

■ CHIEF JUSTICE ROBERTS announced the judgment of the Court and delivered an opinion, in which [JUSTICES] SCALIA, KENNEDY, and ALITO join.

[The] right to participate in democracy through political contributions is protected by the First Amendment, but that right is not absolute. In] a series of cases over the past 40 years, we have spelled out how to draw the constitutional line between the permissible goal of avoiding corruption in the political process and the impermissible desire simply to limit political speech. We have said that government regulation may not target the general gratitude a candidate may feel toward those who support him or his allies, or the political access such support may afford. [Any] regulation must instead target what we have called "quid pro quo" corruption or its appearance. That Latin phrase captures the notion of a direct exchange of an official act for money. [Campaign] finance restrictions that pursue other objectives, we have explained, impermissibly inject the Government into the debate over who should govern. And those who govern should be the last people to help decide who should govern.

The statute at issue in this case imposes two types of limits on campaign contributions. The first, called base limits, restricts how much money a donor may contribute to a particular candidate or committee. 2 U.S.C. § 441a(a)(1).

The second, called aggregate limits, restricts how much money a donor may contribute in total to all candidates or committees. § 441a(a)(3).

This case does not involve any challenge to the base limits, which we have previously upheld as serving the permissible objective of combatting corruption. The Government contends that the aggregate limits also serve that objective, by preventing circumvention of the base limits. We conclude, however, that the aggregate limits do little, if anything, to address that concern, while seriously restricting participation in the democratic process. The aggregate limits are therefore invalid under the First Amendment.

I.B. In the 2011–2012 election cycle, appellant Shaun McCutcheon contributed a total of $33,088 to 16 different federal candidates, in compliance with the base limits applicable to each. He alleges that he wished to contribute $1,776 to each of 12 additional candidates but was prevented from doing so by the aggregate limit on contributions to candidates. McCutcheon also contributed a total of $27,328 to several noncandidate political committees, in compliance with the base limits applicable to each. He alleges that he wished to contribute to various other political committees, including $25,000 to each of the three Republican national party committees, but was prevented from doing so by the aggregate limit on contributions to political committees.

II.B.1. [We] see no need in this case to revisit Buckley's distinction between contributions and expenditures and the corollary distinction in the applicable standards of review. [Because] we find a substantial mismatch between the Government's stated objective and the means selected to achieve it, the aggregate limits fail even under the "closely drawn" test.

III. [The] Government may no more restrict how many candidates or causes a donor may support than it may tell a newspaper how many candidates it may endorse. [The aggregate] limits deny the individual all ability to exercise his expressive and associational rights by contributing to someone who will advocate for his policy preferences. A donor must limit the number of candidates he supports, and may have to choose which of several policy concerns he will advance.

[It] is no answer to say that the individual can simply contribute less money to more people. To require one person to contribute at lower levels than others because he wants to support more candidates or causes is to impose a special burden on broader participation in the democratic process.

IV. [This] Court has identified only one legitimate governmental interest for restricting campaign finances: preventing corruption or the appearance of corruption. We have consistently rejected attempts to suppress campaign speech based on other legislative objectives.

[Moreover], while preventing corruption or its appearance is a legitimate objective, Congress may target only a specific type of corruption—"quid pro quo" corruption. [In] addition to actual quid pro quo arrangements, Congress may permissibly limit the appearance of corruption stemming from public awareness of the opportunities for abuse inherent in a regime of large individual financial contributions to particular candidates.

[Spending] large sums of money in connection with elections, but not in connection with an effort to control the exercise of an officeholder's official duties, does not give rise to such quid pro quo corruption. Nor does the possibility that an individual who spends large sums may garner influence over or access to elected officials or political parties.

[The] definition of corruption that we apply today [has] firm roots in Buckley itself. [The] line between quid pro quo corruption and general influence may seem vague at times, but the distinction must be respected in order to safeguard basic First Amendment rights. [The] dissent laments that our opinion leaves only remnants of FECA and BCRA that are inadequate to combat corruption. Such rhetoric ignores the fact that we leave the base limits undisturbed. Those base limits remain the primary means of regulating campaign contributions—the obvious explanation for why the aggregate limits received a scant few sentences of attention in Buckley.

B.   When the Government restricts speech, the Government bears the burden of proving the constitutionality of its actions.

[If] there is no corruption concern in giving nine candidates up to $5,200 each, it is difficult to understand how a tenth candidate can be regarded as corruptible if given $1,801, and all others corruptible if given a dime. And if there is no risk that additional candidates will be corrupted by donations of up to $5,200, then the Government must defend the aggregate limits by demonstrating that they prevent circumvention of the base limits.

The problem is that they do not serve that function in any meaningful way. In light of the various statutes and regulations currently in effect, Buckley's fear that an individual might "contribute massive amounts of money to a particular candidate through the use of unearmarked contributions" to entities likely to support the candidate is far too speculative.

C.   [Quite] apart from the foregoing, the aggregate limits violate the First Amendment because they are not closely drawn to avoid unnecessary abridgment of associational freedoms. [Because] the statute is poorly tailored to the Government's interest in preventing circumvention of the base limits, it impermissibly restricts participation in the political process.

1.   The Government argues that the aggregate limits are justified because they prevent an individual from giving to too many initial recipients who might subsequently recontribute a donation. [But experience] suggests that the vast majority of contributions made in excess of the aggregate limits are likely to be retained and spent by their recipients rather than rerouted to candidates.

[Likewise, state] parties rarely contribute to candidates in other States. [As] with national and state party committees, candidates contribute only a small fraction of their campaign funds to other candidates. [The] fact is that candidates who receive campaign contributions spend most of the money on themselves, rather than passing along donations to other candidates. In this arena at least, charity begins at home.

2.   Importantly, there are multiple alternatives available to Congress that would serve the Government's anticircumvention interest, while avoiding "unnecessary abridgment" of First Amendment rights.

The most obvious might involve targeted restrictions on transfers among candidates and political committees. There are currently no such limits. [Other] alternatives might focus on earmarking. Many of the scenarios that the Government and the dissent hypothesize involve at least implicit agreements to circumvent the base limits—agreements that are already prohibited by the earmarking rules. The FEC might strengthen those rules further by, for example, defining how many candidates a PAC must support in order to ensure that "a substantial portion" of a donor's contribution is not rerouted to a certain candidate.

D.   Finally, disclosure of contributions minimizes the potential for abuse of the campaign finance system. [Disclosure] requirements burden speech, but—unlike the aggregate limits—they do not impose a ceiling on speech. For that reason, disclosure often represents a less restrictive alternative to flat bans on certain types or quantities of speech.

With modern technology, disclosure now offers a particularly effective means of arming the voting public with information. [Today], given the Internet, disclosure offers much more robust protections against corruption. [Because] massive quantities of information can be accessed at the click of a mouse, disclosure is effective to a degree not possible at the time Buckley, or even McConnell, was decided.

V.   At oral argument, the Government shifted its focus from Buckley's anticircumvention rationale to an argument that the aggregate limits deter corruption regardless of their ability to prevent circumvention of the base limits. [That] new rationale for the aggregate limits—embraced by the dissent—does not wash. [When] donors furnish widely distributed support within all applicable base limits, all members of the party or supporters of the cause may benefit, and the leaders of the party or cause may feel particular gratitude. That gratitude stems from the basic nature of the party system, in which party members join together to further common political beliefs, and citizens can choose to support a party because they share some, most, or all of those beliefs. To recast such shared interest, standing alone, as an opportunity for quid pro quo corruption would dramatically expand government regulation of the political process.

■ JUSTICE THOMAS, concurring in the judgment.

I adhere to the view that this Court's decision in Buckley v. Valeo denigrates core First Amendment speech and should be overruled.

[I] would overrule Buckley and subject the aggregate limits in BCRA to strict scrutiny, which they would surely fail.

■ JUSTICE BREYER, with whom [JUSTICES] GINSBURG, SOTOMAYOR, and KAGAN join, dissenting.

[The] Buckley Court focused upon the same problem that concerns the Court today, and it wrote:

"The overall $25,000 ceiling does impose an ultimate restriction upon the number of candidates and committees with which an individual may associate himself by means of financial support. But this quite modest restraint upon protected political activity serves to prevent evasion of the $1,000 contribution limitation by a person who might otherwise contribute massive amounts of money to a particular candidate through the use of unearmarked contributions to political committees likely to contribute to that candidate, or huge contributions to the candidate's political party. The limited, additional restriction on associational freedom imposed by the overall ceiling is thus no more than a corollary of the basic individual contribution limitation that we have found to be constitutionally valid."

Today a majority of the Court overrules this holding. It is wrong to do so.

II.   [The] plurality's first claim—that large aggregate contributions do not give rise to corruption—is plausible only because the plurality defines "corruption" too narrowly. [As] the history of campaign finance reform shows and as our earlier cases on the subject have recognized, the anticorruption interest that drives Congress to regulate campaign contributions is a far broader, more important interest than the plurality acknowledges. It is an interest in maintaining the integrity of our public governmental institutions. And it is an interest rooted in the Constitution and in the First Amendment itself.

Consider at least one reason why the First Amendment protects political speech. Speech does not exist in a vacuum. Rather, political communication seeks to secure government action. A politically oriented "marketplace of ideas" seeks to form a public opinion that can and will influence elected representatives.

[The] First Amendment advances not only the individual's right to engage in political speech, but also the public's interest in preserving a democratic order in which collective speech matters.

[Corruption] breaks the constitutionally necessary "chain of communication" between the people and their representatives. It derails the essential speech-to-government-action tie. Where enough money calls the tune, the general public will not be heard. Insofar as corruption cuts the link between political thought and political action, a free marketplace of political ideas loses its point. That is one reason why the Court has stressed the constitutional importance of Congress' concern that a few large donations not drown out the voices of the many.

[The] "appearance of corruption" can make matters worse. It can lead the public to believe that its efforts to communicate with its representatives or to help sway public opinion have little purpose. And a cynical public can lose interest in political participation altogether.

The upshot is that the interests the Court has long described as preventing "corruption" or the "appearance of corruption" are more than ordinary factors to be weighed against the constitutional right to political speech. Rather, they are interests rooted in the First Amendment itself. They are rooted in the constitutional effort to create a democracy responsive to the people—a government where laws reflect the very thoughts, views, ideas, and sentiments, the expression of which the First Amendment protects. Given that end, we can and should understand campaign finance laws as resting upon a broader and more significant constitutional rationale than the plurality's limited definition of "corruption" suggests.

III. The plurality invalidates the aggregate contribution limits for a second reason. It believes they are no longer needed to prevent contributors from circumventing federal limits on direct contributions to individuals, political parties, and political action committees.

[The] plurality is wrong. Here, as in Buckley, in the absence of limits on aggregate political contributions, donors can and likely will find ways to channel millions of dollars to parties and to individual candidates, producing precisely the kind of "corruption" or "appearance of corruption" that previously led the Court to hold aggregate limits constitutional. Those opportunities for circumvention will also produce the type of corruption that concerns the plurality today. The methods for using today's opinion to evade the law's individual contribution limits are complex, but they are well known, or will become well known, to party fundraisers.

IV. [The] plurality concludes that even if circumvention were a threat, the aggregate limits are "poorly tailored" to address it. The plurality, however, does not show, or try to show, that [its] hypothetical alternatives could effectively replace aggregate contribution limits.

[The] conclusion is simple: There is no "substantial mismatch" between Congress' legitimate objective and the "means selected to achieve it." The Court, as in Buckley, should hold that aggregate contribution limits are constitutional.

V. In the past, when evaluating the constitutionality of campaign finance restrictions, we have typically relied upon an evidentiary record amassed below to determine whether the law served a compelling governmental objective.

[Determining] whether anticorruption objectives justify a particular set of contribution limits requires answering empirically based questions, and applying significant discretion and judgment. To what extent will unrestricted giving lead to corruption or its appearance? What forms will any such corruption take? To what extent will a lack of regulation undermine public confidence in the democratic system? To what extent can regulation restore it?

These kinds of questions, while not easily answered, are questions that Congress is far better suited to resolve than are judges. [Without] further development of the record, however, I fail to see how the plurality can now find grounds for overturning Buckley. The justification for aggregate contribution restrictions is strongly rooted in the need to assure political integrity and ultimately in the First Amendment itself.

———

6. **Doctrinal reach of anticorruption rationale.** In **McDonnell v. United States**, 579 U.S. 550 (2016), the Court had to determine whether the former governor of Virginia had violated the Hobbs Act by taking gifts and cash in exchange for setting up meetings and hosting events. The Court held that McDonnell's actions did not count as "official acts" under the statute. It supported its holding in part on the basis of constitutional avoidance. Chief Justice ROBERTS wrote: "[T]he Government's expansive interpretation of 'official act' would raise significant constitutional concerns. Section 201 prohibits quid pro quo corruption—the exchange of a thing of value for an 'official act. In the Government's view, nearly anything a public official accepts—from a campaign contribution to lunch—counts as a quid; and nearly anything a public official does—from arranging a meeting to inviting a guest to an event—counts as a quo. But conscientious public officials arrange meetings for constituents, contact other officials on their behalf, and include them in events all the time. The basic compact underlying representative government assumes that public officials will hear from their constituents and act appropriately on their concerns— whether it is the union official worried about a plant closing or the homeowners who wonder why it took five days to restore power to their neighborhood after a storm. The Government's position could cast a pall of potential prosecution over these relationships if the union had given a campaign contribution in the past or the homeowners invited the official to join them on their annual outing to the ballgame. Officials might wonder whether they could respond to even the most commonplace requests for assistance, and citizens with legitimate concerns might shrink from

participating in democratic discourse. [None] of this, of course, is to suggest that the facts of this case typify normal political interaction between public officials and their constituents. Far from it. But the Government's legal interpretation is not confined to cases involving extravagant gifts or large sums of money, and we cannot construe a criminal statute on the assumption that the Government will use it responsibly."

SECTION 4. JOURNALISM AND MEDIA

The First Amendment protects not only the "freedom of speech" but also the "freedom of the press." Does that specific reference to the "press" entitle the media to special constitutional protection? Or are press claims more properly analyzed as an aspect of the general freedom of expression guaranteed by the "speech" clause? This section focuses on the constitutional protection of the press. Should the press merit any protections more extensive than those generally available to disseminators of information and opinion? May government compel journalists to divulge information they possess, in aid of such state interests as criminal law enforcement? Does the press enjoy a constitutional right of access to such places as jails and courtrooms in order to obtain newsworthy information? Are the media exempt from tax laws, regulations or civil liability that extend to others? Does it matter whether these laws single out the "press" for special treatment or treat it the same as everyone else? Finally, the Court has read the First Amendment to confer lesser protection on broadcasters than on the print media. Why should this be so? Is such differential treatment still warranted in light of technological change? How should we think about the press and its protections in an age of ubiquitous and diverse media?

Does the Press Clause simply reiterate the Speech Clause or does it provide some protection to the institutional media beyond that enjoyed by other speakers? Consider two alternative views. On the first view, the press occupies a special status as a metaphorical "fourth branch" of government. The most prominent advocate of special significance for the Press Clause was Justice Stewart. He argued that "the Free Press guarantee is, in essence, a *structural* provision of the Constitution. [It] extends protection to an institution. The publishing business [is] the only organized private business that is given explicit constitutional protection. [If] the Free Press guarantee meant no more than freedom of expression, it would be a constitutional redundancy. [It] is [a] mistake to suppose that the only purpose of the constitutional guarantee of a free press is to insure that a newspaper will serve as a neutral forum for debate, a 'market place for ideas,' a kind of Hyde Park Corner for the community. A related theory sees the press as a neutral conduit of information between the people and their elected leaders. These theories, in my view, again give insufficient weight to the institutional autonomy of the press that it was the purpose of the Constitution to guarantee." Justice Stewart also noted that the system of separation of powers "deliberately created an internally competitive system" and argued that the "primary purpose [of the Press Clause was to] create a fourth institution outside the Government as an additional check on the three official branches. [The] relevant metaphor [is that] of the Fourth Estate." In his view, then, the First Amendment protected "the institutional autonomy of the press." Stewart, "Or of the Press," 26 Hast. L.J. 631 (1975).

On the alternative view, the institutional press is just another speaker, with no greater or lesser First Amendment privileges than other nonmedia speakers. Is this view even more plausible in the age of the internet and the blogosphere, where the lines between the institutional press and other sources of information have blurred? For an argument along these lines and contrary to Justice Stewart's, consider dicta in Chief Justice BURGER's concurring opinion in **First National Bank of Boston v. Bellotti**, 435 U.S. 765 (1978): "Because the First Amendment was meant to guarantee freedom to express and to communicate ideas, I can see no difference between the right of those who seek to disseminate ideas by way of a newspaper and those who give lectures or speeches that seek to enlarge the audience by publication and wide dissemination. [I] perceive two fundamental difficulties with a narrow reading of the Press Clause. First although certainty on this point is not possible, the history of the Clause does not suggest that the authors contemplated a 'special' or 'institutional' privilege. [Indeed] most pre-First Amendment commentators 'who employed the term "freedom of speech" with great frequency used it synonymously with freedom of the press.' Those interpreting the Press Clause as extending protection only to, or creating a special role for, the 'institutional press' must either (a) assert such an intention on the part of the Framers for which no supporting evidence is available; (b) argue that events after 1791 somehow operated to 'constitutionalize' this interpretation; or (c) candidly acknowledging the absence of historical support, suggest that the intent of the Framers is not important today.

"To conclude that the Framers did not intend to limit the freedom of the press to one select group is not necessarily to suggest that the Press Clause is redundant. The Speech Clause standing alone may be viewed as a protection of the liberty to express ideas and beliefs, while the Press Clause focuses specifically on the liberty to disseminate expression broadly and 'comprehends every sort of publication which affords a vehicle of information and opinion.' Lovell v. Griffin. Yet there is no fundamental distinction between expression and dissemination. The liberty encompassed by the Press Clause, although complementary to and a natural extension of Speech Clause liberty, merited special mention simply because it had been more often the object of official restraints. [The] second fundamental difficulty with interpreting the Press Clause as conferring special status on a limited group is one of definition. The very task of including some entities within the 'institutional press' while excluding others, whether undertaken by legislature, court or administrative agency, is reminiscent of the abhorred licensing system of Tudor and Stuart England—a system the First Amendment was intended to ban from this country. Further, the officials undertaking that task would be required to distinguish the protected from the unprotected on the basis of such variables as content of expression, frequency or fervor of expression, or ownership of the technological means of dissemination. Yet nothing in this Court's opinions supports such a confining approach to the scope of Press Clause protection.[1] [In short], the First Amendment does not 'belong' to any definable category of persons or entities: it belongs to all who exercise its freedoms."

Chief Justice Burger's disinclination to rest media protections on the Press Clause has been the typical position of the Court. Most press claims

---

[1] "Near v. Minnesota, which examined the meaning of freedom of the press, did not involve a traditional institutionalized newspaper but rather an occasional publication (nine issues) more nearly approximating the product of a pamphleteer than the traditional newspaper." [Footnote by Chief Justice Burger.]

have been adjudicated by analysis of the Speech Clause and of general principles of freedom of expression. Would it be preferable to rest any "special status" rights of the press on further elaboration of the Press Clause, or does the press receive adequate protection under the Court's readings of the Speech Clause and the First Amendment generally? Consider these questions in reviewing the materials that follow.

————

PRESS ACCESS TO GOVERNMENT INFORMATION

Does the First Amendment entitle the press to obtain information the government seeks to withhold? On the view that the press has special institutional responsibility as a watchdog of government, such access rights would appear indispensable. But claims of a special press right of access in general have not fared well, with the exception of the right of access to criminal trials, in the Richmond Newspapers case. What is the proper scope of that newly recognized access? For commentary on press rights of access in order to obtain government information, see BeVier, "An Informed Public, An Informing Press: The Search for a Constitutional Principle," 68 Calif. L. Rev. 482 (1980) (arguing that courts may recognize press rights to publish and disseminate information without also recognizing a right of access to government information); Baker, "Press Rights and Government Power to Structure the Press," 34 U. Miami L. Rev. 819 (1980) (noting a distinction between "offensive" and "defensive" press claims and suggesting that defensive rights of the press against government intrusions are more persuasive than offensive, right-of-access claims); Dyk, "Newsgathering, Press Access, and the First Amendment," 44 Stan. L. Rev. 927 (1992) (arguing for heightened press access to check government).

1. ***Press access to prisons.*** The Court first confronted press demands for access to jails in companion cases, **Pell v. Procunier**, 417 U.S. 817 (1974), and **Saxbe v. Washington Post Co.**, 417 U.S. 843 (1974). In Pell, the majority rejected an attack on a California rule providing that "press and other media interviews with specific individual inmates will not be permitted." And in Saxbe, the Court turned back a challenge to a very similar Federal Bureau of Prisons prohibition of press interviews of individually designated prisoners in most federal prisons. Justice STEWART delivered the majority opinion in each case. Central to his rejection of the journalists' claim was his assertion that, although the First Amendment bars "government from interfering in any way with the free press," it does not "require government to accord the press special access to information not shared by members of the public generally." He explained: "It is one thing to say that a journalist is free to seek out sources of information not available to members of the general public, that he is entitled to some constitutional protection of the confidentiality of such sources, and that government cannot restrain the publication of news emanating from such sources. It is quite another thing to suggest that the Constitution imposes upon government the affirmative duty to make available to journalists sources of information not available to members of the public generally."

Justice POWELL found that approach unduly simplistic. He concluded in Pell that an absolute ban on interviews "impermissibly restrains the ability of the press to perform its constitutionally established function of informing the people on the conduct of their government." Elaborating that position in Saxbe in a lengthy dissent joined by Justices Brennan and Marshall, he stated: "I cannot follow the Court in concluding that *any* governmental restriction on press access to information, so long as it is nondiscriminatory, falls outside the purview of First Amendment concern. [At] some point official restraints on access to news sources, even though not directed solely at the press, may so undermine the function of the First Amendment that it is both appropriate and necessary to require the Government to justify such regulations in terms more compelling than discretionary authority and administrative convenience. [In] seeking out the news the press [acts] as an agent of the public at large." In a separate dissent, Justice DOUGLAS, joined by Justices Brennan and Marshall, similarly rested on the right "of the people": "the public's interest in being informed about prisons [is] paramount." Accordingly, the interview bans were "an unconstitutional infringement on the public's right to know protected by the free press guarantee of the First Amendment."

Press access claims similar to those rejected in Pell and Saxbe resurfaced four years later. But in **Houchins v. KQED, Inc.**, 438 U.S. 1 (1978), the 7-person Court, in an unusual division, sustained a portion of the claim of access to jails. The case arose from an action filed by San Francisco public television station KQED, which sought to gain access to a county jail to investigate allegedly shocking conditions. After the suit was filed, Sheriff Houchins modified his "no-access" policy of barring the general public and the media from Santa Rita and launched a monthly tour program limited to groups of 25 persons. Those on the tour were not permitted to take photographs or interview inmates. The lower court awarded KQED preliminary relief, giving the news media access to the jail "at reasonable times and hours" and authorizing inmate interviews and the use of photographic and sound equipment.

The Court, dividing 3–1–3 (Justices Marshall and Blackmun did not participate in the case), held the order proper in part. Chief Justice BURGER's opinion viewed the case as governed by Pell and Saxbe and found no basis for judicial relief: "[Until] the political branches decree otherwise, [the media have] no right of special access to the [jail] different from or greater than that accorded the public generally." Justice STEVENS's dissent, joined by Justices Brennan and Powell, insisted that Pell was distinguishable because in Pell there had been "substantial press and public access" to the jail; there, the rejected media claim asserted the additional right "to interview specifically designated inmates." He asserted that "the Court has never intimated that a nondiscriminatory policy of excluding entirely both the public and the press from access to information about prison conditions would avoid constitutional scrutiny." He emphasized "the special importance of allowing a democratic community access to knowledge about how its servants were treating [prisoners]." KQED, accordingly, should have prevailed in his view not because of any special press privilege but as an advocate of "the public's right to be informed."

Justice STEWART's decisive concurrence agreed with Chief Justice Burger's basic premises that the press had no special access rights, but differed in applying those principles here: "Whereas [Chief Justice Burger] appears to view 'equal access' as meaning access that is identical in all respects, I believe that the concept of equal access must be accorded more flexibility in order to accommodate the practical distinctions between the press and the general public." That "practical accommodations" approach permitted him to find a basis for limited relief for KQED. Emphasizing the "critical role played by the press in American society," he explained: "[T]erms of access that are reasonably imposed on individual members of the public may, if they impede effective reporting without sufficient justification, be unreasonable as applied to journalists who are there to convey to the general public what the visitors see." Accordingly, the First Amendment "required the Sheriff to give members of the press *effective* access" to all areas open to the public. Simply permitting reporters to sign up for the monthly tours "on the same terms as the public" was inadequate "as a matter of constitutional law." Accordingly, the trial court's order permitting press access "on a more flexible and frequent basis than scheduled monthly tours" was justified in order "to keep the public informed," as was the order permitting the media to bring cameras and recording equipment into the jail.

2. ***Press access to pretrial hearings.*** In **Gannett Co. v. Depasquale**, 443 U.S. 368 (1979), a divided Court rejected a newspaper publisher's attack on an order barring the public, including the press, from a pretrial hearing on suppression of evidence in a murder case. The prevailing opinion held that the press and the public had no independent constitutional right to insist upon access to such pretrial proceedings when the accused, the prosecutor, and the trial judge all had agreed to close the hearing in order to assure a fair trial. Although the Justices focused primarily on the Sixth Amendment provision that, in "all criminal prosecutions, the accused shall enjoy the right to [a] public trial," some comments on First Amendment issues surfaced in most of the opinions. Justice STEWART, writing for the Court, accepted that the Sixth Amendment's public trial guarantee reflected the public as well as the defendant's interest, but held that "our adversary system of criminal justice is premised upon the proposition that the public interest is fully protected by the participants of the litigation," who had agreed to the closure order here. He found nothing in the structure, text or history of the Sixth Amendment to support "any correlative right in members of the public to insist upon a public trial." He found it unnecessary to decide whether there was any First Amendment right to attend criminal trials: "[E]ven assuming, arguendo, that the [First Amendment] may guarantee such access in some situations, a question we do not decide, this putative right was given all appropriate deference by the [trial judge] in the present case."

Justice POWELL's concurring opinion considered the First Amendment issue more fully and concluded, relying on his approach in Saxbe: "Because of the importance of the public's having accurate information concerning the operation of its criminal justice system, I would hold explicitly that petitioner's reporter had an interest protected by the [First Amendment] in being present at the pretrial suppression hearing." But he suggested that a closure motion would be appropriate if "a fair trial for the defendant is likely to be jeopardized by publicity." Applying this standard, Justice Powell found that the First Amendment right of access had been "adequately respected" by the trial judge in this case. Justice REHNQUIST's concurring opinion took a narrower view of the First Amendment. He stated: "Despite the Court's seeming reservation of the [question], it is clear that this Court repeatedly has held that there is no First Amendment right of access in the public or the press to judicial or other governmental proceedings." In his view, the Court had "emphatically" rejected Justice Powell's view "that the First Amendment is some sort of constitutional 'sunshine law' that requires notice, an opportunity to be heard and substantial reasons before a governmental proceeding may be closed to the public and press."

Justice BLACKMUN's partial dissent, joined by Justices Brennan, White and Marshall, derived a public right of access from the Sixth Amendment and argued that states could not exclude the public "from a proceeding within the ambit of the Sixth Amendment's guarantee without affording full and fair consideration to the public's interest in maintaining an open proceeding." Emphasizing the "societal interest in the public trial that exists separately from, and at times in opposition to, the interests of the accused," he argued that a court may not give effect to "an accused's attempt to waive his public trial right" in all circumstances: "[The] public trial interest cannot adequately be protected by the prosecutor and judge in conjunction, or connivance, with the defendant." Justice Blackmun recognized, however, that "the publication of information learned in an open proceeding may harm irreparably, under certain circumstances, the ability of the defendant to obtain a fair trial," and suggested that "limited exceptions to the principle of publicity" would be acceptable if "necessary" in such cases.

3. *Press access to criminal trials.* A year after Gannett, the 7–1 decision in **Richmond Newspapers, Inc. v. Virginia**, 448 U.S. 555 (1980), held that, "[a]bsent an overriding interest articulated in findings, the trial of a criminal case must be open to the public." Chief Justice BURGER's opinion announcing the judgment (joined by Justices White and Stevens) stated that the "narrow question" was "whether the right of the public and press to attend criminal trials is guaranteed under [the] Constitution," a question not reached in Gannett. After reviewing the historical practice of having trials "open to all who cared to observe," he concluded that, when the Constitution was adopted, "criminal trials both here and in England had long been presumptively open." He noted the "nexus between openness, fairness, and the perception of fairness" and commented: "To work effectively, it is important that society's criminal process 'satisfy the appearance of justice,' and the appearance of justice can best be provided by allowing people to observe it." Although attendance at trials "is no longer a wide-spread pastime," that merely validated "the media claim of functioning as surrogates for the public" in the modern context. The "unbroken, uncontradicted history" supported his conclusion that "a presumption of openness inheres in the very nature of a criminal trial under our system of justice."

Turning to the constitutional sources for an access claim not explicitly guaranteed, he concluded that "the right to attend criminal trials is implicit in the guarantees of the First Amendment." The First Amendment protections of speech, press, and the right to assemble "share a common core purpose of assuring freedom of communication on matters relating to the functioning of government. Plainly it would be difficult to single out any aspect of government of higher concern and importance to the people than the manner in which criminal trials are conducted." Accordingly, the First Amendment could be read "as protecting the right of everyone to attend trials so as to give meaning to those explicit guarantees"; thus, "the First Amendment guarantees of speech and press, standing alone, prohibit government from summarily closing courtroom doors." He distinguished Pell and Saxbe as involving "penal institutions which, by definition [and tradition], are not 'open' or public places."

Chief Justice Burger conceded that the Constitution did not spell out a "right of the public to attend trials." But he noted that this had not "precluded recognition of important rights not enumerated": "Notwithstanding the appropriate caution against reading into the Constitution rights not explicitly defined, the Court has acknowledged that certain unarticulated rights are implicit in enumerated guarantees. For example, the rights of association and of privacy [as well as] the right to travel appear nowhere in the Constitution or Bill of Rights. Yet these important but unarticulated rights have nonetheless been found to share constitutional protection in common with explicit guarantees." He also noted that the Ninth Amendment had been adopted "to allay the fears of those who were concerned that expressing certain guarantees could be read as excluding others." In short, "fundamental rights, even though not expressly guaranteed, have been recognized by the Court as indispensable to the enjoyment of rights explicitly defined," and "the right to attend criminal trials" could accordingly be found "implicit in the guarantees of the First Amendment."

On the facts of the case, Chief Justice Burger found no "overriding interest articulated in findings" for closing the criminal trial here. The defendant had requested the closure; the prosecution had not objected. The trial judge made no findings to support closure, nor any inquiry "as to whether alternative solutions would have met the need to ensure fairness," such as witnesses' exclusion from the courtroom or their sequestration during the trial. He cautioned: "We have no occasion here to define the circumstances in which all or parts of a criminal trial may be closed to the [public]." A trial judge could impose "reasonable limitations on access to a trial" in the interests of the fair administration of justice. Moreover, "since courtrooms have limited capacity, there may be occasions when not every person who wishes to attend can be accommodated. In such situations, reasonable restrictions on general access are traditionally imposed, including preferential seating for media representatives."

In a brief separate statement Justice WHITE, who joined Chief Justice Burger's opinion, noted that this decision would have been unnecessary if the majority had adopted the dissent's Sixth Amendment position in Gannett. Justice STEVENS, who joined Chief Justice Burger's opinion, also submitted a separate concurrence viewing the Court as recognizing for the first time a broad First Amendment right of access to "newsworthy matter": "the First Amendment protects the public and the press from abridgment of their rights of access to information about the operation of their government, including the Judicial Branch; given the total absence of any record justification for the closure order entered in this case, that order violated the First Amendment."

In an opinion concurring in the judgment, Justice BRENNAN, joined by Justice Marshall, stated: "Because I believe that the First Amendment [secures a] public right of access [to trial proceedings], I agree with those of my Brethren who hold that, without more, agreement of the trial judge and the parties cannot constitutionally close a trial to the public." Justice Brennan relied in part on his "Address," 32 Rutgers L. Rev. 173 (1979), arguing that "the First Amendment embodies more than a commitment to free expression and communicative interchange for their own sakes; it has a *structural* role to play in securing and fostering our republican system of self-government. Implicit in this structural role is not only 'the principle that debate on public issues should be uninhibited, robust, and wide open,' but the antecedent assumption that valuable public debate [must] be informed. The structural model links the First Amendment to that process of communication necessary for a democracy to survive, and thus entails solicitude not only for communication itself, but for the indispensable conditions of meaningful communication."

Applying this approach, he found, perusing materials similar to those relied on by Chief Justice Burger, that, "[a]s a matter of law and virtually immemorial custom, public trials have been the essentially unwavering rule in ancestral England and in our own Nation." Moreover, publicity served several "particular purposes" of the judicial process. He noted, for example, that "judges are not mere umpires, but, in their own sphere, lawmakers—a coordinate branch of *government*. [Thus,] so far as the trial is the mechanism for judicial factfinding, as well as the initial forum for legal decisionmaking, it is a genuine governmental proceeding. It follows that the conduct of the trial is preeminently a matter of public interest. [Popular] attendance at trials, in sum, substantially furthers the particular public purposes of that critical judicial proceeding. In that sense, public access is an indispensable element of the trial process itself." He concluded: "What countervailing interest might be sufficiently compelling to reverse this presumption of openness need not concern us now, for the statute at stake here authorizes trial closures at the unfettered discretion of the judge and parties."

A separate opinion by Justice STEWART concurring in the judgment emphasized that Gannett had left open the First Amendment issues reached here and concluded: "Whatever the ultimate answer to [the First Amendment] question may be with respect to pretrial suppression hearings in criminal cases, the [First Amendment] clearly give[s] the press and the public a right of access to trials themselves, civil as well as criminal. [With] us, a trial is by very definition a proceeding open to the press and to the public. [Even] more than city streets, sidewalks, and parks as areas of traditional First Amendment activity, a trial courtroom is a place where representatives of the press and of the public are not only free to be, but where their presence serves to assure the integrity of what goes on." He added, however, that the access right was not "absolute": "[Much] more than a city street, a trial courtroom must be a quiet and orderly place. Moreover, every courtroom has a finite physical capacity, and there may be occasions when not all who wish to attend a trial may do so. And while there exist many alternative ways to satisfy the constitutional demands of a fair trial, those demands may also sometimes justify limitations upon the unrestricted presence of spectators in the courtroom." Here, reversal was in order because "the trial judge appears to have given no recognition to the right of representatives of the press and members of the public to be present at [the] murder trial."

In still another opinion concurring in the judgment, Justice BLACKMUN reiterated his Sixth Amendment position in Gannett and went beyond: "[W]ith the Sixth Amendment set to one side in this case, I am driven to conclude, as a secondary position, that the First Amendment must provide some measure of protection for public access to the trial. [It] is clear and obvious to me, on the approach the Court has chosen to take, that, by closing this criminal trial, the trial judge abridged [the] First Amendment interests of the public."

Justice REHNQUIST, the sole dissenter, adhered to his position in Gannett and found nothing in the First, Sixth, or Ninth Amendments, or in any other constitutional provision, to prohibit what the state trial judge had done in this case.

What is the scope of Richmond Newspapers? Was it the watershed that Justice Stevens depicted? To what extent should it extend beyond criminal trials to other governmental information and proceedings? For comments on the implications of Richmond Newspapers, see, e.g., Cox, "Foreword—Freedom of Expression in the Burger Court," 94 Harv. L. Rev. 1 (1980), and Lewis, "A Public Right to Know About Public Institutions: The First Amendment as Sword," 1980 Sup. Ct. Rev. 1 (arguing that Richmond Newspapers "put to rest [the] claim that the Press Clause [gives journalists] a distinct and preferred status. As a practical matter it has not been a winning argument anyway. [Most] future cases seeking access to government information will probably be brought by press organizations, but they will be based on the rights of the public.").

4. *Extension of Richmond Newspapers.* In **Globe Newspaper Co. v. Superior Court**, 457 U.S. 596 (1982), the Court concluded that the First Amendment had been violated by a Massachusetts law which had been construed to *require* the exclusion of the press and the general public from the courtroom during the testimony of a minor who had allegedly been a victim of a sex offense. The case arose when the Boston Globe unsuccessfully sought access to a state court trial where the defendant had been charged with the rape of three girls who were minors. In upholding the State's mandatory closure rule, the highest state court had distinguished Richmond Newspapers by emphasizing "at least one notable exception" to the tradition of "openness" in criminal trials: "cases involving sexual assault." The mandatory closure law accordingly operated "in an area of traditional sensitivity to the needs of victims."

Justice BRENNAN, writing for the majority, found the law invalid under the principles of Richmond Newspapers. In his view, Richmond Newspapers "firmly established for the first time that the press and general public have a constitutional right of access to criminal trials," even though no such right was "explicitly mentioned [in] the First Amendment." Protecting "the free discussion of governmental affairs" was a major purpose of the Amendment; offering such protection served "to ensure that the individual citizen can effectively participate in and contribute to our republican system of self-government." A "right of access to *criminal trials*" was properly afforded by the First Amendment because "the criminal trial historically has been open to the press and general public" and because "the right of access to criminal trials plays a particularly significant role in the functioning of the judicial process and the government as a whole." This constitutional right of access, though not "absolute," was entitled to protection unless the State showed "that the denial [of access] is necessitated by a compelling governmental interest, and is narrowly tailored to serve that interest." Massachusetts' defense of its law could not survive that strict scrutiny.

Justice Brennan conceded that the first of the two interests put forth by the state—protecting the physical and psychological well-being of minor victims of sex crimes from further trauma and embarrassment—was "a compelling one." But the closure law was not "a narrowly tailored means of accommodating the State's asserted interest: That interest could be served just as well by requiring the trial court to determine on a case-by-case basis whether the State's legitimate concern for the well-being of the minor victim necessitates closure." Nor could the closure law be sustained on the basis of the State's second asserted interest—"the encouragement of minor victims of sex crimes to come forward and provide accurate testimony." In rejecting that argument, Justice Brennan stated: "Not only is the claim speculative in empirical terms, but it is also open to serious question as a matter of logic and common sense. [Even if the law] effectively advanced the State's interest, it is doubtful that the interest would be sufficient to overcome the constitutional attack, for that same interest could be relied on to support an array of mandatory-closure rules designed to encourage victims to come forward: Surely it cannot be suggested that minor victims of sex crimes are the *only* crime victims who, because of publicity, [are] reluctant to come forward and testify."

Justice O'CONNOR concurred only in the judgment. She stated that she did not interpret Richmond Newspapers "to shelter every right that is 'necessary to the enjoyment of other First Amendment rights.' Instead, Richmond Newspapers rests upon our long history of open criminal trials and the special value, for both public and accused, of that openness. [Thus] I interpret neither Richmond Newspapers nor [today's decision] to carry any implications outside the context of criminal trials."

Chief Justice BURGER, joined by Justice Rehnquist, dissented, objecting to the Court's "expansive interpretation" of Richmond Newspapers and "its cavalier rejection of the serious interests supporting Massachusetts' mandatory closure rule." He claimed that Richmond Newspapers had *not* established "a First Amendment right of access to all aspects of all criminal trials under all circumstances." Although that case had emphasized the traditional openness of criminal trials in general, there was "clearly a long history of exclusion of the public from trials involving sexual assaults, particularly those against minors. [It] would misrepresent the historical record to state that there is an 'unbroken, uncontradicted history' of open proceedings in cases involving the sexual abuse of minors"; and such a specific "history of openness" was necessary to invoke Richmond Newspapers.

Chief Justice Burger also found the majority's "wooden application" of strict scrutiny "inappropriate." He emphasized: "Neither the purpose of the law nor its effect is primarily to deny the press or public access to information; the verbatim transcript is made available to the public and the media and may be used without limit. We therefore need only examine whether the restrictions imposed are reasonable and whether the interests of the [State] override the very limited incidental effects of the law on First Amendment rights." To him, it seemed "beyond doubt, considering the minimal impact of the law on First Amendment rights and the overriding weight of the [State's] interest in protecting child rape victims, that the Massachusetts law is not unconstitutional." Moreover, there was adequate justification for making the law mandatory rather than discretionary: "[V]ictims and their families are entitled to assurance [of] protection. The legislature did not act irrationally in deciding not to leave the closure determination to the idiosyncracies of individual judges subject to the pressures available to the media."

In another broad interpretation of Richmond Newspapers, the Court in **Press-Enterprise Co. v. Superior Court**, 464 U.S. 501 (1984), held

Richmond Newspapers applicable to voir dire examination of prospective jurors in a criminal trial—in this instance, a trial involving charges of rape and murder of a teenage girl. Chief Justice BURGER's opinion for the Court rejected a generalized interest in protecting the privacy of prospective jurors, relying extensively on history to show that public jury selection has long been an integral part of public trials. As in both Richmond Newspapers and Globe, however, the Court did not hold the right of public access to this facet of a trial to be absolute: "The presumption of openness may be overcome only by an overriding interest based on findings that closure is essential to preserve higher values and is narrowly tailored to serve that interest. The interest is to be articulated along with findings specific enough that a reviewing court can determine whether the closure order was properly entered." Chief Justice Burger found this standard unmet in this case, especially in light of the trial court's failure to consider alternatives to closure to protect the privacy of prospective jurors. And he suggested a specific alternative: "The jury selection process may, in some circumstances, give rise to a compelling interest of a prospective juror when interrogation touches on deeply personal [matters]. For example a prospective juror might privately inform the judge that she, or a member of her family, had been raped but had declined to seek prosecution because of the embarrassment and emotional trauma from the very disclosure of the [episode]. By requiring the prospective juror to make an affirmative request, the trial judge can ensure that there is in fact a valid basis for a belief that disclosure infringes a significant interest in privacy."

Richmond Newspapers was extended even further in another Press-Enterprise case two years later, **Press-Enterprise Co. v. Superior Court**, 478 U.S. 1 (1986) (Press-Enterprise II). Relying entirely on the First Amendment, the Court held that a newspaper had a right of access to the transcripts of a preliminary hearing in a criminal case, despite the objections of the trial judge, the prosecutor and the defendant, all of whom believed that pretrial publicity would jeopardize the defendant's right to a fair trial. Writing for the Court, Chief Justice BURGER refused to view the right of access and the right to a fair trial as necessarily in tension. Although the defendant clearly had a right to a fair trial, "one of the important means of assuring a fair trial is that the process be open to neutral observers." He went on to conclude that the preliminary hearing in a criminal case should be treated as a trial for First Amendment access purposes: "[T]he First Amendment question cannot be resolved solely on the label we give the event, i.e., 'trial' or otherwise, particularly where the preliminary hearing functions much like a full scale trial." Because of a tradition of access to preliminary hearings of the type at issue here and because public access plays a positive and important role in the functioning of the process (since "the preliminary hearing is often the final and most important step in the criminal proceeding"), there was a presumptive First Amendment right of access here. It followed that access could not be denied in the absence of specific findings that there was a substantial probability of injury to the accused's right to a fair trial and that there were no reasonable alternatives to closure adequate to protect the defendant's rights: "The First Amendment right of access cannot be overcome by the conclusory assertion that publicity might deprive the defendant of [a fair trial]." Justice STEVENS, joined in part by Justice Rehnquist, dissented: "[The] freedom to obtain information that the Government has a legitimate interest in not disclosing [is] far narrower than the freedom to disseminate information. [In] this case, the risk of prejudice to the defendant's right to a fair trial is perfectly obvious," and "that risk is far more significant than the countervailing interest in publishing the transcript of the preliminary hearing sooner rather than later. [I] fear that today's decision will simply further unsettle the law in this area."

5. *Press interference with judicial proceedings.* Is the government interest in the administration of justice ever sufficient to justify punishing publication, as opposed to excluding the press from judicial proceedings? In **Landmark Communications, Inc. v. Virginia**, 435 U.S. 829 (1978), the Court invalidated the conviction of a newspaper publisher for printing an accurate report of a pending inquiry by the Virginia Judicial Inquiry and Review Commission that had identified the state judge under investigation. A state law deemed information before the Commission confidential and made disclosure a crime. Chief Justice BURGER, writing for the Court, noted that the information published lay near "the core of the First Amendment" and that the "interests advanced by the imposition of criminal sanctions [were] insufficient to justify the actual and potential encroachments on freedom of speech and of the press." Noting that the operation of judicial inquiry commissions, like the operation of the judicial system itself, was a matter of public interest, he insisted that the State's "legitimate" interests were not "sufficient to justify the subsequent punishment of speech at issue here." The asserted interests were promoting efficient Commission proceedings, protecting the reputation of Virginia's judges, and maintaining the institutional integrity of its courts. In the course of his discussion, Chief Justice Burger commented that "injury to official reputation is an insufficient reason 'for repressing speech that would otherwise be free.' "

In Landmark, the Court relied heavily on a line of cases involving the application of contempt sanctions to publications, even though the state sanctions in Landmark rested on a legislative finding of clear and present danger rather than on the inherent contempt power of the courts. That line of cases began with **Bridges v. California**, 314 U.S. 252 (1941), which reversed contempt convictions in two companion cases. In the first, a newspaper, the Los Angeles Times, was found guilty of contempt for publishing editorials about the pending sentencing of two union members who had previously been convicted of assaulting nonunion workers. One editorial, for example, criticized the defendants as "thugs" and "gorillas," urged the judge to sentence them to San Quentin, and stated that the judge would "make a serious mistake if he grants probation." In the second, union leader Harry Bridges—while a motion for a new trial in a labor dispute was pending—had caused the newspaper publication of his telegram to the Secretary of Labor threatening a strike if the "outrageous" court decision were enforced. The newspaper and Bridges were convicted of contempt. The lower courts had rested their contempt findings on the "tendency" of the publications to interfere with the "orderly administration of justice." Justice BLACK's majority opinion in the 5–4 decision concluded that punishment was permissible only where there was a clear and present danger that justice would be obstructed, and described the clear and present danger standard as "a working principle that the substantive evil must be extremely serious and the degree of imminence extremely high before utterances can be punished." Justice FRANKFURTER's dissent stated: "A trial is not 'a free trade in ideas.' "

In **Pennekamp v. Florida**, 328 U.S. 331 (1946), the Court reaffirmed that the "essential right of the courts to be free of intimidation and coercion [is] consonant with a recognition that freedom of the press must be allowed in the broadest scope compatible with the supremacy of order." In Pennekamp v. Florida, a newspaper involved in an anti-vice crusade published editorials and a cartoon implying that the judges were using legal technicalities to hinder the prosecution of several rape and gambling cases. The newspaper and its associate editor, Pennekamp, were held in contempt and fined by a Florida court. As in Bridges, the Court applied the clear and present danger test and reversed.

In **Craig v. Harney**, 331 U.S. 367 (1947), the Court held that to warrant a sanction, "[t]he fires which [the expression] kindles must constitute an imminent, not merely a likely, threat to the administration of justice. The danger must not be remote or even probable; it must immediately imperil." Craig v. Harney reversed contempt convictions of a newspaper editor who, in an effort to influence an elected lay judge on a pending motion for a new trial in a private lawsuit, published inaccurate reports and unfair criticisms of the judge's action in directing a verdict for a landlord. Justice DOUGLAS's majority opinion commented: "[T]he law of contempt is not made for the protection of judges who may be sensitive to the winds of public opinion. Judges are supposed to be men of fortitude, able to thrive in a hardy climate." One of the dissenters, Justice JACKSON, retorted: "From our sheltered position, fortified by life tenure, [it] is easy to say that this local judge ought to have shown more fortitude in the face of criticism. [Of] course, the blasts of these little papers in this small community do not jolt us, but I am not so confident that we would be indifferent if a news monopoly in our entire jurisdiction should perpetrate this kind of an attack on us."

And in **Wood v. Georgia**, 370 U.S. 375 (1962), the Court invalidated a contempt citation against an elected sheriff in Bibb County, Georgia, who publicly criticized judges who had ordered a grand jury investigation into black voting practices, charging them with an attempt to intimidate black voters and analogizing them to the Ku Klux Klan. Chief Justice WARREN, writing for the Court, held that the state's showing had fallen far short of meeting the clear and present danger standard: "The type of 'danger' evidenced by the record is precisely one of the types of activity envisioned by the [framers of the First Amendment]. Men are entitled to speak as they please on matters vital to them; errors in judgment or unsubstantiated opinions may be exposed, of course, but not through punishment for contempt for the expression. [In] the absence of some other showing of a substantive evil actually designed to impede the course of justice, [his] utterances are entitled to be protected." Justice HARLAN, joined by Justice Clark, dissented, distinguishing Bridges, Pennekamp and Harney on the ground that here the speaker was an elected official and his intended audience a jury rather than a presumably hardier judge.

In Landmark, Chief Justice Burger found the state courts' efforts to distinguish the Bridges line of cases "unpersuasive" and added: "The threat to the administration of justice posed by the speech and publications in Bridges [et al.] was, if anything, more direct and substantial than the threat posed by Landmark's article."

6. ***Press access to sensitive government information.*** In 2010, WikiLeaks, an online news organization that focuses on making sensitive

and classified government documents publicly available, set off a firestorm by releasing hundreds of cables from U.S. embassies and a series of government documents describing the war in Afghanistan known as the Afghan War Diary to established news outlets including the New York Times and the Guardian. Army private Bradley Manning, the source of many of the documents disclosed in 2010, has been charged and tried in military court for giving more than 250,000 documents to WikiLeaks. The United States has not brought charges against the founder and editor-in-chief of WikiLeaks, Julian Assange.

Three years later, a flurry of leaks by former NSA contractor Edward Snowden focused attention once more on the role of the press. Snowden handed over more than 10,000 classified NSA documents to reporters at the Guardian, New York Times, and Washington Post that revealed vast data collection and surveillance programs run by the NSA. Leaked documents also disclosed that the United States had spied on Britain, France, Germany, and China, as well as 114 high-ranking world leaders. The Justice Department charged Snowden, who fled to Russia seeking temporary asylum, with violation of the Espionage Act but did not file charges against the journalists who published the leaks.

Could the U.S. bring charges against Assange or the Snowden journalists consistent with the freedom of the press? For an argument that such a prosecution would violate the freedom of the press and should be protected under First Amendment values, see Yochai Benkler, "A Free Irresponsible Press: Wikileaks and the Battle Over the Soul of the Networked Fourth Estate," 46 Harv. C.R.-C.L. L. Rev. 311 (2011).

Recall Bartnicki v. Vopper (2001; p. 95), in which Justice Stevens wrote for the majority that, "As a general matter, 'state action to punish the publication of truthful information seldom can satisfy constitutional standards.' [And] 'if a newspaper lawfully obtains truthful information about a matter of public significance then state officials may not constitutionally punish publication of the information, absent a need . . . of the highest order.' [We have not] resolve[d] the question 'whether, in cases where information has been acquired *unlawfully* by a newspaper or by a source, government may ever punish not only the unlawful acquisition, but the ensuing publication as well.' " Would the prosecution of Assange or other journalists raise precisely that question? What result?

GOVERNMENTAL DEMANDS FOR INFORMATION FROM THE PRESS

Restraints against publication are not the only sanctions that may confront the press because of information in its possession. The materials that follow arise from situations in which government, typically in the interest of law enforcement, demands that journalists disclose information they have obtained in the course of their newsgathering activities. Can the First Amendment be read to grant to journalists a special immunity from governmental inquiries? The Branzburg case raises that question in the context of grand jury investigations. The Zurcher case involves a claimed press privilege against newsroom searches based on ex parte warrants.

Branzburg v. Hayes

408 U.S. 665, 92 S. Ct. 2646, 33 L. Ed. 2d 626 (1972).

[Branzburg arose from the claims of three journalists: Branzburg, Pappas, and Caldwell. Branzburg, a Louisville reporter, had written articles about drug activities he had observed. He declined to testify before a state grand jury, refusing to identify the persons he had seen possessing marijuana or making hashish. Pappas, a Massachusetts television reporter covering a "civil disorder," was allowed to remain in Black Panther headquarters for several hours on the condition that he disclose nothing. He broadcast no report and refused to tell a grand jury about what had taken place inside the headquarters. Caldwell was a New York Times reporter who had written articles about the Black Panthers after interviewing their leaders. He refused to appear before a federal grand jury investigating "possible violations of a number of criminal statutes" (including those protecting the President against assassination). The trial court issued a protective order stating that he was not required to reveal confidential information unless the government showed "a compelling national interest" in his testimony "which cannot be served by any alternative means." Caldwell thought that limited privilege inadequate, refused to appear, and was sentenced for contempt. Caldwell's conviction was set aside by the Court of Appeals. The Branzburg and Pappas convictions were affirmed by state courts. The reporters sought a conditional privilege that would have barred their mandatory appearance before the grand jury unless the government could demonstrate that they possessed information relevant to a crime and that the information they possessed was unavailable from other sources. The Supreme Court rejected their arguments.]

■ Opinion of the Court by JUSTICE WHITE.

The issue in these cases is whether requiring newsmen to appear and testify before state or federal grand juries abridges the freedom of speech and press guaranteed by the First Amendment. We hold that it does not.

[The journalists] press First Amendment claims that may be simply put: that to gather news it is often necessary to agree either not to identify the source of information published or to publish only part of the facts revealed, or both; that if the reporter is nevertheless forced to reveal these confidences to a grand jury, the source so identified and other confidential sources of other reporters will be measurably deterred from furnishing publishable information, all to the detriment of the free flow of information protected by the First Amendment.

[News] gathering [qualifies] for First Amendment protection; without some protection for seeking out the news, freedom of the press could be eviscerated. But these cases involve no intrusions upon speech or assembly, [and] no penalty, civil or criminal, related to the content of published material, is at issue here. The use of confidential sources by the press is not forbidden or restricted. [No] attempt is made to require the press to publish its sources of information or indiscriminately to disclose them on request. The sole issue [is] the obligation of reporters to respond to grand jury subpoenas as other citizens do and to answer questions relevant to an investigation into the commission of crime. [The Constitution does not protect] the average citizen from disclosing to a grand jury information that he has received in confidence. The claim is, however, that reporters are [exempt].

[The] great weight of authority is that newsmen are not exempt from the normal duty of appearing before a grand jury and answering questions relevant to a criminal [investigation]. The prevailing constitutional view of the newsman's privilege is very much rooted in the ancient role of the grand jury. [I]ts investigative powers are necessarily broad. [The] longstanding principle that "the public has a right to every man's evidence," except for those persons protected by a constitutional, common law, or statutory privilege, is particularly applicable to grand jury proceedings. A [minority] of States have provided newsmen a statutory privilege of varying breadth; [none] has been provided by federal statute.

[We] are asked to [interpret] the First Amendment to grant newsmen a testimonial privilege that other citizens do not enjoy. This we decline to do. [On] the records now before us, we perceive no basis for holding that the public interest in law enforcement and in ensuring effective grand jury proceedings is insufficient to override the consequential, but uncertain, burden on news gathering which is said to result from insisting that reporters, like other citizens, respond to relevant questions put to them in the course of a valid grand jury investigation or criminal trial. This conclusion [does not] threaten the vast bulk of confidential relationships between reporters and their sources. [Only] where news sources themselves are implicated in crime or possess information relevant to the grand jury's task need they or the reporter be concerned about grand jury subpoenas. Nothing before us indicates that a large number or percentage of *all* confidential news sources fall into either category and would in any way be deterred by our [holding].

There remain those situations where a source is not engaged in criminal conduct but has information suggesting illegal conduct by others. Newsmen frequently receive information from such sources pursuant to a tacit or express agreement to withhold the source's name and suppress any information that the source wishes not published. [The] argument that the flow of news will be diminished by compelling reporters to aid the grand jury in a criminal investigation is not irrational, nor are the records before us silent on the matter. But we remain unclear how often and to what extent informers are actually deterred from furnishing information when newsmen are forced to testify before a grand jury. [The] evidence fails to demonstrate that there would be a significant constriction of the flow of news to the public if this Court reaffirms the prior common-law and constitutional rule regarding the testimonial obligations of newsmen. Estimates of the inhibiting effect of such subpoenas on the willingness of informants to make disclosures to newsmen are widely divergent and to a great extent speculative. It would be difficult to canvass the views of the informants themselves; surveys of reporters on this topic are chiefly opinions of predicted informant behavior and must be viewed in the light of the professional self-interest of the interviewees. [Accepting] the fact, however, that an undetermined number of informants not themselves implicated in crime will nevertheless [refuse] to talk to newsmen if they fear identification by a reporter in an official investigation, we cannot accept the argument that the public interest in possible future news about crime from undisclosed, unverified sources must take precedence over the public interest in pursuing and prosecuting those crimes reported to the press by informants and in thus deterring the commission of such crimes in the [future].

We are admonished that refusal to provide a First Amendment reporter's privilege will undermine the freedom of the press to collect and disseminate news. But this is not the lesson history teaches us. [From] the beginning of our country the press has operated without constitutional protection for press informants, and the press has flourished. [It] is said that currently press subpoenas have multiplied, that mutual distrust and tension between press and officialdom have increased, that reporting styles have changed, and that there is now more need for confidential sources. [These] developments, even if true, are treacherous grounds for a far-reaching interpretation of the [First Amendment].

[The] requirements of those cases [e.g., NAACP v. Alabama] which hold that a State's interest must be "compelling" or "paramount" to justify even an indirect burden on First Amendment rights, are also met here. As we have indicated, the investigation of crime by the grand jury implements a fundamental governmental role of securing the safety of the person and property of the [citizen]. If the test is that the government "convincingly show a substantial relation between the information sought and a subject of overriding and compelling state interest" it is quite apparent (1) that the State has the necessary interests in extirpating the traffic in illegal drugs, in forestalling assassination attempts on the President, and in preventing the community from being disrupted by violent disorders endangering both persons and property; and (2) that, based on the stories Branzburg and Caldwell wrote and Pappas' admitted conduct, the grand jury called these reporters as they would others—because it was likely that they could supply information to help the government determine whether illegal conduct had occurred and, if it had, whether there was sufficient evidence to return an indictment.

We are unwilling to embark the judiciary on [the] administration of a constitutional newsman's privilege[, which] would present practical and conceptual difficulties of a high order. Sooner or later, it would be necessary to define those categories of newsmen who qualified for the privilege, a questionable procedure in light of the traditional doctrine that liberty of the press is the right of the lonely pamphleteer [just] as much as of the large metropolitan publisher who utilizes the latest photocomposition methods. [Almost] any author may quite accurately assert that he is contributing to the flow of information to the public, that he relies on confidential sources of information, and that these sources will be silenced if he is forced to make disclosures before a grand jury. [In] each instance where a reporter is subpoenaed to testify, the courts would also be embroiled in preliminary factual and legal determinations with respect to whether the proper predicate had been laid for the reporter's appearance. [In] the end, by considering whether enforcement of a particular law served a "compelling" governmental interest, the courts would be inextricably involved in distinguishing between the value of enforcing different criminal laws. [At] the federal level, Congress has freedom to determine whether a statutory newsman's privilege is necessary and desirable and to fashion standards and rules as narrow or broad as deemed necessary [and], equally important, to re-fashion those rules as experience from time to time may dictate. There is also merit in leaving state legislatures free, within First Amendment limits, to fashion their own standards. [In addition], there is much force in the pragmatic view that the press has at its disposal powerful mechanisms of communication and is far from helpless to protect itself from harassment or substantial [harm].

[Finally,] news gathering is not without its First Amendment protections, and grand jury investigations, if instituted or conducted other than in good faith, would pose wholly different issues for resolution under the First Amendment. Official harassment of the press undertaken not for purposes of law enforcement but to disrupt a reporter's relationship with his news sources would have no justification. Grand juries are subject to judicial control and subpoenas to motions to quash. We do not expect courts will forget that grand juries must operate within the limits of the First Amendment as well as the Fifth.

■ JUSTICE POWELL, concurring in the opinion of the Court.

I add this brief statement to emphasize what seems to me to be the limited nature of the Court's holding. The Court does not hold that newsmen, subpoenaed to testify before a grand jury, are without constitutional rights with respect to the gathering of news or in safeguarding their sources. [As] indicated in the concluding portion of the opinion, the Court states that no harassment of newsmen will be tolerated. If a newsman believes that the grand jury investigation is not being conducted in good faith he is not without remedy. Indeed, if the newsman is called upon to give information bearing only a remote and tenuous relationship to the subject of the investigation, or if he has some other reason to believe that his testimony implicates confidential source relationships without a legitimate need of law enforcement, he will have access to the Court on a motion to quash and an appropriate protective order may be entered. The asserted claim to privilege should be judged on its facts by the striking of a proper balance between freedom of the press and the obligation of all citizens to give relevant testimony with respect to criminal conduct. The balance of these vital constitutional and societal interests on a case-by-case basis accords with the tried and traditional way of adjudicating such questions. In short, the courts will be available to newsmen under circumstances where legitimate First Amendment interests require protection.

■ JUSTICE STEWART, with whom JUSTICES BRENNAN and MARSHALL join, dissenting.

The Court's crabbed view of the First Amendment reflects a disturbing insensitivity to the critical role of an independent press in our society. [While] Justice Powell's enigmatic concurring opinion gives some hope of a more flexible view in the future, the Court in these cases holds that a newsman has no First Amendment right to protect his sources when called before a grand jury. The Court thus invites state and federal authorities to undermine the historic independence of the press by attempting to annex the journalistic profession as an investigative arm of [government].

The reporter's constitutional right to a confidential relationship with his source stems from the broad societal interest in a full and free flow of information to the public. It is this basic concern that underlies the Constitution's protection of a free press. [A] corollary of the right to publish must be the right to gather news. [This right] implies, in turn, a right to a confidential relationship between a reporter and his source. [This] follows as a matter of simple logic once three factual predicates are recognized: (1) newsmen require informants to gather news; (2) confidentiality [is] essential to the creation and maintenance of a news-gathering relationship with informants; and (3) the existence of an unbridled subpoena power [will] either deter sources from divulging information or deter reporters from gathering and publishing information. After today's decision, the potential [source must] choose between risking exposure by giving information or avoiding the risk by remaining [silent].

The impairment of the flow of news cannot, of course, be proved with scientific precision, as the Court seems to demand. [But] we have never before demanded that First Amendment rights rest on elaborate empirical studies demonstrating beyond any conceivable doubt that deterrent effects [exist]. Rather, on the basis of common sense and available information, we have asked, often implicitly, (1) whether there was a rational connection between the cause (the governmental action) and the effect (the deterrence or impairment of First Amendment activity) and (2) whether the effect would occur with some regularity, i.e., would not be de minimis. And in making this determination, we have shown a special solicitude towards the "indispensable liberties" protected by the First Amendment. [Once] this threshold inquiry has been satisfied, we have then examined the competing interests in determining whether there is an unconstitutional infringement of First Amendment freedoms. [E.g., NAACP v. Alabama.] Surely the analogous claim of deterrence here is as securely grounded in evidence and common sense as the claims in [earlier cases], although the Court calls the claim "speculative." [To] require any greater burden of proof is to shirk our duty to protect values securely embedded in the Constitution. [We] cannot escape the conclusion that when neither the reporter nor his source can rely on the shield of confidentiality against unrestrained use of the grand jury's subpoena power, valuable information will not be published and the public dialogue will inevitably be impoverished.

[As our cases hold with respect to witnesses called before legislative investigations, I would hold that,] when a reporter is asked to appear before a grand jury and reveal confidences, [the] government must (1) show that there is probable cause to believe that the newsman has information which is clearly relevant to a specific probable violation of law; (2) demonstrate that the information sought cannot be obtained by alternative means less destructive of First Amendment rights; and (3) demonstrate a compelling and overriding interest in the information. [Both] the "probable cause" and "alternative means" requirements [would] serve the vital function of mediating between the public interest in the administration of justice and the constitutional protection of the full flow of information. These requirements would avoid a direct conflict between these competing concerns, and they would generally provide adequate protection for newsmen. No doubt the courts would be required to make some delicate judgments in working out this accommodation. But that, after all, is the function of courts of law. Better such judgments, however difficult, than the simplistic and stultifying absolutism adopted by the Court in denying any force to the First Amendment in these cases.

■ JUSTICE DOUGLAS, dissenting.

[There] is no "compelling need" that can be shown which qualifies the reporter's immunity from appearing or testifying before a grand jury, unless the reporter himself is implicated in a crime. His immunity in my view [is] quite complete.

————

JOURNALISTIC PRIVILEGE AFTER BRANZBURG

1. ***The aftermath of Branzburg.*** In response to Branzburg, numerous bills to establish a journalists' privilege were introduced in state legislatures and in Congress. Some forty states and the District of Columbia have enacted "press shield" laws providing at least a qualified free speech privilege against compelled revelation of journalists' anonymous sources. A federal press shield law pending in Congress as of 2010 would bar the compelled disclosure from news providers in federal proceedings of information identifying confidential sources absent a government showing of need and exhaustion and a judicial balancing of the public interest in news gathering and dissemination against the public interest in compelling disclosure (with the burden on the press in criminal cases and on the government in civil cases).

Many lower courts after Branzburg emphasized Justice Powell's concurrence rather than Justice White's opinion for the Court, finding in the concurrence some ground for affording journalists greater-than-normal protection from compulsion to divulge confidential sources. In recent years, however, federal prosecutors have more aggressively demanded confidential source information from journalists in connection with pending criminal investigations, including with respect to leaks of classified or otherwise secret government information, and courts have proved more deferential to the prosecution, reading Branzburg more in line with Justice White's than Justice Powell's opinion. See, e.g., In re Grand Jury Subpoena: Judith Miller, 397 F.3d 964 (D.C. Cir. 2005) (rejecting a claim of journalist privilege against a grand jury subpoena to reveal confidential sources in connection with investigation of possible illegal exposure of an undercover CIA officer's identity).

How should the balance be struck between government need in criminal cases and the press interest in the free flow of information given on a confidential basis? Should courts be permitted to weigh the relative value of the story? Or to look only at the government's need and the extent to which it has exhausted alternative sources? In the Judith Miller case, supra, Judge David Tatel's influential concurrence in the judgment suggested that a court deciding whether to enforce a press privilege in a leak case "must weigh the public interest in compelling disclosure, measured by the harm the leak caused, against the public interest in newsgathering, measured by the leaked information's value." Should courts be permitted thus to balance when leaked information does more harm than good? Are courts institutionally capable of making such judgments?

To what extent is any such balance changed by the rise of the internet? At the time Branzburg was decided, journalism was concentrated in large, organized institutional outlets such as daily newspapers and broadcasting networks. Such organizations adhered to codes and practice of self-regulation such as corroboration and sourcing requirements. With the rise of the internet, news is communicated by a vast array of decentralized sources. Should non-professional "journalists" such as bloggers be permitted to invoke any privilege against disclosure of anonymous sources? How should the scope of any statutory or constitutional reporter's privilege be defined? For discussion, see Papandrea, "Citizen Journalism and the Reporter's Privilege," 91 Minn. L. Rev. 515 (2007).

2.   *Searches of newsrooms pursuant to warrants.* The Court once more rejected a press claim for special protection from law enforcement demands for information in **Zurcher v. Stanford Daily**, 436 U.S. 547 (1978). In that case, the Court upheld execution of a warrant authorizing a search of a campus newspaper office for photographs of a violent demonstration.[1] The police obtained an ex parte warrant for a search of the Daily's offices for pictures and negatives that might help them to identify the demonstrators. The Daily's civil suit claimed that the police decision to engage in a search rather than proceed by subpoena violated the First Amendment. In rejecting the claim, Justice WHITE's majority opinion emphasized the Fourth Amendment rather than the First. His opinion in 'Zurcher was as skeptical as that in Branzburg about press allegations of chilling effects and risks to confidential sources. His reasoning contained only one sentence suggesting that First Amendment considerations be taken into account in applying Fourth Amendment search warrant criteria in the media context: "[Prior cases insist] that courts apply the warrant requirements with particular exactitude when First Amendment interests would be endangered by the search."

As in Branzburg, Justice POWELL's concurrence built upon a passing remark in the prevailing opinion and elaborated the relevance of First Amendment concerns, stating: "This is not to say that a warrant which would be sufficient to support the search of an apartment or an automobile necessarily would be reasonable in supporting the search of a newspaper office. [While] there is no justification for the establishment of a separate Fourth Amendment procedure for the press, a magistrate asked to issue a warrant for the search of press offices can and should take cognizance of the independent values protected by the First Amendment—such as those highlighted by Mr. Justice Stewart—when he weighs such factors." And he added in a footnote that his separate opinion here, like that in Branzburg, could be read as supporting the view "that under the warrant requirement of the Fourth Amendment, the magistrate should consider the values of a free press as well as the societal interests in enforcing the criminal law." Justice STEWART's dissent argued that warrants to search newspaper offices should issue only when a magistrate finds probable cause to believe that it would be impractical to obtain the evidence by a subpoena. He emphasized that subpoena applications permit the press to obtain an adversary hearing prior to producing the information, by making a motion to quash; ex parte warrants, by contrast, provide "no opportunity to challenge the necessity for the search until after it has occurred and the constitutional protection of the newspaper has been irretrievably invaded."

As a result of legislative efforts that began in the wake of the Stanford Daily decision, Congress adopted the Privacy Protection Act in 1980. 42 U.S.C. § 2000aa. The Act requires state and federal law enforcement officers to use subpoena procedures to obtain documents from persons engaged in the communications industry. Search warrants are permitted only in

---

[1]   The division on the Court was strikingly similar to that in Branzburg. Justice Powell once again supplied the critical vote for the majority with a separate concurrence putting a more speech-protective gloss on Justice White's opinion; Justice Stewart once again dissented on First Amendment grounds, this time joined only by Justice Marshall. (Justice Brennan did not participate in the case.) Justice Stevens, who had replaced Justice Douglas since Branzburg, submitted a separate dissent, based on the Fourth Amendment.

exceptional circumstances, such as when there is a fear that the needed materials would be destroyed.

––––––––

LAWS SINGLING OUT THE PRESS

In the discussion in this section so far, the Court has tended to treat the press on a par with other speakers for First Amendment purposes, and declined to carve out special protections for the institutional media. In one line of cases, however, the Court has suggested that even a content-neutral law requires special scrutiny when it singles out the press, or a small subset of the press, for special treatment. In the case that follows, this result obtained even where the special treatment arguably benefited the press:

––––––––

Minneapolis Star & Tribune Co. v. Minnesota Comm'r of Revenue

460 U.S. 575, 103 S. Ct. 1365, 75 L. Ed. 2d 295 (1983).

■ JUSTICE O'CONNOR delivered the opinion of the Court.

This case presents the question of a State's power to impose a special tax on the press and, by enacting exemptions, to limit its effect to only a few newspapers.

I.   Since 1967, Minnesota has imposed a sales tax on most sales of goods. In general, the tax applies only to retail sales. [As] part of this general system of taxation and in support of the sales tax, Minnesota also enacted a tax on the "privilege of using, storing or consuming in Minnesota tangible personal property." This use tax applies to any nonexempt tangible personal property unless the sales tax was paid on the sales price. Like the classic use tax, this use tax protects the State's sales tax by eliminating the residents' incentive to travel to States with lower sales taxes to buy goods rather than buying them in Minnesota.

The appellant [is] the publisher of a morning [and] an evening newspaper (until 1982) in Minneapolis. From 1967 until 1971, it enjoyed an exemption from the sales and use tax provided by Minnesota for periodic publications. In 1971, however, while leaving the exemption from the sales tax in place, the legislature amended the scheme to impose a "use tax" on the cost of paper and ink products consumed in the production of a publication. Ink and paper used in publications became the only items subject to the use tax that were components of goods to be sold at retail. In 1974, the legislature again amended the statute, this time to exempt the first $100,000 worth of ink and paper consumed by a publication in any calendar year, in effect giving each publication an annual tax credit of $4,000. Publications remained exempt from the sales tax. After the enactment of the $100,000 exemption, 11 publishers, producing 14 of the 388 paid circulation newspapers in the State, incurred a tax liability in 1974. [Appellant] was one of the 11, and, of the $893,355 collected, it paid $608,634, or roughly two-thirds of the total revenue raised by the tax. In 1975, 13 publishers, producing 16 out of 374 paid circulation papers, paid a tax. That year, [appellant] again bore roughly two-thirds of the total receipts from the use tax on ink and paper. [Appellant] instituted this action to seek a refund of the use taxes it paid from January 1, 1974 to May 31, 1975. [The] Minnesota Supreme Court upheld the [tax]. [The Court held that this taxing system violated appellant's First Amendment rights.]

II.   Star Tribune argues that we must strike this tax on the authority of Grosjean v. American Press Co., 297 U.S. 233 (1936). Although there are similarities, [we] agree with the State that Grosjean is not controlling. In Grosjean, [Louisiana] imposed a license tax of 2% of the gross receipts from the sale of advertising on all newspapers with a weekly circulation above 20,000. Out of at least 124 publishers in the State, only 13 were subject to the tax. After noting that the tax was "single in kind" and that keying the tax to circulation curtailed the flow of information, this Court held the tax invalid as an abridgment of the freedom of the press. [The argument of the publishers] emphasized the events leading up to the tax and the contemporary political climate in Louisiana. All but one of the large papers subject to the tax had "ganged up" on Senator Huey Long, and a circular distributed by Long and the governor to each member of the state legislature described "lying newspapers" as conducting "a vicious campaign" and the tax as "a tax on lying." [Although] the Court's opinion did not describe this history, it stated, "[The tax] is bad because, in the light of its history and of its present setting, it is seen to be a deliberate and calculated device in the guise of a tax to limit the circulation of information," an explanation that suggests that the motivation of the legislature may have been significant. Our subsequent cases have not been consistent in their reading of Grosjean on this point. [We] think that the result in Grosjean may have been attributable in part to the perception on the part of the Court that the state imposed the tax with an intent to penalize a selected group of newspapers. In the case currently before us, however, there is no legislative history and no indication, apart from the structure of the tax itself, of any impermissible or censorial motive on the part of the legislature. We cannot resolve the case by simple citation to Grosjean. Instead, we must analyze the problem anew under the general principles of the First Amendment.

III.   Clearly, the First Amendment does not prohibit all regulation of the press. It is beyond dispute that [government] can subject newspapers to generally applicable economic regulations without creating constitutional problems. Minnesota, however, has not chosen to apply its general sales and use tax to newspapers. Instead, it has created a special tax that applies only to certain publications protected by the First Amendment. Although the State argues now that the tax on paper and ink is part of the general scheme of taxation, the use tax provision is facially discriminatory, singling out publications for treatment that [is] unique in Minnesota tax law.

[By] creating this special use tax, [Minnesota] has singled out the press for special treatment. We then must determine whether the First Amendment permits such special taxation. A tax that burdens rights protected by the First Amendment cannot stand unless the burden is necessary to achieve an overriding governmental interest.

[There] is substantial evidence that differential taxation of the press would have troubled the Framers of the First Amendment. [The] fears of the [Framers] were well-founded. A power to tax differentially, as opposed to a power to tax generally, gives a government a powerful weapon against the taxpayer selected. When the State imposes a generally applicable tax, there is little cause for concern. We need not fear that a government will destroy a selected group of taxpayers by burdensome taxation if it must impose the same burden on the rest of its constituency. When the State singles out the press, though, the political constraints that prevent a legislature from passing crippling taxes of general applicability are weakened, and the threat of burdensome taxes becomes acute. That threat can operate as effectively as a censor to check critical comment by the press, undercutting the basic assumption of our political system that the press will often serve as an important restraint on government. [Differential] treatment, unless justified by some special characteristic of the press, suggests that the goal of the regulation is not unrelated to suppression of expression, and such a goal is presumptively unconstitutional. Differential taxation of the press, then, places such a burden on the interests protected by the First Amendment that we cannot countenance such treatment unless the State asserts a counterbalancing interest of compelling importance that it cannot achieve without differential taxation.

IV. The main interest asserted by Minnesota in this case is the raising of revenue. [Standing alone], however, it cannot justify the special treatment of the press, for an alternative means of achieving the same interest without raising concerns under the First Amendment is clearly available: the State could raise the revenue by taxing businesses generally, avoiding the censorial threat implicit in a tax that singles out the press. Addressing the concern with differential treatment, Minnesota invites us to look beyond the form of the tax to its substance. The tax is, according to the State, merely a substitute for the sales tax, which, as a generally applicable tax, would be constitutional as applied to the press. There are two fatal flaws in this reasoning. First, the State has offered no explanation of why it chose to use a substitute for the sales tax rather than the sales tax itself. [Further,] even assuming that the legislature did have valid reasons for substituting another tax for the sales tax, we are not persuaded that this tax does serve as a substitute. The State asserts that this scheme actually *favors* the press over other businesses, because the same rate of tax is applied, but, for the press, the rate applies to the cost of components rather than to the sales price. We would be hesitant to fashion a rule that automatically allowed the State to single out the press for a different method of taxation as long as the effective burden was no different from that on other taxpayers or the burden on the press was lighter than that on other businesses. One reason for this reluctance is that the very selection of the press for special treatment threatens the press not only with the current *differential* treatment, but with the possibility of subsequent differentially *more burdensome* treatment. Thus, even without actually imposing an extra burden on the press, the government might be able to achieve censorial effects, for "[t]he threat of sanctions may deter [the] exercise of [First Amendment] rights almost as potently as the actual application of sanctions." NAACP v. Button.

A second reason to avoid the proposed rule is that courts as institutions are poorly equipped to evaluate with precision the relative burdens of various methods of taxation. The complexities of factual economic proof always present a certain potential for error, and courts have little familiarity with the process of evaluating the relative economic burden of taxes. In sum, the possibility of error inherent in the proposed rule poses too great a threat to concerns at the heart of the First Amendment, and we cannot tolerate that possibility.[1] Minnesota, therefore, has offered no adequate justification for the special treatment of newspapers.

V.   Minnesota's ink and paper tax violates the First Amendment not only because it singles out the press, but also because it targets a small group of newspapers. The effect of the $100,000 exemption [is] that only a handful of publishers pay any tax at [all]. The State explains this exemption as part of a policy favoring an "equitable" tax system, although there are no comparable exemptions for small enterprises outside the press. [Whatever] the motive of the legislature in this case, we think that recognizing a power in the State not only to single out the press but also to tailor the tax so that it singles out a few members of the press presents such a potential for abuse that no interest suggested by Minnesota can justify the [scheme].

VI. We need not and do not impugn the motives of the Minnesota legislature in passing the ink and paper tax. Illicit legislative intent is not the sine qua non of a violation of the First Amendment. We have long recognized that even regulations aimed at proper governmental concerns can restrict unduly the exercise of rights protected by the First Amendment. A tax that singles out the press [places] a heavy burden on the State to justify its action. Since Minnesota has offered no satisfactory justification for its tax on the use of ink and paper, the tax violates the First Amendment. [Reversed.]

■ JUSTICE REHNQUIST, dissenting.

Today we learn from the Court that a State runs afoul of the First Amendment [where] the State structures its taxing system to the advantage of newspapers. [The Court recognizes that Minnesota] could avoid constitutional problems by imposing on newspapers the 4% sales tax that it imposes on other retailers. Rather than impose such a tax, however, the Minnesota legislature decided to provide newspapers with an exemption from the sales tax and impose a 4% use tax on ink and paper; thus, while both taxes are part of one [system], newspapers are classified differently within that system. The problem the Court finds too difficult to deal with is whether this difference in treatment results in a significant burden on newspapers. [Had] a 4% sales tax been imposed, the Minneapolis Star & Tribune would have been liable for $1,859,950 in 1974. The same "complexities of factual economic proof" can be analyzed for 1975. [Had] the sales tax been imposed, as the Court agrees would have been permissible, the Minneapolis Star & Tribune's liability for 1974 and 1975 would have been $3,685,092. The record further indicates that the Minneapolis Star & Tribune paid $608,634 in use taxes in 1974 and $636,113 in 1975—a total liability of $1,244,747. We need no expert testimony from modern day Euclids or Einsteins to determine that the $1,224,747 paid in use taxes is significantly less burdensome than the $3,685,092 that could have been levied by a sales tax. A fortiori, the Minnesota taxing scheme which singles

---

[1]   If a State employed the same *method* of taxation but applied a lower *rate* to the press, so that there could be no doubt that the legislature was not singling out the press to bear a more burdensome tax, we would, of course, be in a position to evaluate the relative burdens. And, given the clarity of the relative burdens, as well as the rule that differential methods of taxation are not automatically permissible if less burdensome, a lower tax rate for the press would not raise the threat that the legislature might later impose an extra burden that would escape detection by the courts. Thus, our decision does not, as the dissent suggests, require Minnesota to impose a greater tax burden on publications. [Footnote by Justice O'Connor.]

out newspapers for "different treatment" has benefited, not burdened, the "freedom of speech, [and] of the press."

[No] First Amendment issue is raised unless First Amendment rights have been [infringed]. [The] State is required to show that its taxing scheme is rational. But in this case that showing can be made easily. [So] long as the State can find another way to collect revenue from the newspapers, imposing a sales tax on newspapers would be to no one's advantage; not the newspaper and its distributors who would have to collect the tax, not the State who would have to enforce collection, and not the consumer who would have to pay for the paper in odd amounts. The reasonable alternative Minnesota chose was to impose the use tax on ink and paper.

[The] Court finds in very summary fashion that the exemption newspapers receive for the first $100,000 of ink and paper used also violates the [First Amendment]. I cannot agree. [The] exemption is in effect a $4,000 credit which benefits all newspapers. Minneapolis Star & Tribune was benefited to the amount of $16,000 in the two years in question; $4,000 each year for its morning paper and $4,000 each year for its evening paper. Absent any improper motive on the part of the Minnesota legislature in drawing the limits of this exemption, it cannot be construed as violating the First Amendment. [There] is no reason to conclude that the State, in drafting the $4,000 credit, acted other than reasonably and rationally to fit its sales and use tax scheme to its own local needs and usages. To collect from newspapers their fair share of taxes under the sales and use tax scheme and at the same time avoid abridging the freedoms of speech and press, the Court holds today that Minnesota must subject newspapers to millions of additional dollars in sales tax liability. Certainly this is a hollow victory for the newspapers and I seriously doubt the Court's conclusion that this result would have been intended by the ["Framers of the First Amendment"]. [Justice White concurred in part and dissented in part; Justice Blackmun joined the majority opinion except for one footnote.]

THE IMPLICATIONS AND LIMITS OF MINNEAPOLIS STAR

1. *Is the press special?* The Court in Minneapolis Star Tribune emphasizes the dangers involved in singling out "the press" for special regulatory treatment. Yet, as the preceding materials in this section illustrate, the Court typically has refused to recognize claims of the press to special protection beyond that available to anyone who exercises First Amendment rights by communicating information and opinion. Is the Court's focus on "the press" in Minneapolis Star Tribune therefore superfluous? Is it inconsistent with prior decisions? Or does this case suggest that in some areas the press *will* receive more protection than other claimants under the First Amendment?

If the latter reading is unwarranted and there remains nothing constitutionally special about the press, what was the Court's ground for employing strict scrutiny in Minneapolis Star Tribune? That singling out the press presumptively risks content discrimination, as exemplified by the overt bias of Huey Long in Grosjean? Does Minneapolis Star Tribune suggest that certain subjects—e.g., criticism of government in a broad sense—will receive special protection? Does Minneapolis Star Tribune treat the press as an especially highly protected format of communication? Should it be permissible, by analogy, for zoning regulations to single out bookstores or billboards for special treatment?

2. ***Slippery slopes.*** Although couched in different terms, Justice Rehnquist's objections to the majority's creation of a prophylactic rule to safeguard the press against future abuses of the taxing power raise the perennial problem of the use and misuse of "slippery slope" arguments. The same argument appears in numerous guises, including the search for a "stopping point," the fear of "a foot in the door," the question of "Where do you draw the line?," and the wariness of abuse of power. Regardless of how phrased, the point is the same—if we permit this seemingly innocuous exercise of a power, we are on a slippery slope leading inevitably to much more dangerous exercises of that same power. See generally Schauer, "Slippery Slopes," 99 Harv. L. Rev. 361 (1985).

The contrast between the majority and Justice Rehnquist's dissent makes Minneapolis Star an appropriate vehicle for reconsidering under what circumstances, if any, a currently innocuous exercise of power should be precluded for fear that it will lead to a far less innocuous abuse. Is Court review of every abuse likely? Will such review be timely? If the Court cannot check every abuse, can lower courts serve that function? Can nonjudicial bodies be trusted to follow the spirit as well as the letter of constitutional decisions? But does eagerness to decide cases on the basis of where a currently innocuous policy might lead fly in the face of the Court's reluctance to decide anything other than the case before it? Is a slippery slope argument a variant of an advisory opinion, in the sense that the basis for the decision is a hypothetical scenario that may never occur? Could we not prevent all abuses of power by granting no power whatsoever?

3. ***Antimedia, intramedium and intermedia discrimination.*** In **Arkansas Writers' Project, Inc. v. Ragland**, 481 U.S. 221 (1987), the Court relied on Minneapolis Star in striking down an Arkansas sales tax scheme that exempted newspapers and "religious, professional, trade and sports journals" but not other types of magazines. Part V of Justice O'Connor's opinion in Minneapolis had relied on the existence of discrimination *within* the class of publications, as opposed to distinctions between newspapers and other commodities. This more overt form of content discrimination was the basis for the Court's decision in Ragland. Justice MARSHALL found that the Arkansas exemption not only resembled the $100,000 exemption in Minneapolis Star, but also was even more troublesome because "a magazine's tax status depends entirely on its *content*." He noted that this type of content-based regulation "does not evade the strictures of the First Amendment merely because it does not burden the expression of particular *views* by specific magazines." Justice SCALIA, joined by Chief Justice Rehnquist, dissented, for reasons paralleling those articulated in Justice Rehnquist's dissent in Minneapolis Star. He argued as well that the selective tax exemption should not be subject to strict scrutiny because it amounted to a subsidy that infringed no one's rights. He commented: "Are government research grant programs or the funding activities of the Corporation for Public Broadcasting subject to strict scrutiny because they provide money for the [study] of some subjects but not others? Because there is no principled basis to distinguish the subsidization of speech in [such an area]—which we would surely uphold—from the subsidization that we strike down here, our decision today places the granting or denial of protection within our own idiosyncratic discretion."

Contrast with Arkansas Writers' Project the decision in **Leathers v. Medlock**, 499 U.S. 439 (1991), upholding a selective sales tax exemption scheme. Arkansas imposed a sales tax on most goods and services, including cable television, but exempted newspapers, magazines and direct satellite broadcast services. Cable operators and subscribers challenged the selective exemption under the First Amendment. The Court rejected the challenge. Justice O'CONNOR, writing for the Court, found Arkansas' tax scheme distinguishable from the ones struck down in Minneapolis Star and Ragland: "[Those] cases demonstrate that differential taxation of First Amendment speakers is constitutionally suspect when it threatens to suppress the expression of particular ideas or viewpoints. Absent a compelling justification, the government may not exercise its taxing power to single out the press. [A] tax is also suspect if it targets a small group of speakers. [Finally,] for reasons that are obvious, a tax will trigger heightened scrutiny under the First Amendment if it discriminates on the basis of the content of taxpayer speech.

"The Arkansas tax at issue here presents none of these types of discrimination. The Arkansas sales tax is a tax of general applicability. It applies to receipts from the sale of all tangible personal property and a broad range of services, unless within a group of specific exemptions. [The] tax does not single out the press. [Furthermore,] there is no indication in this case that Arkansas has targeted cable television in a purposeful attempt to interfere with its First Amendment activities. [Unlike] the taxes involved in Grosjean and Minneapolis Star, the Arkansas tax has not selected a narrow group to bear fully the burden of the tax. The danger from a tax scheme that targets a small number of speakers is the danger of censorship; a tax on a small number of speakers runs the risk of affecting only a limited range of views. The risk is similar to that from content-based regulation: It will distort the market for ideas. [There] is no comparable danger from a tax on the services provided by a large number of cable operators offering a wide variety of programming throughout the State. [This] is not a tax structure that resembles a penalty for particular speakers or particular ideas." Finally, Justice O'Connor rejected cable's argument that the "intermedia discrimination" effected by the tax scheme was impermissible: "Regan v. Taxation with Representation stands for the proposition that a tax scheme that discriminates among speakers does not implicate the First Amendment unless it discriminates on the basis of ideas."

Justice MARSHALL dissented, joined by Justice Blackmun. He would have found that the intermedia discrimination here triggered strict scrutiny no less than the intramedium discrimination struck down in Minneapolis Star and Ragland: "Because cable competes with members of the print and electronic media in the larger information market, the power to discriminate between these media triggers the central concern underlying the nondiscrimination principle: the risk of covert censorship. [By] imposing tax burdens that disadvantage one information medium relative to another, the State can favor those media that it likes and punish those that it dislikes. [We] have previously recognized that differential taxation within an information medium distorts the marketplace of ideas by imposing on some speakers costs not borne by their competitors. Differential taxation across different media likewise 'limits the circulation of information to which the public is entitled,' where, as here, the relevant media compete in the same information market."

In **Turner Broadcasting v. FCC,** 512 U.S. 622 (1994) (Turner I), which held that requirements that cable operators carry broadcast signals were subject only to the level of scrutiny appropriate to content-neutral regulations, the Court found no impermissible discrimination against cable operators or programmers. First, it rejected the cable *operators'* argument "that strict scrutiny applies because the must-carry provisions single out certain members of the press—here, cable operators—for disfavored treatment." Justice KENNEDY wrote for the Court: "Regulations that discriminate among media, or among different speakers within a single medium, often present serious First Amendment concerns. [Minneapolis Star, Arkansas Writers' Project.] It would be error to conclude, however, that the First Amendment mandates strict scrutiny for any speech regulation that applies to one medium (or a subset thereof) but not others. [Leathers.] As Leathers illustrates, the fact that a law singles out a certain medium, or even the press as a whole, 'is insufficient by itself to raise First Amendment concerns.' The taxes invalidated in Minneapolis Star and Arkansas Writers' Project [targeted] a small number of speakers, and thus threatened to 'distort the market for ideas.' But such heightened scrutiny is unwarranted when the differential treatment is 'justified by some special characteristic of' the particular medium being regulated. The must-carry provisions [are] justified by special characteristics of the cable medium: the bottleneck monopoly power exercised by cable operators and the dangers this power poses to the viability of broadcast television. Appellants do not argue, nor does it appear, that other media [that] transmit video programming such as [satellite] are subject to bottleneck monopoly control, or pose a demonstrable threat to the survival of broadcast television. It should come as no surprise, then, that Congress decided to impose the must-carry obligations upon cable operators only. [Moreover,] the regulations are broad-based, applying to almost all cable systems in the country, rather than just a select few. As a result, the provisions do not pose the same dangers of suppression and manipulation that were posed by the more narrowly targeted regulations in Minneapolis Star and Arkansas Writers' Project [and thus] do not call for strict scrutiny."

Second, the Court likewise rejected cable *programmers'* argument that strict scrutiny was called for "because the must-carry provisions favor one set of speakers (broadcast programmers) over another (cable programmers). [Not] all speaker-partial laws are presumed invalid. Rather, [speaker-based] laws demand strict scrutiny when they reflect the Government's preference for the substance of what the favored speakers have to say (or aversion to what the disfavored speakers have to say). [Congress] granted must-carry privileges to broadcast stations on the belief that the broadcast television industry is in economic peril due to the physical characteristics of cable transmission and the economic incentives facing the cable industry. Thus, the fact that the provisions benefit broadcasters and not cable programmers does not call for strict scrutiny under our precedents."

4. *Laws of general applicability.* In **Cohen v. Cowles Media Co.,** 501 U.S. 663 (1991), the Court held that the First Amendment did not bar an action in state court for promissory estoppel against a newspaper that breached its promise of confidentiality to a source. Dan Cohen, who worked for the Republican candidate for governor in the 1982 election, leaked to the Minneapolis Star and another paper documents indicating that a Democratic candidate for lieutenant governor had had two criminal charges brought against her. The papers promised him confidentiality, but later made the editorial judgment to identify him as the source in their stories. He was fired

by his employer as a result. Cohen sued the papers for breach of contract and fraud and won $200,000 in compensatory and $500,000 in punitive damages from a jury. The Minnesota Supreme Court found the fraud and contract theories untenable but held that the compensatory damages judgment could be sustained on a promissory estoppel theory, except that it would violate the newspapers' First Amendment rights. The Supreme Court reversed and remanded, finding no First Amendment bar to a promissory estoppel action.

Justice WHITE wrote for the Court: "Respondents [rely on a line of cases holding] that 'if a newspaper lawfully obtains truthful information about a matter of public significance then state officials may not constitutionally punish publication of the information, absent a need to further a state interest of the highest order.' [E.g., Landmark, Fla. Star.] [This] case, however, is not controlled by this line of cases but, rather, by the equally well-established line of decisions holding that generally applicable laws do not offend the First Amendment simply because their enforcement against the press has incidental effects on its ability to gather and report the news. As the cases relied on by respondents recognize, the truthful information sought to be published must have been lawfully acquired. The press may not with impunity break and enter an office or dwelling to gather news. Neither does the First Amendment relieve a newspaper reporter of the obligation shared by all citizens to respond to a grand jury subpoena and answer questions relevant to a criminal investigation, even though the reporter might be required to reveal a confidential source. [Branzburg.] The press, like others interested in publishing, may not publish copyrighted material without obeying the copyright laws. [Zacchini.] Similarly, the media must obey the National Labor Relations Act, Associated Press v. NLRB, 301 U.S. 103 (1937), and the Fair Labor Standards Act, Oklahoma Press Publishing Co. v. Walling, 327 U.S. 186 (1946); may not restrain trade in violation of the antitrust laws, Associated Press v. United States, 326 U.S. 1 (1945); Citizen Publishing Co. v. United States, 394 U.S. 131 (1969); and must pay non-discriminatory taxes, [Murdock; Minneapolis Star.] Accordingly, enforcement of such general laws against the press is not subject to stricter scrutiny than would be applied to enforcement against other persons or organizations.

"There can be little doubt that the Minnesota doctrine of promissory estoppel is a law of general applicability. It does not target or single out the press. Rather, [the] doctrine is generally applicable to the daily transactions of all the citizens of Minnesota. The First Amendment does not forbid its application to the press. [Respondents] and amici argue that permitting Cohen to maintain a cause of action for promissory estoppel will inhibit truthful reporting because news organizations will have legal incentives not to disclose a confidential source's identity even when that person's identity is itself newsworthy. [But] if this is the case, it is no more than the incidental, and constitutionally insignificant, consequence of applying to the press a generally applicable law that requires those who make certain kinds of promises to keep them."

Justice BLACKMUN, joined by Justices Marshall and Souter, dissented. He regarded the lawsuit as penalizing the content of the newspapers' speech and thus as controlled by such cases as Hustler v. Falwell: "There, we found that the use of a claim of intentional infliction of emotional distress to impose liability for the publication of a satirical critique violated the First Amendment. There was no doubt that Virginia's tort of intentional infliction of emotional distress was 'a law of general applicability' unrelated to the suppression of speech. Nonetheless, a unanimous Court found that, when used to penalize the expression of opinion, the law was subject to the strictures of the First Amendment. [As] in Hustler, the operation of Minnesota's doctrine of promissory estoppel in this case cannot be said to have a merely 'incidental' burden on speech; the publication of important political speech is the claimed violation. Thus, as in Hustler, the law may not be enforced to punish the expression of truthful information or opinion."

Justice SOUTER, joined by Justices Marshall, Blackmun and O'Connor, also dissented, finding that, even if the promissory estoppel law did have general applicability, "it [is still] necessary to articulate, measure, and compare the competing interests involved [to] determine the legitimacy of burdening constitutional interests." He emphasized the "importance of the information to public discourse" and argued that "[t]he importance of this public interest is integral to the balance that should be struck in this case. There can be no doubt that the fact of Cohen's identity expanded the universe of information relevant to the choice faced by Minnesota voters in that State's 1982 gubernatorial election, the publication of which was thus of the sort quintessentially subject to strict First Amendment. The propriety of his leak to respondents could be taken to reflect on his character, which in turn could be taken to reflect on the character of the candidate who had retained him as an adviser. An election could turn on just such a factor; if it should, I am ready to assume that it would be to the greater public good, at least over the long run."

Was the newspapers' argument in Cowles Media consistent with the journalists' argument in Branzburg? In Branzburg, the press claimed that any pressure to reveal the names of confidential sources would dry up those sources, reducing the flow of information to the public. In Cowles, the press claimed that it had a First Amendment right to reveal its sources' names, and that this revelation would serve the interest in ensuring the flow of information to the public—an argument Justice Souter endorsed in his dissent. How can both these arguments hold simultaneously? Was the press trying to have its cake and eat it too? For exploration of the issues raised in Cowles, see Levi, "Dangerous Liaisons: Seduction and Betrayal in Confidential Press-Source Relations," 43 Rutgers L. Rev. 609 (1991).

THE FIRST AMENDMENT AND THE BROADCAST MEDIA

To what extent are constitutional restrictions on regulation of the print media applicable to the broadcast media? To what extent may broadcasters be treated differently? That issue has arisen in materials covered earlier. Recall, e.g., FCC v. Pacifica (1978; p. 172), which justified regulation of an indecent radio broadcast on the ground that broadcasting is uniquely intrusive into the home and accessible to children. Recall also the emphasis on the unique nature of broadcasting in Red Lion (1969; p. 488), in which the Court permitted government to enforce rights of access to broadcasting based on the scarcity of the over-the-air spectrum.

In both Pacifica and Red Lion, the Court upheld restrictions upon broadcasters that would have been impermissible if imposed on those seeking to communicate by print or the non-broadcast spoken word. For example, the Court held, in contrast to Pacifica, that offended audiences must simply avert their eyes or ears if they saw Cohen's jacket at a courthouse or received Bolger Drug Products' condom advertisements in the mail. And the Court held, in contrast to Red Lion, that a governmentally imposed right of access violated the First Amendment rights of the Miami Herald newspaper in Tornillo (1974; p. 488). In contrast, the Court allowed government to impose greater access obligations on the broadcast media, rejecting First Amendment challenges beginning with Red Lion.

To understand the cases that follow, it is helpful to consider briefly the background of broadcast regulation. As the Court recounted in Red Lion: "Before 1927, the allocation of frequencies was left entirely to the private sector, and the result was chaos. It quickly became apparent that broadcast frequencies constituted a scarce resource whose use could be regulated and rationalized only by the Government. Without government control, the medium would be of little use because of the cacophony of competing voices, none of which could be clearly and predictably heard." Accordingly, Congress enacted the Radio Act of 1927 and the Communications Act of 1934. As the Court recounted in Turner Broadcasting: "In the Communications Act of 1934, Congress created a system of free broadcast service and directed that communications facilities be licensed across the country in a 'fair, efficient, and equitable' manner. Congress designed this system of allocation to afford each community of appreciable size an over-the-air source of information and an outlet for exchange on matters of local concern. [It] has long been a basic tenet of national communications policy that 'the widest possible dissemination of information from diverse and antagonistic sources is essential to the welfare of the public.' " The 1934 Act created the Federal Communications Commission (FCC) and authorized it to confer licenses on broadcasters and to regulate the broadcast spectrum "as public convenience, interest, or necessity requires." Licenses provide for use but not ownership of a portion of the broadcast spectrum. The Court upheld broadcast licensing in National Broadcasting Co. v. United States, 319 U.S. 190 (1943). For an overview of the tension between broadcasting law and ordinary free speech principles, see Weinberg, "Broadcasting and Speech," 81 Calif. L. Rev. 1101 (1993). For commentary critical of broadcast licensing in particular, see Coase, "The Federal Communications Commission," 2 J. L. & Econ. 1 (1959); Spitzer, "The Constitutionality of Licensing Broadcasters," 64 N.Y.U. L Rev. 990 (1989).

SCARCITY AND ACCESS

1.   *Right-of-reply obligations on the broadcasting media.* May government safeguard individual reputations by requiring a broadcaster to afford reply time to the target of an attack? When government has sought to vindicate the interest in private reputation by authorizing defamation actions, the Court has sharply curtailed suits against the press. But when the FCC sought to provide rights of access for individuals attacked on the air and imposed requirements that radio and television stations give reply time, the Court sustained the regulations against the claim that they violated the First Amendment rights of the broadcaster. May government regulate the media with the aim of improving the marketplace of ideas?

Red Lion Broadcasting Co. v. FCC, 395 U.S. 367 (1969), rejected broadcasters' First Amendment challenge to the FCC "fairness doctrine," which required licensed broadcast stations to present discussion of public issues, to assure fair coverage for each side, and to provide free reply time in response to certain personal attacks and political editorials. In sustaining those regulations in Red Lion, Justice WHITE's opinion for a unanimous Court reasoned that restricting the editorial discretion of the broadcasting media would "enhance rather than abridge the freedoms of speech and press." He emphasized the "scarcity of broadcast frequencies, the Government's role in allocating those frequencies, and the legitimate claims of those unable without governmental assistance to gain access to those frequencies for expression of their views." He began from the supposition that "differences in the characteristics of news media justify differences in the First Amendment standards applied to them. Just as the Government may limit the use of sound amplifying equipment potentially so noisy that it drowns out civilized private speech, so may the Government limit the use of broadcast equipment." He continued:

"Where there are substantially more individuals who want to broadcast than there are frequencies to allocate, it is idle to posit an unabridgeable First Amendment right to broadcast comparable to the right of every individual to speak, write, or publish. If 100 persons want broadcast licenses but there are only 10 frequencies to allocate, all of them may have the same 'right' to a license; but if there is to be any effective communication by radio, only a few can be licensed and the rest must be barred from the airwaves. It would be strange if the First Amendment, aimed at protecting and furthering communications, prevented the Government from making radio communication possible by requiring licenses to broadcast and by limiting the number of licenses so as not to overcrowd the spectrum.

"[A] license permits broadcasting, but the licensee has no constitutional right to be the one who holds the license or to monopolize a radio frequency to the exclusion of his fellow citizens. There is nothing in the First Amendment which prevents the Government from requiring a licensee to share his frequency with others and to conduct himself as a proxy or fiduciary with obligations to present those views and voices which are representative of his community and which would otherwise, by necessity, be barred from the airwaves. [It] is the right of the viewers and listeners, not the right of the broadcasters, which is paramount. It is the purpose of the First Amendment to preserve an uninhibited marketplace of ideas in which truth will ultimately prevail, rather than to countenance monopolization of that market, whether it be by the Government itself or a private licensee. [It]is the right of the public to receive suitable access to social, political, esthetic, moral, and other ideas and experiences which is crucial here.

"[We cannot] say that it is inconsistent with the First Amendment goal of producing an informed public capable of conducting its own affairs to require a broadcaster to permit answers to personal attacks occurring in the course of discussing controversial issues, or to require that the political opponents of those endorsed by the station be given a chance to communicate with the public. Otherwise, station owners and a few networks would have unfettered power to make time available only to the highest bidders, to communicate only their own views on public issues, people and candidates, and to permit on the air only those with whom they agreed. There is no sanctuary in the First Amendment for unlimited private censorship operating in a medium not open to all.

"It is strenuously argued, however, that if political editorials or personal attacks will trigger an obligation in broadcasters to afford the opportunity for expression to speakers who need not pay for time and whose views are unpalatable to the licensees, then broadcasters will be irresistibly forced to self-censorship and their coverage of controversial public issues will be eliminated or at least rendered wholly ineffective. Such a result would indeed be a serious matter, for should licensees actually eliminate their coverage of controversial issues, the purposes of the doctrine would be stifled. [At] this point, however, as the Federal Communications Commission has indicated, that possibility is at best speculative."

"[It] does not violate the First Amendment to treat licensees given the privilege of using scarce radio frequencies as proxies for the entire community, obligated to give suitable time and attention to matters of great public concern. To condition the granting or renewal of licenses on a willingness to present representative community views on controversial issues is consistent with the ends and purposes of those constitutional provisions forbidding the abridgment of freedom of speech and freedom of the press. In view of the scarcity of broadcast frequencies, the Government's role in allocating those frequencies, and the legitimate claims of those unable without governmental assistance to gain access to those frequencies for expression of their views, we hold the regulations and ruling at issue here are both authorized by statute and constitutional." Justice White noted in a footnote: "We need not deal with the argument that even if there is no longer a technological scarcity of frequencies limiting the number of broadcasters, there nevertheless is an economic scarcity in the sense that the Commission could or does limit entry to the broadcasting market on economic grounds and license no more stations than the market will support. [A] related argument, which we also put aside, is that quite apart from scarcity of frequencies, technological or economic, Congress does not abridge freedom of speech or press by legislation directly or indirectly multiplying the voices and views presented to the public through timesharing, fairness doctrines, or other devices which limit or dissipate the power of those who sit astride the channels of communication with the general public."

For commentary on the problems raised by Red Lion, see, e.g., Bollinger, "Freedom of the Press and Public Access: Toward a Theory of Partial Regulation of the Mass Media," 75 Mich. L. Rev. 1 (1976); Van Alstyne, "The Mobius Strip of the First Amendment: Perspectives on Red Lion," 29 S.C. L. Rev. 539 (1978); and Krattenmaker & Powe, "The Fairness Doctrine Today: A Constitutional Curiosity and An Impossible Dream," 1985 Duke L.J. 151; Powe, "Or of The [Broadcast] Press," 55 Tex. L. Rev. 39 (1976).

2. *The limits of Red Lion: technological versus economic scarcity.* Note that the Red Lion opinion emphasized technological scarcity and expressly declined to reach the broader argument that government may compel access or otherwise regulate speech in order to solve problems of economic scarcity. In Tornillo, Chief Justice BURGER reviewed and rejected, with respect to the print press, arguments for "an enforceable right of access to the press" and the concomitant claim "that Government has an obligation to ensure that a wide variety of views reach the public." Access advocates emphasized the concentration of power in the newspaper business and the shrinking number of newspapers, noted the disappearance of real

opportunity to form competing newspapers by dissidents, and accordingly urged "that the only effective way to insure fairness and accuracy" is "for government to take affirmative action." But the Court in Tornillo was not persuaded: "However much validity may be found in these arguments, at each point the implementation of a remedy such as an enforceable right of access necessarily calls for some mechanism, either governmental or consensual. If it is governmental coercion, this at once brings about a confrontation with the [First Amendment]." For the position of "access advocates," see Barron, "Access to the Press—A New First Amendment Right," 80 Harv. L. Rev. 1641 (1967), and Lange, "The Role of the Access Doctrine in the Regulation of the Mass Media," 52 N. Car. L. Rev. 1 (1973). For reflections on Tornillo, see Powe, "Tornillo," 1987 Sup. Ct. Rev. 345. For a later effort to generalize the holding of Red Lion to broader settings, see Fiss, "Free Speech and Social Structure," 71 Iowa L. Rev. 1405 (1986).

3.   *Repeal of the fairness doctrine.* The fairness doctrine, despite its validation in Red Lion, was subject to considerable criticism. Broadcasters resisted being treated less protectively than other media. Some observers charged that the doctrine perversely made television and radio blander rather than more diverse because it gave stations an incentive to avoid controversial editorials and pointed attacks. Others criticized it as unadministrable. Above all it was criticized for obsolescence: the expanded capacity of the electromagnetic spectrum and the growth of programming competition from cable and satellite diminished the "scarcity" rationale.

In August 1987, the FCC repealed the fairness doctrine, after an extensive administrative proceeding noting the rise of competition in information services markets and finding that the doctrine "chilled" the First Amendment rights of broadcasters. See Syracuse Peace Council, 2 FCC Rec. 5043 (1987); FCC, Fairness Doctrine Obligations of Broadcast Licensees, 102 F.C.C.2d 142 (1985). In announcing the repeal, then-FCC chairman Mark Fowler stated: "The First Amendment does not guarantee a fair press, only a free press."

4.   *A constitutional right of access to the broadcasting media for editorial advertisements?* Red Lion held that the First Amendment permitted access obligations to be imposed on broadcasters. But does the First Amendment compel such access? The Court answered this question in the negative three years after Red Lion in **Columbia Broadcasting, Inc. v. Democratic National Comm.**, 412 U.S. 94 (1973). The CBS case originated with complaints filed before the FCC in 1970 by the Democratic National Committee and an anti-war group challenging certain broadcasters' policies of refusing all editorial advertisements. The FCC sustained the broadcasters' position, but the Court of Appeals reversed, holding that "a flat ban on paid public issue announcements is in violation of the First Amendment, at least when other sorts of paid announcements are accepted." The Supreme Court held that, even assuming the broadcasters' refusal amounted to state action, broadcasters were not constitutionally required to accept such advertisements.

Chief Justice BURGER's opinion for the Court rejected the argument that a broad right of access could be drawn from the Red Lion ruling. Instead, he emphasized the statutory indications "that Congress intended to permit private broadcasting to develop with the widest journalistic freedom consistent with its public obligations." He emphasized that even broadcasters have substantial editorial discretion, and concluded: "To agree that debate on public issues should be 'robust, and wide-open' does not mean that we should exchange 'public trustee' broadcasting, with all its limitations, for a system of self-appointed editorial commentators." Chief Justice Burger cautioned against constitutionally mandating an extension of the fairness doctrine: "The Commission's responsibilities under a right-of-access system would tend to draw it into a continuing case-by-case determination of who should be heard and when." Moreover, he noted "the reality that in a very real sense listeners and viewers constitute a 'captive audience.'"

Justice DOUGLAS's concurrence took a far firmer constitutional position on the side of the broadcasters: "My conclusion is that TV and radio stand in the same protected position under the First Amendment as do newspapers and magazines." The Red Lion case, in which he had not participated, curtailed broadcasters' rights unduly, he insisted, since "the First Amendment puts beyond the reach of government federal regulation of news agencies save only business or financial practices which do not involve First Amendment rights." Justice BRENNAN's extensive dissent, joined by Justice Marshall, concluded, in "balancing" the competing interests, that the broadcasters' "absolute ban on editorial advertising" could "serve only to inhibit, rather than to further" robust public debate. He insisted that the fairness doctrine was "insufficient" to provide that kind of debate. He noted not only the interests of broadcasters and of the listening and viewing public, "but also the independent First Amendment interest of groups and individuals in effective self-expression." Drawing on access principles developed in the public forum context, he commented: "[F]reedom of speech does not exist in the abstract. On the contrary, the right to speak can flourish only if it is allowed to operate in an effective forum—whether it be a public park, a schoolroom, a town meeting hall, a soapbox, or a radio and television frequency. For in the absence of an effective means of communication, the right to speak would ring hollow indeed." Accordingly, "in light of the current dominance of the electronic media as the most effective means of reaching the public, any policy that *absolutely* denies citizens access to the airwaves" was unjustifiable.

5. *A statutory right of access to the broadcasting media for candidates seeking federal elective office.* Sec. 312(a)(7) of the Communications Act of 1934, as added by the Federal Election Campaign Act of 1971, authorizes the FCC to revoke a broadcaster's license "for willful or repeated failure to allow reasonable access to or to permit purchase of reasonable amounts of time for the use of a broadcasting station by a legally qualified candidate for Federal elective office on behalf of his candidacy." The 6–3 decision in **CBS, Inc. v. FCC**, 453 U.S. 367 (1981), found that this provision created a major new statutory right of access—a right that enlarged the political broadcasting responsibilities of licensees. The Court also held that the FCC's interpretation and application of the provision did not violate broadcasters' First Amendment rights. The controversy originated in October 1979, when the Carter-Mondale Presidential Committee asked each of the three major television networks to sell the Committee a half-hour of early December 1979 air time. The Committee sought to broadcast a documentary on the record of the Carter Administration, to augment President Carter's planned announcement of his candidacy for re-election. All three networks denied the request, relying on their across-the-board rules about political broadcasts. The Committee filed a complaint, and the FCC ruled that the networks' reasons were "deficient"

under the FCC's interpretation of the statute. The FCC concluded that the networks had violated the law by failing to provide "reasonable access." Chief Justice BURGER—who had emphasized "the widest journalistic freedom" for broadcasters in CBS v. DNC (p. 636)—wrote the majority opinion. Justice WHITE's dissent, joined by Justices Rehnquist and Stevens, strongly disagreed with Chief Justice Burger's broad reading of the law and with the Court's endorsement of the FCC standards and their application.

Can CBS v. DNC and CBS v. FCC be reconciled? Are broadcasters better viewed as conduits for speech or as speakers and editors in their own right? Are they both? Do the two CBS decisions simply reflect consistent judicial deference to the expertise of the FCC?

6.   *The standard of review in broadcasting cases.* Recall that the Court, in **FCC v. League of Women Voters**, 468 U.S. 364 (1984), invalidated 47 U.S.C. § 399, which prohibited "editorializing" by noncommercial educational broadcasting stations receiving public funds from the Corporation for Public Broadcasting. The Court found the law to be content-based, but nonetheless held that the special features of broadcasting dictated applying a standard lower than strict scrutiny. Justice BRENNAN, writing for the Court, stated that regulation of the content of broadcasting would be upheld "only when we [are] satisfied that the restriction is narrowly tailored to further a substantial governmental interest, such as ensuring adequate and balanced coverage of public issues." Because the restriction on expression of editorial opinion was found to lie "at the heart of First Amendment protection," the Court applied its standard carefully and found the government's justifications insufficient to justify the restriction.

7.   *Speaker access to public television.* **Arkansas Educational Television Comm'n (AETC) v. Forbes**, 523 U.S. 666 (1998), which rejected a free speech challenge to the exclusion of a candidate from a candidate debate televised by a public broadcasting station, raised the question of what First Amendment constraints apply to the exercise of journalistic judgment by public broadcasters. Justice KENNEDY, writing for the majority, suggested that First Amendment obligations of neutrality might not apply at all to most decisions by public broadcasters to exclude speakers: "In the case of television broadcasting, [broad] rights of access for outside speakers would be antithetical, as a general rule, to the discretion that stations and their editorial staff must exercise to fulfill their journalistic purpose and statutory obligations. [Television] broadcasters enjoy the 'widest journalistic freedom' consistent with their public responsibilities. Among the broadcaster's responsibilities is the duty to schedule programming that serves the 'public interest, convenience, and necessity.' Public and private broadcasters alike are not only permitted, but indeed required, to exercise substantial editorial discretion in the selection and presentation of their programming." As a general rule, the nature of editorial discretion counsels against subjecting broadcasters to claims of viewpoint discrimination. Programming decisions would be particularly vulnerable to claims of this type because even principled exclusions rooted in sound journalistic judgment can often be characterized as viewpoint-based. Much like a university selecting a commencement speaker, a public institution selecting speakers for a lecture series, or a public school prescribing its curriculum, a broadcaster by its nature will facilitate the expression of some viewpoints instead of others. Were the judiciary to require, and so to define and approve, pre-established criteria for access, it would risk implicating the

courts in judgments that should be left to the exercise of journalistic discretion. [This] is not to say the First Amendment would bar the legislative imposition of neutral rules for access to public broadcasting. Instead, we say that, in most cases, the First Amendment of its own force does not compel public broadcasters to allow third parties access to their programming." The majority in AETC nonetheless applied a First Amendment requirement of viewpoint neutrality in the particular context of a televised candidate debate, finding it satisfied as Forbes was excluded on the basis of popularity, not platform.

In dissent, Justice STEVENS wrote that a public broadcaster ought to be subject to greater obligations of neutrality than the majority had enforced. Echoing his dissent in FCC v. League of Women Voters (p. 407), he wrote: "Because AETC is owned by the State, deference to its interest in making ad hoc decisions about the political content of its programs necessarily increases the risk of government censorship and propaganda in a way that protection of privately owned broadcasters does not."

THE INFORMATION AGE

The past fifty years have produced rapid changes in media technology and modes of mass communication. Are traditional First Amendment principles applicable to the internet and ever-changing modes of communication? Or are new principles needed to suit changing technologies?

1. *Cable television and the First Amendment.* The First Amendment status of cable was long unsettled. The cable industry argued against application of Red Lion or any other lesser standard of protection, reasoning that technological scarcity is not an issue on cable systems. On the other hand, cable is in part a vehicle for broadcasting transmission, and cable systems depend on the grant of municipal franchises, including rights-of-way over streets and utility poles. Government has sometimes taken the position that cable is more like broadcasting than like print media by virtue of these facts, and therefore more regulable.

The Supreme Court put to rest this debate in **Turner Broadcasting v. FCC, 512 U.S. 622 (1994)** (Turner I). In the course of rejecting the cable industry's argument for strict scrutiny of the requirement that it carry certain broadcast signals, the Court rejected any argument for applying Red Lion or extending it by analogy to the cable context. Justice KENNEDY wrote for the Court: "There can be no disagreement on an initial premise: Cable programmers and cable operators engage in and transmit speech, and they are entitled to the protection of the speech and press provisions of the First Amendment. [Leathers.] Through 'original programming or by exercising editorial discretion over which stations or programs to include in its repertoire,' cable programmers and operators 'seek to communicate messages on a wide variety of topics and in a wide variety of formats.' Los Angeles v. Preferred Communications, Inc., 476 U.S. 488 (1986). [The] Government [contends] that regulation of cable television should be analyzed under the same First Amendment standard that applies to regulation of broadcast television. It is true that our cases have permitted more intrusive regulation of broadcast speakers than of speakers in other media. Compare [Red Lion with Tornillo.] But the rationale for applying a less rigorous standard of First Amendment scrutiny to broadcast regulation, whatever its validity in the cases elaborating it, does not apply in the context of cable regulation.

"The justification for our distinct approach to broadcast regulation rests upon the unique physical limitations of the broadcast medium. As a general matter, there are more would-be broadcasters than frequencies available in the electromagnetic spectrum. And if two broadcasters were to attempt to transmit over the same frequency in the same locale, they would interfere with one another's signals, so that neither could be heard at all. The scarcity of broadcast frequencies thus required the establishment of some regulatory mechanism to divide the electromagnetic spectrum and assign specific frequencies to particular broadcasters. In addition, the inherent physical limitation on the number of speakers who may use the broadcast medium has been thought to require some adjustment in traditional First Amendment analysis to permit the Government to place limited content restraints, and impose certain affirmative obligations, on broadcast licensees.

"[Although] courts and commentators have criticized the scarcity rationale since its inception, we have declined to question its continuing validity as support for our broadcast jurisprudence, and see no reason to do so here. The broadcast cases are inapposite in the present context because cable television does not suffer from the inherent limitations that characterize the broadcast medium. Indeed, given the rapid advances in fiber optics and digital compression technology, soon there may be no practical limitation on the number of speakers who may use the cable medium. Nor is there any danger of physical interference between two cable speakers attempting to share the same channel. In light of these fundamental technological differences between broadcast and cable transmission, application of the more relaxed standard of scrutiny adopted in Red Lion and the other broadcast cases is inapt when determining the First Amendment validity of cable regulation.

"[Although] the Government acknowledges the substantial technological differences between broadcast and cable, it advances a second argument for application of the Red Lion framework to cable regulation. It asserts that the foundation of our broadcast jurisprudence is not the physical limitations of the electromagnetic spectrum, but rather the 'market dysfunction' that characterizes the broadcast market. Because the cable market is beset by a similar dysfunction, the Government maintains, the Red Lion standard of review should also apply to cable. While we agree that the cable market suffers certain structural impediments, the Government's argument is flawed in two respects. First, as discussed above, the special physical characteristics of broadcast transmission, not the economic characteristics of the broadcast market, are what underlies our broadcast jurisprudence. Second, the mere assertion of dysfunction or failure in a speech market, without more, is not sufficient to shield a speech regulation from the First Amendment standards applicable to nonbroadcast media. See, e.g., [Austin, MCFL, Tornillo.]"

Accordingly, Justice Kennedy proceeded to use ordinary First Amendment principles—in particular, the distinction between content-based and content-neutral laws—to analyze the must-carry rules. He did, however, find cable's particular characteristics relevant in applying those principles, and thus found cable's "chokehold" monopoly relevant to the determination that the must-carry rules were content-neutral: "When an individual subscribes to cable, the physical connection between the television set and the cable network gives the cable operator bottleneck, or gatekeeper, control over most (if not all) of the television programming that is channeled into the subscriber's home. Hence, simply by virtue of its ownership of the essential pathway for cable speech, a cable operator can prevent its subscribers from obtaining access to programming it chooses to exclude. A cable operator, unlike speakers in other media, can thus silence the voice of competing speakers with a mere flick of the switch. The potential for abuse of this private power over a central avenue of communication cannot be overlooked. The First Amendment's command that government not impede the freedom of speech does not disable the government from taking steps to ensure that private interests not restrict, through physical control of a critical pathway of communication, the free flow of information and ideas."

In **Denver Area Educational Telecommunications Consortium v. FCC**, 518 U.S. 727 (1996), which struck down some but not other cable indecency regulations (see p. 181), the plurality opinion expressly declined to decide whether cable is more analogous to print or to broadcasting. As Justice BREYER explained for the plurality in declining to analogize cable either to a common carrier or to a bookstore: "Both categorical approaches suffer from the same flaws: they import law developed in very different contexts into a new and changing environment, and they lack the flexibility necessary to allow government to respond to very serious practical problems without sacrificing the free exchange of ideas the First Amendment is designed to protect." Justice SOUTER elaborated in concurrence: "All of the relevant characteristics of cable are presently in a state of technological and regulatory flux. [Thus] we should be shy about saying the final word today about what will be accepted as reasonable tomorrow." Justice THOMAS, joined by Chief Justice Rehnquist and Justice Scalia in partial dissent, found the plurality's approach unsatisfactory and would have preferred to state directly that cable's First Amendment protection was equivalent to that of the print press: "Our First Amendment distinctions between media, dubious from their infancy, placed cable in a doctrinal wasteland in which regulators and cable operators alike could not be sure whether cable was entitled to the substantial First Amendment protections afforded the print media or was subject to the more onerous obligations shouldered by the broadcast media. Over time, however, we have drawn closer to recognizing that cable operators should enjoy the same First Amendment rights as the nonbroadcast media. [In] Turner, we stated expressly what we had implied in Leathers: The Red Lion standard does not apply to cable television. [In] Turner, by adopting much of the print paradigm, and by rejecting Red Lion, we adopted with it a considerable body of precedent that governs the respective First Amendment rights of competing speakers. In Red Lion, we had legitimized consideration of the public interest and emphasized the rights of viewers, at least in the abstract. Under that view, 'it is the right of the viewers and listeners, not the right of the broadcasters, which is paramount.' After Turner, however, that view can no longer be given any credence in the cable context. It is the operator's right that is preeminent."

Municipal governments have typically exacted from cable operators the requirement that they dedicate one or more channels to the government as public access channels to be used for public, educational or governmental purposes. Federal legislation governing the cable industry has explicitly permitted such arrangements, and has additionally required that cable operators dedicate a certain number of "leased access" channels for programming from sources unaffiliated with them. Does compulsion to provide public access and leased access channels raise any serious First Amendment issue? Although this issue was not directly presented in Denver Area, Justice Thomas's opinion questioned the constitutionality of requiring public access and leased access channels in the first place: "There is no getting around the fact that leased and public access are a type of forced speech. Though the constitutionality of leased and public access channels is not directly at issue in these cases, the position adopted by the Court in Turner ineluctably leads to the conclusion that the federal access requirements are subject to some form of heightened scrutiny. Following Turner, some commentators have questioned the constitutionality of leased and public access. Such questions are not at issue here." But he argued that even if such access were assumed to be constitutional, cable programmers and viewers had no First Amendment right to insist that any particular programming be shown.

If public access channels are constitutionally created, then do they function as public forums? Justice KENNEDY's opinion in Denver Area took such a view, and thus concluded that government could not authorize content-based discrimination on such channels: "Public access channels meet the definition of a public forum. We have recognized two kinds of public forums. The first and most familiar are traditional public forums, like streets, sidewalks, and parks, which by custom have long been open for public assembly and discourse. 'The second category of public property is the designated public forum, whether of a limited or unlimited character— property that the State has opened for expressive activity by part or all of the public.' Public access channels fall in the second category. Required by the franchise authority as a condition of the franchise and open to all comers, they are a designated public forum of unlimited character. The House Report for the 1984 Cable Act [characterized] public access channels as 'the video equivalent of the speaker's soapbox or the electronic parallel to the printed leaflet. They provide groups and individuals who generally have not had access to the electronic media with the opportunity to become sources of information in the electronic marketplace of ideas.' "

On this view, must a public access channel permit a program by a racist speaker whose speech does not rise to the level of Brandenburg incitement? An indecent program that is not obscene or otherwise proscribed by law? Note Justice Thomas's reply to Justice Kennedy in Denver Area: "Public access channels are [not] public fora. [Cable] systems are not public property. Cable systems are privately owned and privately managed, and [no] case [holds] that government may designate private property a public forum [absent] at least some formal easement or other property interest."

2. *Net neutrality and the First Amendment.* Though the questions raised in Turner and Denver Area may seem quaint in the internet age, do they foreshadow potential First Amendment issues with net neutrality policies? The principle of "net neutrality," adopted by the Federal Communications Commission most recently in 2015, requires internet service providers to provide access to all content on the internet so that the internet would remain open to all users and uses. Does net neutrality vindicate the "the right of the public to receive suitable access to social, political, [and] esthetic" ideas that the Court highlighted in Red Lion? Does it resemble the must-carry provision at stake in Turner? Do internet service providers present the same "potential for abuse of [private power] over a

central avenue of communication" as did the cable operators in Turner? Or would the providers' lack of monopoly power—at least in some places—mean that they could prevail on their own First Amendment challenge to such policies?

3. ***The internet and the First Amendment.*** The rapid expansion of the internet presents numerous questions about the parameters of free speech protection and the proper extent of government regulation and control. Proponents of regulation cite the potential for uncontrolled dissemination of pornography, rampant copyright infringement, and the proliferation of harassment and unwanted invasions of privacy. Critics of regulatory frameworks argue that the legislative and judicial response cannot keep pace with the growth of technology; thus, the market should be allowed to develop technological solutions to these problems on its own.

The internet allows individuals to be their own content publishers. An important threshold issue is how to characterize the nature of the speech that occurs in these mediums. A single web page can contain commercial advertisements, political speech, and obscene material. The information can either be contained in the website, or it can take the form of links to other web pages.

On-line postings can also present difficult issues about the responsibility for the content of the postings if found to be libelous or defamatory. Should internet service providers be considered conduits for the distribution of information or publishers with editorial control? What about the companies on whose platforms or sites the communications appear? Who should bear the liability for harassment through threatening postings either to newsgroups or directly to personal e-mail accounts? Does the fact that members of the university community have access to e-mail and campus newsgroups as part of the educational mission of the university alter the level of administrative responsibility (and hence liability) for objectionable conduct perpetuated over the network? Is it constitutionally permissible for a university to restrict students' access to protected material, for example, by prohibiting students from downloading indecent material?

The issue of transmission of obscene as well as indecent material over the internet is complicated by its technological mechanics. How should a court determine the proper forum for evaluating whether a particular transmission is obscene? At the point of origin (the server where the information is stored)? At various points along the message route? At the point where the user downloads the material? See United States v. Thomas, 74 F.3d 701 (6th Cir.1996), cert. denied, 519 U.S. 820 (1996). Whose community standards should be used in evaluating whether a transmission is obscene? The community of internet users? The community where the download occurs? Where the upload occurs? Who will be ultimately liable for the transmission? The individuals who upload the material onto a web site or newsgroup, the individuals who download the material onto their individual hard drives, or the internet service providers through whose servers and networks these transmissions take place?

Should questions about speech on the internet be resolved by finding the most appropriate analogies between existing law on the protection of speech rights and the characteristics of this new medium? For instance, are websites more like bookstores or newspapers? Are internet service providers more like common carriers or do they have some responsibility to regulate the content that passes through their networks? Are online service providers (e.g., Google) more like distributors of information provided by third parties or publishers of content? Are social media platforms public squares or company towns? Is the internet a pervasive and invasive medium like broadcasting (Pacifica) and cable (Denver Area) where content is pushed into the eyes and ears of viewers? Or is the internet best understood as more of a "pull" technology where participants must venture out and subscribe to newsgroups and mailing lists, download data from remote sites, and type in web addresses in order to view particular pages? If this pull interpretation prevails, regulation of speech on the internet may require the development of entirely new analogies and constitutional frameworks. On the other hand, if the internet comes to be dominated by "push" technologies, which allow subscribers to request and receive custom content, analogies to broadcast and cable may appear more applicable. Push services go to favorite web sites, automatically download data, send updates, and push the data directly onto the subscriber's hard drive, thereby alleviating the need for subscribers to venture out onto the web in order to pull the data themselves. Push technologies further complicate the search for parallels to prior methods of constitutional analysis. Just as web pages and bulletin boards give everyone the opportunity to be a publisher, so push technologies promise everyone the opportunity to be his or her own broadcaster. Does this vast communication potential demand the imposition of a regulatory scheme to prevent abuses or does it represent the ultimate free marketplace of ideas where speech can best be countered by more speech?

The Court first addressed such questions in **Reno v. ACLU**, 521 U.S. 844 (1997), reported in full at p. 183. Writing for the Court, Justice STEVENS exhaustively recounted the three-judge district court's findings about the characteristics of the internet, and expressly rejected any analogy between the internet and the broadcasting medium: "[Decisions such as Red Lion v. FCC and FCC v. Pacifica] relied on the history of extensive government regulation of the broadcast medium; the scarcity of available frequencies at its inception; and its 'invasive' nature. Those factors are not present in cyberspace. [The] vast democratic fora of the Internet [have never] been subject to the type of government supervision and regulation that has attended the broadcast industry. Moreover, the Internet is not as 'invasive' as radio or television. The District Court specifically found that 'communications over the Internet do not 'invade' an individual's home or appear on one's computer screen unbidden. Users seldom encounter content 'by accident.' [Finally,] unlike the conditions that prevailed when Congress first authorized regulation of the broadcast spectrum, the Internet can hardly be considered a 'scarce' expressive commodity. It provides relatively unlimited, low-cost capacity for communication of all kinds, [including] not only traditional print and news services, but also audio, video, and still images, as well as interactive, real-time dialogue. Through the use of chat rooms, any person with a phone line can become a town crier with a voice that resonates farther than it could from any soapbox. Through the use of Web pages, mail exploders, and newsgroups, the same individual can become a pamphleteer. As the District Court found, 'the content on the Internet is as diverse as human thought.' We agree with its conclusion that our cases provide no basis for qualifying the level of First Amendment scrutiny that should be applied to this medium."

In **Packingham v. North Carolina**, 582 U.S. ___, 137 S. Ct. 1730 (2017), discussed at p. 345, the Court addressed state exclusion of a sex offender from social media platforms. Acknowledging the limits of the

Court's understanding, Justice KENNEDY wrote: "While we now may be coming to the realization that the Cyber Age is a revolution of historic proportions, we cannot appreciate yet its full dimensions and vast potential to alter how we think, express ourselves, and define who we want to be. The forces and directions of the Internet are so new, so protean, and so far reaching that courts must be conscious that what they say today might be obsolete tomorrow."

Does the Court's view of technology demonstrate a valid sense of humility in engaging with changing technology? Or is it unnecessarily fatalistic in forgoing any attempt to impose a comprehensive doctrine? As technological change increasingly leads to the convergence of media, all accessed from a single device, does it any longer make sense to treat First Amendment freedoms as varying by medium?

CHAPTER 4

THE RELIGION CLAUSES: FREE EXERCISE AND ESTABLISHMENT

The role that religion should play in public life has often been a divisive problem in American society. Religious values often determine where citizens stand on issues like abortion, civil rights protections for gay and transgender people, mandated contraceptive care, and other controversial social issues. Sometimes, the government takes a clear stance on these issues, either through laws banning or requiring certain conduct or through government funding of certain activities. These government actions raise difficult questions about what if any accommodations the Constitution guarantees to people whose religious beliefs are burdened by the law. Should an evangelical baker opposed to same-sex marriage have to comply with ordinary civil rights protections and bake a wedding cake for a gay wedding if he believes that doing so is sinful? Should a group of nuns receive an exception from a law that normally requires employers to pay for their employees' birth control? Should a member of a Native American religion that uses otherwise illegal substances in its sacraments be able to use them? These questions have raised fierce debates that have divided courts and the public alike. They have also inspired a gradual political reversal as popular conceptions of who benefits from accommodations for religious minorities has shifted.

The closely related issue of the proper relationship between church and state leads to an equally vitriolic debate: Must the government subsidize religious private education if it subsidizes secular private education? Must religious student groups be allowed to meet on public school grounds? Should courthouses be able to display the Ten Commandments? Although the answers to these questions and others are doctrinally controversial, they lie at the heart of the country's identity—and the country's divisions.

The First Amendment provides that "Congress shall make no law respecting an establishment of religion, or prohibiting the free exercise thereof." The two clauses, commonly referred to as the "Establishment Clause" and the "Free Exercise Clause," have given rise to separate bodies of case law. But this should not obscure the fact that the two clauses are interrelated. They protect overlapping values, yet sometimes exert conflicting pressures. Consider the common practice of exempting church property from taxation. Does the benefit conveyed by government to religion via that exemption constitute an "establishment"? Would the "free exercise" of religion be unduly burdened if church property were not exempted from taxation? Articulating satisfactory criteria to accommodate the potentially conflicting emanations of the two religion clauses is a recurrent challenge in this chapter.

Sections 1 and 2 consider respectively the original history of the religion clauses and the problem of defining religion. Section 3 examines ways in which government may be said to abridge the free exercise of religion. The most direct way is by deliberately prohibiting or disadvantaging a religious sect or its central practices. While such laws are rare in contemporary society, the Court has subjected them to the strictest scrutiny. A harder case is presented when religious objections are raised to the application of general regulations that as applied restrict religious exercise in particular situations. For example, may the Amish claim constitutional exemption from compulsory education laws? The story of the Court's answer to this question has undergone dramatic twists and turns. Such an exemption was denied by the Court for Mormon plural marriage in 1878, the very first time it decided a free exercise case. The principle of non-exemption was reaffirmed in the first flag salute case, Minersville School Dist. v. Gobitis (1940), which itself was repudiated (though not overturned) in West Virginia v. Barnette (1942). In Shebert v. Verner (1963), the Warren Court held free exercise to require some religious exemptions from generally applicable laws. In Employment Division v. Smith (1990), the Rehnquist Court drastically narrowed the scope of such compelled exemptions. Congress sought to reverse Smith by providing for statutory religious exemption claims under the Religious Freedom Restoration Act of 1993, but the Court struck down that law as exceeding Congress's power as applied to state practices in City of Boerne. Congress subsequently enacted the Religious Land Use and Institutionalized Persons Act of 2000, which partially restored exemptions in state zoning matters and for prisoners, and the doctrinal trend may now be tending back toward exemptions. In Fulton v. City of Philadelphia (2021; p. 699), the Court declined to overrule Smith, but left its future in doubt.

Section 4 focuses on three Establishment Clause issues: the rendering of government financial aid to activities conducted by religious organizations; religion in the public schools; and the use or apparent endorsement of religious teachings or symbols by governmental bodies. Lastly, Section 5 considers how the two clauses may be reconciled: it asks when government is *permitted* to exempt religiously motivated practices from general laws, even if it is not compelled to do so, and whether government ever *must* exempt certain practices despite the fact that the government believes that, in doing so, it would violate the Establishment Clause.

The principal tension in the Establishment Clause cases is among conceptions of government neutrality: Does the clause require a "wall of separation" between church and state? Does it require formal neutrality, whereby government never adverts to religion, for advantage or for disadvantage? Or does it require simply that government treat religious organizations and activities equally, including them in any benefit schemes generally enjoyed by others?

SECTION 1. A BRIEF HISTORY OF THE RELIGION CLAUSES

One of the primary ways in which courts interpret the religion clauses is through the lens of original understanding. Just as controversial as the Supreme Court's jurisprudence interpreting the religion clauses, then, are the historical narratives upon which those interpretations are based. Over the past century, two competing narratives have emerged: The first, "separationism," argues that the Framers intended a secular government and strong divisions between church and state. The second, "nonpreferentialism," asserts that the Framers established a Christian nation and sought only to restrict the national government from preferring one sect over another. This section attempts to set forth a brief, more neutral history of the religion clauses. It then discusses the two narratives constructed by the Court in greater depth, casting doubt on both interpretations.

1. *The broad outlines of a history of the religion clauses.* The American movement toward institutional separation of church and state began with the Declaration of Independence in 1776, when the states began the process of drafting new constitutions to replace their colonial charters. In New England, the stronghold of the Congregationalist Church, the states had long collected mandatory taxes to support local ministers, subject to exemptions for religious dissenters who obtained certificates. Rhode Island, founded by dissenter Roger Williams, and Pennsylvania, founded by Quaker William Penn, never had established churches. In the rest of the country, colonial charters had established the Church of England. Now, throughout the country, the religious minorities of the time—mainly Baptists, Presbyterians, and Quakers—began to advocate for the elimination of state policies requiring them to support churches with their tax dollars.

These dissenters made little headway in New England, but in Virginia, a constitutional convention passed a Declaration of Rights stating that "religion, or the duty which we owe to our Creator, and the manner of discharging it, can be directed only by reason and conviction, not by force or violence; and therefore all men are equally entitled to the free exercise of religion according to the dictates of consciences." The law also freed Virginians from any sort of mandatory church attendance, guaranteed freedom of belief, and exempted them from mandatory tax assessments to support religion.

But some Virginians, including Patrick Henry, were concerned about the potential poverty of ministers and the stability of the state, which was often thought at the time to depend on strong religious institutions. They therefore proposed a new assessment that would tax citizens in support of the ministry of their choice. The proposal faced strong opposition from a coalition that included James Madison, who wrote his famous Memorial and Remonstrance in support of his position. Madison devoted almost the entirety of his argument in the Remonstrance to advocating for religious liberty. He argued that coercion on matters of conscience is wrong because true, meaningful belief is purely voluntary and cannot result from force. Government cannot coerce individuals to make decisions regarding their beliefs, as even the government cannot logically have control over beliefs. Accordingly, the right to liberty of conscience is "in its nature an inalienable right." Government and religion, then, must occupy two separate spheres.

Madison developed these views from his reading of seventeenth-century British philosopher John Locke, who believed that the human conscience should be left free and that consequently religion must occupy a sphere of its own, protected from the coercive power of the state. At the time of the Revolution, many Americans took the further step of arguing that the government must not forcibly collect taxes to support religion against citizens' liberty of conscience.

Madison's opposition to any coerced tax assessment in Virginia succeeded. In 1786 the legislature passed The Virginia Bill for Religious Freedom, originally drafted by Thomas Jefferson in 1779, which enacted: "That no man shall be compelled to frequent or support any religious worship, place or ministry whatsoever, nor shall be enforced, restrained, molested, or burthened in his body or goods, nor shall otherwise suffer on account of his religious opinions or [belief]." Jefferson's preamble to the Bill declared that: "Almighty God hath created the mind free; that all attempts to influence it by temporal punishments or burthens, or by civil incapacitations, tend only to beget habits of hypocrisy and meanness, and are a departure from the plan of the Holy author of our religion, who being Lord both of body and mind, yet chose not to propagate it by coercions on [either]; that to compel a man to furnish contributions of money for the propagation of opinions which he disbelieves, is sinful and tyrannical; that even the forcing him to support this or that teacher of his own religious persuasion, is depriving him of the comfortable liberty of giving his contributions to the particular pastor, whose morals he would make his [pattern]." The Virginia statute, then, focused on protecting religion from the state, not the state from religion. The writings of Madison and his contemporaries are likewise directed at protecting the church from the state. Indeed, many thinkers at this time believed that religious belief actually supported the state by promoting honesty, loyalty and obedience.

By the time the Constitution was ratified, every state constitution guaranteed the liberty of conscience. No such provision, however, appeared in the U.S. Constitution. Madison himself argued that the Bill of Rights was useless: "[E]xperience proves the inefficacy of a bill of rights on those occasions when its controul is most needed. Repeated violations of these parchment barriers have been committed by overbearing majorities in every state." He also argued that the Bill of Rights was unnecessary, urging that, in a country of such size and diversity as the United States, opposed factions would control one another and prevent any single faction from gaining a majority. These structural protections were more efficacious than paper ones: "If there were a majority of one sect, a bill of rights would be a poor protection of liberty." See Finkelman, "James Madison and the Bill of Rights: A Reluctant Paternity," 1990 S. Ct. L. Rev. 301.

Nevertheless, the same religious minorities who had opposed compulsory tax assessments for religion protested the omission of guaranteed liberty of conscience during the ratification debates. Giving into political pressure, Madison spearheaded the effort to amend the Constitution. His draft Bill of Rights provided that "the civil rights of none shall be abridged on account of religious belief or worship, nor shall any national religion be established, nor shall the full and equal rights of conscience be in any manner, or on any pretext, infringed." The House Committee changed the language to read that "no religion shall be established by law, nor shall the equal rights of conscience be infringed." One Connecticut Congressman objected to the first clause of this draft language on the basis that his state's law, which compelled tax assessments for religion but allowed citizens to allocate those assessments to a church of their choice, might be construed as an establishment—a term with an almost universally negative connotation at this time. Madison responded that the Congressman should not be concerned; the Amendment would not apply to the states.

The draft language was then changed to read: "Congress shall make no laws touching religion, or infringing the rights of conscience," and then "Congress shall make no law establishing Religion, or prohibiting the free exercise thereof, nor shall the rights of conscience be infringed." It is unclear why the First Congress deleted the final phrase, but the remaining clauses guaranteed that no one would be compelled to support religion with which he or she disagreed and that Congress could not stop anyone from worshipping as he or she chose. Thomas Jefferson famously described the clauses as "building a wall of separation between Church & State" in his 1802 letter to the Baptists of Danbury, Connecticut.

2. ***The separationist view.*** One major historical interpretation emerging from this evidence is "separationism," which has two components: voluntarism and separatism. Proponents of this view argue that the Founders established a secular state walled off from religion and place particular emphasis on the writings and beliefs of Thomas Jefferson and James Madison.

Separationism was first hinted at by the Supreme Court in the 1878 case of **Reynolds v. United States**, 98 U.S. 145 (1878; p. 671). Chief Justice WAITE quoted Jefferson's letter to the Danbury Baptist Association, in which he wrote that the Establishment Clause "buil[t] a wall of separation between church and State." The view was later and most famously expounded by Justice BLACK, writing for the Court in **Everson v. Board of Education**, 330 U.S. 1 (1947; p. 711). Justice Black reviewed historical evidence, once again citing Jefferson to suggest that the Framers favored "a wall of separation":

"A large proportion of the early settlers of this country came here from Europe to escape the bondage of laws which compelled them to support and attend government-favored churches. The centuries immediately before and contemporaneous with the colonization of America had been filled with turmoil, civil strife, and persecutions generated in large part by established sects determined to maintain their absolute political and religious supremacy. With the power of government supporting them, at various times and places, Catholics had persecuted Protestants, Protestants had persecuted Catholics, Protestant sects had persecuted other Protestant sects, Catholics of one shade of belief had persecuted [other Catholics], and all of these had from time to time persecuted Jews. In efforts to force loyalty to whatever religious group happened to be on top and in league with the government of a particular time and place, men and women had been fined, cast in jail, cruelly tortured, and [killed].

"These practices of the old world were transplanted and began to thrive in the soil of the new America. The very charters granted by the English Crown to the individuals and companies designated to make the laws which would control the destinies of the colonials authorized these individuals and companies to erect religious establishments which all, whether believers or nonbelievers, would be required to support and attend. [These] practices became so commonplace as to shock the freedom-loving colonials into a feeling of abhorrence. The imposition of taxes to pay ministers' salaries and to build and maintain churches and church property aroused their indignation. It was these feelings which found expression in the First Amendment. [Virginia provided] able leadership for the movement. The people there, as elsewhere, reached the conviction that individual religious liberty could be achieved best under a government which was stripped of all power to tax, to support, or otherwise to assist any or all religions, or to interfere with the beliefs of any religious individual or group."

Justice RUTLEDGE, who dissented in Everson, nonetheless agreed with Justice Black about the original understanding of the religion clauses. Justice Rutledge's dissent put heavy emphasis on Madison's Remonstrance: "As the Remonstrance discloses throughout, Madison opposed every form and degree of official relation between religion and civil authority. For him religion was a wholly private matter beyond the scope of civil power either to restrain or to support. Denial or abridgment of religious freedom was a violation of rights both of conscience and of natural equality. State aid was no less obnoxious or destructive to freedom and to religion itself than other forms of state interference. 'Establishment' and 'free exercise' were correlative and coextensive ideas, representing only different facets of the single great and fundamental freedom. The Remonstrance, following the Virginia statute's example, referred to the history of religious conflicts and the effects of all sorts of establishments, current and historical, to suppress religion's free exercise. With Jefferson, Madison believed that to tolerate any fragment of establishment would be by so much to perpetuate restraint upon that freedom. Hence he sought to tear out the institution not partially but root and branch, and to bar its return forever."

Consider the following comment on the Black and Rutledge opinions: "What emerges from the Court's examination of history is a pair of fundamental principles [animating] the first amendment: voluntarism and separatism. [Voluntarism means] that the advancement of a church would come only from the voluntary support of its followers and not from the political support of the state. [Separatism means] that both religion and government function best if each remains independent of the other." Tribe, American Constitutional Law § 14–3 (2d ed. 1988). See also Van Alstyne, "Trends in the Supreme Court: Mr. Jefferson's Crumbling Wall—A Comment on Lynch v. Donnelly," 1984 Duke L.J. 770 ("Voluntarism [was] the principle of personal choice. Separatism was the principle of non-entanglement."). But consider also Feldman, Divided By God, 174–75 (2005) ("[T]he period of the framing was not characterized by general religious persecution. [By] contrast, recognition of the extent of Nazi persecution in Europe had indeed produced a shock to reasonable American minds by 1947 and was playing a real part in pushing Black and his colleagues to believe that the federal Constitution should be interpreted to protect religious minorities.").

3. *The nonpreferentialist view.* The historical account set forth in Everson by Justices Black and Rutledge has been relied upon as authoritative in many later decisions. But some dispute that account of the history of the religion clauses. One major account suggests that the First Amendment was intended merely to prevent "the establishment of a national church or religion, or the giving of any religious sect or denomination a preferred status." Cord, Separation of Church and State (1982). On this view, government might support religion in general so long as it does not prefer one religion over another. The First Amendment was intended not to protect the government from religion, but to protect religion from government by preventing the government from favoring one religion over another. In addition to the writings of Madison and Jefferson cited by Justice Black, nonpreferentialist scholars point to arguments made by Madison's and Jefferson's contemporaries, who scholars claim sought mainly to protect religious dissenters from government coercion. Although they had different

reasons for doing so, then, these dissenters had banded together with Madison and Jefferson to fight for nonpreferentialism and nothing more.

Several Justices have found the nonpreferentialist view persuasive, though it has never commanded a majority of the Court. For example, in **Wallace v. Jaffree**, 472 U.S. 38 (1985; p. 736), Justice REHNQUIST wrote a dissent taking issue with the "wall of separation" metaphor. He read the history to indicate that Madison did not embrace a strict separationist view of the religion clauses at the time the religion clauses were framed. He emphasized that Madison originally proposed constitutional language barring the establishment of a "*national* religion" and argued that this proposal "obviously does not conform to the 'wall of separation' between church and State idea which latter-day commentators have ascribed to him." Justice Rehnquist concluded: "It seems indisputable from [glimpses] of Madison's thinking, as reflected by actions on the floor of the House in 1789, that he saw the Amendment as designed to prohibit the establishment of a national religion, and perhaps to prevent discrimination among sects. He did not see it as requiring neutrality on the part of government between religion and irreligion. Thus the Court's opinion in Everson—while correct in bracketing Madison and Jefferson together in their exertions in their home State leading to the enactment of the Virginia Statute of Religious Liberty— is totally incorrect in suggesting that Madison carried these views onto the floor of the United States House of Representatives when he proposed the language which would ultimately become the Bill of Rights." Justice Rehnquist also noted that the First Congress had provided for financial aid to sectarian schools in the Northwest Territory and for a presidential proclamation and prayer on the Thanksgiving holiday.

Similarly, concurring in **Rosenberger v. Rector**, 515 U.S. 819 (1995; p. 410), Justice THOMAS found "much to commend" in the view that "the Framers saw the Establishment Clause simply as a prohibition on governmental preferences for some religious faiths over others." He emphasized that the Virginia assessment that Madison opposed in the Remonstrance was a "Bill Establishing a Provision for Teachers of the Christian Religion." Thus, in Justice Thomas's view, "Madison's objection to the assessment bill did not rest on the premise that religious entities may never participate on equal terms in neutral government programs. [Rather, according] to Madison, the Virginia assessment was flawed because it 'violated that equality which ought to be the basis of every law.' [The] bill singled out religious entities for special benefits. [The] funding provided by the Virginia assessment was to be extended only to Christian sects, and the Remonstrance seized on this defect: 'Who does not see that the same authority which can establish Christianity, in exclusion of all other Religions, may establish with the same ease any particular sect of Christians, in exclusion of all other Sects.' " Justice Thomas also cited Justice Rehnquist's Jaffree dissent for evidence of Madison's nonpreferentialism in the House debates on the First Amendment, and cited "historical examples of [public] funding [of religion] that date back to the time of the founding. To take but one famous example, both Houses of the First Congress elected chaplains, [Congress] enacted legislation providing for an annual salary of $500 to be paid out of the Treasury, [and] Madison himself was a member of the committee that recommended the chaplain system in the House."

In several opinions, Justice SOUTER has sought to refute the nonpreferentialist arguments made by Justices Rehnquist and Thomas, relying in part upon Laycock, " 'Nonpreferential' Aid to Religion: A False Claim About Original Intent," 27 Wm. & Mary L. Rev. 875 (1986). In his concurrence in **Lee v. Weisman**, 505 U.S. 577 (1992; p. 737), Justice SOUTER wrote: "When James Madison arrived at the First Congress with a series of proposals to amend the National Constitution, one of the provisions read that 'the civil rights of none shall be abridged on account of religious belief or worship, nor shall any national religion be established, nor shall the full and equal rights of conscience be in any manner, or on any pretext, infringed.' Madison's language did not last long. It was [changed] to read that 'no religion shall be established by law, nor shall the equal rights of conscience be infringed' [and then] 'Congress shall make no laws touching religion, or infringing the rights of conscience' [and then] 'Congress shall make no law establishing Religion, or prohibiting the free exercise thereof, nor shall the rights of conscience be infringed.' [The] House [thus] rejected [a] version [that] arguably ensured only that 'no religion' enjoyed an official preference over others, and deliberately chose instead a prohibition extending to laws establishing 'religion' in general. [Indeed, the] Framers repeatedly considered and deliberately rejected such narrow language and instead extended their prohibition to state support for 'religion' in general."

4. ***The interpretations disputed.*** Some commentators have argued that both views are flawed. As an initial matter, both interpretations rely heavily on the writings of Jefferson and Madison. But Jefferson was not even in the country when the First Amendment was voted upon, and Madison, although he spearheaded the congressional effort to pass the Bill of Rights, did not initially believe the Constitution needed to be amended to protect religious freedom.

Commentators also point out that it is not clear that the Founders—at least at the time when they passed the First Amendment—were universally opposed to *any* "entanglement" of the state with religion. Indeed, at the time the First Amendment was passed, both Jefferson and Madison focused on protecting religion from the state. Consider the following argument: "[Jefferson's] focus was on the liberty of conscience and the necessity of individual judgment in finding truth, which he feared that the state might infringe. [At] the same time, Madison and his supporters in opposing [tax assessments supporting religion] and urging religious freedom also had the goal of protecting religion, not the state. [In] America, the establishment of religion by the government came to be seen as posing a fundamental danger to the liberty of conscience by threatening dissenters with the possibility of coercion. The constitutional guarantee of nonestablishment sought to protect conscience from coercion by guaranteeing a division between the institutional spheres of organized religion and government." Feldman, Divided by God 38, 47 (2005).

Nor is it clear that the Founders were concerned solely with nonpreferentialism. First, as noted above, the Founders appear to have been in substantial agreement that all should respect the liberty of conscience. Second, the bill against which Madison wrote his famous Remonstrance was nonpreferentialist in the sense that it treated all religious sects equally: it assessed taxes to support religious establishments, but taxpayers could choose to which religious establishment they directed their payments. Indeed, many of the New England states assessed taxes in similar fashion until 1820 on the ground that religion would fade without mandatory taxation to support it. Despite supporters' protestations to the contrary, dissenters derided the practice as both "establishing" whatever church was dominant and infringing on their liberty. Indeed, as noted above, one Connecticut Congressman objected to draft language of the First Amendment that "no religion shall be established by law" on the basis that his state's law might be construed as an establishment—to which Madison responded only that the Amendment would not apply to the states.

Are these historical debates at all relevant to contemporary interpretation of the religion clauses? Consider Justice BRENNAN's concurrence in Abington School Dist. v. Schempp (p. 735): "A too literal quest for the advice of the Founding Fathers [seems] to me futile and misdirected. [The] historical record is at best ambiguous, and statements can readily be found to support either side of the proposition." Moreover, he added, "[o]ur religious composition makes us a vastly more diverse people than were our forefathers. They knew differences chiefly among Protestant sects. Today the Nation is far more heterogeneous religiously."

5. *The incorporation of the religion clauses against the states.* Free exercise of religion, like freedom of speech, is easily understood as the type of "liberty" that might be encompassed by the Fourteenth Amendment and thus applied to the states. The Establishment Clause presents a more difficult case for incorporation—particularly with regard to the nonpreferentialist interpretation of the religion clauses. At the time the First Amendment was adopted, several states, unlike Virginia, had established official churches; under one nonpreferentialist view, one of the motivations of the Establishment Clause was to bar Congress from interfering with state establishments. Thus Cord, supra, argues that the First Amendment was meant to "safeguard the right of freedom of conscience in religious beliefs against invasion solely by the national government [but] to allow the states, unimpeded, to deal with religious establishments and aid to religious institutions as they saw fit." See also Howe, The Garden and the Wilderness (1965). Similarly, Justice Thomas, later joined by Justice Gorsuch, has expressed the view in his opinions that the text and history of the Establishment Clause "resist incorporation" against the states.

Nonetheless, the Court, beginning with Everson, has assumed that the Establishment Clause was incorporated into the Fourteenth Amendment and was therefore applicable to the states—without serious discussion of the federalism problem, or the additional textual difficulty of using the "liberty" of the Fourteenth Amendment as the incorporation route. Justice Brennan sought to fill these gaps in his concurrence in Schempp, supra: "It has been suggested, with some support in history, that [incorporation of the Establishment Clause] is conceptually impossible because the Framers meant the [clause] also to foreclose any attempt by Congress to disestablish the existing official state churches. [But] the last of the formal state establishments was dissolved more than three decades before the Fourteenth Amendment was ratified, and thus the problem of protecting official state churches from federal encroachments could hardly have been any concern of those who framed the post-Civil War Amendments.

"[It] has also been suggested that the 'liberty' guaranteed by the Fourteenth Amendment logically cannot absorb the Establishment Clause because that clause is not one of the provisions of the Bill of Rights which in terms protects a 'freedom' of the individual. The fallacy in this contention [is] that it underestimates the role of the Establishment Clause as a coguarantor, with the Free Exercise Clause, of religious liberty. The Framers did not entrust the liberty of religious beliefs to either clause alone."

SECTION 2. THE DEFINITION OF "RELIGION"

How should religion be distinguished from secular moral or philosophical beliefs? From matters of mere personal preference? How should religious organizations be distinguished from other nongovernmental associations commanding significant loyalty and adherence? These questions can be important in delimiting the scope of religious exemptions or in identifying when government benefits constitute establishments.

Although the Court has never given a definitive meaning to the word "religion" as it appears in the Constitution, it considered the scope of a statutory definition of "religion" in a series of cases arising in the Vietnam era under draft laws that provided for a conscientious objector exemption. Section 6(j) of the Universal Military Training and Service Act of 1948 exempted from combatant military service those persons who were conscientiously opposed to participation in "war in any form" by reason of their "religious training and belief." The latter phrase was defined by the law as a "belief in a relation to a Supreme Being involving duties superior to those arising from any human relation, but [not including] essentially political, sociological, or philosophical views or a merely personal moral code." (A 1967 amendment deleted the statutory reference to a "belief in a relation to a Supreme Being," after the 1966 conviction and three-year sentence that gave rise to Welsh, which follows.)

In **United States v. Seeger**, 380 U.S. 163 (1965), the Court interpreted the statutory term "religion" very broadly. Seeger stated on his selective service form that he preferred to leave the question about his belief in a Supreme Being "open" and that he believed in "goodness and virtue for their own sakes" and had "a religious faith in a purely ethical creed [without] belief in God, except in the remotest sense." Justice CLARK's opinion for the Court found Seeger entitled to the exemption: "[The] test of belief 'in a relation to a Supreme Being' is whether a given belief that is sincere and meaningful occupies a place in the life of its possessor parallel to that filled by the orthodox belief in God of one who clearly qualifies for the exemption. Where such beliefs have parallel positions in the lives of their respective holders we cannot say that one is 'in a relation to a Supreme Being' and the other is not." Justice Clark emphasized "the richness and variety of spiritual life in our country" and noted the writings of modern theologians, whose definitions of God differed from traditional theism. In a concurring opinion, Justice DOUGLAS stated that he "would have difficulties" if he "read the statute differently" from the Court: "For then those who embraced one religious faith rather than another would be subject to penalties; and that kind of discrimination, as we held in [Sherbert], would violate the Free Exercise Clause [and] would also result in a denial of equal protection by preferring some religions over others."

In **Welsh v. United States**, 398 U.S. 333 (1970), Justice BLACK's plurality opinion, joined by Justices Douglas, Brennan and Marshall, found an exemption appropriate even though Welsh had struck the word "religious" on his application: "[V]ery few registrants are fully aware of the broad scope of the word 'religious' as used in § 6(j)." Moreover, Welsh's claim was not barred by the exclusion in § 6(j) of those persons with "essentially political, sociological, or philosophical views or a merely personal moral code." That language, Justice Black concluded, should not be read "to exclude those who hold strong beliefs about our domestic and foreign affairs or even those whose conscientious objection to participation in all wars is founded to a substantial extent upon considerations of public policy. The two groups of registrants that obviously do fall within these exclusions from the exemption are those whose beliefs are not deeply held and those whose objection to war does not rest at all upon moral, ethical, or religious principle but instead rests solely upon considerations of policy, pragmatism, or expediency." Justice HARLAN, concurring in the result, found that § 6(j) must be read as limited to "those opposed to war in general because of theistic beliefs" but that, so read, § 6(j) was unconstitutional: Congress "cannot draw the line between theistic or nontheistic religious beliefs on the one hand and secular beliefs on the other. Any such distinctions are not, in my view, compatible with the Establishment Clause." He concluded that the Court, rather than nullifying the exemption entirely, should extend its coverage to those who, like Welsh, had been unconstitutionally excluded. Justice WHITE's dissent concluded that, whether or not Seeger was an accurate reflection of legislative intent, he could not join a "construction of § 6(j) extending draft exemption to those who disclaim religious objections to war and whose views about war represent a purely personal code arising not from religious training and belief as the statute requires but from readings in philosophy, history, and sociology." And he would have found that the "religious training and belief" requirement did not violate the Establishment Clause even were it not required by the Free Exercise Clause: "It is very likely that § 6(j) is a recognition by Congress of free exercise values. [That] judgment is entitled to respect."

The 8–1 decision in **Gillette v. United States**, 401 U.S. 437 (1971), held that Congress could constitutionally refuse to exempt those who did not oppose all wars but only particular conflicts. One such selective objector, for example, claimed that it was his duty as a faithful Catholic to discriminate between "just" and "unjust" wars, and to refuse to participate in the latter. Justice MARSHALL's majority opinion read the statute to require that "conscientious scruples relating to war and military service must amount to conscientious opposition to participating personally in any war and all war." He found the exemption constitutional as so construed. While "the Establishment Clause forbids subtle departures from neutrality, 'religious gerrymanders,' as well as obvious abuses, [still,] a claimant alleging 'gerrymander' must be able to show the absence of a neutral, secular basis for the lines government has drawn." And that showing had not been made here: "We conclude not only that the affirmative purposes underlying § 6(j) [such as the government's interest in 'fairness'] are neutral and secular, but also that valid neutral reasons exist for limiting the exemption to objectors to all war, and that the section therefore cannot be said to reflect a religious preference." He also found the government's interest sufficient to justify any burden on selective objectors' rights of free exercise. Justice DOUGLAS dissented, emphasizing the "implied First Amendment right" of "conscience" and arguing that the law worked "an invidious discrimination in favor of religious persons and against others with like scruples."

What distinguishes a religious pacifist from a pacifist whose beliefs rest only on "essentially political, sociological, or philosophical views or a merely personal moral code"? A belief in a "supreme being"? Why should that matter? Because it suggests a source of countervailing sovereignty to that of the state? A belief in a transcendent reality? A belief that one's activity will have consequences beyond one's lifetime? Participation in rituals such as prayer? Adherence to a sacred text? The fact that one is born into a religious "way of life" rather than acquiring it through individual choice? Doesn't that leave out converts to a faith? A belief that not all questions in the universe can be answered through human rationality? Why should that matter? Because it disables the religionist from participating fully in rationalist political debate? Is a religious exemption a kind of compensation for the disadvantage religious arguments suffer in secular politics? Is any of these features common to all religions?

Assuming that it is possible to define religion at all, should it be defined the same way for free exercise and establishment purposes? Consider the argument that religion should be defined broadly for free exercise but narrowly for Establishment Clause purposes. See Tribe, American Constitutional Law § 14–6 (1st ed. 1978). Such an approach would allow broad religious exemptions, but would not jeopardize every government action that reflects some arguably religious precept. Thus, for example, Mr. Seeger might receive his draft exemption on the ground that his pacifist beliefs were adequately "religious" for that purpose, but then teach his beliefs in a public school classroom without running afoul of the Establishment Clause. But a dual definition of religion "presents a number of problems, most importantly the first amendment's text." Tribe, American Constitutional Law § 14–6 (2d ed. 1988) (departing from his earlier approach). As Justice Rutledge wrote in his Everson dissent, " 'Religion' appears only once in the Amendment. But the word governs two prohibitions and governs them alike. It does not have two meanings." Might the Seeger problem be solved not by defining "religion" narrowly for Establishment Clause purposes, but rather by defining narrowly what constitutes an "establishment"?

———

THE LIMITS OF JUDICIAL INQUIRY INTO RELIGIOUS BELIEF

Why insist on an objective definition of religion? Why not allow religion to be subjectively defined by its adherents? One danger is that such a definition might invite fraud, and create the problem of religious "impostors." It might also expand the definition of religion so greatly that courts would respond by curtailing the substantive scope of free exercise protection. Cf. Fallon, "The Linkage Between Justiciability and Remedies—And Their Connections to Substantive Rights," 92 Va. L. Rev. 633, 637 (2006) (arguing that courts balance and adjust justiciability doctrines, available remedies, and the scope of substantive rights in order to avoid "practically intolerable or disturbingly sub-optimal" outcomes). On the other hand, secular inquiry into the truth or falsity of religious beliefs would appear to be a core violation of free exercise and nonestablishment. The Court tried to steer between these difficulties in **United States v. Ballard**, 322 U.S. 78 (1944). The defendants in Ballard were indicted under the federal mail fraud laws. They had solicited funds for the "I Am" movement. Among their representations were the claims that they had been selected as "divine messengers" to communicate the message of the "alleged divine entity, Saint Germain" and that they had, "by reason of supernatural attainments, the power to heal persons of ailments and diseases." Justice DOUGLAS's majority opinion stated that the First Amendment barred submission to the jury of "the truth or verity of respondents' religious doctrines or beliefs," though it did not bar submission to the jury of the question whether the defendants sincerely believed their representations. He commented: "Men may believe what they cannot prove. They may not be put to the proof of their religious doctrines or beliefs. [The] miracles of the New Testament, the Divinity of Christ, life after death, the power of prayer are deep in the religious convictions of many. If one could be sent to jail because a jury in a hostile environment found those teachings false, little indeed would be left of religious freedom." Justice Jackson, dissenting, expressed doubt whether the "sincerity" of beliefs could be examined without evaluating their content: "I do not see how we can separate an issue as to what is believed from considerations as to what is believable." Chief Justice Stone also dissented, joined by Justices Roberts and Frankfurter.

Is the Court's resolution of the difficulty here satisfactory? Can a jury find that defendants knew that their representations were false *without* inquiring into the truth or falsity of the underlying beliefs? Some argue that courts are competent to evaluate a claimant's sincerity because courts regularly consider questions of mental state in other contexts and can evaluate objective evidence such as whether a claimant tries to act in ways consistent with her claimed belief. See, e.g., Adams & Barmore, "Questioning Sincerity: The Role of the Courts After Hobby Lobby," 67 Stan. L. Rev. Online 59 (2014). For an argument that courts must look carefully at a claimant's sincerity in order to prevent fraud and reduce frivolous lawsuits, see Chapman, "Adjudicating Religious Sincerity," 92 Wash. L. Rev. 1185 (2017). Questions of sincerity are particularly relevant regarding groups whose beliefs may be satirical. For instance, the Church of the Flying Spaghetti Monster, or "Pastafarianism," proclaims that a Flying Spaghetti Monster created the universe, and its founder has been an outspoken advocate against teaching creationism and intelligent design in schools. In 2016 a federal judge in the District of Nebraska ruled that Pastafarianism is not a religion, but rather "a parody, intended to advance an argument about science, the evolution of life, and the place of religion in public education." Cavanaugh v. Bartelt, 178 F. Supp.3d 819, 824 (D. Neb. 2016). Consider also the comedian John Oliver's Our Lady of Perpetual Exemption, a church he founded to draw attention to religious organizations' tax-exempt status and sometimes questionable fundraising.

Another source of controversy regarding judicial power to decide questions of religious doctrine has been the recurrent effort to draw courts into disputes arising from church schisms. Typically, the posture is that a church splits and both factions claim ownership of existing church property as the genuine "closest continuer" of the church; the court is asked to adjudicate the property dispute, which may entail ruling on which faction is the true church. The normal rule is that courts should try to stay out of internal church disputes. But "marginal judicial involvement" is permissible, so long as the courts do not decide church property disputes by "resolving underlying controversies [of] religious doctrine." The Court has said that courts may apply "[n]eutral principles of law, developed for use in all property disputes," in adjudicating church property controversies, but that the religion clauses preclude determining matters "at the very core of a religion—the interpretation of particular church doctrines and the importance of those doctrines to religion." See Presbyterian Church v. Hull

Church, 393 U.S. 440 (1969). The Court has been sharply divided over the application of these guidelines. See, e.g., Jones v. Wolf, 443 U.S. 595 (1979).

While courts may apply "neutral principles of law" to decide church property disputes, there is less clarity about when courts may hear certain tort claims against religious organizations. Resolving some tort cases, such as whether a church negligently supervised a pastor who abused parishioners, could conceivably entangle the court in religion: determining what duty of care a church owes its congregation, or what the relationship between a pastor and a church should look like, could involve questions of religious doctrine. The Supreme Court has never directly addressed tort suits against religious groups, and state courts have split on which tort claims are permissible. See, e.g., Gibson v. Brewer, 952 S.W.2d 239 (Mo. 1997) (en banc) (holding a claim for negligent supervision of clergy would entangle the court in religion); Malicki v. Doe, 814 So.2d 347 (Fla. 2002) (holding a negligent supervision claim was permissible because the church did not claim its supervision of clergy was a religious question).

SECTION 3. THE FREE EXERCISE OF RELIGION

To some extent, claims based on the free exercise of religion overlap with free speech claims. For example, recall the free speech objections raised by members of Jehovah's Witnesses in cases such as Cantwell v. Connecticut, Lovell v. Griffin, Martin v. Struthers and Wooley v. Maynard. But the "free exercise" guarantee raises distinctive problems. *First*, "exercise" implies more than belief or expression; it often implies conduct or action. In many of the cases that follow, the free exercise claimant argues that a general law resting on state interests not related to religion either interferes with behavior dictated by religious belief or compels conduct forbidden by religious belief. Should government have more leeway to regulate conduct than belief? *Second*, the Establishment Clause has no parallel in the Speech Clause. In the religion context, however, it places limits on how far either legislatures or courts can go in exempting religious believers from general regulations, or otherwise accommodating free exercise values. The free exercise cases that follow look first at the question whether government may deliberately disadvantage religion or a particular religion, and second at whether religious practitioners are entitled to exemptions from generally applicable laws that conflict with dictates of their faith.

LAWS DISCRIMINATING AGAINST RELIGION

Free exercise clearly bars outlawing or compelling belief in a particular religious faith. As Chief Justice Burger stated in McDaniel v. Paty, which follows, "The Free Exercise Clause categorically prohibits government from regulating, prohibiting, or rewarding religious beliefs as such." Perhaps because this principle is so basic, free exercise controversies over such attempts at thought control are rare. In Torcaso v. Watkins, 367 U.S. 488 (1961), the Court struck down a Maryland requirement that all holders of public office declare their belief in the existence of God. The decision stated: "Neither the State nor the Federal Government can constitutionally force a person 'to profess a belief or disbelief in any religion,'" nor could they "aid those religions based on a belief in the existence of God as against those religions founded on different beliefs." Torcaso rested principally on the Free Exercise Clause, but also noted by way of analogy the religious test clause of Article VI: "[N]o religious Test shall ever be required as a Qualification to any Office or public Trust under the United States."

In **McDaniel v. Paty**, 435 U.S. 618 (1978), the Court invalidated, under the Free Exercise Clause, a Tennessee provision disqualifying clergy from being legislators or constitutional convention delegates. (Tennessee was the last state to retain the disqualification, once commonplace in state laws.) Chief Justice BURGER's plurality opinion, joined by Justices Powell, Rehnquist and Stevens, found the absolute bar on interference with religious *beliefs* inapplicable, because the state barrier referred to "*status* [as] 'minister' or 'priest' " and ministerial status was "defined in terms of conduct and activity rather [than] belief." The plurality nonetheless applied strict scrutiny to the disqualification's burden on religious practice, and found the State's rationale that it was preventing establishment of religion inadequate to support the ban: "[T]he American experience provides no persuasive support for the fear that clergymen in public office will be less careful of anti-establishment interests or less faithful to their oaths of civil office than their unordained counterparts." Separate concurrences by Justice BRENNAN, joined by Justice Marshall, and by Justice STEWART found that the disqualification did directly burden religious belief and thus was absolutely prohibited under Torcaso, without any further balancing. Justice Brennan wrote: "Clearly freedom of belief protected by the Free Exercise Clause embraces freedom to profess or practice that belief, even including doing so to earn a livelihood." Justice Stewart wrote: "The disability imposed on McDaniel, like the one imposed on Torcaso, implicates the 'freedom to believe' more than the less absolute 'freedom to act.' " (Note that both Torcaso and McDaniel rejected the government's argument that a public job or office is a mere "privilege" to which the state may attach conditions that would otherwise violate the First Amendment.)

Free exercise challenges arise more commonly when laws regulate religious practice or conduct. While previous eras have witnessed various forms of overt discrimination against disfavored religions, modern legislation rarely evinces outright hostility to particular religions or religious practices. Like overt racial bigotry, overt religious prejudice rarely appears on the face of contemporary laws. The Court has proved willing, however, to look behind the face of a statute to discern religiously discriminatory purpose, as illustrated in the Lukumi case, which follows. In Lukumi, the Court unanimously invalidated a city ordinance prohibiting the ritual slaughter of animals, finding that the law, while apparently neutral on its face, actually was targeted against practitioners of the Santería faith and thus violated the Free Exercise Clause:

Church of the Lukumi Babalu Aye v. City of Hialeah

508 U.S. 520, 113 S. Ct. 2217, 124 L. Ed. 2d 472 (1993).

■ JUSTICE KENNEDY delivered the opinion of the Court, except as to Part II-A-2.

[This] case involves practices of the Santeria religion, which originated in the nineteenth century. When hundreds of thousands of members of the Yoruba people were brought as slaves from eastern Africa to Cuba, their traditional African religion absorbed significant elements of Roman Catholicism. The resulting syncretion, or fusion, is Santeria, "the way of the saints." The Cuban Yoruba express their devotion to spirits, called orishas. [The] Santeria faith teaches that every individual has a destiny from God, a destiny fulfilled with the aid and energy of the orishas. The basis of the Santeria religion is the nurture of a personal relation with the orishas, and one of the principal forms of devotion is an animal sacrifice. [According] to Santeria teaching, the orishas are powerful but not immortal. They depend for survival on the sacrifice. Sacrifices are performed at birth, marriage, and death rites, for the cure of the sick, for the initiation of new members and priests, and during an annual celebration. Animals sacrificed in Santeria rituals include chickens, pigeons, doves, ducks, guinea pigs, goats, sheep, and turtles. The animals are killed by the cutting of the carotid arteries in the neck. The sacrificed animal is cooked and eaten, except after healing and death rituals. Santeria adherents faced widespread persecution in Cuba, so the religion and its rituals were practiced in secret. The open practice of Santeria and its rites infrequent.

[The Church's] announcement of plans to open a Santeria church in Hialeah[, Florida,] prompted the city council to hold an emergency public session on June 9, 1987. [The] city council adopted Resolution 87–66, which noted the "concern" expressed by residents of the city "that certain religions may propose to engage in practices which are inconsistent with public morals, peace or safety," and declared that "the City reiterates its commitment to a prohibition against any and all acts of any and all religious groups which are inconsistent with public morals, peace or safety." [In] September 1987, the city council adopted three substantive ordinances addressing the issue of religious animal sacrifice. Ordinance 87–52 defined "sacrifice" as "to unnecessarily kill, torment, torture, or mutilate an animal in a public or private ritual or ceremony not for the primary purpose of food consumption," and prohibited owning or possessing an animal "intending to use such animal for food purposes." It restricted application of this prohibition, however, to any individual or group that "kills, slaughters or sacrifices animals for any type of ritual, regardless of whether or not the flesh or blood of the animal is to be consumed." The ordinance contained an exemption for slaughtering by "licensed establishments" of animals "specifically raised for food purposes." [Ordinance] 87–71 [defined] sacrifice as had Ordinance 87–52, and then provided that "it shall be unlawful for any person, persons, corporations or associations to sacrifice any animal within the corporate limits of the City of Hialeah, Florida." The final Ordinance, 87–72, defined "slaughter" as "the killing of animals for food" and prohibited slaughter outside of areas zoned for slaughterhouse use. The ordinance provided an exemption, however, for the slaughter or processing for sale of "small numbers of hogs and/or cattle per week in accordance with an exemption provided by state law." All ordinances and resolutions passed the city council by unanimous vote. Violations [were] punishable by fines not exceeding $500 or imprisonment not exceeding 60 days, or both.

[At] a minimum, the protections of the Free Exercise Clause pertain if the law at issue discriminates against some or all religious beliefs or regulates or prohibits conduct because it is undertaken for religious reasons. Indeed, it was "historical instances of religious persecution and intolerance that gave concern to those who drafted the Free Exercise Clause." [If] the object of a law is to infringe upon or restrict practices because of their religious motivation, the law is not neutral; and it is invalid unless it is justified by a compelling interest and is narrowly tailored to advance that interest.

To determine the object of a law, we must begin with its text, for the minimum requirement of neutrality is that a law not discriminate on its face. [Petitioners] contend that three of the ordinances fail this test of facial neutrality because they use the words "sacrifice" and "ritual," words with strong religious connotations. We agree that these words are consistent with the claim of facial discrimination, but the argument is not conclusive. The words "sacrifice" and "ritual" have a religious origin, but current use admits also of secular meanings. [But] facial neutrality is not determinative. [The] Free Exercise Clause protects against governmental hostility which is masked, as well as overt.

[The] record in this case compels the conclusion that suppression of the central element of the Santeria worship service was the object of the ordinances. [The June 9 resolution aimed at] "certain religions" [and] it cannot be maintained that city officials had in mind a religion other than Santeria. It is [also] a necessary conclusion that almost the only conduct subject to Ordinances 87–40, 87–52, and 87–71 is the religious exercise of Santeria church members. [Ordinance] 87–71 excludes almost all killings of animals except for religious sacrifice, and the primary purpose requirement narrows the proscribed category even further, in particular by exempting Kosher slaughter. Operating in similar fashion is Ordinance 87–52, which prohibits the "possession, sacrifice, or slaughter" of an animal with the "intent to use such animal for food purposes" [but exempts] "any licensed [food] establishment" with regard to "any animals which are specifically raised for food purposes," if the activity is permitted by zoning and other laws. This exception, too, seems intended to cover Kosher slaughter. [Ordinance] 87–40 incorporates the Florida animal cruelty statute. Its prohibition is broad on its face, punishing "whoever . . . unnecessarily . . . kills any animal." The city claims that this ordinance is the epitome of a neutral prohibition. [But the city] deem[s] [k]illings for religious reasons [unnecessary but] deems hunting, slaughter of animals for food, eradication of insects and pests, and euthanasia as necessary. [The city's] application of the ordinance's test of necessity devalues religious reasons for killing by judging them to be of lesser import than nonreligious reasons. Thus, religious practice is being singled out for discriminatory treatment.

[The] legitimate governmental interests in protecting the public health and preventing cruelty to animals could be addressed by restrictions stopping far short of a flat prohibition of all Santeria sacrificial practice. [Counsel] for the city conceded at oral argument that, under the ordinances, Santeria sacrifices would be illegal even if they occurred in licensed, inspected, and zoned slaughterhouses. [With] regard to the city's interest in ensuring the adequate care of animals, regulation of conditions and treatment, regardless of why an animal is kept, is the logical response to the city's concern, not a prohibition on possession for the purpose of sacrifice.

[In Part II-A-2 of Justice Kennedy's opinion, which was joined only by Justices Stevens, Blackmun and O'Connor, he added: "In determining if the object of a law is a neutral one under the Free Exercise Clause, we can also find guidance in our equal protection cases. [Here], as in equal protection cases, we may determine the city council's object from both direct and circumstantial evidence. [Arlington Heights.] [The] minutes and taped excerpts of the June 9 session, both of which are in the record, evidence significant hostility exhibited by residents, members of the city council, and other city officials toward the Santeria religion and its practice of animal sacrifice. The public crowd that attended the June 9 meetings interrupted statements by council members critical of Santeria with cheers and the brief comments of [the Church's leader] with taunts. When [a council member supporting the ordinances] stated that in prerevolution Cuba 'people were put in jail for practicing this religion,' the audience applauded. [One council member said that the] 'Bible says we are allowed to sacrifice an animal for consumption,' [and] continued, 'but for any other purposes, I don't believe that the Bible allows that.' [The] chaplain of the Hialeah Police Department told the city council that Santeria was a sin, 'foolishness,' 'an abomination to the Lord,' and the worship of 'demons.' [This] history discloses the object of the ordinances to target animal sacrifice by Santeria worshippers because of its religious motivation." Resuming his opinion for the Court, Justice Kennedy continued:]

In sum, [the] ordinances had as their object the suppression of religion. The pattern we have recited discloses animosity to Santeria adherents and their religious practices; the ordinances by their own terms target this religious exercise; the texts of the ordinances were gerrymandered with care to proscribe religious killings of animals but to exclude almost all secular killings; and the ordinances suppress much more religious conduct than is necessary in order to achieve the legitimate ends asserted in their defense.

[A] law burdening religious practice that is not neutral or not of general application must undergo the most rigorous of scrutiny. [It] follows from what we have already said that these ordinances cannot withstand this scrutiny. First, even were the governmental interests compelling, [all] four ordinances are overbroad or underinclusive. [The] absence of narrow tailoring suffices to establish the invalidity of the ordinances. [Moreover,] [w]here government restricts only conduct protected by the First Amendment and fails to enact feasible measures to restrict other conduct producing substantial harm or alleged harm of the same sort, the interest given in justification of the restriction is not compelling. [Reversed.]

■ JUSTICE SCALIA, joined by CHIEF JUSTICE REHNQUIST, concurring in part and concurring in the judgment.

I do not join [Part II-A-2] because it departs from the opinion's general focus on the object of the laws at issue to consider the subjective motivation of the lawmakers, i.e., whether the Hialeah City Council actually intended to disfavor the religion of Santeria. [But] it is virtually impossible to determine the singular "motive" of a collective legislative body, and this Court has a long tradition of refraining from such inquiries. [The] First Amendment does not refer to the purposes for which legislators enact laws, but to the effects of the laws enacted: "Congress shall make no law . . .

prohibiting the free exercise [of religion]. . . . " This does not put us in the business of invalidating laws by reason of the evil motives of their authors. Had the Hialeah City Council set out resolutely to suppress the practices of Santeria, but ineptly adopted ordinances that failed to do so, I do not see how those laws could be said to "prohibit the free exercise" of religion. Nor, in my view, does it matter that a legislature consists entirely of the pure-hearted, if the law it enacts in fact singles out a religious practice for special burdens. Had the ordinances here been passed with no motive on the part of any councilman except the ardent desire to prevent cruelty to animals (as might in fact have been the case), they would nonetheless be invalid.

[Justice SOUTER filed an opinion concurring in part and in the judgment and Justice BLACKMUN, joined by Justice O'Connor, filed an opinion concurring in the judgment. Both these opinions found this an easy case for invalidation, reasoning that, in Justice Souter's words, Hialeah had enacted "a rare example of a law actually aimed at suppressing religious exercise," and that such a law is nearly always invalid. Justices Souter and Blackmun declined to join all of Justice Kennedy's opinion, however, because it referred in dicta to aspects of Employment Division v. Smith (1997; p. 684) that they found objectionable.]

IDENTIFYING ANTIRELIGIOUS PURPOSE

1. ***Lukumi and religious gerrymanders.*** Justice Kennedy called the law in Lukumi a "religious gerrymander"—that is, "an impermissible attempt to target petitioners and their religious practices." Like drawing a district boundary so as to include or exclude members of a particular race or political party, the Hialeah law was drawn with definitions and exceptions that in practice singled out Santería for adverse treatment.

Hialeah's law was struck down under the Free Exercise Clause. But the Court has also struck down "religious gerrymanders" under the Establishment Clause. For example, in **Larson v. Valente**, 456 U.S. 228 (1982), the Court struck down a Minnesota law imposing registration and reporting requirements for charitable solicitations and exempting some, but not all, religious organizations from the law. The requirements applied only to religious organizations that solicit more than 50% of their funds from nonmembers. The law was challenged by the Unification Church, which consists of followers of Rev. Sun Myung Moon, on the ground that it preferred traditional over untraditional religions.

The Court found that this scheme violated the "clearest command of the Establishment Clause," namely that "one religious denomination cannot be officially preferred over another." In invalidating the 50% rule, Justice BRENNAN's majority opinion applied strict scrutiny and found the law not closely tailored to any government interest in preventing fraudulent or abusive solicitation practices. He emphasized Minnesota's "*selective* legislative imposition of burdens and advantages upon particular denominations," noting that "the provision was drafted with the explicit intention of including particular religious denominations and excluding others." One state senator observed that other lawmakers seemed to have a religious animus toward groups that were included, stating, " 'I'm not sure why we're so hot to regulate the Moonies anyway.' " By contrast, an earlier version of the law was eliminated when "the legislators perceived that [it] would bring a Roman Catholic Archdiocese within the Act." Justice Brennan found that the 50% rule's "capacity—indeed, its express design—to burden or favor selected religious denominations led the Minnesota Legislature to discuss the characteristics of various sects with a view towards 'religious gerrymandering.' "

Note that Larson, like Lukumi, looked behind the facial neutrality of the law to discern a religiously discriminatory purpose. Why was Larson litigated under the Establishment rather than the Free Exercise Clause? Because its selective favoritism toward mainstream religions was more apparent than its selective burdens on unorthodox ones? Because the selective burdens did not fall upon practices central to the free exercise of the Unification faith? Was animal sacrifice more central to Santeria practitioners than solicitation was to Unification Church members? Is solicitation an aspect of the free exercise of religion at all? Should prosecutors, juries and judges be entrusted with deciding such questions?

Conversely, why was Lukumi litigated as a free exercise rather than an establishment case? Justice Kennedy noted several times Hialeah's careful exemption of the kosher slaughter practices used by Orthodox Jews. Did such exemptions for one religious tradition in particular create religious favoritism in violation of the Establishment Clause? Justice Kennedy expressly declined to reach that issue in Lukumi: "We need not discuss whether [the] differential treatment of two religions is itself an independent constitutional violation. Cf. Larson. It suffices to recite this feature of the law as support for our conclusion that Santeria alone was the exclusive legislative concern." Does it seem implausible to imagine that Hialeah had "established" Orthodox Judaism, itself a minority faith? The Court has suggested that religious favoritism might violate the Establishment Clause whether it favors mainstream or minority faiths. See Kiryas Joel (1994; p. 810).

2.   ***Singling out religion for denial of public funding.*** Lukumi shows that even a law that makes no mention of religion can be found discriminatory against religion. Interestingly, the Court has held that even a law that singles out religion to deny government funding might not be discriminatory. This issue was addressed in Locke v. Davey (2004; p. 794). There, the Court held, in an opinion by Chief Justice Rehnquist, that a Washington state educational scholarship that could not be used to pursue a degree in devotional theology did not unconstitutionally single out religion for disfavor under Lukumi. The Court explained that neither the Washington constitutional provision denying public money for religious instruction nor the program "suggest[ed] animus towards religion." Justice Scalia, in dissent, argued that legislative animus did not matter, a position in keeping with his general rejection of the use of legislative history to establish intent. But the Court distinguished Locke in its decision in Trinity Lutheran Church of Columbia v. Comer (2017; p. 796) and in Espinoza v. Montana Department of Revenue (2020; p. 800). In both cases, Chief Justice Roberts wrote for the Court that denying a religious organization funds for secular purposes solely because of the organization's religious status violated the organization's religious rights.

3.   ***Religious or racial animosity?*** The Lukumi case demonstrates that it is not always possible to separate laws motivated by religious animosity from laws motivated by racial, or other, considerations. Such laws often stem from a variety of sources at once. The Church of Lukumi Babalu

Aye is a Santería church composed predominately of Cuban-Americans of Afro-Caribbean descent. Much of the opposition to the animal-sacrifice elements of Santería stemmed from the white Cuban population of the Miami area. "Whenever the carcasses of dead animals appeared on beaches or in trash bins, residents blamed the [predominantly Afro-Caribbean] working class. [Cuban] [e]migrees who criticized santería tended to be the white elite, who were embarrassed and resentful of the negative attention." García, Havana USA 96 (1996).

4. *Expressions of bias and differential results.* In **Masterpiece Cakeshop v. Colorado Civil Rights Commission**, 584 U.S. ___, 138 S. Ct. 1719 (2018), a Colorado baker, Jack Phillips, told a same-sex couple that he would not create a cake for their wedding celebration because of his religious opposition to same-sex marriages. The couple filed a charge with the Colorado Civil Rights Commission pursuant to the Colorado Anti-Discrimination Act (CADA), which prohibits discrimination based on sexual orientation in a "place of business engaged in any sales to the public and any place offering services . . . to the public." The Colorado Civil Rights Division first found probable cause for a violation and referred the case to the Commission. The Commission then referred the case for a formal hearing before a state Administrative Law Judge, who ruled in the couple's favor.

The case received wide public attention as the first major post-Obergefell clash between religious liberty and marriage equality. Justice KENNEDY's opinion for a 7–2 Court avoided the major issues of whether the baker was entitled to a religious exemption from Colorado's anti-discrimination law and whether requiring the baker to make a cake would violate his free speech rights. Instead, the Court found a Lukumi violation:

"[Our] society has come to the recognition that gay persons and gay couples cannot be treated as social outcasts or as inferior in dignity and worth. For that reason the laws and the Constitution can, and in some instances must, protect them in the exercise of their civil rights. The exercise of their freedom on terms equal to others must be given great weight and respect by the courts. At the same time, the religious and philosophical objections to gay marriage are protected views and in some instances protected forms of expression. [Nevertheless,] while those religious and philosophical objections are protected, it is a general rule that such objections do not allow business owners and other actors in the economy and in society to deny protected persons equal access to goods and services under a neutral and generally applicable public accommodations law. When it comes to weddings, it can be assumed that a member of the clergy who objects to gay marriage on moral and religious grounds could not be compelled to perform the ceremony without denial of his or her right to the free exercise of religion. This refusal would be well understood in our constitutional order as an exercise of religion, an exercise that gay persons could recognize and accept without serious diminishment to their own dignity and worth. Yet if that exception were not confined, then a long list of persons who provide goods and services for marriages and weddings might refuse to do so for gay persons, thus resulting in a community-wide stigma inconsistent with the history and dynamics of civil rights laws that ensure equal access to goods, services, and public accommodations.

"[The] neutral and respectful consideration to which Phillips was entitled was compromised here, however. The Civil Rights Commission's treatment of his case has some elements of a clear and impermissible hostility toward the sincere religious beliefs that motivated his objection. That hostility surfaced at the Commission's formal, public hearings. [During the Commission's first public meeting,] [one] commissioner suggested that Phillips can believe 'what he wants to believe,' but cannot act on his religious beliefs 'if he decides to do business in the state.' A few moments later, the commissioner restated the same position: '[I]f a businessman wants to do business in the state and he's got an issue with the—the law's impacting his personal belief system, he needs to look at being able to compromise.' Standing alone, these statements are susceptible of different interpretations. On the one hand, they might mean simply that a business cannot refuse to provide services based on sexual orientation, regardless of the proprietor's personal views. On the other hand, they might be seen as inappropriate and dismissive comments showing lack of due consideration for Phillips' free exercise rights and the dilemma he faced. In view of the comments that followed, the latter seems the more likely.

"[At the Commission's second public meeting,] another commissioner made specific reference to the previous meeting's discussion but said far more to disparage Phillips' beliefs. The commissioner stated: ['Freedom] of religion and religion has been used to justify all kinds of discrimination throughout history, whether it be slavery, whether it be the holocaust, whether it be—I mean, we—we can list hundreds of situations where freedom of religion has been used to justify discrimination. And to me it is one of the most despicable pieces of rhetoric that people can use to—to use their religion to hurt others.' To describe a man's faith as 'one of the most despicable pieces of rhetoric that people can use' is to disparage his religion in at least two distinct ways: by describing it as despicable, and also by characterizing it as merely rhetorical—something insubstantial and even insincere. The commissioner even went so far as to compare Phillips' invocation of his sincerely held religious beliefs to defenses of slavery and the Holocaust. This sentiment is inappropriate for a Commission charged with the solemn responsibility of fair and neutral enforcement of Colorado's antidiscrimination law—a law that protects discrimination on the basis of religion as well as sexual orientation.

"The record shows no objection to these comments from other commissioners. And the later state-court ruling reviewing the Commission's decision did not mention those comments, much less express concern with their content. Nor were the comments by the commissioners disavowed in the briefs filed in this Court. For these reasons, the Court cannot avoid the conclusion that these statements cast doubt on the fairness and impartiality of the Commission's adjudication of Phillips' case. Members of the Court have disagreed on the question whether statements made by lawmakers may properly be taken into account in determining whether a law intentionally discriminates on the basis of religion. See Lukumi (Scalia, J., concurring in part and concurring in judgment). In this case, however, the remarks were made in a very different context—by an adjudicatory body deciding a particular case.

"Another indication of hostility is the difference in treatment between Phillips' case and the cases of other bakers who objected to a requested cake on the basis of conscience and prevailed before the Commission. [On] at least three other occasions the Civil Rights Division considered the refusal of bakers to create cakes with images that conveyed disapproval of same-sex marriage, along with religious text. Each time, the Division found that the baker acted lawfully in refusing service. It made these determinations because, in the words of the Division, the requested cake included 'wording and images [the baker] deemed derogatory.' The treatment of the conscience-based objections at issue in these three cases contrasts with the Commission's treatment of Phillips' objection. The Commission ruled against Phillips in part on the theory that any message the requested wedding cake would carry would be attributed to the customer, not to the baker. Yet the Division did not address this point in any of the other cases with respect to the cakes depicting anti-gay marriage symbolism. Additionally, the Division found no violation of CADA in the other cases in part because each bakery was willing to sell other products, including those depicting Christian themes, to the prospective customers. But the Commission dismissed Phillips' willingness to sell 'birthday cakes, shower cakes, [and] cookies and brownies,' to gay and lesbian customers as irrelevant. The treatment of the other cases and Phillips' case could reasonably be interpreted as being inconsistent as to the question of whether speech is involved, quite apart from whether the cases should ultimately be distinguished."

Justice KAGAN concurred, joined by Justice Breyer: "I write separately to elaborate on one of the bases for the Court's holding. The Court partly relies on the disparate consideration of Phillips' case compared to the cases of [three] other bakers who objected to a requested cake on the basis of conscience. [What] makes the state agencies' consideration [disquieting] is that a proper basis for distinguishing the cases was available—in fact, was obvious. The Colorado Anti-Discrimination Act (CADA) makes it unlawful for a place of public accommodation to deny 'the full and equal enjoyment' of goods and services to individuals based on certain characteristics, including sexual orientation and creed. The three bakers in the cases [brought by William Jack] did not violate that law. Jack requested them to make a cake (one denigrating gay people and same-sex marriage) that they would not have made for any customer. In refusing that request, the bakers did not single out Jack because of his religion, but instead treated him in the same way they would have treated anyone else—just as CADA requires. By contrast, the same-sex couple in this case requested a wedding cake that Phillips would have made for an opposite-sex couple. In refusing that request, Phillips contravened CADA's demand that customers receive 'the full and equal enjoyment' of public accommodations irrespective of their sexual orientation. The different outcomes in the Jack cases and the Phillips case could thus have been justified by a plain reading and neutral application of Colorado law—untainted by any bias against a religious belief. I read the Court's opinion as fully consistent with that view."

Justice GORSUCH concurred, joined by Justice Alito, to disagree with Justice Kagan: "In both cases, the effect on the customer was the same: bakers refused service to persons who bore a statutorily protected trait (religious faith or sexual orientation). But in both cases the bakers refused service intending only to honor a personal conviction. To be sure, the bakers knew their conduct promised the effect of leaving a customer in a protected class unserved. But there's no indication the bakers actually intended to refuse service because of a customer's protected characteristic. We know this because all of the bakers explained without contradiction that they would not sell the requested cakes to anyone, while they would sell other cakes to members of the protected class (as well as to anyone else). So, for example, the bakers in the first case would have refused to sell a cake denigrating same-sex marriage to an atheist customer, just as the baker in the second case would have refused to sell a cake celebrating same-sex marriage to a heterosexual customer. And the bakers in the first case were generally happy to sell to persons of faith, just as the baker in the second case was generally happy to sell to gay persons. In both cases, it was the kind of cake, not the kind of customer, that mattered to the bakers.

Justice GINSBURG dissented, joined by Justice Sotomayor: "The different outcomes the Court features do not evidence hostility to religion of the kind we have previously held to signal a free-exercise violation, nor do the comments by one or two members of one of the four decisionmaking entities considering this case justify reversing the judgment below. [The] bakeries' refusal to make Jack cakes of a kind they would not make for any customer scarcely resembles Phillips' refusal to serve Craig and Mullins: Phillips would *not* sell to Craig and Mullins, for no reason other than their sexual orientation, a cake of the kind he regularly sold to others. When a couple contacts a bakery for a wedding cake, the product they are seeking is a cake celebrating *their* wedding—not a cake celebrating heterosexual weddings or same-sex weddings—and that is the service Craig and Mullins were denied. [Jack,] on the other hand, suffered no service refusal on the basis of his religion or any other protected characteristic. He was treated as any other customer would have been treated—no better, no worse.

"[Statements] made at the Commission's public hearings on Phillips' case provide no firmer support for the Court's holding today. [The] proceedings involved several layers of independent decisionmaking, of which the Commission was but one. [What] prejudice infected the determinations of the adjudicators in the case before and after the Commission? The Court does not say. Phillips' case is thus far removed from the only precedent upon which the Court relies, Lukumi, where the government action that violated a principle of religious neutrality implicated a sole decisionmaking body, the city council."

Does the Masterpiece Cakeshop decision break new ground in identifying antireligious animus? How searching was the Court's inquiry into animus in Masterpiece compared to Lukumi? Has the Court broadened the category of considerations that could count as animus? How much of a role did the allegedly disparate treatment between Phillips and the other bakers' cases play in the Court's decision? Recall that Justice Scalia refused to look to the legislative history of the ordinance in Lukumi, meaning the majority of the Court looked only to the ordinance itself. Can that be reconciled with Justice Kennedy's consideration of adjudicators' motives and statements in Masterpiece? Is his distinction between the adjudicatory versus legislative natures of the proceedings in Masterpiece and Lukumi convincing? Furthermore, were the commissioners' statements genuinely antireligious? For an argument that the Court misread them, see Kendrick & Schwartzman, "The Etiquette of Animus," 132 Harv. L. Rev. 133 (2018).

While the Court left open the questions whether someone can claim a religious exemption to antidiscrimination laws and whether there is a free speech issue in requiring someone to engage in an arguably artistic project, does the language in Justice Kennedy's opinion provide support for a particular outcome on those questions? How might Justices Kagan and Gorsuch's concurrences be used to argue those issues?

Consider also how Masterpiece Cakeshop fits with another important case from same Term, Trump v. Hawaii, 585 U.S. ___, 138 S. Ct. 2392 (2018), which declined to apply Lukumi analysis to President Donald Trump's allegedly anti-Muslim statements associated with his executive order banning travel from a several majority-Muslim countries. Is there tension between the two decisions? While the majority in Trump v. Hawaii did not directly address the potential establishment violation, Justice Breyer's dissent argued that if the decision to implement the ban were "significantly affected by religious animus," it would violate the First Amendment. Justice Sotomayor, also in dissent, found explicitly that "the primary purpose of the Proclamation is to disfavor Islam and its adherents."

———

RELIGIOUS EXEMPTIONS

Free exercise claims are more commonly raised against facially neutral laws that are not targeted at a religious practice, but which have a disproportionately adverse impact on religious practitioners. Such laws might either require conduct that is incompatible with religious practice or forbid conduct that is religiously required. The free exercise claimant typically seeks an exemption from, not invalidation of the law. Are religious exemptions ever constitutionally compelled?

The Court's first major decision on free exercise exemptions was **Reynolds v. United States**, 98 U.S. 145 (1878), which upheld application of a federal law making bigamy a crime in the territories to a Mormon claiming that polygamy was his religious duty. As Chief Justice WAITE read the First Amendment, "Congress was deprived of all legislative power over mere opinion, but was left free to reach actions which were in violation of social duties or subversive of good order." He reviewed the traditional condemnation of multiple marriages in modern western society, and cited work by Francis Lieber (better known as the author of the Civil War-era "Lieber Code" on the laws of war) suggesting that "polygamy leads to the patriarchal principle, which, when applied to large communities, fetters the people in stationary despotism, while that principle cannot long exist in connection with monogamy." Chief Justice Waite concluded: "Laws are made for the government of actions, and while they cannot interfere with mere religious belief and opinions, they may with practices. Suppose one believed that human sacrifices were a necessary part of religious worship, would it be seriously contended that the civil government under which he lived could not interfere to prevent a sacrifice? Or if a wife religiously believed it was her duty to burn herself upon the funeral pile of her dead husband, would it be beyond the power of the civil government to prevent her carrying her belief into practice? So here, as a law of the organization of society under the exclusive dominion of the United States, it is provided that plural marriages shall not be allowed. Can a man excuse his practices to the contrary because of his religious belief? To permit this would be to make the professed doctrines of religious belief superior to the law of the land, and in effect to permit every citizen to become a law unto himself. Government could exist only in name under such circumstances."

Cantwell v. Connecticut, 310 U.S. 296 (1940; p. 61), which incorporated the Free Exercise Clause against the states, suggested that religious conduct was not wholly outside the protection of the Free Exercise Clause, even if it was subject to greater regulation than belief. Justice ROBERTS wrote: "[Free exercise] embraces two concepts—freedom to believe and freedom to act. The first is absolute, but in the nature of things, the second cannot be. [In] every case the power to regulate must be so exercised as not, in attaining a permissible end, unduly to infringe the protected freedom."

That same year, in **Minersville School Dist. v. Gobitis**, 310 U.S. 586 (1940; p. 476), the Court refused to grant a free exercise exemption to Lillian and William Gobitis, Jehovah's Witnesses who had been expelled from a Pennsylvania public school for refusing to salute the flag. In his opinion for the Court, Justice FRANKFURTER wrote: "In the judicial enforcement of religious freedom we are concerned with a historic concept. The religious liberty which the Constitution protects has never excluded legislation of general scope not directed against doctrinal loyalties of particular sects. Judicial nullification of legislation cannot be justified by attributing to the framers of the Bill of Rights views for which there is no historic warrant. Conscientious scruples have not, in the course of the long struggle for religious toleration, relieved the individual from obedience to a general law not aimed at the promotion or restriction of religious beliefs. The mere possession of religious convictions which contradict the relevant concerns of a political society does not relieve the citizen from the discharge of political responsibilities. The necessity for this adjustment has again and again been recognized. In a number of situations the exertion of political authority has been sustained, while basic considerations of religious freedom have been left inviolate. Reynolds. In [previous] cases the general laws in question, upheld in their application to those who refused obedience from religious conviction, were manifestations of specific powers of government deemed by the legislature essential to secure and maintain that orderly, tranquil, and free society without which religious toleration itself is unattainable."

Just three years later, the Court effectively reversed Gobitis, which had been widely criticized, in **West Virginia State Bd. of Educ. v. Barnette**, 319 U.S. 624 (1943; p. 478), but did so on free-speech grounds, leaving the free exercise holding unchanged. And in **Braunfeld v. Brown**, 366 U.S. 599 (1961), the Court rejected a free exercise challenge to a Pennsylvania Sunday closing law. The challengers were Orthodox Jews whose religion required that they close their stores on Saturdays. They alleged that the Sunday closing laws would place them at such a severe competitive disadvantage as to force them out of business. Chief Justice WARREN's plurality opinion, joined by Justices Black, Clark and Whittaker, rejected the free exercise challenge. Citing Reynolds and Cantwell, Chief Justice Warren emphasized that, unlike the freedom to hold religious beliefs and opinions, the "freedom to act, even when the action is in accord with one's religious convictions, is not totally free from legislative restrictions." He added that the law here did not "make criminal the holding of any religious belief or opinion, nor force anyone to embrace any religious belief. [It simply made] the practice of their religious beliefs more expensive. To strike down [legislation] which imposes only an indirect burden on the exercise of religion, i.e., legislation which does not make unlawful the religious practice itself, would radically restrict the operating latitude of the [legislature]. We are a cosmopolitan nation made up of people of almost every conceivable religious preference. [Consequently,] it cannot be expected, much less required, that legislators enact no law regulating conduct that may in some way result in an economic disadvantage to some religious sects and not to others because of the special practices of the various religions. [If] the State regulates conduct by enacting a general law within its power, the purpose and effect of which is to advance the State's secular goals, the statute is valid despite its indirect burden on religious observance unless the State may accomplish its purpose by means which do not impose such a burden.

"As we pointed out in [McGowan v. Maryland (1961; p. 759), rejecting an Establishment Clause challenge to Sunday closing laws], we cannot find a State without power to provide a weekly respite from all labor and, at the same time, to set one day of the week apart from the others as a day of rest, repose, recreation and tranquility. [To] permit the exemption [sought by the challengers] might well undermine the State's goal of providing a day that, as best possible, eliminates the atmosphere of commercial noise and activity. [E]nforcement problems would be more difficult [and Saturday observers] might well [receive] an economic advantage over their competitors who must remain closed on that day. [Competitors might] assert that they have religious convictions which compel them to close their businesses on what had formerly been their least profitable day. This might make necessary a state-conducted inquiry into the sincerity of the individual's religious beliefs, a practice which a State might believe would itself run afoul of the spirit of constitutionally protected religious guarantees." Justice Frankfurter, joined by Justice Harlan, also rejected the free exercise claim in a separate opinion.

Justice BRENNAN's dissent argued that the law violated the Free Exercise Clause because it "put an individual to a choice between his business and his religion." He argued that the state's interest was "the mere convenience of having everyone rest on the same day. It is to defend this interest that the Court holds that a State need not follow the alternative route of granting an exemption for those who in good faith observe a day of rest other than Sunday. [The Court] conjures up several difficulties with such a system which seem to me more fanciful than real. [The] Court [has] exalted administrative convenience to a constitutional level high enough to justify making one religion economically disadvantageous." Justices Stewart and Douglas also dissented.

Compare with the decision in Braunfeld the Court's decision in the following case, which held that a state must pay unemployment benefits to a Saturday sabbatarian:

Sherbert v. Verner
374 U.S. 398, 83 S. Ct. 1790, 10 L. Ed. 2d 965 (1963).

[Appellant Sherbert, a Seventh-day Adventist, was discharged by her employer "because she would not work on Saturday, the Sabbath Day of her faith." She was unable to obtain other employment because she would not take Saturday work. Her claim for South Carolina state unemployment compensation was denied because the state compensation law barred benefits to workers who failed, without good cause, to accept "suitable work when offered." The highest state court sustained the denial of benefits and the Supreme Court reversed.]

■ JUSTICE BRENNAN delivered the opinion of the [Court].

[If the state decision is to stand] it must be either because [appellant's] disqualification as a beneficiary represents no infringement by the State of her constitutional rights of free exercise; or because any incidental burden on the free exercise of appellant's religion may be justified by a "compelling state interest in the regulation of a subject within the State's constitutional power to regulate." We turn first to the question whether the disqualification for benefits imposes any burden on the free exercise of appellant's religion. We think it is clear that it does. In a sense the consequences of such a disqualification to religious principles and practices may be only an indirect result of welfare legislation within the State's general competence to enact; it is true that no criminal sanctions directly compel appellant to work a six-day week. But this is only the beginning, not the end, of our inquiry. [Here] not only is it apparent that appellant's declared ineligibility for benefits solely derives from the practice of her religion, but the pressure upon her to forego that practice is unmistakable. The ruling forces her to choose between following the precepts of her religion and forfeiting benefits, on the one hand, and abandoning one of the precepts of her religion in order to accept work, on the other hand. Governmental imposition of such a choice puts the same kind of burden upon the free exercise of religion as would a fine imposed against appellant for her Saturday worship.

[We] must next consider whether some compelling state interest [justifies] the substantial infringement of appellant's First Amendment right. [The] appellees suggest no more than a possibility that the filing of fraudulent claims by unscrupulous claimants feigning religious objections to Saturday work might not only dilute the unemployment compensation fund but also hinder the scheduling by employers of necessary Saturday work. [But] no such objection appears to have been made before the [state courts, and] there is no proof whatever to warrant such fears of malingering or deceit. [Even if] there were such risks, it would plainly be incumbent upon the appellees to demonstrate that no alternative forms of regulation would combat such abuses without infringing First Amendment rights. In these respects, then, the state interest asserted in the present case is wholly dissimilar to the interests which were found to justify the less direct burden upon religious practices in [Braunfeld]. [That statute was] saved by a countervailing factor which finds no equivalent in the instant case—a strong state interest in providing one uniform day of rest for all workers. That secular objective could be achieved, the Court found, only by declaring Sunday to be that day of rest. [Here] no such justifications underlie the determination of the state court that appellant's religion makes her ineligible to receive [benefits].

In holding as we do, plainly we are not fostering the "establishment" of the Seventh-day Adventist religion in South Carolina, for the extension of unemployment benefits to Sabbatarians in common with Sunday worshippers reflects nothing more than the governmental obligation of neutrality in the face of religious differences, and does not represent that involvement of religious with secular institutions which it is the object of the Establishment Clause to forestall. [Nor] do we, by our decision today, declare the existence of a constitutional right to unemployment benefits on the part of all persons whose religious convictions are the cause of their unemployment. This is not a case in which an employee's religious convictions serve to make him a nonproductive member of society. [Our] holding today is only that South Carolina may not constitutionally apply the eligibility provisions so as to constrain a worker to abandon his religious convictions respecting the [day of rest]. [Reversed and remanded.]

■ JUSTICE STEWART, concurring in the result.

[I] think that the guarantee of religious liberty embodied in the Free Exercise Clause affirmatively requires government to create an atmosphere of hospitality and accommodation to individual belief or disbelief. [Yet] in cases decided under the Establishment Clause the Court [has] decreed that government must blind itself to the differing religious beliefs and traditions of the people. With all respect, I think it is the Court's duty to face up to the dilemma posed by the conflict between the [religion clauses].

[I] cannot agree that today's decision can stand consistently with [Braunfeld]. The Court says that there was a "less direct burden upon religious practices" in that case than in this. With all respect, I think the Court is mistaken simply as a matter of fact. The Braunfeld case involved a *criminal* statute [and a drastic impact on the challenger's business]. The impact upon the appellant's religious freedom in the present case is considerably less onerous [than in Braunfeld]. Even upon the unlikely assumption that the appellant could not find suitable non-Saturday employment, the appellant at the worst would be denied a maximum of 22 weeks of compensation payments. I agree with the Court that the possibility of that denial is enough to infringe upon the appellant's constitutional right to the free exercise of her religion. But it is clear to me that in order to reach this conclusion the Court must explicitly reject the reasoning of [Braunfeld]. I think [Braunfeld] was wrongly decided and should be overruled, and accordingly I concur in the result [here].

■ JUSTICE HARLAN, whom JUSTICE WHITE joins, dissenting.

[In] no proper sense can it be said that the State discriminated against the appellant on the basis of her religious beliefs or that she was denied benefits *because* she was a Seventh-day Adventist. She was denied benefits just as any other claimant would be denied benefits who was not "available for work" for personal reasons. With this background, this Court's decision comes into clearer focus. What the Court is holding is that if the State chooses to condition unemployment compensation on the applicant's availability for work, it is constitutionally compelled to *carve out an exception*—and to provide benefits—for those whose unavailability is due to their religious convictions. Such a holding has particular significance in two respects.

First, despite the Court's protestations to the contrary, the decision necessarily overrules [Braunfeld]. Clearly, any differences between this case and Braunfeld cut against the present appellant. *Second,* the implications of the present decision are far more troublesome than its apparently narrow dimensions would indicate at first glance. [The meaning of the holding is that the State] must *single out* for financial assistance those whose behavior is religiously motivated, even though it denies such assistance to others whose identical behavior [is] not religiously motivated. It has been suggested that such singling out of religious conduct for special treatment may violate the constitutional limitations on state action. See Kurland, "Of Church and State and the Supreme Court," 29 U. Chi. L. Rev. 1 (1961). My own view, however, is that at least under the circumstances of this case it would be a permissible accommodation of religion for the State, if it *chose* to do so, to create an exception to its eligibility requirements for persons like the appellant. The constitutional obligation of "neutrality" is not so narrow a channel that the slightest deviation from an absolutely straight course leads to condemnation. [There is] enough flexibility in the Constitution to permit a legislative judgment accommodating an unemployment compensation law to the exercise of religious beliefs such as appellant's. [I] cannot subscribe to the conclusion that the State is constitutionally *compelled* to carve out an exception to its general rule of eligibility in the present case. Those situations in which the Constitution may require special treatment on account of religion are, in my view, few and far between. [Such] compulsion in the present case is particularly inappropriate in light of the indirect, remote, and insubstantial effect of the decision below on the exercise of appellant's religion and in light of the direct financial assistance to religion that today's decision [requires].

————

LIMITING THE SCOPE OF MANDATORY RELIGIOUS EXEMPTIONS?

In the wake of Sherbert, religious objectors to general regulations repeatedly came to the Court, invoking Sherbert's strict scrutiny in claiming constitutionally mandated exemptions. Although the Court typically adhered to the Sherbert analysis in form, it quite frequently rejected the religious objectors' claims in fact. The major cases in which the free exercise claims succeeded arose in the unemployment compensation context following Sherbert, and in the education setting following Wisconsin v. Yoder. In other cases, the Court, despite lip service to Sherbert's strict scrutiny standard, in fact exercised a quite deferential variety of review and accordingly refused to carve out exemptions from general regulations.

1.   *Unemployment compensation cases after Sherbert.* **Thomas v. Review Board**, 450 U.S. 707 (1981), a case factually very close to Sherbert, relied on it to strike down Indiana's denial of unemployment compensation to a Jehovah's Witness who quit his job in a munitions factory because of his religious objections to war. A state court upheld the denial of compensation, because the law denied compensation to all employees who voluntarily left employment for personal reasons without good cause. Chief Justice Burger's majority opinion, however, found the coercive impact here "indistinguishable from Sherbert" and rejected an argument that the grant of benefits to the employee would violate the Establishment Clause. Justice Rehnquist was the sole dissenter, insisting that the majority had read free exercise "too broadly" and had failed "to squarely acknowledge that such a reading conflicts with many of our Establishment Clause cases." He urged that Sherbert be overruled. **Hobbie v. Unemployment Appeals Comm'n**, 480 U.S. 136 (1987), likewise followed Sherbert in upholding the unemployment compensation claim of an employee whose religious beliefs had changed during the course of her employment.

2.   *Compulsory education laws.* In **Wisconsin v. Yoder**, 406 U.S. 205 (1972), Yoder, a member of the Old Order Amish, was convicted and fined $5 for refusing to send his 15-year-old daughter to school after she had completed the eighth grade, in violation of Wisconsin's requirement of school attendance until age sixteen. The Amish object to high school education because of their "fundamental belief that salvation requires life in a church community separate and apart from the world and worldly influence." They believe that high school exposes their children to worldly influence and emphasizes "intellectual and scientific accomplishments, self-distinction, competitiveness, worldly success, and social life with other students." The Amish society, by contrast, emphasizes "informal learning-through-doing"

and "wisdom, rather than technical knowledge; community welfare, rather than competition; and separation [from] contemporary worldly society." Attendance at school through the eighth grade is acceptable to the Amish because it "prepares children to read the Bible [and] to be good farmers and citizens," and because such education does not "significantly expose their children to worldly values." The Wisconsin Supreme Court overturned Yoder's conviction because it violated the Free Exercise Clause. The Court affirmed, with six Justices joining the majority opinion and only one Justice dissenting in part.

Chief Justice BURGER's majority opinion insisted that "a State's interest in universal education" must be strictly scrutinized "when it impinges on fundamental rights and interests" such as the right of free exercise. The State could not prevail unless it showed that its requirement served "a state interest of sufficient magnitude to override the [free exercise claim]." And "only those interests of the highest order and those not otherwise served can overbalance legitimate claims of free exercise. [E.g., Sherbert.]" Applying this analysis, Chief Justice Burger began by asking whether the Amish claim was "rooted in religious belief" (the sincerity of the Amish was conceded), and found it was "not merely a matter of personal preference, but one of deep religious conviction, shared by an organized group, and intimately related to daily living." Compulsory school-attendance laws required the Amish "to perform acts undeniably at odds with fundamental tenets of their religious beliefs" and carried with them "a very real threat of undermining the Amish community and religious practice."

Chief Justice Burger proceeded to reject the State's attempted reliance on the "belief"-"action" distinction: "in this context belief and action cannot be neatly confined in logic-tight compartments." Nor could the case be disposed of because the law was facially nondiscriminatory, for such a regulation might nevertheless "offend the constitutional requirement for governmental neutrality if it unduly burdens the free exercise of religion. [E.g., Sherbert.]" Accordingly exercising the heightened scrutiny demanded by this case as well as Sherbert, the Court examined the interests asserted by the State. Chief Justice Burger noted the State's claim that "some degree of education is necessary to prepare citizens to participate [effectively] in our open political system [and] to be self-reliant and self-sufficient participants in society," but replied that an additional one or two years of formal high school would do "little to serve those interests."

Turning to the State's argument that the Amish position fostered "ignorance," Chief Justice Burger replied that "the Amish community has been a highly successful social unit within our society, even if apart from the conventional 'mainstream.' Its members are productive and very law-abiding members of society." The State also argued that children "may choose to leave the Amish community, and that if this occurs they will be ill-equipped for life." Chief Justice Burger found this argument "highly speculative": "There is nothing in this record to suggest that the Amish qualities of reliability, self-reliance and dedication to work would fail to find ready markets in today's society." Accordingly, the State's interest here "emerges as somewhat less substantial than requiring such attendance for children generally." The Court added that it was "not dealing with a way of life and mode of education by a group claiming to have recently discovered some 'progressive' [process] for rearing children for modern life." In view of the long history of the Amish as a "successful and self-sufficient segment of

American society" and their showing of "the adequacy of their alternative mode of continuing informal vocational education in terms of precisely those overall interests that the State advances," a showing that "probably few other religious groups or sects could make, and weighing the minimal difference between what the State would require and what the Amish already accept, it was incumbent on the State to show with more particularity how its admittedly strong interest in compulsory education would be adversely affected by granting an exemption to the Amish. [Sherbert.]" The Court dismissed in a footnote the claim that a mandatory exemption for the Amish would violate the Establishment Clause: "Accommodating the religious beliefs of the Amish can hardly be characterized as sponsorship or active involvement."

Justice DOUGLAS dissented in part, emphasizing the potential conflict of interest between Amish parents and their children. He insisted that the free exercise rights of Amish children had to be reached here. Some Amish children might want to attend high school in order to be able to choose whether to adhere or break with the Amish tradition. (The majority opinion, as well as the concurring notations by Justices Stewart and White, insisted that this issue was not presented by the record.) Justice Douglas also objected to the majority's emphasis on the "law and order record" of the Amish, finding it "quite irrelevant."

3. ***The New Glarus Amish in Yoder v. Wisconsin.*** The Old Order Amish families in Wisconsin v. Yoder were among the least likely groups of people to participate in a precedent-setting legal case. "The Amish feel that 'going to the law' violates their faith's tradition of nonresistance." The great attention brought to the New Glarus community by the Yoder case sparked division between Amish in favor of the litigation and those against it. It also pitted more progressive members of the community against traditionalists. The Amish plaintiffs had "repeatedly argued that [they] would flee the community if the courts ruled against them and thus burdened their religious practice. As it happened, almost all the Amish did leave New Glarus—but after the U.S. Supreme Court ruled *in favor* of their faith. [Far] from preserving their community, the litigation sparked discord that contributed to its disintegration." Peters, The Yoder Case: Religious Freedom, Education, and Parental Rights 2, 6 (2003).

4. ***Denials of free exercise exemption claims between Sherbert and Smith.*** Even though Sherbert and Yoder held that the Free Exercise Clause mandated exemptions from government regulations in certain circumstances, a much larger number of cases during this period rejected such claims. The heightened scrutiny announced by such decisions as Sherbert and Yoder proved quite deferential in fact.

a. **United States v. Lee**, 455 U.S. 252 (1982): Lee, a member of the Old Order Amish, employed several Amish to work on his farm and in his carpentry shop. He objected, on religious grounds, to paying the Social Security tax for his employees, arguing that "the Amish believe it sinful not to provide for their own elderly." Chief Justice BURGER's majority opinion found Yoder distinguishable and rejected Lee's claim. Chief Justice Burger conceded that "there is a conflict between the Amish faith and the obligations imposed by the social security system" and accepted that heightened scrutiny was appropriate. In nevertheless upholding application of the tax law to Lee, he noted that "the State may justify a limitation on religious liberty by showing that it is essential to accomplish an overriding governmental interest"; here, mandatory participation in the Social Security system was indispensable to the fiscal vitality of the system. Chief Justice Burger distinguished Yoder on the ground that here "it would be difficult to accommodate the comprehensive social security system with myriad exceptions flowing from a wide variety of religious beliefs." He also noted that there was "no principled way" to distinguish between general taxes and Social Security taxes, so that, if Lee's claim were granted, a religious opponent to war "would have a similarly valid claim to be exempt from paying [a] percentage of the income tax." "The tax system could not function if denominations were allowed to challenge [it] because tax payments were spent in a manner that violates their religious beliefs."

In a separate opinion concurring only in the judgment, Justice STEVENS criticized the majority for imposing upon the Government "a heavy burden of justifying the application of neutral general laws [to] individual conscientious objectors. In my opinion, it is the objector who must shoulder the burden of demonstrating that there is a unique reason for allowing him a special exemption from a valid law of general applicability." The Amish ought to prevail under strict scrutiny, which he opposed, because an exemption to them would be costless to the government: "[T]he nonpayment of these taxes by the Amish would be more than offset by the elimination of their right to collect benefits. [Since] the Amish have demonstrated their capacity to care for their own, the social cost of eliminating this relatively small group of dedicated believers would be minimal." Nor was there a great risk of myriad similar claims: "[T]he Amish claim applies only to a small religious community within an established welfare system of its own." Nevertheless, he agreed with the majority's result because of the difficulties involved in processing claims to religious exemption from taxes.

b.   **Bob Jones University v. United States**, 461 U.S. 574 (1983): This decision rejected a free exercise challenge to IRS denials of tax-exempt status to two educational institutions that practiced racial discrimination in accordance with the religious beliefs upon which they were founded. The IRS claimed that the schools were disqualified as "charities" because their racial policies were "contrary to settled public policy." After finding that the IRS policy was authorized by Congress, Chief Justice BURGER's opinion for the Court rejected the free exercise claim despite formal application of strict scrutiny. Under the Lee standard that "[t]he state may justify a limitation on religious liberty by showing that it is essential to accomplish an overriding governmental interest," the Court found the governmental interest in eradicating racial discrimination in education sufficiently "compelling."

c.   **Goldman v. Weinberger**, 475 U.S. 503 (1986): In rejecting a free exercise challenge in this case, involving military service, the Court abandoned any reliance on heightened scrutiny and instead adopted an openly deferential approach. Goldman was an Orthodox Jew, a clinical psychologist in the Air Force, who was disciplined for wearing a yarmulke in violation of uniform dress regulations barring the wearing of headgear indoors. He sought an exemption from the Air Force regulation under the strict scrutiny standard of Sherbert. Justice REHNQUIST's majority opinion answered: "Our review of military regulations challenged on First Amendment grounds is far more deferential than constitutional review of similar [regulations] designed for civilian society. The military need not encourage debate or tolerate protest to the extent that such tolerance is required of the civilian state by the First Amendment; to accomplish its mission the military must foster instinctive obedience, unity, commitment, and esprit de corps." Accordingly, "when evaluating whether military needs justify a particular restriction on religiously motivated conduct, courts must give great deference to the professional judgment of military authorities concerning the relative importance of a particular military interest." In this case, the military judgment was that "the traditional outfitting of personnel in standardized uniforms encourages the subordination of personal preferences and identities in favor of the overall group mission. [The] First Amendment does not require the military to accommodate such practices as the wearing of [the yarmulke] in the face of its view that they would detract from the uniformity sought by the dress regulations."

In a concurring opinion, Justice STEVENS, joined by Justices White and Powell, admitted that Goldman presented "an especially attractive case for an exception" but worried about the application of such an exemption to members of other religious groups who wished to wear, e.g., turbans and dreadlocks. He accordingly insisted on testing the validity of the regulation "as it applied to all service personnel who have sincere religious beliefs." The interest in uniformity was important because it was an interest "in uniform treatment for the members of all religious faiths"; yet the "very strength of [Captain Goldman's] claim creates the danger that a similar claim on behalf of a Sikh or a Rastafarian might readily be dismissed as 'so extreme, so unusual, or so faddish an image that public confidence in his ability to perform his duties will be destroyed.' If exceptions from dress code regulations are to be granted, [inevitably] the decisionmaker's evaluation of the character and the sincerity of the requester's faith—as well as the probable reaction of the majority to the favored treatment of a member of that faith—will play a critical part in the decision. [Yet the] Air Force has no business drawing distinctions between such persons when it is enforcing commands of universal application."

Justice BRENNAN's dissent, joined by Justice Marshall, attacked the majority's "subrational-basis standard—absolute, uncritical 'deference to the professional judgment of military authorities.'" He rejected as "totally implausible" the claim that the "group identity of the Air Force would be threatened" by the wearing of yarmulkes. In response to the Government's fear of "a classic parade of horribles, the specter of a brightly-colored, 'rag-tag band of soldiers,'" he stated: "Although turbans, saffron robes, and dreadlocks are not before us [and] must each be evaluated against the reasons a service branch offers for prohibiting personnel from wearing them while in uniform, a reviewing court could legitimately give deference to dress and grooming rules that have a *reasoned* basis in, for example, functional utility, health and safety considerations, and the goal of a polished, professional appearance. It is the lack of any reasoned basis for prohibiting yarmulkes that is so striking here."

Justice BLACKMUN's dissent stated that the Air Force was justified in considering "the cumulative costs of accommodating constitutionally indistinguishable requests for religious exemptions" and also shared Justice Stevens's concern about discriminating in favor of mainstream religions. He nevertheless joined the dissenters because the "Air Force simply has not shown any reason to fear that a significant number of enlisted [people] would request religious exemptions that could not be denied on neutral grounds such as safety, let alone that granting these requests would noticeably impair the overall image of the service." Justice O'CONNOR's dissent, joined by Justice Marshall, found "two consistent themes" in the precedents: "First, when the government attempts to deny a free exercise claim, it must show that an unusually important interest is at stake, whether that interest is denominated 'compelling,' 'of the highest order,' or 'overriding.' [Sherbert, Yoder, and Lee.] Second, the government must show that granting the requested exemption will do substantial harm to that interest, whether by showing that the means adopted is the 'least restrictive' or 'essential,' or that the interest will not 'otherwise be served.' These two requirements are entirely sensible [and there is no reason why they] should not apply in the military, as well as the civilian, context." Applying these standards here, she stated that she "would require the Government to accommodate the sincere religious belief of Captain Goldman."

After Goldman, Congress enacted a law permitting members of the military to "wear an item of religious apparel while wearing the uniform," unless "the wearing of the item would interfere with the performance [of] military duties [or] the item of apparel is not neat and conservative." 10 U.S.C. § 774.

d. **Bowen v. Roy**, 476 U.S. 693 (1986): The Court by a vote of 8–1 rejected a free exercise challenge to a requirement in the federal AFDC and Food Stamp programs that applicants for welfare benefits be identified by Social Security numbers. The challengers claimed that assignment of a number for their two-year-old daughter, Little Bird of the Snow, would violate their religious beliefs because it would "rob the spirit" of the child. Chief Justice BURGER's majority opinion rejected the claim regarding the *government*'s use of the number by distinguishing free exercise claims with respect to personal conduct from such claims with respect to the government's conduct: "Never to our knowledge has the Court interpreted the First Amendment to require the Government *itself* to behave in ways that the individual believes will further his or her spiritual development. [Free exercise] does not afford an individual a right to dictate the conduct of the Government's internal procedures."

The Court did not rule definitively on the requirement that the *applicant* furnish a Social Security number as a condition of receiving aid, but five Justices indicated that they thought that free exercise warranted an exception here. Chief Justice BURGER, writing on this issue only for himself and Justices Powell and Rehnquist, would have rejected both aspects of the free exercise claim, asserting that scrutiny should be more deferential in the case of a condition on benefits than in the case of "governmental action [that] criminalizes religiously inspired activity or inescapably compels conduct that some find objectionable for religious reasons." Justice WHITE's brief dissent apparently would have granted both aspects of the free exercise claim, finding that the case was controlled by Sherbert and Thomas. Justice O'CONNOR, joined by Justices Brennan and Marshall, disputed Chief Justice Burger's distinction between "conditions" and "compulsion," arguing that the fact that the "underlying dispute involves an award of benefits rather than an exaction of penalties does not grant the Government license to apply a different version of the Constitution." Applying heightened scrutiny, she would have exempted Roy from providing the number. Justices BLACKMUN and STEVENS filed separate partial concurrences, agreeing that free exercise did not bar the government's own use of the Social Security number, but claiming that the record was insufficient to allow consideration of the claims with respect to Roy's furnishing the number. However, Justice Blackmun appended to his concurrence a comment that, if forced to reach the latter issue, he would agree with Justice O'Connor's position. Given Justice Blackmun's comment, and the view of the four dissenters, there was apparently a majority on the Court to uphold a free exercise claim regarding the furnishing of the number.

e. **Lyng v. Northwest Indian Cemetery Protective Ass'n**, 485 U.S. 439 (1988): This was an unsuccessful free exercise challenge to the U.S. Forest Service's plan to build a road through and permit timber harvesting in an area of national forest traditionally used by several Indian tribes as sacred areas for religious rituals. In a 5–3 decision, the Court rejected the free exercise claim. Justice O'CONNOR's majority opinion acknowledged that the challengers' beliefs were "sincere" and that "the Government's proposed actions [would] have severe adverse effects on the practice of their religion," but insisted that the burden was not sufficiently great to trigger any form of heightened scrutiny. Accordingly, the Government did not have to meet a "compelling interest" standard of justification for the project. Relying heavily on Bowen v. Roy (p. 681), she stated: "The building of a road or the harvesting of timber on publicly owned land cannot meaningfully be distinguished from the use of a Social Security number in Roy. In both cases, the challenged Government action would interfere significantly with private persons' ability to pursue spiritual fulfillment according to their own religious beliefs. In neither case, however, would the affected individuals be coerced by the Government's action into violating their religious beliefs; nor would either governmental action penalize the religious activity by denying any person an equal share of the rights, benefits, and privileges enjoyed by other citizens." She acknowledged that "indirect coercion or penalties on the free exercise of religion, not just outright prohibitions, are subject to scrutiny under the First Amendment. [But] this does not and cannot imply that incidental effects of governmental programs, which may make it more difficult to practice certain religions but which have no tendency to coerce individuals into acting contrary to their religious beliefs, require government to bring forward a compelling justification for otherwise lawful actions. The crucial word in the constitutional text is 'prohibit.' "

Justice O'Connor went on to rely heavily on the possibility that many similar claims might impair the operation of government: "[Government] simply could not operate if it were required to satisfy every citizen's religious needs and desires. [The] First Amendment must apply to all citizens alike, and it can give to none of them a veto of public programs that do not prohibit the free exercise of religion. The Constitution does not, and courts cannot, offer to reconcile the various competing demands on Government, many of them rooted in sincere religious belief, that inevitably arise in so diverse a society as ours. That task [is] for the legislatures and other institutions." Thus, though the Government could not forbid the Indian challengers from visiting the area, these rights "do not divest the Government of its right to use what is, after all, *its* land."

Justice BRENNAN, joined by Justices Marshall and Blackmun, dissented. He objected to the majority's limitation of free exercise claims to cases of direct or indirect "coercion": "The constitutional guarantee [draws] no such fine distinctions between types of restraints on religious exercise, but rather is directed against any form of governmental action that frustrates or inhibits religious practice. [I] cannot accept the Court's premise that the form of the Government's restraint on religious practice, rather than its effect, controls our constitutional analysis. [Ultimately,] the Court's coercion test turns on a distinction between governmental actions that compel affirmative conduct inconsistent with religious belief, and those governmental actions that prevent conduct consistent with religious belief. [Such] a distinction is without constitutional significance. The crucial word in the constitutional text, as the Court itself acknowledges, is 'prohibit,' a comprehensive term that in no way suggests that the intended protection is aimed only at governmental actions that coerce affirmative conduct." He accordingly insisted that the Sherbert "compelling interest" standard was appropriate here.

5. ***The Court's methodology in applying Sherbert.*** In the preceding cases, the Court used three techniques to distinguish Sherbert and Yoder. In some cases, it found an overriding government interest in uniformity, for example in the administration of the tax laws. In others, it found that free exercise interests were attenuated and government interests paramount in specialized environments such as the military. And in others, it applied a narrow definition of what constitutes a burden on religious practice, rejecting free exercise claims seeking to alter "internal" government operations such as the use of Social Security numbers and the development of federal property.

Can these findings be reconciled with Sherbert and Yoder? In particular, can the narrow definition of burdens on free exercise set forth in Roy and Lyng be reconciled with Sherbert? Didn't Sherbert itself compel a change in "internal government operations," and in the use of government "property"? Can government actions even with respect to "internal" operations have negative external effects on religious practitioners? See Williams & Williams, "Volitionalism and Religious Liberty," 76 Cornell L. Rev. 769 (1991) (arguing that the Court undervalues the beliefs of "nonvolitionalist" religions, i.e., those that believe that negative religious consequences can attach even to events over which the religious adherent exercised no personal control). Should the fact that the government had a monopoly over use of a unique worship site have mattered in Lyng? Could the Native American worshippers in Lyng themselves have asserted a countervailing property right? See Lupu, "Where Rights Begin: The Problem of Burdens on the Free Exercise of Religion," 102 Harv. L. Rev. 933 (1988) (arguing that government actions that are comparable to harms actionable at common law should count as burdens on religion, and that in Lyng, the government interfered, in effect, with a prescriptive easement of access to the worship site). In reading the 1990 Smith case, which follows, consider whether the pattern of decisions after Sherbert and Yoder had already abandoned in all but name strict scrutiny of most neutral government regulations challenged as violations of free exercise:

Employment Division, Dept. of Human Resources v. Smith

494 U.S. 872, 110 S. Ct. 1595, 108 L. Ed. 2d 876 (1990).

■ JUSTICE SCALIA delivered the opinion of the Court.

This case requires us to decide whether the Free Exercise Clause [permits] Oregon to include religiously inspired peyote use within the reach of its general criminal prohibition on use of that drug, and thus permits the State to deny unemployment benefits to persons dismissed from their jobs because of such religiously inspired use.

I.   Oregon law prohibits the knowing or intentional possession of a "controlled substance," [including] the drug peyote, a hallucinogen derived from [a plant]. Respondents Alfred Smith and Galen Black were fired from their jobs with a private drug rehabilitation organization because they ingested peyote for sacramental purposes at a ceremony of the Native American Church, of which both are members. When respondents applied to petitioner Employment Division for unemployment compensation, they were determined to be ineligible for benefits because they had been discharged for work-related "misconduct". [The Oregon Supreme Court, after a first round of litigation that went up to the Supreme Court, found on remand that respondents' peyote use fell within the prohibition of Oregon's criminal laws, that those laws made no exception for sacramental use of the drug, but that that the ban on sacramental peyote use was invalid under the Free Exercise Clause. Thus, the state court ruled, Oregon could not deny unemployment benefits for engaging in conduct that was constitutionally protected. The Court again granted certiorari.]

II.   Respondents' claim for relief rests on our decisions in Sherbert, Thomas, and Hobbie, in which we held that a State could not condition the availability of unemployment insurance on an individual's willingness to forgo conduct required by his religion. As we observed in Smith I, however, the conduct at issue in those cases was not prohibited by law. [Now that it is clear] that Oregon does prohibit the religious use of peyote, we proceed to consider whether that prohibition is permissible under the Free Exercise Clause.

A.   [The] free exercise of religion means, first and foremost, the right to believe and profess whatever religious doctrine one desires. [But] the "exercise of religion" often involves not only belief and profession but the performance of (or abstention from) physical acts: assembling with others for a worship service, participating in sacramental use of bread and wine, proselytizing, abstaining from certain foods or certain modes of transportation. It would be true, we think (though no case of ours has involved the point), that a state would be "prohibiting the free exercise [of religion]" if it sought to ban such acts or abstentions only when they are engaged in for religious reasons, or only because of the religious belief that they display. It would doubtless be unconstitutional, for example, to ban the casting of "statues that are to be used for worship purposes," or to prohibit bowing down before a golden calf.

Respondents in the present case, however, seek to carry the meaning of "prohibiting the free exercise [of religion]" one large step further. They contend that their religious motivation for using peyote places them beyond the reach of a criminal law that is not specifically directed at their religious practice, and that is concededly constitutional as applied to those who use the drug for other reasons. They assert, in other words, that "prohibiting the free exercise [of religion]" includes requiring any individual to observe a generally applicable law that requires (or forbids) the performance of an act that his religious belief forbids (or requires). As a textual matter, we do not think the words must be given that meaning. It is no more necessary to regard the collection of a general tax, for example, as "prohibiting the free exercise [of religion]" by those citizens who believe support of organized government to be sinful, than it is to regard the same tax as "abridging the freedom [of] the press" of those publishing companies that must pay the tax as a condition of staying in business. It is a permissible reading of the text, in the one case as in the other, to say that if prohibiting the exercise of religion (or burdening the activity of printing) is not the object of the tax but merely the incidental effect of a generally applicable and otherwise valid provision, the First Amendment has not been offended.

Our decisions reveal that the latter reading is the correct one. We have never held that an individual's religious beliefs excuse him from compliance with an otherwise valid law prohibiting conduct that the State is free to regulate. On the contrary, the record of more than a century of our free exercise jurisprudence contradicts that proposition. [We] first had occasion to assert that principle in [Reynolds], where we rejected the claim that criminal laws against polygamy could not be constitutionally applied to those whose religion commanded the practice. [Subsequent] decisions have consistently held that the right of free exercise does not relieve an individual of the obligation to comply with a "valid and neutral law of general applicability on the ground that the law proscribes (or prescribes) conduct that his religion prescribes (or proscribes)." United States v. Lee (Stevens, J., concurring in judgment). [See also Prince; Braunfeld; Gillette.]

The only decisions in which we have held that the First Amendment bars application of a neutral, generally applicable law to religiously motivated action have involved not the Free Exercise Clause alone, but the Free Exercise Clause in conjunction with other constitutional protections, such as freedom of speech and of the press, see [Cantwell; Murdock]; or the right of parents, acknowledged in Pierce v. Society of Sisters, to direct the education of their children, see Wisconsin v. Yoder. Some of our cases prohibiting compelled expression, decided exclusively upon free speech grounds, have also involved freedom of religion [see Wooley v. Maynard; Barnette.]

[The] present case does not present such a hybrid situation, but a free exercise claim unconnected with any communicative activity or parental right. Respondents urge us to hold, quite simply, that when otherwise prohibitable conduct is accompanied by religious convictions, not only the convictions but the conduct itself must be free from governmental regulation. We have never held that, and decline to do so now. There being no contention that Oregon's drug law represents an attempt to regulate religious beliefs, the communication of religious beliefs, or the raising of one's children in those beliefs, the rule to which we have adhered ever since Reynolds plainly controls.

B.   [Respondents] argue that even though exemption from generally applicable criminal laws need not automatically be extended to religiously motivated actors, at least the claim for a religious exemption must be evaluated under the balancing test set forth in Sherbert. Under the Sherbert test, governmental actions that substantially burden a religious practice must be justified by a compelling governmental interest. [We] have never invalidated any governmental action on the basis of the Sherbert test except the denial of unemployment compensation. Although we have sometimes purported to apply the Sherbert test in contexts other than that, we have always found the test satisfied [United States v. Lee; Gillette v. United States]. In recent years we have abstained from applying the Sherbert test (outside the unemployment compensation field) at all. [Roy; Lyng; Goldman.]

Even if we were inclined to breathe into Sherbert some life beyond the unemployment compensation field, we would not apply it to require exemptions from a generally applicable criminal law. The Sherbert test, it must be recalled, was developed in a context that lent itself to individualized governmental assessment of the reasons for the relevant conduct. As a plurality of the Court noted in Roy, a distinctive feature of unemployment compensation programs is that their eligibility criteria invite consideration of the particular circumstances behind an applicant's unemployment. [Our] decisions in the unemployment cases stand for the proposition that where the State has in place a system of individual exemptions, it may not refuse to extend that system to cases of "religious hardship" without compelling reason.

Whether or not the decisions are that limited, they at least have nothing to do with an across-the-board criminal prohibition on a particular form of conduct. [Although] we have sometimes used the Sherbert test to analyze free exercise challenges to such laws, we have never applied the test to invalidate one. We conclude today that the sounder approach, and the approach in accord with the vast majority of our precedents, is to hold the test inapplicable to such challenges. The government's ability to enforce generally applicable prohibitions of socially harmful conduct, like its ability to carry out other aspects of public policy, "cannot depend on measuring the effects of a governmental action on a religious objector's spiritual development." [Lyng.] To make an individual's obligation to obey such a law contingent upon the law's coincidence with his religious beliefs, except where the State's interest is "compelling"—permitting him, by virtue of his beliefs, "to become a law unto himself," Reynolds—contradicts both constitutional tradition and common sense.

The "compelling government interest" requirement seems benign, because it is familiar from other fields. But using it as the standard that must be met before the government may accord different treatment on the basis of race, or before the government may regulate the content of speech, is not remotely comparable to using it for the purpose asserted here. What it produces in those other fields—equality of treatment, and an unrestricted flow of contending speech—are constitutional norms; what it would produce here—a private right to ignore generally applicable laws—is a constitutional anomaly.[1]

---

[1] [Just] as we subject to the most exacting scrutiny laws that make classifications based on race or on the content of speech, so too we strictly scrutinize governmental classifications based on religion. But we have held that race-neutral laws that have the *effect* of disproportionately disadvantaging a particular racial group do not thereby become subject to compelling-interest analysis under the Equal Protection Clause, see Washington v. Davis; and we have held that generally applicable laws unconcerned with regulating speech that have the *effect* of interfering with speech do not thereby become subject to compelling-interest analysis under the First Amendment, see Citizen Publishing Co. v. United States, 394 U.S. 131 (1969) (antitrust laws). Our conclusion that generally applicable, religion-neutral laws that have the

Nor is it possible to limit the impact of respondents' proposal by requiring a "compelling state interest" only when the conduct prohibited is "central" to the individual's religion. Cf. [Lyng (Brennan, J., dissenting).] It is no more appropriate for judges to determine the "centrality" of religious beliefs before applying a "compelling interest" test in the free exercise field, than it would be for them to determine the "importance" of ideas before applying the "compelling interest" test in the free speech field. What principle of law or logic can be brought to bear to contradict a believer's assertion that a particular act is "central" to his personal faith? Judging the centrality of different religious practices is akin to the unacceptable "business of evaluating the relative merits of differing religious claims." United States v. Lee (Stevens, J., concurring). [Repeatedly] and in many different contexts, we have warned that courts must not presume to determine the place of a particular belief in a religion or the plausibility of a religious claim. [E.g., Thomas; Ballard.]

If the "compelling interest" test is to be applied at all, then, it must be applied across the board to all actions thought to be religiously commanded. Moreover, if "compelling interest" really means what it says (and watering it down here would subvert its rigor in the other fields where it is applied), many laws will not meet the test. Any society adopting such a system would be courting anarchy, but that danger increases in direct proportion to the society's diversity of religious beliefs, and its determination to coerce or suppress none of them. Precisely because [we] value and protect [religious] divergence, we cannot afford the luxury of deeming *presumptively invalid,* as applied to the religious objector, every regulation of conduct that does not protect an interest of the highest order. The rule respondents favor would open the prospect of constitutionally required religious exemptions from civic obligations of almost every conceivable kind—ranging from compulsory military service [e.g., Gillette] to the payment of taxes [United States v. Lee] to health and safety regulation such as manslaughter and child neglect laws, compulsory vaccination laws, drug laws, and traffic laws; to social welfare legislation such as minimum wage laws, child labor laws, animal cruelty laws, environmental protection laws, and laws providing for equality of opportunity for the races [Bob Jones University]. The First Amendment's protection of religious liberty does not require this.

Values that are protected against government interference through enshrinement in the Bill of Rights are not thereby banished from the political process. Just as a society that believes in the negative protection accorded to the press by the First Amendment is likely to enact laws that affirmatively foster the dissemination of the printed word, so also a society that believes in the negative protection accorded to religious belief can be expected to be solicitous of that value in its legislation as well. It is therefore not surprising that a number of States have made an exception to their drug laws for sacramental peyote use. But to say that a nondiscriminatory religious-practice exemption is permitted, or even that it is desirable, is not to say that it is constitutionally required, and that the appropriate occasions for its creation can be discerned by the courts. It may fairly be said that leaving accommodation to the political process will place at a relative disadvantage those religious practices that are not widely engaged in; but that unavoidable

---

effect of burdening a particular religious practice need not be justified by a compelling governmental interest is the only approach compatible with these precedents. [Footnote by Justice Scalia.]

consequence of democratic government must be preferred to a system in which each conscience is a law unto itself or in which judges weigh the social importance of all laws against the centrality of all religious beliefs. [Reversed.]

■ JUSTICE O'CONNOR, concurring in the judgment [joined by JUSTICES BRENNAN, MARSHALL, and BLACKMUN as to Parts I and II of the opinion, but not as to the judgment].

Although I agree with the result the Court reaches, [I] cannot join its opinion. In my view, today's holding dramatically departs from well-settled First Amendment jurisprudence, appears unnecessary to resolve the question presented, and is incompatible with our Nation's fundamental commitment to individual religious [liberty].

II. A.   The Court today [interprets] the [Free Exercise] Clause to permit the government to prohibit, without justification, conduct mandated by an individual's religious beliefs, so long as that prohibition is generally applicable. But a law that prohibits certain conduct—conduct that happens to be an act of worship for someone—manifestly does prohibit that person's free exercise of his religion. A person who is barred from engaging in religiously motivated conduct is barred from freely exercising his religion. [The] First Amendment [does] not distinguish between laws that are generally applicable and laws that target particular religious practices. Indeed, few States would be so naive as to enact a law directly prohibiting or burdening a religious practice as such.

[To] say that a person's right to free exercise has been burdened, of course, does not mean that he has an absolute right to engage in the conduct. Under our established First Amendment jurisprudence, we have recognized that the freedom to act, unlike the freedom to believe, cannot be absolute. Instead, we have respected both the First Amendment's express textual mandate and the governmental interest in regulation of conduct by requiring the Government to justify any substantial burden on religiously motivated conduct by a compelling state interest and by means narrowly tailored to achieve that interest.

[The] Court attempts to support its narrow reading of the Clause by claiming that "[w]e have never held that an individual's religious beliefs excuse him from compliance with an otherwise valid law prohibiting conduct that the State is free to regulate." But as the Court later notes, as it must, in cases such as Cantwell and Yoder we have in fact interpreted the Free Exercise Clause to forbid application of a generally applicable prohibition to religiously motivated conduct. [The] Court endeavors to escape from our decisions in Cantwell and Yoder by labeling them "hybrid" decisions, but there is no denying that both cases expressly relied on the Free Exercise Clause, and that we have consistently regarded those cases as part of the mainstream of our free exercise jurisprudence. Moreover, in each of the other cases cited by the Court to support its categorical rule, we rejected the particular constitutional claims before us only after carefully weighing the competing interests. [Prince; Braunfeld; Gillette; Lee.] That we rejected the free exercise claims in those cases hardly calls into question the applicability of First Amendment doctrine in the first place. Indeed, it is surely unusual to judge the vitality of a constitutional doctrine by looking to the win-loss record of the plaintiffs who happen to come before us.

B. [In] my view, [the] essence of a free exercise claim is relief from a burden imposed by government on religious practices or beliefs, whether the burden is imposed directly through laws that prohibit or compel specific religious practices, or indirectly through laws that, in effect, make abandonment of one's own religion or conformity to the religious beliefs of others the price of an equal place in the civil community. [A] State that makes criminal an individual's religiously motivated conduct burdens that individual's free exercise of religion in the severest manner possible. [I] would have thought it beyond argument that such laws implicate free exercise concerns. Indeed, we have never distinguished between cases in which a State conditions receipt of a benefit on conduct prohibited by religious beliefs and cases in which a State affirmatively prohibits such conduct. The Sherbert compelling interest test applies in both kinds of cases. [E.g., Lee; Gillette; Yoder.]

[Legislatures], of course, have always been "left free to reach actions which were in violation of social duties or subversive of good order." [Reynolds.] [But once] it has been shown that a government regulation or criminal prohibition burdens the free exercise of religion, we have consistently asked the Government to demonstrate that unbending application of its regulation to the religious objector "is essential to accomplish an overriding governmental interest" [Lee] or represents "the least restrictive means of achieving some compelling state interest" [Thomas]. To me, the sounder approach—the approach more consistent with our role as judges to decide each case on its individual merits—is to apply this test in each case to determine whether the burden on the specific plaintiffs before us is constitutionally significant and whether the particular criminal interest asserted by the State before us is compelling.

[The] Court today gives no convincing reason to depart from settled First Amendment jurisprudence. There is nothing talismanic about neutral laws of general applicability or general criminal prohibitions, for laws neutral toward religion can coerce a person to violate his religious conscience or intrude upon his religious duties just as effectively as laws aimed at religion. [A] law that makes criminal such an activity therefore triggers constitutional concern—and heightened judicial scrutiny—even if it does not target the particular religious conduct at issue. Our free speech cases similarly recognize that neutral regulations that affect free speech values are subject to a balancing, rather than categorical, approach. See e.g., [O'Brien, p. 252]. [The] Court's parade of horribles not only fails as a reason for discarding the compelling interest test, it instead demonstrates just the opposite: that courts have been quite capable of applying our free exercise jurisprudence to strike sensible balances between religious liberty and competing state interests.

Finally, the Court today suggests that the disfavoring of minority religions is an "unavoidable consequence" under our system of government and that accommodation of such religions must be left to the political process. In my view, however, the First Amendment was enacted precisely to protect the rights of those whose religious practices are not shared by the majority and may be viewed with hostility. The history of our free exercise doctrine amply demonstrates the harsh impact majoritarian rule has had on unpopular or emerging religious groups such as the Jehovah's Witnesses and the Amish. [The] compelling interest test reflects the First Amendment's mandate of preserving religious liberty to the fullest extent possible in a pluralistic society. For the Court to deem this command a "luxury" is to denigrate "[t]he very purpose of a Bill of Rights."

III. The Court's holding today not only misreads settled First Amendment precedent; it appears to be unnecessary to this case. I would reach the same result applying our established free exercise jurisprudence. [In Part III, Justice O'Connor, writing only for herself, found that Oregon had "a compelling interest in prohibiting the possession of peyote by its citizens." The critical question thus was "whether exempting respondents from the State's general criminal prohibition 'will unduly interfere with fulfillment of the governmental interest.' [Lee.]" She concluded: "Although the question is [close,] uniform application of Oregon's criminal prohibition is 'essential to accomplish' its overriding interest in 'preventing the physical harm'" caused by drug use. She rejected the argument that any incompatibility between the general law and an exemption was "belied by the fact that the Federal Government and several States provide exemptions for the religious use of peyote," finding that such other exemptions did not mean that Oregon was *required* to grant an exemption by the First Amendment. She added moreover, that the constitutionality of applying Oregon's general criminal prohibition "cannot, and should not turn on the centrality of the particular religious practice at issue."]

■ JUSTICE BLACKMUN, with whom JUSTICES BRENNAN and MARSHALL join, dissenting.

[I] agree with Justice O'Connor's analysis of the applicable free exercise doctrine, and I join parts I and II of her opinion. As she points out, "the critical question in this case is whether exempting respondents from the State's general criminal prohibition 'will unduly interfere with fulfillment of the governmental interest.' " I do disagree, however, with her specific answer to that question.

I.   In weighing respondents' clear interest in the free exercise of their religion against Oregon's asserted interest in enforcing its drug laws, it is important to articulate in precise terms the state interest involved. It is not the State's broad interest in fighting the critical "war on drugs" that must be weighed against respondents' claim, but the State's narrow interest in refusing to make an exception for the religious, ceremonial use of peyote. [E.g., Thomas; Yoder.] Failure to reduce the competing interests to the same plane of generality tends to distort the weighing process in the State's favor.

[Oregon] has never sought to prosecute respondents, and does not claim that it has made significant enforcement efforts against other religious users of peyote. The State's asserted interest thus amounts only to the symbolic preservation of an unenforced prohibition. [But] a government interest in ["symbolism"] cannot suffice to abrogate the constitutional rights of individuals. [The] State proclaims an interest in protecting the health and safety of its citizens from the dangers of unlawful drugs. It offers, however, no evidence that the religious use of peyote has ever harmed anyone. [The] carefully circumscribed ritual context in which respondents used peyote is far removed from the irresponsible and unrestricted recreational use of unlawful [drugs]. [Moreover,] just as in Yoder, the values and interests of those seeking a religious exemption in this case are congruent, to a great degree, with those the State seeks to promote through its drug laws. Not only does the Church's doctrine forbid nonreligious use of peyote; it also generally advocates self-reliance, familial responsibility, and abstinence from alcohol.

III. [Finally], although I agree with Justice O'Connor that courts should refrain from delving into questions of whether, as a matter of religious doctrine, a particular practice is "central" to the religion, I do not think this means that the courts must turn a blind eye to the severe impact of a State's restrictions on the adherents of a minority religion. Respondents believe, and their sincerity has *never* been at issue, that the peyote plant embodies their deity, and eating it is an act of worship and communion. Without peyote, they could not enact the essential ritual of their religion. [This] potentially devastating impact must be viewed in light of the federal policy—reached in reaction to many years of religious persecution and intolerance—of protecting the religious freedom of Native Americans. See American Indian Religious Freedom Act, 42 U.S.C. § 1996 ("it shall be the policy of the United States to protect and preserve for American Indians their inherent right of freedom to believe, express, and exercise the traditional religions . . . , including but not limited to access to sites, use and possession of sacred objects, and the freedom to worship through ceremonials and traditional rites"). [The] American Indian Religious Freedom Act, in itself, may not create rights enforceable against government action restricting religious freedom, but this Court must scrupulously apply its free exercise analysis to the religious claims of Native Americans, however unorthodox they may be. Otherwise, both the First Amendment and the stated policy of Congress will offer to Native Americans merely an unfulfilled and hollow promise.

———

SMITH AND RELIGIOUS EXEMPTIONS

1. ***Smith's story.*** Smith was a Native American who had become a serious alcoholic after a lifetime of harsh treatment by federal authorities. "As a young child he was the unwilling recipient of the U.S. government's policy to deprive American Indians of their native heritage and assimilate them into U.S. society. [As] a young man he lived on the city streets and was unwillingly drafted into the army [only] to come home several years later to a life of alcohol abuse." One day in 1957, after waking up in an alley on some cardboard boxes after a drinking binge, Smith gave up drinking. Smith embraced his Native American heritage and became an alcohol treatment counselor at a Native American alcohol program. The practice of Native American rituals, including the ritual consumption of peyote at issue in the case, was an important part of his recovery from alcoholism. As Smith described his peyote consumption, "I took the medicine—the communion, the sacrament, and I survived. I didn't have to go back to have a relapse." The position from which Smith was fired for peyote use was a counseling position in an alcohol treatment program which required employees to promise they would not drink or use drugs. Long, Religious Freedom and Indian Rights 22–35 (2000).

2. ***The history of religious exemptions.*** The opinions in Smith allude to the text of the First Amendment and the Court's free exercise precedents, but do not discuss whether the Framers might have viewed some religious exemptions as mandatory. In "The Origins and Historical Understanding of Free Exercise of Religion," 103 Harv. L. Rev. 1409 (1990), Michael McConnell traces the historical origins of the Free Exercise Clause, notes that pressure for the Free Exercise Clause came from the evangelical

religious movements of the colonial and founding periods, and argues that evangelicals viewed the constitutional guarantee of free exercise as protecting their right actively to fulfill religious obligations without state interference. He concludes that an interpretation of free exercise to mandate religious exemptions was both within the contemplation of the Framers and consistent with then-popular views about religious liberty and limited government. While he concedes that "exemptions were not common enough to compel the inference that the term 'free exercise of religion' necessarily included an enforceable right to exemption," he concludes nonetheless that "the modern doctrine of free exercise exemptions [before Smith] is more consistent with the original understanding than is a position that leads only to the facial neutrality of legislation." In "Free Exercise Revisionism and the Smith Decision," 57 U. Chi. L. Rev. 1109 (1990), McConnell criticizes the Court for failing to undertake in Smith "even a cursory inquiry into the history of the clause." For an alternative view of the same history, see Hamburger, "A Constitutional Right of Religious Exemption: An Historical Perspective," 60 Geo. Wash. L. Rev. 915 (1992), and Hamburger, Separation of Church and State (2002).

In **City of Boerne v. Flores**, 521 U.S. 507 (1997), which held that Congress lacked authority under the civil rights enforcement clauses to enact a statute applying the Sherbert rather than the Smith standard to claims of religious exemption from generally applicable state laws, Justices O'Connor and Scalia engaged in a lively colloquy on whether or not historical evidence supported the Smith standard:

Justice O'CONNOR's dissent argued that "the historical evidence casts doubt on the Court's current interpretation of the Free Exercise Clause." She noted that various colonial charters and acts had stated that religious practice should not be interfered with unless it caused some specified public harm: for example, because it was "unfaithfull to the Lord Proprietary, or molest[ed] or conspire[d] against the civil Government" (Maryland Act Concerning Religion, 1649); or was "us[ed] to licentiousness and profaneness [or] to the civil injury, or outward disturbance of others" (Charter of Rhode Island, 1663). "In other words," she argued, "when religious beliefs conflicted with civil law, religion prevailed unless important state interests militated otherwise." Likewise, she noted, early state constitutions quite commonly "guaranteed free exercise of religion or liberty of conscience, limited by particular defined state interests." For example, the New York Constitution of 1777 guaranteed free exercise but provided that it "shall not be so construed as to excuse acts of licentiousness, or justify practices inconsistent with the peace or safety of this State." Other states similarly provided for free exercise subject to the constraints of "the public peace" (New Hampshire) or the "peace or safety of the State" (Maryland, Georgia). Justice O'Connor also cited the Northwest Ordinance of 1787, which established a bill of rights for the Northwest Territory providing that: "No person, demeaning himself in a peaceable and orderly manner, shall ever be molested on account of his mode of worship or religious sentiments."

From this evidence, Justice O'Connor concluded that, "around the time of the drafting of the Bill of Rights, it was generally accepted that the right to 'free exercise' required, where possible, accommodation of religious practice." She suggested that otherwise, "there would have been no need to specify" licentiousness or other justifications for interference. Rather, she argued, "these documents make sense only if the right to free exercise was viewed as generally superior to ordinary legislation, to be overridden only when necessary to secure important government purposes." A particularly protective example, she noted, could be found in James Madison's draft Free Exercise Clause for the Virginia Declaration of Rights, which, though not ultimately adopted, would have provided that "no man [ought] on account of religion to be [subjected] to any penalties or disabilities, unless under color of religion the preservation of equal liberty, and the existence of the State be manifestly endangered."

Justice O'Connor next cited early examples of religious accommodation in the colonies and states. For example, some colonial governments created alternatives to oath requirements to accommodate Quakers and other Protestant sects that did not permit the swearing of allegiance to civil government; some colonies and the Continental Congress exempted Quakers and Mennonites from military service; some states with established churches exempted religious objectors from tithes. From these examples she concluded that state legislatures favored religious accommodations when possible, and that "it is reasonable to presume that the drafters and ratifiers of the First Amendment—many of whom served in state legislatures—assumed courts would apply the Free Exercise Clause similarly."

Finally, Justice O'Connor interpreted the writings of various framers as supporting this interpretation. For example, she read Madison's Memorial and Remonstrance as suggesting that religious duty might prevail over civil law whether that law was directed at religion or was more generally applicable. She concluded: "As the historical sources [show,] the Free Exercise Clause is properly understood as an affirmative guarantee of the right to participate in religious activities without impermissible governmental interference, even where a believer's conduct is in tension with a law of general application."

Justice SCALIA, the author of Smith, wrote a separate concurrence in Boerne disputing Justice O'Connor's historical claims. He argued that "[t]he material that the dissent claims is at odds with Smith either has little to say about the issue or is in fact more consistent with Smith than with the dissent's interpretation of the Free Exercise Clause." As he read the early colonial and state Free Exercise Clauses, they were "a virtual restatement of Smith: Religious exercise shall be permitted so long as it does not violate general laws governing conduct." On his reading, avoiding "licentiousness" or disturbance of public "peace" or "order" simply meant "obeying the laws" or avoiding " 'the occurrence of illegal actions.' " He argued that it was impossible to derive Sherbert's compelling interest test from caveats about mere "peace and order."

Justice Scalia also discounted evidence of early legislative accommodations: "that legislatures sometimes (though not always) found it 'appropriate' to accommodate religious practices does not establish that accommodation was understood to be constitutionally mandated by the Free Exercise Clause." Likewise, as to writings such as Madison's Remonstrance, there was "no reason to think they were meant to describe what was constitutionally required (and judicially enforceable), as opposed to what was thought to be legislatively or even morally desirable."

He concluded that "the most telling point made by the dissent is to be found, not in what it says, but in what it fails to say. Had the understanding in the period surrounding the ratification of the Bill of Rights been that the various forms of accommodation discussed by the dissent were constitutionally required (either by State Constitutions or by the Federal Constitution), it would be surprising not to find a single state or federal case refusing to enforce a generally applicable statute because of its failure to make accommodation. Yet the dissent cites none—and to my knowledge, [none] exists." Accordingly, he found, the "historical evidence does nothing to undermine the conclusion" in Smith that "the people" rather than the Court should decide questions of religious exemption.

3.   *Impact of exemptions for secular activities.* During the height of the COVID-19 pandemic in the United States, all states and many municipalities adopted various restrictions on gatherings in furtherance of public health. Numerous free exercise challenges were brought to these restrictions, the great majority of which were addressed by the lower federal courts. When parties applied for emergency review, the Supreme Court sometimes intervened in the form of orders issued without argument or complete briefing. During the early stages of the pandemic, the Court was relatively deferential to State restrictions, but became less so after Justice Barrett replaced Justice Ginsburg some eight months after restrictions began. In **Tandon v. Newsom**, 141 S. Ct. 1294 (2021), the Court issued a 5–4 per curiam opinion in such a case in which it sought to sum up the principles that had emerged its cases: "This Court's decisions have made the following points clear. First, government regulations are not neutral and generally applicable, and therefore trigger strict scrutiny under the Free Exercise Clause, whenever they treat any comparable secular activity more favorably than religious exercise. It is no answer that a State treats some comparable secular businesses or other activities as poorly as or even less favorably than the religious exercise at issue. Second, whether two activities are comparable for purposes of the Free Exercise Clause must be judged against the asserted government interest that justifies the regulation at issue. Third, the government has the burden to establish that the challenged law satisfies strict scrutiny. To do so in this context, it must do more than assert that certain risk factors 'are always present in worship, or always absent from the other secular activities' the government may allow. Instead, narrow tailoring requires the government to show that measures less restrictive of the First Amendment activity could not address its interest in reducing the spread of COVID. Where the government permits other activities to proceed with precautions, it must show that the religious exercise at issue is more dangerous than those activities even when the same precautions are applied. Otherwise, precautions that suffice for other activities suffice for religious exercise too. These principles dictated the outcome in this case. [California] treats some comparable secular activities more favorably than at-home religious exercise, permitting hair salons, retail stores, personal care services, movie theaters, private suites at sporting events and concerts, and indoor restaurants to bring together more than three households at a time."

Justice KAGAN dissented, joined by Justices Breyer and Sotomayor (Chief Justice Roberts did not join either opinion but stated he would have denied the application): "[The] First Amendment requires that a State treat religious conduct as well as the State treats comparable secular conduct. Sometimes finding the right secular analogue may raise hard questions. But not today. California limits religious gatherings in homes to three households. If the State also limits all secular gatherings in homes to three households, it has complied with the First Amendment. And the State does exactly that: It has adopted a blanket restriction on at-home gatherings of all kinds, religious and secular alike. California need not [treat] at-home religious gatherings the same as hardware stores and hair salons—and thus unlike at-home secular gatherings, the obvious comparator here. As the per curiam's reliance on separate opinions and unreasoned orders signals, the law does not require that the State equally treat apples and watermelons."

4. *The political economy of religious exemptions.* In the famous footnote four of the Carolene Products case, the Court suggested that judicial intervention is appropriate where the political process is unlikely to protect "discrete and insular" minorities. Are religious practitioners "discrete and insular minorities" in need of such judicial protection? Large denominations are often able to obtain exemptions through the political process. Sacramental wine used in Catholic and some Protestant ceremonies, for example, was exempted by statute from Prohibition. Recall too the legislative exemption of the Catholic church from the solicitation restrictions in Larson v. Valente (1982; p. 665). Should the Court presume that members of minority faiths, like racial minorities and political dissenters, are unable similarly to protect their religious practices through the political process and are in need of judicial protection from majority prejudice?

Justice O'Connor took this view in Smith, suggesting that religious minorities are politically powerless and thus in need of judicial solicitude: "[T]he First Amendment was enacted precisely to protect the rights of those whose religious practices are not shared by the majority and may be viewed with hostility. The history of our free exercise doctrine amply demonstrates the harsh impact majoritarian rule has had on unpopular or emerging religious groups." Justice Scalia, in contrast, noted that "a number of States have made an exception to their drug laws for sacramental peyote use," suggesting that even minority faiths may obtain legislative exemptions without resort to the courts. He conceded that "leaving accommodation to the political process will place at a relative disadvantage those religious practices that are not widely engaged in," but viewed that as an "unavoidable consequence of democratic government." Which of these views is more persuasive? Which view is borne out by Congress's passage of RFRA by overwhelming majorities, see p. 702?

Are judges more likely than legislatures to be free of bias or selectivity toward minority religions? One empirical survey found the results of pre-Smith judicial accommodation cases skewed ("Minority religionists bring and lose more cases; majority religionists bring fewer cases and win a larger percentage of them"), and concludes that "Smith had the effect of increasing religious equality because overall it significantly reduced the differential success rates that prevailed under the pre-Smith regime." Krotoszynski, "If Judges Were Angels: Religious Equality, Free Exercise, and the (Underappreciated) Merits of Smith," 102 Nw. L. Rev. 1189 (2008).

Should judicially mandated religious exemptions be required to compensate for a special structural disadvantage the religious suffer in politics—namely, that the Establishment Clause disables them from using religious arguments as a basis for legislation? For such an argument, see Sullivan, "Religion and Liberal Democracy," 59 U. Chi. L. Rev. 195 (1992); Greene, "The Political Balance of the Religion Clauses," 102 Yale L.J. 1611 (1993). For the countervailing view that religion should not enjoy any special exemption from laws that reflect the majority's indifference or neglect, but rather should enjoy exemptions only insofar as similarly situated nonreligious practices would receive them, see Eisgruber & Sager, Religious

Freedom and the Constitution (2007) (arguing for a theory of "equal liberty" that "denies that religion is a constitutional anomaly, a category of human experience that demands special benefits and/or necessitates special restrictions").

Is religious argument truly excluded from political debate? For expansive views of its permissibility, see Carter, The Culture of Disbelief (1993); Perry, Love and Power (1991); Perry, "Religious Arguments in Public Political Debate," 29 Loyola L. Rev. 1421 (1996). For a more cautiously approving view, see Greenawalt, Religious Convictions and Political Choice (1988); Greenawalt, "Religious Expression in the Public Square," 29 Loyola L. Rev. 1411 (1996). For arguments for greater restraint on religious participation in politics because the Establishment Clause forbids translation of religious commitments into public policy, see Teitel, "A Critique of Religion as Politics in the Public Sphere," 78 Cornell L. Rev. 747 (1993); Audi, "The Separation of Church and State and the Obligations of Citizenship," 18 Phil. & Pub. Affairs 259 (1989). Consider the following observations on this issue by Justice Scalia in his dissent in Edwards v. Aguillard (1987; p. 754): "Our cases in no way imply that the Establishment Clause forbids legislators merely to act upon their religious convictions. We surely would not strike down a law providing money to feed the hungry or shelter the homeless if it could be demonstrated that, but for the religious beliefs of the legislators, the funds would not have been approved. [We] do not presume that the sole purpose of a law is to advance religion merely because it was supported strongly by organized religions or by adherents of particular faiths. To do so would deprive religious men and women of their right to participate in the political process. [Such] religious activism [resulted, for example,] in the abolition of slavery."

5. *A ministerial exemption from antidiscrimination laws?* Where the Americans with Disabilities Act (ADA) would otherwise permit an action against a religious congregation for employment discrimination against a religious instruction teacher, do the First Amendment Religion Clauses compel a "ministerial" exception to the Act? In **Hosanna-Tabor Evangelical Lutheran Church and School v. Equal Employment Opportunity Commission**, 565 U.S. 171 (2012), the Supreme Court unanimously answered that question "yes." The EEOC and a teacher brought suit under the ADA against the Hosanna-Tabor Evangelical Lutheran Church and School, alleging that the teacher had been fired in retaliation for threatening to file an ADA lawsuit after the church did not reinstate her after a disability leave. In finding that action foreclosed by both the Free Exercise and Establishment Clauses, Chief Justice ROBERTS wrote for a unanimous Court:

"Until today, we have not had occasion to consider whether [the] freedom of a religious organization to select its ministers is implicated by a suit alleging discrimination in employment. The Courts of Appeals, in contrast, have had extensive experience with this issue, [and have] uniformly recognized the existence of a 'ministerial exception,' grounded in the First Amendment, that precludes application of such legislation to claims concerning the employment relationship between a religious institution and its ministers. We agree that there is such a ministerial exception. The members of a religious group put their faith in the hands of their ministers. Requiring a church to accept or retain an unwanted minister, or punishing a church for failing to do so, intrudes upon more than a mere employment decision. Such action interferes with the internal governance of the church, depriving the church of control over the selection of those who will personify its beliefs. By imposing an unwanted minister, the state infringes the Free Exercise Clause, which protects a religious group's right to shape its own faith and mission through its appointments. According the state the power to determine which individuals will minister to the faithful also violates the Establishment Clause, which prohibits government involvement in such ecclesiastical decisions."

The Chief Justice rejected the EEOC's argument that Employment Division v. Smith precludes recognition of a ministerial exception: "It is true that the ADA's prohibition on retaliation, like Oregon's prohibition on peyote use, is a valid and neutral law of general applicability. But a church's selection of its ministers is unlike an individual's ingestion of peyote. Smith involved government regulation of only outward physical acts. The present case, in contrast, concerns government interference with an internal church decision that affects the faith and mission of the church itself." Based on the record in the case, he held that the teacher qualified as a minister, noting that she had undergone extensive religious training, examination, and certification as a "called" teacher and that her "job duties reflected a role in conveying the Church's message and carrying out its mission." He concluded that, because the teacher "was a minister within the meaning of the exception, the First Amendment requires dismissal of this employment discrimination suit against her religious employer."

Justice THOMAS filed a brief concurrence noting that he would "defer to a religious organization's good-faith understanding of who qualifies as its minister" out of respect for the autonomy of religious decision-making. Justice ALITO, joined by Justice KAGAN, filed a concurrence noting that, given the variety of religious practices protected by the Religion Clauses, the "ministerial" exception should turn on an employee's religious function rather than formal title or any specific process of "ordination": "The 'ministerial' exception should [apply] to any 'employee' who leads a religious organization, conducts worship services or important religious ceremonies or rituals, or serves as a messenger or teacher of its faith. If a religious group believes that the ability of such an employee to perform these key functions has been compromised, then the constitutional guarantee of religious freedom protects the group's right to remove the employee from his or her position."

What do you make of Chief Justice Roberts's suggested distinction under Smith between the "outward act" of ingesting peyote for religious purposes and "government interference with an internal church decision"? For an argument that the religion clauses prohibit the government from interfering with international church affairs—the increasingly influential "church autonomy" theory—see Laycock, "Towards a General Theory of the Religion Clauses: The Case of Church Labor Relations and the Right to Church Autonomy," 81 Colum. L. Rev. 1373 (1981). What else might qualify as an "internal church decision"? Does Hosanna-Tabor carve out a new exception to Smith? If so, what is its nature?

In **Our Lady of Guadalupe School v. Morrissey-Berru**, 140 S. Ct. 2049 (2020), the Court, by a 7–2 vote, extended the ministerial exception to foreclose employment discrimination claims by two teachers against the Catholic elementary schools where they taught. The teachers' duties included both secular and religious instruction. Justice ALITO wrote for the

Court: "Although these teachers were not given the title of 'minister,' [we] hold that their cases fall within the same rule that dictated our decision in Hosanna-Tabor. The religious education and formation of students is the very reason for the existence of most private religious schools, and therefore the selection and supervision of the teachers upon whom the schools rely to do this work lie at the core of their mission. Judicial review of the way in which religious schools discharge those responsibilities would undermine the independence of religious institutions in a way that the First Amendment does not tolerate."

Justice Alito went on to offer a justification that had not appeared in Chief Justice Roberts's majority opinion in Hosanna-Tabor, namely a principle of church autonomy: "The independence of religious institutions in matters of faith and doctrine is closely linked to independence in what we have termed 'matters of church government.' This does not mean that religious institutions enjoy a general immunity from secular laws, but it does protect their autonomy with respect to internal management decisions that are essential to the institution's central mission. And a component of this autonomy is the selection of the individuals who play certain key roles." Turning to the term "minister," Justice Alito wrote that "[s]imply giving an employee the title of 'minister' is not enough to justify the exception. And by the same token, since many religious traditions do not use the title 'minister,' it cannot be a necessary requirement. [What] matters, at bottom, is what an employee does. And implicit in our decision in Hosanna-Tabor was a recognition that educating young people in their faith, inculcating its teachings, and training them to live their faith are responsibilities that lie at the very core of the mission of a private religious school."

Justice THOMAS, joined by Justice Gorsuch, concurred to "reiterate" his view that "the Religion Clauses require civil courts to defer to religious organizations' good-faith claims that a certain employee's position is ministerial."

Justice SOTOMAYOR, joined by Justice Ginsburg, dissented: "Two employers fired their employees allegedly because one had breast cancer and the other was elderly. [The] majority shields those employers from disability and age-discrimination claims. [The] Court reaches this result even though the teachers taught primarily secular subjects, lacked substantial religious titles and training, and were not even required to be Catholic. In foreclosing the teachers' claims, the Court [collapses] Hosanna-Tabor's careful analysis into a single consideration: whether a church thinks its employees play an important religious role. [That] simplistic approach has no basis in law and strips thousands of schoolteachers of their legal protections. [Until] today, no court had held that the ministerial exception applies [to] lay teachers like respondents. [To] be sure, [the teachers] taught religion for a part of some days in the week. But that should not transform them automatically into ministers. [Nor] is it dispositive that both teachers prayed with their students."

6. **Smith and constitutional jurisprudence.** Justice Scalia's opinion for the Court in Smith reflects a strong mistrust of judicial balancing. Indeed, in a footnote, Justice Scalia suggested that "it is horrible to contemplate that federal judges will regularly balance against the importance of general laws the significance of religious practice." He found any judicial inquiry into the significance or "centrality" of a religious practice offensive to free exercise. For elaboration of Justice Scalia's general

antipathy toward balancing, see Scalia, "The Rule of Law as a Law of Rules," 56 U. Chi. L. Rev. 1175 (1989). How warranted is Justice Scalia's concern that balancing in the free exercise area will invite subjective or arbitrary judicial discretion? See Marshall, "In Defense of Smith and Free Exercise Revisionism," 58 U. Chi. L. Rev. 308 (1990) ("Exemption analysis threatens free exercise values because it requires courts to consider the legitimacy of the religious claim."). But see McConnell, "Free Exercise Revisionism," supra: "Why is the Free Exercise Clause a particular target? [Unless] Smith is the harbinger of a wholesale retreat from judicial discretion across the range of constitutional law, there should be some explanation of why the problem in this field is more acute than it is elsewhere."

Justice O'Connor, in contrast, endorsed a "balancing, rather than categorical, approach," and argued that courts had adequately protected state interests even though they engaged in balancing under Sherbert, Yoder and their progeny. She favored continued case-by-case determination of "whether the burden on the specific plaintiffs before us is constitutionally significant and whether the particular criminal interest asserted by the State before us is compelling." She denied any need to inquire into the centrality of religious practices. But can the Court determine whether a burden is "constitutionally significant" without making such a centrality inquiry? Is there a danger that courts making such an inquiry will exhibit unconscious bias, viewing minority religions through the lens of mainstream practices? Similarly to Justice O'Connor, Justice Barrett has now stated that she is "skeptical" of a categorical approach and called for a standard that is "much more nuanced." Does her caution suggest that these questions may have no good answer?

Was Smith consistent with the doctrine of stare decisis? Note that Justice Scalia sought to distinguish rather than overrule prior cases inconsistent with the deferential rule embraced in Smith. Are these distinctions persuasive? See McConnell, "Free Exercise Revisionism," supra (arguing that the Court's distinction of Yoder and the unemployment compensation cases "appears to have one function only: to enable the Court to reach the conclusion it desired in Smith without openly overruling any prior decisions"). Would candid overrule have been preferable? Did the pre-Smith decisions themselves lack candor? Did Smith simply state the rule immanent in the earlier decisions? Should Smith's relationship with the cases that come before it, especially Sherbert, affect how the Court thinks about whether to overrule Smith?

7. *The end of Smith?* In **Fulton v. City of Philadelphia**, 141 S. Ct. 1868 (2021), the Court considered a free exercise challenge brought by Catholic Social Services in Philadelphia against city ordinances that, as applied by the city, barred CSS from participating in the placement of foster children or adoptees because CSS would not place the children with same-sex couples. In the run-up to the decision, many observers expected the Court to take the opportunity to overturn Smith. Instead, in an opinion by Chief Justice ROBERTS, the Court avoided the issue by holding that the ordinances were not generally applicable: "A law is not generally applicable if it invites the government to consider the particular reasons for a person's conduct by providing a mechanism for individualized exemptions. Smith. The current version of section 3.21 specifies in pertinent part: 'Rejection of Referral. Provider shall not reject a child or family including, but not limited to, . . . prospective foster or adoptive parents, for Services based upon . . .

their ... sexual orientation ... unless an exception is granted by the Commissioner or the Commissioner's designee, in his/her sole discretion.' [Like] the good cause provision in Sherbert, section 3.21 incorporates a system of individual exemptions, made available in this case at the 'sole discretion' of the Commissioner. [In] addition to relying on the contract, the City argues that CSS's refusal to certify same-sex couples constitutes an 'Unlawful Public Accommodations Practice' in violation of the Fair Practices Ordinance. But [we] conclude that it does not because foster care agencies do not act as public accommodations in performing certifications."

In a concurrence, Justice BARRETT, joined by Justice Kavanaugh and by Justice Breyer for all but the first paragraph, wrote that she found "the historical record more silent than supportive on the question whether the founding generation understood the First Amendment to require religious exemptions from generally applicable laws in at least some circumstances. In my view, the textual and structural arguments against Smith are more compelling. As a matter of text and structure, it is difficult to see why the Free Exercise Clause—lone among the First Amendment freedoms—offers nothing more than protection from discrimination." She then asked "[What] should replace Smith? The prevailing assumption seems to be that strict scrutiny would apply whenever a neutral and generally applicable law burdens religious exercise. But I am skeptical about swapping Smith's categorical antidiscrimination approach for an equally categorical strict scrutiny regime, particularly when this Court's resolution of conflicts between generally applicable laws and other First Amendment rights—like speech and assembly—has been much more nuanced. There would be a number of issues to work through if Smith were overruled. To name a few: Should entities like Catholic Social Services—which is an arm of the Catholic Church—be treated differently than individuals? Cf. Hosanna-Tabor. Should there be a distinction between indirect and direct burdens on religious exercise? Cf. Braunfeld. What forms of scrutiny should apply? Compare Sherbert (assessing whether government's interest is compelling), with Gillette (assessing whether government's interest is substantial). And if the answer is strict scrutiny, would pre-Smith cases rejecting free exercise challenges to garden-variety laws come out the same way?"

Justice ALITO, joined by Justices Thomas and Gorsuch, concurred in the judgment only and laid out at great length why Smith should be overturned: "There is no question that Smith's interpretation can have startling consequences. [Suppose] that the Volstead Act, which implemented the Prohibition Amendment, had not contained an exception for sacramental wine. The Act would have been consistent with Smith even though it would have prevented the celebration of a Catholic Mass anywhere in the United States. Or suppose that a State, following the example of several European countries, made it unlawful to slaughter an animal that had not first been rendered unconscious. That law would be fine under Smith even though it would outlaw kosher and halal slaughter. Or suppose that a jurisdiction in this country, following the recommendations of medical associations in Europe, banned the circumcision of infants. A San Francisco ballot initiative in 2010 proposed just that. A categorical ban would be allowed by Smith even though it would prohibit an ancient and important Jewish and Muslim practice. Or suppose that this Court or some other court enforced a rigid rule prohibiting attorneys from wearing any form of head covering in court. The rule would satisfy Smith even though it would prevent Orthodox Jewish men, Sikh men, and many Muslim women from appearing. Many other

examples could be added. [The] present case shows that the dangers posed by Smith are not hypothetical. The city of Philadelphia (City) has issued an ultimatum to an arm of the Catholic Church: Either engage in conduct that the Church views as contrary to the traditional Christian understanding of marriage or abandon a mission that dates back to the earliest days of the Church—providing for the care of orphaned and abandoned children. [RFRA and RLUIPA] are no substitute for a proper interpretation of the Free Exercise Clause.

"[Smith] paid shockingly little attention to the text of the Free Exercise Clause. Instead of examining what readers would have understood its words to mean when adopted, the opinion merely asked whether it was 'permissible' to read the text to have the meaning that the majority favored. This strange treatment of the constitutional text cannot be justified—and is especially surprising since it clashes so sharply with the way in which Smith's author, Justice Scalia, generally treated the text of the Constitution (and, indeed, with his entire theory of legal interpretation). [The] ordinary meaning of 'prohibiting the free exercise of religion' was (and still is) forbidding or hindering unrestrained religious practices or worship. That straightforward understanding [does] not suggest a distinction between laws that are generally applicable and laws that are targeted. As interpreted in Smith, the Clause is essentially an anti-discrimination provision: It means that the Federal Government and the States cannot restrict conduct that constitutes a religious practice for some people unless it imposes the same restriction on everyone else who engages in the same conduct. Smith made no real attempt to square that equal-treatment interpretation with the ordinary meaning of the Free Exercise Clause's language. [The] key point for present purposes is that the text of the Free Exercise Clause gives a specific group of people (those who wish to engage in the exercise of religion) the right to do so without hindrance. The language of the Clause does not tie this right to the treatment of persons not in this group. [Not] only is it difficult to square Smith's interpretation with the terms of the Free Exercise Clause, the absence of any language referring to equal treatment is striking. If equal treatment was the objective, why didn't Congress say that?" Justice Alito then turned to the historical record in the colonies and States and found "one predominant model. This model extends broad protection for religious liberty but expressly provides that the right does not protect conduct that would endanger 'the public peace' or 'safety.' [This model] is antithetical to Smith. If, as Smith held, the free-exercise right does not require any religious exemptions from generally applicable laws, it is not easy to imagine situations in which a public-peace-or-safety carveout would be necessary. Legislatures enact generally applicable laws to protect public peace and safety. If those laws are thought to be sufficient to address a particular type of conduct when engaged in for a secular purpose, why wouldn't they also be sufficient to address the same type of conduct when carried out for a religious reason? Smith's [defenders'] chief response is that the free-exercise provisions that included these carveouts were tantamount to the Smith rule because any conduct that is generally prohibited or generally required can be regarded as necessary to protect public peace or safety. This argument gives 'public peace and safety' an unnaturally broad interpretation."

Justice GORSUCH, joined by Justices Thomas and Alito, concurred to point out how implausible was the majority's reading of Philadelphia ordinances: "Given all the maneuvering, it's hard not to wonder if the majority is so anxious to say nothing about Smith's fate that it is willing to say pretty much anything about municipal law and the parties' briefs. One way or another, the majority seems determined to declare there is no 'need' or 'reason' to revisit Smith today. But tell that to CSS. [The] majority's course guarantees that this litigation is only getting started. As the final arbiter of state law, the Pennsylvania Supreme Court can effectively overrule the majority's reading of the Commonwealth's public accommodations law. The City can revise its FPO to make even plainer still that its law does encompass foster services. Or with a flick of a pen, municipal lawyers may rewrite the City's contract to close the § 3.21 loophole. Once any of that happens, CSS will find itself back where it started."

Three Justices have explicitly called for Smith to be overruled, and Justices Kavanaugh and Barrett have stated that it is "difficult to see" how Smith can be reconciled with the text and structure of the First Amendment. Given the Marks rule, these two Justices may have total control over the future of the doctrine. This makes the answers to Justice Barrett's questions about what should replace Smith especially important to the future of religious exemptions. How would you answer Justice Barrett's questions about what should replace Smith? Might she be alluding to the intermediate scrutiny regime that applies in the free speech context when a law aimed at conduct burdens expressive conduct? See United States v. O'Brien.

Since 2017, Our Lady of Guadalupe, Fulton, Tandon, Espinosa, Trinity Lutheran, and Masterpiece have all significantly bolstered free exercise rights without formally disturbing Smith. Do these cases render the question whether Smith is ever formally overruled moot? The weakening of Smith in recent years arguably resembles the weakening of Sherbert in cases like Lee, Bob Jones, Goldman, Bowen, and Lyng. Does this history suggest that— when it comes to religious exemptions—the Supreme Court will always be tempted to weaken its rules into more flexible standards? If so, does that suggest that the Court lacks the courage of its convictions, or does it show that more flexible standards are necessary to deal with the questions posed by religious exemptions?

CONSTITUTIONAL LAW BY STATUTE: LEGISLATIVE RESPONSES TO SMITH

1. ***The federal Religious Freedom Restoration Act of 1993 and its invalidation.*** After the Court issued the Smith decision, a broad coalition of religious groups began working on legislation that would contain Smith's effects by restoring a range of religious exemptions. The coalition attracted strong bipartisan support in Congress, and in 1993, the Congress overwhelmingly passed and the President signed the Religious Freedom Restoration Act (RFRA), 42 U.S.C. §§ 2000bb et seq. The Act contained formal findings that "laws 'neutral' toward religion may burden religious exercise without compelling justification," and that Smith had "virtually eliminated the requirement that the government justify burdens on religious exercise imposed by laws neutral toward religion." The Act identified as one of its purposes "to restore the compelling interest test as set forth in [Sherbert] and [Yoder]."

The Act, 42 U.S.C. § 2000bb–1, provided that: "(a) Government shall not substantially burden a person's exercise of religion even if the burden results from a rule of general applicability, except as provided in subsection (b) of this section. (b) Government may substantially burden a person's exercise of religion only if it demonstrates that application of the burden to the person (1) is in furtherance of a compelling governmental interest; and (2) is the least restrictive means of furthering that compelling governmental interest."

Did Congress have the authority to enact RFRA under § 5 of the Fourteenth Amendment, which permits Congress to "enforce, by appropriate legislation," the substantive guarantees of the Fourteenth Amendment? The Court ruled that it did not in **City of Boerne v. Flores**, 521 U.S. 507 (1997). The Boerne decision reasoned that RFRA had rewritten rather than merely enforced the protections of free exercise as the Court had previously interpreted them, exceeding Congress's authority and infringing the prerogatives of the states. At least as to state legislation, RFRA now furnishes no cause of action; but RFRA still binds federal actors.

2. *The continuing constraints of RFRA on the federal government.* While Boerne held the application of RFRA to the States to be beyond Congress' legislative authority under § 5 of the Fourteenth Amendment, it did not invalidate RFRA's application to the federal government. In **Gonzales v. O Centro Espirita Beneficente Uniao do Vegetal**, 546 U.S. 418 (2006), Chief Justice ROBERTS reaffirmed the stringency of RFRA's test for denial of free exercise exemptions in an 8–0 opinion (Justice Alito was not yet sitting when the case was heard.) The case involved a small religious sect (UDV) that receives communion by drinking a hallucinogenic tea called *hoasca*, brewed from Amazon rainforest plants and containing DMT, a controlled substance under the federal narcotics laws. The Court permitted a suit challenging a U.S. Customs interception of a shipment of *hoasca* to proceed. The Court held that the Government had failed to demonstrate a compelling interest in barring the tea's sacramental use: "Under the [focused] inquiry required by RFRA and the compelling interest test, the Government's mere invocation of [the] Controlled Substances Act cannot carry the day. It is true, of course, that Schedule I substances such as DMT are exceptionally dangerous. [But] there is no indication that Congress, in classifying DMT, considered the harms posed by the particular use at issue here—the circumscribed, sacramental use of *hoasca* by the UDV. [For] the past 35 years, there has been a regulatory exemption for use of peyote—a Schedule I substance—by the Native American Church. [If] such use is permitted [for] hundreds of thousands of Native Americans practicing their faith, it is difficult to see how those same findings alone can preclude any consideration of a similar exception for the 130 or so American members of the UDV who want to practice theirs."

RFRA engendered greater judicial disagreement—and public controversy—in **Burwell v. Hobby Lobby**, 573 U.S. 682 (2014), a case that raised so many distinct issues it reads like a law school exam. The case arose from the so-called contraceptive mandate derived from the Patient Protection and Affordable Care Act of 2010 (ACA), popularly known as Obamacare. The ACA requires employers with 50 or more full-time employees to offer "a group health plan or group health insurance coverage" that provides "minimum essential coverage" including "preventive care and screenings" for women without "any cost sharing requirements." Congress authorized the Health Resources and Services Administration (HRSA), a part of the Department of Health and Human Services (HHS), to further define these provisions. HRSA promulgated guidelines under which nonexempt employers are generally required to provide "coverage, without cost sharing" for "all FDA approved contraceptive methods, sterilization procedures, and patient education and counseling."

HHS through the HRSA exempted certain "religious employers" from the contraceptive mandate, including "churches, their integrated auxiliaries, and conventions or associations of churches," as well as "the exclusively religious activities of any religious order." When an insurer receives notice that one of its clients has invoked this provision, the insurer must exclude contraceptive coverage from the employer's insurance plan while bearing the costs of separately paying for contraceptive coverage for plan recipients. HHS determined this provided no net expense to insurers due to the savings created from decreased medical costs down the road.

Hobby Lobby is a for-profit chain of 500 arts-and-crafts stores with more than 13,000 employees. It is a closely held corporation controlled by David and Barbara Green and their children. The firm's statement of purpose says the owners will "honor[ ] the Lord in all [they] do by operating the company in a manner consistent with Biblical principles." As a for-profit corporation, Hobby Lobby could not invoke the "religious employers" exemption, and it challenged the contraceptive mandate as applied to it under RFRA.

The Court held 5–4 that Hobby Lobby was entitled to an exception from the mandate under RFRA. Justice ALITO, joined by Chief Justice Roberts and Justices Scalia, Kennedy, and Thomas, wrote the opinion for the Court. Relying on the Dictionary Act's definition of "person" to include artificial persons, the Court first held that corporations were persons for purposes of RFRA analysis. It then rejected the argument that for-profit corporations were not protected by RFRA on the ground that Braunfeld v. Brown (1961; p. 672) had considered (and rejected on the merits) the free exercise claims of Sabbath-observant Jewish business owners. The Court further rejected the view that RFRA necessarily encompassed only claims that could have been made under the Free Exercise Clause before Smith.

Next, the Court considered and rejected the argument that the sincere beliefs of a for-profit corporation could not be ascertained. Justice Alito also emphasized that Hobby Lobby was a closely held corporation, and that "numerous practical restraints" made the idea of unrelated shareholders agreeing to run a corporation under the same religious beliefs improbable."

After finding that the law imposed a substantial burden on the "ability of the objecting parties to conduct business in accordance with their religious beliefs," the Court bracketed the question of compelling government interest and turned to whether HHS had adopted the least restrictive means of furthering the government's interest. It held that HHS had not: "The most straightforward way of doing this would be for the Government to assume the cost of providing the four contraceptives at issue to any women who are unable to obtain them under their health-insurance policies due to their employers' religious objections. This would certainly be less restrictive of the plaintiffs' religious liberty, and HHS has not shown that this is not a viable alternative. HHS has not provided any estimate of the average cost per employee of providing access to these contraceptives, two of which, according to the FDA, are designed primarily for emergency use. Nor has HHS provided any statistics regarding the number of employees who might be affected because they work for corporations like Hobby Lobby. [Nor] has HHS told us that it is unable to provide such statistics. It seems likely, however, that the cost of providing the forms of contraceptives would be minor when compared with the overall cost of ACA.

"[HHS] contends that RFRA does not permit us to take this option into account because 'RFRA cannot be used to require creation of entirely new programs.' But we see nothing in RFRA that supports this argument, and drawing the line between the 'creation of an entirely new program' and the modification of an existing program (which RFRA surely allows) would be fraught with problems. We do not doubt that cost may be an important factor in the least-restrictive-means analysis, but both RFRA and its sister statute, RLUIPA, may in some circumstances require the Government to expend additional funds to accommodate citizens' religious beliefs. HHS's view that RFRA can never require the Government to spend even a small amount reflects a judgment about the importance of religious liberty that was not shared by the Congress that enacted that law."

Beyond cost, Justice Alito continued, there was a further indication that the government had not adopted the least restrictive means: "In the end, however, we need not rely on the option of a new, government-funded program in order to conclude that the HHS regulations fail the least-restrictive-means test. HHS itself has demonstrated that it has at its disposal an approach that is less restrictive than requiring employers to fund contraceptive methods that violate their religious beliefs. HHS has already established an accommodation for nonprofit organizations with religious objections. We do not decide today whether an approach of this type complies with RFRA for purposes of all religious claims. At a minimum, however, it does not impinge on the plaintiffs' religious belief that providing insurance coverage for the contraceptives at issue here violates their religion, and it serves HHS's stated interests equally well."

Justice KENNEDY concurred to insist that "that the Court's opinion does not have the breadth and sweep ascribed to it by the respectful and powerful dissent." Referring to the existing accommodations, Justice Kennedy wrote that "the Government has not met its burden of showing that it cannot accommodate the plaintiffs' similar religious objections under this established framework. RFRA is inconsistent with the insistence of an agency such as HHS on distinguishing between different religious believers—burdening one while accommodating the other—when it may treat both equally by offering both of them the same accommodation."

Justice GINSBURG, joined in full by Justice Sotomayor and partly by Justices Breyer and Kagan, dissented. "In a decision of startling breadth," she began, "the Court holds that commercial enterprises, including corporations, along with partnerships and sole proprietorships, can opt out of any law (saving only tax laws) they judge incompatible with their sincerely held religious beliefs. Compelling governmental interests in uniform compliance with the law, and disadvantages that religion-based opt-outs impose on others, hold no sway, the Court decides, at least when there is a 'less restrictive alternative.' And such an alternative, the Court suggests, there always will be whenever, in lieu of tolling an enterprise claiming a religion-based exemption, the government, i.e., the general public, can pick up the tab. [In] the Court's view, RFRA demands accommodation of a for-profit corporation's religious beliefs no matter the impact that accommodation may have on third parties who do not share the corporation owners' religious faith—in these cases, thousands of women employed by Hobby Lobby and [their] dependents. Persuaded that Congress enacted RFRA to serve a far less radical purpose, and mindful of the havoc the Court's judgment can introduce, I dissent."

Justice Ginsburg explained the background of the contraceptive mandate in the Women's Health Amendment to the ACA. "The genesis of this coverage should enlighten the Court's resolution of these cases," she argued. "While the Women's Health Amendment succeeded, a countermove proved unavailing. The Senate voted down the so-called 'conscience amendment,' which would have enabled any employer or insurance provider to deny coverage based on its asserted 'religious beliefs or moral convictions.' "

Justice Ginsburg then characterized RFRA: "RFRA's purpose is specific and written into the statute itself. The Act was crafted to restore the compelling interest test as set forth in Sherbert and Yoder, and to guarantee its application in all cases where free exercise of religion is substantially burdened. [In] short, the Act reinstates the law as it was prior to Smith, without 'creat[ing] . . . new rights for any religious practice or for any potential litigant.' Given the Act's moderate purpose, it is hardly surprising that RFRA's enactment in 1993 provoked little controversy."

The dissent then addressed the majority's approach to RFRA: "Despite these authoritative indications, the Court sees RFRA as a bold initiative departing from, rather than restoring, pre-Smith jurisprudence. [T]he Court points first to the Religious Land Use and Institutionalized Persons Act of 2000 (RLUIPA), which altered RFRA's definition of the term 'exercise of religion.' RFRA, as originally enacted, defined that term to mean 'the exercise of religion under the First Amendment to the Constitution.' As amended by RLUIPA, RFRA's definition now includes 'any exercise of religion, whether or not compelled by, or central to, a system of religious belief.' That definitional change, according to the Court, reflects 'an obvious effort to effect a complete separation from First Amendment case law.' The Court's reading is not plausible. RLUIPA's alteration clarifies that courts should not question the centrality of a particular religious exercise. But the amendment in no way suggests that Congress meant to expand the class of entities qualified to mount religious accommodation claims, nor does it relieve courts of the obligation to inquire whether a government action substantially burdens a religious exercise."

Turning to RFRA, Justice Ginsburg first rejected the idea that a for-profit corporation had rights under the law: "Until this litigation, no decision of this Court recognized a for-profit corporation's qualification for a religious exemption from a generally applicable law, whether under the Free Exercise Clause or RFRA. The absence of such precedent is just what one would expect, for the exercise of religion is characteristic of natural persons, not artificial legal entities. As Chief Justice Marshall observed nearly two centuries ago, a corporation is 'an artificial being, invisible, intangible, and existing only in contemplation of law.' Dartmouth College v. Woodward (1819). Corporations, Justice Stevens more recently reminded [in dissent], 'have no consciences, no beliefs, no feelings, no thoughts, no desires.' Citizens United (2010; p. 583). The Court's special solicitude to the rights of religious organizations [is] just that. No such solicitude is traditional for commercial organizations. Indeed, until today, religious exemptions had never been extended to any entity operating in the commercial, profit-making world. The reason why is hardly obscure. Religious organizations exist to foster the interests of persons subscribing to the same religious faith. Not so of for-profit corporations. Workers who sustain the operations of those corporations commonly are not drawn from one religious community. Indeed, by law, no religion-based criterion can restrict the work force of for-profit corporations. The distinction between a community made up of believers in the same religion and one embracing persons of diverse beliefs, clear as it is, constantly escapes the Court's attention. One can only wonder why the Court shuts this key difference from sight. [Had] Congress intended RFRA to initiate a change so huge, a clarion statement to that effect likely would have been made in the legislation."

Justice Ginsburg then challenged the Court's substantial burden analysis: "I agree with the Court that the Green famil[y's] religious convictions regarding contraception are sincerely held. But those beliefs, however deeply held, do not suffice to sustain a RFRA claim. RFRA, properly understood, distinguishes between factual allegations that [plaintiffs'] beliefs are sincere and of a religious nature, which a court must accept as true, and the legal conclusion that [plaintiffs'] religious exercise is substantially burdened, an inquiry the court must undertake. That distinction is a facet of the pre-Smith jurisprudence RFRA incorporates. Bowen. Undertaking the inquiry that the Court forgoes, I would conclude that the connection between the famil[y's] religious objections and the contraceptive coverage requirement is too attenuated to rank as substantial. The requirement carries no command that Hobby Lobby purchase or provide the contraceptives they find objectionable. Instead, it calls on the companies covered by the requirement to direct money into undifferentiated funds that finance a wide variety of benefits under comprehensive health plans. [Importantly,] the decisions whether to claim benefits under the plans are made not by Hobby Lobby, but by the covered employees and dependents, in consultation with their health care providers. [It] is doubtful that Congress, when it specified that burdens must be substantial, had in mind a linkage thus interrupted by independent decisionmakers (the woman and her health counselor) standing between the challenged government action and the religious exercise claimed to be infringed."

Justice Ginsburg went on to argue that "the Government has shown that the contraceptive coverage for which the ACA provides furthers compelling interests in public health and women's well being. Those interests are concrete, specific, and demonstrated by a wealth of empirical evidence. To recapitulate, the mandated contraception coverage enables women to avoid the health problems unintended pregnancies may visit on them and their children. The coverage helps safeguard the health of women for whom pregnancy may be hazardous, even life threatening. And the mandate secures benefits wholly unrelated to pregnancy, preventing certain cancers, menstrual disorders, and pelvic pain."

Finally, Justice Ginsburg rejected the Court's least restrictive means analysis: "A least restrictive means cannot require employees to relinquish benefits accorded them by federal law in order to ensure that their commercial employers can adhere unreservedly to their religious tenets. [T]he ACA [requires] coverage of preventive services through the existing employer-based system of health insurance 'so that [employees] face minimal logistical and administrative obstacles.' Impeding women's receipt of benefits 'by requiring them to take steps to learn about, and to sign up for, a new [government] health benefit' was scarcely what Congress contemplated. [And] where is the stopping point to the 'let the government pay' alternative? Suppose an employer's sincerely held religious belief is offended by health coverage of vaccines, or paying the minimum wage, or according women equal pay for substantially similar work. Does it rank as a less restrictive alternative to require the government to provide the money or benefit to which the employer has a religion-based objection? Because the Court cannot easily answer that question, it proposes something else: Extension to commercial enterprises of the accommodation already afforded to nonprofit religion-based organizations. [I] have already discussed the 'special solicitude' generally accorded nonprofit religion-based organizations that exist to serve a community of believers, solicitude never before accorded to commercial enterprises comprising employees of diverse faiths.

"[Would] the exemption the Court holds RFRA demands for employers with religiously grounded objections to the use of certain contraceptives extend to employers with religiously grounded objections to blood transfusions (Jehovah's Witnesses); antidepressants (Scientologists); medications derived from pigs, including anesthesia, intravenous fluids, and pills coated with gelatin (certain Muslims, Jews, and Hindus); and vaccinations (Christian Scientists, among others)? [The] Court, however, sees nothing to worry about. Today's cases, the Court concludes, are 'concerned solely with the contraceptive mandate.' [But] the Court has assumed, for RFRA purposes, that the interest in women's health and well being is compelling and has come up with no means adequate to serve that interest, the one motivating Congress to adopt the Women's Health Amendment. There is an overriding interest, I believe, in keeping the courts out of the business of evaluating the relative merits of differing religious claims, or the sincerity with which an asserted religious belief is held. Indeed, approving some religious claims while deeming others unworthy of accommodation could be perceived as favoring one religion over another, the very risk the Establishment Clause was designed to preclude. The Court, I fear, has ventured into a minefield by its immoderate reading of RFRA. I would confine religious exemptions under that Act to organizations formed for a religious purpose, engaged primarily in carrying out that religious purpose, and not engaged substantially in the exchange of goods or services for money beyond nominal amounts."

3. ***The continuing constraints of RLUIPA on state governments.*** In 2000, three years after City of Boerne, Congress enacted the Religious Land Use and Institutionalized Persons Act (RLUIPA), which requires a compelling interest for denying free exercise exemptions in a narrower range of contexts than RFRA: prisons and zoning. RLUIPA applies if the substantial burden on religious exercise arises from a federally funded program; if the substantial burden affects interstate commerce; or if "the substantial burden is imposed in the implementation of a land use regulation or system of land use regulations, under which a government makes, or has in place formal or informal procedures or practices that permit the government to make individualized assessments of the proposed uses for the property involved." How may Congress permissibly regulate this final situation consistent with Smith and City of Boerne?

The Court applied RLUIPA in **Holt v. Hobbs**, 574 U.S. 352 (2015). In an opinion by Justice ALITO, a unanimous Court ruled that the Arkansas Department of Correction could not forbid a Muslim prisoner from growing a half-inch beard in accordance with his faith. The Court found that while the Department had a compelling interest in being able to identify prisoners and prevent them from hiding contraband in their hair, it was not clear the policy would actually further those interests, and at the very least it was not narrowly tailored: prisoners with dermatological conditions were permitted to grow short beards, and all prisoners could have more than half an inch of hair on their heads.

4. *State RFRAs and the changing politics of religious exemptions.* As evidenced by the overwhelming margins by which RFRA and RLUIPA were passed in Congress, there was a robust political consensus on the importance of religious exemptions not so long ago. This consensus produced legislation at the state as well as the federal level: as of 2019, 21 states had passed RFRAs of their own (including "majority-Democratic" states such as Connecticut, Illinois, and Pennsylvania), thereby re-imposing on themselves the constraint that City of Boerne lifted. Other states have developed RFRA-like free-exercise standards through judicial interpretation of their state constitutions.

The early state RFRAs were passed with little opposition. However, two recent judicial developments have dramatically changed the politics of state RFRAs, and of religious exemptions more generally. The first is the Supreme Court's decision to grant a religious exemption from the Affordable Care Act's contraceptive coverage mandate in Hobby Lobby. The second development was the rapid success of the gay-rights movement, culminating in the Supreme Court's decision in Obergefell. As same-sex marriage was legalized in more and more jurisdictions in the run-up to Obergefell, some religious bakers, photographers, and others have argued for a free exercise right to refuse to provide their services in connection with same-sex weddings. In 2013, the New Mexico Supreme Court rejected such an argument in Elane Photography v. Willock, 296 P. 3d 491 (2012), holding that the state Human Rights Act required a Christian wedding photographer to serve a same-sex wedding, despite the state's RFRA, which did not apply to disputes between private parties. After Elane Photography and Hobby Lobby, several state RFRAs were proposed that would have applied to for-profit corporations and disputes between private parties. National controversy erupted over a proposed bill in Arizona, which was ultimately vetoed by the governor, and later one in Indiana, which was passed and signed into law.

The debates over Hobby Lobby and the state RFRAs reflect a notable change in substance and tone from the 1990s and 2000s. Religious exemptions were then primarily about accommodating the beliefs of minority religious groups; now, the discussion of religious exemptions centers around claims by Protestant and Catholic Christians, members of the largest religious groups in America. Many have come to believe that all religious people, even Christians, need protection from a secular state that will otherwise "vilify" those who refuse to assent to "the new orthodoxy," as Justice Alito put it in his Obergefell dissent. On the other side, some liberals have come to see religious exemptions as a way for social conservatives to evade the consequences of political battles that they have lost. For more on the changing politics of religious exemptions, and in particular liberals' waning commitment to exemptions, see Paul Horwitz, The Hobby Lobby Moment, 128 Harv. L. Rev. 154 (2014). For an early version of the liberal case against religious exemptions, see Marci Hamilton, God vs. the Gavel (2005).

SECTION 4. THE ESTABLISHMENT CLAUSE

All interpretations of the Establishment Clause agree that it prohibits the creation of an official national church and the mandating of religious conduct. Thus, requiring oaths of fidelity to a faith, or tithes, or other financial support for a church would be paradigmatic violations of the clause. There, however, agreement ends. Modern debates over the scope of the Establishment Clause have centered on what the clause might prohibit beyond official oaths or tithes. Does the Establishment Clause bar official sponsorship of religious tenets or symbols, even if no citizen is coerced to support them? Should psychological "coercion" count? Is government "endorsement" of religion troubling even in the absence of coercion? Must religious entities and functions be excluded from all forms of public financial support? May they be included on an equal footing with other recipients of government largesse? Or should there be an absolute bar on government aid to religious evangelism? This section explores these questions in the context of three kinds of Establishment Clause claims: claims that government has impermissibly provided aid to religion, claims that government has impermissibly allowed religion to intrude into public schools, and claims that government has impermissibly sponsored religious doctrines or symbols.

At the outset, it must be noted that the Court set forth an influential test for Establishment Clause violations in **Lemon v. Kurtzman**, 403 U.S. 602 (1971), that is often referred to in the materials that follow as the "Lemon test." Lemon struck down certain types of financial aid to nonpublic schools. Summarizing past decisions, Lemon held that a statute must meet three criteria in order to withstand Establishment Clause attack: "First, the statute must have a secular legislative purpose; second, its principal or primary effect must be one that neither advances nor inhibits religion; finally, the statute must not foster 'an excessive government entanglement with religion.'"

The Lemon test was sharply criticized for decades even as the test remained on the books. The principal criticisms were: (1) that the "purpose" requirement, taken literally, would invalidate all deliberate government accommodation of religion, even though such accommodation is sometimes required by the Free Exercise Clause, and has sometimes been held permissible under the Establishment Clause even if not constitutionally compelled; (2) that legislative "purpose" is in any case difficult to ascertain in a multimember body, and (3) that the "entanglement" prong contradicts the previous two—*some* administrative "entanglement" is essential to ensure that government aid does not excessively promote religious purposes. Faced with these criticisms, the Court did not formally renounce the Lemon test until 2022, in Kennedy v. Bremerton School Dist. (p. 746). Instead, the Court's decisions increasingly employed different analytical devices for distinguishing establishments, most particularly the so-called endorsement test first described by Justice O'Connor in her Lynch v. Donnelly concurrence (p. 764) and first applied by the Court's majority in Allegheny County v. ACLU (p. 771). The Bremerton decision also repudiated the endorsement test.

PUBLIC FINANCIAL AID TO RELIGIOUS INSTITUTIONS

In recent decades, sharp Establishment Clause debate has arisen over religious subsidies. The problem is older than the Constitution: Recall that James Madison wrote his 1785 polemic Memorial and Remonstrance Against Religious Assessments, a classic expression of principles of religious liberty, in response to Patrick Henry's proposal to the Virginia legislature that a property tax be imposed to raise funds to be distributed, as the taxpayer directed, to churches for payment of clergy and maintenance of houses of worship. In that document, Madison wrote, "Religion [of] every man must be left to the conviction and conscience of every man," and queried, "Who does not see that the same authority which can establish Christianity, in exclusion of all other Religions, may establish with the same ease any particular sect of Christians, in exclusion of all other Sects? That the same authority which can force a citizen to contribute three pence only of his property for the support of any one establishment, may force him to conform to any other establishment in all cases whatsoever?" Madison, Memorial and Remonstrance Against Religious Assessments, in James Madison: Writings 29 (J. Rakove ed., 1999).

The Court itself did not become fully engaged in deciding issues of financial assistance to religious institutions until the late 1940s. Before that, the issue was of central national importance, but focused on state constitutions. From the 1840s through the 1930s, American Catholics sought state funding for Catholic institutions such as schools, orphanages and hospitals, arguing (with much justification) that equivalent state-supported institutions were de facto Protestant. With rare and typically short-lived exceptions, states refused such funding on the ground that states should not fund "sectarian" (i.e. Roman Catholic) institutions. Struggles over these issues reached a climax in 1875 and 1876, when national Republicans proposed a federal constitutional amendment that would have barred states from funding "sectarian" institutions. Known as the "Blaine Amendment" for presidential aspirant and Republican Congressman James G. Blaine of Maine, the amendment would not have changed the legal landscape much, and was designed to place a wedge between Democratic congressmen and Catholic voters. The federal amendment failed, but in its wake, dozens of states adopted either constitutional amendments or statutes (sometimes called "Baby Blaines") similarly prohibiting funding of sectarian institutions.

The Court's occasional early encounters with the issue were inconclusive. Thus, Bradfield v. Roberts, 175 U.S. 291 (1899)—the Court's first decision in the area—sustained a federal appropriation for the construction of a public ward to be administered as part of a hospital under the control of sisters of the Catholic church; but the Court in Bradfield did not reach the issue of whether aid to religious institutions is permissible, because it held that the hospital was not a religious body. See also Reuben Quick Bear v. Leupp, 210 U.S. 50 (1908) (upholding federal disbursement to Catholic schools of funds held in trust for education of Sioux Indians).

Several decades later, the issue of aid to religious institutions produced the Court's first full-scale examination of constitutional guidelines, in Everson v. Board of Education:

Everson v. Board of Education

330 U.S. 1, 67 S. Ct. 504, 91 L. Ed. 711 (1947).

[This case arose from a challenge to a New Jersey statute that authorized school districts to make rules and contracts to transport children to and from school, "including the transportation of school children to and from school other than a public school, except such school as is operated for profit." Pursuant to that law, a local school board adopted a resolution authorizing reimbursement to parents for money spent to transport their children on public buses. A local taxpayer challenged those payments going to parents of Roman Catholic parochial school students. The highest state court denied relief. The Supreme Court affirmed, but not before setting forth the influential statements that "no tax large or small" may be used to support religion and that there must be a "wall of separation between church and state" (recall the dueling historical accounts given by the majority and dissenters at p. 648):]

■ JUSTICE BLACK delivered the opinion of the Court.

The only contention here is that the state statute and the resolution, insofar as they authorized reimbursement to parents of children attending parochial schools, violate the Federal Constitution [including by] forc[ing] inhabitants to pay taxes to help support and maintain schools which are dedicated to, and which regularly teach, the Catholic Faith. This is alleged to be a use of state power to support church schools contrary to the prohibition of the First Amendment which the 14th Amendment made applicable to the states.

[The] "establishment of religion" clause of the First Amendment means at least this: Neither a state nor the Federal Government can set up a church. Neither can pass laws which aid one religion, aid all religions, or prefer one religion over another. Neither can force nor influence a person to go to or to remain away from church against his will or force him to profess a belief or disbelief in any religion. No person can be punished for entertaining or professing religious beliefs or disbeliefs, for church attendance or non-attendance. No tax in any amount, large or small, can be levied to support any religious activities or institutions, whatever they may be called, or whatever form they may adopt to teach or practice religion. Neither a state nor the Federal Government can, openly or secretly, participate in the affairs of any religious organizations or groups and vice versa. In the words of Jefferson, the clause against establishment of religion by law was intended to erect "a wall of separation between church and State."

We must [not strike down the New Jersey law] if it is within the State's constitutional power even though it approaches the verge of that power. New Jersey cannot consistently with the Establishment Clause of the First Amendment contribute tax-raised funds to the support of an institution which teaches the tenets and faith of any church. On the other hand, other language of the amendment commands that New Jersey cannot hamper its citizens in the free exercise of their own religion. Consequently, it cannot exclude individual Catholics, Lutherans, Mohammedans, Baptists, Jews, Methodists, Non-believers, Presbyterians, or the members of any other faith, *because of their faith, or lack of it,* from receiving the benefits of public welfare legislation. While we do not mean to intimate that a state could not provide transportation only to children attending public schools, we must be careful, in protecting the citizens of New Jersey against state-established churches, to be sure that we do not inadvertently prohibit New Jersey from extending its general state law benefits to all its citizens without regard to their religious belief.

Measured by these standards, we cannot say that the First Amendment prohibits New Jersey from spending tax-raised funds to pay the bus fares of parochial school pupils as a part of a general program under which it pays the fares of pupils attending public and other schools. It is undoubtedly true that children are helped to get to church schools. There is even a possibility that some of the children might not be sent to the church schools if the parents were compelled to pay their children's bus fares out of their own pockets when transportation to a public school would have been paid for by the State. [Similarly,] parents might be reluctant to permit their children to attend schools which the state had cut off from such general government services as ordinary police and fire protection, connections for sewage disposal, public highways and sidewalks. Of course, cutting off church schools from these services, so separate and so indisputably marked off from the religious function, would make it far more difficult for the schools to operate. But such is obviously not the purpose of the First Amendment. That Amendment requires the state to be neutral in its relations with groups of religious believers and non-believers; it does not require the state to be their adversary. State power is no more to be used so as to handicap religions than it is to favor them.

This Court has said that parents may, in the discharge of their duty under state compulsory education laws, send their children to a religious rather than a public school if the school meets the secular educational requirements which the state has power to impose. See Pierce v. Society of Sisters, 268 U.S. 510 (1925). It appears that these parochial schools meet New Jersey's requirements. The State contributes no money to the schools. It does not support them. Its legislation, as applied, does no more than provide a general program to help parents get their children, regardless of their religion, safely and expeditiously to and from accredited schools.

The First Amendment has erected a wall between church and state. That wall must be kept high and impregnable. We could not approve the slightest breach. New Jersey has not breached it here. Affirmed.

■ JUSTICE JACKSON, joined by JUSTICE FRANKFURTER, dissenting.

[The] Court's opinion marshals every argument in favor of state aid and puts the case in its most favorable light, but much of its reasoning confirms my conclusions that there are no good grounds upon which to support the present legislation. In fact, the undertones of the opinion, advocating complete and uncompromising separation of Church from State, seem utterly discordant with its conclusion yielding support to their commingling in educational matters.

■ JUSTICE RUTLEDGE, joined by JUSTICES FRANKFURTER, JACKSON and BURTON, dissenting.

The Amendment's purpose was [to] create a complete and permanent separation of the spheres of religious activity and civil authority by comprehensively forbidding every form of public aid or support for religion. [Does] New Jersey's action furnish support for religion by use of the taxing power? Certainly it does, if the test remains undiluted as Jefferson and Madison made it, that money taken by taxation from one is not to be used or given to support another's religious training or belief, or indeed one's own. [T]he prohibition is [absolute].

Two great drives are constantly in motion to abridge, in the name of education, the complete division of religion and civil authority which our forefathers made. One is to introduce religious education and observances into the public schools. The other, to obtain public funds for the aid and support of various private religious schools. [Both] avenues were closed by the Constitution. Neither should be opened by this Court. The matter is not one of quantity, to be measured by the amount of money expended. Now as in Madison's day it is one of principle, to keep separate [spheres] as the First Amendment drew them, to prevent the first experiment upon our [liberties].

––––––

MAINTAINING A "WALL OF SEPARATION"?

1. ***"No tax large or small."*** Everson classically recognizes the tension between antiestablishment and free exercise values. The aid challenged in Everson—provision of free school bus access to parochial school students—was aid directed to individuals (as distinguished from direct aid to the parochial institutions themselves). Since Everson, the Court has often accorded great weight to the identity of the immediate recipient of aid in determining whether an aid program violates the Establishment Clause. Should that be determinative? Madison's Remonstrance objected to sectarian aid even if directed to the church of the taxpayer's choice. The aid program in Everson was also directed to transportation rather than theology. The majority likens the program to the provision of fire, police and sanitation services to parochial schools. The dissent, on the other hand, rejects this comparison and instead analogizes the Everson aid program to the provision of "textbooks, of school lunches, of athletic equipment, [and] of writing and other materials." Which attempts at classification are more persuasive?

2. ***The "wall of separation."*** In Establishment Clause cases in the years immediately following Everson, the Court repeatedly cited the "wall of separation" metaphor approvingly. Later Courts, however, have been less enthusiastic about the metaphor. In his 1971 majority opinion in Lemon v. Kurtzman, for example, Chief Justice Burger commented: "[We] must recognize that the line of separation, far from being a 'wall,' is a blurred, indistinct, and variable barrier depending on all the circumstances of a particular relationship." And in Lynch v. Donnelly (1984; p. 764), Chief Justice Burger's opinion for the Court called the "wall of separation" metaphor "a useful figure of speech," but went on to say that "the metaphor itself is not a wholly accurate description of the practical aspects of the relationship that in fact exists between church and state."

3. ***Forms of aid: texts, tests, teachers, teaching aids and tuition.*** Everson held, on the one hand, that "[n]o tax in any amount, large or small, can be levied to support any religious activities or institutions," and, on the other hand, that the Establishment Clause does not bar the extension of "general state law benefits to all its citizens without regard to their religious belief." The Court was silent on the issue of aid to parochial education for two decades after Everson. But it returned to the issue in Board of Education v. Allen, 392 U.S. 236 (1968), holding that a state may lend books on secular subjects to parochial school students without violating the Establishment Clause. In Lemon v. Kurtzman, 403 U.S. 602 (1971), better known for its

restatement of the three-pronged Establishment Clause test, the Court concluded that the state's reimbursement of nonpublic schools for the cost of teachers' salaries, textbooks, and instructional materials, and its payment of a salary supplement to teachers in nonpublic schools, resulted in excessive entanglement of church and state.

The Court's decisions involving aid to parochial education after Allen and Lemon were far from consistent. In Meek v. Pittenger, 421 U.S. 349 (1975), and Wolman v. Walter, 433 U.S. 229 (1977), for example, the Court held that states may not constitutionally lend instructional materials such as maps, magazines, transparencies, tape recorders and laboratory equipment to parochial school students, despite its holding in Allen that lending *books* to such students is permissible. This aspect of Meek and Wolman was expressly overruled in Mitchell v. Helms (2000; p. 728), which held state loans of textbooks to religious schools constitutionally indistinguishable from state loans of instructional materials, and held such loans permissible. Wolman also held that states may not provide transportation for parochial school students to take field trips, despite its holding in Everson that states *may* provide such students with transportation to and from school. In Levitt v. Committee for Public Education, 413 U.S. 472 (1973), the Court held that states may not reimburse parochial schools for the cost of administering tests that are state-required but teacher-prepared. In Committee for Public Education v. Regan, 444 U.S. 646 (1980), however, the Court held that states *may* subsidize parochial schools for the expense of administering state-prepared examinations. And in Mueller v. Allen (1983; p. 718), the Court upheld a form of financial aid to parents of parochial school students (tax deductions) despite its rejection of a similar type of aid (tuition rebates and tax deductions) in Committee for Public Education v. Nyquist, 413 U.S. 756 (1973). For an effort to find coherence in the parochial education cases, see Tribe, American Constitutional Law 1219–21 (2d ed. 1988).

4. *Permissible subsidies: general beneficiary class and decentralized choice.* In attempting to reconcile its decisions in the religious subsidy context, the Court has relied upon several distinctions. First, it has looked at the breadth of the statutory class of beneficiaries: the broader the class, the more likely the Court is to uphold the statute. Is a distinction on the basis of breadth of statutory class a tenable one? The Court has upheld statutes that provide aid to private school students, as opposed to *all* students, on several occasions, presumably because the public school students were already receiving the aid in question. If this reasoning is extended, however, does it not suggest that financial aid to parochial school students is permissible, so long as the statutory class includes all private school students? If this is the case, does the defense that the beneficiary class is a general one require anything more than that parochial school students not receive benefits that students in other schools do not receive?

A second distinction upon which the Court has repeatedly relied is based upon the identity of the initial recipient of the aid. The Court has been far more receptive to programs that channel aid to parochial school students and their parents than it has been to programs that give aid directly to parochial schools. Is this distinction a helpful one? Does it not ignore the economic reality that money is fungible, parochial schools benefit whenever parents of parochial school students benefit, and religious practice benefits anytime a religious institution is relieved of nonreligious costs?

5. ***Other forms of public aid to religion.*** In **McCollum v. Board of Education**, 333 U.S. 203 (1948), the Court struck down a school board's practice of permitting students to attend sectarian classes held in the public schools during school hours by parochial school instructors. Justice Black's majority opinion found two problems: first, public school buildings were used for the purpose of providing religious education, and second, the program afforded "sectarian groups an invaluable aid in that it help[ed] to provide pupils for their religious classes through use of the state's compulsory public school machinery."

Just four years later, however, the Court held in **Zorach v. Clauson**, 343 U.S. 306 (1952), that releasing children during school hours to attend sectarian classes *outside* the public school did *not* violate the Establishment Clause. In his opinion for the Court, Justice DOUGLAS emphasized: "This 'released time' program involves neither religious instruction in public school classrooms nor the expenditure of public funds. All costs, including the application blanks, are paid by the religious organizations.

"[Appellants, taxpayers and residents whose children attend public schools, challenge the law], contending it is in essence not different from the one involved in [McCollum]. Their [argument] reduces itself to this: the weight and influence of the school is put behind a program for religious instruction; public school teachers police it, keeping tab on students who are released; the classroom activities come to a halt while the students who are released for religious instruction are on leave; the school is a crutch on which the churches are leaning for support in their religious training; without the cooperation of the schools this 'released time' program, like the one in [McCollum], would be futile and ineffective.

"[No] one is forced to go to the religious classroom and no religious exercise or instruction is brought to the classrooms of the public schools. A student need not take religious instruction. He is left to his own desires as to the manner or time of his religious devotions, if any. There is a suggestion that the system involves the use of coercion to get public school students into religious classrooms. There is no evidence in the record before us that supports that conclusion.

"[Apart] from that claim of coercion, we do not see how New York by this type of 'released time' program has made a law respecting an establishment of [religion]. There cannot be the slightest doubt that the First Amendment reflects the philosophy that Church and State should be [separated]. The First Amendment, however, does not say that in every and all respects there shall be a separation of Church and State. Rather, it studiously defines the manner, the specific ways, in which there shall be no concert or union or dependency one on the other. That is the common sense of the matter. Otherwise the state and religion would be aliens to each other—hostile, suspicious, and even unfriendly. Churches could not be required to pay even property taxes. Municipalities would not be permitted to render police or fire protection to religious groups. Policemen who helped parishioners into their places of worship would violate the Constitution. Prayers in our legislative halls; the appeals to the Almighty in the messages of the Chief Executive; the proclamations making Thanksgiving Day a holiday; 'so help me God' in our courtroom oaths—these and all other references to the Almighty that run through our laws, our public rituals, our ceremonies would be flouting the First Amendment. A fastidious atheist or agnostic could even object to the supplication with which the Court opens each session: 'God save the United

States and this Honorable Court.' We would have to press the concept of separation of Church and State to these extremes to condemn the present law on constitutional grounds. [We] are a religious people whose institutions presuppose a Supreme Being. We guarantee the freedom to worship as one chooses. We make room for as wide a variety of beliefs and creeds as the spiritual needs of man deem necessary. We sponsor an attitude on the part of government that shows no partiality to any one group and that lets each flourish according to the zeal of its adherents and the appeal of its dogma. When the state encourages religious instruction or cooperates with religious authorities by adjusting the schedule of public events to sectarian needs, it follows the best of our traditions. For it then respects the religious nature of our people and accommodates the public service to their spiritual needs. To hold that it may not would be to find in the Constitution a requirement that the government show a callous indifference to religious groups. That would be preferring those who believe in no religion over those who do believe. [Government] may not coerce anyone to attend church, to observe a religious holiday, or to take religious instruction. But it can close its doors or suspend its operations as to those who want to repair to their religious sanctuary for worship or instruction. No more than that is undertaken here. [The] constitutional standard is the separation of Church and State. The problem [is] one of degree.

"In the McCollum case the classrooms were used for religious instruction and the force of the public school was used to promote that instruction. Here, [the] public schools do no more than accommodate their schedules to a program of outside religious instructions. We follow [McCollum]. But we cannot expand it to cover the present released time program unless separation of Church and State means that public institutions can make no adjustments of their schedules to accommodate the religious needs of the people. We cannot read into the Bill of Rights such a philosophy of hostility to religion."

In dissent, Justice BLACK maintained that the released-time program constituted public aid to religion: "[Here as in McCollum], the school authorities release some of the children on the condition that they attend the religious classes, get reports on whether they attend, and hold the other children in the school building until the religious hour is over. As we attempted to make categorically clear, the McCollum decision would have been the same if the religious classes had not been held in the school buildings. [New York] is manipulating its compulsory education laws to help religious sects get pupils. This is not separation but combination of [Church and State]."

Justice JACKSON also dissented: "This released time program is founded upon a use of the State's power of coercion, which, for me, determines its unconstitutionality. Stripped to its essentials, the plan has two stages, first, that the State compel each student to yield a large part of his time for public secular education and, second, that some of it be 'released' to him on condition that he devote it to sectarian religious purposes. [If] public education were taking so much of the pupils' time as to injure the public or the students' welfare by encroaching upon their religious opportunity, simply shortening everyone's school day would facilitate voluntary and optional attendance at Church classes. But that suggestion is rejected upon the ground that if they are made free many students will not go to the Church. Hence, they must be deprived of freedom for this period, with Church attendance put to them as one of the two permissible ways of using it. The distinction attempted between [McCollum] and this is trivial, almost to the point of cynicism. [The] wall which the Court was professing to erect between Church and State has become even more warped and twisted than I expected. Today's judgment will be more interesting to students of psychology and of the judicial processes than to students of constitutional law." Justice Frankfurter agreed with Justice Jackson and also filed a separate dissent.

Thirty years later, the Court would articulate a similarly religion-inclusive view of the Establishment Clause in the context of explicitly financial public aid to religion:

———

Mueller v. Allen

463 U.S. 388, 103 S. Ct. 3062, 77 L. Ed. 2d 721 (1983).

[This case arose from a challenge to Minnesota's income tax law, which permitted its taxpayers to deduct from gross income actual expenses incurred for "tuition, textbooks and transportation" for the education of their dependents attending elementary or secondary schools. The deduction was available for expenses incurred in sending children to both public and nonpublic schools. The deduction was limited to $500 per child in primary school and $700 per child in secondary school. At the time, about 820,000 children attended Minnesota public schools and about 91,000 attended nonpublic schools; about 95% of the latter group attended religious schools. The Court upheld the deduction:]

■ JUSTICE REHNQUIST delivered the opinion of the Court.

Minnesota allows taxpayers, in computing their state income tax, to deduct certain expenses incurred in providing for the education of their children. The [Court of Appeals] held that the Establishment Clause [was] not offended by this arrangement. We now affirm.

One fixed principle in this field is our consistent rejection of the argument that "any program which in some manner aids an institution with a religious affiliation" violates the Establishment Clause. For example, it is now well-established that a state may reimburse parents for expenses incurred in transporting their children to school [Everson], and that it may loan secular textbooks to all school-children within the state. [Allen.] Notwithstanding the repeated approval given programs such as those in Allen and Everson, our decisions also have struck down arrangements resembling, in many respects, these forms of assistance. See, e.g., [Lemon; Levitt; Meek; Wolman.] In this case we are asked to decide whether Minnesota's tax deduction bears greater resemblance to those types of assistance to parochial schools we have approved, or to those we have struck down. Petitioners place particular reliance on our decision in [Nyquist], where we held invalid a New York statute providing public funds for the maintenance and repair of the physical facilities of private schools and granting thinly disguised "tax benefits," actually amounting to tuition grants, to the parents of children attending private schools. [We] conclude that [the provision here] bears less resemblance to the arrangement struck down in Nyquist than it does to [Everson and Allen].

[We] turn to the specific challenges raised [here] under the Lemon framework. Little time need be spent on the question of whether the Minnesota tax deduction has a secular purpose. [A] state's decision to defray the cost of educational expenses incurred by parents—regardless of the type of schools their children attend—evidences a purpose that is both secular and understandable. An educated populace is essential to the political and economic health of any community, and a state's efforts to assist parents in meeting the rising cost of educational expenses plainly serves this secular purpose of ensuring that the state's citizenry is well-educated. [We] turn therefore to the more difficult but related question whether the Minnesota statute has "the primary effect of advancing the sectarian aims of the nonpublic schools." In concluding that it does not, we find several features of the Minnesota tax deduction particularly significant. First, an essential feature of Minnesota's arrangement is the fact that [the provision] is only one among many deductions [available] under the Minnesota tax laws. Our decisions consistently have recognized that traditionally "[l]egislatures have especially broad latitude in creating classifications and distinctions in tax statutes." [The] Minnesota legislature's judgment that a deduction for educational expenses fairly equalizes the tax burden of its citizens and encourages desirable expenditures for educational purposes is entitled to substantial deference. Other characteristics of [the provision] argue equally strongly for the provision's constitutionality. Most importantly, the deduction is available for educational expenses incurred by *all* parents, including those whose children attend public schools and those whose children attend non-sectarian private schools or sectarian private [schools].

[By] channeling whatever assistance it may provide to parochial schools through individual parents, Minnesota has reduced the Establishment Clause objections to which its action is subject. It is true, of course, that financial assistance provided to parents ultimately has an economic effect comparable to that of aid given directly to the schools attended by their children. It is also true, however, that under Minnesota's arrangement public funds become available only as a result of numerous, private choices of individual parents of school-age children. [All] of our recent cases invalidating state aid to parochial schools [except Nyquist] have involved the direct transmission of assistance from the state to the schools themselves. [Where], as here, aid to parochial schools is available only as a result of decisions of individual parents no "imprimatur of State approval" can be deemed to have been conferred on any particular religion, or on religion generally.

The historic purposes of the clause simply do not encompass the sort of attenuated financial benefit, ultimately controlled by the private choices of individual parents, that eventually flows to parochial schools from the neutrally available tax benefit at issue in this case.

Petitioners argue that, notwithstanding [its facial neutrality], in application the statute primarily benefits religious institutions. Petitioners contend that most parents of public school children incur no tuition expenses, and that other expenses deductible under [the provision] are negligible in value; moreover, they claim that 96% of the children in private schools in 1978–1979 attended religiously-affiliated institutions. Because of all this, they reason, the bulk of deductions taken [will] be claimed by parents of children in sectarian schools.

We need not consider these contentions in detail. We would be loath to adopt a rule grounding the constitutionality of a facially neutral law on annual reports reciting the extent to which various classes of private citizens claimed benefits under the law. Such an approach would scarcely provide the certainty that this field stands in need of, nor can we perceive principled standards by which such statistical evidence might be evaluated. Moreover, the fact that private persons fail in a particular year to claim the tax relief to which they are entitled—under a facially neutral statute—should be of little importance in determining the constitutionality of the statute permitting such relief.

Finally, [if] parents of children in private schools choose to take especial advantage of the relief provided by [the law], it is no doubt due to the fact that they bear a particularly great financial burden in educating their children. More fundamentally, whatever unequal effect may be attributed to the statutory classification can fairly be regarded as a rough return for the benefits [provided] to the state and all taxpayers by parents sending their children to parochial schools. In the light of all this, we believe it wiser to decline to engage in the type of empirical inquiry into those persons benefited by state law which petitioners urge. Thus, we hold that the Minnesota tax deduction for educational expenses satisfies the primary effect inquiry of our Establishment Clause cases.

Turning to the third part of the Lemon inquiry, we have no difficulty in concluding that the Minnesota statute does not "excessively entangle" the state in religion. The only plausible source of the "comprehensive, discriminating, and continuing state surveillance" necessary to run afoul of this standard would lie in the fact that state officials must determine whether particular textbooks qualify for a deduction. In making this decision, state officials must disallow deductions taken from "instructional books and materials used in the teaching of religious tenets, doctrines or worship, the purpose of which is to inculcate such tenets, doctrines or worship." [Affirmed.]

■ JUSTICE MARSHALL, with whom JUSTICES BRENNAN, BLACKMUN and STEVENS join, dissenting.

The Establishment Clause [prohibits] a State from subsidizing religious education, whether it does so directly or indirectly. In my view, this principle of neutrality forbids [any] tax benefit, including the tax deduction at issue here, which subsidizes tuition payments to sectarian schools. [Indirect] assistance in the form of financial aid to parents for tuition payments is [impermissible] because it is not "subject [to] restrictions" which " 'guarantee the separation between secular and religious educational functions [and] ensure that State financial aid supports only the former.' " [Nyquist, quoting Lemon.] By ensuring that parents will be reimbursed for tuition payments they make, the Minnesota statute requires that taxpayers in general pay for the cost of parochial education and extends a financial "incentive to parents to send their children to sectarian schools." Nyquist. [That] parents receive a reduction of their tax liability, rather than a direct reimbursement, is of no greater significance here than it was in Nyquist. [It] is equally irrelevant whether a reduction in taxes takes the form of a tax "credit," a tax "modification," or a tax "deduction." What is of controlling significance is not the form but the "substantive impact" of the [financial aid].

[That] the Minnesota statute makes some small benefit available to all parents cannot alter the fact that the most substantial benefit provided by the statute is available only to those parents who send their children to schools that charge tuition. [The] bulk of the tax benefits afforded by the Minnesota scheme are enjoyed by parents of parochial school children not because parents of public school children fail to claim deductions to which they are entitled, but because the latter are simply *unable* to claim the largest tax deduction that Minnesota authorizes. [Parents] who send their children to free public schools are simply ineligible to obtain the full benefit of the deduction except in the unlikely event that they buy $700 worth of pencils, notebooks, and bus rides for their school-age children. Yet parents who pay at least $700 in tuition to nonpublic, sectarian schools can claim the full deduction even if they incur no other educational expenses.

That this deduction has a primary effect of promoting religion can easily be determined without any resort to the type of "statistical evidence" that the majority fears would lead to constitutional uncertainty. [In] this case, it is undisputed that well over 90% of the children attending tuition-charging schools in Minnesota are enrolled in sectarian schools. History and experience likewise instruct us that any generally available financial assistance for elementary and secondary school tuition expenses mainly will further religious education because the majority of the schools which charge tuition are sectarian. [T]ax assistance for tuition payments inevitably redounds to the benefit of nonpublic, sectarian schools and parents who send their children to those schools.

[For] the first time, the Court has upheld financial support for religious schools without any reason at all to assume that the support will be restricted to the secular functions of those schools and will not be used to support religious instruction. This result is flatly at odds with the fundamental principle that a State may provide no financial support whatsoever to promote [religion].

————

RELIGIOUS INCLUSION IN PUBLIC SUBSIDIES: EVERSON VS. MUELLER

1. ***The competing theories in Everson and Mueller.*** If Everson articulated, at least in theory, a separationist view of church and state, Mueller v. Allen articulated an alternative, more inclusionary view. On Everson's strict separationist view, no financial benefit "large or small" could flow from government to religious institutions. In Mueller's more inclusionary view, religious individuals or institutions may receive unlimited government financial aid so long as they do so on the same terms as other comparable beneficiaries. The latter approach would conceive neutrality under the Establishment Clause as requiring equal access for religion, not a wall of separation between church and state. On this view, exclusion of religious participants from the programs of the welfare state may discourage religious choices people would have made in the absence of the state or its programs. Which view of the religion clauses is more persuasive? More administrable? For elaboration of the inclusionary approach and its premises, see McConnell, "Religious Freedom at a Crossroads," 59 U. Chi. L. Rev. 115 (1992); see also Laycock, "Formal, Substantive, and Disaggregated Neutrality Toward Religion," 39 DePaul L. Rev. 993 (1990) (endorsing "substantive neutrality" toward religion that "[n]either encourages nor discourages religious belief or disbelief, practice or nonpractice"). For

competing views, see Sullivan, "Religion and Liberal Democracy," 59 U. Chi. L. Rev. 195 (1992); Lupu, "The Lingering Death of Separationism," 62 Geo. Wash. L. Rev. 230 (1994).

2. *Antecedents to Mueller.* The Court never embraced completely the separationist view, as the holding, as opposed to the rhetoric, of Everson itself demonstrated. Indeed, a pre-Mueller precursor of the assimilationist view may be found in **Walz v. Tax Commission**, 397 U.S. 664 (1970), which upheld a state tax exemption for "real or personal property used exclusively for religious, educational or charitable purposes." Writing for the Court, Chief Justice Burger noted that the tax exemption conferred "indirect economic benefit" upon churches, but emphasized that the state had "granted exemption to all houses of religious worship within a broad class of property owned by nonprofit, quasi-public corporations which include hospitals, libraries, playgrounds, scientific, professional, historical and patriotic groups."

Likewise, in another pre-Mueller case, Widmar v. Vincent (1981; p. 360), the Court struck down a state university's ban on the use of its facilities for prayer and religious discussion by student groups. In reaching that conclusion, the Court rejected the university's claim that permitting use of the university forum by the student groups would have violated the Establishment Clause. Justice POWELL's majority opinion found that an "equal access" policy would not violate the Establishment Clause. In applying the "effect" part of the Lemon test, he insisted that any aid to religious groups from a policy of "nondiscrimination against religious speech" would be only "incidental," because "an open forum in a public university does not confer any imprimatur of State approval on religious sects or practices" and the forum "was available to a broad class of non-religious as well as religious speakers."

3. *Aid to higher education: a different standard?* Prior to Mueller, the Court also had found fewer Establishment Clause barriers to financial aid to colleges and universities than to elementary and secondary schools. Although the Court has applied the three-part Lemon test developed in the elementary and secondary school context, the Justices have found it more readily satisfied in higher education cases and have been less prone to find excessive "entanglement" in state supervision schemes. The distinction between the levels of education was first articulated in Chief Justice BURGER's plurality opinion in **Tilton v. Richardson**, 403 U.S. 672 (1971): "There are generally significant differences between the religious aspects of church-related institutions of higher learning and parochial elementary and secondary schools. [C]ollege students are less impressionable and less susceptible to religious indoctrination. [Furthermore], by their very nature, college and postgraduate courses tend to limit the opportunities for sectarian influence by virtue of their own internal disciplines. [Since] religious indoctrination is not a substantial purpose [of] these church-related colleges, [there] is less likelihood than in primary and secondary schools that religion will permeate the area of secular education. This reduces the risk that government aid will in fact serve to support religious activities. Correspondingly the necessity for intensive government surveillance is diminished and the resulting entanglements between government and religion lessened. Such inspection as may be necessary to ascertain that the facilities are devoted to secular education is minimal."

Tilton upheld federal construction grants to church-related colleges. The funds had to be used for facilities devoted exclusively to secular educational purposes. The pattern of Tilton was followed two years later in Hunt v. McNair, 413 U.S. 734 (1973), where a divided Court sustained a construction aid program using state-issued revenue bonds to permit colleges to borrow funds at low interest. In **Roemer v. Maryland Public Works Board**, 426 U.S. 736 (1976), the majority went a step further: it approved annual noncategorical grants to eligible private colleges, including some church-related ones, subject only to the restriction that the funds not be used for "sectarian purposes." Justice BLACKMUN's plurality opinion conceded that the "entanglement" problem (arising from the supervision needed to assure that funds were used only for secular purposes) was more serious in the context of annual grants than with "one-time" aid. He nevertheless found the program permissible.

4. *Increasing deference to the inclusion of religion in public subsidies.* Did the principles of Mueller eventually prevail over those in Everson? Did the Court increasingly abandon separationism for a version of substantive neutrality that considered religion capable of inclusion in the public order so long as it was on a par with other social entities? Consider the Court's deference to the inclusion of religion in public subsidies in the following series of cases:

Witters v. Washington Department of Services for Blind, 474 U.S. 481 (1986), unanimously held that the "effect" prong of the Lemon test was not violated by a law authorizing payment to a visually handicapped person for vocational rehabilitation services, where the recipient sought to use the funds to pay his tuition at a Christian college in order to prepare himself for a career as a "pastor, missionary, or youth director." Justice MARSHALL's opinion emphasized that the aid program provided "no financial incentive for students to undertake sectarian education" and did not "tend to provide greater or broader benefits for recipients who apply their aid to religious education." Moreover, there was no showing that any "significant portion of the aid expended under the Washington program as a whole will end up flowing to religious education." Justice Marshall's reliance on the small quantity of aid that found its way into religious education, however, did not seem to represent the views of the majority. Concurring opinions by Justices WHITE, POWELL (joined by Chief Justice Burger and Justice Rehnquist) and O'CONNOR all emphasized their reliance on Mueller v. Allen (p. 718). Justice Powell criticized the Court for not relying directly on Mueller. He insisted that Mueller meant that "state programs that are wholly neutral in offering educational assistance to a class defined without reference to religion do not violate the [effect] part of the [Lemon] test, because any aid to religion results from the private choices of individual beneficiaries."

Bowen v. Kendrick, 487 U.S. 589 (1988): This was a challenge to the Adolescent Family Life Act of 1982, which authorizes federal grants to public and nonpublic organizations, including organizations with ties to religious denominations, for counseling services and research "in the area of premarital adolescent sexual relations and pregnancy." Some of the grants, the Court noted, went "to various organizations that were affiliated with religious denominations and that had corporate requirements that the organizations abide by religious doctrines." The Court, in a majority opinion by Chief Justice REHNQUIST, rejected an on-the-face attack on the Act and remanded the as-applied challenge for further proceedings. As in Mueller, the court readily found a secular purpose (preventing teenage pregnancy) but conceded the question of effect was more difficult. There were two problems. The first was the specific mention of religious organizations in the law itself. But since various institutions in the public and private sector were also mentioned, the Court found that any effect of advancing religion was "incidental and remote." Second, the law permitted "religious institutions to participate as recipients of federal funds." But again Justice Rehnquist found this permissible: "[This] Court has never held that religious institutions are disabled by the First Amendment from participating in publicly sponsored social welfare programs." Moreover, "nothing on the face of the [law] indicates that a significant proportion of the federal funds will be disbursed to 'pervasively sectarian' institutions." The Court also rejected a claim that the Act necessarily advanced religion because religiously affiliated grantees provided the counseling services: although the Establishment Clause bars government-financed indoctrination into "the beliefs of a particular religious faith," the Court insisted that when aid goes to religiously affiliated institutions that are not "pervasively sectarian," it would not "presume that [it will] be used in a way that would have the primary effect of advancing religion." Finally, the Court did not find a violation of the "excessive entanglement" prong of Lemon, concluding that there was no reason to fear that the monitoring involved here would "cause government to intrude unduly into the day-to-day operations of the religiously affiliated [grantees]." In remanding the as-applied challenge to the trial court, the Court suggested that the validity of the law as applied would turn on such issues as the "pervasive[ly] sectarian" nature of the grantees and whether any of the aid was used to finance "specifically religious activit[ies] in an otherwise substantially secular setting."

Justice O'CONNOR's concurrence emphasized that the majority opinion should not read as tolerating "the kind of improper administration that seems to have occurred [here]." She insisted that "*any* use of public funds to promote religious doctrines" was unconstitutional and that "*extensive* violations—if they can be proved in this case—will be highly relevant in shaping an appropriate remedy that ends such abuses." Justice KENNEDY, joined by Justice Scalia, also submitted a concurrence, arguing that a finding that funds went to a pervasively sectarian institution would still not be a sufficient condition for unconstitutionality, but only a preliminary step in determining the way federal funds were used: "The question in an as-applied challenge is not whether the entity is of a religious character, but how it spends its grant."

Justice BLACKMUN, joined by Justices Brennan, Marshall and Stevens, dissented, insisting the law was unconstitutional under the "effect" prong of Lemon. He would have found the law invalid on its face, because the involvement of religious organizations in teaching and counseling create an unacceptable risk that the message would in fact be religious. Although the Court had "recognized that the Constitution does not prohibit the government from supporting secular social-welfare services solely because they are provided by a religiously affiliated organization," he argued, there is "a very real and important difference between running a soup kitchen or a hospital, and counseling pregnant teenagers on how to make the difficult decisions facing them. The risk of advancing religion at public expense, and of creating an appearance that the government is endorsing the medium and the message, is much greater when the religious organization is directly engaged in pedagogy, with the express intent of shaping belief and changing behavior, than when it is neutrally dispensing medication, food, or shelter."

In **Zobrest v. Catalina Foothills School District**, 509 U.S. 1 (1993), the Court, relying on Mueller and Witters, held that the provision of a publicly funded sign language interpreter to a deaf student in a parochial school classroom did not violate the Establishment Clause. The Individuals with Disabilities Education Act and its state equivalent provided for funding such interpreters for hearing-impaired students generally. Writing for the Court, Chief Justice REHNQUIST held that the Establishment Clause did not mandate exclusion from such funding of an otherwise eligible student attending parochial school: "[W]e have consistently held that government programs that neutrally provide benefits to a broad class of citizens defined without reference to religion are not readily subject to an Establishment Clause challenge just because sectarian institutions may also receive an attenuated financial benefit." He emphasized that the Act did not distinguish between public and parochial schools, and found that it thus "creates no financial incentive for parents to choose a sectarian school." He rejected the argument that the Establishment Clause absolutely barred the presence of a public employee on parochial school premises. And he found no danger that the sign language interpreter would personally assist in religious instruction: "Nothing in this record suggests that a sign language interpreter would do more than accurately interpret whatever material is presented to the class as a whole." He concluded: "[Zobrest's] parents have chosen of their own free will to place him in a pervasively sectarian environment. The sign language interpreter they have requested will neither add to nor subtract from that environment, and hence the provision of such assistance is not barred by the Establishment Clause."

Justice BLACKMUN, joined by Justice Souter, dissented, objecting that "[u]ntil now, the Court never has authorized a public employee to participate directly in religious indoctrination. Yet that is the consequence of today's decision." Justice O'Connor, joined by Justice Stevens, also dissented, on statutory grounds.

Recall that in **Rosenberger v. Rector and Visitors of The Univ. of Virginia**, 515 U.S. 819 (1995, p. 410), the Court held that the Free Speech Clause required inclusion of an otherwise eligible student-edited evangelical Christian magazine called "Wide Awake" in a public university program that authorized payments from a mandatory Student Activities Fund to outside contractors for the printing costs of a variety of student-authored publications. The Court rejected the contention that such inclusion would violate the Establishment Clause. Justice KENNEDY, writing for the Court, found the Establishment Clause issue similar to that in Widmar: "The governmental program here is neutral toward religion. There is no suggestion that the University created it to advance religion or adopted some ingenious device with the purpose of aiding a religious cause. The object of the [funding program] is to open a forum for speech and to support various student enterprises, including the publication of newspapers, in recognition of the diversity and creativity of student life. [The] neutrality of the program distinguishes the student fees from a tax levied for the direct support of a church or group of churches.

"Government neutrality is apparent [also because the] University has taken pains to disassociate itself from the private speech involved in this case. [There] is no real likelihood that the speech in question is being either endorsed or coerced by the State. [We] do not confront a case where, even under a neutral program that includes nonsectarian recipients, the government is making direct money payments to an institution or group that is engaged in religious activity. [It is undisputed] that no public funds flow directly to [the Christian magazine's] coffers.

"It does not violate the Establishment Clause for a public university to grant access to its facilities on a religion-neutral basis to a wide spectrum of student groups, including groups which use meeting rooms for sectarian activities, accompanied by some devotional exercises. See [Widmar, Lamb's Chapel.] [A] public university may maintain its own computer facility and give student groups access to that facility, including the use of the printers, on a religion neutral, say first-come-first-served, basis. [There] is no difference in logic or principle, and no difference of constitutional significance, between a school using its funds to operate a facility to which students have access, and a school paying a third-party contractor to operate the facility on its behalf. [Any] benefit to religion is incidental to the government's provision of secular services for secular purposes on a religion-neutral basis. [By] paying outside printers, the University in fact attains a further degree of separation from the student publication, for it avoids the duties of supervision, escapes the costs of upkeep, repair, and replacement attributable to student use, and has a clear record of costs. [Moreover,] the student publication is not a religious institution. [It] is instead a publication involved in a pure forum for the expression of ideas."

Justice O'CONNOR wrote a concurrence, noting that "particular features of the University's program—such as the explicit disclaimer, the disbursement of funds directly to third-party vendors, the vigorous nature of the forum at issue, and the possibility for objecting students to opt out— convince me that providing such assistance in this case would not carry the danger of impermissible use of public funds to endorse Wide Awake's religious message." Justice THOMAS likewise concurred, emphasizing the historical pedigree of tax exemptions for religious institutions and arguing that the direct subsidy here posed no greater Establishment Clause problem: "The historical evidence of government support for religious entities through property tax exemptions is [overwhelming]. [Walz.] [This] tradition puts to rest the notion that the Establishment Clause bars monetary aid to religious groups even when the aid is equally available to other groups. A tax exemption in many cases is economically and functionally indistinguishable from a direct monetary subsidy. In one instance, the government relieves religious entities (along with others) of a generally applicable tax; in the other, it relieves religious entities (along with others) of some or all of the burden of that tax by returning it in the form of a cash subsidy. Whether the benefit is provided at the front or back end of the taxation process, the financial aid to religious groups is undeniable. The analysis under the Establishment Clause must also be the same."

Justice SOUTER, joined by Justices Stevens, Ginsburg and Breyer, dissented, arguing that funding Wide Awake would violate the Establishment Clause because it would employ "public funds for the direct subsidization of preaching the word. [If] the Clause was meant to accomplish nothing else, it was meant to bar this use of public money." He criticized the majority for "blanch[ing] the patently and frankly evangelistic character of the magazine." He also found it no defense that the "University's funding scheme is 'neutral,' in the formal sense that it makes funds available on an evenhanded basis to secular and sectarian applicants alike": "Evenhandedness as one element of a permissibly attenuated benefit is, of course, a far cry from evenhandedness as a sufficient condition of constitutionality for direct financial support of religious proselytization, and our cases have unsurprisingly repudiated any such attempt to cut the Establishment Clause down to a mere prohibition against unequal direct aid." He distinguished other cases permitting the inclusion of religious beneficiaries in funding programs: "Witters, Mueller, and Zobrest [explicitly] distinguished the indirect aid in issue from contrasting examples in the line of cases striking down direct aid, and each thereby expressly preserved the core constitutional principle that direct aid to religion is impermissible." He found unconvincing the argument that payment to the third-party printer broke the chain of direct aid: "If this indeed were a critical distinction, the Constitution would permit a State to pay all the bills of any religious institution." He also found unconvincing the argument that the mandatory student fee somehow differed for Establishment Clause purposes from a general tax: "[O]ur cases on direct government aid have frequently spoken in terms in no way limited to tax revenues." He concluded: "The Court is ordering an instrumentality of the State to support religious evangelism with direct funding. This is a flat violation of the Establishment Clause."

The strong trend of deference toward inclusion of religious beneficiaries in public programs in the above cases raised some doubt about two 1985 decisions that had invalidated public educational programs carried out at parochial schools. In **Grand Rapids School District v. Ball**, 473 U.S. 373 (1985), and **Aguilar v. Felton**, 473 U.S. 402 (1985), the Court struck down programs in which public school teachers, paid from public funds, offered supplementary classes such as remedial math and reading in parochial school classrooms, and conducted community education in parochial school buildings.

In **Agostini v. Felton**, 521 U.S. 203 (1997), a case involving the use at private religious schools of public remedial education funds under Title I of the Elementary and Secondary Education Act of 1965, the Court overruled those decisions, declaring Aguilar "no longer good law." Justice O'CONNOR wrote for the 5–4 majority of the Court. She began by noting that, after Aguilar had invalidated the use of public funds to teach publicly funded remedial courses inside parochial school classrooms, the New York school board had resorted to teaching parochial school students "at public school sites, at leased sites, and in mobile instructional units (essentially vans converted into classrooms) parked near the sectarian school," all at significant additional cost. She now rejected Aguilar's and Ball's assumptions: "[First,] we have abandoned the presumption [that] the placement of public employees on parochial school grounds inevitably results in the impermissible effect of state-sponsored indoctrination or constitutes a symbolic union between government and religion. [Zobrest] expressly rejected the notion—relied on in Ball and Aguilar—that, solely because of her presence on private school property, a public employee will be presumed to inculcate religion in the students. Zobrest also implicitly repudiated [the] assumption [that] the presence of a public employee on private school property creates an impermissible 'symbolic link' between government and religion. [Second,] we have departed from the rule relied on in Ball that all government aid that directly aids the educational function of religious schools is invalid. In Witters, we held that the Establishment Clause did not bar a State from issuing a vocational tuition grant to a blind person who wished to use the grant to attend a Christian college and become a pastor, missionary, or youth director. [The] same logic applied in Zobrest. [We] do not see any perceptible (let alone dispositive) difference in the degree of symbolic union between a student receiving remedial instruction in a classroom on his sectarian school's campus and one receiving instruction in a van parked just at the school's curbside. Nor under current law can we conclude that a program placing full-time public employees on parochial campuses to provide Title I instruction would impermissibly finance religious indoctrination. In all relevant respects, the provision of instructional services under Title I is indistinguishable from the provision of sign-language interpreters [in Zobrest]. Both programs make aid available only to eligible recipients. That aid is provided to students at whatever school they choose to attend. [And,] as in Zobrest, Title I services are by law supplemental to the regular curricula. [They] do not, therefore, 'relieve sectarian schools of costs they otherwise would have borne in educating their students.'

"[Where] aid is allocated on the basis of neutral, secular criteria that neither favor nor disfavor religion, and is made available to both religious and secular beneficiaries on a nondiscriminatory basis, [the] aid is less likely to have the effect of advancing religion. [We] therefore hold that a federally funded program providing supplemental, remedial instruction to disadvantaged children on a neutral basis is not invalid under the Establishment Clause when such instruction is given on the premises of sectarian schools."

Justice SOUTER dissented, joined by Justices Stevens, Ginsburg and, in part, Breyer: "[The] flat ban on subsidization antedates the Bill of Rights and has been an unwavering rule in Establishment Clause cases. [The] rule expresses the hard lesson learned over and over again in the American past and in the experiences of the countries from which we have come, that religions supported by governments are compromised just as surely as the religious freedom of dissenters is burdened when the government supports religion. [If] a State may constitutionally enter the schools to teach [remedial education,] it must in constitutional principle be free to assume, or assume payment for, the entire cost of instruction provided in any ostensibly secular subject in any religious school. [Zobrest] is no [sanction] for overruling Aguilar or any portion of Ball. In Zobrest [the] signer could [be] seen as more like a hearing aid than a teacher, and the signing could not be understood as an opportunity to inject religious content in what was supposed to be secular instruction. [In] Zobrest and Witters, it was fair to say that individual students were themselves applicants for individual benefits. [But] under Title I, a local educational agency [may] receive federal funding by proposing programs approved to serve individual students who meet the criteria of need, which it then uses to provide such programs at the religious schools; students eligible for such programs may not apply directly for Title I funds." Justice Ginsburg filed a separate dissent.

In its first major test of the scope of Agostini, **Mitchell v. Helms**, 530 U.S. 793 (2000), the Court upheld against establishment challenge a program that provided publicly funded computers and other teaching aids to public and private elementary and secondary schools, including parochial schools. Justice THOMAS, announcing the judgment of the Court and writing for himself, Chief Justice Rehnquist and Justices Scalia and Kennedy, held that the only issue in the case was whether the program had an impermissibly religious effect, and outlined a comprehensive approach to how neutrality should be assessed in challenges to parochial aid: "As a way of assuring neutrality, we have repeatedly considered whether any governmental aid that goes to a religious institution does so 'only as a result of the genuinely independent and private choices of individuals.' Agostini. [For] if numerous private choices, rather than the single choice of a government, determine the distribution of aid pursuant to neutral eligibility criteria, then a government cannot, or at least cannot easily, grant special favors that might lead to a religious establishment." Justice O'CONNOR, joined by Justice Breyer, filed a separate concurrence only in the judgment, objecting that "the plurality's treatment of neutrality comes close to assigning that factor singular importance in the future adjudication of Establishment Clause challenges to government school-aid programs." Justice SOUTER, joined by Justices Stevens and Ginsburg, dissented: "It is beyond question that the plurality's notion of evenhandedness [as] a practical guarantee of the validity of aid to sectarian schools would be the end of the principle of no aid to the schools' religious mission. [To] the plurality there is nothing wrong with aiding a school's religious mission; the only question is whether religious teaching obtains its tax support under a formally evenhanded criterion of distribution. [In] rejecting the principle of no aid to a school's religious mission the plurality is attacking the most fundamental assumption underlying the Establishment Clause, that government can in fact operate with neutrality in its relation to religion."

––––––––––

SCHOOL VOUCHER SCHEMES AND PAROCHIAL SCHOOLS

1. *The debate over voucher programs.* Mitchell gave rise to speculation about the Court's likely reaction to head-on constitutional challenges to voucher schemes that permitted the use of public monies by parents to send their children to religious schools. The Supreme Court found such schemes did not violate the Establishment Clause in **Zelman v. Simmons-Harris**, 536 U.S. 639 (2002). Cleveland, Ohio, had adopted a voucher program where 96% of participants in the program used the funds to enroll in religious schools. THE CHIEF JUSTICE wrote for a 5–4 court: "[The] Establishment Clause prevents a State from enacting laws that have the 'purpose' or 'effect' of advancing or inhibiting religion. There is no dispute that the program challenged here was enacted for the valid secular purpose of providing educational assistance to poor children in a demonstrably failing public school system. [T]he question presented is whether the Ohio program nonetheless has the forbidden 'effect' of advancing or inhibiting religion.

"To answer that question, our decisions have drawn a consistent distinction between government programs that provide aid directly to religious schools [Mitchell, Agostini, Rosenberger], and programs of true private choice, in which government aid reaches religious schools only as a result of the genuine and independent choices of private individuals. While our jurisprudence with respect to the constitutionality of direct aid programs has 'changed significantly' over the past two decades, our jurisprudence with respect to true private choice programs has remained consistent and unbroken. Three times [Mueller, Witters, Zobrest] we have confronted Establishment Clause challenges to neutral government programs that provide aid directly to a broad class of individuals, who, in turn, direct the aid to religious schools or institutions of their own choosing. Three times we have rejected such challenges.

"[These cases] thus make clear that where a government aid program is neutral with respect to religion, and provides assistance directly to a broad class of citizens who, in turn, direct government aid to religious schools wholly as a result of their own genuine and independent private choice, the program is not readily subject to challenge under the Establishment Clause. A program that shares these features permits government aid to reach religious institutions only by way of the deliberate choices of numerous individual recipients. The incidental advancement of a religious mission, or the perceived endorsement of a religious message, is reasonably attributable to the individual recipient, not to the government, whose role ends with the disbursement of benefits.

"[We] believe that the program challenged here is a program of true private choice, consistent with Mueller, Witters, and Zobrest, and thus constitutional. As was true in those cases, the Ohio program is neutral in all respects toward religion. It is part of a general and multifaceted undertaking by the State of Ohio to provide educational opportunities to the children of a failed school district. It confers educational assistance directly to a broad class of individuals defined without reference to religion, i.e., any parent of a school-age child who resides in the Cleveland City School District. The program permits the participation of *all* schools within the district, religious or nonreligious. Adjacent public schools also may participate and have a financial incentive to do so. Program benefits are available to participating families on neutral terms, with no reference to religion.

"In sum, the Ohio program is entirely neutral with respect to religion. It provides benefits directly to a wide spectrum of individuals, defined only by financial need and residence in a particular school district. It permits such individuals to exercise genuine choice among options public and private, secular and religious. The program is therefore a program of true private choice. In keeping with an unbroken line of decisions rejecting challenges to similar programs, we hold that the program does not offend the Establishment Clause."

JUSTICE THOMAS concurred to highlight the plight of minority children in inner city schools and the importance of school choice as an effort to realize the promise of Brown v. Board of Education. He stated it would be a "tragic irony" to "convert[ ] the Fourteenth Amendment's guarantee of individual liberty into a prohibition on the exercise of individual choice."

JUSTICE SOUTER, joined by Justices Stevens, Ginsburg, and Breyer, dissented: "The record indicates that [Cleveland's public] schools are failing to serve their objective, and the vouchers in issue here are said to be needed to provide adequate alternatives to them. If there were an excuse for giving short shrift to the Establishment Clause, it would probably apply here. But there is no excuse. Constitutional limitations are placed on government to preserve constitutional values in hard cases, like these.

"[The] applicability of the Establishment Clause to public funding of benefits to religious schools was settled in Everson. 'No tax in any amount, large or small, can be levied to support any religious activities or institutions, whatever they may be called, or whatever form they may adopt to teach or practice religion.' The Court has never in so many words repudiated this statement, let alone, in so many words, overruled Everson. Today, however, the majority holds that the Establishment Clause is not offended by Ohio's Pilot Project Scholarship Program, under which students may be eligible to receive as much as $2,250 in the form of tuition vouchers transferable to religious schools. In the city of Cleveland the overwhelming proportion of large appropriations for voucher money must be spent on religious schools if it is to be spent at all, and will be spent in amounts that cover almost all of tuition. The money will thus pay for eligible students' instruction not only in secular subjects but in religion as well, in schools that can fairly be characterized as founded to teach religious doctrine and to imbue teaching in all subjects with a religious dimension. Public tax money will pay at a systemic level for teaching the covenant with Israel and Mosaic law in Jewish schools, the primacy of the Apostle Peter and the Papacy in Catholic schools, the truth of reformed Christianity in Protestant schools, and the revelation to the Prophet in Muslim schools, to speak only of major religious groupings in the Republic. Can a Court consistently leave Everson on the books and approve the Ohio vouchers? The answer is that it cannot. It is only by ignoring Everson that the majority can claim to rest on traditional law in its invocation of neutral aid provisions and private choice to sanction the Ohio law.

"[There is] no way to interpret the 96.6% of current voucher money going to religious schools as reflecting a free and genuine choice by the families that apply for vouchers. The 96.6% reflects, instead, the fact that too few nonreligious school desks are available and few but religious schools can afford to accept more than a handful of voucher students. And contrary to the majority's assertion, public schools in adjacent districts hardly have a financial incentive to participate in the Ohio voucher program, and none has. For the overwhelming number of children in the voucher scheme, the only alternative to the public schools is religious. And it is entirely irrelevant that the State did not deliberately design the network of private schools for the sake of channeling money into religious institutions. The criterion is one of genuinely free choice on the part of the private individuals who choose, and a Hobson's choice is not a choice, whatever the reason for being Hobsonian.

"[For] perspective on this foot-in-the-door of religious regulation, it is well to remember that the money has barely begun to flow. Prior examples of aid, whether grants through individuals or in-kind assistance, were never significant enough to alter the basic fiscal structure of religious schools; state aid was welcome, but not indispensable. But given the figures already involved here, there is no question that religious schools in Ohio are on the way to becoming bigger businesses with budgets enhanced to fit their new stream of tax-raised income. [The] intensity of the expectable friction can be gauged by realizing that the scramble for money will energize not only contending sectarians, but taxpayers who take their liberty of conscience seriously. Religious teaching at taxpayer expense simply cannot be cordoned from taxpayer politics, and every major religion currently espouses social positions that provoke intense opposition. Not all taxpaying Protestant citizens, for example, will be content to underwrite the teaching of the Roman Catholic Church condemning the death penalty. Nor will all of America's Muslims acquiesce in paying for the endorsement of the religious Zionism taught in many religious Jewish schools. Nor will every secular taxpayer be content to support Muslim views on differential treatment of the sexes, or, for that matter, to fund the espousal of a wife's obligation of obedience to her husband, presumably taught in any schools adopting the articles of faith of the Southern Baptist Convention. Views like these, and innumerable others, have been safe in the sectarian pulpits and classrooms of this Nation not only because the Free Exercise Clause protects them directly, but because the ban on supporting religious establishment has protected free exercise, by keeping it relatively private. With the arrival of vouchers in religious schools, that privacy will go, and along with it will go confidence that religious disagreement will stay moderate."

JUSTICE BREYER, joined by Justice Stevens and Justice Souter, also dissented: "I write separately [to] emphasize the risk that publicly financed voucher programs pose in terms of religiously based social conflict. I do so because I believe that the Establishment Clause concern for protecting the Nation's social fabric from religious conflict poses an overriding obstacle to the implementation of this well-intentioned school voucher program.

"[Cleveland's] program insists that the religious school accept students of all religions. Does that criterion treat fairly groups whose religion forbids them to do so? The program also insists that no participating school 'advocate or foster unlawful behavior or teach hatred of any person or group on the basis of race, ethnicity, national origin, or religion.' And it requires the State to 'revoke the registration of any school if, after a hearing, the superintendent determines that the school is in violation" of the program's rules.) [I]t is difficult to imagine a more divisive activity than the appointment of state officials as referees to determine whether a particular religious doctrine 'teaches hatred or advocates lawlessness.'

"How are state officials to adjudicate claims that one religion or another is advocating, for example, civil disobedience in response to unjust laws, the use of illegal drugs in a religious ceremony, or resort to force to call attention to what it views as an immoral social practice? What kind of public hearing will there be in response to claims that one religion or another is continuing to teach a view of history that casts members of other religions in the worst possible light? How will the public react to government funding for schools that take controversial religious positions on topics that are of current popular interest—say, the conflict in the Middle East or the war on terrorism? Yet any major funding program for primary religious education will require criteria. And the selection of those criteria, as well as their application, inevitably pose problems that are divisive."

2. *The scope of permissible conditions on voucher programs.* The Cleveland plan permitted public funds to be transferred to religious schools only if they agreed not to discriminate on the basis of race, religion or ethnic background, or to "advocate or foster unlawful behavior or teach hatred of any person or group on the basis of race, ethnicity, national origin, or religion." Are such prerequisites for public funding required by the Establishment Clause? The Equal Protection Clause? Or are they forbidden by the Free Exercise or Free Speech Clauses as unconstitutional conditions on the distribution of public funds?

How far may public values be required to govern the life of religious entities? May the energy of faith-based services be harnessed to the public values of the state without depleting the normative pluralism that religious diversity provides as a check on government in the first place? Are public strings on privatized services a desirable vehicle for liberalizing the private religious realm? Will government's introduction of public values into the religious sphere, in the form of inducements rather than coercion, have a beneficial civilizing and liberalizing influence on religion, helping to curb religious rivalries that tear societies apart and to guide the potentially unruly private religious sector toward ever greater peace? For suggestions along these lines, see Macedo, "Constituting Civil Society: School Vouchers, Religious Nonprofit Organizations, and Liberal Public Values," 75 Chi.-Kent L. Rev. 417 (2000); Minow, "Public and Private Partnerships: Accounting for the New Religion," 116 Harv. L. Rev. 1229, 1261 (2003). Or are such conditions on religious recipients of public funds a pernicious and colonizing force, likely to homogenize the rich diversity of religious viewpoints and ways of life, leveling all faiths to a bland common denominator and bleeding normative pluralism of its color and vibrancy? See Sullivan, "The New Religion and the Constitution," 116 Harv. L. Rev. 1397 (2003).

Do founding principles of religious liberty offer any guidance on these questions? Consider the view that perhaps "we—and Madison—cannot have it both ways: a multiplicity of politically mobilized but nevertheless distinctive and uncorrupted religious sects that serve as a check on government, combined with a politics of civility, moderation, mutual respect, equal civic status, and significant common ground. [Madison's] philosophy of church-state relations cannot decide for us the constitutionality of school vouchers. But his Memorial and Remonstrance at least should convince us that we cannot resolve this momentous issue in peremptory fashion by giving controlling weight to the features of inclusiveness and parental choice (to uphold a voucher scheme) or the direct subsidization of purely sectarian teaching (to strike it down)." Blasi, Essay, "School Vouchers and Religious Liberty: Seven Questions from Madison's Memorial and Remonstrance," 87 Cornell L. Rev. 783 (2002).

3. *Continuing barriers to voucher programs.* Many predicted a rapid proliferation of voucher programs in the immediate wake of Zelman, but this growth failed to materialize. For one explanation of voucher programs' limited political success immediately after Zelman, see James Forman, Jr., The Rise and Fall of School Vouchers: A Story of Religion, Race, and Politics, 54 U.C.L.A. L. Rev. 547 (2007) (citing, among other things, the rise of the "accountability movement" in education and the No Child Left Behind Act).

After Republicans took control of statehouses across the country in the 2010 midterm elections, voucher programs gained renewed popularity, with statewide programs enacted in Louisiana, Indiana, Nevada and Wisconsin. But the constitutions of the latter three states contain "Baby Blaine" amendments (see p. 710) which prohibit the states from giving financial aid to any sectarian institution. The Florida Supreme Court struck down the nation's first state-wide voucher program in Bush v. Holmes, 919 So. 2d 392 (2006), under the state's Blaine Amendment, and the Colorado Supreme Court issued a similar ruling in 2015. On the other hand, the Wisconsin and Indiana Supreme Courts have heard and rejected Blaine Amendment challenges to the states' voucher programs.

———

RELIGION IN PUBLIC SCHOOLS

Recall that in McCollum v. Board of Education (p. 716), the Court struck down a school board's practice of permitting students to attend sectarian classes held in public schools during school hours by parochial instructors. The Court stated that the practice not only constituted aid to religion but also was problematic for its use of public school buildings. In Zorach v.

Clauson (p. 716), however, the Court upheld a New York City "released time" program that permitted its public schools to release students to go to religious institutions for religious instruction. The Court distinguished Zorach from McCollum on the ground that, in McCollum, "the classrooms were used for religious instruction and the force of the public school was used to promote that instruction." As the materials that follow indicate, the Court has found that additional considerations must be taken into account when addressing Establishment Clause challenges in the context of public schools.

PRAYER IN PUBLIC SCHOOLS

1.   *Teacher-led prayers, Bible readings and moments of silence.* The Court has consistently struck down school prayer initiated by school officials as a violation of the Establishment Clause. The Court's first encounter with the problem came in **Engel v. Vitale**, 370 U.S. 421 (1962). There, the New York Board of Regents had prepared a "nondenominational" prayer for use in the public schools, which read: "Almighty God, we acknowledge our dependence upon Thee, and we beg Thy blessings upon us, our parents, our teachers and our Country." A local school board directed that the prayer be recited daily by each class. That practice was challenged by parents of a number of students who claimed that it was "contrary to the beliefs, religions, or religious practices of both themselves and their children." The highest state court upheld the practice, so long as the schools did not compel any student to join in the prayer over a parent's objection. Justice BLACK's majority opinion held the practice "wholly inconsistent with the Establishment Clause." The practice was clearly "a religious activity" and the Establishment Clause "must at least mean that [it] is no part of the business of government to compose official prayers for any group of the American people to recite as a part of a religious program carried on by government."

Justice Black added: "Neither the fact that the prayer may be denominationally neutral, nor the fact that its observance on the part of the students is voluntary, can serve to free it from the limitations of the Establishment Clause, as it might from the Free Exercise [Clause]. Although these two clauses may in certain instances overlap, they forbid two quite different kinds of governmental encroachment upon religious freedom. The Establishment Clause, unlike the Free Exercise Clause, does not depend upon any showing of direct governmental compulsion and is violated by the enactment of laws which establish an official religion whether those laws operate directly to coerce nonobserving individuals or not. This is not to say, of course, that laws officially prescribing a particular form of religious worship do not involve coercion of such individuals. When the power, prestige and financial support of government is placed behind a particular religious belief, the indirect coercive pressure upon religious minorities to conform to the prevailing officially approved religion is plain. But the purposes underlying the Establishment Clause go much further than that. [Its] most immediate purpose rested on the belief that a union of government and religion tends to destroy government and to degrade religion. [Another] purpose [rested upon] an awareness of the historical fact that governmentally established religions and religious persecutions go hand in hand."

Justice STEWART's dissent relied on Zorach in concluding that New York's practice merely recognized "the deeply entrenched and highly cherished spiritual traditions of our Nation"—and that the references to religion and to God in such practices as congressional prayers and official oaths were similarly justified. Justice Douglas concurred separately; Justices Frankfurter and White did not participate.

One year after Engel, the Court extended the principles of that case beyond state-composed prayers. **Abington School District v. Schempp**, 374 U.S. 203 (1963), held that the Establishment Clause prohibits state laws and practices "requiring the selection and reading at the opening of the school day of verses from the Holy Bible and the recitation of the Lord's Prayer by the students in unison." The Pennsylvania law in Schempp provided: "At least ten verses from the Holy Bible shall be read, without comment, at the opening of each public school on each school day. Any child shall be excused from such Bible reading, or attending such Bible reading, upon the written request of his parent or guardian." The Schempp family, members of the Unitarian Church, successfully challenged the law.

Justice CLARK's opinion for the Court stated: "The wholesome 'neutrality' of which this Court's cases speak [stems] from a recognition of the teachings of history that powerful sects or groups might bring about a fusion of governmental and religious functions or a concert or dependency of one upon the other to the end that official support of the State or Federal Government would be placed behind the tenets of one or of all orthodoxies. This the Establishment Clause prohibits. [The] test may be stated as follows: what are the purpose and the primary effect of the enactment? If either is the advancement or inhibition of religion then the enactment exceeds the scope of legislative power as circumscribed by the Constitution." Applying those principles (which foreshadowed the Lemon test), Justice Clark noted that "it is no defense to urge that the religious practices here may be relatively minor encroachments on the First Amendment. The breach of neutrality that is today a trickling stream may all too soon become a raging torrent." He pointed out that the decision did not bar the "study of the Bible or of religion, when presented objectively as part of a secular program of education." But that was not the case here: these were "religious exercises, required by the State in violation of the command of the First Amendment that the Government maintain strict neutrality, neither aiding nor opposing religion." Justices Douglas, Goldberg and Brennan filed separate concurrences.

Justice STEWART, the sole dissenter, insisted that "religion and government must necessarily interact in countless ways" and that "there are areas in which a doctrinaire reading of the Establishment Clause leads to irreconcilable conflict with the Free Exercise Clause." He elaborated: "The dangers both to government and to religion inherent in official support of instruction in the tenets of various religious sects [see McCollum] are absent in the present cases, which involve only a reading from the Bible unaccompanied by comments which might otherwise constitute instruction. [In] the absence of coercion upon those who do not wish to [participate], such provisions cannot [be] held to represent the type of support of religion barred by the [Establishment Clause]. [W]hether [the exercises] are constitutionally invalid [turns] on the question of coercion. [Certain] types of exercises would present situations in which no possibility of coercion on the part of secular officials could be claimed to exist. [But] a law which provided for religious exercises during the school day and which contained no excusal provision would obviously be unconstitutionally coercive upon those who did not wish to participate. And even under a law containing an excusal provision, if the exercises were held during the school day, and no equally desirable alternative were provided by the school authorities, the likelihood that children might be under at least some psychological compulsion to participate would be great. In a case such as the latter, however, I think we would err if we *assumed* such coercion in the absence of any evidence. Viewed in this light, it seems to be clear that the [record here is] wholly inadequate to support an informed or responsible decision."

The issue of school prayer returned to the Court in **Wallace v. Jaffree**, 472 U.S. 38 (1985). The decision struck down an Alabama law authorizing schools to set aside one minute at the start of each day "for meditation or voluntary prayer." The statute was an amendment of an earlier law which had authorized a one-minute period of silence in all public schools merely "for meditation." Justice STEVENS's opinion for the Court stated that "the individual freedom of conscience protected by the First Amendment embraces the right to select any religious faith or none at all." He found that the law "was not motivated by any clearly secular purpose," thus violating the Lemon test. He noted that the state legislator sponsoring the amendment had said that it was an "effort to return voluntary prayer" to the public schools. He elaborated: "The legislative intent to return prayer to the public schools is, of course, quite different from merely protecting every student's right to engage in voluntary prayer during an appropriate moment of silence during the school day." The earlier law "already protected that right, containing nothing that prevented any student from engaging in voluntary prayer during a silent minute of meditation." Hence, the amendment to that law must have been enacted "to convey a message of State endorsement and promotion of prayer. [The] addition of 'or voluntary prayer' indicates that the State intended to characterize prayer as a favored practice. Such an endorsement is not consistent with the established principle that the Government must pursue a course of complete neutrality toward religion."

Justice O'CONNOR concurred in the result. She did not view all moment-of-silence requirements as unconstitutional. She suggested that the crucial question was whether the state had endorsed religion. "By mandating a moment of silence, the State does not necessarily endorse any activity that might occur during the period," nor "encourage[ ] prayer over other specified alternatives." But in this case, "the purpose and likely effect" of the Alabama amendment was "to endorse and sponsor voluntary prayer in the public schools." Here the state had "conveyed or attempted to convey the message that children should use the moment of silence for prayer." Chief Justice Burger and Justices White and Rehnquist dissented.

2. ***School prayer and "coercion."*** Do the school prayer cases, like the released-time cases (McCollum and Zorach), turn on the principle that coercion into a profession of belief violates the Establishment Clause, and the assumption that the public school setting is inherently coercive? What makes the school setting coercive? The fact that attendance is compulsory? The psychological immaturity of children, and their lack of fully developed faculties of resistance and consent? See Stone, "In Opposition to the School Prayer Amendment," 50 U. Chi. L. Rev. 823 (1983) (noting that children are especially vulnerable to peer pressure).

Why should coercion be a prerequisite to a finding of establishment? The Free Exercise Clause already prohibits coercion into faith or out of it. As Justice Clark noted in Schempp, "the Free Exercise Clause [recognizes] the right of every person to freely choose his own [religious] course, free of any compulsion from the state." Would limiting establishment to cases of "coercion" make the Establishment Clause mere surplusage, redundant of the Free Exercise Clause? What else beyond coercion might the Establishment Clause prohibit? One possibility is religious incentives or inducements that fall short of coercion. See, e.g., Choper, "Religion in the Schools," 47 Minn. L. Rev. 329 (1963) (arguing that the Establishment Clause is violated in public schools when the state engages in "solely religious activity that is likely to result in (1) compromising the student's religious or conscientious beliefs or (2) influencing the student's freedom of religious or conscientious choice"). Why should it not be enough that the school practices are "solely religious"? Why should it also be necessary to demonstrate impact on student beliefs or choice?

Another possibility is suggested by Justice O'Connor's Jaffree concurrence: she argues that the state may not "endorse" religion. Does endorsement cover a broader range of cases than coercion? Why should government have to refrain from religious speech or symbolism if it is not coercing or influencing a citizen to change his or her faith? Justice O'Connor suggested in Jaffree, citing her concurrence in Lynch v. Donnelly (1984; p. 764), that endorsement sends a message of symbolic civic excommunication to nonmembers of the endorsed faith. Why should such a message constitute establishment in the absence of a showing that religious beliefs will be altered as a result? Consider which principle, coercion or endorsement, animates the various opinions in the following case, which invalidated an official prayer at a middle school graduation ceremony.

Lee v. Weisman

505 U.S. 577, 112 S. Ct. 2649, 120 L. Ed. 2d 467 (1992).

[The case arose when the principal of a Providence public middle school invited a rabbi to deliver prayers at the school's graduation ceremony, pursuant to the school district's longstanding custom of inviting members of the clergy for this purpose. The principal advised the rabbi that his prayers should be nonsectarian. The rabbi's invocation read:

"God of the Free, Hope of the Brave: For the legacy of America where diversity is celebrated and the rights of minorities are protected, we thank You. May these young men and women grow up to enrich it. For the liberty of America, we thank You. May these new graduates grow up to guard it. For the political process of America in which all its citizens may participate, for its court system where all may seek justice we thank You. May those we honor this morning always turn to it in trust. For the destiny of America we thank You. May the graduates of Nathan Bishop Middle School so live that they might help to share it. May our aspirations for our country and for these young people, who are our hope for the future, be richly fulfilled. AMEN."

The rabbi's benediction read:

> "O God, we are grateful to You for having endowed us with the capacity for learning which we have celebrated on this joyous commencement. Happy families give thanks for seeing their children achieve an important milestone. Send Your blessings upon the teachers and administrators who helped prepare them. The graduates now need strength and guidance for the future, help them to understand that we are not complete with academic knowledge alone. We must each strive to fulfill what You require of us all: To do justly, to love mercy, to walk humbly. We give thanks to You, Lord, for keeping us alive, sustaining us and allowing us to reach this special, happy occasion. AMEN."

Deborah Weisman, a student at the school, raised an Establishment Clause challenge to the prayer and benediction:]

■ JUSTICE KENNEDY delivered the opinion of the Court.

These dominant facts mark and control the confines of our decision: State officials direct the performance of a formal religious exercise at promotional and graduation ceremonies for secondary schools. Even for those students who object to the religious exercise, their attendance and participation in the state-sponsored religious activity are in a fair and real sense obligatory, though the school district does not require attendance as a condition for receipt of the diploma. [The] controlling precedents as they relate to prayer and religious exercise in primary and secondary public schools compel the holding here that the policy of the city of Providence is an unconstitutional one. [It] is beyond dispute that, at a minimum, the Constitution guarantees that government may not coerce anyone to support or participate in religion or its exercise. [The] State's involvement in the school prayers challenged today violates these central principles.

[We] are asked to recognize the existence of a practice of nonsectarian prayer, prayer which is more acceptable than one which, for example, makes explicit references to the God of Israel, or to Jesus Christ, or to a patron saint. [But] though the First Amendment does not allow the government to stifle prayers which aspire to [a civic religion], neither does it permit the government to undertake that task for itself. The First Amendment's Religion Clauses mean that religious beliefs and religious expression are too precious to be either proscribed or prescribed by the State. The design of the Constitution is that preservation and transmission of religious beliefs and worship is a responsibility and a choice committed to the private sphere, which itself is promised freedom to pursue that mission. [The] suggestion that government may establish an official or civic religion as a means of avoiding the establishment of a religion with more specific creeds strikes us as a contradiction that cannot be accepted.

The degree of school involvement here made it clear that the graduation prayers bore the imprint of the State and thus put school-age children who objected in an untenable position. [As] we have observed before, there are heightened concerns with protecting freedom of conscience from subtle coercive pressure in the elementary and secondary public schools. Our decisions in [Engel and Schempp] recognize, among other things, that prayer exercises in public schools carry a particular risk of indirect coercion. [What] to most believers may seem nothing more than a reasonable request that the nonbeliever respect their religious practices, in a school context may appear to the nonbeliever or dissenter to be an attempt to employ the machinery of the State to enforce a religious orthodoxy.

The undeniable fact is that the school district's supervision and control of a high school graduation ceremony places public pressure, as well as peer pressure, on attending students to stand as a group or, at least, maintain respectful silence during the Invocation and Benediction. This pressure, though subtle and indirect, can be as real as any overt compulsion. [F]or the dissenter of high school age, who has a reasonable perception that she is being forced by the State to pray in a manner her conscience will not allow, the injury is no less real. There can be no doubt that for many, if not most, of the students at the graduation, the act of standing or remaining silent was an expression of participation in the Rabbi's prayer. That was the very point of the religious exercise. It is of little comfort to a dissenter, then, to be told that for her the act of standing or remaining in silence signifies mere respect, rather than participation. What matters is that, given our social conventions, a reasonable dissenter in this milieu could believe that the group exercise signified her own participation or approval of it.

Finding no violation under these circumstances would place objectors in the dilemma of participating, with all that implies, or protesting. We do not address whether that choice is acceptable if the affected citizens are mature adults, but we think the State may not, consistent with the Establishment Clause, place primary and secondary school children in this position. Research in psychology supports the common assumption that adolescents are often susceptible to pressure from their peers towards conformity, and that the influence is strongest in matters of social convention. To recognize that the choice imposed by the State constitutes an unacceptable constraint only acknowledges that the government may no more use social pressure to enforce orthodoxy than it may use more direct means.

[Although] attendance at graduation [ceremonies] is voluntary, [the argument] that the option of not attending the graduation excuses any inducement or coercion in the ceremony itself [lacks] all persuasion. Law reaches past formalism. And to say a teenage student has a real choice not to attend her high school graduation is formalistic in the extreme. [Everyone] knows that in our culture high school graduation is one of life's most significant occasions. A school rule which excuses attendance is beside the point. Attendance may not be required by official decree, yet it is apparent that a student is not free to absent herself from the graduation exercise in any real sense of the term "voluntary," for absence would require forfeiture of those intangible benefits which have motivated the student through youth and all her high school years.

[The government argues] that the prayers are an essential part of these ceremonies because for many persons an occasion of this significance lacks meaning if there is no recognition, however brief, that human achievements cannot be understood apart from their spiritual essence. [But this] fails to acknowledge that what for many of Deborah's classmates and their parents was a spiritual imperative was for [her] religious conformance compelled by the State. [The] Constitution forbids the State to exact religious conformity from a student as the price of attending her own high school graduation.

[We] do not hold that every state action implicating religion is invalid if one or a few citizens find it offensive. People may take offense at all manner of religious as well as nonreligious messages, but offense alone does not in every case show a violation. We know too that sometimes to endure social isolation or even anger may be the price of conscience or nonconformity. But, by any reading of our cases, the conformity required of the student in this case was too high an exaction to withstand the test of the Establishment Clause. The prayer exercises in this case are especially improper because the State has in every practical sense compelled attendance and participation in an explicit religious exercise at an event of singular importance to every student, one the objecting student had no real alternative to avoid. [No] holding by this Court suggests that a school can persuade or compel a student to participate in a religious exercise. That is being done here, and it is forbidden by the Establishment Clause. [Affirmed.]

[Justice BLACKMUN, joined by Justices STEVENS and O'CONNOR, concurred to argue that, while government pressure to engage in a religious activity "is sufficient" to establish an Establishment Clause violation "it is not enough that the government restrain from compelling religious practices" because "[the] mixing of government and religion can be a threat to free government, even if no one is forced to participate."]

■ JUSTICE SOUTER, with whom JUSTICES STEVENS and O'CONNOR join, concurring.

[Petitioners] rest most of their argument on a theory that [the] Establishment Clause [does] not forbid the state to sponsor affirmations of religious belief that coerce neither support for religion nor participation in religious observance. I appreciate the force of some of the arguments supporting a "coercion" analysis of the Clause. [See] McConnell, "Coercion: The Lost Element of Establishment," 27 Wm. & Mary L. Rev. 933 (1986). But we could not adopt that reading without abandoning our settled law, a course that, in my view, the text of the Clause would not readily permit. Nor does the extratextual evidence of original meaning stand so unequivocally at odds with the textual premise inherent in existing precedent that we should fundamentally reconsider our course.

[T]his Court has declared the invalidity of many noncoercive state laws and practices conveying a message of religious endorsement. [For example,] in Wallace v. Jaffree, we struck down a state law requiring a moment of silence in public classrooms not because the statute coerced students to participate in prayer (for it did not), but because the manner of its enactment "conveyed a message of state approval of prayer activities in the public schools." [Our] precedents [cannot] support the position that a showing of coercion is necessary to a successful Establishment Clause claim.

[While] petitioners insist that the prohibition extends only to the "coercive" features and incidents of establishment, they cannot easily square that claim with the constitutional text. The First Amendment forbids not just laws "respecting an establishment of religion," but also those "prohibiting the free exercise thereof." Yet laws that coerce nonadherents to "support or participate in any religion or its exercise," would virtually by definition violate their right to religious free exercise. Thus, a literal application of the coercion test would render the Establishment Clause a virtual nullity. [Without] compelling evidence to the contrary, we should presume that the Framers meant the Clause to stand for something more than petitioners attribute to it.

Petitioners argue from the political setting in which the Establishment Clause was framed, and from the Framers' own political practices following ratification, that government may constitutionally endorse religion so long as it does not coerce religious conformity. [They contend, for example,] that because the early Presidents included religious messages in their inaugural and Thanksgiving Day addresses, the Framers could not have meant the Establishment Clause to forbid noncoercive state endorsement of religion. [But Jefferson] steadfastly refused to issue Thanksgiving proclamations of any kind, in part because he thought they violated the Religion Clauses. [He] accordingly construed the Establishment Clause to forbid not simply state coercion, but also state endorsement, of religious belief and observance. [During] his first three years in office, James Madison also refused to call for days of thanksgiving and prayer, though later, amid the political turmoil of the War of 1812, he did so on four separate occasions. Upon retirement, in an essay condemning as an unconstitutional "establishment" the use of public money to support congressional and military chaplains, he concluded that "religious proclamations by the Executive recommending thanksgivings & fasts are shoots from the same root with the legislative acts reviewed." [To] be sure, the leaders of the young Republic engaged in some of the practices that separationists like Jefferson and Madison criticized. The First Congress did hire institutional chaplains, and Presidents Washington and Adams unapologetically marked days of "public thanksgiving and prayer." [Yet this proves] at worst that [the framers,] like other politicians, could raise constitutional ideals one day and turn their backs on them the next.

[Regardless,] religious invocations in Thanksgiving Day addresses and the like, rarely noticed, ignored without effort, conveyed over an impersonal medium, and directed at no one in particular, inhabit a pallid zone worlds apart from official prayers delivered to a captive audience of public school students and their families. [When] public school officials, armed with the State's authority, convey an endorsement of religion to their students, they strike near the core of the Establishment Clause. However "ceremonial" their messages may be, they are flatly unconstitutional.

■ JUSTICE SCALIA, with whom CHIEF JUSTICE REHNQUIST and JUSTICES WHITE and THOMAS join, dissenting.

[In] holding that the Establishment Clause prohibits invocations and benedictions at public-school graduation ceremonies, the Court—with nary a mention that it is doing so—lays waste a tradition that is as old as public-school graduation ceremonies themselves, and that is a component of an even more longstanding American tradition of nonsectarian prayer to God at public celebrations generally. As its instrument of destruction, the bulldozer of its social engineering, the Court invents a boundless, and boundlessly manipulable, test of psychological coercion.

[From] our Nation's origin, prayer has been a prominent part of governmental ceremonies and proclamations. The Declaration of Independence, the document marking our birth as a separate people, "appealed to the Supreme Judge of the world for the rectitude of our intentions" and avowed "a firm reliance on the protection of divine Providence." In his first inaugural address, after swearing his oath of office on a Bible, George Washington deliberately made a prayer a part of his first official act as President, [offering] "fervent supplications to that Almighty Being who rules over the universe." [Such] supplications have been a characteristic feature of inaugural addresses ever since. [Our] national celebration of Thanksgiving likewise dates back to President Washington. [This] tradition of Thanksgiving Proclamations—with their religious theme of prayerful gratitude to God—has been adhered to by almost every

President. The other two branches of the Federal Government also have a long-established practice of prayer at public events. [Congressional] sessions have opened with a chaplain's prayer ever since the First Congress. And this Court's own sessions have opened with the invocation "God save the United States and this Honorable Court" since the days of Chief Justice Marshall.

[The] Court presumably would separate graduation invocations and benedictions from other instances of public "preservation and transmission of religious beliefs" on the ground that they involve "psychological coercion." [But a] few citations of "research in psychology" that have no particular bearing upon the precise issue here cannot disguise the fact that the Court has gone beyond the realm where judges know what they are doing. The Court's argument that state officials have "coerced" students to take part in the invocation and benediction at graduation ceremonies is, not to put too fine a point on it, incoherent.

[The] Court's notion that a student who simply sits in "respectful silence" during the invocation and benediction (when all others are standing) has somehow joined—or would somehow be perceived as having joined—in the prayers is nothing short of ludicrous. [Surely] "our social conventions" have not coarsened to the point that anyone who does not stand on his chair and shout obscenities can reasonably be deemed to have assented to everything said in his presence. [But] let us assume the very worst, that the nonparticipating graduate is "subtly coerced" . . . to stand! Even that [does] not remotely establish a "participation" (or an "appearance of participation") in a religious exercise. [It is] a permissible inference that one who is standing is doing so simply out of respect for the prayers of others that are in progress.

[The] deeper flaw in the Court's opinion does not lie in its wrong answer to the question whether there was state-induced "peer-pressure" coercion; it lies, rather, in the Court's making violation of the Establishment Clause hinge on such a precious question. The coercion that was a hallmark of historical establishments of religion was coercion of religious orthodoxy and of financial support by force of law and threat of penalty. Typically, attendance at the state church was required; only clergy of the official church could lawfully perform sacraments; and dissenters, if tolerated, faced an array of civil disabilities. [Thus,] while I have no quarrel with the Court's general proposition that the Establishment Clause "guarantees that government may not coerce anyone to support or participate in religion or its exercise," I see no warrant for expanding the concept of coercion beyond acts backed by threat of penalty—a brand of coercion that, happily, is readily discernible to those of us who have made a career of reading the disciples of Blackstone rather than of Freud. The Framers understood that "speech is not coercive; the listener may do as he likes."

The Court relies on our "school prayer" cases, [Engel and Schempp.] But whatever the merit of those cases, they do not support, much less compel, the Court's psycho-journey. [School] instruction is not a public ceremony. [And] we have made clear our understanding that school prayer occurs within a framework in which legal coercion to attend school (i.e., coercion under threat of penalty) provides the ultimate backdrop. [Finally,] our school-prayer cases turn in part on the fact that the classroom is inherently an instructional setting, and daily prayer there—where parents are not present to counter "the students' emulation of teachers as role models and the children's susceptibility to peer pressure," might be thought to raise special concerns regarding state interference with the liberty of parents to direct the religious upbringing of their children. [Voluntary] prayer at graduation—a one-time ceremony at which parents, friends and relatives are present—can hardly be thought to raise the same concerns.

[Given] the odd basis for the Court's decision, invocations and benedictions will be able to be given at public-school graduations next June, as they have for the past century and a half, so long as school authorities make clear that anyone who abstains from screaming in protest does not necessarily participate in the prayers. All that is seemingly needed is an announcement, or perhaps a written insertion at the beginning of the graduation Program, to the effect that, while all are asked to rise for the invocation and benediction, none is compelled to join in them, nor will be assumed, by rising, to have done so. That obvious fact recited, the graduates and their parents may proceed to thank God, as Americans have always done, for the blessings He has generously bestowed on them and on their country. [The] founders of our Republic knew the fearsome potential of sectarian religious belief to generate civil dissension and civil strife. And they also knew that nothing, absolutely nothing, is so inclined to foster among religious believers of various faiths a toleration—no, an affection— for one another than voluntarily joining in prayer together, to the God whom they all worship and seek. [To] deprive our society of that important unifying mechanism, in order to spare the nonbeliever what seems to me the minimal inconvenience of standing or even sitting in respectful nonparticipation, is as senseless in policy as it is unsupported in law.

COERCION VS. ENDORSEMENT

1. ***The Court's division in Lee.*** For decades after the early school prayer decisions, some segments of the religious community had vocally called for them to be overruled, and hoped that the appointment of conservative justices would turn the tide. Lee v. Weisman was a bitter disappointment to them; President Reagan's nominee Justice Kennedy provided the fifth vote to hold once again that establishment principles barred prayer in schools, even where studiously nondenominational. Note the vigorous division on the Court between those who advocate reducing establishment interventions to cases of "coercion," and those who insist that establishment can also occur through "endorsement." Which camp did Justice Kennedy ally with? Did he define "coercion" so loosely that it blurred into "endorsement?" Lee was viewed at the time as a propitious case in which to announce a new, more deferential coercion test; indeed, the Solicitor General filed an amicus curiae brief advocating such a test. As the later cases show, the endorsement test survived this close brush with extinction and continues today. Why is that so, when there were at least nominally five votes for the coercion test in Lee?

2. ***Student-led invocations at school football games.*** Relying on Lee, the Court struck down as facially unconstitutional another version of school prayer in **Santa Fe Independent School District v. Doe**, 530 U.S. 290 (2000). Under the public high school program at issue in the case, which replaced a previous program providing for a student "chaplain" to provide "prayer at football games," the student body was empowered to vote each year on whether to have a student speaker preceding varsity football games

who would "deliver a brief invocation and/or message [to] solemnize the event," and on who the student speaker would be.

Writing for the Court, Justice STEVENS, joined by Justices O'Connor, Kennedy, Souter, Ginsburg and Breyer, concluded that "the specific purpose of the policy was to preserve a popular 'state-sponsored religious practice,' that 'invites and encourages religious messages,' which are 'the most obvious method of solemnizing an event.'" He explained that the mere fact that the speech was student-initiated did not make it private student speech rather than official speech: "[T]hese invocations are authorized by a government policy and take place on government property at government-sponsored school-related events. [T]he majoritarian process implemented by the District guarantees, by definition, that minority candidates will never prevail and that their views will be effectively silenced. [While] Santa Fe's majoritarian election might ensure that most of the students are represented, it does nothing to protect the minority; indeed, it likely serves to intensify their offense." Although the chosen speaker was not obligated to deliver a prayer, "the expressed purposes of the policy encourage the selection of a religious message, and that is precisely how the students understand the policy."

He explained: "[The] invocation is [delivered] to a large audience assembled as part of a regularly scheduled, school-sponsored function conducted on school property. The message is broadcast over the school's public address system, [subject] to the control of school officials. [In] this context the members of the listening audience must perceive the pregame message as a public expression of the views of the majority of the student body delivered with the approval of the school administration. [Regardless] of the listener's support for, or objection to, the message, an objective Santa Fe High School student will unquestionably perceive the inevitable pregame prayer as stamped with her school's seal of approval."

Justice Stevens rejected the school district's attempt to distinguish the case from Lee v. Weisman on basis of relative coerciveness: "The District [argues] that attendance at the commencement ceremonies at issue in Lee 'differs dramatically' from attendance at high school football games. [Attendance] at a high school football game, unlike showing up for class, is certainly not required in order to receive a diploma. [There] are some students, however, such as cheerleaders, members of the band, and, of course, the team members themselves, for whom seasonal commitments mandate their attendance, sometimes for class credit. The District also minimizes the importance to many students of attending and participating in extracurricular activities as part of a complete educational experience. [But to] assert that high school students do not feel immense social pressure, or have a truly genuine desire, to be involved in the extracurricular event that is American high school football is 'formalistic in the extreme.' [For] many [students], the choice between whether to attend these games or to risk facing a personally offensive religious ritual is in no practical sense an easy one. The Constitution [demands] that the school may not force this difficult choice upon these students for '[i]t is a tenet of the First Amendment that the State cannot require one of its citizens to forfeit his or her rights and benefits as the price of resisting conformance to state-sponsored religious practice.' Even if we regard every high school student's decision to attend a home football game as purely voluntary, we are nevertheless persuaded that the delivery of a pregame prayer has the improper effect of coercing those present to participate in an act of religious worship. For 'the government may no more use social pressure to enforce orthodoxy than it may use more direct means.' As in Lee, '[w]hat to most believers may seem nothing more than a reasonable request that the nonbeliever respect their religious practices, in a school context may appear to the nonbeliever or dissenter to be an attempt to employ the machinery of the State to enforce a religious orthodoxy.' The constitutional command will not permit the District 'to exact religious conformity from a student as the price' of joining her classmates at a varsity football game."

Chief Justice REHNQUIST, dissenting along with Justices Scalia and Thomas, objected that the majority's decision "bristles with hostility to all things religious in public life. [Respondents] in this case challenged the [program] before it had been put into practice. [The] fact that a policy might 'operate unconstitutionally under some conceivable set of circumstances is insufficient to render it wholly invalid.' [Therefore], the question is not whether the district's policy may be applied in violation of the Establishment Clause, but whether it inevitably will be." Because it was possible for the school district's policy to be applied in nonreligious ways, Chief Justice Rehnquist saw no reason to invalidate the program on its face.

3. *Student-led prayer in extracurricular school settings.* By contrast, the Court in the next Term held permissible under the Establishment Clause the use of school facilities for worship and prayer when led by a private evangelical Christian club as part of an extracurricular afterschool program for elementary school students that was open to other groups such as the Boy and Girl Scouts and the 4-H Club. In **Good News Club v. Milford Central School**, 533 U.S. 98 (2001), the Court held that it was unconstitutional viewpoint discrimination under the Free Speech Clause to exclude such religious speech from a "limited public forum" that had been opened up non-selectively to a wide range of groups (see p. 360). The Court also, by a vote of 6–3, rejected the school's defense that such exclusion was compelled by the Establishment Clause.

Justice THOMAS, writing for the Court, found "unpersuasive" the school's argument that elementary school students would be especially vulnerable to "coercive pressure to participate": "The Good News Club seeks nothing more than to be treated neutrally and given access to speak about the same topics as are other groups. [Allowing] the Club to speak on school grounds would ensure neutrality, not threaten it. [Because] the children cannot attend without their parents' permission, they cannot be coerced into engaging in the Good News Club's religious activities. [Whatever] significance we may have assigned in the Establishment Clause context to the suggestion that elementary school children are more impressionable than adults, we have never extended our Establishment Clause jurisprudence to foreclose private religious conduct during nonschool hours merely because it takes place on school premises where elementary school children may be present. [We] decline to employ Establishment Clause jurisprudence using a modified heckler's veto, in which a group's religious activity can be proscribed on the basis of what the youngest members of the audience might misperceive."

Justice SCALIA concurred, emphasizing that there was no coercion and that endorsement of religion cannot be found in private religious speech expressed in a traditional or designated public forum open to all on equal terms. Justice BREYER concurred in the free speech ruling, but, as to the

Establishment Clause defense, noted that children's reasonable perceptions of endorsement would be relevant and that facts relevant to such perceptions required more factual development on remand. Justices STEVENS and SOUTER, each writing in dissent, agreed with Justice Breyer that there should have been a remand on the establishment issue, which the courts below had not reached because they had ruled for the school on the free speech issue. Justice Souter concluded that "there is a good case that Good News's exercises blur the line between public classroom instruction and private religious indoctrination, leaving a reasonable elementary school pupil unable to appreciate that the former instruction is the business of the school while the latter evangelism is not."

4. ***The end of endorsement, and of Lemon.*** After decades of criticizing Lemon and years of using the endorsement test intermittently, the Court announced a new approach in 2022:

———

Kennedy v. Bremerton School District

597 U.S. ___, 142 S. Ct. 2407 (2022).

■ JUSTICE GORSUCH delivered the opinion of the Court.

Joseph Kennedy lost his job as a high school football coach because he knelt at midfield after games to offer a quiet prayer of thanks. Mr. Kennedy prayed during a period when school employees were free to speak with a friend, call for a reservation at a restaurant, check email, or attend to other personal matters. He offered his prayers quietly while his students were otherwise occupied. [The] Bremerton School District disciplined him anyway [because] it thought anything less could lead a reasonable observer to conclude (mistakenly) that it endorsed Mr. Kennedy's religious beliefs. That reasoning was misguided. Both the Free Exercise and Free Speech Clauses of the First Amendment protect expressions like Mr. Kennedy's.

[Did] Mr. Kennedy offer his prayers in his capacity as a private citizen, or did they amount to government speech attributable to the District? [Applying Garcetti and Lane], it seems clear to us that Mr. Kennedy has demonstrated that his speech was private speech, not government speech. When Mr. Kennedy uttered the three prayers that resulted in his suspension, he was not engaged in speech "ordinarily within the scope" of his duties as a coach. He did not speak pursuant to government policy. He was not seeking to convey a government-created message. He was not instructing players, discussing strategy, encouraging better on-field performance, or engaged in any other speech the District paid him to produce as a coach. [During] the postgame period when these prayers occurred, coaches were free to attend briefly to personal matters—everything from checking sports scores on their phones to greeting friends and family in the stands. We find it unlikely that Mr. Kennedy was fulfilling a responsibility imposed by his employment by praying during a period in which the District has acknowledged that its coaching staff was free to engage in all manner of private speech. That Mr. Kennedy offered his prayers when students were engaged in other activities like singing the school fight song further suggests that those prayers were not delivered as an address to the team, but instead in his capacity as a private citizen. Nor is it dispositive that Mr. Kennedy's prayers took place "within the office" environment—here, on the field of play.

Instead, what matters is whether Mr. Kennedy offered his prayers while acting within the scope of his duties as a coach. And taken together, both the substance of Mr. Kennedy's speech and the circumstances surrounding it point to the conclusion that he did not.

Of course, acknowledging that Mr. Kennedy's prayers represented his own private speech does not end the matter. So far, we have recognized only that Mr. Kennedy has carried his threshold burden. [A] second step remains where the government may seek to prove that its interests as employer outweigh even an employee's private speech on a matter of public concern.

[The] District argues that its suspension of Mr. Kennedy was essential to avoid a violation of the Establishment Clause. To defend its approach, the District relied on Lemon and its progeny. What the District [overlooked], however, is that the shortcomings associated with this ambitious, abstract, and ahistorical approach to the Establishment Clause became so apparent that this Court long ago abandoned Lemon and its endorsement test offshoot. American Legion (plurality opinion); town of Greece. The Court has explained that these tests invited chaos in lower courts, led to differing results in materially identical cases, and created a minefield for legislators. This Court has since made plain, too, that the Establishment Clause does not include anything like a "modified heckler's veto, in which religious activity can be proscribed based on perceptions or "discomfort." Good News Club.

[In] place of Lemon and the endorsement test, this Court has instructed that the Establishment Clause must be interpreted by reference to historical practices and understandings. Town of Greece. The line that courts and governments must draw between the permissible and the impermissible has to accord with history and faithfully reflect the understanding of the Founding Fathers. An analysis focused on original meaning and history, this Court has stressed, has long represented the rule rather than some exception within the Court's Establishment Clause jurisprudence.

[To] be sure, this Court has long held that government may not, consistent with a historically sensitive understanding of the Establishment Clause, make a religious observance compulsory. Zorach. Government may not coerce anyone to attend church, nor may it force citizens to engage in a formal religious exercise. Lee v. Weisman. No doubt, too, coercion along these lines was among the foremost hallmarks of religious establishments the framers sought to prohibit when they adopted the First Amendment. Members of this Court have sometimes disagreed on what exactly qualifies as impermissible coercion in light of the original meaning of the Establishment Clause. But in this case Mr. Kennedy's private religious exercise did not come close to crossing any line one might imagine separating protected private expression from impermissible government coercion.

[The] District did not discipline Mr. Kennedy for engaging in prayer while presenting locker-room speeches to students. [He] also willingly ended his practice of postgame religious talks with his team. The only prayer Mr. Kennedy sought to continue was the kind he had "started out doing" at the beginning of his tenure—the prayer he gave alone. He made clear that he could pray "while the kids were doing the fight song" and "take a knee by [him]self and give thanks and continue on." Mr. Kennedy did not seek to direct any prayers to students or require anyone else to participate. His plan was to wait to pray until athletes were occupied, and he "told everybody" that's what he wished "to do." It was for three prayers of this sort alone in October 2015 that the District suspended him.

[Of] course, some will take offense to certain forms of speech or prayer they are sure to encounter in a society where those activities enjoy such robust constitutional protection. But offense does not equate to coercion. Town of Greece.

[The] District suggests that *any* visible religious conduct by a teacher or coach should be deemed—without more and as a matter of law—impermissibly coercive on students. In essence, the District asks us to adopt the view that the only acceptable government role models for students are those who eschew any visible religious expression. [Such] a rule would be a sure sign that our Establishment Clause jurisprudence had gone off the rails. [Not] only could schools fire teachers for praying quietly over their lunch, for wearing a yarmulke to school, or for offering a midday prayer during a break before practice. Under the District's rule, a school would be *required* to do so. It is a rule that would defy this Court's traditional understanding that permitting private speech is not the same thing as coercing others to participate in it.

[This] case looks very different from [Lee and Santa Fe Independent School Dist. v. Doe]. [The] prayers for which Mr. Kennedy was disciplined were not publicly broadcast or recited to a captive audience. Students were not required or expected to participate. And, in fact, none of Mr. Kennedy's students did participate in any of the three October 2015 prayers that resulted in Mr. Kennedy's discipline.

■ JUSTICE THOMAS, concurring.

[The] Court's opinion does not resolve two issues related to Kennedy's free-exercise claim. First, the Court refrains from deciding whether or how public employees' rights under the Free Exercise Clause may or may not be different from those enjoyed by the general public. [We] have held that the First Amendment protects public employee speech only when it falls within the core of First Amendment protection—speech on matters of public concern. It remains an open question, however, if a similar analysis can or should apply to free-exercise claims in light of the "history" and "tradition" of the Free Exercise Clause. [Second], the Court also does not decide what burden a government employer must shoulder to justify restricting an employee's religious expression because the District had no constitutional basis for reprimanding Kennedy under any possibly applicable standard of scrutiny. [The] Court has never before applied Pickering balancing to a claim brought under the Free Exercise Clause. A government employer's burden therefore might differ depending on which First Amendment guarantee a public employee invokes.

■ JUSTICE ALITO, concurring.

The expression at issue in this case is unlike that in any of our prior cases involving the free-speech rights of public employees. Petitioner's expression occurred while at work but during a time when a brief lull in his duties apparently gave him a few free moments to engage in private activities. When he engaged in this expression, he acted in a purely private capacity. The Court does not decide what standard applies to such expression under the Free Speech Clause but holds only that retaliation for this expression cannot be justified based on any of the standards discussed.

■ JUSTICE SOTOMAYOR, with whom JUSTICE BREYER and JUSTICE KAGAN join, dissenting.

This case is about whether a public school must permit a school official to kneel, bow his head, and say a prayer at the center of a school event. The Constitution does not authorize, let alone require, public schools to embrace this conduct. [The] Court now charts a different path, yet again paying almost exclusive attention to the Free Exercise Clause's protection for individual religious exercise while giving short shrift to the Establishment Clause's prohibition on state establishment of religion. To the degree the Court portrays petitioner Joseph Kennedy's prayers as private and quiet, it misconstrues the facts. The record reveals that Kennedy had a longstanding practice of conducting demonstrative prayers on the 50-yard line of the football field. Kennedy consistently invited others to join his prayers and for years led student athletes in prayer at the same time and location. The Court ignores this history. The Court also ignores the severe disruption to school events caused by Kennedy's conduct, viewing it as irrelevant because the [District] stated that it was suspending Kennedy to avoid it being viewed as endorsing religion. Under the Court's analysis, presumably this would be a different case if the District had cited Kennedy's repeated disruptions of school programming and violations of school policy regarding public access to the field as grounds for suspending him. As the District did not articulate those grounds, the Court assesses only the District's Establishment Clause concerns. It errs by assessing them divorced from the context and history of Kennedy's prayer practice.

Today's decision goes beyond merely misreading the record. The Court overrules Lemon, and calls into question decades of subsequent precedents that it deems "offshoots" of that decision. In the process, the Court rejects longstanding concerns surrounding government endorsement of religion and replaces the standard for reviewing such questions with a new "history and tradition" test. In addition, while the Court reaffirms that the Establishment Clause prohibits the government from coercing participation in religious exercise, it applies a nearly toothless version of the coercion analysis, failing to acknowledge the unique pressures faced by students when participating in school-sponsored activities.

Properly understood, this case is not about the limits on an individual's ability to engage in private prayer at work. This case is about whether a school district is required to allow one of its employees to incorporate a public, communicative display of the employee's personal religious beliefs into a school event, where that display is recognizable as part of a longstanding practice of the employee ministering religion to students as the public watched. A school district is not required to permit such conduct; in fact, the Establishment Clause prohibits it from doing so. [Kennedy's] tradition of a 50-yard line prayer thus strikes at the heart of the Establishment Clause's concerns about endorsement. For students and community members at the game, Coach Kennedy was the face and the voice of the District during football games. [Permitting] a school coach to lead students and others he invited onto the field in prayer at a predictable time after each game could only be viewed as a postgame tradition occurring with the approval of the school administration.

Kennedy's prayer practice also implicated the coercion concerns at the center of this Court's Establishment Clause jurisprudence. [Students] look up to their teachers and coaches as role models and seek their approval.

Students also depend on this approval for tangible benefits. Players recognize that gaining the coach's approval may pay dividends small and large, from extra playing time to a stronger letter of recommendation to additional support in college athletic recruiting. In addition to these pressures to please their coaches, this Court has recognized that players face "immense social pressure" from their peers in the "extracurricular event that is American high school football."

[Kennedy] accepted certain limitations on his freedom of speech when he accepted government employment. Garcetti.

[The] District has a strong argument that Kennedy's speech, formally integrated into the center of a District event, was speech in his official capacity as an employee that is not entitled to First Amendment protections at all. It is unnecessary to resolve this question, however, because, even assuming that Kennedy's speech was in his capacity as a private citizen, the District's responsibilities under the Establishment Clause provided adequate justification for restricting it. Similarly, Kennedy's free exercise claim must be considered in light of the fact that he is a school official and, as such, his participation in religious exercise can create Establishment Clause conflicts. Accordingly, his right to pray at any time and in any manner he wishes while exercising his professional duties is not absolute. [The] District's directive prohibiting Kennedy's demonstrative speech at the 50-yard line was narrowly tailored to avoid an Establishment Clause violation.

The Court relies on an assortment of pluralities, concurrences, and dissents by Members of the current majority to effect fundamental changes in this Court's Religion Clauses jurisprudence, all the while proclaiming that nothing has changed at all. [The] Court now says for the first time that endorsement simply does not matter, and completely repudiates the test established. [Precedent] long has recognized that endorsement concerns under the Establishment Clause, properly understood, bear no relation to a heckler's veto. [The] endorsement inquiry considers the perspective not of just any hypothetical or uninformed observer experiencing subjective discomfort, but of the reasonable observer who is aware of the history and context of the community and forum in which the religious speech takes place. [The] endorsement inquiry is not about the perceptions of particular individuals or saving isolated nonadherents from discomfort but concern with the political community writ large.

The Court now goes much further [than it has before] overruling Lemon entirely and in all contexts. It is wrong to do so. [To] put it plainly, the purposes and effects of a government action matter in evaluating whether that action violates the Establishment Clause, as numerous precedents beyond Lemon instruct in the particular context of public schools.

Upon overruling one "grand unified theory," the Court introduces another: It holds that courts must interpret whether an Establishment Clause violation has occurred mainly "by reference to historical practices and understandings." [While] the Court has long referred to historical practice as one element of the analysis in specific Establishment Clause cases, the Court has never announced this as a general test or exclusive focus. The Court reserves any meaningful explanation of its history-and-tradition test for another day, content for now to disguise it as established law and move on. It should not escape notice, however, that the effects of the majority's new rule could be profound. The problems with elevating history and tradition over purpose and precedent are well documented. [For] now, it suffices to say that the Court's history-and-tradition test offers essentially no guidance for school administrators. If even judges and Justices, with full adversarial briefing and argument tailored to precise legal issues, regularly disagree (and err) in their amateur efforts at history, how are school administrators, faculty, and staff supposed to adapt?

———

THE AFTERMATH OF BREMERTON

1. ***The historical test.*** The Bremerton majority stated that its "historical practices and understandings" test had already replaced Lemon and endorsement. The dissent rejoined that the majority opinion had overruled the two tests and substituted a new one, albeit without specifying its precise contours. Squabbling aside, what *is* the new test? Is the presence of coercion the new Establishment Clause test? If so, is that consistent with the original meaning of the Establishment Clause, which according to one scholar can be "captured in a simple slogan: no coercion and no money"? Feldman, Divided By God 237 (2005). Or is the test broader than coercion, given that the Bremerton court did not specify that coercion was the only possible component in its historical test?

2. ***Retrospective Establishment Clause doctrine with Lemon or endorsement.*** What now is the status of the Establishment Clause cases decided under the Lemon or endorsement tests? Do they remain valid as a matter of precedent? Or must similar cases now be relitigated under the historical practices and understandings test? If they are valid precedent, what does that say about the passing of the Lemon and endorsement tests? If not, does the Establishment Clause doctrine of the last half-century have to be rewritten? Are there reliance interests in play?

3. ***School prayer and employee speech.*** The Bremerton majority held that Kennedy's prayer was "private" speech, not uttered in his official capacity. In reaching that conclusion, the majority opinion applied Garcetti and Lane, two leading employee speech cases. This elicited sperate statements by Justices Thomas and Alito hinting that the standard for government employees' free exercise might be more prayer-protective than normal employee speech standards. What is, or should be, the (subtle) relationship between employee prayer and employee speech standards?

———

RELIGION AND THE PUBLIC SCHOOL CURRICULUM

1. ***The Ten Commandments.*** In **Stone v. Graham**, 449 U.S. 39 (1980), the Court held unconstitutional a Kentucky law that required the posting of a copy of the Ten Commandments, purchased with private contributions, in public school classrooms. In sustaining the law, the state trial court had emphasized that the law's "avowed purpose" was "secular and not religious." The Court reversed summarily, without hearing argument on the merits. The majority's per curiam opinion concluded that the law had "no secular legislative purpose," even though it required that each display of the Ten Commandments have a notation in small print stating: "The secular application of the Ten Commandments is clearly seen in its adoption as the

fundamental legal code of Western Civilization and the Common Law of the United States." The majority viewed the predominant purpose of the posting requirement as "plainly religious," since the Ten Commandments are "undeniably a sacred text in the Jewish and Christian faiths." Even though some of the Commandments address secular matters, "the first part of the Commandments concerns the religious duties of believers."

Justice Rehnquist's dissent insisted that the Court's ruling was "without precedent in Establishment Clause jurisprudence." He noted: "The fact that the asserted secular purpose may overlap with what some may see as a religious objective does not render [the law] unconstitutional." Justice Stewart also dissented on the merits; Chief Justice Burger and Justice Blackmun objected to the summary disposition, arguing that the case should have been given plenary consideration.

2. ***The pledge of allegiance.*** Under the school prayer precedents, is the Establishment Clause violated when teachers in a public school classroom lead students in joint recitation of the Pledge of Allegiance, as modified by Congress in 1954, at the height of anti-communist political fervor, to include the words "one nation *under God*"? In **Elk Grove Unified School District v. Newdow**, 542 U.S. 1 (2004), the court of appeals gave an affirmative answer to that question, but on appeal, the Supreme Court reversed the decision on the ground that the challenger—an atheist father who did not wish his daughter to have to undergo recitation of the Pledge as written at her public elementary school—lacked prudential standing to sue based on state court rulings conferring custody upon the girl's mother.

Chief Justice REHNQUIST, joined by Justice O'Connor and in part by Justice Thomas, concurred in the judgment but would have found standing and reached the merits, finding no Establishment Clause violation. Citing precedents for invoking God in presidential inaugurations from Washington to Wilson, and the motto "In God We Trust" on the national currency, Chief Justice Rehnquist concluded that "our national culture allows public recognition of our Nation's religious history and character." He continued: "I do not believe that the phrase 'under God' in the Pledge converts its recital into a 'religious exercise' of the sort described in Lee. Instead, it is a declaration of belief in allegiance and loyalty to the United States flag and the Republic that it represents. The phrase 'under God' is in no sense a prayer, nor an endorsement of any religion, but a simple recognition of the fact [that] 'from the time of our earliest history our peoples and our institutions have reflected the traditional concept that our Nation was founded on a fundamental belief in God.' Reciting the Pledge, or listening to others recite it, is a patriotic exercise, not a religious one; participants promise fidelity to our flag and our Nation, not to any particular God, faith, or church."

Justice O'CONNOR concurred separately in the judgment, noting that the Pledge did not violate her "endorsement" test: "For centuries, we have marked important occasions or pronouncements with references to God and invocations of divine assistance. Such references can serve to solemnize an occasion instead of to invoke divine provenance. The reasonable observer, [fully] aware of our national history and the origins of such practices, would not perceive these acknowledgments as signifying a government endorsement of any specific religion, or even of religion over non-religion." Justice THOMAS concurred in the judgment as well, but conceded that the court of appeals had acted reasonably under the Court's school prayer precedents, and thus reiterated his view that the Establishment Clause should not be incorporated against the States.

3. *Teaching evolution and creationism.* In **Epperson v. Arkansas**, 393 U.S. 97 (1968), the Court invalidated the Arkansas version of the Tennessee "anti-evolution" law that gained national notoriety in the Scopes "monkey law" trial in 1927. The Court found the law to be in conflict with the Establishment Clause mandate of "neutrality." The Arkansas law prohibited teachers in state schools from teaching "the theory or doctrine that mankind ascended or descended from a lower order of animals." The highest state court had expressed "no opinion" on "whether the Act prohibits any explanation of the theory of evolution or merely prohibits teaching that the theory is true." On either interpretation, Justice FORTAS's majority opinion concluded, the law could not stand: "The overriding fact is that Arkansas' law selects from the body of knowledge a particular segment which it proscribes for the sole reason that it is deemed to conflict with a particular religious doctrine; that is, with a particular interpretation of the Book of Genesis by a particular religious group. Government in our democracy, state and national, must be neutral in matters of religious theory, doctrine, and practice. It may not be hostile to any religion or to the advocacy of no religion; and it may not aid, foster, or promote one religion or religious theory against another or even against the militant opposite. [The] vigilant protection of constitutional freedoms is nowhere more vital than in the community of American schools. [The] State's undoubted right to prescribe the curriculum for its public schools does not carry with it the right to prohibit, on pain of criminal penalty, the teaching of a scientific theory or doctrine where that prohibition is based upon reasons that violate the First Amendment. In the present case, there can be no doubt that Arkansas has sought to prevent its teachers from discussing the theory of evolution because it is contrary to the belief of some that the Book of Genesis must be the exclusive source of doctrine as to the origin of man. No suggestion has been made that Arkansas' law may be justified by considerations of state policy other than the religious views of some of its citizens. It is clear that fundamentalist sectarian conviction was and is the law's reason for existence. Its antecedent, Tennessee's 'monkey law,' candidly stated its purpose: to make it unlawful 'to teach any theory that denies the story of the Divine Creation of man as taught in the Bible, and to teach instead that man has descended from a lower order of animals.' Perhaps the sensational publicity attendant upon the Scopes trial induced Arkansas to adopt less explicit language. It eliminated Tennessee's reference to 'the story of the Divine Creation of man' as taught in the Bible, but there is no doubt that the motivation for the law was the same: to suppress the teaching of a theory which, it was thought, 'denied' the divine creation of man. Arkansas' law cannot be defended as an act of religious neutrality. Arkansas did not seek to excise from the curricula of its schools and universities all discussion of the origin of man. The law's effort was confined to an attempt to blot out a particular theory because of its supposed conflict with the Biblical account, literally read."

In separate opinions, Justices BLACK and STEWART explained that they concurred solely on the ground of vagueness. Justice Black criticized the majority for reaching out to "troublesome" First Amendment questions: "It is plain that a state law prohibiting all teaching of human development or biology is constitutionally quite different from a law that compels a teacher to teach as true only one theory of a given doctrine. [A] question that arises for me is whether this Court's decision forbidding a State to exclude the subject of evolution from its schools infringes the religious freedom of those who consider evolution an anti-religious doctrine. If the theory is considered anti-religious, as the Court indicates, how can the State be bound by the Federal Constitution to permit its teachers to advocate such an 'anti-religious' doctrine to schoolchildren? The very cases cited by the Court as supporting its conclusion that the State must be neutral, not favoring one religious or anti-religious view over another. The Darwinian theory is said to challenge the Bible's story of creation; so too have some of those who believe in the Bible, along with many others, challenged the Darwinian theory. Since there is no indication that the literal Biblical doctrine of the origin of man is included in the curriculum of Arkansas schools, does not the removal of the subject of evolution leave the State in a neutral position toward these supposedly competing religious and anti-religious doctrines? [I] am also not ready to hold that a person hired to teach schoolchildren takes with him into the classroom a constitutional right to teach sociological, economic, political, or religious subjects that the school's managers do not want discussed."

In the following case the Court definitively rejected Justice Black's "neutrality" approach, striking down a state law that mandated that the theories of evolution and creation be taught alongside one another, if at all.

Edwards v. Aguillard

482 U.S. 578, 107 S. Ct. 2573, 96 L. Ed. 2d 510 (1987).

■ JUSTICE BRENNAN delivered the opinion of the Court.

The question for decision is whether Louisiana's "Balanced Treatment for Creation-Science and Evolution-Science in Public School Instruction" Act (Creationism Act) is facially invalid as violative of the Establishment Clause. The Creationism Act forbids the teaching of the theory of evolution in public schools unless accompanied by instruction in "creation science." No school is required to teach evolution or creation science. If either is taught, however, the other must also be taught. The theories of evolution and creation science are statutorily defined as "the scientific evidences for (creation or evolution) and inferences from those scientific evidences." Appellees, who include parents of children attending Louisiana public schools, Louisiana teachers, and religious leaders, challenged the constitutionality of the Act. [The] District Court [granted summary judgment to appellees, holding] that the Creationism Act violated the Establishment Clause either because it prohibited the teaching of evolution or because it required the teaching of creation science with the purpose of advancing a particular religious doctrine. The Court of Appeals affirmed. [We affirm.]

[The] Court has been particularly vigilant in monitoring compliance with the Establishment Clause in elementary and secondary schools. [Families] entrust public schools with the education of their children, but condition their trust on the understanding that the classroom will not purposely be used to advance religious views that may conflict with the private beliefs of the student and his or her family. Students in such institutions are impressionable and their attendance is involuntary. The State exerts great authority and coercive power through mandatory attendance requirements, and because of the students' emulation of teachers as role models and the children's susceptibility to peer pressure.

Lemon's first prong focuses on the purpose that animated adoption of the Act. [In] this case, appellants have identified no clear secular purpose for the Louisiana Act. True, the Act's stated purpose is to protect academic freedom. This phrase might, in common parlance, be understood as referring to enhancing the freedom of teachers to teach what they will. The Court of Appeals, however, correctly concluded that the Act was not designed to further that goal. [Even] if "academic freedom" is read to mean "teaching all of the evidence" with respect to the origin of human beings, the Act does not further this purpose. The goal of providing a more comprehensive science curriculum is not furthered either by outlawing the teaching of evolution or by requiring the teaching of creation science. While the Court is normally deferential to a State's articulation of a secular purpose, it is required that the statement of such purpose be sincere and not a sham. It is [clear] that requiring schools to teach creation science with evolution does not advance academic freedom. The Act does not grant teachers a flexibility that they did not already possess to supplant the present science curriculum with a presentation of theories, besides evolution, about the origin of life.

[Furthermore,] the goal of basic "fairness" is hardly furthered by the Act's discriminatory preference for the teaching of creation science and against the teaching of evolution. While requiring that curriculum guides be developed for creation science, the Act says nothing of comparable guides for evolution. Similarly, research services are supplied for creation science but not for evolution. Only "creation scientists" can serve on the panel that supplies the resource services. The Act forbids school boards to discriminate against anyone who "chooses to be a creation-scientist" or to teach "creationism," but fails to protect those who choose to teach evolution or any other non-creation science theory, or who refuse to teach creation science. [Moreover,] the Act fails even to ensure that creation science will be taught, but instead requires the teaching of this theory only when the theory of evolution is taught. Thus we agree with the Court of Appeals' conclusion that the Act does not serve to protect academic freedom, but has a distinctly different purpose of discrediting "evolution by counterbalancing its teaching at every turn with the teaching of creationism. . . ."

[We] need not be blind in this case to the legislature's preeminent religious purpose in enacting this statute. There is a historic and contemporaneous link between the teachings of certain religious denominations and the teaching of evolution. It was this link that concerned the Court in [Epperson]. [The] same historic and contemporaneous antagonisms between the teachings of certain religious denominations and the teaching of evolution are present in this case. The preeminent purpose of the Louisiana legislature was clearly to advance the religious viewpoint that a supernatural being created humankind. The term "creation science" was defined as embracing this particular religious doctrine by those responsible for the passage of the Creationism Act. Senator Keith's leading expert on creation science, Edward Boudreaux, testified at the legislative hearings that the theory of creation science included belief in the existence of a supernatural creator.

[Furthermore,] it is not happenstance that the legislature required the teaching of a theory that coincided with this religious view. The legislative history documents that the Act's primary purpose was to change the science curriculum of public schools in order to provide persuasive advantage to a particular religious doctrine that rejects the factual basis of evolution in its entirety. The sponsor of the Creationism Act, Senator Keith, explained during the legislative hearings that his disdain for the theory of evolution resulted from [his] own religious beliefs. [The] state senator repeatedly stated that scientific evidence supporting his religious views should be included in the public school curriculum to redress the fact that the theory of evolution incidentally coincided with what he characterized as religious beliefs antithetical to his own. The legislation therefore sought to alter the science curriculum to reflect endorsement of a religious view that is antagonistic to the theory of evolution. In this case, the purpose of the Creationism Act was to restructure the science curriculum to conform with a particular religious viewpoint. Out of many possible science subjects taught in the public schools, the legislature chose to affect the teaching of the one scientific theory that historically has been opposed by certain religious sects. As in Epperson, the legislature passed the Act to give preference to those religious groups which have as one of their tenets the creation of humankind by a divine creator.

[Because] the primary purpose of the Creationism Act is to advance a particular religious belief, the Act endorses religion in violation of the First Amendment. We do not imply that a legislature could never require that scientific critiques of prevailing scientific theories be taught. [Teaching] a variety of scientific theories about the origins of humankind to schoolchildren might be validly done with the clear secular intent of enhancing the effectiveness of science instruction. But because the primary purpose of the Creationism Act is to endorse a particular religious doctrine, the Act furthers religion in violation of the Establishment Clause. [Affirmed.]

■ JUSTICE POWELL, with whom JUSTICE O'CONNOR joins, concurring.

I write separately to note certain aspects of the legislative history, and to emphasize that nothing in the Court's opinion diminishes the traditionally broad discretion accorded state and local school officials in the selection of the public school curriculum. [A] religious purpose alone is not enough to invalidate an act of a state legislature. The religious purpose must predominate. [Here,] it is clear that religious belief is the Balanced Treatment's Act's "reason for existence." [Whatever] the academic merit of particular subjects or theories, the Establishment Clause limits the discretion of state officials to pick and choose among them for the purpose of promoting a particular religious belief. The language of the statute and its legislative history convince me that the Louisiana legislature exercised its discretion for this purpose in this [case].

■ JUSTICE SCALIA, with whom CHIEF JUSTICE REHNQUIST joins, dissenting.

[There] is ample evidence that the majority is wrong in holding that the Balanced Treatment Act is without secular purpose. [Senator] Keith and his witnesses testified essentially: (1) [There] are two and only two scientific explanations for the beginning of life—evolution and creation [science]. (2) The body of scientific evidence supporting creation science is as strong as that supporting evolution. In fact, it may be [stronger]. (3) Creation science is educationally valuable. Students exposed to it better understand the current state of scientific evidence about the origin of [life]. (4) Although creation science is educationally valuable and strictly scientific, it is now being censored from or misrepresented in the [public schools]. (5) The censorship of creation science [has] harmful effects. [E.g., it] deprives students of knowledge of one of the two scientific explanations for the origin of life and leads them to believe that evolution is proven [fact]. [We] have no way of knowing, of course, how many legislators believed the testimony of Senator Keith and his witnesses. But in the absence of evidence to the contrary, we have to assume that many of them [did].

[Moreover, the] Louisiana Legislature explicitly set forth its secular purpose ("protecting academic freedom") in the very text of the Act. [If] one adopts the obviously intended meaning of the statutory terms "academic freedom," there is no basis whatever for concluding that the purpose they express is a "sham." [The] legislative history gives ample evidence of the sincerity of the Balanced Treatment Act's articulated purpose. Witness after witness urged the legislators to support the Act so that students would not be "indoctrinated" but would instead be free to decide for themselves, based upon a fair presentation of the scientific evidence, about the origin of life. [It] is undoubtedly true that what prompted the Legislature to direct its attention to the misrepresentation of evolution in the schools (rather than the inaccurate presentation of other topics) was its awareness of the tension between evolution and the religious beliefs of many children. But [a] valid secular purpose is not rendered impermissible simply because its pursuit is prompted by concern for religious [sensitivities].

[Criticizing the Court's inquiry into legislative motivation under the Lemon "purpose" test, Justice Scalia continued:] [While] it is possible to discern the objective "purpose" of a statute, [discerning] the subjective motivation of those enacting the statute is, to be honest, almost always an impossible task. The number of possible motivations, to begin with, is not binary, or indeed even finite. To look for the sole purpose of even a single legislator is probably to look for something that does not exist.

Putting that problem aside, however, where ought we to look for the individual legislator's purpose? We cannot of course assume that every member present (if, as is unlikely, we know who or even how many they were) agreed with the motivation expressed in a particular legislator's preenactment floor or committee statement. Quite obviously, "what motivates one legislator to make a speech about a statute is not necessarily what motivates scores of others to enact it." Can we assume, then, that they all agree with the motivation expressed in the staff-prepared committee reports they might have read—even though we are unwilling to assume that they agreed with the motivation expressed in the very statute that they voted for? Should we consider postenactment floor statements? Or postenactment testimony from legislators, obtained expressly for the lawsuit? Should we consider media reports on the realities of the legislative bargaining? All of these sources, of course, are eminently manipulable. Legislative histories can be contrived and sanitized, favorable media coverage orchestrated, and postenactment recollections conveniently distorted. Perhaps most valuable of all would be more objective indications—for example, evidence regarding the individual legislators' religious affiliations. And if that, why not evidence regarding the fervor or tepidity of their beliefs?

Having achieved, through these simple means, an assessment of what individual legislators intended, we must still confront the question (yet to be addressed in any of our cases) how many of them must have the invalidating intent. If a state senate approves a bill by vote of 26 to 25, and only one of the 26 intended solely to advance religion, is the law unconstitutional? What if 13 of the 26 had that intent? What if 3 of the 26 had the impermissible intent, but 3 of the 25 voting against the bill were motivated by religious hostility or were simply attempting to "balance" the votes of their impermissibly motivated colleagues? Or is it possible that the intent of the bill's sponsor is alone enough to invalidate it—on a theory, perhaps, that even though everyone else's intent was pure, what they produced was the fruit of a forbidden tree? Because there are no good answers to these questions, this Court has recognized from Chief Justice Marshall, see Fletcher v. Peck, to Chief Justice Warren, United States v. O'Brien, that determining the subjective intent of legislators is a perilous enterprise.

Given the many hazards involved in assessing the subjective intent of governmental decisionmakers, the first prong of Lemon is defensible, I think, only if the text of the Establishment Clause demands it. That is surely not the case. [In] the past we have attempted to justify our embarrassing Establishment Clause jurisprudence on the ground that it "sacrifices clarity and predictability for flexibility." [I] think it time that we sacrifice some "flexibility" for "clarity and predictability." Abandoning Lemon's purpose test—a test which exacerbates the tension between the Free Exercise and Establishment Clauses, has no basis in the language or history of the amendment, and, as today's decision shows, has wonderfully flexible consequences—would be a good place to start.

DEFINING RELIGION VS. SCIENCE

In Kitzmiller v. Dover Area School District, 400 F. Supp. 2d 707 (M.D. Pa. 2004), a federal district court invalidated a requirement that teachers must read aloud a statement to ninth graders identifying Intelligent Design as an alternative explanation to evolution regarding the origins of life. The court first rejected the requirement under the endorsement test: "The history of the intelligent design (hereinafter ID) movement [and] the development of the strategy to weaken education of evolution by focusing students on alleged gaps in the theory of evolution is the historical and cultural background against which the Dover School Board acted in adopting the challenged ID Policy. [A] reasonable observer, whether adult or child, would be aware of this social context in which the ID Policy arose. [The] concept of intelligent [design], in its current form, came into existence after [Edwards] and [in] addition to the [ID movement] itself describing ID as a religious argument, ID's religious nature is evident because it involves a supernatural designer. [The] evidence at trial demonstrates that ID is nothing less than the progeny of creationism. [Edwards held] that the Constitution forbids teaching creationism as science. [Furthermore, we find that] ID is not science. We find that ID fails on three different levels, any one of which is sufficient to preclude a determination that ID is science. They are: (1) ID violates the centuries-old ground rules of science by invoking and permitting supernatural causation; (2) the argument of irreducible complexity, central to ID, employs the same flawed and illogical contrived dualism that doomed creation science in the 1980's; and (3) ID's negative attacks on evolution have been refuted by the scientific community. [It] is additionally important to note that ID has failed to gain acceptance in the scientific community, it has not generated peer-reviewed publications, nor has it been the subject of testing and research."

The court also held that the requirement failed the Lemon test: "[A] wealth of evidence [reveals] that the District's purpose [in introducing the requirement] was to advance creationism, an inherently religious view, both by introducing it directly under the label ID and by disparaging the scientific theory of evolution, so that creationism would gain credence by default as the only apparent alternative to evolution. [Furthermore, the] effect of Defendants' actions in adopting the curriculum change was to impose a religious view of biological origins into the biology course, in violation of the Establishment Clause."

PUBLIC DISPLAYS OF RELIGIOUS SYMBOLS

Outside the context of the public schools, the Court has been more tolerant of governmental sponsorship of religious symbolism. No justice has seriously questioned, for example, the permissibility of the motto "In God We Trust" on the national currency (on coins since 1864 and paper currency since 1957), or the recitation of the phrase "one nation under God" in the Pledge of Allegiance (added in 1954). What explains this deferential view? That these practices have lost their religious significance over time? That they were civic rather than religious to begin with? That they merely commemorate historical "fact" about the piety of the founding generation? That the nonbelieving observer can readily ignore them? What is the Court's basis for rejecting most Establishment Clause challenges in the following cases?

1. *Sunday closing laws.* **McGowan v. Maryland**, 366 U.S. 420 (1961), was one of four companion cases in which the Court rejected claims that Sunday closing laws violated the religion clauses. Chief Justice WARREN wrote the majority opinion. He noted in McGowan that there is "no dispute that the original laws which dealt with Sunday labor were motivated by religious forces." But he concluded: "In light of the evolution of our Sunday Closing Laws through the centuries, and of their more or less recent emphasis upon secular considerations, it is not difficult to discern that as presently written and administered, most of them, at least, are of a secular rather than of a religious character, and that presently they bear no relationship to establishment of religion as those words are used in the [Constitution]. The present purpose and effect of most of them is to provide a uniform day of rest for all citizens; the fact that this day is Sunday, a day of particular significance for the dominant Christian sects, does not bar the State from achieving its secular [goals]. Sunday is a day apart from all others. The cause is irrelevant; the fact exists."

2. *Legislative prayer.* In **Marsh v. Chambers**, 463 U.S. 783 (1983), the Court upheld "the Nebraska Legislature's practice of opening each legislative day with a prayer by a chaplain paid by the State." Chief Justice BURGER's majority opinion relied largely on history to sustain the practice despite the fact that the position of chaplain had been held for 16 years by a Presbyterian, that the chaplain was paid at public expense, and that all of the prayers were "in the Judeo-Christian tradition." This was the first case since Lemon in 1971 that did not apply the three-pronged test. Instead, the majority looked at the specific features of the challenged practice in light of a long history of acceptance of legislative and other official prayers. The majority concluded: "Weighed against the historical background, [the allegedly vulnerable] factors do not serve to invalidate Nebraska's practice."

Chief Justice Burger viewed prayer in this context as "unique" in its historical roots: "The opening of sessions of legislative and other deliberative public bodies with prayer is deeply embedded in the history and tradition of this country. From colonial times through the founding of the Republic and ever since, the practice of legislative prayer has coexisted with the principles of disestablishment and religious freedom. In the very courtrooms in which the United States District Judge and later three Circuit Judges heard and decided this case, the proceedings opened with an announcement that concluded, 'God save the United States and this Honorable Court.' The same invocation occurs at all sessions of this Court. [Although] prayers were not offered during the Constitutional Convention, the First Congress, as one of its early items of business, adopted the policy of selecting a chaplain to open each session with prayer. [On] April 25, 1789, the Senate elected its first chaplain; the House followed suit on May 1, 1789. A statute providing for the payment of these chaplains was enacted into law on September 22, 1789. [In] light of the unambiguous and unbroken history of more than 200 years, there can be no doubt that the practice of opening legislative sessions with a prayer has become part of the fabric of our society. [It] is simply a tolerable acknowledgment of beliefs widely held among the people of this country."

Justice BRENNAN, joined by Justice Marshall, filed a lengthy dissent: "Legislative prayer clearly violates the principles of neutrality and separation that are embedded within the Establishment Clause. It is contrary to the fundamental message of Engel and Schempp. It intrudes on the right to conscience by forcing some legislators either to participate in a 'prayer opportunity,' with which they are in basic disagreement, or to make their disagreement a matter of public comment by declining to participate. It forces all residents of the State to support a religious exercise that may be contrary to their own beliefs. It requires the State to commit itself on fundamental theological issues. It has the potential for degrading religion by allowing a religious call to worship to be intermeshed with a secular call to order. And it injects religion into the political sphere by creating the potential that each and every selection of a chaplain, or consideration of a particular prayer, or even reconsideration of the practice itself, will provoke a political battle along religious lines and ultimately alienate some religiously identified group of citizens." Under the Lemon test, he argued, the practice could not be sustained, since the purpose and effect were "clearly religious" and there was also excessive political entanglement.

Justice STEVENS also dissented: "In a democratically elected legislature, the religious beliefs of the chaplain tend to reflect the faith of the majority of the lawmakers' constituents. Prayers may be said by a Catholic priest in the Massachusetts Legislature and by a Presbyterian minister in the Nebraska Legislature, but I would not expect to find a Jehovah's Witness or a disciple of Mary Baker Eddy or the Reverend Moon serving as the official chaplain in any state legislature. Regardless of the motivation of the majority that exercises the power to appoint the chaplain, it seems plain to me that the designation of a member of one religious faith to serve as the sole official chaplain of a state legislature for a period of 16 years constitutes the preference of one faith over another in violation of the Establishment Clause of the First Amendment."

Note that in Marsh, Chief Justice Burger relied heavily on the legislative chaplaincies established by the First Congress as a historical precedent supporting the rejection of the Establishment Clause claim. Was that reliance justified? James Madison, principal author of the religion clauses, was a member of that Congress, but he later stated in correspondence that "it was not with my approbation" that Congress had thus deviated from the " 'immunity of Religion from civil jurisdiction.' " He explained in an essay that " '[t]he law appointing Chaplains establishes a religious worship for the national representatives, to be performed by Ministers of religion, elected by a majority of them, and these are to be paid out of the national taxes. [The] establishment of the chaplainship to Cong[res]s is a palpable violation of equal rights, as well as of Constitutional principles: The tenets of the chaplains elected in [by the Majority] shut the door of worship ag[ain]st the members whose creeds & consciences forbid a participation in that of the majority.' " For an in-depth account of Madison's views on the topic, see Olree, "James Madison and Legislative Chaplains," 102 Nw. U. L. Rev. 145 (2008). For a history of appointments to the congressional chaplaincies, noting controversies sparked by the appointments of Catholic, Unitarian and guest Hindu chaplains and suggesting that such appointments have been more religiously divisive than the Marsh opinion suggests, see Lund, "The Congressional Chaplaincies," 17 Wm. & Mary Bill of Rights J. 1171 (2009).

In **Town of Greece v. Galloway**, 573 U.S. 565 (2014), the Court revisited legislative prayer at a distance of more than thirty years—and upheld it. At issue was the practice in Greece, New York, of asking a series of volunteer clergy to offer prayers at town meetings after the Pledge of Allegiance and roll call. According to the Court's 5–4 opinion by Justice KENNEDY, the town had compiled "a list of willing 'board chaplains.' [The] town at no point excluded or denied an opportunity to a would-be prayer giver. Its leaders maintained that a minister or layperson of any persuasion, including an atheist, could give the invocation. But nearly all of the congregations in town were Christian; and from 1999 to 2007, all of the participating ministers were too. Greece neither reviewed the prayers in advance of the meetings nor provided guidance as to their tone or content. [Some] of the ministers spoke in a distinctly Christian idiom; and a minority invoked religious holidays, scripture, or doctrine."

The Court held that Marsh controlled, though not precisely for the reasons given in the case. "Marsh is sometimes described as 'carving out an exception' to the Court's Establishment Clause jurisprudence, because it sustained legislative prayer without subjecting the practice to any of the formal tests that have traditionally structured this inquiry. The Court in Marsh found those tests unnecessary because history supported the conclusion that legislative invocations are compatible with the Establishment Clause. [Yet] Marsh must not be understood as permitting a practice that would amount to a constitutional violation if not for its historical foundation. The case teaches instead that the Establishment Clause must be interpreted by reference to historical practices and understandings. That the First Congress provided for the appointment of chaplains only days after approving language for the First Amendment demonstrates that the Framers considered legislative prayer a benign acknowledgment of religion's role in society."

Justice Kennedy rejected the argument that under Marsh, legislative prayer must be nonsectarian. "One of the Senate's first chaplains, the Rev. William White, gave prayers in a series that included the Lord's Prayer, the Collect for Ash Wednesday, prayers for peace and grace, a general thanksgiving, St. Chrysostom's Prayer, and a prayer seeking 'the grace of our Lord Jesus Christ, &c.' The decidedly Christian nature of these prayers must not be dismissed as the relic of a time when our Nation was less pluralistic than it is today. Congress continues to permit its appointed and visiting chaplains to express themselves in a religious idiom. It acknowledges our growing diversity not by proscribing sectarian content but by welcoming ministers of many creeds. [Marsh] nowhere suggested that the constitutionality of legislative prayer turns on the neutrality of its content." However, "[i]n rejecting the suggestion that legislative prayer must be nonsectarian, the Court does not imply that no constraints remain on its content. The relevant constraint derives from its place at the opening of legislative sessions, where it is meant to lend gravity to the occasion and reflect values long part of the Nation's heritage. Prayer that is solemn and respectful in tone, that invites lawmakers to reflect upon shared ideals and common ends before they embark on the fractious business of governing, serves that legitimate function. If the course and practice over time shows that the invocations denigrate nonbelievers or religious minorities, threaten damnation, or preach conversion, many present may consider the prayer to fall short of the desire to elevate the purpose of the occasion and to unite lawmakers in their common effort. That circumstance would present a different case than the one presently before the Court."

Justice Kennedy went on to explain that the fact that the town asked "a predominantly Christian set of ministers to lead the prayer" did not invalidate it. "The town made reasonable efforts to identify all of the congregations located within its borders and represented that it would welcome a prayer by any minister or layman who wished to give one. That nearly all of the congregations in town turned out to be Christian does not reflect an aversion or bias on the part of town leaders against minority faiths. So long as the town maintains a policy of nondiscrimination, the Constitution does not require it to search beyond its borders for non-Christian prayer givers in an effort to achieve religious balancing. The quest to promote a diversity of religious views would require the town to make wholly inappropriate judgments about the number of religions [it] should sponsor and the relative frequency with which it should sponsor each, a form of government entanglement with religion that is far more troublesome than the current approach."

Justice Kennedy rejected the argument that the prayers coerced attendees at town council meetings by exerting "subtle pressure to participate in prayers that violate their beliefs in order to please the board members from whom they are about to seek a favorable ruling." He said that "[t]he inquiry remains a fact-sensitive one that considers both the setting in which the prayer arises and the audience to whom it is directed. [The] principal audience for these invocations is not, indeed, the public but lawmakers themselves, who may find that a moment of prayer or quiet reflection sets the mind to a higher purpose and thereby eases the task of governing. [The] analysis would be different if town board members directed the public to participate in the prayers, singled out dissidents for opprobrium, or indicated that their decisions might be influenced by a person's acquiescence in the prayer opportunity. No such thing occurred in the town of Greece. [Nothing] in the record indicates that town leaders allocated benefits and burdens based on participation in the prayer, or that citizens were received differently depending on whether they joined the invocation or quietly declined. In no instance did town leaders signal disfavor toward nonparticipants or suggest that their stature in the community was in any way diminished." And while some participants might have felt offended, offense "does not equate to coercion. Adults often encounter speech they find disagreeable; and an Establishment Clause violation is not made out any time a person experiences a sense of affront from the expression of contrary religious views in a legislative forum, especially where, as here, any member of the public is welcome in turn to offer an invocation reflecting his or her own convictions."

Finally, Justice Kennedy distinguished Lee v. Weisman (p. 737): "Nothing in the record suggests that members of the public are dissuaded from leaving the meeting room during the prayer, arriving late, or even, as happened here, making a later protest. [Should] nonbelievers choose to exit the room during a prayer they find distasteful, their absence will not stand out as disrespectful or even noteworthy. And should they remain, their quiet acquiescence will not, in light of our traditions, be interpreted as an agreement with the words or ideas expressed. Neither choice represents an unconstitutional imposition as to mature adults, who presumably are not readily susceptible to religious indoctrination or peer pressure."

Justice KAGAN dissented at length, joined by Justices Ginsburg, Breyer and Sotomayor. Taking Marsh as settled law, she distinguished the facts: "The practice at issue here differs from the one sustained in Marsh because Greece's town meetings involve participation by ordinary citizens, and the invocations given—directly to those citizens—were predominantly sectarian in content. Still more, Greece's Board did nothing to recognize religious diversity: In arranging for clergy members to open each meeting, the Town never sought (except briefly when this suit was filed) to involve, accommodate, or in any way reach out to adherents of non-Christian religions. So month in and month out for over a decade, prayers steeped in only one faith, addressed toward members of the public, commenced meetings to discuss local affairs and distribute government benefits."

Justice Kagan further distinguished Marsh on the ground that the town council was not only a legislative body: "The town hall here is a kind of hybrid. Greece's Board indeed has legislative functions, as Congress and state assemblies do—and that means some opening prayers are allowed there. But [the] Board's meetings are also occasions for ordinary citizens to engage with and petition their government, often on highly individualized matters. That feature calls for Board members to exercise special care to ensure that the prayers offered are inclusive—that they respect each and every member of the community as an equal citizen. But the Board, and the clergy members it selected, made no such effort. Instead, the prayers given in Greece, addressed directly to the Town's citizenry, were more sectarian, and less inclusive, than anything this Court sustained in Marsh. [Still] more, the prayers betray no understanding that the American community is today, as it long has been, a rich mosaic of religious faiths. The monthly chaplains appear almost always to assume that everyone in the room is Christian (and of a kind who has no objection to government-sponsored worship). The Town itself has never urged its chaplains to reach out to members of other faiths, or even to recall that they might be present."

Justice Kagan concluded that "Greece could not do what it did: infuse a participatory government body with one (and only one) faith, so that month in and month out, the citizens appearing before it become partly defined by their creed—as those who share, and those who do not, the community's majority religious belief. In this country, when citizens go before the government, they go not as Christians or Muslims or Jews (or what have you), but just as Americans (or here, as Grecians). That is what it means to be an equal citizen, irrespective of religion. And that is what the Town of Greece precluded by so identifying itself with a single faith."

The "fact-sensitive" inquiry laid out in Town of Greece has led to some disparate outcomes in the lower courts. For instance, after Town of Greece both the Fourth and the Sixth Circuits addressed the question whether the Establishment Clause prohibits county commissioners from offering sectarian prayers (in both cases Christian prayers), when only the commissioners are permitted to offer invocations. In Bormuth v. County of Jackson, 870 F.3d 494 (6th Cir. 2017), the Sixth Circuit ruled the practice was permissible because there is a history of legislator-led prayer; the opportunity to give the prayers was not restricted by religion, but rather depended only on being elected to the office of commissioner; and the prayers did not denigrate non-Christians. The same year, the Fourth Circuit struck down a similar prayer practice in Lund v. Rowan County, 863 F.3d 268 (4th Cir. 2017). The court stated that legislator-led sectarian prayer did not per se violate the Establishment Clause, but that the prayers offered by the commissioners in that case sometimes proselytized and evangelized, thus violating Town of Greece's proscription on denigrating minority faiths and "preach[ing] conversion," and that the local government setting made the risk of coercion greater.

3. *Public religious displays.* Clearly, it would violate the Establishment Clause for government to place a Latin cross on the dome of the state capitol. Such symbolism would clearly constitute religious "endorsement." Even under a narrow nonpreferentialist view, government is barred from the symbolic union of a church and the state. The Establishment Clause, at a minimum, prohibits theocracy. But may a government place, or permit others to place, elsewhere on public property a display depicting the birth of Christ at Christmas or a menorah commemorating the Jewish festival of Chanukah? Does such a display implicate the Establishment Clause to the same extent as the cross on the capitol? Will its predominant meaning appear religious? Regardless of the surrounding context? What if private parties finance the display? Will such a display likely be attributed to the government? The following cases consider the constitutionality of such public displays.

Lynch v. Donnelly

465 U.S. 668, 104 S. Ct. 1355, 79 L. Ed. 2d 604 (1984).

■ CHIEF JUSTICE BURGER delivered the opinion of the Court.

[Each] year, in cooperation with the downtown retail merchants' association, the City of Pawtucket, Rhode Island, erects a Christmas display as part of its observance of the Christmas holiday season. The display is situated in a park owned by a nonprofit organization and located in the heart of the shopping district. The display is essentially like those to be found in hundreds of towns or cities across the Nation—often on public grounds—during the Christmas season. The Pawtucket display comprises many of the figures and decorations traditionally associated with Christmas, including, among other things, a Santa Claus house, reindeer pulling Santa's sleigh, candy-striped poles, a Christmas tree, carolers, cutout figures representing such characters as a clown, an elephant, and a teddy bear, hundreds of colored lights, a large banner that reads "SEASONS GREETINGS," and the crèche at issue here. All components of this display are owned by the City. The crèche, which has been included in the display for 40 or more years, consists of the traditional figures, including the Infant Jesus, Mary and Joseph, angels, shepherds, kings, and animals, all ranging in height from 5 inches to 5 feet. In 1973, when the present crèche was acquired, it cost the City $1365; it now is valued at $200. The erection and dismantling of the crèche costs the City about $20 per year; nominal expenses are incurred in lighting the crèche. No money has been expended on its maintenance for the past 10 years. The District Court held that the City's inclusion of the crèche in the display violates the Establishment Clause. [A] divided panel of the [First] Circuit affirmed. [We] reverse.

[There] is an unbroken history of official acknowledgment by all three branches of government of the role of religion in American life from at least 1789. [Our] history is replete with official references to the value and invocation of Divine guidance in deliberations and pronouncements of the Founding Fathers and contemporary leaders. [Long] before Independence, a day of Thanksgiving was celebrated as a religious holiday to give thanks for the bounties of Nature as gifts from God. [Executive Orders] and other official announcements of Presidents and of the Congress have proclaimed both Christmas and Thanksgiving National Holidays in religious terms. [Thus,] it is clear that Government has long recognized—indeed it has subsidized—holidays with religious significance. Other examples of reference to our religious heritage are found in the statutorily prescribed national motto "In God We Trust," which Congress and the President mandated for our currency, and in the language "One nation under God," as part of the Pledge of Allegiance to the [American flag]. [One] cannot look at even this brief resume without finding that our history is pervaded by expressions of religious beliefs such as are found in Zorach. Equally pervasive is the evidence of accommodation of all faiths and all forms of religious expression, and hostility toward [none].

This history may help explain why the Court consistently has declined to take a rigid, absolutist view of the Establishment Clause. [In] our modern, complex society, whose traditions and constitutional underpinnings rest on and encourage diversity and pluralism in all areas, an absolutist approach in applying the Establishment Clause is simplistic and has been uniformly rejected by the Court. Rather than mechanically invalidating all governmental conduct or statutes that confer benefits or give special recognition to religion in general or to one faith—as an absolutist approach would dictate—the Court has scrutinized challenged legislation or official conduct to determine whether, in reality, it establishes a religion or religious faith, or tends to do so. In each case, the inquiry calls for line drawing; no fixed, per se rule can be framed. [In] the line-drawing process we have often found it useful to inquire whether the challenged law or conduct has a secular purpose, whether its principal or primary effect is to advance or inhibit religion, and whether it creates an excessive entanglement of government with religion. [Lemon.] But, we have repeatedly emphasized our unwillingness to be confined to any single test or criterion in this sensitive area.

[In] this case, the focus of our inquiry must be on the crèche in the context of the Christmas season. [Viewed in this context,] there is insufficient evidence to establish that the inclusion of the crèche is a purposeful or surreptitious effort to express some kind of subtle governmental advocacy of a particular religious message. In a pluralistic society a variety of motives and purposes are implicated. [The] crèche in the display depicts the historical origins of this traditional event long recognized as a National Holiday. [The] display is sponsored by the City to celebrate the Holiday and to depict the origins of that Holiday. These are legitimate secular purposes.

[The] District Court found that the primary effect of including the crèche is to confer a substantial and impermissible benefit on religion in general and on the Christian faith in particular. [But we] are unable to discern a greater aid to religion deriving from inclusion of the crèche than from [endorsements] previously held not violative of the Establishment Clause [e.g., in McGowan, Zorach, and Marsh.] The dissent asserts that some observers may perceive that the City has aligned itself with the Christian faith by including a Christian symbol in its display and that this serves to advance religion. We can assume, arguendo, that the display advances religion in a sense; but our precedents plainly contemplate that on occasion some advancement of religion will result from governmental action. [Here,] whatever benefit to one faith or religion or to all religions, is indirect, remote and incidental; display of the crèche is no more an advancement or endorsement of religion than the Congressional and Executive recognition of the origins of the Holiday itself as "Christ's Mass", or the exhibition of literally hundreds of religious paintings in governmentally supported [museums].

[To] forbid the use of this one passive symbol—the crèche—at the very time people are taking note of the season with Christmas hymns and carols in public schools and other public places [would] be a stilted over-reaction contrary to our history and to our holdings. If the presence of the crèche in this display violates the Establishment Clause, a host of other forms of taking official note of Christmas, and of our religious heritage, are equally offensive to the Constitution. The Court has acknowledged that the "fears and political problems" that gave rise to the Religion Clauses in the 18th century are of far less concern today. [Everson.] We are unable to perceive the Archbishop of Canterbury, the Vicar of Rome, or other powerful religious leaders behind every public acknowledgment of the religious heritage long officially recognized by the three constitutional branches of government. Any notion that these symbols pose a real danger of establishment of a state church is farfetched indeed. [Reversed.]

■ JUSTICE O'CONNOR, concurring.

I concur in the opinion of the Court. I write separately to suggest a clarification of our Establishment Clause doctrine. The suggested approach leads to the same result in this case as that taken by the Court, and the Court's opinion, as I read it, is consistent with my analysis.

The Establishment Clause prohibits government from making adherence to a religion relevant in any way to a person's standing in the political community. Government can run afoul of that prohibition in two principal ways. One is excessive entanglement with religious institutions, which may interfere with the independence of the institutions, give the institutions access to government or governmental powers not fully shared by nonadherents of the religion, and foster the creation of political constituencies defined along religious lines. The second and more direct infringement is government endorsement or disapproval of religion. Endorsement sends a message to nonadherents that they are outsiders, not full members of the political community, and an accompanying message to adherents that they are insiders, favored members of the political community. Disapproval sends the opposite message.

[The] central issue in this case is whether Pawtucket has endorsed Christianity by its display of the crèche. To answer that question, we must examine both what Pawtucket intended to communicate in displaying the crèche and what message the City's display actually conveyed. The purpose and effect prongs of the Lemon test represent these two aspects of the meaning of the City's action. [The] proper inquiry under the purpose prong of Lemon, I submit, is whether the government intends to convey a message of endorsement or disapproval of religion. Applying that formulation to this case, I would find that Pawtucket did not intend to convey any message of endorsement of Christianity or disapproval of non-Christian religions. The evident purpose of including the crèche in the larger display was not promotion of the religious content of the crèche but celebration of the public holiday through its traditional symbols. Celebration of public holidays, which have cultural significance even if they also have religious aspects, is a legitimate secular [purpose].

[The] effect prong of the Lemon test [requires] that a government practice not have the effect of communicating a message of government endorsement or disapproval of religion. It is only practices having that effect, whether intentionally or unintentionally, that make religion relevant, in reality or public perception, to status in the political community. Pawtucket's display of its crèche, I believe, does not communicate a message that the government intends to endorse the Christian beliefs represented by the crèche. Although the religious and indeed sectarian significance of the crèche [is] not neutralized by the setting, the overall holiday setting changes what viewers may fairly understand to be the purpose of the display—as a typical museum setting, though not neutralizing the religious content of a religious painting, negates any message of endorsement of that content. The display celebrates a public holiday, and no one contends that declaration of that holiday is understood to be an endorsement of religion. The holiday itself has very strong secular components and traditions. Government celebration of the holiday [generally] is not understood to endorse the religious content of the holiday. [The] crèche is a traditional symbol of the holiday that is very commonly displayed along with purely secular symbols, as it was in Pawtucket.

These features combine to make the government's display of the crèche in this particular physical setting no more an endorsement of religion than such governmental acknowledgments of religion as [printing] "In God We Trust," on coins, and opening court sessions with "God save the United States and this honorable court." Those government acknowledgments of religion serve, in the only ways reasonably possible in our culture, the legitimate secular purposes of solemnizing public occasions, expressing confidence in the future, and encouraging the recognition of what is worthy of appreciation in society. For that reason, and because of their history and ubiquity, those practices are not understood as conveying government approval of particular religious beliefs. The display of the crèche likewise [cannot] fairly be understood to convey a message of government endorsement of [religion].

■ JUSTICE BRENNAN, with whom JUSTICES MARSHALL, BLACKMUN and STEVENS join, dissenting.

[In] my view, Pawtucket's maintenance and display at public expense of a symbol as distinctively sectarian as a crèche simply cannot be squared with our prior cases. [The] City's inclusion of the crèche in its Christmas display simply does not reflect a "clearly secular purpose." [The] nativity scene, unlike every other element of the Hodgson Park display, reflects a sectarian exclusivity that the avowed purposes of celebrating the holiday season and promoting retail commerce simply do not encompass. [The] inclusion of a distinctively religious element like the crèche [demonstrates] that a narrower sectarian purpose lay behind the decision to include a nativity scene.

[The] "primary effect" of including a nativity scene in the City's display [is] to place the government's imprimatur of approval on the particular religious beliefs exemplified by the crèche. [The] effect on minority religious groups, as well as on those who may reject all religion, is to convey the message that their views are not similarly worthy of public recognition nor entitled to public support. [Finally], it is evident that Pawtucket's inclusion of a crèche [does] pose a significant threat of fostering "excessive entanglement."

[The] Court, by focusing on the holiday "context" in which the nativity scene appeared, seeks to explain away the clear religious import of the crèche. [It] blinks reality to claim, as the Court does, that by including such a distinctively religious object as the crèche in its Christmas display, Pawtucket has done no more than made use of a "traditional" symbol of the holiday, and has thereby purged the crèche of its religious content and conferred only an "incidental and indirect" benefit on religion. [Even] in the context of Pawtucket's seasonal celebration, the crèche retains a specifically Christian religious meaning. [It] is the chief symbol of the characteristically Christian belief that a divine Savior was brought into the world and that the purpose of this miraculous birth was to illuminate a path toward salvation and redemption. For Christians, that path is exclusive, precious and holy. But for those who do not share these beliefs, the symbolic re-enactment of the birth of a divine being who has been miraculously incarnated as a man stands as a dramatic reminder of their differences with Christian faith. [To] be so excluded on religious grounds by one's elected government is an insult and an injury that, until today, could not be countenanced by the Establishment Clause.

[The] Court apparently believes that once it finds that the designation of Christmas as a public holiday is constitutionally acceptable, it is then free to conclude that virtually every form of governmental association with the celebration of the holiday is also constitutional. The vice of this dangerously superficial argument is that it overlooks the fact that the Christmas holiday in our national culture contains both secular and sectarian elements. To say that government may recognize the holiday's traditional, secular elements of gift giving, public festivities and community spirit, does not mean that government may indiscriminately embrace the distinctively sectarian aspects of the holiday.

When government decides to recognize Christmas day as a public holiday, it does no more than accommodate the calendar of public activities to the plain fact that many Americans will expect on that day to spend time visiting with their families, attending religious services, and perhaps enjoying some respite from pre-holiday activities. The Free Exercise Clause, of course, does not necessarily compel the government to provide this accommodation, but neither is the Establishment Clause offended by such a step. Cf. [Zorach]. [If] public officials go further and participate in the *secular* celebration of Christmas—by, for example, decorating public places with such secular images as wreaths, garlands or Santa Claus figures—they move closer to the limits of their constitutional power but nevertheless remain within the boundaries set by the Establishment Clause. But when those officials participate in or appear to endorse the distinctively religious elements of this otherwise secular event, they encroach upon First Amendment freedoms. For it is at that point that the government brings to the forefront the theological content of the holiday, and places the prestige, power and financial support of a civil authority in the service of a particular faith.

The inclusion of a crèche in Pawtucket's otherwise secular celebration of Christmas clearly violates these principles. Unlike such secular figures as Santa Claus, reindeer and carolers, a nativity scene represents far more than a mere "traditional" symbol of Christmas. The essence of the crèche's symbolic purpose and effect is to prompt the observer to experience a sense of simple awe and wonder appropriate to the contemplation of one of the central elements of Christian dogma—that God sent His son into the world to be a Messiah. Contrary to the Court's suggestion, the crèche is far from a mere representation of a "particular historic religious event." It is, instead, best understood as a mystical re-creation of an event that lies at the heart of Christian faith. To suggest, as the Court does, that such a symbol is merely "traditional" and therefore no different from Santa's house or reindeer is not only offensive to those for whom the crèche has profound significance, but insulting to those who insist for religious or personal reasons that the story of Christ is in no sense a part of "history" nor an unavoidable element of our national ["heritage"].

[The] Court has never comprehensively addressed the extent to which government may acknowledge religion by, for example, incorporating religious references into public ceremonies, [and] I do not presume to offer a comprehensive approach. Nevertheless, [at] least three principles—tracing the narrow channels which government acknowledgments must follow to satisfy the Establishment Clause—may be identified. First, although the government may not be compelled to do so by the Free Exercise Clause, it may, consistently with the Establishment Clause, act to accommodate to some extent the opportunities of individuals to practice their religion. [That] principle would justify government's decision to declare December 25th a public holiday. Second, our cases recognize that while a particular governmental practice may have derived from religious motivations and retain certain religious connotations, it is nonetheless permissible for the government to pursue the practice when it is continued today solely for secular reasons. [McGowan.] Thanksgiving Day, in my view, fits easily within this principle.

Finally, we have noted that government cannot be completely prohibited from recognizing in its public actions the religious beliefs and practices of the

American people as an aspect of our national history and culture. While I remain uncertain about these questions, I would suggest that such practices as the designation of "In God We Trust" as our national motto [and] the references to God contained in the Pledge of Allegiance can best be understood [as] a form of "ceremonial deism," protected from Establishment Clause scrutiny chiefly because they have lost through rote repetition any significant religious content. Moreover, these references are uniquely suited to serve such wholly secular purposes as solemnizing public occasions, or inspiring commitment to meet some national challenge in a manner that simply could not be fully served in our culture if government were limited to purely non-religious phrases. The practices by which the government has long acknowledged religion are therefore probably necessary to serve certain secular functions, and that necessity, coupled with their long history, gives those practices an essentially secular meaning. The crèche fits none of these categories. [By] insisting that such a distinctively sectarian message is merely an unobjectionable part of our "religious heritage," the Court takes a long step backwards to the days when Justice Brewer could arrogantly declare for the Court that "this is a Christian nation." Church of Holy Trinity v. United States, 143 U.S. 457 (1892). Those days, I had thought, were forever put behind us by the Court's decision in [Engel], in which we rejected a similar argument [in defense of the Regents' Prayer].

The American historical experience concerning the public celebration of Christmas, if carefully examined, provides no support for the Court's decision. [Attention] to the details of history should not blind us to the cardinal purposes of the Establishment Clause, nor limit our central inquiry in these cases—whether the challenged practices "threaten those consequences which the Framers deeply feared." [The] intent of the Framers with respect to the public display of nativity scenes is virtually impossible to discern primarily because the widespread celebration of Christmas did not emerge in its present form until well into the [nineteenth century]. [There] is no evidence whatsoever that the Framers would have expressly approved a Federal celebration of the Christmas holiday including public displays of a nativity scene.

[Pawtucket's] action should be recognized for what it is: a coercive, though perhaps small, step toward establishing the sectarian preferences of the majority at the expense of the minority, accomplished by placing public facilities and funds in support of the religious symbolism and theological tidings that the crèche [conveys].

■ JUSTICE BLACKMUN, joined by JUSTICE STEVENS, dissenting.

The crèche has been relegated to the role of a neutral harbinger of the holiday season, useful for commercial purposes, but devoid of any inherent meaning and incapable of enhancing the religious tenor of a display of which it is an integral part. The city has its victory—but it is a Pyrrhic one indeed. The import of [the decision] is to encourage use of the crèche in a municipally sponsored display, a setting where Christians feel constrained in acknowledging its symbolic meaning and non-Christians feel alienated by its presence. Surely, this is a misuse of a sacred symbol.

———

APPLYING THE ENDORSEMENT TEST

1. *Holiday displays.* In **Allegheny County v. American Civil Liberties Union [ACLU]**, 492 U.S. 573 (1989), a majority of the Court held unconstitutional a freestanding display of a nativity scene on the main staircase of a county courthouse. Unlike the display in the Lynch case, the crèche belonged to a Catholic organization and was not surrounded by figures of Santa Claus or other Christmas decorations. But a different majority in the same case upheld the display of a Jewish Chanukah menorah placed next to a Christmas tree and a sign saying "Salute to Liberty" in the City-County Building, a block away from the courthouse. The menorah was owned by a Jewish group, but stored, erected, and removed annually by the city.

In the course of reaching these holdings, the Court, by a 5–4 majority, adopted Justice O'Connor's "no endorsement" analysis as a general approach to Establishment Clause adjudication. Justice BLACKMUN, joined by Justices Brennan, Marshall, O'Connor and Stevens, noted: "In recent years, we have paid particularly close attention to whether the challenged governmental practice either has the purpose or effect of 'endorsing' religion. [Of course,] the word 'endorsement' is not self-defining. [But whether] the key word is 'endorsement,' 'favoritism,' or 'promotion,' the essential principle remains the same. The Establishment Clause, at the very least, prohibits government from appearing to take a position on questions of religious belief or from 'making adherence to a religion relevant in any way to a person's standing in the political community.' [Lynch (O'Connor, J., concurring).]"

Justice KENNEDY, joined by Chief Justice Rehnquist and Justices White and Scalia, rejected the majority's "endorsement" analysis, viewing it as reflecting "an unjustified hostility toward religion." The dissent argued for a narrower test of establishment: "government may not coerce anyone to support or participate in any religion or its exercise; and it may not, in the guise of avoiding hostility or callous indifference, give direct benefits to religion in such a degree that it in fact 'establishes a [state] religion or religious faith, or tends to do so.' [Lynch.] [But] non-coercive government action within the realm of flexible accommodation or passive acknowledgement of existing symbols does not violate the Establishment Clause unless it benefits religion in a way more direct and more substantial than practices that are accepted in our national heritage." He also objected that Justice O'Connor's endorsement test disregarded history: "Few of our traditional practices recognizing the part religion plays in our society [such as Thanksgiving Proclamations and legislative prayer] can withstand scrutiny under a faithful application of this formula." Finally, he argued, the "endorsement" approach was "unworkable in practice": it "threatens to trivialize constitutional adjudication [by embracing] a jurisprudence of minutiae" governing the detailed context of governmental displays.

Justice O'CONNOR, joined by Justices Brennan and Stevens, defended the endorsement test against Justice Kennedy's attack and criticized his proposed narrower test: "An Establishment Clause standard that prohibits only 'coercive' practices or overt efforts at government proselytization, but fails to take account of the numerous more subtle ways that government can show favoritism to particular beliefs or convey a message of disapproval to others, would not, in my view, adequately protect the religious liberty or respect the religious diversity of the members of our pluralistic political community. Thus, this Court has never relied on coercion alone as the touchstone of Establishment Clause analysis. To require a showing of coercion, even indirect coercion, as an essential element of an Establishment Clause violation would make the Free Exercise Clause a redundancy."

A 5–4 majority of the Court found the crèche display here unconstitutional. Justice BLACKMUN, joined by Justices Brennan, Marshall, O'Connor and Stevens, noted that "here, unlike in Lynch, nothing in the context of the display detracts from the crèche's religious message." The display in Lynch, for example, was accompanied by Santa's house, reindeer and a talking wishing well; here, the crèche "stands alone." To the majority, the crèche conveyed an essentially religious message and constituted an endorsement of Christian doctrine. Justice KENNEDY, joined by Chief Justice Rehnquist and Justices White and Scalia, dissented from this holding. In his view, the crèche display was a permissible, noncoercive accommodation of religious faith: "The crèche [is a] purely passive symbol[ ] of [a] religious holiday. Passersby who disagree with [its] message are free to ignore [it], or even to turn their backs, just as they are free to do so when they disagree with any other form of government speech." Justice Kennedy conceded that "[s]ymbolic recognition or accommodation of religious faith may violate the Clause in an extreme case, [such as] the permanent erection of a large Latin cross on the roof of city hall." But the crèche here, in his view, represented no similar "effort to proselytize on behalf of a particular religion."

By a vote of 6–3, however, the Court upheld the display of the menorah. Justice BLACKMUN, writing here only for himself, found that the menorah, while "a religious symbol," conveyed a message that was "not exclusively religious." He emphasized that it stood next to a Christmas tree and a sign saluting liberty and thus had "an 'overall holiday setting' that represents both Christmas and Chanukah—two holidays, not one." He acknowledged that a simultaneous endorsement of Judaism and Christianity would still violate the Establishment Clause, but insisted that government may acknowledge both Christmas and Chanukah as secular holidays. Moreover, he argued, "the relevant question [is] whether the combined display of the tree, the sign, and the menorah has the effect of endorsing both Christian and Jewish faiths, or rather simply recognizes that both Christmas and Chanukah are part of the same winter-holiday season, which has attained a secular status in our society. [The] latter seems far more plausible and is also in line with Lynch." Justice O'CONNOR agreed that the menorah display was constitutional but criticized Justice Blackmun for obscuring the religious nature of the menorah and the holiday of Chanukah. She added: "One need not characterize Chanukah as a 'secular holiday' or strain to argue that the menorah has a 'secular dimension' in order to conclude that [the] display does not convey a message of endorsement of Judaism or of religion in general." She concluded that the joint display as a whole "conveyed a message of pluralism and freedom of belief during the holiday season" and was therefore permissible.

Justice BRENNAN, joined by Justices Marshall and Stevens, dissented with respect to the menorah, finding that it was "indisputably a religious symbol, used ritually in a celebration that has deep religious significance." He concluded that government may not "promote pluralism by sponsoring or condoning displays having strong religious associations on its property." Justice STEVENS, joined by Justices Brennan and Marshall, also dissented with respect to the menorah, arguing that the Establishment Clause "should be construed to create a strong presumption against the display of religious symbols on public property. There is always a risk that such symbols will offend nonmembers of the faith being advertised as well as adherents who consider the particular advertisement disrespectful."

Are the distinctions drawn in Allegheny between the crèche and the menorah display persuasive? Which matters more, the location or the surrounding elements? Is it fair to criticize the opinion as more about "interior decorating" than law? Or does the Court's focus on the perceptions of the reasonable observer capture accurately the concerns animating the Establishment Clause?

2. *Ku Klux Klan cross.* In **Capitol Square Review Board v. Pinette**, 515 U.S. 753 (1995), the Court held that the Free Speech Clause compelled the city of Columbus, Ohio, to permit the Ku Klux Klan to erect a large unattended Latin cross on a public square adjacent to the Statehouse, and that the Establishment Clause did not forbid it. Having found that the Free Speech Clause otherwise barred content-based discrimination against the cross because the setting was a public forum (see p. 360), the Court held, by a vote of 7–2, that permitting the cross equal access to public property along with other unattended private symbols would not, as the city argued, violate the Establishment Clause, even assuming that the Klan cross was an entirely religious and not political symbol (Justice Thomas alone would have treated it as the latter). The Court was divided on the appropriate Establishment Clause analysis, but there were still five votes—those of the concurring and dissenting justices—for applying the "endorsement" test.

While Justice SCALIA wrote for seven Justices on the result, he wrote only for a four-Justice plurality in his reasoning. Joined by Chief Justice Rehnquist and Justices Kennedy and Thomas, he acknowledged that the endorsement test had been applied in previous cases but would not have applied it here. He would have paid no attention to what any observer would have thought, reasonably or otherwise, about whether the Christian symbolism of the Klan cross ought to be attributed to the city government of Columbus: "Petitioners argue [that], because an observer might mistake private expression for officially endorsed religious expression, [permitting the cross would violate the Establishment Clause.] [Petitioners] rely heavily on Allegheny County and Lynch, but each is easily distinguished. In Allegheny County we held that the display of a privately-sponsored crèche on the 'Grand Staircase' of the Allegheny County Courthouse violated the Establishment Clause. That staircase was not, however, open to all on an equal basis, so the County was favoring sectarian religious expression. [In] Lynch we held that a city's display of a crèche did not violate the Establishment Clause because, in context, the display did not endorse religion. [The] case neither holds nor even remotely assumes that the government's neutral treatment of private religious expression can be unconstitutional. [What] distinguishes Allegheny County and [Lynch] is the difference between government speech and private speech. Petitioners assert, in effect, that that distinction disappears when the private speech is conducted too close to the symbols of government [and thus] private speech can be mistaken for government speech. That proposition cannot be accepted, at least where, as here, the government has not fostered or encouraged the mistake. [It] has radical implications for our public policy to suggest that neutral laws are invalid whenever hypothetical observers may—even reasonably—confuse an incidental benefit to religion with state endorsement." The plurality would have adopted instead a per se rule: "Religious expression cannot violate the Establishment Clause where it (1) is purely private and (2) occurs in a traditional or designated public forum, publicly announced and open to all on equal terms."

Justice O'CONNOR wrote a concurrence joined by Justices Souter and Breyer, and Justice SOUTER wrote a concurrence joined by Justices O'Connor and Breyer. The three concurring Justices expressly reaffirmed Justice O'Connor's endorsement test. Justice O'Connor wrote: "I part company with the plurality on a fundamental point: I disagree that 'it has radical implications for our public policy to suggest that neutral laws are invalid whenever hypothetical observers may—even reasonably—confuse an incidental benefit to religion with State endorsement.' On the contrary, when the reasonable observer would view a government practice as endorsing religion, I believe that it is our duty to hold the practice invalid. The plurality today takes an exceedingly narrow view of the Establishment Clause that is out of step both with the Court's prior cases and with well-established notions of what the Constitution requires. The Clause is more than a negative prohibition against certain narrowly defined forms of government favoritism; it also imposes affirmative obligations that may require a State, in some situations, to take steps to avoid being perceived as supporting or endorsing a private religious message."

The concurring Justices would have required Columbus to exclude the cross from the public square if they had thought its message would be attributed to the city, but they did not view such attribution as likely in the circumstances of this case. Justice O'Connor emphasized that the cross was in the public square rather than upon a government building and that "the reasonable observer" would be "fully aware that Capitol Square is a public space in which a multiplicity of groups, both secular and religious, engage in expressive conduct." Justice Souter noted that the Klan, in support of its application, had stated that the cross would be accompanied by a disclaimer, "legible 'from a distance,' explaining that the cross was erected by private individuals 'without government support,' " and stressed that the city could easily have required the Klan to affix a sign to the cross disclaiming any government endorsement of the Christian faith.

Justices STEVENS and GINSBURG each filed a dissent. Justice Stevens wrote that "the Constitution generally forbids the placement of a symbol of a religious character in, on, or before a seat of government." In his view, "the Establishment Clause prohibits government from allowing, and thus endorsing, unattended displays that take a position on a religious issue. If the State allows such stationary displays in front of its seat of government, viewers will reasonably assume that it approves of them. [A] reasonable observer would likely infer endorsement from the location of the cross erected by the Klan in this case. Even if the disclaimer at the foot of the cross (which stated that the cross was placed there by a private organization) were legible, that inference would remain, because a property owner's decision to allow a third party to place a sign on her property conveys the same message of endorsement as if she had erected it herself." Justice Ginsburg emphasized that the disclaimer offered here was inadequate, deferring the question whether a disclaimer could ever dispel the Establishment Clause problem.

3. *Coercion, endorsement, acknowledgment and the Lemon test.* Do the religious symbolism cases from Lynch to Allegheny and Pinette retain any continuing analytic role for the three-part Lemon test? Or did the

Court in these cases effectively adopt a different three-part test: coercion and endorsement are impermissible under the Establishment Clause, but mere acknowledgment of religion is not? On this analysis, the school cases are treated as instances of coercion, even if it means stretching that concept quite far to embrace even psychological coercion. The crèche in Allegheny is invalidated as endorsement. But Sunday closings, legislative prayer, and crèches or menorahs in secularized contexts each count as mere government acknowledgments of religion, comparable to religious allusions in holiday proclamations, on the currency, in the Pledge of Allegiance, and in the art on the walls of public museums. Are such holdings sufficiently respectful toward religion? See Kurland, "The Religion Clauses and the Burger Court," 34 Cath. U. L. Rev. 1 (1984) (arguing that the Court's treatment of the crèche in Lynch "further detracts from the religious significance of the Christmas holiday, [which] every year [pays] more homage to Mammon than to God").

Can the endorsement test be objectively administered, or will it always tend to be administered from the perspective of members of majority faiths? See Van Alstyne, "Trends in the Supreme Court: Mr. Jefferson's Crumbling Wall—A Comment on [Lynch]," 1984 Duke L.J. 770 (suggesting that Lynch reflected "religious ethnocentrism"); Tushnet, "The Constitution of Religion," 18 Conn. L. Rev. 701 (1986) ("Judges will always be broadly representative of the general population, and will be susceptible to all the distortions of interpretation that membership in the majority entails."). Can the endorsement test be consistently administered? Why is a crèche less of an endorsement when surrounded by reindeer and talking wishing wells than when it is standing alone? For commentary favorable toward the endorsement test, see Beschle, "The Conservative as Liberal: The Religion Clauses, Liberal Neutrality, and the Approach of Justice O'Connor," 62 Notre Dame L. Rev. 151 (1987) and Marshall, " 'We Know It When We See It': The Supreme Court and Establishment," 59 S. Cal. L. Rev. 495 (1986). For commentary critical of the test, see Smith, "Symbols, Perceptions, and Doctrinal Illusions: Establishment Neutrality and the 'No Endorsement' Test," 86 Mich. L. Rev. 266 (1987).

4. ***The Ten Commandments.*** Recall that the Court in Stone v. Graham invalidated the posting of the Ten Commandments in a public school classroom. Is the posting or placement of the Ten Commandments in other public settings more permissible? Less coercive? Less likely to appear to be an endorsement? Several prominent public controversies over Ten Commandments displays culminated in a pair of cases decided by the Court at the end of Justice O'Connor's last full Term on the Court. Justice Breyer provided the decisive vote yielding opposite outcomes in the two cases. On what grounds does he distinguish the two Ten Commandment displays for Establishment Clause purposes? What test does the Court apply in the cases that follow? Does the Lemon test make a comeback?

McCreary County v. ACLU of Kentucky

545 U.S. 844, 125 S. Ct. 2722, 162 L. Ed. 2d 729 (2005).

■ JUSTICE SOUTER delivered the opinion of the Court [in which JUSTICES STEVENS, O'CONNOR, GINSBURG, and BREYER joined].

I.   [In] the summer of 1999, petitioners McCreary County and Pulaski County, Kentucky (hereinafter Counties), put up in their respective courthouses large, gold-framed copies of an abridged text of the King James version of the Ten Commandments, including a citation to the Book of Exodus. [In] each county, the hallway display was "readily visible to . . . county citizens who use the courthouse to conduct their civic business." [In] November 1999, respondents American Civil Liberties Union of Kentucky sued the Counties in Federal District Court. Within a month, [the] legislative body of each County authorized a second, expanded display, by nearly identical resolutions reciting that the Ten Commandments are "the precedent legal code upon which the civil and criminal codes of . . . Kentucky are founded." [After] the District Court [ordered] that the "display . . . be removed from [each] County Courthouse," [the] Counties [installed] another display in each courthouse, [consisting] of nine framed documents of equal size, one of them setting out the Ten Commandments explicitly identified as the "King James Version" at Exodus 20:3–17. Assembled with the Commandments are framed copies of the Magna Carta, the Declaration of Independence, the Bill of Rights, the lyrics of the Star Spangled Banner, the Mayflower Compact, the National Motto, the Preamble to the Kentucky Constitution, and a picture of Lady Justice.

II.   [Despite] the intuitive importance of official purpose to the realization of Establishment Clause values, the Counties ask us to abandon Lemon's purpose test, or at least to truncate any enquiry into purpose here. [They argue] true "purpose" is unknowable, and its search merely an excuse for courts to act selectively and unpredictably in picking out evidence of subjective intent. The assertions are [unconvincing.] Governmental purpose is a key element of a good deal of constitutional doctrine. [In] Establishment Clause analysis [an] understanding of official objective emerges from readily discoverable fact, without any judicial psychoanalysis of a drafter's heart of hearts. The eyes that look to purpose belong to an " 'objective observer,' " one who takes account of the traditional external signs that show up in the " 'text, legislative history, and implementation of the statute,' " or comparable official act. [The] Counties [want] an absentminded objective observer, not one presumed to be familiar with the history of the government's actions and competent to learn what history has to show. The Counties' position just bucks common sense: reasonable observers have reasonable memories, and our precedents sensibly forbid an observer "to turn a blind eye to the context in which [the] policy arose."

III.   We take Stone v. Graham (1980; p. 751), as the initial legal benchmark, our only case dealing with the constitutionality of displaying the Commandments. Stone recognized that the Commandments are an "instrument of religion." [The] display rejected in Stone had two obvious similarities to the first one in the sequence here: both set out a text of the Commandments as distinct from any traditionally symbolic representation, and each stood alone, not part of an arguably secular display. Stone stressed the significance of integrating the Commandments into a secular scheme to forestall the broadcast of an otherwise clearly religious message and for good reason, the Commandments being a central point of reference in the religious and moral history of Jews and Christians. They proclaim the existence of a monotheistic god (no other gods). They regulate details of religious obligation (no graven images, no sabbath breaking, no vain oath swearing). And they unmistakably rest even the universally accepted prohibitions (as against murder, theft, and the like) on the sanction of the divinity proclaimed at the beginning of the text. [The] Counties' solo exhibit here did nothing more to counter the sectarian implication than the postings at issue in Stone. [When] the government initiates an effort to place this statement alone in public view, a religious object is unmistakable.

[In the] second display, unlike the first, the Commandments were not hung in isolation, [but] include[d] the statement of the government's purpose expressly set out in the county resolutions, and underscored it by juxtaposing the Commandments to other documents with highlighted references to God as their sole common element. The display's unstinting focus was on religious passages, showing that the Counties were posting the Commandments precisely because of their sectarian content. That demonstration of the government's objective was enhanced by serial religious references and the accompanying resolution's claim about the embodiment of ethics in Christ. Together, the display and resolution presented an indisputable, and undisputed, showing of an impermissible purpose.

[After] the Counties changed lawyers, they mounted a third display. The result was the "Foundations of American Law and Government" exhibit, which placed the Commandments in the company of other documents the Counties thought especially significant in the historical foundation of American government. [The] extraordinary resolutions for the second display passed just months earlier were not repealed or otherwise repudiated. Indeed, the sectarian spirit of the common resolution found enhanced expression in the third display, which quoted more of the purely religious language of the Commandments than the first two displays had done. No reasonable observer could swallow the claim that the Counties had cast off the objective so unmistakable in the earlier displays. [He] would probably suspect that the Counties were simply reaching for any way to keep a religious document on the walls of courthouses constitutionally required to embody religious neutrality.

[We] do not decide that the Counties' past actions forever taint any effort on their part to deal with the subject matter. We hold only that purpose needs to be taken seriously under the Establishment Clause and needs to be understood in light of context; an implausible claim that governmental purpose has changed should not carry the day in a court of law any more than in a head with common sense. [Nor] do we have occasion here to hold that a sacred text can never be integrated constitutionally into a governmental display on the subject of law, or American history. We do not forget, and in this litigation have frequently been reminded, that our own courtroom frieze include[s] the figure of Moses holding tablets exhibiting a portion of the Hebrew text of the later, secularly phrased Commandments; in the company of 17 other lawgivers, most of them secular figures, there is no risk that Moses would strike an observer as evidence that the National Government was violating neutrality in religion.

IV. [Justice Souter then cited Jefferson and Madison to disagree with Justice Scalia's view of the founding, largely echoing the views in his concurrence in Lee v. Weisman (see p. 737)]

[While] the dissent fails to show a consistent original understanding from which to argue that the neutrality principle should be rejected, it does manage to deliver a surprise [in saying] that the deity the Framers had in mind was the God of monotheism, with the consequence that government may espouse a tenet of traditional monotheism. This is truly a remarkable view. [It] apparently means that government should be free to approve the core beliefs of a favored religion over the tenets of others, a view that should trouble anyone who prizes religious liberty. Certainly history cannot justify it; on the contrary, history shows that the religion of concern to the Framers was not that of the monotheistic faiths generally, but Christianity in particular, a fact that no member of this Court takes as a premise for construing the Religion Clauses.

[We] are centuries away from the St. Bartholomew's Day massacre and the treatment of heretics in early Massachusetts, but the divisiveness of religion in current public life is inescapable. This is no time to deny the prudence of understanding the Establishment Clause to require the Government to stay neutral on religious belief, which is reserved for the conscience of the individual. [Affirmed.]

■ JUSTICE O'CONNOR, concurring.

[Given] the history of this particular display of the Ten Commandments, the Court correctly finds an Establishment Clause violation. The purpose behind the counties' display conveys an unmistakable message of endorsement to the reasonable observer. [M]any Americans find the Commandments in accord with their personal beliefs. But we do not count heads before enforcing the First Amendment. Nor can we accept the theory that Americans who do not accept the Commandments' validity are outside the First Amendment's protections. [It] is true that the Framers lived at a time when our national religious diversity was neither as robust nor as well recognized as it is now. They may not have foreseen the variety of religions for which this Nation would eventually provide a home. They surely could not have predicted new religions, some of them born in this country. But they did know that line-drawing between religions is an enterprise that, once begun, has no logical stopping point. [The] Religion Clauses protect adherents of all religions, as well as those who believe in no religion at all.

■ JUSTICE SCALIA, with whom CHIEF JUSTICE REHNQUIST and JUSTICE THOMAS join, and with whom JUSTICE KENNEDY joins as to Parts II and III, dissenting.

I.   On September 11, 2001 I was attending in Rome, Italy an international conference of judges and lawyers. That night and the next morning virtually all of the participants watched, in their hotel rooms, the address to the Nation by the President of the United States concerning the murderous attacks upon the Twin Towers and the Pentagon, in which thousands of Americans had been killed. The address ended, as Presidential addresses often do, with the prayer "God bless America." The next afternoon I was approached by one of the judges from a European country, who, after extending his profound condolences for my country's loss, sadly observed "How I wish that the Head of State of my country, at a similar time of national tragedy and distress, could conclude his address 'God bless _____.' It is of course absolutely forbidden." That is one model of the relationship between church and state—a model spread across Europe by the armies of Napoleon, and reflected in the Constitution of France, which begins "France is [a] . . . secular . . . Republic." Religion is to be strictly excluded from the public forum. This is not, and never was, the model adopted by America. [Justice Scalia then reiterated his view, stated in his dissent in Lee v. Weisman (p. 737), that George Washington, Chief Justice Marshall, and the First Congress's prayers in an official capacity indicate that such prayers do not violate the Establishment Clause.] [And] of course the First Amendment itself accords religion (and no other manner of belief) special constitutional protection.

These actions of our First President and Congress and the Marshall Court were not idiosyncratic; they reflected the beliefs of the period. Those who wrote the Constitution believed that morality was essential to the well-being of society and that encouragement of religion was the best way to foster morality. [Nor] have the views of our people on this matter significantly changed. Presidents continue to conclude the Presidential oath with the words "so help me God." Our legislatures, state and national, continue to open their sessions with prayer led by official chaplains. The sessions of this Court continue to open with the prayer "God save the United States and this Honorable Court." Invocation of the Almighty by our public figures, at all levels of government, remains commonplace. Our coinage bears the motto "IN GOD WE TRUST." And our Pledge of Allegiance contains the acknowledgment that we are a Nation "under God." With all of this reality (and much more) staring it in the face, how can the Court possibly assert that " 'the First Amendment mandates governmental neutrality between . . . religion and nonreligion,' " and that "manifesting a purpose to favor . . . adherence to religion generally," is unconstitutional?

[T]oday's opinion [also] suggests that the posting of the Ten Commandments violates the principle that the government cannot favor one religion over another. That is indeed a valid principle where public aid or assistance to religion is concerned, or where the free exercise of religion is at issue, but it necessarily applies in a more limited sense to public acknowledgment of the Creator. If religion in the public forum had to be entirely nondenominational, there could be no religion in the public forum at all. One cannot say the word "God," or "the Almighty," without contradicting the beliefs of some people that there are many gods, or that God or the gods pay no attention to human affairs. Historical practices [demonstrate] that there is a distance between the acknowledgment of a single Creator and the establishment of a religion. [The] three most popular religions in the United States, Christianity, Judaism, and Islam—which combined account for 97.7% of all believers—are monotheistic. All of them, moreover (Islam included), believe that the Ten Commandments were given by God to Moses, and are divine prescriptions for a virtuous life. Publicly honoring the Ten Commandments is thus indistinguishable, insofar as discriminating against other religions is concerned, from publicly honoring God. [Neither can] be reasonably understood as a government endorsement of a particular religious viewpoint.[1]

[Justice Stevens asserts] that I would "marginalize the belief systems of more than 7 million Americans" who adhere to religions that are not

---

[1] This is not to say that a display of the Ten Commandments could never constitute an impermissible endorsement of a particular religious view. The Establishment Clause would prohibit, for example, governmental endorsement of a particular version of the Decalogue as authoritative. Here the display of the Ten Commandments alongside eight secular documents, and the plaque's explanation for their inclusion, make clear that they were not posted to take sides in a theological dispute. [Footnote by Justice Scalia.]

monotheistic. Surely that is a gross exaggeration. The beliefs of those citizens are entirely protected by the Free Exercise Clause, and by those aspects of the Establishment Clause that do not relate to government acknowledgment of the Creator. [Justice Stevens] fails to recognize that in the context of public acknowledgments of God there are legitimate competing interests: On the one hand, the interest of that minority in not feeling "excluded"; but on the other, the interest of the overwhelming majority of religious believers in being able to give God thanks and supplication as a people, and with respect to our national endeavors. Our national tradition has resolved that conflict in favor of the majority.

II. [As] bad as the Lemon test is, it is worse for the fact that, since its inception, its seemingly simple mandates have been manipulated to fit whatever result the Court aimed to achieve. Today's opinion is no different. In two respects it modifies Lemon to ratchet up the Court's hostility to religion. First, the Court justifies inquiry into legislative purpose, not as an end itself, but as a means to ascertain the appearance of the government action to an "'objective observer.'" [Under] this approach, even if a government could show that its actual purpose was not to advance religion, it would presumably violate the Constitution as long as the Court's objective observer would think otherwise. [Second,] the Court replaces Lemon's requirement that the government have "a secular . . . purpose," with the heightened requirement that the secular purpose "predominate" over any purpose to advance religion. [The] new demand that secular purpose predominate contradicts Lemon's more limited requirement, and finds no support in our cases. In all but one of the five cases in which this Court has invalidated a government practice on the basis of its purpose to benefit religion, it has first declared that the statute was motivated entirely by the desire to advance religion. See Santa Fe, Wallace, Stone, Epperson. [I] have urged that Lemon's purpose prong be abandoned, because [even] an exclusive purpose to foster or assist religious practice is not necessarily invalidating. But today's extension makes things even worse.

III. [Even] accepting the Court's Lemon-based premises, the displays at issue here were constitutional. The walls of both courthouses were already lined with historical documents and other assorted portraits; each Foundations Display was exhibited in the same format as these other displays and nothing in the record suggests that either County took steps to give it greater prominence.

[On] its face, the Foundations Displays manifested the purely secular purpose that the Counties asserted before the District Court: "to display documents that played a significant role in the foundation of our system of law and government." That the Displays included the Ten Commandments did not transform their apparent secular purpose into one of impermissible advocacy for Judeo-Christian beliefs. [The] acknowledgment of the contribution that religion in general, and the Ten Commandments in particular, have made to our Nation's legal and governmental heritage is surely no more of a step towards establishment of religion than was the practice of legislative prayer we approved in Marsh, and it seems to be on par with the inclusion of a crèche or a menorah in a "Holiday" display that incorporates other secular symbols, see Lynch, Allegheny.

[In] any event, the Court's conclusion that the Counties exhibited the Foundations Displays with the purpose of promoting religion is doubtful. [If] the Commandments have a proper place in our civic history, even placing them by themselves can be civically motivated—especially when they are placed, not in a school (as they were in the Stone case upon which the Court places such reliance), but in a courthouse. [The] first [and second] displays did not necessarily evidence an intent to further religious practice; nor did the resolutions authorizing them; and there is no basis for attributing whatever intent motivated the first and second displays to the third.

Van Orden v. Perry

545 U.S. 677, 125 S. Ct. 2854, 162 L. Ed. 2d 607 (2005).

■ CHIEF JUSTICE REHNQUIST announced the judgment of the Court and delivered an opinion, in which JUSTICES SCALIA, KENNEDY, and THOMAS join.

[The] 22 acres surrounding the Texas State Capitol contain 17 monuments and 21 historical markers commemorating the "people, ideals, and events that compose Texan identity." The monolith challenged here stands 6-feet high and 3-feet wide. It is located to the north of the Capitol building, between the Capitol and the Supreme Court building. Its primary content is the text of the Ten Commandments.

[This case presents] us with the difficulty of respecting both faces [of the Religion Clauses]. Our institutions presuppose a Supreme Being, yet these institutions must not press religious observances upon their citizens. One face looks to the past in acknowledgment of our Nation's heritage, while the other looks to the present in demanding a separation between church and state. Reconciling these two faces requires that we neither abdicate our responsibility to maintain a division between church and state nor evince a hostility to religion by disabling the government from in some ways recognizing our religious heritage.

[Whatever] may be the fate of the Lemon test in the larger scheme of Establishment Clause jurisprudence, we think it not useful in dealing with the sort of passive monument that Texas has erected on its Capitol grounds. Instead, our analysis is driven both by the nature of the monument and by our Nation's history. [In] this case we are faced with a display of the Ten Commandments on government property outside the Texas State Capitol. Such acknowledgments of the role played by the Ten Commandments in our Nation's heritage are common throughout America. We need only look within our own Courtroom. [Chief Justice Rehnquist then described the Supreme Court's frieze, as well as other references to the Ten Commandments throughout the Supreme Court building.]

[Of course,] the Ten Commandments are religious—they were so viewed at their inception and so remain. The monument, therefore, has religious significance. According to Judeo-Christian belief, the Ten Commandments were given to Moses by God on Mt. Sinai. But Moses was a lawgiver as well as a religious leader. And the Ten Commandments have an undeniable historical meaning, as the foregoing examples demonstrate. Simply having religious content or promoting a message consistent with a religious doctrine does not run afoul of the Establishment Clause.

There are, of course, limits to the display of religious messages or symbols. For example, we held unconstitutional a Kentucky statute requiring the posting of the Ten Commandments in every public schoolroom.

Stone v. Graham. [Neither] Stone itself nor subsequent opinions have indicated that Stone's holding would extend to a legislative chamber. The placement of the Ten Commandments monument on the Texas State Capitol grounds is a far more passive use of those texts than was the case in Stone, where the text confronted elementary school students every day. [Texas] has treated her Capitol grounds monuments as representing the several strands in the State's political and legal history. The inclusion of the Ten Commandments monument in this group has a dual significance, partaking of both religion and government. We cannot say that Texas' display of this monument violates the Establishment Clause. [Affirmed.]

■ JUSTICE SCALIA, concurring.

I join the opinion of the Chief Justice because I think it accurately reflects our current Establishment Clause jurisprudence. [I] would prefer to reach the same result by adopting an Establishment Clause jurisprudence that is in accord with our Nation's past and present practices, and that can be consistently applied—the central relevant feature of which is that there is nothing unconstitutional in a State's favoring religion generally, honoring God through public prayer and acknowledgment, or, in a nonproselytizing manner, venerating the Ten Commandments.

■ JUSTICE THOMAS, concurring.

[Justice Thomas began his opinion by reiterating his view that the Establishment Clause ought not be incorporated against the States.]

Even if the Clause is incorporated, or if the Free Exercise Clause limits the power of States to establish religions, our task would be far simpler if we returned to the original meaning of the word "establishment" than it is under the various approaches this Court now uses. The Framers understood an establishment "necessarily [to] involve actual legal coercion." There is no question that, based on the original meaning of the Establishment Clause, the Ten Commandments display at issue here is constitutional. In no sense does Texas compel petitioner Van Orden to do anything. The mere presence of the monument along his path involves no coercion and thus does not violate the Establishment Clause.

■ JUSTICE BREYER, concurring in the judgment.

[If] the relation between government and religion is one of separation, but not of mutual hostility and suspicion, one will inevitably find difficult borderline cases. And in such cases, I see no test-related substitute for the exercise of legal judgment. That judgment is not a personal judgment. Rather, as in all constitutional cases, it must reflect and remain faithful to the underlying purposes of the Clauses, and it must take account of context and consequences measured in light of those purposes. [The] case before us is a borderline case. [On] the one hand, the Commandments' text undeniably has a religious message, invoking, indeed emphasizing, the Deity. On the other hand, focusing on the text of the Commandments alone cannot conclusively resolve this case. Rather, to determine the message that the text here conveys, we must examine how the text is used. And that inquiry requires us to consider the context of the display.

In certain contexts, a display of the tablets of the Ten Commandments can convey not simply a religious message but also a secular moral message (about proper standards of social conduct). And in certain contexts, a display of the tablets can also convey a historical message (about a historic relation between those standards and the law)—a fact that helps to explain the display of those tablets in dozens of courthouses throughout the Nation, including the Supreme Court of the United States. Here the tablets have been used as part of a display that communicates not simply a religious message, but a secular message as well. The circumstances surrounding the display's placement on the capitol grounds and its physical setting suggest that the State itself intended the latter, nonreligious aspects of the tablets' message to predominate. And the monument's 40-year history on the Texas state grounds indicates that that has been its effect.

The group that donated the monument, the Fraternal Order of Eagles, a private civic (and primarily secular) organization, while interested in the religious aspect of the Ten Commandments, sought to highlight the Commandments' role in shaping civic morality as part of that organization's efforts to combat juvenile delinquency. [The] physical setting of the monument, moreover, suggests little or nothing of the sacred. The monument sits in a large park containing 17 monuments and 21 historical markers, all designed to illustrate the "ideals" of those who settled in Texas and of those who have lived there since that time. [If] these factors provide a strong, but not conclusive, indication that the Commandments' text on this monument conveys a predominantly secular message, a further factor is determinative here. As far as I can tell, 40 years passed in which the presence of this monument, legally speaking, went unchallenged (until the single legal objection raised by petitioner). [Those] 40 years suggest more strongly than can any set of formulaic tests [that] the public visiting the capitol grounds has considered the religious aspect of the tablets' message as part of what is a broader moral and historical message reflective of a cultural heritage.

This case, moreover, is distinguishable from instances where the Court has found Ten Commandments displays impermissible. The display is not on the grounds of a public school, where, given the impressionability of the young, government must exercise particular care in separating church and state. This case also differs from McCreary County, where the short (and stormy) history of the courthouse Commandments' displays demonstrates the substantially religious objectives of those who mounted them, and the effect of this readily apparent objective upon those who view them. That history there indicates a governmental effort substantially to promote religion, not simply an effort primarily to reflect, historically, the secular impact of a religiously inspired document. And, in today's world, in a Nation of so many different religious and comparable nonreligious fundamental beliefs, a more contemporary state effort to focus attention upon a religious text is certainly likely to prove divisive in a way that this longstanding, pre-existing monument has not.

[At] the same time, to reach a contrary conclusion here, based primarily upon on the religious nature of the tablets' text would, I fear, lead the law to exhibit a hostility toward religion that has no place in our Establishment Clause traditions. Such a holding might well encourage disputes concerning the removal of longstanding depictions of the Ten Commandments from public buildings across the Nation. [I]t could thereby create the very kind of religiously based divisiveness that the Establishment Clause seeks to avoid.

■ JUSTICE STEVENS, with whom JUSTICE GINSBURG joins, dissenting.

The sole function of the monument on the grounds of Texas' State Capitol is to display the full text of one version of the Ten Commandments. The monument is not a work of art and does not refer to any event in the history of the State. It is significant because, and only because, it communicates the following message: "I AM the LORD thy God. Thou shalt have no other gods before me. Thou shalt not make to thyself any graven images. Thou shalt not take the Name of the Lord thy God in vain. Remember the Sabbath day, to keep it holy. Honor thy father and thy mother, that thy days may be long upon the land which the Lord thy God giveth thee. Thou shalt not kill. Thou shalt not commit adultery. Thou shalt not steal. Thou shalt not bear false witness against thy neighbor. Thou shalt not covet thy neighbor's house. Thou shalt not covet thy neighbor's wife, nor his manservant, nor his maidservant, nor his cattle, nor anything that is thy neighbor's."

Viewed on its face, Texas' display has no purported connection to God's role in the formation of Texas or the founding of our Nation; nor does it provide the reasonable observer with any basis to guess that it was erected to honor any individual or organization. The message transmitted by Texas' chosen display is quite plain: This State endorses the divine code of the "Judeo-Christian" God.

1.   [At] the very least, the Establishment Clause has created a strong presumption against the display of religious symbols on public property. [Government's] obligation to avoid divisiveness and exclusion in the religious sphere is compelled by the Establishment and Free Exercise Clauses, which together erect a wall of separation between church and state. [The] wall that separates the church from the State does not prohibit the government from acknowledging the religious beliefs and practices of the American people, nor does it require governments to hide works of art or historic memorabilia from public view just because they also have religious significance. This case, however, is not about historic preservation or the mere recognition of religion. The monolith displayed on Texas Capitol grounds cannot be discounted as a passive acknowledgment of religion, nor can the State's refusal to remove it upon objection be explained as a simple desire to preserve a historic relic. This Nation's resolute commitment to neutrality with respect to religion is flatly inconsistent with the plurality's wholehearted validation of an official state endorsement of the message that there is one, and only one, God.

II.   When the Ten Commandments monument was donated to the State of Texas in 1961, it was not for the purpose of commemorating a noteworthy event in Texas history, signifying the Commandments' influence on the development of secular law, or even denoting the religious beliefs of Texans at that time. To the contrary, the donation was only one of over a hundred largely identical monoliths, and of over a thousand paper replicas, distributed to state and local governments throughout the Nation over the course of several decades. This ambitious project was the work of the Fraternal Order of Eagles, a well-respected benevolent organization whose good works [including combating juvenile delinquency] have earned the praise of several Presidents. Cecil B. DeMille, who at that time was filming the movie The Ten Commandments teamed up with the Eagles to produce the type of granite monolith now displayed in front of the Texas Capitol and at courthouse squares, city halls, and public parks throughout the Nation.

[Though] the State of Texas may genuinely wish to combat juvenile delinquency, and may rightly want to honor the [Fraternal Order of the] Eagles for their efforts, it cannot effectuate these admirable purposes through an explicitly religious medium.

[T]he Decalogue is a venerable religious text. [For] many followers, the Commandments represent the literal word of God as spoken to Moses. The message conveyed by the Ten Commandments thus cannot be analogized to an appendage to a common article of commerce ("In God we Trust") or an incidental part of a familiar recital ("God save the United States and this honorable Court"). Thankfully, the plurality does not attempt to minimize the religious significance of the Ten Commandments. Attempts to secularize what is unquestionably sacred defy credibility and disserve people of faith.

[Moreover,] the Ten Commandments display projects not just a religious, but an inherently sectarian message. There are many distinctive versions of the Decalogue, ascribed to by different religions and even different denominations within a particular faith; to a pious and learned observer, these differences may be of enormous religious significance. In choosing to display this version of the Commandments, Texas tells the observer that the State supports this side of the doctrinal religious debate. [Even] if, however, the message of the monument, despite the inscribed text, fairly could be said to represent the belief system of all Judeo-Christians, it would still run afoul of the Establishment Clause by prescribing a compelled code of conduct from one God, namely a Judeo-Christian God, that is rejected by prominent polytheistic sects, such as Hinduism, as well as nontheistic religions, such as Buddhism. [Today] there are many Texans who do not believe in the God whose Commandments are displayed at their seat of government. Many of them worship a different god or no god at all. [Recognizing] the diversity of religious and secular beliefs held by Texans and by all Americans, it seems beyond peradventure that allowing the seat of government to serve as a stage for the propagation of an unmistakably Judeo-Christian message of piety would have the tendency to make nonmonotheists and nonbelievers "feel like [outsiders] in matters of faith, and [strangers] in the political community."

III. [Justice Stevens distinguished between government symbols and religious proclamations and also repeated the separationist citations to Jefferson and Madison's refusal to give proclamations.]

[Many] of the Framers understood the word "religion" in the Establishment Clause to encompass only the various sects of Christianity. [For] nearly a century after the Founding, many accepted the idea that America was not just a religious nation, but "a Christian nation." The original understanding of the type of "religion" that qualified for constitutional protection under the Establishment Clause likely did not include those followers of Judaism and Islam who are among the preferred "monotheistic" religions Justice Scalia embraced in McCreary County. [Justice Scalia's] inclusion of Judaism and Islam is a laudable act of religious tolerance, but it is unmoored from the Constitution's history and text and patently arbitrary in its inclusion of some, but exclusion of other (e.g., Buddhism), widely practiced non-Christian religions. [Such a] reading of the First Amendment [would] eviscerate the heart of the Establishment Clause. It would replace Jefferson's "wall of separation" with a perverse wall of exclusion [and] would permit States to construct walls of their own choosing. A Clause so understood might be faithful to the expectations of some of our Founders, but it is plainly not worthy of a society whose enviable hallmark over the course of two centuries has been the continuing expansion of religious pluralism and tolerance.

[It] is our duty, therefore, to interpret the First Amendment's command that "Congress shall make no law respecting an establishment of religion" not by merely asking what those words meant to observers at the time of the founding, but instead by deriving from the Clause's text and history the broad principles that remain valid today. [The] principle that guides my analysis is neutrality. The basis for that principle is firmly rooted in our Nation's history and our Constitution's text. I recognize that the requirement that government must remain neutral between religion and irreligion would have seemed foreign to some of the Framers. [Fortunately,] we are not bound by the Framers' expectations—we are bound by the legal principles they enshrined in our Constitution. The Establishment Clause [forbids] Texas from displaying the Ten Commandments monument.

■ JUSTICE O'CONNOR, dissenting.

For essentially the reasons given by Justice Souter, as well as the reasons given in my concurrence in McCreary County, I respectfully dissent.

■ JUSTICE SOUTER, with whom JUSTICES STEVENS and GINSBURG join, dissenting.

[A] governmental display of an obviously religious text cannot be squared with neutrality, except in a setting that plausibly indicates that the statement is not placed in view with a predominant purpose on the part of government either to adopt the religious message or to urge its acceptance by others. [A] pedestrian happening upon the monument at issue here needs no training in religious doctrine to realize that the statement of the Commandments, quoting God himself, proclaims that the will of the divine being is the source of obligation to obey the rules. [Nothing] on the monument [detracts] from its religious nature. [The] government of Texas is telling everyone who sees the monument to live up to a moral code because God requires it, with both code and conception of God being rightly understood as the inheritances specifically of Jews and Christians.

The monument's presentation of the Commandments with religious text emphasized and enhanced stands in contrast to any number of perfectly constitutional depictions of them, the frieze of our own Courtroom providing a good example, where the figure of Moses stands among history's great lawgivers. While Moses holds the tablets of the Commandments showing some Hebrew text, no one looking at the lines of figures in marble relief is likely to see a religious purpose behind the assemblage or take away a religious message from it. Only one other depiction represents a religious leader, and the historical personages are mixed with symbols of moral and intellectual abstractions like Equity and Authority. [V]iewers can readily take him to be there as a lawgiver in the company of other lawgivers.

[Texas] says that the Capitol grounds are like a museum for a collection of exhibits. [The] Government of the United States does not violate the Establishment Clause by hanging Giotto's Madonna on the wall of the National Gallery. But 17 monuments with no common appearance, history, or esthetic role scattered over 22 acres is not a museum, and anyone strolling around the lawn would surely take each memorial on its own terms without any dawning sense that some purpose held the miscellany together more coherently than fortuity and the edge of the grass.

[Our] numerous discussions of Stone have never treated its holding as restricted to the classroom. [A] state capitol building [is] the civic home of every one of the State's citizens. If neutrality in religion means something, any citizen should be able to visit that civic home without having to confront religious expressions clearly meant to convey an official religious position.

How convincing is Justice Breyer's distinction between the Ten Commandments exhibit in McCreary County and the monument on the Texas capitol grounds in Van Orden? How much does, or should, a monument's age affect what a reasonable observer would think of it? Is the Court's approach to religious monuments simply "we know it when we see it," or is there a workable legal standard that incorporates age, history and physical context? Consider these issues in the following case.

The American Legion v. American Humanist Association

588 U.S. ___, 139 S. Ct. 2067, 204 L. Ed. 2d 452 (2019).

[After World War I, residents of Prince George's County, Maryland, formed a committee to erect a memorial for the county's soldiers who fell in World War I. The local American Legion completed the project in 1925: a 32-foot tall Latin cross on the highway in Bladensburg, Maryland, outside Washington DC that displays the American Legion's emblem at its center and sits on a large pedestal bearing, *inter alia*, a bronze plaque that lists the names of the 49 county soldiers who had fallen in the war. In 1961, the Maryland-National Capital Park and Planning Commission acquired the Cross and the land where it sits, now a busy crossroads. It uses public funds for upkeep. The American Legion reserves the right to continue using the site for ceremonies. The monument was challenged in 2014. The district court upheld it; the Fourth Circuit reversed.]

■ JUSTICE ALITO announced the judgment of the Court and delivered the opinion of the Court with respect to Parts I, II-B, II-C, III, and IV, and an opinion with respect to Parts II-A and II-D, in which the CHIEF JUSTICE and JUSTICES BREYER and KAVANAUGH join.

[Although] the cross has long been a preeminent Christian symbol, its use in the Bladensburg memorial has a special significance. After the First World War, the picture of row after row of plain white crosses marking the overseas graves of soldiers who had lost their lives in that horrible conflict was emblazoned on the minds of Americans at home, and the adoption of the cross as the Bladensburg memorial must be viewed in that historical context. For nearly a century, the Bladensburg Cross has expressed the community's grief at the loss of the young men who perished, its thanks for their sacrifice, and its dedication to the ideals for which they fought. It has become a prominent community landmark, and its removal or radical alteration at this date would be seen by many not as a neutral act but as the manifestation of "a hostility toward religion that has no place in our Establishment Clause traditions." [There] is no evidence of discriminatory intent in the selection of the design of the memorial or the decision of a Maryland commission to maintain it. The Religion Clauses of the Constitution aim to foster a society in which people of all beliefs can live together harmoniously, and the presence of the Bladensburg Cross on the land where it has stood for so many years is fully consistent with that aim.

I. The cross came into widespread use as a symbol of Christianity by the fourth century, and it retains that meaning today. But there are many contexts in which the symbol has also taken on a secular meaning. Indeed, there are instances in which its message is now almost entirely secular. A cross appears as part of many registered trademarks held by businesses and secular organizations, including Blue Cross Blue Shield, the Bayer Group, and some Johnson & Johnson products. [The] familiar symbol of the Red Cross—a red cross on a white background—shows how the meaning of a symbol that was originally religious can be transformed. [The] image used in the Bladensburg memorial—a plain Latin cross—also took on new meaning after World War I. "During and immediately after the war, the army marked soldiers' graves with temporary wooden crosses or Stars of David"—a departure from the prior practice of marking graves in American military cemeteries with uniform rectangular slabs. The vast majority of these grave markers consisted of crosses, and thus when Americans saw photographs of these cemeteries, what struck them were rows and rows of plain white crosses. As a result, the image of a simple white cross "developed into a 'central symbol'" of the conflict. Contemporary literature, poetry, and art reflected this powerful imagery. [After] the 1918 armistice, the War Department announced plans to replace the wooden crosses and Stars of David with uniform marble slabs like those previously used in American military cemeteries. But the public outcry against that proposal was swift and fierce. [When] the American Battle Monuments Commission took over the project of designing the headstones, it responded to this public sentiment by opting to replace the wooden crosses and Stars of David with marble versions of those symbols. [This] national debate and its outcome confirmed the cross's widespread resonance as a symbol of sacrifice in the war.

[Since] its dedication, the Cross has served as the site of patriotic events honoring veterans, including gatherings on Veterans Day, Memorial Day, and Independence Day. Like the dedication itself, these events have typically included an invocation, a keynote speaker, and a benediction. Over the years, memorials honoring the veterans of [several] other conflicts have been added to the surrounding area, which is now known as Veterans Memorial Park. Because the Cross is located on a traffic island with limited space, the closest of these other monuments is about 200 feet away in a park across the road.

II.A. [If] the Lemon Court thought that its test would provide a framework for all future Establishment Clause decisions, its expectation has not been met. In many cases, this Court has either expressly declined to apply the test or has simply ignored it. This pattern is a testament to the Lemon test's shortcomings. As Establishment Clause cases involving a great array of laws and practices came to the Court, it became more and more apparent that the Lemon test could not resolve them. [The] Lemon test presents particularly daunting problems in cases, including the one now before us, that involve the use, for ceremonial, celebratory, or commemorative purposes, of words or symbols with religious associations. Together, these considerations counsel against efforts to evaluate such cases under Lemon and toward application of a presumption of constitutionality for longstanding monuments, symbols, and practices.

B. First, these cases often concern monuments, symbols, or practices that were first established long ago, and in such cases, identifying their original purpose or purposes may be especially difficult. [Second,] as time goes by, the purposes associated with an established monument, symbol, or practice often multiply. [The] existence of multiple purposes is not exclusive to longstanding monuments, symbols, or practices, but this phenomenon is more likely to occur in such cases. Even if the original purpose of a monument was infused with religion, the passage of time may obscure that sentiment. As our society becomes more and more religiously diverse, a community may preserve such monuments, symbols, and practices for the sake of their historical significance or their place in a common cultural heritage. Third, just as the purpose for maintaining a monument, symbol, or practice may evolve, the message conveyed may change over time. [With] sufficient time, religiously expressive monuments, symbols, and practices can become embedded features of a community's landscape and identity. The community may come to value them without necessarily embracing their religious roots. Familiarity itself can become a reason for preservation. Fourth, when time's passage imbues a religiously expressive monument, symbol, or practice with this kind of familiarity and historical significance, removing it may no longer appear neutral, especially to the local community for which it has taken on particular meaning. A government that roams the land, tearing down monuments with religious symbolism and scrubbing away any reference to the divine will strike many as aggressively hostile to religion. These four considerations show that retaining established, religiously expressive monuments, symbols, and practices is quite different from erecting or adopting new ones. The passage of time gives rise to a strong presumption of constitutionality.

C. The role of the cross in World War I memorials is illustrative of each of the four preceding considerations. [This] is not to say that the cross's association with the war was the sole or dominant motivation for the inclusion of the symbol in every World War I memorial that features it. But today, it is all but impossible to tell whether that was so. The passage of time means that testimony from those actually involved in the decisionmaking process is generally unavailable, and attempting to uncover their motivations invites rampant speculation. And no matter what the original purposes for the erection of a monument, a community may wish to preserve it for very different reasons, such as the historic preservation and traffic-safety concerns the Commission has pressed here.

III. [Due] in large part to the image of the simple wooden crosses that originally marked the graves of American soldiers killed in the war, the cross became a symbol of their sacrifice, and the design of the Bladensburg Cross must be understood in light of that background. That the cross originated as a Christian symbol and retains that meaning in many contexts does not change the fact that the symbol took on an added secular meaning when used in World War I memorials.

Not only did the Bladensburg Cross begin with this meaning, but with the passage of time, it has acquired historical importance. [As] long as it is retained in its original place and form, it speaks as well of the community that erected the monument nearly a century ago and has maintained it ever since. The memorial represents what the relatives, friends, and neighbors of the fallen soldiers felt at the time and how they chose to express their sentiments. And the monument has acquired additional layers of historical meaning in subsequent years. The Cross now stands among memorials to veterans of later wars. It has become part of the community.

The monument would not serve that role if its design had deliberately disrespected area soldiers who perished in World War I. More than 3,500

Jewish soldiers gave their lives for the United States in that conflict, and some have wondered whether the names of any Jewish soldiers from the area were deliberately left off the list on the memorial or whether the names of any Jewish soldiers were included on the Cross against the wishes of their families. There is no evidence that either thing was done, and we do know that one of the local American Legion leaders responsible for the Cross's construction was a Jewish veteran.

IV. The cross is undoubtedly a Christian symbol, but that fact should not blind us to everything else that the Bladensburg Cross has come to represent. For some, that monument is a symbolic resting place for ancestors who never returned home. For others, it is a place for the community to gather and honor all veterans and their sacrifices for our Nation. For others still, it is a historical landmark. For many of these people, destroying or defacing the Cross that has stood undisturbed for nearly a century would not be neutral and would not further the ideals of respect and tolerance embodied in the First Amendment. For all these reasons, the Cross does not offend the Constitution.

■ JUSTICE BREYER, with whom JUSTICE KAGAN joins, concurring.

I have long maintained that there is no single formula for resolving Establishment Clause challenges. The Court must instead consider each case in light of the basic purposes that the Religion Clauses were meant to serve: assuring religious liberty and tolerance for all, avoiding religiously based social conflict, and maintaining that separation of church and state that allows each to flourish in its separate sphere.

I agree with the Court that allowing the State of Maryland to display and maintain the Peace Cross poses no threat to those ends. [The] case would be different, in my view, if there were evidence that the organizers had deliberately disrespected members of minority faiths or if the Cross had been erected only recently, rather than in the aftermath of World War I. [Nor] do I understand the Court's opinion today to adopt a "history and tradition test" that would permit any newly constructed religious memorial on public land. The Court appropriately looks to history for guidance, but it upholds the constitutionality of the Peace Cross only after considering its particular historical context and its long-held place in the community. A newer memorial, erected under different circumstances, would not necessarily be permissible under this approach.

■ JUSTICE KAVANAUGH, concurring.

[Consistent] with the Court's case law, the Court today applies a history and tradition test. [As] this case again demonstrates, this Court no longer applies the old test articulated in Lemon. [The] opinion identifies five relevant categories of Establishment Clause cases: (1) religious symbols on government property and religious speech at government events; (2) religious accommodations and exemptions from generally applicable laws; (3) government benefits and tax exemptions for religious organizations; (4) religious expression in public schools; and (5) regulation of private religious speech in public forums. The Lemon test does not explain the Court's decisions in any of those five categories.

[I] have great respect for the Jewish war veterans who in an *amicus* brief say that the cross on public land sends a message of exclusion. I recognize their sense of distress and alienation. Moreover, I fully understand the deeply religious nature of the cross. It would demean both believers and nonbelievers to say that the cross is not religious, or not all that religious. A case like this is difficult because it represents a clash of genuine and important interests. Applying our precedents, we uphold the constitutionality of the cross. In doing so, it is appropriate to also restate this bedrock constitutional principle: All citizens are equally American, no matter what religion they are, or if they have no religion at all.

■ JUSTICE KAGAN, concurring in part.

[Although] I agree that rigid application of the Lemon test does not solve every Establishment Clause problem, I think that test's focus on purposes and effects is crucial in evaluating government action in this sphere—as this very suit shows. [I] prefer at least for now to do so case-by-case, rather than to sign on to any broader statements about history's role in Establishment Clause analysis.

[Justice THOMAS concurred only in the judgment, restating his views that the Establishment Clause should not be incorporated against the States, that it even still may not apply against the States without legislative action, and that Establishment can only occur with coercion.]

■ JUSTICE GORSUCH, with whom JUSTICE THOMAS joins, concurring in the judgment.

The American Humanist Association wants a federal court to order the destruction of a 94 year-old war memorial because its members are offended. [This] "offended observer" theory of standing has no basis in law. [Imagine] if a bystander disturbed by a police stop tried to sue under the Fourth Amendment. Suppose an advocacy organization whose members were distressed by a State's decision to deny someone else a civil jury trial sought to complain under the Seventh Amendment. Or envision a religious group upset about the application of the death penalty trying to sue to stop it. Does anyone doubt those cases would be rapidly dispatched for lack of standing?

Proceeding on these principles, this Court has held offense alone insufficient to convey standing in analogous—and arguably more sympathetic—circumstances. [An] African-American offended by a Confederate flag atop a state capitol would lack standing to sue under the Equal Protection Clause, but an atheist who is offended by the cross on the same flag could sue under the Establishment Clause. Who really thinks *that* could be the law? In fact, this Court has already expressly rejected "offended observer" standing under the Establishment Clause itself. Valley Forge. [With] Lemon now shelved, little excuse will remain for the anomaly of offended observer standing, and the gaping hole it tore in standing doctrine in the courts of appeals should now begin to close. Nor does this development mean colorable Establishment Clause violations will lack for proper plaintiffs. By way of example only, a public school student compelled to recite a prayer will still have standing to sue. So will persons denied public office because of their religious affiliations or lack of them. And so will those who are denied government benefits because they do not practice a favored religion or any at all. On top of all that, States remain free to supply other forms of relief consistent with their own laws and constitutions.

■ JUSTICE GINSBURG, with whom JUSTICE SOTOMAYOR joins, dissenting.

[The] Latin cross is the foremost symbol of the Christian faith, embodying the "central theological claim of Christianity: that the son of God died on the cross, that he rose from the dead, and that his death and resurrection offer the possibility of eternal life." Precisely because the cross symbolizes these sectarian beliefs, it is a common marker for the graves of Christian soldiers. For the same reason, using the cross as a war memorial does not transform it into a secular symbol. [Just] as a Star of David is not suitable to honor Christians who died serving their country, so a cross is not suitable to honor those of other faiths who died defending their nation.

By maintaining the Peace Cross on a public highway, the Commission elevates Christianity over other faiths, and religion over nonreligion.

[As] I see it, when a cross is displayed on public property, the government may be presumed to endorse its religious content. The venue is surely associated with the State; the symbol and its meaning are just as surely associated exclusively with Christianity. [A] presumption of endorsement, of course, may be overcome. [The] typical museum setting, for example, though not neutralizing the religious content of a religious painting, negates any message of endorsement of that content. Lynch (O'Connor, J., concurring). Similarly, when a public school history teacher discusses the Protestant Reformation, the setting makes clear that the teacher's purpose is to educate, not to proselytize. The Peace Cross, however, is not of that genre.

[At] the dedication ceremony, the keynote speaker analogized the sacrifice of the honored soldiers to that of Jesus Christ, calling the Peace Cross "symbolic of Calvary," where Jesus was crucified. Local reporters variously described the monument as "[a] mammoth cross, a likeness of the Cross of Calvary, as described in the Bible"; "a monster [C]alvary cross," and "a huge sacrifice cross." The character of the monument has not changed with the passage of time.

The cross was never perceived as an appropriate headstone or memorial for Jewish soldiers and others who did not adhere to Christianity. [Throughout] the headstone debate [after World War I,] no one doubted that the Latin cross and the Star of David were sectarian gravemarkers, and therefore appropriate only for soldiers who adhered to those faiths. [The] overwhelming majority of World War I memorials contain no Latin cross. In fact, the "most popular and enduring memorial of the [post-World War I] decade" was "[t]he mass-produced Spirit of the American Doughboy statue." [Like] cities and towns across the country, the United States military comprehended the importance of paying equal respect to all members of the Armed Forces who perished in the service of our country, and therefore avoided incorporating the Latin cross into memorials. The construction of the Tomb of the Unknown Soldier is illustrative. When a proposal to place a cross on the Tomb was advanced, the Jewish Welfare Board objected; no cross appears on the Tomb.

SECTION 5. RECONCILING THE RELIGION CLAUSES

As this chapter illustrates, the two religion clauses are sometimes in tension. Some accommodations may appear to have the effect of establishing religion, and a fastidious application of establishment principles might burden free exercise. In the face of these frictions, how much leeway should government have to "accommodate" free exercise concerns, when the Free Exercise Clause does not compel such accommodation? And how much leeway should government have to refuse accommodations on establishment grounds before free exercise compels an exemption? Although several of the above cases deal with these issues, this section addresses them explicitly. It first asks what values might serve to reconcile the clauses. The section then explores, in the words of Chief Justice Rehnquist, how much "play in the joints" there is between the two clauses.

VALUES RECONCILING THE RELIGION CLAUSES

Some commentators have suggested that the two religion clauses can be harmonized by recognizing that "establishment" and "free exercise" serve a single value—protecting the individual's freedom of religious belief and practices, with "free exercise" barring the curbing of that freedom through penalties and "establishment" barring inhibitions on individual choice that arise from governmental aid to religion. Yet viewing the clauses as protecting that single goal does not eliminate the potential tensions. If either the anti-penalties or anti-rewards theme is taken as an absolute, the competing theme will be unduly denigrated: if all penalties are barred, undue benefit to religion may result; if all benefits are barred, undue burdens on religion may be the consequence. Identifying a single "freedom" value, then, does not eliminate the need for accommodation.

Would "neutrality" be a better reconciling theme? Can the religion clauses be read as making the Constitution "religion-blind"? Philip Kurland proposed as a unifying principle that "the freedom and separation clauses should be read as a single precept that government cannot utilize religion as a standard for action or inaction because these clauses prohibit classification in terms of religion either to confer a benefit or to impose a burden." Kurland, "Of Church and State and the Supreme Court," 29 U. Chi. L. Rev. 1 (1961). This view would limit government decisionmaking to secular criteria and would forbid any deliberate accommodation of religion. The Court has never embraced such a strict "neutrality" approach, as the materials below demonstrate. For critical commentary on Kurland's position, see Choper, "The Religion Clauses of the First Amendment: Reconciling the Conflict," 41 U. Pitt. L. Rev. 673 (1980); Pfeffer, "Religion-Blind Government," 15 Stan. L. Rev. 389 (1963).

As another possibility, consider the view that the two clauses might be reconciled by a broad view of permissible accommodation. On this view, free exercise compels some accommodation of religion, establishment forbids other accommodation of religion, and between these two areas lies a broad zone where religious accommodation by government is neither forbidden nor required. This was the view expressed by Justice HARLAN in dissent from **Sherbert v. Verner**, 374 U.S. 398 (1963), which held that free exercise compelled the grant of unemployment benefits to a person who lost her job because she observed Saturday as her sabbath. Justice Harlan expressly noted his disagreement with Kurland that all religious accommodations were forbidden. He viewed a religious exemption from the definition of voluntary unemployment as constitutionally permissible but not compelled: "[There] is, I believe, enough flexibility in the Constitution to permit a legislative judgment accommodating an unemployment compensation law to the exercise of religious beliefs such as appellant's. [But] I cannot subscribe to the conclusion that the State is constitutionally compelled to carve out an exception to its general rule of eligibility in the present case. Those situations in which the Constitution may require special treatment on account of religion are, in my view, few and far between." Consider whether Justice Harlan's view has prevailed in the cases that follow.

FUNDING FOR RELIGIOUS EDUCATION AND INSTITUTIONS

1. ***State funding for religious education and "play in the joints."*** In **Locke v. Davey**, 540 U.S. 712 (2004), the Court upheld the State of Washington's refusal, in accordance with its state constitutional ban on the appropriation of public money for "any religious worship exercise or instruction," to allow student recipients of its Promise Scholarship Program to "use the scholarship at an institution where they are pursuing a degree in devotional theology." Although the court of appeals held that Washington's action impermissibly "singled out religion for unfavorable treatment," the Court reversed.

In his opinion for the Court, Chief Justice REHNQUIST stated: "[There] are some state actions permitted by the Establishment Clause but not required by the Free Exercise Clause. [There] is no doubt that the State could, consistent with the [Establishment Clause], permit Promise Scholars to pursue a degree in devotional theology. The question before us, however, is whether Washington, pursuant to its own constitution, [can] deny them such funding without violating the Free Exercise Clause. [The religion clauses] are frequently in tension. Yet we have long said that 'there is room for play in the joints' between them. In other words, there are some state actions permitted by the Establishment Clause but not required by the Free Exercise Clause.

"[Davey] contends that under the rule we enunciated in Lukumi (1993; p. 662), the program is presumptively unconstitutional because it is not facially neutral with respect to religion. [This] would extend the Lukumi line of cases well beyond not only their facts but their reasoning. [In] the present case, the State's disfavor of religion (if it can be called that) [imposes] neither criminal nor civil sanctions on any type of religious service or rite. [The] State has merely chosen not to fund a distinct category of instruction.

"[Because] the Promise Scholarship Program funds training for all secular professions, Justice Scalia contends the State must also fund training for religious professions. But training for religious professions and training for secular professions are not fungible. Training someone to lead a congregation is an essentially religious endeavor. And the subject of religion is one in which both the United States and state constitutions embody distinct views—in favor of free exercise, but opposed to establishment—that find no counterpart with respect to other callings or professions. That a State would deal differently with religious education for the ministry than with education for other callings is a product of these views, not evidence of hostility toward religion.

"[There are] few areas in which a State's antiestablishment interests come more into play. Since the founding of our country, there have been popular uprisings against procuring taxpayer funds to support church leaders, which was one of the hallmarks of an 'established' religion. [Most] States that sought to avoid an establishment of religion around the time of the founding placed in their constitutions formal prohibitions against using tax funds to support the ministry. That early state constitutions saw no problem in explicitly excluding only the ministry from receiving state dollars reinforces our conclusion that religious instruction is of a different ilk.

"Far from evincing the hostility toward religion which was manifest in Lukumi, we believe that the entirety of the Promise Scholarship Program goes a long way toward including religion in its benefits. The program permits students to attend pervasively religious schools, so long as they are accredited. [And] under the Promise Scholarship Program's current guidelines, students are still eligible to take devotional theology courses. [In] short, we find neither in the history or text of Article I, § 11 of the Washington Constitution, nor in the operation of the Promise Scholarship Program, anything that suggests animus towards religion. The State's interest in not funding the pursuit of devotional degrees is substantial and the exclusion of such funding places a relatively minor burden on Promise Scholars. If any room exists between the two Religion Clauses, it must be here."

Justice SCALIA, joined by Justice Thomas, dissented: "The [Lukumi] opinions are irreconcilable with today's decision, which sustains a public benefits program that facially discriminates against religion. [When] the State makes a public benefit generally available, that benefit becomes part of the baseline against which burdens on religion are measured; and when the State withholds that benefit from some individuals solely on the basis of religion, it violates the Free Exercise Clause no less than if it had imposed a special tax.

"That is precisely what the State of Washington has done here. It has created a generally available public benefit, whose receipt is conditioned only on academic performance, income, and attendance at an accredited school. It has then carved out a solitary course of study for exclusion: theology. No field of study but religion is singled out for disfavor in this fashion. [The] Court's reference to historical 'popular uprisings against procuring taxpayer funds to support church leaders,' is therefore quite misplaced. That history involved not the inclusion of religious ministers in public benefits programs like the one at issue here, but laws that singled them out for financial aid. [One] can concede the Framers' hostility to funding the clergy specifically, but that says nothing about whether the clergy had to be excluded from benefits the State made available to all.

"[The] interest to which the Court defers is not fear of a conceivable Establishment Clause violation, budget constraints, avoidance of endorsement, or substantive neutrality. [It] is a pure philosophical preference: the State's opinion that it would violate taxpayers' freedom of conscience not to discriminate against candidates for the ministry. This has no logical limit and can justify the singling out of religion for exclusion from public programs in virtually any context. The Court never says whether it deems this interest compelling (the opinion is devoid of any mention of standard of review) but, self-evidently, it is not.

"[The] other reason the Court thinks this particular facial discrimination less offensive is that the scholarship program was not motivated by animus toward religion. The Court does not explain why the legislature's motive matters, and I fail to see why it should. [We] rejected the Court's methodology in McDaniel v. Paty. The State [there] defended [its clergy-disqualification] statute as an attempt to be faithful to its constitutional separation of church and state, and we accepted that claimed benevolent purpose as bona fide. Nonetheless, because it did not justify facial discrimination against religion, we invalidated the restriction.

"[What next?] Will we deny priests and nuns their prescription-drug benefits on the ground that taxpayers' freedom of conscience forbids medicating the clergy at public expense? This may seem fanciful, but recall that France has proposed banning religious attire from schools, invoking interests in secularism no less benign than those the Court embraces today. When the public's freedom of conscience is invoked to justify denial of equal treatment, benevolent motives shade into indifference and ultimately into repression."

Justice THOMAS filed a separate dissent noting that in his view, "the study of theology does not necessarily implicate religious devotion or faith."

2.   *Vouchers and establishment vs. free exercise.* Recall that in Zelman v. Simmons-Harris (2002; p. 729), the Court held that the Establishment Clause permits inclusion of religions schools in public education funding schemes. After Locke and Zelman, is it fair to say that the Establishment Clause permits but the Free Exercise Clause does not compel the inclusion of parochial schools in voucher schemes? Are these positions consistent?

―――――

FUNDING FOR RELIGIOUS ENTITIES

―――――

Trinity Lutheran Church of Columbia, Inc. v. Comer
582 U.S. ___, 137 S. Ct. 2012, 198 L. Ed. 2d 551 (2017).

■ ROBERTS, C. J., delivered the opinion of the Court, except as to footnote 3.

The Missouri Department of Natural Resources offers state grants to help public and private schools, nonprofit daycare centers, and other nonprofit entities purchase rubber playground surfaces made from recycled tires. Trinity Lutheran Church applied for such a grant for its preschool and daycare center and would have received one, but for the fact that Trinity Lutheran is a church. The Department had a policy [based on Article I, Section 7 of the Missouri Constitution] of categorically disqualifying churches and other religious organizations from receiving grants under its playground resurfacing program. The question presented is whether the Department's policy violated the rights of Trinity Lutheran under the Free Exercise Clause of the First Amendment.

II.   [The] parties agree that the Establishment Clause [does] not prevent Missouri from including Trinity Lutheran in [its] Program. That does not, however, answer the question under the Free Exercise Clause, because we have recognized that there is "play in the joints" between what the Establishment Clause permits and the Free Exercise Clause compels.

III. A.   [The] Department's policy expressly discriminates against otherwise eligible recipients by disqualifying them from a public benefit solely because of their religious character. [Such] a policy imposes a penalty on the free exercise of religion that triggers the most exacting scrutiny. [Like] the disqualification statute in McDaniel, the Department's policy puts

Trinity Lutheran to a choice: It may participate in an otherwise available benefit program or remain a religious institution. Of course, Trinity Lutheran is free to continue operating as a church, just as McDaniel was free to continue being a minister. But that freedom comes at the cost of automatic and absolute exclusion from the benefits of a public program for which the Center is otherwise fully qualified. And when the State conditions a benefit in this way, [the] State has punished the free exercise of religion. [It] is true the Department has not criminalized the way Trinity Lutheran worships or told the Church that it cannot subscribe to a certain view of the Gospel. But [as] the Court put it more than 50 years ago, "[i]t is too late in the day to doubt that the liberties of religion and expression may be infringed by the denial of or placing of conditions upon a benefit or privilege." Sherbert.

B.   [The] Department [argues] that the free exercise question in this case is instead controlled by our decision in Locke v. Davey. It is not. [Davey] was not denied a scholarship because of who he was; he was denied a scholarship because of what he proposed to do—use the funds to prepare for the ministry. Here there is no question that Trinity Lutheran was denied a grant simply because of what it is—a church.

The Court in Locke also stated that Washington's choice was in keeping with the State's antiestablishment interest in not using taxpayer funds to pay for the training of clergy; in fact, the Court could "think of few areas in which a State's antiestablishment interests come more into play." [Here] nothing of the sort can be said about a program to use recycled tires to resurface playgrounds.

[The] Department emphasizes Missouri's similar [tradition] of not furnishing taxpayer money directly to churches. But Locke took account of Washington's antiestablishment interest only after determining [that] the scholarship program did not "require students to choose between their religious beliefs and receiving a government benefit." [In] this case, there is no dispute that Trinity Lutheran is put to the choice between being a church and receiving a government benefit. The rule is simple: No churches need apply.[1]

C.   Under [the "most rigorous" scrutiny] standard, only a state interest "of the highest order" can justify the Department's discriminatory policy. Yet the Department offers nothing more than Missouri's policy preference for skating as far as possible from religious establishment concerns. In the face of the clear infringement on free exercise before us, that interest cannot qualify as compelling.

■ JUSTICE THOMAS, with whom JUSTICE GORSUCH joins, concurring in part.

[This] Court's endorsement in Locke of even a "mild kind" of discrimination against religion remains troubling. But because the Court today appropriately construes Locke narrowly and because no party has asked us to reconsider it, I join nearly all of the Court's opinion.

■ JUSTICE GORSUCH, with whom JUSTICE THOMAS joins, concurring in part.

[I] offer only two modest qualifications.

First, the Court leaves open the possibility a useful distinction might be drawn between laws that discriminate on the basis of religious status and

---

[1]   [Footnote 3, for a plurality of the Court]: This case involves express discrimination based on religious identity with respect to playground resurfacing. We do not address religious uses of funding or other forms of discrimination.

religious use. Respectfully, I harbor doubts about the stability of such a line. Does a religious man say grace before dinner? Or does a man begin his meal in a religious manner? Is it a religious group that built the playground? Or did a group build the playground so it might be used to advance a religious mission? The distinction blurs in much the same way the line between acts and omissions can blur when stared at too long, leaving us to ask (for example) whether the man who drowns by awaiting the incoming tide does so by act (coming upon the sea) or omission (allowing the sea to come upon him).

[Second] and for similar reasons, I am unable to join the footnoted observation, n. 3, that "[t]his case involves express discrimination based on religious identity with respect to playground resurfacing." Of course the footnote is entirely correct, but I worry that some might mistakenly read it to suggest that only "playground resurfacing" cases, or only those with some association with children's safety or health, or perhaps some other social good we find sufficiently worthy, are governed by the legal rules recounted in and faithfully applied by the Court's opinion. [And] the general principles here do not permit discrimination against religious exercise—whether on the playground or anywhere else.

■ JUSTICE BREYER, concurring in the judgment.

[I] find relevant, and would emphasize, the particular nature of the "public benefit" here at issue. The Court stated in Everson that "cutting off church schools from" such "general government services as ordinary police and fire protection . . . is obviously not the purpose of the First Amendment." Here, the State would cut Trinity Lutheran off from participation in a general program designed to secure or to improve the health and safety of children. I see no significant difference. [I] would leave the application of the Free Exercise Clause to other kinds of public benefits for another day.

■ JUSTICE SOTOMAYOR, with whom JUSTICE GINSBURG joins, dissenting.

[This] case is about nothing less than the relationship between religious institutions and the civil government—that is, between church and state. The Court today profoundly changes that relationship by holding, for the first time, that the Constitution requires the government to provide public funds directly to a church.

[This] is a case about whether Missouri can decline to fund improvements to the facilities the Church uses to practice and spread its religious views. [The] Court has repeatedly warned that [payments] from the government to a house of worship would cross the line drawn by the Establishment Clause. [The] Establishment Clause does not allow Missouri to grant the Church's funding request because the Church uses the Learning Center, including its playground, in conjunction with its religious mission. [The] Court may simply disagree with this account of the facts and think that the Church does not put its playground to religious use. If so, its mistake is limited to this case. But if it agrees that the State's funding would further religious activity and sees no Establishment Clause problem, then it must be implicitly applying a rule other than the one agreed to in our precedents. [Such] a break with precedent would mark a radical mistake.

[Even] assuming the absence of an Establishment Clause violation and proceeding on the Court's preferred front—the Free Exercise Clause—the Court errs. It claims that the government may not draw lines based on an entity's religious "status." But we have repeatedly said that it can. [The] play in the joints between the Free Exercise and Establishment Clauses gives government some room to recognize the unique status of religious entities and to single them out on that basis for exclusion from otherwise generally applicable laws. [The] State need not, for example, fund the training of a religious group's leaders, those "who will preach their beliefs, teach their faith, and carry out their mission." It may instead avoid the historic "antiestablishment interests" raised by the use of "taxpayer funds to support church leaders." Locke.

Missouri has decided that the unique status of houses of worship requires a special rule when it comes to public funds. [Missouri's] decision, which has deep roots in our Nation's history, reflects a reasonable and constitutional judgment. [The] use of public funds to support core religious institutions can safely be described as a hallmark of the States' early experiences with religious establishment. Every state establishment saw laws passed to raise public funds and direct them toward houses of worship and ministers. And as the States all disestablished, one by one, they all undid those laws. [In] Locke, this Court expressed an understanding of, and respect for, this history.

[Like] the use of public dollars for ministers at issue in Locke, turning over public funds to houses of worship implicates serious anti-establishment and free exercise interests. [As] was true in Locke, a prophylactic rule against the use of public funds for houses of worship is a permissible accommodation of these weighty interests. The rule has a historical pedigree identical to that of the provision in Locke. [Today,] thirty-eight States have a counterpart to Missouri's Article I, § 7.10. The provisions, as a general matter, date back to or before these States' original Constitutions. That so many States have for so long drawn a line that prohibits public funding for houses of worship, based on principles rooted in this Nation's understanding of how best to foster religious liberty, supports the conclusion that public funding of houses of worship "is of a different ilk." Locke.

[The Court also] suggests that this case is different because it involves "discrimination" in the form of the denial of access to a possible benefit. But in this area of law, a decision to treat entities differently based on distinctions that the Religion Clauses make relevant does not amount to discrimination.

At bottom, the Court creates the following rule today: The government may draw lines on the basis of religious status to grant a benefit to religious persons or entities but it may not draw lines on that basis when doing so would further the interests the Religion Clauses protect in other ways. Nothing supports this lopsided outcome.

————

1. ***Footnote 3 and secular use.*** Much of the discussion around Trinity Lutheran has focused on footnote 3: "This case involves express discrimination based on religious identity with respect to playground resurfacing. We do not address religious uses of funding or other forms of discrimination." Only Chief Justice Roberts and Justices Kennedy, Alito, and Kagan signed on; Justices Thomas and Gorsuch did not. Commentators have pointed to this plurality footnote as a way in which the Court has left itself the option of letting states decline to provide funds when the activity involved seems more "religious" than playground resurfacing. How important to the Court's reasoning is the secular nature of the funds' use?

What other things could count as "secular" uses of money? Could a church be eligible for a state grant program that helps weatherproof buildings if the church wants to use the funds to renovate its sanctuary, as opposed to a related school? How do you weigh the arguments of Justice Sotomayor and Justice Gorsuch that the church conceives of the school as part of its religious mission (and which Justice would be correct about the implications?)

2. *Locke v. Davey after Trinity Lutheran.* The Court did not overrule Locke; instead, it distinguished the case by saying Locke addressed the religious *use* of funds, while the issue in Trinity Lutheran involved the church's *status* as religious. How convincing is this distinction? Is Justice Gorsuch correct that status and use are not coherent categories? Trinity Lutheran is the first case in which the Court has required the government to give money directly to a religious organization. How much of Locke's reasoning still stands after Trinity Lutheran? Is there still room for play in the joints between the religion clauses, or does Trinity Lutheran narrow the gap between what the Establishment Clause permits and the Free Exercise Clause requires? For an analysis of Trinity Lutheran's consideration of, and potential effect on, Locke and other areas of religion clauses jurisprudence, including vouchers, see Laycock, "Churches, Playgrounds, Government Dollars—And Schools?", 131 Harv. L. Rev. 133 (2017).

In **Espinoza v. Montana Department of Revenue**, 140 S. Ct. 2246 (2020), the Court revisited the Locke v. Davey question in a slightly different form, and by a 5–4 vote sustained a Free Exercise challenge to a state rule barring the use of tax-subsidized scholarships for attendance at religious schools. Chief Justice ROBERTS wrote the opinion of the Court: "The Montana Legislature established a program to provide tuition assistance to parents who send their children to private schools. The program grants a tax credit to anyone who donates to certain organizations that in turn award scholarships to selected students attending such schools. When petitioners sought to use the scholarships at a religious school, the Montana Supreme Court struck down the program. The Court relied on the no-aid provision of the State Constitution, which prohibits any aid to a school controlled by a 'church, sect, or denomination.' The question presented is whether the Free Exercise Clause of the United States Constitution barred that application of the no-aid provision. [The] parties do not dispute that the scholarship program is permissible under the Establishment Clause. [The] government support makes its way to religious schools only as a result of Montanans independently choosing to spend their scholarships at such schools. [We] accept the Montana Supreme Court's interpretation of state law—including its determination that the scholarship program provided impermissible 'aid' within the meaning of the Montana Constitution—and we assess whether excluding religious schools and affected families from that program was consistent with the Federal Constitution. [As in Trinity Lutheran,] Montana's no-aid provision bars religious schools from public benefits solely because of the religious character of the schools. [This] case also turns expressly on religious status and not religious use. The Montana Supreme Court applied the no-aid provision solely by reference to religious status. [Status-based] discrimination remains status based even if one of its goals or effects is preventing religious organizations from putting aid to religious uses."

Chief Justice Roberts then distinguished Locke, which, he wrote, "differs from this case in two critical ways. First, Locke explained that

Washington had merely chosen not to fund a distinct category of instruction: the essentially religious endeavor of training a minister to lead a congregation. Thus, Davey was denied a scholarship because of what he proposed to do—use the funds to prepare for the ministry. Apart from that narrow restriction, Washington's program allowed scholarships to be used at 'pervasively religious schools' that incorporated religious instruction throughout their classes. By contrast, Montana's Constitution does not zero in on any particular 'essentially religious' course of instruction at a religious school. Rather, [the] no-aid provision bars all aid to a religious school 'simply because of what it is,' putting the school to a choice between being religious or receiving government benefits. At the same time, the provision puts families to a choice between sending their children to a religious school or receiving such benefits. Second, Locke invoked a 'historic and substantial' state interest in not funding the training of clergy. As evidence of that tradition, the Court in Locke emphasized that the propriety of state-supported clergy was a central subject of founding-era debates, and that most state constitutions from that era prohibited the expenditure of tax dollars to support the clergy. But no comparable 'historic and substantial' tradition supports Montana's decision to disqualify religious schools from government aid. In the founding era and the early 19th century, governments provided financial support to private schools, including denominational ones. 'Far from prohibiting such support, the early state constitutions and statutes actively encouraged this policy.'

"[The] Department argues that a tradition against state support for religious schools arose in the second half of the 19th century, as more than 30 States—including Montana—adopted no-aid provisions. Such a development, of course, cannot by itself establish an early American tradition. [In] addition, many of the no-aid provisions belong to a more checkered tradition shared with the Blaine Amendment of the 1870s. That proposal—which Congress nearly passed—would have added to the Federal Constitution a provision similar to the state no-aid provisions, prohibiting States from aiding 'sectarian' schools. It was an open secret that 'sectarian' was code for 'Catholic.' The Blaine Amendment was born of bigotry and arose at a time of pervasive hostility to the Catholic Church and to Catholics in general; many of its state counterparts have a similarly shameful pedigree. The no-aid provisions of the 19th century hardly evince a tradition that should inform our understanding of the Free Exercise Clause."

Justice THOMAS concurred separately to reiterate his view that the Establishment Clause should not be incorporated against the states. He was joined by Justice Gorsuch, marking the first time any other justice espoused this view. Justice ALITO concurred to offer an account of the anti-Catholic nature of the state Blaine amendments such as Montana's. Justice GORSUCH concurred to restate the criticisms he made of the religious status/religious use distinction in his concurrence in Trinity Lutheran.

Justice GINSBURG, joined by Justice Kagan, dissented on the grounds that the Montana Supreme Court had struck down the entire scholarship program, thus nullifying any claim of differential treatment for religion.

Justice BREYER also dissented: "Although the majority refers in passing to the 'play in the joints' between that which the Establishment Clause forbids and that which the Free Exercise Clause requires, its holding leaves that doctrine a shadow of its former self. [I] think the majority is wrong to replace the flexible, context-specific approach of our precedents with a test of 'strict' or 'rigorous' scrutiny. And it is wrong to imply that courts should use that same heightened scrutiny whenever a government benefit is at issue. [Government] benefits come in many shapes and sizes. The appropriate way to approach a State's benefit-related decision may well vary depending upon the relation between the Religion Clauses and the specific benefit and restriction at issue. [Disagreements] that concern religion may involve small but important details of a particular benefit program. Does one detail affect one religion negatively and another positively? What about a religion that objects to the particular way in which the government seeks to enforce mandatory (say, qualification-related) provisions of a particular benefit program?"

Justice SOTOMAYOR also dissented: "Until Trinity Lutheran, the right to exercise one's religion did not include a right to have the State pay for that religious practice. That is because a contrary rule risks reading the Establishment Clause out of the Constitution. [A] State may refuse to extend certain aid programs to religious entities when doing so avoids historic and substantial antiestablishment concerns."

The Supreme Court subsequently granted certiorari in Carson v. Makin, in which Petitioners called for Locke v. Davy to be overruled.

Carson v. Makin

596 U.S. ___, 142 S. Ct. 1987 (2022).

■ CHIEF JUSTICE ROBERTS delivered the opinion of the Court.

[The] "unremarkable" principles applied in Trinity Lutheran and Espinoza suffice to resolve this case. Maine offers its citizens a benefit: tuition assistance payments for any family whose school district does not provide a public secondary school. Just like the wide range of nonprofit organizations eligible to receive playground resurfacing grants in Trinity Lutheran, a wide range of private schools are eligible to receive Maine tuition assistance payments here. And like the daycare center in Trinity Lutheran, BCS and Temple Academy are disqualified from this generally available benefit solely because of their religious character. [In Espinoza,] as here, that program specifically carved out private religious schools from those eligible to receive such funds. [A] neutral benefit program in which public funds flow to religious organizations through the independent choices of private benefit recipients does not offend the Establishment Clause. Zelman. [An] interest in separating church and state more fiercely than the Federal Constitution cannot qualify as compelling in the face of the infringement of free exercise. [There] is nothing neutral about Maine's program. The State pays tuition for certain students at private schools—so long as the schools are not religious. That is discrimination against religion.

The Court of Appeals [and the dissent] distinguish this case from Trinity Lutheran and Espinoza on the ground that the funding restrictions in those cases were solely status-based religious discrimination, while the challenged provision here imposes a use-based restriction. [That] premise, however, misreads our precedents. In Trinity Lutheran and Espinoza, we held that the Free Exercise Clause forbids discrimination on the basis of religious status. But those decisions never suggested that use-based discrimination is any less offensive to the Free Exercise Clause. This case illustrates why.

Educating young people in their faith, inculcating its teachings, and training them to live their faith are responsibilities that lie at the very core of the mission of a private religious school. Any attempt to give effect to such a distinction by scrutinizing whether and how a religious school pursues its educational mission would also raise serious concerns about state entanglement with religion and denominational favoritism. Indeed, Maine concedes that the Department barely engages in any such scrutiny. [That] suggests that any status-use distinction lacks a meaningful application not only in theory, but in practice as well. In short, the prohibition on status-based discrimination under the Free Exercise Clause is not a permission to engage in use-based discrimination.

Our opinions in Trinity Lutheran and Espinoza [explain] why Locke can be of no help to Maine here. [The] funding in Locke was intended to be used to prepare for the ministry. Funds could be and were used for theology courses; only pursuing a vocational religious *degree* was excluded. Locke's reasoning expressly turned on what it identified as the "historic and substantial state interest" against using "taxpayer funds to support church leaders." But [it] is clear that there is no 'historic and substantial' tradition against aiding private religious schools comparable to the tradition against state-supported clergy invoked by Locke. Locke cannot be read beyond its narrow focus on vocational religious degrees to generally authorize the State to exclude religious persons from the enjoyment of public benefits on the basis of their anticipated religious use of the benefits.

■ JUSTICE BREYER, with whom JUSTICE KAGAN joins, and with whom JUSTICE SOTOMAYOR joins except as to Part I-B, dissenting.

[In] applying [the religion] Clauses, we have often said that there is room for play in the joints between them. [The] Court today nowhere mentions, and I fear effectively abandons, this longstanding doctrine. [To] interpret the two Clauses as if they were joined at the hip will work against their basic purpose: to allow for an American society with practitioners of over 100 different religions, and those who do not practice religion at all, to live together without serious risk of religion-based social divisions.

[We] have never previously held what the Court holds today, namely, that a State *must* (not *may*) use state funds to pay for religious education as part of a tuition program designed to ensure the provision of free statewide public school education. What happens once "may" becomes "must"? Does that transformation mean that a school district that pays for public schools must pay equivalent funds to parents who wish to send their children to religious schools? Does it mean that school districts that give vouchers for use at charter schools must pay equivalent funds to parents who wish to give their children a religious education? What other social benefits are there the State's provision of which means—under the majority's interpretation of the Free Exercise Clause—that the State must pay parents for the religious equivalent of the secular benefit provided? The concept of "play in the joints" means that courts need not, and should not, answer with "must" these questions that can more appropriately be answered with "may."

[Cities] and States normally pay for police forces, fire protection, paved streets, municipal transport, and hosts of other services that benefit churches as well as secular organizations. But paying the salary of a religious teacher as part of a public school tuition program is a different matter. [Schools] were excluded from the playground resurfacing program at issue in Trinity Lutheran because of the mere fact that they were owned or controlled by a church, sect, or other religious entity. Here, by contrast, [Maine] chooses not to fund only those schools that promote the faith or belief system with which the schools are associated and/or present the academic material taught through the lens of this faith—*i.e.*, schools that will use public money for religious purposes. Maine thus excludes schools from its tuition program not because of the schools' religious character but because the schools will use the funds to teach and promote religious ideals. [In] Espinoza, [the] State prohibited families from using the scholarship at any private school owned or controlled in whole or in part by any church, religious sect, or denomination.

[These] distinctions are important. The very point of the Establishment Clause is to prevent the government from sponsoring religious activity itself. [State] funding of religious activity risks the very social conflict based upon religion that the Religion Clauses were designed to prevent.

■ JUSTICE SOTOMAYOR, dissenting.

[The] Court's analysis does leave some options open to Maine. For example, under state law, school administrative units (SAUs) that cannot feasibly operate their own schools may contract directly with a public school in another SAU, or with an approved private school, to educate their students. I do not understand today's decision to mandate that SAUs contract directly with schools that teach religion, which would go beyond Zelman's private-choice doctrine and blatantly violate the Establishment Clause.

[In Trinity Lutheran], I feared that the Court was leading us to a place where separation of church and state is a constitutional slogan, not a constitutional commitment. Today, the Court leads us to a place where separation of church and state becomes a constitutional violation. If a State cannot offer subsidies to its citizens without being required to fund religious exercise, any State that values its historic antiestablishment interests more than this Court does will have to curtail the support it offers to its citizens.

———

1. *Locke v. Davey after Carson v. Makin.* Formally, Carson v. Makin did not overrule Locke v. Davey. But what remains of that decision? Is Locke's play-in-the-joints theory still in play? Why did Justice Breyer's dissent say that he feared the theory had been "effectively abandon[ed]"?

2. *Reconciling Trinity Lutheran and Carson v. Makin.* If Chief Justice Roberts in Carson repudiated the status-use distinction, what is the correct reading of Trinity Lutheran today? If it rests, as Chief Justice Roberts wrote in Carson, on a history of state non-support of clergy, then is the correct test a purely historical one? And if so, why isn't the unbroken practice of the states not directly funding tuition for religious education decisive in Carson?

3. *The law in practice after Carson v. Makin.* States often fund various cultural institutions such as libraries, not all of which are fully public. After Carson, would a state's refusal to fund a private religious cultural institution associated with a church violate the Free Exercise Clause? Will the Supreme Court eventually hold that a state that funds public schools violates the Free Exercise Clause if it does not also fund private religious education?

———

LEGISLATIVE ACCOMMODATION OF RELIGION

1. ***Accommodation.*** Statutory accommodations in the interest of free exercise values present recurrent problems of tension between the goals of the Free Exercise and Establishment Clauses. Statutory exemptions are widespread in legislation in such areas as social security and labor. Recall that, in Sherbert, Justice Harlan's dissent argued that legislators have broad discretion to promote free exercise values by enacting statutory accommodations. By what standards should statutory accommodations of religious practices be judged? Might some legislative accommodations amount to the impermissible establishment of religion? The following cases explore this question.

2. ***Accommodation vs. delegation.*** One clear limit on religious accommodation is that government may not, consistent with the Establishment Clause, delegate to a religious entity the power to exercise civic authority. **Larkin v. Grendel's Den, Inc.**, 459 U.S. 116 (1982), struck down a Massachusetts law that gave churches and schools the power to veto the issuance of liquor licenses to restaurants within 500 feet of the church or school buildings. By a vote of 8–1, the Court balked at the notion that governmental authority could so be conferred on religious organizations. Chief Justice BURGER's majority opinion conceded a church's "valid interest in being insulated from certain kinds of commercial establishments, including those dispensing liquor," but concluded that the delegation of a veto power to churches had the effect of "advancing religion," impermissible under the Lemon standards. He added that "the mere appearance of a joint exercise of legislative authority by Church and State provides a significant symbolic benefit to religion in the minds of some." Moreover, turning to the "entanglement" prong of the Lemon test, he found that the law "enmeshes churches in the exercise of substantial governmental powers contrary to our consistent interpretation of the Establishment Clause." Justice REHNQUIST, the sole dissenter, argued that because the state could have banned all liquor establishments within 500 feet of a church, the Constitution did not prevent the state from electing a less drastic alternative of allowing each church to decide whether it wished to be "unmolested by activities at a neighboring bar."

3. ***Permissible statutory accommodations and their limits.*** Title VII of the Civil Rights Act of 1964, which forbids employment discrimination on the basis of, inter alia, race, gender or religion, requires employers to make reasonable accommodations to the religious practices of employees. (For an interpretation of the statutory "reasonable accommodation" requirement, see Trans World Airlines v. Hardison, 432 U.S. 63 (1977).) The Court has never questioned the permissibility of that accommodation provision. But **Estate of Thornton v. Caldor, Inc.**, 472 U.S. 703 (1985), struck down a Connecticut law providing: "No person who states that a particular day of the week is observed as his Sabbath may be required to work on such day. An employee's refusal to work on his Sabbath shall not constitute grounds for his dismissal." The law was the result of a substantial revision of the state's Sunday closing laws; under the revision, many businesses were allowed to remain open on Sundays. Chief Justice BURGER's opinion for the Court held that this mandatory, absolute deference to the Sabbath observer constituted an impermissible establishment of religion because the statute clearly advanced "a particular religious practice." The law gave employees an "absolute and unqualified

right" not to work on their Sabbath. "The State thus commands that Sabbath religious concerns automatically control over secular interests at the workplace; the statute takes no account of the convenience or interests of the employer or those of other employees who do not observe a Sabbath. [Moreover], there is no exception when honoring the dictates of Sabbath observers would cause the employer substantial economic burdens or when the employer's compliance would require the imposition of significant burdens on other employees required to work in place of the Sabbath observers. Finally, the statute allows for no consideration as to whether the employer has made reasonable accommodation proposals. This unyielding weighting in favor of Sabbath observers over all other interests contravenes a fundamental principle of the Religion Clauses." Justice O'CONNOR, joined by Justice Marshall, filed a concurring opinion in which she sought to distinguish the exception here from that in Title VII. To her, the crucial distinctions were the exclusive religious orientation and absolute character of the Connecticut law: "[A] statute outlawing employment discrimination based on race, color, religion, sex, or national origin has the valid secular purpose of assuring employment opportunity to all groups in our pluralistic society. Since Title VII calls for reasonable rather than absolute accommodation and extends that requirement to all religious beliefs rather than protecting only the Sabbath observance, I believe an objective observer would perceive it as an anti-discrimination law rather than an endorsement of religion or a particular religious provision."

In **Corporation of Presiding Bishop v. Amos**, 483 U.S. 327 (1987), the Court upheld a different provision of Title VII, this one accommodating religious employers rather than employees. Title VII generally prohibits discrimination in employment on the basis of religion, but exempts religious organizations. The exemption, 42 U.S.C. § 702, provides that the antidiscrimination provision "shall not apply [to] a religious corporation [with] respect to the employment of individuals of a particular religion to perform work connected with a carrying on by such corporation [of] its activities." An employee of the Mormon Church who had been discharged from his job as a janitor at a gymnasium run by the Church for failing to qualify as a church member claimed that his firing on the basis of religion violated the Act. The Church claimed that its action was permitted by the exemption in § 702. The employee in turn claimed that if § 702 were "construed to allow religious employers to discriminate on religious grounds in hiring for nonreligious jobs," it violated the Establishment Clause.

Without dissent, the Court rejected the Establishment Clause attack on § 702. Justice WHITE's opinion defended the constitutionality of the general principle underlying the exemption: "We find unpersuasive the District Court's reliance on the fact that [§ 702] singles out religious entities for a benefit. Although the Court has given weight to this consideration in its past decisions [e.g., Mueller; Nyquist] it has never indicated that statutes that give special consideration to religious groups are per se invalid. That would run contrary to the teaching of our cases that there is ample room for accommodation of religion under the Establishment Clause. Where [government] acts with the proper purpose of lifting a regulation that burdens the exercise of religion, we see no reason to require that the exemption come packaged with benefits to secular entities." Justice White insisted that the exemption was "in no way questionable under the Lemon analysis." Under its "purpose" prong, the law need not be "unrelated to religion"; rather, "Lemon's 'purpose' requirement aims at preventing the [governmental] decisionmaker [from] abandoning neutrality and acting with the intent of promoting a particular point of view in religious matters." Nor did the exemption violate the "effect" prong: "A law is not unconstitutional simply because it *allows* churches to advance religion. [For] a law to have forbidden 'effects,' [it] must be fair to say that the *government itself* has advanced religion through its own activities and influence."

Justice BRENNAN, joined by Justice Marshall, concurred in the judgment. He emphasized that "religious organizations have an interest in autonomy in ordering their internal affairs" and must be free to discriminate on a religious basis with respect to religious activities. He was willing to uphold the extension of the exemption to nonreligious activities because distinguishing religious from nonreligious activities would necessitate "ongoing government entanglement in religious affairs," which in turn would have a chilling effect on free exercise. Justice O'CONNOR also concurred only in the judgment, emphasizing her "endorsement" approach set forth in Lynch v. Donnelly. She urged the Court to recognize that laws such as this *do* advance religion, but that the Constitution permits such advancement unless the government's purpose was to endorse religion and "the statute actually conveys a message of endorsement." Justice BLACKMUN also concurred in the judgment, indicating substantial agreement with Justice O'Connor's opinion.

Two years later, however, in **Texas Monthly, Inc. v. Bullock**, 489 U.S. 1 (1989), the Court refused to accept an "accommodation" argument in the context of a tax exemption available only to religious publications. The decision struck down a Texas law exempting from the sales tax "[p]eriodicals that are published or distributed by a religious faith and that consist wholly of writings promulgating the teaching of the faith and books that consist wholly of writings sacred to a religious faith." Justice BRENNAN's plurality opinion, joined by Justices Marshall and Stevens, held that the statute violated the Establishment Clause, relying heavily on the fact that the exemption was not available to any similarly situated nonreligious publication. He thus distinguished such cases as Mueller and Widmar, for in each of these the benefit to religious organizations was one also available to secular organizations: "In all of these cases, [we] emphasized that the benefits derived by religious organizations flow to a large number of nonreligious groups as well. Indeed were those benefits confined to religious organizations, they could not have appeared other than as state sponsorship of religion. [How] expansive the class of exempt organizations or activities must be to withstand constitutional assault depends upon the State's secular aim in granting a tax exemption." For example, if the State chose "to subsidize, by means of a tax exemption, all groups that contributed to the community's cultural, intellectual, and moral betterment, than the exemption for religious publications could be retained." The plurality distinguished the Amos case on the ground that there, but not here, granting the exemption "prevented potentially serious encroachments on protected religious freedoms," since in most cases the payment of a sales tax would not violate the religious tenets of a religious organization.

Justice BLACKMUN, joined by Justice O'Connor, concurred in the judgment. He stressed the inevitable tension between free exercise and Establishment Clause values and insisted that the plurality had gone too far in preferring the latter over the former. He therefore would hold only that "a tax exemption *limited* to the sale of religious literature by religious organizations violates the Establishment Clause." The exemption here constituted a "preferential support for the communication of religious messages. Although some forms of accommodating religion are constitutionally permissible, this one surely is not." Justice White also concurred in the judgment.

Justice SCALIA, joined by Chief Justice Rehnquist and Justice Kennedy, dissented. He argued that the decision would invalidate many religiously targeted tax exemptions, e.g., for church-owned residences for members of the clergy, motor vehicles owned by religious organizations, and meals served at church functions. He relied heavily on Walz, arguing that its sustaining of a tax exemption for religious property did not depend on the availability of a similar exemption for property owned by nonreligious charitable organizations. More broadly, he rejected the conclusion in both the plurality and the concurring opinions that "no law is constitutional whose 'benefits [are] confined to religious organizations' except, of course, those laws that are unconstitutional *unless* they contain benefits confined to religious organizations. Our jurisprudence affords no support for this unlikely proposition." He added that the Court had "often made clear that '[t]he limits of permissible state accommodation of religion are by no means coextensive with a noninterference mandated by the Free Exercise Clause.' " Although it was "not always easy to determine when accommodation slides over into promotion, and neutrality into favoritism," the "withholding of a tax upon the dissemination of religious materials is not even a close case." He argued that where an exemption "comes so close to being a constitutionally required accommodation, there is no doubt that it is at least a permissible one."

Three years after Widmar, Congress enacted the Equal Access Act of 1984, 28 U.S.C. § 4071. The Act extended the access rights recognized for university students in Widmar to secondary school students. The Act provided, inter alia: "It shall be unlawful for any public secondary school which receives Federal financial assistance and which has a limited open forum to deny equal access [to] any students who wish to conduct a meeting within that limited open forum on the basis of the religious, political, philosophical or other content of the speech at such meetings." The Senate Report accompanying the bill contained a finding that high school students are capable of understanding the difference between student-initiated religious speech and state-sponsored religious activity. In **Board of Education v. Mergens**, 496 U.S. 226 (1990), the Court interpreted the Act broadly and rejected the argument that the law violated the Establishment Clause by mandating school sponsorship of religious organizations. The Court held that the school officials' denial of a request for formation of a student Christian club violated the Act and that the application of the law here did not violate the Establishment Clause. There was no majority opinion on the Establishment Clause analysis. Justice O'CONNOR's plurality opinion, joined by Chief Justice Rehnquist and Justices White and Blackmun, found that requiring the school to recognize the religious club did not violate the three-pronged Lemon test. On the "effect" issue, she stated: "Because the Act on its face grants equal access to both secular and religious speech, we think it clear that the Act's purpose was not to 'endorse or disapprove of religion,' Wallace v. Jaffree (quoting Lynch v. Donnelly, O'Connor, J., concurring). [There] is a crucial difference between *government* speech endorsing religion, which the Establishment Clause forbids, and *private* speech endorsing religion, which the Free Speech and Free Exercise

Clauses protect. We think that secondary school students are mature enough and are likely to understand that a school does not endorse or support student speech that it merely permits on a nondiscriminatory basis."

Justice KENNEDY, joined by Justice Scalia, concurred only in the judgment on the Establishment Clause issue. He rejected Justice O'Connor's endorsement test and argued instead that the Establishment Clause is violated only where government either gives such direct benefits to a religion that it has the effect or tendency of establishing a state religion, or "coerce[s] any student to participate in a religious activity." He found no such "coercion" here. Justice MARSHALL's concurrence in the judgment, joined by Justice Brennan, emphasized that the Act as applied could be sustained only if a school took special steps to disassociate itself from religious speech and "to avoid appearing to endorse [a religious group's] goals." He insisted that the plurality approach dismissed "too lightly the distinctive pressures created by [the school's] highly structured environment." Justice STEVENS, the sole dissenter, relied solely on statutory grounds, arguing that the Act's requirements were triggered only if other "controversial or partisan" groups were granted access, which was not the case here.

In **Cutter v. Wilkinson**, 544 U.S. 709 (2005), the Court rejected an Establishment Clause defense raised by prison officials against prisoners' attempts to enforce section 3 of the Religious Land Use and Institutionalized Persons Act of 2000 (RLUIPA), which provides: "No government shall impose a substantial burden on the religious exercise of a person residing in or confined to an institution," unless the burden furthers "a compelling governmental interest," and does so by "the least restrictive means." Congress enacted the statute in reaction to the Court's ruling in Employment Division v. Smith (1990; p. 684), which held that the Free Exercise Clause did not require religious exemptions from generally applicable laws, and to the Court's invalidation in City of Boerne v. Flores (1997), as exceeding Congress's civil rights enforcement authority, of the Religious Freedom Restoration Act, which had attempted to correct Smith by providing statutory religious exemptions across the board.

In Cutter, the Court held unanimously that that the much narrower exemption provisions of RLUIPA on their face qualified as a permissible accommodation of religion. Justice GINSBURG wrote the opinion of the Court: "Just last Term, in Locke v. Davey, the Court reaffirmed that 'there is room for play in the joints between' the Free Exercise and Establishment Clauses, allowing the government to accommodate religion beyond free exercise requirements, without offense to the Establishment Clause. [We] hold that § 3 of RLUIPA fits within the corridor between the Religion Clauses: On its face, the Act qualifies as a permissible legislative accommodation of religion that is not barred by the Establishment Clause. Foremost, we find RLUIPA's institutionalized-persons provision compatible with the Establishment Clause because it alleviates exceptional government-created burdens on private religious exercise. Kiryas Joel, Amos. Furthermore, the Act on its face does not founder on shoals our prior decisions have identified: Properly applying RLUIPA, courts must take adequate account of the burdens a requested accommodation may impose on nonbeneficiaries, see Thornton, and they must be satisfied that the Act's prescriptions are and will be administered neutrally among different faiths, see Kiryas Joel. [RLUIPA] protects institutionalized persons who are unable freely to attend to their religious needs and are therefore dependent on the government's permission and accommodation for exercise of their religion.

"We do not read RLUIPA to elevate accommodation of religious observances over an institution's need to maintain order and safety. Our decisions indicate that an accommodation must be measured so that it does not override other significant interests. [We] have no cause to believe that RLUIPA would not be applied in an appropriately balanced way, with particular sensitivity to security concerns. [Lawmakers] supporting RLUIPA were mindful of the urgency of discipline, order, safety, and security in penal institutions. They anticipated that courts would apply the Act's standard with 'due deference to the experience and expertise of prison and jail administrators in establishing necessary regulations and procedures to maintain good order, security and discipline, consistent with consideration of costs and limited resources.' [Should] inmate requests for religious accommodations become excessive, impose unjustified burdens on other institutionalized persons, or jeopardize the effective functioning of an institution, the facility would be free to resist the imposition. In that event, adjudication in as-applied challenges would be in order." Justice THOMAS filed a concurrence reiterating his position that the Establishment Clause should not be incorporated against the states.

4. ***Accommodation and public officials.*** Soon after the Court's decision in Obergefell, a Kentucky county clerk named Kim Davis entered the national spotlight when she began refusing to issue marriage licenses to any couple in order to avoid issuing them to same-sex couples, which she believed would be contrary to her Christian faith. Several couples brought suit against Davis, and a federal district court ordered her to resume issuing marriage licenses. Davis refused to comply even after the Supreme Court denied her request for a stay of the order, and the district judge ordered her jailed for contempt of court. After five days, the judge ordered Davis released on the condition that she not interfere with her deputies issuing marriage licenses. However, Davis was not required to sign the licenses herself, as she had previously done.

Meanwhile, North Carolina enacted a law that permitted public officials to recuse themselves from performing all duties related to marriage ceremonies due to a sincerely held religious objection. Several clerks in North Carolina have invoked the law to avoid issuing marriage licenses to same-sex couples. The statute granted public officials an absolute right to recuse themselves, subject to no balancing test that might take into account the inconvenience to the state or to couples seeking marriage licenses. Does this unqualified accommodation run afoul of the Court's decision in Estate of Thornton v. Caldor, (p. 805)?

5. ***Accommodation and religious gerrymandering.*** May a legislature accommodate a religious community by gerrymandering a school district to keep its students isolated from other students in a distinctive religious community? The Court answered that question negatively in **Board of Education of Kiryas Joel v. Grumet**, 512 U.S. 687 (1994). The case involved a community of ultra-orthodox Jews, the Satmar Hasidim, living in the town of Kiryas Joel, New York, which was named for Grand Rebbe Joel Teitelbaum, the founder of the sect. The boundaries of the town had been drawn carefully under New York's general village incorporation law to exclude all but Satmars, but the town was part of the broader Monroe-Woodbury school district.

The Satmar children in the community attended religious schools with the exception of schoolchildren with special needs. Those children were originally educated by the state in a special annex to one of the private religious schools in Kiryas Joel. But after the then-governing decision in Aguilar v. Felton (1985; p. 727, overruled in 1997 by Agostini v. Felton, p. 727), the special needs children were sent to public schools. Parents of most of these children soon withdrew them from the secular public schools, citing "the panic, fear and trauma [the children] suffered in leaving their own community and being with people whose ways were so different." The Satmar community then turned to the state legislature, which passed a law designating Kiryas Joel as its own school district in order to create a special needs school that would not include students other than Satmar orthodox Jews. In signing the bill into law, Governor Mario Cuomo called it "a good faith effort to solve the unique problem" of providing special education services to the village. By a vote of 6–3, the Court invalidated the special law creating the new school district.

Justice SOUTER, writing for the Court, found the law carving out the separate school district to serve the Satmar community to violate the Establishment Clause under Larkin v. Grendel's Den, which "teaches that a State may not delegate its civic authority to a group chosen according to a religious criterion. [It] is [not] dispositive that the recipients of state power in this case are a group of religious individuals united by common doctrine, not the group's leaders or officers. Although some school district franchise is common to all voters, the State's manipulation of the franchise for this district limited it to Satmars, giving the sect exclusive control of the political subdivision. In the circumstances of this case, the difference between thus vesting state power in the members of a religious group as such instead of the officers of its sectarian organization is one of form, not substance. [If] New York were to delegate civic authority to 'the Grand Rebbe,' Larkin would obviously require invalidation (even though under McDaniel the Grand Rebbe may run for, and serve on his local school board), and the same is true if New York delegates political authority by reference to religious belief. [There is a difference] between a government's purposeful delegation on the basis of religion and a delegation on principles neutral to religion, to individuals whose religious identities are incidental to their receipt of civic authority." He looked behind the facial neutrality of the state law to find a legislative history indicating the state's intent to draw "boundary lines of the school district that divide residents according to religious affiliation."

Justice O'CONNOR concurred in part and in the judgment, emphasizing the particularity of the accommodation here: "Accommodations may [justify] treating those who share [a deeply held] belief differently; but they do not justify discriminations based on sect. A state law prohibiting the consumption of alcohol may exempt sacramental wines, but it may not exempt sacramental wine used by Catholics but not by Jews." She argued that a more generally drafted statute might survive Establishment Clause challenge: "A district created under a generally applicable scheme would be acceptable even though it coincides with a village which was consciously created by its voters as an enclave for their religious group." Justice KENNEDY concurred in the judgment, objecting to New York's "religious gerrymandering," which drew "political boundaries on the basis of religion."

Justice SCALIA, joined by Chief Justice Rehnquist and Justice Thomas, dissented: "The Court today finds that the Powers That Be, up in Albany, have conspired to effect an establishment of the Satmar Hasidim. I do not know who would be more surprised at this discovery: the Founders of our Nation or Grand Rebbe Joel Teitelbaum, founder of the Satmar. The Grand Rebbe would be astounded to learn that after escaping brutal persecution and coming to America with the modest hope of religious toleration for their ascetic form of Judaism, the Satmar had become so powerful, so closely allied with Mammon, as to have become an 'establishment' of the Empire State. And the Founding Fathers would be astonished to find that the Establishment Clause—which they designed 'to insure that no one powerful sect or combination of sects could use political or governmental power to punish dissenters,' has been employed to prohibit characteristically and admirably American accommodation of the religious practices (or more precisely, cultural peculiarities) of a tiny minority sect." He distinguished Larkin v. Grendel's Den on the ground that here there was no delegation to a religious entity, and emphasized the facial neutrality of the law. He found no basis for finding a religious preference here, nor for presuming that New York would not be "as accommodating toward other religions (presumably those less powerful than the Satmar Hasidim) in the future."

What distinguishes the act of incorporation originally creating Kiryas Joel in an area occupied exclusively by Satmar Hasidim from the New York State Legislature's act designating the town as a school district to accommodate special needs children? What implications, if any, does Kiryas Joel have for other accommodations? What Establishment Clause values underlay Justice Souter's opinion?

INDEX

References are to Pages

RELIGIOUS FREEDOM RESTORATION ACT

REPOSE

REPUTATION